W9-BEJ-546

Glencoe

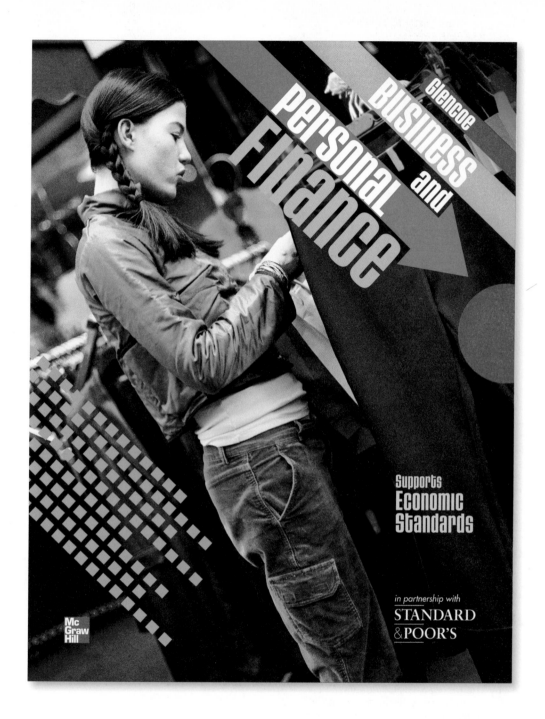

Business and Personal Finance

Supports Economic Standards

in partnership with STANDARD & POOR'S

Jack R. Kapoor
Les R. Dlabay
Robert J. Hughes

Bothell, WA • Chicago, IL • Columbus, OH • New York, NY

Notice: Information on featured companies, organizations, and their products and services is included for educational purposes only and does not present or imply endorsement of the *Business and Personal Finance* program.

glencoe.com

Copyright © 2012 by The McGraw-Hill Companies, Inc.

Send all inquiries to:
McGraw-Hill Education
4400 Easton Commons
Columbus, OH 43219

ISBN: 978-0-07-894580-9 (Student Edition)
MHID: 0-07-894580-1 (Student Edition)

Printed in the United States of America.

2 3 4 5 6 7 8 9 DOW 17 16 15 14 13 12 11

The McGraw-Hill Companies

About the Authors

Jack R. Kapoor

Jack Kapoor is a professor of business and economics in the Business and Technology Division of the College of DuPage, Glen Ellyn, Illinois, where he has taught business and economics since 1969. He received his BA and MS from San Francisco State College and his EdD from Northern Illinois University. He previously taught at Illinois Institute of Technology's Stuart School of Management, San Francisco State University's School of World Business, and other colleges. Professor Kapoor was awarded the Business and Technology Division's Outstanding Professor Award for 1999-2000. He served as an assistant national bank examiner for the U.S. Treasury Department and has been an international trade consultant to Bolting Manufacturing Co., Ltd., Bombay, India. Dr. Kapoor has been an author, content consultant and developer for books, television series, and audio courses, and has studied business practices in capitalist, socialist, and communist countries.

Les R. Dlabay

Les Dlabay is a professor of business at Lake Forest College, Lake Forest, Illinois. Sharing resources with the less fortunate is an ongoing financial goal of his. Through child sponsorship programs, world hunger organizations and community service activities, he believes the extensive wealth in our society should be used to help others. In addition to writing several textbooks, Dr. Dlabay teaches various international business courses. His "hobbies" include collecting cereal packages from over 100 countries and paper currency from 200 countries, which are used to teach about economic, cultural, and political aspects of foreign business environments. Professor Dlabay also uses many field research activities with his students, conducting interviews, surveys, and observations of business activities.

Robert J. Hughes

Bob Hughes, professor of business at Dallas County Community Colleges, believes two words, Financial Literacy!, can literally change people's lives. Whether you want to be rich or just manage the money you have, the ability to analyze financial decisions and gather financial information are skills that can always be improved upon. In addition to writing several textbooks, Dr. Hughes has taught personal finance, introduction to business, business math, small business management, small business finance, and accounting since 1972. He also served as a content consultant for two popular national television series, and is the lead author for a business math project utilizing computer-assisted instruction funded by the ALEKS Corporation. He received his BBA from Southern Nazarene University and his MBA and EdD from the University of North Texas. His hobbies include writing, investing, collecting French antiques, art, and travel.

Contributors and Reviewers

Dustin Dayley
Hurricane High School
Hurricane, UT

Traquel Dayley
Financial & Economic Education Consultant
Hurricane, UT

Kathy Kagay, retired
Maysville High School
Maysville, MO

Ariane Biba S. Kavass
Economics/Personal Finance Teacher
Southwind High School
Memphis, TN

Mindy Robison
Mathematics Teacher
Midvale Middle School, Canyons School District
Midvale, UT

Deborah Crosby
Business Instructor
Glencliff High School
Nashville, TN

Teresa Harmon
Crystal City High School
Crystal City, MO

Melinda Sloan
McGavock High School
Mount Juliet, TN

Rhonda Bradby
Business Education Teacher
Surry County High School
Dendron, VA

Sally Martin
Brentsville District High School
Nokesville, VA

Paul Jussila
South Windsor High School
South Windsor, CT

Mike Kelly
Hazelwood East High School
St. Louis, MO

Jason Lee
Olympia High School
Orlando, FL

Natalie Schaublin
Westerville North High School
Westerville, OH

Ken Schnitzer
Montclair High School
Montclair, NJ

Susie Wright
Walnut Ridge High School
Columbus, OH

Steven Gearhart
CTE Business Teacher
John F. Kennedy High School
San Antonio, TX

Ryan Moore
North Springs Charter High School
Sandy Springs, GA

Patty Wamble
Cape Central High School
Cape Girardeau, Missouri

Glen Zipfel
Christian Brothers High School
St. Louis, Missouri

Jeff Noyes
Minnetonka High School
Minnetonka, Minnesota

Mark Van Hoy
Hazelwood West High School
Hazelwood, Missouri

Alana Eaton
Kennard-Dale High School
Fawn Grove, PA

Tracy Kelly
Coolidge High School
Coolidge, AZ

Table of Contents

Table of Contents

Table of Contents

Table of Contents

Table of Contents

Table of Contents

Table of Contents

Features Table of Contents

Real-World Applications

Can you create and develop a budget? Do you know how to develop a financial career goal? These Unit Project features will help you get involved in the world of business and personal finance.

Unit Project

Discovery Project

College and Career Readiness

College & Career READINESS

Features Table of Contents

Life Skills You Can Use

These features allow you to learn about many different finance-related careers as well as finance-related skills and information you will need to successfully meet your financial goals.

Careers That Count!

reality bytes

Common Cents

Features Table of Contents

Improve Your Financial Skills

Do you know how a deficit can affect your own personal finances? Can you create a personal balance sheet? These features will help you improve your financial skills.

Economics and You

GO FIGURE Mathematics

Document Detective

Features Table of Contents

Finance in the Real World

It is important to know how business and personal finance actually works in United States and global economies. These features will show you how financial topics affect real-world companies and individuals, and how financial topics affect people in different parts of the world.

ASK STANDARD & POOR'S

Around the World

National Academic Standards

By improving your academic skills, you improve your ability to learn and achieve success now and in the future. It also improves your chances of landing a high-skill, high-wage job. The features and assessments in *Business and Personal Finance* provide many opportunities for you to strengthen your academic skills.

National English Language Arts Standards	
To help incorporate literacy skills (reading, writing, listening, and speaking) into Business and Personal Finance, each section contains a listing of the language arts skills covered. These skills have been developed into standards by the National Council of Teachers of English and International Reading Association.	
NCTE 1	Students read a wide range of print and nonprint texts to build an understanding of texts, of themselves, and of the cultures of the United States and the world; to acquire new information; to respond to the needs and demands of society and the workplace; and for personal fulfillment. Among these texts are fiction and nonfiction, classic and contemporary works.
NCTE 2	Students read a wide range of literature from many periods in many genres to build an understanding of the many dimensions (e.g., philosophical, ethical, aesthetic) of human experience.
NCTE 3	Students apply a wide range of strategies to comprehend, interpret, evaluate, and appreciate texts. They draw on their prior experience, their interactions with other readers and writers, their knowledge of word meaning and of other texts, their word identification strategies, and their understanding of textual features (e.g., sound-letter correspondence, sentence structure, context, graphics).
NCTE 4	Students adjust their use of spoken, written, and visual language (e.g., conventions, style, vocabulary) to communicate effectively with a variety of audiences and for different purposes.
NCTE 5	Students employ a wide range of strategies as they write and use different writing process elements appropriately to communicate with different audiences for a variety of purposes.
NCTE 6	Students apply knowledge of language structure, language conventions (e.g., spelling and punctuation), media techniques, figurative language, and genre to create, critique, and discuss print and nonprint texts.
NCTE 7	Students conduct research on issues and interests by generating ideas and questions, and by posing problems. They gather, evaluate, and synthesize data from a variety of sources (e.g., print and nonprint texts, artifacts, people) to communicate their discoveries in ways that suit their purpose and audience.
NCTE 8	Students use a variety of technological and informational resources (e.g., libraries, databases, computer networks, video) to gather and synthesize information and to create and communicate knowledge.
NCTE 9	Students develop an understanding of and respect for diversity in language use, patterns, and dialects across cultures, ethnic groups, geographic regions, and social roles.
NCTE 10	Students whose first language is not English make use of their first language to develop competency in the English language arts and to develop understanding of content across the curriculum
NCTE 11	Students participate as knowledgeable, reflective, creative, and critical members of a variety of literacy communities.
NCTE 12	Students use spoken, written, and visual language to accomplish their own purposes (e.g., for learning, enjoyment, persuasion, and the exchange of information).

Prepare for Academic Success!

National Math Standards	
National Council of Teachers of Mathematics Standards for Grades 9–12	
You also have opportunities to practice math skills indicated by standards developed by the National Council of Teachers of Mathematics	
Number and Operations	Understand numbers, ways of representing numbers, relationships among numbers, and number systems.
	Understand the meanings of operations and how they relate to one another.
	Compute fluently and make reasonable estimates.
Algebra	Understand patterns, relations, and functions.
	Represent and analyze mathematical situations and structures using algebraic symbols.
	Use mathematical models to represent and understand quantitative relationships.
	Analyze change in various contexts.
Geometry	Analyze characteristics of two- and three-dimensional geometric shapes and develop mathematical arguments about geometric relationships.
	Use visualization, spatial reasoning, and geometric modeling to solve problems.
Measurements	Understand measurable attributes of objects and the units, systems, and processes of measurement.
	Apply appropriate techniques, tools, and formulas to determine measurements.
Data Analysis and Probability	Formulate questions that can be addressed with data and collect, organize, and display relevant data to answer them.
	Select and use appropriate statistical methods to analyze data.
	Develop and evaluate inferences and predictions that are based on data.
	Understand and apply basic concepts of probability.
Problem Solving	Apply and adapt a variety of appropriate strategies to solve problems.
	Solve problems that arise in mathematics and in other contexts.
	Build new mathematical knowledge through problem solving.
	Monitor and reflect on the process of problem solving.
Reasoning and Proof	Recognize reasoning and proof as fundamental aspects of mathematics.
	Make and investigate mathematical conjectures.
	Develop and evaluate mathematical arguments and proofs.
	Select and use various types of reasoning and methods of proof.
Communication	Organize and consolidate their mathematical thinking through communication;
	Communicate their mathematical thinking coherently and clearly to peers, teachers, and others.
	Analyze and evaluate the mathematical thinking and strategies of others.
	Use the language of mathematics to express mathematical ideas precisely.
Connections	Recognize and use connections among mathematical ideas.
	Understand how mathematical ideas interconnect and build on one another to produce a coherent whole.
	Recognize and apply mathematics in contexts outside of mathematics.
Representation	Create and use representations to organize, record, and communicate mathematical ideas.
	Select, apply, and translate among mathematical representations to solve problems.
	Use representations to model and interpret physical, social, and mathematical phenomena.

Prepare for Academic Success!

National Science Standards	
The National Science Educational Standards outline these science skills that you can practice in this text.	
Unifying and Concepts and Processes	Students should develop an understanding of science unifying concepts and processes: systems, order, and organization; evidence, models, and explanation; change, constancy, and measurement; evolution and equilibrium; and form and function.
Content Standard A	Students should develop abilities necessary to do scientific inquiry, understandings about scientific inquiry.
Content Standard B	Students should develop an understanding of the structure of atoms, structure and properties of matter, chemical reactions, motions and forces, conservation of energy and increase in disorder, and interactions of energy and matter.
Content Standard C	Students should develop understanding of the cell; molecular basis of heredity; biological evolution; interdependence of organisms; matter, energy, and organization in living systems; and behavior of organisms.
Content Standard D	Students should develop an understanding of energy in the earth system, geochemical cycles, origin and evolution of the earth system, origin and evolution of the universe.
Content Standard E	Students should develop abilities of technological design, understandings about science and technology.
Content Standard F	Students should develop understanding of personal and community health; population growth; natural resources; environmental quality; natural and human-induced hazards; science and technology in local, national, and global challenges.
Content Standard G	Students should develop understanding of science as a human endeavor, nature of scientific knowledge, historical perspectives.

Reprinted with permission from the National Academy of Sciences, Courtesy of the National Academies Press, Washington, D.C.

National Social Studies Standards	
The National Council for the Social Studies is another organization that provides standards to help guide your studies. Activities in this text relate to these standards.	
I. Culture	
A	Analyze and explain the ways groups, societies, and cultures address human needs and concerns.
B	Predict how data and experiences may be interpreted by people from diverse cultural perspectives and frames of reference.
C	Apply an understanding of culture as an integrated whole that explains the functions and interactions of language, literature, the arts, traditions, beliefs and values, and behavior patterns.
D	Compare and analyze societal patterns for preserving and transmitting culture while adapting to environmental or social change.
E	Demonstrate the value of cultural diversity, as well as cohesion, within and across groups.
F	Interpret patterns of behavior reflecting values and attitudes that contribute or pose obstacles to cross-cultural understanding.
G	Construct reasoned judgments about specific cultural responses to persistent human issues.
H	Explain and apply ideas, theories, and modes of inquiry drawn from anthropology and sociology in the examination of persistent issues and social problems.
II. Time, Continuity, and Change	
A	Demonstrate that historical knowledge and the concept of time are socially influenced constructions that lead historians to be selective in the questions they seek to answer and the evidence they use.
B	Apply key concepts such as time, chronology, causality, change, conflict, and complexity to explain, analyze, and show connections among patterns of historical change and continuity.

Prepare for Academic Success!

C	Identify and describe significant historical periods and patterns of change within and across cultures, such as the development of ancient cultures and civilizations, the rise of nation-states, and social, economic, and political revolutions.
D	Systematically employ processes of critical historical inquiry to reconstruct and reinterpret the past, such as using a variety of sources and checking their credibility, validating and weighing evidence for claims, and searching for causality.
E	Investigate, interpret, and analyze multiple historical and contemporary viewpoints within and across cultures related to important events, recurring dilemmas, and persistent issues, while employing empathy, skepticism, and critical judgment.
F	Apply ideas, theories, and modes of historical inquiry to analyze historical and contemporary developments, and to inform and evaluate actions concerning public policy issues.
III. People, Places, and Environment	
A	Refine mental maps of locales, regions, and the world that demonstrate understanding of relative locations, direction, size, and shape.
B	Create, interpret, use, and synthesize information from various representations of the earth, such as maps, globes, and photographs.
C	Use appropriate resources, data sources, and geographic tools such as aerial photographs, satellite images, geographic information systems (GIS), map projections, and cartography to generate, manipulate, and interpret information such as atlases, databases, grid systems, charts, graphs, and maps.
D	Calculate distance, scale, area, and density, and distinguish spatial distribution patterns.
E	Describe, differentiate, and explain the relationships among various regional and global patterns of geographic phenomena such as landforms, soils, climate, vegetation, natural resources, and population.
F	Use knowledge of physical system changes such as seasons, climate and weather, and the water cycle to explain geographic phenomena.
G	Describe and compare how people create places that reflect culture, human needs, government policy, and current values and ideals as they design and build specialized buildings, neighborhoods, shopping centers, urban centers, industrial parks, and the like.
H	Examine, interpret, and analyze physical and cultural patterns and their interactions, such as land use, settlement patterns, cultural transmission of customs and ideas, and ecosystem changes.
I	Describe and assess ways that historical events have been influenced by, and have influenced, physical and human geographic factors in local, regional, national, and global settings.
J	Analyze and evaluate social and economic effects of environmental changes and crises resulting from phenomena such as floods, storms, and drought.
K	Propose, compare, and evaluate alternative policies for the use of land and other resources in communities, regions, nations, and the world.
IV. Individual Development and Identity	
A	Articulate personal connections to time, place, and social/cultural system.
B	Identify, describe, and express appreciation for the influence of various historical and contemporary cultures on an individual's daily life.
C	Describe the ways family, religion, gender, ethnicity, nationality, socioeconomic status, and other group and cultural influences contribute to the development of a sense of self.
D	Apply concepts, methods, and theories about the study of human growth and development, such as physical endowment, learning, motivation, behavior, perception, and personality.
E	Examine the interaction of ethnic, national, or cultural influences in specific situations or events.
F	Analyze the role of perceptions, attitudes, values, and beliefs in the development of personal identity.
G	Compare and evaluate the impact of stereotyping, conformity, acts of altruism, and other behaviors on individuals and groups.
H	Work independently and cooperatively within groups and institutions to accomplish goals.
I	Examine factors that contribute to and damage one's mental health and analyze issues related to mental health and behavioral disorders in contemporary society.

Prepare for Academic Success!

V. Individuals, Groups, and Institutions	
A	Apply concepts such as role, status, and social class in describing the connections and interactions of individuals, groups, and institutions in society.
B	Analyze group and institutional influences on people, events, and elements of culture in both historical and contemporary settings.
C	Describe the various forms institutions take, and explain how they develop and change over time.
D	Identify and analyze examples of tensions between expressions of individuality and efforts used to promote social conformity by groups and institutions.
E	Describe and examine belief systems basic to specific traditions and laws in contemporary and historical movements.
F	Evaluate the role of institutions in furthering both continuity and change.
G	Analyze the extent to which groups and institutions meet individual needs and promote the common good in contemporary and historical settings.
H	Explain and apply ideas and modes of inquiry drawn from behavioral science and social theory in the examination of persistent issues and social problems.
VI. Power, Authority, and Governance	
A	Examine persistent issues involving the rights, roles, and status of the individual in relation to the general welfare.
B	Explain the purpose of government and analyze how its powers are acquired, used, and justified.
C	Analyze and explain ideas and mechanisms to meet needs and wants of citizens, regulate territory, manage conflict, establish order and security, and balance competing conceptions of a just society.
D	Compare and analyze the ways nations and organizations respond to conflicts between forces of unity and forces of diversity.
E	Compare different political systems (their ideologies, structure, institutions, processes, and political cultures) with that of the United States, and identify representative political leaders from selected historical and contemporary settings.
F	Analyze and evaluate conditions, actions, and motivations that contribute to conflict and cooperation within and among nations.
G	Evaluate the role of technology in communications, transportation, information-processing, weapons development, or other areas as it contributes to or helps resolve conflicts.
H	Explain and apply ideas, theories, and modes of inquiry drawn from political science to the examination of persistent ideas and social problems.
I	Evaluate the extent to which governments achieve their stated ideals and policies at home and abroad.
J	Prepare a public policy paper and present and defend it before an appropriate forum in school or community.
VII. Production, Distribution, and Consumption	
A	Explain how the scarcity of productive resources (human, capital, technological, and natural) requires the development of economic systems to make decisions about how goods and services are to be produced and distributed.
B	Analyze the role that supply and demand, prices, incentives, and profits play in determining what is produced and distributed in a competitive market system.
C	Consider the costs and benefits to society of allocating goods and services through private and public sectors.
D	Describe the relationships among the various economic institutions that comprise economic systems such as households, business firms, banks, government agencies, labor unions, and corporations.
E	Analyze the role of specialization and exchange in economic processes.
F	Compare how values and beliefs influence economic decisions in different societies.
G	Compare basic economic systems according to how rules and procedures deal with demand, supply, prices, the role of government, banks, labor and labor unions, savings and investments, and capital.
H	Apply economic concepts and reasoning when evaluating historical and contemporary social developments and issues.
I	Distinguish between the domestic and global economic systems, and explain how the two interact.

J	Apply knowledge of production, distribution, and consumption in the analysis of a public issue such as the allocation of health care or the consumption of energy, and devise an economic plan for accomplishing a socially desirable outcome related to that issue.
K	Distinguish between economics as a field of inquiry and the economy.
VIII. Science, Technology, and Society	
A	Identify and describe both current and historical examples of the interaction and interdependence of science, technology, and society in a variety of cultural settings.
B	Make judgments about how science and technology have transformed the physical world and human society and our understanding of time, space, place, and human-environment interactions.
C	Analyze how science and technology influence the core values, beliefs, and attitudes of society, and how core values, beliefs, and attitudes of society shape scientific and technological change.
D	Evaluate various policies that have been proposed as ways of dealing with social changes resulting from new technologies, such as genetically engineered plants and animals.
E	Recognize and interpret varied perspectives about human societies and the physical world using scientific knowledge, ethical standards, and technologies from diverse world cultures.
F	Formulate strategies and develop policies for influencing public discussions associated with technology-society issues, such as the greenhouse effect.
IX. Global Connections	
A	Explain how language, art, music, belief systems, and other cultural elements can facilitate global understanding or cause misunderstanding.
B	Explain conditions and motivations that contribute to conflict, cooperation, and interdependence among groups, societies, and nations.
C	Analyze and evaluate the effects of changing technologies on the global community.
D	Analyze the causes, consequences, and possible solutions to persistent, contemporary, and emerging global issues, such as health, security, resource allocation, economic development, and environmental quality.
E	Analyze the relationships and tensions between national sovereignty and global interests, in such matters as territory, economic development, nuclear and other weapons, use of natural resources, and human rights concerns.
F	Analyze or formulate policy statements demonstrating an understanding of concerns, standards, issues, and conflicts related to universal human rights.
G	Describe and evaluate the role of international and multinational organizations in the global arena.
H	llustrate how individual behaviors and decisions connect with global systems.
X. Civic Ideals and Practices	
A	Explain the origins and interpret the continuing influence of key ideals of the democratic republican form of government, such as individual human dignity, liberty, justice, equality, and the rule of law.
B	Identify, analyze, interpret, and evaluate sources and examples of citizens' rights and responsibilities.
C	Locate, access, analyze, organize, synthesize, evaluate, and apply information about selected public issues—identifying, describing, and evaluating multiple points of view.
D	Practice forms of civic discussion and participation consistent with the ideals of citizens in a democratic republic.
E	Analyze and evaluate the influence of various forms of citizen action on public policy.
F	Analyze a variety of public policies and issues from the perspective of formal and informal political actors.
G	Evaluate the effectiveness of public opinion in influencing and shaping public policy developments and decision making.
H	Evaluate the degree to which public policies and citizen behaviors reflect or foster the stated ideals of a democratic republican form of government.
I	Construct a policy statement to achieve one or more goals related to an issue of public concern.
J	Participate in activities to strengthen the "common good," based upon careful evaluation of possible options for citizen action.

National Council for the Social Studies, *Expectations of Excellence: Curriculum Standards for Social Studies (Washington, D.C.: NCSS, 1994).*

Prepare for Academic Success!

Business and Economics Standards

The features and assessments in *Business and Personal Finance* provide many opportunities to strengthen your knowledge of finance concepts with integrated economic content.

National Business Education Association Economic Standards	
NBEA I	**Allocation of Resources Achievement Standard** Assess opportunity costs and trade-offs involved in making choices about how to use scarce economic resources.
NBEA II	**Economic Systems Achievement Standard** Explain why societies develop economic systems, identify the basic features of different economic systems, and analyze the major features of the U.S. economic system.
NBEA III	**Economic Institutions and Incentives Achievement Standard** Analyze the role of core economic institutions and incentives in the U.S. economy.
NBEA IV	**Markets and Prices Achievement Standard** Analyze the role of markets and prices in the U.S. economy.
NBEA V	**Market Structures Achievement Standard** Analyze the different types of market structures and the effect they have on the price and the quality of the goods and services produced.
NBEA VI	**Productivity Achievement Standard** Explain the importance of productivity and analyze how specialization, division of labor, investment in physical and human capital, and technological change affect productivity and global trade.
NBEA VII	**The Role of Government Achievement Standard** Analyze the role of government in economic systems, especially the role of government in the U.S. economy.
NBEA VIII	**Global Economic Concepts Achievement Standard** Examine the role of trade, protectionism, and monetary markets in the global economy.
NBEA IX	**Aggregate Supply and Aggregate Demand Achievement Standard** Analyze how the U.S. economy functions as a whole and describe selected macroeconomic measures of economic activity.
National Business Education Association Personal Finance Standards	
NBEA I	**Personal Decision Making** Use a rational decision-making process as it applies to the roles of citizens, workers, and consumers.
NBEA II	**Earning a Living** Identify various forms of income and analyze factors that affect income as a part of the career decision-making process.
NBEA III	**Managing Finances and Budgeting** Develop and evaluate a spending/savings plan.
NBEA IV	Saving and Investing Evaluate savings and investment options to meet short- and long-term goals.
NBEA V	**Buying Goods and Services** Apply a decision-making model to maximize consumer satisfaction when buying goods and services.
NBEA VI	**Banking** Evaluate services provided by financial deposit institutions to transfer funds.
NBEA VII	**Using Credit** Analyze factors that affect the choice of credit, the cost of credit, and the legal aspects of using credit.
NBEA VIII	**Protecting Against Risk** Analyze choices available to consumers for protection against risk and financial loss.

Council for Economic Education (CEE) Standards	
Scarcity	Productive resources are limited. Therefore, people cannot have all the goods and services they want; as a result, they must choose some things and give up others.
Marginal Cost/ Benefit	Effective decision making requires comparing the additional costs of alternatives with the additional benefits. Most choices involve doing a little more or a little less of something: few choices are "all or nothing" decisions.
Allocation of Goods and Services	Different methods can be used to allocate goods and services. People acting individually or collectively through government, must choose which methods to use to allocate different kinds of goods and services.

Prepare for Academic Success!

Role of Incentives	People respond predictably to positive and negative incentives.
Gain from Trade	Voluntary exchange occurs only when all participating parties expect to gain. This is true for trade among individuals or organizations within a nation, and among individuals or organizations in different nations.
Specialization and Trade	When individuals, regions, and nations specialize in what they can produce at the lowest cost and then trade with others, both production and consumption increase.
Markets – Price and Quantity Determination	Markets exist when buyers and sellers interact. This interaction determines market prices and thereby allocates scarce goods and services.
Role of Price in Market System	Prices send signals and provide incentives to buyers and sellers. When supply or demand changes, market prices adjust, affecting incentives.
Role of Competition	Competition among sellers lowers costs and prices, and encourages producers to produce more of what consumers are willing and able to buy. Competition among buyers increases prices and allocates goods and services to those people who are willing and able to pay the most for them.
Role of Economic Institutions	Institutions evolve in market economies to help individuals and groups accomplish their goals. Banks, labor unions, corporations, legal systems, and not-for-profit organizations are examples of important institutions. A different kind of institution, clearly defined and enforced property rights, is essential to a market economy.
Role of Money	Money makes it easier to trade, borrow, save, invest, and compare the value of goods and services.
Role of Interest Rates	Interest rates, adjusted for inflation, rise and fall to balance the amount saved with the amount borrowed, which affects the allocation of scarce resources between present and future uses.
Role of Resources in Determining Income	Income for most people is determined by the market value of the productive resources they sell. What workers earn depends, primarily, on the market value of what they produce and how productive they are.
Profit and the Entrepreneur	Entrepreneurs are people who take the risks of organizing productive resources to make goods and services. Profit is an important incentive that leads entrepreneurs to accept the risks of business failure.
Growth	Investment in factories, machinery, new technology, and in the health, education, and training of people can raise future standards of living.
Role of Government	There is an economic role for government in a market economy whenever the benefits of a government policy outweigh its costs. Governments often provide for national defense, address environmental concerns, define and protect property rights, and attempt to make markets more competitive. Most government policies also redistribute income.
Using Cost/ Benefit Analysis to Evaluate Government Programs	Costs of government policies sometimes exceed benefits. This may occur because of incentives facing voters, government officials, and government employees, because of actions by special interest groups that can impose costs on the general public, or because social goals other than economic efficiency are being pursued.
Macroeconomy- Income/ Employment, Prices	A nation's overall levels of income, employment, and prices are determined by the interaction of spending and production decisions made by all households, firms, government agencies, and others in the economy.
Unemployment and Inflation	Unemployment imposes costs on individuals and nations. Unexpected inflation imposes costs on many people and benefits some others because it arbitrarily redistributes purchasing power. Inflation can reduce the rate of growth of national living standards because individuals and organizations use resources to protect themselves against the uncertainty of future prices.
Monetary and Fiscal Policy	Federal government budgetary policy and the Federal Reserve System's monetary policy influence the overall levels of employment, output, and prices.

Begin the Unit

Discover the World of Business and Personal Finance

Successful readers first set a purpose for reading. *Business and Personal Finance* teaches you the skills you will need to make plans for your future. Think about why you are reading this book. Consider how you might be able to use what you learn as you plan for your future both at home and at work.

In Your World Prepare for college and the real world by considering how unit topics relate to your own experiences. Understanding how you can use these topics in your own life can help you prepare for your future.

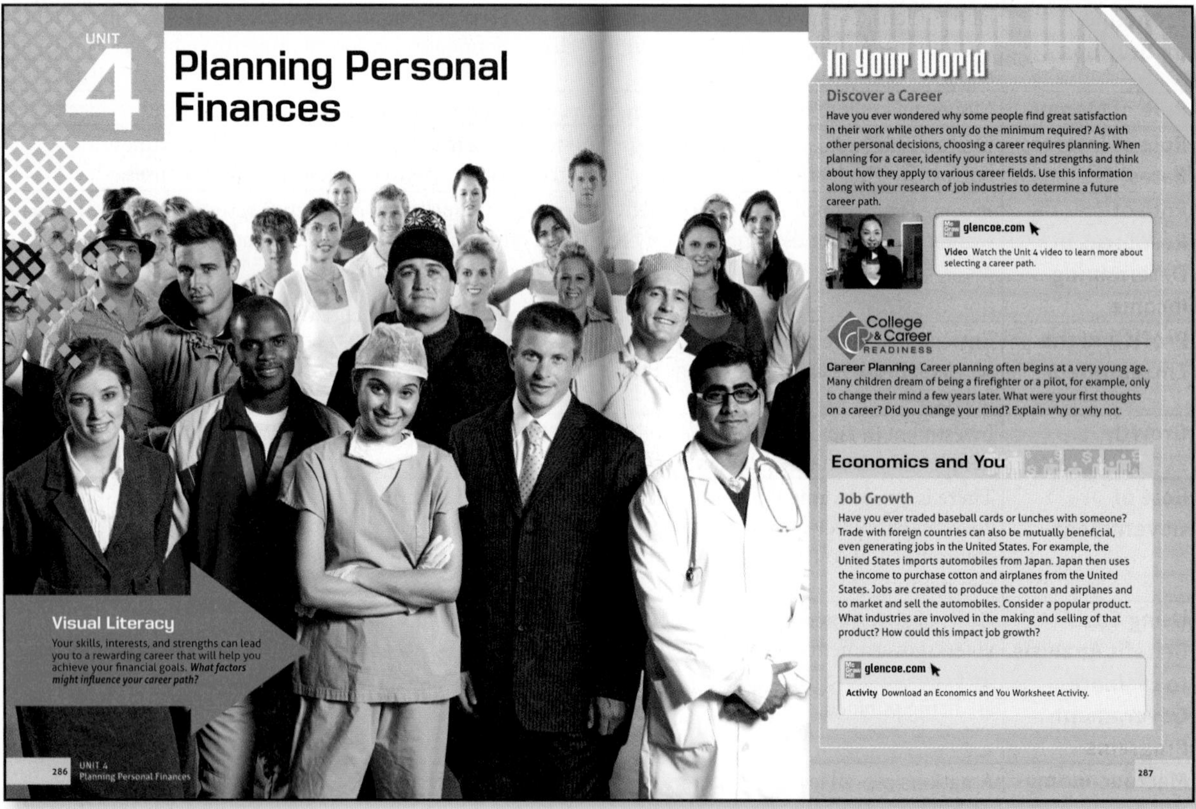

UNIT 4

Planning Personal Finances

In Your World

Discover a Career

Have you ever wondered why some people find great satisfaction in their work while others only do the minimum required? As with other personal decisions, choosing a career requires planning. When planning for a career, identify your interests and strengths and think about how they apply to various career fields. Use this information along with your research of job industries to determine a future career path.

glencoe.com

Video Watch the Unit 4 video to learn more about selecting a career path.

College & Career READINESS

Career Planning Career planning often begins at a very young age. Many children dream of being a firefighter or a pilot, for example, only to change their mind a few years later. What were your first thoughts on a career? Did you change your mind? Explain why or why not.

Economics and You

Job Growth

Have you ever traded baseball cards or lunches with someone? Trade with foreign countries can also be mutually beneficial, even generating jobs in the United States. For example, the United States imports automobiles from Japan. Japan then uses the income to purchase cotton and airplanes from the United States. Jobs are created to produce the cotton and airplanes and to market and sell the automobiles. Consider a popular product. What industries are involved in the making and selling of that product? How could this impact job growth?

glencoe.com

Activity Download an Economics and You Worksheet Activity.

Visual Literacy

Your skills, interests, and strengths can lead you to a rewarding career that will help you achieve your financial goals. ***What factors might influence your career path?***

286 UNIT 4 Planning Personal Finances

287

Visual Literacy Use the photo to predict what the unit will be about. Answer the question to help you prepare for learning new finance concepts.

Economics and You Understand the financial skills that will be featured in the unit by answering the questions in this unit feature.

glencoe.com Use online resources such as videos and worksheets to help you better understand the unit information.

To the Student

Begin the Chapter

What Is the Chapter All About?

Use the information in the chapter opener to help you prepare to learn about chapter topics and connect what you already know to the information you will find. Use the reading guide at the beginning of each section to preview what you will learn in the section.

Discovery Project Use your skills to create a project that previews topics you will learn in the chapter.

The Big Idea Know the main idea of each chapter to help you better understand what you will read.

Standard & Poors Improve your writing by expanding on the Standard & Poor's question and answer in each chapter.

The Essential Question Before you read provides you with a question that will provide a personal connection to the chapter content and lead to other questions and inquiry.

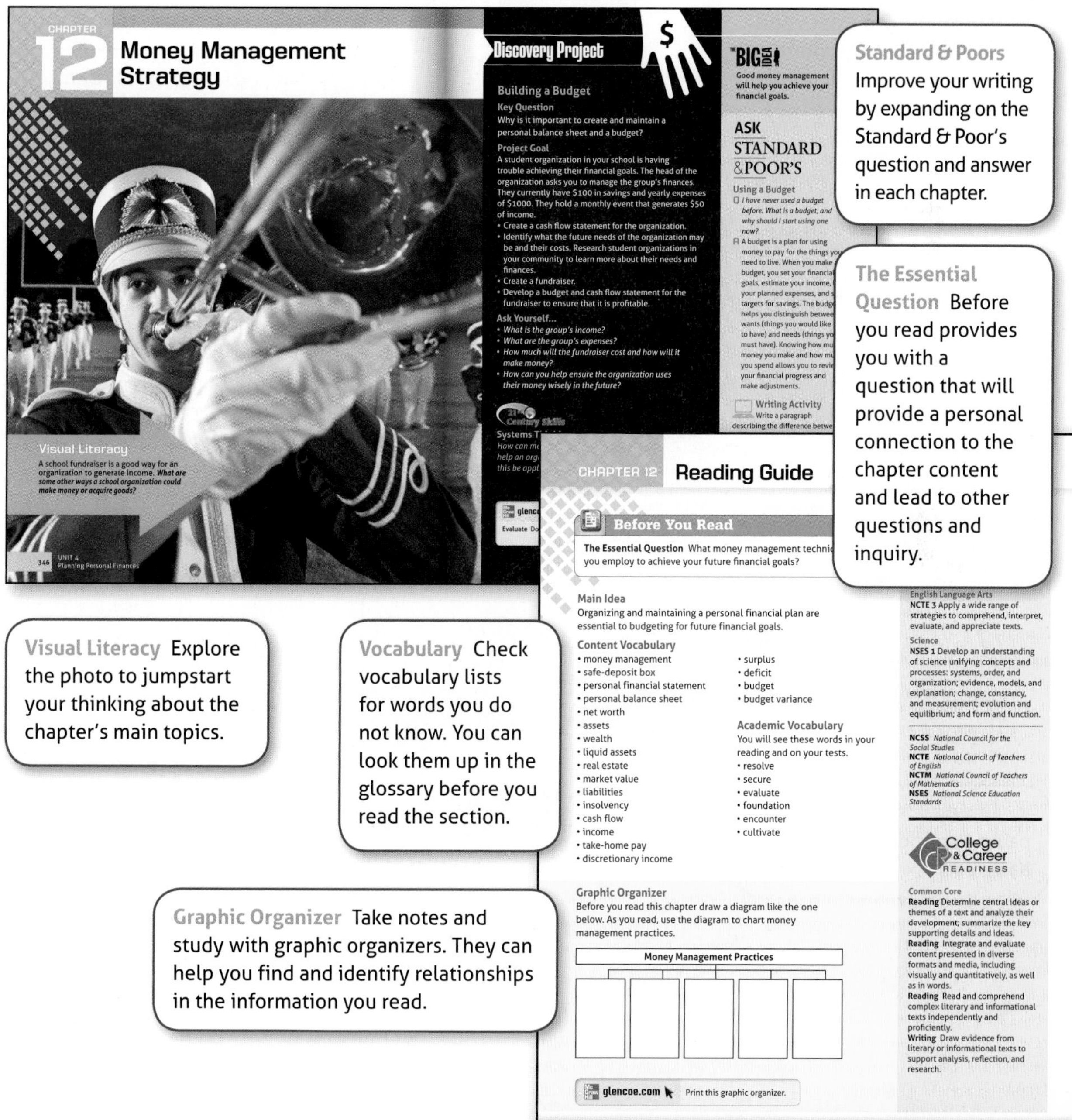

CHAPTER 12 Money Management Strategy

Visual Literacy
A school fundraiser is a good way for an organization to generate income. *What are some other ways a school organization could make money or acquire goods?*

346 UNIT 4 Planning Personal Finances

Discovery Project

Building a Budget

Key Question
Why is it important to create and maintain a personal balance sheet and a budget?

Project Goal
A student organization in your school is having trouble achieving their financial goals. The head of the organization asks you to manage the group's finances. They currently have $100 in savings and yearly expenses of $1000. They hold a monthly event that generates $50 of income.
- Create a cash flow statement for the organization.
- Identify what the future needs of the organization may be and their costs. Research student organizations in your community to learn more about their needs and finances.
- Create a fundraiser.
- Develop a budget and cash flow statement for the fundraiser to ensure that it is profitable.

Ask Yourself...
- *What is the group's income?*
- *What are the group's expenses?*
- *How much will the fundraiser cost and how will it make money?*
- *How can you help ensure the organization uses their money wisely in the future?*

21st Century Skills
Systems T...

BIG IDEA
Good money management will help you achieve your financial goals.

ASK STANDARD & POOR'S

Using a Budget
Q *I have never used a budget before. What is a budget, and why should I start using one now?*
A A budget is a plan for using money to pay for the things you need to live. When you make a budget, you set your financial goals, estimate your income, your planned expenses, and s... targets for savings. The budg... helps you distinguish betwee... wants (things you would like to have) and needs (things yo... must have). Knowing how mu... money you make and how mu... you spend allows you to revie... your financial progress and make adjustments.

Writing Activity
Write a paragraph describing the difference betwe...

CHAPTER 12 Reading Guide

Before You Read

The Essential Question What money management techni... you employ to achieve your future financial goals?

Main Idea
Organizing and maintaining a personal financial plan are essential to budgeting for future financial goals.

Content Vocabulary
- money management
- safe-deposit box
- personal financial statement
- personal balance sheet
- net worth
- assets
- wealth
- liquid assets
- real estate
- market value
- liabilities
- insolvency
- cash flow
- income
- take-home pay
- discretionary income
- surplus
- deficit
- budget
- budget variance

Academic Vocabulary
You will see these words in your reading and on your tests.
- resolve
- secure
- evaluate
- foundation
- encounter
- cultivate

Graphic Organizer
Before you read this chapter draw a diagram like the one below. As you read, use the diagram to chart money management practices.

Money Management Practices

glencoe.com Print this graphic organizer.

English Language Arts
NCTE 3 Apply a wide range of strategies to comprehend, interpret, evaluate, and appreciate texts.
Science
NSES 1 Develop an understanding of science unifying concepts and processes: systems, order, and organization; evidence, models, and explanation; change, constancy, and measurement; evolution and equilibrium; and form and function.

NCSS *National Council for the Social Studies*
NCTE *National Council of Teachers of English*
NCTM *National Council of Teachers of Mathematics*
NSES *National Science Education Standards*

College & Career READINESS

Common Core
Reading Determine central ideas or themes of a text and analyze their development; summarize the key supporting details and ideas.
Reading Integrate and evaluate content presented in diverse formats and media, including visually and quantitatively, as well as in words.
Reading Read and comprehend complex literary and informational texts independently and proficiently.
Writing Draw evidence from literary or informational texts to support analysis, reflection, and research.

348 UNIT 4 Planning Personal Finances

Visual Literacy Explore the photo to jumpstart your thinking about the chapter's main topics.

Vocabulary Check vocabulary lists for words you do not know. You can look them up in the glossary before you read the section.

Graphic Organizer Take notes and study with graphic organizers. They can help you find and identify relationships in the information you read.

Begin the Section

Prepare with Reading Guides and Study Tools

In addition to the reading guide at the beginning of each chapter, each section contains many reading strategies that can help you comprehend the text. See if you can predict the information and skills you will learn in the section by using clues and information that you already know.

SECTION 1 Organizing Financial Records

Opportunity Costs and Money Management

How do you decide when to spend money?

Your daily spending and saving decisions are at the center of financial planning. Each decision you make involves a choice or a trade-off. You choose one thing and reject another. If you decide to go to the movies instead of working on your science fair project, you make a choice. Every decision you make between two or more possibilities has an opportunity cost. Decisions about money management involve making numerous trade-offs.

Money management is the day-to-day financial activities necessary to get the most from your money. In order to manage your money wisely, you have to consider many financial trade-offs. Good money management can help you keep track of where your money goes so you can make it go farther. You need to consider whether to spend your paycheck on entertainment or to deposit some of it where it can contribute to your long-term financial security. If you spend the money now, you do not have the opportunity to earn interest on your money.

When buying a cell phone, should you shop around for a better price or is that a waste of time? You may be able to save some money by checking prices at other stores, but you would also use something you can never replace—your time. Trade-offs are difficult to **resolve** or reach a decision about, because you may like both options.

How can you be sure to make the right decisions when you are faced with tough opportunity costs? You may never be sure, but you can become a better judge of your options. Consider how those options fit your values, your current financial situation, and your goal of effective money management.

By considering your values, your goals, and the state of your bank account, you can make better spending decisions. For example, if your goal is to save as much money as you can for college, then you might borrow a book from the library rather than buy it from a bookstore. On the other hand, if your goal is to put aside only a certain amount of your paycheck each month, you might be able to buy the book with the money you have left.

Reading Check

Relate How is managing opportunity costs, or trade-offs, important to effective money management?

Section Objectives

- **Discuss** the relationship between opportunity costs and money management.
- **Explain** the benefits of keeping financial records and documents.
- **Describe** a system to maintain personal financial documents.

As You Read

Relate Have you ever been in a situation where you asked yourself, "Where did my money go?"

Chapter 12 Money Management Strategy 349

Headings Skim the headings to help identify the main idea and supporting details.

Section Objectives Preview section topics before you read to help you understand important concepts.

As You Read Relate concepts to your experiences as you read through each section by considering the answer to the question.

Reading Checks These let you pause to respond to what you have read.

To the Student

Review the Section

Check Your Understanding with Self-Assessments

After you read, use the self-assessment at the end of the section to check your understanding. Make sure that you can answer the questions in your own words before moving on in the text.

Review Key Concepts Confirm your understanding of key concepts and skills found in the section.

Critical Thinking Use critical thinking to stretch your knowledge of section concepts further.

Academic and 21st Century Skills These cross-curricular activities will help you build your skills as you learn about business and personal finance.

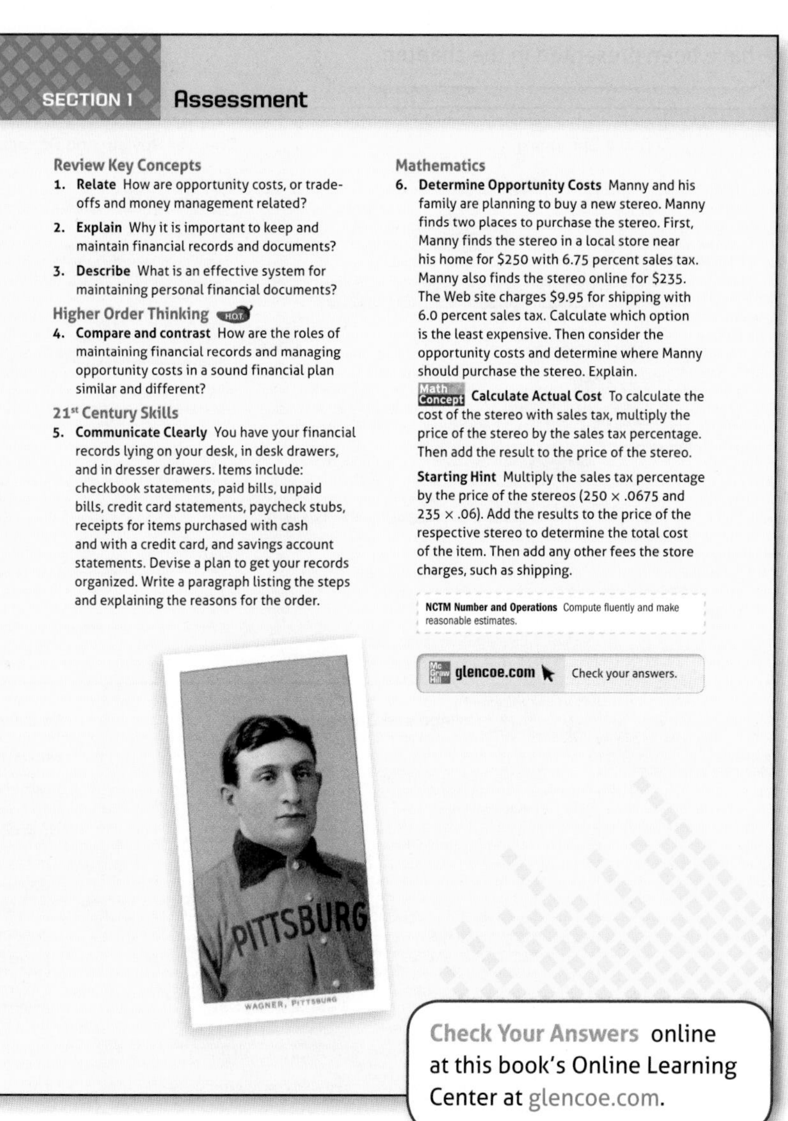

SECTION 1 **Assessment**

Review Key Concepts

1. **Relate** How are opportunity costs, or trade-offs and money management related?
2. **Explain** Why it is important to keep and maintain financial records and documents?
3. **Describe** What is an effective system for maintaining personal financial documents?

Higher Order Thinking HOT

4. **Compare and contrast** How are the roles of maintaining financial records and managing opportunity costs in a sound financial plan similar and different?

21st Century Skills

5. **Communicate Clearly** You have your financial records lying on your desk, in desk drawers, and in dresser drawers. Items include: checkbook statements, paid bills, unpaid bills, credit card statements, paycheck stubs, receipts for items purchased with cash and with a credit card, and savings account statements. Devise a plan to get your records organized. Write a paragraph listing the steps and explaining the reasons for the order.

Mathematics

6. **Determine Opportunity Costs** Manny and his family are planning to buy a new stereo. Manny finds two places to purchase the stereo. First, Manny finds the stereo in a local store near his home for $250 with 6.75 percent sales tax. Manny also finds the stereo online for $235. The Web site charges $9.95 for shipping with 6.0 percent sales tax. Calculate which option is the least expensive. Then consider the opportunity costs and determine where Manny should purchase the stereo. Explain.

Math Concept **Calculate Actual Cost** To calculate the cost of the stereo with sales tax, multiply the price of the stereo by the sales tax percentage. Then add the result to the price of the stereo.

Starting Hint Multiply the sales tax percentage by the price of the stereos (250 × .0675 and 235 × .06). Add the results to the price of the respective stereo to determine the total cost of the item. Then add any other fees the store charges, such as shipping.

NCTM Number and Operations Compute fluently and make reasonable estimates.

glencoe.com Check your answers.

Check Your Answers online at this book's Online Learning Center at glencoe.com.

Review the Chapter

Know and Understand the Chapter Concepts

Review what you learned in the chapter and see how this learning applies to your other subjects and real-world situations.

Visual Summary See the concepts that have been presented in the chapter.

Vocabulary Review Check your recall of important ideas and terms.

Critical Thinking These questions take your knowledge of the chapter further. If you have trouble answering these questions, reread the related parts of the chapter.

Your Financial Portfolio Consider real-world situations with business and personal financial scenarios.

Academics and 21st Century Skills These activities connect what you have learned to other classes and in the real world.

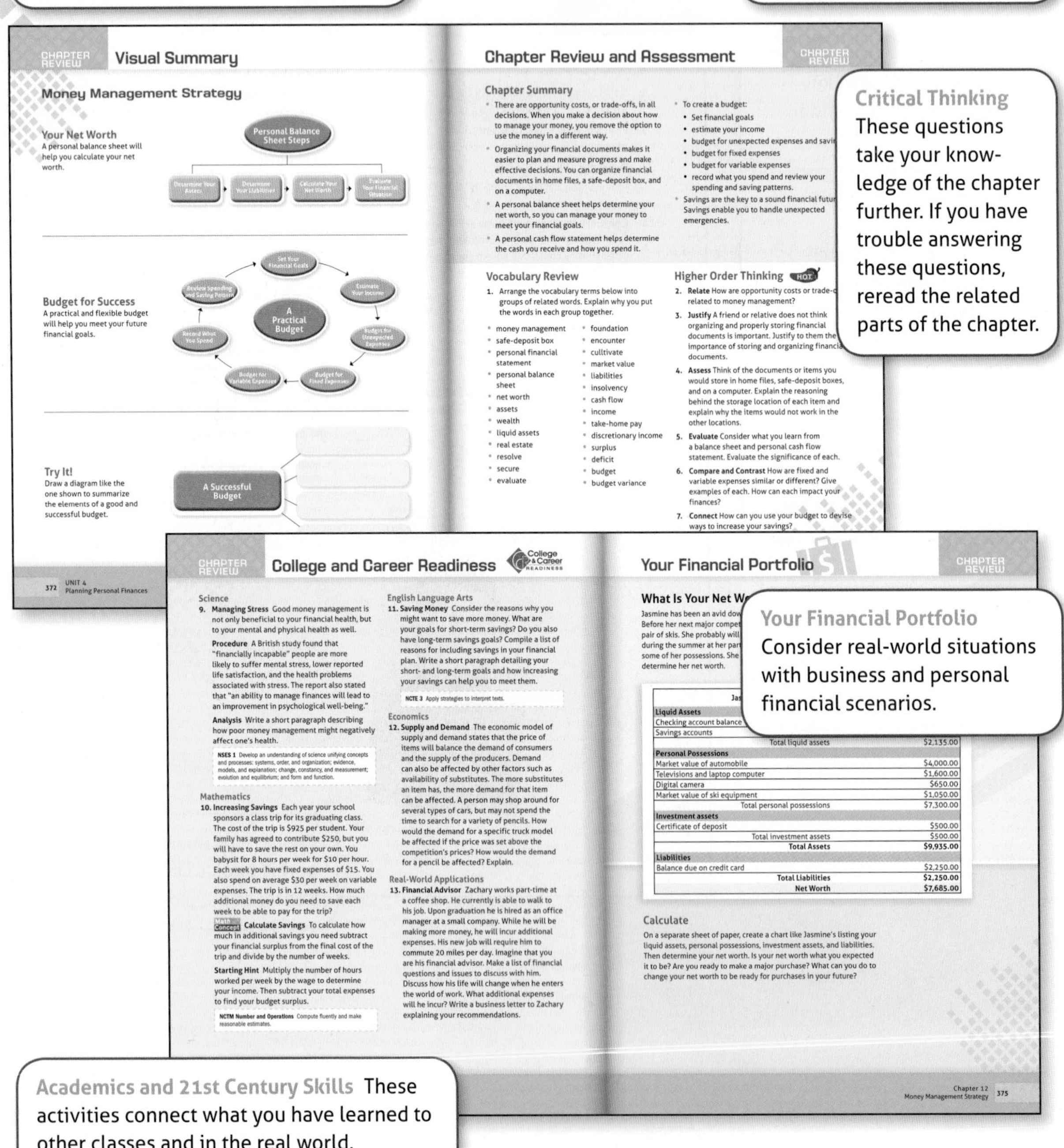

Close the Unit

What Have You Learned About Business and Personal Finance?

Every unit ends with a project that lets you apply an important skill from the unit. To complete each project, you will perform research, plan your project, connect with your community, create a presentation, and share what you have learned.

Project Objective Ask yourself the questions to determine what you will need to do for the project.

Project Checklist Make sure that you have done everything you need to complete your project.

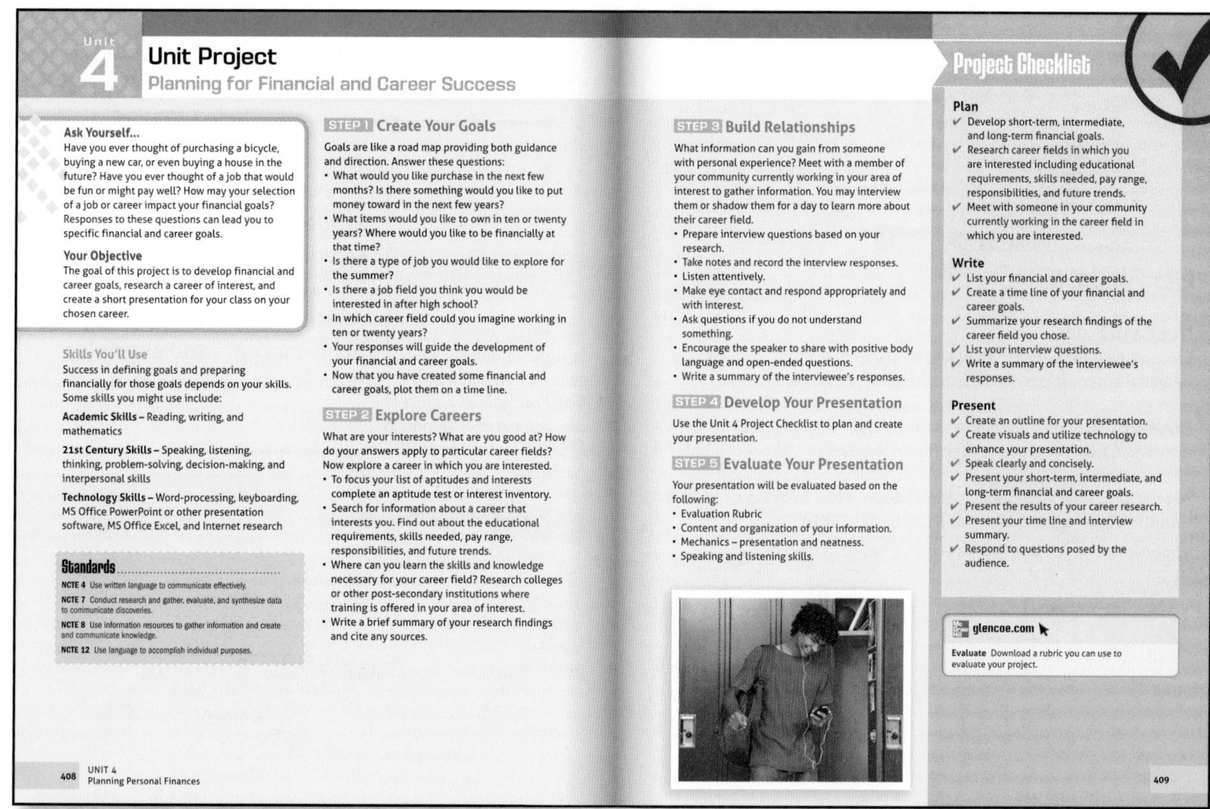

Unit 4

Unit Project

Planning for Financial and Career Success

Ask Yourself...
Have you ever thought of purchasing a bicycle, buying a new car, or even buying a house in the future? Have you ever thought of a job that would be fun or might pay well? How may your selection of a job or career impact your financial goals? Responses to these questions can lead you to specific financial and career goals.

Your Objective
The goal of this project is to develop financial and career goals, research a career of interest, and create a short presentation for your class on your chosen career.

Skills You'll Use
Success in defining goals and preparing financially for those goals depends on your skills. Some skills you might use include:

Academic Skills – Reading, writing, and mathematics

21st Century Skills – Speaking, listening, thinking, problem-solving, decision-making, and interpersonal skills

Technology Skills – Word-processing, keyboarding, MS Office PowerPoint or other presentation software, MS Office Excel, and Internet research

Standards

NCTE 4 Use written language to communicate effectively.

NCTE 7 Conduct research and gather, evaluate, and synthesize data to communicate discoveries.

NCTE 8 Use information resources to gather information and create and communicate knowledge.

NCTE 12 Use language to accomplish individual purposes.

STEP 1 Create Your Goals

Goals are like a road map providing both guidance and direction. Answer these questions:
- What would you like purchase in the next few months? Is there something would you like to put money toward in the next few years?
- What items would you like to own in ten or twenty years? Where would you like to be financially at that time?
- Is there a type of job you would like to explore for the summer?
- Is there a job field you think you would be interested in after high school?
- In which career field could you imagine working in ten or twenty years?
- Your responses will guide the development of your financial and career goals.
- Now that you have created some financial and career goals, plot them on a time line.

STEP 2 Explore Careers

What are your interests? What are you good at? How do your answers apply to particular career fields? Now explore a career in which you are interested.
- To focus your list of aptitudes and interests complete an aptitude test or interest inventory.
- Search for information about a career that interests you. Find out about the educational requirements, skills needed, pay range, responsibilities, and future trends.
- Where can you learn the skills and knowledge necessary for your career field? Research colleges or other post-secondary institutions where training is offered in your area of interest.
- Write a brief summary of your research findings and cite any sources.

408 UNIT 4 Planning Personal Finances

STEP 3 Build Relationships

What information can you gain from someone with personal experience? Meet with a member of your community currently working in your area of interest to gather information. You may interview them or shadow them for a day to learn more about their career field.
- Prepare interview questions based on your research.
- Take notes and record the interview responses.
- Listen attentively.
- Make eye contact and respond appropriately and with interest.
- Ask questions if you do not understand something.
- Encourage the speaker to share with positive body language and open-ended questions.
- Write a summary of the interviewee's responses.

STEP 4 Develop Your Presentation

Use the Unit 4 Project Checklist to plan and create your presentation.

STEP 5 Evaluate Your Presentation

Your presentation will be evaluated based on the following:
- Evaluation Rubric
- Content and organization of your information.
- Mechanics – presentation and neatness.
- Speaking and listening skills.

Project Checklist

Plan
- ✔ Develop short-term, intermediate, and long-term financial goals.
- ✔ Research career fields in which you are interested including educational requirements, skills needed, pay range, responsibilities, and future trends.
- ✔ Meet with someone in your community currently working in the career field in which you are interested.

Write
- ✔ List your financial and career goals.
- ✔ Create a time line of your financial and career goals.
- ✔ Summarize your research findings of the career field you chose.
- ✔ List your interview questions.
- ✔ Write a summary of the interviewee's responses.

Present
- ✔ Create an outline for your presentation.
- ✔ Create visuals and utilize technology to enhance your presentation.
- ✔ Speak clearly and concisely.
- ✔ Present your short-term, intermediate, and long-term financial and career goals.
- ✔ Present the results of your career research.
- ✔ Present your time line and interview summary.
- ✔ Respond to questions posed by the audience.

glencoe.com

Evaluate Download a rubric you can use to evaluate your project.

409

Apply the Academic, 21st Century, and Technology Skills Learn about the skills that will be used as the basis of the project.

Evaluation Rubric A rubric is a scoring tool that lists the project criteria. You can find an evaluation rubric for each project at this book's Online Learning Center at glencoe.com .

To the Student

Study with Features

Skills You Can Use at School, at Home, and in the Workplace

As you read, look for feature boxes throughout each chapter. These features build academic skills and critical thinking skills that relate to real-world finance topics to prepare you for the workplace.

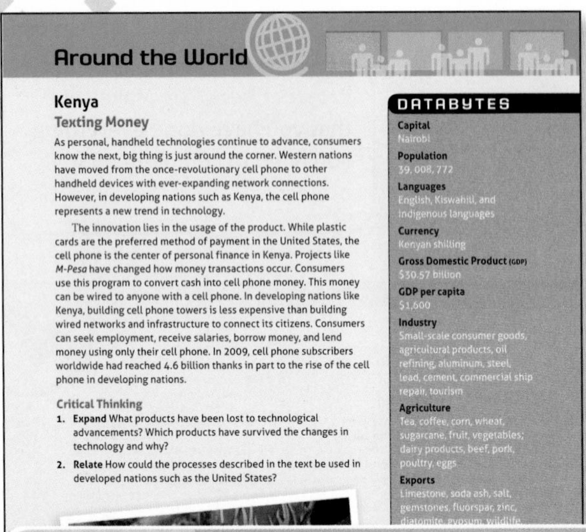

Around the World

Kenya

Texting Money

As personal, handheld technologies continue to advance, consumers know the next, big thing is just around the corner. Western nations have moved from the once-revolutionary cell phone to other handheld devices with ever-expanding network connections. However, in developing nations such as Kenya, the cell phone represents a new trend in technology.

The innovation lies in the usage of the product. While plastic cards are the preferred method of payment in the United States, the cell phone is the center of personal finance in Kenya. Projects like *M-Pesa* have changed how money transactions occur. Consumers use this program to convert cash into cell phone money. This money can be wired to anyone with a cell phone. In developing nations like Kenya, building cell phone towers is less expensive than building wired networks and infrastructure to connect its citizens. Consumers can seek employment, receive salaries, borrow money, and lend money using only their cell phone. In 2009, cell phone subscribers worldwide had reached 4.6 billion thanks in part to the rise of the cell phone in developing nations.

Critical Thinking

1. **Expand** What products have been lost to technological advancements? Which products have survived the changes in technology and why?
2. **Relate** How could the processes described in the text be used in developed nations such as the United States?

DATABYTES

Capital
Nairobi

Population
39,008,772

Languages
English, Kiswahili, and indigenous languages

Currency
Kenyan shilling

Gross Domestic Product (GDP)
$30.57 billion

GDP per capita
$1,600

Industry
Small-scale consumer goods, agricultural products, oil refining, aluminum, steel, lead, cement, commercial ship repair, tourism

Agriculture
Tea, coffee, corn, wheat, sugarcane, fruit, vegetables; dairy products, beef, pork, poultry, eggs

Exports
Limestone, soda ash, salt, gemstones, fluorspar, zinc, diatomite, gypsum, wildlife,

Around the World Have you ever wondered what financial systems are like in other countries? In this feature, you will discover information about a country's exports, economy, and fast facts about its financial systems. You will also use this information to answer critical thinking questions.

GO FIGURE Mathematics

Net Cash Flow

Calculating your net cash flow will help you determine your current financial status. It is a quick assessment of your income and expenses.

EXAMPLE Calculate your net cash flow if your total income for the month is $1,675 and your expenses are $1,425.

Formula	Income –	Expenses	=	Net Cash Flow
Application	$1,675 –	$1,425	=	$250
Solution	You have a positive net cash flow of $250.			

Your Turn

You work 12 hours a week, weeks a month, at a part-ti job after school at a grocer store. You earn $8 an hour. pay $60 a month for gas, $80 a car payment, and $52 a month

Go Figure You can use your academic skills to solve math, science, English language, and social studies problems related to financial topics. Main concepts and examples help you work through the answers.

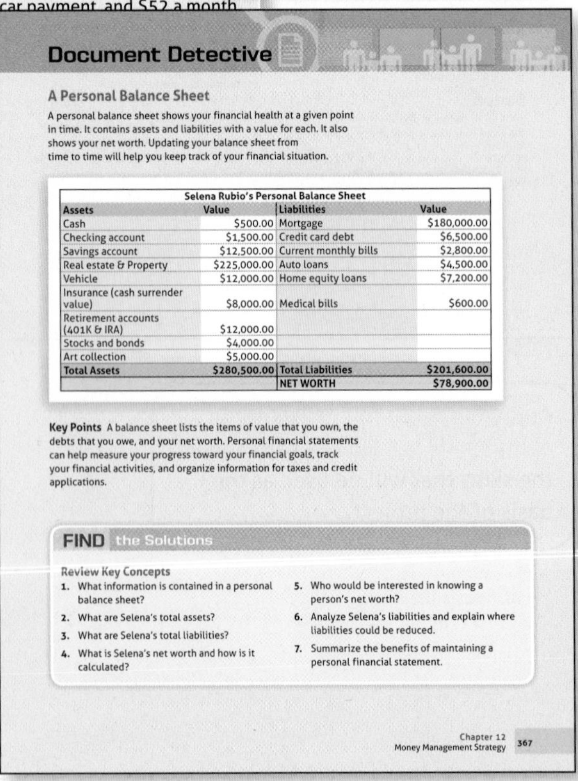

Document Detective

A Personal Balance Sheet

A personal balance sheet shows your financial health at a given point in time. It contains assets and liabilities with a value for each. It also shows your net worth. Updating your balance sheet from time to time will help you keep track of your financial situation.

Selena Rubio's Personal Balance Sheet

Assets	Value	Liabilities	Value
Cash	$500.00	Mortgage	$180,000.00
Checking account	$1,500.00	Credit card debt	$6,500.00
Savings account	$12,500.00	Current monthly bills	$2,800.00
Real estate & Property	$225,000.00	Auto loans	$4,500.00
Vehicle	$12,000.00	Home equity loans	$7,200.00
Insurance (cash surrender value)	$8,000.00	Medical bills	$600.00
Retirement accounts (401K & IRA)	$12,000.00		
Stocks and bonds	$4,000.00		
Art collection	$5,000.00		
Total Assets	**$280,500.00**	**Total Liabilities**	**$201,600.00**
		NET WORTH	**$78,900.00**

Key Points A balance sheet lists the items of value that you own, the debts that you owe, and your net worth. Personal financial statements can help measure your progress toward your financial goals, track your financial activities, and organize information for taxes and credit applications.

FIND the Solutions

Review Key Concepts

1. What information is contained in a personal balance sheet?
2. What are Selena's total assets?
3. What are Selena's total liabilities?
4. What is Selena's net worth and how is it calculated?
5. Who would be interested in knowing a person's net worth?
6. Analyze Selena's liabilities and explain where liabilities could be reduced.
7. Summarize the benefits of maintaining a personal financial statement.

Chapter 12
Money Management Strategy 367

Document Detective These features will help you identify and understand the financial documents you will use for family and business finances. Each feature has questions for you to answer that will help you know how to use the documents in the real world.

To the Student

Careers That Count!

Samir Parikh • Financial Accountant

I am a financial accountant for an insurance brokerage firm. I prepare, analyze, and present the various financial statements, supporting schedules, and budgets to the accounting manager and company president. A typical workday begins the night before, when I look at my schedule for any urgent items that require immediate attention. The next morning, once those tasks are completed, I move onto daily activities, such as monitoring the daily cash flow, evaluating employee expense reimbursements, and reconciling the cash deposits to our general ledger. Having proficient computer skills goes a long way in making my day easier, and being able to communicate effectively with the staff is another crucial skill. You may want to get an internship or part-time job at an accounting firm or in an accounting department to help you decide if you like this type of work and its culture.

EXPLORE CAREERS

Visit the Web site of the U.S. Department of Labor's Bureau of Labor Statistics and obtain information about a career as an accountant.

1. What is the special certification that can be obtained by an accountant?
2. What are the requirements of this certification?

CAREER FACTS

Skills	Education	Career Path
Finance, math, problem solving skills, proficiency in accounting and auditing software	Bachelor's degree or higher in accounting	Accountants can become CPAs, start their own businesses, or work for the Federal Government.

glencoe.com

Activity Download a Career Exploration Activity.

Careers That Count! Have you ever considered entering a career in finance? Each of these features interviews a professional in the financial career cluster and lists the skills and education needed for different financial careers.

Economics and You

Balance of Trade

Also called net exports, balance of trade is the difference between the total value of exports (goods made in a country and transported to other countries for sale) and the total value of imports (goods a country brings in from other countries). In simple terms, balance of trade is determined by subtracting total imports from total exports over a period of time, typically a month or a year. Surpluses might signal a strong manufacturing base, high tariffs, or overseas demand for U.S. products, but they can also mean that consumers have less disposable income to spend.

Personal Finance Connection In your personal finances, you have a surplus when you have a positive net cash flow and a deficit when you spend more than you earn. In trade, surpluses occur when exports exceed imports; deficits occur when imports exceed exports.

Critical Thinking Compare and contrast deficits and surpluses and how they affect your personal finances and international trade.

Import and Exports of Goods and Services

Billions of Dollars: 2000, 1750, 1500, 1250, 1000, 750, 500, 250, 0

Imports (Goods) 1575; Imports (Services) 381; Total Imports 1956; Exports (Goods) 1038; Exports (Services) 525; Total Exports 1563; Balance of Trade 393

glencoe.com

Activity Download an Economics and You Worksheet Activity.

Economics and You Learn how economic concepts affect real-world situations in business and personal finance. A critical thinking question in each of these features helps you expand on your understanding of the topic.

reality bytes

Protecting Financial Records on Your Computer

It is a good idea to duplic... or "back up," financial an... other personal data to an... external source in case your computer is damage... or stolen. Options includ... large-capacity hard drive... smaller flash drives. Ano... alternative is a fee-based... online backup service; files can be easily downloaded onto a new computer.

Reality Bytes Discover how using technology such as computer software, Web sites, and computer backups can help companies and families track and improve their finances.

COMMON CENTS

Pay or Save?

Be a smart consumer and pay off your credit card bills before you put mone... away in a savings account... The interest rate charged on credit cards is usually higher than the interest y... can earn from your saving... account.

Concept Application

How would this approach impact your budget? What specific areas of the budget will be affected?

Common Cents This feature shows you how to use knowledge and experience in financial situations. You will use this information to determine the best approach in real-life scenarios.

To the Student

Online Learning Center

Use the Internet to Extend Your Learning

Look for the glencoe.com icon throughout the text that directs you to additional content and activities on the Business and Personal Finance Online Learning Center.

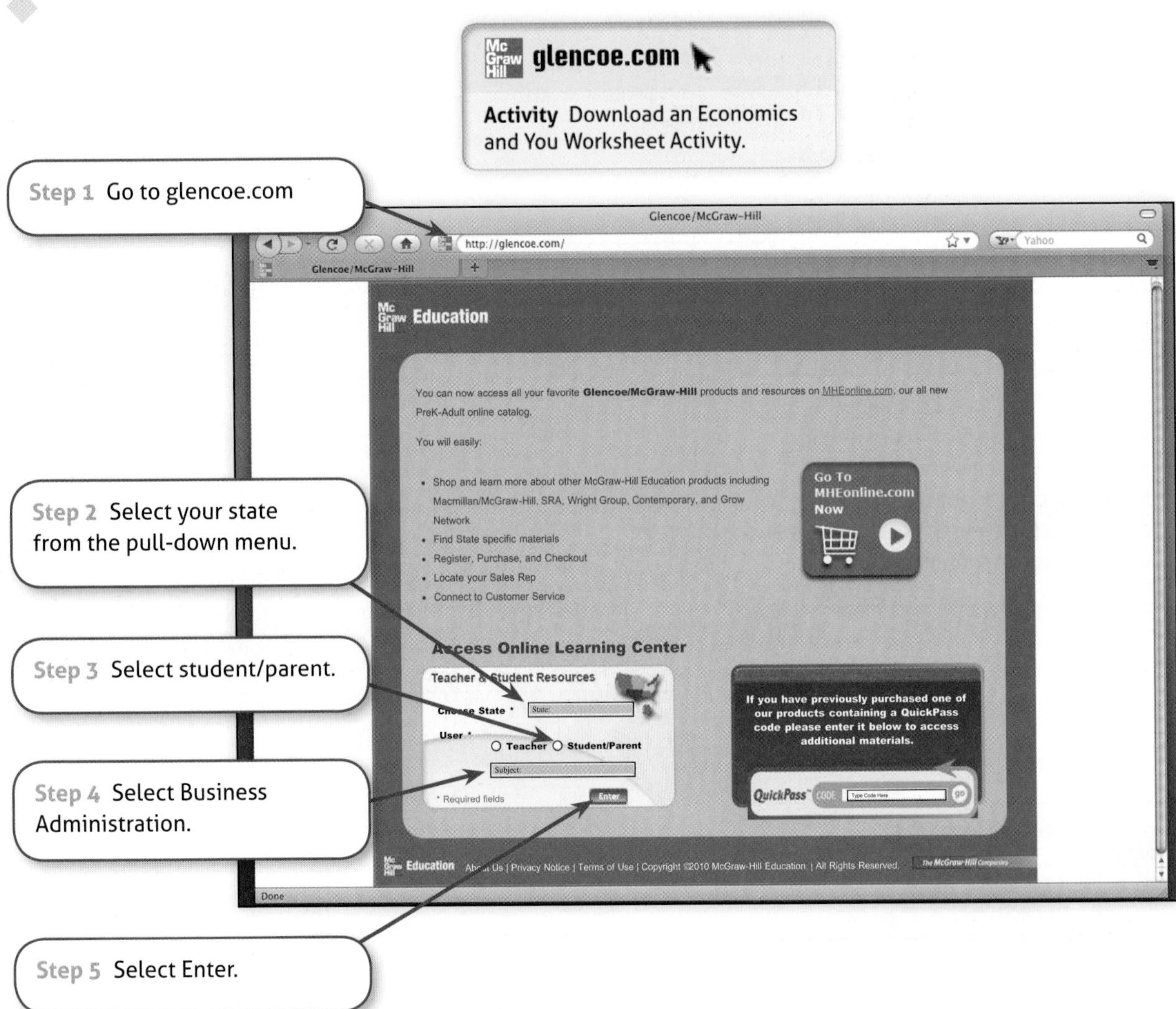

To the Student

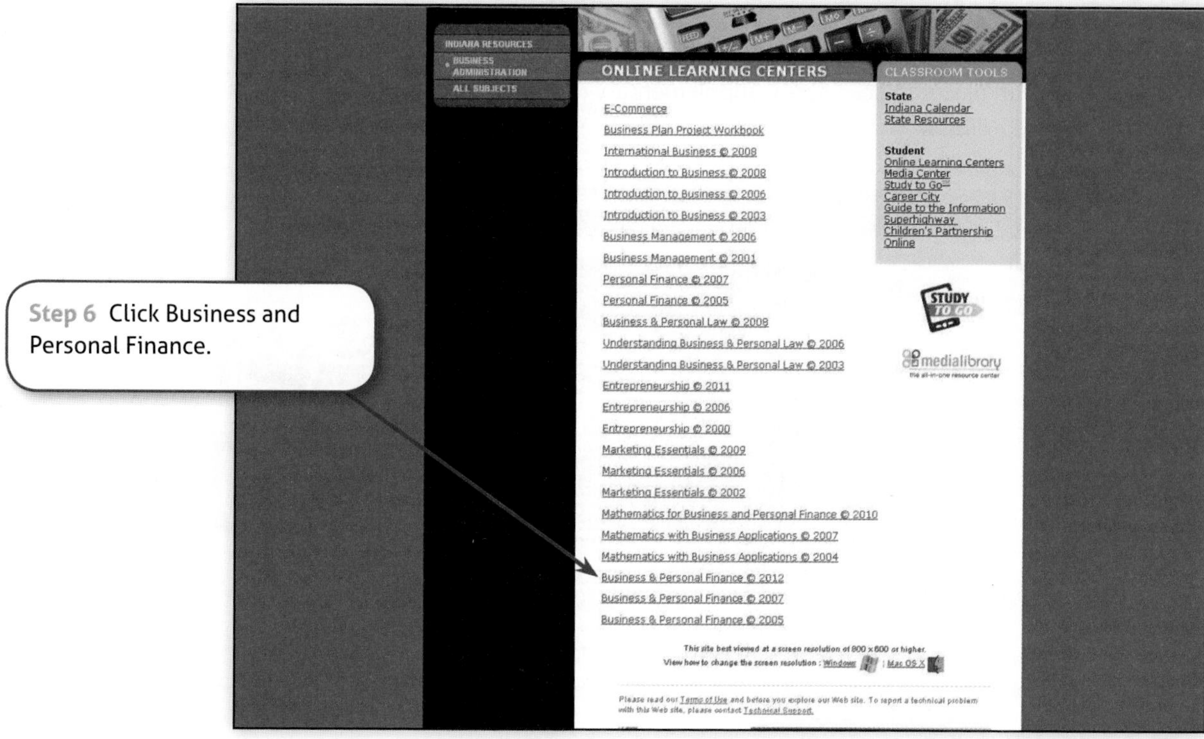

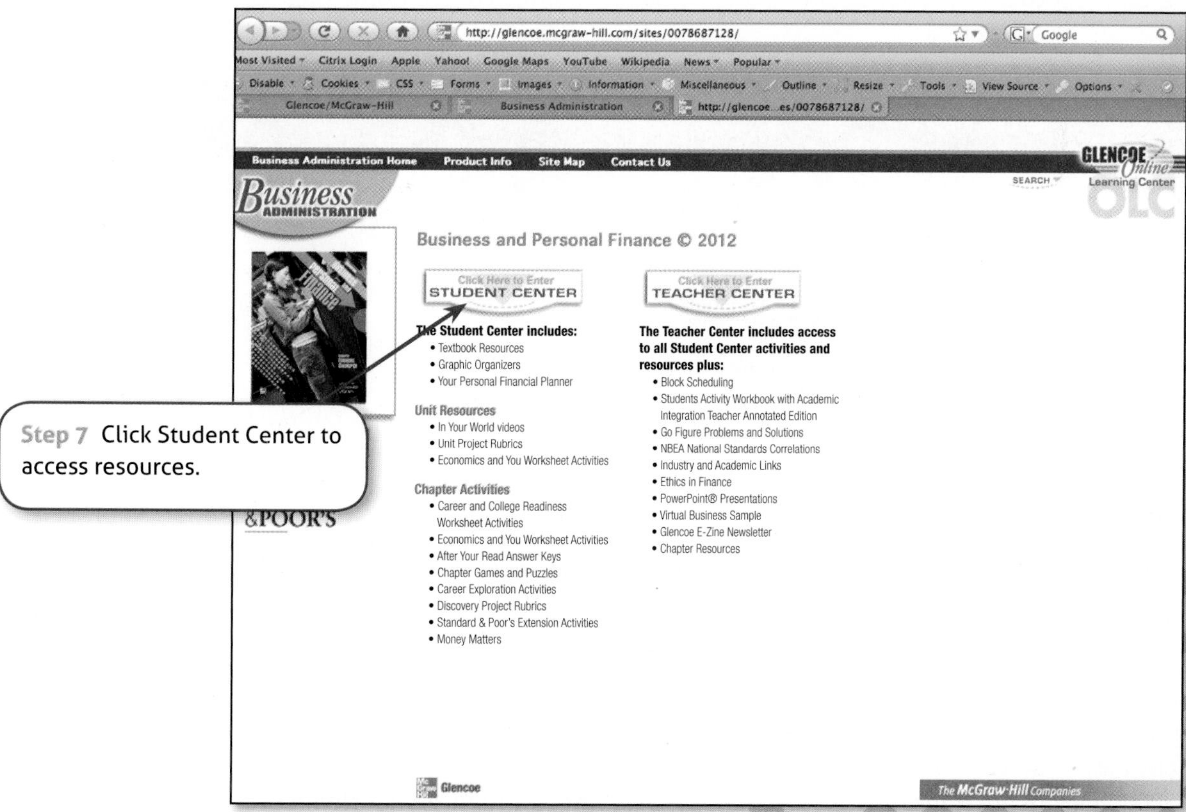

connect™

CONNECT is an innovative Web-based program designed to help you succeed in your coursework and in the workplace. You can access supplementary resources for *Business and Personal Finance* through CONNECT.

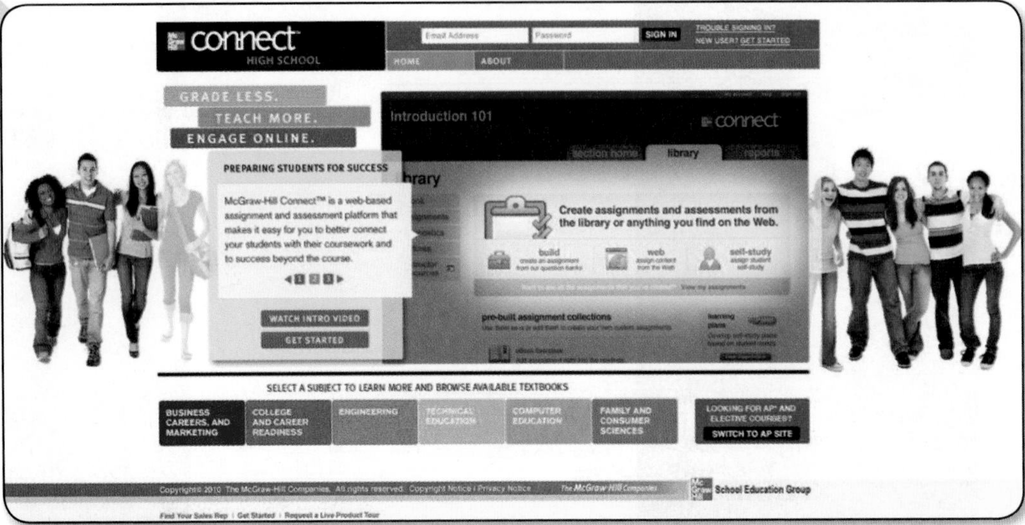

CONNECT

Use Connect to access your Business and Personal Finance course home page.

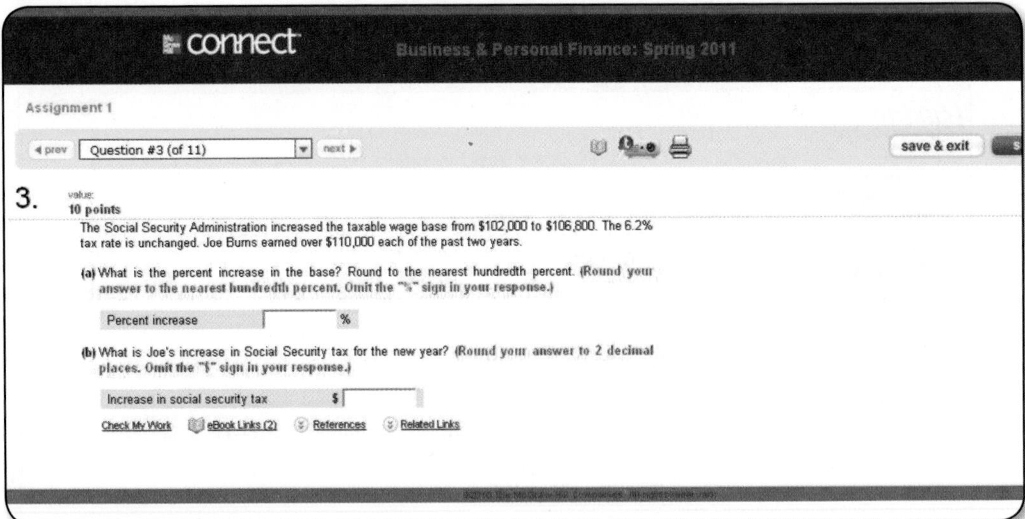

LEARN

- Complete your homework online.
- Get immediate feedback on your work.
- Link back to sections of the book to review business and personal finance concepts.

Easy to access!

Connect to Glencoe Business and Personal Finance at mcgrawhillconnect.com/k12

SUCCEED

Use CONNECT to access the Business and Personal Finance Online Learning Center for these resources:

- Unit videos
- Self-checks
- Practice tests
- Chapter Summaries
- Chapter Visual Summaries with Content and Academic Vocabulary
- Chapter Graphic Organizers
- Chapter Games and Puzzles

Access your eBook anywhere!

- Store class notes.
- Highlight and bookmark material online.
- Full book coverage, including all topics and every relevant figure from the textbook.

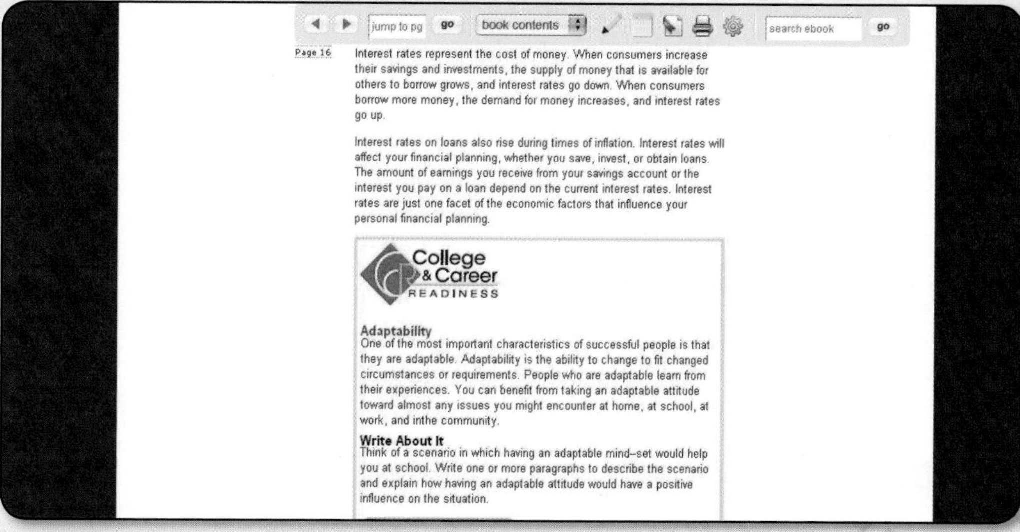

Interest rates represent the cost of money. When consumers increase their savings and investments, the supply of money that is available for others to borrow grows, and interest rates go down. When consumers borrow more money, the demand for money increases, and interest rates go up.

Interest rates on loans also rise during times of inflation. Interest rates will affect your financial planning, whether you save, invest, or obtain loans. The amount of earnings you receive from your savings account or the interest you pay on a loan depend on the current interest rates. Interest rates are just one facet of the economic factors that influence your personal financial planning.

College & Career READINESS

Adaptability
One of the most important characteristics of successful people is that they are adaptable. Adaptability is the ability to change to fit changed circumstances or requirements. People who are adaptable learn from their experiences. You can benefit from taking an adaptable attitude toward almost any issues you might encounter at home, at school, at work, and inthe community.

Write About It
Think of a scenario in which having an adaptable mind-set would help you at school. Write one or more paragraphs to describe the scenario and explain how having an adaptable attitude would have a positive influence on the situation.

with ConnectPlus

Reading: What's in It for You?

What role does reading play in your life? The possibilities are countless. Are you on a sports team? Perhaps you like to read about the latest news and statistics in sports or find out about new training techniques. Are you looking for a part-time job? You might be looking for advice about résumé writing, interview techniques, or information about a company. Are you enrolled in an English class, an algebra class, or a business class? Then your assignments require a lot of reading.

Improving or Fine-Tuning Your Reading Skills Will:

- Improve your grades.
- Allow you to read faster and more efficiently.
- Improve your study skills.
- Help you remember more information accurately.
- Improve your writing.

The Reading Process

Good reading skills build on one another, overlap, and spiral around in much the same way that a winding staircase goes around and around while leading you to a higher place. This handbook is designed to help you find and use the tools you will need **before, during,** and **after** reading.

Strategies You Can Use

- Identify, understand, and learn
- Understand why you read.
- Take a quick look at the whole text.
- Try to predict what you are about to read.Take breaks while you read and ask yourself questions about the text.
- Take notes.
- Keep thinking about what will come next.
- Summarize.

Vocabulary Development

Word identification and vocabulary skills are the building blocks of the reading and the writing process. By learning to use a variety of strategies to build your word skills and vocabulary, you will become a stronger reader.

Use Context to Determine Meaning

The best way to expand and extend your vocabulary is to read widely, listen carefully, and participate in a rich variety of discussions. When reading on your own, though, you can often figure out the meanings of new words by looking at their **context,** the other words and sentences that surround them.

Tips for Using Context

Look for clues like these:

- **A synonym or an explanation of the unknown word in the sentence:** *Elise's shop specialized in millinery, or hats for women.*
- A reference to what the word is or is not like: *An archaeologist, like a historian, deals with the past.*
- A general topic associated with the word: *The cooking teacher discussed the best way to braise meat.*
- A description or action associated with the word: *He used the shovel to dig up the garden.*

Predict a Possible Meaning

Another way to determine the meaning of a word is to take the word apart. If you understand the meaning of the **base,** or **root,** part of a word, and also know the meanings of key syllables added either to the beginning or end of the base word, you can usually figure out what the word means.

Word Origins Since Latin, Greek, and Anglo-Saxon roots are the basis for much of our English vocabulary, having some background in languages can be a useful vocabulary tool. For example, *astronomy* comes from the Greek root *astro,* which means "relating to the stars." *Stellar* also has a meaning referring to stars, but its origin is Latin. Knowing root words in other languages can help you determine meanings, derivations, and spellings in English.

Prefixes and Suffixes A prefix is a word part that can be added to the beginning of a word. For example, the prefix *semi* means "half" or "partial," so *semicircle* means "half a circle." A suffix is a word part that can be added to the end of a word. Adding a suffix often changes a word from one part of speech to another.

Using Dictionaries A dictionary provides the meaning or meanings of a word. Look at the sample dictionary entry on the next page to see what other information it provides.

Thesauruses and Specialized Reference Books A thesaurus provides synonyms and often antonyms. It is a useful tool to expand your vocabulary. Remember to check the exact definition of the listed words in a dictionary before you use a thesaurus. Specialized dictionaries such as *Barron's Dictionary of Business Terms* or *Black's Law Dictionary* list terms and expressions that are not commonly included in a general dictionary. You can also use online dictionaries.

Glossaries Many textbooks and technical works contain condensed dictionaries that provide an alphabetical listing of words used in the text and their specific definitions.

Dictionary Entry

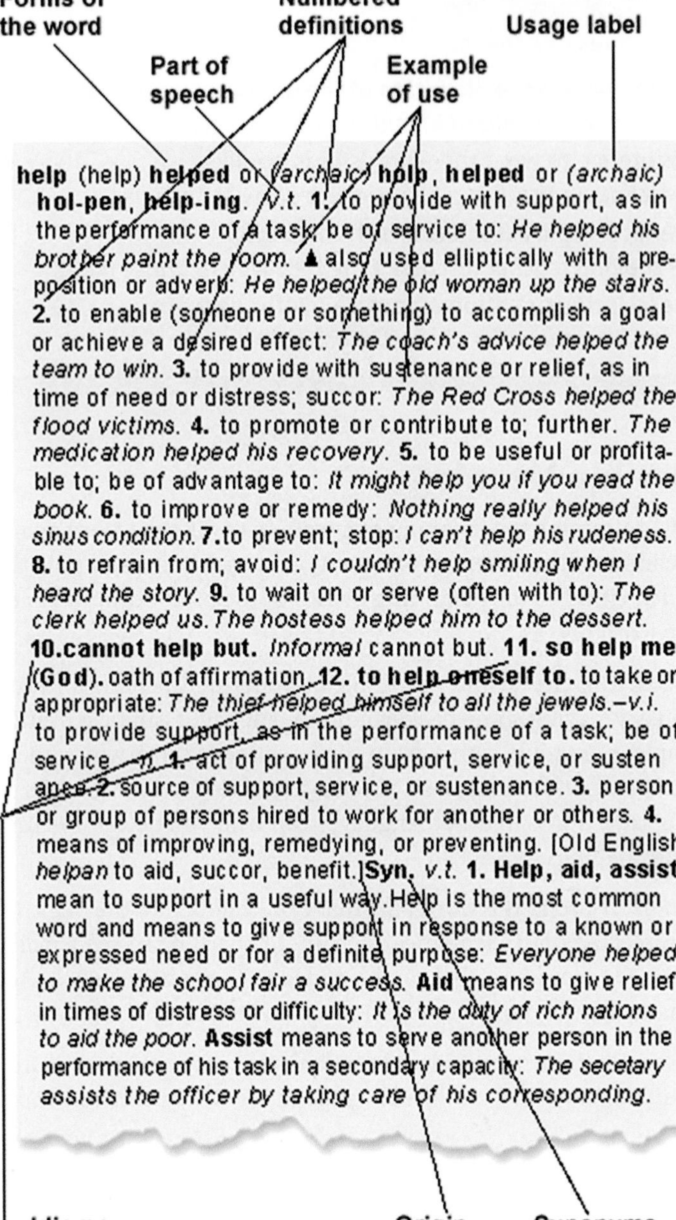

help (help) **helped** or *(archaic)* **holp**, **helped** or *(archaic)* **hol-pen**, **help-ing**. *v.t.* **1.** to provide with support, as in the performance of a task; be of service to: *He helped his brother paint the room.* ▲ also used elliptically with a preposition or adverb: *He helped the old woman up the stairs.* **2.** to enable (someone or something) to accomplish a goal or achieve a desired effect: *The coach's advice helped the team to win.* **3.** to provide with sustenance or relief, as in time of need or distress; succor: *The Red Cross helped the flood victims.* **4.** to promote or contribute to; further. *The medication helped his recovery.* **5.** to be useful or profitable to; be of advantage to: *It might help you if you read the book.* **6.** to improve or remedy: *Nothing really helped his sinus condition.* **7.** to prevent; stop: *I can't help his rudeness.* **8.** to refrain from; avoid: *I couldn't help smiling when I heard the story.* **9.** to wait on or serve (often with to): *The clerk helped us. The hostess helped him to the dessert.* **10. cannot help but.** *Informal* cannot but. **11. so help me (God).** oath of affirmation. **12. to help oneself to.** to take or appropriate: *The thief helped himself to all the jewels.* —*v.i.* to provide support, as in the performance of a task; be of service —*n.* **1.** act of providing support, service, or sustenance. **2.** source of support, service, or sustenance. **3.** person or group of persons hired to work for another or others. **4.** means of improving, remedying, or preventing. [Old English *helpan* to aid, succor, benefit.] **Syn.** *v.t.* **1. Help, aid, assist** mean to support in a useful way. Help is the most common word and means to give support in response to a known or expressed need or for a definite purpose: *Everyone helped to make the school fair a success.* **Aid** means to give relief in times of distress or difficulty: *It is the duty of rich nations to aid the poor.* **Assist** means to serve another person in the performance of his task in a secondary capacity: *The secetary assists the officer by taking care of his corresponding.*

Recognize Word Meanings Across Subjects Have you learned a new word in one class and then noticed it in your reading for other subjects? The word might not mean exactly the same thing in each class, but you can use the meaning you already know to help you understand what it means in another subject area. For example:

Math Each digit represents a different place **value.**

Health Your **values** can guide you in making healthful decisions.

Economics The **value** of a product is measured in its cost.

Understanding What You Read

Reading comprehension means understanding—deriving meaning from—what you have read. Using a variety of strategies can help you improve your comprehension and make reading more interesting and more fun.

Read for a Reason

To get the greatest benefit from your reading, **establish a purpose for reading.** In school, you have many reasons for reading, such as:

- to learn and understand new information.
- to find specific information.
- to review before a test.
- to complete an assignment.
- to prepare (research) before you write.

As your reading skills improve, you will notice that you apply different strategies to fit the different purposes for reading. For example, if you are reading for entertainment, you might read quickly, but if you read to gather information or follow directions, you might read more slowly, take notes, construct a graphic organizer, or reread sections of text.

Draw on Personal Background

Drawing on personal background may also be called activating prior knowledge. Before you start reading a text, ask yourself questions like these:

- What have I heard or read about this topic?
- Do I have any personal experience relating to this topic?

Using a K-W-L Chart A K-W-L chart is a good device for organizing information you gather before, during, and after reading. In the first column, list what you already **know,** then list what you **want** to know in the middle column. Use the third column when you review and assess what you **learned.** You can also add more columns to record places where you found information and places where you can look for more information.

K (What I already know)	W (What I want to know)	L (What I have learned)

Adjust Your Reading Speed Your reading speed is a key factor in how well you understand what you are reading. You will need to adjust your speed depending on your reading purpose.

Scanning means running your eyes quickly over the material to look for words or phrases. Scan when you need a specific piece of information.

Skimming means reading a passage quickly to find its main idea or to get an overview. Skim a text when you preview to determine what the material is about.

Reading for detail involves careful reading while paying attention to text structure and monitoring your understanding. Read for detail when you are learning concepts, following complicated directions, or preparing to analyze a text.

Techniques to Understand and Remember What You Read

Preview

Before beginning a selection, it is helpful to **preview** what you are about to read.

Previewing Strategies

- Read the title, headings, and subheadings of the selection.
- Look at the illustrations and notice how the text is organized.
- Skim the selection: Take a glance at the whole thing.
- Decide what the main idea might be.
- Predict what a selection will be about.

Predict

Have you ever read a mystery, decided who committed the crime, and then changed your mind as more clues were revealed? You were adjusting your predictions. Did you smile when you found out that you guessed who committed the crime? You were verifying your predictions.

As you read, take educated guesses about story events and outcomes; that is, **make predictions** before and during reading. This will help you focus your attention on the text and it will improve your understanding.

Determine the Main Idea

When you look for the **main idea,** you are looking for the most important statement in a text. Depending on what kind of text you are reading, the main idea can be located at the very beginning (news stories in newspaper or a magazine) or at the end (scientific research document). Ask yourself the following questions:

- What is each sentence about?
- Is there one sentence that is more important than all the others?
- What idea do details support or point out?

Taking Notes

Cornell Note-Taking System There are many methods for note taking. The **Cornell Note-Taking System** is a well-known method that can help you organize what you read. To the right is a note-taking activity based on the Cornell Note-Taking System.

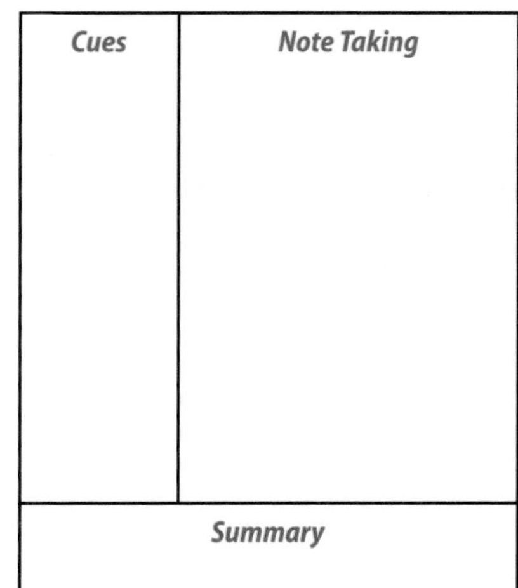

Graphic Organizers Using a graphic organizer to retell content in a visual representation will help you remember and retain content. You might make a **chart** or **diagram,** organizing what you have read. Here are some examples of graphic organizers:

Venn diagrams When mapping out a compare-and-contrast text structure, you can use a Venn diagram. The outer portions of the circles will show how two characters, ideas, or items contrast, or are different, and the overlapping part will compare two things, or show how they are similar.

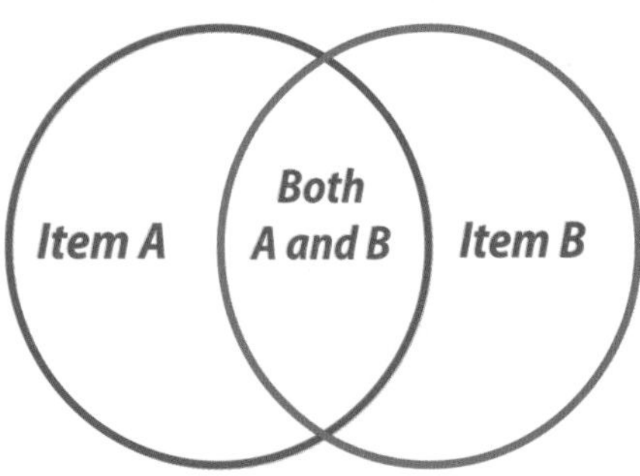

Flow charts To help you track the sequence of events, or cause and effect, use a flow chart. Arrange ideas or events in their logical, sequential order. Then, draw arrows between your ideas to indicate how one idea or event flows into another.

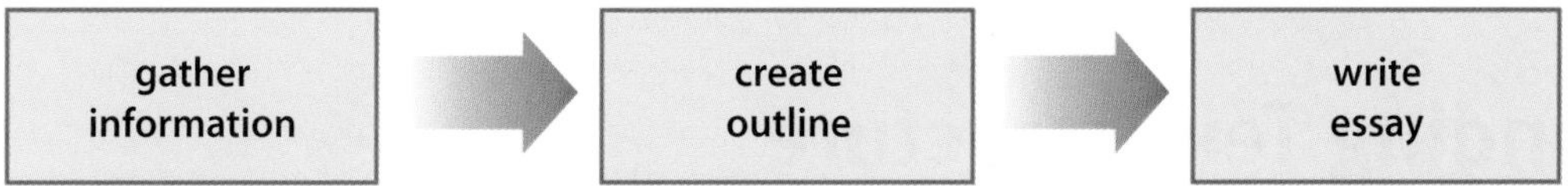

Visualize

Try to form a mental picture of scenes, characters, and events as you read. Use the details and descriptions the author gives you. If you can **visualize** what you read, it will be more interesting and you will remember it better.

Question

Ask yourself questions about the text while you read. Ask yourself about the importance of the sentences, how they relate to one another, if you understand what you just read, and what you think is going to come next.

Clarify

If you feel you do not understand meaning (through questioning), try these techniques:

What to Do When You Do Not Understand

- Reread confusing parts of the text.
- Diagram (chart) relationships between chunks of text, ideas, and sentences.
- Look up unfamiliar words.
- Talk out the text to yourself.
- Read the passage once more.

Review

Take time to stop and review what you have read. Use your note-taking tools (graphic organizers or Cornell notes charts). Also, review and consider your K-W-L chart.

Monitor Your Comprehension

Continue to check your understanding by using the following two strategies:

Summarize Pause and tell yourself the main ideas of the text and the key supporting details. Try to answer the following questions: Who? What? When? Where? Why? How?

Paraphrase Pause, close the book, and try to retell what you have just read in your own words. It might help to pretend you are explaining the text to someone who has not read it and does not know the material.

Understanding Text Structure

Good writers do not just put together sentences and paragraphs, they organize their writing with a specific purpose in mind. That organization is called text structure. When you understand and follow the structure of a text, it is easier to remember the information you are reading. There are many ways text may be structured. Watch for signal words. They will help you follow the text's organization (also, remember to use these techniques when you write).

Compare and Contrast

This structure shows similarities and differences between people, things, and ideas. This is often used to demonstrate that things that seem alike are really different, or vice versa.

Signal words: similarly, more, less, on the one hand / on the other hand, in contrast, but, however

Cause and Effect

Writers use the cause-and-effect structure to explore the reasons for something happening and to examine the results or consequences of events.

Signal words: so, because, as a result, therefore, for the following reasons

Problem and Solution

When they organize text around the question "how?" writers state a problem and suggest solutions.

Signal words: how, help, problem, obstruction, overcome, difficulty, need, attempt, have to, must

Sequence

Sequencing tells you in which order to consider thoughts or facts. Examples of sequencing are:

Chronological order refers to the order in which events take place.

Signal words: first, next, then, finally

Spatial order describes the organization of things in space (to describe a room, for example).

Signal words: above, below, behind, next to

Order of importance lists things or thoughts from the most important to the least important (or the other way around).

Signal words: principal, central, main, important, fundamental

▶ Reading for Meaning

It is important to think about what you are reading to get the most information out of a text, to understand the consequences of what the text says, to remember the content, and to form your own opinion about what the content means.

Interpret

Interpreting is asking yourself, "What is the writer really saying?" and then using what you already know to answer that question.

Infer

Writers do not always state exactly everything they want you to understand. By providing clues and details, they sometimes imply certain information. An **inference** involves using your reason and experience to develop the idea on your own, based on what an author implies or suggests. What is most important when drawing inferences is to be sure that you have accurately based your guesses on supporting details from the text. If you cannot point to a place in the selection to help back up your inference, you may need to rethink your guess.

Draw Conclusions

A conclusion is a general statement you can make and explain with reasoning, or with supporting details from a text. If you read a story describing a sport where five players bounce a ball and throw it through a high hoop, you may conclude that the sport is basketball.

Analyze

To understand persuasive nonfiction (a text that discusses facts and opinions to arrive at a conclusion), you need to analyze statements and examples to see if they support the main idea. To understand an informational text (a text, such as a textbook, that gives you information, not opinions), you need to keep track of how the ideas are organized to find the main points.

Hint: Use your graphic organizers and notes charts.

Distinguish Facts from Opinions

This is one of the most important reading skills you can learn. A fact is a statement that can be proven. An opinion is what the writer believes. A writer may support opinions with facts, but an opinion cannot be proven. For example:

Fact: California produces fruit and other agricultural products.

Opinion: California produces the best fruit and other agricultural products.

Evaluate

Would you take seriously an article on nuclear fission if you knew it was written by a comedic actor? If you need to rely on accurate information, you need to find out who wrote what you are reading and why. Where did the writer get information? Is the information one-sided? Can you verify the information?

▶ Reading for Research

You will need to **read actively** in order to research a topic. You might also need to generate an interesting, relevant, and researchable **question** on your own and locate appropriate print and nonprint information from a wide variety of sources. Then, you will need to **categorize** that information, evaluate it, and **organize** it in a new way in order to produce a research project for a specific audience. Finally, **draw conclusions** about your original research question. These conclusions may lead you to other areas for further inquiry.

Locate Appropriate Print and Nonprint Information

In your research, try to use a variety of sources. Because different sources present information in different ways, your research project will be more interesting and balanced when you read a variety of sources.

Literature **and Textbooks** These texts include any book used as a basis for instruction or a source of information.

Book Indices A book index, or a bibliography, is an alphabetical listing of books. Some book indices list books on specific subjects; others are more general. Other indices list a variety of topics or resources.

Periodicals Magazines and journals are issued at regular intervals, such as weekly or monthly. One way to locate information in magazines is to use the *Readers' Guide to Periodical Literature.* This guide is available in print form in most libraries.

Technical Manuals A manual is a guide or handbook intended to give instruction on how to perform a task or operate something. A vehicle owner's manual might give information on how to operate and service a car.

Reference Books Reference books include encyclopedias and almanacs, and are used to locate specific pieces of information.

Electronic Encyclopedias, Databases, and the Internet There are many ways to locate extensive information using your computer. Infotrac, for instance, acts as an online reader's guide. CD encyclopedias can provide easy access to all subjects.

Organize and Convert Information

As you gather information from different sources, taking careful notes, you will need to think about how to **synthesize** the information, that is, convert it into a unified whole, as well as how to change it into a form your audience will easily understand and that will meet your assignment guidelines.

1. First, ask yourself what you want your audience to know.
2. Then, think about a pattern of organization, a structure that will best show your main ideas. You might ask yourself the following questions:
   - When comparing items or ideas, what graphic aids can I use?
   - When showing the reasons something happened and the effects of certain actions, what text structure would be best?
   - How can I briefly and clearly show important information to my audience?
   - Would an illustration or even a cartoon help to make a certain point?

UNIT 1

Economics and Personal Finance

Visual Literacy

The integration of world economies provides new opportunities, but it also can put nations at risk. ***With the rapidly increasing exchange of information, culture, and resources how can nations protect their individual and global interests?***

In Your World

The Global Village

Global transformation began centuries ago when ambitious traders left home to seek new resources and new markets. This continues today with advancements in technology, trade, and connectivity. Today's world is a global village with a global economy. This increase in connectivity and competition has provided many opportunities for consumers, but it also has drawbacks. For example, it has led in part to many jobs shifting to other nations with lower labor costs.

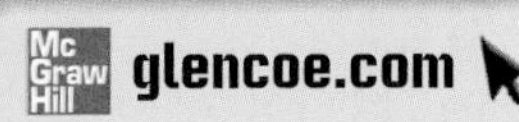

Video Watch the Unit 1 video to learn more about the impact of globalization.

Global Integration Global integration provides increased access and more opportunities, but it also presents additional risks to the global economy. Explain the benefits and drawbacks of global integration. How will technology impact the global economy?

Economics and You

Globalization

Developments in telecommunications have made the same sporting events and television shows you watch available to people all over the world. This improved access has changed the cultural choices and buying habits of other nations. Viewers demand foreign products they see advertised and used on television. Opinions vary on globalization. Some believe it will lead to the loss of American jobs. Others believe it will provide global unity and increased wealth. Search online to find a company that has outsourced jobs. Write a brief paragraph explaining why you would or would not pay more for goods if it meant preserving jobs in America.

glencoe.com

Activity Download an Economics and You Worksheet Activity.

CHAPTER 1

The Fundamentals of Economics

Visual Literacy

Businesses and consumers must make choices due to limited resources. ***What choices do you have to make because of limited resources?***

Discovery Project

Teaching Financial Literacy

Key Question

What economic concepts can children understand that can help them learn about financial literacy?

Project Goal

Research indicates that it is never too early to learn about economic concepts related to financial literacy.

- Work in small groups to develop three activities for 4th grade students that will teach them about economics, the government, and global trade. Assume that the children have never participated in activities on these topics.
- Write a script that tells the students the reason for each activity by identifying the objectives.
- Use concepts and examples appropriate for the children's level of education.
- Design props and other visual aids that younger children can relate to and enjoy.
- Present the activities to your classmates to get feedback. This will give you an opportunity to revise the activities if necessary.
- Be willing to accept constructive criticism.

Ask Yourself...

- *What concepts should be incorporated in the activities?*
- *What are the objectives for each activity?*
- *What types of props and visual aids will keep the attention of a 4th grader?*
- *How will you determine if the activities achieved the objectives?*

Economic Literacy

Why is it important to begin learning about financial literacy and economics at an early age?

glencoe.com

Evaluate Download an assessment rubric.

THE BIG IDEA

The more you know about economics, the more informed decisions you will make regarding your current and future finances.

ASK STANDARD & POOR'S

Regulation in a Market Economy

Q *Why does the government regulate the market in a market economy?*

A Ideally everyone would deal honestly and fairly with one another. However, this is not the case, so there is government regulation. Government regulation is designed to set and enforce standards and rules, settle disputes, and make improvements to keep transactions fair and efficient. There are supporters and opponents of government regulation. Those in favor of regulation believe the market cannot protect, monitor, and police itself. Opponents of regulation believe the market will regulate itself and the funding for regulation could be used for other purposes.

Writing Activity

Make a list of wants and needs for an individual, a family, a business, and a government. Write one sentence next to each want and need explaining how scarcity impacts each item.

Reading Guide

Before You Read

The Essential Question How do economic concepts and policies affect your personal finances?

Main Idea

The more you know about how an economy operates and the impact economic factors can have on your finances, the better educated you will be when making life decisions about the use of your financial resources and planning for the future.

Content Vocabulary

- economics
- opportunity cost
- scarcity
- factors of production
- land
- labor
- capital
- entrepreneurship
- economy
- traditional economy
- bartering
- command economy
- market economy
- supply
- demand
- equilibrium point
- price ceiling
- price floor
- demand elasticity
- elastic demand
- inelastic demand
- financial market
- depository institutions
- non-depository institutions
- incentive

Academic Vocabulary

You will see these words in your reading and on your tests.

- allocates
- discretion
- fungible
- derivatives

Graphic Organizer

Before you read this chapter, draw a diagram like the one shown. As you read, use the web to summarize the questions each type of economy must address.

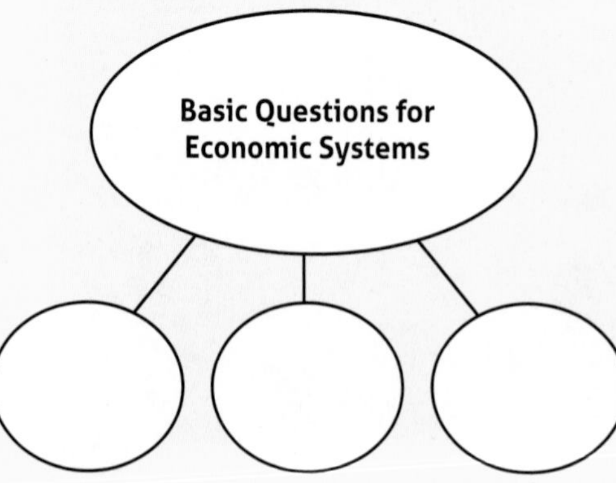

  glencoe.com Print this organizer.

Standards

Academic

Mathematics

NCTM Algebra Represent and analyze mathematical situations and structures using algebraic symbols.

NCTM Problem Solving Apply and adapt a variety of appropriate strategies to solve problems.

NCTM Problem Solving Solve problems that arise in mathematics and in other contexts.

English Language Arts

NCTE 12 Use language to accomplish individual purposes.

NCTE 1 Read texts to acquire new information.

Social Studies

NCSS VI E Compare different political systems (their ideologies, structure, institutions, processes, and political cultures) with that of the United States.

NCTM *National Council of Teachers of Mathematics*

NCTE *National Council of Teachers of English*

NCSS *National Council for the Social Studies*

NSES *National Science Education Standards*

Common Core

Reading Determine central ideas or themes of a text and analyze their development; summarize the key supporting details and ideas.

Reading Read and comprehend complex literary and informational texts independently and proficiently.

Writing Write routinely over extended time frames (time for research, reflection, and revision) and shorter time frames (a single sitting or a day or two) for a range of tasks, purposes, and audiences.

Scarcity and Economics

How might limited funds affect your financial decisions?

How much money do you have? Your decision on what to do with that money is the essence of economics and personal finance. **Economics** is the study of the decisions that go into making, distributing, and using goods and services.

Section Objectives

- **Explain** opportunity cost.
- **Discuss** the concept of scarcity and factors of production.
- **Compare** different economic systems and their methods for allocating goods and services.
- **Explain** how prices are determined through supply and demand.
- **Distinguish** between elastic and inelastic demand.

As You Read

Connect What roles do you and your family members play in the country's economy?

Opportunity Costs and Trade-offs

In order to make a decision, you need to distinguish between wants and needs. A need is a necessity, like food and clothing. A want is something you desire but can live without. Imagine that you earned $200. You can save the money in an account established for college. You could also invest it in hopes of earning a large return. Maybe you choose to spend all of it on something you want or need immediately.

Each action has an opportunity cost and a trade-off. An **opportunity cost** is what you give up to get something else. Your $200 is not enough money to satisfy all your needs and wants. If you spend the money, it will take you longer to collect the money you need to build the funds needed for college. If you save the money, you will give up the satisfaction of owning a new product that you may really want right now. So you must compare those alternatives when making a decision, as there are costs and benefits to each one. These costs and benefits are also called marginal costs and benefits. A marginal cost is the cost of obtaining one more of an item. In this case, it is the cost of purchasing the product you want. A marginal benefit is the benefit of purchasing one more of an item. It is the benefit you receive from purchasing the item you want. Evaluating the marginal costs and benefits will help you to make effective decisions.

From a business perspective, the marginal cost is what is given up by producing one more of a product. The marginal benefit is what the consumer is willing to give up to obtain one more of a product. Businesses use this information to maximize profits by comparing the costs and benefits of producing additional quantities of a product.

Scarcity and Society

If you think about all your needs and wants, you realize that they cannot be satisfied with the $200 you earned from shoveling snow. This problem is an economic principle called scarcity. **Scarcity** requires that people decide which goods and services to use or not use due to limited resources and unlimited wants.

reality bytes

To the Highest Bidder
Concerts and sporting events fill stadiums and arenas all over the world. Tickets for these events are often difficult to get. If you are unable to get tickets to an event, there are many online auction sites available that offer tickets to popular events that are sold out. These sites operate as a free market where the consumer determines the price of the item. A ticket is worth whatever a consumer is willing to spend. For this reason, tickets on auction sites can sometimes be very expensive, and you will often pay significantly more than the face value of the ticket.

The economic principle of scarcity should not be confused with the term *shortage*. Scarcity will always exist in an economy because of competition for resources and alternative uses for these resources. A shortage is temporary, for example if a drought were to destroy a particular crop.

Scarcity can also affect businesses. Because resources are in limited supply, to have one thing may mean giving up something else. For example a restaurant owner may want a costly new décor and more money to put into kitchen equipment. The owner must evaluate the opportunity costs of the new décor and the kitchen equipment and determine what he or she should give up.

Factors of Production

Scarce resources require choices. When economists discuss scarce resources they are referring to the factors of production. (See **Figure 1.**) **Factors of production** are resources needed to produce goods and services. The four factors of production are land, labor, capital, and entrepreneurship.

Land In economic terms, **land** refers to natural resources that exist and were not created by people. It includes actual surface land and water as well as animals, trees, mineral, and other products of nature. Because a finite amount of "land" exists, economists consider land to be in limited supply.

Labor **Labor** is the work that people do and includes all of their abilities, efforts, and skills. It includes any work that people do to produce goods and services. This category includes all people except entrepreneurs who have a special role in the economy.

Capital The manufactured goods used to produce other goods and services are **capital.** For example, machines, buildings, and tools used in a plant to produce certain products are examples of capital. When land, labor, and capital are combined the value of all three factors will increase. For example, if you combine an uncut diamond (land), a diamond cutter (labor), and a diamond-cutting machine (capital) you end up with a valuable good.

Entrepreneurship The fourth factor of production is entrepreneurship. **Entrepreneurship** refers to the ability of individuals to start new businesses, introduce new products, and improve business processes. It involves the willingness to take risks to make profit, but entrepreneurs must incur the costs of failed efforts.

Everything we make requires the four factors of production. The amount of each factor you own determines your wealth. The more capital and land you own, the richer you will be. The same is true for nations as well. Nations with an abundance of natural resources on hand, for example, tend to be wealthier than nations with fewer national resources.

FIGURE 1 Factors of Production

Economic Necessity The four factors of production are necessary to be able to produce the items consumers want. *What are examples of the factors of production for producing shoes?*

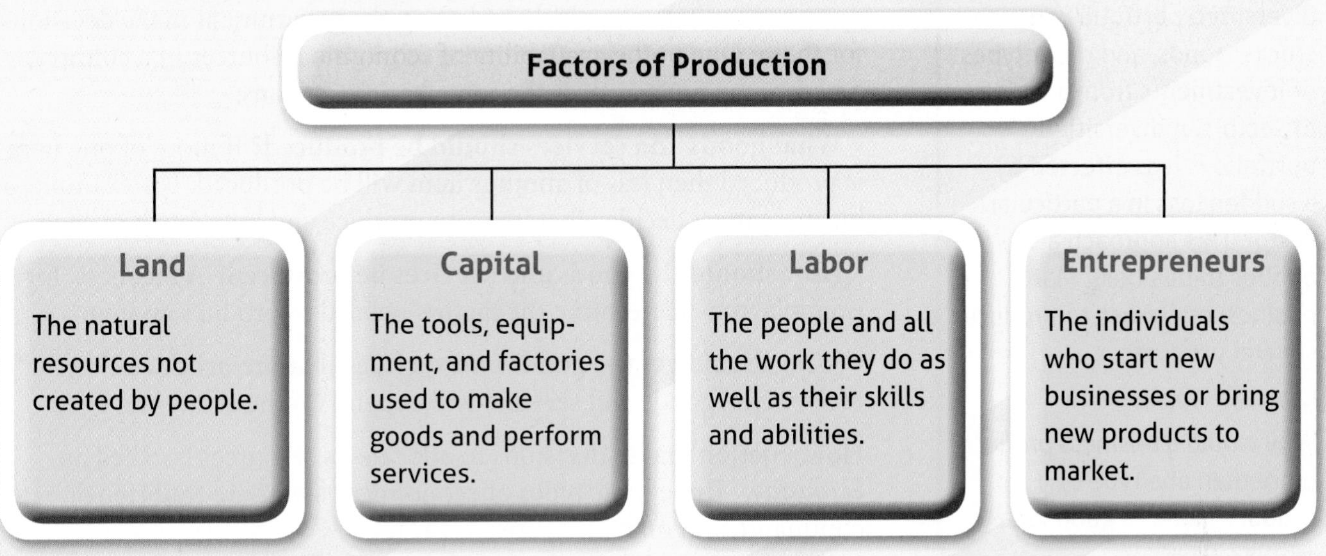

Factors of Production
Land
The natural resources not created by people.
Capital
The tools, equipment, and factories used to make goods and perform services.
Labor
The people and all the work they do as well as their skills and abilities.
Entrepreneurs
The individuals who start new businesses or bring new products to market.

Scarcity and the Government

A nation's government must also manage the use of limited resources. For example, the United States government has to decide how to spend the money it receives from taxpayers. When you buy goods, you may pay sales tax. When you start working, you will pay income tax.

The government is responsible for choosing how to spend taxpayers' money. The elected officials who represent taxpayers in local, state, and national governments make those choices. As soon as you are 18 years old, you will have the opportunity to vote for these government officials. Their decisions determine the policies that will affect your personal finances and other areas of your life. This is why it is important to understand the views of those who want to be elected to represent you.

How a government **allocates,** or distributes, the limited resources it has to provide the goods and services you need and want differs based on the economic system under which it governs. An economic opportunity cost is what an economy must sacrifice to provide for its people. Each decision involves giving up something else. The decisions government officials make affect you as an investor, a worker, and a consumer.

Reading Check

Define What does scarcity mean in terms of economics?

Diversify

Investors try to keep a diversified portfolio. A diversified portfolio contains stocks, bonds, and other types of investments from a variety of sectors. A diversified portfolio is less affected by a sudden loss in a particular sector. This approach also applies to business. Many businesses choose to produce several products.

Concept Application

Why would a business produce more than one type of product? Is this a good idea?

Types of Economic Systems

Why should you understand the economic systems in other countries?

Economic systems vary depending on government involvement. In some systems people have more options as individuals, while in other systems they act collectively by letting the government make decisions for them. Due to the availability of economic resources in a country, an economy must answer the same basic questions:

- **What goods and services should be produced?** If more of one item is produced then less of another item will be produced. For example, a business must decide what items to produce and how much of each.
- **How should the goods and services be produced?** A business, for example, must determine the factors needed to produce an item.
- **Who should get the goods and services that are produced?** Who receives the goods and services will depend on the economic system.

How a nation makes decisions to allocate its resources is called an **economy.** Three basic types of economic systems are traditional, command, and market.

Traditional Economy

In a **traditional economy,** all three economic questions are answered by customs and tradition. Members of the society engage in activities required for survival. They produce tools needed for hunting and gathering, as well as goods needed for shelter and cooking. How they go about the production is based on what their ancestors did. Since their main concern is survival, extra goods are not available for sale. If there are extra goods, members of a traditional economy may barter. **Bartering** is the exchange of products without the use of money.

Today, examples of traditional economies are limited. The Inuit people who live in the cold environment of the Arctic Circle are one example. The roles played by each member of that society are based on survival in an extreme environment. Bhutan in Africa is an underdeveloped country where agriculture is important for survival. With few roads or other means of transporting goods, those who farm the land generally consume the farmed products.

Command Economy

A **command economy** is a system in which a central authority controls all economic decisions. Either a dictator or a central planning committee decides what products are produced. The government also decides how the products are produced because the government controls all the economic resources in the country. It controls the land, housing, public utilities, factories, and stores. Therefore, the government is the employer for all people in that society.

Everyone Contributes
A traditional economy is an economy based on custom and tradition. *What are some advantages and disadvantages of a traditional economy?*

In a command economy, the selection of consumer products is limited to the basic needs. You will not see a variety of choices or different brands of products. Individuals in a command economy have no influence over what is produced or how it is produced. For special luxuries, like a washing machine or an automobile, consumers are often put on a waiting list. Though the selection of products is minimal, prices for necessities, such as food, shelter, and clothing, are low in command economies so the people collectively can benefit from government control.

Only a few countries in the world today still possess the characteristics of a true command economy. North Korea and parts of China are the two main examples. In these countries, a large amount of the economic activity is government-planned.

Market Economy

In a **market economy**, supply, demand, and a system of pricing allow people to make the economic decisions through free interaction. The marketplace, not the government, has control over economic decisions. What is produced is based on consumer demand. This is called consumer sovereignty. Every time an individual buys a product, the question of what should be produced is answered. The businesses who take the risk of making the products decide how products are produced. Individuals determine who gets the products that are produced. They work and invest their earnings so they have money to buy the products they need and want. The more income individuals have, the more goods and services they can buy.

In a market economy, consumers have a variety of products from which to choose. Prices are established in the marketplace based on the interaction of buyers and sellers and competition plays a role in the quality, variety, and pricing. Market economies are common in developed nations, such as Japan and the United States.

Careers That Count!

Ileana Bromfield • Legislative Assistant

It would be impossible for state legislators to complete their workloads without reliable help. As a legislative assistant, I respond to requests from constituents, read and research bills, speak with the press, and work with researchers, attorneys, constituent aides, and committee staff. I may also assist with re-election tasks. Legislative staffers have to be willing to work behind the scenes and understand that the credit for our work will likely go to the legislators. I have a degree in political science, but my colleagues come from a variety of backgrounds, including social studies, law, economics, and foreign languages. My time-management and multi-tasking skills are put to the test every day. This is a fast-paced, high-energy job. It is not always secure, because assistants often lose their jobs when the legislators move on or do not get re-elected. However, it can be a great stepping stone to other jobs, and knowing what I do has an impact makes this a very rewarding job.

EXPLORE CAREERS

Visit the Web site of the U.S. Department of Labor's Bureau of Labor Statistics and learn more about the responsibilities of legislators.

1. What are some specific tasks that require both the legislator and his or her assistants to be excellent communicators and team players?
2. How could you address the job-security concerns if you were a legislative assistant?

Skills	Education	Career Path
Diplomacy, communication, multi-tasking, leadership, time-management, and conflict resolution skills	Bachelor's degree; age, residence, and voter registration requirements may apply	Legislative assistants can become legislators, lawyers, or politicians.

glencoe.com

Activity Download a Career Exploration Activity.

Mixed Economic Systems

As you learned about the three economic systems, you may have realized that no nation is a purely traditional, command, or market economy. There are aspects of each type of economic system found in all nations. For example, in the United States the government has laws and regulations that affect how businesses operate. Therefore, how something is produced is not solely at the **discretion,** or judgment, of the business owner. There are laws that protect consumers that businesses must follow. The United States also offers free public education, and programs such as Medicare and Medicaid, which are paid for by taxpayers. The classification of an economic system is based on the degree to which it conforms to the three basic systems.

Reading Check

Summarize What is a market economy?

FIGURE 2 **Economic Systems**

Mixed Economies Most economies in the world are a mixture of traditional, command, and market economic systems. *What aspects of each system can be found in the U.S. economy?*

	Traditional	Command	Market
Advantages	• Each person's role in the economy is set and well-defined • Stable and predictable	• Change and improvements in the economy can occur rapidly • Public services such as education and health care cost very little or nothing at all	• Individual freedoms for everyone • Adjust to change gradually • Limited government interference • Not controlled by a central decision maker • Variety of goods and services • Higher level of consumer satisfaction
Disadvantages	• New ideas and changes in procedures are discouraged • Limited progress • Standard of living is often lower	• Does not address the needs and wants of consumers • Limited incentive for people to work • A large ruling body is needed and often consumes resources • Limited flexibility to address change • Does not encourage initiative in individuals	• Only productive resources are rewarded • Does not provide for people who are unable to work due to age for example • Does not produce enough public goods such as health care • Workers and businesses face uncertainty due to competition and change

Supply and Demand

How can knowledge of pricing theories improve your personal finances?

The concepts of supply and demand operate together in a market economy. As the price of a particular item goes down, more consumers will demand the product, increasing demand. If the price of the item increases consumers will demand less of the product, reducing demand. This correlation is the law of supply.

In a market economy, prices and wages are determined by supply and demand. **Supply** is how much producers are willing and able to produce at a certain price. **Demand** is how much consumers are willing and able to buy at a certain price. **Figure 3** shows how price is related to the quantity demanded or supplied.

Influences on Supply

Price is not the only factor that can affect supply. There are four factors that can influence the supply of a particular product: price of inputs, number of suppliers, taxes, and technology.

Price of Inputs Inputs are all of the materials, wages, etc. that are necessary to produce a product. As the price of inputs decreases, a producer can make more of a product at a lower cost. This increases the supply available at each price. However, if the price of inputs increases, producers will make fewer products reducing the supply.

Number of Suppliers As suppliers in a particular industry enter and leave the market, supply is affected. When additional suppliers enter an industry, more of a product is supplied, increasing supply at each price. However, when suppliers leave an industry, supply is reduced.

Taxes If the government places more taxes on a product, the cost of producing that product will increase. A business will produce less of the product due to the increased cost, and the supply will decrease.

Technology Advancements in technology will increase supply. Technology allows suppliers to produce more products at a lower cost.

When you plot supply and demand on a graph, the price at which consumers and producers agree is called the **equilibrium point.** When prices are at the equilibrium point, there are no overages or shortages of goods. This same principle can be applied to jobs and wages. When there are as many employees as employers need and they agree on a wage, there is no shortage or surplus of employees.

Surpluses

A surplus occurs when supply exceeds demand. To get rid of their products quickly, producers lower prices to encourage consumers to buy. That action provides an incentive for consumers to buy larger quantities when prices are low. For example, at the end of a season, you often find excess products on sale in clothing stores. When there is a surplus of employees in a given career area, workers may accept lower wages because they want to be employed.

Shortages

A shortage occurs when demand exceeds supply. Consumers drive the price up when there is a shortage and producers are willing to sell at a higher price since they earn more profit. For example, when there is an oil shortage, gasoline prices often increase and consumers are forced to pay the higher prices. When there is a shortage of employees in a given career area, workers can often negotiate higher wages because the employer has a need for those workers. Some employers may even offer a signing bonus if they elect to work for them.

Government Intervention

In some cases, the government will get involved in setting prices if it believes it is necessary to protect consumers or suppliers. A **price ceiling** is a maximum price set by the government that can be charged for goods and services. Price ceilings often result in shortages of goods

FIGURE 3 **Demand, Supply, and Price**

Demand and Supply Curves These graphs show how price is related to the quantity demanded or supplied. *When the price goes down, what happens to the quantity demanded? What happens to the quantity supplied?*

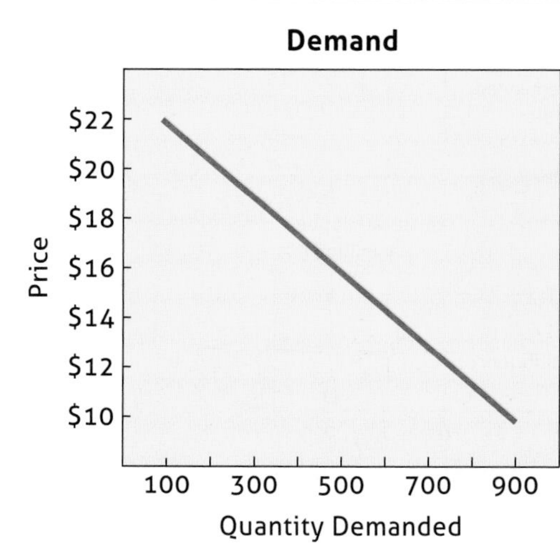

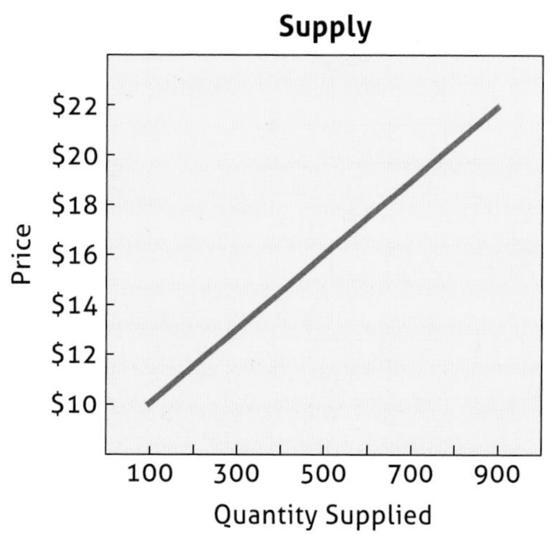

or services. The shortage may lead to the government limiting the sale or distribution of goods and services in short supply. For example, a local government could set a price ceiling on rent for apartments in a certain area. More people would like to rent at the government-set price, but property owners would be less likely to build additional units if they could not charge higher rent. This would result in a shortage of apartments. See **Figure 4.**

In contrast, a **price floor** is a minimum price set by the government that can be charged for goods and services. The minimum wage is an example of a price floor. It is the lowest legal wage that can be paid to most workers. If a local business was prepared to hire 50 workers at $6.00 an hour, but the minimum wage was set at $7.25 an hour, the price floor would cause the business to hire less, creating a surplus of unemployed workers. See **Figure 4.**

Demand Elasticity

The degree to which demand is affected by price is called **demand elasticity.** Just like an elastic band that stretches when you pull it, the demand for elastic goods changes as the price changes for that product. Thus, **elastic demand** is when demand for a product is affected by price. For example, as the price of movies increases, people attend fewer movies. When prices decrease, more people attend movies.

FIGURE 4 **Price Ceilings and Floors**

Government Intervention In some cases, the government will set price ceilings or price floors. *What are the effects of the price ceiling and the price floor?*

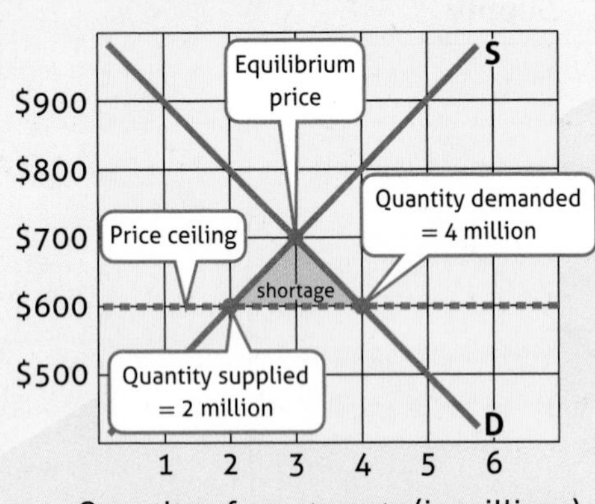

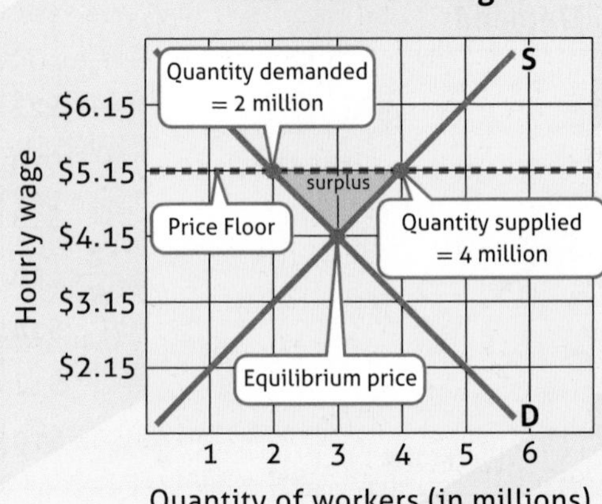

Demand is also affected by available substitutes. When there are many available brands of detergent, demand tends to be more elastic. For example, if the price of one brand of detergent increases, consumers will buy other less expensive brands. So the demand for the higher-priced detergent would decline.

A person's financial situation will have a bearing on choices as well. The price relative to a person's income will affect demand for a product. Consumers on a budget will react to changes in price and seek out available lower-priced substitutes. However, higher-priced items may not affect high-income earners because the increase in price would be small in relation to their income.

With **inelastic demand,** price has little influence on demand. Most products that have inelastic demand are necessities. For example, electricity and prescription drugs are items that people need. Therefore, when the prices of these products change, demand does not change much.

Inelastic demand is also apparent with brand loyal consumers and situations when you must make an immediate purchase without regard to price. Brand-loyal consumers do not accept substitutes and so they opt to pay a premium price. For example, if you had a favorite brand of athletic shoes and the price went up, you may still buy them because you are loyal to that brand. If you approach a sign that indicates a gas station is the last one for miles and you are running low, you will pay whatever the price of the gasoline is at that service station.

Denmark

High Income Tax

While most people do not like taxes, they have accepted them as a part of life. Many people frequently vote in elections to try and lower taxes or prevent them from being raised. So imagine how it would feel to live in the country with the highest taxes in the world. Denmark has some of the highest tax rates in the world with a tax-to-GDP (gross domestic product) ratio of 48.9 percent. This calculation includes all forms of taxes, including social contribution (or gross tax), municipal tax, health tax, state tax, sales tax, church tax, and corporate tax. In spite of this, surveys regularly report a high level of satisfaction among Danish citizens. This is probably partially due to the way government uses those taxes. Among other things, Denmark provides free education and health care and boasts low unemployment rates and steady economic growth. If you do lose your job, the government offers unemployment insurance for up to four years.

Critical Thinking

1. **Expand** Research to find the type of state tax used in Denmark. What are the various income brackets for state tax?
2. **Relate** People in the United States are constantly seeking lower taxes. Do you think we should have lower taxes? Or do you think we should follow Denmark's model and raise taxes?

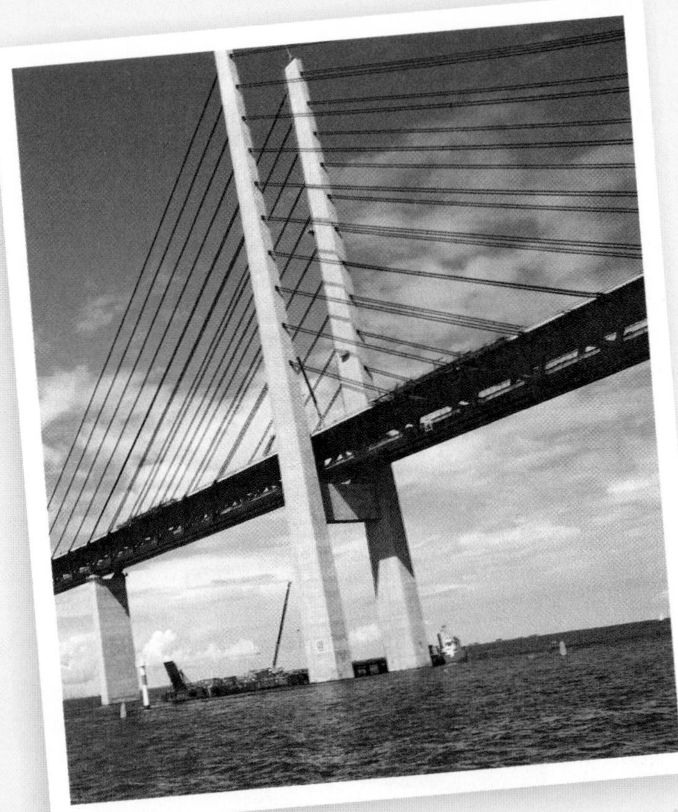

DATABYTES

Capital
Copenhagen

Population
5,515,575

Languages
Danish, Faroese, English, Greenlandic (an Inuit dialect), German (small minority)

Currency
Danish krone

Gross Domestic Product (GDP)
$311.9 billion

GDP per capita
$36,000

Industry
Iron, steel, nonferrous metals, chemicals, food processing, machinery and transportation equipment, textiles and clothing, electronics, construction, furniture and other wood products, shipbuilding and refurbishment, windmills, pharmaceuticals, medical equipment

Agriculture
Barley, wheat, potatoes, sugar beets; pork, dairy products; fish

Exports
Machinery and instruments, meat and meat products, dairy products, fish, pharmaceuticals, furniture, windmills

Natural Resources
Petroleum, natural gas, fish, salt, limestone, chalk, stone, gravel and sand

SECTION 1 Assessment

Review Key Concepts

1. **Define** What is an opportunity cost?
2. **Summarize** What is the role of marginal cost and benefit when making decisions?
3. **List** What are the four factors of production?
4. **Describe** What is scarcity? Why is it a basic problem in economics?
5. **Explain** How are prices determined through supply and demand? What is consumer sovereignty?
6. **Distinguish** What is elastic demand? What is inelastic demand?
7. **Compare and Contrast** Compare and Contrast the economic systems.

Higher Order Thinking H.O.T.

8. **Theorize** Can businesses create inelastic demand for their products? Explain your answer and, if yes, provide examples.

English Language Arts

9. **Synthesize** Consumers, businesses, and governments face scarcity of resources. Research how each group addresses scarcity. What are the marginal costs and benefits? What are the long-term consequences of the choices? How do businesses respond to consumer sovereignty? Prepare a brief summary of your research.

NCTE 12 Use language to accomplish individual purposes.

Mathematics

10. **Opportunity Cost** Tom took a job at a grocery store during his summer break. At the end of the summer, he managed to save $500 from the job. Tom would like to purchase a new television for his bedroom, while his parents have advised him to open a savings account. A new savings account earns 2 percent interest per year. If Tom chooses to purchase the television instead, what is the marginal cost or marginal benefit after one year?

Math Concept **Calculate Cost** To calculate the marginal cost or benefit, you determine the total benefit of the option that was not taken.

Starting Hint Multiply the total dollar amount by the annual interest rate in order to determine the interest earned after one year.

NCTM Problem Solving Apply and adapt a variety of appropriate strategies to solve problems.

Check your answers.

The Financial System

When you start earning money, how will you save or invest it?

When you listen to the news you may hear reports on how the "market did today." The market in this case is the financial market. If you own stocks or bonds, you would be interested in that news. The market responds to changes in the economy in the United States and abroad, as well as changes in government policies.

Financial Markets

A **financial market** is a mechanism that provides the means for purchasing and selling stocks, bonds, commodities, and other financial instruments. Stocks are ownership shares in a corporation. A bond is money loaned to a company or government. A commodity is a good that is **fungible,** can be easily substituted for a good of equal value, and has demand. Commodities include goods such as agricultural (i.e. wheat, sugar) and mining products (i.e. coal, iron ore).

In the United States, there are two financial markets or exchanges that bring buyers and sellers together. They are the New York Stock Exchange and the electronic NASDAQ. There are other types of financial markets as well that involve money markets, **derivatives** (involves managing financial risk), insurance markets, and foreign exchange markets.

Financial markets provide the means for companies to find investors and lenders. When companies do well, investors may be paid dividends (portion of the company's profits). Lenders are paid interest.

The sale prices for stocks change constantly as a result of trading. When a large number of investors start buying a stock the price generally goes up. When investors start selling stocks, the price goes down. So, you can make money buying and selling stocks if you buy when the stock price is low and sell when it is higher. You can also lose money if the opposite occurs.

Advancements in technology and telecommunications have made the world one large financial market. United States government securities, foreign exchanges, and stocks are traded continuously across the world. In addition, countries like Britain, Germany, and Japan have separate financial markets as well. In today's global economy other countries' financial markets can influence the United States financial market. The economy, political unrest, government policies, and a host of other factors can influence the market.

Section Objectives

- **Explain** financial markets and financial institutions.
- **Identify** incentives.
- **Describe** how different groups respond to incentives.

As You Read

Observe Look around your community for examples of the financial system and the roles of the government that affect your life.

Financial Institutions

Financial institutions provide services for their clients or members so they can save, borrow, or invest their money. For example, the money you put into your bank is used to provide loans to the bank's customers that need to borrow money. This process keeps the money supply moving through the economy.

There are two broad categories of financial institutions in the United States: depository institutions and non-depository institutions.

Depository Institutions **Depository institutions** manage money deposited in their institution. Examples of depository institutions include:

- Commercial Banks
- Credit unions
- Savings and Loan Associations

The money deposited is used to provide other customers and members with loans. Savers are paid interest on the money they deposited. Depository institutions borrow money (money deposited) at one interest rate and then lend money at a higher rate.

There are many laws and regulations that govern how these depository institutions may function. The Federal Reserve Board oversees this industry.

Non-depository Institutions **Non-depository institutions** do not handle deposits, but they do act as an intermediary between savers and borrowers. They sell securities and insurance policies in order to generate income for their institutions and they either invest or lend the funds they collect. Non-depository institutions include firms such as: insurance companies, investment bankers, mutual funds, and stock brokerage firms. The Securities and Exchange Commission (SEC) is the regulatory agency that oversees the sale of stocks and bonds.

Commercial Banks
A bank is one of the most common financial institutions for consumers. *What type of institution is a commercial bank? Why?*

Brokerage Companies
A stock brokerage firm helps consumers to purchase and trade stocks and bonds and other securities. *What other services do brokerage firms offer?*

Insurance companies sell insurance to companies and individuals to protect them from financial risks. For example, you may purchase homeowner's insurance or automobile insurance. In both cases you pay for the reassurance that if something should happen to your home or auto, you have insurance that will cover some of the repair costs. Life insurance is purchased to defray funeral costs and to provide money to family members who may need it to pay family debts. The owner of the purchased policy will pay premiums for the life of the policy. Because insurance companies collect these payments on a regular schedule, they may lend surplus funds to others.

Investment bankers are licensed brokers that specialize in helping companies and governments issue new securities to the investing public. They help investors by purchasing and trading stocks and bonds, as well as providing advice and managing the assets of a company. They are often used when companies merge.

Mutual fund companies create portfolios of stocks. Each mutual fund contains stocks from several different corporations. Mutual fund companies manage those funds, some of which carry more risk than others. An individual or company may purchase shares in a mutual fund that suits their needs and tolerance for risk.

Brokerage firms and stock brokers are agents that buy and sell securities for individuals. They advise investors and conduct the trading of securities on the investors' behalf for a fee. They may also provide software to allow traders to select a trade and complete the transactions on their own.

Reading Check

Summarize What is the difference between depository and non-depository institutions?

Economics and You

Adam Smith

Adam Smith was born in Scotland in 1723. His most famous and influential work was *The Wealth of Nations.* In it, he introduced the concept of "division of labor" meaning labor becomes more productive as each worker becomes more skilled at a single job. Smith defined a nation's wealth as the sum of the goods produced by labor.

Smith's main argument was that a society is most successful when individuals are free to pursue self-interests without government regulation. He suggested that the role of government should be limited to enforcing contracts, granting patents and copyrights, and providing public works such as roads and bridges. Smith's idea of a "laissez-faire" (French for "let it be") approach marked the beginning of modern economics. In fact, this premise still serves as the basis of the U.S. economy in which competition, division of labor, and limited government involvement are believed to lead to increased productivity and output.

Personal Finance Connection A free market economy provides many benefits to the consumer. The consumer drives the economy and is provided with many options for purchases and investing. Considering and evaluating the opportunity costs and trade-offs for each option is critical to managing your personal finances.

Critical Thinking List examples of how Smith's ideas are evident in the workings of the modern U.S. economy. Explain how a person's pursuit of his or her own self-interests might benefit society as a whole.

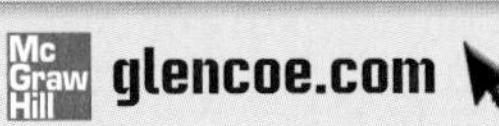

Activity Download an Economics and You Worksheet Activity.

Incentives

How do incentives affect how you manage your personal finances?

An **incentive** encourages specific behavior and helps to motivate individuals to take specific action. There is generally a reward attached to incentives. An example of a positive incentive would be getting bonus points for doing extra credit on a school project or a rebate for buying a particular product. A negative incentive would involve getting a zero as a test grade for not completing an assignment.

How Businesses Use Incentives

Businesses use incentives to motivate workers and to encourage consumers to buy their products. Businesses offer incentives to workers through recognition and wages and to consumers through savings and rewards programs.

Workers To encourage workers to do their very best, businesses may offer a reward, such as "Employee of the Month." Salespeople may be encouraged to reach or exceed certain sales goals to receive a bonus. Employees may receive a bonus if productivity exceeds a goal. A negative incentive may involve not following a business's regulations or rules. If employees break any rules, they can be fired.

Businesses also offer incentives through wages. The higher the wage offered by a business the higher the quantity or work supplied. For example, if an employee earns $10 an hour at his or her current job, the decision to work 3 hours less incurs an opportunity cost of $30. If a business increases the wage to $15 an hour, the cost of the 3 hours increases to $45. The cost to the employee of working less is an incentive for him or her to work more.

Consumers To entice consumers to buy their products, businesses will offer special sales and loyalty programs. Loyalty program incentives may be special discounts and free products or services after a certain number of purchases. Some incentives to encourage restaurant patronage may be offering free toys for children or free appetizers with dinner. Some restaurants even offer "children eat free" if adults purchase dinners. Businesses may be very creative with the incentives they offer consumers. However, consumers must be aware of "scams". Some incentives may be too good to be true. For example, you may be offered a $500 gift card if you complete a survey. However, when you read the fine print, you learn that not everyone who completes the survey receives the incentive. Also, you may be asked to supply personal information. Identity theft is a serious crime that often uses consumer incentives to gather information.

How Governments Use Incentives

Most government-sponsored incentives involve tax benefits for producers, citizens, savers, and investors. Two types of tax incentives are tax deductions and tax credits. Tax deductions reduce the taxable income upon which tax payers calculate the amount they owe the state or federal government. A tax credit is a dollar amount that reduces the total tax owed after all tax deductions have been applied. It is important to keep abreast of any changes in the laws with regard to income taxes; as they change all the time.

Producers A state may offer tax relief in the form of no taxes or a lower tax rate for companies that build a new facility that will help a depressed area by hiring new workers. Some companies may receive tax incentives to create energy efficient buildings or for repairing historic buildings. A federal government may offer tax relief to foreign companies that are willing to open a new manufacturing facility in the United States (foreign direct investment). A negative incentive for producers would be fines for not following government regulations. For example, a company may be fined if it is found to exceed the air pollution requirements set by a community and corrective action would be required.

Civic Literacy

Civic literacy combines the knowledge and skills necessary to effectively participate in government and your community. It is important for you to understand your rights and duties as a citizen at the local, state, and national level. For example, voting is both a right and duty of citizens. Whether you are voting on school issues or in national elections, it is important to stay informed on the issues and understand the processes of the government because your vote may affect national and global issues.

Write About It

Consider how you can stay informed on candidates as well as national and local issues. Write a summary of sources and methods for staying informed on civic issues.

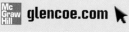

Activity Download a Career and College Readiness Worksheet Activity.

Endless Options
There are many options and incentives to encourage saving for college and for retirement. *What factors would help you decide on how to save your money and plan for the future?*

Savers and Investors To encourage employees to save for their retirement, the government allows them to create special accounts, such as 401K and individual retirement accounts (IRAs). The government incentive is that the money saved in those accounts is not considered income for tax purposes. Thus, money saved in a 401K reduces the income upon which income tax is computed.

Specific stocks and bonds may also provide tax incentives because they may be taxed at a different rate than others. To encourage saving for college, all states have special college savings programs (529 fund) that parents can begin when a child is very young. The 529 contributions are not tax deductible when they are made. However, the actual fund is tax-deferred. When a child uses the money for college it is tax-free.

A disincentive for savers is low interest rates. For example in 2010, savings account interest rates were less than one percent. A weak economy with many companies reporting poor results may create a negative incentive or disincentive for investing in securities.

Citizens To encourage citizens to recycle, local government may provide residents with recycling bins to use. Tax deductions may be allowed for children, college tuition, and a portion of charitable donations, as well as interest paid on mortgages. Negative incentives for citizens that encourage them to pay their state and federal taxes, are fines and possible imprisonment.

To encourage citizens to buy energy-efficient hybrid vehicles and appliances, they may be offered tax credits. To encourage home sales, new home buyers may be offered a tax credit for specific periods of time. In 2010 the amount of the tax credit was $8,000 for new home buyers. "Cash for Clunkers" was a special program established in 2009 for a short period of time to encourage citizens to trade in their gas-guzzling autos for new autos. These types of incentives are often created to increase consumer spending and improve the economy.

After You Read

Connect Why is learning about economic concepts important to managing your personal finances?

Assessment

Review Key Concepts

1. **Identify** What are incentives? Provide examples.
2. **Explain** What are financial markets?
3. **Describe** What are the types of financial institutions? How are they similar? How are they different?
4. **Summarize** Describe how workers, producers, consumers, savers, investors, and citizens respond to incentives.

Higher Order Thinking 

5. **Relate** How do incentives for each group impact the economy?

21st Century Skills

6. **Make Judgments and Decisions** During an economic downturn, or recession, businesses cut back on production and lay off workers. When a recession is coupled with a meltdown of the financial markets and housing markets, the economy gets even worse. Recently in the United States many homeowners lost their homes because they could not pay their mortgages. Some people took out mortgages on homes they could not afford. In other cases, home values declined dramatically, and as a result mortgages were greater than the value of the homes. Banks that held delinquent mortgages foreclosed homes. What recommendations would you make to your generation and to your government so this does not happen again?

Mathematics

7. **Local Income Tax and Sales Tax** You want to determine how much you pay in local tax and sales tax over a year. Local tax is based on your annual salary while sales tax is based on goods that are purchased. Research to determine the local tax rate of your city or assume your locality has a tax rate of 2.25 percent. The local sales tax where you have purchased all of your goods is 6.25 percent. Calculate the local income tax you pay if your annual salary is $43,000. If you purchased $12,350 worth of goods during the year, what is the sales tax you would have paid?

Math Concept **Calculate Tax** To calculate the tax that is owed first identify the tax rate for the specific tax. Determine what the tax is based on and multiply the rate by the base amount.

Starting Hint Determine the sales tax you would have paid by first determining the total amount you paid for consumer goods during the period. Identify the sales tax rate and multiply this by the total amount spent on consumer goods.

NCTM Problem Solving Solve problems that arise in mathematics and in other contexts.

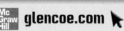

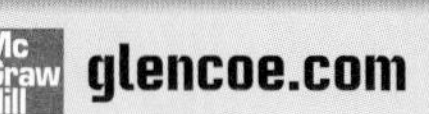

Check your answers.

CHAPTER REVIEW

Visual Summary

The Fundamentals of Economics

Economy Overlap

Most modern economies are mixed economies, combining elements of the different economic systems.

Command Economy
- Government decides what products to produce and how
- Government owns land, utilities, factories, stores
- Products limited to necessities

Mixed Economy
- Regulations to protect consumers
- Programs for low-income families and the elderly

Market Economy
- No government involvement in the production of goods and services
- Marketplace determines production
- Large selection of products

Incentives

Businesses and governments use incentives to positively impact the economy.

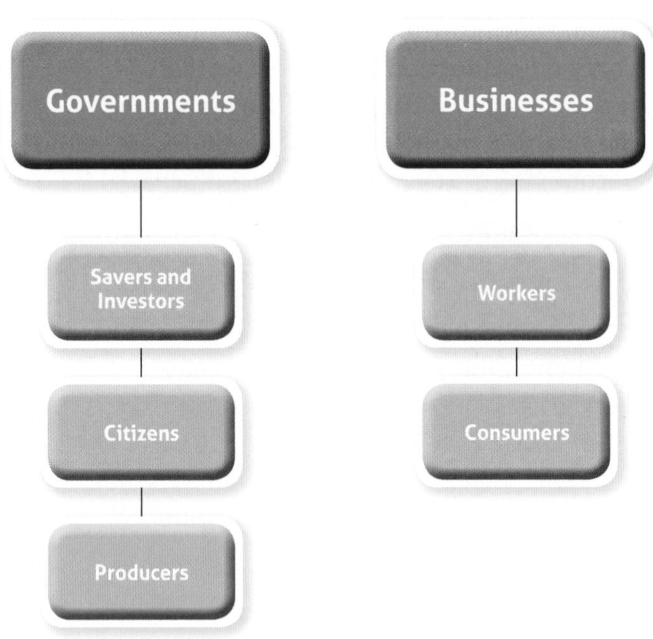

Try It!

Draw a diagram like the one shown to identify the factors of production.

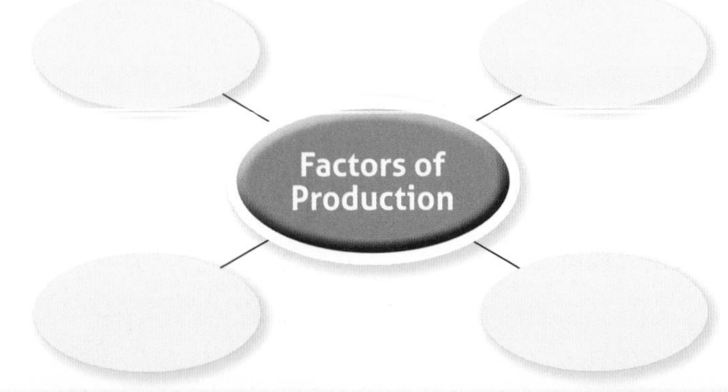

Chapter Review and Assessment

Chapter Summary

- Due to scarcity, individuals and nations must make decisions based on limited economic resources to satisfy their unlimited wants and needs.
- Opportunity costs help in the decision-making process.
- Due to the principle of scarcity, the three types of economic systems (traditional, command, and market) must make decisions on what, how, and who should get the goods that are produced in a nation to meet the unlimited needs and wants of its people.
- Supply and demand interact in the marketplace to determine prices.
- The four factors of production are land, labor, capital, and entrepreneurship.
- Financial institutions provide services for their clients or members so they can save, borrow, or invest their money.
- The economy, political unrest, government policies, and a host of other factors can influence financial markets.
- Businesses use incentives to motivate workers and to encourage consumers to buy their products.
- Most government-sponsored incentives involve tax benefits for producers, citizens, savers, and investors.

Vocabulary Review

1. Write each of the vocabulary terms below on an index card, and the definitions on separate index cards. Work in pairs or small groups to match each term to its definition.

- economics
- opportunity cost
- scarcity
- factors of production
- land
- labor
- capital
- entrepreneurship
- economy
- traditional economy
- bartering
- command economy
- market economy
- supply
- demand
- equilibrium point
- price ceiling
- price floor
- demand elasticity
- elastic demand
- inelastic demand
- financial market
- depository institutions
- non-depository institutions
- incentive
- allocates
- discretion
- fungible
- derivatives

Higher Order Thinking 

2. **Describe** What are needs and wants and provide examples of each?
3. **Summarize** What role do financial institutions serve in the economy?
4. **Relate** How do incentives benefit a business, the government, and the consumer?
5. **Distinguish** How are depository and non-depository institutions different? What is the purpose of each to the economy?
6. **Synthesize** Select a popular product. Identify examples for each factor of production for the manufacturing and selling of the product.
7. **Hypothesize** If an economy were to lose one of the four factors of production, how would it be affected? Consider this for each factor of production.
8. **Compare and contrast** Explain how businesses, consumers, and governments face scarcity of resources. What are the trade-offs and opportunity costs for each?
9. **Defend** Explain a recent decision you made based on the concept of opportunity cost.

College and Career Readiness

Social Studies

10. Economic Systems Imagine that you moved to a new home in a traditional or command economy. Consider what your life would be like. What things would be the same and what things would be different? Consider topics such as your daily activities, current and future finances, education, career choices, and personal goals. Write an essay to explain the comparisons between the economy in which you live, and your imaginary home in either a traditional or command economy.

NCSS VI E Compare different political systems (their ideologies, structure, institutions, processes, and political cultures) with that of the United States.

Mathematics

11. Equilibrium Price and Quantity Market equilibrium is the price at which consumers wish to purchase the same amount that producers are willing to offer for sale. It is the point at which there is no incentive for producers or consumers to change their behavior. Assume the following supply and demand equations: supply is given by $Qs = 90 + 10P$ and demand is $Qd = 150 - 5P$. Find the equilibrium price where the quantity demanded (Qd) is equal to the quantity supplied (Qs). Also solve for the quantity demanded (Qd) and the quantity supplied (Qs).

Math Concept **Calculate Equilibrium Quantity** To calculate the equilibrium quantity solve for the equilibrium price and substitute this figure with "P" in either of the quantity demanded or quantity supplied formulas. Solve for Qd or Qs to determine the quantity.

Starting Hint Determine the equilibrium price by setting the quantity demanded and quantity supplied formulas equal to each other as follows: $Qs = Qd$ or $90 + 10P = 150 - 5P$. Solve this equation for P.

NCTM Algebra Represent and analyze mathematical situations and structures using algebraic symbols.

English Language Arts

12. Financial Planning Keeping up with current news is a good practice. The more you know about the state of the U.S. economy, the better position you are in to make intelligent decisions about your current well being and your financial future. Find a current news article about the economy. Cite your source by including the name of the publication, author, date, and page number. Summarize the article in one paragraph, and in a second paragraph indicate how that information may have an impact on you and your family now or in the future.

NCTE 1 Read texts to acquire new information.

Economics

13. Production Why do countries trade? Countries have different resources. Climates, growing seasons, and natural resources vary. No two countries have the same degree of efficiency when using resources. It is more efficient to produce goods with lower opportunity costs, and then use the increased production of those goods to trade for goods with higher opportunity costs. How would an increase in trade result in more efficient use of the world's scarce resources? How will standards of living be affected? Explain in a one-page essay.

Real-World Applications

14. Take-home Pay Juan has been offered a job working 16 hours per week for $12.50 per hour. His auto insurance is $175 per month. His parents prefer that he concentrate on school and not work more than 16 hours per week. (A) Calculate Juan's weekly net pay if he works 16 hours per week by applying these deductions: federal income tax rate 10 percent; state income tax rate 2 percent; Social Security rate 7 percent; unemployment insurance 3 percent. (B) How much money would Juan have left at the end of the month after paying for his car insurance? (C) How can Juan use the concept of opportunity cost to make a decision?

Do Your Financial and Educational Goals Work Together?

Rory's parents had saved enough money for her tuition at a state-funded college. However, Rory was responsible for all other college costs, like books, housing, food, and activities. If she wanted to go to a private college, she would have to take out a student loan to pay the difference. Rory decided on the state-funded college so she would not go into debt. During college, she continued to work part-time. By the time she finished college, she was debt-free and still had money in her bank account.

Comparison of Costs Between State-Funded and Privately-Funded Colleges for One Year*

State-Funded College		Privately-Funded College		Notes
Tuition	$	Tuition	$	
Books	$	Books	$	
Food	$	Food	$	
Fun Activities	$	Fun Activities	$	
Subtotal	$	Subtotal	$	
If staying on campus		If staying on campus		
Housing	$	Housing	$	
Total	$	Total	$	
If commuting		If commuting		
Gasoline, Tolls	$	Gasoline, Tolls	$	
Total	$	Total	$	

**Note: These costs are for one year. Multiply totals by four to complete the financial plan for college.*

Financial Plan for College

State-Funded College		Privately-Funded College		Notes
Cost for 4 years	$	Cost for 4 years	$	
Financing		Financing		
Savings	$	Savings	$	
Wages	$	Wages	$	
Student Loans	$	Student Loans	$	
Total	$	Total	$	

Calculate

Research the cost of tuition at a state-funded and privately-funded college. Calculate the costs involved if you live on campus and if you commute to college. On a separate sheet of paper, create a chart like the one above to illustrate the financial costs involved. What can you do now to plan for the finances you will need for college? In your chart, include the savings, wages, and student loans that may be necessary to finance a four-year college education for both the state-funded and privately-funded college you researched.

CHAPTER 2

Economics and the Global Economy

Visual Literacy

The right to vote is a fundamental principle of American democracy. ***Why do you need to be concerned about the views of those running for government offices?***

Discovery Project

Develop a Financial Plan

Key Question

What options are available, and what factors should be considered when developing a financial plan?

Project Goal

Work with a partner or in small groups to design a financial plan for a client. Create a profile of your client with regard to age, marital status, number of children, and occupation. Create a name for your team and decide on a strategy for managing $100,000 of your client's money. Assign members of the team responsibilities such as monitoring the economy and reporting news about government policies, foreign financial markets, and current events that impact financial markets. In essence your team is the financial advisor for the client you described. So, you must be able to support your financial game plan with research and knowledge of your client's needs now and in the future. Create a presentation detailing your financial plan and the reasons for your choices and present it to the class.

Ask Yourself...

- *How are you going to describe your client?*
- *Where can you find current information on saving and investing money?*
- *What factors should be considered when deciding on a financial strategy for your client?*
- *How should the $100,000 be allocated to meet your client's current and future needs?*
- *How would you present the financial plan to your client?*

Reason Effectively

Why do you need to understand economics and politics in order to create a financial plan?

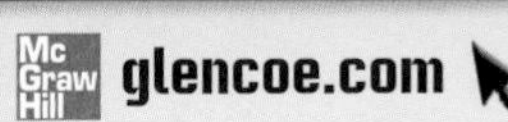

Evaluate Download an assessment rubric.

THE BIG IDEA

The more you know about economics and government policies, the more informed your decisions will be regarding your current and future finances.

ASK STANDARD & POOR'S

Government Policies and Economics

Q *If I cannot vote yet, why should I be concerned with economics and government policies?*

A Government policies can impact your future earnings and savings through income tax guidelines, interest rates, and government sponsored programs that must be funded with your tax dollars. The more you know about government policies and the health of the economy, the better choices you will make regarding your finances. Knowledge of government policies and the economy will also help you when you decide on a career and when you vote.

Writing Activity

Write a letter to an elected official about a policy that will affect you now or in the near future. To find a topic of interest visit a government Web site to see recent legislation, such as the recent credit card legislation.

CHAPTER 2

Reading Guide

Before You Read

The Essential Question How can your understanding of economic principles and government policies influence your financial decisions?

Main Idea

The more you know about how an economy operates and the government's role in the economy, the better educated you will be when making life decisions about the use of your financial resources, voting for government officials, and planning your future career.

Content Vocabulary

- fiat money
- money supply
- budget deficit
- budget surplus
- patent
- copyright
- trademark
- Gross Domestic Product (GDP)
- Consumer Price Index (CPI)
- inflation
- deflation
- recession
- trough
- specialization
- international trade
- absolute advantage
- comparative advantage
- balance of trade
- protectionism
- tariff
- quota
- embargo

Academic Vocabulary

You will see these words in your reading and on your tests.

- regulator
- intellectual property
- indicators
- interdependent

Graphic Organizer

Before you read this chapter draw a diagram like the one shown. As you read, use the diagram to chart economic concepts as they relate to the government and the community.

Economics and Community	Economics and Government

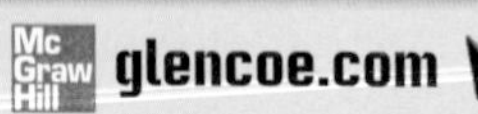

Print this organizer.

Standards

Academic

Mathematics

NCTM Representations Create and use representations to organize, record, and communicate mathematical ideas.

NCTM Number and Operations Understand meanings of operations and how they relate to one another.

English Language Arts

NCTE 5 Use different writing process elements to communicate effectively.

NCTE 8 Use information resources to gather information and create and communicate knowledge.

Social Studies

NCSS VI C Power, Authority, & Governance Analyze and explain ideas and mechanisms to meet needs and wants of citizens, regulate territory, manage conflict, establish order and security, and balance competing conceptions of a just society.

NCTM *National Council of Teachers of Mathematics*
NCTE *National Council of Teachers of English*
NCSS *National Council for the Social Studies*
NSES *National Science Education Standards*

Common Core

Reading Determine central ideas or themes of a text and analyze their development; summarize the key supporting details and ideas.

Speaking and Listening Prepare for and participate effectively in a range of conversations and collaborations with diverse partners, building on others' ideas and expressing their own clearly and persuasively.

Role of Money

Why is a stable money supply important to your personal savings and future financial plans?

Money is something that is used for trading, saving, lending, and investing. You can use it to make purchases and pay off debts. You can also save it for future use.

Money has little value unless people accept it as representing value. For example, when you play a board game with play money, you give it value for the purpose of the board game.

Similarly, money in the United States is **fiat money,** which means the government has deemed it to be money or legal tender. Legal tender means you can use it to pay a debt. Just as play money is used in the game, you could use beads or stones to represent money. However, these items do not work as well as the money used in the United States. Money also works better than the barter system because it can be used for a variety of different exchanges in the market place. You do not have to worry about not having the goods someone else wants in order to make the exchange of goods work. See **Figure 1** for some examples of the value of currency in other nations.

Functions of Money

Money has three main functions. It serves as a medium of exchange, a unit of value, and a store of value.

Medium of Exchange When you purchase the things you want, you use money as the medium of exchange. You do not use rocks or shells or play money; you use money the government has designated as currency. Thus, money makes it easier to trade and do business.

Unit of Value As a unit of value, money helps you compare prices on the goods and services you may want to buy. You can compare the prices of automobiles, candy bars, and haircuts. A monetary value is placed on those items so you can be the judge of the items that have more value in comparison to the others on the market.

Store of Value Money also serves as a store of value, which means you can accumulate and save money without losing value. As a store of value, money may lose value if an economy experiences high inflation. Inflation is increased prices of the goods and services you buy. When there is inflation, the value of money decreases. When that happens, you pay more for the things you buy. For example, if it costs you $100 for your weekly household food, that same grocery bill may be $110 or more with inflation. Thus, your money loses value when there is inflation.

Section Objectives

- **Name** the three main functions and properties of money.
- **Discuss** the roles government plays in the United States economy.
- **Explain** the Federal Budget.
- **Cite** examples of government agencies established to protect investors, workers, consumers, and the environment.
- **Describe** the structure, purpose, and function of the Federal Reserve System.

As You Read

Connect When you think of the word *money* what comes to mind? What purpose does money serve in your personal finances, with the government, and with the economy?

FIGURE 1 **Exchange Rates**

Ebb and Flow The currency exchange rate is the rate at which one nation's currency can be exchanged for another. *Why do exchange rates fluctuate?*

Foreign Exchange Rates											
U.S. Dollar Equivalent											
Country (Currency)	**2000**	**2001**	**2002**	**2003**	**2004**	**2005**	**2006**	**2007**	**2008**	**2009**	**2010**
AUSTRALIA (Dollar)	0.5815	0.5169	0.5437	0.6524	0.7365	0.7627	0.7535	0.8391	0.8537	0.7927	0.8928
EURO (Euro)	0.9232	0.8952	0.9454	1.1321	1.2438	1.2449	1.2563	1.3711	1.4726	1.3935	1.3194
UNITED KINGDOM (Pound)	1.5156	1.4396	1.5025	1.6347	1.833	1.8204	1.8434	2.002	1.8545	1.5661	1.529
BRAZIL (Real)	1.8301	2.3527	2.9213	3.075	2.9262	2.4352	2.1738	1.9461	1.8326	1.9976	1.7903
CANADA (Dollar)	1.4855	1.5487	1.5704	1.4008	1.3017	1.2115	1.134	1.0734	1.066	1.1412	1.0345
CHINA (Yuan)	8.2784	8.277	8.2771	8.2772	8.2768	8.1936	7.9723	7.6058	6.9477	6.8307	6.8155
DENMARK (Kroner)	8.0953	8.3323	7.8862	6.5774	5.9891	5.9953	5.9422	5.4413	5.0885	5.3574	5.6553
INDIA (Rupees)	44.9975	47.22	48.6257	46.5908	45.261	44.0002	45.1861	41.1774	43.3859	48.3324	45.8795
JAPAN (Yen)	107.804	121.568	125.2204	115.9387	108.1508	110.1069	116.3121	117.7623	103.3906	93.6827	90.5096
KOREA (Won)	1130.8975	1292.0149	1250.314	1192.0817	1145.2364	1023.7492	954.321	928.9717	1098.7061	1274.6252	1161.8882
MEXICO (Pesos)	9.4586	9.3366	9.6633	10.7925	11.2897	10.8938	10.9056	10.9281	11.1425	13.4979	12.673
SWEDEN (Kroner)	9.1735	10.3425	9.7233	8.0787	7.348	7.471	7.3718	6.755	6.5846	7.6539	7.3782

Properties of Money

For money to function in an economy, it should possess certain properties or characteristics. It should be divisible, usable, and stable.

Divisible You need to be able to divide money into smaller units. In the U.S. a quarter is one-fourth of one dollar—four quarters equal one dollar.

The Euro

The euro is the official currency of the European Union (EU), and is currently used in more than half of the countries in the EU (about 327 million people). *What are some benefits of adopting a single currency among nations?*

The Value of Money
In the past, money was in the form of coins, generally made of precious metals like gold and silver. *Why is paper money, which has no inherent value, worth so much?*

Usable You also need money that is usable. You should be able to move it from your home to the store. Thus, money in the U.S. is in the form of paper bills ($1, $5, $20, $50, $100) and coins (penny, nickel, dime, quarter).

Stable Lastly, money should have stable value. You should be able to use the same amount of money from week to week or month to month to buy the goods and services you need. The stability of money is important to an economy. Therefore, the government takes measures to keep prices stable to avoid inflation (high prices) or deflation (low prices).

Money Supply

When you add all the money individuals have to the money businesses and the government have, you know how much money is in circulation. The total amount of money in circulation in a country is called its **money supply.** This money supply also includes money in checking and savings accounts in banks. Bank money increases the money supply because banks use the money deposited to provide loans for businesses and individuals. The money supply increases each time the same money is deposited and paid out in loans.

Effect on Prices When the money supply in a nation is equal to the production of goods and services, there is no inflation or deflation. When the money supply increases more than production, there is too much money for too few goods, so prices go up. This occurs when there is too much borrowed money in circulation. When there is an abundance of productivity and a low money supply, prices do down, causing deflation. Inflation and deflation are both bad for an economy.

Reading Check

Identify What is the role of money in the economy?

Economics and You

Economic Activity

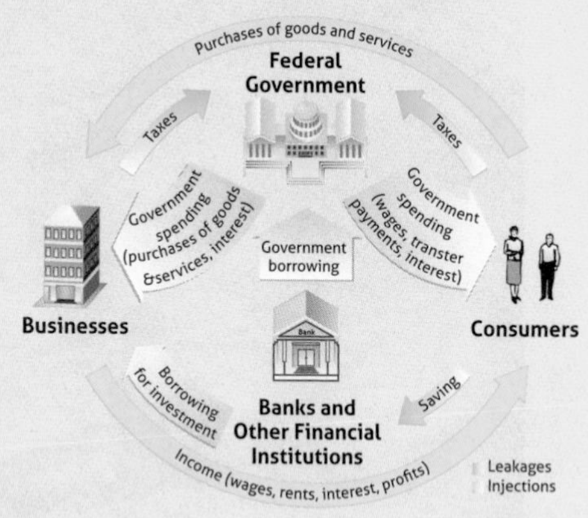

In a market economy, the flow of economic resources, income, and goods and services is circular. Dollars flow from businesses to individuals and from the individuals back to the businesses. Individuals sell their resources to businesses; for example, a business pays for the skills of its employees. Then, individuals buy the goods and services produced by businesses. Not all income is a part of this cycle. Some money is removed through taxation, for example. This loss of money from the cycle is called *leakage.* Leakage is balanced through investments, or injections, such as government spending. This spending is usually in the form of infrastructure projects such as maintaining national parks.

Personal Finance Connection Consumers are just one aspect of economic activity. Consumers pay for the goods and services created by businesses. Consumers are able to purchase these goods and services because they are able to sell their resources, both goods and services, to businesses.

Critical Thinking How do leakages and the balancing of the leakages by the government affect consumers as buyers of goods and services and as sellers of resources to businesses? Research to find other examples of leakages in the circular flow of economic activity. What injections are used to balance the loss of money?

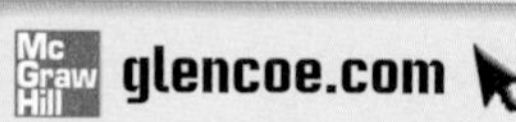

Activity Download an Economics and You Worksheet Activity.

Role of Government in the Economy

Which government policies and taxes impact your financial plans?

The United States government has several roles to play in an effort to do what is best for the safety and welfare of its people. In order to do so the government prepares a Federal Budget that projects the revenue expected to be generated and the costs involved in running the government. See **Figure 2** for revenue sources and **Figure 3** for a perspective on the Federal Budget over several years.

When the government spends more than it gets in revenue there is a **budget deficit.** The budget deficit creates national debt because to cover the deficit, the government must borrow money. This borrowing is similar to an individual overspending his or her income.

When the government spends the same amount it gets in revenue, the budget is said to be balanced. When a government gets more revenue than it spends there is a **budget surplus.**

FIGURE 2 **Government Revenue**

Give and Take This pie chart shows the percentages of government revenue from a recent year. *What types of services are funded with this money?*

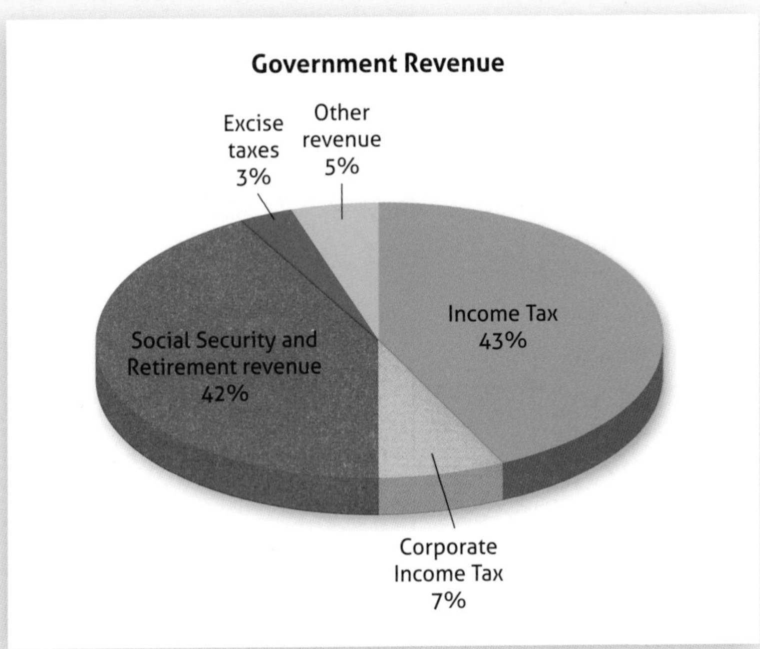

The government makes decisions on how to spend the revenue it gets from taxpayers in order to provide regulation, protection, and assistance to its citizens.

Regulation

To safeguard the economy and protect investors, workers, consumers, and the environment, the government plays the role of **regulator,** or controller. All the expenses incurred by these agencies are paid for through tax revenue (See **Figure 2**). The following federal regulatory agencies are in place for the safety and health of citizens:

Investors The Securities and Exchange Commission (SEC) regulates the sale of stocks and bonds. The Federal Reserve System (The Fed) regulates the U.S. banking system. It also guides monetary policy with regard to interest rates and foreign exchange rates. Depending on the current economy, the U.S. dollar may be weak or strong when exchanged for a different currency. For example, a weak dollar would make U.S. exports more desirable to people in another country.

Workers The Occupational Safety and Health Administration (OSHA) issues guidelines for worker safety. The Equal Employment Opportunity Commission (EEOC) regulates hiring, firing, and promotions to ensure employees receive equal treatment based on ability and not on other factors, such as age or gender.

Rwanda

One Laptop per Child

How can a developing country expect to thrive in the 21st century if its children do not have access to computers? The things we take for granted, like computers in homes and schools, are unheard of in many parts of the world. Yet this is exactly what children need to help keep up with the pace of change in today's digital world. One Laptop Per Child (OLPC) was developed to address this need. Rwanda has embraced this initiative by purchasing over 100,000 laptops and becoming the largest OLPC customer in Africa. The OLPC's XO computer is durable and capable of withstanding extreme weather conditions and high humidity. It consumes little power, weighs less than 3.5 pounds, and has features such as a built-in wireless adapter and video camera. Preinstalled content educates children in an engaging way. Rwanda plans to give these laptops to every child between the ages of 9 and 12. The government intends to create a wireless broadband network covering the entire capitol of Kigali, and will install fiber-optic cable throughout the country for broadband access. After years of civil unrest, Rwanda's goal is stability and prosperity, and educating its children will go far in achieving this.

Critical Thinking

1. **Expand** The One Laptop Per Child computers are uniquely designed to be durable and cost-effective. Research the XO laptops. What problems commonly befall laptop computers, and how has OLPC addressed these problems?
2. **Relate** Why are computers so important to a child's education? How does providing free laptops help impoverished children?

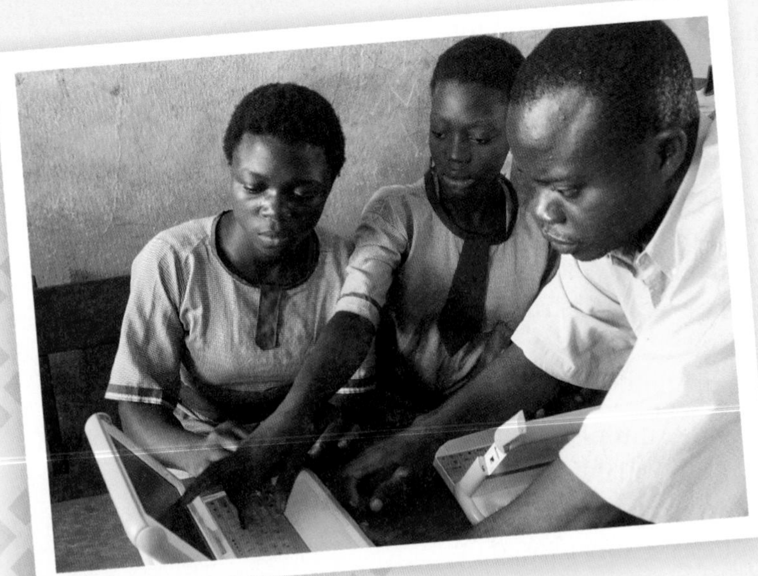

DATABYTES

Capital
Kigali

Population
11,055,976

Languages
Kinyarwanda (official) universal Bantu vernacular, French (official), English (official), Kiswahili (Swahili) used in commercial centers

Currency
Rwandan franc

Gross Domestic Product (GDP)
$5.07 billion

GDP per capita
$900

Industry
Cement, agricultural products, small-scale beverages, soap, furniture, shoes, plastic goods, textiles, cigarettes

Agriculture
Coffee, tea, pyrethrum (insecticide made from chrysanthemums), bananas, beans, sorghum, potatoes; livestock

Exports
Coffee, tea, hides, tin ore

Natural Resources
Gold, cassiterite (tin ore), wolframite (tungsten ore), methane, hydropower, arable land

FIGURE 3 The Federal Deficit

Budget Ups and Downs A budget deficit occurs when an entity spends more money than it brings in, and the opposite is a budget surplus. *What are some economic trends that can influence budget deficits and surpluses?*

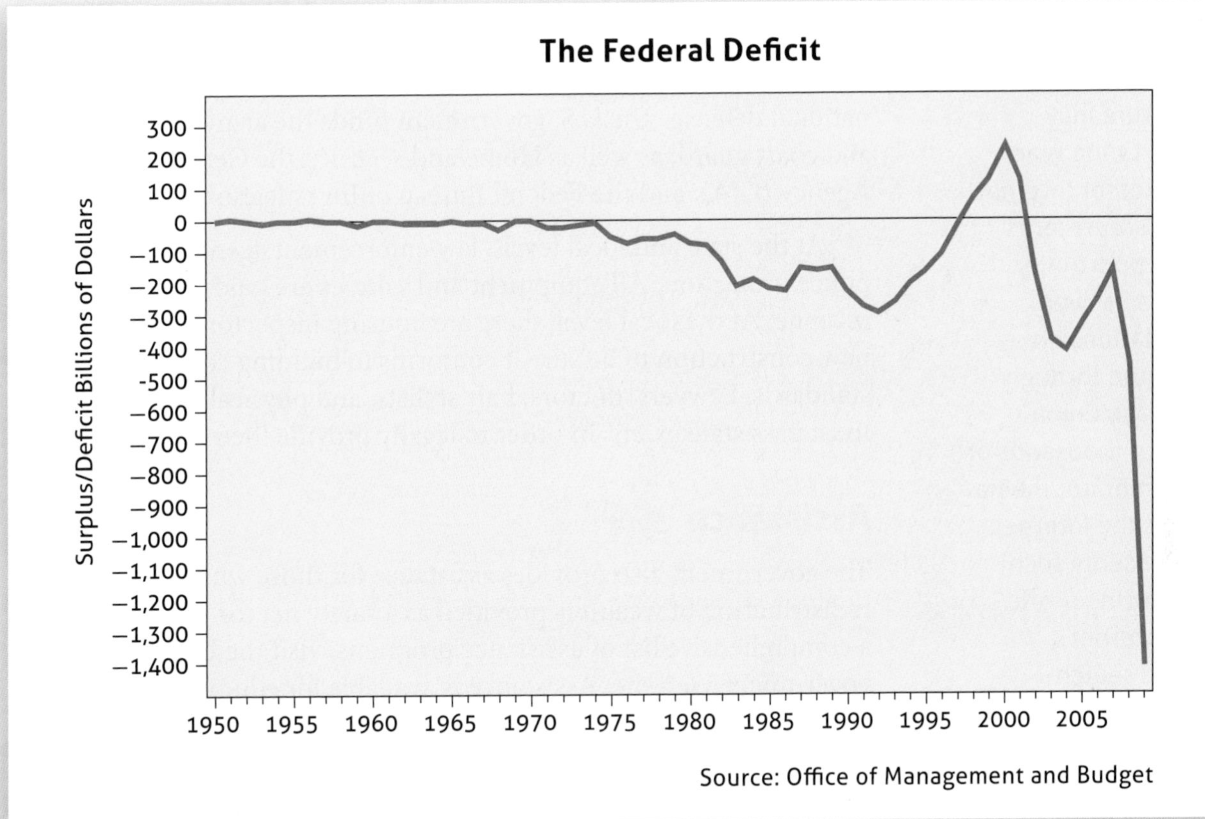

Consumers The Food and Drug Administration (FDA) regulates the safety and labeling of food, drugs, and cosmetics. The Consumer Product Safety Commission regulates products other than food, drugs, and cosmetics. It sets standards for products, and it has the power to recall unsafe products. The Federal Trade Commission (FTC) protects consumers by enforcing the laws that regulate competition, consumer protection, and the economy.

Environment The Environmental Protection Agency (EPA) was established to protect the health of people in the United States and the environment.

Protection

The legal structure in the United States protects citizens and businesses. For example, a party in a contract may sue the other party if all the requirements noted in the contract are not fulfilled. Courts uphold laws as well and listen to cases involving legal and criminal cases.

reality bytes

Globalization and the Internet

While tariffs and embargoes are examples of barriers to international trade, another barrier to international trade in the future may be censorship. China is an immense market for Internet companies and represents a large profit opportunity. However, China has very stringent regulations on what is presented through the media. In fact, China employs tens of thousands of employees to monitor media outlets such as the Internet. Since China presents such a large and growing profit opportunity, Internet companies and search engines such as Google and Yahoo! have made and will continue to make adjustments to accommodate China's requirements.

Some legal cases in addition to contracts may involve laws that protect a company from imposters. Those laws involve patents and copyrights. A **patent** is an exclusive right granted by the government to an inventor to prevent anyone else from using the invention for a period of time. A **copyright** is the exclusive right granted to an author. In order to use the rights to **intellectual property,** an idea or invention, the user must get permission and generally pay a fee to do so. A **trademark,** such as a company logo, protects a company's name and reputation.

Protection of the people in the United States is a priority at all levels of government. A portion of federal spending goes toward national defense. The U.S. government funds the army, navy, marines, and coast guard, as well as Homeland security, the Central Intelligence Agency (CIA), and the Federal Bureau of Investigation (FBI).

At the state and local levels, law enforcement agencies provide police protection. All equipment and salaries are paid for through tax revenue. At the local level, there are housing inspectors that check new construction to be sure it conforms to building codes and safety standards. Lawyers, doctors, hair stylists, and physical therapists, all must pass state exams in order to legally provide their services.

Assistance

The government also provides assistance for those who need it. This redistribution of wealth is provided as a safety net for citizens. To see a comprehensive list of assistance programs, visit the United States government Web site. Assistance is available for education, disaster relief, energy, food, housing, insurance, and health care.

Under the Social Security Act, the government established the means for the welfare of individuals. When you begin to earn wages, you will notice that a portion of your paycheck goes to FICA, which stands for Federal Insurance Contribution Act. You pay into a fund that provides income for retirees and survivors and dependents of deceased and disabled workers who paid into the fund, as well as health care for seniors (Medicare) and for those with low income (Medicaid).

Some additional programs for those with little or no income are childcare, food stamps, National School Lunch Program and Breakfast Program, and housing assistance. For qualified students, there are grants, scholarships, and fellowships, as well as student loans.

When you see tornadoes, hurricanes, or other disasters that devastate an area and local and state governments need assistance, the federal government lends a hand. The Federal Emergency Management Agency (F.E.M.A.) provides experts and relief funds needed to rebuild the area's infrastructure. Low interest loans are granted to individuals and businesses to help them as well.

Reading Check

Define What are a budget deficit and a budget surplus?

Federal Reserve System

How might the actions of the Federal Reserve impact your financial decisions?

As the central bank of the United States, the Federal Reserve System (The Fed) regulates the U.S. banking system. It also guides monetary policy with regard to interest rates and foreign exchange rates. Among the functions of the Federal Reserve System are check clearing, acting as the federal government's fiscal agent, supervising banks, holding reserves and setting reserve requirements, supplying paper currency, and regulating the money supply. Let's take a look at the Fed's structure, function, and role in the economy.

Structure & Function

The Federal Reserve System is made up of a Board of Governors, which is a government agency, and twelve Federal Reserve Banks. Members of the Board of Governors are appointed by the President and confirmed by the U.S. Senate. Each member serves for fourteen years. Each of the twelve banks is responsible for a specific geographic area within the United States.

The Board and Federal Reserve banks work together to supervise and regulate depository institutions and other financial institutions. Other functions include: provide banking services to member banks and the government; write regulations and implement consumer credit protection laws; and offer statistics and information on the economy, consumer credit, and the monetary policy to government officials, as well as publish related reports.

Role in the Economy

The primary responsibility of the Fed is regulating the money supply. This function of the Fed is crucial to the stability of the economy. It influences the economy through its control over the federal funds rate, which is the rate banks borrow money from the Federal Reserve System. For example, if the economy is growing too fast and inflation needs to be curbed, the Fed may increase the federal funds rate, which in turn forces banks to increase their interest rates. If the economy is in a recession, the Fed may lower interest rates to encourage borrowing and consumer spending.

The Fed is also involved with international affairs and the foreign exchange markets. The Chairman serves on several international monetary boards and attends international monetary and financial meetings as one of the United States delegates. Changes in monetary policies affect international relations and trade. For example, the U.S. dollar may be weak or strong when exchanged for a different currency. A weak dollar would make U.S. exports more desirable to people in another country. The reverse would be true if the dollar were too strong.

Strong Dollar Versus a Weak Dollar

As supply of and demand for the dollar change in the global economy, the value of the dollar changes as well. Neither a strong dollar nor a weak dollar are better for the economy. As the value of the dollar increases, U.S. imports become less expensive and U.S. exports become more costly to other nations. This helps to create a trade deficit. When the value of the dollar decreases, imports to the U.S. become more costly, and exports are less expensive. This helps to create a trade surplus. In either case, one sector of the economy is negatively affected. In most cases, trade deficits tend to correct themselves through the price system.

Concept Application

What is the relationship between international trade and the value of the dollar? What is the economic impact?

SECTION 1 Assessment

Review Key Concepts

1. **List** What are the three main functions and properties of money?
2. **Identify** What roles does the government play in the United States economy?
3. **Describe** Explain the Federal Budget and what a balanced budget is.
4. **Cite** What are some examples of government agencies established to protect investors, workers, consumers, and the environment? What services do they provide?
5. **Summarize** What is the structure, purpose, and function of the Federal Reserve?
6. **Explain** Identify sources of government revenue and explain the national debt.

Higher Order Thinking H.O.T.

7. **Relate** What is the government's role in supporting and stabilizing the economy? How do these actions impact your personal finances?

21st Century Skills

8. **Property Rights** There are laws to protect intellectual property rights in the United States and in many other countries. Conduct research on the laws governing intellectual property. For example, music is considered an intellectual property. When is downloading music from the Internet considered illegal? What could happen to individuals that download music illegally in the United States?

Mathematics

9. **Government Budget** The government earns money in various ways, including taxes, tariffs and issuing bonds. When the government spends more money than it earns, it incurs a budget deficit. A budget surplus is when the government spends less than it earns. When it spends what it earns, the budget is in balance. A small country has collected income taxes in the amount of $2,500,000; tariffs of $4,750,000; and money from bond issuance in the amount of $6,420,000. If it spent $13,340,000 does it have a deficit, surplus, or balanced budget? If the budget is not balanced, how could the country balance the budget.

   Math Concept **Calculate Budget Surplus and Deficit** To calculate the status of a government budget determine the total amount of income the government has collected or earned during the period and subtract this from the total amount spent.

   Starting Hint Determine the total amount of money the government has collected or earned by identifying the total taxes, tariffs, money collected from bond issuance, and any other income and adding them together.

NCTM Problem Solving Solve problems that arise in mathematics and in other contexts.

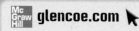

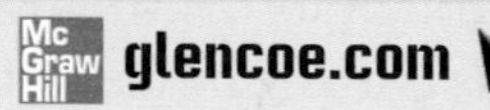

Check your answers.

Economic Indicators and You

How does the economy affect you as a consumer and worker?

The goals of an economy are economic growth, stable prices, and full employment. When a nation reaches those goals, businesses, consumers, and workers have confidence in the economy. Businesses invest in new machinery and research. They hire more workers. As more and more workers are employed the goal of full employment is reached. Stable prices are created by selling goods and service at prices that consumers are willing and able to pay.

To measure economic goals and study the state of the economy, government and private economists use economic **indicators,** or statistical values**.** These indicators measure variables in the economy and provide insight into how well the economy is doing. Some economic indicators include: gross domestic product (GDP), consumer price index, and unemployment rates.

Section Objectives

- **Cite** the three basic goals of an economy.
- **Describe** economic indicators and their significance.
- **Discuss** the segments of the business cycle.
- **Examine** the reasons nations trade with one another.
- **Explain** balance of trade.
- **Compare** free trade and protectionism.

As You Read

Connect What do you think the roles of individuals, businesses, and the government in the circular flow of economic activity are?

Gross Domestic Product

To measure the productivity in a nation, many countries use Gross Domestic Product. According to the U.S. government's definition, the "**Gross Domestic Product** (GDP) is the value of all final goods and services produced inside a country in a given period of time." It includes private investment, government and personal spending, and the difference between imports and exports; as well as the difference between expanding and shrinking inventories. The largest percentage of the GDP is consumer spending, at around 70 percent. GDP growing significantly each year could indicate a strong economy.

Consumer Price Index

The **Consumer Price Index** (CPI) measures the cost of a basket of goods and services for an urban family. The Bureau of Labor Statistics (BLS) publishes the CPI on a monthly basis and is seasonally adjusted. From the CPI economists are able to determine if there is inflation, deflation, or stable prices. **Inflation** is when prices go up. When prices are inflated, it costs more to buy the goods you need and want. Thus, your dollar does not stretch as far as it did before. **Deflation** is when prices go down. Although it sounds good to hear that prices go down with deflation, it is not good for the economy. Companies require a certain amount of profit to stay in business. If prices have to be reduced too much, companies may shut down because they may not have enough money to buy new products or pay their bills. Therefore, the goal of an economy is to have stable prices.

Unemployment Rate

According to the U.S. government's definition, "the unemployment rate is a percentage of the total work force of people actively seeking employment who are currently unemployed." The rate that is acceptable as an economic goal for the United States is around five percent. A low unemployment rate is a goal because employed workers are consumers that buy goods and services. A low unemployment rate is also good for the government because employed workers pay taxes. Additionally, unemployment payments for people out of work are low.

Reading Check

Identify What are economic indicators, and what are some examples?

Business Cycles

How do business cycles impact you, the consumer?

In addition to economic indicators, economists study the fluctuations in the economy to determine in which phase of the business cycle the economy is in at a given point in time. The four main segments of a business cycle are expansion, recession, trough, and recovery. This cyclical movement from one step to the next is determined after the step occurs. See **Figure 4** for a representation of the circular flow of economic activity.

Expansion

When an economy is growing and economic indicators are positive, a nation is in the expansion phase. Some economists consider this a period of prosperity. Businesses are doing well, unemployment is low, and consumers are spending to fuel this economic period. When this phase of the business cycle reaches its peak and begins to decline, the next phase begins, which is a recession.

Recession

A **recession** marks a period of economic downturn for a period of six months. During a recession the economy slows down. Unemployment rises. Lack of consumer demand forces businesses to cut back production and any future business improvement. As the economy declines, the government suffers from a loss of revenue and increased costs for unemployed workers. A very long recession is called a depression. In a depression, businesses shut their doors and many workers become unemployed. Consumer spending is greatly reduced and poverty increases. The United States experienced a depression in the early 1930s.

FIGURE 4 **Economic Activity**

Circular Flow The government, businesses, and consumers are all connected in the flow of economic activity. *How do the activities of businesses impact the consumer?*

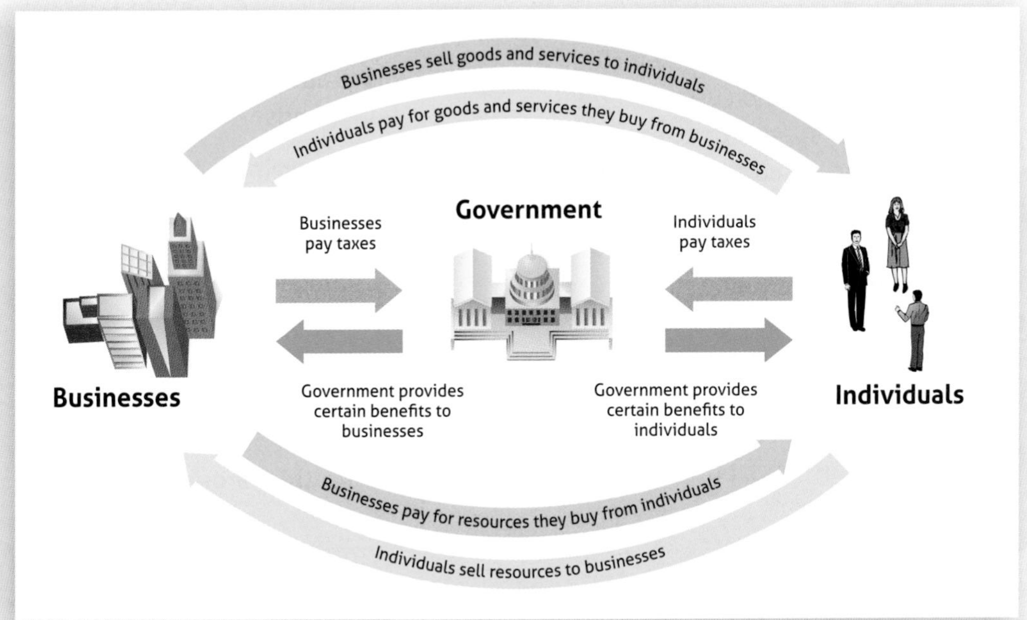

Businesses sell goods and services to individuals
Individuals pay for goods and services they buy from businesses
Government
Businesses pay taxes
Individuals pay taxes
Businesses
Individuals
Government provides certain benefits to businesses
Government provides certain benefits to individuals
Businesses pay for resources they buy from individuals
Individuals sell resources to businesses

Trough

The low point in a business cycle is called a **trough.** It is between a recession or depression and the recovery phase. Economic indicators begin to pick up as more workers are employed and spending increases. At this point the next segment begins—recovery.

Recovery

The recovery phase of a business cycle occurs after a recession or depression when the economy improves. With economic growth, businesses invest in more capital goods and hire more workers to keep up with consumer demand. In this segment, you would see lower unemployment, stable prices, and increased productivity.

Achieving Economic Goals

In order to achieve economic goals, the government may intervene. For example, to stimulate spending during a recession, the government may reduce taxes so consumers and businesses have more money to spend. In order to help reduce unemployment, the government may pass legislation that provides incentives for businesses to hire new employees and training for unemployed workers. In addition, to combat inflation, interest rates may be raised by the Federal Reserve to discourage credit purchases.

Careers That Count!

Brenda Wellington • Budget Analyst

As a budget analyst for a private organization, I find the most efficient ways to increase profits and to distribute funds among various departments and programs. I develop, analyze, and execute budgets, and estimate future financial needs. My typical workday includes reviewing financial requests, examining past and current budgets, and researching developments that affect spending. I examine budget estimates and proposals for completeness, accuracy, and compliance with procedures, regulations, and organizational objectives. Then I consolidate individual departmental budgets into budget summaries that argue for or against funding requests. Throughout the year, I monitor the budget to determine if funds are being spent as planned. If they are not, I write a report that explains the variations, and I recommend revisions. This job can be stressful, but rewarding. If you are interested in this kind of work, I recommend a bachelor's or master's degree in accounting, finance, business, public administration, economics, or statistics.

EXPLORE CAREERS

Visit the Web site of the U.S. Department of Labor's Bureau of Labor Statistics and learn more about a career as a budget analyst.

1. For example, in a graphic design firm what are unique challenges faced by the budget analyst compared to the artists or sales staff?
2. In what sector do most budget analysts work? What are the future opportunities for this career?

Skills	Education	Career Path
Analytical skills, math skills, statistics, accounting, and computer science; knowledge of financial analysis software; strong oral and written communication skills	Bachelor's degree, but most firms require a master's degree; professional development classes are taken over a career	A budget analyst can become a controller, auditor, CFO (chief financial officer), tax examiner, or chief revenue agent.

glencoe.com

Activity Download a Career Exploration Activity.

Sometimes drastic measures are needed when an economy falters. President Roosevelt established the New Deal to help the United States recover from the depression. Two components of the New Deal were Social Security and the Securities and Exchange Commission. In response to the recent financial crisis, the government passed legislation to help banks, mortgage companies, and auto makers. For example, Troubled Asset Relief Program (TARP) helped lending institutions, while the American Recovery and Reinvestment Act of 2009 helped consumers and unemployed workers. Both acts were intended to bring life back to a weak economy.

Reading Check

Summarize What are the segments of the business cycle?

Role of Trade

How can your personal finances benefit from international trade?

Individuals, organizations, and nations trade for the things they want and need. Individuals trade their skills for wages. They trade their wages for the products they need and want. Organizations trade the goods and services they produce for revenue and hopefully a profit. Nations trade with one another because they are dependent on each other's resources to provide the goods and services their people need. In theory, everyone gains from trading.

Division of Labor and Specialization

Specialization in manufacturing occurs when tasks are divided among different workers. Each worker contributes to making the final product. The goal of production specialization is increased productivity. When all the workers do their part, a final product is manufactured. An assembly line in a manufacturing plant is an example of production specialization. Today, robots that specialize in one or more aspects of the manufacturing process have replaced many of the jobs that were once done by people.

Specialization can be applied to economics. For trading to be accomplished efficiently there is a division of labor and specialization. Individuals specialize in the work they choose. Organizations specialize in the goods and services they offer and nations do the same. Trade is necessary because everyone is economically **interdependent,** or they need each other to create the goods and services produced in a nation.

Production and consumption should increase with specialization because everyone is doing their best to produce what society wants. The more workers produce, the more money they earn to buy products. The more organizations earn, the more products they can make and sell. The more both individuals and organizations earn, the more money the government earns in taxes to provide the social services a nation needs and wants.

International Trade

If you look at the labels on the goods you buy, you will see that many of them are constructed or produced in another country. Grapes may come from Chile, clothing from Sri Lanka, toys from China, and electronics from Japan. People in other countries may buy goods made in the U.S., like wheat, airplanes, and advanced technologies. This exchange of goods and services among nations is **international trade.** The goods coming into a country are called imports. Goods sold to other nations are called exports. The importing and exporting of goods helps to create a global marketplace, where all countries involved in international trade benefit with a larger selection of goods, increased competition, improved standard of living, and opportunities that would not exist without such trade.

Global Awareness

With globalization and the interdependence of the world's economies, global awareness is more important than ever. Global awareness involves understanding and addressing global issues including other nations' cultures and languages. Developing global awareness includes respectfully working with and learning from people from diverse cultures and lifestyles. Being globally aware will help you to be successful in the increasingly globalized world.

Write About It

Research to find a current global economic issue. How do various nations view the issue? What are their solutions? Write one or more paragraphs to describe the differences or similarities between the nations regarding the chosen global issue.

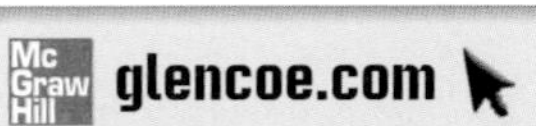

Activity Download a Career and College Readiness Worksheet Activity.

Balance of Trade
Countries benefit from trade when each country concentrates on the goods and services it produces most efficiently. *Why do you think the United States exports so many engineering and scientific instruments?*

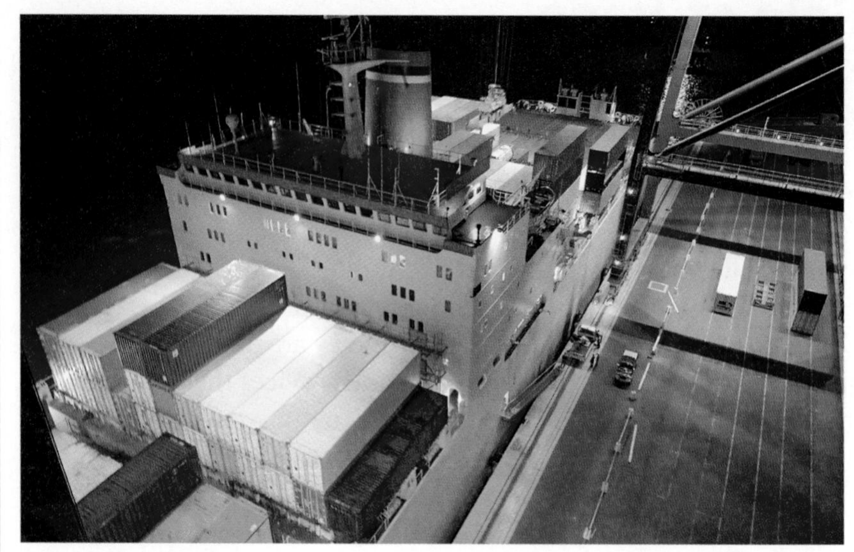

Why Nations Trade

Some countries can produce certain goods more efficiently depending on the resources available. Economic resources (or factors of production) include: land (raw materials), labor (workers), entrepreneurship (business owners), and capital (tools, equipment).

Scarcity of resources creates interdependency among nations. For example, nations with limited fertile land, but abundant capital need to trade to acquire food supplies for their citizens. Even when a country has abundant economic resources, it may be more economical to trade with other countries. For example, due to the low employee wages in some countries, it is more profitable to import goods than to produce them in the U.S. where labor costs are higher.

The particular resources in a nation often give it an advantage in the production of one or more products. For example, Brazil's climate makes it ideally suited for growing bananas. Countries with more moderate climates will produce fewer bananas giving Brazil an advantage in banana production. A country has an **absolute advantage** when it can produce more of a product than can another country.

An absolute advantage in the production of a particular product is not necessary for a country to benefit from specialization and trade with other countries. Trade is also beneficial whenever a country has a comparative advantage. **Comparative advantage** is the ability of a country to produce a product more efficiently and at a lower opportunity cost than another country. For example, two countries, Country A and Country B, both produce corn and soybeans. Country A is able to produce more of both products, but is able to produce significantly more corn than Country B. Country A should not continue to take land from the more efficient production of corn to use for the less efficient production of soybeans. Country A's opportunity cost is less if it focuses on the production of corn, and imports soybeans. Country A has a comparative advantage.

Balance of Trade **Balance of trade** is the difference between the value of a country's imports and exports during a specific period of time. (See **Figure 5.**) A trade deficit occurs whenever the value of the products a country imports exceeds the value of the products it exports. A country has a trade surplus whenever the value of its exports exceeds the value of its imports.

It is important to realize that a continued trade deficit is not necessarily a bad thing. A trade deficit continues because there are opportunities for foreign investors in a country's economy. For example, many Japanese automobile companies have built factories in the United States to satisfy demand for Japanese cars. This creates supporting industries that benefit U.S. citizens by providing domestic jobs. See **Figure 6** for an example of fluctuation in the U.S. trade deficit.

Free Trade vs. Protectionism Many economists believe that international trade works best when there is free trade. Free trade is based on market economic principles and no regulations. Without regulation, total output and international competition increases. Nations create alliances and agreements with one another to encourage free trade. These agreements lay the groundwork for companies to compete in the global marketplace without trade restrictions. For example, the United States has a trade agreement with its neighbors, Canada and Mexico called the North American Free Trade Agreement (NAFTA). In Europe many countries belong to the European Union (EU), which unites countries for trading and economic purposes. In its agreement, the EU even established one currency called the euro.

FIGURE 5 **Imports and Exports**

Trade Balance This chart shows total imports and exports in dollars in a recent year. *What are some factors that might affect the balance of trade?*

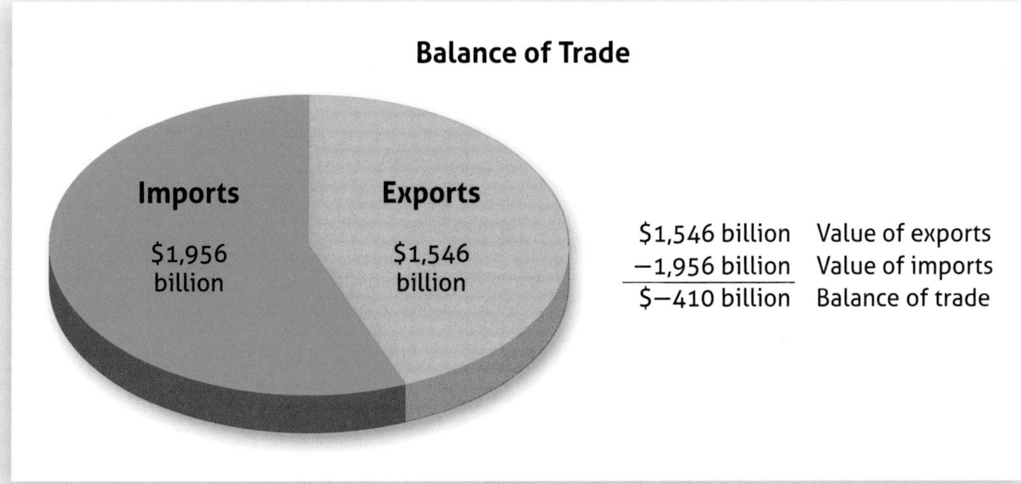

After You Read

Connect Why is it important to be aware of global economic policies when making your personal financial decisions?

The largest trade agreement that involves countries from all around the world is the World Trade Organization (WTO). The WTO establishes rules for fair trade among its member nations. If a country believes one of the member nations is not following the rules it may bring the infraction to the WTO for review and request for action. The WTO created the framework for our global marketplace.

Sometimes, however, nations find it necessary to restrict trade, thus creating a barrier to free trade. **Protectionism** is the practice of using barriers to free trade. Trade barriers that may be used include tariffs, quotas, and embargoes. Protectionism attempts to protect domestic industries from global competition.

A **tariff** is a tax on imports. Today, tariffs are often imposed on products when the government wants to help domestic companies to better compete with foreign made goods. Tariffs increase the price of the imported product, which helps the domestic company compete.

A **quota** is a restriction on the quantity or value of goods that can be imported. Once a quota is reached for a particular product, no more products in that category can be imported into a country. Quotas protect domestic suppliers of those products that had quotas placed on them. Domestic businesses benefit from quotas on imports.

An **embargo** restricts imports and exports to and from a country. Embargoes are imposed when there is a health issue, such as tainted food. This complete ban on goods may also be done for political reasons.

FIGURE 6 **Balance of Trade**

The Impact In 2009, the largest decreases in services exports were in travel and transportation. *What do you think accounts for the decrease?*

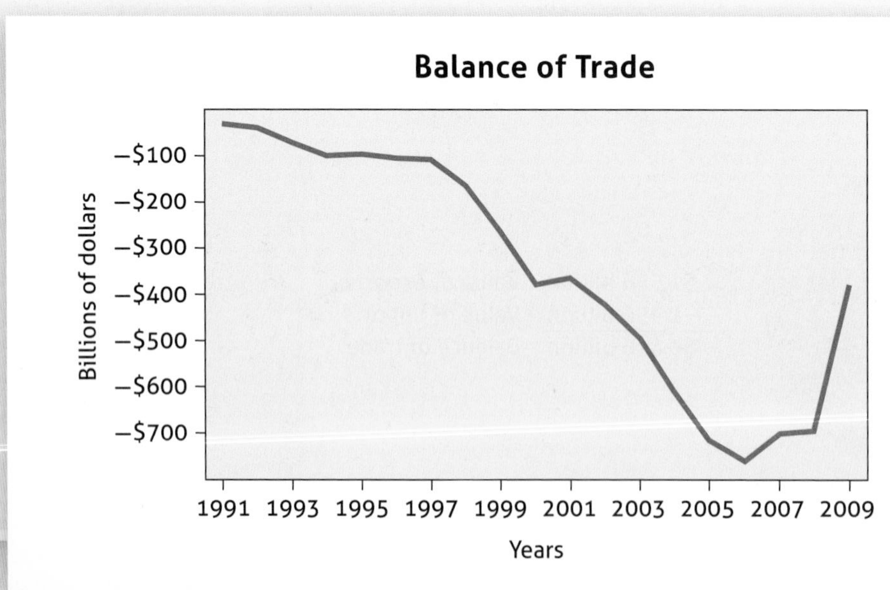

Review Key Concepts

1. **List** What are the three basic goals of an economy?
2. **Describe** What are some economic indicators, and what information do they provide about the economy?
3. **Identify** What are the segments of the business cycle? Explain each segment.
4. **Explain** What are the reasons nations trade with one another?
5. **Identify** What is a trade surplus and trade deficit? How do they relate to balance of trade?
6. **Compare** How are free trade and protectionism similar or different?
7. **Distinguish** What is the difference between comparative and absolute advantage?

Higher Order Thinking H.O.T.

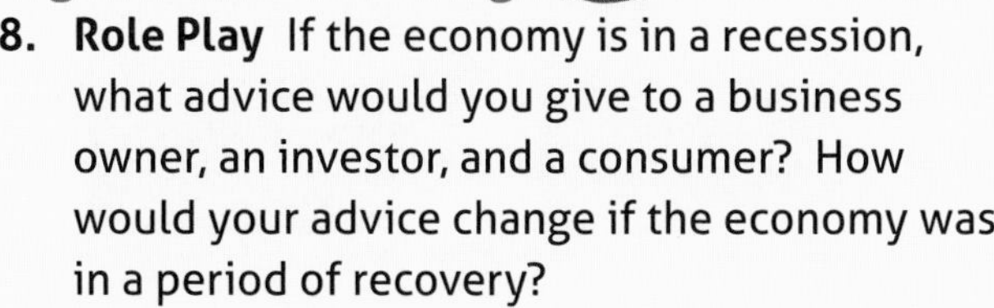

8. **Role Play** If the economy is in a recession, what advice would you give to a business owner, an investor, and a consumer? How would your advice change if the economy was in a period of recovery?

English Language Arts

9. **Pros and Cons of Free Trade** The North American Free Trade Agreement (NAFTA) was created to expand trade among the United States, Canada, and Mexico, and make these countries more competitive in the global marketplace. NAFTA reduces and, in some cases, eliminates trade barriers all together. Gather information from print and online resources about NAFTA. How do you as a consumer benefit from free trade agreements like NAFTA? How do businesses in the United States benefit? What are the negative outcomes of this agreement? What are the effects of the World Trade Organization? Present your findings in a one-page report, and identify your information sources.

NCTE 8 Use information resources to gather information and create and communicate knowledge.

Mathematics

10. **Currency Exchange** Jennifer, who lives in Ohio, spent a week with her family in Canada last month. She spent one of those days shopping, when the exchange rates made the American dollar worth more than the Canadian dollar. During the trip, Jennifer purchased a shirt priced at $25.99, a purse priced at $45.00, and two pairs of shoes priced at $35.99 for each pair. On that day, the American dollar was equal to $1.10 in Canadian dollars. Note that currency exchange rates change daily. Calculate the total cost of the goods purchased in Canada in American dollars.

Math Concept **Calculate Cost of Goods** To calculate the cost of goods purchased in another country, divide the total cost in the foreign currency by the exchange rate.

Starting Hint Multiply the quantity purchased for each item by the price of that item to determine total cost for each item. Divide the total cost in Canadian dollars by the exchange rate to determine the total cost in American dollars.

NCTM Representations Create and use representations to organize, record, and communicate mathematical ideas.

glencoe.com Check your answers.

Visual Summary

Economics and the Global Economy

Role of Currency

Money can be used for a variety of exchanges in the market place and is easier than bartering.

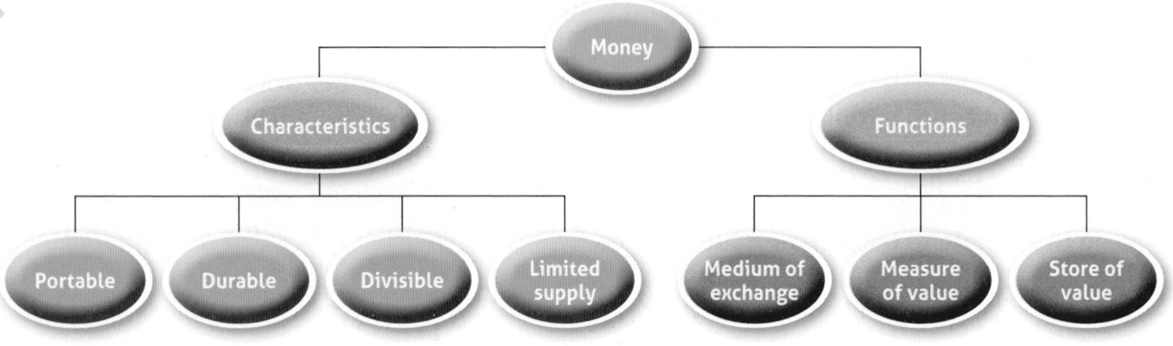

Balance of Trade

A trade deficit occurs when the value of imports exceeds the value of exports. A trade surplus occurs when the value of exports exceeds the value of imports.

Balance of Trade = Value of Exports – Value of Imports

Try It!

Draw a diagram like the one shown to illustrate the flow of the segments of the business cycle.

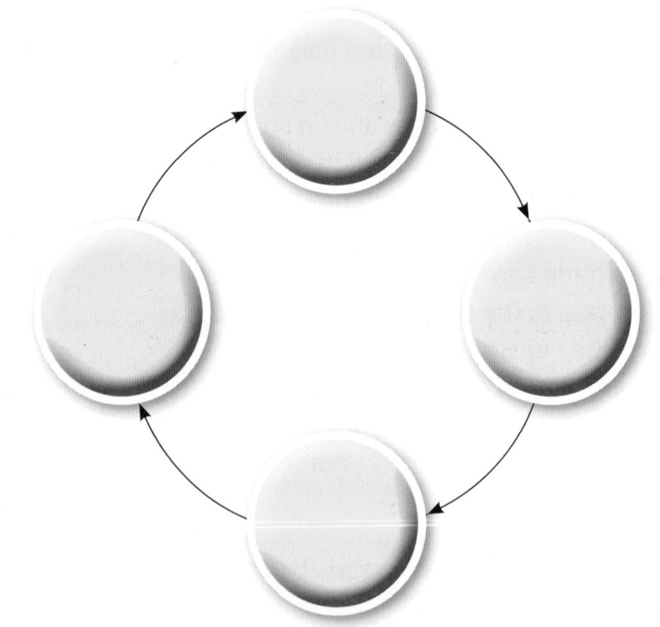

Chapter Review and Assessment

Chapter Summary

- Money functions to provide a medium of exchange, a unit of value, and a store of value.
- The United States money supply affects prices. The federal government attempts to control the money supply to create price stability.
- The government plays three important roles: regulation, protection, and assistance.
- There are government agencies established to protect investors, workers, consumers, and the environment.
- The Federal Reserve System regulates banking and guides monetary policy.
- Three basic goals of an economy are stable prices, low unemployment, and high productivity.
- Gross Domestic Product (GDP), Consumer Price Index (CPI), and unemployment rates help monitor an economy's health.
- Economies go through ups and downs, called business cycles with the following fluctuations: expansion, recession, trough, and recovery.
- Nations trade with one another due to interdependency and the efficiency created by a global marketplace.

Vocabulary Review

1. Use at least ten of these vocabulary terms to write an essay on globalization and the benefits and drawbacks of a global economy.

- fiat money
- money supply
- budget deficit
- budget surplus
- patent
- copyright
- trademark
- Gross Domestic Product (GDP)
- Consumer Price Index (CPI)
- inflation
- deflation
- recession
- trough
- specialization
- international trade
- absolute advantage
- comparative advantage
- balance of trade
- protectionism
- tariff
- quota
- embargo
- regulator
- intellectual property
- interdependent
- indicators

Higher Order Thinking

2. **Relate** What is globalization? How does international trade and technology impact globalization?
3. **Associate** Discuss how specialization and division of labor contribute to trade as well as absolute and comparative advantage.
4. **Determine** Explain the effect that the United States money supply has on prices. How does the government regulate this?
5. **Examine** Why is the unemployment rate not a completely accurate account of the number of people actually unemployed?
6. **Project** In which phase of the business cycle are businesses most likely to lay off workers and cut back on production? Explain.
7. **Extend** How is consumer confidence important to the U.S. economy? How does it affect businesses and the government?
8. **Evaluate** How do fluctuations in economic indicators impact stock brokers, consumers, and the government? How would reduced economic growth impact these groups?
9. **Justify** Explain and defend the significance of government agencies. How are they funded?

College and Career Readiness

Social Studies

10. Government Assistance Discuss the government's fiscal policy for government spending and taxation when instituting government programs, such as TARP and auto industry bailouts, used to help privately-held companies during a financial or economic crisis. Write a fair and balanced written report. Include citations from reliable sources to support the pros and cons for the policies.

NCSS VI C Power, Authority, & Governance Analyze and explain ideas and mechanisms to meet needs and wants of citizens, regulate territory, manage conflict, establish order and security, and balance competing conceptions of a just society.

Mathematics

11. Tariffs Country A imports SUVs from Country B. In order to help the domestic car companies better compete with foreign ones, Country A places a tariff on the imported SUVs. The domestic company prices its SUV at $43,250 while the imported SUV is priced at $43,900 which includes the tariff. Without the tariff, the two SUVs would have the same price. Calculate the tariff percentage placed on the imported SUVs. If 35,000 of Country B's SUVs are sold in Country A, how much tariff is collected by Country A's government?

Math Concept **Calculate Tariff Percentage** To calculate the tariff imposed by a country on foreign goods, compare the difference in price between foreign and domestic goods.

Starting Hint To calculate the tariff percentage placed on the foreign goods by Country A, determine the dollar amount of the tariff. Divide this amount by the SUV price without the tariff.

NCTM Number and Operations Understand meanings of operations and how they relate to one another.

English Language Arts

12. Television Advertising Sweden prohibits advertising to children on television. Assuming the same type of legislation is pending in Congress, write a letter to the Federal Trade Commission that supports or disagrees with the ban on children's television advertising. You must take a stand one way or the other.

NCTE 5 Use different writing process elements to communicate effectively.

Economics

13. Government Programs Universal health care is government-run medical care, and it continues to be a topic of debate in politics and medicine. In universal health care, hospitals and doctors are paid by the government for the medical services provided to a nation's citizens. In countries that offer universal health care, citizens do not pay directly for their medical expenses. The government pays for them through taxes, which are higher than in countries where medical services are not provided. Research the pros and cons of universal health care. Write a newspaper-style article to express your opinion and persuade readers to consider your viewpoint.

Real-World Applications

14. Labeling Laws The labels on food products provide nutritional facts and ingredients. The ingredient with the highest percentage is listed first, next highest next, and so on. Advertising claims can provide additional information such as low sodium, high fiber, sugar-free, and high in calcium. Research the ingredients and calories, as well as the costs for five of your favorite packaged foods. Check out substitutes for those five items that cost less, but that have the same ingredients or nutritional value. Write a summary of your findings and note any revelations about costs and product labeling that may help you to be a better consumer. Are any of the items produced in another country? Do these items differ in their labeling approach?

Your Financial Portfolio

Securities Portfolio

Chris decided to begin investing the money earned from odd jobs and gifts at an early age. Chris read the newspaper, watched the news, and paid attention to products that appeared to be popular with teens. After researching the companies that produced those products, Chris decided on which ones were worth investing in. At age 13, Chris bought stock in one of those companies and followed its price for several months. When Chris had enough money he bought stock in another company. His research indicated that it is a good idea to diversify when investing money. So he made sure that the stock he selected was in a different field. Someone told him about mutual funds, which sounded good too. So he invested some money in a health-related mutual fund. By the time Chris was 21 he had a diversified portfolio of stocks, bonds, and mutual funds that was doing quite well. He never sold any of the securities he purchased. He did earn dividends on some of the stock. Luckily he did not have to touch his investments while in college. Some stocks had split (two for one), so he had more stock than he originally purchased. At this point in his life he wanted to begin selling and buying stocks as investors do to make money. So, he hired a stock broker to handle his investments. In his research he learned that some stock brokers charge a percentage of the sale price or purchase price, while others offer a flat fee. Chris opted for a flat fee of $8.95 per transaction.

Research

Research stock prices and stock brokerage firms to see how much money you would need to begin investing in securities (stock and bonds) and mutual funds. Make a plan. How much money do you need to begin your own securities portfolio? Which stocks, bonds, or mutual funds would you like to purchase? Should you include any international securities? On a separate sheet of paper, create a chart with at least ten securities that you would like to purchase. Note the number of shares, the current price, and total amount needed. Identify the stock broker or brokerage firm that would handle your trades and include the cost of the trades in your chart. How much money do you need to make this hypothetical securities portfolio a reality?

Unit 1

Unit Project

Understanding Global Trade

Ask Yourself...

Have you ever looked at product labels to see where products were made? Have you ever thought about the cost of importing products from another country? Does the origin of a product ever affect your purchasing decision? Responses to these questions can help you understand and appreciate the importance of global trade.

Your Objective

The goal of this project is to develop an understanding of the role and importance of global trade in our society today.

Skills You'll Use

Success in defining goals and preparing financially for those goals depends on your skills. Some skills you might use include:

Academic Skills—Reading, writing, and research

21st Century Skills—Critical thinking, decision making, speaking, listening, and role-playing

Technology Skills—Word processing, keyboarding, presentation software, and Internet research

Standards

NCTE 7 Conduct research and gather, evaluate, and synthesize data to communicate discoveries.

NCTE 8 Use information resources to gather information and create and communicate knowledge.

NCSS VII A Production, Distribution, and Consumption Explain how the scarcity of productive resources (human, capital, technological, and natural) requires the development of economic systems to make decisions about how goods and services are to be produced and distributed.

STEP 1 Research a Product

Choose a product that you have purchased recently or are considering buying, such as an article of clothing, a game, or a media player, that was made in a foreign country. Answer these questions:

- Where was the product manufactured?
- Is there a similar product available that is made in the United States?
- What factors affected your decision to purchase that particular product over competing brands?
- How does the imported product benefit your life?

Your responses will help you consider the origin of a product as well as the end use. Use your answers to create an information sheet about the product you purchased. You may choose to include a spreadsheet or chart that compares the product you purchased with a competing similar product.

STEP 2 Explore Laws

Conduct research using print and online resources to find out more about the import laws that affect the product you purchased.

- Does the country that made the product have an absolute or comparative advantage for producing that product?
- Is the country that manufactured the product allowed free trade or protectionism with the United States?
- If protectionism applies, what tariffs or quotas are placed on the product? How might these affect the price you paid for the product?
- Research the history of the product to determine if embargoes have ever been placed on it. If so, why?

Write a one-page report that explains how the product you purchased was affected by global trade laws. Be sure to cite the sources of your information.

STEP 3 Build Relationships

Follow your teacher's directions to divide into pairs. One person will play the part of a salesperson selling the product you chose. The other person will be a business owner who is trying to decide whether he should stock the product or a comparable product made in the United States.

- Prepare for your role-play by meeting with a trusted adult in your community who is knowledgeable about your product. Ask him or her what factors influence customers to buy the imported product or its competition. Take note of the answers.
- Develop speaking points based on the information you gathered in Steps 1 and 2 and in your interview.
- During the role-play, listen to and note the business owner's concerns. Address them politely.
- Act in a professional manner.
- Show respect for the business owner's decision and thank him for his time.

Use your notes to develop a graphic organizer comparing the benefits and drawbacks of your product and its American-made competition.

STEP 4 Develop Your Presentation

Use the Unit 1 Project Checklist to plan and create your presentation.

STEP 5 Evaluate Your Presentation

Your presentation will be evaluated based on the following:

- Evaluation rubric
- Extent of your research
- Mechanics—clarity of your presentation
- Speaking and listening skills

Project Checklist

Plan

- ✔ Choose and evaluate an imported product that you have or might purchase.
- ✔ Research trade laws affecting your chosen imported product.
- ✔ Interview a local salesperson to compare and contrast your product with a competitive brand.
- ✔ Role-play a salesperson representing your chosen product to a business owner.

Write

- ✔ Create an information sheet about your chosen product.
- ✔ Report your research findings about global trade laws that affect your product.
- ✔ Type up the responses from your interview in a question and answer format.
- ✔ List benefits of the imported product to use as speaking points in your role-play.
- ✔ Draw a graphic organizer to compare and contrast the imported product with a product made in the United States.

Present

- ✔ Create an outline for your presentation.
- ✔ Create visuals and use technology to enhance your presentation.
- ✔ Speak clearly and concisely.
- ✔ Share the information sheet about your chosen product.
- ✔ Present your findings about global trade laws and how your product was affected by them.
- ✔ Present your graphic organizer comparing the imported and American-made product.
- ✔ Respond to questions from your classmates.

McGraw Hill **glencoe.com**

Evaluate Download a rubric you can use to evaluate your project.

UNIT 2

Business Ownership and Planning

Visual Literacy

Clear-cut business and financial plans are crucial elements in any new business venture, but there are personal characteristics that can also determine business success or failure. ***What personal traits and skills would be good to have when starting a new business?***

In Your World

Be Your Own Boss

Have you ever thought about starting your own business? As an entrepreneur, you need to understand and accept the risks before you can reap the rewards. One out of two small businesses fails in the first year. However, if you have a great idea, know how to write a business plan, get funding, and work hard, you may be one of the lucky business owners who can tell a great success story.

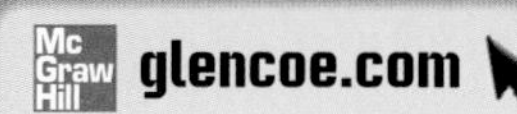

Video Watch the Unit 2 video to learn more about what it takes to make a success out of a small business.

Start-Up Costs Think about a business you would like to own. Write down a "to do" list that you would need to complete before investing any money in your venture. Does the list inspire you, or does it make you wonder if owning a small business may not be worth the effort? Explain your answer.

Economics and You

Economic Systems and Taxes

In a command economy that has socialism as the political philosophy, taxes are high. High taxes are needed to provide the social services that a government provides. In socialistic countries taxes pay for free education from kindergarten through college, free medical care for all citizens, and for subsidies to certain industries to keep prices low for consumers. Higher taxes reduce the amount of net profit for business owners in a command economy. In a market economy, the government does not provide the wealth of social programs one would see in a socialized country. Therefore, taxes are not as high in market economies and that encourages people to open their own businesses. Write one or more paragraphs to explain in which economic system you would rather be a citizen, taxpayer, and business owner.

glencoe.com

Activity Download an Economics and You Worksheet Activity.

CHAPTER 3

Types of Business Ownership

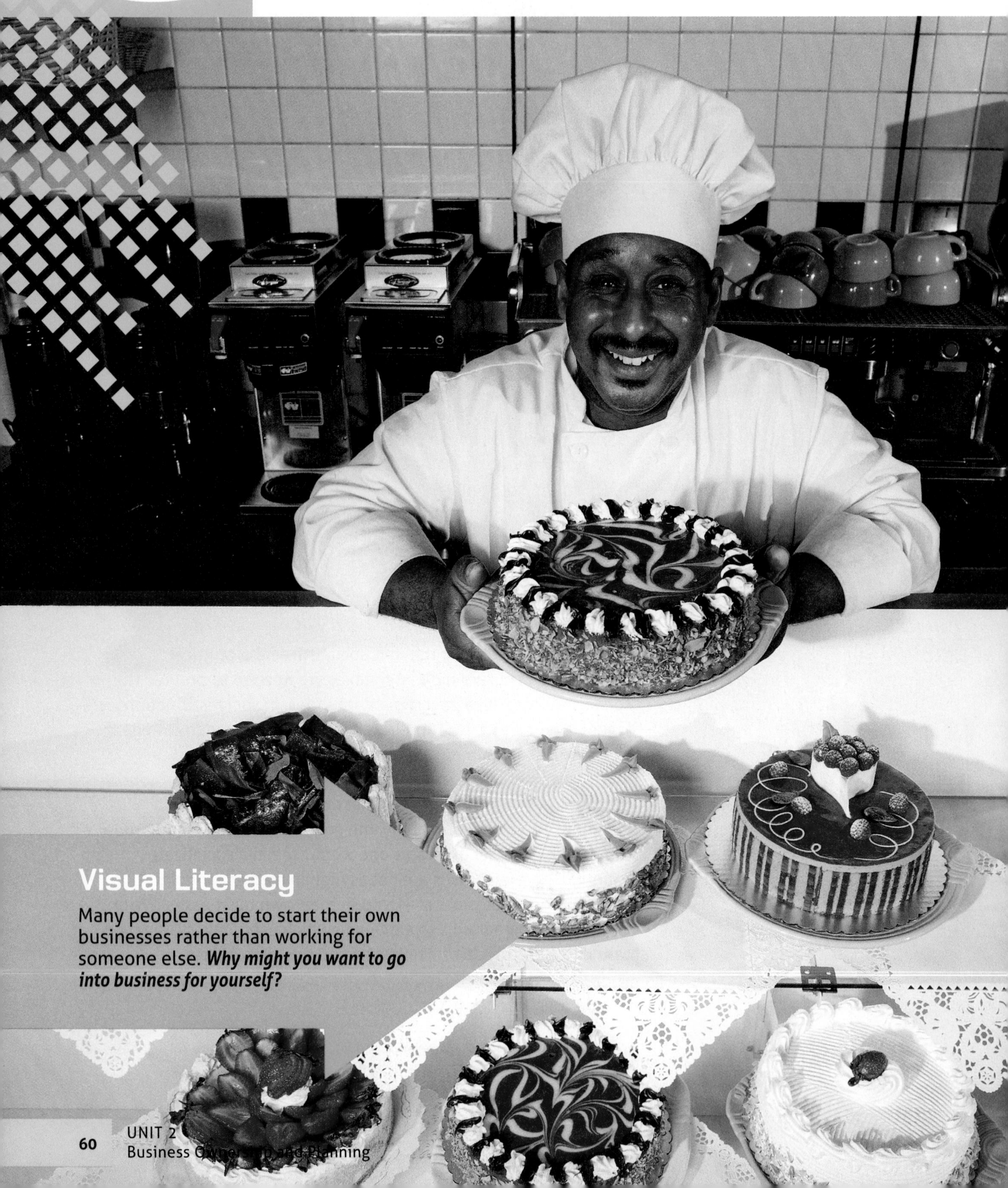

Visual Literacy

Many people decide to start their own businesses rather than working for someone else. ***Why might you want to go into business for yourself?***

Discovery Project

Filing for Incorporation

Key Question

Why is it important to thoroughly understand all aspects of a business when applying for incorporation?

Project Goal

Rose and Alice have a partnership in their cake decorating business, called The Icing. They have decided that their business is growing and they would like to operate as a corporation. Suppose they have hired you to research and complete their application, known as the articles of incorporation, and write their corporate bylaws. Conduct research to find sample articles of incorporation and corporate bylaws. Evaluate each document carefully to ensure that you understand what is expected. These forms may vary slightly from state to state but generally ask for the same pieces of information. If necessary, interview your teacher or another adult for clarification. Once you thoroughly understand what is expected and necessary, complete the articles of incorporation and develop corporate bylaws for Rose and Alice to review.

Ask Yourself...

- *What will the official corporate name be?*
- *What is the purpose of the business?*
- *Will this be a closely held corporation or a publicly held corporation?*
- *If it is a publicly held corporation, what is the maximum number of shares that it can issue?*
- *What process will be used to elect the board of directors?*
- *How often will stockholders meet?*

Apply Technology Effectively

How could you use technology to make the board of directors more efficient?

 glencoe.com 

Evaluate Download an assessment rubric.

THE BIG IDEA

There are several types of business ownership available to businesses.

ASK STANDARD & POOR'S

Business Ownership

Q *In a sole proprietorship, you get to keep all the profits for yourself. Why would I want to have all the hassles of setting up a corporation?*

A Each type of business structure offers advantages and disadvantages. The net income from a sole proprietorship is taxed at personal income tax rates, but a corporation's profits are taxed at lower, corporate tax rates. However, a sole proprietorship is easier to set up, so you could be in business more quickly.

Writing Activity

Write a list of pros and cons for a sole proprietorship and a corporation. In one paragraph summarize your results and identify which type of business ownership you would prefer.

Reading Guide

Before You Read

The Essential Question If you owned a small business, what type of business ownership would best suit your needs and future goals?

Main Idea

Understanding and selecting the proper form of organization for your business can be an essential factor in its success.

Content Vocabulary

- public sector
- private sector
- competition
- price competition
- nonprice competition
- market
- oligopoly
- monopoly
- profit
- sole proprietorship
- entrepreneur
- Employer Identification Number (EIN)
- unlimited liability
- limited life
- partnership
- partnership agreement
- general partner
- limited partner
- cooperative
- corporation
- articles of incorporation
- corporate bylaws
- corporate charter
- board of directors
- limited liability company (LLC)
- franchise

Academic Vocabulary

You will see these words in your reading and on your tests.

- operate
- generate
- elect
- stockholders

Graphic Organizer

Before you read this chapter, create a numbered list like the one shown. As you read, note the basic pieces of information that should be included in a partnership agreement.

Partnership Agreement

1. ______
2. ______
3. ______
4. ______
5. ______
6. ______

 **glencoe.com**  Print this graphic organizer.

Standards

Academic

Mathematics

NCTM Connections Recognize and apply mathematics in contexts outside of mathematics.

NCTM Algebra Represent and analyze mathematical situations and structures using algebraic symbols.

English Language Arts

NCTE 7 Conduct research and gather, evaluate, and synthesize data to communicate discoveries.

NCTE 12 Use language to accomplish individual purposes.

Science

NSES F Develop understanding of personal and community health; population growth; natural resources; environmental quality; natural and human-induced hazards; science and technology in local, national, and global challenges.

NCTM *National Council of Teachers of Mathematics*
NCTE *National Council of Teachers of English*
NCSS *National Council for the Social Studies*
NSES *National Science Education Standards*

Common Core

Reading Determine central ideas or themes of a text and analyze their development; summarize the key supporting details and ideas.

Reading Read and comprehend complex literary and informational texts independently and proficiently.

Writing Write routinely over extended time frames (time for research, reflection, and revision) and shorter time frames (a single sitting or a day or two) for a range of tasks, purposes, and audiences.

Private Enterprise System

How does living in a free-enterprise system affect your financial decisions?

The United States is often referred to as a private system because individuals, not the government, own the majority of the resources. The **public sector** is all government-funded services. Public schools are part of the public sector because they are paid for by tax dollars. The **private sector** in an economy is all businesses not funded by the government. Your local supermarket is part of the private sector and an example of private enterprise.

Section Objectives

- **Describe** the effects of competition on businesses and consumers.
- **Explain** how competition impacts the consumer.
- **Identify** the advantages and disadvantages of a sole proprietorship.
- **Explain** the differences between general and limited partners.
- **Identify** the advantages and disadvantages of a partnership.
- **Identify** the advantages and disadvantages of a cooperative.

As You Read

Predict What might be an advantage of owning your own business? A disadvantage?

Freedom to Compete

Competition is the struggle among businesses for customers. Competition is necessary in a private enterprise system to encourage businesses to provide quality products at prices consumers want to pay. Businesses work hard to get and keep their customers because if they do not, another business will take those customers away.

Price and Nonprice Competition **Price competition** assumes consumers will choose the lowest priced products available. You observe price competition whenever a company states—"We will beat all competitors' prices." Discounts, coupons, rebates, and special sales are examples of price competition. With price competition, businesses compete by offering lower prices than their competitors.

Nonprice competition relies on factors other than price to attract and keep customers. Excellent service, free shipping, quality construction, and brand reliability are examples of nonprice competition. You may frequent a certain restaurant because of its location, food quality, and excellent wait staff. Based on all those factors, you may pay more for your food than in another restaurant. Thus, businesses that use nonprice competition can sometimes charge more than their competitors and still be successful.

Levels of Competition A **market** is where an exchange takes place between buyers and sellers. Market structures are based on levels of competition. The U.S. government ensures that there is competition through its laws. Perfect competition is when you have many competitors vying for many customers. There are two other situations in which competition is not perfect.

An **oligopoly** is characterized by a few large businesses in a market and many consumers that want or need those firms' products. An example of an oligopoly in the U.S. could be the mobile phone services. Verizon, AT&T and Sprint are three companies that dominate the mobile phone industry. As a consumer, your vendor, or retailer, choices may be limited. However, competition is still intense among these three giants. So, products, prices, and services must be competitive.

A **monopoly** is characterized by the existence of only one supplier in a market. In this case, there is no competition. If many consumers want the product produced by this one supplier, they have no choice but to pay the price charged by the supplier. Monopolies are prohibited in the U.S. and other market economies unless there is government control. The U.S. postal service is an example of a government-controlled monopoly for first-class mail.

Risk

There are no guarantees for success in a private enterprise system. Risk, which is the potential for failure, is always present. Entrepreneurs are the risk takers in a private enterprise system. Statistics tell us that only one in every three new businesses in the U.S. succeed during their first year.

Risks of doing business involve competition, changes in economic conditions, new government regulations, new technologies, natural disasters, and lawsuits due to unforeseen circumstances.

Profit

The money left after paying the expenses of doing business is called **profit.** Businesses generate income, which is sometimes called revenue, by selling their goods and services. However, it also costs them money to run their businesses. For example, they pay rent on the buildings where they operate, and employees must be paid. The difference between revenue and expenses is profit. Profit helps to motivate business owners to operate more efficiently. This incentive encourages businesses to reinvest some of their profits in human capital, new machinery, and product innovation.

Profitable businesses keep an economy going by employing workers and paying taxes. When there is high employment in an economy, workers have the means to buy more goods and services. That, in turn, generates revenue for other businesses. The government benefits, too. All the workers and successful businesses pay taxes. When a company is profitable it is also able to contribute to society through charitable donations and projects that help citizens and communities.

Reading Check

Summarize How do price and competition interact in a market and impact businesses and consumers?

Document Detective

An Application for an Employer ID Number

You may decide in the future to start your own business. When you establish a business, you are required by law to apply to the federal government for an employer identification number. An IRS Form SS-4 contains the following information:

- Name and address of the business
- Type of business
- Date the business started
- Principal activity of the business

Form **SS-4** (Rev. December 20--) Department of the Treasury Internal Revenue Service

Application for Employer Identification Number

(For use by employers, corporations, partnerships, trusts, estates, churches, government agencies, Indian tribal entities, certain individuals, and others.)

► See separate instructions for each line. ► Keep a copy for your records.

EIN

OMB No. 1545-0003

Type or print clearly.

1 Legal name of entity (or individual) for whom the EIN is being requested: Callahan Tree Service

2 Trade name of business (if different from name on line 1)

3 Executor, trustee, "care of" name: Lee Callahan

4a Mailing address (room, apt., suite no. and street, or P.O. box): 1537 Hayden Road

5a Street address (if different) (Do not enter a P.O. box.)

4b City, state and ZIP code: Lee, TX

5b City, state, and ZIP code

6 County and state where principal business is located: Tarrant

7a Name of principal officer, general partner, grantor, owner, or trustor: Lee Callahan

7b SSN, ITIN, or EIN

8a Type of entity (check only one box)

- ☒ Sole proprietor (SSN)
- ☐ Partnership
- ☐ Corporation (enter form number to be filed) ►
- ☐ Personal service corp.
- ☐ Church or church-controlled organization
- ☐ Other nonprofit organization (specify) ►
- ☐ Other (specify) ►
- ☐ Estate (SSN of decedent)
- ☐ Plan administrator (SSN)
- ☐ Trust (SSN of grantor)
- ☐ National Guard
- ☐ State/local government
- ☐ Farmers' cooperative
- ☐ Federal government/military
- ☐ REMIC
- ☐ Indian tribal governments/enterprises

Group Exemption Number (GEN) ►

8b If a corporation, name the state or foreign country (if applicable) where incorporated | State | Foreign country

9 Reason for applying (check only one box)

- ☒ Started new business (specify type) ► Tree maintenance
- ☐ Hired employees (Check the box and see line 12.)
- ☐ Compliance with IRS withholding regulations
- ☐ Other (specify) ►
- ☐ Banking purpose (specify purpose) ►
- ☐ Changed type of organization (specify new type) ►
- ☐ Purchased going business
- ☐ Created a trust (specify type) ►
- ☐ Created a pension plan (specify type) ►

10 Date business started or acquired (month, day, year): 03/15/--

11 Closing month of accounting year: December

12 First date wages or annuities were paid or will be paid (month, day, year). **Note:** *If applicant is a withholding agent, enter date income will first be paid to nonresident alien. (month, day, year)* . . . ► 4/15/--

13 Highest number of employees expected in the next 12 months. **Note:** *If the applicant does not expect to have any employees during the period, enter "-0-."* ►

Agricultural	Household	Other
		3

14 Check **one** box that best describes the principal activity of your business.

- ☐ Construction
- ☐ Rental & leasing
- ☐ Transportation & warehousing
- ☐ Health care & social assistance
- ☐ Wholesale–agent/broker
- ☐ Real estate
- ☐ Manufacturing
- ☐ Finance & insurance
- ☐ Accommodation & food service
- ☐ Wholesale–other
- ☐ Retail
- ☒ Other (specify) Tree Trimming

15 Indicate principal line of merchandise sold; specific construction work done; products produced; or services provided. Cut and trim trees

Has the applicant ever app... ☒ No

Key Points An employer sends an IRS Form SS-4 to the federal government. When received, the government assigns the employer a number. This process can also be completed online at the IRS Web site. A number is assigned instantly if completed online. The Employer Identification Number (EIN) helps the government monitor taxes that a business is required to pay. Whenever taxes are paid, a business must provide its identification number.

FIND the Solutions

Review Key Concepts

1. Who should use the Form SS-4?
2. What is the purpose of this form?
3. What was the date that this business started?
4. In what state was this business incorporated?
5. What is the principal activity of the business?

Business Ownership Organization

Are there different kinds of business ownership?

Understanding how to handle your personal finances can help prepare you for managing your own business. The abilities to plan, manage, and keep track of your own money can be applied to handling a business. If you decide to start a business and manage its finances, it is important to become familiar with the different types of ownership.

When you start a business, you have a choice as to how the ownership is legally organized. Business ownership can take one of three legal forms:

- sole proprietorship
- partnership
- corporation

It is important to select the most appropriate form of ownership that best suits your needs and the needs of your business. This section will examine the first two forms of business ownership—sole proprietorship and partnership.

Reading Check

Recall What three personal finance skills can be applied to a business?

Sole Proprietorship

What are the characteristics of a sole proprietorship?

The word *sole* means "single" or "one." The word *proprietor* means "owner." A **sole proprietorship,** therefore, is a business owned by one person. The sole proprietorship is the oldest and most common form of business ownership. Approximately 75 percent of all businesses in the United States today are organized as sole proprietorships. Although many people think of corporations when they think about business in the United States, the sole proprietorship is the backbone of American business.

Most sole proprietorships are small-business operations, each owned by an individual. An individual who takes the risk of starting a new business is known as an **entrepreneur.** Many of these businesses provide services, such as auto repair, house cleaning, carpentry, or plumbing. They generally **operate,** or perform, out of homes, small offices, or storefronts. Some sole proprietorships become quite successful, but many go out of business. In all cases, however, the owners of sole proprietorships are pursuing their dreams of running their own businesses.

For example, Debbi Fields had a dream of selling cookies. She created a highly successful business called Mrs. Fields Cookies. John Johnson wanted to start a magazine. So he borrowed $500 from his family and created the successful magazine *Ebony*. Even some major corporations began as risky ventures by entrepreneurs. The company Corning would not exist without Amory Houghton, and there would be no Colgate-Palmolive without the determination of William Colgate.

Advantages of Sole Proprietorship

Organizing a business as a sole proprietorship has several advantages. The most important advantage is having the freedom to make all the decisions. Also, you receive all profits and pay tax once a year as an individual. This type of business has easy set-up, simple licensing and paperwork, and few government regulations.

Easy Set-Up A sole proprietorship is the easiest form of business organization to set up. Although local and state governments require some paperwork, you can usually complete this without much difficulty. Starting a sole proprietorship does take some effort, but because a minimal amount of documentation is required, the cost of organizing a sole proprietorship is relatively low.

Licensing and Paperwork In many cases, you can organize a sole proprietorship by simply obtaining a license to do business from your local or state government. You might also need to obtain a state sales tax number because you may be required to collect sales tax on any products you sell to customers.

If you are planning to operate under a business name other than your own name, you must apply for a *Certificate of Doing Business Under an Assumed Name*. This is also referred to as a DBA, which stands for "Doing Business As." For example, Celia Jontos wants to start a personalized wedding planning service, *Time to Remember*. In order to operate legally under this business name, Ms. Jontos will need to get a DBA certificate.

If you intend to hire one or more employees to work in your business, you will need an Employer Identification Number. An **Employer Identification Number (EIN)** is a number assigned by the Internal Revenue Service, which is used for income tax purposes. Many sole proprietors hire managers and several employees. Some large companies, which are also organized as sole proprietorships, have hundreds of employees.

Total Control As a sole proprietor, you can run your business as you wish. This is a great advantage because you do not have to convince partners, stockholders, or other people that your business decisions are sound. You can choose what merchandise to sell or services to provide, what prices to charge, and what hours you will work. As the sole owner of your own business, you make all management and financial decisions.

Financial Literacy

Financial literacy is the ability to make personal economic and financial decisions and effectively manage your money. Financial literacy involves budgeting and increasing your savings, but it also involves retirement planning, managing credit, tax strategies, and insurance. Basic financial literacy will not only improve your personal finances, but it will also impact the nation. Financially literate citizens will make better financial and economic decisions that will help to establish a more efficient and stable economy.

Write About It

Research financial literacy and any resources. How can you become financially literate? Summarize your results for achieving financial literacy in a brief report and present it to the class.

Activity Download a Career and College Readiness Worksheet Activity.

Careers That Count!

Chris Jackson • General Contractor

Some general contractors own contracting firms in charge of construction; others are salaried employees of property owners and developers. I started out as an apprentice during college, and now I own a small firm. As a general contractor, I help homeowners, landlords, and businesses construct, remodel, or repair their buildings. I may bid to take part of a job—for example, fixing a kitchen—or oversee an entire project. I have to know prices and be able to plan for expenses. Whether I handle the entire job or subcontract parts of the job to electrical, heating, and plumbing specialists, I am responsible for the job being done on time and according to the budget. While some general contractors will do all types of work, most of us specialize in one type of construction project. For example, residential contractors like me may oversee some commercial buildings, but we rarely take on large-scale projects like bridges, sewage systems, and industrial sites.

EXPLORE CAREERS

Before contractors begin a project, they must submit a bid or price quote to the individual, company, or government agency that needs the work done.

1. How do contractors make an accurate bid?
2. Do you think the lowest bidder always gets to take on the project? Explain your answer.

Skills	Education	Career Path
Accounting, communication, leadership, decision-making, sales, math, negotiation, organization, problem-solving, and time-management skills	High school diploma or equivalent; bachelor's degree in construction science; experience in the field; contractor's license exam	General contractors can become cost estimators, specification writers, urban planners, civil engineers, surveyors, and architects.

glencoe.com

Activity Download a Career Exploration Activity.

Profits to Owner With a sole proprietorship, when your business makes a profit, you can keep all of it (after you pay taxes). As your business grows and becomes more successful, you will receive larger profits. A sole proprietorship allows the owner to reap the rewards of hard work and determination.

Profits Taxed Once A business organized as a sole proprietorship does not pay income taxes as a company. You, as the owner, must declare the profits of the business on your personal income tax return. Tax is computed on your total income for the year. If you operate your business full-time, any profits you make will be counted as taxable income. If your business operates part-time and you also have a full-time job, your taxable income will include income from your job as well as the net income from your business.

Few Government Regulations Another benefit of operating as a sole proprietorship is that you do not have to complete and file many forms and reports with the state and federal governments. There may be some government regulations regarding the particular business, but most sole proprietors experience little government red tape.

Disadvantages of Sole Proprietorship

With most choices people make, there is a positive side and a negative side. Though organizing your business as a sole proprietorship has advantages, this form of organization also has several drawbacks.

Limited Capital When you start a sole proprietorship, the only source of working capital, besides money you borrow, is your own money. Generally, no one else helps you finance the business. Moreover, the amount of cash available to you may be limited. Adequate funding and a positive cash flow are essential for a business. Without a sufficient amount of money to establish the business, begin operations, and expand, you could have serious difficulties.

Unlimited Liability A major disadvantage of a sole proprietorship is that if your business is not successful, you are responsible for all losses. **Unlimited liability** is a situation in which the owner of the business is responsible to pay the business debts out of personal assets. In other words, if your business is unsuccessful, you could lose your car, home, savings, and other assets. If your business's financial situation is bad, you might have to declare personal bankruptcy.

Starting a new business involves a high risk. More than half of all new businesses fail within the first five years. If your business fails, your financial position and credit rating could be seriously damaged.

Limited Human Resources An advantage of a sole proprietorship is that you are the only decision maker in the business. However, when you are the sole owner of a business, you cannot rely on other individuals to help carry the load.

Most people have limited knowledge and talents. Perhaps you know a lot about certain goods or services, but your basic business skills are weak. For example, if you start a painting business, you may have skills in painting, be able to identify different types of paint, and know the proper way to apply paint to different surfaces. At the same time, you may have limited business experience in pricing, record-keeping, or advertising and marketing.

Starting Small
Small businesses have traditionally been the backbone of the American economy. *What small businesses can you name in your neighborhood?*

Poor decisions in purchasing, accounting, or marketing could ruin your business. A sole proprietor must be willing to hire the people whose diverse talents and skills will improve the business.

Limited Life A sole proprietorship has a **limited life,** a situation in which a business's life span or existence is determined by the owner's life span or the owner's decision to terminate the business. The business may also legally end if sold to someone else. In that case, the new owner creates a new business in his or her name.

Reading Check

Define What is an Employer Identification Number?

The Partnership

What are the characteristics of a partnership?

Some people choose to form a partnership when starting a business. A **partnership** is a business owned by two or more persons. Partners as co-owners agree voluntarily to operate the business for profit. When a partnership is formed, the partners sign a special legal agreement: A **partnership agreement** is a written document that states how the partnership will be organized. The agreement includes:

- Names of the partners
- Name and nature of the business
- Amount of investment by each partner
- Duties, rights, and responsibilities of each partner
- Procedures for sharing profits and losses
- How assets will be divided when and if the partnership is dissolved

In a partnership, you and your co-owners decide how to divide profits and losses from the business. You also outline the duties and responsibilities of each partner. All partners must agree to the conditions stated in the partnership agreement. Some large companies began as partnerships before becoming corporations. For example, in 1876, an icebox maker named Abram Anderson started a partnership with a fruit merchant named Joseph Campbell. Their small partnership grew to become the Campbell Soup Company.

General Partners and Limited Partners

There are two basic types of partners: general partners and limited partners. In many partnerships, all partners are general partners. A **general partner** is a business partner who has decision-making authority, takes an active role in the operation of the business, and has unlimited liability for all losses or debts of the partnership. Every partnership has at least one general partner.

All general partners have what is known as agency power. Agency power, also known as mutual agency, is the right to sign contracts that are legally binding on the partnership. For example, suppose that Dylan, Juanita, and Charles form a partnership to make bookcases. Dylan goes to Clinton Wood Products and signs a contract to purchase wood from that company. Dylan acted on behalf of the business with agency power, and so the partnership is legally obligated under the contract.

A partnership can also add limited partners. A **limited partner** is a business partner who does not take an active role in decision making or in running the business. A limited partner's liability in the partnership is limited to the amount of his or her investment in the business. For example, Christa Clark, a limited partner in Low Country Furniture, invested $25,000 in the business. Christa is not involved in running the business. Moreover, her financial liability is limited to her $25,000 investment. That means if the business fails, the most she can lose is $25,000.

Advantages of the Partnership

Many of the advantages of a partnership are similar to the advantages of a sole proprietorship. However, instead of being the only decision maker in a business, you would share decision making with your partners. More people can **generate,** or make, more ideas and possibly more money.

There are several advantages of a partnership:

- Easy set-up
- More skills and knowledge
- Available capital
- Total control by partners
- Profits taxed once

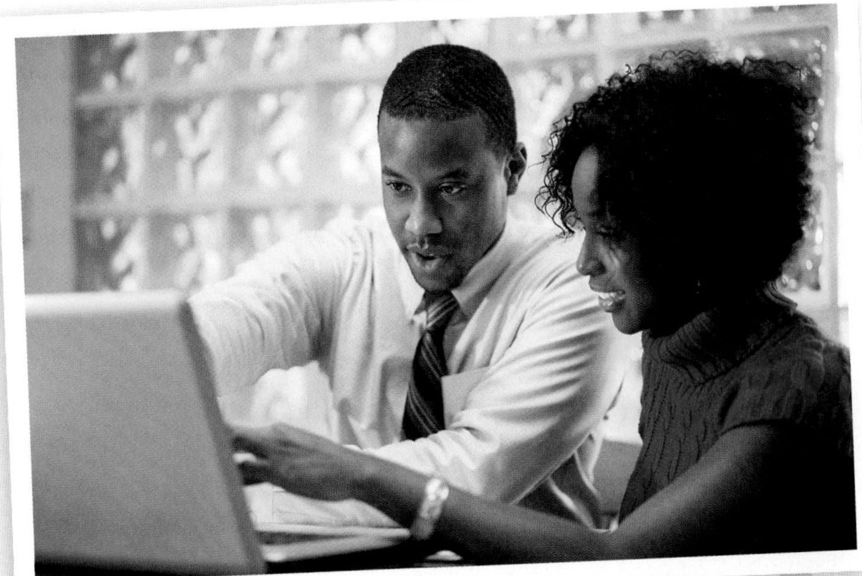

Two Is Company
A partnership allows you to benefit from the skills and knowledge of more than just yourself. *Why is a partnership agreement important?*

reality bytes

Virtual Consultants
Using technology can help you plan your business strategy. Smart software allows you to strategize about how to build your business. For example, the MBA Wizard is intelligent software created with the capacity to learn. It has accurately evaluated over 20,000 business plans, and thus, its expanding knowledge is accessible to the user.

Around the World

Estonia

Tiger Leap Foundation

Improving education is a goal of most countries. Estonia has developed a unique way to meet this challenge. The Estonian government developed the Tiger Leap program to improve the quality of school education through the use of modern information and communication technology. Funded by the Ministry of Education, the initial aim of the program was to modernize the information and communication technologies (ICT) infrastructure of educational establishments. The focus then shifted to e-learning initiatives of schools and universities. By using ICT and e-learning as a part of the daily curriculum, the Tiger Leap Foundation hopes to increase the curriculum quality and effectiveness of Estonian schools.

The effectiveness of the Foundation can be seen in the specific projects that they do. The ScienceTiger project is a three-year project, begun in 2008, aimed at getting students interested in science by encouraging teachers to make experiments with innovative devices. For example, many school gyms were provided with dataloggers and sensors to be used for physics lessons. In addition to physics, the ScienceTiger project will also focus on areas of biology and chemistry.

Critical Thinking

1. **Expand** Research to find how teachers are trained to support the Tiger Leap program. Explain the process.
2. **Relate** The State assists local municipalities who are unable to afford the required ICT equipment for their schools. Do you feel the federal and state governments of the United States should do more to ensure consistent and minimal computer equipment to public schools?

DATABYTES

Capital
Tallinn

Population
1,291,170

Languages
Estonian (official), Russian, other

Currency
Estonian kroon

Gross Domestic Product (GDP)
$18.26 billion

GDP per capita
$18,700

Industry
Engineering, electronics, wood and wood products, textiles; information technology, telecommunications

Agriculture
Potatoes, vegetables; livestock and dairy products; fish

Exports
Machinery and equipment, wood and paper, metals, food products, textiles, chemical products

Natural Resources
Oil shale, peat, phosphorite, clay, limestone, sand, dolomite, arable land, sea mud

Easy Set-Up A partnership is also relatively easy to set up. Although some paperwork is required, it is generally minimal. You may need to obtain certain local or state business permits or licenses. For some types of business operations, you must also know and follow various government regulations.

The most important legal document of a partnership is the partnership agreement. All the terms and conditions of the partnership must be clearly stated in this written document. Taking care to make the agreement as complete and clear as possible can help you to avoid misinterpretations and misunderstandings between partners as the partnership and business grow.

More Skills and Knowledge The skills and knowledge needed to operate the business in a sole proprietorship are the responsibility of just one person. In a partnership, however, the various partners can contribute different skills and experience. One person may have previous experience running a similar type of business. Another partner might have extensive business or accounting experience. A third partner might have excellent sales and marketing skills. The pooling of talent and knowledge is an advantage that partnerships have over sole proprietorships.

Available Capital Several individuals in a business partnership can contribute more money to a business venture than one person acting alone with only personal assets. Moreover, if additional cash is needed to maintain or expand business operations, it can be easier to raise capital when several people are working to do so.

For example, in 1872, dry goods merchant Levi Strauss received a letter from one of his customers, a Nevada tailor named Jacob Davis. Davis had been making overalls for miners and had created a way to strengthen the pants by adding rivets to the seams. He wanted to patent his idea but could not afford the $68 he needed to file the papers. He wrote to Strauss to suggest that they hold the patent together. Strauss agreed, and after the two teamed up in 1873, Levi's® jeans became a reality.

Obtaining bank financing may be more feasible when more than one individual is responsible for the loan. For example, a bank may be more willing to approve a loan, or a bank may also be more willing to loan greater sums of money to a partnership than to a sole proprietorship because the risk is shared among the partners.

The partners' credit ratings are very important. Avoid entering a partnership agreement with anyone who has a questionable credit rating. The ability of all partners to borrow money can be an important factor in the success or failure of a business.

Total Control by Partners In a partnership, the operation of the business is the sole responsibility of the general partners, who can do as they want. However, the partners are also responsible for the success or failure of the business.

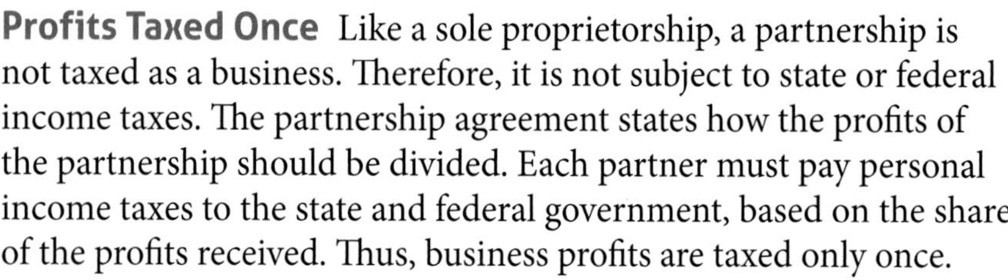

Profits Taxed Once Like a sole proprietorship, a partnership is not taxed as a business. Therefore, it is not subject to state or federal income taxes. The partnership agreement states how the profits of the partnership should be divided. Each partner must pay personal income taxes to the state and federal government, based on the share of the profits received. Thus, business profits are taxed only once.

Disadvantages of the Partnership

While a partnership can offer many advantages, a number of problems can arise when several people own and operate a business. This form of business ownership can avoid some of the problems associated with sole proprietorships, but it also has disadvantages:

- Unlimited liability
- Possible disagreement among partners
- Shared profits
- Limited life

In 1975, two young men named Bill Gates and Paul Allen formed a partnership to produce computer software. Today their company, Microsoft, is a major corporation, and Bill Gates and Paul Allen are two of the wealthiest people in the world. Microsoft is a partnership that turned into one of America's greatest success stories. However, most people never come close to this level of achievement. Many partnerships have very little success or eventually fail. Entering a partnership can involve large financial risks.

Unlimited Liability Earlier in this section, you learned that the owner of a sole proprietorship has unlimited liability. The same is true of the general partners in a partnership. If the partnership loses money or has financial problems, each co-owner is personally responsible for all of the debts of the business. In other words, if your partnership fails and the debts of the business cannot be covered by its assets, you and your partners are responsible for paying the bills out of your own personal assets.

For example, two friends ask you to join them in forming a partnership. You have a large amount of personal assets. Your two partners have very few assets. If the business fails, you could end up being personally responsible for the majority of the business debts. You could even lose everything you own. It is very important to choose your business partners carefully. Know the personal financial position and credit ratings of each partner. Remember, each general partner has unlimited liability for the entire business, not just part of it.

Disagreement Among Partners When several people manage a business, they may not always agree on important business decisions. A common reason for failed partnerships is that the partners have serious conflicts about how the business should operate, and they allow the business to suffer financially from these conflicts.

Shared Profits Hard work on your part may be the crucial factor in the success of the business. Nevertheless, you still must share the profits with your partners. The way in which the profits of the business are divided is outlined in the partnership agreement.

Limited Life The life of a partnership depends on the willingness and ability of the partners to continue in business together. A partnership has a limited life, and partnerships can end for a number of reasons. Perhaps a partner dies or decides to retire or withdraw from the partnership due to illness. The partners may disagree and decide to end their partnership, or they may decide to add new partners. In these situations, the original partnership dissolves. The remaining partners and any new partners should then draw up a new partnership agreement, which will create a new business.

Reading Check

Differentiate How are a general and limited partner different?

The Cooperative

What are the characteristics of a cooperative?

Another way to organize a business venture is a cooperative. A **cooperative** is an organization that is owned and operated by its members. Cooperatives provide a wide range of products and services from utilities to grocery stores.

Advantages of the Cooperative

A cooperative provides benefits, control, and ownership to the user. Members of a cooperative elect a board of directors or membership group to oversee the management of the business. Each member has an equal vote. This gives each member some control over the business. In addition, a cooperative is often able to save money on purchases of certain goods and services. Groups of people and small businesses can pool their resources and contacts to increase purchasing power. Another benefit to this pooling of resources is a cooperative can make marketing of goods and services more efficient and profitable.

Disadvantages of the Cooperative

There are also disadvantages to this type of business. While a cooperative has a manager, he or she is responsible to the membership group or board of directors. All decisions must be approved by this organization. This may limit the flexibility of the business and slow decisions on profit opportunities. Due to limited capital the potential for growth is limited. It can be difficult to maintain the membership group as members may lose interest or find other ventures.

SECTION 1 Assessment

Review Key Concepts

1. **List** What are the costs, advantages, and disadvantages of a partnership? Of a sole proprietorship?
2. **Describe** What are the costs, advantages, and disadvantages to starting a cooperative?
3. **Distinguish** What is the difference between a general partner and a limited partner?
4. **Relate** How does competition affect consumers, sellers, and producers?
5. **Assess** How does a monopoly affect businesses and consumers?
6. **Evaluate** How do taxes affect the different types of businesses?

Higher Order Thinking 

7. **Conclude** You are starting your own business repairing bicycles. Your uncle is supplying money for start-up costs. Decide whether your uncle should be a general partner or limited partner.

21st Century Skills

8. **Collaborate with Others** Jacob and his friend, Seth, have decided to form a partnership and start their own business. They both plan to be general partners in the business. They have determined that the business will require $500 for equipment and supplies to get started. Write a partnership agreement detailing how Jacob and Seth will divide the investment; profits and losses; and duties, rights, and responsibilities. Be sure to include all the basic information required in a partnership agreement.

Mathematics

9. **Partnership** Sam, Beth, and Sanjay have created a partnership in order to start a small real estate investment company. They did this in order to be able to pool their finances as well as their expertise. Sam is the general partner while Beth and Sanjay are both limited partners. The partnership agreement states that Sam owns 45 percent of the business, Beth owns 30 percent and Sanjay owns 25 percent which is based on their percentage of initial investment. If the total initial investment was $250,000 how much did each partner invest?

Math Concept **Calculate Partnership Investment** To calculate the initial investment in a partnership, identify the percent of ownership and basis of this percentage per the partnership agreement. Determine the total amount invested in order to calculate each partner's original contribution.

Starting Hint Determine the original investment for the general partner by identifying his or her ownership percentage. Per the partnership agreement, percent ownership is based on each partners' original investment. Multiply the general partner's percent ownership by the initial investment.

NCTM Problem Solving Solve problems that arise in mathematics and in other contexts.

glencoe.com Check your answers.

What Is a Corporation?

What is the difference between a corporation and other businesses?

You have probably heard the word *corporation.* A number of large corporations exist nationally and globally, such as IBM, Volkswagen, Sony, Xerox, and Goodyear. A corporation is another form of business ownership that is different from a sole proprietorship or a partnership.

A **corporation** is a business organization that operates as a legal entity that is separate from its owners and is treated by law as if it were an individual person. A corporation can do everything that a sole proprietorship or a partnership can do—own property, buy and sell merchandise, pay bills, and make contracts. It can also sue and be sued in the court system. About 20 percent of businesses in the United States are organized as corporations, but they produce about 90 percent of the total business revenue in the United States.

Reading Check

State What is a corporation?

Starting a Corporation

What is the process of forming a corporation?

When you form a corporation, you create a legal entity. This process is more complex than starting a sole proprietorship or a partnership.

Paperwork and Documents

To create a corporation, you must file an application with the state for permission to operate. The application to operate as a corporation is called the **articles of incorporation.** The application includes information such as the corporate name and the type of business in which the corporation will be involved.

In addition, you must write a set of corporate bylaws. **Corporate bylaws** are the rules by which a corporation will operate. Items in the bylaws may include how the company will **elect,** or choose, directors of the corporation and when stockholders will meet.

When the state approves the application, it issues a corporate charter. A **corporate charter** is a license to operate a corporation. It states the purpose of the business and spells out the laws and guidelines under which the business will operate.

Section Objectives

- **Describe** two types of corporations.
- **Summarize** the process of forming a corporation.
- **Discuss** the advantages and disadvantages of a corporation.
- **Discuss** the advantages and costs of a franchise.

As You Read

Question What is the advantage of separating ownership and management?

Big Business
Even though corporations make up only about 20 percent of businesses in the United States, they produce about 90 percent of the business revenue. *Why do you think they account for such a large portion of the revenue?*

Issuing Stock

The ownership of a corporation is divided into units, which are shares of stock. These shares of stock are bought by people who become known as **stockholders.** Stockholders are the legal owners of the corporation. If you buy even one share of stock in Xerox, for example, you are legally an owner of the company and have all the rights of ownership. Small corporations usually have only a few stockholders. Larger corporations, such as Google, have thousands of stockholders.

Closely Held Corporations A closely held, or private, corporation is one whose shares are owned by a small group of people. The shares are not traded openly in stock markets. Many small and family businesses are organized as closely held corporations. A closely held corporation can be opened to the general public if the stockholders decide in favor of this move. When a corporation decides to sell its stock on the open market, the decision is known as "going public."

Publicly Held Corporations A publicly held corporation is one that sells its shares openly in stock markets, where anyone can buy them. Most of these corporations trade their stock on an exchange, such as the New York Stock Exchange or the American Stock Exchange. Almost all major corporations are publicly held.

Reading Check

Rephrase Explain what articles of incorporation and a corporate charter are.

Advantages of the Corporation

What are the benefits of forming a corporation?

Establishing your business as a corporation has a number of advantages over a sole proprietorship and a partnership such as the ability to raise capital; limited liability; continued life; and the separation of ownership and management.

Ability to Raise Capital

A major advantage of a corporation is the ability to sell its stock and generate capital, or money. If the corporation needs money for growth, expansion, or other purposes, the company can sell additional shares of stock to raise the necessary funds. If a large amount of capital is needed to start a business, the company may begin as a closely held corporation rather than as a partnership. Examples of this kind of corporation might include an automobile dealership, a restaurant, or an amusement park.

Limited Liability

A great advantage to the stockholders, or owners, of a corporation is that they have limited liability. This means that if the corporation has debts or financial problems, the owners may lose only the amount of their investment—the price they paid for their stock.

Consider the following example: You own $20,000 worth of stock in the Family Fun Restaurant. The restaurant is not successful and goes out of business while owing $150,000 dollars to its creditors. As a stockholder, you can lose only up to $20,000, or the amount of your investment, to help repay these debts. You are not personally responsible for any debt beyond that amount.

Unlike a sole proprietorship or a general partnership, a corporation leaves your personal assets protected. You are not legally responsible for all the debts owed by the corporation.

Continued Life

When a sole proprietor retires, dies, or sells his or her business to someone else, that business ceases to exist. Each time partners enter or leave a partnership, a new partnership must be created. In a corporation, however, a change of owners does not end the legal operation of the business. Stockholders may enter or leave at any time without affecting the existence of the corporation. Its legal status as a business continues indefinitely.

Separation of Ownership and Management

The owners do not run the business in most publicly held corporations. Instead, they elect a **board of directors,** a group of individuals who are responsible for overseeing the general affairs of the corporation. Corporate officers and professional managers are hired to make day-to-day decisions in running the business. Other specialists, such as lawyers and accountants, advise the professional managers. By separating management from ownership, the corporation can take advantage of the skills, knowledge, and experience of various individuals to ensure that the business will run successfully. (See **Figure 1** for corporate advantages.)

Shop by Phone

Instead of driving from store to store, use your telephone to see if a store has the item that you want and compare prices. You will save gas and time. Also, use the Internet to see if the store sells merchandise online.

Concept Application

What type of business ownership might an online store have? What would be the advantage of this type of ownership for the store?

FIGURE 1 Corporate Advantages

Separation of Power Some sole proprietorships or partnerships eventually decide to become a corporation to help ensure the continued life of the business. *How can the separation of ownership and management help ensure continued life?*

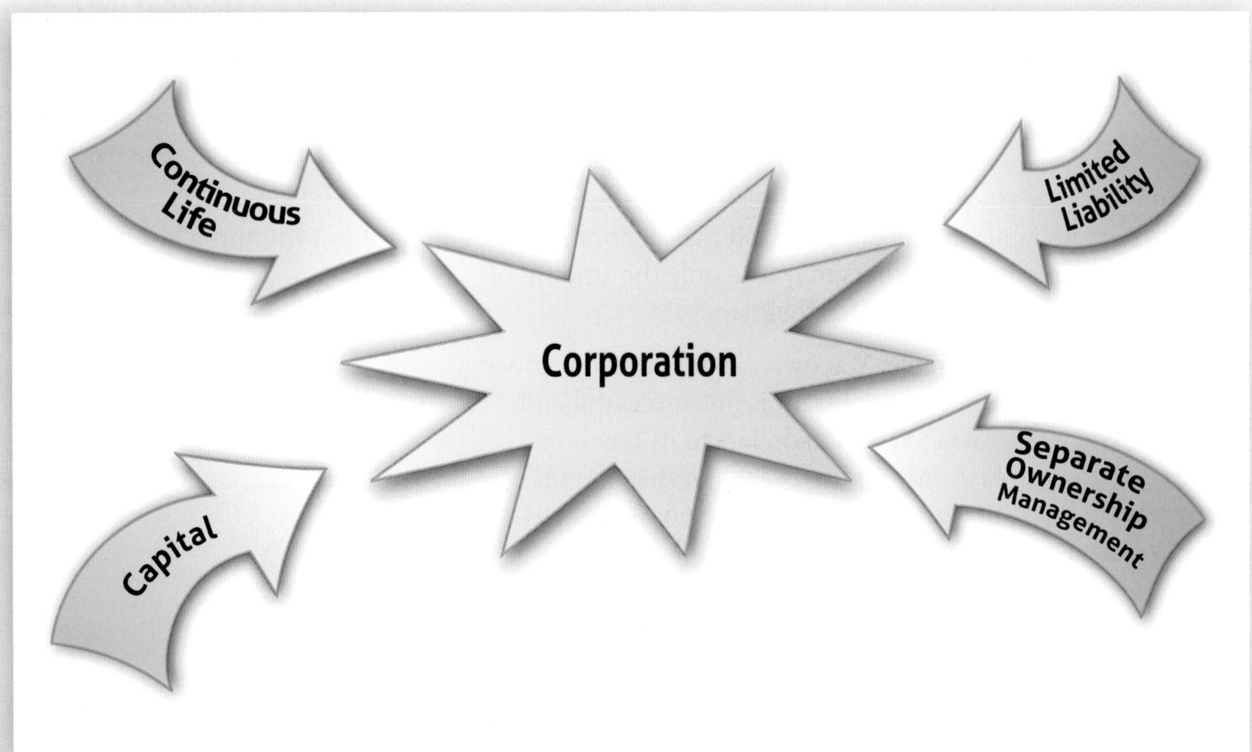

In smaller, closely held corporations, the owners often act as the managers who run the business. Some closely held corporations are family-run businesses. A family-run business has some connection between a family and the policies of the business. In many cases, families maintain control by holding senior management positions in the business. The separation of ownership and management usually does not occur until a company grows large and goes public.

For example, Apple Computer was established originally as a partnership. It was managed and run by its co-owners, Steve Jobs and Steve Wozniak. To expand, they formed a closely held corporation. After it became a publicly held corporation, the company hired professional managers and other specialists to run the business. (See **Figure 2** for an example of a publicly held corporation as well as other forms of business ownership.)

Reading Check

Identify Who are the board of directors, and what role do they play in a business?

Economics and You

Economic Systems

Two types of economic systems are command and market. In a command economy, the government makes the economic decisions of what to produce, how it should be produced, and for whom it should be produced. Prices for necessities are kept low so everyone in the nation can afford them. In a market economy, the three economic decisions are made in the marketplace. Consumers through their purchases determine what should be produced, businesses decide how to most efficiently produce the products consumers want, and consumers decide for whom they should be produced by working and earning the money needed to make purchases. In reality most economies are mixed; each containing some characteristics of market and command economies. For example, a government may encourage free enterprise in a market system, but still regulate how a business functions by imposing guidelines for food and product safety.

Personal Finance Connection A business owner in a market system may still face government regulations. For example, pollution controls require sophisticated machinery to monitor and reduce pollutants. Accurate recordkeeping is required for tax purposes. Nonetheless, business owners in a market system get to earn a profit, which they can keep or reinvest to improve their business operations.

Critical Thinking As a consumer which type of economic system do you prefer—a command economy or a market economy? Explain. If you wanted to be a business owner, which type would you prefer? Why?

Market and Command Economies

Planning in Market and Command Economies	
Market System	Command System
In a market system planning is undertaken by private firms, individuals, and elected government representatives. Economic activity is coordinated by private businesses and individuals responding to market signals.	In pure socialist systems central planners undertake the planning on behalf of everyone. Planners also control the movement of resources, particularly labor.

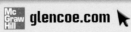

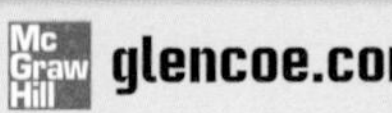

Activity Download an Economics and You Worksheet Activity.

Disadvantages of a Corporation

What are the drawbacks of corporate ownership?

Though the corporate form of ownership has a number of advantages, it also has several disadvantages. Some disadvantages to a corporation include:

- Complex and expensive set-up
- Slow decision-making process
- Taxes

Complex and Expensive Set-Up

You have learned that sole proprietorships and partnerships are fairly easy to set up, but each type of business also has its disadvantages. In contrast, a great deal of work is required to create a corporation. You must complete many forms, file reports, and adhere to many laws and regulations.

As a result of the great amount of work and organization required, forming a corporation costs a large amount of money. Some costs of creating a corporation include legal fees, licensing costs, filing fees, costs of issuing stock certificates, and administrative costs.

Slow Decision-Making Process

A major disadvantage of the corporation is the slowness of the decision-making process. In sole proprietorships and partnerships, only a few people determine how the business is run. As a result, decisions may be made quickly. However, in corporations, especially large ones, many different people study the issues and discuss and debate them before making a decision. The process can take even more time if disagreements occur. Thus, corporations may not respond quickly to issues or situations that affect business.

Taxes

Another major disadvantage of a corporation concerns taxes. Because a corporation is a separate legal entity, it must pay state and federal income taxes on its profits. Dividends that stockholders receive are then taxed again.

Reading Check

Recall What are some of the costs that make starting a corporation expensive?

Limited Liability Company

What is another type of ownership?

The federal government also allows another form of business ownership—a **limited liability company (LLC),** which is a business that operates and pays taxes as a partnership but has limited liability for the owners. It combines some advantages of both the partnership and the corporation. In an LLC, the liability of the owners is limited to their investments. The profits are taxed only once. This form of business is intended for smaller businesses.

Most states allow the creation of LLCs, and they are becoming very popular. The Internal Revenue Service approves of this new form of business organization if the company is small. This form of ownership is not intended for large business operations.

Reading Check

Recognize What are two advantages of an LLC?

FIGURE 2 Forms of Business Ownership

Consider Your Options When deciding to form a business, you should carefully consider the advantages of each type before deciding what form your business will take. *What type of business might you form if you wanted to teach people a skill that you possess?*

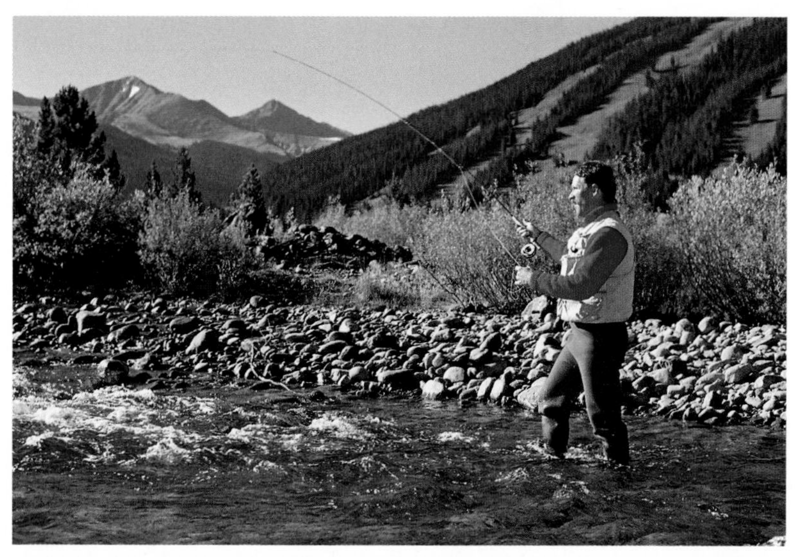

1 Sole Proprietorships A hobby such as fly-fishing could turn into an ideal sole proprietorship. An avid fisherman could offer his or her services as a fishing guide or instructor.

2 Partnerships Some businesses may be too large for one person to operate. For example, a floral-design business that specializes in events might be a good enterprise for a partnership whose owners contribute different talents.

3 Closely Held Corporations Some businesses are organized as closely held corporations. The owners could be a group with a common interest, such as kayaking.

4 Publicly Held Corporations Walt Disney World is part of the The Walt Disney Company, a publicly held corporation with thousands of stockholders.

Franchise Owner
Any type of business may purchase a franchise. *What is a parent corporation?*

Franchise

What are the advantages of a franchise?

A franchise is not necessarily a form of business ownership, but it is important to understand its legal status. A **franchise** is a contractual agreement to sell a company's products or services in a designated geographic area. Franchises are very popular in fast-food businesses, such as McDonald's, Subway, Burger King, Wendy's, and Taco Bell, all of which have franchises. Franchises such as these offer a well-known and established name and a business plan to follow.

If you start a franchise, you first organize your business as a sole proprietorship, partnership, corporation, or LLC. You then purchase a franchise from a corporation, known as a parent corporation. You are now licensed, and the franchise is an asset of your business.

Smaller franchises may cost only a few thousand dollars, but large ones, such as Midas Muffler, cost hundreds of thousands of dollars.

Reading Check

State Explain what a franchise is.

After You Read

Relate Imagine you and a few friends decide to start a business making and selling baked goods decorated to order. What type of business organization would suit you best?

Choosing the Form of Ownership

Which form of business ownership is best?

No magic formula exists for deciding which form of ownership is the best. You must carefully consider the advantages and disadvantages of each. Then you can decide which one is best for your particular business and personal needs. Many people feel that a small start-up business is best established as a sole proprietorship or a partnership. These forms of ownership are easy to establish. If the business is successful, you can consider creating a corporation to gain increased capital and limited liability.

Assessment

Review Key Concepts

1. **Identify** What are the three main documents and paperwork that must be completed when forming a corporation?
2. **List** What are the costs and the four advantages that a corporation has over a partnership or sole proprietorship?
3. **Describe** What is the difference between a closely held corporation and a publicly held corporation?
4. **Explain** What are the advantages and costs of a franchise?

Higher Order Thinking H.O.T.

5. **Judge** It is now possible to buy "do-it-yourself" incorporation kits. Judge whether you think this is a good idea or if an attorney should be used to handle the legal aspects of incorporating.

English Language Arts

6. **Evaluating Forms of Corporations** Cathy Masen and Edgar Hale own an online retail business that they founded as a partnership. The business is becoming more successful. They have asked for your advice on whether to become a closely held corporation or an LLC. They do not intend to hire more employees at this time. Conduct research to find out more about the advantages and disadvantages of each form and write a letter to Cathy Masen and Edgar Hale with your recommendation. Be sure to clearly outline the reasons for your decision.

NCTE 7 Conduct research and gather, evaluate, and synthesize data to communicate discoveries.

Mathematics

7. **Issuing Stock** Sanbar City Consultants is a privately owned company. They have decided to go public by selling shares of stock in order to raise enough capital to expand the business internationally. If the initial offering of their stock sells for $17.25 per share, and they want to raise $1.5 million, how many shares of stock do they need to sell? If the initial offering of the stock sells for $25.50, and they want to raise the same amount of capital, how many shares do they need to sell now?

Math Concept **Calculate Shares Needed** To calculate the number of shares needed to sell in order to gain a specific amount of capital, divide the total amount of capital needed by the initial offering price.

Starting Hint Determine the total amount of capital needed for Sanbar City Consultants to expand internationally by identifying the initial offering price of the stock and divide the total capital needed by this price.

NCTM Connections Recognize and apply mathematics in contexts outside of mathematics.

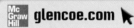

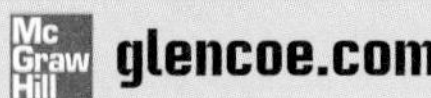

Check your answers.

CHAPTER REVIEW

Visual Summary

Types of Business Ownership

Comparing Advantages

Both a sole proprietorship and a partnership have several advantages as a form of business ownership.

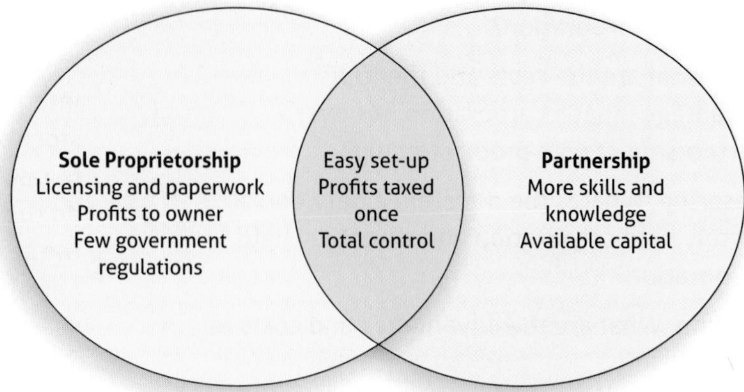

A Corporation

It is important to carefully consider the advantages and disadvantages of corporate ownership.

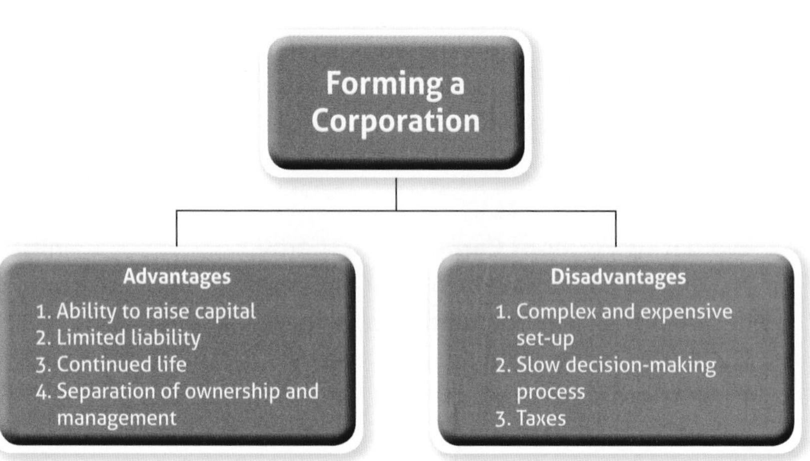

Forming a Corporation
Advantages
1. Ability to raise capital
2. Limited liability
3. Continued life
4. Separation of ownership and management
Disadvantages
1. Complex and expensive set-up
2. Slow decision-making process
3. Taxes

Try It!

Draw a Web diagram like the one shown to organize the different forms of business ownership available.

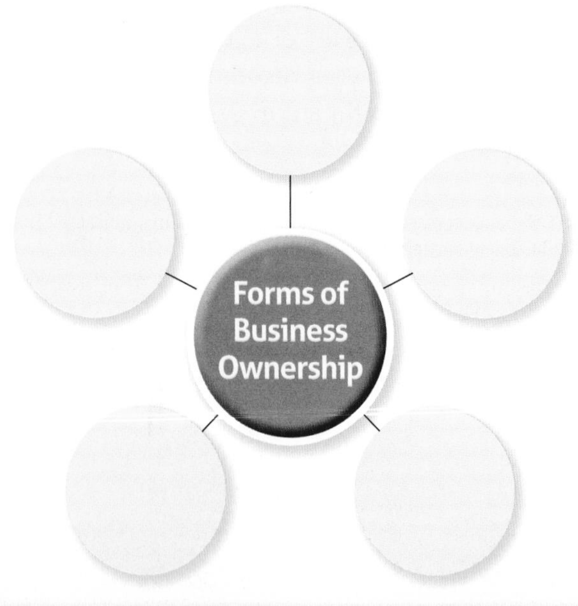

Chapter Review and Assessment

Chapter Summary

- Sole proprietorships are easy to set up; the owner retains control and profits; there are few government regulations; and profits are taxed once as personal income.
- The disadvantages include limited capital, unlimited liability, limited human resources, and a limited life.
- In partnerships, general partners have decision-making authority, are active in the business, and have unlimited liability.
- Limited partners rarely take an active role in the business, and their liability is limited to their investment.
- Partnerships are easy to set up and bring more skills, knowledge, and capital to the business.
- Partners retain control, and profits are taxed once as personal income.
- Disadvantages include unlimited liability; potential disagreements; shared profits; and limited life of the business.
- Closely held corporations have shares held by a few individuals, and shares are not traded in stock markets.
- Publicly held corporations sell shares on stock exchanges, and shares are held by many individuals and institutions.
- To form a corporation, you must file articles of incorporation and write corporate bylaws.
- The state issues a corporate charter.
- Corporations operate as legal entities separate from owners and issue stock; stockholders have limited liability. However, corporations are difficult and expensive to establish; decision making can be slow; and profits are taxed twice.

Vocabulary Review

1. Imagine that you are a lawyer specializing in business law. Use the terms below to write a memo explaining the different forms of ownership to a new client.

- public sector
- private sector
- competition
- price competition
- nonprice competition
- market
- oligopoly
- monopoly
- sole proprietorship
- Employer Identification Number (EIN)
- unlimited liability
- limited life
- partnership
- partnership agreement
- general partner
- limited partner
- cooperative
- corporation
- articles of incorporation
- corporate bylaws
- corporate charter
- board of directors
- limited liability company (LLC)
- franchise
- operate
- generate
- elect
- stockholders

Higher Order Thinking 

2. **Predict** What effect might an increase of stockholders have on a corporation?
3. **Analyze** Why might it be a disadvantage to make all the decisions in a business?
4. **Infer** In a large corporation, many people are involved in making decisions. Infer who might be involved in the decision-making process.
5. **Create** One item included in corporate bylaws is the election of the board of directors. Design a plan a company could use for this process.
6. **Hypothesize** Why do you think many sole proprietorships provide services over goods?
7. **Theorize** What skills and knowledge might a sole proprietor lack that would make a partnership a good idea?
8. **Judge** Determine if there is a benefit to purchasing a franchise rather than opening a similar business on your own.
9. **Justify** What do you feel is the most important element of a partnership agreement?

College and Career Readiness

Science

10. Managing Stress Entrepreneurs often realize that the responsibility of running a company is much greater than anticipated. It can easily drain the owner of both time and money. But many entrepreneurs are now learning how to use stress as an asset, rather than a liability.

Procedure Conduct research to learn more about "good stress" and entrepreneurs.

Analysis Create an oral report to share your findings, including a definition of good stress and how entrepreneurs can use good stress while avoiding stress that can become a health risk.

NSES F Develop understanding of personal and community health; population growth; natural resources; environmental quality; natural and human-induced hazards; science and technology in local, national, and global challenges.

Mathematics

11. A Partnership Tom and Juan are in a partnership in which Tom is a general partner and Juan is a limited partner. They are thinking about expanding their business and raising the capital to do so by going public. They are also in the middle of a lawsuit in which they could possibly owe up to $350,000. Tom's current ownership percentage is 55 percent giving him $95,000 of the entire business value. Calculate Juan's ownership percentage and his dollar portion of the entire business value. How much is the entire business worth? If the partnership loses the lawsuit, how much will each partner stand to lose? Explain you answer.

Math Concept **Calculate Ownership Value** Calculate the ownership value of a partner by identifying the total value of the company and then subtracting the values of the other partners.

Starting Hint Calculate the total value of the partnership by setting up an algebraic equation as follows: $0.55 \times A = \$95{,}000$ where A is the total value of the business.

NCTM Algebra Represent and analyze mathematical situations and structures using algebraic symbols.

English Language Arts

12. Entrepreneurship There are many advantages and disadvantages to consider when trying to decide what form your business should take. Use the information found in your text and in print or online resources to create a pamphlet that clearly and simply outlines and compares the benefits and drawbacks to sole proprietorships, partnerships, and corporations. Your pamphlet should include clear, easy-to-understand language. Feel free to add graphics to add to the appeal of your pamphlet.

NCTE 12 Use language to accomplish individual purposes.

Economics

13. Human Capital Business owners must constantly re-invest in their businesses in order to grow and thrive. One of the most controversial investments is that of employee training. Many companies provide only on-the-job training, while other companies happily provide employees with classroom training, Web training, or seminars. In addition, many larger corporations reimburse employees for continued education. Conduct research to find out the advantages and disadvantages of investing in employee training. Do you feel it is a worthwhile investment? If you owned a company, would you budget for new employee training or continued education? Write a paragraph with your answers.

Real-World Applications

14. Advertising Think of a hobby or skill that you do well. Now imagine that you are forming a sole proprietorship to teach others how to do this skill. Consider how you might advertise your new business and research the cost. Would you use online or print ads? Flyers? Build a Web page? Decide what medium you would use and then use the appropriate software to create an advertisement. Write copy for your ad that will effectively convey the service you are offering, as well as give necessary details such as time, place, and cost. Include art or photos if appropriate.

Your Financial Portfolio

Setting Up a Partnership

Mary has been teaching yoga classes at a gym for the past three years. She feels she now has enough experience to open her own yoga studio. Since she is concerned about costs and responsibilities, she spoke with one of the other yoga instructors, Tony, about starting a yoga business together. Tony thinks it is a great idea. Together, they outlined their partnership plan:

Location: One of Tony's friends works at an art gallery, which has a peaceful environment and ample floor space. Mary spoke with the owner of the gallery and negotiated using the gallery weekday evenings and Saturday and Sunday mornings. Mary and Tony agreed to pay the gallery owner 25 percent of all class fees.

Competition: The only yoga classes presently being offered in the area are at the health club where they both work.

Start-Up Costs: Mary and Tony must purchase 25 yoga mats at $20 per mat. They also will have insurance costs of $1,200 per year, plus $150 in fees and licenses. They will each contribute an equal amount of money from their personal savings to open the business.

Schedule: They will begin their business with eight classes per week: one each weekday evening, two classes on Saturday morning, and one on Sunday morning. Each class will be one hour in length. They agree that each person will teach four classes a week and cover for the other during illness or vacation.

Responsibilities: Mary is responsible for maintaining accounting records and paying bills. Tony is responsible for advertising and promotion.

Revenue: They decide to charge $15 per class. They project the weekend classes might bring in 25 students at each class ($375). Weekday classes might average 5 to 10 students ($75–150). Mary and Tony agree to share revenue and expenses equally.

Creating the Partnership: To establish a legal partnership, they write a document that outlines the organization of the business, the responsibilities of each partner, and the division of profits and losses.

Analyze

What kind of business would you start with a partner? With another student, choose a business and discuss how you would share responsibilities if you started a partnership together. Ask: What ways might you finance the business? What skills and traits do each of you have that might complement each other in a partnership? Outline your plan, using Mary and Tony's outline as a model for your business partnership.

CHAPTER 4

Developing a Business Plan

Visual Literacy

Independent business owners work hard to make their ventures successful. ***How can having a business plan help increase a business's chances of being profitable?***

Discovery Project

Preparing a Strategic Plan

Key Question

Why is it important to have a documented, strategic plan for any business?

Project Goal

You have decided to start a party planning business to help others organize and plan events. You realize the importance of having a written business plan for your venture. Create a strategic plan for your business that includes a mission statement, company description, and product and service plan. You may want to locate some samples online to learn more about how to develop an effective strategic plan and what information is useful or necessary. Your mission statement should include both the vision and the values of your business. Be sure that your company description is detailed, explaining your business's goals, challenges, and potential customers. Your product and service plan should outline the specific products and services you will offer to your clients, and how you will deliver them.

Ask Yourself...

- *Will you work alone or hire employees?*
- *Will you purchase needed decorations, food, and other items for your client's events?*
- *What goals will you set for your business?*
- *What action steps will be needed to achieve your goals?*
- *Who will you market your services to?*
- *What values are important to incorporate into your business?*

Solve Problems

What might you do if you had two clients request your services for events on the same evening?

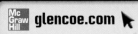

glencoe.com

Evaluate Download an assessment rubric.

THE BIG IDEA

A documented business plan is necessary for any business to grow and succeed.

ASK STANDARD & POOR'S

Business Plan

Q *My older sister and I are running a very successful business making children's birthday cakes. Since we are already doing well, why do we need a business plan?*

A Just because your business is successful now does not mean that it will remain successful. By creating a business plan, you can define clear goals for things like sales and profitability that will help you keep your business on track. Your business plan can help you to assess how inflation may affect your business over time.

Writing Activity

There are many other advantages to having a written business plan in addition to keeping your goals in focus. Write an analysis of some of the other advantages.

CHAPTER 4 **Reading Guide**

Before You Read

The Essential Question What type of research might you conduct to help develop a business plan?

Main Idea

For a business to grow and succeed, a sound business plan and effective financial management are essential.

Content Vocabulary

- free enterprise system
- business plan
- strategic plan
- marketing plan
- financial plan
- accounting
- transaction
- generally accepted accounting principles (GAAP)
- budget
- merchandise
- inventory
- cash flow
- negative cash flow

Academic Vocabulary

You will see these words in your reading and on your tests.

- contingency
- components
- monotonous
- project

Graphic Organizer

Before you read this chapter, draw a pie chart like the one shown. As you read, look for the four guidelines that will help you set your business goals.

Guidelines for Goals

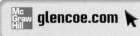

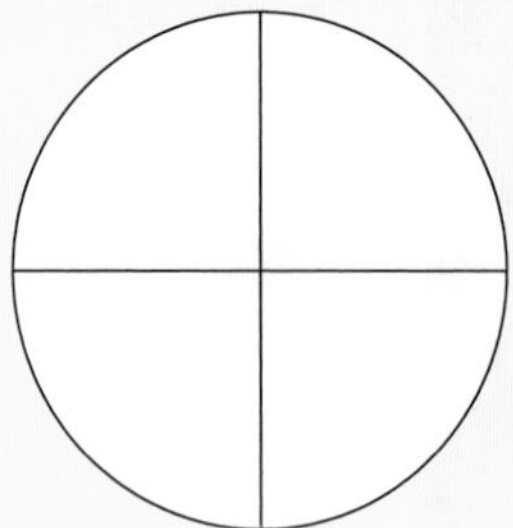

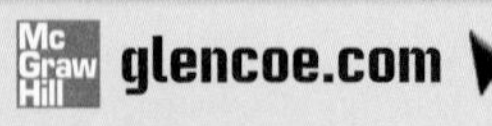

Print this graphic organizer.

Standards

Academic

Mathematics

NCTM Problem Solving Build new mathematical knowledge through problem solving.
NCTM Connections Understand how mathematical ideas interconnect and build on one another to produce a coherent whole.
NCTM Number and Operations Compute fluently and make reasonable estimates.

English Language Arts

NCTE 5 Use different writing process elements to communicate effectively.
NCTE 12 Use language to accomplish individual purposes.

Social Studies

NCSS I A Analyze and explain the ways groups, societies, and cultures address human needs and concerns.

NCTM *National Council of Teachers of Mathematics*
NCTE *National Council of Teachers of English*
NCSS *National Council for the Social Studies*
NSES *National Science Education Standards*

Common Core

Reading Determine central ideas or themes of a text and analyze their development; summarize the key supporting details and ideas.
Reading Read and comprehend complex literary and informational texts independently and proficiently.
Writing Draw evidence from literary or informational texts to support analysis, reflection, and research.
Writing Conduct short as well as more sustained research projects based on focused questions, demonstrating understanding of the subject under investigation.

A Plan for Business

The Business Environment

What do all businesses have in common?

When you hear the word *business,* do you think of large businesses, such as Microsoft, Ford, Coca-Cola, Disney, or IBM? Maybe you think of smaller businesses, such as your neighborhood flower shop or hardware store. All of these businesses are part of the **free enterprise system,** which is an economic system in which people can choose what they buy, what they produce and sell, and where they work. Businesses in such a system must compete to attract customers.

One of the main measurements of success for a business is the amount of profit it generates. Remember, profit is the amount of money earned over and above the amount spent to keep the business operating. Large and small businesses must do two things to survive: 1) operate at a profit with effective financial management and 2) attract and keep individuals who will run the business.

Reading Check

Define What is a free enterprise system?

Section Objectives

- **Discuss** the importance of financial management for a business.
- **Explain** the components of a business plan.
- **Describe** the aspects of a financial plan.

As You Read

Question Why is a good marketing plan necessary for any business?

Developing a Business Plan

What is a Business Plan?

Whether you are starting your own business or taking over a family business, you must first develop a business plan. A **business plan** is a written proposal that describes a new business and strategies to launch that business. It helps you focus on exactly what you want to do, how you will do it, and what you expect to accomplish. It sets goals for the business just as you set goals for yourself. A business plan is an important part of a proposal to secure funding from investors. Before they invest or loan money, they want to see that prospective owners have fully developed ideas.

Components of a Business Plan

A business plan can have as many as 15 components: an executive summary, mission statement, company description, product and service plan, management team plan, industry overview, market analysis, competitive analysis, marketing plan, operational plan, organizational plan, financial plan, growth plan, **contingency** (or emergency) plan, and supporting documents, as well as a cover page, title page, and table of contents.

FIGURE 1 **Business Plan Components**

Planning Your Business Any business should have a thorough, documented business plan. *How will a business plan help you?*

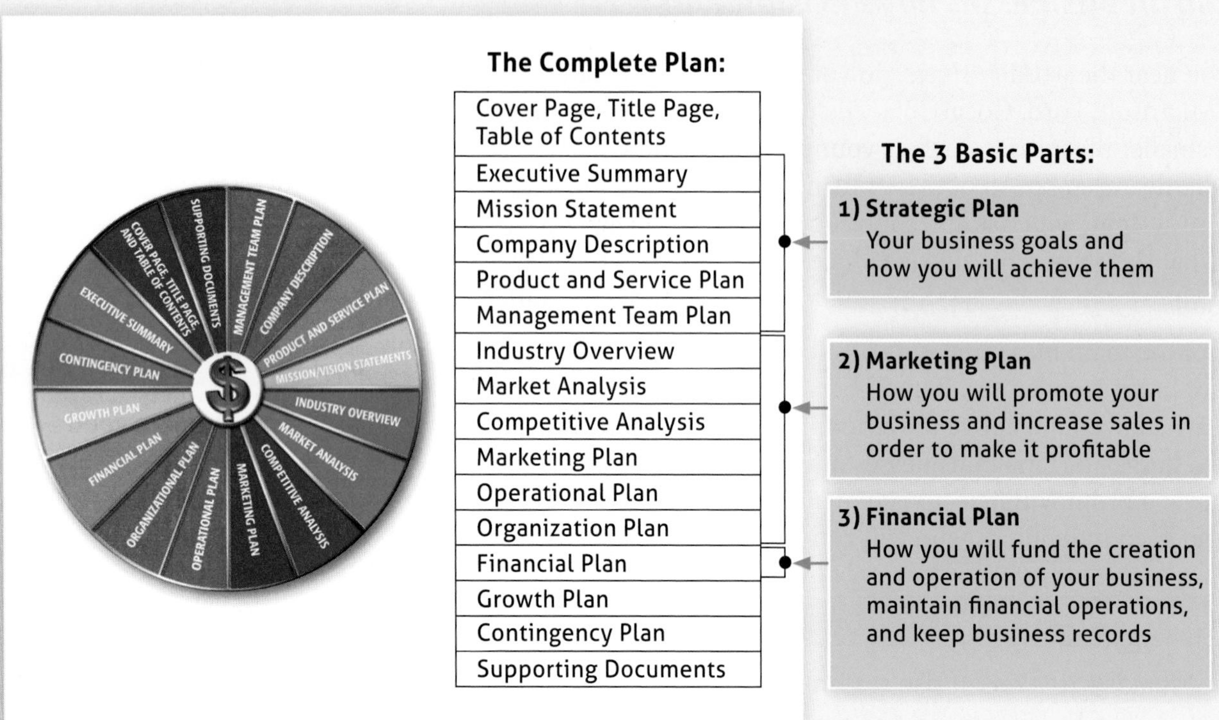
The Complete Plan:
Cover Page, Title Page, Table of Contents
Executive Summary
Mission Statement
Company Description
Product and Service Plan
Management Team Plan
Industry Overview
Market Analysis
Competitive Analysis
Marketing Plan
Operational Plan
Organization Plan
Financial Plan
Growth Plan
Contingency Plan
Supporting Documents
The 3 Basic Parts:
1) Strategic Plan
Your business goals and how you will achieve them
2) Marketing Plan
How you will promote your business and increase sales in order to make it profitable
3) Financial Plan
How you will fund the creation and operation of your business, maintain financial operations, and keep business records

Three basic parts of a business plan, that can include many of the 15 components, focus on a strategic plan, a marketing plan, and a financial plan. The overall **strategic plan** is a written outline of the business goals and the steps to take to achieve them. The second part is the **marketing plan,** a written outline of how the business will be promoted to increase customers and sales. The third part is the **financial plan,** which is a written outline of how the business will get money to start up and operate, and how the business will maintain financial operations and business records. Basically, the financial plan determines how you will keep track of your money. **Figure 1** illustrates the components of a business plan.

The Strategic Plan

Both new and ongoing businesses must have sound strategic plans to be successful. In the classic novel, *Alice in Wonderland,* Alice asks the Cheshire Cat which way she should walk. The Cheshire Cat replies, "That depends a good deal on where you want to get to." This is an appropriate observation about decision making and planning. Every person and every business needs goals and a specific course of action to achieve those goals.

Document Detective

A Job Description

When you write a business plan, it is important to think about how you will build a staff of employees. You start by defining the positions and listing the qualifications of the people who will fill those positions. A job description contains the following information:

- Job title
- Description of responsibilities
- List of required skills and education

Premier Building Company		
Title/Compensation	**Description**	**Job Specifications**
Entrepreneur/Owner • Full time • Salary/Wage: Varies based on revenues; 20% of sales • Estimated after year one: $120,000	• Oversees all operations • Responsible for setting up all policies, procedures, and guidelines • Performs all hiring and employee evaluation functions • Responsible for setting long-and short-term organizational goals • Allocates resources	• Excellent communication skills • Ability to motivate and lead
Accountant • Part-time contract professional; 12 hours per week • Pro-rated salary: $30,000	• Responsible for supervising payroll, accounts payable, and accounts receivable functions • Responsible for, and coordinates with, vendors and subcontractors • Works with owner to obtain financing and lines of credit • Responsible for payment and compliance with local, state, and federal requirements	• Excellent verbal and written communication skills • Ability to work with others • At least 2 years experience in construction or a related service or manufacturing industry • Certification as a CPA
Director of Operations • Full time • Salary: $55,000 per year	• Develops operational procedures • Responsible for implementing all policies, procedures, and guidelines • Manages all operations and assists with hiring and employee evaluation • Troubleshoots all problems, customer service issues, and employee complaints	• Ability to work with people of all backgrounds and skills • Ability to motivate and lead • At least 4 years experience in the construction industry or 2-year degree in management • A minimum of 2 years management experience

Key Points Job descriptions are an important part of a business plan because investors will want to know how you will staff your organization. The descriptions can be advertised in the classified section of a newspaper or magazine, or posted on Internet job sites.

FIND the Solutions

Review Key Concepts

1. How will the owner be compensated?
2. What skills and background are required for the job of accountant?
3. What are the job functions of the director of operations?
4. Why is the accountant's salary pro-rated over the year?
5. How much experience does the director of operations need?

Business Planning Software
There is a variety of software available to help the budding entrepreneur write a business plan. These programs, such as Business Plan Pro, help you develop a professional business plan for any size or type of business. Many of these programs also provide sample business plans that you can review for ideas.

If you are a business owner, your ultimate goal is to have a successful and profitable business. In order to realize that objective, you must first determine the strategic plan you will follow to keep the business growing and moving in the right direction.

A strategic plan is similar to a game plan you might have for your sports team. Simply saying "We want to win!" will not bring a victory. The coach must devise a plan that outlines how the team will achieve the big win. The team must work together to apply the strategies that the coach has developed. Similarly, a business owner or operator may say that he or she wants the business to succeed, but without a sound business plan, it probably will not happen. The first step in writing a strategic plan is to set goals.

Setting Goals Businesses set both short-term and long-term goals. In the business world, short-term goals are goals you expect to reach within one or two years. Long-term goals are those that may take three or more years to reach. Because long-term goals require a considerable amount of time, they may be less specific than short-term goals. You will probably revise them as you go.

Goals for businesses have the same guidelines as goals you might establish for your personal finances:

- They should be realistic.
- They should be specific.
- They should have a clear time frame.
- They should help you decide what type of action to take.

Whether you own a small convenience store in the city or run a multinational corporation such as Kodak, the goals can be similar. Common objectives might include increasing sales, adding new customers, or updating equipment.

Business, Big and Small
Both large and small business can be successful and profitable, even side by side. *How might this location actually help the small business to succeed?*

Personalized Goals Just as people have personalized goals, businesses must also set individual goals to meet their specific needs. *What are three goals that this small business might have?*

However, goals can also differ, depending on the size of the business. For example, the goals of a small business might include buying a computer system, introducing a new line of merchandise, or moving to a better location. Medium-sized businesses may want to open more stores or begin operating online to increase sales. Larger corporations have more complex goals. They may want to expand their international markets; change distribution systems; or acquire other, smaller corporations.

Businesses should design goals according to the basic guidelines, regardless of the size of the business. Goals should be well thought out and compatible with the philosophy of the business. In all cases, a business needs to determine if its goals are financially possible.

Identify Steps to Achieve Your Goals For personal finances, people set financial goals and then decide on ways to achieve those goals. For example, suppose that you have a short-term personal goal of making the honor roll. This is an admirable goal, but how do you accomplish it? You analyze the situation and plan your course of action. You identify specific actions you can take, such as taking better notes, doing your homework more carefully, and asking more questions in class.

Long-term goals involve more steps over a longer period of time. Suppose that your long-term goal is to become a successful graphic designer. What must you do to become a designer? You will need a career plan. Then you will have to identify short-term steps, such as taking related high school courses, selecting schools or colleges to attend, and completing the application process. Later you may focus your attention on long-term steps, such as graduating, getting a job, and acquiring professional experience. Hopefully, by taking these steps, you will achieve your goal of becoming a designer.

When developing a strategic plan for your business, you should use the same technique. First, identify your short-term and long-term goals. Then create a plan that consists of specific steps toward each goal.

Economics and You

Economic Indicators

Unemployment figures and the Consumer Price Index are economic indicators that help economists determine how well the economy is doing. As unemployment rises, the economy slows down because consumer spending and confidence drops. The Consumer Price Index (CPI) is a market basket of some 400 goods and services that an urban household purchases, such as food, housing, utilities, clothing, entertainment, and gasoline. Changes in the CPI provide insight into whether prices are going up, which is inflation, or if they are going down, which is deflation. The goal for an economy is stable prices; prices that do not fluctuate significantly.

Consumer Price Index

Item	Description	Price Base Period (1982–1984)	Price Second Period (1998)	Price Third Period (January 2006)
1	Toothpaste (7 oz.)	$1.40	$1.49	$2.25
2	Milk (1 gal.)	$1.29	$1.29	$1.79
3	Peanut Butter (2-lb. jar)	$2.50	$2.65	$3.73
4	Lightbulb (60 walt)	$.45	$.48	$.65

Personal Finance Connection When developing a business plan, economic indicators, like unemployment figures and the CPI, help in setting realistic goals. The current state of the economy needs to be part of your analysis of the industry, market, and competition, as well as your marketing, financial, and operational plans. In a robust economy, your goals will be different than when the economy is faltering. On a personal level economic indicators need to be part of your financial plans as well. If the economy is in a recession and job security is not guaranteed, your spending habits need to be adjusted accordingly. You may save more and watch your investments very closely; as you adjust your financial goals to reflect the current economic times.

Critical Thinking Why do business plans and personal household plans need to be reviewed periodically and revised? What changes would you make in your household plans if you lost your job and became one of the unemployed?

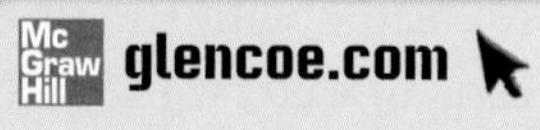

Activity Download an Economics and You Worksheet Activity.

A Strategic Plan Case Study Mike and Erin have plans to start up an eco-friendly landscape business. They realize the importance of setting realistic, achievable goals. Because their business would be new, their short-term goals include getting a new business loan with a low interest rate, purchasing basic equipment, locating suppliers for plants and flowers, and purchasing a low-cost phone system.

Long-term goals include acquiring a storage facility, purchasing a hybrid (gas/electric) vehicle to transport equipment, and increasing the number of customers by 20 percent each year.

Steps to Achieve Business Goals Mike and Erin have worked with other landscapers and have experience taking care of a variety of flowers, plants, and trees. They plan to start their business as a service, and then open a retail nursery as well. In their strategic plan, Mike and Erin identify the steps they will take to achieve each of their goals. One of their short-term goals is to show a profit after two years. To reach that goal, they plan to increase the number of customers and keep expenses low.

The Marketing Plan

A marketing plan outlines the ways in which you will promote your business. Promotional activities include advertising and promotions. Advertising is any paid message that a business sends about its products. Promotion is any form of communication a business uses to inform, persuade, or remind people about its products or to enhance its image. You will show a profit or expand your operations by increasing customers. Therefore, you want to communicate with as many potential customers as possible to tell them about your goods or services. For example, Mike and Erin plan to place ads with photographs of their projects in a local newspaper.

As with the creation of a strategic plan, you have to address some specific questions. If you have something to sell, how do you sell it? How do you reach people in an efficient manner? What promotions or advertising can you afford? To begin to answer these questions, you should research the existing market for your goods or services. See **Figure 2** for an illustration of this process.

Larger corporations may hire private marketing firms to assist them in developing marketing plans. Some corporations, such as Levi-Strauss, McDonald's, and Ford, have been very successful over the years. Effective marketing plans have allowed these corporations to introduce new products, maintain sales of existing products, and keep their names in the public eye.

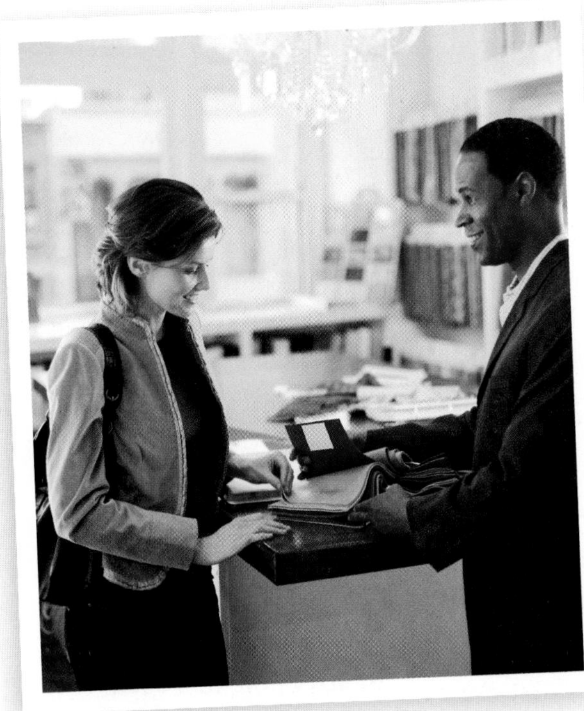

Marketing Money
A good marketing plan is essential to help a business bring in new customers and gain an edge over its competitors. *What forms of advertising can you think of that small businesses use?*

FIGURE 2 Steps to Prepare a Marketing Plan

Do Your Research Before developing a marketing plan, you must first do your research. *What types of information should you look for in your marketing research?*

To prepare a marketing plan, you first need to research the existing market. By seeing what is out there, you can better develop an effective marketing plan. This plan will become your road map for reaching new customers and expanding your business. Take these steps to prepare your marketing plan, an important component of your overall business plan.

1 **Assess** the competition.

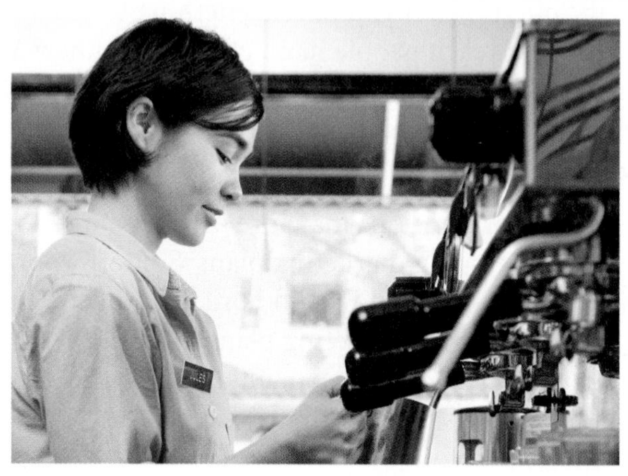

2 **Identify** services offered.

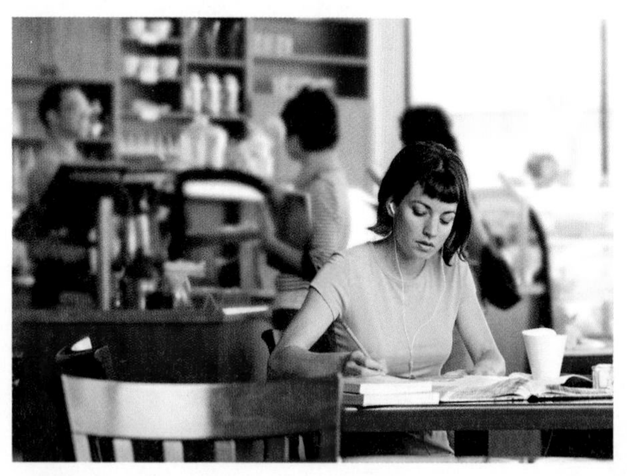

3 **Research** the current pricing and advertising.

4 **Identify** potential customers.

The Financial Plan

You have probably noticed that the elements in the strategic plan and the marketing plan involve the need for the efficient management of money. In order to make intelligent financial decisions regarding the direction and future of your business, you must record and report your finances in an orderly, consistent manner. Many people consider a financial plan to be the most important document for a successful business venture. Sound financial decisions provide the opportunity for:

- Sales to rise
- Expenses to fall
- Profits to increase
- Assets to be acquired
- Liabilities to be paid
- Credit to expand
- Customers to increase
- New products to develop

Aspects of a Financial Plan A financial plan outlines the essential elements for starting and running a business. An effective plan addresses three aspects of operating your business (See **Figure 3**):

- Assets needed
- Purchasing methods
- Daily financial operations

First, it identifies the assets you will need to purchase in order to begin or continue operating the business. Assets are property or items of value owned by a business. These might include products to sell or machines, supplies, office equipment, and transportation necessary for operations.

Second, your financial plan should address the method that you will use to acquire or purchase these items. How will your business pay for the things it needs? Do you have sufficient cash available? Should you borrow money from a bank or credit union?

The third and most important aspect of the financial plan involves the daily financial operations of the business. This feature addresses the recording, summarizing, reporting, and analyzing of your business's finances.

Identifying Needed Assets The first aspect of creating a financial plan is to identify the assets that are necessary to start the business and then to make it grow and increase its profits.

Suppose that the two entrepreneurs, Mike and Erin, want to buy a computer system. The system should be able to handle their present business operations as well as increased business activity in the future. They should consider features such as processing speed, memory capacity, upgradeability, and the software that is included.

COMMON CENTS

The Advertising Dollar
Many businesses, large and small, plan to spend a certain amount of their budgets (about 5 percent or more of their net sales) on promotional activities, such as advertising promotions. This expense pays off with more customers and profits.

Concept Application

If a surf and skateboard shop earns $35,000 a month in net sales, what might be a good annual advertising budget for the store?

FIGURE 3 **The Financial Plan**

A Three-Step Plan The first step in a financial plan should be to identify what assets are needed. *What type of assets should be considered for a business?*

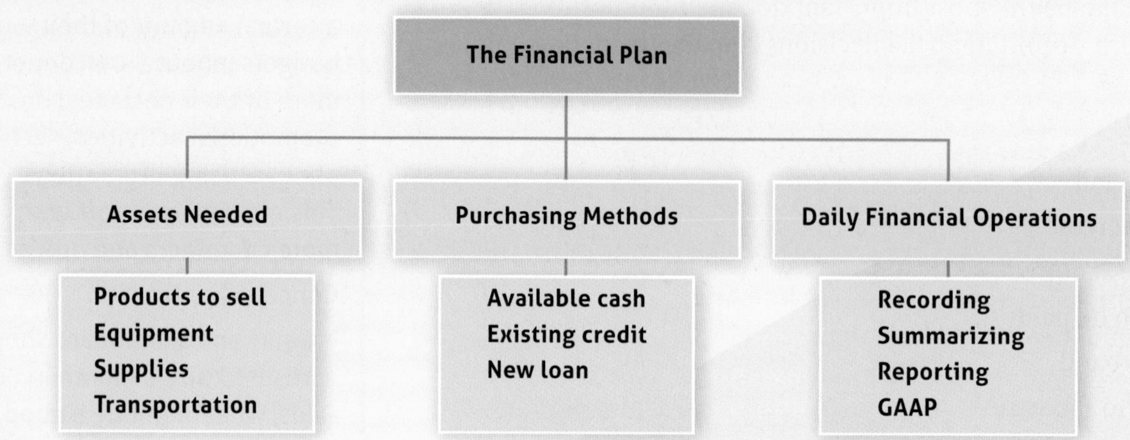

After Mike and Erin have determined the computer **components,** or parts, that their business needs, they should analyze the prices of different systems. They will need to purchase the best system for the best price. When their analysis is complete, Mike and Erin can decide what computer system to buy. This research process should be a part of buying any major asset.

Asset Analysis
Before purchasing new assets for your business, you should adequately research product features and prices. *Can you name five assets that a business owner might research prior to purchase?*

France

Auto-Entrepreneurship

Before beginning a business of your own, you must first decide what form of business ownership you will establish. Unfortunately, one consideration for this decision is often the amount of legal fees and paperwork involved. In an effort to encourage more small businesses, France introduced a new class of business ownership in 2009, called *auto-entrepreneur.* This new system of business ownership is designed to make it easier, quicker, and cheaper for individuals to start a small business. Under the new system, there are no required courses or registration fees to register your new business. Another major highlight of the auto-entrepreneur system is that new business owners will be exempt from paying *taxe professionnelle,* or the French business tax, for the first three years and social charges and taxes will be deferred until the business begins to generate sales. Once sales are generated, the business will be required to make monthly or quarterly payments to the French social security authorities. These charges will include a payment for affiliation to the French health system, as well as pension, invalidity, benefits, and the welfare levy (CSG/CRDS).

Critical Thinking

1. **Expand** Research business ownership in France. What other two options are there for business ownership status for individuals starting a business in France?
2. **Relate** Do you think a business plan would differ based on the type of business ownership?

DATABYTES

Capital
Paris

Population
64,057,792

Language
French

Currency
Euro

Gross Domestic Product (GDP)
$2.666 trillion

GDP per capita
$32,800

Industry
Machinery, chemicals, automobiles, metallurgy, aircraft, electronics; textiles, food processing; tourism

Agriculture
Wheat, cereals, sugar beets, potatoes, wine grapes; beef, dairy products; fish

Exports
Machinery and transportation equipment, aircraft, plastics, chemicals, pharmaceutical products, iron and steel, beverages

Natural Resources
Coal, iron ore, bauxite, zinc, uranium, antimony, arsenic, potash, feldspar, fluorspar, gypsum, timber, fish

Purchasing Assets The second step of a financial plan is to determine the method to use to purchase the items. Mike and Erin need to ask several specific questions: Can they purchase the computer system with their available cash or should they get a loan? Will they be able to get a reasonable interest rate? Can they take advantage of alternatives to purchasing, such as leasing? Can they get a better deal if they wait? In answering these questions, Mike and Erin will have to perform a careful analysis of their existing finances regarding their debts, available cash, and future expenses.

They must also investigate all sources of credit. Will the company that is selling them the computer extend credit to them? Should they apply for a short-term loan from a bank? By examining these and other questions, Mike and Erin are practicing effective financial management.

As a high school student, you make similar decisions about your personal finances. If you want to buy an inexpensive item, such as a CD, you might pay cash. You will give the purchase little financial consideration. However, if it is a more expensive item, such as a sound system or a used car, you should examine your situation more carefully. Consider some of the following questions: Do you really need it? What is the most you can spend? How much money do you have now? Is there anything else you might need? By considering these questions, you are performing a financial analysis of your purchase—and practicing effective financial management.

As a business owner or operator, you might find that some items you want to purchase are beyond your means. You may not have enough cash. Especially when you are starting a business, you will have to accept the fact that you will not be able to obtain everything that you want immediately. You will have to work within your financial resources until your business begins to make a profit and you can afford to expand your assets. If you are working with limited resources, you must make decisions based on your need for the items and your ability to pay for them, whether with cash or credit.

Recording and Reporting Business Finances The third aspect of a financial plan involves the financial operation of a business. How will Mike and Erin keep daily financial records? Will sales cover their expenses and produce a profit? Will cash be available for unexpected costs? Will they be able to pay their bills on time?

Mike and Erin must know where their business stands financially at all times. The recording and handling of financial information, in an accurate and efficient manner, is essential. It includes using accepted accounting procedures, analyzing financial statements, controlling cash, and paying debts. If data is not recorded in a timely manner, or if the information is not analyzed correctly, inappropriate financial decisions can result. For a new business or a small existing business, this could be disastrous. Thousands of small businesses close each year due to poor financial decisions.

Assessment

Review Key Concepts

1. **Identify** What are the three aspects of a financial plan?
2. **Explain** How can you practice good financial management when purchasing assets for a business?
3. **Describe** What are the three main parts of a business plan? What is the role of each part?

Higher Order Thinking H.O.T.

4. **Determine** The mission statement is one component of the strategic plan part of a business plan. Determine how the mission statement is important to the marketing plan as well.

21st Century Skills

5. **Work Creatively with Others** Follow your teacher's instructions to divide into pairs. Choose a local business, such as a book store, a bicycle repair shop, a florist, or a deli. Now imagine that you are the new owners. You need to develop a sound business plan to help your business grow and succeed. Begin by considering the strategic plan. Work together to develop two short-term and two long-term goals for the chosen business. Be sure as you develop your goals that they are realistic and specific, and that they have a clear time frame.

Mathematics

6. **Business Plan** Terrell and Troy have created a business plan for their trophy manufacturing business. They have identified multiple goals including increasing their customer base by 15 percent per year for the next 5 years and 10 percent per year for another 5 years. They have also determined that they will increase revenues by 10 percent per year for the next 5 years and then 5 percent per year for another 5 years. If they start with 50 customers and $9,500 in revenue, what will their customer base and revenues be in 10 years?

Calculate Business Plan Growth To calculate the customer base and revenue growth over a period of time, multiply the prior period by the growth percentage and add the result to the prior period for each period.

Starting Hint Determine the customer base after year 5 by using the following formula. $P \times (1 + g)^n$ where P is prior period or base number of customers, g is the growth rate and n is the number of periods expected to grow at rate g.

NCTM Problem Solving Build new mathematical knowledge through problem solving.

McGraw Hill **glencoe.com** Check your answers.

Section Objectives

- **Explain** the importance of accounting in financial management.
- **Describe** how investments in your business can improve productivity.
- **Identify** the primary functions of accounting.

As You Read

Predict What do you think the term *cash flow* means?

Aspects of Financial Management

What economic theories and principles should you know for effective financial management?

As you learned in the first section of this chapter, sound financial management is critical to the survival of any business. Financial management includes all aspects of operating a business. It is the glue that holds the business together. At the same time, it is the oil that helps it run smoothly.

Also remember, business cycles occur regularly. There are periods of expansion as well as periods of contraction. If the contraction of the economy lasts long enough and is deep enough it can develop into a recession. If the recession is bad enough it can turn in to a depression. Eventually the economy will hit the low point in the business cycle, or the trough. The increase in economic activity following the trough is the recovery. (See **Figure 4**)

Many business functions and procedures are based on economic theories and principles. Supply and demand, pricing, market segments, and competition are just a few of the economic principles you need to know about. An understanding of basic accounting principles and procedures is also useful. You should have the financial knowledge and skills to be able to collect, summarize, and analyze financial data.

Reading Check

Identify List four economic principles you should be familiar with to practice sound financial management?

Accounting: The Backbone of Financial Management

What is accounting?

Accounting is the systematic process of recording and reporting the financial position of a business. The financial position depends on the transactions that occur in the daily operation of the business. A **transaction** is any activity that has an effect on the financial situation of a business. Every time you buy supplies, sell merchandise, buy a photocopier, or pay utility bills, your business is making a transaction. Accounting records and reports can help a business operate efficiently—and profitably—by keeping track of how much the business earns and spends.

Accounting is often referred to as the "language of business." Accounting plays a vital role in the day-to-day activities of every business. The influence of accounting is demonstrated by the fact that many of its terms have become commonplace. You have probably heard terms such as *assets, liabilities, expenses, revenue,* and *inventory.* These are all accounting terms. Business owners use this language to communicate with other owners of the business, their creditors, and customers. They do this by issuing financial statements.

GAAP

When recording and reporting financial changes in a business, owners, bookkeepers, and accountants must use a standard set of guidelines, which are referred to as **generally accepted accounting principles (GAAP)** (pronounced "gap"). If General Motors, Ford, and DaimlerChrysler all prepared their financial reports in different ways, no one could compare the three corporations financially. Using the GAAP guidelines allows investors, banks, suppliers, and government agencies to make comparisons of the financial condition of various companies. They can determine which businesses are financially stable, which ones have the highest percentage of profit, and which ones are growing the fastest.

Every business must have an accurate accounting system, either manual or computerized. Computer software programs can handle much of the basic accounting work for most businesses. By using modern technology, owners and managers can spend more time analyzing their finances and planning for the future, and spend less time doing **monotonous,** or boring and unchanging, paperwork.

The accounting system has many functions and procedures. However, some of the most essential functions of accounting that most businesses use include budgeting, inventory, payroll, cash flow, and investments.

FIGURE 4 **Business Cycles**

Trough and Recovery Improved economic activity will follow the low point in a business cycle. *What factors could cause a recession to become a depression?*

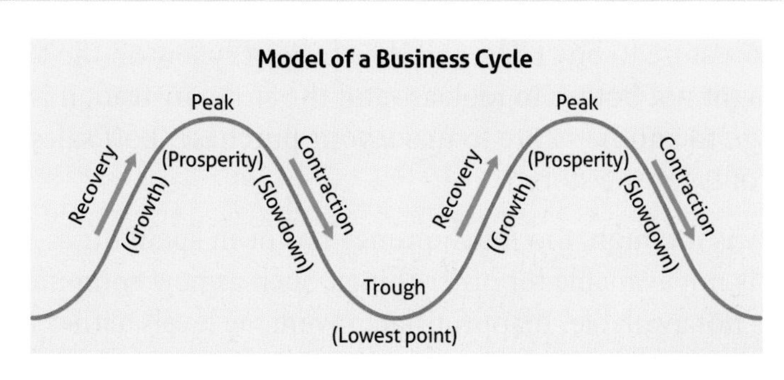

Creativity

Learning and innovation skills now separate candidates in the workplace. Creativity is an innovation skill that will prepare you for a more complex work environment that continues to progress. Those who are able to think creatively produce constructive and innovative ideas. These ideas may refine a current process or even drastically change an established approach. Creative thinkers are also able to assess and adjust their ideas as well as the ideas of others to get the most out of creative work.

Write About It

Think of a situation in school which required creativity. Write one or more paragraphs to describe the scenario and explain how thinking creatively impacted the situation.

 **glencoe.com** 

Activity Download a Career and College Readiness Worksheet Activity.

Budgeting

One important function of accounting is budgeting. A **budget** for a business is a formal, written statement of expected income and expenses for a future period of time. For example, the entrepreneurs Mike and Erin can write a budget to **project,** or predict, the amount of money they think they will earn through sales or other income in their landscaping business. They also project their production or operating costs (expenses) for the same period. The difference between these two amounts will be their projected profit or loss for the period. This gives them a glimpse into the financial future of their business. It provides the information they will need to make decisions.

To be practical, you should regularly compare a budget with actual income and expenses. If you are working with a yearly budget, you should make monthly comparisons of the budgeted amounts to the actual amounts. If the actual amounts are not reasonably close to the budgeted figures, you need to make adjustments. If the actual amounts are far greater than the projected figures, you must take immediate action to avoid further financial problems. An important aspect of financial management is to recognize a problem and take action to remedy it. Accurate, current accounting statements and reports allow you to recognize a problem when it first develops so that you can make financial decisions and take corrective measures.

Inventory

The largest asset of many businesses is the merchandise they have on hand to sell. **Merchandise** is the goods retailers buy with the intent to resell to customers. The **inventory** is the merchandise retailers have for sale. Most cash transactions involve the purchase, control, and sale of merchandise. Therefore, it is essential that inventory be carefully maintained and examined. By tracking inventory, businesses know the following facts about their merchandise:

- Amount of merchandise sold
- Merchandise that is selling well
- When to reorder merchandise
- Merchandise that should not be reordered

Amount of Inventory The wrong level, or amount, of inventory can be costly for a business. Having too little inventory means that the business may not be able to satisfy its customers' wants. For example, when you go to a store to buy CDs, and they have very few on the shelves, you might not bother to look around the store. Instead, it is likely you will go to another store to make your purchase. Lost sales mean lower profits for the store.

If inventory is too high, too much money has been spent on inventory and is not available for other things, such as new computers, because cash is not available. Inappropriate inventory levels, either too high or too low, are signs of poor management.

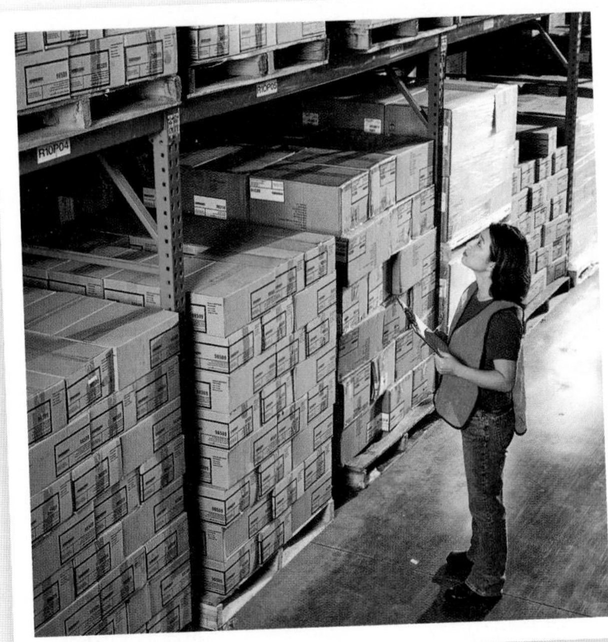

Tracking Inventory
By keeping accurate accounts of your inventory, you will know which merchandise is selling well. *Why is it important to know which merchandise is selling and which is not?*

Most stores use computer programs to monitor inventory. These programs provide daily reports that detail what items have been sold, what is still available, and what must be reordered.

Payroll

While merchandise is usually the largest asset of a business, payroll is usually the largest expense of a business. Large companies such as AT&T, Coca-Cola, and American Airlines employ thousands of people. Weekly payrolls are in the millions of dollars. Some small businesses employ fewer than a hundred people, and some very small businesses might employ fewer than ten people. Whether your business is large or small, payroll is usually your greatest expense.

Because payroll involves so much cash, it is regulated by state and federal laws and must be prepared according to generally accepted accounting principles (GAAP). Most businesses use computer programs to process payroll checks, to complete payroll reports, and to examine payroll information. Efficient payroll management involves two important activities.

Determining Number of Employees First, you must determine whether you have the proper number of employees working at the proper times. Having too many employees or employees working at the wrong times means that you are paying more in wages and salaries than you should. Your payroll expense must be reduced. If you do not have enough employees or are understaffed at certain times, your company risks losing sales. Both situations are indicators of poor management.

Using GAAP The second activity that ensures efficient payroll management is using generally accepted accounting principles (GAAP) to prepare payrolls. Paychecks must be issued on time. All payroll taxes must be paid, and voluntary deductions must be taken.

Careers That Count!

Marianne Cole • Bookkeeper

In my first part-time bookkeeping job in a small retail store, I learned to balance cash registers, determine if registers are over or short, complete daily reports, and count and deposit daily receipts. Now, as a full-time bookkeeper for a large company, I handle payroll, accounts payable and receivable, and profit and loss. I balance ledgers, tag and log invoices and claims, and forward pertinent paperwork to the general offices. I make numerous computations each day, so I use specialized accounting software, spreadsheets, and databases. If you love working with numbers and have a good eye for detail, you may enjoy bookkeeping. Take courses like business math, consumer math, and applied math, and computer classes, and then continue your preparation in college with a strong emphasis on topics like accounts payable and receivable, general ledger balancing, and quarterly tax preparation. You may also want to become a notary public so you can notarize financial documents.

EXPLORE CAREERS

Visit the Web site of the U.S. Department of Labor's Bureau of Labor Statistics and obtain information about a career as a bookkeeper.

1. What are some of the health and safety risks encountered in this profession?
2. What measures should a bookkeeper take to stay safe at work?

Skills	Education	Career Path
High aptitude for numbers; accounting, computer, math, organizational, customer service, and problem-solving skills	High school diploma, plus some accounting courses or relevant work experience; certification is recommended for advancement and higher pay	Bookkeepers can become auditors, tax preparers, accountants, and tax examiners.

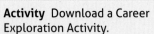

glencoe.com 

Activity Download a Career Exploration Activity.

All payroll records should also be available for managers and owners to evaluate immediately. Accurate, complete, and readily available payroll information is essential.

Cash Flow

Every person needs cash. Every business needs cash. Available cash often determines what a business can or cannot do. An adequate amount of available cash allows your business to pay its debts, take advantage of discounts, and pay for expansion.

In personal finance, cash flow refers to the amount of money that actually goes into and out of a person's wallet or bank accounts. For a business, **cash flow** is the amount of cash that is available at any given time. Money comes in, and money goes out—this is cash flow. A goal of effective financial management is to maintain a constant flow of cash through the business. This is easy to say, but it is not always easy to do. Economic and financial conditions constantly change. Sometimes sales are high, and then they may suddenly drop off. Expenses may also vary. When a business spends more money than it receives, it experiences a condition known as a **negative cash flow,** also called a *cash crunch.* When your cash flow is negative, your business suffers.

As a student, you have probably experienced similar cash crunches. For example, suppose that you want to go to the movies on Friday night with your friends, but on Wednesday you buy the wool sweater you want. So, on Friday night, you discover that you do not have enough money to go out. For you, this is a short-term disappointment. For a business, however, a shortage of money could mean serious problems. Without a sufficient flow of cash, merchandise cannot be replaced, bills cannot be paid, and funds for future growth and expansion cannot be invested. Maintaining a positive cash flow is a primary goal of financial management.

Investments

Successful businesses invest for the future. As profits increase, money should be set aside or invested for future business needs. This reserve cash may be needed to purchase new equipment, relocate the business operation, or sell a new line of merchandise. For example, suppose that Mike and Erin form a business partnership. Their goal is to purchase a building for their landscaping business within the next five years. They should set aside a certain amount of money each year to ensure that sufficient funds will be available to buy the building or make a down payment.

Successful businesses invest funds to improve productivity. Productivity is the measure of the amount of goods produced in a specific period of time using a specific amount of resources. It is the most important factor contributing to economic growth. Productivity goes up when more goods are produced using the same amount of resources in the same amount of time.

A few of the areas in which a business can invest include:

- human capital
- capital goods
- technology

Human Capital Improvement to productivity can come from investing in human capital. Human capital is the sum of people's skills, abilities, health, knowledge, and motivation.

Businesses can invest in human capital by providing training that improves the skills of their workers. A business may also choose to pay for an employee to further his or her education in a related field. When a business invests in human capital, its workers are more skilled and motivated. Increased productivity allows for more products to be produced at the same cost to the business. This increase in output causes the price of goods for the consumer to decrease.

Capital Goods Another way to improve productivity is to invest in capital goods. Capital goods are resources used to produce goods and services, such as buildings, materials, and equipment. Capital goods include delivery trucks, cash registers, and medical supplies. A farmer may choose to invest in a new tractor or a corporation may invest in a new, larger building.

Technology The introduction of a new machine or a new industrial process can lower the cost of production and increase productivity. Lower production costs mean a business is able to produce more goods at all prices in the market. For example, improvements in the fuel efficiency of aircraft engines have lowered the costs of travel for air travelers. Many business leaders believe that an organization that does not invest in technology cannot survive. Imagine an office without computers and the negative effect this would have on productivity.

Investments and Reserve Funds

Businesses need reserve cash for emergencies or unexpected costs. If equipment breaks and needs repair, sales take an unexpected drop, or a natural disaster hits your area, you will need cash. Cash reserves, also called *reserve funds,* could save your business when any type of disaster strikes.

Cash should be carefully invested and closely monitored. Investments by businesses are similar to personal savings. You should save money for unexpected bills or events, such as a broken water heater or a medical bill. You would also need to save for a new car, summer vacation, or computer for your personal needs.

Reading Check

Recall What is a cash crunch?

The Importance of Financial Management

What are some aspects of financial management?

Businesses must make a profit and invest part of that profit for future use. Making and monitoring investments is an important aspect of financial management. In addition to investments, sound financial management relies on accounting. You will learn more about accounting functions and managing a business's finances in the remaining chapters of this book.

After You Read

React Is having a reserve fund as important as having a regular savings account? Why or why not?

Assessment

Review Key Concepts

1. **Identify** What are the five essential functions of accounting that most businesses use?
2. **Explain** How can accounting help a business run efficiently and profitably?
3. **Describe** Why are investments important to a business?
4. **Relate** How can investing in human capital, technology, and capital goods improve the productivity of a business? What are the costs to the business of each?

Higher Order Thinking 

5. **Propose** Suppose your office discovered it had a cash crunch one month. Prepare a list of three suggestions for ways to help cut office expenses.

English Language Arts

6. **Budget Planning** A budget is a written statement of expected income and expenses for a given period of time. A budget is important for individuals as well as businesses. Consider your personal finances. Write a list of income and expenses you might include on a personal budget. Then suppose you were the owner of a fast-food restaurant. Write another list of the income and expenses you might include on a budget for your business. Write a summary identifying how these budgets might be similar.

NCTE 12 Use language to accomplish individual purposes.

Mathematics

7. **Accounting Help Needed** Randy is an accountant at XYZ Store Co. In January the store had $150,000 in sales, $35,000 in payroll, $20,000 in rent and utilities, and $20,000 in inventory purchased. In February it had $175,000 in sales, $39,000 in payroll, $25,000 in rent and utilities, and $45,000 in inventory purchased. Randy has been asked to provide the net cash flow for each of the two months. He also needs to determine the percentage growth of cash flow from January to February. He has asked for your help in calculating these figures.

Calculate Net Cash Flow To calculate the net cash flow for a period identify the total sales for the given period and subtract from this figure the total expenses paid by cash for the same period.

Starting Hint Determine the percentage growth from January to February by first identifying the net cash flow for each month. Divide the net cash flow in February by the net cash flow in January and subtract the result by 1.

NCTM Connections Understand how mathematical ideas interconnect and build on one another to produce a coherent whole.

Mc Graw Hill **glencoe.com** Check your answers.

Visual Summary

Developing a Business Plan

Effective Business Plan

Each of the three basic parts of a business plan help lead and direct the other parts. They must be developed together to be effective.

Accurate Accounting

Accounting records and reports allow business owners and managers to accurately analyze their finances and plan for the future of the business.

Try It!

Draw a diagram like the one shown to document the steps for successfully preparing a marketing plan.

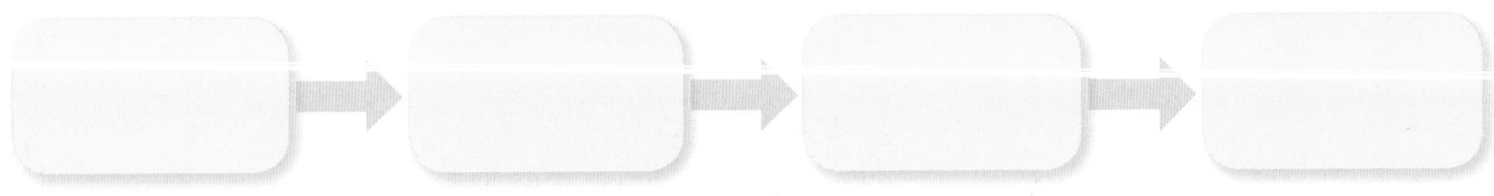

Chapter Review and Assessment

Chapter Summary

- One of the measures of success for a business is the amount of profit it earns.
- Businesses must do two things to survive: operate at a profit with effective financial management and attract customers.
- The components of a business plan include: executive summary, mission statement, company description, product and service plan, management team plan, industry overview, market analysis, competitive analysis, marketing plan, operational plan, organizational plan, financial plan, growth plan, contingency plan, and supporting documents—plus a cover page, title page, and table of contents.
- The three basic parts of a business plan focus on a strategic plan, a marketing plan, and a financial plan.
- The financial plan identifies the assets you need, how you will acquire these assets, and how you will handle daily financial operations.
- Accounting is the systematic process of recording and reporting a business's financial position, including all transactions involving money.
- Accounting functions include the preparation of financial statements, auditing, budgeting, payroll, inventory, cash flow, and investments.

Vocabulary Review

1. Arrange the vocabulary terms below into groups of related words. Explain why you put the words together.

- free enterprise system
- business plan
- strategic plan
- marketing plan
- financial plan
- accounting
- transaction
- generally accepted accounting principles (GAAP)
- budget
- merchandise
- inventory
- cash flow
- negative cash flow
- contingency
- components
- monotonous
- project

Higher Order Thinking 

2. **Predict** What might the consequences be if a company's business plan did not include the strategic plan, marketing plan, and financial plan?
3. **Infer** How is having proper inventory levels important to financial management?
4. **Hypothesize** What research might you do for preparing a marketing plan for a local florist?
5. **Theorize** It is important for business owners to know where their business stands financially at all times. Theorize what might happen if an owner analyzed a business's finances only twice a year.
6. **Assess** If you were to invest in your business, would you invest in human capital, capital goods, or technology? Why?
7. **Recommend** Your catering business has been showing steady profits for the last six months. Prepare a list of three suggestions for how to responsibly handle the profits.
8. **Deduce** What might happen if a budget is not regularly compared to actual income and expenses?
9. **Evaluate** A small business owner sets a goal to double her profits. Point out why this is not a good goal and how the owner could revise it.

College and Career Readiness

Social Studies

10. Cultural Research Imagine you are starting a business. Choose what product or service you will sell. In order to expand your business, you will need to sell to a broad market. As part of your marketing plan, conduct research about who will buy your product or service. Consider different cultures that might value your product or service. Determine if other regions, states, or countries would provide a good market. Conduct research to find three countries or cultures that would be a good source of potential customers for you. Write a summary of your findings, including an explanation of why those three markets might purchase your product or service.

NCSS I A Analyze and explain the ways groups, societies, and cultures address human needs and concerns.

Mathematics

11. Inventory Penny's toy store requires 3-weeks worth of merchandise on hand. 2-weeks are on the shelves while 1-week is in the warehouse. They have a system in place where an order is processed once the total merchandise on hand reaches a level of 2-weeks. At this point, 2-weeks of merchandise is ordered which typically takes 1 week to arrive at the store. If Penny's toy store currently has 2-weeks of merchandise on hand, in 1 week, how many cases of product should the store have on hand? Assume 1-week of merchandise is equivalent to 100 cases.

Math Concept **Calculate Inventory Levels** Calculate the expected level of merchandise on hand by first determining the current level on hand. Adjust this amount by any merchandise depletion as well as purchases.

Starting Hint First identify the current level of merchandise on hand. Subtract 1-week of merchandise from the current amount in order to arrive at the level of merchandise on hand prior to any reorders. Multiply this figure by 100 to arrive at the number of cases.

NCTM Number and Operations Compute fluently and make reasonable estimates.

English Language Arts

12. Web Site Design Sam and Billy own a small business making and selling hand-carved wooden charms in the shapes of various animals. They began their business six months ago and have been selling locally. They would like to build a larger customer base and have decided to build a Web site to try and market their products. Sketch out a proposed plan for the Web site, including graphics and copy for the home page, as well as proposed links to other pages that you would recommend they include.

NCTE 5 Use different writing process elements to communicate effectively.

Ethics

13. Whistleblowing Many businesses have a code of ethics, many of which include a section on "whistleblowing." Companies want employees to feel that if they witness inappropriate behavior, they can report it without fear of retaliation. The guidelines may encourage you to speak with your supervisor but also offer guidance if the situation is not resolved or you are uncomfortable speaking to your supervisor. Suppose that you have a good working relationship with your supervisor but witnessed him bullying your coworkers. Would you speak to him about his actions? Would you keep silent to maintain your relationship? What other actions could you take?

Real-World Applications

14. Evaluating Expenses Imagine that you and a partner have decided to start a business selling customized t-shirts. Follow your teacher's instructions to form into pairs. With your partner, consider the assets and inventory you would need to start your business. Once you have developed your list of assets and inventory, research cost estimates for each item. Are there any expenses that you could put off until later? For example, do you need software to manage your accounting or can it be done manually? Could you buy the t-shirts as orders are placed or would you need to have them in stock? Note which items are mandatory and revise your start-up cost estimate.

Your Financial Portfolio

Planning for Success

For several years Tom has been going with his father to yard sales. His father buys old clocks and radios. He fixes them if they need repairs and sells them at the Millerton Flea Market. Tom wants to start his own business and organize his plans.

Oldies but Goodies

Type of business:	Selling used CDs, DVDs, videos, and video games
Location:	Millerton Flea Market
Target customers:	All ages, but mainly ages 10 to 35 for the CDs, DVDs, and videos; and ages 10 to 25 for the video games
Potential number of customers:	About 300 to 800 people visit the flea market each day, which is open Fridays through Sundays.
Competition:	No one has been selling these products at the flea market since the Albertsons moved away.
Other competition:	The nearest place to buy used CDs is about 10 miles away; three local video stores sell used DVDs, videos, and video games.
Challenges:	Getting enough products to sell: Jaimie McKerry buys surplus stock for Franklin's Discounts, and he will sell me used CDs for about $2.50 each if I buy at least 100 at a time.
Costs:	Purchasing the products, Dad will share expenses with me for renting the table ($50 for the weekend), and gas for when we go look at garage sales.
Potential profit:	I used to look at all the DVDs, CDs, and videos when Vin Albertson had his table, and he seemed to move a lot of merchandise. I think I can make a profit of $3 a unit and sell 30 to 50 units a weekend.
Background and special skills:	I have been going to garage sales with Dad for several years. There are always old DVDs, CDs, videos, and video games that I can pick up at low prices. I like negotiating when I buy and sell, and I like helping Dad at his table. I also know popular titles.

Prepare a Plan

Select a merchandising business that you think you would like to own. On a separate sheet of paper, describe the type of business, the product(s) involved, and the factors you think would make it successful, and explain why you think you could make this business a success.

CHAPTER 5

Developing a Financial Plan

Visual Literacy

Starting and operating a business requires equipment and often space and inventory, all of which require money. ***How might you raise the money to start your own business?***

Developing a Statement of Required Start-Up Capital

Key Question

How can you determine the amount of start-up capital required for a new business?

Project Goal

The first step to developing a strong financial plan is to create a statement of required start-up capital. This will require careful consideration of your proposed business, as well as a lot of research. Suppose you are opening a toy store. Begin by determining what assets are needed for your business. Once you have a list of assets, you must research the price for each to develop an estimate of the asset's cost. Then conduct research to determine what start-up costs are required and estimate the cost for each of these. Once you have all the estimates, add them together to determine your total required start-up capital.

Ask Yourself...

- *How can you determine what equipment you will need?*
- *How will your business differ from your competition?*
- *Who can help you identify start-up costs?*
- *How will you determine the cost for each asset and start-up cost?*

Interact Effectively with Others

Why is it important to dress professionally when conducting the research for your financial plan?

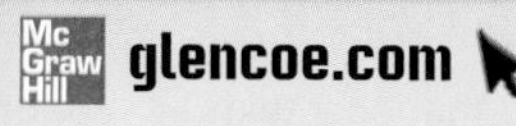

Evaluate Download an assessment rubric.

THE BIG IDEA

A solid financial plan will give you a complete financial picture of your business.

ASK STANDARD & POOR'S

Financial Plan

Q *Since the projections in a financial plan are just guesses, why is the plan so important? Why should I bother spending time making financial predictions that might not come true?*

A A financial plan is essential to understanding what will make your business profitable, how much cash you will need to operate the business, and the future value of the business. Even though your financial plan will need to be updated regularly, it still provides you with a solid idea of where your business should be headed.

Writing Activity

In addition to the projected financial statements that make up the financial plan, a business owner will also need to maintain financial statements showing actual transactions. Write an explanation of how you would use your financial predictions and why you would need to update your financial plan regularly.

CHAPTER 5

Reading Guide

Before You Read

The Essential Question Why is it important to create a well-thought-out and realistic financial plan?

Main Idea

A good financial plan shows financial projections of your income and expenses and how much capital is needed.

Content Vocabulary

- capital
- start-up capital
- start-up costs
- operating capital
- financial forecasting
- projected financial statements
- gross profit on sales
- fixed expenses
- variable expenses
- reserve capital
- chart of accounts

Academic Vocabulary

You will see these words in your reading and on your tests.

- complex
- revenue
- preliminary
- framework

Graphic Organizer

Before you read this chapter, draw a graphic organizer like the one below. As you read, note the four basic steps involved in preparing to open a new business.

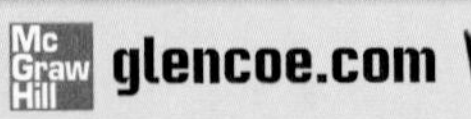

glencoe.com Print this graphic organizer.

Standards

Academic

Mathematics

NCTM Connections Recognize and apply mathematics in contexts outside of mathematics.

NCTM Problem Solving Apply and adapt a variety of appropriate strategies to solve problems.

NCTM Problem Solving Build new mathematical knowledge through problem solving.

English Language Arts

NCTE 5 Use different writing process elements to communicate effectively.

NCTE 7 Conduct research and gather, evaluate, and synthesize data to communicate discoveries.

Science

NSES E Develop abilities of technological design, understandings about science and technology.

NCTM *National Council of Teachers of Mathematics*

NCTE *National Council of Teachers of English*

NCSS *National Council for the Social Studies*

NSES *National Science Education Standards*

Common Core

Reading Determine central ideas or themes of a text and analyze their development; summarize the key supporting details and ideas.

Reading Read and comprehend complex literary and informational texts independently and proficiently.

Writing Draw evidence from literary or informational texts to support analysis, reflection, and research.

Writing Conduct short as well as more sustained research projects based on focused questions, demonstrating understanding of the subject under investigation.

Identifying Required Capital

Elements of a Financial Plan

Why is a financial plan an important part of a business plan?

A financial plan is often considered the most important part of an overall business plan. Without adequate planning and cash, your business may not survive. **Figure 1** shows how wise financial planning can help you make your business dream a reality.

An effective financial plan enables you to determine required capital. **Capital** is the money you will need to establish a business, operate it for the first few months, and expand it once it stabilizes. The process of determining required capital will include identifying and analyzing the assets and costs that are involved in starting a new business and assigning each an estimated dollar value.

A financial plan addresses the sources of funding you will use to acquire or purchase needed items. In addition, the plan outlines how you will record, summarize, and report the finances of your business.

Section Objectives

- **Explain** start-up capital.
- **Identify** start-up costs.
- **Describe** operating capital.
- **Explain** projected income statements.
- **Discuss** the role of reserve capital.

As You Read

Predict What is the difference between start-up capital and operating capital?

Reading Check

Define What is capital?

Determining Required Capital

Why is it necessary to have a clear, concise, and realistic financial plan?

The first aspect of a financial plan is to determine how much capital you will need. You may be shocked at the amount of money that is required to start a successful business. The purpose of a financial plan is to give you a realistic idea of what you will need. The quality of your plan will affect the success of your business. It will also impact your ability to qualify for financing. A concise and realistic financial plan will give lenders confidence in your business knowledge and skills.

There are three types of required capital: start-up capital, operating capital, and reserve capital. To begin a financial plan, you will need to analyze carefully all three types of required capital and estimate the amount of each needed to start up your business.

Reading Check

Recall What is the first step in developing a financial plan?

Cross-Cultural Skills

Successful people both in and outside of business possess strong cross-cultural skills. Cross-cultural skills include the ability to work effectively with people from a variety of cultural backgrounds. It is important to respect cultural differences and approach ideas and values with an open mind. Utilizing cross-cultural skills will lead to the creation of new ideas and increase innovation.

Write About It

Think of a situation in which you used or saw someone use cross-cultural skills. Write one or more paragraphs to describe the scenario and explain how these skills positively impacted the situation.

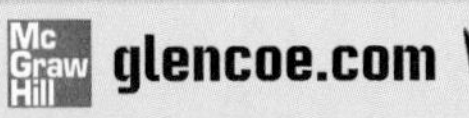

Activity Download a Career and College Readiness Worksheet Activity.

Start-Up Capital

Why do many start-up businesses fail within the first five years of operation?

The first type of required capital is **start-up capital**—the money required to start your business. Sufficient start-up capital is essential to the survival of a new business.

Establishing a business is an expensive and risky venture. The U.S. Small Business Administration reports that most small businesses fail in the first one to five years of operation. One of the reasons these businesses fail is that they lack sufficient start-up capital. If money is not available to purchase necessary merchandise or to pay current bills, a business will not survive.

Start-up capital is divided into two basic categories. The first category is the capital required to purchase the assets you will need to start your business. Before you can open the doors of your business, you will need to buy various items. These items may include equipment, display racks, and inventory.

The second category of start-up capital is **start-up costs**—the costs or fees involved in establishing your business. Start-up costs may include permits, legal and accounting fees, and security deposits. Some start-up costs are one-time expenses, such as permits, legal fees, and deposits for telephone service. Other costs are continuing expenses, such as rent, maintenance, and insurance.

Identifying Required Assets

Some assets are common to all businesses, both new and established. These are the items that most businesses need in order to operate. Other assets are unique to specific types of businesses or to certain geographic areas.

When preparing a financial plan, you will need to identify both common and unique assets. Be sure to record the types and quantities of items that you will need. To start, list the assets that are commonly needed by businesses. Assets might include office furniture, such as desks and file cabinets; computer hardware and software; display cases or shelves; store equipment, such as copiers and cash registers; merchandise inventory; transportation or delivery equipment, such as cars or vans; store and office supplies; carpeting and lighting; and security and communication systems.

Next, list the assets you will need that may be unique to your specific type of business or to your geographic area. Such assets might include unique pieces of production or repair equipment; special types of display equipment; special electronic, security, or maintenance equipment; special raw materials; or required health or safety equipment.

FIGURE 1 Creating a Business

Foundation for Success A financial plan must be detailed and accurate to ensure a successful business. *How might you research what supplies your business will need?*

Creating a new business requires lots of preparation and hard work. By creating a thorough and realistic financial plan, you will ensure that your business has the money it needs to prosper and grow.

1 **Analyze your needs and costs.** Research the supplies your business will need and the fees and costs that you will have to pay to get started.

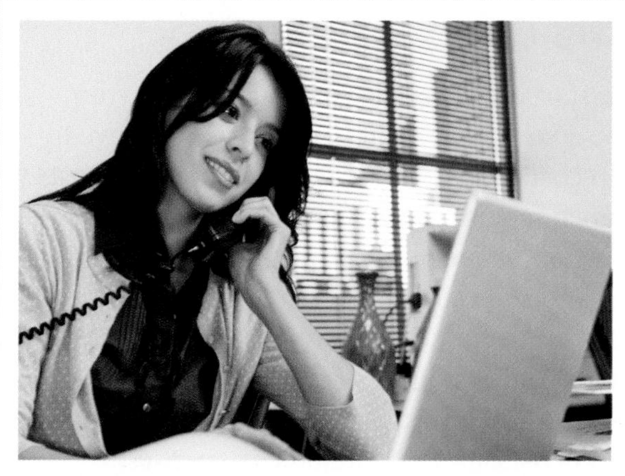

2 **Secure funding.** Your plan will describe how each business expense will be paid. Financial institutions will consider the accuracy of your financial plan before agreeing to lend money to your business.

3 **Plan your process.** In your financial plan, you will show how you will record, summarize, and report your business's finances once you get started.

4 **Prepare for opening.** A good financial plan will ensure that you have money to cover all the supplies and preparations necessary to open your business.

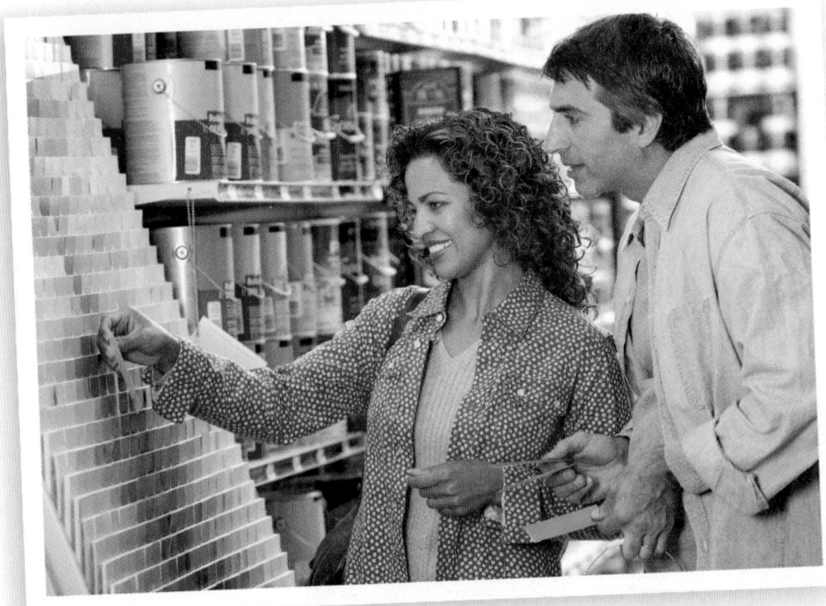

Amassing Assets
Many business, such as a hardware store, require substantial start-up capital to cover the cost of inventory. *What types of businesses would not require inventory?*

When you make these lists, it is a good idea to observe established businesses that are similar to your business, read trade journals, and consult with vendors in the industry. This will give you a better idea of what assets you will need.

Identifying Start-Up Costs

Next, identify and list the start-up costs for your business in your financial plan. This can be a **complex,** or difficult, task. You have to identify common start-up costs and determine which of those costs you should include in your financial plan. You must also become familiar with required local and state licenses, permits, and fees. Local trade associations, banks, and the U.S. Small Business Administration can help you identify these costs. Some common start-up costs include business insurance; legal and professional fees; licenses and permits; bank fees; marketing and advertising costs; security deposits; remodeling and renovation costs; and maintenance expenses.

Unidentified costs are a serious problem for entrepreneurs who are beginning new businesses, so be sure to include any type of cost that you feel you may encounter in starting up your business. Too often, unexpected or hidden costs consume start-up funds. If that happens, money may not be available for other needed items.

Assigning Costs to Identified Items

Once you have identified your required assets and start-up costs, you must estimate how much you will have to pay for each item. Be careful to assign a realistic dollar value to each required asset and start-up cost. If you underestimate, you may have to reduce costs in other areas, and then you may not have enough cash to pay for essential items. If this occurs often, your business may face a serious cash flow problem.

Document Detective

A Personal Financial Statement

When you apply for a loan, you must present an accurate personal financial statement so that banks and lenders can review your current financial status. They want to be sure that you have resources to pay off a loan. This form lists the following information:

- Name and contact information
- Assets and income
- Liabilities and loans
- Source of income
- Noteholder contact information

U.S. SMALL BUSINESS ADMINISTRATION

OMB APPROVAL NO. 3245-0188
EXPIRATION DATE: 3/31/2008

PERSONAL FINANCIAL STATEMENT

As of April, 20--

Complete this form for: (1) each proprietor, or (2) each limited partner who owns 20% or more interest and each general partner, or (3) each stockholder owning 20% or more of voting stock, or (4) any person or entity providing a guaranty on the loan.

Name Sarah Dean — Business Phone (303) 555-8941

Residence Address 10 West Cleveland Rd. — Residence Phone (303) 555-1527

City, State, & Zip Code Twinsburg, OH 44218

Business Name of Applicant/Borrower Interiors by Design

ASSETS	(Omit Cents)	LIABILITIES	(Omit Cents)
Cash on hand & in Banks	$ 15,000	Accounts Payable	$ 2,500
Savings Accounts	$ 3,000	Notes Payable to Banks and Others (Describe in Section 2)	$ –
IRA or Other Retirement Account	$ 35,000	Installment Account (Auto)	$ 2,500
Accounts & Notes Receivable	$ –	Mo. Payments	$ 500
Life Insurance-Cash Surrender Value Only (Complete Section 8)	$ 3,000	Installment Account (Other)	$ –
Stocks and Bonds (Describe in Section 3)	$ 4,000	Mo. Payments	$
		Loan on Life Insurance	$ –
Real Estate (Describe in Section 4)	$ 75,000	Mortgages on Real Estate (Describe in Section 4)	$ 100,000
Automobile-Present Value	$ 7,000	Unpaid Taxes (Describe in Section 6)	$ 8,000
Other Personal Property (Describe in Section 5)	$ –	Other Liabilities (Describe in Section 7)	$ –
Other Assets (Describe in Section 5)	$ –	Total Liabilities	$ 113,000
		Net Worth	$ 29,000
Total	$ 142,000	Total	$ 142,000

Section 1. Source of Income		Contingent Liabilities	
Salary	$ 55,000	As Endorser or Co-Maker	$
Net Investment Income	$	Legal Claims & Judgments	$
Real Estate Income	$	Provision for Federal Income Tax	$
Other Income (Describe below)*	$	Other Special Debt	$

Description of Other Income in Section 1.

Key Points The Small Business Administration (SBA) developed a personal financial statement for loan applicants to complete when applying for an SBA loan. Similar to a personal balance sheet, the form details a person's assets, liabilities, and net worth.

FIND the Solutions

Review Key Concepts

1. What is the purpose of a personal financial statement?
2. What is Sarah's net worth?
3. How was her net worth calculated?
4. What is Sarah's salary?
5. Why would the SBA want to know the names and addresses of noteholders?

Play it safe by estimating on the high side. For example, suppose that your business will need a photocopier machine. You determine that it will cost between $1,400 and $1,800. When you assign costs to your required assets, you should use the higher estimate, $1,800. If you pay only $1,600 for the photocopier, you can apply the additional budgeted amount ($200) to other costs.

The final step in calculating how much money you will need to launch your business is to prepare a statement of required start-up capital. For example, Amanda Woodland is opening a new business called "The Silver Lining Gift Shop." She has developed a statement of required start-up capital. Amanda's statement is shown in **Figure 2.**

FIGURE 2 Required Start-Up Capital

Calculating Costs Writing out a list of expected assets and start-up costs will help ensure that all start-up costs are considered. *Why is it important to know start-up costs before starting a business?*

The Silver Lining Gift Shop

Statement of Required Start-Up Capital

Item	Cost	
ASSETS		
Display equipment	$11,400	
Office furniture	3,100	
Computer system	4,400	
Photocopier	1,800	
Merchandise	37,000	
Supplies	3,500	
Alarm system	2,700	
Carpet, lights, fans	12,400	
Maintenance equipment	2,900	
Total Assets		**79,200**
START-UP COSTS		
Insurance	3,100	
Professional/legal fees	2,700	
Business permits/licenses	200	
Utility deposits	700	
Advertising	1,300	
Repairs/Maintenance	2,200	
Banking fees	200	
Total Start-Up Costs		**10,400**
Total Required Start-Up Capital		**$89,600**

Amanda realizes that there will be unexpected costs and small items that she will need to purchase, which are not on this statement. But she thinks that she has identified all major required assets and start-up costs. After listing the items, she realizes that she will need approximately $90,000 in start-up capital. If Amanda had not researched and analyzed all her costs carefully, she probably would have guessed that she could start her gift shop with much less than $90,000.

Reading Check

Summarize What are some of the start-up costs that might be required for a business?

Operating Capital

Why should you predict the operating capital you will need?

Next, you must focus on the second type of required capital needed to start your business. This is called **operating capital**—the amount of capital needed to operate a business for the first few months or years.

Although the sale of your products or services will generate revenue, this money is often not enough to cover business expenses and expansion plans. You will need money to purchase additional merchandise and increase sales to keep your business running. Also, cash must be available to carry out your strategic and marketing plan.

As part of your financial plan, you must do **financial forecasting**, which is the process of estimating a business's operating capital. This future financial picture of your business is reported in **projected financial statements**—statements that predict the financial position of a business in the months and years to come. The projected financial statements will include income statements, balance sheets, and statements of cash flows.

Financial Forecasting A key component of a financial plan is estimating a business's operating capital. *What type of documents are used to report financial forecasting?*

Economics and You

Free Trade vs. Trade Barriers

Free trade occurs when there are no trade restrictions or taxes on goods traded among member nations of a trade agreement. Businesses flourish because their products can be purchased and sold in each others' countries easily. Trade barriers, such as quotas and tariffs make it more difficult for businesses to be involved in the global marketplace. For example, if a quota is reached for a specific product, no more of that product may be brought into the country. Tariffs are taxes on products entering a country; thus increasing the price of an imported product.

Personal Finance Connection If business owners want to import goods from a foreign country they must know the effect of trade barriers on their financial plans. If quotas are imposed, shipping costs may need to be adjusted to ensure deliveries arrive well before a quota for that type of good is reached. If tariffs are imposed, costs associated with the purchase of those products must reflect the increased costs on their financial plans. When purchasing imported products, consumers may not notice price differences unless an item is a lot more than the same type of domestic product. In that case, the imported item may have had a tariff on it to allow domestic producers to sell the product more competitively in the United States.

Critical Thinking What are the pros and cons for free trade for businesses, workers, and consumers?

U.S. Exports and Imports

Toys, games, and sporting goods
TVs, DVD players, etc.
Fuel oil
Airplanes
Computers
Iron and steel mill products
Household appliances
Books and printed matter
Exports
Imports
10 30 50 70 90 110 130
Value in billions of dollars

Activity Download an Economics and You Worksheet Activity.

Projected Income Statement

An income statement for a merchandising business will report **revenue** (income), cost of merchandise sold, operating expenses, and net income or loss. This statement will also include gross profit on sales. **Gross profit on sales** is the profit made from selling merchandise before operating expenses are deducted. This type of statement usually reports what happened in the previous period.

In contrast, a projected income statement is an estimate of the way in which income amounts will change over the next few months or years. You create this statement before you begin business operations. This statement reveals where you expect your business to be in the future.

Estimating figures for a projected income statement can be a challenge. You must analyze all information regarding revenue and expenses for your type of business. You can obtain this information from trade associations, vendors, local business organizations, and government agencies such as the U.S. Small Business Administration and the Bureau of the Census. The information from these sources is based on facts and averages. However, to create figures for your projected income statement, you will have to apply that information to your business and make educated guesses.

It is better to estimate projected revenues on the low side and to estimate projected expenses on the high side. This approach will allow some flexibility if sales do not reach your expectations or if expenses are higher than you had originally estimated. If you project yearly sales of between $130,000 and $150,000, use the lower estimate of $130,000. If you estimate your heating bill might be between $3,000 and $4,000, use the higher amount of $4,000.

It is important to determine the correct amount for a start-up company's expenses. Expenses are often classified as fixed or variable.

Fixed Expenses Expenses that remain the same regardless of business activity are **fixed expenses.** These might include rent, insurance, or interest on a loan. Fixed expenses are fairly easy to project because they remain constant, or fixed, for a stated length of time. For example, no matter how much your business earns from sales in a particular month, you will still pay the same amount in rent for the duration of your lease.

Variable Expenses Expenses that may change are **variable expenses.** Sometimes variable expenses can be adjusted depending on sales. Such expenses might include supplies, advertising, wages, and sometimes utilities. For example, if sales are lower than you had predicted, you could purchase fewer supplies or reduce your employees' hours. It is more difficult to project variable expenses.

Some variable expenses, such as maintenance and repairs, have nothing to do with sales. These also cannot be projected accurately. When your computer or cash register no longer works, you must have it repaired or replaced. The main characteristic of variable expenses is that they change with business conditions and other situations.

reality bytes

Easy Planning
Many entrepreneurs are skilled at sales and promoting their businesses but have trouble applying financial math. However, when you must create a financial plan to start or expand a business, technology is available to help. Financial plan software can analyze a financial situation, make projections, and create financial statements for a financial plan.

Marketing Expenses
Businesses often struggle with how much money to spend on marketing and advertising. *Why is it important for businesses to allot money for advertising and promotions?*

Figure 3 shows a projected income statement for Skelly's Craft Shop for the first four months of operation. You can see that the statement is projecting losses in each month. This is not unusual for a new business. In fact, it is common for a new business to go for several months or even a year without reporting a profit. Notice, however, that the estimated loss for Skelly's Craft Shop decreases each month.

Figure 4 shows a projected income statement for Skelly's Craft Shop for the first five years of operation. It provides a long-range view of business activity. If the amounts are projected realistically, they may indicate the potential success of the business.

Notice that by the end of the second year, the craft shop anticipates a profit. This is good news for the owners. It is also important information to include in a financial plan for banks or other financial institutions that might provide funding.

FIGURE 3 Projected Income Statement

Predicted Income A projected income statement shows the expected expenses as well as the anticipated profits. *Why should you project expenses on the high side?*

Skelly's Craft Shop
Projected Income Statement

MONTH	1	2	3	4
REVENUE				
Sales	$9,000	$10,600	$12,500	$14,600
Cost of Merchandise Sold	– 5,400	– 6,400	– 7,300	– 8,700
Gross Profit on Sales	**$3,600**	**$4,200**	**$5,200**	**$5,900**
EXPENSES				
Rent	3,800	3,800	3,800	3,800
Electricity	200	200	200	200
Heat/AC	300	325	340	350
Telephone	100	140	175	195
Insurance	290	290	290	290
Maintenance/Repairs	100	160	230	250
Miscellaneous	100	140	170	200
Wages	400	490	575	680
Taxes	250	250	250	250
Supplies	475	550	630	720
Interest	510	510	530	530
Advertising	875	875	960	760
Total Expenses	**$7,400**	**$7,730**	**$8,150**	**$8,225**
Net Income/<Loss>	**<$3,800>**	**<$3,530>**	**<$2,950>**	**<$2,325>**

FIGURE 4 Projected 5-Year Income Statement

Long-Term Predictions A financial plan should include a projected income statement for the first few months as well as one for the first few years of your business. *Why would financial institutions want to see a projected income statement for years rather than months?*

Skelly's Craft Shop
Projected 5-Year Income Statement

YEAR	1	2	3	4	5
REVENUE					
Sales	$172,000	$224,600	$258,500	$298,000	$370,000
Cost of Merchandise Sold	– 103,200	– 125,400	– 147,100	– 169,000	– 205,000
Gross Profit on Sales	**$68,800**	**$99,200**	**$111,400**	**$129,000**	**$165,000**
EXPENSES					
Rent	45,600	47,300	48,200	51,800	55,000
Electricity	4,600	4,800	5,000	5,200	5,600
Heat/AC	3,500	3,900	4,400	4,700	5,000
Telephone	1,200	1,400	1,600	1,800	2,200
Insurance	3,500	3,600	3,700	3,800	4,000
Maintenance/Repairs	1,200	1,600	2,300	2,500	2,800
Miscellaneous	1,000	1,400	1,700	1,900	2,200
Wages	4,800	6,100	7,200	8,000	9,900
Taxes	2,900	3,500	3,900	4,200	7,600
Supplies	4,900	5,500	6,300	7,000	7,900
Interest	5,800	5,400	5,000	4,800	4,100
Advertising	5,900	5,100	4,300	4,000	5,000
Total Expenses	**$84,900**	**$89,600**	**$93,600**	**$99,700**	**$111,300**
Net Income/<Loss>	**<$16,100>**	**$9,600**	**$17,800**	**$29,300**	**$53,700**

Projected Balance Sheet

Financial institutions will also want to see a forecast of the overall financial position of your business. You provide this with a projected balance sheet. It shows an estimate of the future assets, liabilities, and net worth of your business in one year, three years, or five years from now. A projected balance is shown in **Figure 5.**

Review the projected balance sheet for Ramos T-Shirts. The net worth of the business is projected to increase over the next three years, with the owner's equity increasing from $37,600 at the end of the first year to $50,600 at the end of the third year. You will also notice that in this same period, assets are projected to increase ($71,200 to $83,100), and liabilities to decrease ($33,600 to $32,500).

New Zealand

Science Spending

When a company develops a financial plan, it must estimate its capital and start-up costs. One area of capital that many businesses might overlook is the costs associated with research and development. The New Zealand government has recognized the importance of science and the need for research and development (R&D) in order to further technology. Prime Minister John Key says on his Web site, "To grow our economy, we need to generate and use new ideas." To this end, Prime Minister Key announced in 2010 that the government would be awarding more than $300 million to businesses for R&D and science. About $20 million of that is intended specifically for small businesses.

The money will be given in the form of technology transfer vouchers. These vouchers would typically be worth $100,000 to $200,000 each. Prime Minister Key believes that the vouchers will allow smaller firms that do not have the resources for research and development to access public research institutes for that purpose. The expectation is that science will help the firms develop new products and improve the way they do business.

Critical Thinking

1. **Expand** Research to find other steps that the New Zealand government has taken to help promote science. Describe them.
2. **Relate** More than half of the science funding is allocated for technology grants to larger companies doing valuable research. Do you agree that this is the best use of the money to boost science in their country? Are there other ways that you might suggest a country could promote science?

DATABYTES

Capital
Wellington

Population
4,252,277

Languages
English (official), Maori (official), Sign Language (official)

Currency
New Zealand dollar

Gross Domestic Product (GDP)
$110.9 billion

GDP per capita
$27,300

Industry
Food processing, wood and paper products, textiles, machinery, transportation equipment, banking and insurance, tourism, mining

Agriculture
Dairy products, lamb and mutton; wheat, barley, potatoes, pulses, fruits, vegetables; wool, beef; fish

Exports
Dairy products, meat, wood and wood products, fish, machinery

Natural Resources
Natural gas, iron ore, sand, coal, timber, hydropower, gold, limestone

Projected Statement of Cash Flows

A statement of cash flows reports how much cash a business has taken in and where the cash has gone. This document shows how the cash position of a business changed during an accounting period.

Many consider the projected statement of cash flows to be the most important projected financial statement. When you prepare a projected statement of cash flows, you analyze the amount of cash that you anticipate will be available for your business in the future. Will you have sufficient cash if your business operates on its projected path? Remember, success and growth depend on available cash.

Figure 6 shows a projected statement of cash flows for Westport Sporting Goods for a period of three months. You can see that the business predicts a positive cash flow for the three-month period. In other words, more money is shown coming into Westport Sporting Goods each month than is shown going out.

FIGURE 5 **Projected 3-Year Balance Sheet**

Financial Position A projected balance sheet clearly shows the anticipated assets and liabilities of your business. *Why do you want to show an increase in assets each year?*

Ramos T-Shirts

Projected 3-Year Balance Sheet			
YEAR	**1**	**2**	**3**
ASSETS			
Cash in Bank	$13,200	$15,000	$12,000
Accounts Receivable	2,300	3,100	4,000
Store Equipment	18,400	22,100	27,000
Office Equipment	7,200	6,500	6,700
Merchandise Inventory	24,900	26,000	30,000
Supplies	1,000	1,100	1,100
Computer Equipment	4,200	3,500	2,300
Total Assets	**$71,200**	**$77,300**	**$83,100**
	$7,400	$8,100	$8,800
Accounts Payable			
Notes Payable	26,200	25,300	23,700
Total Liabilities	**$33,600**	**$33,400**	**$32,500**
OWNER'S EQUITY			
Jon Ramos, Capital	37,600	43,900	50,600
Total Liabilities	**$71,200**	**$77,300**	**$83,100**

It should be noted for this example that these three months—April, May, and June—are probably a particularly high sales period for a sporting goods store. Therefore, the business might not have such a positive cash flow throughout the entire year.

Reading Check

Recall Which projected financial statement is often considered the most important?

FIGURE 6 **Projected Statement of Cash Flow**

Coming and Going It is important for a business to know how much cash is coming in and where it is going. *What is the biggest cash expense for Westport Sporting Goods?*

Westport Sporting Goods
Projected Statement of Cash Flow

	APRIL	MAY	JUNE
CASH RECEIVED			
Cash Sales	$33,500	$37,400	$39,500
Interest Income	170	175	180
Total Cash Inflow	**$33,670**	**$37,575**	**$39,680**
CASH DISBURSED			
Rent	$4,600	$4,600	$4,600
Utilities	1,300	1,375	1,420
Supplies	450	450	460
Advertising	2,800	3,000	3,700
Bank Charges/Fees	220	250	270
Interest Expense	3,400	3,300	3,200
Telephone	510	530	540
Maintenance	950	1,075	1,100
Credit Card Fees	390	425	460
Payroll	9,200	10,100	10,300
Taxes	4,800	6,000	7,300
Delivery Charges	1,040	1,260	1,290
Miscellaneous	520	600	600
Insurance	675	675	675
Total Cash Outflow	**$30,855**	**$33,640**	**$35,915**
NET OPERATING CASH FLOW	**2,815**	**3,935**	**3,765**
BEGINNING CASH BALANCE	**5,860**	**8,675**	**12,610**
ENDING CASH BALANCE	**$8,675**	**$12,610**	**$16,375**

Careers That Count!

Kent Rolfes • Controller

Does business math and problem solving interest you? I enjoy both, so I worked hard to become a controller for a large retail chain. My career requires many different skills. Interpersonal skills are important because I manage people and work as part of a team to solve problems. I need to have strong communication skills so I can explain complex financial data. I work extensively with various departments, such as accounting, auditing, and budgeting, so a broad understanding of business is essential. As controller, I am responsible for all aspects of the company's finances. My daily responsibilities include banking, profit and loss statements, balance sheets, payroll, accounts payable, accounts receivable, collections, cost accounting, inventory valuation, and government filing. I also prepare and analyze weekly cash management reports, monthly expense reports, and quarterly financial statements complete with management analysis. I use all of this information to summarize and forecast the company's financial position.

EXPLORE CAREERS

Visit the Web site of the U.S. Department of Labor's Bureau of Labor Statistics and obtain information about a career as a controller.

1. In what other areas do controllers need expertise, and why?
2. Other than academic skills, what skills would be essential to a controller?

Skills	Education	Career Path
Accounting, analytical, communication, computer, decision-making, management, math, organizational, and problem-solving skills	Bachelor's or master's degree in accounting, finance, or business administration; Certified Public Accountant (CPA)	Controllers can become tax examiners, financial analysts, budget analysts, treasurers, tax preparers, economists, and auditors.

 glencoe.com 

Activity Download a Career Exploration Activity.

Reserve Capital

Why is it important for a start-up business to have reserve capital available?

The third type of capital is called **reserve capital**—money that is set aside for unexpected costs or opportunities. Reserve capital is like cash in a savings account. If and when you need money, it is there.

When emergencies arise, reserve capital can be a lifeline for small businesses. Unexpected costs can occur at any time and usually require immediate attention. Examples of unexpected costs include repair bills and the expense of replacing broken equipment. Without immediate access to cash, your business could face financial problems.

Reserve capital is also needed to take advantage of business opportunities. Suppose that a competitor is going out of business and has offered you inventory at a great price if you pay for it in cash. You can use your reserve fund to take advantage of the opportunity. Good financial planning includes taking advantage of these opportunities.

Cash Only
Businesses are sometimes required to pay cash for merchandise deliveries.
Why might vendors prefer cash payments?

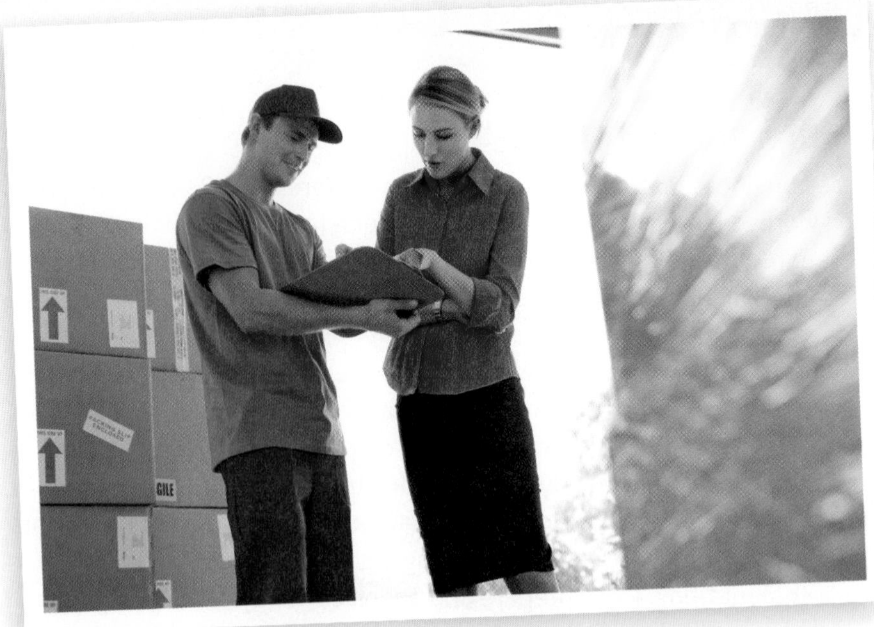

In addition, business owners use reserve capital to expand and grow their businesses. For example, you might use cash from the reserve fund to buy new lines of merchandise or to purchase more up-to-date equipment. Such forward-thinking investments allow your business to develop and become financially successful.

The amount of capital set aside in a reserve fund will vary from business to business. Many businesses set up this fund as a line of credit at the bank. It can also come from your personal funds.

You should not use your reserve capital for the normal operation of your business. It should be used only for unexpected costs and worthwhile business opportunities. By keeping a reasonable amount of money in your reserve fund, you will be able to take care of your business even in crisis situations and be able to take advantage of opportunities that require money from your business.

Reading Check

Recognize What is reserve capital?

Using Technology

How can technology assist in preparing financial information?

Recording, summarizing, and reporting financial information can be an extremely time-consuming activity. Computers offer small business owners the ability to automate all the accounting functions. Daily, weekly, monthly, and annual reports can be generated quickly and accurately. With software and hardware being very affordable, most small businesses use some form of automated accounting.

Review Key Concepts

1. **Describe** What is operating capital used for?
2. **Explain** Where can you find the financial information needed to create a projected income statement?
3. **Identify** What type of business opportunities might require the use of reserve capital?
4. **Distinguish** What is the difference between start-up capital and start-up costs?

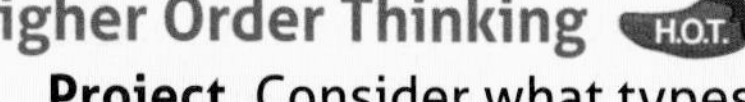

Higher Order Thinking H.O.T.

5. **Project** Consider what types of businesses might require large amounts of capital to begin operating. Explain your answer.

21st Century Skills

6. **Solve Problems** Sam and Emily own a local flower shop. They have been in business for about a year. When Emily visited the wholesale flower market this week, she found that the prices were higher on many of the flowers that she usually purchases for the flower shop. Develop a list of suggestions for Sam and Emily of how they might keep the same number of flowers in stock while staying within their operating budget.

Mathematics

7. **Projected Income Statement** You are starting a business and need to project for your future sales and expenses. Develop a 3-year income statement using the following estimations. Year 1 revenue will be $165,000 and will grow at 20 percent per year. Cost of merchandise sold is 50 percent of revenues. All rent, utilities, and supplies will stay flat each year at $25,000 per year. Year 1 payroll will be $5,000 and will increase at 4 percent per year. Taxes are 35 percent of revenues. Assume no other items aside from the revenues and expenses detailed above. Calculate net income for years 1-3.

Math Concept **Calculate Net Income** To calculate the net income, identify the total revenues and total expenses for each year. Subtract total expenses from total revenues to determine total net income. Repeat for each year.

Starting Hint Determine the cost of merchandise sold for each year by first identifying the revenues for the year. Multiply the revenues by the percentage that cost of merchandise sold makes up of revenues. Repeat this process for each year.

NCTM Connections Recognize and apply mathematics in contexts outside of mathematics.

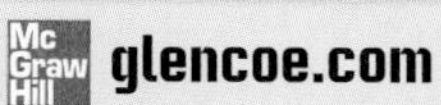

Check your answers.

Section Objective

- **Identify** the elements of a financial plan.

As You Read

Predict What is the advantage of having a thorough and solid financial plan?

Starting a Business

What are some requirements to start a business?

For the past five years, Molly Singer has worked at King Point Florist, a local flower and garden store. During that time, Molly learned to create fresh flower arrangements, fruit and gourmet baskets, and dried flower displays. She has read several books on floral design and has received numerous compliments on her arrangements.

Because of her work at the florist shop, Molly has experience in purchasing flowers and arrangements, advertising, pricing, sales procedures, and recordkeeping. She has taken several business courses at the local community college and has attended two seminars on running a small business.

Molly now feels that she is ready to open her own florist business. She realizes that running her own business will be very different from working for someone else. She is a little nervous about the challenges she will face as a business owner. However, she is confident that she has the knowledge and skills she needs to operate a successful flower shop.

Molly has decided to call her business "Cricket Lane Flowers." After researching locations and potential markets for a shop, she has found a small store that will fit her needs. It is located on a main street with a steady traffic flow and high visibility. No other flower shops are in the area, but there are several small businesses nearby that seem to attract customers. The store is in good condition, the monthly rent is reasonable, and the required decorating should be affordable.

Reading Check

Paraphrase What are some areas of experience that will help a potential new business owner?

A Business Plan for Cricket Lane Flowers

What is an example of a business plan?

With some **preliminary,** or early, research completed, Molly is ready to create her business plan for Cricket Lane Flowers. Her overall business plan consists of three parts: a strategic plan, a marketing plan, and a financial plan. This section provides brief summaries of Molly's strategic and marketing plans as well as all elements of her financial plan.

The Strategic Plan

For her strategic plan, Molly researched the local flower market, identified the competition, and decided on the line of flowers and services that her shop will provide. After careful analysis, she set the following short-term and long-term goals. Molly's strategic plan also outlines the steps that she will take to achieve each of her short-term and long-term goals.

Short-Term Goals:

- Rent a store in a good location.
- Secure a good telecommunication system.
- Computerize all accounting functions.
- Increase sales by 5 percent or more each month in the first year
- Utilize all local advertising outlets.

Long-Term Goals:

- Increase sales by 30 percent or more in each of the first three years.
- Show a profit by the end of the second year.
- Expand inventory to include fruit and gift items.
- Develop business clients.

The Marketing Plan

In her marketing plan, Molly analyzed the competition, identified advertising outlets, developed promotional activities, and established an advertising budget for Cricket Lane Flowers. The success of her goals depends on an effective marketing plan. Molly has decided to spend $2,000 in each of the first three months on advertising.

Reading Check

Recall What research should be completed for the strategic plan before finalizing a business's offered goods and services?

The Financial Plan

What must Molly do before she prepares her financial plan?

With her strategic and marketing plans completed, Molly is ready to develop her financial plan. Remember, the success of her strategic and marketing plans depends on the accuracy of her financial plan.

Before preparing a financial plan, Molly must be sure that she has set realistic goals for herself and her business. She knows that although her figures are only estimates, they must be attainable. Also, Molly realizes that it will take time to earn a profit.

COMMON CENTS

Saving Is Better

Spending money is easy, especially when you have a credit card. Resist the temptation to use your card to buy something you want but cannot really afford. Instead, be patient and save your money for that special item.

Concept Application

Why is it important to use your credit cards wisely for business or personal expenses?

Background Information

To help start her business, Molly has saved money over the past five years, and her family will lend her some money. She needs to borrow additional funds, but she is confident that she will qualify for loans because of her well-established credit history. She has financed two cars and uses her credit cards wisely and makes payments on time.

Molly has decided to organize her new business as a sole proprietorship. Although she will have unlimited liability, this form of ownership is easier and less costly to establish than others. She has consulted with an attorney and an accountant. Molly will continue to work with her accountant. She will need to consult him regarding issues such as expansion, taxes, and hiring employees.

Elements of the Financial Plan

Molly's financial plan includes the following reports:

- Statement of Required Start-Up Capital
- Projected 12-Month Income Statement
- Projected 12-Month Statement of Cash Flows
- Projected 3-Year Income Statement
- Projected 3-Year Statement of Cash Flows
- Projected 3-Year Balance Sheet

Cricket Lane Flowers-Financial Plan
Prepared by Molly Singer

Business Objective: To open and operate a financially successful flower shop.

Required Capital:	
Start-Up Capital	$89,000
Operating Capital	12,000
Reserve Capital	15,000
Total Required Capital	$116,000
Sources of Capital:	
Cash from Owner	$30,000
Personal Loans	6,000
Short-Term Commercial Loan	
(SBA Guaranteed)	30,000
Home Equity Loan	50,000
Total Available Capital	$116,000

Molly's complete financial plan for Cricket Lane Flowers appears on the following pages. By reading and analyzing her six projected financial statements in **Figures 7** through **11,** you will see how she expects her business to develop over time.

FIGURE 7 Cricket Lane Flowers—Statement of Required Start-Up Capital

Necessary Funds A statement of required start-up capital will detail how much money is needed and where it will be spent. *What are the two most expensive assets for Molly's business?*

Cricket Lane Flowers

Statement of Required Start-Up Capital	
Item	**Cost**
ASSETS	
Refrigeration equipment	$9,600
Display equipment	8,100
Maintenance equipment	2,900
Delivery van	19,000
Office furniture	1,900
Rugs, lights, ventilation	5,200
Computer system	3,500
Phone systems	750
Photocopier	1,800
Merchandise	17,000
Supplies	1,100
Alarm system	900
Total Assets	**$71,750**
START-UP COSTS	
Rent deposit	3,500
Insurance	1,400
Building signs	3,000
Artists' fees	150
Professional/legal fees	2,200
Business permits/licenses	250
Stationery/business cards	400
Flowers/wire fees	500
Utility deposits	700
Phone lines	450
Advertising	2,000
Repairs/fix-up costs	1,800
Banking fees	200
Other	500
Total Start-Up Costs	**17,050**
Total Required Start-Up Capital	**$88,800**

FIGURE 8 **Projected 12-Month Income Statement**

The First Year This statement shows the revenue and expenses anticipated for the first year of business. *In which month does the business first expect a net income rather than a loss?*

Cricket Lane Flowers

Projected 12-Month Income Statement						
MONTH	**1**	**2**	**3**	**4**	**5**	**6**
REVENUE						
Sales	$11,000	$12,000	$13,600	$15,100	$15,800	$16,500
Cost of Merchandise Sold	4,900	5,300	5,850	6,500	6,800	7,400
Gross Profit on Sales	**$6,100**	**$6,700**	**$7,750**	**$8,600**	**$9,000**	**$9,100**
EXPENSES						
Rent	3,500	3,500	3,500	3,500	3,500	3,500
Electricity	180	180	185	185	185	185
Heat/AC	340	375	390	395	395	370
Telephone	130	040	175	205	225	225
Insurance	480	480	480	480	480	480
Maintenance/Repairs	100	130	150	150	150	155
Miscellaneous	100	140	160	180	180	180
Wages	350	400	475	500	500	600
Taxes	250	360	400	450	475	490
Supplies	460	530	590	620	640	640
Interest	680	680	680	680	680	680
Advertising	2,000	2,000	2,000	1,800	1,700	1,500
Other	100	100	100	100	100	125
Total Expenses	**$8,670**	**$9,015**	**$9,285**	**$9,245**	**$9,210**	**$9,130**
Net Income/<Loss>	<$2,570>	<$2,315>	<$1,535>	<$645>	<$210>	<$30>

Projected 12-Month Statement of Cash Flows						
MONTH	**1**	**2**	**3**	**4**	**5**	**6**
CASH RECEIPTS						
Cash Sales	$10,400	$11,900	$13,400	$15,000	$15,600	$16,500
Total Cash Receipts	**$10,400**	**$11,900**	**$13,400**	**$15,000**	**$15,600**	**$16,500**
CASH PAYMENTS						
Purchase of Merchandise	4,600	5,100	6,050	7,100	7,700	8,400
Operating Expenses	7,740	7,975	8,202	8,115	8,055	7,960
Interest Expense	680	680	680	680	680	680
Taxes	250	360	400	450	475	490
Total Cash Payments	**$13,270**	**$14,115**	**$15,335**	**$16,345**	**$16,910**	**$17,530**
NET CASH FLOW	<$2,870>	<$2,215>	<$1,935>	<$1,345>	<$1,310>	<$1,030>

Projected 12-Month Statement of Cash Flows

Expected Cash Flows A business must have enough capital to cover negative cash flows for the first few months. *Which expense does not change from month to month?*

7	8	9	10	11	12
$17,000	$17,800	$18,700	$20,400	$22,300	$24,000
7,900	8,300	9,100	9,900	11,400	12,000
$9,100	**$9,500**	**$9,600**	**$10,500**	**$10,900**	**$12,000**
3,500	3,500	3,500	3,500	3,500	3,500
185	190	190	190	200	200
370	350	340	340	350	360
225	240	240	250	250	250
480	480	480	480	480	480
160	160	160	175	175	175
180	190	190	190	190	190
600	700	700	800	800	900
525	595	615	640	660	675
660	670	670	670	680	680
680	680	680	680	680	680
1,200	1,200	1,200	1,400	1,500	1,500
125	125	125	125	100	130
$8,890	**$9,080**	**$9,090**	**$9,440**	**$9,595**	**$9,720**
$210	$420	$510	$1,060	$1,305	$2,280

7	8	9	10	11	12
$16,500	$17,500	$18,600	$20,300	$21,400	$23,500
$16,500	**$17,500**	**$18,600**	**$20,300**	**$21,400**	**$23,500**
7,500	8,300	9,000	10,100	10,600	11,900
7,685	7,805	7,795	8,120	8,225	8,365
680	680	680	680	680	680
525	595	615	640	660	675
$16,390	**$17,380**	**$18,090**	**$19,540**	**$20,195**	**$21,620**
$110	$120	$510	$760	$1,205	$1,880

Negative Cash Flow for the 12-Month Period <$6,120>

FIGURE 9 Projected 3-Year Income Statement

Increasing Income *What is the anticipated increase of gross profit on sales between year one and year three?*

Cricket Lane Flowers

Projected 3-Year Income Statement			
YEAR	**1**	**2**	**3**
REVENUE			
Sales	$204,200	$264,000	$338,000
Cost of Merchandise Sold	95,350	122,000	159,000
Gross Profit on Sales	**$108,850**	**$142,000**	**$179,000**
EXPENSES			
Rent	42,000	42,000	43,500
Electricity	2,255	2,800	3,000
Heat/AC	4,375	5,400	5,700
Telephone	2,555	3,000	3,100
Insurance	5,760	6,000	6,300
Maintenance/Repairs	1,840	2,500	4,000
Miscellaneous	2,070	2,400	2,700
Wages	7,325	11,200	17,000
Taxes	6,135	8,200	10,000
Supplies	7,510	8,000	9,500
Interest	8,160	9,300	9,700
Advertising	19,000	15,000	14,000
Other	1,385	2,000	2,000
Total Expenses	**$110,370**	**$117,800**	**$130,500**
Net Income/<Loss>	<$1,520>	$24,200	$48,500

Projected 3-Year Statement of Cash Flows

Future Cash Flows While Molly expects an increase in cash receipts, she also expects higher cash payments. *How long does Molly expect to have a negative cash flow?*

Projected 3-Year Statement of Cash Flows			
YEAR	**1**	**2**	**3**
CASH RECEIPTS			
Cash Sales	$200,600	$262,500	$330,000
Total Cash Receipts	**$200,600**	**$262,500**	**$330,000**
CASH PAYMENTS			
Purchase of Merchandise	96,350	151,000	148,000
Operating Expenses	96,075	100,300	110,800
Interest Expense	8,160	9,300	9,700
Taxes	6,135	8,200	10,000
Total Cash Payments	**$206,720**	**$268,800**	**$278,500**
NET CASH FLOW	– $6,120	– $6,300	+ $51,500

FIGURE 10 Projected 3-Year Balance Sheet

Assets and Liabilities *The value of which assets remains constant for the first three years? Why?*

Cricket Lane Flowers

Projected 3-Year Balance Sheet

YEAR	1	2	3
ASSETS			
Cash in Bank	$13,000	$6,700	$58,200
Accounts Receivable	2,900	4,400	12,400
Display Equipment	8,000	8,000	8,000
Refrigeration Equipment	9,000	9,000	9,000
Delivery Equipment	17,500	17,500	17,500
Office Equipment	9,100	9,100	9,100
Computer Equipment	3,000	3,000	3,000
Merchandise Inventory	21,000	51,700	43,400
Supplies	500	500	500
Total Assets	**$84,000**	**$109,900**	**$161,100**
LIABILITIES			
Accounts Payable	8,400	10,100	12,800
Notes Payable	30,000	30,000	30,000
Total Liabilities	**$38,400**	**$40,100**	**$42,800**
OWNER'S EQUITY			
Molly Singer, Capital	45,600	69,800	118,300
Total Liabilities $ O.E.	**$84,000**	**$109,900**	**$161,100**

FIGURE 11 Chart of Accounts Sheet

Organized Records The Chart of Accounts assigns a number to each type of income or expense to accurately track transactions. *Could a software program help keep track of these accounts?*

CRICKET LANE FLOWERS
Chart of Accounts

ASSETS
101 Cash in Bank
105 Accounts Receivable
110 Merchandise Inventory
115 Supplies
120 Prepaid Insurance
125 Display Equipment
130 Refrigeration Equipment
140 Computer Equipment
145 Delivery Equipment

LIABILITIES
201 Accounts Payable
205 Notes Payable

OWNER'S EQUITY
301 Molly Singer, Capital
302 Molly Singer, Withdrawals
303 Income Summary

REVENUE
401 Sales Revenue
405 Sales Returns

COST OF MERCHANDISE
501 Purchases
505 Purchases Returns

EXPENSES
601 Advertising
605 Bank Card Fees
610 Delivery
615 Insurance
620 Interest
625 Maintenance
630 Miscellaneous
635 Rent
640 Supplies
645 Utilities
650 Tax

After You Read

React Do you think that you could develop a reasonable financial plan for a business using the information provided in this chapter?

Molly will invest the funds from the first three sources of capital (cash from owner, personal loans, and short-term commercial loan) in the business immediately. To cover the initial operation costs of the business, Molly has elected to use a home equity loan. A home equity loan is a loan based on the difference between the current market value of a home and the amount still owed on the mortgage. Home equity loans must be used carefully.

Accounting Procedures

Molly's accountant has set up a **chart of accounts**—a list of all the general ledger accounts that a business will use. This chart of accounts will provide Molly with a **framework,** or structure, for recording and reporting her business transactions. **Figure 11** shows her accounts.

Molly's accountant also recommended purchasing a software program to maintain Cricket Lane Flowers' accounting records, so all accounting procedures will be computerized. By using a software program, Molly will spend less time maintaining her accounting records and will have more time to run her business.

Molly will be responsible for entering all business transactions into the program. At the end of every month, the computer system will generate a trial balance, financial statements, and reports. Molly and her accountant will analyze Cricket Lane Flowers' monthly income statement, statement of cash flows, and balance sheet.

By comparing these financial statements with statements from previous months, Molly and her accountant will be able to evaluate the financial progress and position of her business. If a financial problem is identified, her accountant will make recommendations as to what Molly needs to do to correct the problem. It is only by careful and constant financial analysis that Molly can be assured her business is growing according to the projections outlined in her financial plan.

At the end of each quarter or year, her accountant will also see that all required local, state, and federal reports are submitted.

Budding Business
Molly knows that a solid business plan will help ensure the success of her new venture. *What are the three parts of a business plan that Molly must complete?*

Assessment

Review Key Concepts

1. **Identify** What are the four types of reports that are necessary for a financial plan?
2. **Explain** Why are more than one projected income statement and projected statement of cash flows included in a thorough financial plan?
3. **Describe** What is a chart of accounts?

Higher Order Thinking H.O.T.

4. **Evaluate** Review Molly's short-term and long-term goals developed for her strategic plan. Evaluate how her financial plan will support these goals.

English Language Arts

5. **Reviewing Rivals** A marketing plan helps a business owner to predict the cost of promoting and marketing her new company. An important part of developing a marketing plan is analyzing the competition. By doing this, the business owner can determine the competition's strengths and weaknesses and plan his or her marketing strategy accordingly. Write a short essay outlining the process Molly might use for evaluating potential business rivals to her new flower shop.

NCTE 5 Use different writing process elements to communicate effectively.

Mathematics

6. **Forecast Sensitivity** Use the projected 3-year income statement for Cricket Lane Flowers in Figure 9 to answer the following questions.
   a) What is the percentage of the cost of merchandise sold to sales for each year?
   b) If sales in year 1 were lower than projected and landed at $195,000 and sales then grew at 15 percent per year, what would the net income/(loss) be each year? Assume the same percentage calculated in part a) for cost of merchandise sold and all other expenses remain the same.

Math Concept **Calculate Revised Forecasts** To calculate the revised net income/(loss) replace the original sales figures with the revised ones and do the same for any expenses which have been impacted. Subtract total expense from sales.

Starting Hint Determine the revised sales forecast in year 2 by first identifying the new sales in year 1. Multiply this amount by the percentage of expected sales growth each year and add the result to the sales in year 1.

NCTM Problem Solving Apply and adapt a variety of appropriate strategies to solve problems.

Check your answers.

CHAPTER REVIEW

Visual Summary

Developing a Financial Plan

Determine Needed Capital

It is important to factor in all three types of capital to build an accurate and realistic financial plan.

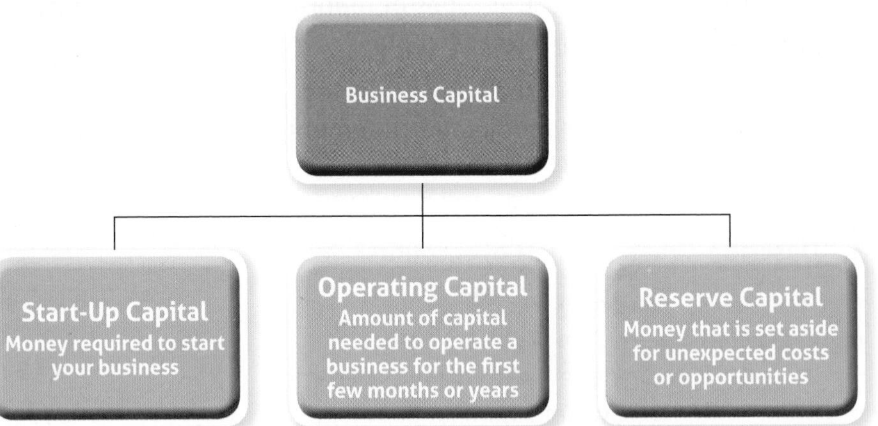

Business Capital
Start-Up Capital
Money required to start your business
Operating Capital
Amount of capital needed to operate a business for the first few months or years
Reserve Capital
Money that is set aside for unexpected costs or opportunities

Financial Forecasting

Projected financial statements can help you predict the future financial position of your business so that you can more accurately determine how much operating capital is needed.

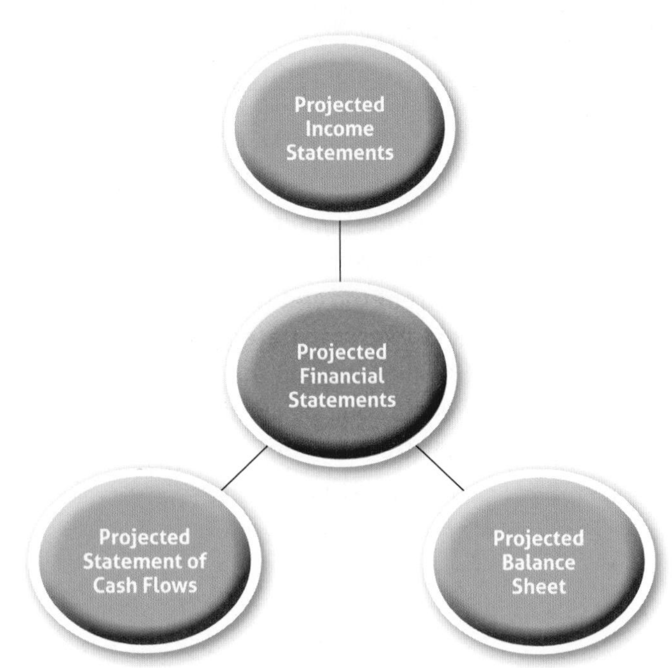

Projected Income Statements
Projected Financial Statements
Projected Statement of Cash Flows
Projected Balance Sheet

Try It!

Draw a chart like the one shown to note the two types of expenses that a business must consider. Then list examples of each type of expense.

________ Expenses	________ Expenses

Chapter Review and Assessment

Chapter Summary

- Start-up capital is money required to purchase assets for a business plus start-up costs.
- Start-up costs include legal, professional, and banking fees, licenses, permits, insurance, marketing costs, and maintenance costs.
- Estimates of start-up costs should be on the high side, as new business owners often underestimate or miss some of these costs.
- Operating capital is the money needed to operate the business for the first few years.
- Projected income statements are an estimate of the way in which income amounts will change over the next few months or years.
- Estimates of fixed expenses and variable expenses are included in the projected income statement.
- Lending institutions see these statements when you apply for commercial loans.
- Reserve capital is money set aside for unexpected costs or opportunities.
- The elements of a financial plan include a statement of required start-up capital, a projected 12-month income statement, a projected 12-month statement of cash flows, a projected 3-year income statement, a projected 3-year statement of cash flows, and a projected 3-year balance sheet.

Vocabulary Review

1. Create multiple-choice test questions for each content and academic vocabulary term.

- capital
- start-up capital
- start-up costs
- operating capital
- financial forecasting
- projected financial statements
- gross profit on sales
- fixed expenses
- variable expenses
- reserve capital
- chart of accounts
- complex
- revenue
- preliminary
- framework

Higher Order Thinking 

2. **Predict** What might happen if you estimate $1,200 for computer hardware but actually spend $2,000?
3. **Determine** Imagine you are helping a friend prepare a projected income statement for her new business. Determine what questions you will need to ask to prepare the statement.
4. **Outline** In one month, your business has $264,000 in sales, the merchandise sold cost $122,000, and total expenses were $117,800. Demonstrate calculating net income or loss.
5. **Categorize** Decide whether each of the following expenses are fixed or variable: rent, electricity, insurance, repairs, wages, taxes, supplies, loan interest, and advertising. Explain.
6. **Construct** If you were opening a used book store. What start-up assets would you need?
7. **Synthesize** How would you use an income and a projected income statement together?
8. **Theorize** What problems might a business owner face if he has insufficient start-up capital?
9. **Consider** What different advertising venues do you see on a regular basis? Which ones might you use to attract customers to a new business?

College and Career Readiness

Science

10. Small Business Software Technology has helped make starting a small business easier. There are now software programs available for such tasks as accounting, taxes, and even business planning.

Procedure Conduct research to learn more about the software programs available to small business owners.

Analysis What types of software are available? Compare the features and prices for different titles that perform the same tasks. Develop a spreadsheet to organize the information you find.

NSES E Develop abilities of technological design, understandings about science and technology.

Mathematics

11. Start-up Costs Use this information to answer the questions: What are total expected expenses in year 1 including all one-time start up costs? If revenues are $50,000 per year, how many years will it take to break-even?

One-time start-up costs		Assets	
Rent deposit	$4,000	Computer system	$2,500
Legal fees	$2,000	Truck	$20,000
Permits/Licenses	$300	Furniture	$1,500
		Other	$3,500
	Monthly recurring costs		
Insurance	$150	Rent	$2,500
Phone/Utilities	$400	Truck maintenance	$150

Math Concept **Calculate Break-Even** Calculate the break-even point by dividing the total start-up costs by the total net income to determine the number of years needed to break-even.

Starting Hint Calculate the total net income per year excluding start-up costs by first identifying the expected monthly expenses. Multiply this by 12 months to determine the expected annual expense. Subtract this from the estimated revenues in order to calculate total net income.

NCTM Problem Solving Build new mathematical knowledge through problem solving.

English Language Arts

12. Starting a Business To start your business you must consider where you will obtain capital. It is not unusual for a new business owner to borrow some of their start-up and operating capital from a financial institution. There are different types of loans available. Conduct research to discover what options are available to someone wanting to start a new business. What are some of the requirements to qualify for the loans? Write a summary of the information you gather. Might you be eligible for any of these loans if you decided to open your own business?

NCTE 7 Conduct research and gather, evaluate, and synthesize data to communicate discoveries.

Economics

13. Economic Factors Remember, projected revenues should be estimated low. Likewise, when estimating variable expenses, you should always estimate high. Fixed expenses generally remain constant. Consider though that interest rates go up after you have prepared your projected financial statements. This means that your interest payments would increase. What adjustments could you make to your already completed financial plan to accommodate the higher interest, without needing to find additional capital? Write a letter to your loan officer explaining how you would handle this.

Real-World Applications

14. Consultants Many small business owners need consultants to help deal with various business issues that arise. Research consultant services in your area. How much do these services cost? What types of services do they offer? Would they come to your business or would you have to go to them, for example would you have to take computer equipment to them for service? How quickly can they respond to issues? Is this an expense that you would include in your financial forecasting? Why or why not? Prepare a brief report to share your findings and answers with the class.

Your Financial Portfolio

Start with a Plan

Three brothers, Collin, Kyle, and J.C., plan to start a house painting business. All of them have experience painting, and they have identified plenty of work in an area downtown that is being renovated. They want to know how much start-up capital they will need to get their business going and to keep it going until it is solidly established.

Start-Up Costs

One-time costs:		
Equipment: 3 ladders	$305	
Paint sprayers	120	
Rollers, brushes, drop cloths, and other supplies (ongoing supplies will be expensed per job)	250	
Down payment for van	$3,000	
Total one-time costs		**$3,675**
Continuing costs (monthly):		
Insurance	$120	
Cell phone	25	
Van loan	625	
Van maintenance and gas	100	
Total monthly costs		**$870**
Total monthly costs × 12 months		**10,440**
Total start-up costs		**$14,115**

Identify

Start-up costs depend on the type of business, the size of the business, and the amount and kind of inventory and operating expenses. On a separate sheet of paper, give an example of the following types of businesses: service, retail, and manufacturing. Which might have the most expensive start-up costs? Why?

Unit 2

Unit Project

Evaluating Entrepreneurship

Ask Yourself...

Have you ever considered owning your own business? Have you thought about the advantages and disadvantages involved in being your own boss? Do you think you have what it takes to establish a successful business? Responses to these questions can help you consider whether entrepreneurship is right for you.

Your Objective

The goal of this project is to consider becoming an entrepreneur, explore possible business opportunities, evaluate whether your strengths and weaknesses are a good fit for entrepreneurship, and create a short presentation to share your findings.

Skills You'll Use

Success in defining goals and preparing financially for those goals depends on your skills. Some skills you might use include:

Academic Skills—Reading, writing, and research

21st Century Skills—Entrepreneurial literacy, creative thinking, decision making, speaking, listening, and interpersonal skills

Technology Skills—Word processing, keyboarding, Internet research, presentation software

Standards

NCTE 2 Read literature to build an understanding of the human experience.

NCTE 5 Use different writing process elements to communicate effectively.

NCTE 8 Use information resources to gather information and create and communicate knowledge.

NCTE 12 Use language to accomplish individual purposes.

STEP 1 Plan Your Business

Before you can be your own boss, there are many questions to be carefully considered.

- What type of product or service would you like your business to offer?
- Would you begin with a franchise, buy an existing business, or start one from scratch?
- Who would your competition be?
- Would you need to hire employees to help you run your business?
- In what areas of the business, such as accounting or sales, would you need assistance?

A successful business must begin with a business plan to organize the goals and actions of the company. Write your responses to the questions above and develop a vision statement that states the scope and purpose of your company.

STEP 2 Explore Entrepreneurship

Are you ready to be your own boss? There are resources to help you determine the answer. You can also learn from other people's experiences.

- Visit the Small Business Administration Web site and take their quiz to help you determine if you're ready to start your own business. If you discover you are not yet ready, what can you do to help prepare for owning a business in the future?
- Locate articles about successful entrepreneurs to find out how they prepared, what challenges they faced, and how they overcame the hurdles.
- Try to think about the specific business you would be interested in owning. What challenges do you think might arise to hinder your success? How might you avoid or overcome them?
- What other resources might you use to help you prepare for and plan your own successful business?

Write a brief report to share the results of the SBA quiz and a summary of the other entrepreneurs you researched. Also explain what steps you could take to prepare for entrepreneurship and describe possible challenges and solutions.

STEP 3 Build Relationships

How can you learn from someone else's mistakes and challenges? Arrange to meet with a local business owner to find out more about his or her personal obstacles as an entrepreneur. Ask for any advice he or she might offer on being prepared to own a business and making it a successful venture.

- Prepare a list of interview questions based on your previous research.
- Record your answers and notes legibly.
- Respect the business owner's time.
- Make eye contact and respond appropriately and with interest.
- Based on the information you learn, adjust your vision statement, if necessary.
- Use the responses and advice of the business owner to create a tip sheet for all prospective entrepreneurs.

STEP 4 Develop Your Presentation

Use the Unit 2 Project Checklist to plan and create your presentation.

STEP 5 Evaluate Your Presentation

Your presentation will be evaluated based on the following:

- Evaluation Rubric
- Creativity and organization of your information
- Mechanics—presentation and neatness
- Interview skills

Project Checklist

Plan

- ✔ Consider the type of business you might like to own and the specifics of how it will be organized and established.
- ✔ Research successful entrepreneurs and explore the Small Business Administration Web site for advice and resources to use in starting your own business.
- ✔ Take the quiz on the SBA site to determine readiness for owning a business.
- ✔ Meet with a business owner in your community for advice on preparing for and planning a successful business venture.

Write

- ✔ Develop a vision statement.
- ✔ Write a report sharing the results of the SBA readiness quiz and summarizing your research on entrepreneurs.
- ✔ List your interview questions.
- ✔ Create a tip sheet for prospective entrepreneurs, using the information learned in your research and interview.

Present

- ✔ Create an outline for your presentation.
- ✔ Create visuals and use technology to enhance your presentation.
- ✔ Speak clearly and concisely.
- ✔ Present your vision statement.
- ✔ Present the results of your SBA quiz and your research on entrepreneurs.
- ✔ Share the tip sheet you created with the results of your research and interview.
- ✔ Respond to questions from your classmates.

Mc Graw Hill **glencoe.com**

Evaluate Download a rubric you can use to evaluate your project.

UNIT 3

Business Finance Basics

Visual Literacy

With so many options, customers need a reason to choose one business over another. ***How might a business make itself stand out from similar businesses in the area?***

In Your World

Staying Profitable

Now that you know what it takes to start a business, you need to know how to keep it running. Financial management of a business includes knowing precisely what you are spending and how you are spending it. A critical factor for making a business grow is positive cash flow during the start-up period. This means bringing in more cash than you pay out, and to do this you need to find creative ways to keep your costs and expenses low.

Video Watch the Unit 3 video to learn about the rewards and challenges of managing a business's finances.

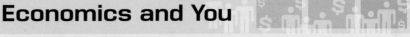

Reducing Costs Business owners set the pricing of their products and services based on a number of factors. For example, when you get a haircut, you are paying for your new look as well as the salon's rent, utilities, maintenance, advertising, and insurance. How can a business owner help keep costs as low as possible?

Economics and You

Economic Indicators

Economic indicators help guide business owners' financial decisions. Business cycles go through ups and downs. To get a sense of where in the business cycle the economy is and may be going, economists study changes in reports on indicators such as Gross Domestic Product and unemployment rates. If the economy is in a recession, a business owner may lay off employees or reduce inventories. When the economy is booming, businesses may expand and hire new employees. How might economic indicators impact your spending habits and budgeting? What adjustments might you have to make with your financial plans?

glencoe.com

Activity Download an Economics and You Worksheet Activity.

CHAPTER 6

Sources of Funding

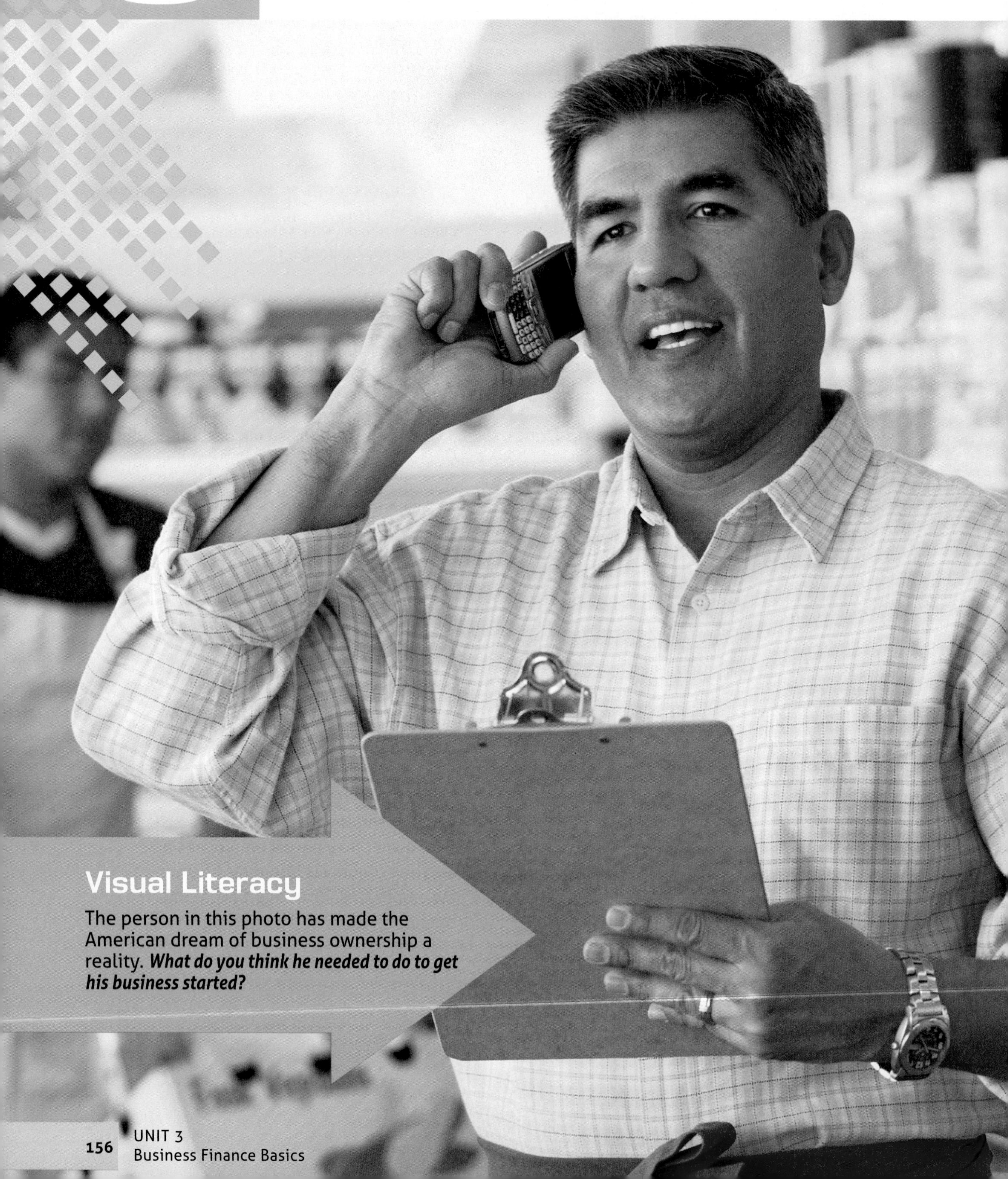

Visual Literacy

The person in this photo has made the American dream of business ownership a reality. ***What do you think he needed to do to get his business started?***

Discovery Project

Starting a Business

Key Question

What is the most important thing an entrepreneur can do before starting any new business venture?

Project Goal

You earned a bachelor's degree in child development and want to run a day care out of your home. Your grandmother, a retired nurse, has volunteered to help you with about 25 percent of your start-up costs. She has also agreed to work with you as a part-time day care assistant, and will collect a small salary once you start making a profit. But before you make any commitments, you need to do your research.

- List the items needed to start a day care business.
- List the licenses, permits, certifications, and insurance required by your state.
- Using these lists as a guide, estimate the start-up and operating costs.
- Identify the future needs and costs of the day care.
- Contact day care centers in your area to learn about their services and fees.
- Determine the sources of funding you will consider.

Ask Yourself...

- *How much money do I need to get started?*
- *What will I need in addition to cash and inventory?*
- *How can I prepare for unanticipated expenses?*
- *What can I offer that other day care centers in the area do not?*

Create Media Products

Using graphics and illustration software, create a flyer to advertise your new day care business.

glencoe.com

Evaluate Download an assessment rubric.

THE BIG IDEA

The success and funding of small businesses and the spirit of entrepreneurship are essential to the American economy.

ASK STANDARD & POOR'S

Fast Cash

Q *My family runs a small business. Recently a lot of unexpected expenses came up, and now we need $4,000 in a hurry. We just expanded our business, so we have no cash in reserves. How can we obtain the money?*

A If you have outstanding (unpaid) invoices from customers whom you have billed for your products, you can take those invoices to a bank and borrow against those receivables. If you have orders to fill but need money for supplies, you can speak to a lender about a short-term commercial loan.

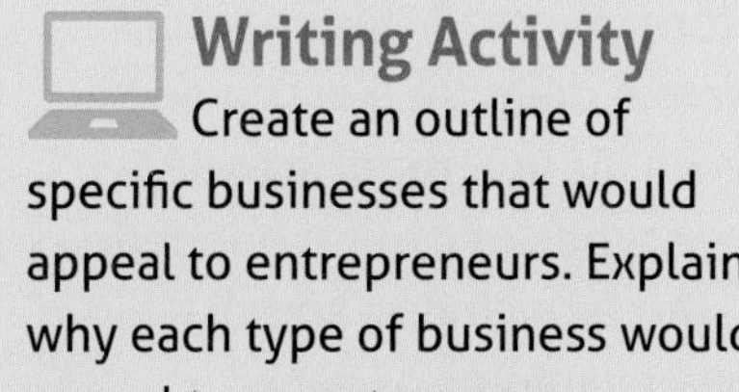

Writing Activity

Create an outline of specific businesses that would appeal to entrepreneurs. Explain why each type of business would appeal to an entrepreneur.

Reading Guide

Before You Read

The Essential Question When you dream of owning a business, you know there will be substantial expenses. But what can you do when you realize the costs go beyond what you can afford?

Main Idea

To start or expand a business, it is crucial that you accurately estimate the amount of funding you will need. There are many sources of funding for entrepreneurs, including the Small Business Administration.

Content Vocabulary

- operating costs
- reserve fund
- private financing
- commercial debt financing
- commercial loan
- line of credit
- secured loan
- unsecured loan
- Small Business Administration (SBA)
- LowDoc Program
- business credit card
- private investor
- commercial finance company
- venture capital firm
- Small Business Investment Companies (SBICs)

Academic Vocabulary

You will see these words in your reading and on your tests.

- routine
- sound
- depressed
- voice

Graphic Organizer

Before you read this chapter, create a diagram like the one shown. As you read, identify three types of capital needed to start a business, and list three examples of each.

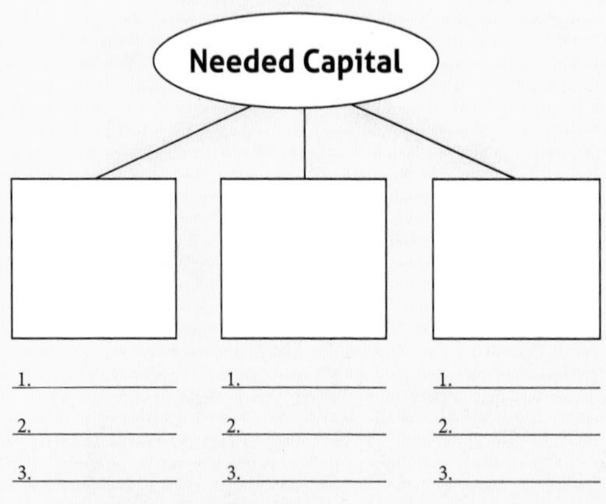

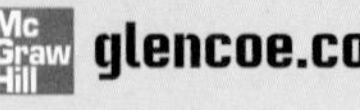

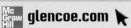

Print this graphic organizer.

Standards

Academic

Mathematics

NCTM Connections Recognize and use connections among mathematical ideas.

NCTM Representation Select, apply, and translate among mathematical representations to solve problems.

NCTM Number and Operations Understand meanings of operations and how they relate to one another.

English Language Arts

NCTE 2 Read literature to build an understanding of the human experience.

NCTE 12 Use language to accomplish individual purposes.

Social Studies

NCSS V G Analyze the extent to which groups and institutions meet individual needs and promote the common good in contemporary and historical settings.

NCTM *National Council of Teachers of Mathematics*

NCTE *National Council of Teachers of English*

NCSS *National Council for the Social Studies*

NSES *National Science Education Standards*

Common Core

Reading Determine central ideas or themes of a text and analyze their development; summarize the key supporting details and ideas.

Writing Draw evidence from literary or informational texts to support analysis, reflection, and research.

Writing Conduct short as well as more sustained research projects based on focused questions, demonstrating understanding of the subject under investigation.

Starting a New Business

What would you need to start a new business?

Jenny, age 8, and Matt, age 7, are going into business. They are going to set up a lemonade stand—called J & M Lemonade—in front of Matt's house. A lot of people walk down that street, which is close to a school and a park and provides plenty of foot traffic. Jenny and Matt figure that their location will provide plenty of customers. It is summer, and people are thirsty. Cold lemonade will be in demand.

Before they begin selling lemonade, however, Jenny and Matt must decide what things they will need to get their business started. In addition to lemonade, Jenny says they will need a large pitcher, a stand or table, and some cups. Matt adds a large sign, a box for their money, and some ice cubes to the list. They agree that they will also need coins to make change for customers.

As with all business operations, Jenny and Matt will need cash, equipment, and supplies, as well as goods or services to sell. How do you think they will get these items? They will probably do what you did when you were their age: They will go home and see what they can find. Their families may help them find a pitcher, a table, and some cardboard to make a sign. They may give them some coins to use for change and buy the lemonade and cups.

Soon Jenny and Matt have all the items they need, and they set up their stand. J & M Lemonade is now part of the free enterprise system.

Reading Check

List What are some basic essentials that all businesses need to get started?

Business Entrepreneurs

What does it take to become an entrepreneur?

When you were younger, you may have had a small business similar to Jenny and Matt's lemonade stand. Like Jenny or Matt, you were an entrepreneur. An entrepreneur is an individual who takes the risk of starting a new business. Entrepreneurs are highly motivated people who transform ideas for products or services into real-world businesses. About 80 percent of the 23 million business operations in the United States are run by one owner. Remember, entrepreneurship is an economic factor of production. In fact, entrepreneurs are the backbone of the American economy.

Section Objectives

- **Explain** the role of entrepreneurs.
- **Differentiate** among start-up costs, operating costs, and reserve funds.
- **Identify** sources of personal and private financing.
- **Discuss** the options available through bank funding.
- **List** the factors banks consider when approving commercial loans.

As You Read

Imagine If you were to open a business to sell a product or service, what would it be? What is the first thing you would do to get started?

High School Entrepreneurs

In a recent Gallup poll, seven out of every ten high school students said that they would like to start a business. It is possible for a high school student to start his or her own business. For example, Fred DeLuca is a successful entrepreneur who started his business shortly after graduating from high school. In 1965, DeLuca borrowed $1,000 from a friend and opened Pete's Super Submarines, a sandwich shop in Bridgeport, Connecticut. Today you may know DeLuca's business as Subway. Subway has over 23,000 restaurants in 82 countries.

Reading Check

Define What is an entrepreneur?

Funding a Business

Why do many entrepreneurs need to find outside sources for funding?

One of the major concerns when starting a business is how it will be financed. People who take on new business ventures usually need far more money than they realize. Jenny and Matt started their lemonade stand with nothing. They had no lemonade, supplies, or cash. They funded their business with cash and other assets that their families provided. They hoped to sell several cups of lemonade and take in some money. Chances are that the money they took in did not cover the cost of the lemonade and other supplies.

Family members supported J & M Lemonade financially, but they did not expect to make a profit on their investment. If it were not for their financial support, Jenny and Matt could not have started their business because other sources of funds were not available.

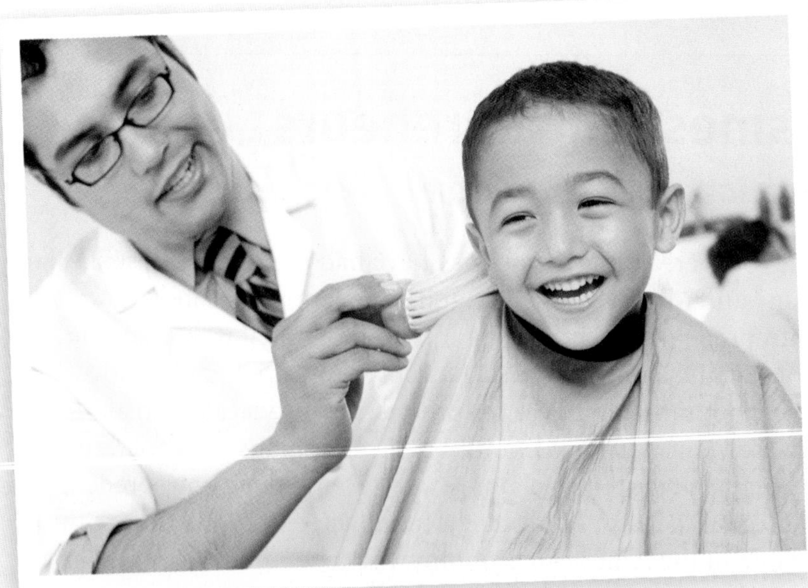

Getting Started
A great idea is just the beginning. *What other factors did the business owner in this photo have to consider before starting out?*

Success Stories
Every successful business you can name needed money to start its operations. *Why is it so important to make a realistic estimate of how much money you will need?*

As a young adult, you would require funding if you decided to start your own business. Unfortunately, it is not easy to get funding for a new business from an outside source. Banks and other financial institutions are very selective about who receives loans. They also expect to get a good return on their investment.

Reading Check

Explain Why are banks and other financial institutions so selective about who receives loans?

Determining Needed Capital

Why is it so important to know how much money is needed to start up a business?

When you are starting a business, the first thing you must do is make a realistic estimate of how much capital you will need. As you know, capital is the money you need to establish a business, to operate it for the first few months, and to expand the business. Determining the capital needed to start up your business is one of the steps of developing a financial plan.

Start-Up Costs

The first goal in determining needed capital is to identify start-up costs. Start-up costs usually require a large amount of cash. If you attempt to estimate the costs without careful analysis, your estimate will probably be too low. To analyze your costs, you should list everything you will require to begin to operate.

Most businesses have some common start-up costs:

- Inventory needed to open the business
- Equipment, fixtures, and display cases
- Security deposit for rented space
- Advertising and promotions
- Insurance
- Professional fees (such as lawyers' fees)
- Remodeling costs (such as creating office space)
- Legal permits and licenses
- Supplies

Your next task is to assign an estimated cost to each item. Unless you list every anticipated cost, your total estimate will not be realistic.

Landscaping firms and convenience stores are different types of businesses, and each has different requirements for operating. Start-up costs vary among businesses and industries. Make sure that you research and explore the industry you are entering.

Operating Costs

Besides determining your start-up costs, you must also estimate your operating costs for the first 90 to 120 days. **Operating costs** are the ongoing expenses for operating a business.

Start-up costs and operating costs are separate cost categories. It is critical that you estimate both types of costs as accurately as possible. If you use all of your money for start-up costs, then you will not have any money available to pay your operating costs. When you start a new business, the amount you earn usually will not be enough to cover your expenses. In many cases, this is especially true for the first couple of years of operation. If you cannot pay your suppliers, rent, or utility bills, your business will be in serious trouble.

When you prepare your budget for the first 90 to 120 days of business, you will include your expected income as well as your estimated monthly costs. Remember it is not unusual for a business to not make a profit for the first couple of years of operation.

Businesses have a number of common operating costs:

- Payroll
- Rent
- Insurance premiums
- Utility bills
- Office expenses
- Advertising
- Delivery charges
- Bank charges and other fees

reality bytes

Internet Finance Education

In order to take advantage of the many loans available to entrepreneurs, you need some basic financial management skills. There are many books and resources available. You can also sign up for online courses and complete them in your spare time. Each online course is sent to you via e-mail on a daily or weekly basis and is designed to help you learn a specific skill or solve a particular problem. There are no grades or degrees, but many courses are free.

Reserve Fund

Before starting a business, you will also have to estimate the amount of money you may need at a later date for growth. A **reserve fund** is money that can be made available for the future expansion of a business. You may need additional money to purchase merchandise or equipment, or perhaps to lease a truck. This money will allow for growth and help you avoid having to borrow additional capital.

Jenny and Matt's lemonade stand stayed in business for only two hours. They did not plan to operate an ongoing business. Of course, you hope that your business will have a much longer life. Therefore, careful financial planning for the future is critical. Consider other expenses when looking ahead and estimating a reserve fund:

- Additional equipment for increased business
- Advertising and other promotional costs
- Capital for any unexpected costs or decreased sales
- Maintaining a positive cash flow
- Expansion of facilities
- Getting and keeping the right amount of inventory

When you have estimated the amounts of your start-up and operating costs and your reserve fund, you will have a good idea of your business's financial needs. You will see what your cash flow will look like during the first months of operation. Then you can estimate the total amount of capital you will need to establish your business and begin to operate.

Reading Check

Describe What is the purpose of a reserve fund?

COMMON CENTS

Paid in Full

When you get your first credit card, use it wisely. Decide how much you can afford to charge each month and stick to that budget. Be sure to pay your bill in full every month. If you do, you will avoid high interest charges and save.

Concept Application

How would good use of personal credit cards help you in starting up a business in the future?

The Perfect Place

Location, location, location is an often-repeated phrase in real estate to emphasize the importance of where you buy a home or business. *What factors would you analyze before settling on the location of your new business?*

Economics and You

Interest Rates and Risk

One of the goals of an economy is stable prices. To stabilize prices, the government controls interest rates. The Federal Reserve System (the Fed) adjusts interest rates by changing the rate it charges for banks to borrow money. The banks then adjust their interest rates for borrowers accordingly. The United States Prime Rate is generally the Fed Funds Target Rate plus three percent. So if the Fed's rate is 1 percent; the Prime Rate is 4 percent. Lenders often use the Prime Rate as a guideline in setting its own rates for loans. If a loan is risky, the lender would increase the interest rate. For secured loans, the interest rate may be closer to the Prime Rate because the risk is lower. Some loans offer an adjustable interest rate that is tied to the Prime Rate. In that case, the monthly payments would vary as the interest portion of the payment changes. There is generally a floor and ceiling rate included in an adjustable rate loan.

	1995	2000	2005	2009
Prime rate—an indication of the rate banks charge large corporations	8.83	9.23	6.19	3.25
Discount rate—the rate financial institutions are charged to borrow funds from Federal Reserve banks	5.21	5.73	4.19	0.50
Treasury bond rate—the yield on long-term (20-year) U.S. government debt obligations	6.95	6.23	4.64	4.11

Personal Finance Connection When borrowing money research the U.S. Prime Rate as it is the base line that banks use when deciding on the interest rates they will offer their customers. Banks add the profit they want to the Prime Rate to arrive at loan interest rates. Shop around for a loan; as banks will offer different rates based on a customer's credit rating and risk (i.e. offering collateral or not offering collateral).

Critical Thinking When would it be advantageous to take out a loan with an adjustable interest rate? When would it be risky? Explain.

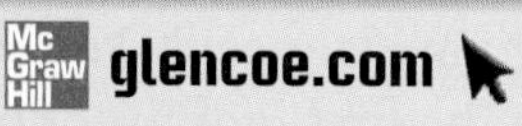

Activity Download an Economics and You Worksheet Activity.

Personal and Private Financing

What is the difference between personal and private financing?

After you have determined the amount of money you require, you will need to figure out how you will get it. Getting affordable and sufficient financing is often a major problem when starting or expanding a business. However, there are many sources of funding available for businesses. Initially, you will probably explore the possibility of personal financing.

Personal Financing

Many people begin small businesses with funds from their own personal assets. In fact, personal assets make up a large part of the start-up funding for most new business ventures in the United States.

The primary reason for using this method is that new small businesses often have difficulty getting affordable funding. Banks and other financial institutions are not interested in risky or unproven business ventures. You cannot just walk into a bank and tell the manager that you have a great idea for a new business and expect the loan officer to hand you money.

Banks are more interested in funding existing businesses that have reported profit over a period of time. These businesses are safer investments and provide banks and other financial institutions with the assurance of a good return on their money.

When starting a small business, you may have to rely on your own assets to finance the start-up and operating costs. You might use your personal savings or investments such as stocks or bonds.

You might also use loans from family members and friends to help finance the business. However, with these sources of capital, you may not have enough cash to get the business going.

Consumer Loans In order to get the funds you need, consider applying for a consumer, or personal, loan. Most financial institutions require that consumer loans be secured with collateral. Collateral is a form of security (usually an asset such as a car or home) that helps guarantee that a loan will be repaid. When you pledge collateral for a loan, the risk to the bank is reduced. As a result, you have a much better chance of getting funding and can receive better interest rates. If you cannot pay back the loan, the financial institution can take the property that you have pledged as collateral.

Home Equity Loans A home equity loan is a loan based on the difference between the current market value of a home and the amount still owed on the mortgage. A home equity loan may also be called a second mortgage.

Home equity loans are fairly safe for financial institutions because they are secured by property. As a result these loans are usually easier to get than consumer loans, and some entrepreneurs who own homes use this source.

To determine the maximum amount of this type of loan, the financial institution will find out the current market value of a home and its equity. Equity is the value of the home less the current balance on the home's mortgage loan.

Suppose a house has a present market value of $175,000, and the mortgage has a balance of $65,000. The equity in the house is $110,000 ($175,000 − $65,000 = $110,000).

Banks will usually allow an owner to borrow up to 80 percent of the current market value of the home. In this example, the maximum amount the bank would loan on a home worth $175,000 would be $140,000 ($175,000 − .80 or 80% = $140,000).

However, there is an existing mortgage with a current balance of $65,000. Therefore, to figure out the amount that the bank would loan, subtract the mortgage balance from $140,000. In this example, the loan cannot exceed $75,000 ($140,000 − $65,000 = $75,000).

Environmental Literacy

To ensure future success you will need to be able to apply an understanding of core subjects to contemporary issues such as the environment. Alternative fuels and other "green" technologies are playing an increasing role in the development of the global landscape. Environmental literacy includes the ability to study and examine environmental issues and make accurate conclusions concerning solutions. Your ability to recognize and address environmental challenges will benefit you as you move forward in school and/or your career.

Write About It

Think of a situation you read about or watched recently that involved environmental issues. Were there aspects of the situation you did not understand? If you are not familiar with any issues, research to find an issue to explore further. Research the environmental issue and prepare a brief report to present to the class.

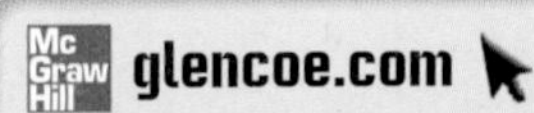

Activity Download a Career and College Readiness Worksheet Activity.

GO FIGURE Mathematics

A Home Equity Loan

Home equity loans are based on the difference between the current market value of a home and the amount still owed on the mortgage.

EXAMPLE Drew wants to apply for a home equity loan at Wilton Bank to start his new Internet company. He presently owns a home that has a market value of $160,000. He has an existing mortgage balance of $90,000. What is the maximum amount the bank will lend to Drew for a home equity loan?

Formula Adjusted Market Value of Home – Existing Mortgage Balance = Home Equity Loan

Solution

A. Find the adjusted market value of the home.

Market Value × .80 or 80% = Adjusted Market Value of Home

$160,000 × .80 or 80% = $128,000

The adjusted market value of the home is $128,000.

B. Find the maximum amount of the home equity loan.

Adjusted Market Value Home – Existing Mortgage Equity Loan Balance = Home equity Loan

$128,000 – $90,000 = $38,000

Wilton Bank will lend Drew up to $38,000 for a home equity loan.

Your Turn

If the adjusted market value of your home is $220,000 and the existing mortgage balance is $142,000, how much would you be allowed to borrow for a home equity loan?

This type of loan is available only if there is a substantial amount of equity in the property. In other words, a home must be worth a lot more than the amount owed on the mortgage. The negative aspect of a home equity loan is that if the business fails, the owner could lose his or her home. A recent study found that more than one-half of new businesses fail during the first five years. Considering this high failure rate, you should think seriously before you finance your business with a home equity loan.

Private Financing

If you cannot get enough capital through personal financing, you must look to other sources. The next option might be private financing. **Private financing** is borrowing money from family or friends. This type of funding is attractive because it involves little paperwork and often requires no collateral and low, or no, interest payments. The disadvantage is that it can lead to personal conflicts if the business is unsuccessful, and you are unable to repay a loan.

Reading Check

Recall Where do many American entrepreneurs find the initial funds for their new ventures?

Bank Funding

What is the difference between a secured and an unsecured loan?

If personal and private financing are insufficient, you may have to apply for a business loan to get additional money. One of your first sources for such financing is your local bank.

Commercial debt financing is borrowing money from a bank or other financial institution to fund a business. Another option is a **commercial loan,** which is a loan that finances a new or ongoing business. Larger banks give out commercial loans, but they are often interested in larger, more established business operations with revenues of millions of dollars. Therefore, when small businesses need money, smaller, local banks are their logical source.

A small bank can better relate to small business needs, and it can offer advice and assist you with other services. Getting funding from local banks has both advantages and disadvantages.

Advantages might include:

- They are highly experienced in dealing with small businesses.
- They offer a wide variety of loan plans.
- They offer advice and other business services.
- They are community-oriented and are interested in seeing local businesses succeed.

Disadvantages might include:

- They are closely regulated by the government.
- There is extensive paperwork, investigation, and documentation involved in the loan process.
- They are conservative by nature and may reject your loan if your business appears too risky.

If you and your local bank are interested in establishing a working relationship, you should know what loan options are available. Most large and even smaller banks offer many online services and provide a wealth of information on loans on their Web sites. All banks offer a wide variety of loans, and a good banker will recommend the loan that is best for you and your business.

Short-Term Commercial Loans

A short-term commercial loan is a business loan that is usually made for a term of one year or less. Most are written for 30-, 60-, or 90-day periods. These loans are typical for small businesses. They are designed to help the business meet short-term financial obligations and help with cash flow during a specific time or season. You could use the money for purchasing merchandise before a peak sales period, acquiring equipment, or paying unexpected bills.

Bank On It
A small, local bank may be an option for many new business owners. *Why might such a bank be motivated to help a new business?*

For example, during the summer months, Durango's Ski Shop begins to prepare its inventory for the upcoming winter season. The owner, Sabrina, decides that she needs a large quantity of new skis. Because the ski shop's sales are typically low in the summer, she has to apply for temporary financing. With a short-term commercial loan, Sabrina can purchase the inventory she needs now and repay the loan with the profits from winter ski sales.

Long-Term Commercial Loans

A long-term commercial loan is a business loan that is made for a term of one to five years. These loans are normally used by larger, established businesses that require great amounts of funding. Because these are large loans, the businesses will need more time to pay them back. They may use the funds for expensive equipment, the relocation of facilities, the expansion of storage areas, or other major expenses.

New or smaller businesses might have trouble getting these loans. Banks consider such businesses to be less stable. Therefore, banks do not want to take the risk that the loan will not be repaid.

Lines of Credit

A **line of credit** is an arrangement in which bank customers can borrow a certain amount of money from the bank immediately. This makes funds available for unexpected costs and **routine,** or regular, expenses. A store owner can borrow all or part of that money at any time and for any purpose. For example, if the plumbing breaks and costs $8,000 to repair, money is available.

The main advantage of this type of funding is that you do not pay any interest unless you access the funds. But once you borrow an amount from the line of credit, the bank will charge you interest.

The bank will review your available credit every so often. Based on your history of accessing the account and repayment pattern, the bank may increase or decrease the amount of credit. This type of funding is intended for short-term costs. For this reason, the bank also expects you to repay the money in a short period of time.

Secured and Unsecured Loans

A **secured loan** is a loan that is backed by collateral. Most short-term and long-term loans must be backed by collateral. Banks will hold the title to the equipment or merchandise used as collateral until the loan is repaid. Most business loans are secured. Usually only a well-established, profitable business can obtain unsecured loans. An **unsecured loan** is a loan that does not require collateral from the borrower. If an unsecured loan is approved, it is usually short-term. Because of the increased risk, the interest rate on an unsecured loan is usually higher.

Reading Check

Extend With so many loan options available, how can you be sure to choose the right loan for you and your business?

Commercial Loan Applications

What are the five C's of credit?

New and expanding small businesses often have difficulty getting necessary funding. Banks use certain standards to judge a company's financial position and determine how much risk to accept. Banks are conservative and selective as to which businesses they approve for financing.

You will learn more about the criteria banks and credit card companies use to determine your creditworthiness in later chapters.

Keeping Busy
A business that depends on seasonal sales will prepare its inventory in advance of the busy season. *Why would the owner of this type of business choose a short-term commercial loan?*

When you fill out an application for credit, you must answer questions regarding your credit history, your annual income, and your valuable assets. These institutions want a complete financial picture. When evaluating commercial loan applications, banks will examine these same factors as well as other information. They want a financial picture of both you and your business.

The Five C's of Credit

If you apply for a commercial loan, the bank will first examine the five C's of credit: character, capacity, capital, collateral, and conditions (see **Figure 1**).

Character Banks want to make sure that you are capable of paying off the loan on time. They will consider your business experience, and your dealings with other local businesses. Your prior history with the bank, your reputation in the local business community, and comments from your creditors will also be important. In addition, proof of your skills as a manager will be essential.

Capacity The bank will determine whether your business has or will have enough cash to repay the loan on time. It will also examine your sales history, statements of cash flow, and profits reported by your business.

Capital The bank will look to see whether you have invested a considerable amount of your personal assets in the business. Some financial institutions require that you use your personal assets for at least 30 percent of the capital needed to start your business.

Collateral The bank will make sure that you have enough business assets to secure the loan. Does your business own office equipment, machinery, delivery equipment, or real estate? Good collateral is also an important element for approval.

Financial Picture
A loan officer will look carefully at the information you provide before deciding to grant you a commercial loan. *What is meant by a "financial picture" of you and your business?*

Conditions Conditions describe the intended purpose of the loan. Will the money be used for working capital, additional equipment, or inventory? The lender will also consider local economic conditions and the overall climate, both within your industry and in other industries that could affect your business.

Business Plan

The bank will also examine your business plan to make sure that your business is financially **sound,** or firm. It looks to see whether you have a clear vision of where you want your business to go and whether you have identified the necessary steps to achieve your goals. Then the bank can better measure your financial needs.

Banks often base loan decisions on the business plan. It is vital that your plan be clear, accurate, and well planned. Include the three basic parts of a business plan that focus on a strategic plan, a marketing plan, and a financial plan. A business plan can include a variety of components, such as an executive summary, mission statement, company description, product and service plan, management team plan, industry overview, market analysis, competitive analysis, marketing plan, operational plan, organization plan, financial plan, growth plan, contingency plan, and supporting documents, as well as a cover page, title page, and table of contents. Spending extra time to make sure that your business plan has accurate information could mean the difference between getting the money you need or not.

FIGURE 1 **The Five C's of Credit**

Current Conditions Banks look at your five C's of credit to determine whether they should grant you a loan. *Considering your local area and the current state of the economy, what are the conditions that a lender will analyze?*

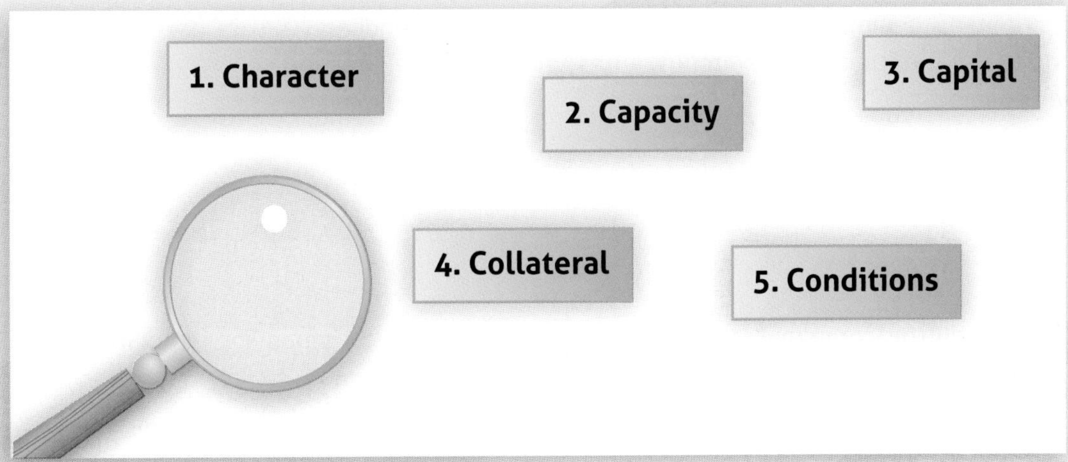

Document Detective

An Application for Business Loan

By applying for a loan through the SBA, you will have a better chance of receiving the funding you need to start your business. An application for a loan from the Small Business Administration (SBA) contains:

- Name and contact information
- Amount requested
- Intended use of loan
- Other outstanding federal loans or debt

U.S. Small Business Administration

APPLICATION FOR BUSINESS LOAN

Individual: *Jason True*
Full Address: *1647 west Alvarez, Phoenix, AZ 85001*

Name of Applicant Business: *True Business Forms*
Tax I.D. No. or SSN:

Full Street Address of Business: *5743 Sun Palm Lane*
Tel. No. (inc. A/C): *480-672-1853*

City: *Phoenix* | County: *Maricopa* | State: *AZ* | Zip: *85001*

Number of Employees (Including subsidiaries and affiliates)
At Time of Application: *14*
If Loan is Approved: *22*
Subsidiaries or Affiliates (Separate for above): ______

Type of Business: *Business to Business*
Date Business Established:

Bank of Business Account and Address: *First Merit # 3006482-1 5812 Tuskan Lane Phoenix, AZ 85001*

Use of Proceeds (Enter Gross Dollar Amount Round to the Nearest Hundreds)	Loan Requested	Use of Proceeds (Enter Gross Dollar Amount Round to the Nearest Hundreds)	Loan Request
Land Acquisition	*$ 150,000*	Pay off SBA Loans	
New Construction/ Expansion Repair	*$ 250,000*	Pay off Bank Loans (Non SBA Associated)	
Acquisition and/or Repair Machinery and Equipment		Other Debit Payment (Non SBA Associated)	
Inventory Purchase		All Other	
Working Capital (including Accounts Payable)		Total Loan Requested	*$ 400,000*
Acquisition of Existing Business		Term of Loan (Requested Mat.)	*10* Yrs.

PREVIOUS SBA OR OTHER FEDERAL GOVERNMENT DEBT: If you or any principles or affiliates have 1) ever requested Government Financing or 2) are delinquent on the repayment of any Federal Debt complete the following:

Name of Agency	Original Amount of Loan	Date of Request	Approved or Declined	Balance	Current or Past Due
SBA	$ *100,000*	*6/28/20--*	*Approved*	$ *12,500*	*Current*
	$			$	

Key Points In order to be granted a loan by the SBA, you need to provide a personal financial history, inform them of the amount of the loan you are requesting, and describe how you intend to use the funds. The example represents just a small portion of the full Application for Business Loan.

FIND the Solutions

Review Key Concepts

1. How many employees will this company have if the loan is approved?
2. How will this company utilize the funds?
3. What is the total amount of the loan?
4. How much does this company owe the SBA for a previous loan?
5. What is the requested term of the loan?

Assessment

Review Key Concepts

1. **List** What factors must banks consider when approving commercial loans?
2. **Identify** What are the sources of personal and private financing?
3. **Explain** What is the role of entrepreneurs?
4. **Discuss** What are some options available through bank funding?
5. **Differentiate** How are start-up costs, operating costs, and reserve funds different?

Higher Order Thinking 

6. **Categorize** Fixed costs do not vary with changes in production or sales. Variable costs respond directly and proportionately to changes in production or sales. What are some typical business expenses that would fall into each cost category?

21st Century Skills

7. **Solve Problems** Katie has operated a résumé writing service out of her home for the past two years. Because she has many new customers, her added equipment and supplies will no longer fit in her extra bedroom. Katie is looking for a new location for the business, but she realizes that the change will bring additional costs. Identify sources of funding that Katie may be able to access. Which sources of funding do you think she should avoid? Which sources do you think would be best?

Mathematics

8. **Starting up** Erin has decided to start a business. She has estimated that her start-up costs will be $11,500. Her operating cost estimate for the first 6-months is $7,500. She also wants to keep a reserve fund of $12,000 in case of emergency or for future expansion. Erin has saved $22,000 for the business so far. How much will she need to borrow in order to have all of the funding she requires? What percentage of the total costs estimated will be borrowed?

Math Concept **Calculate Borrowing Needs** To calculate the total amount needed to borrow for a start-up business determine the total estimated amount of start-up costs and subtract from this figure the total amount already saved.

Starting Hint Determine the total start-up costs needed for the business by identifying the estimates for start-up, 6-months of operating costs as well as any reserve fund desired. Add these figures together.

NCTM Number and Operations Understand meanings of operations and how they relate to one another.

Check your answers.

Section Objectives

- **Describe** the services and benefits of the Small Business Administration.
- **Identify** alternative sources of funding for a business.
- **Explain** why small businesses are important to the American economy.

As You Read

Decide Would you prefer to borrow start-up money from family and friends, or from a financial institution? Explain.

Small Business Administration

What kinds of services does the Small Business Administration provide?

No matter how good your business may look on paper, banks might not provide necessary financing. This is especially true for new or start-up businesses. As a new or start-up business owner, you may not have a sound credit history or enough collateral, managerial experience, or profit from operations. Therefore, you will need some help to get your loan. One option might be the federal government.

The federal government recognizes the importance of small businesses in the American economy and, therefore, provides assistance to them. The **Small Business Administration (SBA)** is an independent agency of the federal government that offers assistance to people who are starting small businesses and to those who want to expand existing businesses. Its services include management training, organizational guidance, and assistance in getting funding.

Almost 99 percent of American businesses are considered "small businesses" under the SBA guidelines. Thousands of businesses take advantage of services offered by the SBA every year. If the SBA did not exist, many small businesses would never get the money they need.

The SBA offers many loan programs to small businesses that have a hard time getting the funding they need through other methods. If you cannot convince the bank that you are a good loan candidate and your business will succeed, you might try the SBA loan programs.

Reading Check

Recall To whom can you turn if you need extra help getting a loan?

Giving Credit
Muhammad Yunus won the Nobel Peace Prize for developing the concept of microcredit, which involves giving loans to entrepreneurs unable to qualify for traditional loans. *What is the number one source of start-up funds for new entrepreneurs?*

Federal Assistance
The SBA's Guaranteed Loan Program is an alternative if your bank denies your loan request. *If you have a great new business idea and a financial plan, why might you still need extra help getting a loan?*

SBA Guaranteed Loans

What is the benefit of receiving an SBA guaranteed loan?

The most common type of SBA loan is obtained through the Guaranteed Loan Program. To get an SBA guaranteed loan for your small business, you apply to a bank or other financial institution for a commercial loan. If the bank denies your request, you can then complete an application for an SBA loan. Your bank submits your application to the SBA under the Guaranteed Loan Program.

The SBA examines your application. If it approves the loan, it authorizes the bank to give you the funding. The SBA then guarantees a major portion of the loan. At present the SBA will guarantee up to 85 percent of a bank loan for $150,000 or less and 75 percent of a loan for more than $150,000. The repayment period usually cannot exceed seven years.

With this guarantee by the federal government, banks are more willing to grant funding to a small business. The bank knows that if you default on the loan, the SBA will repay the majority of the money you owe. Remember, you do not borrow money from the SBA. You get your loan from a bank or some other financial institution, but the SBA guarantees a large portion of the loan.

In the past many people were frustrated by the amount of paperwork and the time it took to process loan applications through the SBA. In response, the SBA introduced the LowDoc (Low Documentation) Program in 1993. The **LowDoc Program** is a government loan program that allows businesses applying for loans of less than $150,000 to submit a one-page application with a small amount of documentation. They receive a reply within 36 hours. This program also features electronic loan processing. Loan maturity is usually 5 to 10 years or up to 25 years.

The SBA also offers a variety of other loans for specific groups or business endeavors. It has special guaranteed loan programs for international trade, pollution control, exporters, and businesses entering markets in economically **depressed,** or disadvantaged, areas. Today the SBA is still the primary source of assistance in getting small business funding. Every year banks and other financial institutions lend billions of dollars to small business operations with SBA guarantees.

Reading Check

Explain Why did the government introduce the LowDoc Program?

Other Sources of Funding

Why might a new business need to obtain funding from other sources?

Some business owners use personal resources or funds from family members or friends to expand their businesses. Many others use short-term commercial loans, which are often guaranteed by the SBA. However, you can also get funding through a business credit card, private investors, commercial finance companies, venture capital firms, and state and local governments.

Business Credit Card

Financial institutions offer alternative funding options to meet the needs of a wide variety of businesses. One of these options is to offer a line of credit through a business credit card. A **business credit card** is a credit card that is issued to a business rather than to an individual. Business credit cards are a major source of short-term financing for small businesses. Commercial loans are another common source.

Business credit cards require the business to have a good credit history. They are suitable for businesses that want to expand or cover unexpected costs, but they are generally not issued for start-up financing. A credit limit on a business credit card is usually under $15,000. The disadvantage of this quick source of funding is high interest rates, similar to those on personal credit cards. Business credit cards are good for emergencies, but balances should be paid as quickly as possible.

Visa, MasterCard, and American Express all offer small business credit cards. Credit card issuers also provide advice and assistance through small business publications.

Another credit option is trade credit. Businesses grant trade credit to other businesses for the purchase of goods or services. Trade credit is a source of short-term financing provided by companies in the same industry. For example, you may purchase goods from a supplier on 60 days of interest-free credit. You must pay the supplier within 60 days of receiving the goods.

Careers That Count!

Sheila O'Dell • Commercial Loan Officer

As a commercial loan officer, it is my job to tend to businesses and corporations that need to borrow money for new equipment or to buy property. I meet with the customers to explain the different types of loans available, and to get basic information to determine their ability to repay the loan. Commercial loans are often too large and complex for me to rely solely on underwriting software, so I have to use my experience and judgment when reviewing financial statements and types of collateral. I use this information, plus a credit report from a credit bureau, and input from my manager to decide whether or not to approve the loan. In many instances, I also act as a salesperson. For example, if a firm is seeking new funds, then I try to persuade the company to obtain the loan from my institution.

EXPLORE CAREERS

Visit the Web site of the U.S. Department of Labor's Bureau of Labor Statistics to learn more about what it takes to become a loan officer.

1. What are some personal traits a loan officer should possess?
2. What can a loan officer do to increase advancement opportunities?

Skills	Education	Career Path
Sales, presentation, communication, math, problem-solving, and organizational skills; good judgment and discretion	High school diploma or equivalent; experience with business accounting, financial statements, and cash flow analysis; familiar with banking and financial software	Commercial loan officers can become credit analysts, debt counselors, and supervisors or managers over other loan officers and clerical staff.

glencoe.com 

Activity Download a Career Exploration Activity.

Private Investors

A **private investor** is a person outside an entrepreneur's circle of friends and relatives who provides funding because he or she is interested in helping a new business to succeed. Typically called "angels," private investors will usually leave the management of the business to the owner. However, they are also interested in getting a good return on their money. This means that you may have to give them a share of ownership.

Private investors typically get involved in businesses they understand or businesses in which they know the entrepreneur. Today, many private investors network with other, like-minded investors, pooling their funds to invest in larger opportunities. These investors typically find opportunities in their local areas through friends and associates.

If you cannot locate private investors in your area, you can turn to the SBA. The SBA has set up the Angel Capital Electronic Network (ACE-Net), which is a Web site that lists small businesses that are looking for investors. The SBA screens both entrepreneurs and investors to assure reliability. Approved investors can access information on thousands of businesses. An investor chooses a business, and then the business owner and the investor can negotiate a deal.

Commercial Finance Companies

A **commercial finance company** is a firm that lends money only to businesses. Commercial finance companies insist that all loans be secured with collateral, such as equipment or inventory. These companies are helpful to existing businesses that need short-term financing.

The government does not regulate commercial finance companies as closely as it does banks, so these companies accept more risk in granting loans. However, if a finance company grants you a riskier loan, it will charge you a higher interest rate. It is easier to get this kind of loan, but you will pay more for it.

Venture Capital Firms

A **venture capital firm** is a company that provides private funding for small businesses that need a substantial amount of immediate cash. Because these small businesses are high-risk in terms of ability to repay loans, they cannot always get adequate funding from lenders such as banks and commercial finance companies. Venture capital firms take the risk, but in turn, they often expect a large return of 25 to 40 percent on their investment.

Venture capital firms usually seek to make investments of at least $500,000. Keep in mind that the venture capital firm is not merely lending money; it is also investing in your business. Therefore, venture capital firms expect to have a **voice,** or right to be heard, in major business decisions and will examine a business's financial position carefully throughout the year.

When looking at investment opportunities, venture capitalists look for businesses with good management teams. They believe a good team is the key to success. They also look for businesses with large, growing markets. The process of obtaining funding from venture capitalists can be slow and often take months. If this type of funding is used, the process should begin long before the money is actually needed.

Most venture capital firms are private, but the SBA created a public venture capital program—the Small Business Investment Company Program. **Small Business Investment Companies (SBICs)** are private investment firms that work with the SBA to provide longer-term funding for small businesses. The advantage in dealing with the SBIC program is that the SBA regulates lenders, and financing terms must meet SBA guidelines. If small businesses need venture capital, they usually go to SBIC firms first.

Reading Check

Identify What is a disadvantage of using a venture capital firm to obtain funding for your business?

United Kingdom

Small-Business Loans

Small business owners often rely on bank loans to get the necessary capital for establishing and operating their new business. Unfortunately, when the economy is having trouble, the banks often cut back approving these loans, reducing the amount of capital available and making the lending criteria stricter. In 2009, the British government decided to step in and assist small-business owners by guaranteeing up to £20 billion (approximately $29 billion) in bank loans. Then Business Secretary Peter Mandelson said the program would specifically address businesses' needs for cash flow, credit, and capital. While the guarantee applies to loans, Mandelson pointed out that companies could also convert existing overdrafts into loans under the program. Former Prime Minister Gordon Brown introduced the program, noting that the decision of which businesses should receive the loans would still fall to the banks rather than the government. The government's role is just to provide the money to the lenders.

The program proved successful when, in 2010, the British Bankers' Association (BBA) reported that four out of every five business loan applications were being approved. Additionally, part-nationalized banks, such as Lloyds Banking Group, pledged extra funding for new business loans in 2010.

Critical Thinking

1. **Expand** Research to learn more about the Financial Services Authority (FSA) which regulates the financial services industry in the United Kingdom. What are the five statutory objectives of the FSA?
2. **Relate** What steps could you take to help assure a bank that you were creditworthy if you were applying for a business loan? What other sources of funding might you consider?

DATABYTES

Capital
London

Population
61, 284, 806

Language
English

Currency
British pound

Gross Domestic Product (GDP)
$2.224 trillion

GDP per capita
$35,200

Industry
Machine tools, electric power equipment, automation equipment, railroad equipment, shipbuilding, aircraft, motor vehicles and parts, electronics and communications equipment, metals, chemicals, coal, petroleum, paper and paper products, food processing, textiles, clothing, other consumer goods

Agriculture
Cereals, oilseed, potatoes, vegetables; cattle, sheep, poultry; fish

Exports
Manufactured goods, fuels, chemicals; food, beverages, tobacco

Natural Resources
Coal, petroleum, natural gas, iron ore, lead, zinc, gold, tin, limestone, salt, clay, chalk, gypsum, potash, silica sand, slate, arable land

State and Local Funding

Why do state and local governments provide funding opportunities for small businesses?

State and local funds are sometimes used to encourage the creation of new businesses and jobs. Because they are not as profit-focused, these funds are more likely to support a small business.

Many states provide opportunities for small businesses to get funding through a variety of programs. These funding programs are available in cities where local and state governments are encouraging individuals to open businesses in economically depressed neighborhoods. Local chambers of commerce or regional offices of the SBA can assist you.

Reading Check

Paraphrase Where can a business owner in an economically depressed area turn for funding sources?

Funding Your Dreams

Why are small businesses essential to the American economy?

The American economy has been built by entrepreneurs who were willing to take risks and explore new ventures. Ray Kroc was 52 years old when he purchased the rights to a hamburger stand owned by the McDonald brothers in San Bernardino, California. His venture would revolutionize the food industry. Robert Pittman was only 26 years old when he combined video and music and created MTV.

Entrepreneurs and small businesses recognize what the consumer wants and see the economic opportunities in developing innovative products and services to satisfy them often creating even more wants that need to be met. Entrepreneurs not only provide jobs but also create a market for venture capital.

The funding of small businesses is essential to the American economy. Almost all of the nation's Fortune 500 companies started as small businesses. They began with little capital and obtained additional funds by using creativity. Today you can get funds through a variety of sources. Through private and public funding, you can pursue your dreams and own your own business.

After You Read

Theorize With so many potential obstacles faced by entrepreneurs and new business owners, why do people continue to dream about business ownership?

Assessment

Review Key Concepts

1. **Identify** What are the alternative sources of funding for a business?
2. **Explain** Why are small businesses important to the American economy?
3. **Describe** What are the services and benefits of the Small Business Administration?

Higher Order Thinking H.O.T.

4. **Determine** You want to expand your new business after six profitable months, and you need $125,000 in additional capital. Would you look for funding from a commercial finance company, a venture capital firm, or an SBIC? Explain your decision.

English Language Arts

5. **Power of Persuasion** Successful entrepreneurs are risk takers, are goal oriented, and are independent. They also know how to secure financing to transform their ideas into products or services that will sell and be profitable. Imagine that you are ready to open your business and you need to borrow $10,000 to get started. Write a letter requesting the funding from a family member, a friend, or a financial institution. Describe the type of business you want to open and explain why you think it will be successful. Your letter should be persuasive, professional, and courteous.

NCTE 12 Use language to accomplish individual purposes.

Mathematics

6. **SBA Loans** Amit went to the bank in order to apply for a loan for his new business venture. Unfortunately, he was denied the loan so he decided to apply for an SBA loan. The SBA loan was approved which authorized the bank to lend Amit the funds he needed while the SBA guaranteed a majority of the loan. If the loan was for $110,000, how much will the SBA guarantee? If the loan was for $175,000 how much would the SBA guarantee?

Math Concept **Calculate Loan Guarantees** To calculate the amount of the loan that is guaranteed by the SBA, first identify the loan amount in order to determine the loan guarantee percentage, multiply this percentage by the loan amount.

Starting Hint Determine the amount guaranteed by the SBA on the $110,000 loan by identifying the guarantee percentage identified in this section and multiplying this percentage by the loan amount.

NCTM Representation Select, apply, and translate among mathematical representations to solve problems.

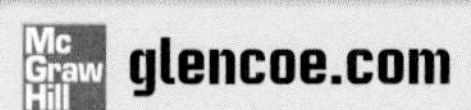

Check your answers.

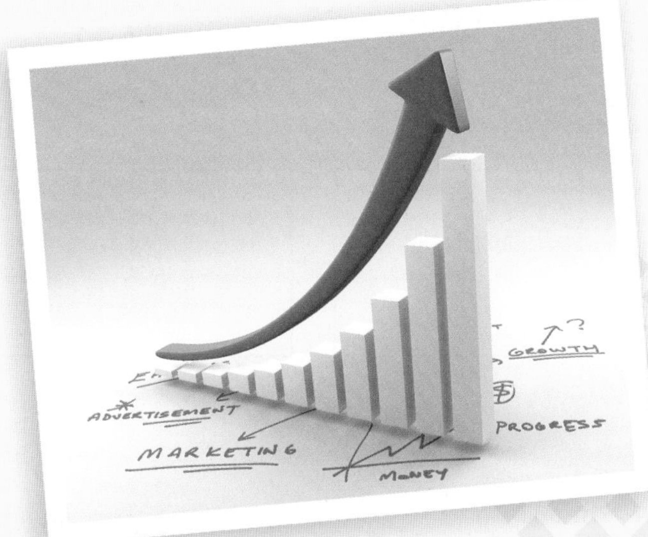

Visual Summary

Sources of Funding

Realize Your Dreams

Through a variety of public and private funding, you can pursue your dream of being your own boss.

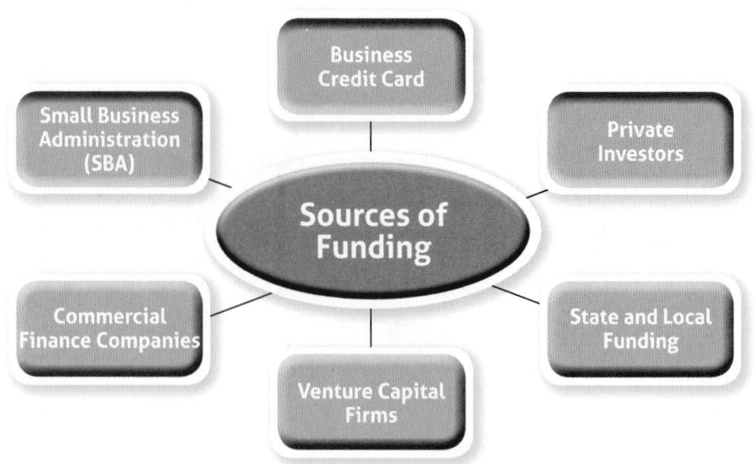

Evaluate Your C's

Banks use certain standards to judge a company's financial position and determine how much risk to take.

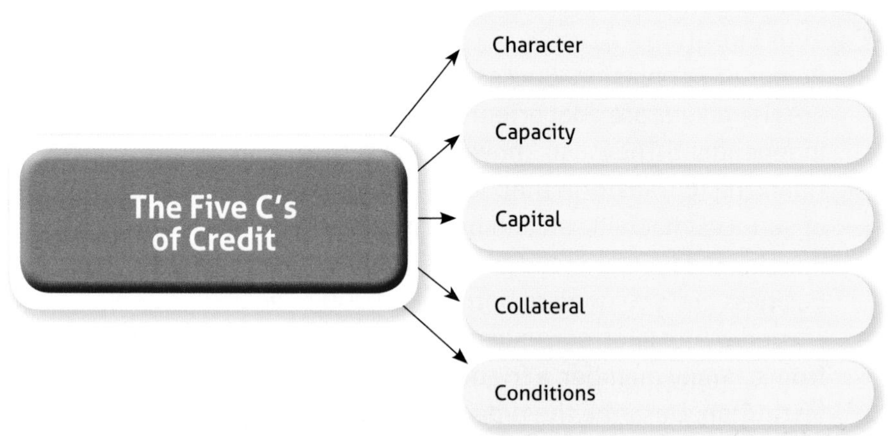

Try It!

The Small Business Administration (SBA) is the primary source of assistance for small business funding. Use a chart like the one shown to outline the steps involved in applying for an SBA loan.

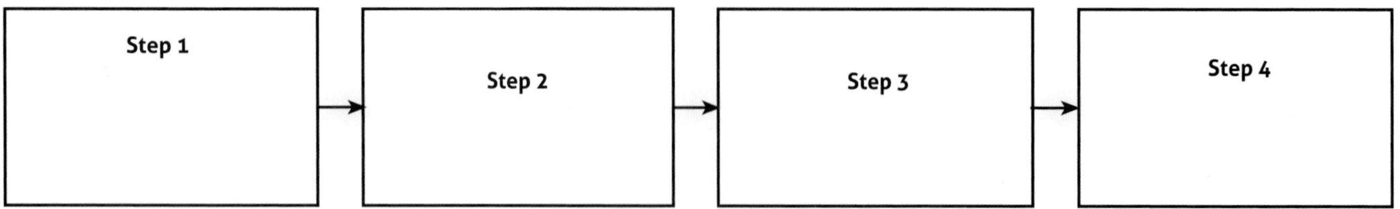

Chapter Review and Assessment

Chapter Summary

- An entrepreneur is a person who takes the risk of starting a new business.
- Start-up costs include money for the purchase of assets needed to run a business, including inventory, equipment, furnishing, supplies, and utilities; costs such as legal, professional, and banking fees; licenses; permits; insurance; marketing costs; and remodeling and maintenance costs. Operating capital is the money needed to operate a business for the first few years. Reserve capital is money set aside for unexpected costs or opportunities.
- Sources of personal financing include personal assets, consumer loans, and home equity loans. Sources of private financing include family and friends.
- Some of the options available through bank funding are short- and long-term commercial loans, lines of credit, and secured and unsecured loans.
- The factors banks consider to approve commercial loans include the five C's: character, capacity, capital, collateral, and conditions.
- The Small Business Administration (SBA) is a major source of funding for new small businesses. This agency can also help with management training and organizational guidance.
- Other sources of funding for a business include business credit cards, private investors (angels), commercial finance companies, venture capital companies, and state and local agencies.

Vocabulary Review

1. Create a fill-in-the-blank sentence for each of these vocabulary terms. You may combine two terms in once sentence if appropriate. The sentences should contain enough information to help determine the missing word(s).

- operating costs
- reserve fund
- private financing
- commercial debt financing
- commercial loan
- line of credit
- secured loan
- unsecured loan
- Small Business Administration (SBA)
- LowDoc Program
- business credit card
- private investor
- commercial finance company
- venture capital firm
- Small Business Investment Companies (SBICs)
- routine
- sound
- depressed
- voice

Higher Order Thinking 

2. **Explain** How can loans guaranteed by the Small Business Administration be a win-win situation for the entrepreneur and the lending institution?
3. **Predict** Based on what you have learned in this chapter, explain how you would raise start-up capital for a new business.
4. **Analyze** When might it be appropriate to use a home equity loan to fund a business?
5. **Compare** Choose the best source of funding for a new business owner: a consumer loan, a home equity loan, or private financing. Explain.
6. **Generalize** Is every business owner an entrepreneur? Why or why not?
7. **Extend** What advantages might the federal government receive by operating the Small Business Administration (SBA)?
8. **Recommend** For what types of expenses should a business use a business credit card? For what expenses should a business not use a credit card? Explain your answers.
9. **Evaluate** How would a bank benefit from approving an unsecured loan?

College and Career Readiness

Social Studies

10. Small Business Advocacy The health of the American economy relies heavily on the success of small businesses. The SBA is an independent agency of the federal government created to help small business owners, but similar organizations, often called small business advocates or lobby groups, have been established outside of the government. Use print or online resources to research these organizations. Create a directory of at least three such organizations, and next to each entry, write a brief description of their purpose and services.

NCSS VG Analyze the extent to which groups and institutions meet individual needs and promote the common good in contemporary and historical settings.

Mathematics

11. Home Equity Loan Joel has been living in his house for 10 years. He would like to purchase a newer house but has decided to make changes to his current one instead. He wants to take out a home equity loan in order to make the renovations. The current market value of Joel's house is $210,000. He has a mortgage balance of $145,000. Calculate the equity Joel has in his house currently. If the bank will allow a maximum of 80 percent of the current market value, what is the maximum amount of home equity loan Joel is able to get?

Math Concept **Calculate Home Equity Amounts** Calculate the amount available to be borrowed on a home equity loan by determining the maximum home equity loan amount available based on market value and subtracting any existing loan balance from this figure.

Starting Hint Calculate the maximum home equity loan amount available based on market value by first identifying the current market value of the home. Next identify the maximum amount that the bank will allow an individual to borrow as a percentage of the current market value.

NCTM Connections Recognize and use connections among mathematical ideas.

English Language Arts

12. Biography The world is full of famous entrepreneurs, past and present. Many of the nation's Fortune 500 companies started as small businesses. Choose one of these individuals and write a one-page biography of him or her. Focus on the business or businesses that this person started. Include details about how the entrepreneur was inspired and, if possible, find out where and how funds were obtained. What obstacles did this person overcome? What characteristics contributed to his or her success?

NCTE 2 Read literature to build an understanding of the human experience.

Ethics

13. Lending Practices Usury, or predatory lending, is defined as the act of lending money at an unreasonably high interest rate. Some lenders dispute whether these practices are unethical, often citing that consumers have choices about where they obtain loans. Some lenders argue that high-risk borrowers should be charged higher rates because they are more likely to go into default. However, some consumer groups argue that higher prices charged to vulnerable consumers are discriminatory and cannot be justified. Why might a new business owner be willing to tolerate usurious lending practices?

Real-World Applications

14. Banking Options When considering banking choices, a new business owner generally has two options: a local bank or a national bank. Both can provide specialized services. Entrepreneurs need to consider their immediate needs as well as how those needs will change. Imagine a business you would like to own. Where is it located? Is it a small local business, a home-based business, or something with the potential to go global? Go online to research a variety of local and national banks. Take notes on the kinds of services each provides, then choose which bank would best suit your needs. Write a short paragraph to explain why you chose this bank.

Your Financial Portfolio

Cost Estimates and Funding

Tanya's mother brings home rejects and remnants of towel fabric from the mill where she works. Tanya's grandmother taught Tanya how to sew the cloth into animal shapes and stuff them. Tanya and her family give these little stuffed animals as presents. She has also sold 25 of them at $8 each to raise money for the high school football team. Tanya and her friend, Lisa, have decided to start a business making and selling "Tanya's Toys." Tanya has listed the expenses of making 100 stuffed animals and the sources of funding.

Item	Cost	Source of Funding
Toweling	$25	She spoke directly to the manager at the mill, who offered a special deal of $25 payable after the animals were sold.
Sewing machines	$430	Tanya was already using the sewing machine she had at home and located another used industrial machine. She and Lisa decided they would buy the second machine after they sold 500 toys.
Other sewing equipment: Sewing shears, tape measure, patterns	$45	Tanya's grandmother offered to loan them the money to buy good sewing shears.
Supplies: Thread, eyes, buttons, ribbon, and felt to decorate the animals	$25	Tanya and Lisa decided to fund the purchase of supplies from their savings.
Wages	0	Tanya and Lisa will not pay themselves wages until they have all the equipment and supplies.

Research

What kind of business could you launch that would require minimal start-up costs? Use the guidelines shown above to describe and name your business and list what equipment and supplies you would need on a separate sheet of paper. Also indicate how you would fund your enterprise. How much would your equipment and supplies cost? How could you persuade family or friends to participate in your business?

CHAPTER 7

Financial Accounting

Visual Literacy

During the accounting cycle, accountants and business owners track, organize, and record a company's financial information. ***What kind of financial information does the owner of the business in this photo need to track and monitor?***

Discovery Project

Analyzing Records

Key Question

How can business owners use accounting records to make financial decisions?

Project Goal

You have finally realized your dream of running a small, neighborhood bakery with local catering service. In the course of business, you have made cupcakes for graduation parties, pastries for picnics, and cakes for weddings. You even have a specialty line of gourmet dog biscuits. Your accountant suggests that you expand the catering aspect of your business because it is more profitable and dependable than the day-to-day operation of the bakery. You have received good advice from your accountant in the past, so you want to consider her suggestion.

- Create a list of your asset accounts and liability accounts.
- Use the first five steps of the accounting cycle to help you identify what you need to analyze.
- Write a summary that explains how you will use this information to decide whether or not to take your accountant's advice.

Ask Yourself...

- *What will I need to do to remain profitable?*
- *What types of accounting records will I need to review and understand before making any decisions?*
- *How will I determine whether or not I made the right decision about expanding the catering services?*

Use Systems Thinking

If you want to buy a new catering truck but your business can only afford to pay 75 percent of the price, would it be acceptable to use money from your personal savings account to pay the difference? Why or why not?

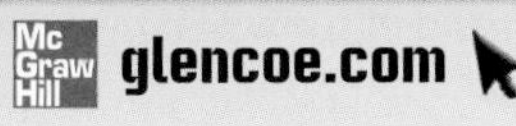

Evaluate Download an assessment rubric.

THE BIG IDEA

Accountants and accounting software can provide the final figures, but it is up to the business owner to interpret the figures and make the decisions.

ASK STANDARD & POOR'S

The Accounting Cycle

Q *When I start my business, I am going to hire an accountant to keep my records. So why do I need to understand the accounting cycle?*

A A professional can help you maintain financial records. However, you still need to understand what information is represented in your financial statements and its relevance to the decisions you will need to make. Also, to communicate with your accountant, you will need to understand what he or she is talking about.

Writing Activity

Imagine that your friend has just started his mobile dog grooming business. Write a persuasive letter that not only convinces him to keep accurate accounting records, but also explains why he needs to analyze the information.

CHAPTER 7 **Reading Guide**

Before You Read

The Essential Question Why is it important for business owners to have a firm grasp of accounting principles?

Main Idea

To make sound financial decisions , all businesses should use the accounting cycle to accurately record, summarize, and analyze their financial transactions.

Content Vocabulary

- financial reports
- accounting period
- accounting cycle
- accounting equation
- account
- accounts receivable
- accounts payable
- double-entry accounting
- T account
- debit
- credit (accounting)
- journal
- general ledger
- posting
- trial balance
- financial statements
- income statement
- cost of merchandise sold
- net income
- balance sheet
- statement of cash flows

Academic Vocabulary

You will see these words in your reading and on your tests.

- claim
- transfer
- primary
- condensed

Graphic Organizer

Before you read this chapter, create a cycle diagram like the one shown. As you read, identify the first five steps of the accounting cycle.

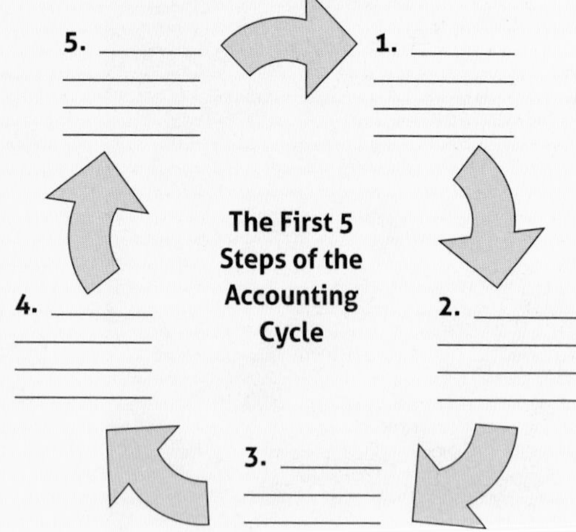

glencoe.com Print this graphic organizer.

Standards

Academic

Mathematics

NCTM Problem Solving Apply and adapt a variety of appropriate strategies to solve problems.

NCTM Number and Operations Understand numbers, ways of representing numbers, relationships among numbers, and number systems.

English Language Arts

NCTE 4 Use written language to communicate effectively.

NCTE 12 Use language to accomplish individual purposes.

Social Studies

NCSS VII I Distinguish between the domestic and global economic systems, and explain how the two interact.

NCTM *National Council of Teachers of Mathematics*
NCTE *National Council of Teachers of English*
NCSS *National Council for the Social Studies*
NSES *National Science Education Standards*

Common Core

Reading Read closely to determine what the text says explicitly and to make logical inferences from it; cite specific textual evidence when writing or speaking to support conclusions drawn from the text.

Speaking and Listening Present information, findings, and supporting evidence such that listeners can follow the line of reasoning and the organization, development, and style are appropriate to task, purpose, and audience.

Speaking and Listening Adapt speech to a variety of contexts and communicative tasks, demonstrating command of formal English when indicated or appropriate.

The Language of Business

How is accounting used in business?

Have you ever wondered how a rap group or a rock band determines how many cities or which cities to play on tour? What types of venues will host the concert? What determines the price of tickets, and how much does a national tour cost? These questions are all answered by accountants and financial advisers.

Accounting plays a vital role in the day-to-day activities of your business—and of every business. Accounting records and reports help a business operate efficiently—and profitably—by keeping track of how much is earned and how much is spent. Accounting is so much a part of the business world that it is often called "the language of business."

Section Objectives

- **Explain** the purpose of the accounting system.
- **Define** the three categories of the accounting equation.
- **Summarize** the reasons for using the accounting cycle.

As You Read

Recognize What is the value of keeping day-to-day track of your financial status?

Reading Check

Interpret Why is accounting called "the language of business"?

The Accounting System

What is the purpose of using the accounting system?

Whether you are keeping financial records for a rock band, a neighborhood bike shop, or a major corporation, accounting principles and procedures are universal. All businesses use the same system, which follows established accounting guidelines called "generally accepted accounting principles," or GAAP. With all businesses using the same system, anyone who is interested in examining the records of a business will be able to understand its financial reports.

The accounting system is designed to collect, record, and report on financial transactions that affect a business. **Financial reports** are written records that summarize the results of financial transactions affecting a business and report its current financial position. They indicate how well your business is doing.

There are many groups and individuals interested in your business's finances:

- Potential buyers
- Government agencies
- Banks or other financial institutions
- Employees and consumers

Careers That Count!

Nicholas Lombardi • Career and Technical Education (CTE) Teacher

I enjoy explaining, giving instruction, and providing inspiration for others. After working behind a desk as an accountant for ten years, I needed a change of pace. I decided to work as a part-time accounting teacher's aide at a vocational school. This turned into a full-time position as a CTE teacher. Traditionally, becoming a CTE teacher required a bachelor's degree and a teaching license, but my state offers alternative routes for people like me who have work experience in the field. In addition to classroom instruction, I teach hands-on computer skills pertaining to the basics of business financial management. I teach courses that are in high demand by area employers, who often provide curriculum input and offer internships or apprenticeships to students. As a vocational teacher, I get to play an active role in building and overseeing these partnerships. I also provide career guidance, help with job placement, and follow up with students after graduation.

EXPLORE CAREERS

Visit the Web site of the U.S. Department of Labor's Bureau of Labor Statistics and obtain information about a career as vocational teacher.

1. What qualities might an accounting teacher need that an accountant may not need?
2. CTE teachers teach a wide variety of subjects, from agriculture to technology. Why do you think most States offer alternative routes to licensure for those who have work experience in their field?

Skills	Education	Career Path
Accounting, math, communication, computer, organizational, and time management	Bachelor's degree in education or business education and/or a master's degree in accounting, finance, or business; alternative routes to licensure depending on state	CTE teachers can become postsecondary-level teachers, senior or mentor teachers, administrators, or supervisors.

 glencoe.com 

Activity Download a Career Exploration activity.

Accounting Assumptions

When you are creating the accounting books for your business, you make two assumptions about the business. The first assumption is that the business will operate as a separate unit, or business entity. This means that the records and reports of your business will be kept completely separate from your personal finances. You never mix your business finances with your personal finances.

The second assumption is that your business will make its financial reports in specific blocks of time. An **accounting period** is a block of time covered by an accounting report. The accounting period can be one month or one quarter (three months), but the most common period is one year.

During this accounting period, you record all financial transactions for your business and report the results. You engage in activities that maintain your accounting records in an orderly manner. The **accounting cycle** is the activities, or steps, that help a business keep its accounting records in an orderly manner.

In this chapter you will learn about the first five steps of the accounting cycle. In each accounting period—whether a month, a quarter, or a year—the entire accounting cycle is completed. You probably have heard news broadcasts such as: "Ford sales are up 4 percent over last quarter and up 6 percent from the same quarter last year." By using a set period of time, such as a quarter, you can compare financial reports from one period to those from another period.

The Accounting Equation

Property is anything of value that you own or control. Both people and businesses have property. You might own a CD player, a computer, clothes, a television set, or maybe a car. For a business, property could include cash, office equipment, supplies, merchandise, or vehicles. When you own an item of property, you have a financial **claim,** or legal right, to that item. In contrast, when you have control over an item, you have only the right to use it. A rented office is property, but a business does not have a financial claim to it. In accounting, property or items of value owned by your business are called *assets.*

Your equity in a piece of property is your share of its value, or your financial claim to the property. This also applies to businesses. For example, suppose that your business owns a truck valued at $16,000. You are the owner of the business, so your equity in the truck is $16,000. If the truck is completely paid for, you have financial claim to the truck. An owner's claim to the assets of a business is called *owner's equity.*

However, what if you still owe $3,000 to the Stratford Savings Bank for the truck? The truck is valued at $16,000, but the creditor (the bank) has $3,000 equity, while your equity is now only $13,000. Both you and the creditor have financial claims to (equity in) the asset.

Property − Creditor's Financial Claim = Owner's Financial Claim
$16,000 − $3,000 = $13,000

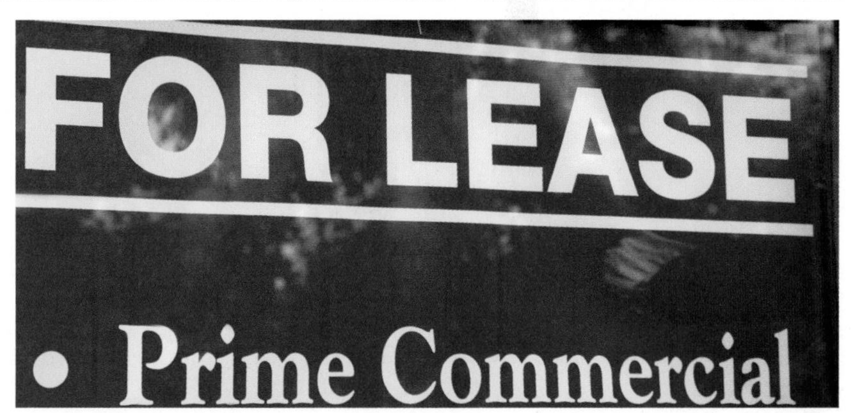

COMMON CENTS

Costly Corrections

When recording transactions manually, never erase errors. The erasure may look like an illegal cover-up. Instead, cross out the error and write the correction above it.

Concept Application

Accounting errors can cost businesses money. In what other ways might a business suffer as a result of accounting errors?

Rented Space

Many businesses rent space where they run their operations. *Since a rented office or retail space is property, is it correct to call it an asset? Why or why not?*

Creditors' claims to the assets of a business are called *liabilities*, or the debts of a business. The relationship between assets and the two types of equity (liabilities and owner's equity) is shown in the accounting equation:

Property − Creditor's Financial Claim = Owner's Financial Claim
Assets − Liabilities = Owner's Equity

The **accounting equation** (Assets − Liabilities = Owner's Equity) is the basis for keeping all accounting records in balance. The entire system of accounting is based on this equation. As your business buys, sells, or exchanges goods and services involving many business transactions, the numbers may change. However, total assets will always equal total liabilities plus owner's equity. As you learn more, you will understand why this equation is so important.

Reading Check

Memorize What is the accounting equation?

Establishing Accounts

What are accounts?

When you set up the books of a business, you create accounts for each of the three categories in the accounting equation:

- Assets
- Liabilities
- Owner's equity

An **account** shows the balance for a specific item, such as cash or equipment. You must look at your business and determine what accounts your business needs.

Businesses create only the accounts they need for their type of business operation. The accounts used by one business may differ from the accounts used by another.

For example, Chris Archer uses the following accounts for his business, Archer Delivery Service:

Assets
Cash in Bank
Accounts Receivable
Office Equipment
Delivery Equipment

Liabilities
Accounts Payable

Owner's Equity
Chris Archer, Capital

An Income Statement

If you own or work in a business, you will want to know if the business is profitable or not. If you are not bringing in enough income to offset your expenses, you will not make a profit. An income statement contains the following information:

- Income generated
- Expenses incurred
- Profit or loss

General Products—Income Statement

Year ending December 31, 20XX

Revenue		
Sales		$450,000
Costs of goods sold		250,000
Gross profit		$200,000
Operating Expenses		
Salaries	$70,000	
Advertising	12,000	
Rent	14,000	
Utilities	3,600	
Maintenance	1,200	
Insurance	1,500	
Misc.	1,000	
Total Expenses		$103,300
Net Profit		$96,700
Taxes	$48,350	
Net Profit		**$48,350**

Key Points An income statement shows how much a company earns after it pays all its expenses, such as salaries, advertising, rent, utilities, maintenance, insurance, and other operating expenses.

FIND the Solutions

Review Key Concepts

1. How is gross profit calculated?
2. What time period is covered in the statement?
3. What percent of net profit does this company pay in taxes?
4. How much did it cost this company to produce the goods it sold?
5. What could this company do to increase its profits?

reality bytes

Computerized Accounting Software

There are many options to consider when looking for computerized accounting software to help you run your business. A businessperson's decision about which one is right for his or her needs is an important choice—one that could mean the difference between success and failure. Looking for the right accounting software solution for your business can be a real challenge.

Asset Accounts

Chris has established four asset accounts. The first account shows all of the cash that enters or leaves the business. It is *Cash in Bank* because all cash received by his business is deposited in a bank account, and all cash paid out is paid by check. In accounting, both cash and checks are considered cash transactions.

The second asset account for the business is *Accounts Receivable.* **Accounts receivable** is the total amount of money owed to a business by customers. Chris completed deliveries for other companies, and they owe his business money. This account represents a future value that will eventually bring cash into the business.

Chris will use the two remaining asset accounts, *Office Equipment* and *Delivery Equipment,* when he buys equipment. If he needs other accounts for other assets, he can create them.

Liabilities Account

Chris listed only one liability account—*Accounts Payable.* **Accounts payable** is the amount of money owed, or payable, to the creditors of a business. The balance owed will remain in Accounts Payable until the business pays the debt.

Owner's Equity Account

The owner's equity account is identified by the owner's name, Chris Archer, followed by the word *Capital.* This account will report the owner's share of assets. Most businesses have more accounts than those presented here for Archer Delivery Service. Businesses often have many accounts, such as revenue or sales, utilities and other expenses, merchandise, payroll, and many more.

T Accounts

When accountants analyze and record business transactions, they use **double-entry accounting,** which is a system of record-keeping in which each business transaction affects at least two accounts. Remember, Archer Delivery Service has six accounts that can be used.

An efficient way to understand double-entry accounting is to use T accounts. A **T account** is a tool to increase or decrease each account that is affected by a transaction.

Account Name		Account Name	
Left Side Debit	Right Side Credit	Left Side Debit	Right Side Credit

As you can see by this illustration, a T account has the account name at the top and has a left side and right side. An amount entered on the left side of a T account is called a **debit.** An amount entered on the right side of a T account is called a **credit.**

Rules of Debit and Credit

Debits and credits are used to record the increases or decreases in accounts affected by a business transaction. Under double-entry accounting, for each debit in one account (or accounts), there must be a credit of an equal amount in another account (or accounts).

The rules of debit and credit vary, depending on whether the account is an asset, a liability, or an owner's equity account. Regardless of the type of account, the left side is always the debit side and the right side is always the credit side. The general rules are:

- An asset account increases on the debit side and decreases on the credit side.
- Liability accounts and owner's equity accounts increase on the credit side and decrease on the debit side.

Reading Check

Restate Explain what is meant by double-entry accounting.

Using the Five Steps

How do businesses use the first five steps of the accounting cycle?

The accounting cycle consists of ten steps. This section describes how businesses apply and benefit from the first five activities, or steps, of the accounting cycle:

1. Collect and verify source documents.
2. Analyze each transaction.
3. Journalize each transaction.
4. Post to the general ledger.
5. Prepare a trial balance.

STEP 1 Collect and Verify Source Documents

When a business transaction occurs, a paper called a source document is prepared. A source document is evidence that a business transaction happened. Common source documents include check stubs, invoices, receipts, and memorandums. Collect and check all source documents before recording anything in your business's books.

STEP 2 Analyze Each Transaction

Applying the rules of debit and credit to analyze transactions using T accounts is simple. Remember that every transaction must have a debit (or debits) and a credit (or credits) of an equal amount of money.

Initiative

Initiative is taking action to start a process without influence from a supervisor or leader. For example, without any direction from a supervisor, a person who shows initiative may decide to develop a new product or service for a business. Successful people often show initiative by developing and improving life and professional skills to prepare for complex and changing life and work environments.

Write About It

Think of a situation in which you took initiative or saw someone exhibit initiative. Write one or more paragraphs to describe the scenario and explain how this skill positively impacted the situation.

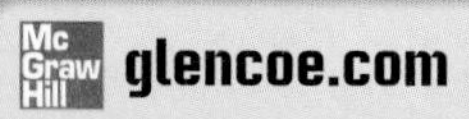

Activity Download a Career and College Readiness Worksheet Activity.

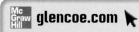

Use these steps to analyze Transaction #1:

1. Identify the two accounts affected.
2. Classify each of the accounts.
3. Decide whether each account is increasing or decreasing.
4. Determine which account is debited and which is credited.

Transaction #1 On May 5, Archer Delivery Service purchased a photocopier for $900. Check 104 was written for the full amount.

Analysis:

1. The accounts affected are Office Equipment and Cash in Bank.
2. Both are asset accounts.
3. The business is buying office equipment. The balance in the Office Equipment account is increasing. Cash in Bank is decreasing.
4. According to the debit-credit rules, increases in asset accounts are recorded as debits. Office Equipment is debited $900. Decreases in asset accounts are recorded as credits. Cash in Bank is credited $900.

Office Equipment		Cash in Bank	
Debit	Credit	Debit	Credit
+900	–	+	−900

Here is another example:

Transaction #2 On May 7, Archer Delivery Service bought a truck for $11,000 from Gail's Auto Land. The entire cost was financed by Wilton Bank.

Analysis:

1. The accounts affected are Delivery Equipment and Accounts Payable.
2. Delivery Equipment is an asset account. Accounts Payable is a liability account. In this transaction, the business is buying a truck.
3. The balance in the account Delivery Equipment is increasing. The balance in Accounts Payable is increasing.
4. The Delivery Equipment account is debited $11,000. Accounts Payable is credited $11,000.

Delivery Equipment		Accounts Payable	
Debit	Credit	Debit	Credit
+11,000	–	–	+11,000

Notice that both Transactions #1 and #2 have a debit to one account and a credit to another account. Every business transaction will have balancing debit and credit entries. This is how the system of double-entry accounting works.

Equipment Equity
Expensive equipment, such as a delivery truck, is usually financed rather than paid for in full. *Would a financed delivery truck be an asset or liability or both? Explain.*

STEP 3 Journalize Each Transaction

Do you keep a diary or journal? Many people do. They write down the day-to-day events that they want to remember. Businesses do the same thing. The financial events of your business are your business transactions, which you record in a journal. You use T accounts to analyze the transactions, but to record the transactions, you use a journal. A **journal** is a record of all of the transactions of a business. Business transactions are recorded in the order in which they occur. The process of recording business transactions in a journal is called *journalizing.*

A business journal uses accounting stationery. The stationery has lined columns for recording dollar amounts. You do not use commas, decimal points, or dollar signs. For example, the amount $1,846.20 is entered as shown in **Figure 1.**

FIGURE 1 Entry on Accounting Stationery

Special Stationery Accountants use specific stationery designed for accounting procedures. *Why would accountants intentionally eliminate dollar signs, commas, and decimals?*

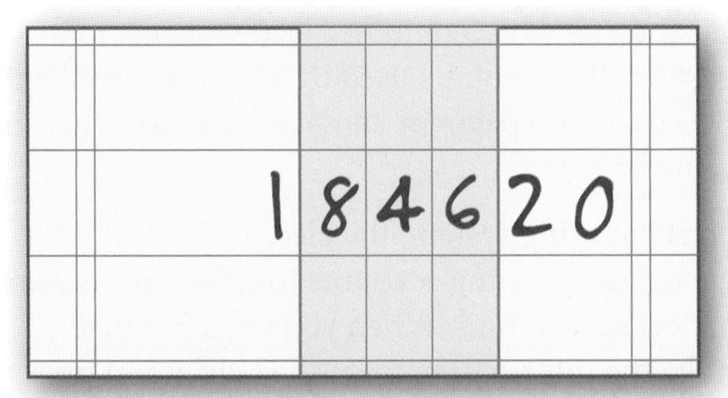

FIGURE 2 **Transactions in a General Journal**

All-Purpose Journal The general journal is one of the most common accounting journals. *What types of entries would anyone be able to locate in a general journal?*

GENERAL JOURNAL — PAGE 4

	DATE		DESCRIPTION	DEBIT	CREDIT	
1	May	5	Office Equipment	900 00		1
2			Cash in Bank		900 00	2
3			Check 104			3
4		7	Delivery Equipment	11 000 00		4
5			Accounts Payable/Wilton Bank		11 000 00	5
6			Promissory Note			6
7						7

One of the most common accounting journals is the general journal. A general journal is an all-purpose journal in which all the transactions of a business may be recorded. When a business transaction occurs, a source document—such as a receipt or invoice—is created. Then you analyze the transaction, using T accounts, and enter it in the general journal. You record the date of the transaction, the accounts affected, and the amount of the debit and credit entries. **Figure 2** shows Transactions #1 and #2 entered in a general journal.

STEP 4 Post to the General Ledger

By looking at a general journal, you cannot easily see what the balance is in each of your accounts. You may want to know how much cash you have, how much your business owes in accounts payable, how much office equipment you have, and most important, whether your business is making a profit.

In order to find the balance of each account, you must **transfer,** or move, the amounts that are in the general journal to a general ledger. A **general ledger** is a book or set of electronic files that contains the accounts used for a business. Each account has its own page. In a manual accounting system, the accounts used by a business are kept on separate pages or cards. These pages or cards are kept together in a book or file, which is the ledger.

In a computerized accounting system, the electronic files of the accounts comprise the ledger. Keeping accounts together in a general ledger makes information easy to find. When you need financial statements, you can take the information from the ledger and present it as well-organized reports. **Figure 3** shows a blank ledger page.

Making Entries The manual accounting system uses a ledger account form, which is accounting stationery for recording financial information about specific accounts. There are several common ledger account forms. These forms are described by the number of amount columns they have. For example, the ledger page in **Figure 3** is a four-column ledger account form. The four-column account form has spaces to enter the account name, the account number, the date, a description of the entry, and the posting reference.

To make entries, next to the title *Account,* you enter one of your business's account names, such as Cash in Bank. As you can see, the page has four amount columns. You use the first two amount columns to enter the debit or credit amounts from the general journal. You use the last two amount columns to enter the new account balance after you make an entry from the general journal.

The type of account determines which balance amount column you will use. For example, asset account balances are recorded on the debit side. Liability and owner's equity account balances are recorded on the credit side.

Posting is the process of recording transfers of amounts from the general journal to individual accounts in the general ledger. **Figure 4** shows how you would post the general journal entry for May 5 to the corresponding accounts in the general ledger.

The date you record on the account in the general ledger is the date on which the transaction occurred. You may also enter a brief description of the transaction. You then transfer the debit entry of $900 from the general journal to the account in the general ledger account called Office Equipment. Because this account had a previous balance of $1,600, it now has a new balance of $2,500. Remember that debit entries increase the balance in asset accounts.

FIGURE 3 **The General Ledger**

The Big Picture The general ledger is the core of a company's financial records. *What is the most important reason for maintaining an accurate, up-to-date general ledger?*

ACCOUNT ______________________ ACCOUNT NO. ________

DATE	DESCRIPTION	DEBIT	CREDIT	BALANCE	
				DEBIT	CREDIT

FIGURE 4 Posting to the General Ledger

In the Details Posting is transferring an amount from the general journal to the general ledger. *Why is posting necessary?*

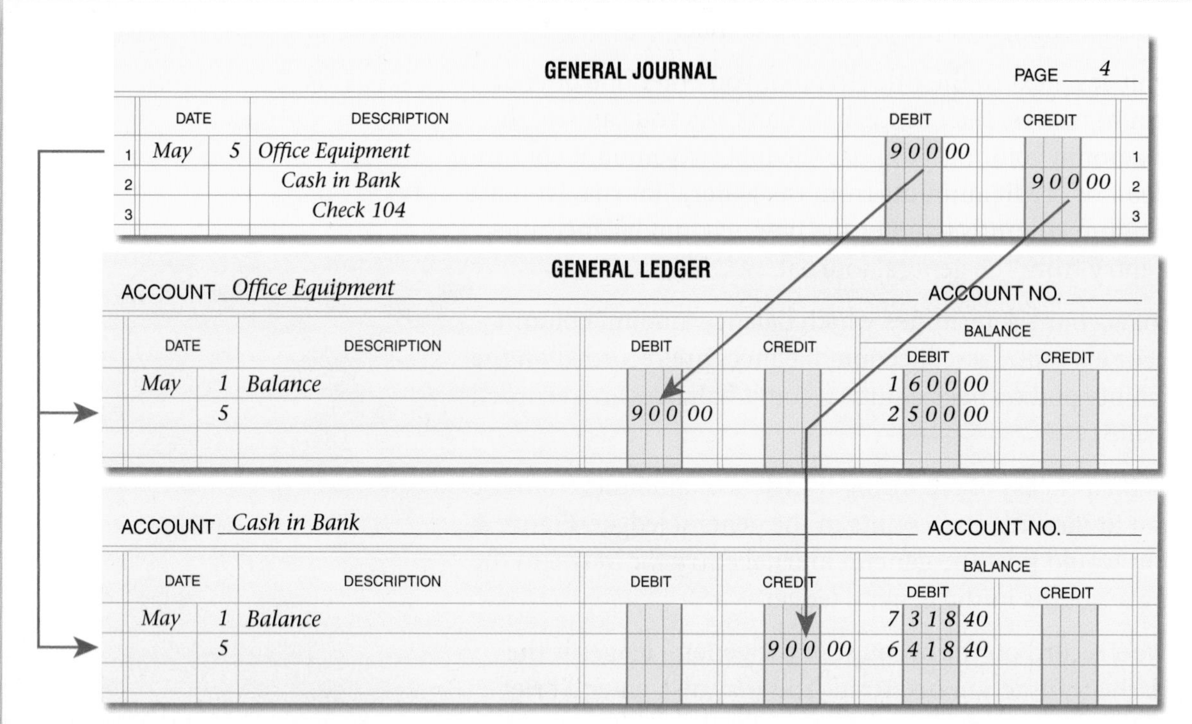

GENERAL JOURNAL — PAGE 4

	DATE		DESCRIPTION	DEBIT	CREDIT	
1	May	5	Office Equipment	900 00		1
2			Cash in Bank		900 00	2
3			Check 104			3

GENERAL LEDGER

ACCOUNT Office Equipment — ACCOUNT NO.

DATE		DESCRIPTION	DEBIT	CREDIT	BALANCE DEBIT	BALANCE CREDIT
May	1	Balance			1 600 00	
	5		900 00		2 500 00	

ACCOUNT Cash in Bank — ACCOUNT NO.

DATE		DESCRIPTION	DEBIT	CREDIT	BALANCE DEBIT	BALANCE CREDIT
May	1	Balance			7 318 40	
	5			900 00	6 418 40	

You then record the credit entry to the general ledger account Cash in Bank. This amount is entered in the credit column. Cash in Bank is an asset account. Remember that credit entries decrease asset account balances. Thus, the balance in the Cash in Bank account decreases by $900. The new debit balance for Cash in Bank is $6,418.40. Both account balances are recorded on the debit side.

Final Balances At the end of an accounting period, you will post the figures from the general journal to the appropriate accounts in the general ledger. After all entries have been posted, the final balance for each account will appear on the general ledger. See **Figure 5.**

This account had a beginning balance of $1,600. Three debit entries were made: $900, $2,350, and $3,680. Each of these entries increased the account balance. On May 18, a credit entry of $400 decreased the balance. So, the account called Office Equipment has a final debit balance of $8,130.

Time to Post The size of the business, the number of transactions, and whether the business uses a manual accounting system or a computerized accounting system will affect how often posting occurs. Ideally, businesses should post daily to keep their accounts up to date.

FIGURE 5 Journal Entries Posted to a General Ledger

Individual Entries A general ledger shows individual expenses and totals for each type of account. *What was the balance of this account after the credit of $400 was deducted?*

GENERAL LEDGER

ACCOUNT *Office Equipment* ACCOUNT NO. ______

DATE		DESCRIPTION	DEBIT	CREDIT	BALANCE DEBIT	BALANCE CREDIT
May	*1*	*Balance*			*1 600 00*	
	5		*900 00*		*2 500 00*	
	12		*2 350 00*		*4 850 00*	
	18			*400 00*	*4 450 00*	
	27		*3 680 00*		*8 130 00*	

STEP 5 Prepare a Trial Balance

When you have journalized all your business transactions and posted each of them to the accounts in the general ledger, you need to know if the account balances are correct. Did you post all the amounts from the general journal to the general ledger accounts? Is the accounting equation still in balance?

FIGURE 6 A Completed Trial Balance

Balancing Act A trial balance statement lists all the separate accounts for a business. *What does it mean if the debit and credit columns are not equal?*

Archer Delivery Service
Trial Balance
For the Month Ended May 31, 20--

Account	Debit	Credit
Cash in Bank	*2 891 00*	
Accounts Receivable	*1 370 00*	
Office Equipment	*8 130 00*	
Delivery Equipment	*4 260 00*	
Accounts Payable		*5 822 00*
Chris Archer, Capital		*10 829 00*
Totals	*16 651 00*	*16 651 00*

To answer these questions, you will prepare a trial balance. A **trial balance** is a list of all the account names for a business and their current balances. After you complete all posting, the total of all the debit balances should equal the total of all the credit balances. If the debit and credit totals are the same, then the general ledger is balanced. You can assume that the posting is complete and that the math is correct. **Figure 6** shows an example of a trial balance for the month of May 20--.

You will notice that the accounting equation is still balanced:

Assets = Liabilities + Owner's Equity

Keeping Records

To summarize, you have learned that businesses keep financial records according to an established set of principles and procedures. Every effective business, large and small, follows GAAP guidelines. The steps of the accounting cycle are universal. **Figure 7** illustrates the first five steps of the accounting cycle that were introduced in this section. Businesses generate their financial statements by following the steps of the accounting cycle.

FIGURE 7 The First Five Steps of the Accounting Cycle

The Backbone The accounting cycle is the basis of all accounting procedures. *Why should all businesses use the same accounting system?*

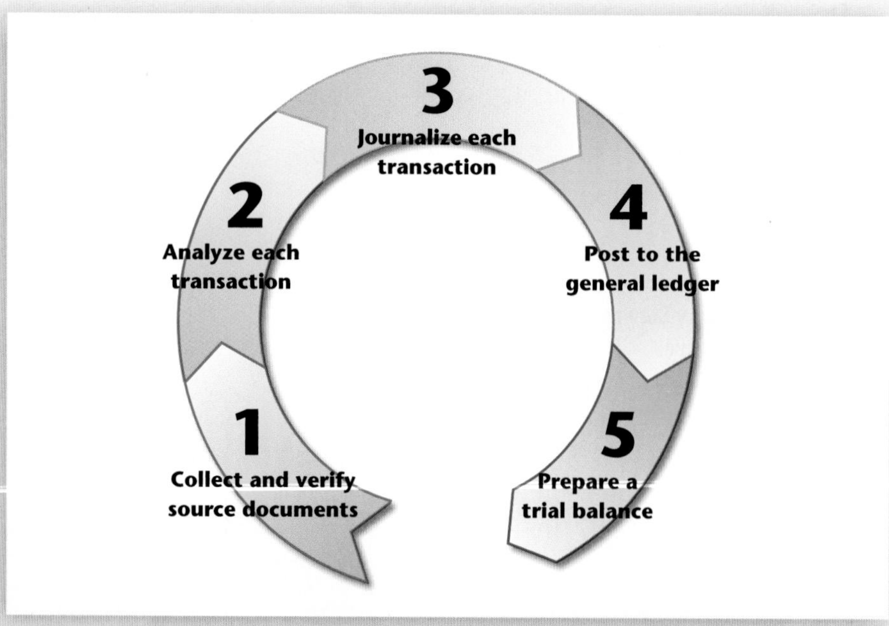
1
Collect and verify source documents
2
Analyze each transaction
3
Journalize each transaction
4
Post to the general ledger
5
Prepare a trial balance

SECTION 1 Assessment

Review Key Concepts

1. **Explain** What is the purpose of the accounting system?
2. **Define** Identify and define the three categories of the accounting equation.
3. **Summarize** Why do businesses use the accounting cycle?

Higher Order Thinking H.O.T.

4. **Extend** As a junior accountant, you have just prepared a trial balance for your supervisor and found that the debit and credit columns are off by over $2,300. What should you do before you submit the information to your supervisor?

21st Century Skills

5. **Work Creatively with Others** Put yourself in the role of bookkeeper, and choose a partner to play a graphic designer who has just started a business. The designer has purchased the equipment, furniture, and supplies needed, and has already begun work for several clients. Set up appropriate accounts for the designer. With your partner, role-play a discussion in which you explain the accounting system that you set up for the business. Have the designer ask questions about how it will work. Use accounting concepts and terms from "the language of business."

Mathematics

6. **Accounting Transactions** ABC Company has made the following transactions in the early part of the year. Create t-accounts for each transaction listed below. Using the t-accounts, calculate the net change in total assets, liabilities, and owners' equity for ABC Company.
   a) ABC Company purchased office equipment for $1,500 in cash
   b) ABC Company purchased a delivery truck for $15,000 on credit
   c) ABC Company sold $7,500 worth of inventory, the purchaser paid 25 percent of the total in cash and 75 percent on credit

Math Concept **Calculate Balance Sheet Changes** To calculate the net changes in the balance sheet identify the debits and credits for each account. Determine the total debit or credit in assets and liabilities, respectively. Assets equals liabilities plus owners' equity.

Starting Hint Determine the net change in total assets by identifying the asset accounts that are impacted by each transaction Calculate total debits minus total credits for each asset account. A positive number is a net debit; negative is a net credit.

NCTM Problem Solving Apply and adapt a variety of appropriate strategies to solve problems.

 glencoe.com  Check your answers.

Section Objectives

- **Define** the meaning and purpose of financial statements.
- **Describe** the functions of an income statement.
- **Explain** why it is necessary to understand the statement of cash flows.

As You Read

List Which merchandising businesses in your community do you frequent?

Financial Statements

Why are financial statements important for operating a business?

To operate a business profitably, you need to have up-to-date financial information. You cannot make decisions if you do not have the current facts. Financial statements provide this information. **Financial statements** are reports that summarize changes that result from business transactions during an accounting period. By preparing and analyzing these statements, you can see if your business is on course, having difficulty, or headed for serious trouble. Preparing financial statements is another step in the accounting cycle.

The **primary,** or most important, financial statements are the income statement (or the statement of operations or statement of earnings) and the balance sheet. A third statement, the statement of cash flows, is also used. The sources of information for your financial statements are the final balances in the general ledger accounts. When you prepared your trial balance, you proved that the posting from the general journal to the general ledger was correct and complete. Now you have to report what happened during this accounting period.

You will now examine financial statements from a small merchandising business—Happy House Card Shop owned by Sheila Henry. A merchandising business is a business that buys goods, marks them up, and sells them to customers. The shop sells a variety of cards, gift wrapping, and small gifts bought from wholesalers or distributors.

Income Statement

At the end of an accounting period, you want to know how much money your business made or lost. You also want to know how much money you took in from sales and where the money went. You report this information on your **income statement,** which is a report of the net income or net loss for an accounting period. An income statement for a merchandising business has five sections: revenue, cost of merchandise sold, gross profit on sales, operating expenses, and net income (or loss). The amounts entered on the income statement will be the ending balances in the accounts in the general ledger. **Figure 8** shows an income statement.

Revenue You will notice that the beginning of the statement reports the total sales (A), or revenue, for the period. Happy House earned $292,619 in sales for the year ending December 31, 20--. This is the total amount of money that the business earned from selling merchandise to customers.

Cost of Merchandise Sold Next, the cost of the merchandise sold (B) is calculated and reported. The **cost of merchandise sold** is the amount of money the business paid for the goods that it sold to customers. To arrive at this amount, Sheila first determines the cost of merchandise in the store at the beginning of the accounting period.

In this case, $83,744 was on hand. Then she adds the cost of the additional merchandise that Happy House purchased during the year, which was $205,813. This means that the store had a total of $289,557 in merchandise available to be sold.

After counting her inventory, Sheila determines that she still has $93,281 in merchandise in the store. This means that the cost of the merchandise sold is $196,276.

FIGURE 8 **Income Statement**

Vital Records An income statement shows profits and losses, and where money was spent. *Who might want to review income statements other than a business owner and his or her accountant?*

HAPPY HOUSE CARD SHOP

Income Statement

For the Year Ended December 31, 20--

Revenue:		
Sales	**292,619 (A)**	
Cost of Merchandise Sold:		
Merchandise on Hand Jan. 1	83,744	
Plus Merchandise Purchased	205,813	
Merchandise Available for Sale	289,557	
Minus Merchandise Still on Hand	93,281	
Total Cost of Merchandise Sold:		**196,276 (B)**
Gross Profit on Sales		**96,343 (C)**
Operating Expenses:		
Advertising Expense	2,734	
Insurance Expense	487	
Maintenance Expense	3,551	
Miscellaneous Expense	762	
Rent Expense	18,500	
Salaries Expense	26,931	
Supplies Expense	1,024	
Utilities Expense	4,107	
Total Operating Expenses:		**58,096 (D)**
Net Income		**38,247 (E)**

Gross Profit Sheila then subtracts the cost of the merchandise sold ($196,276) from the amount earned from sales ($292,619) to arrive at (C), the gross profit on sales ($96,343). The gross profit on sales is the profit made from selling merchandise before operating expenses are deducted. This is the profit Sheila made by marking up her merchandise and selling it.

Net Income **Net income** is the amount of revenue that remains after expenses for the accounting period are subtracted from the gross profit on sales. To calculate the net income for the period, Sheila subtracts the total operating expenses (D = $58,096) from the gross profit on sales (C = $96,343). For this period, Happy House Card Shop reported a net income (E) of $38,247.

Analyzing the Income Statement

You can see that Happy House made a profit. It is a good idea to compare the figures on this income statement to those on last year's statement. A comparison of **condensed,** or summarized, income statements for Happy House is shown in **Figure 9.** By reviewing the changes, Sheila will have an idea of how well her business is doing.

In **Figure 9**, you can see that sales increased by 3.10 percent from last year. Depending on where the business is located and on general economic conditions, this may be good. Notice that the net income rose by 5.44 percent. This could be because the business reduced total operating expenses by 5.19 percent. Sales increased, but the net income increased at a greater rate. This is an example of good financial management.

FIGURE 9 **Comparison of Income Statements**

Progress Check A common method of analysis is using an income statement. *What can a business owner learn by comparing statements from one year to the next?*

HAPPY HOUSE CARD SHOP
Comparative Income Statement
For the Year Ended December 31, 20--

	Previous Year	Current Year	Dollar Change	Percent Change
Sales	283,834	292,619	+8,785	+3.10
Cost of Merchandise Sold	186,283	196,276	+9,993	+5.36
Gross Profit on Sales	97,551	96,343	−1,208	−1.24
Total Operating Expenses	61,277	58,096	−3,181	−5.19
Net Income	36,274	38,247	+1,973	+5.44

Around the World

Germany

Historical Cost Accounting

Businesses in the United States all follow GAAP guidelines for their accounting so that anyone can understand the financial reports. Unfortunately, these guidelines only apply within the United States. There are no international guidelines. Each country develops their own accounting system based on their country's laws and practices.

The German accounting system is based on law and tax codes and is extremely conservative when compared to the United States. For example, the amortization period for intangible items on a financial statement is up to 40 years in the United States but only 5 years in Germany. The German accounting system is greatly influenced by the banks and the reporting system is geared toward the workers and investors. The system is considered to be loyal to historical costs because there is no requirement for information for changing prices. This is because Germany works at keeping inflation low. Another great deviation from U.S. practices is that in addition to the financial statement, German businesses must provide social accounting. This means that they prepare a management report with information about the working environment, personnel, training, environmental concerns, and group activities in the industry.

Critical Thinking

1. **Expand** What steps would you take to ensure that accounting guidelines were being followed for your business?
2. **Relate** Would those steps change if you were doing business in a country other than the United States?

DATABYTES

Capital
Berlin

Population
82,282,988

Language
German

Currency
Euro

Gross Domestic Product (GDP)
$3.273 trillion

GDP per capita
$34,100

Industry
Iron, steel, coal, cement, chemicals, machinery, vehicles, machine tools, electronics, food and beverages, shipbuilding, textiles

Agriculture
Potatoes, wheat, barley, sugar beets, fruit, cabbages; cattle, pigs, poultry

Exports
Machinery, vehicles, chemicals, metals and manufactures, foodstuffs, textiles

Natural Resources
Coal, lignite, natural gas, iron ore, copper, nickel, uranium, potash, salt, construction materials, timber, arable land

Behind the Scenes
Staying in business requires not just great customer service, but ongoing evaluation and good decision making as well. *What are the main kinds of financial statements a business owner should monitor on a regular basis?*

Another common method of analysis is to show figures on an income statement as a percentage of sales. Based on the present income statement and last year's statement from Happy House, a partial analysis is shown in **Figure 10.**

Last year the cost of merchandise sold was 65.63 percent of total sales. This year it increased to 67.08 percent of total sales. Sheila Henry paid more for her merchandise, but her sales did not increase at the same rate.

The gross profit on total sales decreased from 34.37 percent to 32.92 percent. Happy House sold more merchandise but lowered its percentage of gross profit. If it were not for a drop in expenses this year, the business would have reported a lower net income. This analysis provides the owner of Happy House with some of the information that she needs to make decisions regarding the store's pricing.

FIGURE 10 Comparison Using Percentage of Sales

Percentages Financial figures can also be expressed as percentages, and a business can assess and express its progress on a percentage basis. *How would the information in this sample be useful to the business owner in terms of pricing the merchandise?*

	Previous Year		Current Year	
	Amount in Dollars	Percent	Amount in Dollars	Percent
Sales	283,834	100.00	292,619	100.00
Cost of Merchandise Sold	– 186,283	– 65.63	–196,276	–67.08
Gross Profit on Sales	97,551	34.37	96,343	32.92

The Balance Sheet

The other primary financial statement of a business is a balance sheet. A **balance sheet** is a report of the balances of all asset, liability, and owner's equity accounts at the end of an accounting period. The main purpose of the balance sheet is to present a business's financial position by reporting the assets of a business and the claims against those assets (creditor's claims and owner's claims). It reports what the business owns, owes, and is worth on a specific date. It is like taking a financial photo of your business on the last day of the accounting period. This is your present financial situation. The balance sheet for Happy House Card Shop is shown in **Figure 11.**

You learned previously that the basic accounting equation must always be in balance. The balance sheet represents the basic accounting equation.

Assets = Liabilities + Owner's Equity

FIGURE 11 **Balance Sheet**

Financial Snapshot A balance sheet represents the financial status of a business on the last day of an accounting period. *If a business is in balance, what will the balance sheet show?*

HAPPY HOUSE CARD SHOP
Balance Sheet
December 31, 20--

ASSETS		
Cash in Bank	35,372	
Accounts Receivable	14,201	
Merchandise Inventory	93,281	
Supplies	8,285	
Office Equipment	12,187	
Display Equipment	47,883	
TOTAL ASSETS		**211,209**
LIABILITIES		
Accounts Payable	42,722	
Sales Tax Payable	3,621	
Payroll Taxes Payable	2,749	
TOTAL LIABILITIES		**49,092**
OWNER'S EQUITY		
Sheila Henry, Capital		162,117
TOTAL LIABILITIES + OWNER'S EQUITY		**211,209**

Economics and You

Profit Motive

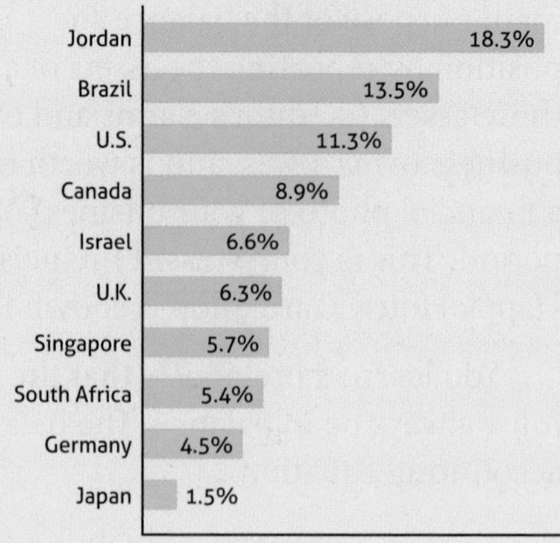

Profit is the revenue left after paying all the costs and expenses associated with running a business. Profit provides the incentive for entrepreneurs to risk their own money to open and run a business. For entrepreneurs to be successful, they must sell the goods and services customers want or need at a competitive price—a price they are willing to pay. That price must be high enough to cover the cost of the item (to make or purchase), as well as enough extra for profit. Profits are needed to buy more goods and make improvements to a company. Profits are taxed, so the actual profit an entrepreneur realizes is less than the one reported on an income statement. Thus, net income on an income statement is really net profit before taxes.

Personal Finance Connection You can share in the profits of a corporation if you are an investor. Corporations pay dividends to stockholders when they make a profit. You can also use the profit motive to improve your ability to budget your money. List your revenue sources and expenses to see how much money you have left (your personal profit). Do you need to make more money to cover all your expenses or what expenses can you reduce so you have more money left for saving and investing?

Critical Thinking If a business did not prepare financial reports, how might you know if it made a profit or suffered a loss? What problems could arise if a business owner did not keep accurate financial records?

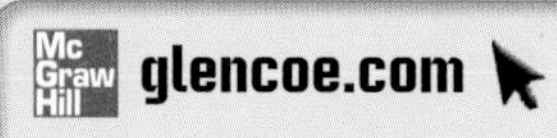

Activity Download an Economics and You Worksheet Activity.

Notice that a balance sheet consists of three sections: an asset section, a liability section, and an owner's equity section. On the Happy House balance sheet, the total assets ($211,209) equal the total liabilities ($49,092) plus the owner's equity ($162,117). This means the accounting equation is still in balance.

Analyzing the Balance Sheet

To analyze these figures, you would compare the current amounts on the balance sheet with figures from last year, as shown in **Figure 12.**

By examining the numbers and percentages, you can see that changes have taken place. Happy House bought various assets during the year. This is shown in various increased balances:

- Supplies
- Office Equipment
- Display Equipment

The business also has more cash and inventory on hand, and higher accounts receivable, than last year.

The balance sheet is an important financial statement, but to make wise decisions, you should always compare the financial data to a previous year's balance sheet.

Remember, the financial statements provide the information about assets, liabilities, and owner's equity. In order to utilize the data provided by financial statements, you must analyze and interpret the data to make recommendations and effective decisions based on that information.

Reading Check

Explain How does the owner of a merchandising business earn a profit on sales?

FIGURE 12 **Comparison of Balance Sheets**

Year-to-Year Comparison To analyze the figures on a current balance sheet, a business owner needs to compare it to those from previous accounting periods. *What can the owner learn from such a comparison? In this sample, have the assets increased or decreased?*

HAPPY HOUSE CARD SHOP
Comparative Balance Sheet
December 31, 20--

	Previous Year	Current Year	Dollar Change	Percent Change
ASSETS				
Cash in Bank	22,743	35,372	+12,629	+55.53
Accounts Receivable	8,338	14,201	+5,863	+70.32
Merchandise Inventory	83,744	93,281	+9,537	+11.93
Supplies	4,631	8,285	+3,654	+78.90
Office Equipment	8,958	12,187	+3,229	+36.05
Display Equipment	41,720	47,883	+6,163	+14.77
TOTAL ASSETS	**170,134**	**211,209**	**+23,075**	**+13.56**
LIABILITIES				
Accounts Payable	39,837	42,722	+2,885	+7.24
Sales Tax Payable	3,506	3,621	+115	+3.28
Payroll Taxes Payable	2,921	2,749	– 172	– 5.88
TOTAL LIABILITIES	**46,264**	**49,092**	**+2,828**	**+6.11**
OWNER'S EQUITY				
Sheila Henry, Capital	**123,870**	**162,117**	**+38,247**	**+30.88**

Statement of Cash Flows

Why are cash flows important?

The income statement and balance sheet provide vital financial information, but neither financial statement shows how cash came into or went out of the business during the period. You will want to know how much cash is available during business operations. You may remember that your personal cash flow is the money that actually goes in and out of your wallet and bank accounts. In a business, cash flow refers to the sources and uses of cash during an accounting period.

Understanding cash flows will help you in cash management. Suppose that your school has a big dance coming up on Friday. All of your friends are going and will probably go somewhere to eat after it is over. You will need cash for Friday night, but you will not get your paycheck from your job until Saturday. In this example, money needs to go out for the dance before money comes in from your job. You have a "cash crunch" problem. Businesses often face similar problems. If a small business experiences a cash crunch situation, it could have serious problems. Good cash control and management means that sufficient cash is available for operating the business on a daily basis and for emergencies.

Cash Inflows and Outflows

A **statement of cash flows** is a financial statement that reports how much cash a business took in and where the cash went. It explains changes in the Cash in Bank account during the accounting period.

Entertainment Expenses
It is often assumed that people in the entertainment industry earn a lot of money, but that is not always true—at least not right away.
Explain why a theatre group would experience a negative cash flow before ticket sales begin.

FIGURE 13 **Statement of Cash Flows**

Show Me the Money A business may look good on paper with assets, such as building and equipment, but income in the form of cash is needed to pay for expenses. *What items would be considered cash inflows for this business?*

HAPPY HOUSE CARD SHOP
Statement of Cash Flows
For the Year Ended December 31, 20--

Cash Flows from Operating Activities		
Cash Receipts from:		
Sales to Customers	$286,756	$286,756
Cash Payments for:		
Purchase of Merchandise	($202,928)	
Operating Expenses	(61,807)	(264,735)
Net Cash Flows from Operating Activities		$22,021
Cash Flows from investing Activities:		
Cash Payments for:		
Purchase of Assets (Equipment)	($9,392)	
Net Cash Flows from Investing Activities		(9,392)
Cash Flows from Financing Activities:		
Net Cash Flows from Financing Activities		0
Net Increase (Decrease) in Cash		**$12,629**
Cash at Beginning of Year		22,743
Cash at End of Year		**$35,372**

Cash flows include both cash inflows (cash that enters a business) and cash outflows (cash that exits a business). Cash inflows may include sales and interest earned from investments or savings. Cash outflows may include operating expenses, merchandise purchases, supplies, and interest and taxes paid.

Figure 13 shows the statement of cash flows for Happy House. Notice that the statement of cash flows has three sections:

- Cash Flows from Operating Activities
- Cash Flows from Investing Activities
- Cash Flows from Financing Activities

Analyzing the Statement of Cash Flows

Happy House has a positive cash flow. During the year, more cash entered the business than was paid out. The difference is $12,629.

When your business has negative cash flows, you will probably experience a lack of available cash. You may not be able to pay your bills or buy goods to resell. The business will not grow. Your statement of cash flows can be a major consideration when you want to borrow money. Potential investors and lenders want to see cash flowing into your business in a constant, positive manner.

Reading Check

Review How can a business owner determine how much cash is available during business operations?

Computerized Accounting

How do businesses use accounting software?

Most businesses use some type of accounting software to record and report their business transactions. Even for an automated system, you still need to collect and keep your source documents. Each business transaction must be separated into its debit and credit parts. However, you will enter the transaction in the computer system by using account numbers rather than the account names. You still need to enter the amounts.

Computerized Posting

When all transactions are entered, you can "tell" the program to post all amounts to the appropriate general ledger accounts. Computerized posting is faster and eliminates accounting errors that you might make by doing it manually.

Reading Check

Identify What are the benefits of using accounting software for posting?

After You Read

React Now that you know about the advantages of having a standardized accounting system, what, if any, disadvantages can you name?

Using Accounting Principles

What are important financial tools for businesses?

You have learned about several basic financial statements that are some of the tools used to apply the first five accounting principles. The basic accounting principles are the backbone of every business. Business owners and investors who risk their money and time depend on accurate accounting records to report the results of the operation and financial condition of their businesses. All businesses use the same practices, which help them analyze their financial positions and make effective business decisions.

Assessment

Review Key Concepts

1. **Define** What are financial statements, and why are they used?
2. **Describe** What are the functions of an income statement?
3. **Explain** Why is it necessary to understand the statement of cash flows?

Higher Order Thinking H.O.T.

4. **Assess** How it is possible for a business to have made a profit during the most recent accounting period but not have enough money to pay its employees this week?

English Language Arts

5. **Sharing Financial Information** Sylvia worked her way through business school at a health food store. Her manager and mentor taught her about the various aspects of operating a business, from ordering stock to evaluating staff performance. When she graduated, she opened her own store and called it Sylvia's Smoothies. Now she is ready to add a partner to her business. Using presentation software, create a few sample slides about the company's financial status that Sylvia could show to potential partners.

NCTE 12 Use language to accomplish individual purposes.

Mathematics

6. **Income Statement** Nina has a Yoga Shop in which she sells books, videos, and accessories as well as teaches classes. She is preparing the annual income statement for the shop. The cost of merchandise at the beginning of the period was $75,750. She purchased merchandise worth $183,000 during the period and her cost of merchandise at the end of the period was $104,500. Calculate the cost of merchandise sold during the period. If sales were $215,000 and total operating expense was $47,000, what is the net income?

Math Concept **Calculate Net Income** To calculate the net income for a specific period, subtract cost of merchandise sold from sales to determine gross profit on sales. Subtract operating expenses from the gross profit on sales to calculate net income.

Starting Hint Determine the cost of merchandise sold during the period by adding the merchandise purchased to the cost of merchandise at the beginning of the period. Subtract the cost of merchandise at the end of the period from this figure.

NCTM Number and Operations Understand numbers, ways of representing numbers, relationships among numbers, and number systems.

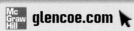

Check your answers.

Visual Summary

Financial Accounting

The Accounting Equation

Use these important equations to confirm that business accounts are in balance.

Assets − Liabilities = Owner's Equity

Assets = Liabilities + Owner's Equity

Statement of Cash Flows

Income statements and balance sheets are important, but it is the statement of cash flows that shows how cash came into or went out of the business during an accounting period.

Cash Inflows (cash entering the business)
- sales
- interest from investments
- interest from savings

The Business

Cash Outflows (cash leaving the business)
- operating expenses
- merchandise purchases
- supplies
- interest paid

Try It!

Create an organizer like the one shown to identify the five sections of an income statement for a merchandising business.

Chapter Review and Assessment

Chapter Summary

- The accounting equation states that Assets − Liabilities = Owner's Equity. Accounts show the balance for a specific item. Accounts are set up as needed by a business, and may vary.
- The first five steps of the accounting cycle are to collect and verify source documents, analyze each transaction, journalize each transaction, post transactions to the general ledger, and prepare a trial balance.
- Business transactions are recorded in the general journal.
- Posting to the general ledger allows you to see the balances in each account.
- A trial balance is a list of all the accounts and their current balances. All the debit balances should equal the total of all the credit balances.
- The income statement is a report of the net income or net loss for an accounting period.
- The balance sheet reports balances for all asset, liability, and owner's equity accounts at the end of an accounting period. It presents the business's financial position.
- The statement of cash flows reports how much cash your business took in and how it was used.

Vocabulary Review

1. Use at least 15 of these terms in a short essay about the basics of financial accounting.

- financial reports
- accounting period
- accounting cycle
- accounting equation
- account
- accounts receivable
- accounts payable
- double-entry accounting
- T account
- debit
- credit (accounting)
- journal
- general ledger
- posting
- trial balance
- financial statements
- income statement
- cost of merchandise sold
- net income
- balance sheet
- statement of cash flows
- claim
- transfer
- primary
- condensed

Higher Order Thinking 

2. **Compare and Contrast** How is balancing your checkbook and bank statements similar or different to steps in the accounting cycle?
3. **Suppose** What might be the advantages and disadvantages of partnering with another accountant in a business venture?
4. **Defend** If you have a receipt, defend whether or not it is necessary to enter a brief description of the transaction in the general journal.
5. **Extend** Why is it important to understand basic accounting procedures, even if you use accounting software to manage accounts?
6. **Ascertain** Last year, the gross profit on sales was 32.38 percent. This year, gross profit on sales is 28.08 percent. Is this enough to justify a price increase? Explain your answer.
7. **Justify** As a business owner, would you hire an accountant or do your own bookkeeping?
8. **Extend** At the end of an accounting period, what documents will a potential investor need?
9. **Speculate** With accounting software available, why do people still choose to hire accountants?

College and Career Readiness

Social Studies

10. International Finance The Internet has spurred an increase in globalization. International business people need to monitor and understand exchange values. The United States uses the dollar, much of Europe uses the euro, and Great Britain still uses the pound. Thanks to the Internet, business people can easily track the exchange rate of multiple currencies. For three days, use online resources to track the dollar exchange rate of the euro, the pound, and a third form of currency. Record how many of each will equal $100. How are international businesses affected by exchange rates?

NCSS VII I Distinguish between the domestic and global economic systems, and explain how the two interact.

Mathematics

11. Balance Sheet Analysis XYZ Co. is a privately owned company that specializes in computer networking and repair. At the end of the year, XYZ Co. had total assets of $305,000. 30 percent of the total assets were made up of cash, 25 percent of accounts receivables, 40 percent of inventory, and 5 percent of supplies. The company also had total liabilities of $245,000 and owner's equity in the amount of $60,000. Calculate the amount of cash, accounts receivables, inventory and supplies on the balance sheet. Is this business in balance?

Math Concept **Calculate Balance Sheet Accounts** Calculate to see if the balance sheet is in balance by using the accounting equation: assets = liabilities + owner's equity. If this equation holds true, the company is in balance.

Starting Hint Calculate the amount of cash on the balance sheet by first identifying the total assets in the assets section of the balance sheet. Cash can be found in this section of the balance sheet, however, the problem provides the percentage of total assets that cash makes up. Multiply this percentage by the total assets.

NCTM Problem Solving Solve problems that arise in mathematics and in other contexts.

English Language Arts

12. Buy or Lease? Sooner or later most businesses have to decide whether to purchase or lease office space. Lavetta is a Certified Public Accountant who has been working from her home for almost four years. She has $15,000 to use for office space, but she does not know if she should buy or lease. Conduct research on leasing versus buying commercial office space. Then write a summary of your findings and include your recommendations for Lavetta.

NCTE 4 Use written language to communicate effectively.

Economics

13. The Role of Economic Institutions Institutions evolve in market economies to help individuals and groups accomplish their goals. The Financial Accounting Standards Board (FASB) is one such organization. The FASB's goal is to improve accounting practices by establishing and enforcing guidelines for reporting accounts, identifying and resolving issues, and creating a uniform standard across the financial markets. FASB standards, known as generally accepted accounting principles (GAAP), govern the preparation of corporate financial reports and are recognized as authoritative by the Securities and Exchange Commission. Why do you think this organization evolved? Give examples of business practices that created a need for the FASB.

Real-World Applications

14. Accounting Software Using software saves time when generating the financial reports needed for evaluating the progress of a business. Search the names of five different accounting software packages. Go to the Web sites for these packages, and look for Web sites that list and compare packages. What sets each system apart from the others? Are some designed for particular industries? Do the users of the systems need to understand accounting? Based on your research, which would you recommend to a small business owner and why? Present your information in an oral report.

Income Statements

Dakota's gardening business now includes gardening for 22 homes and gardening and planting for three commercial properties. She is considering hiring Rashelle for an hourly fee to work with her so she can expand the business. To see if she can afford to hire Rashelle, she has prepared an income statement. In reviewing six months of income statements, Dakota felt she could afford to pay Rashelle, especially if she picked up some new accounts.

Dakota's Gardening

Income Statement for the Month Ended July 31, 20--

Revenue	
Regular gardening fees	$3,460
Charge for plantings	180
Charge for trimming trees	300
Total revenue	$3,940
Operating Expenses	
Buying plantings	$90
Truck loan	150
Equipment: new tree pruner	75
Gas expense	25
Insurance expense	35
Total expenses	$375
Net Income	$3,565

Apply

Choose a service business that you might like to operate. Determine what you would charge for your service. Based on your fee and services, determine what your monthly revenue and expenses would be. Using the same guidelines as shown above, prepare an income statement on a separate sheet of paper. Would you want to hire and supervise help or would you prefer to work alone?

CHAPTER 8

Managing Payroll and Inventory

Visual Literacy

Using an inventory system makes good business sense. ***What are some negative things that could happen as a result of poor inventory management?***

Discovery Project

Explore Payroll and Inventory

Key Question

What are some things employers need to know about payroll and inventory before starting or taking over a business?

Project Goal

Jeremy and Cindy Cole just took over a specialized retail store with 3 full-time employees and 2 part-time workers. They sell gifts imported from India. Cindy plans to run the daily operations of the brick-and-mortar store, and Jeremy will focus on getting their new Web site up and running. About four times a year, they expect to travel to cultural fairs and festivals to sell their products. The previous owner's payroll and inventory records were done by hand, and the Coles would like to update the systems. They have come to you for advice.

- Explain the payroll tasks to perform each pay period. Discuss the payroll information they must record in their accounting records.
- Help them decide if and how they will pay overtime or commissions.
- Explain the types of inventory systems, and offer your suggestions.
- Help them determine which inventory costing method to use.

Ask Yourself...

- *In what way are the employees likely to be paid?*
- *Which employee taxes are the Coles responsible for paying?*
- *What benefits are the Coles likely to offer their staff?*
- *Which type of inventory system and costing method is best for their line of products?*

Think Creatively

How can good inventory management help a business meet its goals? How can you manage your personal inventory at home?

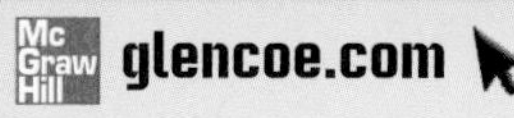

Evaluate Download an assessment rubric.

THE BIG IDEA

Good payroll and inventory management are essential elements for the success of any business.

ASK STANDARD & POOR'S

Social Security and Medicare

Q *I am only 16. Why should I pay Social Security and Medicare taxes? Those programs may not be around when I am old enough to collect.*

A It is true that Social Security programs are projected to run low on funds around the year 2025. Under the present system, the rate of return on your contributions to these programs is lower than what you might earn. However, Congress is working to ensure that Social Security will provide funds for future retirees. Also, Social Security and Medicare offer many other types of benefits including disability benefits.

Writing Activity

Write the title and opening paragraph for an article giving tips on what young workers can do now to supplement Social Security and Medicare. Use the journalistic technique of answering "who, what, when, where, why, and how." Look at newspapers to see how articles are formatted.

Reading Guide

Before You Read

The Essential Question Why is it important for employers to establish and maintain efficient payroll and inventory management systems?

Main Idea

Effective payroll management and inventory maintenance enable businesses to run more profitably, manage cash flow, and consistently meet customer needs.

Content Vocabulary

- payroll
- gross earnings
- salary
- hourly wage
- overtime rate
- commission
- deductions
- Federal Insurance Contributions Act (FICA)
- Social Security tax
- Medicare tax
- total gross earnings
- perpetual inventory system
- point-of-sale terminals
- periodic inventory system
- specific identification method
- first-in, first-out method (FIFO)
- last-in, first-out method (LIFO)

Academic Vocabulary

You will see these words in your reading and on your tests.

- withheld
- allowance
- stock
- staple

Graphic Organizer

Before you read this chapter, create an organizer like the one shown. As you read, use the organizer to identify and describe the four common methods by which employees are paid.

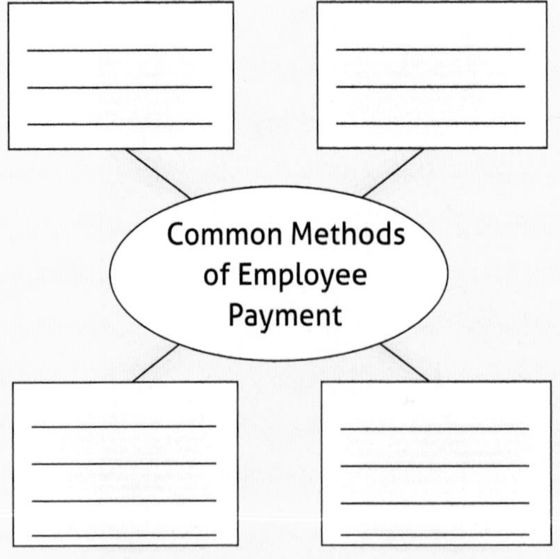

  glencoe.com Print this graphic organizer.

Standards

Academic

Mathematics

NCTM Connections Communicate their mathematical thinking coherently and clearly to peers, teachers, and others.

English Language Arts

NCTE 5 Use different writing process elements to communicate effectively.

NCTE 7 Conduct research and gather, evaluate, and synthesize data to communicate discoveries.

Science

NSES E Students should develop abilities of technological design, understandings about science and technology.

NCTM *National Council of Teachers of Mathematics*
NCTE *National Council of Teachers of English*
NCSS *National Council for the Social Studies*
NSES *National Science Education Standards*

Common Core

Reading Read and comprehend complex literary and informational texts independently and proficiently.

Speaking and Listening Present information, findings, and supporting evidence such that listeners can follow the line of reasoning and the organization, development, and style are appropriate to task, purpose, and audience.

Speaking and Listening Adapt speech to a variety of contexts and communicative tasks, demonstrating command of formal English when indicated or appropriate.

The Importance of Payroll Records

Why do payroll records need to be accurate?

If you own a business, a large and important part of its accounting system will involve payroll. A **payroll** is a list of employees and the payments due to each employee for a specific period of time. The specific period of time during which you pay your employees is known as a pay period. The two most common pay periods are weekly and biweekly (every two weeks). However, some companies pay their employees only once per month.

A good payroll accounting system ensures that employees are paid on time and have the correct amounts on their paychecks. The payroll records and reports need to be very accurate. As with other accounting functions, when you process payroll information, you must follow specific guidelines. As discussed previously, these guidelines are known as generally accepted accounting principles (GAAP). In addition to following GAAP procedures, state and federal governments issue strict guidelines for paying employees and reporting payroll information.

A business has two major goals when setting up a payroll system. The system should perform these functions:

- Collect and process all information needed to prepare and issue payroll checks.
- Maintain payroll records needed for accounting purposes and for preparing reports to government agencies.

Every payroll system has some common tasks or steps. All are important and must be done carefully, accurately, and regularly. If you pay your employees every week, you will complete all of these tasks weekly:

1. Calculate gross earnings.
2. Calculate payroll deductions.
3. Prepare payroll records.
4. Prepare paychecks.
5. Record payroll information in the accounting records.
6. Report payroll information to the government.

Reading Check

Define What is a payroll?

Section Objectives

- **Identify** six steps in managing a payroll system.
- **Explain** how employers calculate employees' gross earnings.
- **Discuss** required and voluntary payroll deductions.
- **Describe** the role of employers in assuring prompt payment to the government.

As You Read

Discover Why is it necessary to keep accurate payroll records?

Careers That Count!

Lorinda Harper • Purchasing Agent

As a purchasing agent for a polymer and electronics manufacturer, I spend my work days finding good sources for products, buying the products, and negotiating the purchasing of raw materials, component parts, equipment, and more. It's my job to develop relationships with suppliers, determine patterns of need, and ensure the best quality and cost of items purchased. I must also understand key market trends and issues that affect the supply of products. I frequently work more than 40 hours a week because of special sales, conferences, or production deadlines, and occasionally I need to travel. I prepared for this career by completing a bachelor's degree program with a business emphasis and several years of on-the-job training, but cultivating business relationships is my strongest skill and my favorite part of my job.

EXPLORE CAREERS

Visit the Web site of the U.S. Department of Labor's Bureau of Labor Statistics and obtain information about a career as a purchasing agent.

1. How might good payroll management affect a company's purchasing abilities?
2. What are some of the requirements for advancing in this career?

Skills	Education	Career Path
Must know how to analyze technical data and to perform financial analyses; communication, negotiation, and math skills; knowledge of supply-chain management	Bachelor's or master's degree in engineering, business, economics, or one of the applied sciences	Purchasing agents can become purchasing managers, wholesale and retail buyers, or supply managers. Other management functions may include production, planning, logistics, and marketing.

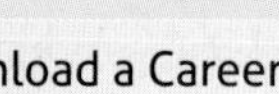

Activity Download a Career Exploration Activity.

Calculating Gross Earnings

What are salaries and wages?

The first step in a payroll system is to calculate the total earnings of all employees for the pay period. The total amount of money an employee earns in a pay period is the **gross earnings.** Three of the most common methods of paying employees are by salary, hourly wage, and salary plus commission.

Salary

A **salary** is a fixed amount of money paid to an employee for each pay period, regardless of the number of hours worked. For example, Catherine Boggs is the manager of the shoe department at Dickinson's Department Store. She earns a fixed weekly salary of $530 even though she may work 40 hours one week and 44 hours another week. Salaries are paid to managers, supervisors, and others.

Hourly Wage

If you work for a local business after school and on the weekends, you probably receive an **hourly wage,** a specific amount of money paid per hour to an employee. Most temporary and part-time jobs pay an hourly wage. Many full-time jobs, such as entry-level jobs, also pay an hourly wage.

For example, Sean McCormick works at a sporting goods outlet on weekday afternoons for $7.25 per hour. Last week he worked 20 hours, and his gross earnings were $145 ($7.25 × 20 = $145). This week he had already worked 20 hours by the end of the day on Wednesday. Sean's gross earnings vary from week to week because he works different amounts of time each week.

Employers may have hourly employees use time cards or a time clock to keep track of each day. They use this information to determine the total hours each employee worked during a pay period. At the end of each period, the employer checks the information on time cards or time sheets for accuracy. If the information is incorrect, paychecks will be inaccurate. That is a problem for both employees and employers.

Overtime Pay

According to state and federal laws, hourly-wage employees generally are paid extra when they work overtime, or more than 40 hours in a pay week. The **overtime rate,** the amount paid above the normal rate, is usually 1.5 times the employee's regular hourly wage. For example, Kelly Robinson's regular hourly wage is $7.40. If she works more than 40 hours in a given week, her overtime rate for the extra hours is $11.10 ($7.40 × 1.5 = $11.10).

Suppose that Kelly worked more than 40 hours last week. To calculate her gross earnings, multiply her regular hourly wage by 40 hours. Then you multiply the overtime rate by the number of overtime hours. By adding the results of these calculations, you can figure out her gross earnings for the week.

Typically, employees might work extra hours during holiday sales or other busy periods. They might also work overtime to cover for other employees who are sick or on vacation. Remember, controlling payroll costs is an important aspect of good financial management.

Commission

A **commission** is an amount of money paid to an employee based on a percentage of the employee's sales. The more the employee sells, the more he or she is paid. Paying commissions to sales employees is a way to encourage them to increase their sales.

reality bytes

Managing Cash Flow

Having enough cash on hand at the right time is key when it comes to managing a growing company. The lag between the time you have to pay your suppliers and employees and the time you collect from your customers is often a problem. The solution is cash flow management. Cash flow management means delaying outlays of cash as long as possible while encouraging anyone who owes you money to pay it as quickly as possible. But how can you encourage people who owe you money to pay on time?

GO FIGURE Mathematics

Gross Earnings and Overtime

Your gross earnings are the total amount of money you receive during a given pay period. Overtime, which you receive if you work more than your allotted number of hours, is 1.5 times your regular hourly rate.

EXAMPLE Kelly worked 43 hours this week. If her regular hourly wage is $7.40 and her overtime wage is $11.10, what are her gross earnings for the week?

Formula (Hourly Rate × Regular Hours) + (Overtime Rate × Overtime Hours) = Gross Earnings

Solution ($7.40 × 40) + ($11.10 × 3) = Gross Earnings
$296 + $33.30 = $329.30
Kelly's gross earnings for the week are $329.30.

Your Turn

If you earn $8.25 an hour and you work 47 hours in one week, what are your gross earnings?

It is very common for employers to pay sales employees a salary plus commission. For example, Olivia Chun is paid a weekly salary of $150 plus a 5 percent commission on all merchandise she sells. This week she recorded sales of $3,725. Olivia's commission for the week is $186.25 ($3,725 × .05 or 5% = $186.25). Her gross earnings for the pay week are $336.25 ($150 + $186.25 = $336.25).

Reading Check

Generalize What types of employees typically receive salaries instead of hourly wages?

Calculating Payroll Deductions

What are some of the deductions that are taken out of employees' paychecks?

If you have ever received a payroll check, you were probably surprised to see that the amount on the check was less than you expected. **Deductions** are the various amounts that are subtracted from an employee's gross earnings. Some deductions are required by local, state, or federal law. Others are voluntary deductions. Employees choose to have these amounts **withheld,** or taken out of, their gross earnings. The calculation of these deductions is the second step in a payroll system.

Typical payroll deductions include:

- Federal Income Tax
- FICA Taxes
- State and local income taxes

Deductions Required by Law

As an employer, you are required by law to deduct certain payroll taxes from the gross earnings of all employees. These include federal income tax, Social Security tax, and Medicare tax. In many states additional taxes are withheld for local and state income taxes. Employers deduct these taxes from employees' paychecks and send the amounts to the appropriate government agencies.

Federal Income Tax Most people pay income tax to the federal government each year. This tax is based on their total income for the year. To ensure that people will have the money to pay these taxes, the government requires employers to withhold an amount of money from employees' paychecks each pay period. This money is sent to the government and is applied to each employee's federal income tax.

After calculating gross earnings, employers use tax tables supplied by the Internal Revenue Service (IRS) to determine the amount of federal tax to withhold from each employee's paycheck. To use the tables, employers must know how many allowances each employee is claiming. An **allowance** is an adjustment to the tax withheld from your paycheck. The more allowances an employee claims, the less tax will be withheld. Allowances are based on marital status and number of dependents. A single person could claim an allowance of zero or one. A married person with two children could claim an allowance of four. **Figure 1** shows an IRS tax table.

For example, Eric Gaus has weekly gross earnings of $235 and claims one allowance. According to the tax table, the amount withheld as his federal income tax is $12. If Eric had too much withheld, the government would refund him the excess amount. If Eric had too little withheld, he would have to send the amount he owed to the IRS.

FICA Taxes In addition to federal income tax, employers also collect Social Security taxes for the federal government by deducting them from their employees' paychecks. The 1935 **Federal Insurance Contributions Act (FICA)** established the present Social Security system. Social Security payments are often referred to as *FICA taxes.*

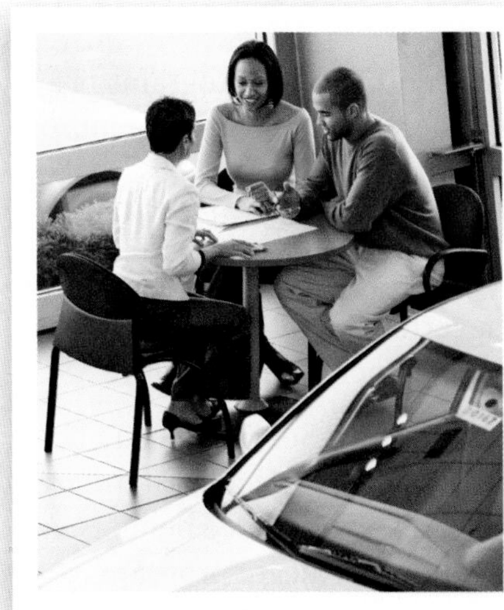

Incentives
Some employees receive a salary, some are paid an hourly wage, and some earn a salary plus commission. *What do you think it means to work for a straight commission?*

FIGURE 1 Internal Revenue Service Tax Table

Uncle Sam's Share Everyone has to pay the correct amount of taxes each year. *How does your employer determine the appropriate amount to withhold from your paycheck?*

SINGLE Persons—**WEEKLY** Payroll Period												
If the wages are		And the number of withholding allowances claimed is										
At least	But less than	0	1	2	3	4	5	6	7	8	9	10
		The amount of income tax to be withheld is										
125	130	8	2	0	0	0	0	0	0	0	0	0
130	135	8	2	0	0	0	0	0	0	0	0	0
135	140	9	3	0	0	0	0	0	0	0	0	0
140	145	9	3	0	0	0	0	0	0	0	0	0
145	150	10	4	0	0	0	0	0	0	0	0	0
150	155	10	4	0	0	0	0	0	0	0	0	0
155	160	11	5	0	0	0	0	0	0	0	0	0
160	165	11	5	0	0	0	0	0	0	0	0	0
165	170	12	6	0	0	0	0	0	0	0	0	0
170	175	12	6	0	0	0	0	0	0	0	0	0
175	180	13	7	1	0	0	0	0	0	0	0	0
180	185	13	7	1	0	0	0	0	0	0	0	0
185	190	14	8	2	0	0	0	0	0	0	0	0
190	195	14	8	2	0	0	0	0	0	0	0	0
195	200	15	9	3	0	0	0	0	0	0	0	0
200	210	16	9	3	0	0	0	0	0	0	0	0
210	220	18	10	4	0	0	0	0	0	0	0	0
220	230	19	11	5	0	0	0	0	0	0	0	0
230	240	21	12	6	1	0	0	0	0	0	0	0
240	250	22	13	7	2	0	0	0	0	0	0	0
250	260	24	15	8	3	0	0	0	0	0	0	0
260	270	25	16	9	4	0	0	0	0	0	0	0
270	280	27	18	10	5	0	0	0	0	0	0	0
280	290	28	19	11	6	0	0	0	0	0	0	0
290	300	30	21	12	7	1	0	0	0	0	0	0
300	310	31	22	13	8	2	0	0	0	0	0	0
310	320	33	24	15	9	3	0	0	0	0	0	0
320	330	34	25	16	10	4	0	0	0	0	0	0
330	340	36	27	18	11	5	0	0	0	0	0	0
340	350	37	28	19	12	6	0	0	0	0	0	0

The FICA taxes pay for programs that provide income to certain individuals:

- The old-age and survivors' benefit programs provide income to retired persons and the spouse and dependents of a deceased worker.
- The disability insurance program provides income to people with disabilities and their families.
- The Medicare program provides health insurance benefits for people 65 or older, certain people with disabilities, and people of any age who have permanent kidney failure.

FICA includes two types of tax: Social Security tax and Medicare tax. **Social Security tax** finances the federal programs that provide retirement, disability, and life insurance benefits. **Medicare tax** is the tax that finances part of the Medicare program.

GO FIGURE Mathematics

FICA Deduction

FICA taxes include the Social Security tax and the Medicare tax. These taxes are used to provide income to a variety of people.

EXAMPLE What is the FICA deduction for Alex Calligros if his gross earnings for the week are $380?

Formula (Gross Earnings × Social Security) + (Gross Earnings × Medicare Tax) = FICA Deduction

Solution ($380 × .062) + ($380 × .0145) = FICA Deduction

$23.56 + $5.51 = $29.07

Alex's FICA taxes amount to $29.07.

Your Turn

If your gross earnings for the month are $550, how much would be deducted from your paycheck for FICA taxes?

All employees pay FICA taxes based on rates established by the United States Congress. The rates can change at any time. In 2010, the FICA tax rates were 6.2 percent for Social Security and 1.45 percent for Medicare. The money from these taxes goes to the Social Security Administration, where it is put into a trust. It is then distributed to people collecting Social Security and Medicare benefits.

Employers use the FICA rates to calculate how much to withhold from the taxable gross earnings of each employee for each pay period. Multiply gross earnings by the Social Security tax, and then multiply gross earnings by the Medicare tax. Add these two figures to determine the FICA deduction.

State and Local Income Taxes Many states and cities tax the earnings of people who live or work within their boundaries. In some states the taxes are simply a percentage of gross earnings. In other states, the amount owed is based on tax tables similar to the federal withholding tables issued by the IRS. Where employees work and/or live determines how state or local taxes are taken from their earnings.

Voluntary Deductions

Many employers also deduct voluntary deductions. An employer will deduct these amounts only if the employee requests it. Once an employee requests a voluntary deduction, it is withheld from each paycheck until the employee asks his or her employer to stop taking it out. Some common voluntary deductions include:

- Health or life insurance premiums
- Union dues
- Contributions to charities
- Pensions and other retirement plans
- Direct deposits to a credit union or bank

Document Detective

A Paycheck Stub

When you receive a check from your employer, a statement will be attached to the check. This statement tells you how your paycheck was calculated. Sometimes employers make mistakes in their payroll. You can check the paycheck stub to make sure the amounts are correct. A paycheck stub contains the following information:

- Name and Social Security number of employee
- Amount earned during the pay period and year-to-date
- Amount of taxes withheld from wages during the pay period and year-to-date

General Products P.O. Box 27806 New York, NY 20012	Michelle Li 101 Second Street Athens, OH 44573	SS no. 299-XX-XXXX
Period beginning: 12/24/20––	Period ending: 01/04/20––	Pay date: 01/11/20––

Pay Summary	
Earnings	$113.07
Less: Taxes	12.93
Deductions	.00
Net Check	$100.14

Earnings-to-Date	**Type**	**Rate**	**Hours**	**Current**	**Year-to-Date**
Holiday	17	6.75	3.25	21.94	89.08
Straight Time	12	6.75	13.50	91.13	368.05

Taxes	**Current**	**Year-to-Date**
Federal income tax	1.11	25.63
Social Security	7.01	65.24
Medicare	1.64	28.43
State income tax	.91	23.06
City tax	2.26	56.97

Key Points A paycheck stub contains information for the current pay period as well as the cumulative total for the calendar year.

FIND the Solutions

Review Key Concepts

1. How much does Michelle make per hour?
2. Does she make more money per hour on holidays?
3. When did Michelle receive this pay?
4. How much in taxes was deducted from her paycheck?
5. What was the total amount Michelle received?

A popular voluntary payroll deduction is a contribution to a 401(k) plan for retirement. Many employees contribute a portion of their gross earnings to a company 401(k) plan. The funds in a 401(k) plan are tax-deferred. Employees do not have to pay taxes on the money that accumulates in their 401(k) plans until they withdraw it.

Reading Check

Compute How do you determine your FICA deduction?

Preparing Payroll Records

What information is included on a payroll register?

The third step in a payroll system is to prepare payroll records. Federal and state laws require all businesses to keep accurate payroll records. Employers are expected to:

- Calculate earnings and deductions correctly.
- Distribute employee paychecks on time.
- Keep accurate payroll records.
- Pay all taxes owed to government agencies on time.
- File all required payroll reports to government agencies on time.

To fulfill these obligations, your business needs an efficient system for collecting, recording, and summarizing payroll information.

Preparing the Payroll Register

After collecting information for the pay period, you record the data on a payroll register. The payroll register is a record that summarizes information about employee earnings and deductions for each pay period. **Figure 2** shows an example of a completed payroll register for Ezra's Sport Clothes.

A payroll register has three main sections pertaining to money: earnings, deductions, and net pay. The earnings section records the regular pay, overtime pay, and gross earnings of each employee for the pay period. The deductions section of the payroll register lists and totals the required and voluntary deductions withheld from each employee. The number of columns varies from business to business. The net pay section records the amount that remains after the total deductions are subtracted from gross earnings. For Ezra's Sport Clothes, the total net pay for this week's payroll is $1,338.31.

Reading Check

Identify What is listed on the deductions section of the payroll register?

Preparing Paychecks

What are some of the benefits of direct deposit?

After checking the accuracy of the payroll register, you prepare a payroll check for each employee. This is the fourth step in a payroll system. The amount on each payroll check—often referred to as *take-home pay*—should equal the net pay listed for each employee. Along with the check, each employee receives a written or printed explanation that shows how the net pay is calculated. The stubs attached to payroll checks provide this explanation and serve as a record for employees. An example of a paycheck that lists gross earnings, deductions, and net pay is shown in **Figure 3.**

Direct Deposit

Instead of issuing paychecks, many businesses offer direct deposit of employee earnings. With direct deposit, net pay is deposited automatically in an employee's designated bank account. Employers do not have to prepare a paycheck if they offer direct deposit. However, they must give employees a written record of their payroll information.

Employees and employers generally prefer direct deposit. Employees do not have to go to the bank to deposit their paychecks; they do not risk misplacing or losing a check; and funds are usually available faster. Employers can reduce the expenses of paper and labor for processing checks by using direct deposit.

FIGURE 2 **Completed Payroll Register for Ezra's Sport Clothes**

Payroll Prep The third step in the payroll system is preparing payroll records. *What is the purpose of a payroll register?*

PAYROLL REGISTER

PAY PERIOD ENDING May 18 20 -- DATE OF PAYMENT May 18

EMPLOYEE NUMBER	NAME	MAR. STATUS	ALLOW.	TOTAL HOURS	RATE	EARNINGS			DEDUCTIONS								NET PAY	CK. NO.
						REGULAR	OVERTIME	TOTAL	SOC. SEC. TAX	MED. TAX	FED. INC. TAX	STATE INC. TAX	HOSP. INS.	UNION DUES	TOTAL			
3	Drummond, R.	S	0	37	7.80	288 60		288 60	17 89	4 18	35 00	5 77		5 00	67 84		220 76	186
7	Feld, D.	M	2	41	7.40	296 00	11 10	307 10	19 04	4 45	14 00	6 14	12 00		55 63		251 47	187
4	Monsalves, D.	S	0	33	8.10	267 30		267 30	16 57	3 88	32 00	5 35	7 00		64 80		202 50	188
9	Simon, J.	S	1	28	7.40	207 20		207 20	12 85	3 00	15 00	4 14		5 00	39 99		167 21	189
11	Turner, J.	S	0	42	8.20	328 00	24 60	352 60	21 86	5 11	52 00	7 05	7 00	5 00	98 02		254 58	190
6	Wyman, B.	M	2	39	7.60	296 40		296 40	18 38	4 30	14 00	5 93	12 00		54 61		241 79	191
					TOTALS	1683 50	35 70	1719 20	106 59	24 92	162 00	34 38	38 00	15 00	380 89		1338 31	

FIGURE 3 **Completed Payroll Check and Stub**

Take-Home Pay The amount on each payroll check should equal the net pay listed for each employee on the payroll register. *What were Ryan Drummond's gross earnings for the period ending May 18? What was his take-home pay (net pay)?*

Ezra's Sport Clothes 186
155 Gateway Blvd. 91-182/1721
Sacramento, CA 94230

Date May 18 20 --

Pay to the Order of Ryan Drummond $ 220.76

Two hundred twenty dollars and 76/100 *Dollars*

American National Bank
SACRAMENTO, CALIFORNIA

Agnes Werman

A172109182A 085 015 1189064C 186

Employee Pay Statement
Detach and retain this statement. 186

Period Ending	Earnings			Deductions							Net Pay
	Regular	Overtime	Total	Social Security Tax	Med. Tax	Federal Income Tax	State Income Tax	Hosp. Ins.	Union Dues	Total	
5/18	288.60		288.60	17.89	4.18	35.00	5.70	–	5.00	67.84	220.76

Automated Payroll Preparation

Today almost all businesses use some type of automated system to prepare payroll records. Computer-generated records provide an efficient and accurate system. A variety of software packages is available. The employer enters the number of hours each employee worked, and the computer produces a payroll register and paychecks.

Reading Check

Describe How does an employee benefit by using direct deposit?

Recording Payroll Information

What payroll information is recorded in a company's accounting records?

After you complete the payroll register and prepare individual paychecks, the payroll must be recorded in the accounting system of your business. This is the fifth step in the payroll process.

User Friendly
Most employees appreciate the convenience of using direct deposit. *Why do many employers prefer to use direct deposit for paying their staff?*

In recording the payroll, you are recording only the total amounts for the pay period. The individual amounts for each employee have already been recorded on the payroll register.

The Salaries Expense Account

Each pay period, you pay out a certain amount of money to your employees in wages or salaries. The amount you pay to all employees before any deductions are taken out is called **total gross earnings.** This is a basic operating expense of your business. You record the total gross earnings in a general ledger account titled *Expense.* On the payroll register in **Figure 2**, the earnings for the period are $1,719.

Deductions to Liabilities

The amount you deduct from employee earnings for Social Security, Medicare, and other taxes or payments is subtracted from total gross earnings. This money does not belong to your company. You must pay it to the proper agencies or organizations on behalf of your employees. Therefore, all deductions taken from employees' gross earnings immediately become liabilities of your business.

Remember when setting up your accounting system, you create only the accounts that your business needs. These accounts are assets, liabilities, and owner's equity. The liabilities of your business are identified in the account title by the word *payable.*

Based on the deductions shown on its payroll register in **Figure 2**, Ezra's Sport Clothes has the following liability accounts:

- Social Security Tax Payable
- Medicare Tax Payable
- Employees' Federal Income Tax Payable
- Employees' State Income Tax Payable
- Hospital Insurance Premium Payable
- Union Dues Payable

These items remain liabilities until the business makes the required payments to the government, insurance companies, local unions, and any other agencies or organizations.

Ireland

Minimum Wages

To help prevent businesses from exploiting the workforce, most countries have some form of minimum wage laws. Ireland is a bit different. In fact, there is no comprehensive statutory minimum wage in Ireland. However, some workers are protected against low wages. Some industries establish Joint Labour Committees (JLCs) to set legally binding minimum levels of pay. In order to create a JLC, there should be little or no effective collective bargaining in that industry.

Trade unions are sometimes able to raise wages of workers but that ability is dependent on various factors. For example, a trade union for skilled manual workers may be more capable of protecting their members' pay than a union representing unskilled workers. While there has been pressure from the trade union movement and other groups for the Irish government to introduce a national statutory minimum wage, the idea has been strongly resisted by the government and employers. The trade unions argue that the current, selective system is not adequate to meet the needs of all those receiving low pay.

Critical Thinking

1. **Expand** One group promoting a national statutory minimum wage is the Combat Poverty Agency. Research to find out more about this agency. What are the four general functions of this agency?
2. **Relate** Do you agree that governments should set minimum wages? Do these laws infringe on the rights of businesses in a free market economy?

DATABYTES

Capital
Dublin

Population
4,250,163

Languages
English, Irish

Currency
Euro

Gross Domestic Product (GDP)
$229.4 billion

GDP per capita
$42,200

Industry
Steel, lead, zinc, silver, aluminum, barite, and gypsum mining processing; food products, brewing, textiles, clothing; chemicals, pharmaceuticals; machinery, rail transportation equipment; glass and crystal; software, tourism

Agriculture
Turnips, barley, potatoes, sugar beets, wheat; beef, dairy product

Exports
Machinery and equipment, computers, chemicals, pharmaceuticals; live animals, animal products

Natural Resources
Natural gas, peat, copper, lead, zinc, silver, barite, gypsum, limestone, dolomite

Smart Management
A store such as the one in this photo employs many people working in many different areas of the business. *How can accurate payroll records help employers manage their business expenses?*

Cash in Bank

After salary expenses and deductions have been recorded, the last account to be affected by payroll is Cash in Bank. Cash in Bank is the account that records all of the cash that enters or leaves the business. For the pay period shown in **Figure 2**, the cash account is reduced by the total amount of net pay, which is $1,338.31. Your cash account balance will be reduced further as you make payments on your payroll liabilities.

Reading Check

Explain Why do the deductions taken from employees' gross earnings immediately become liabilities of a business?

Employer's Payroll Taxes

How do employers help pay for benefits such as Social Security?

The amounts in the various payroll liability accounts of a business represent the taxes that employees paid on their earnings. The state and federal governments also require employers to pay additional taxes that are based on the total taxable gross earnings each pay period. This money goes toward benefits such as Social Security and unemployment and disability insurance.

Employer's Share of FICA Taxes

Federal law requires that the employer match the total amount deducted from employees' paychecks for Social Security and Medicare. In other words, if your employee pays $25, you must pay an additional $25. In **Figure 2**, the total Social Security tax deducted from the total gross earnings for the pay period ending May 18 was $106.59. As the employer, Ezra's Sport Clothes must match this amount ($106.59) and send the government a check totaling $213.18 ($106.59 + $106.59 = $213.18). Employers also have to match Medicare deductions with an equal amount. An employer must match and pay Social Security tax and Medicare tax for every pay period.

Federal and State Unemployment Taxes

The employer pays both federal and state unemployment taxes. The maximum federal unemployment tax is 6.2 percent on the first $7,000 of an employee's annual wages. State unemployment tax rates and maximum taxable amounts vary among states. Employers may deduct up to 5.4 percent of the state unemployment taxes from federal unemployment taxes. Most employers, therefore, pay a federal tax of 0.8 percent (6.2% – 5.4% = 0.8%) of taxable gross earnings.

To calculate the amount to pay, you multiply the total gross earnings for the pay period by the federal tax rate. Then multiply the total gross earnings for the pay period by the state tax rate. Finally, add the two figures to calculate the total amount of taxes to pay.

Reading Check

Recall The state and federal governments require employers to pay taxes; where does this money go?

GO FIGURE Mathematics

Unemployment Taxes

Employers are required to pay federal and state unemployment taxes. These taxes provide income to workers who have lost their jobs.

EXAMPLE The total gross earnings of Prairie Pet Store are $3,000 for the pay period. None of the employees has reached the maximum taxable amount. How much money must the owner pay to the federal and state governments, based on the unemployment tax rates?

Formula (Total Gross Earnings × Federal Tax Rate) + (Total Gross Earnings × State Tax Rate) = Total Unemployment Taxes

Solution ($3,000 × .008) + ($3,000 × .054) = Total Unemployment Taxes

$24 + $162 = $186

Prairie Pet Store will have to pay $24 to the federal government and $162 to the state government for a total of $186.

Your Turn

If your company's total gross earnings for a specific pay period were $4,100, how much would you have to pay in federal and state unemployment taxes?

Reporting Payroll Information to the Government

What information is essential in filing reports to the government?

The amount of money a business owes government agencies must be paid according to strict guidelines, outlined in the Internal Revenue Code (IRC). Both the federal and state governments expect prompt payment along with the proper forms and reports. You must file a variety of forms to the different government agencies. Reporting information about payments to the government is the sixth and last step in the payroll process. You need current and accurate payroll information for filing the reports and making the necessary payments.

Employers must comply with employment tax rules and procedures in the IRC or risk civil or criminal penalties.

The IRC addresses a number of issues:

- Determining whether the federal tax coverage rules apply
- Computing an employee's taxable wages
- Calculating the amount of employment taxes to be withheld
- Depositing the correct amount of taxes with the government
- Filing employment tax returns

Reading Check

Explain What is the function of the Internal Revenue Code (IRC)?

Payroll Accounting in Financial Management

Why is it important to analyze payroll information regularly?

Accurate payroll records are essential for controlling business expenses. Good payroll records can pinpoint the labor cost for different areas of your business. They will also indicate how much of the total gross earnings was spent on overtime. Overtime is justified in many cases, but it may also be a sign of a poor use of employees.

Payroll is often the biggest expense of running a business. Therefore, it is very important to carefully analyze the payroll information of every pay period. Payroll costs can dramatically reduce profits. However, payroll is also an area where you can reduce expenses. Good financial management requires constant review of your payroll system.

Assessment

Review Key Concepts

1. **Identify** What are the six steps in managing a payroll system?
2. **Explain** How do employers calculate employees' gross earnings?
3. **Discuss** Identify and describe required and voluntary payroll deductions.
4. **Describe** What is the role of employers in assuring prompt payment to the government?

Higher Order Thinking H.O.T.

5. **Compare and Contrast** From an employer's standpoint, what are some of the advantages and disadvantages of paying a salary instead of an hourly wage? Which would you prefer to receive and why?

21st Century Skills

6. **Solve Problems** Leigh runs a business that is growing very quickly. She must decide whether to continue paying overtime each week to her employees or to hire another employee or two. Each of Leigh's 15 employees earns an hourly wage of $7.50 and works an average of 8 hours of overtime a week. Calculate how much Leigh is paying her current employees in overtime. Calculate how much it would cost for Leigh to hire an additional employee at $7.50/hour. Which would be the most cost-effective solution: hiring a new employee or continuing to pay her current employees overtime?

Mathematics

7. **Earnings and Tax** Carmen has her own small company. She has two salaried employees that earned $750 and $700, respectively this past pay period. She also has two hourly employees that worked 43 and 45 hours, respectively this past pay period. Both hourly employees earn $9.75 per hour and receive 1.5 times their regular hourly wage for overtime. Calculate total gross earnings for the pay period. How much in total do the employees contribute in FICA tax? How much does the company have to send the government for FICA tax?

Math Concept **Calculate FICA Tax** To calculate the total FICA tax a company must send to the government first determine the total gross earnings for a given pay period and multiply by the FICA tax rates. Multiply this amount by two.

Starting Hint Determine gross pay for hourly employees by multiplying the wage by the hours worked during the period, up to 40. Multiply the wage by 1.5; multiply this figure by the hours worked in excess of 40 hours. Add the amounts.

NCTM Problem Solving Solve problems that arise in mathematics and in other contexts.

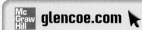

Check your answers.

Section Objectives

- **Identify** information needed for an inventory control system.
- **Summarize** the two main methods of determining inventory quantity.
- **Explain** methods used to calculate cost of inventory.
- **Analyze** inventory turnover.

As You Read

Connect Look at a receipt you received from a recent purchase. Is there an item number listed on the receipt for each item? How might a store owner use these numbers?

Establishing an Inventory System

Why is it important to keep close track of inventory?

Felix Martinez owns a small bookstore that specializes in materials about travel. Business has been very good lately. One of Felix's most challenging tasks is deciding which books to buy and keep in store for his customers. He reviews his **stock,** or supplies and products, regularly to see which books sell well and which ones remain on the shelves. The decisions he makes in purchasing books can have a significant impact on his business's cash flow and profits.

When you own a business, one of the major expenses of your company is the purchasing of merchandise, or the items that you buy with the intent to resell to customers. The amount of merchandise you have on hand at any particular time is known as inventory. Inventory for a manufacturing business can include raw materials or finished goods. For a retail business, products or merchandise in stock, such as books, inventory is often the largest asset of a business.

In order to control the purchase and sale of merchandise, you must establish an inventory control system. This system tracks the quantity and cost of merchandise purchased, the merchandise in stock, and the merchandise sold to customers. See **Figure 4.** Properly tracking the flow of merchandise gives you the up-to-date information that you need to make good management decisions. The essential information for an inventory control system includes the amount of merchandise sold in each accounting period and information about which items are selling well and which items are not selling well.

Tracking and controlling inventory is also a major function of an accounting system. You cannot make good financial decisions without accurate and current inventory information.

Reading Check

Remember What is usually the largest asset of a business?

Controlling Inventory

Why is having too little inventory bad for business?

Because the purchase of merchandise often requires large amounts of money, it has a great impact on cash flow. Therefore, it is essential to maintain proper inventory levels. Your goal is to have enough product to meet customer demand but not have an overstock of items.

FIGURE 4 The Stages of Merchandise

On the Move Merchandise is moving from the time you order it until the time that it is sold to a customer. *What might it mean if items are stored for a long time?*

1 **Ordering Merchandise** Merchandise must be reordered when your inventory runs low in order to meet customer demand.

2 **Storing** Merchandise After you receive merchandise, it must be stored in a safe, efficient manner.

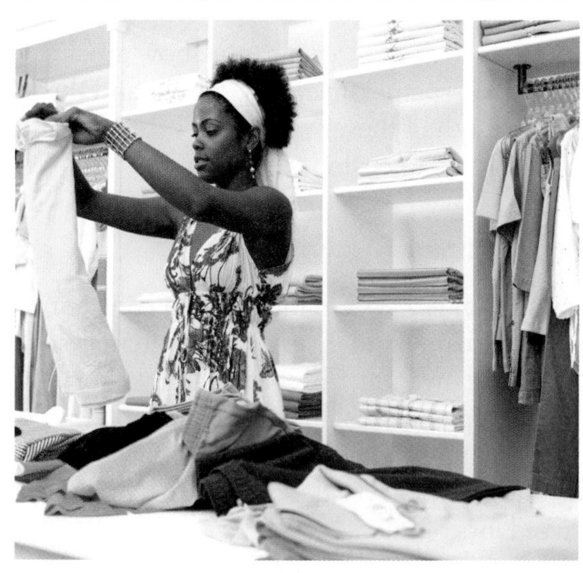

3 **Displaying Merchandise** Merchandise must be displayed in an appealing way that will attract customers.

4 **Selling Merchandise** The sale of merchandise brings in cash for your business and also reduces your inventory, which must be replenished by reordering.

If your inventory is too large, you may have purchased the wrong items or the wrong quantity of items. As a result, cash may not be available for operating expenses, expansion activities, or emergencies. You will also be paying more than necessary for storage. To get rid of excess inventory, you may have to sell it at a loss.

If your inventory is too low, customers will not have enough choices of merchandise. They may shop elsewhere, in which case, you lose sales, and your business receives less cash. Have you ever gone to purchase an item only to find out that the item was out of stock? How did you feel? Disappointed customers often do not return. Satisfied customers, on the other hand, go back to businesses where they find the items they want when they want them. Therefore, maintaining an appropriate level of inventory is good business management.

Reading Check

Explain Why does the purchase of merchandise have a large impact on cash flow?

Determining Amount of Inventory

What systems help determine amount of inventory in stock?

At certain points in each accounting period, businesses need to determine how much merchandise is in stock. They also need to calculate the value of the merchandise. How do you calculate the quantity of merchandise on hand at a given point?

Two accounting methods are used to determine how much merchandise is in stock: the perpetual inventory system and the periodic inventory system. Both of these systems report the quantity of merchandise available for sale to customers.

The Perpetual Inventory System

A **perpetual inventory system** is a system that keeps a constant, up-to-date record of merchandise on hand. Every time an item is sold, the item is deducted from the inventory. A perpetual inventory system allows you to determine the quantity you have on hand and the cost of the items at any time. By having current, up-to-date information, you can reorder and restock items whenever the quantity becomes low. Restocking can help avoid loss of sales.

Before the introduction of computers, this type of inventory system was impossible for most businesses to use. It was just too difficult to keep track of a large quantity of items being bought and sold. Today, however, many businesses use **point-of-sale terminals,** which are electronic cash registers. These terminals are linked to a centralized computer system that keeps track of sales.

Economics and You

Specialization

Individuals, companies, and nations specialize in what they do best. Specialization forces all of them to trade with one another so each gets the good and services needed to satisfy their wants and needs. For example, a company that is good at making clothing will purchase the cloth, thread, buttons, and zippers from companies that make those items. When each company specializes in making specific products, production and consumption increases because each one has the know-how, materials, and machinery to do so. Some companies use just-in-time Inventory systems so suppliers are notified as soon as product reaches a certain quantity. This type of specialization improves inventory control. Nations are also interdependent upon one another due to specialization. A nation that specializes in growing coffee beans will sell them to another nation that does not have the natural resources to do so. The country that buys the coffee beans may have the machinery necessary for processing coffee beans so it sells that machinery to the coffee bean producing country.

Personal Finance Connection In some cases, employees may be responsible for keeping payroll records or managing the company's inventory. Each employee therefore contributes to the business by specializing in what he or she does best. When you decide on your career, you will be specializing in what you do best.

Critical Thinking What facets of payroll recordkeeping and inventory control could make use of specialization of labor? How would specialization improve business operations and chores at home?

Comparative Advantage

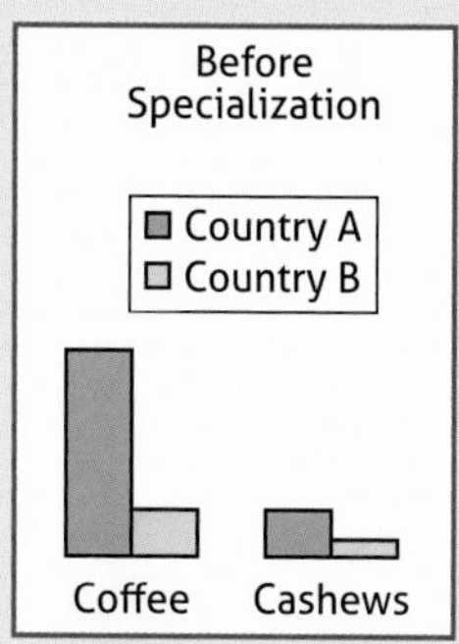

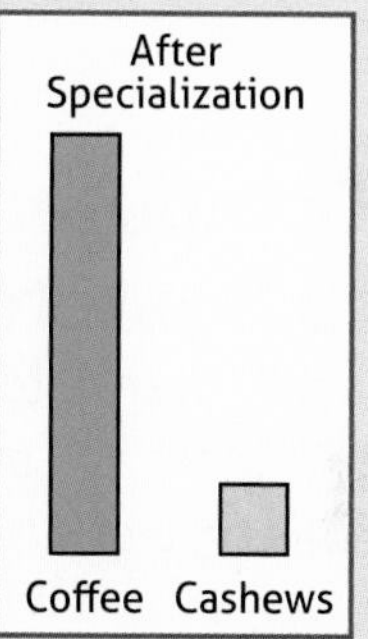

glencoe.com

Activity Download an Economics and You Worksheet Activity.

You have probably bought an item in a store with this kind of system, where the associate passes an electronic gun or scanner over the bar code of the item you are buying. The scanner reads the bar code, you hear a beep, and the item's price appears on the screen of the point-of-sale terminal.

In addition, sales tax is automatically calculated when the items are entered. The sales slip you receive from the store lists the items you just purchased along with their prices.

In addition to recording the prices of items, point-of-sale terminals also identify the items and remove them automatically from the inventory records. When a particular item reaches a predetermined low point, the purchasing manager reorders the item so that the business does not run out of it. With such an automated system, businesses know the number of items sold and the number still on hand at all times. An example of a computer printout of a daily inventory report is shown in **Figure 5.**

It is difficult, but not impossible, for businesses that do not use computers to use a perpetual inventory system. Usually these businesses sell large items, such as cars or furniture. They have fewer items in stock and do not sell many items within a certain time period. As a result, they can keep track of inventory with index cards or inventory sheets that list the items in stock. When the business sells an item, someone pulls the index card for that item from an inventory box or removes the item from an inventory sheet. Because very few items are sold each day, it is possible to maintain a non-computerized perpetual inventory system. For example, a local furniture store may tracks sales using index cards or tracking sheets and total them at the end of each day to track inventory. However, many of these businesses do use computer-based perpetual inventory systems.

FIGURE 5 Computer Printout from a Perpetual Inventory System

What's in Stock? Thanks to computers, a perpetual inventory system is available to almost any business. *How can a merchandise business benefit from this type of system?*

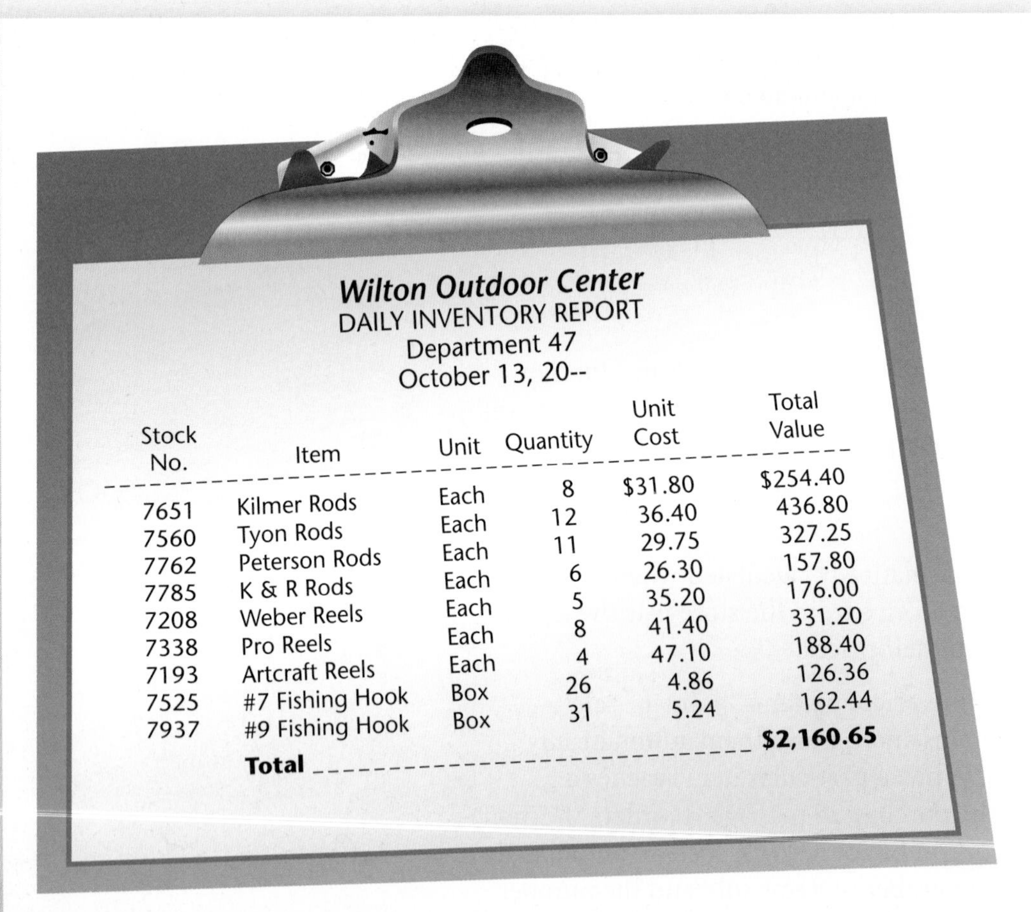

Wilton Outdoor Center
DAILY INVENTORY REPORT
Department 47
October 13, 20--

Stock No.	Item	Unit	Quantity	Unit Cost	Total Value
7651	Kilmer Rods	Each	8	$31.80	$254.40
7560	Tyon Rods	Each	12	36.40	436.80
7762	Peterson Rods	Each	11	29.75	327.25
7785	K & R Rods	Each	6	26.30	157.80
7208	Weber Reels	Each	5	35.20	176.00
7338	Pro Reels	Each	8	41.40	331.20
7193	Artcraft Reels	Each	4	47.10	188.40
7525	#7 Fishing Hook	Box	26	4.86	126.36
7937	#9 Fishing Hook	Box	31	5.24	162.44
	Total				**$2,160.65**

The Periodic Inventory System

Another system used to keep track of merchandise on hand is a periodic inventory system. A **periodic inventory system** is a system in which inventory records are updated only after someone makes an actual physical count of the merchandise on hand. You do not change inventory records every time you purchase or sell something.

Perhaps you have worked in a store and helped take inventory. If not, you may have seen a sign in a store window that read "Closed for Inventory." Businesses take a physical count of merchandise at least once a year. For most businesses, the process of identifying and counting all items of merchandise is time consuming. Therefore, inventory is usually counted when the quantity of merchandise is at its lowest point. For a seasonal business, the count occurs after the peak sales period. In a ski shop, for example, the peak sales period is November through March. You would probably take inventory in May or June, when there is less merchandise to count. After taking the physical count, you can order new merchandise.

Today many businesses use electronic equipment when taking a physical inventory. An employee enters the stock number of each item and the quantity in stock into a handheld computer. When the physical count is complete, he or she prints the inventory record.

Even if a business uses a perpetual inventory system, it must conduct a periodic physical inventory at least once a year to check the accuracy of inventory records. Errors can be made in entering inventory data when purchasing merchandise. Errors can also be made at point-of-sale terminals when the business sells merchandise. Items can be lost, stolen, or identified incorrectly. A periodic physical count ensures that accounting records are accurate and agree with what the business actually has in stock.

Reading Check

Apply Why might a pool supply store in New York take its inventory in November and December?

On the Spot
Many stores use point-of-sale terminals and scanners to record sales. *What is the advantage of using this technology?*

Determining the Cost of Inventory

Why is it important for a business to use its chosen costing method consistently?

You have determined the quantity of merchandise on hand. Now you need to calculate the cost of that merchandise. In other words, the inventory must be assigned a value. You could do this fairly easily if the cost of every item were always the same. However, that is unusual. For example, Heather Martin buys certain items for her pet store several times within a single inventory period. Often the cost of these items changes during that period. Heather might buy a specific brand and size of dog food for $9 per bag in March. She might pay $12 for the same dog food in June. How can she appropriately determine the cost of the remaining bags of dog food she still has on hand? To answer this question, businesses use one of several inventory costing methods approved by GAAP guidelines. All of these methods calculate a value for inventory on hand: the specific identification costing method; the first-in, first-out method; and the last-in, first-out method.

The Specific Identification Costing Method

The **specific identification method** is an inventory costing method in which the exact cost of each item is determined and assigned to an item. The actual cost of each item is obtained from the invoice. This is the most accurate costing method. It is commonly used by businesses that sell a small number of items at high prices. These businesses include appliance stores, car dealerships, and furniture stores. Because every item must be researched, this costing method is not practical for most businesses. You will use it only if you have few items to track and if the cost is easy to look up.

The First-In, First-Out Costing Method

If you cannot determine the exact cost of every item in your inventory, you will have to make a good estimate. One method of estimating cost is the first-in, first-out method. The **first-in, first-out method (FIFO)** is an inventory costing system that assumes the first items purchased (first in) are the first items sold (first out). It also assumes that the items the business purchased most recently are the ones on hand at the end of the period.

For example, Matthew Lee owns a small neighborhood grocery store. One of his bestselling items is milk. Because milk is perishable, the employees stock the shelves first with the milk that was purchased first. As that milk is sold, later purchases are added at the back of the shelves. The first in are the first out.

Here is another example of how the FIFO inventory method works for Lamar's House of Music:

Troy DVD Player–Model #875

Date	Description	Units	Cost	Total
Feb. 4	Beginning Inventory	9	$250	= $2,250
May 12	Purchase	20	253	= 5,060
July 7	Purchase	10	258	= 2,580
Sept. 15	Purchase	12	263	= 3,156
Nov. 9	Purchase	10	265	= 2,650
Total		**61**		**$15,696**

After taking a physical inventory, the employees at Lamar's House of Music discover that there are 12 DVD players still in stock. Using the FIFO method, they assume that the 12 remaining players are the last ones the business purchased, because the "first in" are the "first out." They calculate the cost of the ending inventory as follows:

Sept. 15: 2 units @ $263 = 526
Nov. 9: 10 units @ $265 = $2,650
Cost of ending inventory = $3,176

The Last-In, First-Out Costing Method

Another method for calculating the value of your ending inventory is the last-in, first-out method. The **last-in, first-out method (LIFO)** is a costing method that assumes the last items purchased (last in) are the first items sold (first out). It also assumes that the items purchased first are still on hand at the end of the period.

For example, Stratford Stone Company sells loose stone to contractors. When new stone arrives, it is deposited on top of the existing stone. As the stone is taken from the top of the pile, the first stones sold are the last delivered. The physical flow of the company's product, therefore, is "last-in, first-out."

If the employees at Lamar's House of Music use the LIFO method for calculating the cost of DVD players, they would assume that the last players purchased were sold first. The earliest players are still in stock. This could happen if they pushed older items to the back of the shelves. Using the LIFO method, they would calculate the cost of ending inventory as follows:

Feb. 4: 9 units @ $250 = $2,250
May 12: 3 units @ $253 = $ 759
Cost of ending inventory = $3,009

Choosing a Costing Method

The cost of the ending inventory will vary, depending on which costing method you use. Notice that the inventory at Lamar's House of Music is valued at $3,176 using the FIFO method but at $3,009 using the LIFO method. Similarly, the inventory would be valued at a different amount if the store used the specific identification method.

Inventory Losses

Retail businesses must consider loss of inventory due to human error as they manage their inventory levels. The National Security Survey Final Report found that causes of inventory shortages include employee theft at 48 percent, shoplifting at 32 percent, vendor fraud at 5 percent, and administrative and paper errors at 15 percent.

Concept Application

If a boutique carried 100 dresses and 50 designer handbags, and the store's total inventory shortage was typically 10 percent, how many of each item were lost due to shoplifting?

Management

Successful people both in and outside of business often possess strong management skills. Management is the ability to bring a group of people together to achieve common goals and objectives. In order to lead a group to accomplish goals, you must develop a detailed plan, work effectively with people from a wide range of social and cultural backgrounds, and utilize financial and technological resources. Possessing strong management skills will help to not only achieve personal goals but also prepare you for a career.

Write About It

Think of a situation in which you used or saw someone using management skills. Write one or more paragraphs to describe the scenario and explain how these skills positively impacted the situation.

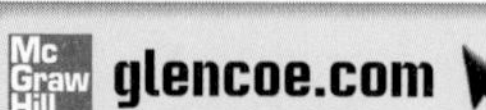

Activity Download a Career and College Readiness Worksheet Activity.

Businesses choose the inventory costing method that seems best for their particular type of business. Once a business chooses a method, however, it must use that method consistently. Consistent reporting helps owners and creditors compare financial reports from one accounting period to another.

Reading Check

Extend Which costing method is most appropriate for a frozen yogurt shop and why?

Analyzing Inventory Turnover

Is it better to have high or low inventory turnover?

In order to evaluate the performance of your business, analyze current inventory information and compare it to data from previous accounting periods.

Inventory Turnover

One type of analysis—the inventory turnover—is the number of times you sell your inventory in a given time period.

Average Inventory The average inventory is the value of beginning inventory plus the value of ending inventory, divided by two. After you have determined the average inventory, you can calculate the inventory turnover. To do so, divide the cost of merchandise sold during that time period by the average inventory.

Inventory Turnover Levels A high inventory turnover means that your business has money tied up in inventory for shorter periods of time. As a result, your financing, storage, and insurance costs are reduced, which benefits your business. On the other hand, a low inventory turnover may mean that sales were lower than expected or that too many items were in stock and remained unsold.

Days in Stock Inventory turnover is used to determine the number of days that merchandise is in stock. You calculate this by dividing the number of days in a calendar year (365) by inventory turnover.

If you find that your merchandise remains in stock for an increasing amount of time from one year to the next, you should determine the reasons and decide whether to change your purchasing practices.

Stock Lists

Another tool that businesses use to plan purchases and manage inventory is stock lists. There are three types of stock lists: the basic stock list, model stock list, and never-out list.

GO FIGURE Mathematics

Average Inventory

You need to determine the average inventory for your company in order to calculate the inventory turnover for a specific period of time.

EXAMPLE Cindy's Fine China had an inventory valued at $65,000 as of January 1, and an inventory valued at $80,000 as of December 31 of the same year. What was the store's average inventory for the year?

Formula (Value of Beginning Inventory + Value of Ending Inventory)/2 = Average Inventory

Solution ($65,000 + $80,000)/2 = $72,500
The store's average inventory for the year was $72,500.

Your Turn

If the value of your beginning inventory was $72,000 and the value of your ending inventory was $100,000, what was your store's average inventory for the year?

Basic Stock List A basic stock list is a form that lists items a store should always keep in stock. A basic stock list is used for **staple,** or basic, merchandise. The basic stock list includes the minimum amount of an item and the quantity to be reordered.

Model Stock List The model stock list is used for fashion merchandise. It is not as specific as the basic stock list. Since fashion merchandise varies more than staple merchandise, the model stock list is shorter, but it specifies quantities of each item.

Never-Out List The never-out list is used for the most popular merchandise. Items are added to the list as their popularity increases or dropped as sales decrease; thus, cash flow can remain steady.

Reading Check

Recall How is inventory turnover calculated?

GO FIGURE Mathematics

Inventory Turnover

Inventory turnover is the number of times you sell your inventory in a given period of time. High inventory turnover is good.

EXAMPLE Cindy's Fine China sold $200,000 of merchandise. If the store's average inventory for the period was $72,500, what was its inventory turnover?

Formula Cost of Merchandise Sold/Average Inventory = Inventory Turnover

Solution $200,000/$72,500 = 2.76
The inventory turnover for Cindy's Fine China was 2.76 times a year.

Your Turn

If you sold $110,000 of merchandise and your average inventory was $80,000, what was your inventory turnover for the year?

GO FIGURE Mathematics

Number of Days in Stock

Inventory turnover is used to determine the number of days that you have merchandise in stock. If merchandise remains in stock for an increasing amount of time, you may want to rethink your purchasing practices.

EXAMPLE Inventory turnover for Cindy's Fine China was 2.76 in 2009 and 3.25 in 2010. How many days did the merchandise remain in stock each year?

Formula 365 Days/Inventory Turnover = Number of Days in Stock

Solution 365/2.76 = about 132 days   365/3.25 = about 112 days
Merchandise remained in stock for about 132 days in 2009 and for about 112 days in 2010.

Your Turn

If you had an inventory turnover of 3.6 for one year, how many days did your merchandise stay in stock?

Payroll, Inventory, and Cash Flow

Why should a business closely monitor its payroll, inventory, and cash flow?

Blood flows through your body, keeping you healthy, active, and alive. Without a steady flow of blood, your body would not function properly, and you would eventually die. Cash has a similar effect on a business. Cash flows through the business, giving it the financial resources it needs to operate in a healthy and profitable manner. A negative cash flow might cause difficulty in a business's daily operations. A negative cash flow means that cash is not available for paying bills, restocking merchandise, or expanding the business. If this happens over an extended period of time, the business may close.

Payroll and inventory are two financial areas that have great influence on your cash flow and on the life of your business. If the inflow of cash is not sufficient to meet the demanding needs of payroll and inventory, financial problems may result. Payroll expenses must be kept to a minimum, and merchandise must be purchased with careful analysis of present and future sales markets. Careful recording, monitoring, and analysis of data involving payroll and merchandise are essential for a positive cash flow and the ability to make sound financial decisions. A successful business carefully monitors its cash flow and constantly analyzes its payroll and inventory costs.

After You Read

Conclude Why do payroll and inventory systems require more careful monitoring and analysis than other aspects of a business?

SECTION 2 Assessment

Review Key Concepts

1. **Identify** What information is needed for an inventory control system?
2. **Summarize** Review the two main methods used to determine inventory quantity.
3. **Explain** What methods are used to calculate cost of inventory? How does cost affect supply?
4. **Analyze** Explain how to analyze inventory turnover.
5. **Relate** How do costs and inventory procedures impact profit?

Higher Order Thinking H.O.T.

6. **Examine** Rick's sandwich shop uses a very successful perpetual inventory system. Explain when and why his business should conduct a physical count of its inventory.

English Language Arts

7. **Inventory Control** Malia is planning to open a small art gallery in New York City, featuring artwork from new and emerging artists in Latin America. As she gets ready to establish her inventory system, she realizes that she will have many decisions to make regarding how to track and control her inventory. Which inventory system should Malia's art gallery use? Which costing method should she use? In a brief statement, explain why these are the best choices. Compare your decisions with those of your classmates.

NCTE 5 Use different writing process elements to communicate effectively.

Mathematics

8. **Average Inventory Turnover** Widget Co. manufactures as well as distributes various widgets to other manufacturers. The company had an inventory value of $225,000 as of January 1. On December 31 of the same year the company had an inventory value of $187,500. Widget Co. sold $475,000 of merchandise during the year. Calculate the average inventory for Widget Co. during the year. Also calculate the inventory turnover for the company for the year. Briefly explain what the inventory turnover figure means for the company.

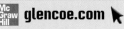

Math Concept **Calculate Inventory Turnover** To calculate the inventory turnover over a period divide the dollar value of the merchandise sold during the period by the average inventory of the company over the same period.

Starting Hint Determine the average inventory by first adding the inventory value at the end of the period to the inventory value at the beginning of the period. Divide the result by two.

NCTM Connections Communicate their mathematical thinking coherently and clearly to peers, teachers, and others.

Check your answers.

CHAPTER REVIEW

Visual Summary

Managing Payroll and Inventory

Voluntary Deductions

An employer will deduct certain amounts when requested by the employee.

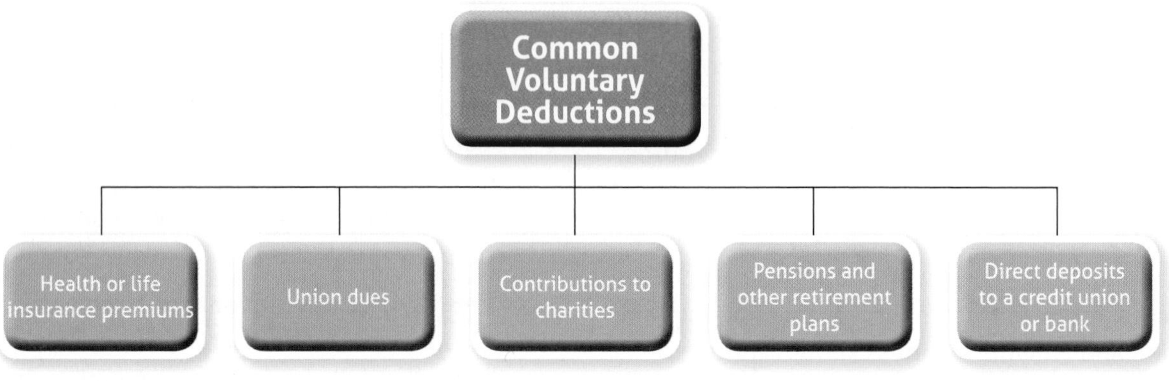

Merchandise Stages

Merchandise is on the move from the time it is ordered until it is sold.

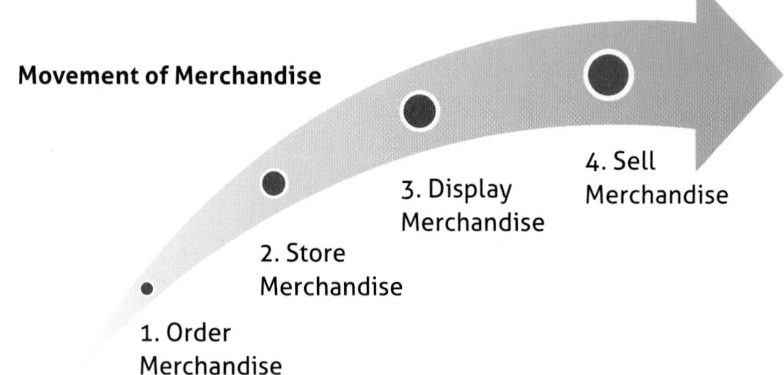

Try It!

Use a graphic organizer like the one shown to list the obligations employers must meet when preparing payroll records.

To Prepare Payroll Records, Employers Must:

1. __________

2. __________

3. __________

4. __________

5. __________

Chapter Review and Assessment

Chapter Summary

- The six steps in managing a payroll system are: (1) calculate gross earnings; (2) calculate payroll deductions; (3) prepare payroll records; (4) prepare paychecks; (5) record payroll information in accounting records; and (6) report payroll information to the government.
- Employees are paid by fixed salary, hourly wages, and commissions based on the value of goods they sell.
- Some payroll deductions are required by law, such as Social Security tax, others are voluntary.
- Payroll information is recorded in the salaries expense account. Deductions become liabilities and are recorded in separate accounts as payables.
- To establish an inventory control system, know the amount of merchandise sold, what items are selling, and what items are not.
- Perpetual inventory systems are possible with bar code scanning and point-of-sale terminals. To keep a periodic inventory system up-to-date, regular physical counts are required.
- The specific identification method works if you sell few, high-priced items. For first in, first out (FIFO) costing, the first items sold are the first bought. For last in, first out (LIFO) costing, the first items sold are the last bought.
- Inventory turnover is calculated by dividing the cost of merchandise sold in a time period by the average inventory.

Vocabulary Review

1. Find, copy, or create visual examples for these vocabulary terms. Use the examples to create a collage.

- payroll
- gross earnings
- salary
- hourly wage
- overtime rate
- commission
- deductions
- Federal Insurance Contributions Act (FICA)
- Social Security tax
- Medicare tax
- total gross earnings
- perpetual inventory system
- point-of-sale terminals
- periodic inventory system
- specific identification method
- first-in, first-out method (FIFO)
- last-in, first-out method (LIFO)
- withheld
- allowance
- stock
- staple

Higher Order Thinking 

2. **Connect** How do the rules of credit and debit apply to employee deductions?
3. **Judge** In order to make more commissions, do you think sales associates might overstate the merits of products just to make a sale?
4. **Research** What are some voluntary deductions an employee might choose to apply to his or her paychecks?
5. **Consider** Why does the IRS charge criminal or civil penalties for failure to properly pay taxes?
6. **Determine** You work at a coffee house from noon to 8:00 p.m. By 4:00 p.m. nearly all of the baked goods have sold. Explain whether this indicates good or poor inventory management.
7. **Categorize** Garrett owns a clothing store geared toward children and young teens. Name the kinds of items that Garrett would keep on a basic stock list, a model stock list, and a never-out list.
8. **Prepare** Imagine you run a store, and your point-of-sale terminals crash. What could you do ahead of time to prepare for such an event?
9. **Justify** Which is worse for a business—too much or too little inventory? Explain.

College and Career Readiness

Science

10. Point-of-Sale Convenience From early electronic cash registers to modern, Web-based point-of-sale (POS) systems, technology has worked to help business owners and retailers improve their inventory management. It also improves the speed and accuracy of sales.

Procedure Research the development of automated point-of-sale systems.

Analysis Prepare a report that outlines the other benefits that a business can experience by taking advantage of the latest POS technology.

NSES E Students should develop abilities of technological design, understandings about science and technology.

Mathematics

11. Cost of Inventory Worldwide Tea Co. had these inventory purchases over the year:

Date	Description	Units	Cost	Total
1/15	Beginning balance	100	$85	$ 8,500
4/25	Purchase	75	$93	$ 6,975
8/31	Purchase	150	$79	$11,850
11/30	Purchase	80	$90	$ 7,200

After completing a physical inventory, the company determined that there are 98 units remaining. Calculate the cost of the ending inventory using the FIFO method. Calculate the cost of ending inventory using the LIFO method.

Math Concept **Calculate Cost of Inventory** Calculate the cost of ending inventory by identifying the inventory level at a given period of time. Determine the particular method being used, and then multiply the units remaining by the purchase cost per unit.

Starting Hint The FIFO method assumes current inventory remains from the most recent purchases. Multiply the number of units by the purchase price for each order to get the total cost.

NCTM Problem Solving Solve problems that arise in mathematics and in other contexts.

English Language Arts

12. Choosing the Right Forms Go to the official Internal Revenue Service Web site to examine the forms businesses use to report payroll information to the government. With your teacher's permission, form small groups and select at least four forms to evaluate. Work together to figure out the information each form requires. Which forms are easy to understand? Which are more difficult to understand? How can a business owner get help with the forms? What additional information is available to business owners regarding how to pay taxes? Present your findings to the class.

NCTE 7 Conduct research and gather, evaluate, and synthesize data to communicate discoveries.

Ethics

13. Revealing Information When you start filling out employment and tax forms, you will need to answer questions about personal information. Examine this scenario: Cathleen completed her online benefits package at work and printed out the summary, which includes her current salary, on a shared printer. She got a phone call and forgot to pick up her printout. Lauren later passed the printer and saw Cathleen's document, which she read. Now Lauren is upset because Cathleen has a higher salary. She wants to discuss this with her manager, but she does not want to reveal how she found the information. What should Lauren do?

Real-World Applications

14. Advertising Art The prices of merchandise are advertised on television, online, and in print ads, and are even painted on store-front windows. Pricing is one of the most important tools retailers use to promote their businesses. Choose a product and then imagine that you are going to place an ad for this item. Research the typical prices for this product and set a reduced price for a clearance sale at the mall. Using markers, crayons, paint, cut-outs from magazines, or illustration software, create an ad displaying the product and its sale price.

Your Financial Portfolio

Keeping Track of Inventory

Janine is helping to count inventory at her mother's jewelry store, The Silver Parrot. She has been working on birthstone pendants. After she counted them, she looked up how many were on order. Then she filled in the number to order, based on the guideline of always keeping at least five pendants in stock.

Description	Number in Stock	Number on Order	Number to Order
January	2	3	0
February	5	0	0
March	0	3	2
April	0	3	2
May	1	3	1
June	4	3	0
July	3	3	0
August	3	0	2
September	2	0	3
October	4	0	1
November	2	3	0
December	1	3	1

Calculate

Before the new products were ordered, Janine's mother decided to change the guideline to "always keep 15 of each pendant in stock," rather than five. On a separate sheet of paper, calculate how many additional birthstone pendants Janine should order for the store.

CHAPTER 9

Pricing, Costing, and Growth

Visual Literacy

Even after opening its doors, a business needs to continually plan for all functions of the business. ***Why must a small business entrepreneur make creative funding decisions when expanding a business?***

Discovery Project

Analyzing Prices

Key Question

What factors go in to pricing beauty and grooming products for teens?

Project Goal

Cosmetic manufacturers target different age groups of males and females because their needs differ. Cosmetic products for teens are significantly different from products for older men and women.

- Work with a partner to analyze the prices of grooming and beauty products for a specific target market.
- Compare competing companies that sell similar products for that target market. The products may be cosmetics, grooming aids, or skin care for males or females.
- Check them out online and in different types of retail outlets (pharmacies, supermarkets, department stores).
- Analyze the prices and explain the goals and factors that must have been considered when pricing these products.

Ask Yourself...

- *How will you select a specific target market?*
- *How will you decide on which product lines to research?*
- *How will you analyze the goals and factors that go into pricing products?*
- *How will you organize and present your report?*

Make Judgments and Decisions

Provide research to back up your analysis of goals and factors that go into pricing beauty and grooming products.

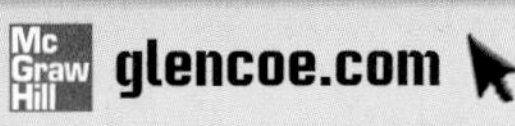

Evaluate Download an assessment rubric.

THE BIG IDEA

Planning for growth is crucial because a bigger business does not necessarily mean a better business.

ASK STANDARD &POOR'S

Selling Price

Q *I started making scarves and hats for my friends for fun, but demand for them has become so high that I am thinking of selling them. How much do I charge?*

A Your selling prices should be close to what your competitors charge. Make sure that your business will be profitable at those prices. For many businesses, profit margins are only in the 10 to 15 percent range. For each $1 in sales, the business keeps ten cents—making accurate pricing essential.

Writing Activity

Expository writing explains and informs. Think about a product you can make or service you can offer. How might you go about putting a price on your product or service? Write a brief statement that explains how much you will charge, and how you came to that decision.

CHAPTER 9

Reading Guide

Before You Read

The Essential Question What does pricing and costing have to do with a business's growth and expansion?

Main Idea

Effective pricing and costing are essential to every business's ability to make a profit and grow.

Content Vocabulary

- pricing
- product cost-plus pricing
- markup
- manufacturing business
- product costing
- cost behavior
- variable costs
- direct materials
- direct labor
- fixed costs
- contribution margin
- break-even point
- market penetration
- target profit
- target sales
- margin of safety

Academic Vocabulary

You will see these words in your reading and on your tests.

- yield
- anticipate
- correspond
- accommodate

Graphic Organizer

Before you read this chapter, create a graphic organizer like the one shown. As you read, take notes about the types of costs that are fixed, and the types of costs that are variable.

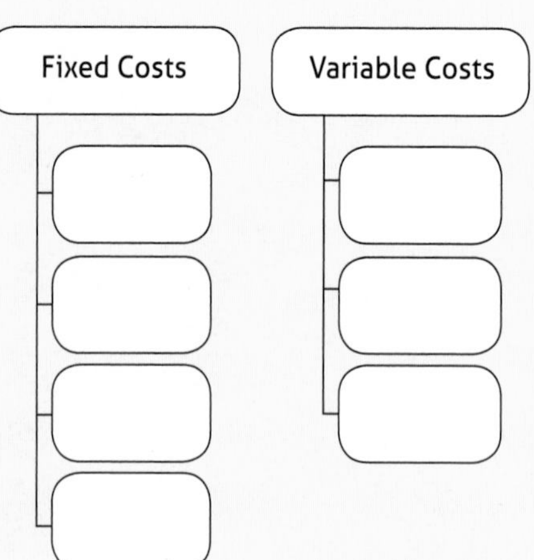

 glencoe.com  Print this organizer.

Standards

Academic

Mathematics

NCTM Problem Solving Solve problems that arise in mathematics and in other contexts.

NCTM Algebra Use mathematical models to represent and understand quantitative relationships.

English Language Arts

NCTE 4 Use written language to communicate effectively.

NCTE 12 Use language to accomplish individual purposes.

Social Studies

NCSS VII G Compare basic economic systems according to how rules and procedures deal with demand, supply, prices, the role of government, banks, labor and labor unions, savings and investments, and capital.

NCTM *National Council of Teachers of Mathematics*
NCTE *National Council of Teachers of English*
NCSS *National Council for the Social Studies*
NSES *National Science Education Standards*

Common Core

Reading Read and comprehend complex literary and informational texts independently and proficiently.

Speaking and Listening Present information, findings, and supporting evidence such that listeners can follow the line of reasoning and the organization, development, and style are appropriate to task, purpose, and audience.

Speaking and Listening Adapt speech to a variety of contexts and communicative tasks, demonstrating command of formal English when indicated or appropriate.

Pricing

Why is pricing important to a business?

Pricing is the process of assigning a selling price to a good or service. Price is usually expressed in monetary terms, such as $60 for a pair of shoes. It can also be expressed in non-monetary terms, such as free goods or services in exchange for the purchase of a product. The oldest form of pricing is the barter system, which involves exchanging a good or service for another good or service without the use of money. For a merchandise business, you must price goods and services appropriately for your business to succeed. If you set monetary prices too high, customers may buy from your competition—or not buy at all. If you set prices too low, you may not be able to cover your costs and operating expenses.

Section Objectives

- **Identify** the goals of pricing.
- **Explain** how retail businesses determine their selling price.
- **Define** product costing.
- **Describe** variable and fixed costs.
- **Explain** the break-even point.

As You Read

Consider If you were going to set prices for a retail business, what factors would you consider?

Goals of Pricing

Many factors influence the prices of goods and services. Pricing decisions must take into account costs, competition, and economic conditions. To make sound pricing decisions, a business owner must consider the goals of pricing.

Every business owner wants to set effective prices that **yield,** or bring in, large profits. Most businesses have three goals that act as guidelines for effective pricing:

- To obtain a given share of the market
- To generate sales that produce a specific profit
- To meet competitors' prices

In establishing prices, a business may have to prioritize these three goals. For example, suppose that a primary goal of your new outdoor sportswear business is to match your competitors' prices. You must remember that if you set your prices too low, you may not produce enough profit for your business to succeed.

Suppose that the primary goal of your business is to increase profits. You can achieve your objective by selling more items at the current price or by selling the same number of items at a higher price. However, if you raise prices to increase profits, you may no longer meet competitors' prices. You must decide which pricing goals are most important to your business.

Reading Check

Explain Why do the three goals of pricing vary among businesses?

reality bytes

Pricing Science
When setting the price for a product, some businesses use product cost-plus pricing; some consider how the competition is priced; and some look at the break-even point. A variety of e-newsletters provide information covering case studies, marketing trends, and the latest product news on pricing strategy. This research can help businesses determine the best price for a product.

Advertising Prices
Newspaper, magazine, and Internet advertisements are sources for information on what competitors are charging for goods. *Do you think a business should always match competitors' selling prices? Explain you answer.*

Merchandise Pricing

How do retail businesses price merchandise they sell?

All the financial procedures you have learned so far have involved merchandising businesses. A merchandising business buys goods, marks them up, and sells them to customers, such as retail stores.

Retail Pricing Methods

A retail business sells goods or services to the consumer. One pricing method used by retailers is product cost-plus pricing. **Product cost-plus pricing** is the process of determining an item's selling price by adding the invoice cost of the item (how much the business paid for the item) to a certain percentage of that cost. This added amount is the **markup,** which is the difference between the cost of an item to a business and the selling price of the item. This markup amount must cover all of the business's expenses and allow for a profit. For example, Luggage World is a retail store that sells travel bags and suitcases. The store manager prices all bags received with a 70 percent markup. Suppose that the Presidential Bag has an invoice cost, or purchase cost, of $48. With a 70 percent markup ($48.00 × .70 or 70% = $33.60) the price of the bag is $81.60. ($48.00 + 33.60 = $81.60)

Adjusting Prices

If you cannot sell an item with a particular markup, you may have to lower the selling price or discontinue stocking the item. The decision how to mark up items will depend on factors such as economic conditions, competition, or the season of the year.

Suppose that you purchase sweatshirts for your sportswear shop at $12 per shirt and price each one with a markup of 60 percent ($12 × .60 or 60% = $7.20). The retail price of each sweatshirt is $19.20

Making Up the Difference A jewelry store may have only a few potential customers each day and will sell merchandise to only a small percentage of them. *Why do stores that sell jewelry and other expensive items have to set high prices on their merchandise?*

(\$12 + \$7.20 = \$19.20). However, if your competitors are selling the same sweatshirts for \$17.99 each, you will probably have difficulty selling your sweatshirts with this markup. If you lower your price, you may not earn enough profit to cover your expenses. If you cannot purchase the same sweatshirts from another supplier at a lower cost, you may have to sell a different line of sweatshirts.

The percentage of markup will vary depending on the line of merchandise you are selling. Stores (such as jewelry stores) that sell very few items in a day have higher markup percentages than stores (such as music stores) that sell many items in a day. The markup must cover expenses and generate a profit for the business.

Reading Check

Explain Why do retail businesses markup the products they sell?

Costing and Pricing in a Manufacturing Business

How does costing affect pricing for manufacturing businesses?

Some businesses produce new merchandise. A **manufacturing business** is a business that buys raw materials or processed goods and transforms them into finished products.

COMMON CENTS

Business Expenses
When planning for expenses that will affect the prices of the products you sell, consider your operating expenses. The top ten small business expenses include: health insurance, Internet fees, cell phone fees, utilities, advertising, accounting services, voice mail, financial planning services, and collection services.

Concept Application

Choose a small business that you would like to own. If you were looking for ways to cut back on your business expenses, what areas would you target and why?

For example, if Tonya decides to sell hand-decorated handbags to her friends, her business will be a manufacturing business. She purchased a plain bag and decorated it to create a desirable new item. Tonya will have to consider the cost of the materials and labor that go into the production of her first bag before she can determine an appropriate price for similar bags. Determining costs and pricing in a manufacturing business is more complicated than in a retail business.

Product Costing

Product costing is the process of analyzing all costs involved in creating products. By product costing, you can establish a selling price that is both competitive and profitable for your business. Product costing will help Tonya decide whether she can sell hand-decorated bags for a reasonable price. If her costs for the first bag are low, she could make and sell similar bags at a profit. However, if making the first bag is expensive, she would have to set a high price to cover costs. The price may be so high that no one would buy the bags. Thus, Tonya could decide that the bags are not worth making.

Reading Check

Recall Which kind of business buys raw materials or processed goods and transforms them into finished products?

Classifying Costs

What are the different types of costs to consider?

Whether you run a large business, such as Apple, or a small business, such as a local bakery, you need complete information about costs to make smart financial decisions. You must identify your costs and determine which costs will increase and which will remain the same.

Hot Sellers
Items like barbecues, bathing suits, air conditioners, and swimming toys rarely go on sale during the summer months. *What might be the reason for this?*

Cost behavior is the way a cost changes in relation to a change in business activity. For example, as your business makes more items, some costs may increase, such as the costs of additional materials or labor. Other costs remain constant and are not influenced by the number of items you produce or the volume of sales. These costs could include rent, taxes, and insurance. In analyzing cost behavior, you will usually classify costs as variable or fixed.

Variable Costs

In product costing, **variable costs** are costs that change in direct proportion to the activity level of production. This means that if production increases, these costs will increase. If production decreases, your variable costs will decrease.

To understand cost behavior, consider the example of Windy River Creations. Wayne and Naomi are Native Americans who want to start a small business producing handmade Native American jewelry. They intend to buy metal bands, beads, leather, and other materials and make items to sell to area stores. They have rented a small shop, purchased a few pieces of equipment, bought materials and supplies, and hired two local artists to make the jewelry.

Windy River has identified three variable costs. These are (1) direct materials used to make the jewelry, (2) direct labor to create the jewelry, and (3) supplies used in processing the jewelry.

Direct Variable Costs **Direct materials** are the raw materials used to make a finished product. For Windy River's jewelry, these materials include metal, beads, leather, pins, packaging, and other items. Wayne and Naomi plan to produce five pieces of jewelry, one of which is the Sunset Bracelet. The direct materials to produce each bracelet cost $4.30.

Direct labor is the work required to convert raw materials into a finished product. To determine the cost of direct labor, multiply the amount of time spent to produce the item by the employee's hourly wage. Wayne and Naomi are paying their employees $12 per hour. It takes approximately 15 minutes (0.25 hours) to make the Sunset Bracelet. Therefore, the cost of direct labor per bracelet is $3 (0.25 × $12 = $3).

Wayne and Naomi now know that the cost of materials and labor needed to make the bracelet is $7.30 ($4.30 direct materials plus $3 direct labor). They must also take into account the cost of the supplies that will be consumed. This cost could include polish, wire, solder, glue, and finishing spray. Wayne and Naomi estimate that the cost of the supplies for one bracelet is $0.35. This brings the total variable cost per bracelet to $7.65, illustrated as follows:

Direct materials	$4.30
Direct labor	$3.00
Supplies	$0.35
Total variable	$7.65

Economics and You

Supply and Demand

When supply is greater than demand business owners may lower the price in hopes of increasing demand. In theory, when a price is reduced demand increases and when a price is increased, demand decreases. There are several exceptions to supply and demand theory because demand is not always that responsive to price changes. When demand is not responsive to price it is called inelastic demand. Inelastic demand occurs when a product is a necessity, when there are no substitutes for the item, and even when customers are very loyal to a particular brand.

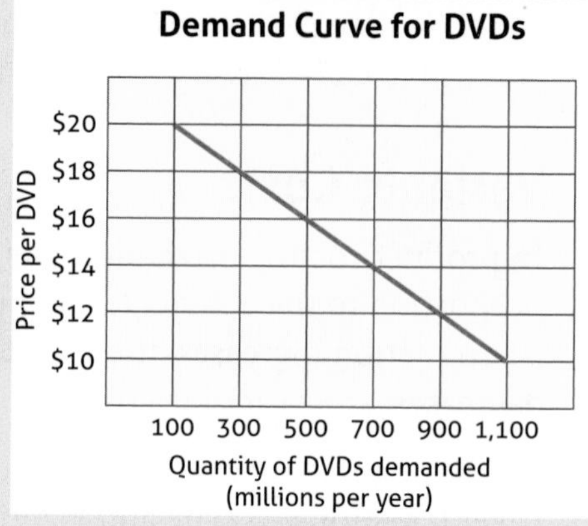

Personal Finance Connection As a consumer, you can become a smarter shopper by taking advantage of those times when supply exceeds demand. On those occasions you are able to buy items that you need at a low price. As long as those items do not have an expiration date, you can stock up on those items and save money.

Critical Thinking How can you apply supply and demand theory to job employment and wages?

Activity Download an Economics and You Worksheet Activity.

As more units are made, the variable cost assigned to each unit remains the same, but the total variable cost for the business increases. When fewer units are made, total variable costs decrease. The table below shows the impact of variable costs for Windy River:

	Unit Variable Cost				Total Variable Cost
7 Bracelets	$7.65	×	7	=	$53.55
10 Bracelets	$7.65	×	10	=	$76.50
18 Bracelets	$7.65	×	18	=	$137.70

Fixed Costs

Rent, insurance, and some utilities are examples of fixed costs. **Fixed costs** are costs that remain constant even if activity or production level changes. The total fixed cost remains the same regardless of the number of units produced. For example, Wayne and Naomi pay $700 per month to rent the shop that Windy River occupies. Regardless of the number of bracelets produced, the fixed cost of rent will remain $700. Remember, the selling price of the bracelets must exceed all fixed costs plus all variable costs in order to make a profit.

Reading Check

Explain What is cost behavior?

Selling Price

How do businesses determine the selling price?

Two methods for setting the price of a product are value basis and cost plus pricing. Value basis is used to set a price based on what the customer will pay for an item as well as the market value of that type of product. The highest level at which value basis prices can be set is determined by the value the customer places on that product including the quality, service, availability and benefits provided by the product.

Cost plus pricing is based upon determining the amount needed to produce a profit based on the expected sales volume and fixed costs to produce the product. A price set would be the amount paid for the product plus a percentage. For example, Wayne and Naomi plan to mark up the variable costs by approximately 70 percent in order to cover the fixed costs and show a profit. The total monthly fixed costs for the business are $1,400. Windy River is selling five types of jewelry, so each type must cover one-fifth, or 20 percent, of the fixed costs per month. Each type of jewelry must cover $280.($1,400 × .20 or 20% = $280). Wayne and Naomi must determine whether this markup is sufficient. They need to determine how many bracelets they must sell to cover fixed and variable costs.

Reading Check

Summarize How would a business owner know whether or not the markup on a product is sufficient?

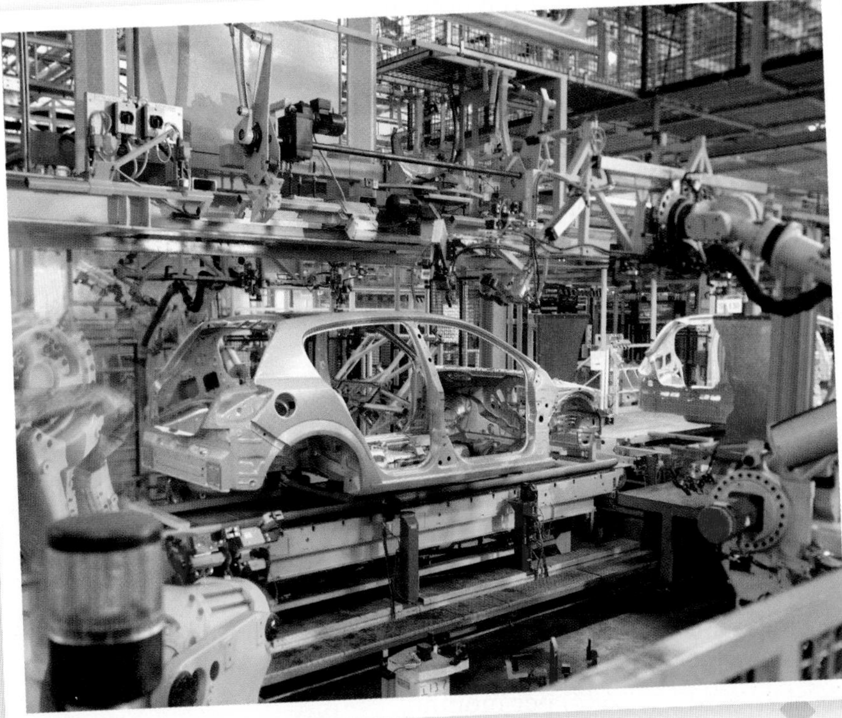

Robots
Many manufacturing companies rely on automation, often robots, to assemble products. *What are some advantages of using robots instead of human beings?*

The Contribution Margin

What is the contribution margin?

The **contribution margin** is the amount of money that the sale of a particular product contributes toward the payment of fixed costs and the profit of a business. The contribution margin equals total sales minus total variable costs. For example, if a product has sales of $13,000 and has variable costs totaling $7,000, it has a contribution margin of $6,000. This is the product's contribution to cover the fixed expenses and provide a profit.

Sales	$13,000
Minus variable costs	−7,000
Contribution margin	$6,000 (Amount available for fixed expenses)

Reading Check

Define What is the contribution margin?

The Break-Even Point

Why do businesses that sell products want to know the break-even point?

The **break-even point** is the point at which total sales equal total costs (variable and fixed costs). The break-even point represents the sales that a business must achieve to break even, or cover all costs. At the break-even point, there is neither a profit nor a loss.

Calculating the break-even point helps a business owner predict how changes in costs and sales will affect the profit earned by the business. The break-even analysis can also determine how many units of a product must be made and sold to cover expenses.

For example, suppose that you wanted to calculate how many units of the Sunset Bracelet that Wayne and Naomi would have to sell to break even, or cover all costs. Represent the number of units needed to break even by a variable such as *n*. On the left side of the equation, multiply unit sales price by *n*. On the right side of the equation, multiply the unit variable costs by *n*, then add the total fixed costs. Solve for *n*. If a product has unit sales of $1,300, unit variable costs of $700, and total fixed costs of $12,000. How many items (n) must be sold to break even?

$$1{,}300\mathbf{n} = 700\text{n} + 12{,}000;\ 1{,}300\mathbf{n} - 700\mathbf{n} = 12{,}000;\ 600\mathbf{n} = 12{,}000$$

$$\mathbf{n} = 20 \text{ items}$$

Break-even sales are the sales, expressed as a dollar amount that a business must make to cover all costs. Using the example from the **Go Figure** box, break-even sales for the Sunset Bracelet are $689 (53 bracelets × $13 = $689) per month.

South Korea

Poised for Growth

When new technologies emerge, the business world quickly takes notice. New companies form to innovate existing products or provide new technology to consumers. Established businesses find ways to integrate technology into their operations in order to streamline production or adapt to changing markets. Technological innovation promotes rapid economic growth. The government and the people of South Korea recognize this. Nowhere is this more evident than in the way that the entire country has embraced broadband. 85 percent of South Korean households subscribe to broadband Internet service, and over two-thirds of the population regularly use the Internet. The government made technology a national initiative by modernizing the country's infrastructure and deregulating policies to encourage competition. The result is that South Korea boasts inexpensive broadband at the fastest speeds on the planet. New telecommunications firms opened to provide service to large populations. Internet gaming has become a national pastime, and successful gamers gain fame similar to American sports stars.

Critical Thinking

1. **Expand** Research South Korean leisure activities. How has innovation in broadband Internet service affected South Korean leisure activities?
2. **Relate** What lessons can the U.S. learn from South Korea's model of implementing broadband? What limits do we face?

DATABYTES

Capital
Seoul

Population
48,636,068

Language
Korean

Currency
South Korean won

Gross Domestic Product (GDP)
$809.7 billion

GDP per capita
$28,000

Industry
Crude oil production, petroleum refining, basic petrochemicals, ammonia, industrial gases, sodium hydroxide (caustic soda), cement, fertilizer, plastics, metals, commercial ship repair, commercial aircraft repair, construction

Agriculture
Wheat, barley, tomatoes, melons, dates, citrus; mutton, chickens, eggs, milk

Exports
Petroleum and petroleum products

Natural Resources
Coal, tungsten, graphite, molybdenum, lead, hydropower potential

GO FIGURE Mathematics

Break-Even Point

By calculating the unit variable cost of products to sell with the monthly fixed costs, a business can figure out how many units of a product must sell to break even.

EXAMPLE Windy River sells each Sunset Bracelet for $13. The unit variable cost for the bracelet is $7.65. The amount of monthly fixed costs that sales of the Sunset Bracelet are expected to contribute is $280. How many units of the Sunset Bracelet must Windy River sell to break even?

Formula Break-Even Sales = Variable Costs + Total Fixed Costs; Unit Sales Price × n = (Unit Variable Costs × n) + Fixed Costs

Solution $\$13.00n = \$7.65n + \$280.00$

$\$13.00n - \$7.65n = \$280.00$

$\$5.35n = \$280.00$

$n = \$280.00 \div \$5.35$

$n = 52.3$ or 53 bracelets

To break even, Windy River must sell 53 Sunset Bracelets each month.

Your Turn

Your sister is selling custom printed T-shirts at the beach on weekends. Fixed costs from sales total $345. How many bracelets should she sell to break even if each T-shirt sells for $20 and the unit variable cost is $11.50 each?

The following calculations show the accuracy of the math.

	Total	Unit
Sales (53 × $13)	$689.00	$13.00
Less variable costs (53 × $7.65)	– $405.45	– $7.65
Contribution margin	$283.55	$5.35
Less fixed costs	–$280.00	
Net income	$3.55	

Fortunately for Wayne and Naomi, Windy River has been averaging sales of 70–80 bracelets per month for the past few months, exceeding their break-even point. At the present rate of sales, the bracelet's contribution margin is covering its share of fixed costs and is contributing to a net income for the business.

By substituting different numbers in the break-even equation, Wayne and Naomi can analyze how changes in sales price, costs, and sales volume affect profit. What if only 45 bracelets are sold? What if the variable costs increase by $2? How much profit is reported if 75 bracelets are sold? Such questions are an important part of financial analysis. If you are a business owner, you must **anticipate,** or predict, changes in the market and be prepared with alternative plans if the changes actually occur. Using the techniques to analyze all financial possibilities and being prepared for change can help keep a business growing.

SECTION 1 Assessment

Review Key Concepts

1. **Identify** What are the goals of pricing?
2. **Explain** How do retail businesses determine their selling price?
3. **Define** What is product costing?
4. **Describe** What are variable costs and fixed costs? Provide examples of each.
5. **Explain** What is the break-even point?

Higher Order Thinking H.O.T.

6. **Examine** Making a profit is always at the top of a business's goals. Explain why an increase in prices may not lead to an increase in profits.

21st Century Skills

7. **Access and Evaluate Information** As someone with a variety of skills in carpentry, plumbing, and general home care, you are considering opening a business providing home maintenance and handyman services. You realize that you will be competing with large plumbing repair companies and other specialists. Make a list of services you plan to offer. Then go online to find sources of similar services in your area to evaluate the competition. Write a plan for marketing the business that explains how you will grow your operation by promoting your services so that potential customers can differentiate you from the competition, and thus, increase your market share.

Mathematics

8. **Variable Costs** A plastic molds company manufactures a product where the raw materials used to make the finished product, or the direct materials cost is $12.50 per unit. The work required to convert the raw materials into a finished product, or the direct labor cost per unit is $5.75. The supplies used in the production process of this specific product cost $1.10 per unit. What is total variable cost per unit of this product? What is the total variable cost if you make 75 units? 125 units?

Math Concept **Calculate Variable Costs** Calculate the total variable cost of a specific product by identifying the variable cost per unit for the product and multiplying this unit cost by the total number of units produced.

Starting Hint Determine the total variable cost per unit by identifying the direct materials, direct labor and supplies cost per unit. Add these together to calculate the total variable cost per unit for the product.

NCTM Problem Solving Solve problems that arise in mathematics and in other contexts.

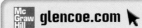

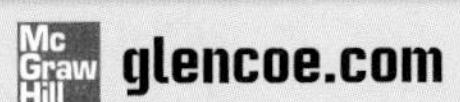

Check your answers.

Section Objectives

- **Identify** and describe the forms of business growth.
- **Summarize** profit planning.
- **Describe** the challenges and the importance of planning for growth.

As You Read

Predict In what ways do you think businesses can grow?

Sources of Business Growth

What are the different sources of business growth?

The key to all successful business operations is growth. Businesses, whether they are small sole proprietorships or large corporations, are much like people. They must grow and mature to achieve success. A business that does not grow can end up far behind its competition.

Business growth can come from many sources and can be measured in many ways. It may develop from an increase in the following:

- the number of customers
- sales
- share of the market
- employees
- lines of merchandise
- profit

These are important aspects of growth for any business as well as indicators of success. However, growth should be carefully planned and directed. Sound financial planning is essential for making decisions regarding expansion. Not every aspect of your business needs to grow every year. For a business, bigger does not necessarily mean better. If a business grows too rapidly or in the wrong area, serious financial problems may result.

Planning growth to **correspond,** or agree, with the business's short-term and long-term goals is essential to financial success. If you have a business, short-term goals for the business reflect the areas to concentrate efforts.

One year you may place an emphasis on increasing the number of customers; the following year, you may explore new lines of merchandise. As one of your target areas grows, others may also increase and grow. For example, if you concentrate on increasing your number of customers this year, your sales and profits should also report increases. Primary growth in one area often leads to secondary growth in other areas.

Customers

Adding new customers usually causes a rise in sales. More sales usually result in greater profits. Increasing the number of customers is always a primary goal in business. Acquiring new customers is often a result of two factors: effective advertising and promotions and referrals by satisfied customers.

Careers That Count!

Maxwell Sebastian • Chief Financial Officer

Every company needs someone to handle the financial aspects of the business. That is me. I like the challenge of making short-term goals that help achieve long-term ones. I am the chief financial officer (CFO) for a chain of motorcycle parts, accessories, and clothing retailers. Among my many daily activities, I'm expected to direct the company's overall financial policies, procedures, and reporting that are required to continue a 30 percent per year growth rate with increasing profitability. I manage all financial functions, including accounting, budgeting, cash flow, bank relationships, risk, inventory management, and taxes. Besides knowledge of accounting, I need to stay abreast of federal and state laws and regulations as well as developments in international trade. The entire accounting department reports to me. I earn a very good living, but the job comes with a lot of responsibility and a lot of pressure. If you are business savvy and love finances, you may want to work toward becoming a CFO.

EXPLORE CAREERS

Visit the Web site of the Bureau of Labor Statistics and obtain information about a career as a top executive.

1. Why would a CFO need to understand pricing principles?
2. In addition to the expected job duties, what other responsibilities might a CFO have that justify the high compensation?

Skills	Education	Career Path
Accounting, analytical, communication, computer, decision-making, math, problem-solving, and long-range planning skills; able to see the big picture, able to cope with stress, flexible, good judgment, independent, likes working with people and numbers	Bachelor's or master's degree in business administration, accounting, economics, finance, or; Certified Public Accountant certification, Seminars, conferences, and training programs can expand job options	Chief financial officers are top executives. This position is not usually reached until after many years of proven work in other positions, such as accountant, CPA, financial planner, and business strategist.

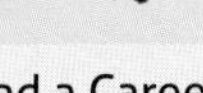
glencoe.com

Activity Download a Career Exploration activity.

Potential customers must know where the business is located, and they must believe that buying from your business will be a positive experience. You can control your advertising and marketing programs, but you have no control over customer referrals. Satisfying your customers' needs is the key to building a solid customer base.

Sales

Growth in sales is also a source of business growth. When sales increase, however, you must be capable of handling the larger volume so that you continue to satisfy your customers. If sales grow too quickly, and you do not have enough employees, the quality of your customer service may suffer seriously. In addition, you must be sure that you have sufficient merchandise to offer.

Market Share

A measurement of growth is the business's share of the existing market. If your business held approximately 15 percent of the potential market last year, and this year your market share has risen to 19 percent, you have achieved positive growth. This is evidence that your business is staying competitive, probably through effective advertising and promotions.

Market Penetration

Market penetration is an attempt to increase sales in your current market. You can do this in a variety of ways. You can find ways to get your customers to use your product more often, possibly by finding other uses and benefits for your product. You can try to attract your competitors' customers. A retail store owner might locate near a competitor to encourage comparison shopping.

Another way to increase sales in your current market is to go after people in your present market who are not using products like yours. Setting up a demonstration of your product in a store is one approach. Customers who would not normally select your product will instantly see and experience the benefits of your product.

Market Development

A business can grow and expand its products to reach new locations locally, nationally, or even internationally. Franchising is one way to grow. Franchisers sell the right to operate a business under the company's name. In exchange for a fee, you the franchiser provide training, hiring, and other assistance such as manuals and market analyses.

Too Much of a Good Thing
If the manager of this store orders too many soccer balls, the unsold balls will have to be stored until the next season. *What are some ongoing challenges for retail stores when ordering products to sell?*

Advantages of Franchising One of the biggest advantages of franchising is that you can expand the business with someone else's money. Franchising also makes it easy for you to manage your growing organization. With franchising, you personally train your franchisees. They, in turn, hire and are responsible for the employees who work for them. You do not have to oversee the workers.

Disadvantages of Franchising Franchising also has its challenges. It is like starting your business all over again. You must prepare training manuals, write operating instructions, and prepare market and competitor analyses.

In addition, the costs of setting up the franchise structure add up. There may be legal, accounting, consulting, and training costs. It may be a long time before a franchise turns a profit. In some cases, you may have to wait three to five years for a profit.

Globalization You should not limit your growth to the United States. Franchises based in the United States can be found throughout Europe and Asia and other parts of the world.

Businesses other than franchises form partnerships and enjoy tremendous success in global markets. Foreign businesspeople come to the United States looking for franchises and partners. They want to take successful business concepts back to their countries.

GO FIGURE Mathematics

Target Sales

Calculating how much product a business must sell to reach a profit is essential for success.

EXAMPLE Windy River sells each Sunset Bracelet for $13. The unit variable cost for the bracelet is $7.65. The amount of monthly fixed costs that sales of the Sunset Bracelet are expected to contribute is $280. The target profit is $500 per month. How many units of the Sunset Bracelet must Windy River sell to reach its target profit?

Formula Target Sales = Variable Costs + Fixed Costs + Target Profit; Unit Sales Price × n = (Unit Variable Costs × n) + Fixed Costs + Target Profit

Solution $\$13.00n = \$7.65n + \$280.00 + \$500.00$

$\$13.00n - \$7.65n + \$280.00 + \$500.00$

$\$5.35n = \$780.00$

$n = \$780.00 \div \$5.35$

$n = 145.7$, or 146 bracelets

Windy River would have to sell 146 Sunset Bracelets to achieve its target profit.

Your Turn

You are selling smoothies at school-sponsored sporting events. You price them at $3.50 each. The unit variable cost is $1.25 each. Your monthly fixed costs by sales should be $150. The target profit is $400 a month. How many smoothies should you sell?

Employees

As your market share grows and your sales increase, you must maintain an appropriate number of employees to contribute to growth. The need to hire more employees to **accommodate,** or provide for, your customers is a sign of positive growth. However, the additional employees should be utilized in the proper manner. Payroll is a major expense of your business.

Product Development

Product development is another way to increase sales to existing customers. When expanding with a new line of merchandise, carefully analyze the potential market and estimate the profits to be made. Expanding for the sake of expansion is not always a source of positive growth.

The new line should assure a new sales market and good profits. Unfortunately, many small businesses experience financial success only to expand to new areas that prove unprofitable.

Profits

One of the key indicators of the success of your business is the rate of growth of your profits. Making a profit is crucial to your business. Profits must grow for your business to survive. However, planning for increased profits is often easier said than done. Businesses may approach profit in several ways.

Reading Check

Identify What is the key to building a solid customer base?

Profit Planning

How can a business plan to make profits?

Business managers frequently evaluate cost and profit data to determine how to maximize profits. They use break-even analysis to test possible changes and to determine how those changes might affect future profits. Using the results of their analysis, managers forecast sales and plan financial activities for their business.

Setting a Target Profit

An important part of the planning process is setting goals. One common goal is to increase the amount of net income, or profit. **Target profit** is the amount of net income that a business sets as a goal. For example, you may want to expand to a new line of merchandise or possibly open another outlet or store. In order to fulfill these objectives, you will need to generate a given amount of profit.

Suppose that Wayne and Naomi want to earn a profit of $500 per month over the next six months on sales of the Sunset Bracelet. Assuming that the selling price and costs remain constant, how many bracelets would they need to sell to achieve this target profit?

Target sales is the number of units a business needs to sell to reach a target profit. The target sales equation is as follows:

Target Sales = Variable Costs + Fixed Costs + Target Profit

Using the target sales equation, you can calculate how many units a business must sell to reach its target profit. Represent the number of units needed to achieve the target profit by a variable such as n. On the left side of the equation, multiply the unit sales price by n. On the right side of the equation, multiply the unit variable costs by n. Then add fixed costs and the required profit. Solve for n.

Windy River has been selling about 70 to 80 bracelets per month, and sales have risen approximately 10 percent per month. By increasing current sales by approximately 10 percent a month for the next six months, Windy River will sell about 124 Sunset Bracelets per month by the sixth month.

Short Shelf Life
Tastes change and trends come and go; new items come out every day. *What are some products that have a short selling period?*

Controlled Expansion
Expanding a small business is generally a good thing, but you should not expand too rapidly. *Can you name a business in your area that expanded but then had financial problems?*

Technology
The ability to apply technology effectively is an important skill both in the classroom and in the workplace. Careers today and in the future will continue to rely heavily on technology. In order to be successful you should be able to use technology to research, organize, assess, and communicate information. In addition, it is important to be familiar with and utilize digital technologies and communication tools, such as smart phones or tablet PCs, to access, create, and present information.

Write About It
Think of a situation in which you used or saw someone use technology to access or present information. Write one or more paragraphs to describe the scenario and explain how using technology impacted the situation.

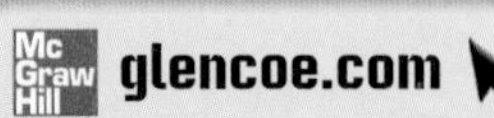

Activity Download a Career and College Readiness Worksheet Activity.

Assuming current sales are 70 per month, projected sales would be as follows:*

Month		
	1	77
	2	85
	3	94
	4	103
	5	113
	6	124

(*Assumes 10 percent increase in current sales per month.)

Windy River would have to sell 146 bracelets per month to reach its target profit of $500. Wayne and Naomi decide that this is an unrealistic expectation. They conclude that a target profit of $400 is more realistic. Using the target sales calculation, they determine that they must sell 128 bracelets each month to achieve the goal of $400.

Margin of Safety

When you are analyzing target sales and profits, you should consider what will happen if you do not reach your target. Your margin of safety will indicate the amount that sales can drop before the business experiences a loss. The **margin of safety** is the target sales minus the break-even sales, which indicates the amount of risk that sales will meet the break-even point. A high margin of safety suggests a minimal risk that sales will fall below the break-even point.

Wayne and Naomi calculate the margin of safety for the Sunset Bracelet as follows:

Target sales (to achieve a profit of $400)	$1,664.00	128 bracelets
Less break-even sales	−689.00	−53 bracelets
Margin of safety	$975.00	75 bracelets

The margin of safety is $975, or 75 bracelets. This means that sales can drop by this amount below target sales before the business experiences a loss on this item. For Windy River, this target sales amount is a fairly safe venture.

Reading Check

Contrast What is the difference between target profit and target sales?

The Challenges of Growth

What are the factors that might affect a business's ability to grow?

If your business is successful, it will probably grow. If you have planned effectively for growth, you will also experience growth.

Document Detective

A Break-Even Analysis

If you manage or own a retail store, you need to analyze your merchandise pricing, costs, and sales to determine when you are making a profit. The Break-Even Analysis Worksheet can help you determine profitability. A break-even analysis contains the following information:

- Names of the products analyzed
- Unit pricing and fixed and variable expenses
- Calculation for number items that must be sold to break even

Break-Even Analysis Worksheet

Store: Sallie's Accessories
Location: 129 Fashion Way
Skokie, Illinois
Product Line: Jewelry
Period: Six months beginning June 20––

Item	Unit Price (P)	Variable Costs per Unit (V)	Fixed Costs (F)	Units to Breakeven (n) $Pn = Vn + F$
Watches	$49.99	$23.25	$2,000	75
Necklaces	$79.95	$29.50	$2,000	40
Rings		$40.00	$2,000	40
Bracelets	$19.95	$4.50	$2,000	130
Earrings	$41.50	$12.00	$2,000	68

Key Points Fixed costs can include such expenses as rent, utilities, insurance, advertising, and administrative expenses.

FIND the Solutions

Review Key Concepts

1. What are the total fixed costs assigned to the jewelry department for the six-month period?
2. What is the break-even point for necklaces?
3. Which item has the highest markup?
4. What would happen to the break-even point if Sallie raised the price of the bracelets?
5. How much does a ring cost at Sallie's?

However, you should consider whether your business is prepared for growth. Several factors affect the ability of a business to grow:

- **Market characteristics**—If your niche market is too small, your business may be unable to grow. To develop further, the business must expand outside into new market areas.
- **Multiple sites**—With more than one location, you must decide where your main operations will be located. You will also need to staff your other locations.
- **Delegation**—Many small business owners are successful at starting their own businesses. However, they may not have the skills to manage others to do expanded tasks. You might consider hiring someone as a manager.
- **Industry innovation**—If your industry's growth is dependent upon innovation or constantly changing ideas and products, you will have to move ahead faster than the trends.
- **Systems and controls**—Effective systems and controls need to be in place for management, marketing, finances, and record keeping.

Reading Check

Expand When is it a good idea to consider hiring a manager?

After You Read

Connect Relate the goals of pricing to the factors involved in making a pricing decision.

Planning and Growth

Why is planning so important?

As you project your business's financial prospects, you must analyze carefully where you will spend your profits. Growth is important, but only if it is carefully analyzed, planned, and controlled. Good planning will usually result in successful growth; poor planning could drive you out of business.

The following guidelines will not guarantee successful decisions, but ignoring them could result in business failure:

- Make sound financial decisions when setting short-term and long-term goals.
- Set realistic financial targets.
- Control expenses and costs.
- Analyze financial statements frequently.
- Analyze your competition.
- Evaluate current economic conditions.
- Maintain a reserve fund.

You may always have limited funds to invest for business growth. However, careful planning and financial analysis should provide you with the knowledge you will need for intelligent investment decisions and well-planned, controlled growth of your business.

Assessment

Review Key Concepts

1. **Identify** Name and describe the forms of business growth.
2. **Summarize** What is profit planning?
3. **Describe** What are the challenges and the importance of planning for growth?
4. **Explain** What are the advantages and disadvantages of franchising?

Higher Order Thinking H.O.T.

5. **Explain** Growth in business is generally considered a good thing. Under what circumstances might it be unwise to expand a small business?

English Language Arts

6. **Growing Pains** A business owner needs to plan for when things go wrong, also to plan for when things go well. When a business is prepared for growth, it can better manage the changes and challenges that growth brings, and the business can achieve the goals that were set when it first started. Choose a business that you would like to start. Create a poster, collage, or other graphic display to visually represent three things that could hamper the growth of your business, and three things that could lead to growth.

NCTE 12 Use language to accomplish individual purposes.

Mathematics

7. **Target Sales and Margin of Safety** Vincent and Marius have started a business selling math flash cards. They have estimated some of the costs associated with their business as well as their selling price. They decided that they would sell the flash cards at $52 per package. Variable costs per package are $20 while fixed costs are $600. Their target profit is $1,000. How many packages do they need to sell in order to reach their target profit? What is the margin of safety in units and sales dollars?

Math Concept **Calculate Margin of Safety** To calculate the margin of safety determine the target sales amount as well as the break-even point. Subtract the break-even point from the target sales to determine the margin of safety.

Starting Hint Determine the target sales by using the formula provided in the chapter: Target sales = variable costs + fixed costs + target profit or: Unit sales price $\times$ n = (unit variable costs $\times$ n) + fixed costs + target profit and solve for n.

NCTM Algebra Use mathematical models to represent and understand quantitative relationships.

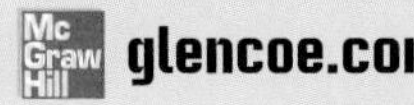

Check your answers.

CHAPTER REVIEW

Visual Summary

Pricing, Costing, and Growth

Grow Your Business

The key to all successful business operations is growth.

Goals of Pricing

A business owner must consider the goals of pricing and take into account costs, competition, and economic conditions before making pricing decisions.

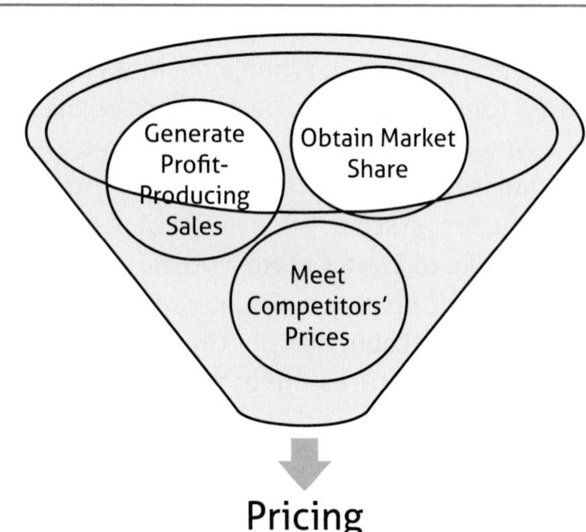

Try It!

Draw a diagram like the one shown to write down guidelines for careful growth planning.

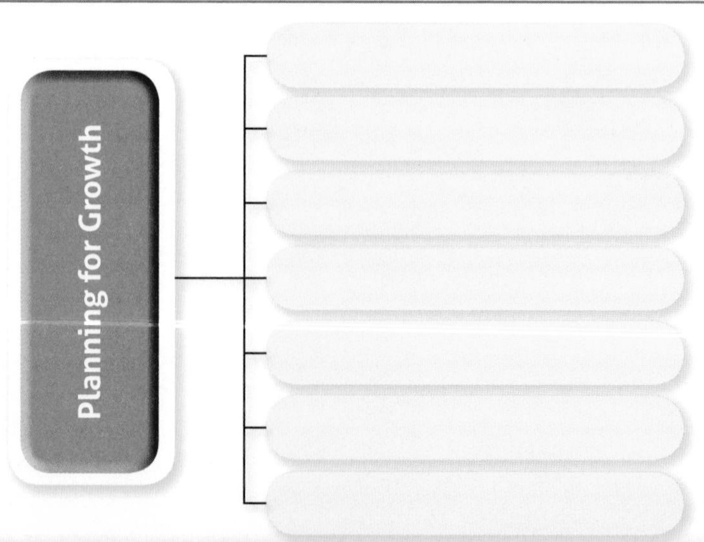

Chapter Review and Assessment

Chapter Summary

- In merchandising businesses, product cost-plus pricing is used: A markup based on the cost of the item is added to the actual cost. The markup percentage covers business expenses plus profit margin. In manufacturing businesses, product costing covers raw materials, plus the cost of processing them, plus profit.
- Variable costs, such as direct materials and direct labor, change in proportion to production levels. Fixed costs remain constant despite production level changes.
- By determining the contribution margin and break-even point, a business can set attractive prices that also ensure a profit for the business.
- Businesses grow by increasing customers, sales, market share, markets, number of employees, lines of merchandise, and profits.
- Profit planning occurs by setting target profit goals and estimating a margin of safety—target sales minus break-even sales.
- Target sales needed to reach a target profit are equal to variable costs, plus fixed costs, plus target profits. The margin of safety is the amount that sales can drop before the business experiences a loss.
- Planning for growth will enable you to grow in a controlled way and to be prepared to take advantage of growth opportunities.

Vocabulary Review

1. Write true-or-false statements using each vocabulary word. Ask a partner to determine whether each statement is true or false and explain why.

- pricing
- product cost-plus pricing
- markup
- manufacturing business
- product costing
- cost behavior
- variable costs
- direct materials
- direct labor
- fixed costs
- contribution margin
- break-even point
- market penetration
- target profit
- target sales
- margin of safety
- yield
- anticipate
- correspond
- accommodate

Higher Order Thinking

2. **Describe** What might happen if a business sold its products for the same price it paid for them?
3. **Analyze** Clothing is often marked up more than 100 percent. What does this mean in terms of the price you pay in the store? What other factors go into the price determination?
4. **Consider** Why do you think it might be common for companies to set prices incorrectly on products or services that are easy to sell?
5. **Propose** If a business is facing increased costs, how can it respond with pricing options?
6. **Extend** Other than price, what means do marketers have to accomplish the goal of improving their market share?
7. **Assess** Sometimes a company must eliminate a successful product as part of a plan for growth. What are some factors that might make a company discontinue a product?
8. **Deduce** How can a business's reserve fund affect growth opportunities?
9. **Defend** Does growth have to be planned and directed, or does growth "just happen"? Defend your answer.

College and Career Readiness

Social Studies

10. Legal and Ethical Pricing Federal and state governments have laws controlling prices. Marketers and retailers must be aware of their rights and responsibilities regarding pricing. One illegal tactic is bait-and-switch advertising. This occurs when a business advertises a low price (the "bait") for an item it has no intention of selling. When the customer comes in and asks for the advertised item, the salesperson says the item is sold out and offers the customer a higher-priced item instead (the "switch"). Go online and find at least three laws that have been enacted to protect consumers and business owners from unfair pricing practices. Write a brief summary of each law and share your findings with the class.

NCSS VII G Compare basic economic systems according to how rules and procedures deal with demand, supply, prices, the role of government, banks, labor and labor unions, savings and investments, and capital.

Mathematics

11. Break-Even Point Justin and Brijesh are thinking about starting a business. Before they move forward they want to see what their break-even point would be to determine if it is a worthwhile project. They decide to sell a specific product for $17 per unit. This product will cost $5 per unit to produce which includes direct materials costs, direct labor costs, and all supplies required. The total fixed costs are $500. Calculate the break-even point and explain what this figure means to them.

Math Concept **Calculate Break-Even Point** To calculate the break-even point of a product determine the number of units needed to be sold to have total sales equal total costs.

Starting Hint First identify the sales price per unit. Next determine the variable costs per unit and the total fixed costs. Use the following formula: Sale price per unit $\times n =$ (Variable costs per unit $\times n$) + Fixed costs. Solve this equation for n.

NCTM Algebra Use mathematical models to represent and understand quantitative relationships.

English Language Arts

12. Customer Relations Michael is one of several department managers in a women's clothing store. A customer approaches him with two dresses that are identical except for the sizes. The one she found in the Juniors department has been marked down to $35.00, but the one she found in the Petites department is still marked at $50.00. None of the Juniors dresses has been marked down because the buyer for that department did not elect to do so. Michael does not want to lose her as a customer. Write a short paragraph that describes what you think Michael should say to the customer when she asks to buy the petite dress for the junior price.

NCTE 4 Use written language to communicate effectively.

Economics

13. Competition Fast-food restaurants that set prices too high, provide inefficient service, or have a staff that is not courteous, risk losing customers. This is because customers will choose other restaurants that offer lower prices, higher-quality food, and better service. Understanding the benefits of competition and the costs of limiting competition helps consumers evaluate public policies. Such policies affect the level of competition in various markets. Why is competition a beneficial and necessary aspect of a successful market economy?

Real-World Applications

14. Cell Phones Cell phone companies advertise in various ways to target very specific markets. Family plans that allow parents and children to stay connected during the day are very popular. Prepaid plans geared toward college students and young people are also popular. What factors would attract you to a cellular plan? Produced in 1983, the world's first commercial portable cell phone had a retail price of $3,995. Think of three reasons why the price of cell phones has changed so much in recent years. Then name at least three other items which have decreased in price over the years.

Your Financial Portfolio

Business Expansion Magic

Under the name of Morgan the Magnificent, Victor Morgan has been performing magic since he was eight years old. Now that he is 16, he wants to branch out from school events and birthday parties for friends and family to perform professionally. He already has his own Web site and a performance video.

To expand the business, he wrote down the following strategies and actions he could take:

Make a flyer and a cover letter I can send out to potential customers.	Contact the human resources department of local companies to let them know I am available to perform at employee functions and holiday parties.
Contact local stores that sell or rent party supplies. Ask if I can post a flyer and if they can recommend me if anybody is looking for an entertainer.	Contact a public relations agency and offer to do free performances in exchange for their helping me get publicity.
Contact local chambers of commerce to find out when they are having street fairs or crafts fairs.	Contact wedding planners to see if they would recommend me to be part of the wedding entertainment.
Call the local newspaper and ask if someone could write an article about me.	Stop by ice cream stores to find out if I can post a flyer.

Analyze

Pick a business in your area. On a separate sheet of paper, list eight strategies and actions that could improve or expand the business. Summarize how the strategies could impact the business.

Unit 3

Unit Project

Finding Funding and Making Money

Ask Yourself...

Where can you get the money needed to start your own business? How can you ensure that the business generates enough profit to stay open? Why do prices vary on a product or service from one business to another? Responses to these questions can help you establish a sound financial plan and a profitable business.

Your Objective

The goal of this project is to begin developing a financial plan for a new business, explore pricing of products and services to help ensure profit, and create a presentation to share your results with the class.

Skills You'll Use

Success in defining goals and preparing financially for those goals depends on your skills. Some skills you might use include:

Academic Skills—Reading and writing

21st Century Skills—Critical thinking, speaking, listening, problem solving, decision making, interpersonal skills

Technology Skills—Word processing, keyboarding, presentation software

Standards

NCTE 4 Use written language to communicate effectively.

NCTE 5 Use different writing process elements to communicate effectively.

NCTE 7 Conduct research and gather, evaluate, and synthesize data to communicate discoveries.

NCTE 12 Use language to accomplish individual purposes.

STEP 1 Explore Sources of Funding

All businesses require some start-up capital to purchase equipment, inventory, or advertising. Think of a type of business you would like to start. What products or services would you sell? Research similar businesses and their finances. Then answer these questions:

- Do you have enough money for start-up costs, operating costs, and a reserve fund?
- What financing options might you consider for a small amount of capital (under $1,000)?
- Where might you turn for more substantial amounts of financing?
- If you needed a large sum, would you attempt to get the entire amount from one source or divide the amount among different sources?

Your responses will help guide you in determining the needs for your new business and in developing your business plan. Consider which sources you would be most likely to turn to for financing and begin to write a financial plan. Keep in mind that this will be an active document which you can update and finalize at a later date, once you have determined the specifics of your new business and can compute actual start-up and operating costs.

STEP 2 Understand Pricing

How will you make a profit in your business? How will you determine what to charge for specific products and services? Search for information on competition and pricing for your products or services.

- How much of your revenue will you need to use to cover payroll or overhead expenses?
- What are your competitors charging for similar products or services?
- What percentage over cost will you add for markup?
- Will you raise your prices if your costs go up?

Write a paragraph explaining how you plan to price your products or services. Then write an explanation of how you might control business expenses to help you retain more of your profits.

STEP 3 Build Relationships

Interview a trusted adult in your community who owns or manages a local business. Ask how the company sets and adjusts its prices to ensure profitability. Talk about your business idea and your pricing plan and ask for his or her opinion as to whether your plans for pricing are realistic.

- Develop interview questions based on your research and plans for ensuring profits.
- Take clear notes and accurately record the responses.
- Practice active listening skills.
- Respond politely and professionally.
- Ask for clarification if you do not understand something.
- Encourage the professional to share by asking open-ended questions.
- Type a summary of your notes and the interviewee's responses.
- Adjust your pricing plan and financial plan as appropriate based on the information learned in your interview.

STEP 4 Develop Your Presentation

Use the Unit 3 Project Checklist to plan and create your presentation.

STEP 5 Evaluate Your Presentation

Your presentation will be evaluated based on the following:

- Evaluation Rubric
- Content and organization of financial plan
- Creativity and logic of pricing plan
- Communication skills

Project Checklist

Plan

- ✔ Select a type of business you would like to start.
- ✔ Explore possible sources of funding for a new business.
- ✔ Research pricing methods and consider possible ways to increase or maintain profits.
- ✔ Interview a trusted adult in your community who owns or manages a local business.

Write

- ✔ Begin developing a financial plan.
- ✔ Write a paragraph to explain the pricing plan for your products or services.
- ✔ Write an explanation of how you can control expenses to help maintain a profit.
- ✔ List your interview questions.
- ✔ Type a summary of the interviewee's responses.

Present

- ✔ Create an outline for your presentation.
- ✔ Create visuals and use technology to enhance your presentation.
- ✔ Speak clearly and concisely.
- ✔ Present your financial plan and your pricing plan.
- ✔ Share your plans to increase or maintain profits.
- ✔ Present the results of your interview.
- ✔ Answer questions posed by the class.

glencoe.com

Evaluate Download a rubric you can use to evaluate your project.

UNIT

4 Planning Personal Finances

Visual Literacy

Your skills, interests, and strengths can lead you to a rewarding career that will help you achieve your financial goals. ***What factors might influence your career path?***

In Your World

Discover a Career

Have you ever wondered why some people find great satisfaction in their work while others only do the minimum required? As with other personal decisions, choosing a career requires planning. When planning for a career, identify your interests and strengths and think about how they apply to various career fields. Use this information along with your research of job industries to help you choose a future career path.

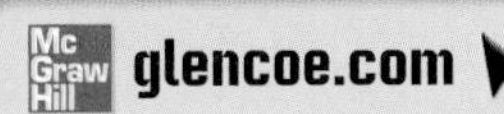

Video Watch the Unit 4 video to learn more about selecting a career path.

Career Planning Career planning often begins at a very young age. Many children dream of being a firefighter or a pilot, for example, only to change their mind a few years later. What were your first thoughts on a career? Did you change your mind? Explain why or why not.

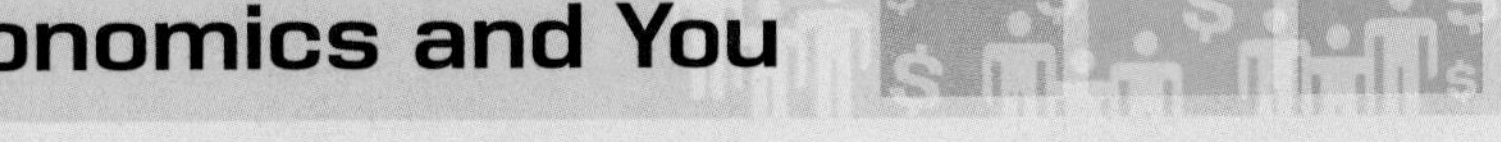

Job Growth

Have you ever traded baseball cards or lunches with someone? Trade with foreign countries can also be mutually beneficial, even generating jobs in the United States. For example, the United States imports automobiles from Japan. Japan then uses the income to purchase cotton and airplanes from the United States. Jobs are created to produce the cotton and airplanes and to market and sell the automobiles. Consider a popular product. What industries are involved in the making and selling of that product? How could this impact job growth?

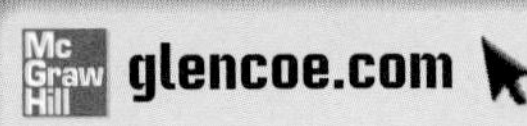

Activity Download an Economics and You Worksheet Activity.

CHAPTER 10

Personal Financial Planning

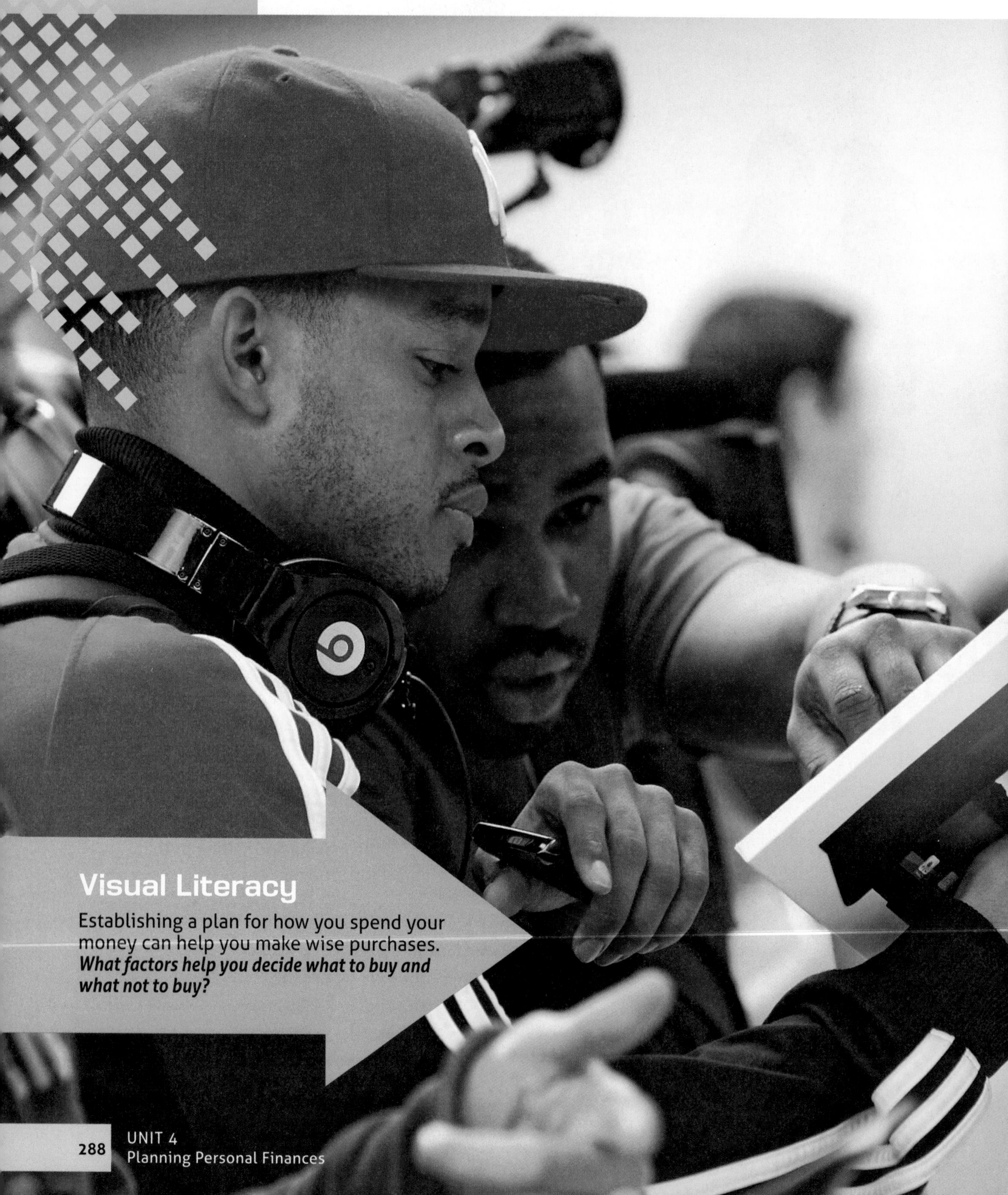

Visual Literacy

Establishing a plan for how you spend your money can help you make wise purchases. ***What factors help you decide what to buy and what not to buy?***

Discovery Project

Creating a Purchase Plan

Key Question

Why is it important to have a plan before making a financial decision?

Project Goal

You have a large family, but only one computer for everyone to use. It can be challenging to coordinate computer time with the other members of your household, so you have decided that it is time to get your own computer. Your family agrees, so they give you $50.00 to help out. You have about $400.00 saved from your part-time job. The computer you want is a laptop that has been advertised on television at a local store for $775.00, but your friend bought the same model directly from the manufacturer for $725.00. Develop a step-by-step financial plan that identifies what you must accomplish to buy the laptop in time for a major research project, which is due at the end of the school year.

Ask Yourself...

- *How much of your current savings can you reasonably contribute to the laptop?*
- *What other expenses will you have in the time frame?*
- *What risks may be associated with the purchase, and will the benefits outweigh the risks?*
- *How much more can you save by the end of the year?*
- *What can you do to find the best price on the laptop?*
- *What steps in your plan ensure that you will accurately track your spending and saving?*

Manage Goals and Time

How can creating a written plan for a significant purchase, such as a laptop, help you manage your time and meet your financial goals?

glencoe.com

Evaluate Download an assessment rubric.

THE BIG IDEA

Financial planning can lead to financial independence and security.

ASK STANDARD &POOR'S

The Money Plan

Q *I am a high school student. I do not have money for investments or buying property. So what difference does it make how I spend my money now?*

A You will not always be a student. Learning to save and use money wisely now will help you know how to achieve financial security in the future. While you are in high school, financial planning can help you decide how to spend, save, and invest your money for special purchases or activities that matter to you. You may even be able to buy stock!

Writing Activity

Make a list of five or more items you would like to purchase. Write a short report comparing the costs and benefits of purchasing each item. How much time do you think it will take to save the money for each? How can this activity be considered financial planning?

Reading Guide

Before You Read

The Essential Question Why is it important to learn now how to plan for your financial future?

Main Idea

The financial planning process can help you reach your financial goals.

Content Vocabulary

- personal financial planning
- goals
- values
- liquidity
- service
- good
- consumer
- interest
- time value of money
- principal
- future value
- annuity
- present value

Academic Vocabulary

You will see these words in your reading and on your tests.

- estimate
- consume
- weigh
- accumulate

Graphic Organizer

Before you read this chapter, create a study organizer like the one below. As you read, identify four guidelines for setting your financial goals.

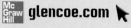

 glencoe.com Print this graphic organizer.

Standards

Academic

Mathematics

NCTM Representation Select, apply, and translate among mathematical representations to solve problems.

NCTM Representation Create and use representations to organize, record, and communicate mathematical ideas.

English Language Arts

NCTE 3 Apply strategies to interpret texts.

NCTE 5 Use different writing process elements to communicate effectively.

Social Studies

NCSS IX H Global Connections Illustrate how individual behaviors and decisions connect with global systems.

NCTM *National Council of Teachers of Mathematics*
NCTE *National Council of Teachers of English*
NCSS *National Council for the Social Studies*
NSES *National Science Education Standards*

Common Core

Reading Integrate and evaluate content presented in diverse formats and media, including visually and quantitatively, as well as in words.

Reading Read and comprehend complex literary and informational texts independently and proficiently.

Speaking and Listening Present information, findings, and supporting evidence such that listeners can follow the line of reasoning and the organization, development, and style are appropriate to task, purpose, and audience.

Personal Financial Decisions

What are the benefits of financial planning?

What is personal finance? It is everything in your life that involves money. **Personal financial planning** is arranging to spend, save, and invest money to live comfortably, have financial security, and achieve goals. Everyone has different financial goals. **Goals** are the things you want to accomplish. For example, getting a college education, buying a car, and starting a business are goals. Planning your personal finances is important because it will help you to reach your goals, no matter what they are. It is up to you to make and follow a financial plan.

Some of the benefits of planning are:

- Increased effectiveness in obtaining, using, and protecting your financial resources throughout your life
- Increased control of your finances by avoiding too much debt, bankruptcy, and dependence on others
- Improved personal relationships gained from well-planned and well-communicated financial decisions
- A sense of freedom from financial worries gained from looking to the future, anticipating expenses, and achieving personal economic goals

We all make hundreds of decisions each day. Most of these decisions are quite simple and have few consequences. However, some are complex and have long-term effects on our personal and financial situations. While everyone makes decisions, few people consider how to make better decisions. The financial planning process can be viewed as a six-step process that can be adapted to any life situation.

STEP 1 Determine Your Current Financial Situation

To figure out your current financial situation, make a list of items that relate to your finances:

- Savings
- Monthly income (job earnings, allowance, gifts, and interest on bank accounts)
- Monthly expenses (money you spend)
- Debts (money you owe to others)

A good way to **estimate,** or make an approximate calculation of, your expenses is to keep a careful record of everything you buy for one month. You can use a small notebook or computer to track your expenses. When you have determined your financial situation, you will be able to start planning.

Section Objectives

- **Define** personal financial planning.
- **List** the six steps of financial planning.
- **Identify** factors that affect personal financial decisions.

As You Read

Relate What are your financial goals? Which goals are needs and which goals are wants?

Careers That Count!

Jason Coupland • Personal Banker

As a personal banker for a national bank, I develop, manage, and build customer relationships. My clients range from high school students opening their first accounts, to businesspeople seeking precise financial products and services. Throughout the week, I oversee the financial operational activities for personal accounts. I process all new account transactions and help customers choose appropriate accounts and banking investment options. My ongoing challenge is to recognize the needs of each individual and match those needs to the bank's services. Thanks to my knowledge of the banking industry and the stock market, I can offer advice to clients and help resolve complaints and issues about their finances. I also provide leadership, training, and support to newly hired staff. If you enjoy working with people and gain satisfaction from helping them reach their financial goals, this may be a good career choice for you.

EXPLORE CAREERS

Visit the Web site of the U.S. Department of Labor's Bureau of Labor Statistics and obtain information about a career as a personal banker.

1. With electronic banking services, explain why personal bankers and loan officers are still in demand.
2. How might this career change in the future?

Skills	Education	Career Path
Communication, customer-service, computer, interpersonal, math, sales, cross-selling, and second language skills	Associate's degree or bachelor's degree with a major in business administration or economics	Personal bankers can become Licensed Private Bankers, District Managers, or Mortgage Consultants

glencoe.com

Activity Download a Career Exploration Activity.

STEP 2 Develop Your Financial Goals

To develop clear financial goals, think about your attitude toward money and ask yourself some questions: Is it more important to spend your money now or to save for the future? Would you rather get a job right after high school or continue your education? Will your chosen career require additional training or education in the future? Do your personal values affect your financial decisions? **Values** are the beliefs and principles you consider important, correct, and desirable. Different people value different things.

Needs and Wants You should periodically analyze your financial values and goals. The purpose of this analysis is to differentiate your needs from your wants. Remember, a need is something you must have to survive, such as food, shelter, and clothing. A want is something you desire or would like to have or do. For example, if you live in an area where the winter is cold, you need a coat. So you may want a leather jacket, but other less expensive coats would also keep you warm. Only you can decide what specific goals to pursue. For example, you might want to save money. So, you could save $50 every month or 15 percent of every paycheck.

STEP 3 Identify Alternative Courses of Action

It is impossible to make a good decision unless you know all your options. Generally, you have several possible courses of action. Suppose that you are saving $50 a month. You might have these options:

- **Continue the same course of action.** You may choose not to change anything.
- **Expand the current situation.** You may decide to increase the amount of money you save every month to $60.
- **Change the current situation.** You could invest in stocks instead of putting your money into a savings account.
- **Take a new course of action.** You could use the $50 to pay off your debts.

Not all of these categories will apply to every decision; however, in each case, be aware that the costs of your decision may outweigh the benefits.

STEP 4 Evaluate Your Alternatives

In this step, you evaluate your alternatives as part of the financial planning process. Use the many sources of financial information that are available. (See **Figure 1.**) Look at your situation in life, your present financial situation, your personal values, and current economic conditions. Consider the consequences and risks of each decision you make.

Sources of Financial Information Relevant and up-to-date information is required at each stage of the decision-making process. Common sources available to help you with your financial decisions include:

- the Internet
- financial institutions such as banks and investment companies
- media sources such as newspapers, magazines, television, and radio
- financial specialists such as financial planners, lawyers, and tax preparers

COMMON CENTS

Pay Yourself First

When you receive your paycheck, pay yourself first. This means that before you pay bills or buy anything, you should put something into your savings account—even a small amount. Think of it as paying yourself. Try saving a percentage of your take-home pay or allowance—1 percent the first month, 2 percent the second month, and so forth. Then sit back and watch your money grow.

Concept Application

If your take-home pay is $860 a month and you save the percentages listed above for 12 months, how much would you have?

Know Your Options
People have a variety of choices when making routine purchases. *What are the benefits of shopping at thrift shops, swap meets, or discount stores?*

Consequences of Choices When you choose one option, you eliminate other possibilities. You cannot choose all options. Suppose that you want to become a full-time college student. You also want the income you would earn at a full-time job. In choosing to pursue your education, you give up the opportunity to work full time, at least for the moment. Remember, an opportunity cost is what is given up when making one choice instead of another. The opportunity cost of going to college would be the benefit of having a full-time job. However, choosing involves more than knowing what you might give up. It also involves knowing what you would gain. For example, by going to college, you could gain a higher-paying job.

Evaluating Risks If you decide to ride your bicycle on a very busy city street, you are taking a risk of having an accident. When you make a financial decision, you also accept certain financial risks. Some types of financial risks include:

- **Inflation Risk** If you wait to buy a car until next year, you accept the possibility that the price may increase.
- **Interest Rate Risk** Interest rates go up or down, which may affect the cost of borrowing or the profits you earn when you save or invest.

FIGURE 1 **Financial Planning Resources**

Get the Facts Information on financial planning can come from many sources. *Which resources might you contact if you want information about saving for college?*

1 **Financial Specialists:** accountants, bankers, financial planners, insurance agents, tax attorneys, and tax preparers

2 **Technology:** computer software and the Internet

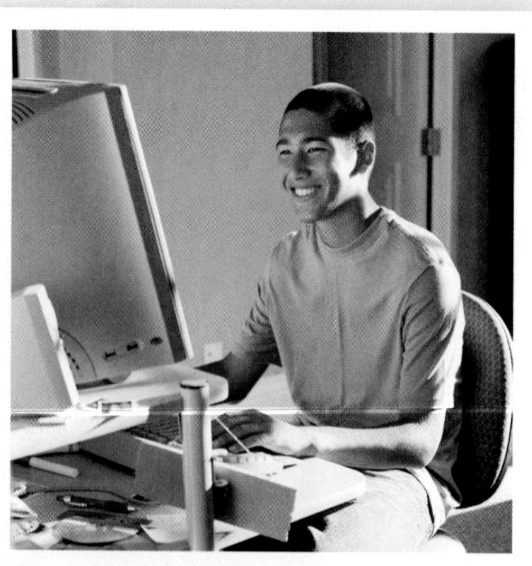

- **Income Risk** You may lose your job due to unexpected health problems, family problems, an accident, or changes in your field of work.
- **Personal Risk** Driving for eight hours on icy mountain roads may be hazardous. The risk may not be worth the money you would save on airfare.
- **Liquidity Risk** **Liquidity** is the ability to easily convert financial assets into cash without loss in value. Some long-term investments, such as a house, can be difficult to convert quickly.

STEP 5 Create and Use Your Financial Plan of Action

A plan of action is a list of ways to achieve your financial goals. If your goal is to increase your savings, a plan of action could be to cut back on spending in a particular area of your budget such as spending on entertainment. If you want to increase your income, you might get a part-time job, work more hours at your present job, or take part of your current income and invest it. You could use the extra money you earn to pay off debts, save money, purchase stocks, or make other investments.

3 **The Media:** books magazines, newsletters, newspapers, radio, and television

4 **Financial Institutions:** banks, credit unions, insurance and investment companies, and savings and loan associations

5 **Education:** high school and college courses and seminars

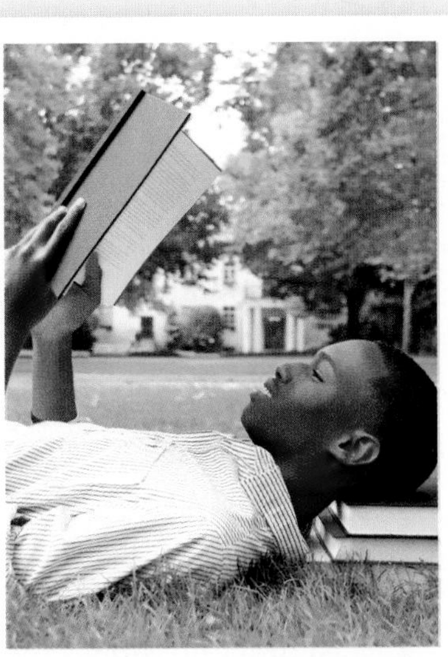

Document Detective

A Monthly Budget Worksheet

A monthly budget worksheet helps you analyze and compare your monthly expenses to the income you receive each month. This analysis helps you plan your spending. A monthly budget worksheet contains the following information:

- Income
- Payroll deductions
- Take-home pay
- Other income
- Expenses
- Income less expenses

Janet Lopez's Monthly Budget Worksheet

Monthly Income	**Amount**	**Variable Monthly Expenses**	**Amount**
Wages (before taxes)	$3500	Utilities (gas, electric)	$75
Allowance	0	Telephone/Cell phone	65
Other income	35	Groceries	135
Payroll Deductions		Clothing	75
Federal tax	$700	Credit card	150
Social Security tax	268	Donations	25
State tax	175	Gasoline	85
Local tax	35	Personal items	45
Other	0		
Total Take-Home Income	**$2357**		
Fixed Monthly Expenses		**Discretionary Monthly Expenses**	
Savings	$100	Movies	$15
Rent/Mortgage	750	Hobbies	35
Car loan	425	Restaurants	55
Vehicle and apartment or house insurance	125	Other	155
Life and health insurance	55		
Cable TV/Internet access	95	**Total Expenses**	**$2465**
		Income Less Expenses	**– $108**

Key Points You create a budget by determining your take-home income. Take-home income is the difference between your wages and deductions. Taxes, union dues, and health insurance are examples of wage deductions. Expenses are also listed. Some expenses are fixed. They do not change. Variable expenses change each month. Discretionary expenses do not include expenses for basic needs.

FIND the Solutions

Review Key Concepts

1. Explain the difference between fixed expenses and variable expenses.
2. List other possible expenses that are not listed on this worksheet.
3. Decide if Janet has enough monthly income for monthly expenses.
4. Explain why utilities are a variable expense.
5. Suggest ways this budget can be balanced.

STEP 6 Review and Revise Your Plan

Financial planning continues as you follow your plan. As you get older, your finances and needs will change. That means that your financial plan will have to change too. You should reevaluate and revise it every year.

Reading Check

Define What is liquidity?

Developing Personal Financial Goals

What should you consider to set financial goals for yourself?

Why do so many people have money problems? The main reason is that they do not plan how they will use their money. You can help to avoid money problems by planning with some clear financial goals in mind.

Types of Financial Goals

Two factors will influence your planning for financial goals. The first factor is the time frame in which you would like to achieve your goals. The second factor is the type of financial need that inspires your goals.

Time Frame of Goals Goals can be defined by the time it takes to achieve them:

- **Short-term goals** take one year or less to achieve (such as saving to buy a computer).
- **Intermediate goals** take two to five years to achieve (such as saving for a down payment on a house).
- **Long-term goals** take more than five years to achieve (such as planning for retirement).

Start with short-term goals that may lead to long-term ones. Some goals, such as having money for the holidays or other special occasions, occur every year. Other goals, such as buying a car, may come up only occasionally. What are some of your short-term, intermediate, and long-term financial goals?

Goals for Different Needs The need to have your hair cut at a salon is different from the need to buy a new car. A haircut is a **service,** or a task that a person or a machine performs for you. A new car is a **good,** or a physical item that is produced and can be weighed or measured. You might buy bottled water every day. You might buy a new car every five or six years.

How you establish and reach your financial goals will depend on whether a goal involves the need for consumable goods, durable goods, or intangible items:

- **Consumable goods** are purchases that you make often and **consume,** or use up, quickly. Food and products, such as shampoo and conditioner, are in this category.
- **Durable goods** are expensive items that you do not purchase often. Most durable goods, such as cars and large appliances, will last three years or more when used on a regular basis.
- **Intangible items** cannot be touched but are often important to your well-being and happiness. Examples of intangibles include your personal relationships, health, education, and free time. Intangibles are often overlooked but can be very expensive.

FIGURE 2 Financial Goals and Activities for Various Life Situations

Financial Goals Your financial needs and goals change at different stages of life. *What are some goals you will have ten years from now that you do not have today?*

Life Situation	Financial Goals and Activities
Young single adult	• Obtain career training. • Become financially independent. • Obtain health insurance. • Develop a savings plan. • Carefully manage your use of credit.
Young couple with no children	• Create an effective financial record-keeping system. • Obtain adequate health and life insurance. • Implement a budget. • Carefully manage your use of credit. • Develop a savings and investment program.
Couple with young children	• Purchase a home. • Obtain adequate health and life insurance. • Start a college fund. • Make a will and name a guardian for your children.
Single parent with young children	• Obtain adequate health, life, and disability insurance. • Make a will and name a guardian for your children. • Establish an emergency fund.
Middle-aged, single adult	• Contribute to a tax-deferred retirement plan. • Evaluate and select appropriate investments. • Accumulate an adequate emergency fund. • Review will and estate plans.
Older couple with no children at home	• Plan retirement housing, living expenses, and activities. • Obtain health insurance for retirement. • Review will and estate plans.

Guidelines for Setting Goals

How can you make good financial decisions? You must identify your goals. Then identify the time frame for achieving each goal and the type of need. However, these factors will change as you go through life. The financial goals you set as a student will be different from the goals you may have if you marry or have children. **Figure 2** shows examples of financial goals and activities related to various life situations.

When setting your financial goals, follow these guidelines:

1. Your financial goals should be realistic.
2. Your financial goals should be specific.
3. Your financial goals should have a clear time frame.
4. Your financial goals should help you decide what type of action to take.

Reading Check

List What are some examples of intangible items?

Influences on Personal Financial Planning

What factors can influence your personal financial planning?

Many factors will influence your day-to-day decisions about finances. The three most important factors are:

- Life situations
- Personal values
- Economic factors

Life Situations and Personal Values

As you enter adulthood, you will experience many changes. You may go to college, start a new career, get married, have children, or move to a new city. These new life situations will affect your financial planning. Your personal values also influence your financial decisions.

For example, Angela just graduated from high school and will be going to college in the fall. She will move out of her parents' house and live in the college dorm. Angela is beginning a new and exciting stage in her life. She values independence, and so she plans to move to an apartment with a roommate in her sophomore year. She will experience more personal freedom, but with her independence will also come more financial responsibility.

Economic Factors

Economic factors across the country and around the world can affect personal finances. They play a role in day-to-day financial planning and decision making for most people. Economics is the study of the decisions that go into making, distributing, and using goods and services. The economy consists of the ways in which people make, distribute, and use their goods and services. To understand economics and the economy, you need to be aware of the market forces, financial institutions, global influences, and economic conditions that affect global as well as personal decisions.

Market Forces The forces of supply and demand determine the prices of products, or goods and services, you purchase. Supply is the amount of goods and services available for sale. Demand is the amount of goods and services people are willing to buy. When there is a high demand for an item, such as a popular toy, or when a company cannot manufacture enough of a certain product to keep up with the demand, the price of the product rises. When there is little demand for a product, or when a company produces more than it can sell, the price of the product drops.

Financial Institutions Most people do business with financial institutions, which include banks, credit unions, savings and loan associations, insurance companies, and investment companies. Financial institutions provide services that increase financial activity in the economy. For example, they handle savings and checking accounts, provide loans, sell insurance, and make investments for their clients.

Among the various government agencies that regulate the financial activities of financial institutions, the Federal Reserve System has a significant responsibility in the U.S. economy. Remember, the Federal Reserve System is the central banking organization of the United States. Its primary role in the U.S. economy is the regulation of the money supply. The Fed controls the money supply by determining interest rates and by buying or selling government securities. Its decisions affect the interest rate you earn on your savings, the interest rate you pay when you borrow money, and to some extent the prices of the products you buy.

Global Influences You and the money you spend are part of the global marketplace, which is another economic factor that can affect financial planning. Look at the items in your home or classroom and you will discover that many of the products were made in other countries.

The economy of every nation is affected by competition with other nations. Each country wants consumers in other countries to buy their products. When other countries sell more goods to the United States than U.S. companies can sell in those markets, more money leaves the United States than enters it. Then less money is available for spending and investing, and interest rates may rise. These global influences also affect financial decisions.

Economic Conditions

Current economic conditions can also affect your personal financial decisions. **Figure 3** shows how economic conditions can influence financial planning. Three important economic conditions are:

1. Consumer prices
2. Consumer spending
3. Interest rates

Consumer Prices Over time the prices of most products go up. Remember, this rise in the level of prices for goods and services is called inflation. During times of rapid inflation, it takes more money to buy the same amount of goods and services. For example, if the rate of inflation is 5 percent, then a computer that cost $1,000 a year ago would now cost $1,050 if the computer price increased at the inflationary rate.

The main cause of inflation is an increase in demand without an increase in supply. For example, if people have more money to spend because of pay increases or borrowing, but the same amounts of goods and services are available, then prices will rise. Inflation can be especially hard on certain groups, such as retired people whose income may not increase. The inflation rate affects consumer prices and varies from year to year. Remember, the consumer price index (CPI) published by the Bureau of Labor Statistics, is a measure of the average change in prices consumers pay for a fixed "basket" of goods and services. In the early 1960s, the annual inflation rate was between 1 and 3 percent. In the late 1970s and early 1980s, the inflation rate climbed to 10–12 percent each year. More recently it slowed to 2–4 percent each year.

Consumer Spending A **consumer** is a person who purchases and uses goods or services. You are a consumer whenever you buy anything—a CD, books, clothes, lunch, or even a haircut. Consumer spending affects the economy by helping to create and maintain jobs. When people buy more goods or services, companies have to hire extra employees to meet the demand. This situation leads to a higher rate of employment, making more jobs available. More people work, and they have more money to spend. However, when consumers buy fewer goods and services, companies have to produce less and lay off workers. Then unemployment rises, making jobs harder to find.

Interest Rates Like everything else, money has a price, and this price is called interest. **Interest** is the price that is paid for the use of another's money. Interest rates also affect the economy. When you deposit your paycheck in a savings account, the interest you receive is money the bank or another financial institution pays you for the use of your money. The bank, in turn, uses your money to make loans to people who want to purchase items such as houses, automobiles, and new businesses. Borrowers who receive the loans must pay a fee, or interest to the bank or lending institution.

Adaptability

One of the most important characteristics of successful people is that they are adaptable. Adaptability is the ability to change to fit changed circumstances or requirements. People who are adaptable learn from their experiences. You can benefit from taking an adaptable attitude toward almost any issue you might encounter at home, at school, at work, and in the community.

Write About It

Think of a scenario in which having an adaptable mind-set would help you at school. Write one or more paragraphs to describe the scenario and explain how having an adaptable attitude would have a positive influence on the situation.

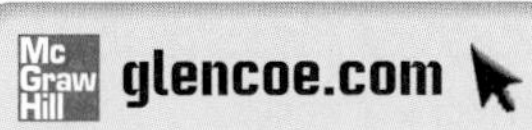

Activity Download a Career and College Readiness Worksheet Activity.

Interest rates represent the cost of money. When consumers increase their savings and investments, the supply of money that is available for others to borrow grows, and interest rates go down. When consumers borrow more money, the demand for money increases, and interest rates go up.

Interest rates on loans also rise during times of inflation. Whether you save, invest, or obtain loans, interest rates will affect your financial planning. The earnings you receive from your savings account or the interest you pay on a loan depend on the current interest rates. Higher interest rates make credit more expensive thus discouraging borrowing and making saving more attractive. Interest rates are just one economic factor that influences your personal financial planning.

FIGURE 3 Economic Conditions and Financial Planning

Economic Conditions Economic conditions will affect your financial planning. *Choose an economic condition from this or previous chapters, and explain how it affects your life today.*

Economic Condition	What It Measures	How It Influences Financial Planning
Consumer prices	The value of a dollar; changes in inflation	If consumer prices increase faster than wages, the value of the dollar decreases—a dollar buys less than it did before. Consumers tend to buy fewer goods and services. Lenders charge higher interest rates.
Consumer spending	Demand for goods and services by individuals and households	Increased consumer spending usually creates more jobs and higher wages. Reduced consumer spending causes unemployment to increase.
Interest rates	Cost of money, cost of credit when you borrow, and the return on your money when you save or invest	Higher interest rates make borrowing money more expensive and make saving more attractive. When interest rates increase, consumer prices tend to increase.
Money supply	The dollars available for spending in our economy	The Federal Reserve System (Fed) sometimes adjusts interest rates in order to increase or decrease the amount of money circulating in the economy. If the Fed lowers interest rates, the money supply increases. If the Fed raises interest rates, the money supply decreases.
Unemployment	The number of people without jobs who are willing and able to work	Low unemployment increases consumer spending. High unemployment reduces consumer spending.
Gross domestic product (GDP)	Total dollar value of all the goods and services produced in a country in one year	The GDP provides an indication of how well people are living in a country.

SECTION 1 Assessment

Review Key Concepts

1. **Define** What is personal financial planning?
2. **List** Name the six steps of financial planning.
3. **Identify** What factors affect personal financial decisions?

Higher Order Thinking H.O.T.

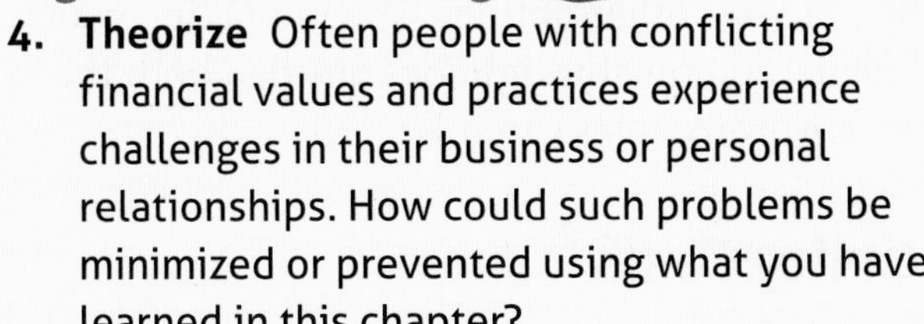

4. **Theorize** Often people with conflicting financial values and practices experience challenges in their business or personal relationships. How could such problems be minimized or prevented using what you have learned in this chapter?

21st Century Skills

5. **Work Creatively with Others** Imagine that your economics class has just ended, and you and a classmate are having lunch together. Your classmate, reflecting on the current chapter, says that she never sets any financial goals and that her financial success or failure happens by luck. With your teacher's permission, work with a partner to role-play a response to your classmate's philosophy. Explain to the classmate how planning, more than luck, determines financial success or failure.

Mathematics

6. **Effects of Inflation** Matthew has been saving money from his summer job for the past two years. He has been doing this in order to purchase a used car so he does not have to rely on his older brother for transportation. Two years ago the price of the car he wanted was $2,600. The inflation rates over the past two years were 3 percent and 2.5 percent, respectively. Assuming the price of the car increased at the inflationary rates, how much did Matthew have to save in order to purchase the used car today?

Math Concept **Calculate the Impact of Inflation** To calculate the impact of inflation, you must first determine the inflation rate and add this percentage increase to the base price.

Starting Hint Multiply the price of the car two years ago by the first year's inflation rate and add this amount to the price two years ago in order to determine the new price after year one.

NCTM Number and Operations Understand meanings of operations and how they relate to one another.

glencoe.com Check your answers.

Section Objectives

- **Explain** the opportunity costs associated with personal financial decisions.
- **Understand** the time value of money.
- **Identify** eight strategies for achieving financial goals at different stages of life.

As You Read

Consider Is it important to start planning your financial future and monitoring your spending now? Why or why not?

Personal and Financial Opportunity Costs

What are personal and financial opportunity costs?

As previously discussed, whenever you make a choice, you have to give up, or trade off, some of your other options. When making your financial decisions and plans, you must **weigh,** or consider, both the personal and financial opportunity costs carefully.

Personal Opportunity Costs

Like financial resources, your personal resources—your health, knowledge, skills, and time—require management. Do you eat a lot of junk food and avoid exercise? Do you get enough sleep each night? The decisions you make about your health now can have consequences as you get older.

In much the same way, the financial decisions you make today will affect your financial health in the future. For example, suppose that you and your friends have tickets to a sold-out concert this Thursday night. On Thursday afternoon your teacher announces an important test for Friday. You must decide whether you will go to the concert, study for the test, or somehow do both. The opportunity cost of going to the concert might be getting a good grade on the test. You have to decide how to use your time to meet your needs, to achieve your goals, and to satisfy your values.

Financial Opportunity Costs

You also must make choices about how you spend money. For example, would you buy the $129 pair of sneakers you saw at the mall or save that money? You cannot do both, because most people have a limited amount of money. To help make choices, consider the **time value of money,** which is the increase of an amount of money due to earned interest or dividends. If you decide to save or invest the $129 instead of buying the sneakers, that money could be worth more later because you would earn interest or dividends on it. On the other hand, perhaps your sneakers are worn out. In that case, your current needs would determine that trading off interest earnings is worthwhile.

Every time you spend, save, or invest money, think about the time value of that money as an opportunity cost. For example, spending money from your savings account means lost interest earning; however, what you buy with that money may have a higher priority than those earnings.

GO FIGURE Mathematics

Annual Interest

Interest is extra money earned from money in an account.

EXAMPLE You just deposited $1,000 in a savings account. The bank will pay you 3 percent annual interest. How much interest will you earn if you keep your money in the bank for one year?

Formula Principal × Annual Interest Rate = Interest Earned for One Year
Solution $1,000 × .03 = $30
You will earn $30 in interest.

Your Turn

What if your sister deposited $50 for one year at the same interest rate? How much would she have?

Calculating Interest You can calculate the time value of your savings by figuring out how much interest you will earn. To do this, you need to know the principal, the annual interest rate, and the length of time your money will be in the account.

For a savings account, the **principal** is the original amount of money on deposit. (For a loan, the principal is the amount that you borrow.) When you open a savings account, the bank or financial institution identifies the interest rate for your account. This is usually given as an annual percentage so that you know how much you will earn each year. By comparing interest rates at several financial institutions, you can figure out which one will make your money grow the fastest.

You can figure out how much interest your money will earn in the first year by multiplying the principal by the annual interest rate.

Future Value of a Single Deposit **Future value** is the amount your original deposit will be worth in the future based on earning a specific interest rate over a specific period of time. Figure out how much your savings will earn and grow by multiplying the principal by the annual interest rate and then adding that interest amount to the principal.

You can determine the future value for two years, three years, and so on. Each year, interest is earned on your principal and on previously earned interest. To calculate the interest earned for the second year, add interest earned in the first year to the principal. Then take that amount and multiply it by the annual interest rate.

Future value computations are also called *compounding*. With compounding, your money increases faster over time. If you make deposits now, your money will have more time to increase. For example, depositing $1,000 at age 40 in an account with 5 percent interest will give you $3,387 at age 65. However, if you deposit the same $1,000 at age 25 you would have a balance of $7,040 at age 65.

Make Time for Fun
As with managing money, you may need to consider trade-offs when managing your time. *What can you do to manage your study time so that you still have time for the activities you enjoy?*

GO FIGURE Mathematics

The Future Value of a Single Deposit

When you earn interest from money you deposit in the bank, your balance increases over time.

EXAMPLE You just deposited $1,000 in a savings account that will pay you 3 percent (.03) annual interest. You earned $30 in interest after the first year. How much will you earn after two years?

Formula (Principal + Previously Earned Interest) × Annual Interest Rate = Interest Earned for the Second Year

Solution ($1,000 + $30) × .03 = $30.90

You will earn $30.90 in interest.

$1,030 + $30.90 = $1,060.90 The future value of your original deposit will be $1,060.90 after two years.

Your Turn

What if you decided to deposit more money, say, $1,500? With 3 percent annual interest, how much would you have after three years?

Future value tables simplify the process of figuring out the effect of compounding. Many online future value calculators are available. The table in Part A of **Figure 4** shows the future value of a single deposit of $1. To use the table, find the annual interest rate that your money is earning. Then see what the future value is at Year 5, Year 6, and so on. Multiply the future value figure by the amount of your deposit. For example, if you deposit $1 in a 7 percent account, at the end of Year 7, you would have $1.61:

$$\$1 \times 1.606 = \$1.606$$

Future Value of a Series of Deposits Some savers like to make regular deposits into their savings. A series of equal regular deposits is sometimes called an **annuity.** Use Part B of the chart in **Figure 4** to find out the future value of $1,000 a year at 5 percent annual interest for six years. At the end of the six years, you would have $6,802:

$$\$1{,}000 \times 6.802 = \$6{,}802$$

Present Value of a Single Deposit You can also calculate the **present value,** which is the amount of money you would need to deposit now in order to have a desired amount in the future. For example, if you want to have $1,000 in five years for a down payment on a car, and your savings account pays 5 percent annual interest, how much money will you need to deposit now to **accumulate,** or collect, $1,000? Part C of **Figure 4** will help you find the answer. Find Year 5 in the left column, and look across to the 5 percent interest-rate column. The value given is 0.784. Multiply this value by the amount of money you want to have in five years:

$$\$1{,}000 \times 0.784 = \$784$$

You need to deposit $784 now to have $1,000 in five years.

FIGURE 4 Future and Present Value Tables

Time Is Money Future value tables can save you time and reduce errors when you compute interest over a long period of time. Present value tables can help you figure out how much you need to deposit now in order to have a certain amount of money in the future. *How much money will you have if you save $2,000 a year for ten years at 9 percent interest?*

A. Future Value of a Single Deposit of $1

	Annual Interest Rate				
Year	**5%**	**6%**	**7%**	**8%**	**9%**
5	1.276	1.338	1.403	1.469	1.539
6	1.340	1.419	1.501	1.587	1.677
7	1.407	1.504	1.606	1.714	1.828
8	1.477	1.594	1.718	1.851	1.993
9	1.551	1.689	1.838	1.999	2.172
10	1.629	1.791	1.967	2.159	2.367

B. Future Value of a Series of Equal Annual Deposits

Year	5%	6%	7%	8%	9%
5	5.526	5.637	5.751	5.867	5.985
6	6.802	6.975	7.153	7.336	7.523
7	8.142	8.394	8.654	8.923	9.200
8	9.549	9.897	10.260	10.637	11.028
9	11.027	11.491	11.978	12.488	13.021
10	12.578	13.181	13.816	14.487	15.193

C. Present Value of a Single Deposit

Year	5%	6%	7%	8%	9%
5	0.784	0.747	0.713	0.681	0.650
6	0.746	0.705	0.666	0.630	0.596
7	0.711	0.665	0.623	0.583	0.547
8	0.677	0.627	0.582	0.540	0.502
9	0.645	0.592	0.544	0.500	0.460
10	0.614	0.558	0.508	0.463	0.422

D. Present Value of a Series of Equal Annual Deposits

Year	5%	6%	7%	8%	9%
5	4.329	4.212	4.100	3.993	3.890
6	5.076	4.917	4.767	4.623	4.486
7	5.786	5.582	5.389	5.206	5.033
8	6.463	6.210	5.971	5.747	5.535
9	7.108	6.802	6.515	6.247	5.995
10	7.722	7.360	7.024	6.710	6.418

Around the World

Malaysia

Licensed Financial Planners

Many people find the idea of personal financial planning to be daunting. The profession of financial planner has developed to help people set their financial goals and take the appropriate actions to meet them. People must be able to trust their financial planner with the personal information that is shared. Malaysia has answered this concern by being the first country to introduce legislation that requires a financial planner to be licensed. As the profession has become more popular, an organization—Financial Planning Association of Malaysia (FPAM)—has been developed to better help the public understand what financial planning is and the role of a financial planner. The organization also aids individuals in finding a trustworthy financial planner to work with.

Included on the FPAM Web site are a list of frequently asked questions, which include a definition of and a six-step process for financial planning; resources such as links to articles and journals about financial planning, information about classes and certifications for financial planners, and a directory of professional financial planners.

Critical Thinking

1. **Expand** Research FPAM and the certification requirements. What are the requirements for becoming a licensed financial planner in Malaysia?
2. **Relate** Do you feel the government should place requirements on specific professions? If so, what other professions do you think should be regulated by the government? If not, why?

DATABYTES

Capital
Kuala Lumpur

Population
25, 715, 819

Language
Bahasa Malaysia, English, Chinese, Tamil, Telugu, Malayalam, Panjabi, Thai, and other indigenous languages

Currency
Malaysian Ringgit

Gross Domestic Product (GDP)
$209.8 billion

GDP per capita
$14, 800

Industry:
Rubber and palm oil processing and manufacturing, electronics, tin melting and smelting, logging, timber processing, petroleum production and refining

Agriculture:
Rubber, palm oil, cocoa, rice, timber, pepper

Exports:
Electronic equipment, petroleum and liquefied natural gas, wood and wood products, palm oil, rubber, textiles, chemicals

Natural Resources:
Tin, petroleum, timber, copper, iron ore, natural gas, bauxite

Present Value of a Series of Deposits You can also use present value calculations to determine how much you would need to deposit so you can take a specific amount of money out of your savings account for a certain number of years. If you want to take $400 out of your account each year for nine years, and your money is earning interest at 8 percent a year, how much money would you need to deposit now? Part D of **Figure 4** will help you find the answer. Find Year 9 in the left column and look across to the 8 percent interest-rate column. The value given is 6.247. Multiply this value by the amount of money that you want to take out every year:

$$\$400 \times 6.247 = \$2,498.80$$

You need to deposit $2,498.80 now to be able to take out $400 each year for nine years. This calculation is used for retirement.

Reading Check

Explain What is meant by the future value of money?

Achieving Your Financial Goals

What strategies can you use to reach your financial goals?

Throughout your life you will have many different financial needs and goals. By learning to use your money wisely now, you will be able to achieve many of those goals.

Financial planning involves choosing a career, and then learning how to protect and manage the money you earn. By using eight strategies, you can avoid many common money mistakes:

1. **Obtain** Obtain financial resources by working, making investments, or owning property. Obtaining money is the foundation of financial planning because you will use that money for all other financial activities.
2. **Plan** The key to achieving your financial goals and financial security is to plan how you will spend your money.
3. **Spend Wisely** Many people spend more than they can afford. Other people buy things they can afford but do not need. Spending less than you earn is the only way to achieve financial security.
4. **Save** Long-term financial security starts with a savings plan. If you save on a regular basis, you will have money to pay your bills, make major purchases, and cope with emergencies.
5. **Borrow Wisely** When you use a credit card or take out another type of a loan, you are borrowing money. Borrowing wisely—and only when necessary—will help you achieve your financial goals and avoid money problems.

reality bytes

Using Software
There are many software products on the market today designed to help you keep track of your personal finances. One of the first and most popular is Quicken®. Features allow you to track and pay bills and see if you have enough money to cover upcoming bills. You can also schedule bill payments and deposits.

Economics and You

Opportunity Cost

An opportunity cost is what you give up to get something else. For example, the government makes decisions about how to spend taxpayers' money. A business owner may have to decide whether to keep profits or spend it on advertising. Keeping the profit may allow the owner to go on a vacation. However, advertising will help generate new customers and possibly more sales. Analysis of the cost and benefit of any action plays an important role in decision making.

Personal Finance Connection You will make many decisions that will require analysis of the costs and benefits. For example, should you use all of your savings to pay college tuition or should you take out a student loan and save your money for living expenses?

Critical Thinking How can opportunity costs be evaluated differently by different people? How do you think a group such as Congress may be challenged evaluating opportunity costs and trade-offs?

Two-year vocational degree — $1.8 million

Bachelor's degree — $2.5 million

Master's degree — $2.8 million

Professional or doctorate degree — $3.8 million

Source: www.collegeboard.com

Activity Download an Economics and You Worksheet Activity.

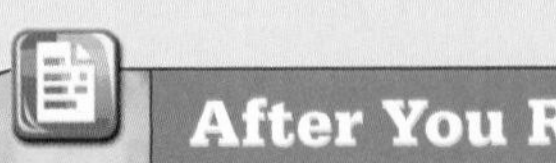

After You Read

Predict Do you think financial planning strategies can help you achieve your goals? If yes, how? If no, why not?

6. **Invest** People invest for two main reasons: to increase their current income and to achieve long-term growth. To increase current income, you can choose investments that pay regular dividends or interest. To achieve long-term growth, you might choose stocks, mutual funds, real estate, and other investments that have the potential to increase in value in the future.
7. **Manage Risk** To protect your resources in case you are ever seriously injured, get sick, or die, you will need insurance coverage. Insurance will protect you and those who depend on you.
8. **Plan for Retirement** When you start to plan for retirement, consider the age at which you would like to stop working full time. You should also think about where you will want to live and how you will want to spend your time: at a part-time job, doing volunteer work, or enjoying hobbies or sports.

Developing and Using a Financial Plan

A good personal financial plan includes assessing your present financial situation, making a list of your current needs, and planning for future needs. You can design a plan on your own, hire a financial planner, or use a money-management software program. Making your financial plan work takes time, effort, and patience, but you will develop habits that will give you a lifetime of satisfaction and security.

Assessment

Review Key Concepts

1. **Explain** What are the opportunity costs associated with personal financial decisions?
2. **Define** What is the time value of money?
3. **Identify** What are the eight strategies for achieving financial goals at different stages of life?

Higher Order Thinking H.O.T.

4. **Evaluate** A common piece of financial advice is "Do not live beyond your means." Explain the meaning of this statement. Do you think it is good advice? Why or why not?

English Language Arts

5. **Weighing Options** Maya is a part-time housekeeper at an assisted living facility, and she is about to graduate from high school. She needs to make a decision about the next step in her continuing education. She enjoys health care, and she is intrigued by the many commercials she sees on television for accelerated degree programs in medical assisting, occupational therapy, and other health care programs. However, these programs are expensive and she wants to keep her job. What are the personal and financial opportunity costs and benefits she faces if she pursues an accelerated degree program? Write your answer in the form of an email you are sending to Maya.

NCTE 5 Use different writing process elements to communicate effectively.

Mathematics

6. **Future Value of a Series of Deposits** Brittany is planning to purchase a house in 6 years. She wants to make a down payment of 15 percent at the time of purchase. She estimates that the purchase price of the house will be $200,000. Brittany is planning to invest $3,500 each year and will earn 8 percent interest annually in her account. What is Brittany's estimated down payment? How much will she have saved at the end of 6 years (use the table in **Figure 4**)? If she did not save enough, how much more will she need?

Math Concept **Calculate the Future Value of a Series of Deposits** To calculate the future value of a series of deposits you find the multiplying factor under the correct length of time and interest rate using the future value table.

Starting Hint Identify the appropriate multiplying factor from the table in **Figure 4.** Multiply this factor by the annual deposit to determine the future value.

NCTM Representation Select, apply, and translate among mathematical representations to solve problems.

Mc Graw Hill **glencoe.com** Check your answers.

Visual Summary

Personal Financial Planning

Be Aware of the Risks

When you make certain financial decisions, you need to be aware of the potential risks associated with each decision you make.

The Time Value of Money

When you understand how different types of deposits earn interest over time, you can make informed financial choices.

Concept	Definition
Future Value of a Single Deposit	The amount your original deposit will be worth in the future based on earning a specific interest rate over a specific period of time.
Future Value of a Series of Deposits	Annual interest made from a series of equal regular deposits.
Present Value of a Single Deposit	The amount of money you would need to deposit now in order to have a desired amount in the future.
Present Value of a Series of Deposits	Use present value calculations to determine how much money you would need to deposit so you can take a specific amount of money out of your savings account for a certain number of years.

Try It!

Draw a diagram like the one shown to illustrate the cycle of economic conditions. Use the blank lines to fill in details about each phase of the cycle.

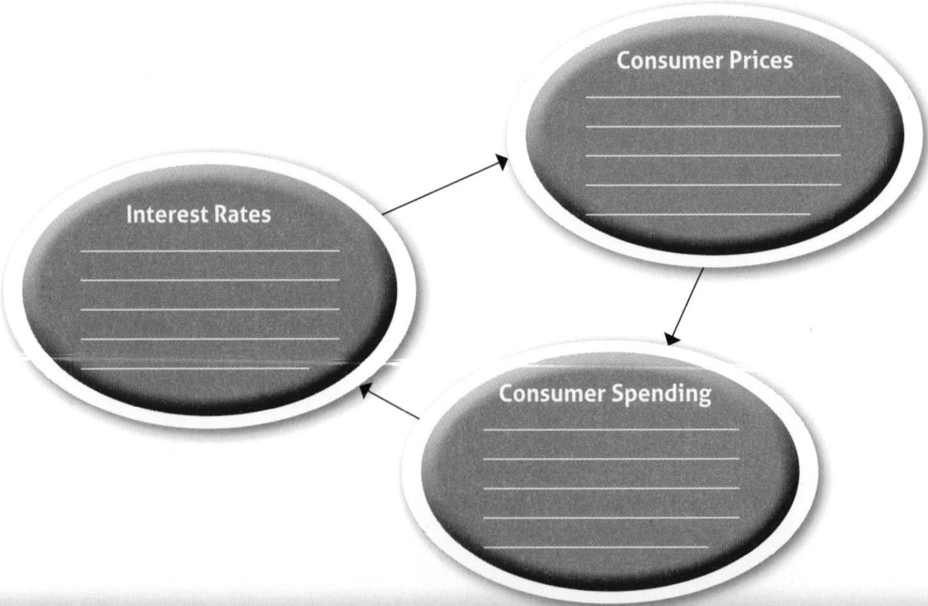

Chapter Review and Assessment

Chapter Summary

- Personal financial planning means managing your money (spending, saving, and investing) so that you can achieve financial independence and security.
- The six steps of financial planning are
  - determine your current financial situation;
  - develop financial goals;
  - identify alternative courses of action;
  - evaluate alternatives;
  - create and use your financial plan of action;
  - review and revise your plan.
- The most important factors that influence personal financial planning are your life situations, your personal values, and outside economic factors.
- For all of your financial decisions, you must make choices and give up something. These opportunity costs, or trade-offs, can be personal or financial.
- The eight strategies for achieving your financial goals and avoiding money problems are: obtain, plan, spend wisely, save, borrow wisely, invest, manage risk, and plan for retirement.

Vocabulary Review

1. Use online or print resources to find an article on unemployment, inflation, interest rates, or the value of the U.S. dollar. Use at least eight of the terms below to write three paragraphs relating the information in the article to personal financial planning.

- personal financial planning
- goals
- values
- liquidity
- service
- good
- consumer
- interest
- time value of money
- principal
- future value
- annuity
- present value
- estimate
- consume
- weigh
- accumulate

Higher Order Thinking

2. **Debate** New and improved versions of electronic devices become available often. Detail arguments for and against upgrading each time a new device becomes available.
3. **Examine** Describe a situation in which a *need* for one person may be a *want* for a different person. Explain how this affects the financial decisions of each person.
4. **Predict** What factors might play a part in the revision of your financial plan as you get older?
5. **Evaluate** Consider three of your financial goals. Write them down, then outline how each goal meets the four guidelines for setting goals.
6. **Justify** Imagine that you are planning an investment for yourself. Would you choose stocks, mutual funds, real estate, or another type of investment? Justify your reasons.
7. **Relate** Interpret the phrase "spend money to make money" and explain how it relates to personal finance.
8. **Pose** Using the time value of money, write an argument in favor of shopping for a good interest rate.
9. **Analyze** What is the relationship between the timing of your goals and the type of good or service that you want?

College and Career Readiness

Social Studies

10. Global Community Imagine that you work as a medical billing and coding specialist for a large medical center. The center has started to outsource services, such as medical transcription, to a country where employees' wages are much lower than in the United States. As a result, the center is in the process of streamlining its record management systems. It also has allowed the center to reduce the number of employees who work in the front and back offices. Staff members believe that more jobs will be lost over the next two years. Using print or online resources, research the trend to outsource medical services to other countries. Based on your findings, would you consider finding another job? Explain your answer.

NCSS IX H Global Connections Illustrate how individual behaviors and decisions connect with global systems.

Mathematics

11. Present Value Randy wants to establish an account in the future where he can withdraw $1,000 per year for 8 years. His account earns 7 percent annual interest. How much money does Randy have to deposit today in order to achieve his goal? If his account only earns 5 percent annual interest, how much does he have to deposit today? If Randy decides that he only wants to withdraw $1,000 per year for 5 years, how much does he have to deposit today if the account earns 7 percent annual interest?

Math Concept **Calculate Present Value** To calculate the present value of a series of deposits find the multiplying factor using **Figure 4.**

Starting Hint To calculate the present value of a series of deposits first identify the appropriate present value factor from the table in **Figure 4.** Multiply this factor by the amount to be withdrawn.

NCTM Representation Create and use representations to organize, record, and communicate mathematical ideas.

English Language Arts

12. Set and Achieve a Goal Review the six steps of the financial planning process. Choose a specific, short-term financial goal that a typical teen might want to achieve, such as saving for a new cell phone or paying a debt. Using the six steps, create a detailed outline that shows how the teen can achieve this goal.

NCTE 3 Apply strategies to interpret texts.

Economics

13. Economic Factors Inflation and interest rates are connected. Both of these economic factors should be considered in your financial planning, especially for long-term goals. Remember, inflation is the rise over time in the level of prices for goods and services. Inflation is measured as an annual percentage rate, like interest rates. Lower interest rates benefit consumers by giving them more borrowing power. When consumers spend more, the economy grows, and inflation is the natural outcome. Inflation, therefore, can be a sign of a healthy, growing economy. Explain why the Federal Reserve would consider raising interest rates during times of economic growth.

Real-World Applications

14. Opportunity Costs When T.J. graduated from high school, he received almost $1,600 in gifts from various family members, and he has about $600 saved from the two seasons he worked as a junior league hockey referee. His parents are urging him to put the money toward college, and his best friend thinks he should use it to get an apartment. Feeling independent and free, T.J. is eager to spend his money on new clothes, a new gaming system, and maybe some hockey equipment. He also needs new brakes for his car. With your teacher's permission, work in a small group to discuss how T.J. should spend his money. Consider the various financial opportunity costs and the time value of money. As a group, present your conclusion to the class in a brief oral report.

Your Financial Portfolio

Getting Your Own Wheels

Are you dreaming of buying your own car? Olivia Johnson is. So far she has saved $3,000. Olivia has her eye on a used car that costs $9,000. Olivia figures she can afford a monthly car payment of no more than $200. Using the interest-rate table below, Olivia calculates the monthly payment needed to repay her car loan by multiplying the amount of the loan by the interest factor. She wants to pay off her loan in three years.

Olivia's Loan Story

Cost of car	$9,000.00
Less the down payment	– 3,000.00
Amount of loan	$6,000.00

Interest Rate of 8%

Months	Interest Factor
12 (one year)	0.08698
24 (two years)	0.04522
36 (three years)	**0.03133**
48 (four years)	0.02441

Multiply loan amount by interest factor (0.03133) for 36 months

$6,000 × 0.03133 = $187.98

Olivia will pay $187.98 a month if she decides to borrow $6,000 for three years.

Calculate

Find an ad for a car you would like to buy. How much will it cost? Suppose you can afford 25 percent of the total price for a down payment. How much money will you need to borrow to pay for the car? On a separate sheet of paper, calculate how much money you will need for your monthly car payment. Calculate what your monthly payment will be if you paid off your loan in 1, 2, 3, and 4 years assuming an interest rate of 8 percent.

1. What is the total amount you will pay for your car if you pay it off in 1, 2, 3, and 4 years?
2. How much interest will you pay on your loan?
3. Which payment plan would enable you to pay the least amount of money for your car?
4. Which payment plan would have the lowest payments?

CHAPTER 11 Finances and Career Planning

Visual Literacy

A well-known expression is, "Choose a job you love, and you will never have to work a day in your life." ***What does this expression mean to you?***

Discovery Project

Building a Career Plan

Key Question

Why is it important to consider more than just salary and other income when planning for your career?

Project Goal

Madeleine will start her first year at the local college next fall. Since she was a little girl, she imagined that she would be a nurse because she likes to take care of people and the pay is good. However, after reading more information about the requirements for nursing school, she is having doubts. Although she is a natural caretaker and she excels in communication and other interpersonal skills, math and science have always been difficult for her. She is worried that she will not do well in nursing school, and that she may have to reconsider her career goals. Develop a plan for Madeleine to use as a starting point as she thinks about her career choices.

Ask Yourself...

- *What are Madeleine's strengths?*
- *What are her weaknesses?*
- *What factors should she consider other than a good salary?*
- *Should Madeleine pursue her dream job? Why or why not?*
- *How can she learn about related career paths that might fit in with her goals?*

Guide and Lead Others

If Madeleine decides to pursue nursing, what would you recommend to her in terms of education and training? What opportunities could she explore to gain hands-on experience?

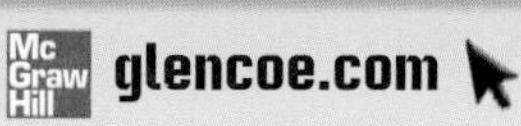

Evaluate Download an assessment rubric.

THE BIG IDEA

Everyone needs income, but the right career is essential for personal satisfaction and fulfillment.

ASK STANDARD &POOR'S

Planning for Life

Q *Career plans are for people who do not know what they want. I know already that I want a high-paying job. So why should I bother thinking about career planning?*

A Money is just one motivation for work. You need to consider many other factors as well. Career planning considers your personal values, goals, and interests—the basics for any career decision. Since you will probably spend the majority of your life working, consider the old adage: "Choose a career you love, and the money will follow."

Writing Activity

Choose a particular job or career that you think you would enjoy doing. Write a cover letter that identifies the abilities, interests, and personal qualities you have that make you an ideal candidate for such a job or career.

Reading Guide

Before You Read

The Essential Question What can you do to make sure the career you choose is personally satisfying and fulfilling?

Main Idea

Choosing and planning for the right career can help you find the job or career that meets your personal and financial goals.

Content Vocabulary

- job
- career
- standard of living
- trends
- potential earning power
- aptitudes
- interest inventories
- demographic trends
- geographic trends
- service industries
- internship
- cooperative education
- networking
- informational interview
- résumé
- cover letter
- cafeteria-style employee benefits
- pension plan
- mentor

Academic Vocabulary

You will see these words in your reading and on your tests.

- flexible
- asset
- wealth
- fixed

Graphic Organizer

Before you read this chapter, create a concept map like the one below. As you read, take note of six sources you can use to find job opportunities.

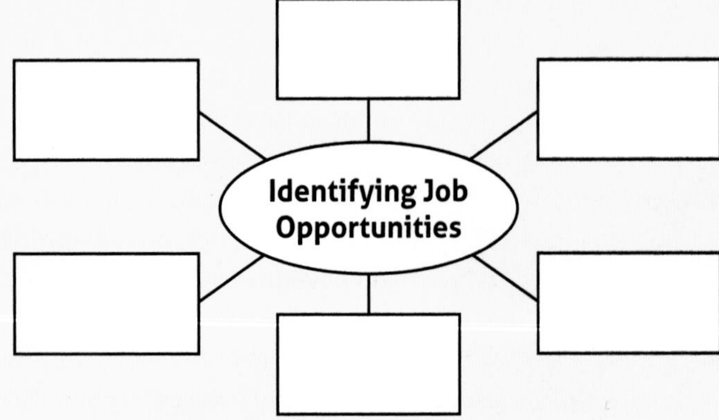

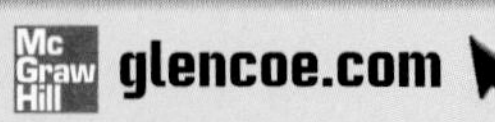

Print this graphic organizer.

Standards

Academic

Mathematics

NCTM Number and Operations Compute fluently and make reasonable estimates.

NCTM Problem Solving Solve problems that arise in mathematics and in other contexts.

English Language Arts

NCTE 5 Use different writing process elements to communicate effectively.

Science

NSES F Develop understanding of personal and community health; population growth; natural resources; environmental quality; natural and human-induced hazards; science and technology in local, national, and global challenges.

NCTM *National Council of Teachers of Mathematics*
NCTE *National Council of Teachers of English*
NCSS *National Council for the Social Studies*
NSES *National Science Education Standards*

Common Core

Reading Determine central ideas or themes of a text and analyze their development; summarize the key supporting details and ideas.

Writing Write informative/explanatory texts to examine and convey complex ideas and information clearly and accurately through the effective selection, organization, and analysis of content.

Speaking and Listening Present information, findings, and supporting evidence such that listeners can follow the line of reasoning and the organization, development, and style are appropriate to task, purpose,and audience.

Choosing a Career

What is the difference between a job and a career?

Some people find true satisfaction in their work, while others work just to make money. Like many people, you may decide to get a **job**—work that you do mainly to earn money. On the other hand, you may decide to prepare for a career. A **career** is a commitment to work in a field that you find interesting and fulfilling. Ensuring that your career will fulfill your personal and financial goals requires planning.

Section Objectives

- **Identify** the personal issues to consider when choosing and planning your career.
- **Explain** how education and training affect career advancement.
- **Discuss** the factors that influence employment.

As You Read

Predict Imagine the job or career you would like to have 15 years from now. How will that job or career fulfill your personal and financial goals?

Career Decision Trade-Offs

Your choice of career will affect the amount of money you make, the people you meet, and how much spare time you have. Some people work just to maintain a **standard of living,** a measure of quality of life based on the amounts and kinds of goods and services a person can buy. They also work to pay for the hobbies and activities they enjoy. Others pursue careers that provide them with both money and personal fulfillment. They select careers that reflect their interests, values, and goals.

Choosing a career will involve trade-offs, or opportunity costs. Many people devote most of their time and energy to their work. As a result, their family lives and personal satisfaction may suffer. Recent **trends**—developments that mark changes in a particular area—indicate that some people are making career decisions, such as declining a promotion, that allow them to spend more time with their families or to enjoy their hobbies and interests.

You may select a career that is challenging and offers you the chance to grow, even if it does not earn you a large salary. On the other hand, you may choose to work in a job that is less satisfying but offers more money. You may look for part-time work or work situations with **flexible,** or adjustable, hours so that you will have more time to spend with your family. You could also decide to give up the security of working for someone else to take on the challenge of running your own business.

The more you know about your own interests, values, needs, and goals, the better you will be able to choose a career that will provide a balance between personal satisfaction and financial rewards.

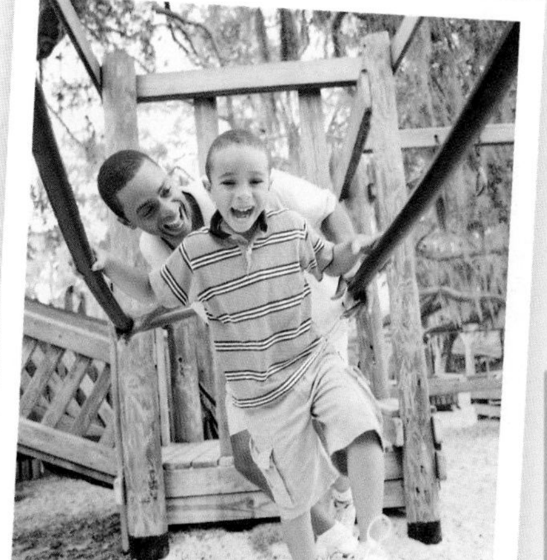

Work and Life Balance
Choosing a career involves trade-offs. *What other trade-offs might a parent choose to make?*

COMMON CENTS

Career Center
At your school's career center or guidance office, you will find a variety of free information that can help you with college choices, résumé preparation, job opportunities, and career counseling.

Concept Application
How can researching different careers that interest you help your financial planning for the future?

Career Training and Skill Development

Obtaining as much formal training as possible will help you meet your financial goals. The more you know, the greater your chances are for success. Having a college degree does not guarantee that you will reach your goals and make a lot of money. However, acquiring more education increases your **potential earning power,** which is the amount of money you may earn over time. Your field of study and the job market will also affect your salary. Some careers, such as law and medicine, offer higher salaries than others, such as the fine arts.

Education is not the only ingredient for success in your job or career. By developing certain habits, you will become an **asset,** or benefit, to any employer. For example, most successful people are able to work well with others. They always strive to do their best. They do not allow conflict with other employees or changes in their duties to affect the quality of their work. They are creative when it comes to solving problems. They communicate well. They understand themselves and other people. These basic qualities and skills make success more likely in most job situations. How do you measure up to this checklist for success? If you think that you might fall short in some areas, what might you do to improve?

Personal Factors

You can take special tests to learn more about your own abilities, interests, and personal qualities. These tests—called *aptitude tests* and *interest inventories*—may give you an edge in choosing a career. You can find out more about such tests from your school guidance counselor or from libraries, bookstores, and on the Internet.

What Do You Do Best? **Aptitudes** are the natural abilities that people possess. For example, you may have a beautiful singing voice, excel at math, or be able to solve puzzles easily. These are all natural aptitudes. Try taking an aptitude test to find out what you do best.

What Do You Enjoy? **Interest inventories** are tests that help you identify the activities you enjoy the most. They match your interests, likes, and dislikes with various kinds of work. For example, someone who enjoys nature and the outdoors could become a science teacher, nature photographer, or landscape designer. What types of careers can you think of that would match your interests?

The Right Fit Aptitude tests and interest inventories may not lead you to the ideal career. They can only point you in the right direction. Another important issue to consider is your personality. For example, do you enjoy large parties? Do you like to take chances, Do you work well under pressure, or do you need time to do a job?

The goal is to find a job or career that gives you the right balance between financial rewards and personal satisfaction. Because your work situation will never stop changing, the key to success is to remain flexible.

Stages of Career Planning

Before you make any decisions about your career, you should review your situation. Changes in your personal life and in society will affect your work life, and the reverse is also true. **Figure 1** shows the stages of career planning, changes, and advancement. If you are getting ready to enter the workforce, you will probably start at Stage 1. That stage will involve determining your personal and career interests.

The diagram in **Figure 2** is only one plan of action. Your progress will depend on your opportunity costs, the choices that are available to you, and your career area. If you are unsure about your direction, talk to people in your field of interest. Ask them what they like and dislike about their work and how they got into the field. Answers to these questions can help you with your career planning.

Reading Check

Rephrase What is potential earning power?

FIGURE 1 **Stages of Career Planning, Changes, and Advancement**

Starting Over *If your career choice became outdated or was no longer in demand, how would you go about making a new choice?*

6. Plan and implement a program for career development.
5. Consider job offers. Accept a job that meets financial and personal requirements.
4. Interview for available positions. Improve interviewing skills.
3. Develop a résumé and cover letter. Apply for jobs.
2. Identify job opportunities in chosen field.
1. Assess personal goals, abilities, and interests. Research careers.
Career Entry
Change to a Different Career
Change Job within Same Career
Career Advancement

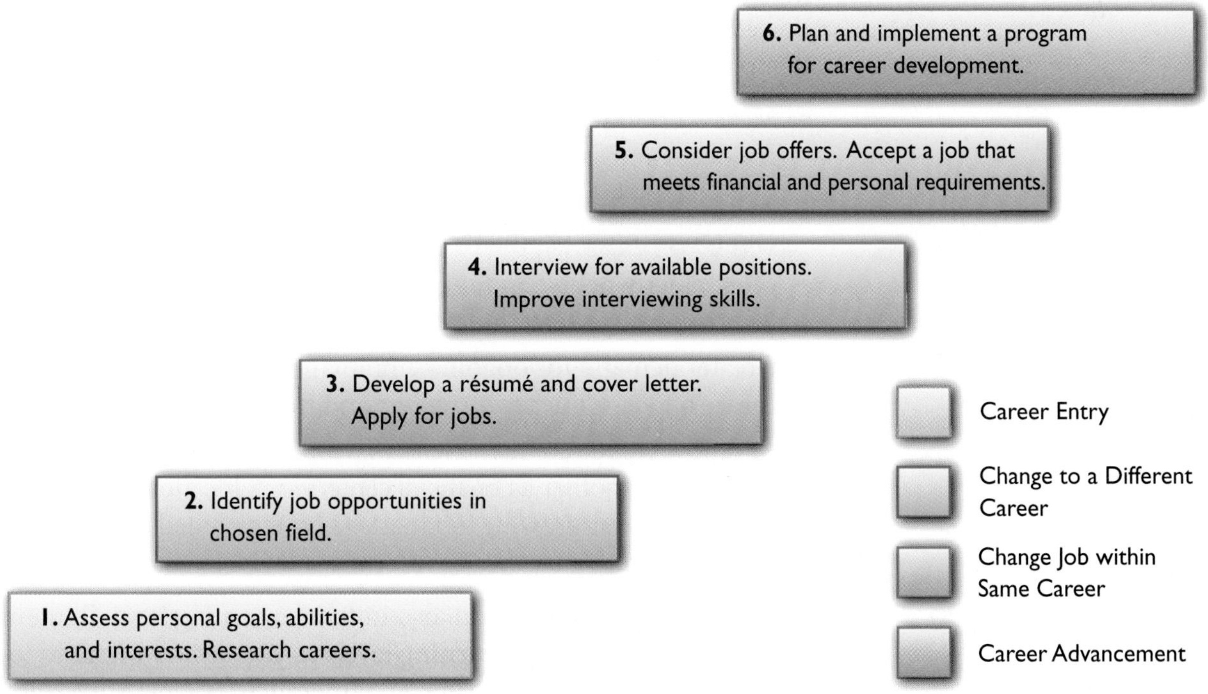

Source: Federal Reserve Bank of Minneapolis

External Factors and Opportunities

Why should you consider external influences when thinking about your career?

Before you begin your job search, you should think about how external factors such as social influences, economic factors, and trends might affect your career. These factors directly affect the job market and the opportunities that are available to you. When you consider your career options, you not only need to focus on your skills, training, and experience, you also need to view the "big picture" on a national and global scale. You may have no control over these particular factors, but you can make some personal decisions based on real-world influences.

Social influences include:

- Demographic trends
- Geographic trends

Other external factors affecting career options include:

- Economic conditions such as interest rates, inflation, and consumer demand
- Industry trends are affected by factors such as foreign competition and technology

Social Influences

Demographic trends are tendencies of people grouped by age, gender, ethnicity, education, or income that change over time. These developments can affect your employment opportunities. Several demographic trends have affected the job market:

- More working parents, which expands the supply of jobs in childcare and food services
- More leisure time, which boosts interest in health, physical fitness, and recreational products
- More elderly people in the overall population, which creates a need for workers in retirement facilities, health care, and travel services
- Greater demand for ongoing employment training, which increases career opportunities for teachers and trainers

Geographic trends are tendencies of people moving from one area of the country to another as financial centers shift location. In recent years, some of the fastest-growing job markets have included cities in Florida, Nevada, Arizona, Arkansas, New Jersey, and California.

Geographic locations can also influence earning level. Remember to consider differences in earning levels as you decide where to look for employment. Big cities, such as San Francisco, New York, and Chicago, usually offer higher salaries, but the cost of living is also higher in such areas.

FIGURE 2 A Career Plan of Action

Transferable Skills Even if you have never held a job, you probably have skills that could transfer to the workplace. *What have you learned that could help you in a working environment?*

1 **Career Interests** Make a list of things you enjoy doing. Think about how you could turn an activity like that into a career.

2 **Career Skills** Think about work experiences you have already had. Which ones did you like? Which ones did not go so well? What skills did you learn?

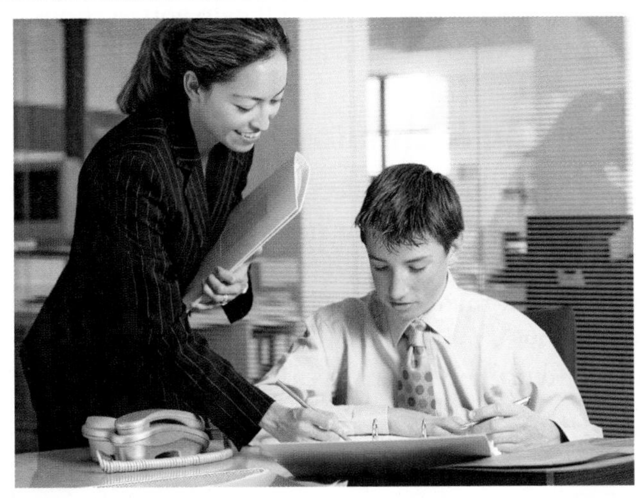

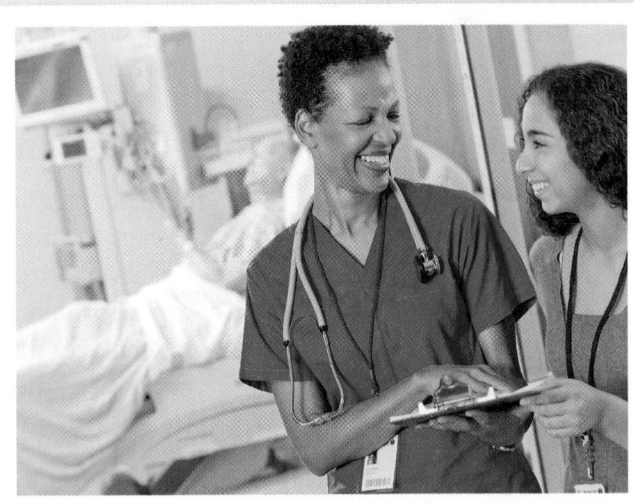

3 **Career Training and Education** What kind of education or training do you need for the career you want?

4 **Employment Position** Now begin to focus. Pinpoint the particular work situation that you would like.

If you accept a high-paying position in a big city with higher living costs, you may actually have a lower standard of living than you would in an area where income levels and the cost of living are lower. You would pay more for items such as food, housing, and other living expenses and your higher salary may not cover the increased costs of these items. For example, in recent years, the cost of living for a single employee earning $30,000 annually was 60 percent higher in the District of Columbia than the national city average. However, the cost of living in Fayetteville, Arkansas was only 10 percent lower than the national city average.

Economic Factors

High interest rates, price increases, or decreased demand for certain goods and services can reduce career opportunities. The job market changes as the economy does, and so the demand for certain types of jobs changes. For example, in the 1990s many companies were looking for people to work in the computer and technology fields. As a result, there were a lot of jobs from which to choose, and salaries were high. As we moved into the 21st century, however, the demand for workers in those industries decreased, and salaries either stayed the same or came down. You cannot control the effects of economic factors on employment trends, so be aware of what jobs are currently in high demand.

In addition, economic factors affect some businesses more than others. For example, high interest rates may reduce employment in housing-related industries, such as construction and real estate, because people are less likely to buy houses when interest rates are high. Being aware of current economic trends will help you to choose a career so that you can achieve your financial goals.

Trends in Industry and Technology

Changes in industry and technology also affect the job market. In recent years, the need for workers in manufacturing has decreased as a result of several trends. First, increased competition from other countries has reduced demand for American-made products. Second, automation has taken over many tasks that used to be done by factory workers. This has decreased the demand for entry-level employees in factories.

While opportunities have dwindled in some areas of the economy, opportunities in other areas have grown. **Service industries** are businesses that provide services for a fee. Service industries are expected to grow and continue to offer employment potential. Perhaps you would like a career in a technology field. You know that your skills are valuable, but you also know that constant technological advances can quickly outdate products and jobs. As a result, you must accept some financial uncertainty. In either case, your career success is likely to depend on communication skills, computer skills, and the ability to communicate in more than one language.

Around the World

Israel

Compulsory Military Service

For many teens and young adults, career planning starts with higher education, such as college or trade school. For Israelis, it starts with military service. Most Israelis are required to serve with the Israel Defense Forces (IDF) at the age of 18. Men serve for three years, and then join the reserve forces. Women serve for two years. This service and the time it takes must be factored into a young Israeli's career planning. In many respects, military service in Israel can be compared to the social and educational rites of passage received in college in other countries. In fact, many Israelis train for their profession while in the IDF. These careers include programming, engineering, and teaching. This training feeds into the growth of the Israeli economy and actually justifies the large cost of the IDF to the government. According to the Mahal IDF Volunteers Web site, "Exporting technology is a pillar of the Israeli economy and engineers who received their formative training in the army's technical units man almost every research and development department in Israel."

Critical Thinking

1. **Expand** Research to discover who is exempt from military service. How does the system of reserves help the Israeli economy?
2. **Relate** Do you think the United States should enforce mandatory military service by its citizens?

DATABYTES

Capital
Jerusalem

Population
7, 233, 701

Language
Hebrew, Arabic, English

Currency
Israeli Shekel

Gross Domestic Product (GDP)
$206.8 billion

GDP per capita
$28, 400

Industry
High-technology products, wood and paper products, potash and phosphates, food, beverages, caustic soda, cement, construction, metals, chemical products, plastics, diamond cutting, textiles, footwear

Agriculture
Citrus, vegetables, cotton, beef, poultry, dairy products

Exports
Machinery and equipment, software, cut diamonds, agricultural products, chemicals, textiles, apparel

Natural Resources
Timber, potash, copper ore, natural gas, phosphate rock, magnesium bromide, clays, sand

Careers That Count!

Brielle Campbell • Customer Service Representative

I work as a customer service representative at a large retailer that sells factory closeouts, such as clothing, furniture, and housewares. I am responsible for providing outstanding service and a friendly environment to each customer. On any given day, my duties include handling money, totaling bills, making change, and giving receipts. I also handle returns, exchanges, and gift card sales. Most of these tasks involve computers, and I received much of my training on the job. I enjoy interacting with all kinds of people, whether it is customers or my coworkers. Even in difficult situations, it is essential that I am respectful and diplomatic. This job works well for me because, as a student, I need scheduling flexibility. I am often able to trade shifts with other cashiers. Sales, holidays, and a varied work schedule provide diversity in the activity and intensity of my job.

EXPLORE CAREERS

In a society that continues to expand its diversity, it is extremely important to work effectively and respectfully with diverse groups of customers and coworkers.

1. Research the meaning of "diversity" in terms of the workplace.
2. What benefits can diversity bring to the workplace?

Skills	Education	Career Path
Communication, organizational, dexterity, computer, and math skills	High school diploma or equivalent, on-the-job training	The skills of a customer service representative are highly transferable and can lead to many career fields, such as retail management and operations, hospitality, and human services.

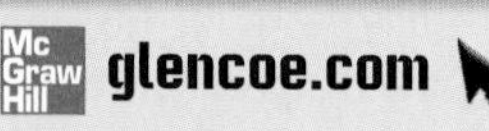

Activity Download a Career Exploration Activity.

There are numerous careers in these industries:

- Information technology—systems analysts, Web-site developers, repair personnel and service technicians, network operation managers
- Health care—medical assistants, physical therapists, home-health workers, laboratory technicians, registered nurses, and health care administrators
- Business services—employee benefit managers, foreign language translators, and trainers
- Social services—child-care workers and eldercare coordinators
- Hospitality services—travel agents and food service managers
- Management and human resources—employment service workers and recruiters
- Education—elementary, secondary, postsecondary, and adult education teachers
- Financial services—insurance agents and investment brokers

Whatever career area you choose, having knowledge of a variety of computer programs and the Internet will be essential.

Document Detective

An IRS Form W-4

By properly filling out a Form W-4, you will ensure that the appropriate amount of tax is deducted from your paychecks. Withholding too little from your pay can result in penalties when you file your yearly income tax return. A Form W-4 asks you for the following:

- Your name and address
- Your marital status
- Number of allowances
- Additional withholdings
- Signature and date

Key Points Employers are required to have each employee complete an IRS Form W-4 to determine the tax withholding. The number of dependents (people you are financially responsible for) you claim on Form W-4 determines the amount of tax withheld from your paychecks. The tax rate varies by the number of dependents you claim. The more dependents, the less you pay in taxes. Because your tax situation may change, review your withholdings each year.

Personal Allowances Worksheet (Keep for your records.)

A Enter "1" for **yourself** if no one else can claim you as a dependent . . . . A ______

B Enter "1" if:
- You are single and have only one job; or
- You are married, have only one job, and your spouse does not work; or
- Your wages from a second job or your spouse's wages (or the total of both) are $1,000 or less. . . B ______

C Enter "1" for your **spouse.** But, you may choose to enter "-0-" if you are married and have either a working spouse or more than one job. (Entering "-0-" may help you avoid having too little tax withheld.) . . . . C ______

D Enter number of **dependents** (other than your spouse or yourself) you will claim on your tax return . . . . D ______

E Enter "1" if you will file as **head of household** on your tax return (see conditions under **Head of household** above) . E ______

F Enter "1" if you have at least $1,500 of **child or dependent care expenses** for which you plan to claim a credit . . F ______
(**Note.** Do **not** include child support payments. See **Pub. 503,** Child and Dependent Care Expenses, for details.)

G **Child Tax Credit** (including additional child tax credit):
- If your total income will be less than $54,000 ($79,000 if married), enter "2" for each eligible child.
- If your total income will be between $54,000 and $84,000 ($79,000 and $119,000 if married), enter "1" for each eligible child plus "1" **additional** if you have four or more eligible children. G ______

H Add lines A through G and enter total here. (**Note.** This may be different from the number of exemptions you claim on your tax return.) ▶ H ______

For accuracy, complete all worksheets that apply.
- If you plan to **itemize or claim adjustments to income** and want to reduce your withholding, see the **Deductions and Adjustments Worksheet** on page 2.
- If you have **more than one job** or are **married and you and your spouse both work** and the combined earnings from all jobs exceed $35,000 ($25,000 if married) see the **Two-Earner/Two-Job Worksheet** on page 2 to avoid having too little tax withheld.
- If **neither** of the above situations applies, **stop here** and enter the number from line H on line 5 of Form W-4 below.

Cut here and give Form W-4 to your employer. Keep the top part for your records.

Form **W-4** | **Employee's Withholding Allowance Certificate** | OMB No. 1545-0010 **2005**

Department of the Treasury Internal Revenue Service

▶ **Whether you are entitled to claim a certain number of allowances or exemption from withholding is subject to review by the IRS. Your employer may be required to send a copy of this form to the IRS.**

1 Type or print your first name and middle initial	Last name	2 Your social security number
Home address (number and street or rural route)	3 ☐ Single ☐ Married ☐ Married, but withhold at higher Single rate. **Note.** If married, but legally separated, or spouse is a nonresident alien, check the "Single" box.	
City or town, state, and ZIP code	4 **If your last name differs from that shown on your social security card, check here. You must call 1-800-772-1213 for a new card.** ▶ ☐	

5 Total number of allowances you are claiming (from line **H** above **or** from the applicable worksheet on page 2) | 5 |

6 Additional amount, if any, you want withheld from each paycheck . . . . | 6 | $

7 I claim exemption from withholding for 2005, and I certify that I meet **both** of the following conditions for exemption.
- Last year I had a right to a refund of **all** federal income tax withheld because I had **no** tax liability **and**
- This year I expect a refund of **all** federal income tax withheld because I expect to have **no** tax liability.

If you meet both conditions, write "Exempt" here . . . . ▶ | 7 |

Under penalties of perjury, I declare that I have examined this certificate and to the best of my knowledge and belief, it is true, correct, and complete.

Employee's signature
(Form is not valid unless you sign it.) ▶ **Date** ▶

8 Employer's name and address (Employer: Complete lines 8 and 10 only if sending to the IRS.)	9 Office code (optional)	10 Employer identification number (EIN)

For Privacy Act and Paperwork Reduction Act Notice, see page 2. Cat. No. 10220Q Form **W-4** (2005)

FIND the Solutions

Review Key Concepts

1. What is the purpose of the Form W-4?
2. On line 6, you may elect to withhold additional money from your pay. Why would someone choose to do this?
3. How could a person be exempt from having withholdings taken from his or her pay?
4. Why is it necessary for the employee to sign the form?
5. Can a married person withhold at the same rate as a single person?

Assessment

Review Key Concepts

1. **Consider** What are some personal issues to consider when choosing and planning your career?
2. **Explain** How do education and training affect career advancement?
3. **List** What are some external factors that influence employment?

Higher Order Thinking H.O.T.

4. **Theorize** Between 1946 and 1964, the U.S. experienced a dramatic population increase of approximately 79 million people. This is called a "baby boom." What employment opportunities might arise if the United States was to experience another significant "baby boom"?

21st Century Skills

5. **Initiative and Self-Direction** Learning more about your own personality can help you choose the best career for you. Typical traits include outgoing, studious, shy, loyal, confident, generous, ambitious, fair, imaginative, patient, athletic, funny, spontaneous, reserved, brave, stubborn, rebellious, and many more. A person who is persistent, outgoing, assertive, energetic, and confident might enjoy working in sales. Someone who is creative, imaginative, inquisitive, and intelligent might enjoy a career in writing. Write down five traits that best describe your personality. With these traits in mind, create a list of jobs and careers that might fit your personality.

Mathematics

6. **Geographic Trends** Janice has been offered a job in Chicago where her current salary of $30,000 will increase by 20 percent. Before accepting the position, Janice wants to understand her potential cost of living. She estimates that rent will be $1,500 per month. She will have to take the train to and from work, which will be $3.50 round trip daily. Her food cost will be $75 per week. If Janice works 5 days a week for 52 weeks per year, what will her annual income be after paying rent, transportation, and food?

Math Concept **Calculate Cost of Living** To calculate the cost of living for a city you must gather information on all applicable costs and determine the annual impact compared to the income.

Starting Hint Gather all applicable expenses including rent, transportation and food. Convert the amounts given for these expenses to an annual equivalent by multiplying by the number of days and weeks and determine the sum.

NCTM Number and Operations Compute fluently and make reasonable estimates.

Career Center
What will your title be?
How many can you handle?

Employment Search Strategies

What steps should you take to search for a job?

Meg filled out dozens of job applications but never received a call for an interview. Douglas went to many interviews and found a challenging and satisfying job. What were the differences between these two people? The answer has to do with how well they communicated the value of the experience they already had and how effectively they used proven employment strategies.

Section Objectives

- **Describe** effective strategies to obtain employment experience.
- **Identify** six sources you can use to find a job opportunity.
- **Explain** the purposes of a résumé and cover letter.
- **Identify** factors to consider after receiving a job offer.
- **Understand** your legal rights during the hiring process.
- **List** steps you can take to improve your long-term career success.

As You Read

Relate List any resources and the people you already know who may be able to help as you prepare for a career.

Obtaining Employment Experience

Many young people who are entering the world of work worry that they do not have enough experience. They may be overlooking the importance of various kinds of work-related training:

- Part-time work
- Volunteer work
- Internships and cooperative education
- Class projects or after-school activities

Part-Time Work Summer and part-time jobs can provide valuable experience. If you have been a camp counselor during the summer, you may decide that you really enjoy working in a day-care center. Perhaps you are a cashier at a drugstore after school. You may want to pursue a career in pharmacology.

Many companies use temporary workers to fill various positions. Working as a "temp" is a good way to gain experience and learn about a particular field. For the same reasons, part-time and temporary work can be worthwhile for people who are changing careers.

Volunteer Work You can learn new skills, develop good work habits, and make professional contacts by volunteering. Many nonprofit community organizations and some government agencies include volunteers on their staffs. You might collect funds for a disaster relief project or build houses with Habitat for Humanity. Volunteering can help you develop skills that you can apply to other work situations. Where could you volunteer in your community?

Internships and Cooperative Education An internship may give you the experience you need to obtain employment. An **internship** is a position in which a person receives training by working with people who are experienced in a particular field. Sometimes it can lead to permanent employment. You also get to practice your application and interviewing skills. Most colleges and universities offer cooperative education and internships as part of their academic programs.

Cooperative education programs allow students to enhance classroom learning with part-time work related to their majors and interests. For example, you would take your high school classes in the morning, and in the afternoon you would work at a local business to apply the workplace skills you learned in class.

Class Projects or After-School Activities Class assignments and school activities can be sources of work-related experience. They can help you gain valuable career skills such as:

- Managing, organizing, and coordinating people
- Public speaking
- Goal setting, planning, and supervising
- Financial planning and budgeting
- Conducting research

Career Information Sources

You need up-to-date information to make the best career decisions. Many sources of information are available to you.

Libraries Most school and public libraries offer a variety of references on careers. Start with such guides as the *Occupational Outlook Handbook*, the *O*NET Dictionary of Occupational Titles*, and Occupational Outlook Quarterly Online.

Mass Media Most newspapers feature business and employment sections with articles on job hunting and career trends.

The Internet Log on to the Internet for a **wealth,** or large amount, of information about jobs and employment. You will find tips and suggestions on everything from filling out applications to job interviewing.

School Guidance Offices Visit your school guidance office for materials and advice on career planning. Take advantage of any services your school may offer.

Community Organizations Almost every community has business and civic groups that can help you in your career search. Attending their meetings gives you an opportunity to meet local businesspeople.

Professional Organizations Many professions have organizations dedicated to sharing information to promote their career areas. The Encyclopedia of Associations can help you find organizations representing careers that interest you.

Volunteer
Giving your time to a local or national nonprofit organization can provide work-related experience. *What types of skills might you gain by helping to build homes?*

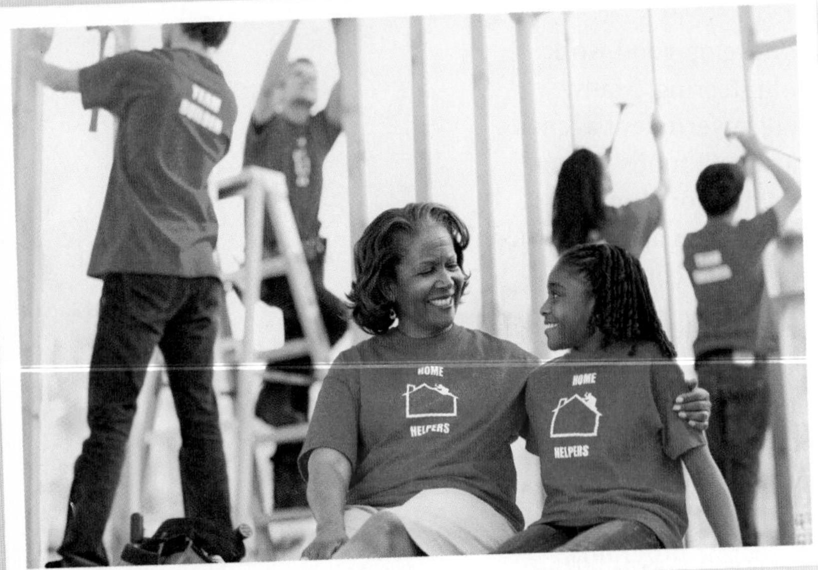

Contacts Family, friends, coworkers, teachers, and former employers are the people you already know who can help you to prepare for your career. Even people whom you do not know can assist you in a job search. That is why it is never too late to begin networking. **Networking** is a way of making and using contacts to get job information and advice. The contacts you make may not be people who can hire you, but they may know someone who can.

They may be able to arrange an **informational interview,** which is a meeting with someone who works in your area of interest who can provide you with practical information about the career or company you are considering.

Identifying Job Opportunities

If you are going to find employment that is right for you, you need to know where to look for job openings. Explore sources such as job advertisements, job fairs, and employment agencies.

Job Advertisements All newspapers have classified ads that include job listings. Although most advertise only jobs that are available locally, some major newspapers, such as *The Wall Street Journal*, list jobs from a wide geographic area.

The Internet is a valuable source for job opportunities. If you are interested in working for a particular company, you can use a search engine to find its Web site and learn more about it. Sometimes you can also find that company's list of current job openings. In addition to company Web sites, the Internet offers job-search Web sites with job advertisements, advice, and résumé services.

Job Fairs At a job fair, recruiters from local and national companies set up tables or booths where you can discuss job opportunities and submit your résumé. To make the most of a job fair, be prepared to make your best impression on several recruiters in a short amount of time. They may call you for an in-depth interview at a later date.

Employment Agencies Employment agencies are businesses that match job hunters with employers. Most often the company that hires you pays the employment agency fee. In some cases, you pay the fee,

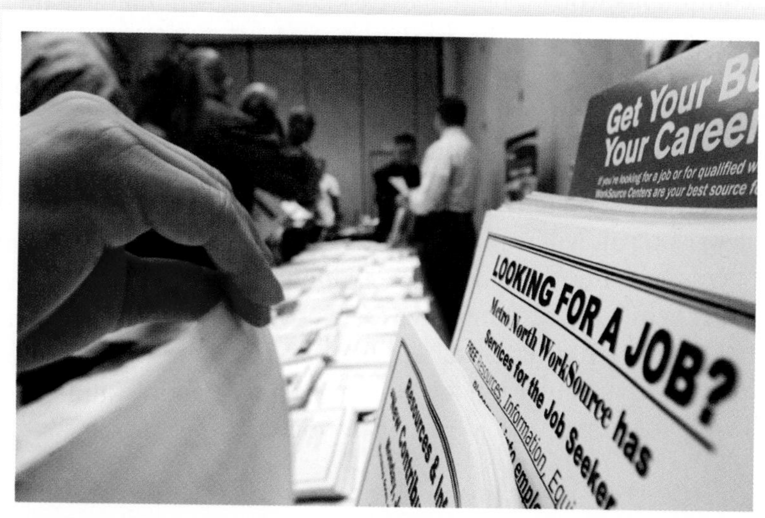

Make It Count
At job fairs, you need to make a good impression on several recruiters in a short time. *What can you do to ensure that you will make a professional and memorable impression on a recruiter?*

reality bytes

Job Hunting Online
A wide selection of online resources awaits job seekers interested in any career. Many Web sites have listings of current job openings. Some sites offer additional features, such as tips on résumé writing and interviewing. These online tools allow job seekers to discover job opportunities locally and nationally.

or you and your new employer share the cost. Do not get involved with agencies that ask you to pay a fee without promising you a job in return. The government also supports employment services. To find out more about them, contact your state's employment service or department of labor.

Other Ways to Find a Job Your ability to find a job is limited only by your imagination and energy. Other ways to find a job include:

- **Visit**—Visit specific companies where you would like to work and ask to speak to someone who might help you.
- **Call**—Check your local telephone directories for the names of businesses in your field of interest, and contact them.
- **Network**—Talk to people with similar interests who have already graduated. They may be able to help you focus your career search.
- **Search**—Search the Web for information about potential jobs and organizations in search of someone with your abilities and skills.

Reading Check

Describe What is the function of an employment agency?

Applying for a Job

What are the steps involved in the job application process?

Making the best possible presentation of your skills and experience is the key to landing a job. Your résumé is your most important tool. A **résumé** is a one- or two-page summary of your education, training, experience, and qualifications. It provides prospective employers with an overview of the contributions you can make to their companies.

The two basic types of résumés are the chronological résumé and the skills résumé. The chronological résumé provides a year-by-year (or longer periods) outline of your education, work experience, and related information. This format is useful for job hunters who have continuous work experience. A skills résumé highlights your skills and abilities in specific categories, such as communications, supervision, or research. If you are a recent graduate or are changing careers, a skills résumé might be the better choice for you. See **Figure 4** for examples of a chronological résumé and a skills résumé.

When you send your résumé to an employer by regular mail, e-mail, or fax, you will want to include a cover letter. A **cover letter** is the personal letter that you present along with your résumé. (See **Figure 3.**) While the résumé serves as an overall summary of your qualifications, a cover letter tells a potential employer why you are interested in a particular job and why you think that it would be worthwhile for him or her to interview you.

The interview is a formal meeting with your potential employer that allows you to express why you think you are the best person for the job. For the interview, you should obtain as much information as you can about the company or industry. Resources include the library, the Internet, or people who are familiar with the company. Here are some typical interview questions:

- What education and training qualify you for this job?
- Why are you interested in working for this company?
- What experiences have helped prepare you for this job?
- What are your major strengths? Major weaknesses?
- What do you plan to be doing five or ten years from now?

Most interviewers will end the interview by telling you when to expect a response. During that time, send that person a note reiterating your interest and thanking him or her for the opportunity to interview.

Reading Check

Plan What should you do if you are granted an interview?

Economics and You

A Nation's Resources

A nation has economic resources that consist of land, labor, capital, and entrepreneurship. Land is a natural resource, such as fertile soil and the right climate to grow things, as well as minerals and oil. Labor includes all people who work in a nation. Capital is money, buildings, and a country's infrastructure (roads, Internet access, and electricity). Capital is an economic resource that makes production of products possible. Entrepreneurs use capital and the other economic resources to produce the goods and services consumers want and need in a nation.

Personal Finance Connection Natural economic resources are similar to your natural abilities, such as being good in sports or math. Workers with more education and/or skills are often paid more for their labor. A consumer's capital is derived from their wages. Consumers need money to buy goods and services they need and want.

Critical Thinking Explain why education and training is an important economic resource for you and for the economic health of the nation.

Income Distribution of U.S. Households

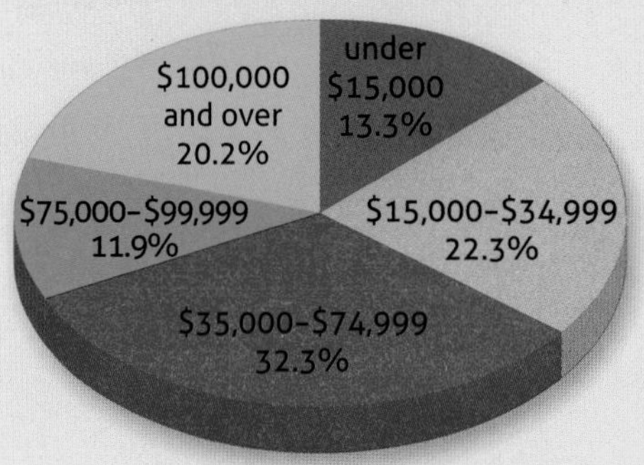

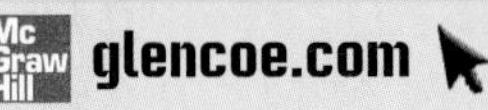

Activity Download an Economics and You Worksheet Activity.

FIGURE 3 **Cover Letter**

Get Noticed Your cover letter should be simple, informative, and direct. *What information in this cover letter might set this applicant apart from others?*

Cover Letter

JERRY HOPKINS
5678 Collins Road
West Barrington, New York 14332

Phone: 914-555-4556
E-mail: jhopkins@internet.com

May 23, 20--

Ms. Hanna Cabral
Human Resources Director
Global Translation Services
3400 Superior Boulevard
Jamestown, New York 13456

Dear Ms. Cabral:

Based on my background and studies in international relations, I am writing to express my interest in the position of associate translator available with your organization. Brenda Kelly, a member of your accounting department, recommended that I contact you. My studies have included courses in global business practices as well as an internship with the exporting department of an electronics company.

My language skills have allowed me to handle customer relations activities with international customers. My ability to work in a cross-cultural environment would provide your organization with a person who can adapt to varied business settings. As a result of my work with companies in other countries, I would be able to meet the diverse needs of your clients.

The enclosed résumé will provide additional information about my qualifications.

I would appreciate the opportunity to meet with you and discuss the ways that my training and background will allow me to contribute to the continued success of your organization. I will call your office on June 1 to determine whether you can arrange a time to see me.

Sincerely,

Jerry Hopkins

Jerry Hopkins
Enclosure

FIGURE 4 Types of Résumés

An Overview Your résumé should give a clear overview of your education, training, experience, and qualifications. *Which of these two résumé formats would be best for a school teacher who wants to obtain an entry-level job at a law firm? Why?*

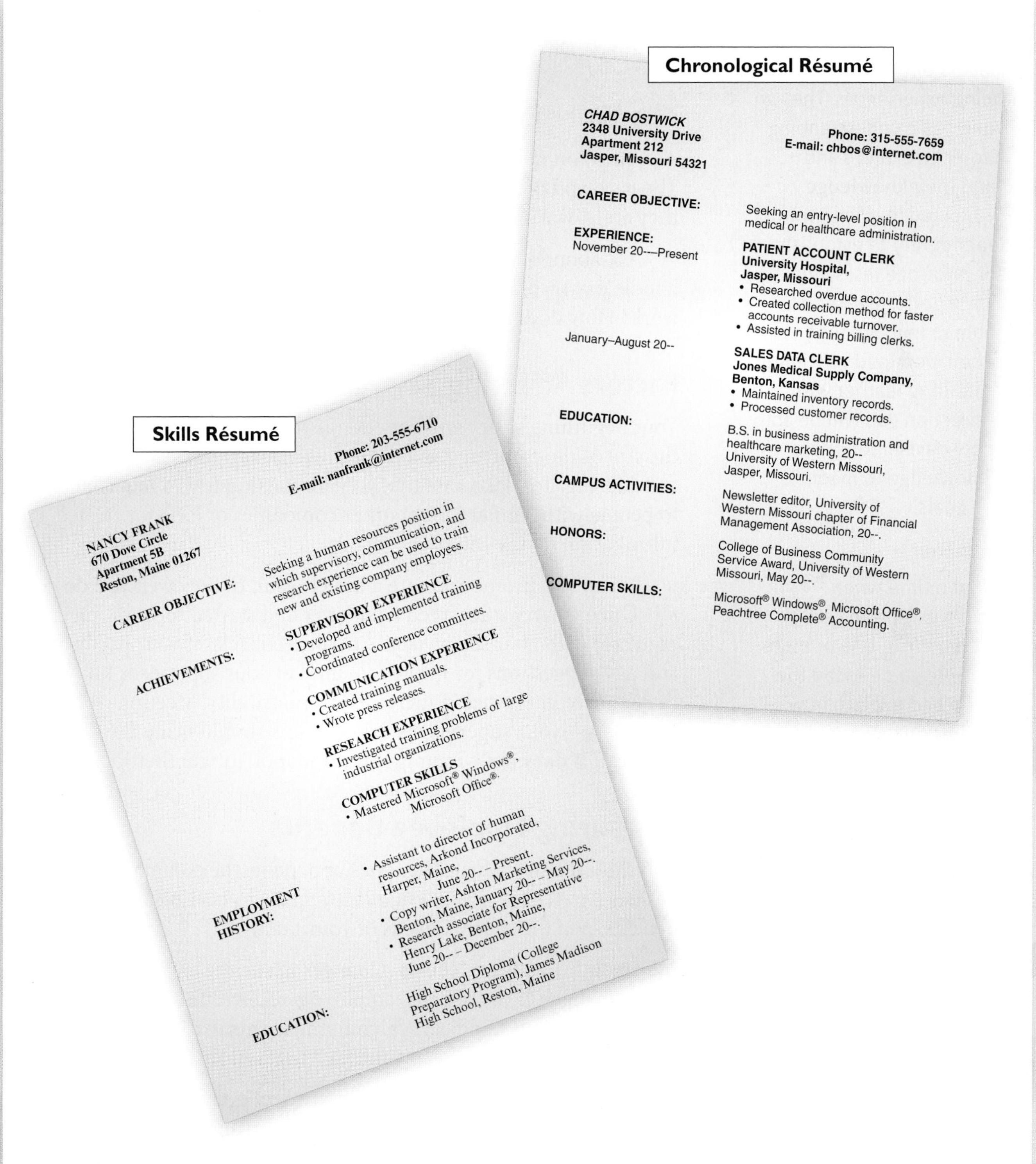

Self-Direction

One characteristic of effective, life-long learners is self-direction. Self-directed learners are owners and managers of their own learning experiences. They go beyond basic understanding of a topic to explore and expand their knowledge. Self-directed learners work independently to establish goals, prioritize tasks, and evaluate performances and are able to manage time and their workload efficiently. As a life-long learner with self-direction you will be able to apply past experiences and knowledge to meet future goals.

Write About It

Think of a time when you have exhibited self-direction. Write one or more paragraphs to describe the scenario and explain how the skills you used in the scenario could be applied to real-world situations.

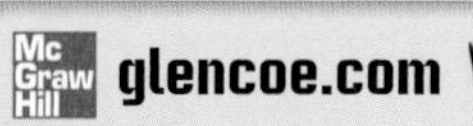

Activity Download a Career and College Readiness Worksheet Activity.

Considering a Job Offer

What factor would be most important to you when considering a job offer?

You may go on several interviews and experience disappointment. Sooner or later, however, someone will say, "We'd like you to work for us." But before you accept an offer, you have to consider several factors. Find out all you can about the company, the job itself, the working environment, the salary, and any other benefits.

The Work Environment

As you go on interviews, you will notice differences in workplaces. The pace and pressure will vary. Even the way people behave when they are at work will depend on the company.

Ask about official company policies. How does the company handle pay increases? How does it measure the quality of employees' work? How does it decide which employees to promote?

Factors Affecting Salary

Your beginning salary will depend on your education and experience, the size of the company, and the average salary for the job you are considering. To make sure that you are starting with a fair salary, talk to people with similar jobs at other companies or look for related information on the Internet.

Raises and promotions are a direct result of how well you do your job. Once you have accepted a job offer and started to work, meet regularly with your supervisor. Ask for feedback on your performance and any suggestions for improvement. Let your supervisor know that you are interested in increased responsibility. Meeting—or exceeding—your supervisor's expectations should bring the reward of a raise. If it does not, you might want to look for another job.

Measuring Employee Benefits

You should also evaluate the types of benefits the company offers besides a paycheck. Pay particular attention to health care, retirement benefits, and the specific needs of your family.

Meeting Employee Needs Changes in society have brought about changes in the benefits employees receive. Today single-parent families and households in which both parents work are common. Businesses have responded to these changes in a variety of ways.

Cafeteria-style employee benefits are programs that allow workers to choose the benefits that best meet their personal needs. A married employee with children may want more life and health insurance, whereas a single parent may also be interested in child-care services.

Because people today live longer, retirement programs are more important than ever. In addition to Social Security benefits, some companies contribute to a **pension plan,** which is a retirement plan that is funded at least in part by an employer. The features of pension plans vary among several basic types. Some plans provide you with a **fixed,** or unchanging, amount of money at retirement. If a business uses a profit-sharing plan, it makes an annual contribution to a retirement fund each year. The money in this fund builds up until you reach retirement age. A third type of pension plan is a 401(k). You set aside a portion of your salary from each paycheck to go into your 401(k). Your employer may match a percentage of your contribution.

Comparing Benefits You can compare the dollar value of employee benefits in several ways. The market value of a benefit is what the benefit would cost if you had to pay for it yourself. For example, the market value of free health insurance is what it would cost you to buy the same insurance. Also, the market value of one week's (five days') paid vacation is one week's salary.

Taxes should also play a part in your decisions about employment benefits. There are two types of employment benefits: tax-exempt and tax-deferred. A tax-exempt benefit is a benefit that is not taxable. For example, medical insurance paid by an employer is tax exempt. For example, if your employer pays $2,000 for your medical insurance, it equals $2,500 before taxes (for the 25 percent tax bracket). A free life insurance policy is an example of a tax-exempt benefit.

A tax-deferred benefit is a benefit for which you will have to pay income tax sometime in the future, most likely after you retire. A 401(k) plan is an example of a tax-deferred benefit. When assessing benefits, remember an untaxed benefit of lower value may be worth more than a benefit of higher value that is subject to taxation.

Reading Check

Distinguish How is a tax-deferred benefit different from a tax-exempt benefit?

Your Rights as an Employee

Why should you know your legal rights as an employee?

As an employee, you have certain legal rights, which can also affect your financial situation. You also have certain legal rights during the hiring process:

- An employer cannot refuse to hire a woman or terminate her employment because she is pregnant. A female employee who stops working because she is pregnant must be given full credit for previous service and for any retirement benefits.

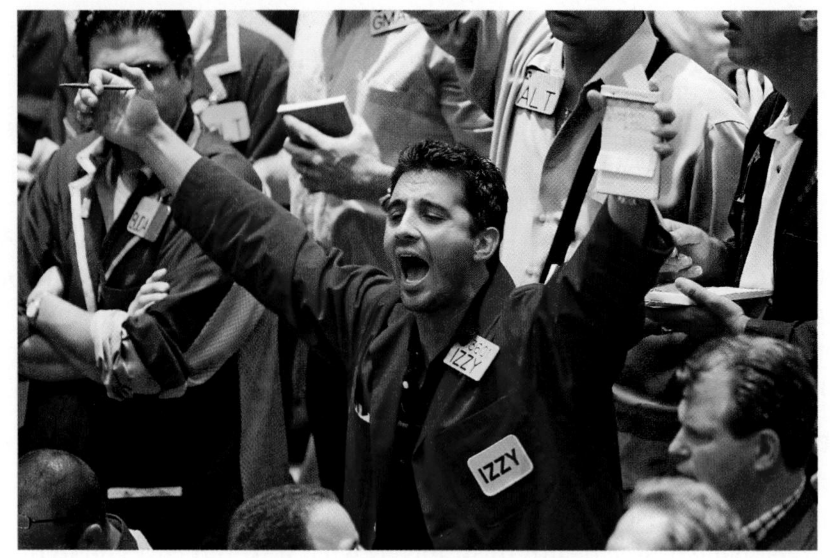

Work Culture
The pace and pressure of work differ from career to career. *How might the pressures faced by a stockbroker differ from the pressures faced by a firefighter?*

- An employer cannot discriminate against a person for any reason related to age, race, color, religion, gender, marital status, national origin, or any mental or physical disabilities.
- An employer must pay for unemployment insurance, contribute to Social Security, and provide for workers' compensation funds in case of a work-related injury or illness.

 **Reading Check**

List What are at least five conditions against which an employer cannot discriminate?

Long-Term Career Development

What steps can you take to help make your career a success?

A job is for today, but a career can last a lifetime. As you enter the world of work, consider: Will you always enjoy the work that you do today? Will you be successful in the career you select? You cannot predict the future, but you can develop skills and attitudes that will increase your chances of being satisfied with your work in years to come. Here are some basic guidelines to follow for career success:

- Make a point of improving your communication skills—both written and oral.
- Do your best to get along with your coworkers.
- Remain flexible and open to new ideas.
- Develop good work habits.
- Combine increased productivity with increased quality.
- Learn to anticipate problems.

- Use lists, note cards, and other time-management techniques. When you have a task to complete, do it as well as you can.
- Be aware that problems may arise, and be ready to take action.
- Be creative in solving your own problems.
- Be willing to learn new techniques and technologies.

Training Opportunities

Advances in technology are changing the world of work at a rapid pace. Many careers that people have today did not exist just a few years ago. These changes will surely continue. A key to your ongoing success will be your ability to keep up with changes in technology and to adapt to the global economy. Remember that you will always be learning new skills and ideas.

How can you make sure that your skills remain up to date? Many companies offer regular training programs, encourage attendance at professional seminars, or help pay for college courses. Read as much as possible on your own. Take advantage of the wealth of information on business, economic, and social trends on the Internet and in newspapers, magazines, and professional journals. Talk with others in your field. Informal meetings with coworkers and associates from other companies can be a valuable source of new information.

Ask Questions
The interview is also a time for you to ask questions. *What are some questions you should and should not ask a potential employer during a job interview?*

Career Paths and Advancement

As time goes by, you will experience changes in your personal interests, values, and goals. Outside factors, such as economic conditions and social trends, will also affect you. These changes will influence your career choices and other financial decisions. You will probably go through a series of career stages, such as those shown in **Figure 5,** and experience specific tasks and concerns with each one.

One way to make sure that your career develops in the right direction is to gain support from someone with more experience and knowledge. A **mentor** is an experienced employee who serves as a teacher and counselor for a less-experienced person. A mentor can give you one-on-one training and help you to meet other knowledgeable people. Many organizations have formal mentoring programs. Some of the best mentors are retired people who are eager to share a lifetime of knowledge and experience.

In addition, you may know a small number of people who can provide opportunities and guidance on a personal basis. Mentors can be role models, or they can be professionals outside your career area who take an interest in your career. They can make suggestions, inform you of opportunities, introduce you to key people, and help guide you through your career. Besides mentors, you probably know other people, friends and/or family, who can serve as role models and supporters as you travel your career path.

After You Read

Extend What will you do in the next six to twelve months that will increase your chances for career success after you graduate?

Changing Careers

Most workers change jobs several times over the course of their lives. About 10 million career changes occur each year. Some seek a better position within the same field. Others move to new careers. Unless a person's current situation is causing excessive stress or illness, most people are reluctant to exchange the security of an existing position for the uncertainty of an unfamiliar one. There are various signs that it is time to move on:

- You feel bored or depressed at work.
- Your job adversely affects you physically or emotionally.
- You receive a series of poor performance evaluations.
- You have little opportunity to obtain a raise or promotion.

At some point you may find yourself out of a job through no fault of your own. This situation can cause emotional and financial stress. While you are looking for another job, continue to eat, sleep, and exercise as usual. Stay involved in family and community activities. You may find new career contacts anywhere. Improve your skills through personal study, classes, or volunteer work. Think about opportunities with nonprofit or government organizations. Whether looking for a new job or your first job, always consider how the financial and personal costs and benefits of your career choice will affect your needs and goals.

FIGURE 5 **Stages of Career Development**

Ongoing Development Each stage of career development brings new tasks and new concerns. *Why might you decide to look at other options during the mid-career adjustment stage?*

Stage	Tasks	Concerns
Pre-entry and career exploration	• Assess personal interests. • Obtain necessary training. • Find an entry-level job.	• Matching interests and abilities to job. • Dealing with disappointment.
Career growth	• Obtain experience, develop skills. • Concentrate on an area of specialization. • Gain respect of colleagues.	• Developing career contacts. • Avoiding career burnout.
Advancement and mid-career adjustment	• Continue to gain experience and knowledge. • Seek new challenges and expanded responsibility.	• Finding continued satisfaction. • Maintaining sensitivity toward colleagues and subordinates.
Late career and preretirement	• Make financial and personal plans for retirement.	• Determining professional involvement after retirement. • Planning participation in community activities.

Assessment

Review Key Concepts

1. **List** What are six effective strategies to obtain employment experience?
2. **Describe** Identify and describe six sources you can use to find a job opportunity.
3. **Explain** What is the purpose of a résumé and a cover letter?
4. **Consider** What are some factors to consider after receiving a job offer?
5. **Explain** What are the legal rights you have during the hiring process?
6. **Identify** What are some steps you can take to improve your long-term career success?

Higher Order Thinking H.O.T.

7. **Compare and contrast** What are the advantages and disadvantages of the career information sources discussed in this chapter?

English Language Arts

8. **Turning Point** Mitchell is in his late thirties. He has been working for his dad, the owner of a construction company, since he was a high school student. Mitchell wanted to work with computer technology, but he started working for his dad because it was convenient and easy. However, after nearly 20 years, Mitchell is wondering if there is something else he could be doing. He is thinking about going back to school. However, his dad will be retiring soon, and he wants Mitchell to take over the company. Write an essay that includes Mitchell's options, and the pros and cons of each option. Conclude with your judgment about what he should do at this turning point in his life.

NCTE 5 Use different writing process elements to communicate effectively.

Mathematics

9. **Employee Benefits Package** James has received a job offer from XYZ Co. The company offered him an annual salary of $35,000. In addition to his salary, James would be given 3 weeks paid vacation as well as 4 paid sick days. He would also be provided with medical and dental insurance with a market value of $6,000 and life insurance with a value of one year's annual salary. Assuming 52 weeks per year and 5 workdays per week, what is James' total compensation package valued at?

Math Concept **Calculate Value of Benefits** To calculate the value of a compensation package you must determine the total value of all benefits the company is offering to you including vacation, sick days, insurance, retirement plans, etc.

Starting Hint Translate vacation days and sick days into a dollar value by dividing the annual salary by the number of weeks in a year (vacation) or the number of work days in a year (sick days).

NCTM Problem Solving Solve problems that arise in mathematics and in other contexts.

Check your answers.

CHAPTER REVIEW

Visual Summary

Finances and Career Planning

Career Planning

The six general steps of career planning can help first-time job hunters, career changers, and those who want to change jobs within the same career.

6. Plan and implement a program for career development.
5. Consider job offers. Accept a job that meets financial and personal requirements.
4. Interview for available positions. Improve interviewing skills.
3. Develop a résumé and cover letter. Apply for jobs.
2. Identify job opportunities in chosen field.
1. Assess personal goals, abilities, and interests. Research careers.

All About You

Choose the right résumé format for your skills and experience, then sell yourself with a great cover letter.

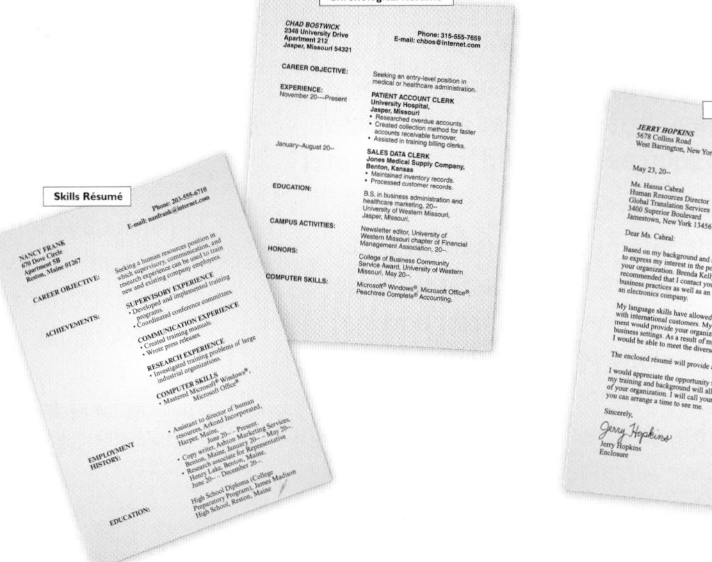

Skills Résumé

NANCY FRANK
670 Dove Circle
Apartment 5B
Reston, Maine 01267

Phone: 203-555-6710
E-mail: nanfrank@internet.com

CAREER OBJECTIVE: Seeking a human resources position in which supervisory, communication, and research experience can be used to train new and existing company employees.

ACHIEVEMENTS:
SUPERVISORY EXPERIENCE
- Developed and implemented training programs.
- Coordinated conference committees.

COMMUNICATION EXPERIENCE
- Created training manuals.
- Wrote press releases.

RESEARCH EXPERIENCE
- Investigated training problems of large industrial organizations.

COMPUTER SKILLS
- Mastered Microsoft® Windows®, Microsoft Office®

EMPLOYMENT HISTORY:
- Assistant to director of human resources, Arkond Incorporated, Harper, Maine, June 20-- – Present.
- Copy writer, Ashton Marketing Services, Benton, Maine, January 20-- – May 20--.
- Research associate for Representative Henry Lake, Benton, Maine, June 20-- – December 20--.

EDUCATION: High School Diploma (College Preparatory Program), James Madison High School, Reston, Maine

Chronological Résumé

CHAD BOSTWICK
2348 University Drive
Apartment 212
Jasper, Missouri 54321

Phone: 315-555-7659
E-mail: chbos@internet.com

CAREER OBJECTIVE: Seeking an entry-level position in medical or healthcare administration.

EXPERIENCE:
November 20---Present
PATIENT ACCOUNT CLERK
University Hospital,
Jasper, Missouri
- Researched overdue accounts.
- Created collection method for faster accounts receivable turnover.
- Assisted in training billing clerks.

January–August 20--
SALES DATA CLERK
Jones Medical Supply Company,
Benton, Kansas
- Maintained inventory records.
- Processed customer records.

EDUCATION: B.S. in business administration and healthcare marketing, 20-- University of Western Missouri, Jasper, Missouri.

CAMPUS ACTIVITIES: Newsletter editor, University of Western Missouri chapter of Financial Management Association, 20--.

HONORS: College of Business Community Service Award, University of Western Missouri, May 20--.

COMPUTER SKILLS: Microsoft® Windows®, Microsoft Office®, Peachtree Complete® Accounting.

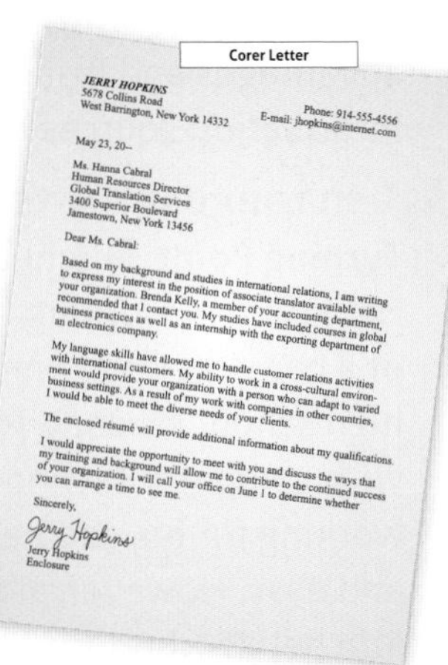

Corer Letter

JERRY HOPKINS
5678 Collins Road
West Barrington, New York 14332

Phone: 914-555-4556
E-mail: jhopkins@internet.com

May 23, 20--

Ms. Hanna Cabral
Human Resources Director
Global Translation Services
3400 Superior Boulevard
Jamestown, New York 13456

Dear Ms. Cabral:

Based on my background and studies in international relations, I am writing to express my interest in the position of associate translator available with your organization. Brenda Kelly, a member of your accounting department, recommended that I contact you. My studies have included courses in global business practices as well as an internship with the exporting department of an electronics company.

My language skills have allowed me to handle customer relations activities with international customers. My ability to work in a cross-cultural environment would provide your organization with a person who can adapt to varied business settings. As a result of my work with companies in other countries, I would be able to meet the diverse needs of your clients.

The enclosed résumé will provide additional information about my qualifications.

I would appreciate the opportunity to meet with you and discuss the ways that my training and background will allow me to contribute to the continued success of your organization. I will call your office on June 1 to determine whether you can arrange a time to see me.

Sincerely,

Jerry Hopkins

Jerry Hopkins
Enclosure

Try It!

Knowing where to find information about jobs is half the battle. Create a cluster map like the one shown to summarize career information sources.

Chapter Review and Assessment

Chapter Summary

- Personal issues to consider when choosing a career include your aptitudes, interests, personality, and current personal situation.
- The more education and training you have, the greater your potential earning power will be. Also, the field of study you select will affect your salary.
- Employment opportunities are affected by social influences, such as demographic trends, geographic trends, and economic factors, as well as industry and technology trends.
- Gain experience through part-time work, volunteer work, internships, cooperative education, and class projects.
- To evaluate career opportunities, use sources such as the Internet, libraries, newspapers, school guidance offices, community organizations, and networking with people working in the field you choose.
- Financial issues to consider when looking for employment are your starting salary, opportunities for promotions and raises, benefits, and the cost of living.
- Legal issues to consider relate to the work environment of the company, its adherence to laws regarding discrimination, minimum wage unemployment insurance, Social Security, and workers' compensation.

Vocabulary Review

1. Create a fill-in-the-blank sentence for each of these vocabulary terms. You may combine two words in one sentence if appropriate. The sentences should contain enough information to help determine the missing word(s).

- job
- career
- standard of living
- trends
- potential earning power
- aptitudes
- interest inventories
- demographic trends
- geographic trends
- service industries
- internship
- cooperative education
- networking
- informational interview
- résumé
- cover letter
- cafeteria-style employee benefits
- pension plan
- mentor
- flexible
- asset
- wealth
- fixed

Higher Order Thinking 

2. **Relate** Your sister has an aptitude for dancing. You love to dance. Are these the same? Explain.
3. **Evaluate** Consider demographic trends and geographic trends. Evaluate the significance of each in terms of career planning.
4. **Defend** Is it important to know about economic factors, such as interest rates and price increases, even when they are beyond your control?
5. **Assess** Explain why the U.S. Bureau of Labor Statistics projects jobs in health care will continue to increase in the next decade.
6. **Examine** A cover letter is about the person you know best—you—so why might it be challenging to write a cover letter? What are some tips you could offer to someone having trouble writing a cover letter?
7. **Compare and Contrast** How are the skills needed to launch a career and those needed to simply get a job similar or different?
8. **Synthesize** Connect the work environment to career paths and advancement.
9. **Judge** If your state was considering raising the minimum wage, would you be in favor of it or against it? Explain your answer.

College and Career Readiness

Science

10. Career Fields The field of science is a growing career field. There are many careers in the science field, such as cancer research, environmental science, pharmaceutical research, and genetic engineering.

Procedure Choose three careers that interest you, including one in the field of science. Using print or online resources, find out the education requirements and the salaries for each career.

Analysis Present your findings to the class in a short oral report. Include answers to the following questions: Which career offers the highest pay? What do you think accounts for the difference in pay? How much do you think salary should affect which choice you make?

NSES F Develop understanding of personal and community health; population growth; natural resources; environmental quality; natural and human-induced hazards; science and technology in local, national, and global challenges.

Mathematics

11. Retirement Benefits You have decided to contribute to your company's 401(k) retirement plan. The plan allows you to contribute up to 50 percent of your annual salary. The company will match $0.75 for each dollar you contribute to the plan for the first 6 percent of your salary. You currently earn $40,000 per year, and you choose to contribute 15 percent of your annual salary. How much will your total contribution be, including your employer's matching contributions, at the end of the year?

Math Concept **Calculate 401(k) Contribution** To calculate the total contribution, you must determine the amount your company will contribute and add this to your contribution.

Starting Hint Calculate the amount that is eligible for company matching by multiplying your annual salary by 6 percent. Multiply this amount by $0.75 in order to determine the total company match.

NCTM Number and Operations Understand numbers, ways of representing numbers, relationships among numbers, and number systems.

English Language Arts

12. Employee Benefits Laura's income is the sole source of support for her two young children. She works full time and sends her children to a daycare center. She recently moved to another state and found a new job. The company offers a variety of employee benefit plans. Laura needs to determine which benefits will be best for her family. Based on the information in the section on employee benefits, what possibilities might Laura have? What will she have to consider in making her decision? Prepare a one-page report to help Laura make her decision.

NCTE 1 Read texts to acquire new information.

Ethics

13. Workplace Relationships As with all aspects of society, most workplaces demand that we coexist and collaborate in order to get the job done. An inevitable outcome of working closely with others is the development of friendships. Suppose you have some personal problems that are troubling you. Is it acceptable to talk about these problems with your friends while at work? To what degree (or under what circumstances) do you believe it is acceptable to deal with your personal issues on company time?

Real-World Applications

14. Applying for Jobs When you were in middle school you offered your babysitting services to neighborhood families. The last few summers, you volunteered every other weekend at an animal shelter. During the week, you worked at a gift shop as a cashier. Throughout high school, you have participated in talent showcases and theatrical productions, both as a performer and as a backstage crew member. In the 10th grade you received a high score in your advanced placement Spanish class, and in the 11th grade you joined the student government. From the information given, develop a list of transferable skills and qualities you can include on a job application or on a résumé.

Your Financial Portfolio

Applying for a Job

Mark Cortez was interested in working at his neighborhood grocery store as a clerk. He wanted to work part-time after school and on weekends to earn money for his personal expenses. He filled out the application at the store and was called back for an interview. Mark interviewed with the store manager and got the job.

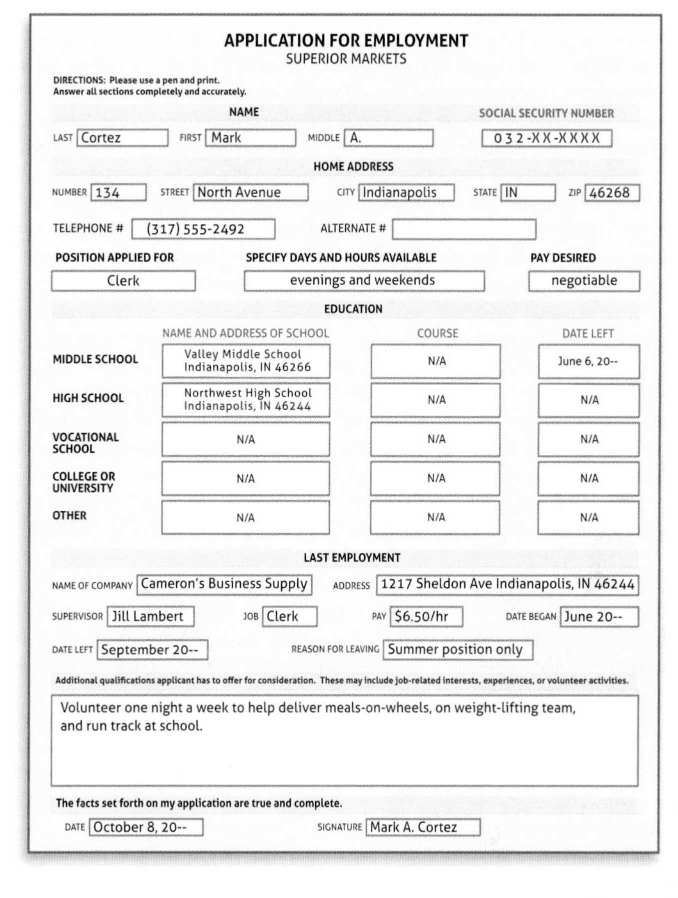

APPLICATION FOR EMPLOYMENT
SUPERIOR MARKETS

DIRECTIONS: Please use a pen and print.
Answer all sections completely and accurately.

NAME
LAST Cortez FIRST Mark MIDDLE A.
SOCIAL SECURITY NUMBER 0 3 2 -X X -X X X X

HOME ADDRESS
NUMBER 134 STREET North Avenue CITY Indianapolis STATE IN ZIP 46268

TELEPHONE # (317) 555-2492 ALTERNATE #

POSITION APPLIED FOR	SPECIFY DAYS AND HOURS AVAILABLE	PAY DESIRED
Clerk	evenings and weekends	negotiable

EDUCATION

	NAME AND ADDRESS OF SCHOOL	COURSE	DATE LEFT
MIDDLE SCHOOL	Valley Middle School Indianapolis, IN 46266	N/A	June 6, 20--
HIGH SCHOOL	Northwest High School Indianapolis, IN 46244	N/A	N/A
VOCATIONAL SCHOOL	N/A	N/A	N/A
COLLEGE OR UNIVERSITY	N/A	N/A	N/A
OTHER	N/A	N/A	N/A

LAST EMPLOYMENT
NAME OF COMPANY Cameron's Business Supply ADDRESS 1217 Sheldon Ave Indianapolis, IN 46244
SUPERVISOR Jill Lambert JOB Clerk PAY $6.50/hr DATE BEGAN June 20--
DATE LEFT September 20-- REASON FOR LEAVING Summer position only

Additional qualifications applicant has to offer for consideration. These may include job-related interests, experiences, or volunteer activities.

Volunteer one night a week to help deliver meals-on-wheels, on weight-lifting team, and run track at school.

The facts set forth on my application are true and complete.
DATE October 8, 20-- SIGNATURE Mark A. Cortez

Complete

Before you interview for a job, you will probably have to fill out an application. Although more and more applications are being taken online, many businesses, especially those that employ young workers, still accept paper applications. Take time to practice "the art" of completing application forms. Always fill out a job application as neatly and accurately as possible. Write "N/A" in any blank for which an answer is not required. N/A means "Not Applicable" and tells the employer that you saw the question, but it does not apply to you. Fill out the application on a separate sheet of paper or make a copy of this application, being sure to fill it out completely. Use a pencil before you complete the application in ink, or use a rough copy. Were there any questions that you could not answer? If so, list those questions and see if you can find answers to them.

Analyze

How does the way in which you complete an application reflect you as a potential employee? List the positive and the negative impressions an application can leave on a potential employer.

CHAPTER 12

Money Management Strategy

Visual Literacy

A school fundraiser is a good way for an organization to generate income. ***What are some other ways a school organization could make money or acquire goods?***

Discovery Project

Building a Budget

Key Question

Why is it important to create and maintain a personal balance sheet and a budget?

Project Goal

A student organization in your school is having trouble achieving their financial goals. The head of the organization asks you to manage the group's finances. They currently have $100 in savings and yearly expenses of $1000. They hold a monthly event that generates $50 of income.

- Create a cash flow statement for the organization.
- Identify what the future needs of the organization may be and their costs. Research student organizations in your community to learn more about their needs and finances.
- Create a fundraiser.
- Develop a budget and cash flow statement for the fundraiser to ensure that it is profitable.

Ask Yourself...

- *What is the group's income?*
- *What are the group's expenses?*
- *How much will the fundraiser cost and how will it make money?*
- *How can you help ensure the organization uses their money wisely in the future?*

Systems Thinking

How can maintaining a budget and cash flow statement help an organization meet their financial goals? How can this be applied to your personal finances?

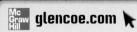

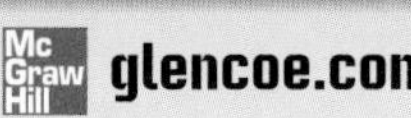

Evaluate Download an assessment rubric.

THE BIG IDEA

Good money management will help you achieve your financial goals.

ASK STANDARD & POOR'S

Using a Budget

Q *I have never used a budget before. What is a budget, and why should I start using one now?*

A A budget is a plan for using money to pay for the things you need to live. When you make a budget, you set your financial goals, estimate your income, list your planned expenses, and set targets for savings. The budget helps you distinguish between wants (things you would like to have) and needs (things you must have). Knowing how much money you make and how much you spend allows you to review your financial progress and make adjustments.

Writing Activity

Write a paragraph describing the difference between wants and needs and how distinguishing between the two can impact your finances. Include examples of wants and needs in your paragraph.

Reading Guide

Before You Read

The Essential Question What money management techniques can you employ to achieve your future financial goals?

Main Idea

Organizing and maintaining a personal financial plan are essential to budgeting for future financial goals.

Content Vocabulary

- money management
- safe-deposit box
- personal financial statement
- personal balance sheet
- net worth
- assets
- wealth
- liquid assets
- real estate
- market value
- liabilities
- insolvency
- cash flow
- income
- take-home pay
- discretionary income
- surplus
- deficit
- budget
- budget variance

Academic Vocabulary

You will see these words in your reading and on your tests.

- resolve
- secure
- evaluate
- foundation
- encounter
- cultivate

Graphic Organizer

Before you read this chapter draw a diagram like the one below. As you read, use the diagram to chart money management practices.

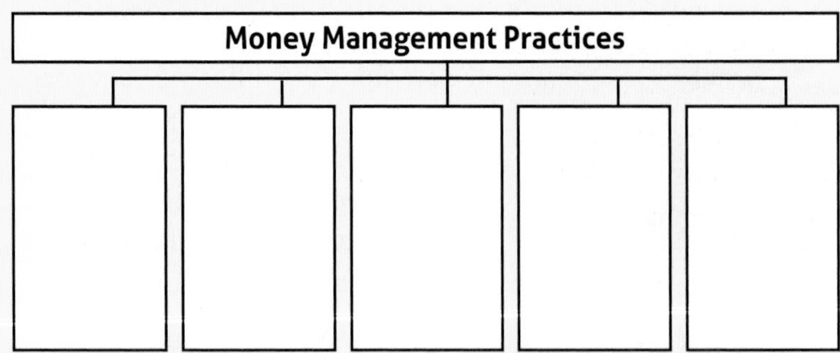

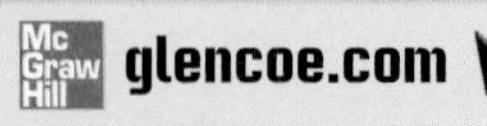

Print this graphic organizer.

Standards

Academic

Mathematics
NCTM Number and Operations Compute fluently and make reasonable estimates.

English Language Arts
NCTE 3 Apply a wide range of strategies to comprehend, interpret, evaluate, and appreciate texts.

Science
NSES 1 Develop an understanding of science unifying concepts and processes: systems, order, and organization; evidence, models, and explanation; change, constancy, and measurement; evolution and equilibrium; and form and function.

NCSS *National Council for the Social Studies*
NCTE *National Council of Teachers of English*
NCTM *National Council of Teachers of Mathematics*
NSES *National Science Education Standards*

Common Core
Reading Determine central ideas or themes of a text and analyze their development; summarize the key supporting details and ideas.
Reading Integrate and evaluate content presented in diverse formats and media, including visually and quantitatively, as well as in words.
Reading Read and comprehend complex literary and informational texts independently and proficiently.
Writing Draw evidence from literary or informational texts to support analysis, reflection, and research.

Opportunity Costs and Money Management

How do you decide when to spend money?

Your daily spending and saving decisions are at the center of financial planning. Each decision you make involves a choice or a trade-off. You choose one thing and reject another. If you decide to go to the movies instead of working on your science fair project, you make a choice. Every decision you make between two or more possibilities has an opportunity cost. Decisions about money management involve making numerous trade-offs.

Money management is the day-to-day financial activities necessary to get the most from your money. In order to manage your money wisely, you have to consider many financial trade-offs. Good money management can help you keep track of where your money goes so you can make it go farther. You need to consider whether to spend your paycheck on entertainment or to deposit some of it where it can contribute to your long-term financial security. If you spend the money now, you do not have the opportunity to earn interest on your money.

When buying a cell phone, should you shop around for a better price or is that a waste of time? You may be able to save some money by checking prices at other stores, but you would also use something you can never replace—your time. Trade-offs are difficult to **resolve** or reach a decision about, because you may like both options.

How can you be sure to make the right decisions when you are faced with tough opportunity costs? You may never be sure, but you can become a better judge of your options. Consider how those options fit your values, your current financial situation, and your goal of effective money management.

By considering your values, your goals, and the state of your bank account, you can make better spending decisions. For example, if your goal is to save as much money as you can for college, then you might borrow a book from the library rather than buy it from a bookstore. On the other hand, if your goal is to put aside only a certain amount of your paycheck each month, you might be able to buy the book with the money you have left.

Reading Check

Relate How is managing opportunity costs, or trade-offs, important to effective money management?

Section Objectives

- **Discuss** the relationship between opportunity costs and money management.
- **Explain** the benefits of keeping financial records and documents.
- **Describe** a system to maintain personal financial documents.

As You Read

Relate Have you ever been in a situation where you asked yourself, "Where did my money go?"

Economics and You

Balance of Trade

Also called net exports, balance of trade is the difference between the total value of exports (goods made in a country and transported to other countries for sale) and the total value of imports (goods a country brings in from other countries). In simple terms, balance of trade is determined by subtracting total imports from total exports over a period of time, typically a month or a year. Surpluses might signal a strong manufacturing base, high tariffs, or overseas demand for U.S. products, but they can also mean that consumers have less disposable income to spend.

Personal Finance Connection In your personal finances, you have a surplus when you have a positive net cash flow and a deficit when you spend more than you earn. In trade, surpluses occur when exports exceed imports; deficits occur when imports exceed exports.

Critical Thinking Compare and contrast deficits and surpluses and how they affect your personal finances and international trade.

Import and Exports of Goods and Services

Billions of Dollars (0, 250, 500, 750, 1000, 1250, 1500, 1750, 2000)

Imports (Goods)	Imports (Services)	Total Imports	Exports (Goods)	Exports (Services)	Total Exports	Balance of Trade
1575	381	1956	1038	525	1563	393

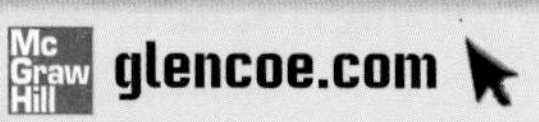

Activity Download an Economics and You Worksheet Activity.

Organization of Financial Documents

How can organizing your financial documents help you in the future?

Today, computers seem to be creating more paperwork than ever. Much of that paperwork relates to financial matters. Personal financial documents, such as pay stubs, bank statements, broker reports, and credit card statements are the basis of financial recordkeeping and personal financial choices. These documents tell you how much you own and how much you owe. Personal financial documents also include automobile titles, birth certificates, marriage license, and tax forms.

The first step in effective money management is to organize your personal financial documents. A well-organized system for handling your personal financial documents has many advantages.

An organized system will help you

- Determine your current financial status.
- Pay your bills on time.
- Complete required tax reports.
- Plan for the future.
- Make sound financial decisions related to your investments.

Storing Financial Documents

Your financial documents can be kept in a file cabinet (preferably a fire-proof model) at home, a safe-deposit box in a bank, or on your computer.

In order to keep your documents safe and to access them in a timely manner, you may want to use a combination of all three places. There are advantages and disadvantages to each place which depend on the types of documents being kept.

Home Files A home file is one place to keep financial documents. A filing system does not need to be elaborate; it just needs to be organized so you can easily file and locate various documents. While a fire-proof file cabinet is preferred, a simple metal one will work. A cardboard box with file folders is better than a shoe box. A filing system is simple to set up and does not take up much space. You need file folders and labels to get started. Follow these steps:

1. Locate your documents and sort them into categories such as payroll stubs, savings account records, checking account statements, utility bills, charge card statements, cash register receipts, birth certificates, car titles, insurance policies, records pertaining to canceled checks, tax records, and copies of all receipts for various payments.
2. Put the documents in file folders and carefully label each folder. You could have a "hanging folder" labeled "Insurance" with several manila file folders labeled "Home," "Auto," and "Life."
3. Actively cultivate the habit of promptly placing your financial documents in the folders. It takes special discipline to maintain your financial records.

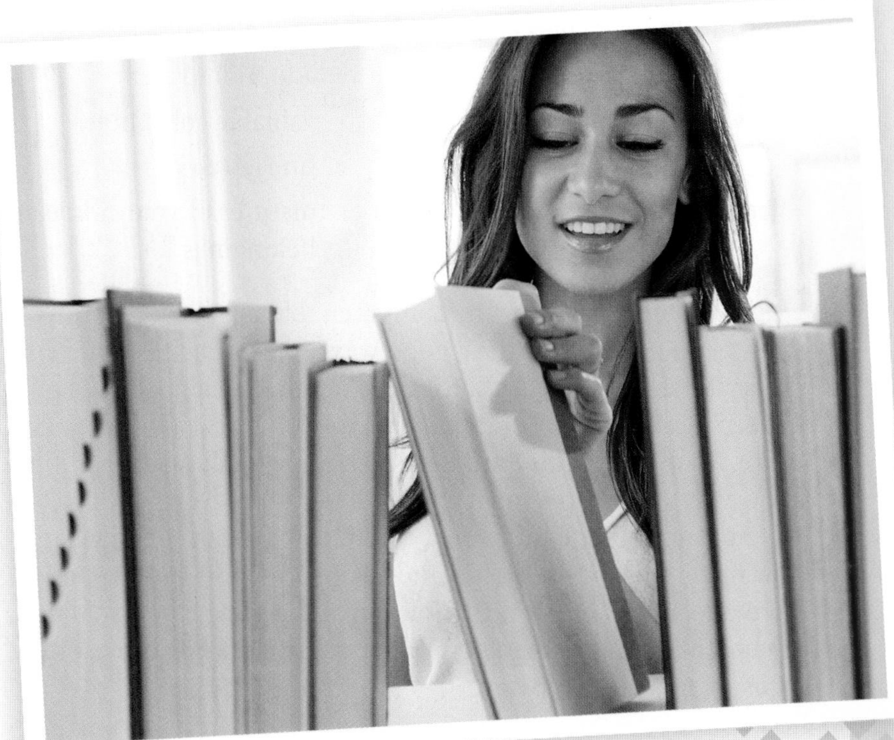

Save or Spend?
Saving and investing reduces the amount of money you can spend now. *Is saving worth the opportunity cost? Why or why not?*

reality bytes

Protecting Financial Records on Your Computer

It is a good idea to duplicate, or "back up," financial and other personal data to an external source in case your computer is damaged or stolen. Options include large-capacity hard drives or smaller flash drives. Another alternative is a fee-based online backup service; files can be easily downloaded onto a new computer.

Most financial documents can be kept in a home file cabinet, giving you convenient access to them. Some items that can be kept in a home file include:

- personal and employment records such as employee benefit information and a resume
- money management records such as a current budget, list of financial goals, and a balance sheet
- financial services records such as a checkbook, bank statements, and canceled checks
- tax records such as W-2 forms and copies of tax returns
- consumer records such as receipts and warranties
- housing records such as home improvement receipts
- insurance records such as policies and a list of premium amounts
- investment records such as brokerage statements
- estate planning and retirement records such as a copy of a will

You should not store difficult-to-replace documents such as mortgage papers, car titles, and insurance policies at home.

Safe-Deposit Box You should keep important documents such as car titles and mortgage loan papers in a **safe-deposit box** - a small, **secure,** or safe, storage compartment that you can rent in a bank, usually for $100 or less. They are kept in a special vault in the bank. Each box has two individual locks and when you rent a box you receive one key and the bank has the other key. Both keys must be used together in order to open the box.

It is a good idea to make a list of the contents of your safe-deposit box as well as copies of the documents contained within. In a safe-deposit box, you may keep important documents such as:

- birth and marriage certificates
- mortgage loan papers
- leases
- stock certificates
- bonds
- certificates of deposit
- contracts
- adoption papers
- valuable collectibles
- fine jewelry
- pictures of your home and belongings

Home Computers A home computer, that is password-protected, with the proper software is a good way to keep track of your financial transactions. You can use software programs specifically designed to keep a running summary of your spending and any deposits you make. Many programs even have electronic banking capabilities that allow you to make payments using the Internet. When you keep track of your monthly spending on a computer, you can see at a glance how much money you spend and easily compare your expenses from one month to the next. You can also generate personal financial documents and statements from the information you have organized by using financial software.

Assessment

Review Key Concepts

1. **Relate** How are opportunity costs, or trade-offs and money management related?
2. **Explain** Why it is important to keep and maintain financial records and documents?
3. **Describe** What is an effective system for maintaining personal financial documents?

Higher Order Thinking

4. **Compare and contrast** How are the roles of maintaining financial records and managing opportunity costs in a sound financial plan similar and different?

21st Century Skills

5. **Communicate Clearly** You have your financial records lying on your desk, in desk drawers, and in dresser drawers. Items include: checkbook statements, paid bills, unpaid bills, credit card statements, paycheck stubs, receipts for items purchased with cash and with a credit card, and savings account statements. Devise a plan to get your records organized. Write a paragraph listing the steps and explaining the reasons for the order.

Mathematics

6. **Determine Opportunity Costs** Manny and his family are planning to buy a new stereo. Manny finds two places to purchase the stereo. First, Manny finds the stereo in a local store near his home for $250 with 6.75 percent sales tax. Manny also finds the stereo online for $235. The Web site charges $9.95 for shipping with 6.0 percent sales tax. Calculate which option is the least expensive. Then consider the opportunity costs and determine where Manny should purchase the stereo. Explain.

Calculate Actual Cost To calculate the cost of the stereo with sales tax, multiply the price of the stereo by the sales tax percentage. Then add the result to the price of the stereo.

Starting Hint Multiply the sales tax percentage by the price of the stereos ($250 \times .0675$ and $235 \times .06$). Add the results to the price of the respective stereo to determine the total cost of the item. Then add any other fees the store charges, such as shipping.

NCTM Number and Operations Compute fluently and make reasonable estimates.

glencoe.com Check your answers.

Section Objectives

- **Describe** a personal balance sheet and cash flow statement.
- **Develop** a personal balance sheet and cash flow statement.

As You Read

Examine What are your assets? How is their value determined?

Personal Balance Sheet

What are your financial goals?

Documents received by banks, businesses, and federal, state, and local governments are only part of your financial picture. Personal financial statements, such as a personal balance sheet and cash flow statement, will give you a complete look at your financial situation. A **personal financial statement** gives information about your current financial position and presents a summary of income and spending.

Personal financial statements can help you:

- determine what you own and what you owe
- measure your progress toward your financial goals
- track your financial activities
- organize information required to file your tax return or apply for credit

To **evaluate,** or determine the value of, your financial situation, you first need to create a balance sheet. A **personal balance sheet,** also known as a net worth statement, is a financial statement that shows what you own and what you owe. Your **net worth** is the difference between the amount you own and the debts you owe. Net worth is a measure of your current financial position. To create a personal balance sheet, follow these steps. **Figure 1** shows an example of a personal balance sheet.

STEP 1 Determine Assets

Available cash and money in bank accounts combined with other items of value are the foundation of your current financial position. **Assets** are any items of value that you own, such as cash, real estate, personal possessions, and investments. **Wealth** is property that has a money value or an exchangeable value. Your assets are an indication of your wealth.

Liquid Assets The first category of wealth is called liquid assets. **Liquid assets** are cash and items that can be quickly converted to cash. The money in your savings and checking accounts is a liquid asset. A life insurance policy with a cash value that can be borrowed if needed is another example of a liquid asset.

If you have $800 in a savings account and $72 in cash, your liquid assets are worth $872 ($800 + $72 = $872).

This money is readily available for you to spend. Most other assets cannot be converted into cash as quickly as writing a check.

FIGURE 1 **A Personal Balance Sheet**

Balance It Out The Duncans' personal balance sheet indicates that they have a positive net worth of $59,950. *What does this amount represent? Explain your answer.*

Melanie and Isaiah Duncan Personal Balance Sheet as of October 31, 20--		
ASSETS		
Liquid Assets		
Checking account balance	$1,800	
Savings account balance	$5,500	
Total liquid assets		$7,300
Real Estate		
Market value of house		$128,000
Personal Possessions		
Car	$8,500	
Furniture and appliances	$5,000	
Stereo/TV	$4,000	
Home computer	$1,500	
Collectibles	$750	
Total personal possessions		$19,750
Investment Assets		
Retirement accounts	$22,000	
Stock investments	$3,500	
Total investments assets		$25,500
TOTAL ASSETS		**$180,550**
LIABILITIES		
Current Liabilities		
Medical bills	$1,750	
Credit Card balances	$4,600	
Total current liabilities		$6,350
Long-Term Liabilities		
Mortgage	$96,000	
Student loan	$7,000	
Equity loan	$8,500	
Car loan	$2,750	
Total long-term liabilities		$114,250
TOTAL LIABILITIES		**$120,600**
Net Worth (assets minus liabilities)		**$59,950**

Careers That Count!

Samir Parikh • Financial Accountant

I am a financial accountant for an insurance brokerage firm. I prepare, analyze, and present the various financial statements, supporting schedules, and budgets to the accounting manager and company president. A typical workday begins the night before, when I look at my schedule for any urgent items that require immediate attention. The next morning, once those tasks are completed, I move onto daily activities, such as monitoring the daily cash flow, evaluating employee expense reimbursements, and reconciling the cash deposits to our general ledger. Having proficient computer skills goes a long way in making my day easier, and being able to communicate effectively with the staff is another crucial skill. You may want to get an internship or part-time job at an accounting firm or in an accounting department to help you decide if you like this type of work and its culture.

EXPLORE CAREERS

Visit the Web site of the U.S. Department of Labor's Bureau of Labor Statistics and obtain information about a career as an accountant.

1. What is the special certification that can be obtained by an accountant?
2. What are the requirements of this certification?

CAREER FACTS

Skills	Education	Career Path
Finance, math, problem solving skills, proficiency in accounting and auditing software	Bachelor's degree or higher in accounting	Accountants can become CPAs, start their own businesses, or work for the Federal Government.

glencoe.com 

Activity Download a Career Exploration Activity.

Real Estate The second category of wealth is **real estate,** which is land and any structures that are on it, such as a house or any other building. The amount recorded on the real estate portion of your balance sheet is the property's **market value,** or the price at which property would sell. If you own a condominium with a market value of $235,000 and a parcel of land valued at $72,000, you list the total value $235,000 + $72,000 or $307,000 under the heading "Real Estate" on your balance sheet.

Personal Possessions Any other valuable belongings that are not real estate are considered personal possessions. Cars, laptop computers, racing bicycles, rare coins, and pieces of fine jewelry are examples of valuable possessions. The emphasis is on "valuable"; old clothes and outdated cell phones are usually not valuable.

The list of personal possessions on the balance sheet may be listed at their original cost, but you will get a better idea of your financial situation by recording their current market value. If you paid $800 for a laptop computer five years ago, it is worth less than that today. In contrast, collectible items, such as old baseball cards and comic books, may increase in value over time. It may not be easy to determine the current values of some items. You can determine the current value of an item by checking Web sites where people buy and sell such items. You may have to look up comparable items in newspaper classified ads or visit thrift stores.

Investment Assets The fourth category of wealth is investment assets. These include retirement accounts and securities such as stocks and bonds. These items are usually for long-term financial needs, such as paying for college, buying a house, or retirement.

STEP 2 Determine Liabilities

Liabilities are the debts that you owe. If you borrow $300 to buy a new surfboard, you record the surfboard as an asset, but you also record the $300 as a liability on your personal balance sheet.

Current Liabilities Current liabilities are short-term debts that have to be paid within one year. The balance on a charge account, insurance premiums, current taxes, utility bills, and medical bills are all considered current liabilities.

Long-Term Liabilities Long-term liabilities are debts that do not have to be fully repaid for at least a year. Loans for home improvement, vehicles, college tuition, and mortgage loans are all considered long-term liabilities.

STEP 3 Calculate Net Worth

To determine your net worth, subtract the value of your liabilities from the value of your assets. Net worth is the amount you would have if all assets were sold for listed values and all debts were paid in full. If you have a net worth of $92,700, that does not mean you have $92,700 to spend. The majority of your net worth may be in investments and real estate that cannot quickly be converted to cash. Net worth is an indication of your general financial situation.

Valuables
Personal possessions such as collectibles are just one type of asset. *What are your assets?*

GO FIGURE Mathematics

Net Worth

Your net worth is determined by your assets and liabilities. Calculating your net worth will help you get an accurate measure of your current financial situation.

EXAMPLE What is your net worth if you have $4,000 in assets and $1,250 in liabilities?

Formula	Assets	–	Liabilities	=	Net Worth
Application	$4,000	–	$1,250	=	$2,750
Solution	Your net worth is $2,750.				

Your Turn

You own a game system worth $250, an amethyst ring worth $160, and a motor bike worth $1,400. You owe your older sister $80 for some clothes she bought for you, and you owe $275 on a credit card. What is your net worth?

It is possible to have a high net worth and still have trouble paying your bills. This is especially true when most of your assets are not liquid, and you do not have enough cash to meet your expenses. This can happen if you purchase a more expensive car than you can afford or spend all of your savings to buy a house.

Insolvency is the inability to pay debts when they are due. If you are unable to pay all your debts, you are considered insolvent. Suppose you owe $5,000 and your assets consist of a 10-year old car and an old computer, both worth a total of $1,800. If you sold all of your assets and put your entire paycheck of $1,100 toward paying your debts, you would still be insolvent.

STEP 4 Evaluate Your Financial Situation

You use a balance sheet to record your financial status and a monthly balance sheet to track changes in your financial position from month to month. An increasing net worth indicates that you are making good financial decisions. If your net worth is decreasing or just holding steady, you may need to make some changes. Remember, your net worth is not money available for use but an indication of your financial position on a given date.

You can increase your net worth by:

- reducing your expenses
- reducing your spending and your debts
- increasing your savings
- increasing your investments

Reading Check

Compile What are three examples of assets and three examples of liabilities?

Cash Flow Statement: Income Versus Expenses

How much do you earn and spend?

Cash flow refers to the movement (cash) in and out of your wallet and/or your bank account. Cash flow is divided into two parts: Cash inflow occurs when you receive **income.** Income includes your paycheck from a job, an allowance from your parents, and interest earned on a savings or checking account or other investments. Cash outflow occurs when you spend money.

A cash flow statement is a summary of your cash inflow and cash outflow during a particular period of time, usually a month or a year. The cash flow statement gives specific, significant information and feedback on where you received income and where you spent money. To create a cash flow statement, such as the one shown in **Figure 2,** follow these steps:

1. Record all your sources of income.
2. Record all your expenses.
3. Calculate your net cash flow.

FIGURE 2 **Cash Flow Statement**

Money Supply Amy's cash flow statement indicates that her expenses total $425. *How might she decrease her variable expenses?*

Amy Grossman Cash Flow Statement for Month Ending July 31, 20--	
Income-Cash Inflow	
Take-home pay	$390
Gift	$75
Investment income	$45
Total Income	$510
Expenses-Cash Outflow	
Fixed expenses	
Student Loans	$80
Transportation	$15
Variable expenses	
Recreation	$100
Clothing	$105
Dining out	$75
Gifts	$50
Total expenses	$425
Net Cash Flow	**$85**

GO FIGURE Mathematics

Net Cash Flow

Calculating your net cash flow will help you determine your current financial status. It is a quick assessment of your income and expenses.

EXAMPLE Calculate your net cash flow if your total income for the month is $1,675 and your expenses are $1,425.

Formula	Income − Expenses = Net Cash Flow
Application	$1,675 − $1,425 = $250
Solution	You have a positive net cash flow of $250.

Your Turn

You work 12 hours a week, 4 weeks a month, at a part-time job after school at a grocery store. You earn $8 an hour. You pay $60 a month for gas, $80 for a car payment, and $52 a month for your cell phone. What is your net cash flow?

STEP 1 Record Your Income

Record all of your sources of income—cash inflow during the month. You need to record the exact amount. Your paycheck will show various deductions for federal, state, and local taxes as well as other deductions such as union dues. The total deductions are withheld from the total amount of money you have earned, or your gross pay. Your **take-home pay,** or net pay, is the amount of income left after taxes and other deductions are subtracted from your gross pay.

If you earn $1,000 a month and have deductions of $300, your take home pay will be $700 ($1,000 − $300). Your cash inflow is the total of your take-home pay plus your interest earnings on savings and checking accounts and other investments.

STEP 2 Record Your Expenses

All expenses are either a fixed expense or a variable expense. Fixed expenses do not vary from month to month, such as rent, cable, Internet charges, and bus fare for commuting to work or school. Variable expenses may change from month to month, such as food, various utilities, clothing, medical costs, and recreation. Your cash outflow is the total of your fixed and variable expenses.

Discretionary income is the money you have left after paying for your essentials, such as rent, utilities, clothing, transportation, and medications. The money left after expenses can be spent at your discretion, or for whatever you want.

STEP 3 Calculate Your Net Cash Flow

To calculate net cash flow, subtract your total expenses from your total income. If your net cash flow is positive, you have a **surplus** or extra money that you can spend or save, depending on your financial goals and values. You could deposit the surplus in a savings and investment account or apply it to your emergency fund for unexpected expenses.

If your net cash flow is negative, you have a **deficit** which means you spent more than you received. A cash flow statement provides the **foundation**, or basis, for carrying out your financial goals.

Reading Check

Explain What is take-home, or net, pay?

Your Financial Position

What is your net worth?

Your net cash flow and your net worth change from month to month. If you have a negative cash flow, you spent more than you earned and you created a deficit. The deficit decreases your net worth. One way to cover the deficit is to take out a loan; however, this increases your liabilities. You could also withdraw funds from your savings which decreases your assets. In either case, your net worth declines.

If you have a positive cash flow, you spent less than you earned and you created a surplus. Ending the month with a surplus should result in an increase in your net worth. You can invest the surplus, increasing your assets, or you can use the surplus to pay off debts and reduce your liabilities. In either event you will increase your net worth. As a general rule, a positive cash flow increases your net worth and a negative cash flow will decrease it. See **Figure 3.**

FIGURE 3 **Evaluating Your Financial Progress**

Expert Advice You have liquid assets of $18,000 and monthly expenses of $5,600. *What is your liquidity ratio? What does this mean? How could you increase the ratio?*

Ratio	Calculation	Example
A **low debt ratio** is desirable.	$\frac{\text{liabilities}}{\text{net worth}}$	$\frac{\$30,000}{\$60,000} = 0.5$
Liquidity ratio indicates number of months you would be able to pay your living expenses in case of a financial emergency.	$\frac{\text{liquid assets}}{\text{monthly expenses}}$	$\frac{\$12,000}{\$5,000} = 2.4$
Debt-payments ratio indicates how much of a person's earnings go to pay debts (excluding a home mortgage). Financial experts recommend a ratio of less than 20 percent.	$\frac{\text{monthly credit payments}}{\text{take home pay}}$	$\frac{\$648}{\$3,600} = 0.18 = 18\%$
Financial experts recommend a **savings ratio** of at least 10 percent.	$\frac{\text{amount saved each month}}{\text{gross monthly income}}$	$\frac{\$700}{\$5,000} = 0.14 = 14\%$

Assessment

Review Key Concepts

1. **Describe** What is a personal balance sheet?
2. **Explain** What is a cash flow statement?
3. **Summarize** How is a cash flow statement created? How is a personal balance sheet created? What are the components of each?

Higher Order Thinking H.O.T.

4. **Compare and contrast** How are a personal balance sheet and cash flow statement similar? How are they different? What role does each play in the development of a personal financial plan?

English Language Arts

5. **Spending Habits** Larry's personal balance sheet shows $1,200 in debts; a savings account balance of $550; and personal property amounting to $3,700 in rare coins. Recently, Larry was promoted at his job and received a salary increase. He had a positive cash flow of $600 last month. What do you think Larry should do with the surplus? Write a short essay comparing and contrasting Larry's options.

NCTE 3 Apply a wide range of strategies to comprehend, interpret, evaluate, and appreciate texts.

Mathematics

6. **Net Worth** Ten years after graduating from college Nitesh would like to create a personal balance sheet. He has a saving accounts, checking account, and cash valued at $33,521.07, a home valued at $488,600, personal possessions with a value of $112,330.50, and an Individual Retirement Account with a value of $198, 658.88. He has expenses totaling $22,564.70. He also has student loans totaling $30,562 and $456,253.65 left on his mortgage. Create a personal balance sheet categorizing Nitesh's assets and liabilities. Then calculate his net worth.

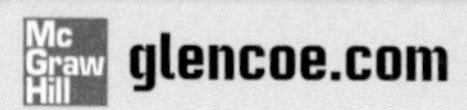

Math Concept Calculate Net Worth To calculate net worth, you subtract the sum of your liabilities from the sum of your assets.

Starting Hint Determine the sum of Nitesh's liabilities. Then determine the sum of his assets.

NCTM Number and Operations Compute fluently and make reasonable estimates.

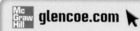

glencoe.com Check your answers.

Budgeting for Financial Goals

Preparing a Budget

What does a budget tell you about your financial situation?

A **budget** is a plan for spending and investing your money to meet your wants and needs. If you want to be successful at financial planning, you must have a budget. A budget will enable you to learn how to live within your income and to spend your money wisely. You cannot reach your financial goals unless you have good money management skills. The following steps will help you develop a budget.

STEP 1 Set Your Financial Goals

Your financial goals are determined by what you want to accomplish with your money. The money you spend and invest today will affect your ability to achieve your financial goals in the future. In order to accomplish your financial goals, you need to know how much money you plan to save, to spend, and to invest.

How you set your financial goals depends on your lifestyle, what you value, and what you plan to do in the future. Your occupation will have a significant impact on your income and your ability to save and invest to reach your financial goals.

It is important to make your financial goals as specific as possible. A definite time frame in which to accomplish your goals will help you achieve them.

STEP 2 Estimate Your Income

Record your estimated income for the next month. Include all sources of income, such as your take-home pay, income on investments and interest on your savings. Do not include estimated bonuses and possible gifts.

Estimating income is easier in some cases than in others. If you work 12 hours each week and take home $90 in net pay, your monthly income is $390 (4 1/3 weeks × $90). In contrast, if you work irregular hours at two part-time jobs, some weeks you could earn $50 and other weeks you might earn $150. In this case you need to estimate your average income for a month. In **Figure 4,** the Thompsons have estimated their income for next month to be $4,300. Use a budget form similar to **Figure 4** and record your estimated net income. A budget should always be a written document or a computer spreadsheet that you can edit.

Section Objectives

- **Identify** the steps to create a personal budget.
- **Discuss** the advantages of increasing your savings.

As You Read

Predict How do you think a budget could benefit your finances?

FIGURE 4 **The Monthly Budget**

Keeping Track The Thompsons have a negative cash flow for the month. *What can they do to have a positive cash flow?*

Financial Goals Pay off student and car loans, save for vacation, and increase investments. ← **Step 1** Set Financial Goals

	Budgeted Amounts	Actual Amounts	Variance
Income			
Salary (Mike)	$3,200.00	$3,200.00	—
Salary (Gina)	$1,100.00	$1,100.00	—
Total Income	$4,300.00	$4,300.00	—
Outflows			
Unexpected Expenses and Savings			
Emergency savings	$200.00	$200.00	—
Vacation savings	$100.00	$100.00	—
College savings	$70.00	$70.00	—
Investment savings	$100.00	$100.00	—
Total Savings	$470.00	$470.00	—
Fixed Expenses			
Mortgage loan	$900.00	$900.00	—
Real Estate Taxes	$200.00	$200.00	—
Car loan	$200.00	$200.00	—
Student loan	$150.00	$150.00	—
Health insurance	$250.00	$250.00	—
Car insurance	$170.00	$170.00	—
Total fixed expenses	$1,870.00	$1,870.00	—
Variable Expenses			
Cell phone	$85.00	$92.00	–$7.00
Groceries	$600.00	$700.00	–$100.00
Gasoline	$450.00	$478.00	–$28.00
Utilities (electric, cable)	$300.00	$350.00	–$50.00
Clothing	$175.00	$150.00	$25.00
Insurance co–pays	$50.00	$20.00	$30.00
Gifts, miscellaneous	$100.00	$75.00	$25.00
Recreation/entertainment	$200.00	$225.00	–$25.00
Total variable expenses	$1,960.00	$2,090.00	–$130.00
Total Outflow	**$4,300.00**	**$4,430.00**	($130)

Step 2 Estimate Your Income

Step 3 Budget for Unexpected Expenses and Savings

Step 4 Budget for Fixed Expenses

Step 5 Budget for Variable Expenses

Step 6 Record What You Spend

Step 7 Review Spending and Savings Patterns

STEP 3 Budget for Unexpected Expenses

Note that the Thompsons have a section labeled "Unexpected Expenses and Savings." One of their financial goals is to save three to six months' worth of living expenses in case someone in the family becomes unemployed, needs medical attention, or runs into some other financial problem. They decide to save $200 each month in an emergency savings account that will earn interest.

The Thompsons are also trying to meet one short-term and two long-term financial goals. Their short-term goal is a trip to Alaska so they set up a vacation fund. They deposit money in their vacation fund each month. Their long-term goals are a college fund for their young children and an investment fund to buy stocks. They put $170 into these other special savings accounts each month, which brings their total monthly savings to $470.

STEP 4 Budget for Fixed Expenses

Fixed expenses are the expenses that do not change from month to month. The Thompsons' monthly fixed expenses include their mortgage, real estate taxes, car loan payment, student loan payments, and insurance premiums. Their budgeted total for fixed expenses is $1,870.

STEP 5 Budget for Variable Expenses

Variable expenses are the expenses that vary from month to month. Budgeting for variable expenses is not as easy as budgeting for fixed expenses. Budget items such as food, medical bills, transportation costs, and utilities change from month to month. The Thompsons' budget for these variable expenses is $1,960.

The data in **Figure 5** is published annually by the U.S. Bureau of Labor Statistics. It shows the dollar amount and percent of the budget spent annually by the average consumer. Comparing your actual annual budget to the U.S. data can indicate when you are spending more or less than the national average. As consumer prices increase due to inflation, people must spend more to buy the same amount. Changes in the cost of living will vary depending on where you live and what you buy.

STEP 6 Record What You Spend

Now that your budget is prepared, begin to keep track of your actual income and expenses. Your variable expenses vary from month to month and the variations need to be recorded. If your car breaks down and you have an $800 repair bill, you will have a definite increase in your transportation costs for the month.

Budget variance is the difference between the budgeted amount and the actual amount spent. The variance can be a surplus which means you spent less than you budgeted.

Teamwork

What does playing on a soccer team, organizing a school function, or working with your family to make a meal at home have in common? Teamwork is central to each activity. Teamwork occurs when the members of a group work together to reach a common goal. To achieve success, you will need to use teamwork skills at home, at school, at work, and in the community.

Write About It

How can you lead by example while collaborating as a team member? Write one or more paragraphs to describe some positive characteristics of successful team members and explain how exhibiting these characteristics could influence others in positive ways.

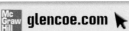

Activity Download a Career and College Readiness Worksheet Activity.

FIGURE 5 **Average Annual Expenditures**

What is Average? It may be useful to compare your spending to the national average. *Why might your housing or other expenses differ from the national average?*

Expenditures	Amount	Percent
Food	$6,133	
At home	3,465	7%
Away from home	2,668	5%
Housing	16,920	34%
Apparel and services	1,881	4%
Transportation	8,758	18%
Health care	2,853	6%
Entertainment	2,698	5%
Personal insurance and pensions	5,336	11%
Other expenditures	5,060	10%
Total	**$49,639**	**100%**

The variance can also be a deficit or a negative amount which means you spent more than you budgeted. A budget variance may also occur if your income is higher or lower than expected. Your income and expenses will not always work out as planned.

In **Figure 4,** the Thompsons have a second column labeled "Actual Amount." This is where they record precisely what they receive in income and how much they spend. Some actual expenses were the same as the budgeted amount and some were not.

The Thompsons have no budget variance on the income category; however they had more expenses than they budgeted in several categories. They had a deficit in those categories and an overall total monthly deficit of $130.

STEP 7 Review Spending and Saving Patterns

Budgeting is a process that must be monitored every month. The following are some budget guidelines to follow:

- keep your records up to date by faithfully recording all transactions
- review your budget at least once a month
- make changes based on your income and expenses

Revise your budget if you are behind on paying your debts or if you have a surplus of money at the end of the month. If your budget always appears to be on target, you still need to prepare a budget summary that shows your transactions over several months or a year.

Revising Goals and Adjusting Your Budget If your budget shows that you consistently have deficits, you need to reduce your expenses or increase your income. To revise your budget you need to identify the areas of over spending and then decide which expenses to cut.

A Personal Balance Sheet

A personal balance sheet shows your financial health at a given point in time. It contains assets and liabilities with a value for each. It also shows your net worth. Updating your balance sheet from time to time will help you keep track of your financial situation.

Selena Rubio's Personal Balance Sheet			
Assets	**Value**	**Liabilities**	**Value**
Cash	$500.00	Mortgage	$180,000.00
Checking account	$1,500.00	Credit card debt	$6,500.00
Savings account	$12,500.00	Current monthly bills	$2,800.00
Real estate & Property	$225,000.00	Auto loans	$4,500.00
Vehicle	$12,000.00	Home equity loans	$7,200.00
Insurance (cash surrender value)	$8,000.00	Medical bills	$600.00
Retirement accounts (401K & IRA)	$12,000.00		
Stocks and bonds	$4,000.00		
Art collection	$5,000.00		
Total Assets	**$280,500.00**	**Total Liabilities**	**$201,600.00**
		NET WORTH	**$78,900.00**

Key Points A balance sheet lists the items of value that you own, the debts that you owe, and your net worth. Personal financial statements can help measure your progress toward your financial goals, track your financial activities, and organize information for taxes and credit applications.

FIND the Solutions

Review Key Concepts

1. What information is contained in a personal balance sheet?
2. What are Selena's total assets?
3. What are Selena's total liabilities?
4. What is Selena's net worth and how is it calculated?
5. Who would be interested in knowing a person's net worth?
6. Analyze Selena's liabilities and explain where liabilities could be reduced.
7. Summarize the benefits of maintaining a personal financial statement.

Pay or Save?

Be a smart consumer and pay off your credit card bills before you put money away in a savings account. The interest rate charged on credit cards is usually higher than the interest you can earn from your savings account.

Concept Application

How would this approach impact your budget? What specific areas of the budget will be affected?

Ask yourself: Is joining Netflix less expensive than going to the movie theater? Could you join a car pool or take public transportation to work? Are you overspending on "wants" or "needs"? Doing without a purchase may be inconvenient, but you will not increase your debt. If you consistently spend $50 a month more than you planned for transportation and cannot find a way to cut back, your budget next month should reflect a $50 increase for transportation and a corresponding $50 decrease in another part of the budget.

Another approach to determine what expenses to cut would be to reevaluate your financial goals. Do all of your expenditures fit into your overall plan for the future? The answer can help you decide where you need to spend less money. Are you making progress toward your objectives? Are your objectives and your goals changing? It may be necessary to revise your goals to meet your needs.

Reading Check

Summarize What are the components of a practical budget?

A Successful Budget

What makes a good budget?

You can prepare a very elaborate budget, but that alone cannot solve your financial problems. You need a realistic spending plan. A budget should be:

- **Carefully planned and related to your goals.** The amounts you use must be based on past spending and your expectations. The spending categories must cover all your expenses.
- **Practical.** If you have a net income of $2,000 a month, it is unrealistic to budget $1,000 a month for rent and utilities and expect to pay for your other needs.
- **Flexible.** Changes in your income, marital status, and new spending habits mean your budget needs revision. You may **encounter,** or experience unexpectedly, unexpected expenses, an increase in your income, and unexpected medical expenses. When you experience these changes, your budget should be easy to revise.
- **Easily accessible.** Use a notebook, file folders, or computer to store your budget. It is almost impossible to keep all your budget information in your head or on random scraps of paper. You will forget or lose the information.

Reading Check

Identify What are the characteristics of a successful budget?

Kenya

Texting Money

As personal, handheld technologies continue to advance, consumers know the next, big thing is just around the corner. Western nations have moved from the once-revolutionary cell phone to other handheld devices with ever-expanding network connections. However, in developing nations such as Kenya, the cell phone represents a new trend in technology.

The innovation lies in the usage of the product. While plastic cards are the preferred method of payment in the United States, the cell phone is the center of personal finance in Kenya. Projects like *M-Pesa* have changed how money transactions occur. Consumers use this program to convert cash into cell phone money. This money can be wired to anyone with a cell phone. In developing nations like Kenya, building cell phone towers is less expensive than building wired networks and infrastructure to connect its citizens. Consumers can seek employment, receive salaries, borrow money, and lend money using only their cell phone. In 2009, cell phone subscribers worldwide had reached 4.6 billion thanks in part to the rise of the cell phone in developing nations.

Critical Thinking

1. **Expand** What products have been lost to technological advancements? Which products have survived the changes in technology and why?
2. **Relate** How could the processes described in the text be used in developed nations such as the United States?

DATABYTES

Capital
Nairobi

Population
39, 008, 772

Languages
English, Kiswahili, and indigenous languages

Currency
Kenyan shilling

Gross Domestic Product (GDP)
$30.57 billion

GDP per capita
$1,600

Industry
Small-scale consumer goods, agricultural products, oil refining, aluminum, steel, lead, cement, commercial ship repair, tourism

Agriculture
Tea, coffee, corn, wheat, sugarcane, fruit, vegetables; dairy products, beef, pork, poultry, eggs

Exports
Limestone, soda ash, salt, gemstones, fluorspar, zinc, diatomite, gypsum, wildlife, hydropower

Natural Resources
Limestone, soda ash, salt, gemstones, fluorspar, zinc, diatomite, gypsum, wildlife, hydropower

Increasing Your Savings

Why should you put money away each payday?

After You Read

React With the information provided in this chapter, would you be able to create a budget and stick to it? Why or why not?

An essential component of a sound financial plan is to open a savings account. Even a small savings account may enable you to handle an unexpected emergency. You may want to establish savings to pay for expensive, unexpected repairs; to buy special items such as a television or computer; or to provide for long-term expenses such as college tuition.

A savings account will help you meet your financial goals. If you save enough, you may be able to retire comfortably. Money that is saved earns interest income. It may not be very much but you need to develop the savings habit. You must resist the temptation to buy whatever you want, whenever you want it. You can increase the amount you save by using several savings strategies.

Pay Yourself First

Each month treat your savings contribution as a monthly fixed expense. When you sit down to pay your bills, write a check to your saving account, and then pay your other bills. As an alternative, have your bank automatically deduct a certain amount from your checking account and deposit it in your savings account.

Payroll Savings

Many employers offer a payroll savings deduction. A portion of your earnings is automatically taken out of your paycheck and put into your savings or retirement account. An advantage of this savings method is that your take-home pay is reduced by the amount of the savings so you never see the money. If you get a pay raise, you can have the increase automatically deducted. Chances are you will not miss the raise because it was not a part of your spendable income.

Spending Less to Save

Another way to save is to start small and spend less each day. If you buy items on sale, place at least a portion of the savings in a "savings jar". If you get a rebate check in the mail place the amount in your jar. It may be a small amount, but you already paid for the item. If you buy coffee on the way to work each day, stop buying coffee and make a cup at home and take it with you. Put the savings in your jar. You may be pleasantly surprised by the amount saved each month. Put the money from the jar into your savings account.

How you save is less important than the action of saving. You need to **cultivate,** or promote the growth of, the savings habit at an early age. Keep in mind that very small amounts increase in value and can help you achieve your financial goals.

Save
Taking public transportation, carpooling, walking, or riding a bike are just some ways to cut expenses.
What are some other ways you could cut expenses?

SECTION 3 Assessment

Review Key Concepts

1. **List** What are the steps for developing a personal budget?
2. **Describe** What items are included in a personal budget?
3. **Explain** What are the advantages of increasing your savings?

Higher Order Thinking H.O.T.

4. **Assess** Explain why it is sometimes difficult for people to increase their savings. How will increasing the amount you put in savings affect your budget?

English Language Arts

5. **Wants and Needs** Tara complains that she cannot seem to get ahead financially. She believes that all expenses, such as her cell phone bill, car payment, gym membership, and subscriptions to several magazines, are absolutely necessary. Write a paragraph persuading Tara to change her financial approach and explaining how to do this. The paragraph should address the importance of sound financial goals, a budget, and fixed and variable expenses.

NCTE 3 Apply a wide range of strategies to comprehend, interpret, evaluate, and appreciate texts.

Mathematics

6. **Budget Variance** Nina is creating her family's monthly budget. Their budgeted monthly variable expenses consist of $600 for food, $300 for transportation, and $200 for personal allowances. This month they actually spent $360 on transportation, $210 for personal allowances, and $590 for food. Calculate the total budget variance for the family's variable expenses.

Math Concept **Calculate Budget Variance** The difference between the sum of the budgeted variable expenses and the sum of the actual variable expenses is the variance.

Starting Hint Add the family's budgeted variable expenses to determine the total budgeted variable expenses for the month. Then add the actual expenses to determine the total actual variable expenses.

NCTM Number and Operations Compute fluently and make reasonable estimates.

Check your answers.

Visual Summary

Money Management Strategy

Your Net Worth
A personal balance sheet will help you calculate your net worth.

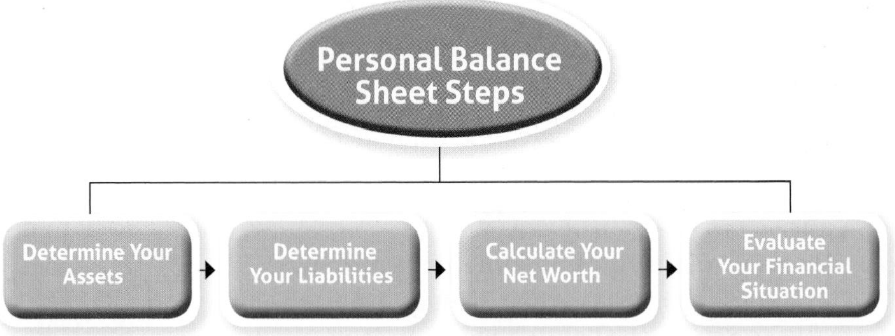

Budget for Success
A practical and flexible budget will help you meet your future financial goals.

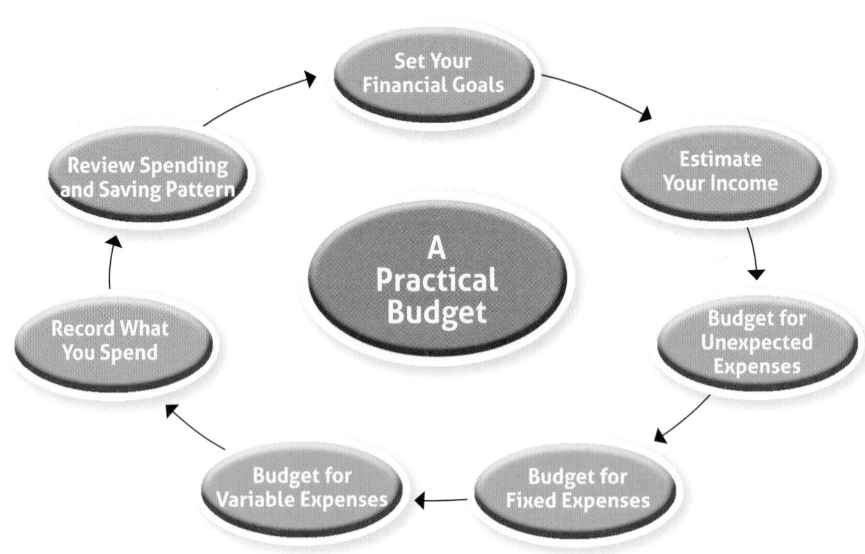

Try It!
Draw a diagram like the one shown to summarize the elements of a good and successful budget.

Chapter Review and Assessment

Chapter Summary

- There are opportunity costs, or trade-offs, in all decisions. When you make a decision about how to manage your money, you remove the option to use the money in a different way.
- Organizing your financial documents makes it easier to plan and measure progress and make effective decisions. You can organize financial documents in home files, a safe-deposit box, and on a computer.
- A personal balance sheet helps determine your net worth, so you can manage your money to meet your financial goals.
- A personal cash flow statement helps determine the cash you receive and how you spend it.
- To create a budget:
  - Set financial goals
  - estimate your income
  - budget for unexpected expenses and savings
  - budget for fixed expenses
  - budget for variable expenses
  - record what you spend and review your spending and saving patterns.
- Savings are the key to a sound financial future. Savings enable you to handle unexpected emergencies.

Vocabulary Review

1. Arrange the vocabulary terms below into groups of related words. Explain why you put the words in each group together.

- money management
- safe-deposit box
- personal financial statement
- personal balance sheet
- net worth
- assets
- wealth
- liquid assets
- real estate
- resolve
- secure
- evaluate
- foundation
- encounter
- cultivate
- market value
- liabilities
- insolvency
- cash flow
- income
- take-home pay
- discretionary income
- surplus
- deficit
- budget
- budget variance

Higher Order Thinking 

2. **Relate** How are opportunity costs or trade-offs related to money management?
3. **Justify** A friend or relative does not think organizing and properly storing financial documents is important. Justify to him or her the importance of storing and organizing financial documents.
4. **Assess** Think of the documents or items you would store in home files, safe-deposit boxes, and on a computer. Explain the reasoning behind the storage location of each item and explain why the items would not work in the other locations.
5. **Evaluate** Consider what you learn from a balance sheet and personal cash flow statement. Evaluate the significance of each.
6. **Compare and Contrast** How are fixed and variable expenses similar or different? Give examples of each. How can each impact your finances?
7. **Connect** How can you use your budget to devise ways to increase your savings?
8. **Analyze** Why is increasing savings challenging for some people?

College and Career Readiness

Science

9. Managing Stress Good money management is not only beneficial to your financial health, but to your mental and physical health as well.

Procedure A British study found that "financially incapable" people are more likely to suffer mental stress, lower reported life satisfaction, and the health problems associated with stress. The report also stated that "an ability to manage finances will lead to an improvement in psychological well-being."

Analysis Write a short paragraph describing how poor money management might negatively affect one's health.

NSES 1 Develop an understanding of science unifying concepts and processes: systems, order, and organization; evidence, models, and explanation; change, constancy, and measurement; evolution and equilibrium; and form and function.

Mathematics

10. Increasing Savings Each year your school sponsors a class trip for its graduating class. The cost of the trip is $925 per student. Your family has agreed to contribute $250, but you will have to save the rest on your own. You babysit for 8 hours per week for $10 per hour. Each week you have fixed expenses of $15. You also spend on average $30 per week on variable expenses. The trip is in 12 weeks. How much additional money do you need to save each week to be able to pay for the trip?

Math Concept **Calculate Savings** To calculate how much in additional savings you need subtract your financial surplus from the final cost of the trip and divide by the number of weeks.

Starting Hint Multiply the number of hours worked per week by the wage to determine your income. Then subtract your total expenses to find your budget surplus.

NCTM Number and Operations Compute fluently and make reasonable estimates.

English Language Arts

11. Saving Money Consider the reasons why you might want to save more money. What are your goals for short-term savings? Do you also have long-term savings goals? Compile a list of reasons for including savings in your financial plan. Write a short paragraph detailing your short- and long-term goals and how increasing your savings can help you to meet them.

NCTE 3 Apply strategies to interpret texts.

Economics

12. Supply and Demand The economic model of supply and demand states that the price of items will balance the demand of consumers and the supply of the producers. Demand can also be affected by other factors such as availability of substitutes. The more substitutes an item has, the more demand for that item can be affected. A person may shop around for several types of cars, but may not spend the time to search for a variety of pencils. How would the demand for a specific truck model be affected if the price was set above the competition's prices? How would the demand for a pencil be affected? Explain.

Real-World Applications

13. Financial Advisor Zachary works part-time at a coffee shop. He currently is able to walk to his job. Upon graduation he is hired as an office manager at a small company. While he will be making more money, he will incur additional expenses. His new job will require him to commute 20 miles per day. Imagine that you are his financial advisor. Make a list of financial questions and issues to discuss with him. Discuss how his life will change when he enters the world of work. What additional expenses will he incur? Write a business letter to Zachary explaining your recommendations.

What Is Your Net Worth?

Jasmine has been an avid downhill skier for as long as she can remember. Before her next major competition, she would like to purchase a new pair of skis. She probably will be able to save enough money by working during the summer at her part-time job. However, she may need to sell some of her possessions. She has made a list of her assets and liabilities to determine her net worth.

Jasmine's Balance Sheets as of April 1, 20--	
Liquid Assets	
Checking account balance	$500.00
Savings accounts	$1,635.00
Total liquid assets	$2,135.00
Personal Possessions	
Market value of automobile	$4,000.00
Televisions and laptop computer	$1,600.00
Digital camera	$650.00
Market value of ski equipment	$1,050.00
Total personal possessions	$7,300.00
Investment assets	
Certificate of deposit	$500.00
Total investment assets	$500.00
Total Assets	**$9,935.00**
Liabilities	
Balance due on credit card	$2,250.00
Total Liabilities	**$2,250.00**
Net Worth	**$7,685.00**

Calculate

On a separate sheet of paper, create a chart like Jasmine's listing your liquid assets, personal possessions, investment assets, and liabilities. Then determine your net worth. Is your net worth what you expected it to be? Are you ready to make a major purchase? What can you do to change your net worth to be ready for purchases in your future?

CHAPTER 13

Consumer Purchasing and Protection

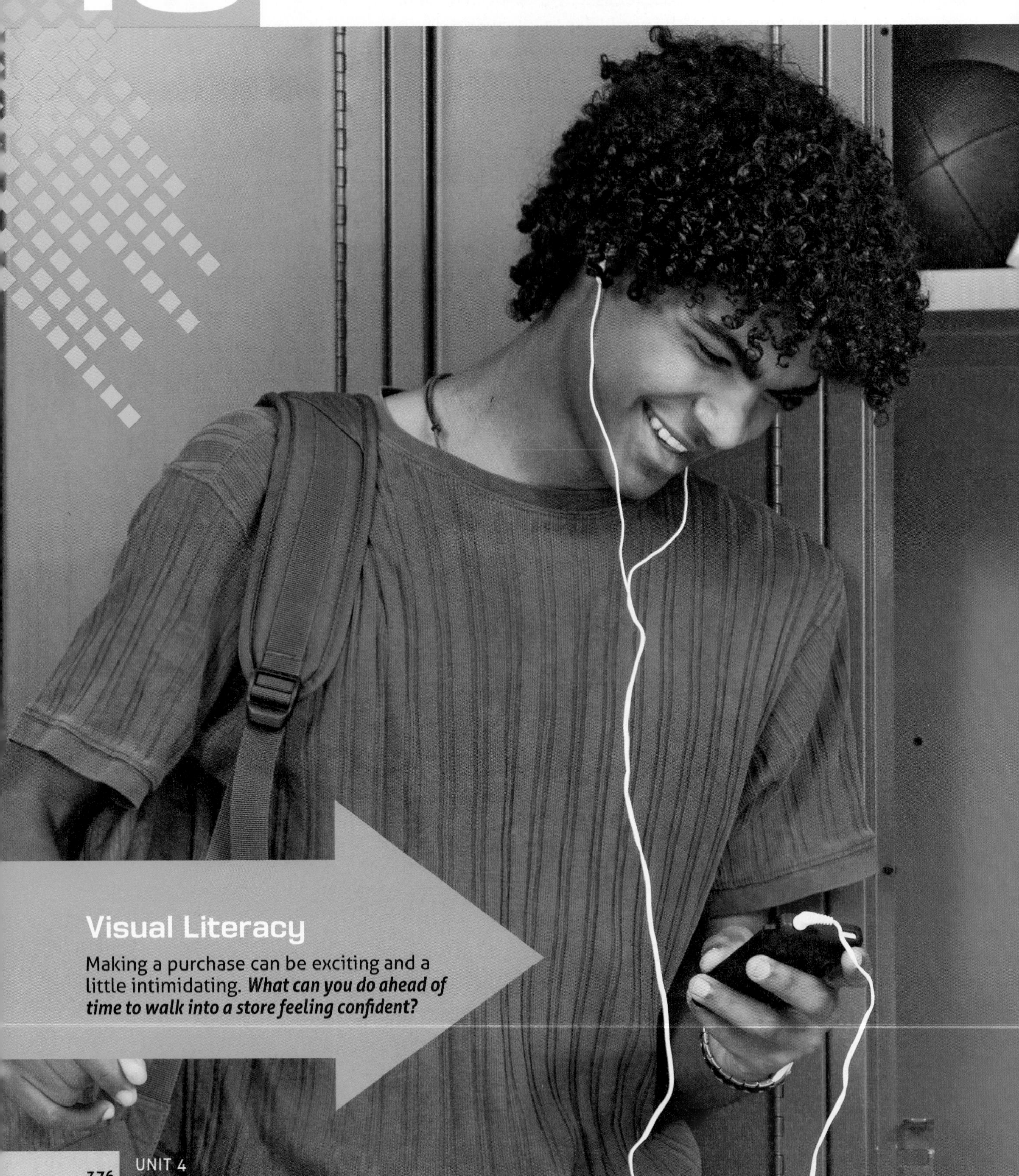

Visual Literacy

Making a purchase can be exciting and a little intimidating. ***What can you do ahead of time to walk into a store feeling confident?***

Discovery Project

Savvy Shopping

Key Question

Why is it important to plan ahead when shopping?

Project Goal

Savvy shopping means getting the most for your money, and it means different things to different people. For some, it means rarely paying full price and always looking for a bargain. For others, it means researching for the best price on the highest quality. A smart idea when shopping for clothes, for example, is that if you are going to spend a significant amount of money on a certain item, it should be high quality and in a classic design. For example, a winter coat, a sturdy pair of work boots, or an item that goes with everything is generally worth the price. Develop a strategy for your next shopping trip that will help you save time, save money, and ensure that you are getting the best value and quality.

Ask Yourself...

- *What are your store options?*
- *How much is your budget?*
- *What can you do before you start shopping?*
- *What can you do during your shopping trip?*
- *What can you do after your purchase to ensure that you get the most for your money?*

Use Systems Thinking

How would you determine the cost per wear of an accessory or item of clothing? How would this information affect your purchasing decisions?

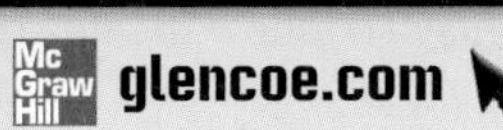

Evaluate Download an assessment rubric.

THE BIG IDEA

Informed consumers know how to get the best value for their money.

ASK STANDARD & POOR'S

Comparison Shopping

Q *I would like to purchase a new stereo. Is it really that important for me to comparison shop?*

A Prices and quality can be very different from one store to another. Particularly with expensive items, it is worthwhile to compare prices on similar items to see if one store has a lower price than the others. If you write down the manufacturer and style information, you can do a lot of this "legwork" by phone or by looking at store advertisements or by doing research on the Internet.

Writing Activity

Research an item that you would like to purchase, such as an entertainment or gaming system, a special occasion outfit, or sports equipment. Where can you get the best deal? What are the advantages and disadvantages of each option? What can you do if the product is defective? Write a summary of your findings.

Reading Guide

Before You Read

The Essential Question How can learning about consumer purchasing and consumer protection benefit you now and in the future?

Main Idea

Understanding the factors that influence your buying decisions can help you get the best value for your money. There are several ways to solve consumer problems, including legal action.

Content Vocabulary

- down payment
- impulse buying
- open dating
- unit pricing
- rebate
- warranty
- service contract
- fraud
- mediation
- arbitration
- small claims court
- class-action suit
- legal aid society

Academic Vocabulary

You will see these words in your reading and on your tests.

- approach
- transactions
- document
- eligible

Graphic Organizer

Before you read this chapter, create an itemized list like the one here. As you read, list six strategies you can use to make informed purchase decisions.

$$ Smart Buying Strategies $$

✔
✔
✔
✔
✔
✔

 glencoe.com  Print this graphic organizer.

Standards

Academic

Mathematics

NCTM Number and Operations Understand meanings of operations and how they relate to one another.
NCTM Problem Solving Solve problems that arise in mathematics and in other contexts.

English Language Arts

NCTE 8 Use information resources to gather information and create and communicate knowledge.
NCTE 12 Use language to accomplish individual purposes.

Science

NSES F Develop an understanding of personal and community health; population growth; natural resources; environmental quality; natural and human-induced hazards; science and technology in local, national, and global challenges.

NCTM *National Council of Teachers of Mathematics*
NCTE *National Council of Teachers of English*
NCSS *National Council for the Social Studies*
NSES *National Science Education Standards*

Common Core

Reading Read and comprehend complex literary and informational texts independently and proficiently.
Speaking and Listening Present information, findings, and supporting evidence such that listeners can follow the line of reasoning and the organization, development, and style are appropriate to task, purpose, and audience.

Factors That Influence Buying Decisions

What influences you to make a purchase?

You may enjoy shopping and do it often, or you might go to the mall only if you need to buy something. In either case, wise buying decisions will help you get the most out of your purchases and will enable you to meet your financial goals. **Figure 1** shows some economic, social, and personal factors that influence purchases.

Marginal Cost and Marginal Benefit

You should consider marginal cost and marginal benefit when making purchasing decisions. Remember, marginal cost is the increase or decrease of the cost of a particular action, and marginal benefit is the increase or decrease of the benefit of a particular action. If two identical items are priced differently, the marginal benefit increases when the lower priced option is selected. If the items were similar but not identical you would have to assess the costs and benefits of purchasing each item. When the marginal cost exceeds the marginal benefit, you should not purchase the item or consider other options.

Trade-Offs and Buying Decisions

To make the most of your buying power, consider trade-offs. Suppose that you buy a sound system with a credit card instead of waiting until you have saved enough money to pay cash for it. You get the pleasure of having the sound system now. However, you might pay a higher price in the long run because of fees and interest the credit card company charges for use of the card.

Perhaps you choose a jacket because it is the cheapest one available. Within a few days, you may discover that it is poorly made or difficult to repair. You may save time by ordering a sweater from a catalog or online. However, if you decide that you do not want it, you may have to pay postage to return it. You might not get your money back for the initial shipping and handling charges. Keep in mind that buying decisions always involve trade-offs, so you will be prepared to make wise choices.

Reading Check

Recognize What are the three factors that influence your purchasing decisions?

Section Objectives

- **Summarize** the factors that influence buying decisions.
- **Describe** marginal cost and marginal benefit.
- **Explain** the phases of a research-based approach to buying goods and services including the role of marginal cost and marginal benefit.
- **List** the types of warranties and their impact.
- **Identify** strategies for making wise buying decisions.

As You Read

Examine What are the economic, social, and personal factors that might influence your car buying decisions?

Economics and You

Consumer Incentives

Businesses provide incentives to encourage consumers to purchase their goods and services. When that incentive is "too good to be true," consider "caveat emptor," which means "let the buyer beware." You must read the fine print to see the restrictions, requirements, or additional actions you need to take in order to qualify for the incentive. For example a discount of $100 off may be the incentive, but it only applies to a specific brand of an item that sells for $1,000 or more. When a product is priced at a very low price and the store sells the item at that low price it is called a loss leader. Loss leaders are legal in most states. However, if you arrive to buy the advertised loss leader and the salesperson tells you that the advertised item is not available and a better version of that product is what you should buy—that is called "bait and switch," and that is against the law.

Personal Finance Connection Whenever you are offered an incentive to buy something it is wise to investigate it first. Do your research to make sure the offer is legitimate.

Critical Thinking Why would a business sell a product as a loss leader if it is not going to make any money on it?

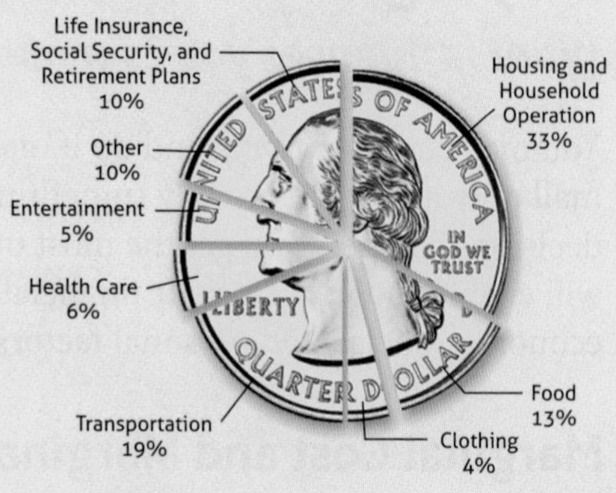

Activity Download an Economics and You Worksheet Activity.

Researching Consumer Purchases

How do you research a product you want to buy?

By taking time to do research and evaluate products you want to buy, you can get more value for your money. By following a research-based **approach,** or method, to buying goods and services, you will gain useful practice in making ordinary purchasing decisions about low-cost items, such as toothpaste. The steps for effective purchasing can also be used for wise buying of major purchases such as motor vehicles.

A research-based approach to buying has four phases:

1. Before you shop—includes preshopping activities such as setting goals and gathering information from other sources
2. Weighing alternatives—includes comparing product features, analyzing prices, and evaluating shopping locations.
3. Making the purchase—includes negotiating lower prices, analyzing payment options, and determining how to acquire the item.
4. After the purchase—includes operating and maintaining the item properly, evaluating post-purchase options, and resolving any purchase concerns.

PHASE 1 Before You Shop

Before you can begin to construct the walls of a house, you need to lay its foundation. In the same way, before you begin to shop, you need to do some background work. A good start to successful shopping involves three steps: identifying your needs, gathering information, and becoming aware of the marketplace. Completing these steps will enable you to get what you really want.

Identify Your Needs Effective decision making should start with an open mind. Some people always buy the same brand when another brand at a lower price would also serve their needs, or when another brand at the same price may provide better quality. If you define your needs clearly, you will be more likely to make the best buying decisions. Remember to evaluate marginal cost and marginal benefit when evaluating needs.

Gather Information The better informed you are, the better buying decisions you will make. For example, suppose that Sarah loses her watch on a white-water rafting trip. She might be able to borrow a watch from a friend for a day or two, but eventually she will need to buy a new watch. To begin her research, she should gather information on the different models and prices of watches.

Information for buying decisions usually falls into three categories: costs, options, and consequences. Sarah might ask questions related to cost, such as "What do watches cost at different stores?" Her options will depend on the brands that the manufacturers produce and where those brands are available. Sarah will also have to consider consequences—how the purchase will affect her budget.

FIGURE 1 Influences on Buying Decisions

Lifetime Financial Adjustments Economic, social, and personal factors vary during the course of a lifetime, but they always have an influence on making financial decisions. *Which factors would be most significant for a married couple who just had their first child?*

Economic Factors	Social Factors	Personal Factors
• Prices	• Lifestyle	• Gender
• Interest rates	• Interests	• Age
• Product quality	• Hobbies	• Occupation
• Supply and demand	• Friends	• Income
• Convenience	• Culture	• Education
• Product safety	• Advertisements	• Family size
• Brand name	• Media (magazines, radio, television, newspapers)	• Geographic region
• Maintenance costs		• Ethnic background
• Warranty		• Religion

Some people do not spend enough time gathering and evaluating information. Others do so much research that they become confused and frustrated. Simple, routine purchases probably do not require much more research than your own experience can provide. Other resources include product advertising and labeling, media sources, consumer publications, such as *Consumer Reports*, government agencies, or the Internet. **Figure 2** illustrates some of these resources. As you research and gather information, take notes on what you learn. Having a written record of the information you collect can be helpful in making comparisons later.

Be Aware of the Marketplace Knowledge is power. Research provides sources for the item you want to buy. In addition, you will be able to identify the make, brand, and features from which you can choose, average prices for an item, and where you can obtain reliable information about similar products or models. Familiarize yourself with common myths about sales, returns, and credits in **Figure 3.**

PHASE 2 Weighing the Alternatives

Every consumer decision may be approached in several effective ways. Instead of buying an item, for example, you might decide to rent it, borrow it, or do without it. You also have alternatives to spending

FIGURE 2 Consumer Information Sources

Information is Power You can gather information to help with purchasing decisions from a variety of sources. *What should you verify before accepting the information from these sources?*

People you know might be able to provide insight on a product's performance, quality, and average price.

Ads and packaging can tell you a lot about a product, so be sure to read the labels.

cash for it. You might take advantage of special deals that allow you to delay payment, or you might choose to pay with a credit card.

Identify What Is Important to You As you evaluate alternatives, decide which characteristics—such as features, performance, or design—are important to you. As you research, you will recognize the characteristics that most closely match your needs. Then evaluate the marginal cost and marginal benefit of each option. You can judge a potential purchase by considering the following factors:

- Your personal values
- Available time for research
- Amount of money you have to spend
- Convenience of buying the item immediately
- Pros and cons of a particular manufacturer

When making a major purchase such as a car you will have to consider a variety of options that will affect the price of the vehicle. Optional equipment for cars can be viewed in three main categories:

- Mechanical devices to improve performance, such as a larger engine, anti-lock brakes, and cruise control
- Convenience options including stereo systems and tinted glass
- Visual options that add to the vehicle's visual appeal

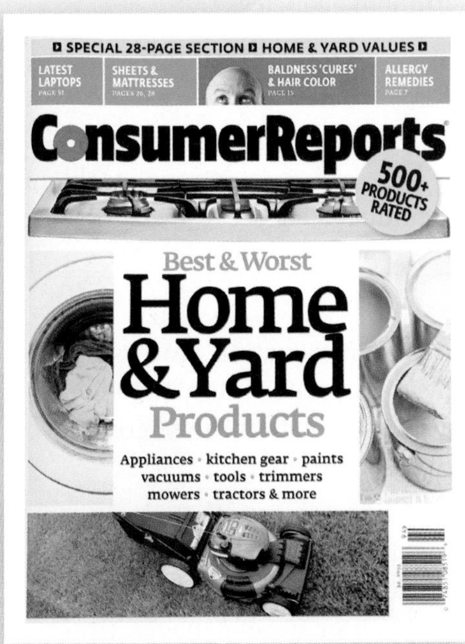

Reports issued by the media and independent testing organizations on the quality of products and services are usually valuable, easily available, and inexpensive.

Web sites for companies, magazines, newspapers, and government agencies have product information and shopping suggestions.

COMMON CENTS

Impulse Buying

Too much impulse buying can ruin a budget. When you are tempted to buy clothes, cool sneakers, CDs, or anything else that you really do not need, give yourself a two-day cool-down period. If you decide you really want it, you can go back to the store and buy it. However, chances are that most things will not seem as necessary a few days later.

Concept Application

How would you plan your budget to allow for some impulse buying?

Compare Prices The price of an item is an important consideration. Prices can vary for all types of products. For example, a watch may cost as little as $15 or as much as $500. Differences in price may be related to quality, but price does not always equal quality. When the quality and quantity are basically the same for an item such as aspirin, sugar, or salt, the lowest-priced item is probably the wisest choice.

When prices and quality vary, you have two options. If you can afford all choices, you can buy the highest-quality item. If not, you should consider buying the item that provides the best value.

Do Comparison Shopping Comparison shopping means you compare prices and features of similar items at different stores. Many people consider comparison shopping a waste of time. However, it can be very useful, especially when making major purchases.

For example, price and features are important considerations when purchasing a motor vehicle. The average used car costs about $10,000 less than the average new car. Common sources of used cars include:

- New-car dealers offer late-model vehicles and may give you a warranty. Prices are usually higher than at other sources.
- Used-car dealers usually have older vehicles. Warranties may be limited or unavailable, but prices are usually lower.
- Individuals selling their own cars can be a bargain if the vehicle was well maintained. Few consumer protection laws apply to these **transactions,** or dealings, so use caution.
- Auctions and dealers that sell cars previously owned by businesses, auto rental companies, and government agencies
- Used-car superstores offer a large inventory of previously owned vehicles.

The appearance of a used car can be deceptive, or misleading. For example, a clean, shiny exterior may hide major operational problems. Be sure to have a trained mechanic conduct a used-car inspection.

PHASE 3 Making the Purchase

After you have completed the research and evaluation process, some other activities and decisions may be appropriate. These include negotiating the price (if possible), deciding whether to use credit or cash, and determining the real price of the product.

Negotiate the Price Certain purchases, such as real estate or cars, may involve price negotiation. To negotiate, research information about the product and the buying situation. Be sure that you are dealing with the person, such as the owner or store manager, who has authority to give you a lower price or additional features.

When negotiating the price of a used car, begin to determine a fair price by checking newspaper ads for the prices of comparable vehicles. Other sources of current used-car prices are *Edmund's Used Car Prices* and *Kelley Blue Book.*

FIGURE 3 Common Consumer Myths

Fact or Fiction? When stories are told over and over again, such as these common consumer beliefs, people tend to accept them as facts. *What can happen to consumers when such myths are allowed to persist?*

Here are some common consumer myths:

"I can return my car within three days of purchase." While many people would say that this statement is true, there is no such time period at most dealers.

"It says right here I've won; it must be true." Fake prize notifications continue to become more convincing. Some consumers actually go to company offices to try to pick up their prizes.

"If I lose my credit cards, I'm liable for purchases." Federal laws limit charges on lost or stolen cards to $50. Most major credit card companies will not even charge you the $50 if you make a reasonable effort to notify the company quickly of lost or stolen cards.

"An auto lease is just like a rental; if I have problems with the car or problems paying, I can just bring it back." Most leases require payments for the duration of the contract. Early termination of the contract can often result in various additional charges.

"You can't repossess my car; it's on private property." While state laws vary, the general rule is that repossession cannot occur if it involves force or entry into a dwelling. However, vehicles in driveways and unlocked garages are usually fair game.

Source: "Ten Top Consumer Law 'Urban Myths,'" National Association of Consumer Agency Administrators

A number of factors influence the basic price of a used car. The number of miles the car has been driven, along with the features and options, affect price. A low-mileage car will have a higher price than a comparable car with high mileage. The condition of the vehicle and the demand for the model also affect price.

When negotiating the price of a new car, the sticker price label printed on the vehicle is your price information source. This label shows the base price of the car with the costs of added features. The dealer's cost is an amount less than the sticker price. The difference between the sticker price and the dealer's cost is the range available for negotiation. Information about dealer's cost is available from *Edmund's New Car Prices* and *Consumer Reports*.

Comparing Financing Options When making a purchase, you usually have two options—pay credit or cash. You need to consider the costs and benefits of each one.

Credit is an arrangement to buy something now and pay for it later. It is a type of loan. To repay the loan, you make monthly payments that often include additional fees or interest. The advantage of paying cash is that you do not have to pay these extra fees or make continuing payments. However, because the cash is no longer in your bank account, you lose the opportunity to earn interest on it. In addition, the money is no longer available for emergencies.

Before deciding to use credit, evaluate its costs, such as interest rates and fees. These costs will differ depending on various factors:

- Source of the loan (for example, parents, bank, or credit card company)
- Type of credit account
- Payment period
- Amount of **down payment**—a portion of the total cost of an item that must be paid at the time of purchase

You may pay cash; however, most people buy cars on credit. Auto loans are available from banks, credit unions, consumer finance companies, and other financial institutions. Many lenders will preapprove you for a certain loan amount, which separates negotiating the price from financing.

The lowest interest rate or the lowest payment does not necessarily mean the best credit plan. Also consider the loan length. Otherwise, after two or three years, the value of your car may be less than the amount you still owe. This is referred to as negative equity.

Leasing a car is another financing option. Leasing is a contractual agreement with monthly payments for the use of the automobile over a set time period. At the end of the lease term, you may return the vehicle to the leasing company, purchase the vehicle, or sell the vehicle. (See **Figure 4.**)

Document Detective 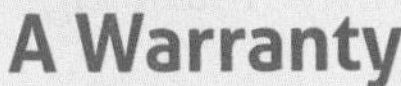

A Warranty

Before making a purchase, you should read the product's warranty to understand exactly what protections the manufacturer offers you. A warranty is an assurance from the seller to the buyer that a product will perform as promised, or it will be replaced or repaired. A warranty for a product contains the following information:

- Name of the seller or manufacturer
- Name of product
- Terms of the warranty
- Instructions for how to get service

FREE FLOW® ONE-YEAR LIMITED WARRANTY

FREE FLOW® plumbing fixture, faucets, and fittings are warranted to be free of defects in material and workmanship for one year from date of installation.

Free Flow will, at its election, repair, replace, or make appropriate adjustments where Free Flow inspection discloses any such defects occurring in normal usage within one year after installation. Free Flow is not responsible for removal or installation costs.

To obtain warranty service, contact Free Flow either through your dealer, plumbing contractor, home center or e-tailer, or by writing to Free Flow, Attn: Customer Service Department, 2525 Highland Drive, Glenview, WI 53044, USA.

IMPLIED WARRANTIES INCLUDING THAT OF MERCHANTABILITY AND FITNESS FOR A PARTICULAR PURPOSE ARE EXPRESSLY LIMITED IN DURATION TO THE DURATION OF THIS WARRANTY. FREE FLOW DISCLAIMS ANY LIABILITY FOR SPECIAL, INCIDENTAL, OR CONSEQUENTIAL DAMAGES. Some states/provinces do not allow limitations on how long an implied warranty lasts, or the exclusion or limitation of special, incidental, or consequential damages so these limitations and exclusions may not apply to you. This warranty gives you specific legal rights. You may also have other rights, which vary from state/province to state/province.

This is our exclusive written warranty.

Notes:
1. There may be variation in color fidelity between catalog images and actual plumbing fixtures.
2. Free Flow reserves the right to make changes in product characteristics, packaging, or availability at any time without notice.

Copyright © 2010.

Key Points A warranty usually covers defects in materials and workmanship, and promises that the product will work properly under normal circumstances. It does not usually cover defects that occur due to the user's carelessness or inappropriate use of the product. It also explains how a buyer can resolve any problems.

FIND the Solutions

Review Key Concepts

1. For how many years are Free Flow fixtures covered by this warranty?
2. If you purchased a Free Flow faucet in November of 2010 and installed it in August of 2011, when would the warranty expire?
3. What will Free Flow do if a product is defective?
4. Who is responsible for the cost of removing a defective faucet and replacing it?
5. If a faucet is replaced under this warranty, will it be the same model faucet?

Innovation

To innovate is to create something new for the first time. This could be a new concept, method, or invention. Innovation can come in small increments or in large advances. For businesses, innovation can create business opportunities. A company can create new products and services or change the competitive landscape. Consider how Apple Computer changed the competitive environment with its iPod, iTunes, iPhone, and iPad innovations.

Write About It

Think of a scenario in which having an innovative mind-set would help you at school. Write one or more paragraphs to describe the scenario and explain how taking an innovative approach would have a positive influence on the situation.

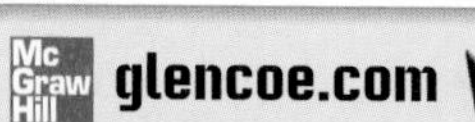

Activity Download a Career and College Readiness Worksheet Activity.

Leasing offers several advantages:

- Only a small cash payment may be required for the deposit.
- Monthly lease payments are usually lower than monthly financing payments.
- You are usually able to obtain a more expensive vehicle more often.

Leasing also has several drawbacks:

- You have no ownership interest in the vehicle.
- You must meet requirements similar to qualifying for credit.
- Additional costs may be incurred for extra mileage, certain repairs, turning the car in early, or even a move to another state.

Know the Real Price Sometimes you may discover that what appears to be a bargain is not such a good deal after extra costs are added to the price. Stores may charge you a fee for installation or delivery. Find out exactly what the purchase price includes and get all costs and conditions in writing.

PHASE 4 After the Purchase

After making a purchase, you may have other costs or tasks. A car, for example, will require additional maintenance and ownership costs. If your car requires repair service, you should follow a process similar to the one you used when you bought the car—investigate, evaluate, and negotiate a variety of servicing options.

Over your lifetime, you can expect to spend more than $200,000 on automobile related expenses. Your driving costs will vary based on two main factors: the size of your vehicle and the number of miles you drive. Costs can be divided into two categories: fixed ownership costs and variable operating costs. Fixed ownership costs include depreciation, interest on the loan, insurance, and various fees such as license and registration fees. Variable operating costs include gas and oil; tires; maintenance and repairs; and parking and tolls.

People who sell, repair, or drive vehicles for a living stress the importance of regular care. While owner's manuals suggest mileage or time intervals for certain services, more frequent oil changes or tune-ups can maximize vehicle life. Maintenance areas to consider are:

- Regular oil changes every 3,000 miles
- Check fluids
- Inspect hoses and belts for wear
- Get a tune-up every 15,000 miles
- Check and clean battery terminals and cables
- Check spark plug wires after 50,000 miles
- Flush radiator and service transmission every 25,000 miles
- Keep lights, turn signals, and horn in good working condition
- Check muffler and exhaust pipes

- Check tires for wear and rotate tires every 7,500 miles
- Check condition of brakes

Remember to deal with reputable auto service businesses. Be sure to get a written, detailed estimate in advance as well as a detailed, paid receipt for the service completed. Studies of consumer problems consistently rank auto repairs as one of the top consumer rip-offs. It is important to know how to handle complaints effectively. The next section explains how to resolve consumer complaints.

Remember that the purchasing process is an ongoing activity. You should rethink and reevaluate your decisions. The information that you gather before you shop, along with your previous buying experiences, will help you make decisions in the future. Also, be sure to consider changes in your needs, lifestyle, values, goals, and financial resources.

Reading Check

Compare What are the advantages and drawbacks of leasing a car?

FIGURE 4 **Buying vs. Leasing**

Do Your Homework To compare the costs of purchasing and leasing a vehicle, use the following sample framework. *Why might a person who uses his or her car for work-related travel choose to purchase rather than lease a car?*

Total vehicle cost, including sales tax ($20,000)		Lease Security deposit ($300)	
Purchasing Costs	**Example**	**Leasing Costs**	**Example**
Down payment (or full amount if paying cash)	$2,000	Monthly lease payments: $385 × 36-month length of lease	$13,860
Monthly loan payment: $385 × 48-month length of financing (this item is zero if vehicle is not financed)	18,480	Opportunity cost of security deposit: $300 security deposit × 3 years × 3 percent	27
Opportunity cost of down payment (or total cost of the vehicle if it is bought for cash): $2,000 × 4 years of financing/ownership × 3 percent	240	End-of-lease charges* (if applicable)	800
Less: Estimated value of vehicle at end of loan term/ownership period	–6,000	Total cost to lease	**$14,687**
Total cost to buy	**$14,720**		

*Such as charges for extra mileage.

Smart Buying Strategies

How can you make an informed purchase decision?

Remember, daily buying decisions involve a trade-off between current spending and saving for the future. A wide variety of economic, social, and personal factors affect daily buying habits. These factors are the basis for achieving personal financial goals. For example, Gordon looks for ways to save on the brands he buys regularly. Anita and Roger buy the lowest-priced brands or look for bargains.

Whatever your style, several strategies can help you get the most value for your dollar—timing of purchases, store selection, brand comparison, information research, price comparison, and warranty evaluation.

Timing Purchases

You are more likely to find a bargain at certain times of the year. Stores traditionally offer reduced prices for seasonal clothing, such as swimsuits and overcoats, about midway through a particular season. You can also find reduced prices at back-to-school sales and other special sales. Timing your purchases can result in big savings.

The law of supply and demand can also affect the timing of purchases. For example, if you wait a few months before buying a popular new CD or DVD, the price may be lower than it was when it first came out because the demand for the item has decreased. When businesses want to reduce the supply of a product, they have clearance sales.

Store Selection

The quality and variety of goods as well as the price at a store may influence your decision to shop there. Store selection may affect the value of the products you purchase. You may also choose a retail store because of its hours, location, reputation, policies, and services such as parking and delivery. **Figure 5** provides an overview of the major types of retailers—businesses that sell directly to consumers.

Over the years, several alternatives to store shopping have emerged. One alternative is the cooperative, a nonprofit organization owned and operated by its members for the purpose of saving money on the purchase of goods and services. Because a cooperative buys large amounts of goods, it can lower prices for its members. The main drawback to cooperatives is that they offer few customer services.

Another alternative to store shopping is direct selling, which includes mail order, TV home shopping, and online shopping. An advantage of these types of shopping is the convenience of not having to leave home. Online shopping sometimes offers lower prices, and you may find excellent product information on the Internet. The possible disadvantages of online direct selling are paying for shipping and handling and difficulty in returning purchases.

Canada

Financial Consumer Agency of Canada

To be a smart consumer, you must first be an educated consumer. The Canadian government developed the Financial Consumer Agency of Canada (FCAC) in an effort to protect and inform consumers in the area of financial services. Over the years, the agency has expanded their services to include a MoneyTools Web site which gives consumers information that helps them shop for financial products and services.

In 2008, the agency launched a financial education Web site, called The Money Belt, aimed specifically at Canadian youth aged 15 to 29. This site offers a wide range of resources for both teachers and students, including links to other financial education programs. The Money Belt helps make the basics of the financial world and personal money management understandable to young consumers. The topics covered include credit cards, bank accounts, credit history, and saving money. In addition to offering practical information and tips, the site also has interactive tools to help youth become money savvy.

Critical Thinking

1. **Expand** Research the Money Belt Web site. What four financial education resources links are available through The Money Belt?
2. **Relate** Review the Quick Tips offered on The Money Belt. Do you feel that these tips are equally relevant in America as they are in Canada? Do you think the United States should offer a similar Web site for financial education of youth?

DATABYTES

Capital
Ottawa

Population
33, 487, 208

Language
English, French

Currency
Canadian dollar

Gross Domestic Product (GDP)
$1.335 trillion

GDP per capita
$38, 400

Industry
Transportation equipment, chemicals, processed and unprocessed minerals, food products, wood and paper products, fish products, petroleum and natural gas

Agriculture
Wheat, barley, oilseed, fruits, vegetables, dairy products, forest products, fish

Exports
Motor vehicles and parts, industrial machinery, aircraft, telecommunications equipment, chemicals, plastics, fertilizers, wood pulp, timber, crude petroleum, natural gas, electricity, aluminum

Natural Resources
Iron ore, nickel, zinc, copper, gold, lead, molybdenum, potash, diamonds, silver, fish, timber, wildlife, coal, petroleum, natural gas, hydropower

Brand Comparison

Most items are sold under a number of well-known brand names that identify the products and their manufacturers. National-brand products are widely advertised and available in many stores. Although they are usually more expensive than non-brand products, national brands usually offer consistent quality or value for your money.

A store-brand, or generic, product is usually sold by one chain of stores and carries the name of that chain on its label. Because store-brand products are often made by the same companies that make national-brand products, their quality is good. However, because they do not carry a brand-name label, they are less expensive.

When you compare brands, remember to consider price and quality. Plan what you are going to buy before you shop and take a list of what you need. Displays may attract your attention and lead to **impulse buying,** which is purchasing items on the spur of the moment. Impulse buying may be fun, but it can cost you more. Also, you may buy products that you do not really need.

Label Information Research

Labels on product packages typically include a great deal of advertising. However, federal laws also require labels to present factual information. For example, food labels must indicate the common name of the product, the name and address of the manufacturer or distributor, the net weight of the product, and a list of the ingredients in decreasing order of weight.

In addition, labels on almost all processed foods must have nutritional information and the specific amounts of nutrients and food substances in the product. Some foods are advertised as being "low in fat" or "high in fiber." Foods must meet government criteria to be labeled with such terms. Manufacturers can include health claims on product packages only if they have scientific evidence to support the claims.

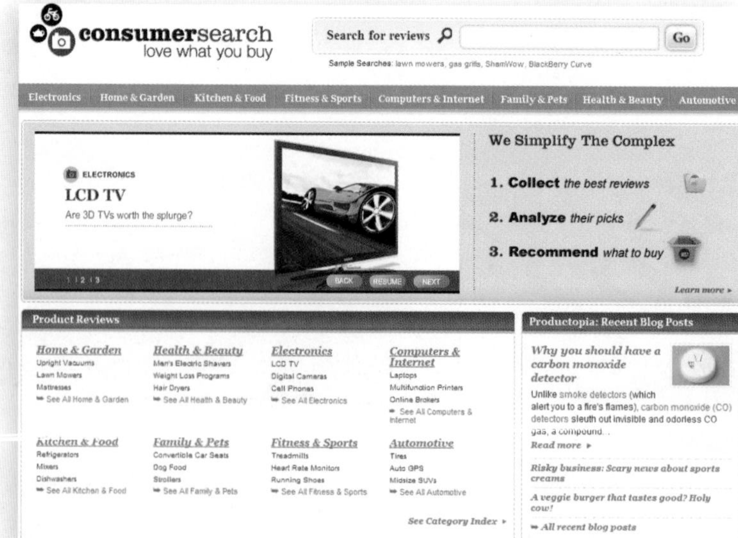

Take Advantage
Consumer Web sites such as the one shown provide a wealth of information for consumers including product reviews. *How would you begin your research for a purchase?*

FIGURE 5 **Types of Retailers**

Shop Around Consumers have a choice of many different types of stores, each of which has pros and cons. *How can competition among stores benefit consumers?*

Traditional Stores	Benefits	Limitations
Department stores	• Wide variety of products grouped by department	• Possible inexperience or limited knowledge of sales staff
Specialty stores	• Wide selection of a specific product line; knowledgeable sales staff	• Prices generally higher; location and shopping hours may not be convenient
Discount stores	• Convenient parking; low prices	• Self-service format; minimal assistance from sales staff
Contemporary Retailers		
Convenience stores	• Convenient location; long hours; fast service	• Prices generally higher than those of other types of retail outlets
Factory outlet	• Brand-name items; low prices	• May offer only "seconds" or "irregulars"; few services; returns may not be allowed
Hypermarket	• Full supermarket combined with general merchandise discount store	• Clerks not likely to offer specialized service or product information
Warehouse, Superstore	• Large quantities of items at discount prices	• May require membership fee; limited services; inventory items may vary

To help consumers determine the freshness of some foods, manufacturers print dates on the labels. **Open dating** is a labeling method that indicates the freshness, or shelf life, of a perishable product, such as milk or bread.

Product labels for appliances, such as refrigerators and washing machines, include information about operating costs, which identify the most energy-efficient models.

Price Comparison

Unit pricing is the use of a standard unit of measurement to compare the prices of packages that are different sizes. For example, Claudia went to the drugstore to buy a bottle of mouthwash and noticed that her favorite brand came in two sizes at different prices. The best way for her to determine which one is the better buy is to use unit pricing. Most grocery stores and drugstores display the unit pricing information for the products they sell. If a store does not provide this information, you can calculate the unit price by dividing the price of the item by the unit of measurement such as ounces, pounds, gallons, or number of sheets (for tissues and paper towels).

Honest Branding
"Reduced calorie," "low in fat and sugar," and "light" or "lite" are common, attention-getting claims on food and drink labels, but the products must meet government criteria to be labeled with such terms. *Why do you think this type of regulation is necessary?*

For example, an 8-ounce can of frozen orange juice that costs $1.60 has a unit price of 20 cents per ounce.

When you know how to calculate the unit price, you can compare the unit prices for various sizes, brands, and stores. Keep in mind that the package with the lowest unit price may not be the best buy for your situation. For example, a 10-pound bag of potatoes might have the lowest unit price, but they may spoil before you can use them.

Two common ways to save money are to take advantage of discount coupons and manufacturers' rebates. By using discount coupons, you save money on products at the time you purchase them. There are many online resources for finding coupons. A **rebate** is a partial refund of the price of a product. To obtain a rebate, you usually have to submit a form, the original receipt, and the package's UPC symbol, or bar code. When comparing prices, the following guidelines can be very helpful:

- More convenience usually means higher prices.
- Ready-to-use products usually have higher prices.
- Large packages are usually the best buy; use unit pricing to compare brands, sizes, and stores.
- Buying items "on sale" may not always mean that you save money; the sale price at one store may be higher than the regular price at another store.

Warranty Evaluation

Many products come with a guarantee of quality called a warranty. A **warranty** is a written guarantee from the manufacturer or distributor that states the conditions under which the product can be returned, replaced, or repaired. Federal law requires sellers of products that cost more than $15 (and that have a warranty) to make the warranty available to customers before purchase. The warranty is often printed directly on the package.

GO FIGURE Mathematics

Unit Pricing

Knowing the unit price of an item can help you determine the best buy.

EXAMPLE The brand of peppermint mouthwash that Claudia likes is offered in two sizes, 12 ounces for $2.89 and 16 ounces for $3.39. Which is the better buy?

Formula Total Price/Unit of Measurement = Unit Price
Solution $2.89/12 oz. = $0.24 oz.
$3.39/16 oz. = $0.21 oz.
The 16-ounce size is the better buy at 21 cents per ounce.

Your Turn

You are considering buying bottles of lemonade for your sister's birthday party. The market is offering a six-pack of 12-ounce bottles for $2.99 and a liter bottle for $1.29. Which is the better buy? (Hint: One liter equals 33.8 ounces.)

Types of Warranties Warranties are divided into two basic types: implied and express. *Implied warranties* are unwritten guarantees that cover certain aspects of a product or its use. An implied warranty of merchantability guarantees that a product is fit for its intended use. For example, a toaster will toast bread, or a CD player will play CDs.

Express warranties, which are usually written, come in two forms. A full warranty states that a defective product will be fixed or replaced at no charge during a reasonable amount of time. A limited warranty covers only certain aspects of the product, such as parts. This type may also require the buyer to pay a portion of the shipping or repair charges.

When you buy a product, you may be offered a **service contract,** which is a separately purchased agreement by the manufacturer or distributor to cover the costs of repairing the item. Service contracts are sometimes called *extended warranties*, but they are not really warranties. You have to pay a fee to obtain a service contract. These contracts insure the buyer against losses not included in the manufacturer's warranty or that occur after the manufacturer's warranty has expired. Service contracts can range from $400 to over $1,000; however, they do not always include everything you might expect. Make sure to read what is covered before purchasing a service contract. Such contracts are generally offered on large, expensive items, such as cars and home appliances.

Because of the costs and exclusions, service contracts are not always worth the cost. You can minimize your concern about expensive repairs by setting aside a fund of money to pay for them. Then, if you need repairs, the money to pay for them will be available. This action can be considered "self-insurance."

Smart shoppers know when to buy, where to buy, what to buy, and how much to pay. In the next section, you will learn some additional rules for smart shoppers: how to resolve consumer complaints and how to use the law to ensure that your rights as a consumer are protected.

Assessment

Review Key Concepts

1. **Summarize** What are the factors that influence buying decisions and what is their impact?
2. **Explain** What are the phases of a research-based approach to buying goods and services? What is the role of marginal cost and marginal benefit in this approach?
3. **Identify** What are the strategies for making wise buying decisions? How do marginal cost and marginal benefit impact decisions?
4. **Describe** What are the types of warranties and contracts? How do they impact purchase decisions?

Higher Order Thinking H.O.T.

5. **Determine** Many consumers are drawn to designer products, brand names, and widely recognized logos, regardless of cost. What are some reasons for this? What are some alternatives?

21st Century Skills

6. **Access and Evaluate Information** Shopping online offers convenience, a variety of products and choices not limited by geographic location, and ease of use. Yet many people limit their online purchases to books, music downloads, and airline tickets. Explain why you would or would not buy these items online:
   1. Expensive tennis shoes
   2. A cell phone
   3. A dress or suit for the prom
   4. Flowers for your mother
   5. Tickets to see your favorite band
   6. A computer
   7. Groceries
   8. A tennis racket

Mathematics

7. **Unit Pricing** Tyler's class is having a class picnic. He has signed up to bring water and cups. Tyler went to the grocery store to buy the water and found that he had a couple of options. The store had 5 gallon water jugs selling for $11.95. They also had cases of $\frac{1}{2}$ liter bottles selling for $8.99. Which option should Tyler choose in order to get the best deal? Note: Each case contains 24 bottles. $\frac{1}{2}$ liter is equivalent to 16.9 ounces, and 1 gallon is equivalent to 128 ounces.

Math Concept **Calculate Price per Unit** To calculate the unit price of water you must first determine a common unit of measure, and then convert the given options to this common unit of measure in order to appropriately compare.

Starting Hint Determine the number of ounces in the water jug by multiplying the number of gallons by the number of ounces per gallon. Divide the price of the jug by the total number of ounces to attain the unit price.

NCTM Number and Operations Understand meanings of operations and how they relate to one another.

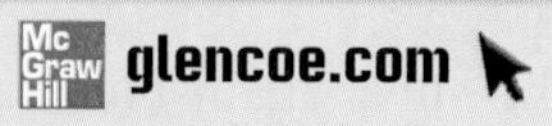

Check your answers.

Sources of Consumer Complaints

What are some examples of consumer complaints?

When you purchase a product, you do not expect to have any problems with it, especially if you have done research and considered the alternatives. Unfortunately, every purchase involves some degree of risk.

Most customer dissatisfaction results from products that are defective or of poor quality. Consumers also complain about unexpected costs, deceptive pricing, and unsatisfactory repair service. Another source of consumer complaints is **fraud**—dishonest business practices that are meant to deceive, trick, or gain an unfair advantage.

Common Types of Fraud

Every year millions of consumers become victims of unethical people who use dishonest business practices to trick or cheat buyers. Experts estimate that fraud costs consumers tens of billions of dollars annually.

As a consumer, you must be aware of various types of fraud. Telephone and mail scams may offer you phony free prizes, travel packages, work-at-home schemes, and investment opportunities. Fraudulent diet products and other remedies attract consumers with phrases such as "scientific breakthrough" or "miraculous cure." The best way to protect yourself from consumer fraud is to recognize it before you become a victim—and to report it if you see it happening.

Reading Check

Recognize What are some examples of fraud?

Section Objectives

- **Explain** the common reasons that lead to consumer complaints.
- **Identify** ways to solve consumer problems.
- **Describe** the legal alternatives for consumers.

As You Read

Recall Have you ever been dissatisfied with the purchase of a good or service? What did you do?

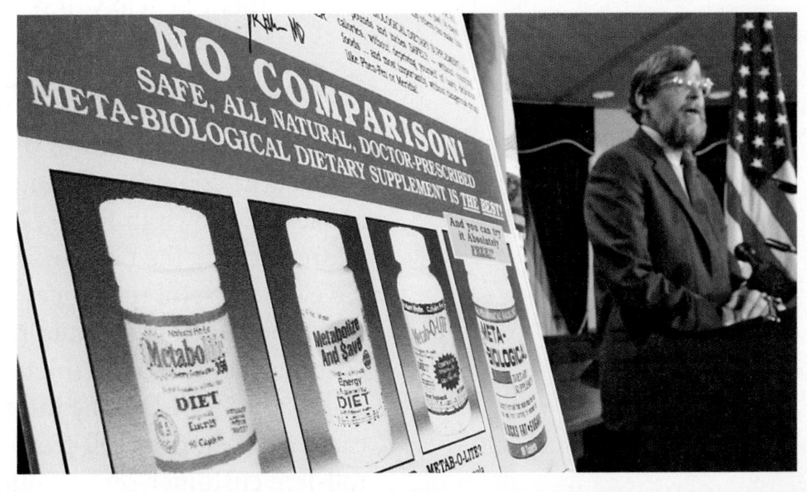

Buyer Beware
Many advertisements, whether in print or online, appeal to the "quick fix" that so many consumers crave. *What should you ask yourself when evaluating an advertisement for a health product?*

Keeping Track
If you experience a problem with a product, it is essential that you document the steps you have taken to resolve it. *What types of records should you keep?*

Resolving Differences Between Buyers and Sellers

What is the best way to resolve a dispute over goods or services?

If you are dissatisfied with a product or service and decide to make a complaint, remember to **document,** or record, the process. Keep a file of receipts, names of people you talk to, dates of attempted repairs, copies of letters you write, and any fees that you have had to pay. Resolving complaints with a business can be handled in five different ways.

Return to the Place of Purchase

Most consumers can resolve their complaints at the original place of purchase. Most businesses care about having a reputation for honesty and fairness and will usually do what is necessary to settle reasonable complaints. Remember to bring sales receipts and other relevant information. Also, keep calm and avoid yelling or threatening the salespeople or managers. Explain the problem as clearly as possible, and ask them to help you resolve it.

Contact Company Headquarters

If you cannot resolve your problem at the local store or business, contact the company's headquarters. Sending a complaint letter such as the one shown in **Figure 6** can be effective. To find a company's address, check the *Consumer's Resource Handbook*. Your library may have other useful references as well. Company Web sites are also good sources. If you would rather talk to someone in the company's customer service department but do not know the telephone number, call 1-800-555-1212, the information number. Your library may also carry a directory of toll-free numbers. Some companies print their toll-free customer-service numbers on their packages.

Consumer Agency Assistance

If the company is not providing the answers you seek, get help from various consumer, business, and government organizations. These groups include national organizations that deal with issues such as nutrition and automobile safety as well as local organizations.

Among the best-known consumer agencies is the Better Business Bureau, a network of offices around the country sponsored by local business organizations. These bureaus deal with complaints against local merchants. However, the merchants are under no obligation to respond to those complaints. Therefore, the bureaus are most useful before you buy a product. They can tell you about the experiences other consumers have had with a certain store or company.

FIGURE 6 **Sample Complaint Letter**

Put It In Writing Sending a letter to a company's headquarters can produce results when you want to resolve a consumer complaint. *When should you take this step to resolve a problem?*

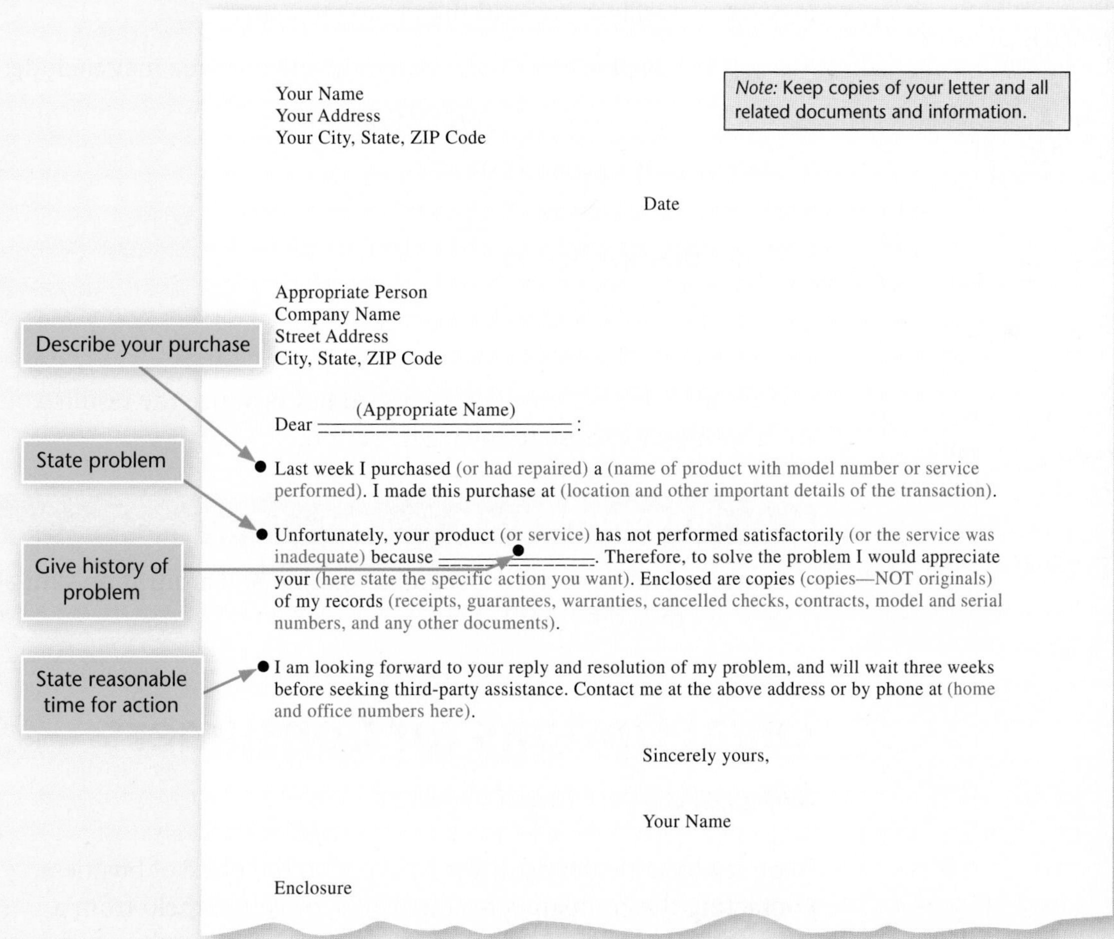

Your Name
Your Address
Your City, State, ZIP Code

Date

Appropriate Person
Company Name
Street Address
City, State, ZIP Code

Dear (Appropriate Name):

• Last week I purchased (or had repaired) a (name of product with model number or service performed). I made this purchase at (location and other important details of the transaction).

• Unfortunately, your product (or service) has not performed satisfactorily (or the service was inadequate) because ________. Therefore, to solve the problem I would appreciate your (here state the specific action you want). Enclosed are copies (copies—NOT originals) of my records (receipts, guarantees, warranties, cancelled checks, contracts, model and serial numbers, and any other documents).

• I am looking forward to your reply and resolution of my problem, and will wait three weeks before seeking third-party assistance. Contact me at the above address or by phone at (home and office numbers here).

Sincerely yours,

Your Name

Enclosure

Source: *Consumer's Resource Handbook,* reprinted by permission of Diana Publishing Co., Collingdale, PA.

reality bytes

Big Mac Index
Should the dollar amount it costs to purchase a Big Mac in the United States equal the cost of a Big Mac in another country? The Big Mac index is published by *The Economist* and is a method for evaluating the purchasing power of currencies around the world. It is based on the idea that the exact same product should cost the same in two different countries. Exchange rates and the value of the dollar constantly fluctuate. The index is a way of determining whether a country's currency is over- or under-valued. For example, suppose a Big Mac costs $3.75 in the U.S. and 250 yen in Japan. If the exchange rate for the Japanese yen is 90 yen for every dollar, then the Big Mac in Japan costs $2.78. According to the Big Mac Index, the yen is under-valued because a Big Mac costs less in Japan. The value of the yen against the dollar would need to increase to make the costs equal.

Government Agencies A large network of local, state, and federal government agencies is also available. These agencies handle all types of problems, from false advertising to illegal business activities. One federal agency is the Food and Drug Administration, which sets safety standards for food, drugs, chemicals, cosmetics, and household and medical devices. The Consumer Product Safety Commission, another federal agency, helps protect consumers against unsafe products. If you do not know which consumer protection agency to choose, contact your U.S. representative locally or in Washington, D.C.

Dispute Resolution

Dispute resolution programs offer other ways to settle disagreements about a product. Working out a complaint may involve **mediation**—the attempt by a neutral third party to resolve a conflict between a customer and a business through discussion and negotiation. However, a decision made in mediation is not legally binding. Sometimes manufacturers and industry organizations use the arbitration process to resolve consumer complaints. **Arbitration** is a process whereby a conflict between a customer and a business is resolved by an impartial third party whose decision is legally binding. Settling a dispute through one of these methods can be quicker, less expensive, and less stressful than going to court.

Sources for dispute resolution programs in your area may include:

- Local or state consumer protection agencies
- State attorney general's office
- Small claims courts
- Better Business Bureau
- trade associations
- local bar associations.

If these dispute resolution methods do not produce the results you want, you may choose to take legal action.

Reading Check

Compare and Contrast How are mediation and arbitration similar? How are they different?

Legal Options for Consumers

What are your legal rights?

First, try to settle your dispute by going to the place of business, contacting the company's headquarters, or getting help from a consumer agency. However, if your previous attempts to resolve an issue have failed, it may be appropriate to pursue legal action through small claims court, a class-action suit, or other legal alternatives.

Careers That Count!

Gloria Maldonado • Retail Sales Specialist

Many retail stores specialize in certain products, such as outdoor clothing and gear for hiking. I started out as a customer in one of these stores, and I knew that someday I would work for them. I started out as a cashier, and worked my way up to retail sales specialist. I have a personal interest in the merchandise and the company's philosophy. I enjoy being surrounded by products that I actually use, it is satisfying to help customers who share similar interests. My typical workday is spent helping outdoor enthusiasts select appropriate gear, and to offer suggestions for other products they might need or want. One thing I especially like about the company is their enthusiasm for protecting the environment. As employees, we are expected to educate ourselves about environmental campaigns, and set an example by recycling all paper, glass, and plastic items.

EXPLORE CAREERS

Go online to find a retail company that is environmentally friendly.

1. What steps has the company taken to be environmentally responsible?
2. How do you think a retail company trains employees to service customers and address complaints?

Skills	Education	Career Path
Sales, interpersonal, communication, computer, product expertise, and customer service	High school diploma or equivalent, sales experience	Retail sales specialists have transferable skills that can lead to careers in marketing, management, and business ownership.

glencoe.com

Activity Download a Career Exploration Activity.

Small Claims Court

Every state has a court system to settle minor disagreements. A **small claims court** is a court that deals with legal disputes that involve amounts below a certain limit. The amount varies from state to state, ranging from about $500 to $10,000. Cases usually do not involve juries or lawyers, so the cost is relatively low. The decision of the judge is final. To effectively use small claims court, experts suggest you

- become familiar with court procedures and filing fees.
- observe other cases to learn about the process.
- present your case in a polite, calm, and concise manner.
- submit evidence such as photographs, receipts, contracts, and other documents.
- use witnesses who can testify on your behalf.

Class-Action Suits

Sometimes many people have the same complaint. For example, several people may have been injured by a defective product. Such a group may qualify for a class-action suit. A **class-action suit** is a legal action on behalf of all the people who have suffered the same injustice. The "class" is represented by a lawyer or group of lawyers.

Legal Action
If you are unable to resolve a complaint with phone calls, personal visits, or letters, you may need to take your complaint to small claims court. *Would you be willing to spend time and money on a case worth $100? Why or why not?*

If a situation qualifies for a class-action suit, all parties must be notified of the suit. An individual may decide to file a separate lawsuit instead. If the court rules in favor of the class action, the money awarded is divided among the claimants or put into public funds.

Other Legal Alternatives

If you do not want to go to small claims court or join in a class-action suit, you may seek the services of a lawyer. Get a referral for a lawyer from someone you know. You can also find the names of lawyers in newspapers, in the yellow pages of the phone book, or by calling a local branch of the American Bar Association (ABA), a professional organization of lawyers. It is important to make sure that the lawyer you choose has experience in handling your type of case. You should also ask about fees and payment policies. Lawyers can be expensive. You may decide that your problem is not worth the time and expense.

After You Read

Connect How does taking action against a defective or poor product produce positive results for both sellers and buyers?

If the cost of lawyers and other legal services is too high, you may seek help from a **legal aid society,** a network of community law offices that provide free or low-cost legal assistance. Supported by public funds, these offices provide a variety of legal services. Not everyone is **eligible,** or qualified, for help from a legal aid society. Your income must fall below a certain amount to qualify.

If you do not qualify to use the legal aid society, and hiring a private attorney is out of your budget, you might visit a legal clinic. In many cases, such businesses can offer basic assistance with advice and filing paperwork. In addition, some private attorneys offer their services at reduced rates and work part time in legal clinics.

Many tools are available to protect your rights. However, they will not be valuable unless you use them. You will have fewer consumer problems if you do business only with companies that have good reputations. You should avoid signing documents you do not understand, and watch out for offers that seem too good to be true.

Assessment

Review Key Concepts

1. **Explain** What are the common reasons that lead to consumer complaints? Why do they lead to complaints?
2. **Identify** What are the ways to solve consumer problems?
3. **Describe** What are consumer rights and the legal alternatives for consumers? How do they work?

Higher Order Thinking H.O.T.

4. **Evaluate** Cases presented in small claims courts are often featured on daytime television shows. Do you think such programs present a realistic portrayal of the American small claims court system? Are such programs beneficial? Explain your answer.

English Language Arts

5. **Making Informed Decisions** About eight weeks ago, you found an out-of-print, very rare CD on an online auction site. You won the item for $45. The seller, located outside of the U.S., sent an email to you asking for a money order for $45, plus $20 for shipping costs, and also asked for your Social Security number. The seller promised the order would arrive in four weeks. After numerous attempts to email the seller, you have not received a response. The seller's ad is no longer on the site. You realize that you have been defrauded. Create a pamphlet to help people make informed decisions when purchasing from Internet auction sites.

NCTE 8 Use information resources to gather information and create and communicate knowledge.

Mathematics

6. **Consumer Complaint** Gerald purchased a washer/dryer set for $450 three months ago. Since then, he had to call for repairs twice. On each of these instances the repair company charged $50 just to go to his house. They also charged $15 per hour. The first time they came out they spent 2.5 hours, and the second time they spent 1.5 hours. Gerald wants to send a complaint letter to the manufacturer. He wants to include his total expense for the washer/dryer in the letter. What amount should be put in his letter? Explain your answer.

Math Concept **Calculate Total Expense** To calculate the total expense incurred for the washer/dryer set determine the cost of each visit from the repair company. Add these costs to the purchase price.

Starting Hint Calculate the cost of the first repair by multiplying the charge per hour by the number of hours spent on the trip. Add this amount to the fee charged by the company to make the trip to the house.

NCTM Number and Operations Understand meanings of operations and how they relate to one another.

Visual Summary

Consumer Purchasing and Protection

How Do You Decide?

There are multiple economic, social, and personal factors that vary throughout your life and have an impact on your purchasing decisions.

Economic Factors	Social Factors	Personal Factors
Prices Interest rates Product quality Supply and demand Convenience Product safety Brand name Maintenance costs Warranty	Lifestyle Interests Hobbies Friends Culture Advertisements Media (magazines, radio, television, newspapers)	Gender Age Occupation Income Education Family size Geographic region Ethic background Religion

Invest the Time

Get more value for your money when you take the time to research and evaluate the products and services you want to buy.

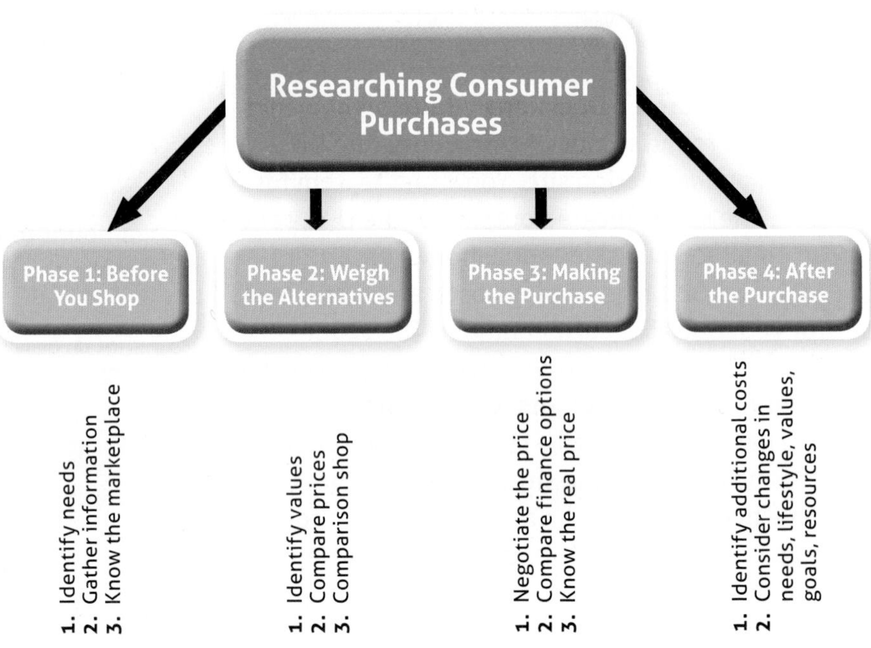

Try It!

Create an organizer like the one shown to highlight the options consumers have to resolve complaints.

Chapter Review and Assessment

Chapter Summary

- Buying decisions are influenced by several factors: economic factors, such as prices, brand names, quality, and maintenance costs; social factors, such as lifestyle and culture; and personal factors, such as age, occupation, and family size.
- A research-based approach to buying involves identifying needs, gathering information, becoming aware of the marketplace, weighing alternatives, and making the purchase.
- The purchase may involve negotiation, plus you will need to determine whether to pay cash or use credit.
- Make buying decisions by using the following strategies: time your purchases, select stores, compare brands, check labels, compare prices, and evaluate warranties.
- To solve consumer problems, return to the place of purchase, contact the company that manufactured the disputed product, obtain help from a consumer agency or dispute resolution program, or initiate legal action.
- Legal alternatives available to consumers include lawsuits in small claims court, joining in a class-action suit, hiring a lawyer, and obtaining assistance from a legal aid society.

Vocabulary Review

1. Use at least eight of these vocabulary terms in a short essay about returning a defective product.

- down payment
- impulse buying
- open dating
- unit pricing
- rebate
- warranty
- service contract
- fraud
- mediation
- arbitration
- small claims court
- class-action suit
- legal aid society
- approach
- transactions
- document
- eligible

Higher Order Thinking 

2. **Determine** What are the factors that contribute to the real price of a computer?
3. **Theorize** Even with all the information that is available, people still become victims of fraud. Why do you think this is so?
4. **Synthesize** Explain how age, education, and occupation affect consumer decisions over one's lifespan.
5. **Compare and contrast** Differentiate between marginal cost and marginal benefit. How might marginal cost and marginal benefit impact purchasing decisions? Provide examples.
6. **Justify** Your friend thinks comparison shopping is a waste of time. Explain comparison shopping and justify to your friend that it is worthwhile.
7. **Evaluate** Consider what motivates you to make purchases. Evaluate whether these influences lead you to make wise decisions.
8. **Judge** What are the common types of contracts for consumers and the impact of each? Are service contracts worthwhile? Explain your position.
9. **Assess** There are many tools available to protect your rights as a consumer. Why might some people choose not to take advantage of these tools? Why is this dangerous?

College and Career Readiness

Science

10. Product Safety Consumer science is the study of providing for the economic and personal well being of individuals and families. Consumer science draws from such fields as economics, sociology, natural science, psychology, law, and business. Consumer protection is one area of consumer science, and knowledge of it is essential when creating safe products.

Procedure Research a product that was recalled for safety concerns.

Analysis What was the product? Why was it recalled? How did the manufacturer address the safety issue? What effect did the safety issue have on consumers and the manufacturer? Summarize your findings in a one-page report.

NSES F Develop an understanding of personal and community health; population growth; natural resources; environmental quality; natural and human-induced hazards; science and technology in local, national, and global challenges.

Mathematics

11. Credit Card Charges Victoria made an impulse purchase and bought a new television for $750 on her credit card. She determined that her budget allowed her to pay $200 per month towards the credit card. The card has a 15 percent annual interest rate which is applied to any outstanding balance greater than one month. Determine how many months it will take Victoria to pay off the credit card assuming no other purchases. Also calculate the total cost of the television including finance charges.

Math Concept **Calculate Credit Card Charges** To calculate the total cost of a credit card purchase determine the ending balance after each month to calculate the monthly finance charge.

Starting Hint Determine the monthly interest rate charge by dividing the annual rate by the number of months in one year. Multiply the monthly interest rate by the ending balance after month 1 to determine the finance charge.

NCTM Problem Solving Solve problems that arise in mathematics and in other contexts.

English Language Arts

12. Consumer Complaints In 2009, the United States Better Business Bureau received nearly one million consumer complaints. The highest number of complaints went to the cell phone industry and the satellite and cable television industry. On a more positive note, these two industries also had the highest percentage of resolutions. If you have a complaint, you should always approach the company first. With a partner, prepare a script you could use when approaching a company with a complaint. Rehearse your script and then present it.

NCTE 12 Use language to accomplish individual purposes.

Economics

13. Pricing Some consumers will pay almost any price to obtain what they value, but others will not. For example, a digital music company recently changed its price from $1.00 per song to $1.39. Although the company continued to experience revenue growth, it was only 8 percent compared to 20 percent in the previous year. Do you think the reduced growth reflected consumers' displeasure with the price increase? Do you think the company will lower its prices? What other options might the company have to increase revenue? What other factors might have contributed to the reduced growth?

Real-World Applications

14. Charitable Donations Giving to charity is an investment in your community, the nation, and the world. The Federal Trade Commission (FTC), the nation's consumer protection agency, says that it is wise to be cautious when making your donation decisions to avoid scam artists who try to make money by taking advantage of your generosity. Visit the FTC's Web site to learn how you can ensure that your charitable donations end up in the right hands. Take notes about the information, then use presentation software to create a presentation for your class. Make your presentation more engaging with handouts, graphics, or other visual aids.

Your Financial Portfolio

Your Budget

David wants a $2,500 laptop computer. At his part-time job at Computer Warehouse, he earns $7 an hour and works an average of 16 hours a week. For ten weeks in the summer, he works 40 hours a week. He also makes money on the side by setting up and troubleshooting computers. By keeping track of his expenses, he has figured his monthly budget.

Average Monthly Income	
Income:	
Monthly take-home pay from Computer Warehouse	$502.50
Income from setting up and troubleshooting computers	50.00
Other income	20.00
Total Income	**$572.50**
Average Monthly Expenses	
Expenses:	
Fixed Expenses	
Online services	$20.00
Car loan and insurance	135.00
Variable Expenses	
Entertainment and personal	90.00
Gifts and contributions	25.00
Total Expenses	**$270.00**

If David sticks to his budget, in a year's time he can save $3,630 ($302.50 × 12 = $3,630). That would be more than enough to buy the computer he wants.

Calculate

What is your budget? A budget can help you see where you are spending your money and assist you in determining how long it will take to save for a special purchase. On a separate sheet of paper, calculate your income and expenses for one month. How much can you save in one month? What is the cost of your desired purchase? How long will it take you to save for what you want?

Unit 4

Unit Project

Planning for Financial and Career Success

Ask Yourself...

Have you ever thought of purchasing a bicycle, buying a new car, or even buying a house in the future? Have you ever thought of a job that would be fun or might pay well? How may your selection of a job or career impact your financial goals? Responses to these questions can lead you to specific financial and career goals.

Your Objective

The goal of this project is to develop financial and career goals, research a career of interest, and create a short presentation for your class on your chosen career.

Skills You'll Use

Success in defining goals and preparing financially for those goals depends on your skills. Some skills you might use include:

Academic Skills – Reading, writing, and mathematics

21st Century Skills – Speaking, listening, thinking, problem solving, decision making, and interpersonal skills

Technology Skills – Word processing, keyboarding, presentation software, and Internet research

Standards

NCTE 4 Use written language to communicate effectively.

NCTE 7 Conduct research and gather, evaluate, and synthesize data to communicate discoveries.

NCTE 8 Use information resources to gather information and create and communicate knowledge.

NCTE 12 Use language to accomplish individual purposes.

STEP 1 Create Your Goals

Goals are like a road map providing both guidance and direction. Answer these questions:

- What would you like to purchase in the next few months? Is there something you would like to put money toward in the next few years?
- What items would you like to own in ten or twenty years? Where would you like to be financially at that time?
- Is there a type of job you would like to explore for the summer?
- Is there a job field you think you would be interested in after high school?
- In which career field could you imagine working in ten or twenty years?
- Your responses will guide the development of your financial and career goals.
- Now that you have created some financial and career goals, plot them on a time line.

STEP 2 Explore Careers

What are your interests? What are you good at? How do your answers apply to particular career fields? Now explore a career in which you are interested.

- To focus your list of aptitudes and interests complete an aptitude test or interest inventory.
- Search for information about a career that interests you. Find out about the educational requirements, skills needed, pay range, responsibilities, and future trends.
- Where can you learn the skills and knowledge necessary for your career field? Research colleges or other post-secondary institutions where training is offered in your area of interest.
- Write a brief summary of your research findings and cite any sources.

STEP 3 Build Relationships

What information can you gain from someone with personal experience? Meet with a member of your community currently working in your area of interest to gather information. You may interview them or shadow them for a day to learn more about their career field.

- Prepare interview questions based on your research.
- Take notes and record the interview responses.
- Listen attentively.
- Make eye contact and respond appropriately and with interest.
- Ask questions if you do not understand something.
- Encourage the speaker to share with positive body language and open-ended questions.
- Write a summary of the interviewee's responses.

STEP 4 Develop Your Presentation

Use the Unit 4 Project Checklist to plan and create your presentation.

STEP 5 Evaluate Your Presentation

Your presentation will be evaluated based on the following:

- Evaluation Rubric
- Content and organization of your information.
- Mechanics – presentation and neatness.
- Speaking and listening skills.

Project Checklist

Plan

- ✔ Develop short-term, intermediate, and long-term financial goals.
- ✔ Research career fields in which you are interested including educational requirements, skills needed, pay range, responsibilities, and future trends.
- ✔ Meet with someone in your community currently working in the career field in which you are interested.

Write

- ✔ List your financial and career goals.
- ✔ Create a time line of your financial and career goals.
- ✔ Summarize your research findings of the career field you chose.
- ✔ List your interview questions.
- ✔ Write a summary of the interviewee's responses.

Present

- ✔ Create an outline for your presentation.
- ✔ Create visuals and utilize technology to enhance your presentation.
- ✔ Speak clearly and concisely.
- ✔ Present your short-term, intermediate, and long-term financial and career goals.
- ✔ Present the results of your career research.
- ✔ Present your time line and interview summary.
- ✔ Respond to questions posed by the audience.

glencoe.com

Evaluate Download a rubric you can use to evaluate your project.

UNIT

5

Banking and Credit

Visual Literacy

There are many options to help you save to purchase your first home or meet other long-term goals. ***What banking services could you use to address short- and long-term financial goals?***

In Your World

Giving Yourself Good Credit

Your credit score and credit reports will stay with you for the rest of your life. Establish good credit now for better purchasing power later. Do you want to buy a new car or home? Then you must be responsible with your credit. A little education about credit can go a long way in helping you plan and enjoy your financial future.

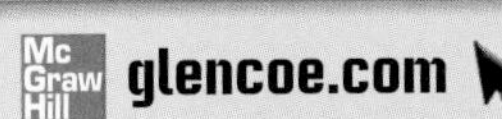

Watch the Unit 5 video to learn more about how to establish and keep good credit.

The Rules of Credit The rules are simple, but you have to follow them. Stick to a realistic budget. If you cannot pay off an item purchased with a credit card in three months, you probably should not purchase it. Why is it dangerous to make only the minimum monthly payments on credit card purchases? Give an example.

Economics and You

Government Regulation

The United States government passes legislation to protect investors, consumers, workers, and the environment. Consumers are protected from unsafe food, drugs, and other products. If any product is unsafe, the regulatory agency in charge will require a company to recall it. However, sometimes government regulations may limit business and consumer freedoms. For example, the Credit Card Act of 2009 prohibits credit card companies from soliciting new credit card owners on college campuses. It also restricts credit to young people under the age of 21, unless they have a co-signer. Are these restrictions fair for businesses? Are they fair for young consumers? Why do you think credit card regulations are imposed on young people?

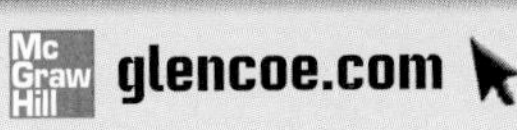

Activity Download an Economics and You Worksheet Activity.

CHAPTER 14

Banking

Visual Literacy

Banks offer more than just checking and savings accounts. ***What other services do banks offer to help you manage your money?***

Discovery Project

Comparing Options

Key Question

What options, other than a savings account, are available to help a person with his or her savings goals?

Project Goal

It is important to know and understand all of the financial services that are available to you when setting your financial goals and managing your money. Before deciding where or how to save your money, you need to research your options.

- Visit several financial institutions in your neighborhood, such as banks or credit unions.
- Obtain information on different accounts and services they offer to help you save money. You might also visit the institution's Web site to find this information.
- Develop a spreadsheet to help you compare the requirements, fees, and benefits of each option.
- Identify which options would be good ones for you now.
- Explain why some of the options would not work for you.

Ask Yourself...

- *How much money do you have for savings?*
- *How much could you add to that each month?*
- *Will any interest you make offset fees for the account?*
- *Will you need immediate access to the money or can you wait for a few months to access it?*

Make Judgments and Decisions

When would a certificate of deposit, or CD, be a better option than a savings account?

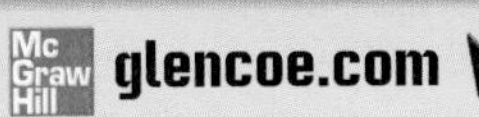

Evaluate Download an assessment rubric.

THE BIG IDEA

Understanding the financial services offered by different institutions can help you get more from your money.

ASK STANDARD & POOR'S

Savings Account

Q *I make only $75 a week at my part-time job and use most of it for movies, food, and music. Because I make so little, do I really need to put my money in a bank?*

A Since you have a small amount of money to take care of, you may not need a bank. However, $75 a week is a large sum to spend on entertainment. You should open a savings account and try to save at least $10 a week. After a year you would have more than $500.

Writing Activity

Write a scene in which you explain to a friend why it is important to save some of your money, rather than spending it all on immediate wants.

Reading Guide

Before You Read

The Essential Question What types of financial services might help you to better manage your cash flow?

Main Idea

Understanding the services provided by financial institutions will help you to choose the best options to manage your money wisely.

Content Vocabulary

- direct deposit
- automated teller machine (ATM)
- debit card
- commercial bank
- savings and loan association (S&L)
- credit union
- certificate of deposit (CD)
- money market account
- rate of return
- compounding
- annual percentage yield (APY)
- overdraft protection
- stop-payment order
- endorsement
- bank reconciliation

Academic Vocabulary

You will see these words in your reading and on your tests.

- authorization
- issuers
- quarterly
- alternative

Graphic Organizer

Before you read this chapter, draw a web diagram like the one below. As you read, note the eight questions you should ask to help you choose a financial institution.

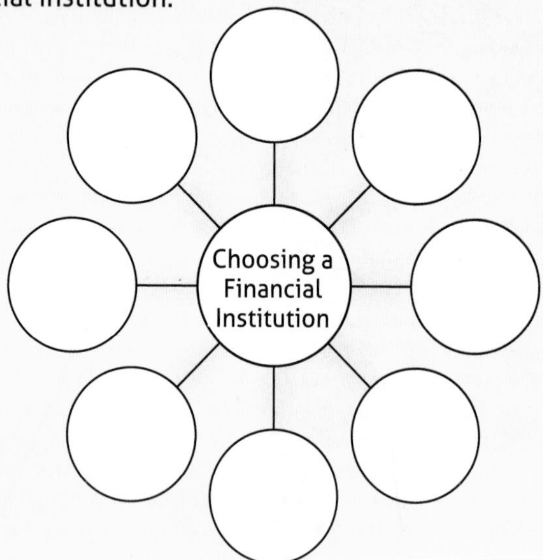

Print this graphic organizer.

Standards

Academic

Mathematics

NCTM Number and Operations Understand numbers, ways of representing numbers, relationships among numbers, and number systems.

NCTM Problem Solving Solve problems that arise in mathematics and in other contexts.

English Language Arts

NCTE 8 Use information resources to gather information and create and communicate knowledge.

Social Studies

NCSS IV D Individual Development & Identity Apply concepts, methods, and theories about the study of human growth and development, such as physical endowment, learning, motivation, behavior, perception, and personality.

NCTM *National Council of Teachers of Mathematics*
NCTE *National Council of Teachers of English*
NCSS *National Council for the Social Studies*
NSES *National Science Education Standards*

Common Core

Reading Read and comprehend complex informational texts independently and proficiently.

Writing Write routinely over extended time frames (time for research, reflection, and revision) and shorter time frames (a single sitting or a day or two) for a range of tasks, purposes, and audiences.

Writing Conduct short as well as more sustained research projects based on focused questions, demonstrating understanding of the subject under investigation.

How to Manage Your Cash

What are your cash needs?

Banking in America began in 1791, soon after the United States declared independence. Congress established the nation's first central bank with eight branches. Today, with more than 11,000 banks, 2,000 savings and loan associations, and 12,000 credit unions in the United States, you have a wide array of financial services from which to choose. A trip to the bank may be a visit to an automated teller machine (ATM) in the mall or a quick look at your savings account balance on the Internet. Your choice of financial services will depend on your daily cash needs and your savings goals. (See **Figure 1.**)

Daily Cash Needs

Your daily cash needs may include buying lunch, going to the movies with friends, filling the car with gasoline, or paying for other routine activities. Of course, you can carry cash, or currency—bills and coins—to pay for these items. You can also use a credit card or go to an ATM, also known as a cash machine.

As you decide which method to use for your everyday cash needs, consider the pros and cons of each one. For example, ATMs may charge a fee for each use. If you pay a $1 fee each time you take out cash, say, twice a week, you will spend $104 on fees each year.

In addition to your short-term cash needs, you need to consider your long-term financial goals. Resist the temptation to overspend and avoid buying on impulse or overusing credit cards. Try not to dip into your savings to pay current bills. Put extra money you have to work for you—in a savings account or an investment plan.

Sources of Quick Cash

Regardless of how well you plan, you may sometimes need more cash than you have available. You have two options: Use your savings or borrow the money. Remember that either choice requires a trade-off. Although you will have immediate access to the funds you need, long-term financial goals—such as paying for college, buying a car, or starting a business—may be delayed.

Reading Check

Recall What are your two options if you need more cash than you currently have available?

Section Objectives

- **Identify** types of financial services.
- **Describe** the various types of financial institutions.
- **Describe** problematic financial businesses.

As You Read

Predict Why might you opt to open a savings account as well as a checking account?

Careers That Count!

Kyle Bielecki • Teller

Handling money is just one part of my job as a teller for a national bank. I am responsible for processing customer transactions in a timely, accurate manner according to established policies and procedures. My day-to-day tasks include tending to checking and savings accounts, ATM/debit cards, telephone and Internet banking, bill payment, certificates of deposit, IRAs, safe-deposit boxes, discount brokerage, credit cards, and merchant processing. Aside from those tasks, I am also expected to uphold the positive image of my bank by providing excellent customer service in a responsible and professional manner. If you want an entry level job in banking, you can usually get a job as a teller with a high school diploma and good communication and math skills. However, if you want a higher level of responsibility and higher pay, you should pursue a college degree, and take courses such as those offered by the Institute of Financial Education and the American Institute of Banking.

EXPLORE CAREERS

Tellers need exceptional customer service skills. Many banks include sales training in orientation programs.

1. Research bank teller jobs online. What qualifications do companies require for this job?
2. Explain why a teller with sales training would be an asset to a bank.

Skills	Education	Career Path
Communication, math, problem-solving, decision-making, and cash-handling skills, as well as proficiency with office machines	High school diploma or equivalent; background check; on-the-job training	Tellers can become loan officers, credit authorizers, sales representatives for financial services, and debt counselors.

Activity Download a Career Exploration Activity.

Types of Financial Services

Which financial services would benefit you?

In order to stay competitive in today's marketplace, banks and other financial institutions have expanded the range of services that they offer. These services can be divided into four main categories:

- Savings
- Payment services
- Borrowing
- Other Financial Services

Savings

Safe storage of funds for future use is a basic need for everyone. Money that is going to be left in a financial institution for months or years is called a *time deposit*. Some examples of time deposit funds include money that you keep in any type of savings account and certificates of deposit or CDs. Having a savings account is essential for any personal finance plan. Selection of a savings plan is commonly based on interest rates, liquidity, safety, and convenience.

FIGURE 1 **Financial Services**

Planning Ahead It is important to consider both short-term and long-term goals when assessing your financial services needs. *How can thinking about your long-term needs help you now?*

Financial Services for Short-Term Needs

- Daily purchases
- Living expenses
- Emergency fund

Daily Cash Needs
- Check cashing
- Automated teller machines (ATMs)
- Prepaid cards

Savings
- Regular savings account
- Money market account

Checking
- Regular checking account
- Online payments
- Automatic preauthorized payments
- Payment by phone
- Cashier's checks
- Money orders

Credit Cards

Financial Services for Long-Term Needs

- Major purchases
- Long-term financial security

Savings
- Certificates of deposit (CDs)
- U.S. Savings Bonds

Credit Services
- Cash loans for cars, education
- Home loans

Investment Services
- Mutual funds
- Financial advice

Other Services
- Tax preparation
- Insurance
- Budgeting

Payment Services

Transferring money from a personal account to businesses or individuals for payments is a basic function of day-to-day financial activity at a bank. The most commonly used payment service is a checking account. Money that you place in a checking account is called a demand deposit because you can withdraw the money at any time, or on demand.

Borrowing

Most people use credit at some time during their lives. If you need to borrow money, financial institutions offer many options. You can borrow money for a short term by using a credit card or taking out a personal cash loan. If you need to borrow for a longer term, say, for the purpose of buying a house or car, you may apply for a mortgage or auto loan.

Other Financial Services

Financial institutions may also offer a variety of services, such as insurance protection; stock, bond, and mutual fund investment accounts; income tax assistance; and financial planning services.

Reading Check

Summarize List the financial services that might be offered by a financial institution.

Electronic Banking Services

How can you use electronic banking services?

When Jeff's older brother was in high school, he had to get to his bank by 3 P.M. on Friday, or he would have to wait until 9 A.M. on Monday to cash his paycheck. Today Jeff's bank is open for longer periods on weekdays as well as on Saturdays. For more convenience, Jeff can use the bank's electronic services 24 hours a day. He can check the status of his account or make a transaction from an ATM, by telephone, or online. Other online services allow customers to get up-to-date account information with personal financial management software to view details about a home loan or a line of credit and to check the amount of interest paid.

FIGURE 2 Electronic Banking

Benefits and Concerns Online banking services provide many benefits and conveniences, but they can also be cause for concern. *What are some benefits of online banking services? What concerns might a person have using these services?*

ELECTRONIC BANKING SERVICES
• Obtain cash; check account balances
• Transfer funds:
• From savings to checking
• From savings to loan
• From checking to loan
• From checking to savings
• Direct deposit of paychecks, government payments
• Preauthorized payments for insurance, mortgage, utilities, and other bills
• Obtain cash; check account balances
• Access "e-banks" with a complete range of financial services
• Debit card retail purchases

Security is the number one issue for online customers. The way to ensure online security is to use a security code, or password, and a customer identification name or number.

Banking online and through electronic systems continues to expand. While most traditional financial institutions offer online banking services, Web-only banks have also become strong competitors. For example, E*Trade Bank operates online while also providing customers with access to ATMs. These "e-banks" and "e-branches" provide nearly every needed financial service, see **Figure 2.**

Direct Deposit

Many businesses offer their employees **direct deposit,** an automatic deposit of net pay to an employee's designated bank account. Instead of a paper paycheck, employees receive a printed statement that lists deductions and information about their earnings. Direct deposit saves time, money, and effort—and offers a safe way to transfer funds.

Automatic Payments

Utility companies, lenders, and other businesses allow customers to use an automatic payment system. With your **authorization,** or permission, your bank will withdraw the amount of your monthly payment or bill from your bank account.

With automatic payments it is important to make sure you have enough money in your account for the payment. Arrange your payments according to when you receive your paycheck. Check your bank statements monthly to make sure payments were made correctly.

ATM Safety
It is important to memorize your PIN and not share it with others. *Why shouldn't you write down your PIN?*

reality bytes

Fingerprints for Cash
Imagine using only your finger to access money at an ATM. Biometrics is the analysis of physical characteristics, especially as a way to verify a person's identity. Biometrics is now being applied to banking security. Fingerprint verification can be used to give individuals access to their banking services at ATMs and online. In 2010, BPS, a Polish bank, was the first bank in Europe to install fingerprint readers at their ATMs as an optional authorization method for cardholders. Customers can place their finger on the reader instead of using their card and entering a PIN.

Automated Teller Machines (ATMs)

A cash machine, or **automated teller machine (ATM),** is a computer terminal that allows a withdrawal of cash from an account. You can also make deposits and transfer money from one account to another. ATMs are located in banks, shopping malls, grocery stores, and even sports arenas.

To use an ATM for banking, you must apply for a card from your financial institution. This card is called a **debit card,** which is a cash card that allows you to withdraw money or pay for purchases from your checking or savings account. The card also allows you to access the machine for other purposes. Some financial institutions may charge a small fee for the use of the card. A debit card is in contrast to a credit card since you are spending your own funds rather than borrowing additional money.

When you use your debit card, the ATM computer will ask you to enter your personal identification number (PIN). Never give this number to any business or individual, or for online transactions. Memorize it and keep a written record in a safe place. Never keep your PIN with your debit card. If your card is lost or stolen along with your PIN, anyone could withdraw money from your account.

In addition, follow simple rules of ATM etiquette when using this banking convenience. If you are in line, stand at least a few feet away from the person using the machine. When you are at the machine, protect the screen as you enter your PIN and other information.

ATM Fees The fees that some financial institutions charge for the convenience of using an ATM can add up over time. You may feel that the benefit is worth the cost. However, you might consider these suggestions:

- Compare ATM fees before opening an account. Get a list of fees in writing.
- Use your bank's ATM machines to avoid the additional fees that other banks charge when you use their machines.
- Consider using traveler's checks, credit cards, personal checks, and prepaid cash cards when you are away from home.

Lost Debit Cards If you lose your debit card, or if it is stolen, notify your bank immediately. Most card **issuers,** or providers, will not hold you responsible for stolen funds. Check with your card issuer. However, some institutions require you to notify them within two days of losing your card. If you wait longer, you may be held responsible for up to $500 for its unauthorized use for up to 60 days. Beyond that time, your liability may be unlimited.

Plastic Payments

Although cash and checks are very common methods of paying for goods and services, various access cards are also available.

Document Detective

A Bank Statement

You need to keep track of deductions and deposits in your check register as you write checks and deposit money. The monthly statement is the bank's record of that activity. It is important that your records and the bank's records are the same so your account will not get overdrawn.

SMITHVILLE BANK N.A.

Tom Jones
21 First Street
Smithville, Florida 55523

ACCOUNT SUMMARY	***Statement Date: 02/24/10***
Balance forwarded from 01/23/10	$41,452.80
Checks	6,310.00
Interest added	50.59
Ending balance	**$35,193.39**

ELECTRONIC CREDITS

Date	Description	
2/24/10	INTEREST PAID	$50.59

CHECKS AND OTHER DEBITS

Date	Check#	Amount
01/27/10	1043	$70.00
02/18/10	1044	100.00
02/12/10	1045	3,600.00
02/10/10	1046	2,440.00
02/19/10	1047	100.00

DAILY BALANCE SUMMARY

Date	Balance
1/27/10	$41,382.80
02/10/10	38,942.80
02/12/10	35,342.80
02/18/10	35,242.80
02/19/10	35,142.80
02/24/10	35,193.39

Key Points If there is a difference between your records and the bank's records, you need to resolve the problem with your bank. If the bank thinks you have less money than you do, your checks may "bounce," or be rejected and go unpaid, causing the bank to charge you penalty fees.

FIND the Solutions

Review Key Concepts

1. What time period does this statement cover?
2. From this statement, what do you think is the meaning of the word *credits*?
3. From this statement, what do you think is the meaning of the word *debits*?
4. On 02/10/10, the balance in this account changed. Why?
5. There is a line on this statement that reads "Checks 6,310.00." What does this mean?
6. What does it mean when a check "bounces"?

Electronic Payments Transactions not involving cash, checks, or credit cards have expanded with technology, improved security, and increased consumer acceptance.

Online Payments Banks and Internet companies serve as third parties to make online bill payments possible. When using these services, you should consider the monthly charge as well as online security and customer service availability. Also on the Web are "cyber cash" services creating their own *e-money* that serves as funding for online transactions.

Stored-Value Cards Prepaid cards for transit fares and school lunches, for example, are common. Some of these stored-value cards are disposable. Others can be reloaded with an additional amount.

Smart Cards These "electronic wallets" are similar to other ATM cards. These cards contain a microchip to store information. The microchip stores prepaid amounts as well as information with account balances, insurance information, and medical history.

Reading Check

Define What is direct deposit?

Evaluating Financial Services

What are the trade-offs when you choose financial services?

When you are making decisions about saving and spending, try to find a balance between your short-term needs and your future financial security. Also, consider the opportunity costs of each choice you make as you select financial services. Ask several questions.

- Is a higher interest rate on a certificate of deposit worth giving up liquidity, or the ability to easily convert it into cash without a cost?
- Would you trade the convenience of getting cash from the ATM near your office for lower ATM fees?
- Is it worth opening a checking account that has no fees—but does not earn interest—if you have to keep a minimum balance of $500?

Remember to consider the value of your time in addition to the money you are saving. Re-evaluate your choices occasionally. You may find a new financial institution that offers you more of the services you need or offers less expensive services.

Reading Check

Paraphrase What are some of the opportunity costs to consider when selecting financial services?

Types of Financial Institutions

What are the differences between financial institutions?

After you have identified the services you want, you can choose from among many types of financial institutions. You may select an institution that offers a wide range of services or one that specializes in certain services. **Figure 3** provides some tips for selecting a financial institution. Almost all institutions provide electronic banking services, or banking via the Internet. Some banks operate exclusively on the Internet.

Safety

When you consider a financial institution consider its safety record. Most savings plans at banks, savings and loan associations, and credit unions are insured by agencies affiliated with the federal government. This protection prevents a loss of money due to the failure of the insured institution. While a few financial institutions have failed in recent years, savers with deposits covered by federal insurance have not lost any money. Depositors of failed organizations either have been paid the amounts in their accounts or have had the accounts taken over by a financially stable institution.

During the Great Depression of the 1930s, many banks failed. The people and businesses that had made deposits in these institutions lost their money. In 1933, the federal government created the Federal Deposit Insurance Corporation (FDIC) to protect deposits in banks. The FDIC insures each account in a federally chartered bank up to $100,000 per account (recently raised to $250,000 temporarily). The FDIC also administers the Savings Association Insurance Fund (SAIF) for savings and loan associations. Like the FDIC, the SAIF insures deposits up to $100,000. All federally chartered banks must participate in the FDIC program. Banks that are not federally chartered may choose to enroll in the program.

Deposit Institutions

Most people use deposit (or depository) institutions to handle their banking needs. These institutions include commercial banks, savings and loan associations, mutual savings banks, and credit unions.

Commercial Banks A **commercial bank** is a for-profit institution that offers a full range of financial services, including checking, savings, and lending. These banks serve individuals and businesses. Commercial banks are organized as corporations with individual investors, or stockholders, contributing the capital the banks need to operate. National banks are authorized to conduct business through a charter, or license, granted by the federal government and state banks by state governments. State-chartered banks are usually subject to fewer restrictions than federally chartered banks.

Savings and Loan Associations A **savings and loan association (S&L)** is a financial institution that traditionally specialized in savings accounts and mortgage loans but now offers many of the same services as commercial banks. Services include checking accounts, business loans, and investment services. S&Ls have either a federal or a state charter.

Mutual Savings Banks Mutual savings banks are owned by depositors and specialize in savings accounts and mortgage loans. Some offer personal and automobile loans as well. The interest rates on loans from a mutual savings bank may be lower than those that a commercial bank charges. In addition, mutual savings banks sometimes pay a higher interest rate on savings accounts.

Credit Unions A **credit union** is a nonprofit financial institution that is owned by its members and organized for their benefit. Traditionally, a credit union's members have some common bond, such as membership in a labor union, college alumni association, or employment by the same company. Today more than 80 million people belong to over 9,000 credit unions in the United States.

Most credit unions offer a full range of services, including checking accounts, loans, credit cards, ATMs, safe-deposit boxes, and investment services. Surveys conducted by consumer organizations and others report lower fees and lower loan rates than those at commercial banks.

FIGURE 3 **Selecting a Financial Institution**

When you are ready to choose a financial institution, plan so that you will have the services you need and will not have to pay for those you will not use. Do your banking homework.

1 **Stop by the bank.** Pick up brochures about the bank's services. While there, speak to a customer service representative about the bank's services.

2 **Take the brochures home.** Study them and discuss the features with your parents.

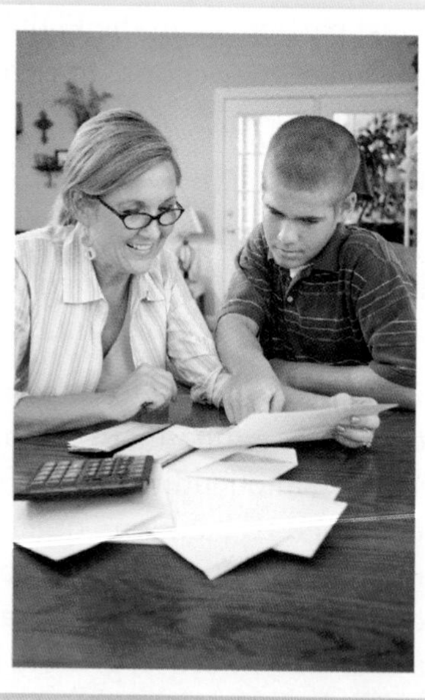

Non-Depository Institutions

Financial services are also available at institutions such as life insurance companies, investment companies, finance companies, and mortgage companies.

Life Insurance Companies Though the main purpose of life insurance companies is to provide financial security for dependents, many insurance policies also contain savings and investment features. In addition, some insurance companies offer retirement planning services.

Investment Companies These firms combine your money with funds from other investors in order to buy stocks, bonds, and other securities. The investment company then manages these combined investments, which are called *mutual funds*. Investment company accounts are not covered by federal deposit insurance.

Finance Companies Finance companies make higher-interest loans to consumers and small businesses that cannot borrow elsewhere because they have below-average credit ratings.

Reading Check

Identify Name four types of deposit institutions.

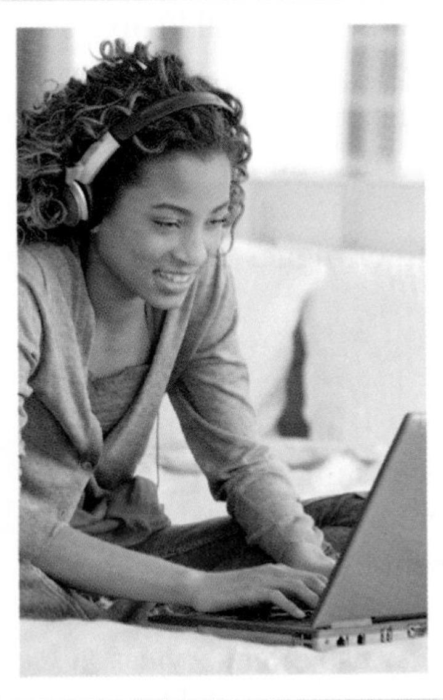

3 **Go online.** Get complete information on the institution's benefits, fees, and charges.

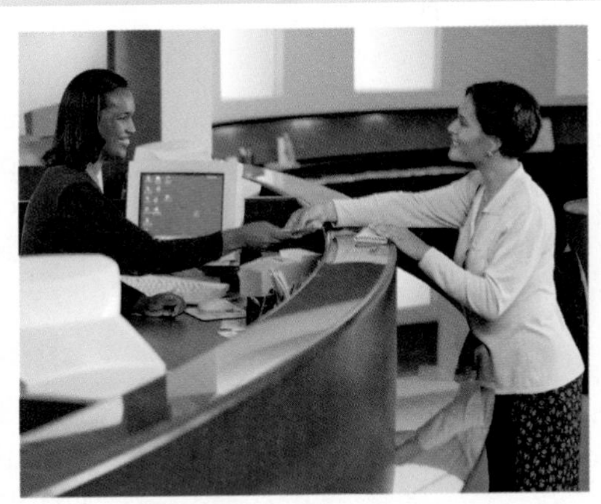

4 **Open your accounts.** Use checking and savings accounts to start managing your money.

Customer Service
It is often helpful to speak to a customer service representative when considering the services of a financial institution. *Why might speaking to a person be more helpful than reading a brochure or Web site?*

Problematic Financial Businesses

What are problematic financial businesses?

Would you pay $20 to borrow $100 for two weeks? Many people without access to financial services use pawnshops, check-cashing outlets, loan stores, and rent-to-own centers.

Pawnshops

Pawnshops make loans based on the value of tangible possessions such as jewelry or other valuable items. Many low- and moderate-income families use these organizations to obtain cash loans quickly. Pawnshops charge higher fees than other financial institutions. Thousands of consumers are increasingly in need of small loans—usually around seventy-five dollars, to be repaid in 30 to 45 days. Pawnshops have become the "neighborhood bankers" and the "local shopping malls," since they provide both lending and retail shopping services, selling items that owners do not redeem. While states regulate rates, three percent interest a month or higher is common.

Check Cashing Outlets

Most financial institutions will not cash a check unless you have an account. The more than six thousand check-cashing outlets (CCOs) charge anywhere from one to twenty percent of the face value of a check; the average cost is two to three percent. For a low-income family, that can be a significant portion of the total household budget. CCOs, sometimes called currency exchanges, also offer services, including electronic tax filing, money orders, private postal boxes, utility bill payment, and the sale of transit tokens.

India

Microloans for Electricity

People in the United States often relate bank loans with major purchases such as a new car or house, or large events such as remodeling a home or starting a business. In India, though, loans have come to mean something as simple as having light.

Many rural areas have no access to electricity. Experts believe this lack of access has contributed to slow economic development, low literacy rates, and poor health. To help combat this problem, many banks are now offering small loans, known as microloans, to provide solar powered devices to bring light to these rural communities. This improvement has increased productivity and improved the health and socio-economic status of the rural citizens. Because the solar-powered devices are offering an alternative to flammable and polluting kerosene lamps, the microloans are also promoting "greener" communities. The "cleaner" light source is good for businesses as well as families. It allows businesses to stay open at night. One vegetable seller noted that, in addition to being cheaper than kerosene, the solar-powered lantern made her vegetables look and smell better than the kerosene lantern. One lantern costs about $66 to $112—the equivalent of a week's wages for the vegetable seller.

Critical Thinking

1. **Expand** How can the solar-powered lights made available through microloans help improve the health of Indians?
2. **Relate** Do you think Americans would use microloans? What alternatives do we have that the rural citizens of India might not?

DATABYTES

Capital
New Delhi

Population
1,173,108,018

Languages
Hindu, Bengali, Telugu, Marathi, Tamil, Urdu, Gujarati, Kannada, Malayalam, Oriya, Punjabi, Assamese, Maithili

Currency
Indian rupee

Gross Domestic Product (GDP)
$1.095 trillion

GDP per capita
$3, 100

Industry
Textiles, chemicals, food processing, steel, transportation equipment, cement, mining, petroleum, machinery, software, pharmaceuticals

Agriculture
Rice, wheat, oilseed, cotton, jute, tea, sugarcane, lentils, onions, potatoes, dairy products, sheep, goats, poultry, fish

Exports
Petroleum products, precious stones, machinery, iron and steel, chemicals, vehicles, apparel

Natural Resources
Coal, iron ore, manganese, mica, bauxite, titanium ore, chromite, natural gas, diamonds, petroleum, limestone, arable land

Payday Loans

Many consumer organizations caution against using payday loans, also referred to as *cash advances, check advance loans*, and *delayed deposit loans*. Desperate borrowers pay annual interest rates of as much as 780 percent and more to obtain needed cash from payday loan companies. These enterprises have increased in recent years. The most frequent users of payday loans are workers who have become trapped by debts or who have been driven into debt by misfortune. In a typical payday loan, a consumer writes a personal check for $115 to borrow $100 for fourteen days. The payday lender agrees to hold the check until the next payday. This $15 finance charge for the fourteen days translates into an annual percentage rate of 391 percent. Some consumers "roll over" their loans, paying another $15 for the $100 loan for the next fourteen days. After a few rollovers, the finance charge can exceed the amount borrowed. The Chicago Department of Consumer Services has reported annual rates ranging from 659 to 1,300 percent for some payday loans.

Rent-to-Own Centers

Years ago, people who rented furniture and appliances found few deluxe items available. Today rental businesses offer big-screen televisions, seven-piece cherrywood bedroom sets, and personal computers. The rent-to-purchase industry is defined as stores that lease products to consumers who can own the item if they complete a certain number of monthly or weekly payments.

Reading Check

Rephrase What is a payday loan?

Comparing Financial Institutions

What should you know to choose a financial institution?

When you compare banks and other financial institutions, you should ask these questions to help choose the best one:

- Where can you get the highest rate of interest on your savings?
- Where can you obtain a checking account with low (or no) fees?
- Will you be able to borrow money from the institution—with a credit card or another type of loan—when you need it?
- Do you need an institution that offers free financial advice?
- Is the institution FDIC- or SAIF-insured?
- Does the institution have convenient locations?
- Does it have online banking services?
- Does it have any special banking services that you might need?

SECTION 1 Assessment

Review Key Concepts

1. **Summarize** What are the types of financial services available for both short-term and long-term needs?
2. **Describe** List the four types of non-depository financial institutions and describe them.
3. **Explain** What are problematic financial businesses? Why are they considered problematic?
4. **Relate** What impact did the Great Depression of the 1930s have on the banking industry?

Higher Order Thinking 

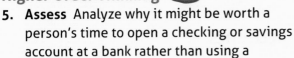

5. **Assess** Analyze why it might be worth a person's time to open a checking or savings account at a bank rather than using a check-cashing outlet.

21st Century Skills

6. **Access and Evaluate Information** Suppose your friend just got a new job and would like to open a checking account with her new wages. She has asked for your help in deciding which bank she should go to. Use a variety of resources to gather information about three different local banks and the services they offer. Use a graphic organizer to help organize and analyze the information you gather. Write an e-mail to your friend with your recommendation and the reasons to support that recommendation.

Mathematics

7. **Checking Account** You want to open a checking account and have gone to two different banks to compare your options. Bank A offers an account with no fees as long as you keep a minimum balance of $300. This account provides an annual interest rate of 1 percent. Bank B's account has no minimum balance requirements but has a fee of $0.75 per month and provides an annual interest rate of 2.75 percent. Which account is better if you plan to keep an average balance of $500 in the account?

Math Concept **Calculate Return Earned** To calculate the annual return earned on a checking account, determine the total amount of interest earned on the account balance and subtract all fees incurred on the account.

Starting Hint Determine the annual return earned on a checking account by first identifying the balance in the account. If monthly balances are not available, the average balance can be used. Multiply this balance by the annual interest rate.

NCTM Number and Operations Understand numbers, ways of representing numbers, relationships among numbers, and number systems.

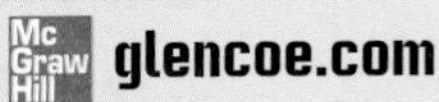

Mc Graw Hill glencoe.com Check your answers.

Section Objectives

- **Compare** the costs and benefits of different savings plans.
- **Explain** features of different savings plans.
- **Compare** the costs and benefits of different types of checking accounts.
- **Use** a checking account effectively.

As You Read

Relate Do you currently have a savings account? Is your interest compounded daily, monthly, or annually? Why does this matter?

Types of Savings Plans

What are some savings program options?

To achieve your financial goals, you will need a savings program. Savings programs may include regular savings accounts, certificates of deposit, money market accounts, and savings bonds. (See **Figure 4.**)

When applying for a savings or a checking account you will need to provide information such as your driver's license number, social security number, home address, phone number, mother's maiden name, and employment information. In addition, some banks have age requirements for certain accounts. With most banks, the application process can be completed at your local branch or online.

Regular Savings Accounts

Regular savings accounts, traditionally called *passbook accounts*, are ideal if you plan to make frequent deposits and withdrawals. They require little or no minimum balance and allow you to withdraw money on demand. The trade-off for this convenience is that the interest you earn will be low compared with other savings plans.

You may receive a passbook that records deposits and withdrawals, but typically, you will get a monthly or quarterly statement in the mail. **Quarterly** means every three months. Commercial banks, savings and loan associations, and other financial institutions offer regular savings accounts. At credit unions they may be called *share accounts*.

Certificates of Deposit

A **certificate of deposit (CD)** is a savings **alternative,** or option, in which money is left on deposit for a stated period of time to earn a specific rate of return. This period of time is called the *term*. The date when the money becomes available to you is called the *maturity date*. This savings plan is a relatively low-risk way to invest your money. It offers a higher interest rate than a regular savings account, but you will have to accept a few trade-offs. To earn the higher interest rate paid by CDs, you must accept three key limitations:

- You may have to leave your money on deposit for one month to five or more years.
- You probably will pay a penalty if you take the money out before the maturity date.
- Financial institutions require that you deposit a minimum amount to buy a certificate of deposit. This amount is usually larger than the balance a regular savings account requires.

CD Investment Strategies Here are some tips for investing in CDs:

- Find out where you can get the best rate. You can put your savings in a bank anywhere in the United States. You can use the Internet to find out what rates banks offer all over the country.
- Consider the economy as you decide what maturity date to choose. You may want to buy a long-term CD if interest rates are relatively high. Then, if interest rates go down because of changes in the economy, your money will continue to earn the higher rate.
- Never let a financial institution "roll over" a CD. For example, if your one-year CD matures, and you do nothing, the bank will redeposit that money in another one-year CD. You may decide to roll over; however, if you know that you will get the best rate possible.
- Consider when you will need the money. If you plan to use the money in two years to help pay for college, then buy a CD with a term of two years or less.
- If you have enough funds to have several accounts, you might consider creating a CD portfolio, which includes CDs that mature at different times. For example, you could have $1,000 in a three-month CD, $1,000 in a six-month CD, and $1,000 in a one-year CD. This way, you would be able to withdraw money at different times and still get better interest rates than you would with a passbook savings account.

Applying for an Account
The process for opening a checking or savings account will vary depending on the bank. However, the required information is often similar. Many banks now allow you to open accounts online.

Concept Application

Search online to find information on applying for a checking and savings account. What information and forms are required? Can you apply online or at a local branch?

FIGURE 4 **Savings Alternatives**

So Many Choices Each type of savings plan has pros and cons that you should consider. *Which type(s) would be best for a person who wants to save frequently but with small amounts?*

Type of Account	Benefits	Drawbacks
Regular savings accounts	• Low minimum balance • Ease of withdrawal • Insured	• Low rate of return
Certificates of deposit (CDs)	• Guaranteed rate of return for time of CD • Insured	• Possible penalty for early withdrawal • Minimum deposit
Money market accounts	• Good rate of return • Some check writing • Insured	• Minimum balance • No interest and possible service charge if below a certain balance
U.S. Savings Bonds	• Low minimum deposit • Guaranteed by the government • Free from state and local taxes	• Lower rate of return when cashed in before bond reaches maturity date

Money Market Accounts

A **money market account** is a savings account that requires a minimum balance and earns interest that varies from month to month. The rates float, or go up and down, as market rates change. Although the interest rate of a money market account is usually higher than that of a regular savings account, a money market account requires a higher minimum balance, typically $1,000. You may have to pay a penalty if your balance goes below the minimum amount. Money market accounts are covered by federal deposit insurance. The FDIC insures money market accounts up to $250,000.

U.S. Savings Bonds

Another savings option is purchasing a U.S. Savings Bond (also called a *Patriot Bond*). For example, when Meagan graduated high school in 2005, her aunt gave her a U.S. Savings Bond as a gift. Her aunt paid $250 for the bond, but it has a face value of $500. This means that if Meagan keeps the bond until the designated maturity date, it will eventually earn enough interest to be worth $500 or even more.

You can purchase Series EE Savings Bonds from the federal government in amounts that range from $25 to $5,000 (face values of $50 to $10,000, respectively). The government limits total purchases per year to $15,000 ($30,000 face value) per person. You may buy savings bonds from banks or through the government's Web site.

The maturity date, or the date a bond reaches its face value, depends on the date it was bought and the interest rate the bond is earning. For some bonds, the rate changes every six months. Because interest rates vary, no official maturity date exists for Series EE Savings Bonds. Bonds purchased after April 1997 and cashed after less than five years are subject to a three-month penalty—that is, you will not receive any interest for the last three months before you cash it.

Long-Term Goals
Some savings options, such as savings bonds, are better for long-term financial goals, such as paying for college. *Why might savings bonds or CDs be better for long-term goals than a savings account?*

Economics and You

The Federal Reserve System

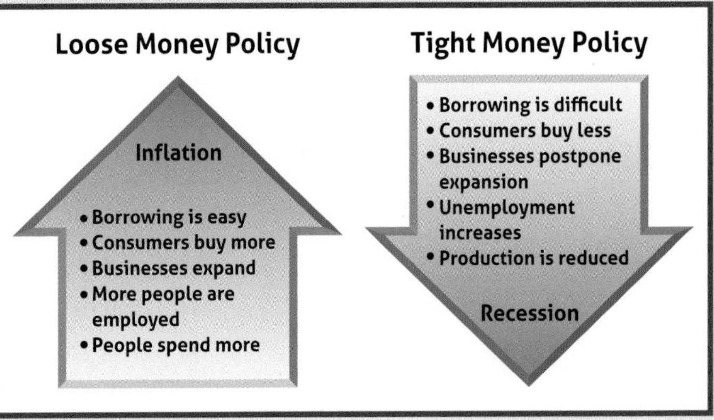

The Federal Reserve System (the Fed) is the United States central bank. There are twelve Federal Reserve Banks that assist the Fed in servicing and regulating depository institutions. The Fed also has the responsibility of monitoring the economy. If the economy is growing too quickly and there is fear of inflation, the Fed may increase interest rates to member banks in an effort to discourage borrowing. This makes it more expensive for other banks to borrow money so they pass the increase onto savers and borrowers. Home mortgages, as well as personal and business loans, decrease because fewer people want to pay the higher interest rates to borrow money, which slows the economy.

Personal Finance Connection If you put your money in a savings account at a local bank and the Fed increases interest rates, you can expect to make more money as your bank increases savings interest rates. However, if you take out a loan when the Fed increases interest rates, the amount of money you will have to pay back to satisfy the loan will be higher.

Critical Thinking What do you think the Fed does when the economy is slowing down and is in a recession? Why?

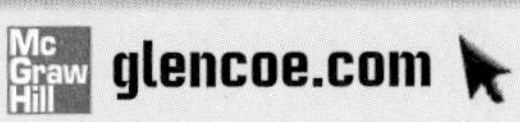

Activity Download an Economics and You Worksheet Activity.

A Series EE Savings Bond continues to earn interest for 30 years if you do not cash it in. The longer you hold it, the more it is worth. Its value may be more than the face value if it is held past maturity.

Meagan kept her bond for ten years. In 2004, she decided to cash it in to help her make a down payment on a condominium. She found out that it was worth a little more than $450. Your bond's worth will depend on current interest rates and on the month and year in which the bond was issued.

Taxes on Savings Bonds The interest you earn on Series EE Bonds is exempt from, or free of, state and local taxes. You do not pay federal taxes on the interest earnings until you cash in the bond. Once a Series EE Bond has reached maturity, you can choose to defer federal taxes further by exchanging it for a Series HH Bond. Low- and middle-income families who use the money from redeemed Series EE Bonds to pay for higher education pay no taxes on the interest.

Reading Check

Recall What is a CD portfolio?

Evaluating Savings Plans

How should you evaluate a savings plan?

Your selection of a savings plan will be influenced by several factors. You should consider the rate of return, inflation, tax considerations, liquidity, restrictions, and fees.

Rate of Return

Earnings on savings can be measured by the rate of return, or yield. The **rate of return** is the percentage of increase in the value of your savings from earned interest. For example, when Emisha put the $75 she earned from babysitting on New Year's Eve into a regular savings account last year, she earned $3 in interest. Therefore, her rate of return was 4 percent. To calculate the rate of return, she divided the total interest by the amount of her deposit ($\$3 \div \$75 = .04$ or 4 percent).

Compounding The yield on your savings will usually be greater than the stated interest rate. **Compounding** is the process in which interest is earned on both the principal—the original amount you deposited—and on any previously earned interest. It is a multistep process for computing interest. First, the interest on the principal is computed. That interest is added to the principal. The next time interest is computed, the new, larger balance is used. Compounding may take place every year, every quarter, every month, or even every day.

How much interest would your account earn in one year if the interest were compounded monthly? To make this calculation, first multiply the principal by the annual interest rate. Divide that figure by 12, the number of months in a year. This is the interest you would earn after the first month. To calculate the interest earned for the second month, add any interest earned in the first month to the principal. Then take that amount and multiply it by the annual interest rate. Next divide that number by 12. This is your interest earned in the second month. After you have repeated this calculation for all 12 months, add the monthly interest totals. The sum of the monthly interest amounts is the interest your account would earn in one year if the interest were compounded monthly.

The more frequently your balance is compounded, the greater your yield, or rate of return, will be. For example, if you deposited $100 in an account with a 4 percent annual interest rate that is compounded annually (once a year), after one year you will earn $4 ($\$100 \times .04$ or $4\% = \$4$). Your rate of return is 4 percent. If you put that same $100 in an account that is compounded monthly at an annual interest rate of 4 percent, your rate of return will be higher.

Remember, your rate of return is the total interest earned divided by the amount of your original deposit. The difference may not seem like much, but compounding can have a great impact on large amounts of money that are held in savings accounts for long periods.

GO FIGURE Mathematics

Interest Compounded Monthly

Savings accounts that pay interest monthly can end up earning more interest than an account that pays once a year.

EXAMPLE You deposit $100 in a savings account. The bank is paying you 4 percent annually, which is compounded monthly. How much interest will you earn for the year?

Formula Find the interest earned for the first month

A. Principal × Annual Interest Rate/12 = Interest Earned for First Month

B. (Principal + Previously Earned Interest) × Annual Interest Rate/12 = Interest Earned for a Given Month

Solution

Month	Calculation
1	($100.00 × 4%) ÷ 12 = $0.33
2	($100.33 × 4%) ÷ 12 = $0.33
3	($100.66 × 4%) ÷ 12 = $0.34
4	($101.00 × 4%) ÷ 12 = $0.34
5	($101.34 × 4%) ÷ 12 = $0.34
6	($101.68 × 4%) ÷ 12 = $0.34
7	($102.02 × 4%) ÷ 12 = $0.34
8	($102.36 × 4%) ÷ 12 = $0.34
9	($102.70 × 4%) ÷ 12 = $0.34
10	($103.04 × 4%) ÷ 12 = $0.34
11	($103.38 × 4%) ÷ 12 = $0.34
12	($103.72 × 4%) ÷ 12 = $0.35

At the end of the year, you will have $104.07 ($100.00 + $4.07 = $104.07). You earned $4.07 in compounded interest for the year.

Your Turn

How much interest would this account earn if interest was paid once for the whole year?

Truth in Savings According to the Truth in Savings law (Federal Reserve Regulation DD), financial institutions have to inform you of the following information:

- Fees on deposit accounts
- Interest rate
- Annual percentage yield (APY)
- Terms and conditions of the savings plan

The **annual percentage yield (APY)** is the amount of interest that a $100 deposit would earn, after compounding, for one year. The interest is based on the annual interest rate and the frequency of compounding for one year. In the **Go Figure** example, the APY is 4.07 percent. The higher the APY is, the better the return. Because the APY is stated as a percentage and as an annual rate, you can compare savings plans that have different rates and compounding frequencies.

GO FIGURE Mathematics

Rate of Return

A compounded rate of return (percentage) is more than the stated year's rate.

EXAMPLE You deposit $100 in a savings account. The bank is paying you 4 percent annually, compounded monthly. After one year, the account has earned $4.07 in interest. What would your rate of return be for one year?

> **Formula** Total Interest Earned/Original Deposit = Rate of Return
>
> **Solution** $4.07/$100 = 0.0407 = 4.07%
> Your rate of return is 4.07 percent.

Your Turn

What would be your rate of return for one year if the account earned $5.14 in interest on a deposit of $100?

Inflation

You should compare the rate of interest you earn on your savings with the rate of inflation. If you open a savings account that offers 3 percent interest, and the inflation rate rises to 6 percent, your money will lose value and buying power. Usually, however, the interest rates offered on savings accounts increase if the rate of inflation increases. The biggest problem with inflation occurs if you are locked into a lower interest rate for a long period.

Tax Considerations

Like inflation, taxes reduce the interest earned on savings. For example, Karim was glad to find a savings account that would pay 5 percent interest. However, he was not happy when he filled out his tax return and had to pay taxes on that interest. He decided to look into tax-exempt and tax-deferred savings plans for some of his money.

Liquidity

Check the savings plans you are considering to determine whether they charge a penalty or pay a lower rate of interest if you withdraw your funds early. If you need to be able to withdraw your money easily, put your money in a liquid account—even if it earns lower interest. On the other hand, if you are saving for long-term goals, a high interest rate is more important than liquidity.

Safety

Most savings plans at banks, savings and loan associations, and credit unions are insured by agencies affiliated with the federal government. This protection prevents a loss of money due to the failure of the insured institution. While a few financial institutions have failed in recent years, savers with deposits covered by federal insurance have not lost any money. Depositors of failed organizations either have been paid the amounts in their accounts or have had the accounts taken over by a financially stable institution.

The Federal Deposit Insurance Corporation (FDIC) administers separate insurance funds: the Bank Insurance Fund and the Savings Association Insurance Fund (SAIF). Credit unions may obtain deposit insurance through the National Credit Union Association (NCUA). Some state-chartered credit unions have opted for a private insurance program.

Restrictions and Fees

Be aware of any restrictions on savings plans, such as a delay between the time when interest is earned and when it is actually paid into your account. Also check for fees for making deposits and withdrawals. Find out about any service charges you may have to pay if your balance drops below a certain amount, or if you do not use your account for a certain period. These fees and service charges can add up.

Reading Check

Define What is the principal?

Types of Checking Accounts

What are the advantages to the different types of checking accounts?

Checking accounts can be divided into three main categories: regular, activity, and interest-earning accounts.

Regular Checking Accounts

Regular checking accounts usually do not require a minimum balance. However, if the account does require a minimum balance, and your account drops below that amount, you will have to pay a monthly service charge. A $10 charge every month can take a bite out of your funds. Some institutions will waive a service charge if you keep a certain balance in your savings account.

Activity Accounts

If you write only a few checks each month and are unable to maintain a minimum balance, this type of checking account may be right for you. The financial institution will charge a fee for each check you write and sometimes a fee for each deposit. In addition, a monthly service fee will be charged. However, you do not need to maintain a minimum balance.

Interest-Earning Checking Accounts

Interest-earning checking accounts are a combination of checking and savings accounts. These accounts pay interest if you maintain a minimum balance. If your account balance goes below the limit, you may not earn any interest, and you may also have to pay a service charge.

Reading Check

Identify What are the three main categories of checking accounts?

Evaluating Checking Accounts

What factors should you consider when choosing a checking account?

Would you rather have a checking account that pays interest and requires a $1,000 minimum balance or one that does not pay interest and has no minimum deposit? How do you decide which will meet your needs? You will need to weigh several factors such as: restrictions, fees and charges, interest, and special services.

Restrictions

The most common restriction is the requirement that you keep a minimum balance. Other restrictions may include the number of transactions allowed and the number of checks you may write in a month.

Fees and Charges

You may pay a monthly service charge as well as fees for check printing, overdrafts, and stop-payment orders.

Interest

Interest rates, frequency of compounding, and the way in which interest is calculated all affect an interest-bearing checking account.

Special Services

Checking account services include ATMs and banking by telephone and online. As a checking account customer, you may also receive **overdraft protection**—an automatic loan made to an account if the balance will not cover checks written. The institution will charge interest on that loan, but the amount may be less than the fee for overdrawing your account. Your bank may also offer an overdraft protection service that transfers money from your savings to your checking account.

The Check Clearing for the 21st Century Act, or "Check 21," took effect in 2004. The Act allows banks to dispense with original paper checks. Banks can now transmit electronic images of checks through the check-clearing process. If you want to receive your cancelled paper check, the bank will provide a substitute check for a fee.

Reading Check

Recall What are three common fees that checking accounts may include?

Using a Checking Account

How do you open and use a checking account?

After you select the type of checking account that best fits your needs, you need to know how to use it effectively. Obtaining and using a checking account involves several activities.

Opening a Checking Account

Before you open a checking account, decide whether you want an individual or joint account. An individual account has one owner; a joint account has two or more. Personal joint accounts are usually "or" accounts, which means only one of the owners needs to sign a check. You sign a signature card at the bank so your signature can be verified.

FIGURE 5 **Check Register**

Keeping Track This sample check register shows how to keep track of checks as you write them. *What other amounts should you record in your check register?*

NUMBER	DATE	DESCRIPTION OF TRANSACTION	PAYMENT/DEBIT (-)		√ T	FEE (IF ANY) (-)	DEPOSIT/CREDIT (+)		BALANCE	
									$ 418	00
106	7/15	Bob's Service Station	$ 25	00		$	$		-25	00
		oil change							393	00
107	7/15	Cutler Enterprises	14	00					-14	00
		magazine subscription							379	00
108	7/16	Motor Vehicles Department	160	00					-160	00
		renewal							219	00
109	7/18	Jack's Music	34	00					-34	00
		gift							185	00

FIGURE 6 **Sample Personal Check**

Personal Check Never write a check in pencil and always write legibly. *Why do you have to write the amount in words and in numerals?*

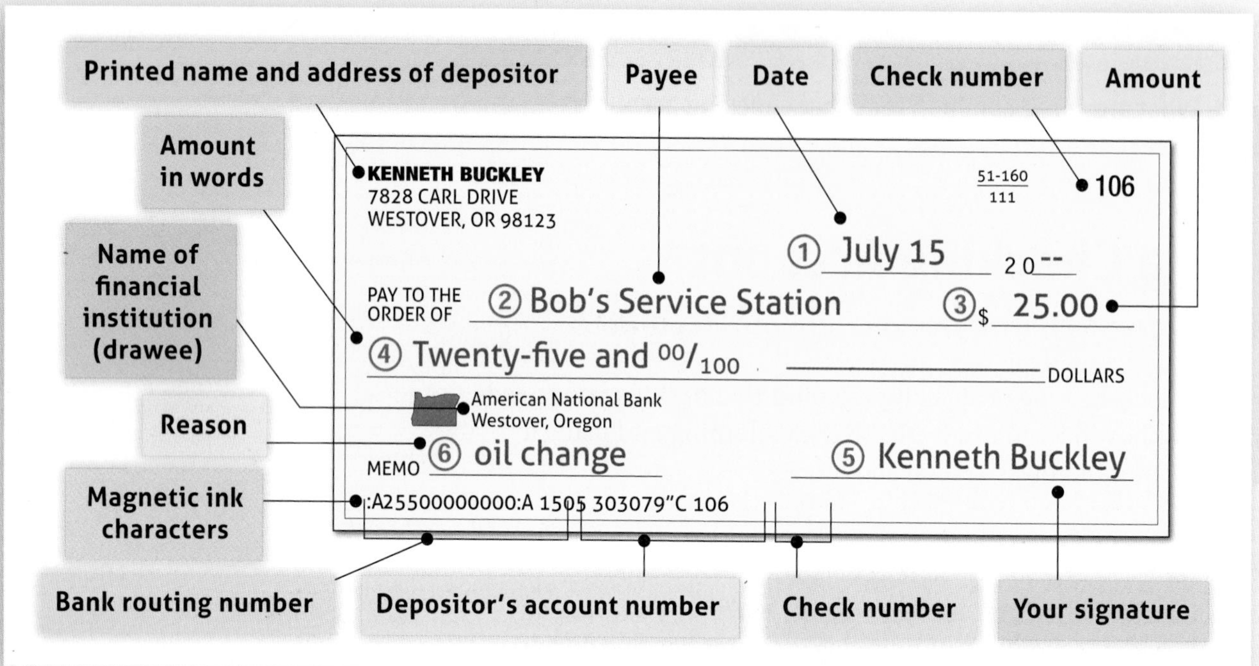

Like a savings account, when applying for a checking account you will need to provide information such as your driver's license number, social security number, home address, phone number, mother's maiden name, and employment information. Check with the bank for other requirements for opening a checking account, such as any age requirements. The application forms can be completed at your local branch or, in many cases, online.

Writing Checks

Before you write a check, write the date, the number of the check, the name of the party who will receive the payment, and the exact amount in your check register. A check register is a small booklet that you use to record activity in your account. You receive it with your supply of blank checks. Record all checks that you write, deposits, ATM withdrawals, debit card charges, interest earned (if any), any fees, and other transactions. Be sure to keep a current balance of the money you have by deducting from or adding to your balance the amount of any check transaction. **Figure 5** shows a sample check register.

Figure 6 shows the correct way to write a check. Follow these steps:

- Write the current date.
- Write the name of the party (payee) who will receive the check.

- Record the amount of the payment in numerals.
- Write the amount in words.
- Sign the check in the same way you signed your signature card at the bank.
- Make a note of the reason for the payment. This is a good place to record an account number if the payment is for a credit card or service, such as electricity or cable television.

If you make a mistake when writing a check, do not erase the error. Write a new check, tear up the old check, and write the word *Void* in your check register. If the mistake is small, you may be able to correct the check and write your initials next to the correction.

If a check is lost or stolen, or if you want to take back your payment for a business transaction, you may ask the bank to issue a stop-payment order. A **stop-payment order** is a request that a bank or other financial institution not cash a particular check. Fees for this service can range from $10 to $20 or more.

Making Deposits

To add money to your checking account, fill out a deposit ticket. Tickets usually include room to list four or five checks and any amount of cash that you are depositing. Endorse, or sign, the back of each check you want to deposit. The **endorsement** is the signature of the payee, the party to whom the check has been written.

There are also different ways to endorse a check. A *blank endorsement* is the most simple. You or the check holder signs the back of the check. This should only be done when you are actually depositing a check since a check may be cashed by anyone once it has been signed.

A *restrictive endorsement* requires the check holder's signature and a restriction on how the paper may be used by the bank. The most common expression used is "For deposit only." This is an instruction that restricts the bank to applying the check amount to the holder's account.

A *special endorsement* allows you to transfer a check to an organization or another person. When you endorse the check, you write the words *pay to the order of*, followed by the name of the organization or person, and then you sign your name.

Here are some tips to follow when endorsing a check:

- Do not endorse a check until you are ready to cash or deposit it.
- Write your signature on the back of the check at the top left end.
- Sign your name exactly as it appears on the front of the check.
- Use a pen so that your signature cannot be erased.
- If depositing a check by mail, write "For deposit only" above your signature.

Media Literacy

Media literacy is the ability to analyze, evaluate, and create media messages. Media literacy involves understanding how, why, and for what purpose media messages are made. Individuals might respond to media messages differently. Understanding how media messages are interpreted and how they can influence opinions and behaviors are important parts of media literacy.

Write About It

Think of a media message you have heard or read about recently. Write one or more paragraphs summarizing the message and its format, describing your reaction to the message, and explaining why another person might react to the message differently.

glencoe.com

Activity Download a Career and College Readiness Worksheet Activity.

Check Clearing

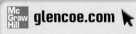

Check clearing is a system that ensures that the money you deposited in the account is available for withdrawal. For example, if you deposit a check for $50 into your account, your bank usually holds that $50 until it clears with the bank on which it was drawn. During this time you cannot withdraw that money. By law, institutions are limited to holding funds from checks drawn on local banks to no more than two business days and on non-local banks to no more than five business days. Check-clearing rules vary, so ask your bank about its rules.

Keeping Track of a Checking Account

Each month your bank will send you a statement that shows your checking account activity for the month.

Your bank statement will list:

- Deposits
- Checks you have written (charged against your account)
- ATM withdrawals
- Debit card charges
- Interest earned and fees

Reconciliation The balance reported on the bank statement may be different from the balance in your check register. You might have written checks that have not yet cleared, or maybe you deposited money into your account after the bank prepared your statement.

To determine your true balance, you can fill out a bank reconciliation form. A **bank reconciliation** is a report that accounts for the differences between the bank statement and a checkbook balance. This process is called *balancing your checkbook*. To balance, or reconcile, your account, follow several steps (See **Figure 7**).

- Compare the checks you have written during the month with those that are listed on the bank statement as paid, or cleared. List all outstanding checks—checks you wrote but have not cleared. Subtract the total amount of outstanding checks from the balance on the bank statement.
- Determine whether any recent deposits are not on the bank statement. If so, add the amounts of those deposits to the bank statement balance.
- Subtract fees and charges listed on the statement from your checkbook balance.
- Add interest earned to your checkbook balance.

Then compare the balance in your check register and the adjusted bank balance on the reconciliation form. They should be the same. If the balances do not match, check your math, and make sure all checks and deposits are entered in your check register and on the statement. If there is a bank error, report it.

FIGURE 7 Bank Account Reconciliation

Balancing Your Checkbook It is important to reconcile your check register with your bank statement each month. *Why is it important for the adjusted bank balance to match your register?*

❖ *American National Bank*
WESTOVER, OREGON

Kenneth Buckley
7828 Carl Drive
Westover, OR 98123

FDIC

Account Number: 303079
Statement Date: 7/15/--

Balance Last Statement	Deposits & Other Credits		Checks & Other Debits		Balance This Statement
	No.	Amount	No.	Amount	
00.00	2	700.00	5	482.00	218.00

Description	Checks & Other Debits	Deposits & Other Credits	Date	Balance
Balance Forward				00.00
Deposit		500.00	7/01	500.00
Check 101	273.00		7/04	227.00
Check 102	27.00		7/07	200.00
Check 103	50.00		7/08	150.00
Deposit		200.00	7/10	350.00
Check 104	100.00		7/14	250.00
Check 105	32.00		7/14	218.00

PLEASE EXAMINE YOUR STATEMENT AT ONCE. IF NO ERROR IS REPORTED IN 10 DAYS THE ACCOUNT WILL BE CONSIDERED CORRECT AND VOUCHERS GENUINE. ALL ITEMS ARE CREDITED SUBJECT TO FINAL PAYMENT.

BANK RECONCILIATION FORM

PLEASE EXAMINE YOUR STATEMENT AT ONCE. ANY DISCREPANCY SHOULD BE REPORTED TO THE BANK IMMEDIATELY.

1. In your checkbook, record any transactions appearing on this statement but not yet listed.
2. List any checks still outstanding in the space provided to the right.

3. Enter the balance shown on this statement here.	218	00
4. Enter deposits recorded in your checkbook but not shown on this statement.	____	—
5. Total lines 3 and 4 and enter here.	218	00
6. Enter total checks outstanding here.	69	00
7. Subtract line 6 from line 5. This adjusted bank balance should agree with your checkbook balance.	149	00

CHECKS OUTSTANDING		
Number	Amount	
106	25	00
107	14	00
108	30	00
TOTAL	69	00

Other Payment Methods

You may make payments by other methods besides using a personal check. A certified check is a personal check with a guaranteed payment. The financial institution deducts the amount from your account when it certifies the check. You can also purchase a cashier's check or money order from a financial institution. You pay the amount of the check or money order plus a fee. Travelers checks allow you to obtain cash in a country's currency when you are away from home.

You sign each check once when you purchase the checks and a second time when you cash them. If you lose a check or it is stolen, it can be replaced with proof of purchase. Prepaid travelers cards allow travelers to get local currency from ATMs throughout the world.

Reading Check

List What information do monthly bank statements list?

Financial Institutions and Your Money

How do banks make money?

The amount of deposits held by a bank affects its ability to loan money. Banks make money by making loans. The amount of money that banks can lend is affected by the reserve requirement set by the Federal Reserve. The reserve requirement is 3 percent to 10 percent of a bank's total deposits, including your deposit. For example, when a bank gets a deposit of $100, the bank can then lend out $90. That $90 goes back into the economy, paying for goods or services, and may end up deposited in another bank. That bank can then lend out $81 of that $90 deposit, and that $81 goes into the economy to pay for goods or services, and is then deposited into another bank that proceeds to lend out a percentage of it. Thus, banking your money benefits you as well as others in the economic system.

After You Read

React What is a bank reconciliation? Why is it important?

Money Options
When travelling in another country, many people feel safer carrying travelers checks rather than cash. *Why are travelers checks more secure than cash?*

Assessment

Review Key Concepts

1. **Explain** What are some of the costs and benefits of the different types of savings accounts?
2. **Describe** What factors can you use to evaluate a savings plan?
3. **List** Identify four factors to evaluate when selecting a checking account.
4. **Identify** What six items on your bank statement will help track your checking account?
5. **Determine** How would you monitor and maintain your savings account? What documents should you use?

Higher Order Thinking H.O.T.

6. **Evaluate** Consider whether you would prefer to have a separate checking and savings account, or an interest-earning checking account. Explain your decision.

English Language Arts

7. **Savings Options** Suppose you received $1,000. You want to save it towards a down payment on a car. Conduct research using your text and other print or online resources to find out more about certificates of deposit and money market accounts. What are the benefits and drawbacks of each? Create a graphic organizer to compare and contrast the two savings options. Based on your findings, write a brief statement indicating which option you would choose for your money and why.

NCTE 8 Use information resources to gather information and create and communicate knowledge.

Mathematics

8. **Annual Percentage Yield** Tori received $300 from her grandmother for her birthday. She wanted to spend the money, but her grandmother convinced her to put it in a savings account. Tori deposited the money into her savings account which provides a 3.5 percent annual interest rate that is compounded monthly. How much money in interest will Tori earn from the bank after 6 months? After one year, Tori will have $310.67 in her account. Calculate the annual percentage yield that she earned on her account.

Math Concept **Calculate Annual Percentage Yield** To calculate the annual percentage yield on a savings account with monthly compounding you must determine the total interest earned for the year and divide this amount by the original deposit.

Starting Hint Calculate the balance in the account after the first month by multiplying the deposit amount by the annual interest rate and dividing the result by 12.

NCTM Problem Solving Solve problems that arise in mathematics and in other contexts.

Check your answers.

Visual Summary

Banking

Know Your Options
When managing your money, it is important to consider the best options for all your financial services needs.

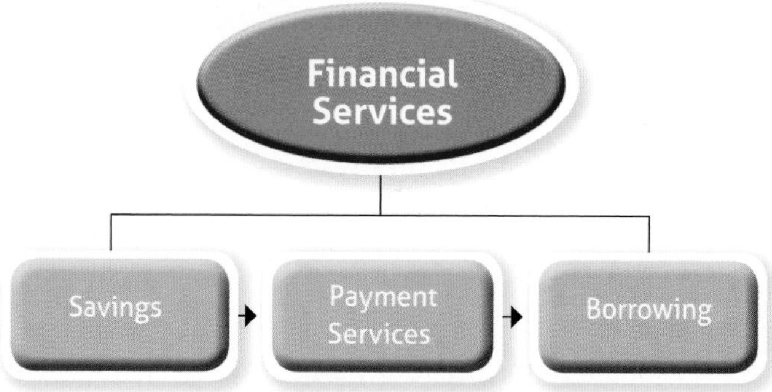

Choose a Financial Institution
Be sure to do your research to accurately compare institutions and select the one that is best for you.

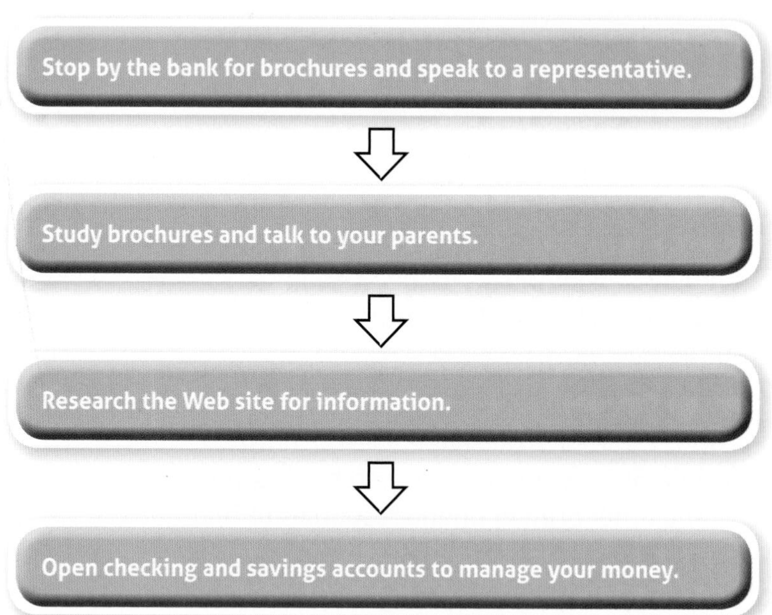

Try It!
Draw a diagram like the one shown and fill in the blank circles with the factors you should compare when selecting a checking account.

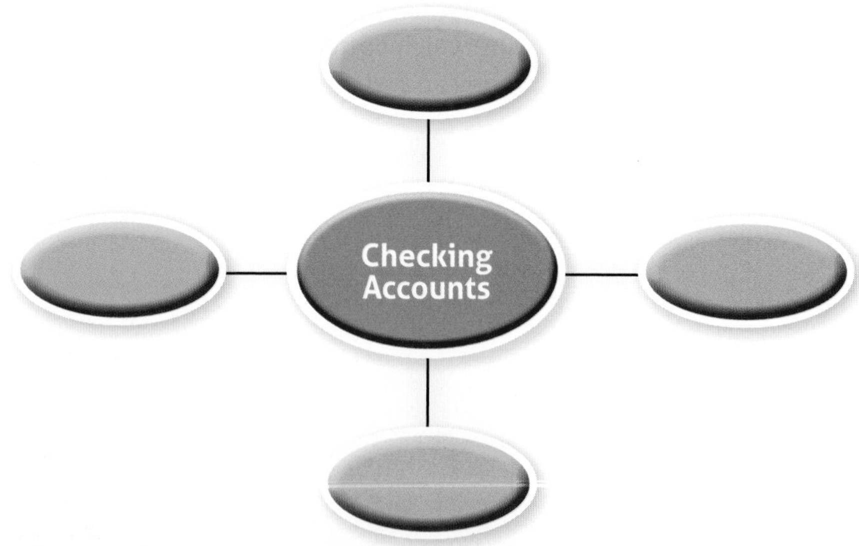

Chapter Review and Assessment

Chapter Summary

- The three primary types of financial services are savings; payment services; and borrowing.
- Commercial banks, savings and loan associations, mutual savings banks, and credit unions are financial institutions that accept secure deposits and provide transfer and lending services.
- Life insurance companies and investment companies accept customers' funds, provide financial security for dependents, and invest and manage funds.
- Finance companies and mortgage companies offer loans.
- Bank savings plans offer the lowest interest rates with the greatest liquidity.
- Higher interest rates are available on certificates of deposit (CDs); money must be on deposit for a specified time.
- Money market accounts and U.S. Savings Bonds are less liquid than bank savings accounts, but may provide greater returns. To evaluate a savings plan, look at its features, such as its rate of return compared with inflation, tax considerations, liquidity, and restrictions and fees.
- Regular, activity, and interest-earning are the three categories of checking accounts. Some of these require minimum balances and/or fees for transactions. Some pay interest on deposits.
- To use a checking account, write checks carefully, endorse checks you deposit, and reconcile your checkbook against bank statements.

Vocabulary Review

1. Write each of the vocabulary terms below on an index card, and the definitions on separate index cards. Work in pairs or small groups to match each term to its definition.

- direct deposit
- automated teller machine (ATM)
- debit card
- commercial bank
- savings and loan association (S&L)
- credit union
- certificate of deposit (CD)
- money market account
- rate of return
- compounding
- annual percentage yield (APY)
- overdraft protection
- stop-payment order
- endorsement
- bank reconciliation
- authorization
- issuers
- quarterly
- alternative

Higher Order Thinking

2. **Relate** What is the process for maintaining a checking and savings account? How are they similar?
3. **Select** Jenny had $5,000 that she wanted to save for six months before using it to pay for her college tuition. Evaluate which type of savings plan would be her best option for a maximum rate of return.
4. **Conclude** Explain why it is important to use financial institutions that are FDIC insured.
5. **Hypothesize** Why do you think the Truth in Savings law was enacted?
6. **Compare and contrast** Research the forms and processes required for applying for a checking and savings account. How are they similar? How are they different?
7. **Evaluate** Why might credit unions offer lower fees and loan rates than a commercial bank?
8. **Assess** What should you know when choosing a financial institution? Why is it important?
9. **Defend** Why do you think electronic services, such as the Check 21 act, may be beneficial?

College and Career Readiness

Social Studies

10. Prepaid Cards Young adults often find themselves struggling with money management. A growing trend is the use of prepaid debit cards to help teach teenagers with money management. A prepaid debit card is generally linked to a parent's checking or savings account. It allows a preset amount of money to be spent and allows the parents to track where the money is being spent. This can then lead to financial discussions between the parent and teen about money management. Conduct additional research as necessary, and write a one-page report with your opinion on whether using prepaid debit cards is a good way to help teenagers learn money management.

NCSS IV D Individual Development & Identity Apply concepts, methods, and theories about the study of human growth and development, such as physical endowment, learning, motivation, behavior, perception, and personality.

Mathematics

11. Interest Earned Sam made $1,300 from his summer internship. He wants to deposit the money into a savings account but is not sure which savings account to open. His first choice earns 2.5 percent annual interest, compounded quarterly while the second choice earns 2.75 percent annual interest, compounded bi-monthly. Which account will earn Sam more money in interest after one year? What is the annual percentage yield on each account?

Math Concept **Calculate Interest Earned** To calculate the annual percentage yield on a savings account with monthly compounding you must determine the total interest earned for the year and divide this amount by the original deposit.

Starting Hint To calculate the interest earned per period on an account that compounds interest bi-monthly, multiply the deposit by the annual interest rate and divide by 6.

NCTM Problem Solving Solve problems that arise in mathematics and in other contexts.

English Language Arts

12. Banking Services Many banks and credit unions now offer financial planning services. Choose a local bank and conduct research to determine what financial planning services that bank offers. These might include one-on-one consultations to help you develop a budget strategy, insurance services, or advice for building a personal business. Create a flyer that lists and briefly describes each service. Which of the services offered do you think you could take advantage of now? Which might you use in the future? Which ones do you not think would benefit you? Why? Write a paragraph summarizing your answers to these questions.

NCTE 8 Use information resources to gather information and create and communicate knowledge.

Economics

13. Subjective Value All goods and services have value. How much any item or service is worth will vary based on factors such as geography, time of year, and intrinsic value to the consumer. For example, fruit costs vary depending on whether it is in season. And a comic book's value will depend a great deal on how important it is to a collector. Conduct research to find a collectible which recently sold for a large amount of money. Why do you think it sold for so much? If you had that amount of money available, would you have been willing to spend it on that item?

Real-World Applications

14. Managing Money Many financial institutions are offering more technology-based services to help consumers manage their money. Suppose your friend Edward just started a new job. He wants to maintain both a checking and savings account so that he can have cash to spend now and start saving for college. Prepare a recommendation for Edward of the online tools that you would suggest he use to help set and attain his short-, intermediate, and long-term goals.

Comparison Shopping for Banking Services

Sean is ready to open some bank accounts and is looking for the bank that best suits his needs. He is deciding between the local bank and the credit union where he works.

Sean's Savings Search

Name of Institution	Kensington Bank	Acme Credit Union
Savings		
Annual interest rate	1.8%	2.5%
Minimum balance required	$100	none
Certificate of Deposit (CD) interest rate for 6 months	5.20%	5.40%
Checking		
Monthly service charge	$8.50	$6.00
Minimum balance for "free" checking	$3,000	$1,000
Fees for ATM	Free	no ATMs
Cost of checks	$10.00	$8.75
Overdraft protection	yes	none
Banking hours	Mon.-Sat. 9-6, Closed Sun.	Mon.-Fri. 9-6, Closed Sat. and Sun.

Sean decided to open a checking account at the bank because he needs the convenience of using the ATM. He opened a savings account at the credit union because it pays higher interest. When he has enough money, he will also purchase a CD at the credit union.

Compare

On a separate sheet of paper, list the banking services that are important to you. Then call or visit several banks in your area and compare services, costs, and interest rates that are available to you. What services are most important to you? Which bank would you choose? Explain why.

CHAPTER 15

Consumer Credit

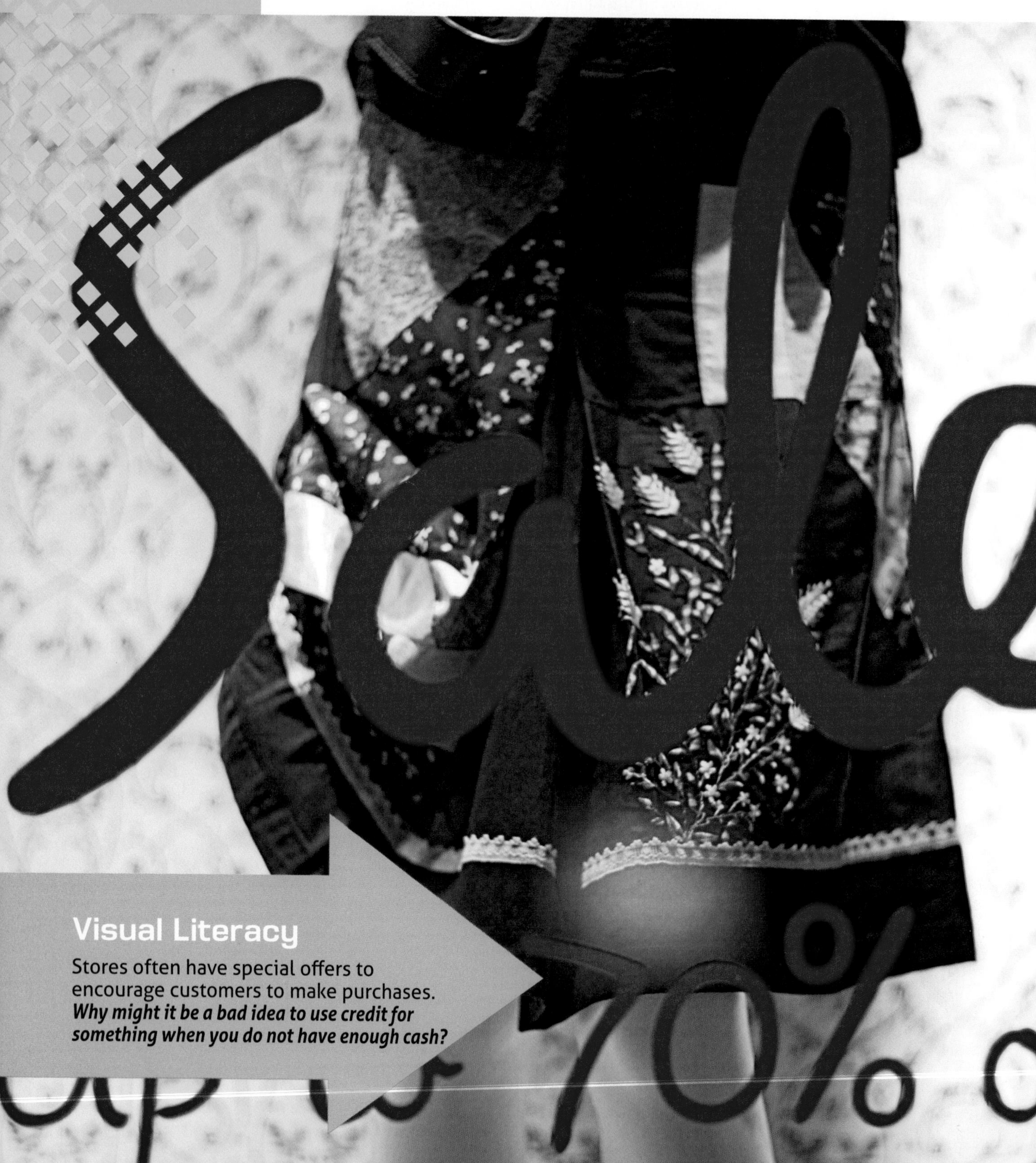

Visual Literacy

Stores often have special offers to encourage customers to make purchases. ***Why might it be a bad idea to use credit for something when you do not have enough cash?***

Discovery Project

Building Good Credit

Key Question

Why is it important to monitor and protect your credit rating?

Project Goal

Imagine you are moving into your first apartment. Your paycheck might cover rent and utilities, but you will be paying for many other things for yourself for the first time, such as furniture, groceries, and gasoline. You decide to use credit cards to make some of these purchases and help build your credit rating.

- Research the types of credit cards that would be useful for you. Is a department store card or gas card worthwhile? Would a smart card or T&E card be a better option?
- Set up a spreadsheet to compare the details of each card you research, including the APR, monthly fees, minimum monthly payment, late fees, and affiliated rewards programs.
- Evaluate your information to identify which card or cards would be best to suit your needs.

Ask Yourself ...

- *How will you use your credit cards?*
- *What types of credit cards will you get?*
- *How did you determine the most cost-effective cards?*
- *Aside from allowing you to buy things you need, what advantages do credit cards offer?*
- *What are the disadvantages of owning credit cards?*

Make Judgments and Decisions

How could you avoid the temptation of overusing your credit card?

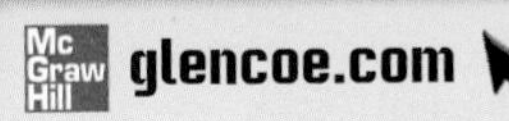

Evaluate Download an assessment rubric.

THE BIG IDEA

Building and maintaining a good credit rating can lead to financial security.

ASK STANDARD & POOR'S

Credit Payments

Q *My brother is going to college and has three credit cards with balances totaling $5,000. He is having trouble paying the minimum monthly payments. What should I tell him?*

A He needs a plan to pay down these debts. Have him contact the credit card companies and tell them that he wants to pay the debt and maintain good credit. They may accept payments of interest only for a few months while he finds ways to increase his income or cut spending.

Writing Activity

Write a one-page description of specific actions the person mentioned above might take to help increase his income and cut his spending. Your descriptions should include the actions he might take, as well as an estimation of the outcome, or how much money he could gain or save.

CHAPTER 15

Reading Guide

Before You Read

The Essential Question What steps can you take now to start building and maintaining a strong credit rating?

Main Idea

There are advantages to using consumer credit if you use it correctly. You must protect your credit and watch for the warning signs of debt problems.

Content Vocabulary

- credit
- consumer credit
- creditor
- closed-end credit
- open-end credit
- line of credit
- grace period
- finance charge
- net income
- annual percentage rate (APR)
- collateral
- simple interest
- minimum monthly payment
- credit rating
- cosigning
- bankruptcy

Academic Vocabulary

You will see these words in your reading and on your tests.

- finance
- title
- portion
- pledged
- promptly
- impostors
- repossess
- confidential

Graphic Organizer

Before you read this chapter, create a numbered list like the one below. As you read, note six questions to ask yourself before using credit.

Questions to Ask

1. ______
2. ______
3. ______
4. ______
5. ______
6. ______

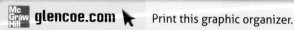

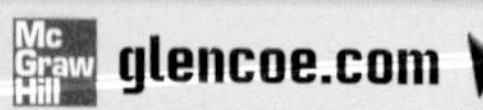

Print this graphic organizer.

Standards

Academic

Mathematics

NCTM Number and Operations Understand numbers, ways of representing numbers, relationships among numbers, and number systems.

NCTM Number and Operations Compute fluently and make reasonable estimates.

NCTM Connections Recognize and apply mathematics in contexts outside of mathematics.

English Language Arts

NCTE 12 Use language to accomplish individual purposes.

Science

NSES F Develop understanding of personal and community health; population growth; natural resources; environmental quality; natural and human-induced hazards; science and technology in local, national, and global challenges.

NCTM *National Council of Teachers of Mathematics*

NCTE *National Council of Teachers of English*

NCSS *National Council for the Social Studies*

NSES *National Science Education Standards*

Common Core

Reading Determine central ideas or themes of a text and analyze their development; summarize the key supporting details and ideas.

Reading Read and comprehend complex literary and informational texts independently and proficiently.

Writing Write routinely over extended time frames (time for research, reflection, and revision) and shorter time frames (a single sitting or a day or two) for a range of tasks, purposes, and audiences.

Using Consumer Credit Wisely

Why is having good credit important?

When you borrow money or charge an item to a credit card, you are using credit. **Credit** is an arrangement to receive cash, goods, or services now and pay for them in the future. **Consumer credit** is the use of credit for personal needs. It is also an indicator of consumer spending and demand. A common form of consumer credit is a credit card account issued by a financial institution. Merchants may also provide financing for products that they sell. Banks may directly finance purchases through loans and mortgages. A financial institution, merchant, or individual can be a **creditor**—an entity that lends money. Good credit is valuable. Having the ability to borrow funds allows us to buy things we would otherwise have to save for years to afford. Credit is an important financial tool, but it can also be dangerous, leading people into debt beyond their ability to repay. That is why using credit wisely is a valuable financial skill.

Today consumer credit is a major force in the American economy. Any forecast or evaluation of the economy includes consumer spending trends and consumer credit as a sustaining force. The use of credit is a basic factor in personal and family financial planning (see **Figure 1**). Paying for an item through credit often involves responsibility and risks.

Credit Uses and Misuses

You can probably think of many good reasons for using credit. For example, maybe you can buy something on credit now for less money than it will cost to pay in cash later. If you live in an area that lacks good public transportation, you may need a vehicle to travel. But when is it appropriate to use credit? If you cannot afford a high monthly payment, it probably is not a good idea to borrow money to buy an expensive sports car when all you need is simple and reliable transportation.

Using credit may increase the amount of money you can spend now, but the cost of credit decreases the amount of money you will have in the future. That is because you will be paying back the money you borrowed along with any charges for borrowing that money. When misused, credit can result in default, bankruptcy, and loss of creditworthiness.

Reading Check

Recognize When is it inappropriate to use credit?

Section Objectives

- **Explain** the meaning of consumer credit.
- **Differentiate** between closed-end credit and open-end credit.

As You Read

Relate Did you ever use credit to buy something you could not afford? What were the consequences?

FIGURE 1 **Consumer Installment Credit**

Rising Credit The use of installment credit has been steadily rising since the mid 1990s. *What is one disadvantage of using credit?*

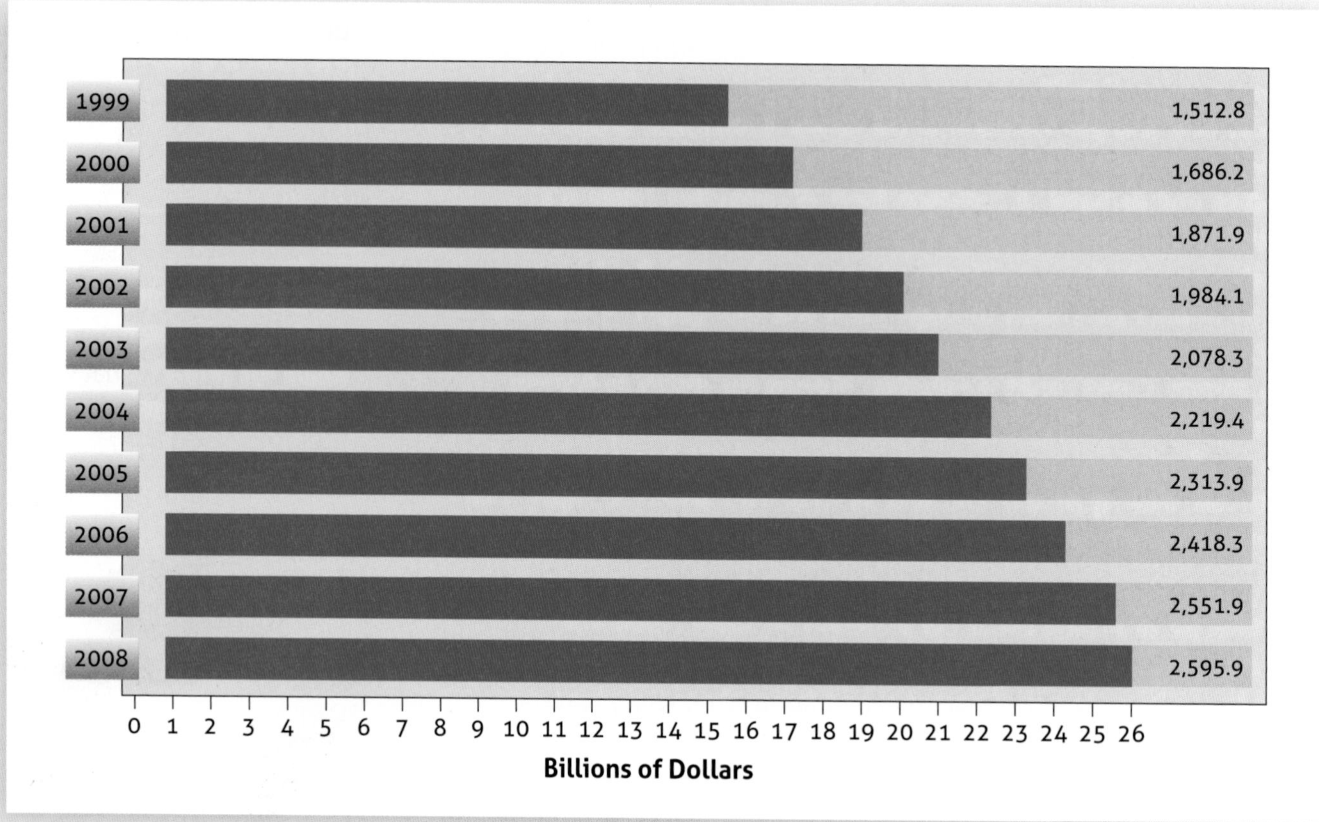

Factors to Consider Before Using Credit

What should you know before using credit?

Imagine you want to **finance**—give or get money for—a used vehicle. Before you decide to finance a major purchase by using credit, consider:

- Do you have the cash you need for the down payment?
- Do you want to use your savings instead of credit?
- Can you afford the item?
- Could you use the credit in some better way?
- Could you put off buying the item for a while?
- What are the opportunity costs of postponing the purchase?
- What are the costs of using credit?

When you buy something on credit, you also agree to pay the fee that a creditor adds to the purchase price. For example, if you do not pay your credit card bill in full every month, you will be charged interest on the amount that you have not paid. It can be a periodic charge for the use of credit. Make sure the benefits of making the purchase now outweigh the costs of credit.

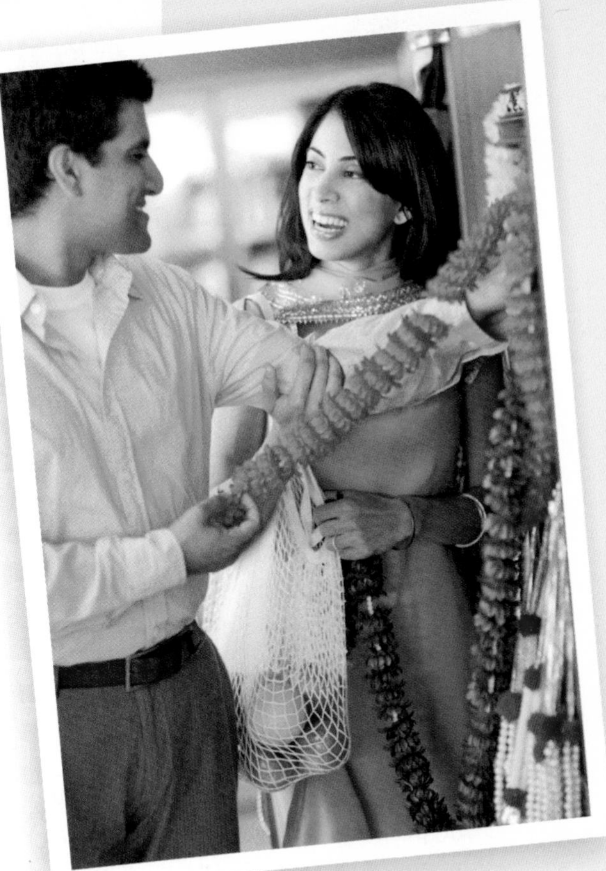

Advantages of Credit

The main advantage of using consumer credit is that it lets you enjoy goods and services now and pay for them later. Credit cards allow you to combine several purchases, making just one monthly payment.

If you are making hotel reservations, renting a car, or shopping by phone or online, you will probably need a credit card. Using credit gives you a record of your expenses. Shopping and traveling without carrying a lot of cash is safer. Finally, if you use credit wisely, other lenders will view you as a responsible person.

Disadvantages of Credit

Always remember that credit costs money. Perhaps the greatest disadvantage of using credit is the temptation to buy more than you can afford. Using credit to buy goods or services you cannot afford can lead to serious trouble. If you fail to repay a loan, or a credit card balance, you can lose your good credit reputation. You may also lose some of your income and property, which may be taken from you in order to repay your debts.

Using credit does not increase your total purchasing power, nor does it mean that you have more money. It just allows you to buy things now for which you must pay later. If your income does not increase, you may have difficulty paying your bills. Therefore, you should always approach credit with caution and avoid using it for more than your budget allows.

Plan Ahead
It is important to plan ahead and budget for items you need or want. *Why should you not view credit as "free money" to shop?*

Reading Check

Summarize What are the advantages of using consumer credit?

Types of Credit

Why would you need more than one type of credit?

There are two basic types of consumer credit: closed-end credit and open-end credit. You may use both types during your lifetime because each has advantages and disadvantages.

Economics and You

Interest Rates

Interest rates vary during fluctuations in the economy. When the economy is in a recession, interest rates are often low to spur economic growth. Low interest rates are good for borrowers but bad for savers. How interest rates are advertised to savers and borrowers is governed by the law. For example, there is a difference between the annual percentage rate (APR) and the annual percentage yield (APY). The APY is higher than the APR because it includes compound interest on savings. Interest rates for borrowers are advertised as the APR. Borrowers must determine if the interest rate is based on the declining balance of the loan or on the total amount of the loan. You will pay less interest during the life of the loan if the interest rate is based on the declining balance.

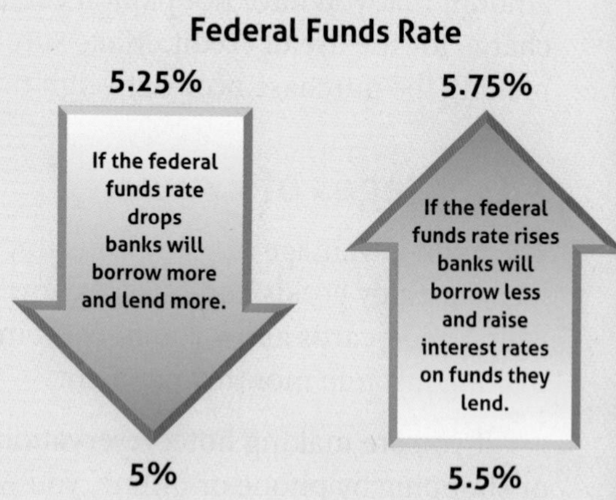

Federal Funds Rate
5.25%
5.75%
If the federal funds rate drops banks will borrow more and lend more.
If the federal funds rate rises banks will borrow less and raise interest rates on funds they lend.
5%
5.5%

Personal Finance Connection When deciding whether to borrow money or use your savings to make a costly purchase. how much you will pay for the item will depend on how the purchase is financed.

Critical Thinking You have $25,000 in savings for which the APY is around one percent. You want to purchase a $30,000 automobile with a down payment of $15,000. The auto loan rate is 10 percent for 4 years with a monthly payment of $380.44. How much will your new automobile cost at the end of four years? If you had to use your savings to make your monthly payments, at what point would you run out of money? What other options do you have if need to buy a vehicle?

Mc Graw Hill
glencoe.com

Activity Download an Economics and You Worksheet Activity.

Closed-End Credit

Closed-end credit is credit as a one-time loan that you will pay back over a specified period of time in payments of equal amounts. An agreement, or contract, lists the repayment terms including: number of payments, payment amount, and the total cost of credit. A mortgage is a common use of closed-end credit. Vehicle loans and installment loans for purchasing furniture or large appliances are other examples. The lender will hold the **title,** or document showing ownership, to the item until all payments have been made.

The three most common types of closed-end credit are installment sales credit, installment cash credit, and single lump-sum credit. Installment sales credit is a loan that allows you to receive merchandise, usually high-priced items. You make a down payment and make payments over a set period of time. Installment cash credit is a direct loan for money for personal purposes, home improvements, or vacation expenses. You may not make a down payment but make payments over a set period of time. Single lump-sum credit is a loan that must be repaid in total on a specified day, usually within 30 to 90 days.

Open-End Credit

What does open-end credit mean? **Open-end credit** is credit as a loan with a certain limit on the amount of money you can borrow for a variety of goods and services. A **line of credit** is the maximum amount of money a creditor will allow a credit user to borrow. Department store and bank credit cards, such as Visa or MasterCard, are examples of open-end credit. After a company has approved your application for credit and you have received the card, you can use it to make purchases, as long as you do not exceed your line of credit. You are then billed periodically for at least partial payment of the total amount you owe. You may have to pay interest or other finance charges.

Many banks offer another type of open end credit called revolving check credit. Also called a bank line of credit, this is a prearranged loan for a specified amount that you can use by writing a special check. Repayment is made in installments over a period. The finance charges are based on the amount of credit used during the month and the outstanding balance.

Reading Check

Recall What is closed-end credit?

Sources of Consumer Credit

What are some sources of consumer credit?

Many sources of consumer credit are available, including commercial banks and credit unions. **Figure 2** summarizes the major sources of consumer credit.

Loans

A loan is borrowed money with an agreement to repay it with interest within a certain amount of time. If you were considering taking out a loan, your immediate thought might be to go to your local bank. However, you might want to explore some other options first.

Inexpensive Loans Parents or other family members are often the source of the least expensive loans—loans with low interest. They may charge only the interest they would have earned on the money if they had deposited it in a savings account. They may even give you a loan without interest. However, loans can complicate family relationships.

Medium-Priced Loans Often you can obtain medium-priced loans—loans with moderate interest—from commercial banks, savings and loan associations, and credit unions. Borrowing from credit unions has several advantages. Credit unions provide personalized service and are sometimes patient with borrowers who can provide good reasons for late or missed payments. You must be a member of a credit union in order to get a loan from one.

Responsibility
One of the most important characteristics of successful people is that they are responsible. Responsibility is a form of trustworthiness. People who are responsible are accountable for their actions. You can benefit from taking a responsible attitude toward almost any issue you might encounter at home, at school, at work, and in the community.

Write About It

Think of a scenario in which having a responsible mind-set would help you at school. Describe the scenario and explain how having a responsible attitude would have a positive influence on the situation. Write one or more paragraphs to describe some positive characteristics of responsible people and explain how exhibiting these characteristics could influence others in positive ways.

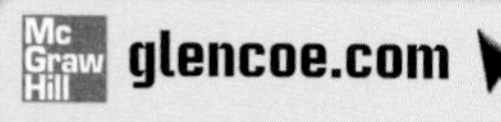

Activity Download a Career and College Readiness Worksheet Activity.

Expensive Loans The easiest loans to obtain are also the most expensive. Finance companies and retail stores that lend to consumers will frequently charge high interest rates, ranging from 12 to 25 percent. Banks also lend money to their credit card holders through cash advances—loans that are billed to the customer's credit card account. Most cards charge higher interest for a cash advance and charge interest from the day the cash advance is made.

Home Equity Loans A home equity loan is a loan based on your home equity—the difference between the current market value of your home and the amount you still owe on the mortgage. Unlike interest on most other types of credit, the interest you pay on a home equity loan is tax-deductible. Use these loans only for major items such as education, home improvements, or medical bills. If you miss payments on a home equity loan, the lender can take your home.

Credit Cards

Credit cards are extremely popular. The average cardholder has more than nine credit cards. Cardholders who pay off their balances in full each month are often known as convenience users. Cardholders who do not pay off their balances every month are known as borrowers.

Most credit card companies offer a **grace period,** a time period during which no finance charges will be added to your account. A **finance charge** is the total dollar amount you pay to use credit. Generally, if you pay your balance before the due date stated on your monthly bill, you do not have to pay a finance charge. Borrowers who carry balances beyond the grace period pay finance charges. The cost of a credit card depends on the type of credit card you have and the terms set forth by the lender. Some credit card companies charge cardholders an annual fee. However, many companies have eliminated annual fees. **Figure 3** gives some tips for choosing a credit card.

Debit Cards Do not confuse credit cards with debit cards. A debit card allows you to electronically subtract money from your savings or checking account to pay for goods or services. A credit card extends credit and delays payment. Debit cards are most commonly used at automated teller machines (ATMs). They are also used to purchase goods in stores and to make other types of payments.

Cobranding The linking of a credit card with a business trade name offering "points" or "premiums" toward the purchase of a product or service is called cobranding. Cobranding has become increasingly popular. Cobranded credit cards offer rebates on products and services such as health clubs, tax preparation services, and gasoline purchases.

Smart Cards Some lenders offer a credit card called a *smart card.* A smart card is a plastic card equipped with a computer chip that can store 500 times as much data as a normal credit card. Smart cards can store a variety of information. A smart card, for example, can be used to buy an airline ticket, store it digitally, and track frequent flyer miles.

FIGURE 2 Sources of Consumer Credit

Obtaining Credit People tend to think of banks when considering loans, but other sources of credit exist. *How does a life insurance company determine how large a loan to give?*

Credit Source	Type of Loan	Lending Policies
Commercial Banks	Single-payment loan Personal installment loans Passbook loans Check-credit loans Credit card loans Second mortgages	• Seek customers with established credit history • Often require collateral or security • Prefer to deal in large loans, such as vehicle, home improvement, and home modernization, with the exception of credit card and check-credit plans • Determine repayment schedules according to the purpose of the loan • Vary credit rates according to the type of credit, time period, customer's credit history, and the security offered • May require several days to process a new credit application
Consumer Finance Companies	Personal installment loans Second mortgages	• Often lend to consumers without established credit history • Often make unsecured loans • Often vary rates according to the size of the loan balance • Offer a variety of repayment schedules • Make a higher percentage of small loans than other lenders • Maximum loan size limited by law • Process applications quickly, frequently on the same day the application is made
Credit Unions	Personal installment loans Share draft-credit plans Credit card loans Second mortgages	• Lend to members only • Make unsecured loans • May require collateral or cosigner for loans over a specified amount • May require payroll deductions to pay off loan • May submit large loan applications to a committee of members for approval • Offer a variety of repayment schedules
Life Insurance Companies	Single-payment or partial payment loans	• Lend on cash value of life insurance policy • No date or penalty on repayment • Deduct amount owed from the value of the policy benefit if death or other maturity occurs before repayment
Federal Savings Banks (Savings and Loan Associations)	Personal installment loans (generally permitted by state-chartered savings associations) Home improvement loans Education loans Savings account loans Second mortgages	• Will lend to all creditworthy individuals • Often require collateral • Loan rates vary depending on size of loan, length of payment, and security involved

FIGURE 3 Choosing and Using a Credit Card

Choose Wisely It is important to carefully consider how you will use a credit card before choosing one. *Why is it important to consider whether you will carry a balance or pay your card in full each month?*

When you choose a credit card, it pays to shop around. Follow these suggestions to find the card that best meets your needs and to use it wisely:

1. Department stores and gasoline companies are good places to obtain your first credit card.
2. Bank credit cards are offered through banks and savings and loan associations. Annual fees and finance charges vary widely, so shop around.
3. If you plan on paying off your balance every month, look for a card that has a grace period and carries no annual fee or a low annual fee. You might have a higher interest rate, but you plan to pay little or no interest anyway.
4. Watch out for creditors that offer low or no annual fees but instead charge a transaction fee every time you use the card.
5. If you plan to carry a balance, look for a card with a low monthly finance charge. Be sure that you understand how the finance charge is calculated.
6. To avoid delays that may result in finance charges, follow the card issuer's instructions as to where, how, and when to make bill payments.
7. Beware of offers of easy credit. No one can guarantee to get you credit.
8. If your card offers a grace period, take advantage of it by paying off your balance in full each month. With a grace period of 25 days, you actually get a free loan when you pay bills in full each month.
9. If you have a bad credit history and have trouble getting a credit card, look for a savings institution that will give you a secured credit card. With this type of card, your line of credit depends on how much money you keep in a savings account that you open at the same time.
10. Travel and entertainment cards often charge higher annual fees than most credit cards. Usually, you must make payment in full within 30 days of receiving your bill, or no further purchases will be approved on the account.
11. Be aware that debit cards are not credit cards but simply a substitute for a check or cash. The amount of the sale is subtracted from your checking account.
12. Think twice before you make a telephone call to a 900 number to request a credit card. You will pay from $2 to $50 for the 900 call and may never receive a credit card.

Sources: American Institute of Certified Public Accountants; U.S. Office of Consumer Affairs; Federal Trade Commission.

Stored-Value (or Gift) Cards Stored-value, gift, or prepaid cards resemble a typical debit card, using technology to store information and track funds. However, unlike traditional debit cards, stored-value cards are prepaid, providing you with immediate money.

Travel and Entertainment (T&E) Cards Travel and Entertainment (T&E) cards are really not credit cards because the balance is due in full each month. However, most people think of T&E cards as credit cards because users do not pay for items when they purchase them.

Assessment

Review Key Concepts

1. **Define** What is consumer credit? Provide an example.
2. **Explain** What is the difference between closed-end credit and open-end credit?
3. **Describe** What are three types of specialty credit cards? What are the characteristics of each?

Higher Order Thinking H.O.T.

4. **Evaluate** Look at the suggestions in **Figure 3.** Which of the factors do you think might be most important in your choice of a credit card?

English Language Arts

5. **Conspicuous Consumption** One of the greatest disadvantages of using credit is the temptation to buy more than you can afford. However, many people argue that this is actually the advantage of credit because you can get a nicer item and pay it off over time. Suppose you need a new car and you must get a loan to buy it. Would you borrow just enough for a simple, reliable car, or more for something with more style and luxury? Write a brief report with your answer and reasons for your position.

NCTE 12 Use language to accomplish individual purposes.

Mathematics

6. **Loan Cost** Vladimir has recently moved into an apartment. Since this is his first time living on his own, he needs to purchase furniture for his new residence. Vladimir does not have enough cash to buy the furniture, and he is not able to use his credit card due to the low credit limit. He decides to take out a loan from a bank for $5,000. The bank charges 6.5 percent annual interest, compounded monthly. Vladimir will pay $300 per month on the loan. What will the loan balance be after 3 months?

Calculate Loan Balance To calculate the balance on a loan add the interest charge for the first period to the original loan amount and subtract the monthly payment. Continue this process for the remaining periods.

Starting Hint Determine the loan balance after month 1 by first multiplying the annual interest rate by the loan amount and dividing by 12. Add the result to the original loan amount and subtract the monthly payment.

NCTM Connections Recognize and apply mathematics in contexts outside of mathematics.

McGraw Hill **glencoe.com** Check your answers.

SECTION 2 The Costs and Methods of Obtaining Credit

Section Objectives

- **Name** the five Cs of credit.
- **Identify** factors to consider when choosing a loan or credit card.
- **Explain** how to build and protect your credit rating.

As You Read

Relate Why should you pay more than the monthly minimum payment on a credit card debt?

Can You Afford a Loan?

What is a loan?

A loan is money that you borrow and must repay. Loans cost money to the borrower in the form of interest. Taking out a loan can be a substantial financial burden. Before you take out a loan, you need to be sure that you can afford it. Will you be able to meet all your usual expenses plus the monthly loan payments you will have to make? You can answer this question in several ways.

One way is to add up all your basic monthly expenses and then subtract the total from your take-home pay. If the difference is not enough to make a monthly loan payment and still have a little left over, you cannot afford the loan.

A second way is to consider what you might give up to make the monthly loan payment. For example, perhaps you are putting some of your monthly income into a savings account. Would you be willing to use that money to make loan payments instead? If not, would you consider cutting back on unnecessary but fun activities, such as going to movies or eating out? Are you prepared to make this trade-off?

Although you cannot measure your credit capacity exactly, you can use the debt payments-to-income ratio formula to decide whether you can safely take on the responsibility of credit.

Debt Payments-to-Income Ratio

The debt payments-to-income ratio is the percentage of debt you have in relation to your net income. **Net income** is the income you receive (take-home pay, allowance, gifts, and interest). Experts suggest that you spend no more than 20 percent of your net income on debt payments. For example, if your net income is $1,000 per month, your monthly debt payments should total no more than $200. Monthly debt payments include credit card and loan payments. You can calculate your debt payments-to-income ratio by dividing your total monthly debt payments (not including housing payments) by your monthly net income.

Twenty percent is the most you should spend on debt payments, but 15 percent is much better. The higher figure does not take into account emergency expenses, and it is based on an average family's average expenses. If you are a young adult who is just beginning to experiment with credit, play it safe and stay below the 20 percent limit.

Reading Check

Identify What is a debt payments-to-income ratio?

GO FIGURE Mathematics

Debt Payments-to-Income Ratio (DPR)

Computing your monthly net income will help you calculate how much to spend on debt payments. Your debt payments-to-income ratio (DPR) will also determine your monthly budget.

EXAMPLE Suppose that your monthly net income is $1,200. Your monthly debt payments include your student loan payment and a gas credit card, and they total $180. What is your debt payments-to-income ratio?

Formula Monthly Debt Payments/Monthly Net Income = Debt Payments-to-Income Ratio (DPR)

Solution $180/$1,200 = 0.15 = 15%

Your Turn

What is your debt payments-to-income ratio if your debt payments total $342 and your net income is $1,000 per month?

The Cost of Credit

What does it cost to apply for credit?

If you are thinking of taking out a loan or applying for a credit card, your first step should be to figure out how much the loan will cost you and whether you can afford it. Then you should shop for the best credit terms. Two key factors will be the finance charge and the annual percentage rate (APR).

The Finance Charge and the Annual Percentage Rate (APR)

The finance charge is the total dollar amount you pay to use credit. In most cases, you will have to pay finance charges to a creditor on any unpaid balance.

The finance charge is calculated using the annual percentage rate. The **annual percentage rate (APR)** is the cost of credit on a yearly basis, expressed as a percentage. For example, an APR of 18 percent means that you pay $18 per year on each $100 you owe. Every organization that extends credit of any kind must state the true APR that it charges its customers. This makes it easy to compare the cost of credit at several businesses or among several different credit cards.

To determine the total amount of finance charges that you will pay on $100 borrowed, look at **Figure 4.** Find the APR at the top of the chart and the number of payments at the left side of the chart. The point at which they meet is the total amount you will pay in finance charges for each $100 borrowed.

For example, find the column showing an APR of 8 percent. Follow it down until it meets the row showing 24 monthly payments. You will see that if you borrow $100 at an APR of 8 percent for two

FIGURE 4 **Annual Percentage Rate Table for Monthly Payments**

Cost of Credit Most creditors charge a finance charge, or interest, on money borrowed. *How much interest would you pay if you borrowed $100 for 6 months at an APR of 9 percent?*

	Annual Percentage Rate—APR (Finance Charge per $100 Borrowed)				
Number of Monthly Payments	**7.0%**	**7.5%**	**8.0%**	**8.5%**	**9.0%**
6	$2.05	$2.20	$ 2.35	$ 2.49	$ 2.64
12	$3.83	$4.11	$ 4.39	$ 4.66	$ 4.94
18	$5.63	$6.04	$ 6.45	$ 6.86	$ 7.28
24	$7.45	$8.00	$ 8.55	$ 9.09	$ 9.64
30	$9.30	$9.98	$10.66	$11.35	$12.04

years (24 months), you will pay $8.55 in finance charges. Under the Truth in Lending Act, the creditor must inform you, in writing and before you sign any agreement, of the finance charge and the APR.

Tackling the Trade-Offs

When you select your financing, you will have to make trade-offs. You will have to choose among various features, including the length of the loan, variable interest rate or fixed interest rate, the size of monthly payments, and the interest rate. Here are some of the major trade-offs you should consider.

Term Versus Interest Costs Many people choose longer-term financing because they want smaller monthly payments. However, the longer the term (the period of time) of a loan at a given interest rate, the greater the amount you will pay in interest charges. Compare the following credit arrangements on a $6,000 loan:

	APR	Term of Loan	Monthly Payment	Total Finance Charge	Total Cost
Creditor A	14%	3 years	$205.07	$1,382.52	$7,382.52
Creditor B	14%	4 years	$163.96	$1,870.08	$7,870.08

How do these choices compare? The answer depends partly on what you need. The lower-cost loan is available from Creditor A. If you are looking for lower monthly payments, you could repay the loan over a longer period of time. However, you would have to pay more in total costs. A loan from Creditor B provides smaller monthly payments but adds about $488 to your total finance charge.

GO FIGURE Mathematics

Simple Interest on a Loan

Simple interest, compounded annually, is a percentage of the amount borrowed. The amount borrowed is called principal. Compound interest may be computed daily, monthly, or yearly.

EXAMPLE Janelle's cousin agreed to lend her $1,000 to purchase a used laptop computer. She has agreed to charge only 5 percent simple interest, and Janelle has agreed to repay the loan at the end of one year. How much interest will she pay for the year? Use the formula below to help compute Janelle's loan interest.

Formula Principal × Interest Rate × Amount of Time = Simple Interest

Solution $1,000 × .05 or 5% × 1 = $50 interest

Your Turn

You just bought a used car for $3,500 from your aunt. She agreed to let you make payments for 3 years with simple interest at 6 percent. How much interest will you pay?

Lender Risk Versus Interest Rate You may prefer financing that requires a minimum down payment, a **portion,** or part, of the total cost of an item that is required at the time of purchase. Another option is to take out a loan that features low, fixed payments with a large, final payment. Keep in mind that the lender's goal is to minimize risk, or make sure that you pay back the loan in full. Both of these financing options can increase your cost of borrowing because they create more risk for the lender. Consumers who want these types of features have to accept the trade-off of a more expensive loan.

To reduce lender risk and increase your chances of getting a loan at a lower interest rate, consider the following options:

- **Variable Interest Rate** A variable interest rate is based on changing rates in the banking system. This means that the interest rate you pay on your loan will vary from time to time. If you have a loan with a variable interest rate and overall interest rates rise, the rate on your loan is adjusted accordingly. Therefore, the lender may offer you a lower beginning interest rate than you would have with a fixed-rate loan.
- **A Secured Loan** You will probably receive a lower interest rate on your loan if you pledge collateral. **Collateral** is a form of security to help guarantee that the creditor will be repaid. It indicates that if you lost your source of income, you could repay your loan with the collateral, such as your savings, or by selling some of your property. If you do not pay back the loan, the lender may have the legal right to take whatever you **pledged,** or promised, as collateral.
- **Up-Front Cash** Many lenders believe that you have a higher stake in repaying a loan if you make a large down payment. Thus, you may have a better chance of getting the other loan features you want.

Around the World

Japan

Cash-Driven Economy

As credit and debit cards are becoming the standard method of payment in many countries, Japan still relies mainly on cash. This is surprising given that Japan is a culture known for its technology. One mindset is that paying in cash indicates wealth, whereas credit cards are used by those with financial limits.

Travelers to Japan are warned that outside of the major cities, cash is frequently the only accepted form of payment for goods and services. Because so many businesses only accept cash payments, citizens of Japan are used to carrying more cash than many Americans are comfortable having on hand. It is common for the average Japanese citizen to carry tens of thousands of yen (the equivalent of hundreds of U.S. dollars) in his or her wallet. In addition to purchases, many transaction fees, such as a deposit for leasing an apartment, are accepted only in cash. Surprisingly, this reliance on cash does not lead to a higher crime rate. Rather, Japanese society in general is known for its honesty. Stories are common about purses or wallets being found on the train and returned to their owner, cash intact.

Critical Thinking

1. **Expand** In Japan, many cash-advance machines allow you take out a personal loan. These loans are often repaid with automatic deductions from your paycheck. Research to determine the limits for these loans and how large the paycheck deductions are.
2. **Relate** Do you think people should be able to get a personal loan so easily? Why or Why not?

DATABYTES

Capital
Tokyo

Population
127, 078, 679

Language
Japanese

Currency
Yen

Gross Domestic Product (GDP)
$5.108 trillion

GDP per capita
$32, 600

Industry
Motor vehicles, electronic equipment, machine tools, steel and nonferrous metals, ships, chemicals, textiles, processed foods

Agriculture
Rice, sugar beets, vegetables, fruit, pork, poultry, dairy products, eggs, fish

Exports
Transport equipment, motor vehicles, semiconductors, electrical machinery, chemicals

Natural Resources
Negligible mineral resources, fish

- **A Shorter Term** The shorter the period of time (or term) for which you borrow, the smaller the chance that something will prevent you from repaying your loan. This lowers the risk to the lender. Therefore, you may be able to borrow at a lower interest rate if you accept a shorter-term loan, but your monthly payments will be higher.

Calculating the Cost of Credit

To assess your trade-offs, you can also compare loans and credit cards by calculating the interest to find the cost of credit. The most common method of calculating interest is the simple interest formula. Other methods, such as simple interest on the declining balance and add-on interest, are variations of this formula.

Simple Interest **Simple interest** is the interest computed only on the principal, the amount that you borrow. It is based on three factors: the principal, the interest rate, and the amount of time for which the principal is borrowed. To calculate the simple interest on a loan, multiply the principal by the interest rate and by the amount of time (in years) for which the money is borrowed. (See the **Go Figure** box.)

Simple Interest on the Declining Balance When a simple interest loan is paid back in more than one payment, the method of computing interest is known as the declining balance method. You pay interest only on the amount of principal that you have not yet repaid. The more often you make payments, the lower the interest you will pay. Most credit unions use this method.

Add-On Interest With the add-on interest method, interest is calculated on the full amount of the original principal, no matter how often you make payments. When you pay off the loan with one payment, this method produces the same APR as the simple interest method. However, if you pay in installments, your actual rate of interest will be higher than the stated rate. Interest payments on this type of loan do not decrease as the loan is repaid. The longer you take to repay the loan, the more interest you will pay.

Cost of Open-End Credit The Truth in Lending Act requires that open-end creditors inform consumers as to how the finance charge and the APR will affect their costs. For example, they must explain how they calculate the finance charge. They must also inform you when finance charges on your credit account begin to accrue so that you know how much time you have to pay your bills before a finance charge is added.

Cost of Credit and Expected Inflation Inflation reduces the buying power of money. Each percentage point increase in inflation means a decrease of about 1 percent in the quantity of goods and services you can buy with the same amount of money. Because of this, lenders incorporate the expected rate of inflation when deciding how much interest to charge.

Phishing

One type of internet fraud is "phishing." With this type of scam you receive fraudulent email messages that appear to be from your financial institution. The messages often appear to be authentic and may even include the institution's logo. The messages usually describe a situation that requires immediate attention and contain a Web link. The link takes you to a screen that requests personal information. The people behind the scam use this information to access your accounts or steal your identity.

To avoid phishing scams:

- If you are not sure that an email is legitimate, type in the company's Web address to access their site. Do not click on an embedded link in a suspicious email.
- If you are a victim of a phishing scam alert your financial institution immediately and place fraud alerts on all of your credit accounts. Make sure to monitor your account statements closely.
- You can report suspicious emails or calls from third parties to the Federal Trade Commission using their Web site or by phone.

Consider the following example: Damon borrowed $1,000 from his aunt at the bargain rate of 5 percent for one year. If the inflation rate was 4 percent that year, his aunt's actual rate of return on the loan would have been only about 1 percent (5 percent stated interest minus 4 percent inflation rate). A professional lender that wanted to receive 5 percent interest on Damon's loan might have charged him 9 percent interest (5 percent interest plus 4 percent—anticipated inflation rate).

The Minimum Monthly Payment Trap On credit card bills and for other forms of credit, the **minimum monthly payment** is the smallest amount you can pay and remain a borrower in good standing. Lenders often encourage you to make the minimum payment because it will then take you longer to pay off the loan. However, if you are paying only the minimum amount on your monthly statement, you need to plan your budget more carefully. The longer it takes for you to pay off a bill, the more interest you pay. The finance charges you pay on an item could end up being more than the item is worth.

For example, suppose that Natasha is buying new books for college. She spends $500 on textbooks, using a credit card that charges 19.8 percent interest per year, and she makes only the minimum monthly payment of $21.67. Based on that payment amount, it will take Natasha approximately two and one-half years to pay off the loan. Interest charges of $150 will be added to the cost of her purchase.

Reading Check

Summarize What is the most common method of calculating interest?

Applying for Credit

Why does a lender need to know about your credit history to extend credit?

Before you take out a loan, ask yourself whether you can meet all of your essential expenses and still afford the monthly loan payments. When you are ready to apply for a loan or a credit card, you should understand the factors that determine whether a lender will extend credit to you.

The Five Cs of Credit

When a lender extends credit to consumers, it takes for granted that some people will be unable or unwilling to pay their debts. Therefore, lenders establish policies for determining who will receive credit. Most lenders build such policies around the "five Cs of credit": character, capacity, capital, collateral, and conditions.

Character: Will You Repay the Loan? Creditors want to know

Know Your Capacity
You should know your finances well enough to ensure that you can repay a loan before you request it of a creditor. *What else will a creditor consider besides capacity?*

Character: Will You Repay the Loan? Creditors want to know what kind of person to whom they will be lending money. They want to know that you are trustworthy and stable. They may ask for personal or professional references, and they may check to see whether you have a history of trouble with the law. Some questions a lender might ask to determine your character are:

- Have you used credit before?
- How long have you lived at your present address?
- How long have you held your current job?

Capacity: Can You Repay the Loan? Your income and the debts you already have will affect your ability to pay additional debts. If you already have a large amount of debt in proportion to your income, lenders probably will not extend more credit to you.

A creditor may ask several questions about your income and expenses:

- What is your job, and how much is your salary?
- Do you have other sources of income?
- What are your current debts?

Capital: What Are Your Assets and Net Worth? You may recall that assets are any items of value that you own, including cash, property, personal possessions, and investments. Your capital is the amount of your assets that exceed your liabilities, or the debts you owe. Lenders want to be sure that you have enough capital to pay back a loan. That way, if you lost your source of income, you could repay your loan from your savings or by selling some of your assets. A lender might ask:

- What are your assets?
- What are your liabilities?

Collateral: What If You Do Not Repay the Loan? Creditors look at what kinds of property or savings you already have, because these can be offered as collateral to secure the loan. If you fail to repay the loan, the creditor may take whatever you pledged as collateral. A creditor might ask:

- What assets do you have to secure the loan (a vehicle, your home, or furniture)?
- Do you have any other assets (bonds or savings)?

Conditions: What If Your Job Is Insecure? General economic conditions, such as unemployment and recession, can affect your ability to repay a loan. The basic question focuses on security—of both your job and the company that employs you.

The information gathered from your application and the credit bureau establishes your credit rating. A **credit rating** is a measure of a person's ability and willingness to make credit payments on time. The factors that determine a person's credit rating are income, current debt, information about character, and how debts have been repaid in the past. If you always make your payments on time and have a low amount of debt, you will probably have a good credit rating. If not, your credit rating will be poor, and a lender probably will not extend credit to you. A good credit rating is a valuable asset that you should protect.

Creditors use different combinations of the five Cs to reach their decisions. Some creditors set unusually high standards, and others simply do not offer certain types of loans. Creditors also use various rating systems. Some rely strictly on their own instincts and experience. Others use a credit scoring or statistical system to predict whether an applicant is a good credit risk. When you apply for a loan, the lender is likely to evaluate your application by asking questions about items such as those included in the checklist in **Figure 6.**

FIGURE 5 **Personal Credit Score**

Average Credit Score According to Experian, the average credit score for Americans is 692 out of a possible 850, though this number can fluctuate from year to year. *How can you improve your credit score?*

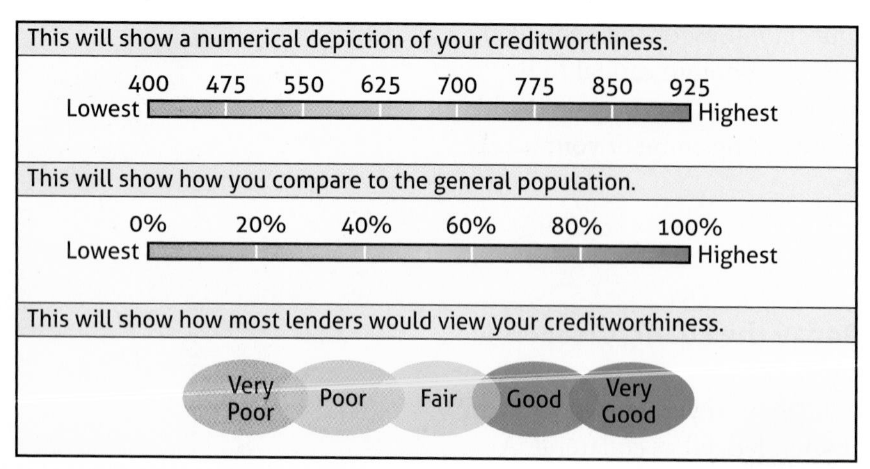

FICO and Vantagescore

Typical questions and information in a credit application appear in **Figure 6.** The information in your credit report is used to calculate your FICO credit score—a number generally between 350 and 850 that rates how risky a borrower is. The higher the score, the less risk you pose to creditors. **Figure 5** shows a numerical depiction and interpretation of your credit worthiness.

Vantagescore is a relatively new scoring technique, the first to be developed collaboratively by the three credit reporting companies. This model allows for a more predictive score for consumers, even for those with limited credit histories, reducing the need for creditors to manually review credit information. Vantagescore features a common score range of 501–990 (higher scores represent lower likelihood of risk). A key benefit of Vantagescore is that as long as the three major credit bureaus have the same information regarding your credit history, you will receive the same score from each of them. A different score alerts you that there are discrepancies in your report.

How Can I Improve My Credit Score? A credit score is a snapshot of the contents of your credit report at the time it is calculated. The first step in improving your score is to review your credit report to ensure it is accurate. Long-term, responsible credit behavior is the most effective way to improve future scores. Pay bills on time, lower balances, and use credit wisely to improve your score over time.

FIGURE 6 Credit Application Information

All About You You are required to provide a lot of personal information on a credit application. *What information does a creditor require about your family?*

- Amount of loan requested
- Proposed use of the loan
- Your name and birth date
- Social Security and driver's license numbers
- Present and previous street addresses
- Present and previous employers and their addresses
- Present salary
- Number and ages of dependents
- Other income and sources of other income
- Have you ever received credit from us?
- If so, when and at which office?
- Checking account number, institution, and branch
- Savings account number, institution, and branch
- Name of nearest relative not living with you
- Relative's address and telephone number
- Your marital status

Credit and Equal Opportunity

You should also know what factors a lender cannot consider, according to the law. The Equal Credit Opportunity Act (ECOA) gives all credit applicants the same basic rights. It states that a lender may not use race, nationality, age, sex, marital status, and certain other factors to discriminate against you.

FIGURE 7 What If You Are Denied Credit?

Understanding Denial The ECOA ensures that you are provided specific reasons for being denied credit. *What are your options if you believe the reasons for a credit denial are invalid?*

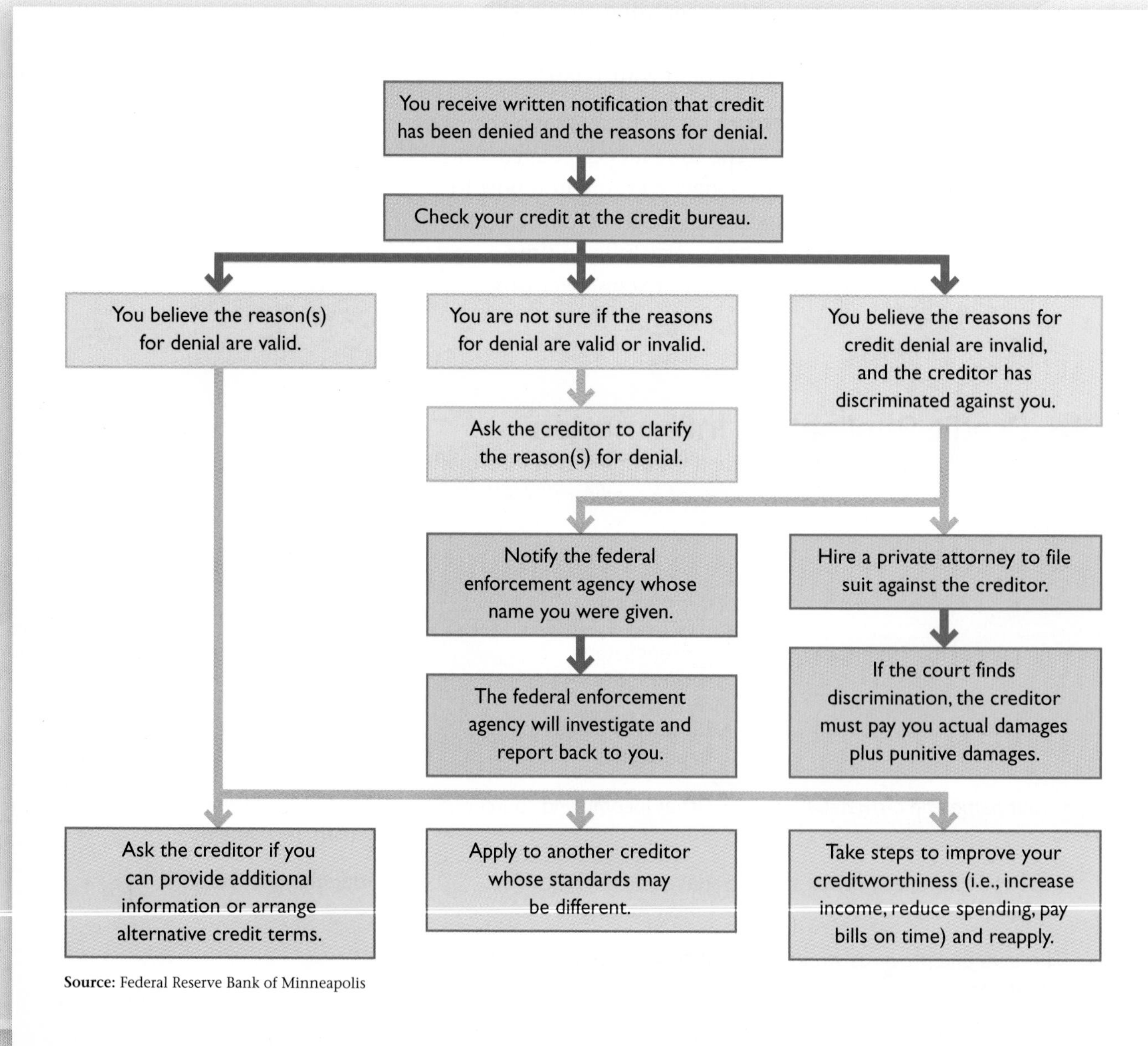

Source: Federal Reserve Bank of Minneapolis

Age The Equal Credit Opportunity Act (ECOA) is very specific about how a person's age may be used as a factor in credit decisions. A creditor may request that you state your age on an application, but if you are old enough to sign a legal contract (usually 18 or 21 years old, depending on state law), a creditor may not

- Turn you down or decrease your credit because of your age
- Ignore your retirement income in rating your application
- Close your credit account because you have retired
- Close your credit account because you reach a certain age

Public Assistance You may not be denied credit because you receive Social Security or public assistance. However, certain information related to this source of income can be considered in determining your creditworthiness.

Housing Loans The ECOA also covers applications for mortgages or home improvement loans. In particular, it bans discrimination against you based on the race or nationality of the people in the neighborhood where you live or want to buy your home, a practice that is called *redlining*.

What If Your Application Is Denied?

If your credit application is denied, the ECOA gives you the right to know the reasons. If the denial is based on a credit report from a credit bureau, you are entitled to know what specific information in the report led to the denial. After you receive this information, you can contact the credit bureau and ask for a copy of your credit report. The bureau cannot charge a fee for this service as long as you ask to see your files within 60 days of notification that your credit application has been denied. You are entitled to ask the bureau to investigate any inaccurate or incomplete information and correct its records. (See **Figure 7.**)

Reading Check

Recall What are FICO and Vantagescore?

Your Credit Report

Why is your credit report important?

When you apply for a loan, the lender will review your credit history closely. The record of your complete credit history is called your credit report, or credit file. Your credit records are collected and maintained by credit bureaus. Most lenders rely heavily on credit reports when they consider loan applications. **Figure 8** provides information on building and protecting your credit history.

Credit Bureaus

A credit bureau is an agency that collects information on how promptly people and businesses pay their bills. The three major credit bureaus are Experian, Trans Union, and Equifax. Each of these bureaus maintains more than 200 million credit files on individuals, based on information they receive from lenders. Several thousand smaller credit bureaus also collect credit information about consumers. These firms make money by selling the information they collect to creditors who are considering loan applications.

Credit bureaus get their information from banks, finance companies, stores, credit card companies, and other lenders. These sources regularly transmit information about the types of credit they extend to customers, the amounts and terms of the loans, and the customers' payment habits. Credit bureaus also collect some information from other sources, such as court records.

Your Credit File

A typical credit bureau file contains your name, address, Social Security number, and birth date as well as other information:

- Your employer, position, and income
- Your previous address

FIGURE 8 **Ways to Build and Protect Your Credit**

Build Good Credit Building a good credit rating means proving that you can be trusted. *Who is allowed to be a cosigner for you on a loan?*

- ☑ Open a checking or savings account, or both.
- ☑ Apply for a local department store credit card.
- ☑ Take out a small loan from your bank.
- ☑ Make payments on time.

Be aware that a creditor must:

1. Evaluate all applicants on the same basis.
2. Consider income from part-time employment.
3. Consider the payment history of all joint accounts, if this accurately reflects your credit history.
4. Disregard information on accounts if you can prove that it does not affect your ability or willingness to repay.

Be aware that a creditor cannot:

1. Refuse you individual credit in your own name if your are creditworthy.
2. Require your spouse to cosign a loan. Any creditworthy person can be your cosigner if one is required.
3. Ask about your family plans or assume that your income will be interrupted to have children.
4. Consider whether you have a telephone listing in your name.

Source: Reprinted by permission of the Federal Reserve Bank of Minneapolis.

- Your previous employer
- Your spouse's name, Social Security number, employer, and income
- Homeowner or renter status
- Checks returned for insufficient funds

Your file also contains detailed information. When you use credit to make a purchase or take out a loan, a credit bureau is informed of your account number, the date, amount, terms, and type of credit.

Your file is updated regularly to show how many payments you have made, how many payments were late or missed, and how much you owe. Any lawsuits or judgments against you may appear as well. Federal law protects your rights if there is incorrect information.

Fair Credit Reporting

Fair and accurate credit reporting is vital to both creditors and consumers. In 1971, the U.S. Congress enacted the Fair Credit Reporting Act, which regulates the use of credit reports. This law requires the deletion of out-of-date information and gives consumers access to their files as well as the right to correct any discrepancies. The act also places limits on who can obtain your credit report.

Who Can Obtain a Credit Report?

Your credit report may be issued only to properly identified persons for approved purposes. It may be supplied in response to a court order or by your own written request. A credit report may also be provided for use in connection with a credit transaction, underwriting of insurance, or some other legitimate business need. Other individuals such as a neighbor or friend cannot be given access to credit information about you. In fact, if they even request such information, they may be subject to a fine, imprisonment, or both. Many consumer organizations believe that credit bureau files are too easy to access.

Equal Opportunity
It is important to have a good credit rating so you can get a mortgage when you decide to buy a home. *What federal law ensures that all applicants for mortgages will be treated equally?*

The credit bureaus contend that current laws protect a consumer's privacy, but many consumer organizations believe that anyone with a personal computer and a modem can easily access credit bureau files.

You may obtain a copy of your credit report free of charge if you have been denied credit. Current law also allows anyone using credit to obtain one free credit report per year.

Time Limits on Unfavorable Data

Most of the information in your credit file may be reported for only seven years. However, if you have declared personal bankruptcy, that fact may be reported for ten years. A credit reporting agency cannot disclose information in your credit file that is more than seven or ten years old unless you are being reviewed for a credit application of $75,000 or more, or unless you apply to purchase life insurance of $150,000 or more.

Incorrect Information

Credit bureaus are required to follow reasonable procedures to make sure that the information in their files is correct. Mistakes can and do occur, however. If you think that a credit bureau may be reporting incorrect data from your file, contact the bureau to dispute the information. The credit bureau must check its records and change or remove the incorrect items. If you challenge the accuracy of an item on your credit report, the bureau must remove the item unless the lender can verify that the information is accurate.

If you are denied credit, insurance, employment, or rental housing based on the information in a credit report, you can get a free copy of your report. Request it within 60 days of the denial. You should review your credit files every year even if you are not planning to apply for a big loan. Individuals should make sure that all accounts for which they are liable, including joint accounts, are listed in their credit files.

Legal Action

You have a legal right to sue a credit bureau or creditor that has caused you harm by not following the rules established by the Fair Credit Reporting Act. If the agency or the user is found guilty, the consumer may be awarded actual damages, court costs, and attorneys' fees. In the case of willful noncompliance, punitive damages in the form of money may also be awarded by the court. The action must be brought within two years of the occurrence or within two years after the discovery of material and willful misrepresentation of the information.

An unauthorized person who obtains a credit report under false pretences may be fined up to $5,000, imprisoned for one year, or both. The same penalties apply to anyone who willfully provides credit information to someone not authorized to receive it.

Review Key Concepts

1. **List** What are the 5 Cs of credit?
2. **Explain** How can you determine if you can afford a loan?
3. **Identify** What are four actions you can take to help build a good credit rating?

Higher Order Thinking

4. **Relate** Suppose you applied for a car loan of $40,000 and were denied for valid reasons. What would your next steps be toward getting a car loan?

21st Century Skills

5. **Analyze Media** Federal law states that anyone who uses credit is now entitled to one free credit report each year. Many companies now advertise in an effort to get consumers to take advantage of this. Visit the Web site for one or more of these organizations that offer to obtain your credit reports for you. Evaluate the Web site and write a brief summary of why people might use these services rather than requesting their own report directly from the credit agencies.

Mathematics

6. **Debt Payments-to-Income Ratio** Seth earns a monthly income of $1,200. He currently carries a balance on his credit card and makes monthly payments of $200. He wants to go on vacation but will have to charge the trip to his credit card. If Seth charges the trip, he will have to pay an additional $120 per month in credit card debt. What is Seth's debt payments-to-income ratio before and after the vacation charge? Should he go on the vacation based on the 20 percent rule?

Math Concept **Calculate Debt Payments-to-Income Ratio** To calculate the debt payments-to-income ratio you must first determine the total monthly debt payments and divide by the total monthly income earned.

Starting Hint Determine the debt payments-to-income ratio before the vacation is charged to the credit card by first identifying the total monthly debt payments. Divide this figure by the monthly income earned.

NCTM Problem Solving Solve problems that arise in mathematics and in other contexts.

glencoe.com Check your answers.

Section Objectives

- **Protect** yourself from fraud and identity theft.
- **Identify** consumer protection laws.

As You Read

Relate Have you ever purchased something online? How do you make sure your online transactions are secure?

Billing Errors and Disputes

What can you do to correct billing errors?

Have you ever received a bill for something you did not buy? Have you ever made a payment that was not credited to your account? If so, you are not alone. You may be a responsible consumer who pays bills **promptly**, or on time, and manages personal finances carefully. Even so, mistakes can happen. If you want to protect your credit rating, your time, and your money, you need to know how to correct mistakes that may pop up in your credit dealings.

What can you do to dispute billing errors? Follow these steps if you think that a bill is wrong or want more information about it. First, notify your creditor in writing, and include any information that might support your case. (A telephone call is not sufficient to protect your rights.) Then pay the portion of the bill that is not in question.

Your creditor must acknowledge your letter within 30 days. Then within two billing periods (but not longer than 90 days), the creditor must either adjust your account or tell you why the bill is correct. If the creditor made a mistake, you do not have to pay any finance charges on the disputed amount. If no mistake is found, the creditor must promptly send you an explanation of the situation and a statement of what you owe, including any finance charges that accumulated and any minimum payments you missed while you were questioning the bill.

Protecting Your Credit Rating

According to law, a creditor may not threaten your credit rating or do anything to damage your credit reputation while you are negotiating a billing dispute. In addition, the creditor may not take any action to collect the amount in question until your complaint has been answered.

Defective Goods and Services

According to the Fair Credit Billing Act, if you purchase a defective item and the store will not accept a return, you may tell your credit card company to stop payment because you made a sincere attempt to resolve, or clear up, the problem.

Reading Check

Recognize Is it sufficient to call a creditor to report a problem?

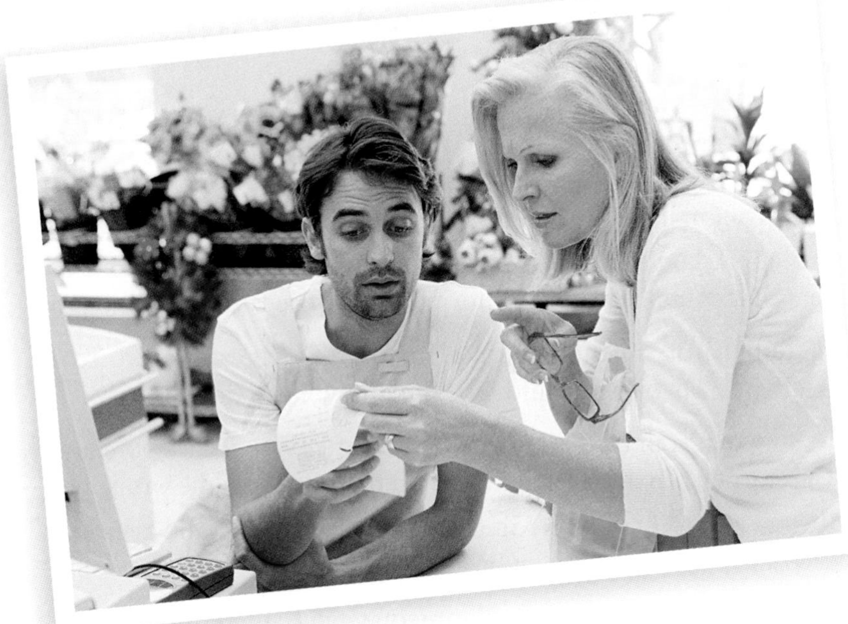

Charge It
Credit cards are convenient, but even the most careful user might encounter issues on a statement. *What would you do about a questionable charge on your bill?*

Credit and Stolen Identity

How can someone steal your identity?

Imagine yourself saying: "I don't remember charging those items. I've never been in that store." Maybe you never charged those goods and services, but someone else did—someone who used your name and personal information to commit fraud. When **impostors,** or people who deceive others by assuming different identities, use your name, Social Security number, credit card number, or other personal information for their own purposes, they are committing a crime, sometimes called "identity theft." Identity theft is the fastest-growing financial crime.

You may not even know that your identity has been stolen until you notice that something is wrong: You may get bills for a credit card account you never opened, or you may see charges to your account for things that you did not purchase. In addition, a thief may access your bank account and withdraw your money using your ATM information.

If you think that your identity has been stolen and that someone is using it to charge purchases or obtain credit in some other way, you can take action. (See **Figure 9** for additional details.) The Federal Trade Commission recommends you:

- Contact the credit bureaus.
- Contact the creditors.
- File a police report.

Reading Check

Describe What are some indications of identity theft?

Protecting Your Credit from Theft or Loss

What should you do if your credit has been stolen?

Some thieves will pick through your trash in search of personal information. You can prevent this from happening by shredding any papers that contain personal information before you throw them out.

Lost credit cards are another key element in credit card fraud. To protect your card, you should take the following actions:

- Be sure that your card is returned to you after you make a purchase. Unreturned cards can sometimes find their way into the wrong hands.
- Keep a record of your credit card numbers. You should keep this record separate from your cards.

Notify the credit card company immediately if your card is lost or stolen. Under the Consumer Credit Protection Act, the maximum amount that you must pay if someone uses your card illegally is $50. If you manage to inform the company before the card is used illegally, you have no obligation to pay at all.

Keeping Track of Your Credit

A big problem with credit or identity theft is that you may not know your credit has been stolen until you notice that something is wrong. You might get bills for a credit card account you never opened. Your credit report may include debts you never knew you had.

Steps to Protect Other Accounts If you believe an identity thief has accessed your bank accounts, checking account, or ATM card, close those accounts immediately. When you open new accounts, insist on password-only access. If your checks have been stolen or misused, stop payment on them. If your ATM card has been lost, stolen, or otherwise compromised, cancel the card and get another one with a new PIN. Stay alert to new instances of identity theft. Notify the company or creditor immediately, and follow up in writing.

Government Agency Protection If you continue to experience identity-theft problems after taking these steps, contact the Privacy Rights Clearinghouse of the Federal Trade Commission (FTC), which provides information on how to network with other victims.

The U.S. Secret Service has jurisdiction over financial fraud cases. Although the service generally investigates cases that involve substantial monetary loss, your information may provide evidence of a larger pattern of fraud that requires its attention.

The Social Security Administration may issue you a new Social Security number if you are still having difficulties after trying to resolve problems resulting from identity theft. Unfortunately, there is no guarantee that a new number will resolve the problem.

FIGURE 9 **Dealing With Stolen Identity**

If someone has stolen your identity, the Federal Trade Commission recommends that you take three actions immediately:

1. **Contact the fraud department of each of the three major Credit Bureaus** Tell them to flag your file with a fraud or security alert, including a statement that creditors should call you for permission before they open any new accounts in your name.
2. **Contact the Creditors** Contact the creditors for any accounts that have been tampered with or opened fraudulently. Follow up in writing.
3. **File a Police Report** Keep a copy of the police report in case your creditors need proof of the crime. If you are still having identity problems, stay alert to new instances of identity theft. You can also contact the Privacy Rights Clearinghouse.

The Federal Trade Commission cannot resolve individual problems for consumers, but it can act against a company if it sees a pattern of possible law violations. You can file a complaint with the FTC through a toll-free consumer help line; by mail; or at its Web site.

Credit Information on the Internet The Internet is becoming almost as important to daily life as the telephone and television. Increasing numbers of consumers use the Internet for financial activities, such as investing, banking, and shopping.

When you make purchases online, make sure that your transactions are secure, that your personal information is protected, and that your "fraud sensors" are sharpened. Although you cannot control fraud or deception on the Internet, you can take steps to recognize it, avoid it, and report it. Here's how:

- Use a secure browser.
- Keep records of your online transactions.
- Review your monthly bank and credit card statements.
- Read the privacy and security policies of Web sites you visit.
- Keep your personal information private.
- Never give your password to anyone online.
- Do not download files sent to you by strangers.

Reading Check

Recall What is the maximum amount you may be required to pay if someone uses your credit card illegally?

Cosigning a Loan

Why would someone ask a friend or relative to cosign a loan?

If a friend or relative ever asks you to cosign a loan, think twice. **Cosigning** a loan means that you agree to be responsible for the loan payments if the other person fails to make them. When you cosign, you are taking a chance that a professional lender will not take. The lender would not require a cosigner if the borrower were considered a good risk.

If you cosign a loan and the borrower does not pay the debt, you may have to pay up to the full amount of the debt as well as any late fees or collection costs. The creditor can even collect the debt from you without first trying to collect from the borrower. The creditor can use the same collection methods against you that can be used against the borrower. If the debt is not repaid, that fact will appear on your credit record.

If you decide to cosign a loan, despite the risks, here are a few things to consider:

1. Be sure you can afford to pay the loan.
2. Consider that even if you are not asked to repay the debt, your liability for this loan may keep you from getting other credit.
3. Before you pledge property to secure the loan, understand that you could lose the property you pledge if the borrower defaults.
4. Check your state law. Some states have laws giving you additional rights as a cosigner.
5. Request that a copy of overdue-payment notices be sent to you so that you can take action to protect your credit history.

Reading Check

Summarize Why should you think twice about cosigning a loan for a friend?

Complaining About Consumer Credit

When should you complain about a lender?

If you believe that a lender is not following the consumer credit protection laws, first try to solve the problem directly with the lender. If that fails, then you should use more formal complaint procedures. This section describes how to file a complaint with the federal agencies that administer consumer credit protection laws.

Careers That Count!

Sandra Murakami • Credit Analyst

After I graduated with a bachelor's degree in accounting, I accepted a credit analyst position for a global organization. As a credit analyst, my job is to consider a company's credit by evaluating financial statements, company statistics, and its managers. With the help of computer programs, I evaluate corporate records and recommend payment plans based on earnings, savings data, payment history, and purchase activity. I help make decisions about the worthiness of corporate customers and credit risk, and then set credit lines. I also advise whether or not to extend credit to a company. My job involves substantial critical thinking, judgment, and decision making—I have to consider the relative costs and benefits of potential actions to ensure that I choose the most appropriate one. Although many employers prefer applicants with a bachelor's degree or with some coursework in credit and loans, some credit analysts can start a career with a high school diploma and learn while on the job.

EXPLORE CAREERS

Visit the Web site of the U.S. Department of Labor's Bureau of Labor Statistics and obtain information about a career as a credit analyst.

1. Why are communication skills, both verbal and written, so important for someone in this position?
2. What type of work experience would benefit someone interested in becoming a credit analyst?

Skills	Education	Career Path
Time-management, accounting, judgment, investigative, analytical, communication, some foreign language, and interpersonal skills	High school diploma in some cases, but a bachelor's degree in accounting, finance, or related field is preferred	Credit analysts, sometimes called risk analysts or underwriters, can become securities underwriters, stockbrokers, financial analysts, or investment advisors.

 glencoe.com 

Activity Download a Career Exploration Activity.

Consumer Credit Protection Laws

If you have a particular problem with a bank in connection with any of the consumer credit protection laws, you can get advice and help from the Federal Reserve System. You do not need to have an account at the bank to file a complaint. You may also take legal action against a creditor. If you decide to file a lawsuit, you should be aware of the various consumer credit protection laws described below.

Credit Card Act In 2009 the United States Congress passed The Credit Card Accountability and Responsibility and Disclosure Act. The bill established fair and clear practices for extending credit to consumers. Some key parts of the bill are:

- Prevents unfair increases in interest rates and changes in terms. The credit card issuer must also give consumers the right to cancel their card before any increases or changes in terms take effect.
- Prohibits excessive and unnecessary fees. Penalty fees must be reasonable and proportional to the violation.

COMMON CENTS

One Is Enough

When you turn 21, you may start receiving applications for credit cards. Be a smart consumer and compare interest rates, annual fees, and any other fees. Decide which credit card best suits your needs and apply for that one. Make sure to shred any other applications and do not simply throw them into the trash.

Concept Application

Why should you get the best (or lowest) interest rate for a credit card?

- Requires fairness in the timing of card payments. Payments that are greater than the minimum amount due must be applied first to the balance with a higher interest rate.
- Provides enhanced disclosures of card terms and conditions. The credit card issuer must provide on your monthly statement the period of time and total interest it will take to pay off the card balance if only the minimum monthly payments are made. In addition, your statement must include the amount needed to pay each month to pay off the card in three years.
- Ensures adequate safeguards for young people. The bill limits prescreened offers to young consumers and requires that an applicant under the age of 21 obtain a cosigner for the credit card.

Truth in Lending and Consumer Leasing Acts If a creditor fails to disclose information as required under the Truth in Lending Act or the Consumer Leasing Act, or gives inaccurate information, you can sue for any money loss you suffer. You can also sue a creditor that does not follow rules regarding credit cards. In addition, the Truth in Lending Act and the Consumer Leasing Act permit class-action lawsuits. A class-action suit is a legal action on behalf of all of the people who have suffered the same injustice.

Equal Credit Opportunity Act (ECOA) If you think that you can prove that a creditor has discriminated against you for any reason prohibited by the ECOA, you may sue for actual damages plus punitive damages—a payment used to punish the creditor who has violated the law—up to $10,000.

Fair Credit Opportunity Act A creditor that fails to follow the rules that apply to correcting any billing errors will automatically give up the amount owed on the item in question and any finance charges on it, up to a combined total of $50. This is true even if the bill was correct. You may also sue for actual damages plus twice the amount of any finance charges.

Fair Credit Reporting Act You may sue any credit bureau or creditor that violates the rules regarding access to your credit records or that fails to correct errors in your credit file. You are entitled to actual damages plus any punitive damages the court allows if the violation is proven to have been intentional.

Consumer Credit Reporting Reform Act The Consumer Credit Reporting Reform Act of 1997 places the burden of proof for accurate credit information on the credit bureau. Under this law, the creditor must prove that disputed information is accurate. If a creditor or the credit bureau verifies incorrect data, you can sue for damages.

The Federal Reserve System has set up a separate office, the Division of Consumer and Community Affairs, in Washington, DC to handle consumer complaints. This division also writes regulations to carry out the consumer credit laws, enforces these laws, and helps banks comply with these laws.

FIGURE 10 **Federal Agencies**

Consumer Rights By law, you are protected as a consumer of credit. *What might lead you to report a creditor to these government agencies?*

If you think you've been discriminated against by:	You may file a complaint with the following agency:
A retailer, nonbank credit card issuer, consumer finance company, state-chartered credit union or bank, and noninsured savings and loan institution	Consumer Response Center Federal Trade Commission (FTC) Washington, DC 20580
A national bank	Comptroller of the Currency Compliance Management Mail Stop 7–5 Washington, DC 20219
A Federal Reserve member bank	Board of Governors of the Federal Reserve System Director, Division of Consumer and Community Affairs Washington, DC 20551
Other insured banks	Federal Deposit Insurance Corporation Consumer Affairs Division Washington, DC 20429
Insured savings and loan institutions and federally chartered state banks	Office of Thrift Supervision Consumer Affairs Program Washington, DC 20552
The FHA mortgage program	Housing and Urban Development (HUD) Department of Health, Education and Welfare Washington, DC 20410
A federal credit union	National Credit Union Administration Consumer Affairs Division Washington, DC 20456

Your Rights Under Consumer Credit Laws

If you believe that you have been refused credit because of discrimination, you can take one or more of the following steps:

1. Complain to the creditor. Let the creditor know that you are aware of the law.
2. File a complaint with the government. You can report any violations to the appropriate government enforcement agency, as shown in **Figure 10.** Although the agencies use complaints to decide which companies to investigate, they cannot handle private cases.
3. If all else fails, sue the creditor. You have the right to bring a case in a federal district court. If you win, you can receive actual damages and punitive damages of up to $10,000. You can also recover reasonable attorneys' fees and court costs.

Assessment

Review Key Concepts

1. **Explain** What two actions can you take to help protect your credit card from theft or loss?
2. **Describe** Identify the three actions you should immediately take if you think you have been a victim of identity theft.
3. **List** Name five consumer credit protection laws you should be aware of.

Higher Order Thinking H.O.T.

4. **Explain** The Consumer Credit Reporting Reform Act states that the burden of proof for accurate information is on the credit bureau rather than on you. How can this benefit you if you find information you feel is wrong on your credit report?

English Language Arts

5. **Write a Letter** When disputing information on a credit bill or credit report, it is important to have that information in writing. For this reason, you should send a letter instead of or as a follow-up to a phone call with your creditor. Suppose you received your credit card statement and it showed a purchase that you had not made. Write a letter to the creditor to dispute the charge. Be sure to clearly state what the charge is and why you feel it was in error, as well as what resolution you would like.

NCTE 4 Use written language to communicate effectively.

Mathematics

6. **Credit Card Billing** Carlos has a credit card which had a balance of $120 on his last statement. He did not make a payment on the card this month. Carlos keeps all of the receipts from his credit card purchases in order to confirm his monthly statements. The receipts show that he spent $45 on food, $25 on clothes, and $20 on other items. The balance shown on his current statement is $225.35 which includes an interest charge (19 percent annual interest rate, compounded monthly). Determine if the balance on the statement is correct.

Math Concept **Calculate Credit Card Balance** To calculate the balance on a credit card, first determine the interest charge on the prior balance. Add the interest charge and any purchases to the prior balance and subtract any payments made.

Starting Hint Determine the interest charged on the credit card by first dividing the annual interest rate by 12 to get the monthly interest rate. Multiply the result by the previous balance on the statement.

NCTM Number and Operations Understand numbers, ways of representing numbers, relationships among numbers, and number systems.

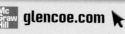

Check your answers.

Managing Your Debts

Signs of Debt Problems

How do you know when you are getting in financial trouble?

Carl Reynolds is a recent college graduate with a steady job earning $40,000 per year. With the latest model sports car parked in the driveway of his new home, Carl appears to have the ideal life. However, Carl is deeply in debt. Almost all of his income is tied up in debt payments. The bank has already begun foreclosure proceedings on his home, and several stores have court orders to **repossess,** or take back, practically all of his new furniture and electronic gadgets.

Carl's situation is called conspicuous consumption. Carl lacks self-discipline. He uses poor judgment or fails to accept responsibility for managing his money. Carl and others like him are not necessarily bad people but simply have not thought about their long-term financial goals.

There are some warning signs of being in financial trouble. If you are experiencing two or more of these warning signs, it is time for you to rethink your priorities.

- You make only the minimum monthly payment on credit cards.
- You struggle to make the monthly payments on your credit bills.
- The total balance on your credit cards increases every month.
- You miss loan payments or often pay late.
- You use savings to pay for necessities such as food and utilities.
- You receive second or third payment due notices from creditors.
- You borrow money to pay off old debts.
- You exceed the credit limits on your credit cards.
- You have been denied credit because of a bad credit report.

Reading Check

Infer Is making only the minimum monthly payment on a credit card a sign of financial trouble?

Debt Collection Practices

Are debt collection practices regulated by laws?

When people are in debt and getting behind in payments, they may worry about debt collection agencies. Creditors will often turn their bad debts over to such companies. However, a federal agency protects certain legal rights of debtors in their dealings with these types of agencies.

Section Objectives

- **Describe** options for managing debt problems.
- **Identify** signs of debt problems.

As You Read

Predict How might filing for bankruptcy negatively impact a person's future?

The Federal Trade Commission enforces the Fair Debt Collection Practices Act (FDCPA). This act prohibits certain practices by debt collectors. The act does not erase the legitimate debts that consumers owe, but it does control the ways in which debt collection agencies do business and deal with consumers in debt.

Reading Check

Recall Is the FDCPA intended to erase a person's legitimate debts?

Financial Counseling Services

What are sources of financial counseling?

If you are having trouble paying your bills and need help, you have several options. You can contact your creditors and try to work out an adjusted repayment plan. In addition, you can contact a nonprofit financial counseling program, such as the Consumer Credit Counseling Service, which operates nationwide.

Consumer Credit Counseling Service

The Consumer Credit Counseling Service (CCCS) is a nonprofit organization affiliated with the National Foundation for Consumer Credit (NFCC). Local branches of the CCCS provide debt counseling services for families and individuals with serious financial problems. The CCCS is not a charity, a lending institution, or a government agency. CCCS counseling is usually free. However, when the organization supervises a debt repayment plan, it sometimes charges a small fee to help pay administrative costs.

Conspicuous Consumption Fancy cars and big houses do not necessarily reflect financial health. *How could using credit for these things endanger your financial future?*

Document Detective

A Credit Card Statement

Understanding how to read your credit card statement is important so you can track where you spend your money each month. You can also verify that the transactions on the statement are accurate. The information listed on a credit card statement includes:

- Payments made
- New balance
- Your available credit
- Transactions for the month
- Minimum payment due

CREDIT CARD STATEMENT

Statement Date 02/03/--
Payment Date 02/28/--

Summary of Account Activity

Previous Balance	Payments	Purchases	Balance Transfers	Cash Advances	Past Due Amount	Fees Charged	Interest Charged	New Balance	Credit Limit	Available Credit	Statement Closing Date	Days in Billing Cycle
$535.07	$450.00	$246.60	$0.00	$0.00	$0.00	$0.00	$1.13	$332.80	$1,000.00	$667.20	2/28/20XX	30

Questions?
Call Customer Service 1-xxx-xxx-xxxx
Lost or Stolen Credit Card 1-xxx-xxx-xxxx

Payment Information

New Balance	Minimum Payment Due	Payment Due Date
$332.80	$15.00	2/20/2010

Late Payment Warning If we do not receive your minimum payment by the date listed above, you may have to pay a $35 late fee and your APRs may be increased up to the Penalty APR of 28.99%.
Minimum Payment Warning If you make only the minimum payment each period, you will pay more in interest and it will take you longer to pay off your balance.

If you make no additional charges using this card and each month you pay ...	You will pay off the balance shown on this statement in about ...	And you will end up paying an estimated total of ...
Only the minimum payment	6 months	$89.04
$40	3 months	$86.91 (Savings=$2.13)

SEND PAYMENTS TO: BANKCENTER P.O. BOX 6575 GOLDEN, NEVADA 88777

Sale Date	Post Date	Reference Number	Type of Activity	Location	Amount
01/05	01/07	24036215006661	Daisy Market	Clover, IL	104.30
01/08	01/10	24692165008000	Chloe's Coffee	Fielding, CT	8.30
01/13	01/13	74046585013013	PAYMENT RECEIVED--THANK YOU		450.00
01/18	01/20	24036215019664	Real Music	Clover, IL	115.50
02/02	02/03	242753050337531	Books 'n' News	Montclair, MO	13.90
02/01	02/03	242753950329000	Nick's Candy	Montclair, MO	4.60

DAYS IN BILLING PERIOD: 25	Purchases	Cash Advance	2012 Totals Year-to-Date	
Balance Subject to Interest Charge >	$85.07	.00	Total fees charged in 20XX	$0.00
ANNUAL PERCENTAGE RATE >	16.00%	27.00%	Total interest charged in 20XX	$1.13

Key Points A credit card statement is sent to you each month. It lists all the purchases you have made using your credit card and the amount of each purchase. It also lists the payments you made during the month. In addition, it indicates how much money you can still borrow from the credit card.

FIND the Solutions

Review Key Concepts

1. How many charges or transactions were completed on this statement?
2. How much more can you charge on the credit card?
3. What is the new balance listed on the statement?
4. What is the minimum payment to be paid?
5. What is the due date of the next payment?

According to the NFCC, millions of consumers contact CCCS offices each year for help with their personal financial problems. To find an office, check your local directory under Consumer Credit Counseling Service. All information is kept **confidential,** or private.

Credit counselors know that most individuals who are overwhelmed with debt are basically honest people who want to clear up their unmanageable indebtedness. The CCCS is concerned with preventing and solving these problems. Its activities are divided into two parts:

- Aiding families with serious debt problems by helping them manage their money better and setting up a realistic budget
- Helping people prevent indebtedness by teaching them the importance of budget planning, educating them about the pitfalls of unwise credit buying, and encouraging credit institutions to withhold credit from people who cannot afford it

Other Counseling Services

In addition, universities, credit unions, military bases, and state and federal housing authorities may provide nonprofit credit counseling services. These organizations usually charge little to nothing for their assistance. You can also check with your bank or consumer protection office for listings of reputable financial counseling services.

Reading Check

Paraphrase What are some ways the CCCS helps consumers prevent debt problems?

Declaring Personal Bankruptcy

Why do people declare personal bankruptcy?

What if an individual suffers from an extreme case of debt problems? Is there any relief? As a last resort, an individual can declare bankruptcy. **Bankruptcy** is a legal process in which some or all of the assets of a debtor are distributed among the creditors because the debtor is unable to pay his or her debts. Bankruptcy may also include a plan for the debtor to repay creditors on an installment basis. Declaring bankruptcy severely damages your credit rating.

For example, Prakrit Singh illustrates the new face of bankruptcy. A 43-year-old freelance photographer from California, she was never in serious financial trouble until she began running up big medical costs. She reached for her credit cards to pay the bills. Because Prakrit did not have health insurance, her debt quickly mounted and soon reached $17,000—too much to pay off with her $25,000-a-year income. Her solution was to declare personal bankruptcy and enjoy the immediate freedom it would bring from creditors' demands.

In 1994, the U.S. Senate passed a bill that reduced the time and cost of bankruptcy proceedings. The bill strengthened creditor rights and enabled more individuals to get through bankruptcy proceedings without selling their assets. Unfortunately, for some debtors, bankruptcy became an acceptable debt management tool.

The U.S. Bankruptcy Act of 1978

Figure 11 illustrates the rate of personal bankruptcy in the United States. The vast majority of bankruptcies in the United States are filed under a part of the U.S. bankruptcy code known as Chapter 7. You have two choices in declaring personal bankruptcy:

- Chapter 7 (a straight bankruptcy)
- Chapter 13 (a wage-earner plan bankruptcy)

Both choices are undesirable, and neither should be considered an easy way to get out of debt.

Chapter 7 Bankruptcy In a Chapter 7 bankruptcy, an individual must draw up a petition listing all assets and liabilities. A person who files for relief under the bankruptcy code is called a debtor. The debtor submits the petition to a U.S. district court and pays a filing fee.

Chapter 7 is a straight bankruptcy in which many, but not all, debts are forgiven. Most of the debtor's assets are sold to pay off creditors. Certain assets, however, receive some protection.

FIGURE 11 **U.S. Bankruptcies**

Rise in Bankruptcies Since the mid-1980s, the number of personal bankruptcies has increased sharply. Bankruptcies decreased after the Bankruptcy Abuse Prevention and Consumer Protection Act was passed in 2005. *What factors may have contributed to the rise in bankruptcies?*

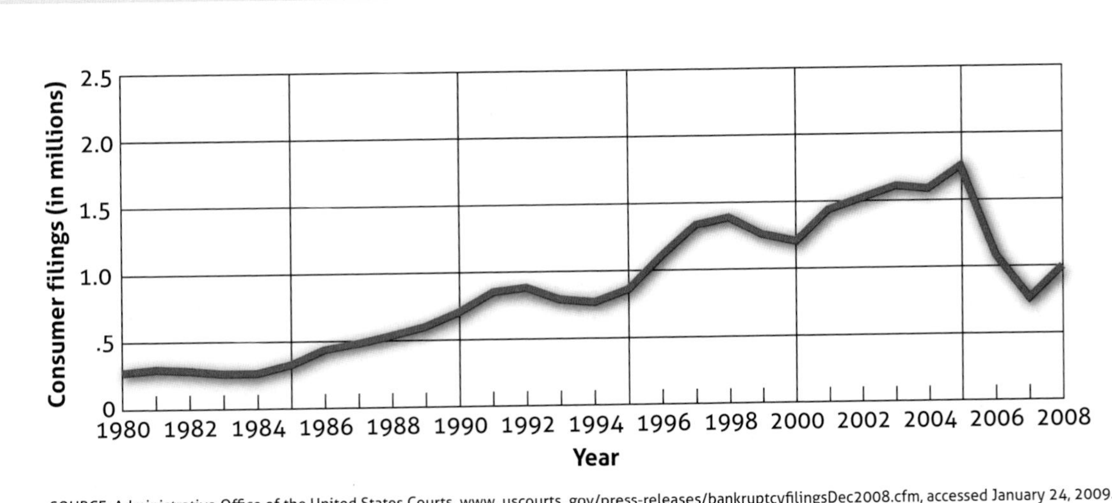

SOURCE: Administrative Office of the United States Courts, www. uscourts. gov/press-releases/bankruptcyfilingsDec2008.cfm, accessed January 24, 2009.

Among the assets usually protected are Social Security payments, unemployment compensation, and the net value of your home, vehicle, household goods and appliances.

The release from debt does not affect alimony, child support, certain taxes, fines, certain debts arising from educational loans, or debts that you fail to disclose properly to the bankruptcy court. Furthermore, debts arising from fraud, driving while intoxicated, or certain other acts or crimes may also be excluded.

Chapter 13 Bankruptcy In a Chapter 13 bankruptcy, a debtor with a regular income proposes a plan to the court for using future earnings or assets to eliminate his or her debts over a specific period of time. In such a bankruptcy, the debtor normally keeps all or most of his or her property.

During the period when the plan is in effect, which can be as long as five years, the debtor makes regular payments to a Chapter 13 trustee, or representative, who then distributes the money to the creditors. Under certain circumstances, the bankruptcy court may approve a plan that permits the debtor to keep all property even though he or she repays less than the full amount of the debts.

The Bankruptcy Abuse Prevention and Consumer Protection Act In 2005, President George W. Bush signed the Bankruptcy Abuse Prevention and Consumer Protection Act. It was perhaps the largest overhaul of the Bankruptcy code since 1978. The law required that:

- The director of the Executive Office for U.S. Trustees develop a financial management training curriculum to educate individual debtors on how to better manage their finances; and test, evaluate, and report to Congress on the curriculum's effectiveness.
- Debtors complete an approved instructional course in personal financial management.
- The clerk of each bankruptcy district keeps a list of credit counseling agencies and courses on financial management.

The law made it more difficult for consumers to file Chapter 7 and forced them to move into a Chapter 13 repayment plan.

Effects of Bankruptcy

People have varying experiences in obtaining credit after they file for bankruptcy. Some find the process more difficult, whereas others find it easier because they have removed the burden of prior debts or because creditors know that they cannot file another bankruptcy case for a certain period of time. Obtaining credit may be easier for people who file a Chapter 13 bankruptcy and repay some of their debts than for those who file a Chapter 7 bankruptcy and make no effort to repay any of their debts. Bankruptcy reports are kept on file in credit bureaus for ten years, a fact that is likely to make getting credit more difficult during that time. Therefore, you should take the extreme step of declaring bankruptcy only when you have no other options.

After You Read

React What would be the best way to avoid credit problems and bankruptcy?

SECTION 4 Assessment

Review Key Concepts

1. **List** Identify five warning signs that you are in financial trouble.
2. **Explain** What are the two main activities of the CCCS?
3. **Describe** What are two options when declaring bankruptcy?

Higher Order Thinking H.O.T.

4. **Relate** Suppose a person is forced to file for bankruptcy. Why might it be easier for someone to get credit if they have filed Chapter 13 bankruptcy, instead of Chapter 7 bankruptcy?

21st Century Skills

5. **Access and Evaluate Information** Suppose a friend comes to you and confides that she has more debt than she can manage and she is not sure where to go for help. Conduct research to locate local nonprofit credit counseling services that your friend might use. CCCS might be one resource, but be sure to look for other, local alternatives. Create a two-column chart, listing the services' names and contact information in the first column, and the services they offer in the second column so that your friend can decide which service is best for her.

Mathematics

6. **Managing Debt** Jameel has an annual income of $26,000. He currently pays $600 in rent, $175 for his car, and $80 in credit card debt each month. Jameel has been thinking about buying a new car. If he purchases the car, he will no longer have his current car payment, but he will have a new payment of $375 per month. What is Jameel's monthly net income before and after the car purchase? Should Jameel purchase the car? Use the tools you have learned in previous sections.

Math Concept **Calculate Net Income** To calculate monthly net income you must first convert annual salary to a monthly figure. Subtract all monthly payments from the monthly salary in order to get monthly net income.

Starting Hint Determine the monthly income by dividing the annual salary by 12. Add all the expenses to calculate the total monthly expense.

NCTM Connections Recognize and apply mathematics in contexts outside of mathematics.

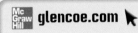

Check your answers.

Visual Summary

Consumer Credit

Earning Credit

Understanding the five Cs can help you determine if a lender will give you credit.

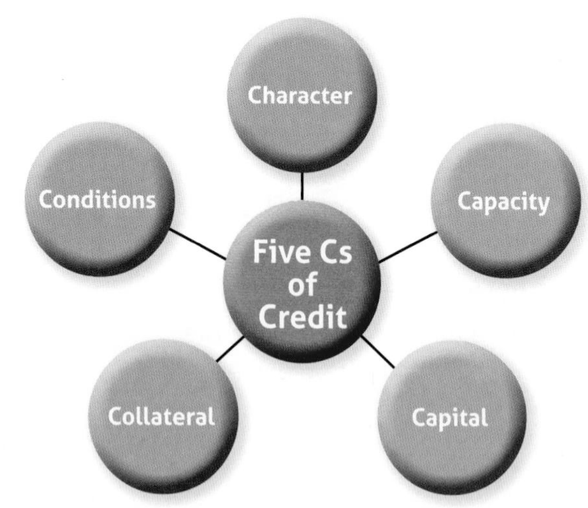

Building Credit

Take steps now to begin building and protecting your credit rating.

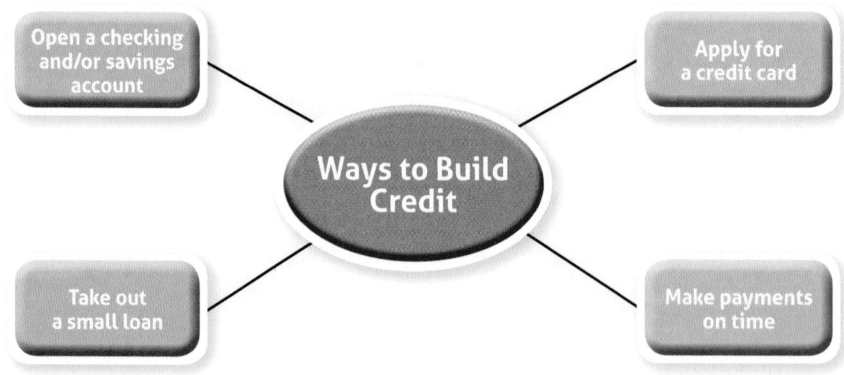

Try It!

Draw a diagram like this one to list the steps you can take to help protect your credit information on the Internet.

Chapter Review and Assessment

Chapter Summary

- Consumer credit is the use of credit for personal needs. Credit is an arrangement to receive cash, goods, or services now and to pay for them later.
- Closed-end credit is credit as a one-time loan that you pay back over a specified period of time in payments of equal amounts.
- Open-end credit is credit as a loan with a limit on the amount of money that you borrow for goods and services.
- The five C's of credit include character, capacity, capital, collateral, and conditions. Creditors use the five C's to determine who will receive credit.
- When choosing a loan or credit card, consider factors such as length of the loan, amount of monthly payments, and interest rate.
- To build and protect good credit, pay your bills and loans promptly and manage your personal finances carefully. Also, correct mistakes related to your credit bills and credit reports.
- Dispute billing errors in writing and pay amounts that are not in question.
- If your credit or identity has been stolen, contact all of your credit card companies; close and open new bank accounts; and change all PINs. Notify law enforcement agencies and credit bureaus.
- If purchasing online, never share your PINs, Social Security numbers, or passwords. Manage debt problems by contacting creditors and/or debt counseling services.
- Bankruptcy is a last resort.

Vocabulary Review

1. Use these vocabulary terms in a short essay about buying a new car.

- credit
- consumer credit
- creditor
- closed-end credit
- open-end credit
- line of credit
- grace period
- finance charge
- net income
- annual percentage rate (APR)
- collateral
- simple interest
- minimum monthly payment
- credit rating
- cosigning
- bankruptcy
- finance
- title
- portion
- pledge
- promptly
- impostors
- repossess
- confidential

Higher Order Thinking 

2. **Analyze** Why might making only the minimum monthly payments on your credit cards be a warning sign of financial trouble?
3. **Predict** What problems might you have if you do not follow the suggested guidelines for protecting your credit information on the Internet?
4. **Infer** Why is it important to keep a record of your credit card numbers separate from the cards? How can this help prevent identity theft?
5. **Deduce** Why is it necessary to differentiate consumer credit from credit?
6. **Differentiate** What are the differences between capital and collateral?
7. **Justify** Explain the advantages of using credit cards, even if you could afford to pay cash.
8. **Evaluate** Would having the same Vantagescore from all three credit unions be preferable to the varying FICO scores?
9. **Judge** Would it be better to use a credit counseling service or declare Chapter 13 bankruptcy to enable you to make one regular monthly payment that will be distributed to your creditors to help pay down debt?

College and Career Readiness

Science

10. Shopping Addiction There are people who use credit cards to support a shopping addiction, which can lead to financial and emotional problems.

Procedure Conduct research to learn more about the causes of shopping addiction and the warning signs, as well as tips on breaking the addiction.

Analysis Write a brief report to share your findings, thoroughly explaining the symptoms and possible treatments for shopping addiction.

NSES F Develop understanding of personal and community health; population growth; natural resources; environmental quality; natural and human-induced hazards; science and technology in local, national, and global challenges.

Mathematics

11. Debt Payment-To-Income Ratio Your friend Sarah wants to buy an ice cream shop. She earns $1,500 per month in her current job, which she will continue to do after purchasing the shop. Sarah pays $350 per month in credit card debt and has no other loans. She will need to borrow $30,000 in order to make the purchase. Sarah has asked you to cosign the loan in order to purchase the ice cream shop. Calculate Sarah's debt payment-to-income ratio before and after the purchase assuming a monthly payment of $468 for the business loan. Should you cosign the loan? Explain why or why not.

Math Concept **Calculate Debt Payment-to-Income Ratio** To calculate the debt payment-to-income ratio you must first determine the total monthly debt payments and the total monthly income earned. Divide the monthly debt payments by the total monthly income.

Starting Hint Calculate the debt payment-to-income ratio before the ice cream shop purchase in order to understand Sarah's current situation. Determine the legal implications of cosigning a loan and also identify all the risks you will assume if you decide to cosign the loan.

NCTM Number and Operations Compute fluently and make reasonable estimates.

English Language Arts

12. Managing Debt One of the services offered by the Consumer Credit Counseling Service is information to help people make better choices and manage their debt responsibly. Visit the CCCS Web site to learn what the top 10 purchasing mistakes are. Use this information to create a poster that illustrates the top 10 mistakes and offers advice on how to avoid them. Use pictures from magazines or draw pictures to illustrate your poster.

NCTE 5 Use different writing process elements to communicate effectively.

Ethics

13. Loan Applications Suppose you and your business partner have decided to expand your business. You need a loan to help finance the new equipment you will need. Your friend has offered to take care of applying for the loan. He researches local financial institutions, and then fills out a loan application request. As you review the application, you notice that he has used some "creative" bookkeeping to make your business look more profitable than it is. How do you feel about what your partner has done? Do you feel that this is ethical? Write a one-page dialogue between you and your partner in which you share your feelings about the misleading information.

Real-World Applications

14. Cosigning a Loan Suppose that a close friend has asked you to cosign a loan she needs to buy a new car. She has spent a lot of money on repairs to her car recently and feels that she should buy a new one rather than repair it again. You would like to help if you can. However, your friend is currently unemployed, and you are concerned that she will not be able to repay the loan. She assures you that once she has the car, she will be able to get a new job and be able to handle the payments. What would you do? Write a letter to your friend explaining your decision.

Credit Cards: Getting the Best Deal

Melanie's parents want to give her a credit card she could use for emergencies. They made it clear that if she could eat it, wear it, or listen to it, it was not an emergency. They asked Melanie to do the homework to find the best deal. She called the bank where she has a savings account and another neighborhood bank and asked about the following credit card information.

Melanie's Credit Card Comparison

Credit Card Company	Peabody Bank	Imperial Bank
Phone number	800/555-1274	800/555-9201
Annual percentage rate (APR)	19.9%	10.9%
Introductory rate	2.9% on transferred balances	5% for first 6 months
Annual fee	$50	none
Grace period	18 days	25 days
Cash advance fee	19.8%	19.9%
Late payment fee	$25	$29
Credit limit for new customers	based on income	based on income
Travel accident insurance	$150,000	$10,000
Other travel-related services	airline miles; lost luggage insurance; emergency travel services	lost luggage insurance; emergency travel services
Protection if the cards are lost or stolen	yes	yes

Melanie chose the credit card with Imperial Bank because there was no annual fee, and the APR was lower. She did not think she would spend enough to make Peabody Bank's offer of airline miles useful. Melanie was surprised at the high penalty for late payments, so she made a mental note to be sure to make her payment on time.

If you wanted a credit card, which company would you choose? Explain why. Would you be influenced by the offer of airline miles?

Research

Research two credit card companies. On a separate sheet of paper, list their fees and any advantages they offer in a similar chart.

CHAPTER 16

The Finances of Housing

Visual Literacy

Many people dream of owning their own home, rather than renting. ***What are some reasons that renting might be preferential to owning?***

Discovery Project

Your First Apartment

Key Question

Why is it important to consider multiple options when choosing a rental property?

Project Goal

Suppose you have decided to rent an apartment after graduation. You will need to research possible locations before you make a decision. Think about what type of neighborhood you would like to live in and how much money you will have to spend on monthly rent and utilities, as well as how much you have saved for a security deposit.

- Compile a list of features and amenities you would like your apartment to have.
- Prioritize these, making sure to include items like location, security features, and price.
- Begin researching possible locations by looking for listings in the newspaper or online, or by visiting some apartment complexes.
- Use your list and your research to build a spreadsheet to compare your top three options side by side.

Ask Yourself ...

- *How much can you afford for your monthly rent?*
- *What is your preferred location? Does it need to be close to work or public transportation?*
- *How many bedrooms and bathrooms do you need? Will you have a roommate?*
- *Do you want any special security features, such as a gated community or an alarm system?*
- *Do you need or want extra amenities such as a gym?*
- *Are there extra features you would require or prefer?*

Use and Manage Information

What could you do if no apartments in your price range met your criteria?

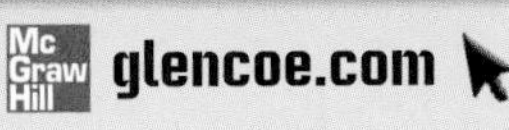

Evaluate Download an assessment rubric.

THE BIG IDEA

There are many factors to consider before renting or buying a home.

ASK STANDARD & POOR'S

Housing Options

Q *My older sister loves her new job and has decided that she would like to work for her company at least five years. Is this a good time for her to buy a house, or should she continue renting?*

A A home can be an excellent investment, but your sister will need to take some things into consideration before she makes this decision. For example, she will need to assess her finances to determine if she can afford to buy a house. She must also consider whether she wants to spend time maintaining a house; if not, it may be best for her to continue renting.

Writing Activity

Build a spreadsheet to analyze the advantages and disadvantages of buying a house. Be sure to include financial considerations, as well as time and lifestyle factors.

CHAPTER 16

Reading Guide

Before You Read

The Essential Question What are some factors that should be included in the decision of whether renting or buying a home is the best action for you?

Main Idea

It is important to understand all of your options and to consider the advantages, disadvantages, and costs of each when making housing decisions. You should understand the processes involved with homeownership before buying or selling.

Content Vocabulary

- mobility
- tenant
- landlord
- lease
- security deposit
- renters insurance
- equity
- escrow account
- private mortgage insurance (PMI)
- mortgage
- points
- amortization
- fixed-rate mortgage
- adjustable-rate mortgage (ARM)
- home equity loan
- refinance
- closing
- title insurance
- deed
- appraisal

Academic Vocabulary

You will see these words in your reading and on your tests.

- lifestyle
- consideration
- complex
- sublet
- dwelling
- foreclose

Graphic Organizer

Before you read this chapter, build a Web diagram like the one shown. As you read, look for six sources of information to use when researching housing options.

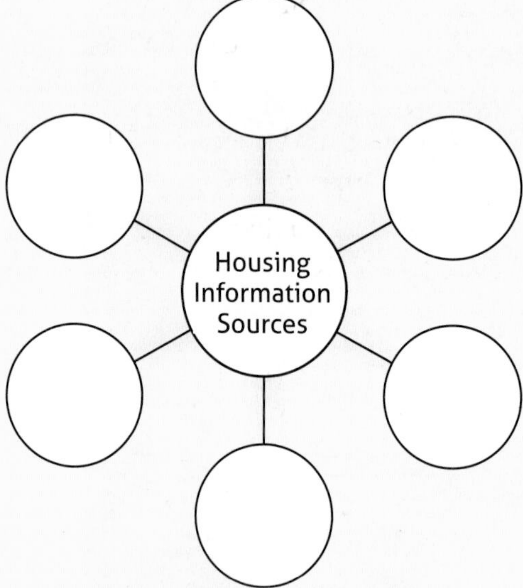

glencoe.com Print this graphic organizer.

Standards

Academic

Mathematics

NCTM Connections Recognize and apply mathematics in contexts outside of mathematics.

NCTM Problem Solving Build new mathematical knowledge through problem solving.

NCTM Number and Operations Compute fluently and make reasonable estimates.

English Language Arts

NCTE 7 Conduct research and gather, evaluate, and synthesize data to communicate discoveries.

NCTE 12 Use language to accomplish individual purposes.

Social Studies

NCSS I F Culture Interpret patterns of behavior reflecting values and attitudes that contribute or pose obstacles to cross-cultural understanding.

NCTM *National Council of Teachers of Mathematics*

NCTE *National Council of Teachers of English*

NCSS *National Council for the Social Studies*

NSES *National Science Education Standards*

Common Core

Reading Determine central ideas or themes of a text and analyze their development; summarize the key supporting details and ideas.

Reading Read and comprehend complex literary and informational texts independently and proficiently.

Writing Write routinely over extended time frames (time for research, reflection, and revision) and shorter time frames (a single sitting or a day or two) for a range of tasks, purposes, and audiences.

Your Lifestyle and Choice of Housing

What are some opportunity costs to consider when evaluating housing options?

Finances play an important role in housing decisions. Whether you are renting an apartment or buying a house, you will have to consider your financial situation. Use your budget and other personal financial statements to determine how much you should spend for housing.

One major factor you will need to consider when making housing decisions is your **lifestyle,** which is the way you choose to spend your time and money. See **Figure 1**. Your lifestyle will determine how close to work you want to live, how long you plan to stay in one place, and how much privacy you would like to have.

Opportunity Costs of Housing Choices

A housing decision requires many trade-offs, or opportunity costs. For example, buying a "handyman's special"—a home that is priced lower because it needs repairs and improvements—may allow you to purchase a larger property for less money, but it also means that you will have to work on the house. Renting an apartment may give you more **mobility,** which is the ability to move easily from place to place. However, you will give up the tax advantages that homeowners enjoy. When you make choices about housing, you cannot look at only the benefits. You also have to consider what you will be giving up. Some common trade-offs include:

- The interest earnings lost on the money used for a down payment on a home or the security deposit for an apartment.
- The time and cost of commuting to work when you live in an area that offers less expensive housing or more living space.
- The loss of tax advantages when you rent a city apartment to be close to your work.
- The time and money you spend when you repair and improve a lower-priced home.

Like every other financial choice, a housing decision requires consideration of what you give up in time, effort, and money.

Reading Check

Recall Why is a "handyman's special" generally priced lower than other homes?

Section Objective

- **Evaluate** various housing alternatives.

As You Read

Predict Do you plan to own or rent a residence? Explain your choice.

FIGURE 1 **Housing for Different Life Situations**

Rent or Own? Your lifestyle and life situation will factor into your housing decision. *Why might a young couple with no children decide to rent?*

Life Situation	Possible Types of Housing
Young single	• Rent an apartment or house because mobility is important and finances are low. • Buy a small home for tax advantages and possible increase in value.
Single parent	• Rent an apartment or house because time for maintenance is at a premium, playmates for children may be nearby, and finances are low. • Buy a home to build long-term financial security.
Young couple, no children	• Rent an apartment or house because mobility is important and finances are low • Buy a home to build long-term financial security.
Couple with children	• Rent an apartment or house because time for maintenance is at a premium and playmates for children may be nearby. • Buy a house to build long-term financial security and to provide more space and privacy.
Retired person	• Rent an apartment or house to meet financial, social, and physical needs. • Buy a home that needs little maintenance, offers convenience, and provides different services.

Renting versus Buying

Why would you rent a home if you could buy one?

One basic **consideration,** or matter for thought, about housing is whether to rent or buy. Your decision will depend on your lifestyle and on financial factors.

Renting is a good choice for young adults who are beginning their careers. It also appeals to people who want or need mobility and do not want to devote time or money to maintenance. Because renting can be cheaper, it appeals to people whose funds are limited.

In contrast, owning property also has advantages. It is a wise choice for people who want a certain amount of stability in their lives. Buying a home also gives the owner privacy and some freedoms that may not be available to a renter. (See **Figure 2**.)

Housing Information Sources

Housing information is plentiful and often free. You can begin researching on your own, using a variety of sources:

- **Libraries**—The public library will probably have books and other basic resources on the subject.

FIGURE 2 Evaluating Housing Alternatives

Pros and Cons When considering your housing options, you must evaluate all the advantages and disadvantages of each option. *How are the pros and cons of renting a home different from renting an apartment?*

	Advantages	Disadvantages
Renting an Apartment	• easy to move • low maintenance responsibility • low financial commitment	• no tax advantage • limitations on activities • less privacy
Renting a House	• easy to move • low maintenance responsibility • low financial commitment • more space	• higher utility expenses • some limitations on activities • no tax advantage
Owning a House	• pride of ownership • plenty of space • tax benefits	• financial commitment • high living expenses • limited mobility
Owning a Condominium	• pride of ownership • fewer maintenance costs or responsibilities than a house • tax benefits • access to recreation and businesses	• financial commitment • less privacy than in a house • need to get along with others • typically small and limited space • may be hard to sell
Owning a Mobile Home	• less expensive than other ownership options	• may be hard to sell • possible poor construction quality

- **Newspapers**—You can find articles on renting, buying, and other housing topics in the real estate section of a newspaper.
- **Internet**—The Internet can provide home buying tips, the latest mortgage rates, and information on available housing.
- **Real Estate Agents**—You might seek the services of an experienced real estate agent who is familiar with the local housing market.
- **Government Agencies**—You can write to government agencies, such as the U.S. Department of Housing and Urban Development.

Any combination of these sources will provide the information you need to make wise housing decisions, whether renting or buying.

Review Key Concepts

1. **List** What three decisions about housing will be determined by your lifestyle?
2. **Summarize** What are the advantages of owning property?
3. **Identify** What are five sources for housing information?

Higher Order Thinking H.O.T.

4. **Compare and contrast** What are the benefits and disadvantages of owning a house and a condominium? Who might benefit more from owning a condominium rather than a house?

English Language Arts

5. **Rental Options** Suppose that you and a friend are going to rent a place to live together. Use the newspaper or Internet to locate listings for at least three apartments or houses for rent. Build a spreadsheet to compare the prices, locations, and features of each option. Evaluate the information in your spreadsheet to determine which location you might choose. Write a paragraph to explain your choice. Were there features that you preferred but had to give up for your choice? If so, why?

NCTE 7 Conduct research and gather, evaluate, and synthesize data to communicate discoveries.

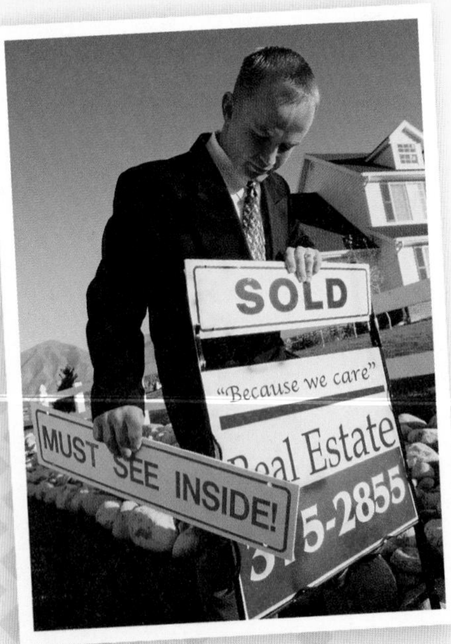

Mathematics

6. **Cost of Purchasing a Home** Teela is purchasing a house for $150,000. Her down payment is 10 percent of the purchase price and monthly payments are $724.00. Annual property taxes are $5,000. The total interest Teela will pay each year on her mortgage will be $6,705, $6,603, and $6,496 for years 1 through 3, respectively. The tax savings she will realize each year is 35 percent of the interest paid. Teela plans to sell the house in 3 years for $165,000. Total principal (or the orginal amount of the loan) paid will be $6,286. Calculate her total out of pocket cost over 3 years.

Math Concept **Calculate Cost of a House** To calculate the out of pocket costs of purchasing a house, first determine the gain or loss on the sale of the house. Add tax savings and subtract down payment, monthly payments, and property taxes from the result.

Starting Hint Determine the gain on sale of the house by first subtracting total principal payments from the loan amount to calculate the loan balance. Subtract the loan balance from the sale price of the home.

NCTM Connections Recognize and apply mathematics in contexts outside of mathematics.

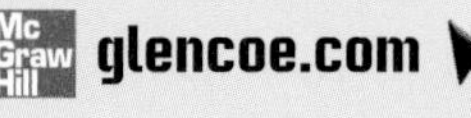

Check your answers.

Selecting a Rental Unit

What should you know before signing a lease?

Are you interested in a "3-bdrm apt., a/c, w/w carpet, pvt back ent, $800 + utils, ref reqd"? This is not a secret code. It is just a short way of describing an apartment for rent listed in the classified ads of a newspaper. Decoded, the message reads: "Three-bedroom apartment for rent. It has air conditioning, wall-to-wall carpeting, and a private back entrance. The rent is $800, and the renter must also pay for utilities. The renter must provide references." The ability to read and understand such ads is one of the skills you will need if you are going to look for some type of rental housing.

When you rent the place where you live, you become a **tenant**—a person who pays for the right to live in a residence owned by someone else. Your **landlord** is the person who owns the property that is rented. At some point in your life, you are likely to rent your residence. You may rent when you are first on your own or later in life when you want to avoid the activities required to maintain your home. About 35 percent of U.S. households live in rental units. You should consider the differences in the size, cost, and location of rental units when making a selection.

Size and Cost

Most people who rent live in apartments. These units may be located in a two-story house, in a high-rise building, or in an apartment complex. A **complex** is a building or group of buildings with housing units. An apartment building contains a number of separate living units that can range in size from one room (an efficiency or studio) to three-bedroom or larger units.

If a unit features a patio and a bit of lawn, it may be called a garden apartment. Some apartments are located in complexes with on-site conveniences such as swimming pools and laundry facilities.

A family or individual who needs more space than an apartment provides may prefer to rent a house. The trade-off for the extra space is usually higher rent. A single person with very few possessions might choose to rent a private room in a house. He or she may have to share common areas, such as the kitchen and bathroom. **Figure 3** describes what to look for when selecting an apartment.

Reading Check

Identify What are categories you should consider when choosing an apartment?

Section Objectives

- **Assess** the advantages and disadvantages of renting.
- **Identify** the costs of renting.

As You Read

Predict How would you begin a search for an apartment?

FIGURE 3 **Selecting an Apartment**

Apartment Options When choosing an apartment, you should consider location, finances, the building, and the layout and facilities. *What factors are included in the finances?*

Location	Finances	Building	Layout and Facilities
• Near school or work • Near place of worship • Near shopping • Near public transportation • Near recreation: parks and museums	• Amount of monthly rent • Amount of security deposit • Cost of utilities • Length of lease	• Condition of building and grounds • Parking facilities • Recreation on premises • Security system • Condition of hallways, stairs, and elevators • Access to mailboxes	• Size and condition of unit • Type and controls of heating and cooling systems • Plumbing and water pressure • Type and condition of appliances • Condition of doors, locks, windows, closets, and floors

Advantages of Renting

What are some of the advantages of renting?

The three main advantages of renting over buying a home are:

- greater mobility
- fewer responsibilities
- lower initial costs

Mobility

For many people, the appeal of renting is the mobility it offers. If you want to move, you can usually notify your landlord 30 days before you plan to leave, and he or she can find a new tenant. If you are offered a job in another town, you can move quickly and simply. If your landlord increases your rent beyond the amount you have budgeted, or if you decide that you want to live in a different community, making a change will be fairly easy if you rent an apartment.

Fewer Responsibilities

Tenants do not have many of the responsibilities that homeowners have. Making major repairs and maintaining the property are the landlord's concern. Tenants do not have to worry about property taxes or property insurance. Of course, they must pay the rent and any utility bills on time, and keep their homes clean.

Benefits of Renting
Renting a home or apartment offers more mobility than owning a home. *What are some other advantages to renting?*

Low Initial Costs

Buying a house typically requires many thousands of dollars for the down payment and other costs. In contrast, you usually pay the equivalent of only one or two months' rent to move into a rental unit.

Reading Check

Recall What are some of the responsibilities that homeowners have that tenants do not?

Disadvantages of Renting

What are some of the disadvantages of renting?

Renting is a good option for many people, but it has some disadvantages. Renting offers few financial benefits and may involve various legal issues for tenants.

Financial and Lifestyle Restrictions

Although it has lower initial costs, renting may actually be more expensive than owning property in some cases. Certain financial benefits are available to homeowners but not to tenants. Homeowners, for example, are eligible for various tax deductions. After many years, homeowners can eliminate their monthly housing payments. Tenants, on the other hand, must continue to pay housing costs each month for as long as they continue to rent. They are also subject to rent increases.

Tenants must accept certain limitations regarding their activities in the places they rent. For example, you might not be allowed to paint your walls without permission from your landlord. Homeowners have more freedom to alter or improve the property.

reality bytes

Virtual Tour Software
Online virtual tours are making selling a home easier than ever. Virtual tour software allows you to create, with a digital camera, rotating, 360-degree photographs that show all the features of a home. Virtual tours can be uploaded to Web sites or distributed to potential buyers on CDs.

Legal Issues

If you decide to rent, you will probably have to sign a **lease,** a legal document that defines the conditions of the rental agreement between the tenant and the landlord (see **Figure 4** for an example of a lease).

Never sign a lease without making sure that you understand and agree with what it says. Pay special attention to the amount and due date of the monthly rent and the length of the rental period. Also, check to see whether you have the right to sublet the property if you want to move before the lease expires. To **sublet** is to have a person other than the original tenant take over the rental unit and payments for the remaining term of the lease. If you disagree with the terms of the lease, discuss it with the landlord before you sign the lease.

A lease is designed to protect the rights of both the landlord and the tenant. The tenant is usually protected from rent increases during the lease term. However, the lease gives the landlord the right to take legal action against a tenant for example who does not pay rent.

Reading Check

Summarize Why might renting be more expensive than owning?

The Cost of Renting

What other factors affect the cost of renting?

Several factors affect and determine the price of renting a home: location, living space, utilities, security deposit, and insurance.

Location

The amount of your monthly rent will depend on the location, or neighborhood, in which you choose to live (see **Figure 5**). You may be willing to live near the freeway if it costs less, or you may be willing to pay more for an apartment that is close to a park or work.

Living Space

The price of a rental unit will also depend on the amount of living space. The least expensive choice might be a private room in a house, but you have to be willing to share common areas. Apartments, which are more expensive, often feature one to four bedrooms. Your most costly option might be to rent a townhouse or single-family house.

Utilities

You may also have to pay for utilities, such as electricity, gas, water, and trash. Before you sign a lease, be sure to ask your landlord if the rent payment includes any utilities.

FIGURE 4 A Typical Lease Agreement

Rental Agreements It is important to thoroughly read and understand all parts of a lease before signing. *Which parts of a lease are most likely to be negotiable?*

- Description of the property, including its address
- Names of owners and tenants
- Dates during which the lease is valid
- Amount of the security deposit
- Amount and due date of monthly rent and penalties for late payment
- List of restrictions regarding pets, remodeling, activities, and so on
- Tenant's right to sublet the rental unit
- Conditions under which the landlord may enter the apartment
- Charges to the tenant for damage or for moving out of the unit early or refusing to pay rent

RENTAL AGREEMENT OF PROPERTY
AT 4744 LEMONA STREET, EAST TROY, WISCONSIN 53120

Parties in agreement are Blanca Romero and April Shullman. Blanca Romero has rented the second floor apartment to be used as a private residence, for his or her (one person) use only and for no other purpose, for a term of six months.

The term of this agreement will be from June 1, 20--, to November 30, 20--, at which time another six-month agreement will be drawn.

The rent will be $650 per month. There will be a security deposit of one and one-half months' rent, for a total of $975. The monies held as security will be held until such time that the tenant desires to move or until he/she is asked to vacate the premises. The security deposit along with any interest it accrues will be returned to the tenant, minus any monies held for repair of damages, rubbish removal, or cleaning to be done.

Rent will be due from the tenant on the first of each month and not later than five days after the first of each month. A late penalty of 5% of the monthly rent will be assessed for any rent not paid by the end of the five-day grace period.

The tenant is personally responsible for paying the monthly expenses, including electric, telephone, and cable service. These expenses are not included in any monthly rent payment.

The tenant was advised that there is to be NO SMOKING in the apartment, while he/she is in residence at this address.

There will be no pets allowed at any time in the apartment while he/she resides here.

If the tenant or landlord decides that the tenant must vacate the apartment, a thirty (30) day notice must be given before the first of the month.

The tenant may not sublease (rent to another person) this property without the landlord's written permission.

The tenant must provide his/her own insurance on the contents of the apartment, such as furniture, jewelry, clothes, etc. The tenant will not hold the landlord or landlord's agent responsible in the event of a loss.

The tenant agrees to let landlord enter property at reasonable hours to inspect or repair the property. Landlord will notify the tenant 24 hours in advance and give the time and reason for the visit.

This place of residence shall be occupied by no more than one (1) person.

At the expiration of tenancy, the tenant will surrender the premises to the landlord in as good condition as when received. The tenant will remove all rubbish from the premises. Failing to do so, the tenant will forfeit part of the security deposit in order for the landlord to pay for removal. If tenant breaks the lease for any reason, the landlord may keep the security deposit.

This agreement is between Blanca Romero and April Shullman. On this day, this agreement is signed by both parties.

Tenant *Blanca Romero* Date *6/1/--* Landlord *A Shore* Date *6/1/--*

FIGURE 5 Finding and Living in Rental Housing

Rules of Renting Your responsibilities do not end once you sign the lease. *How does the lease protect the tenant and the landlord?*

Step 1: The Search

- Choose a location and a price that fits your needs.
- Compare costs and features among possible rental units.
- Talk to people who live in the apartment complex or the neighborhood where the units are located.

Step 2: Before Signing a Lease

- Be sure that you understand and agree with all aspects of the lease.
- Note the condition of the rental unit in writing; have the unit's owner sign it.

Step 3: Living in Rental Property

- Notify the owner of any necessary repairs.
- Respect the rights of neighbors.
- Obtain renters insurance to protect personal belongings.

Step 4: At the End of the Lease

- Leave the unit in good condition.
- Tell your landlord where to send your refunded security deposit.
- Ask that any deductions from your deposit be explained in writing.

Security Deposits

When you sign a lease, you may have to pay a **security deposit,** an amount of money paid to the owner of the property by a tenant to guard against any financial loss or damage that the tenant might cause. Security deposits usually equal one or two months' rent.

When you move out, your landlord must return the security deposit, minus any charges for damage you may have caused or for any unpaid rent. Most states require landlords to return the security deposit within one month. In California, however, it must be returned within three weeks. If money is deducted from your security deposit you have the right to an itemized list of repair costs.

Renters Insurance

Another expense is **renters insurance,** a type of insurance that covers the loss of a tenant's personal property as a result of damage or theft. Many tenants neglect to buy renters insurance, wrongly assuming that their possessions are covered by their landlord's insurance. Most tenants who buy it find the cost worth the peace of mind it brings.

Assessment

Review Key Concepts

1. **Identify** What are the three main advantages of renting a home?
2. **Explain** What are the three disadvantages of renting?
3. **List** What five factors are involved in the cost of renting?

Higher Order Thinking H.O.T.

4. **Explain** Suppose you and a friend decide to rent an apartment together. Explain why it might be important to have both of your names listed on the lease agreement.

21st Century Skills

5. **Solve Problems** It is important to accurately and thoroughly evaluate all the advantages and disadvantages of a residence prior to signing a lease agreement. Carefully consider the factors shown in **Figure 3** such as location, finances, building, and layout and facilities. Write a list of what you would look for in an apartment and prioritize these items. Then develop a list of questions based on those priorities that you could take with you when viewing an apartment to ask the landlord.

Mathematics

6. **Sharing Costs** Jerome currently lives in an apartment by himself. He pays $815 per month in rent which includes all utilities. Jerome's friend recently purchased a house and wants Jerome to move in with him. If he does so, they would split the mortgage payment and all utilities. His friend's monthly mortgage payment is $1,250 and utilities are an additional $275 per month. Calculate what Jerome's new monthly cost would be if he moves into the house. After one year, how much would Jerome save or lose?

Math Concept **Calculate the Cost/Benefit of Sharing Rent** To calculate the cost or benefit of sharing rent in an apartment or house determine the total monthly payment and multiply this amount by the percent share owed by the individual.

Starting Hint Multiply the percentage owed by the individual by the total monthly cost or divide the total cost by the number of people sharing the cost.

NCTM Problem Solving Solve problems that arise in mathematics and in other contexts.

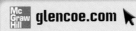

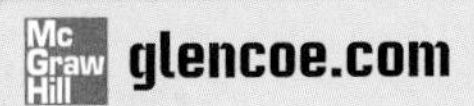
glencoe.com Check your answers.

Section Objectives

- **Identify** the advantages and disadvantages of owning a residence.
- **Explain** how to evaluate a property.
- **Discuss** the financing involved in purchasing a home.
- **Describe** a plan for selling a home.

As You Read

Question Lenders want to know how much money you owe. What other information do they look for?

The Home-Buying Process

How do you buy a home?

Many people dream of owning a home. Buying a home, however, is a huge financial commitment. It will probably be the most costly purchase you will ever make. There are a number of steps that you will need to take to purchase a home. You will need to determine your home ownership needs, find and evaluate a property to purchase, price the property, obtain financing, and close the transaction.

Reading Check

Recall What are the five basic steps involved in purchasing a home?

Step 1: Determine Your Home Ownership Needs

What are some of the benefits and drawbacks of owning a home?

To make an informed decision about whether to buy a home, you will need to consider the benefits and drawbacks of ownership. You will also need to consider the types of homes that are available and how much you can afford to spend.

Owning Your Residence: Benefits

While renters may be attracted to the idea of mobility, homeowners may enjoy a sense of stability and permanence. Home ownership also allows individual expression. You have more freedom to decorate and change your own home and to have pets. Many people find this type of flexibility very appealing.

As a homeowner, you will also gain financial benefits. You can deduct the interest charges on your loan payments from your federal income taxes each year. Your property taxes are also deductible. Moreover, the value of many homes rises steadily. Therefore, homeowners can usually sell their homes for a profit, depending on their **equity**, which is the value of the home less the amount still owed on the money borrowed to purchase it. In addition, once the borrowed money is paid off, homeowners have no further payments to make other than property taxes, homeowners insurance, and maintenance costs.

Owning Your Residence: Drawbacks

Of course, buying a home does not guarantee happiness. Home ownership can involve financial risk. Saving money for a down payment to buy a home is very difficult for many people. Moreover, the tax deductions may not make up for high loan payments. Property values do not always go up; in some cases, they may even decline.

A second drawback is limited mobility. A homeowner who wants to move must either sell his or her property or arrange to rent it to tenants. These processes can be slow and may result in financial loss.

Owning a home can involve high expenses. Homeowners must pay for all maintenance and repairs, such as fixing a leaky roof, cleaning out a flooded basement, putting up new wallpaper, and replacing or repairing broken appliances. The cost of taking care of a home can be quite high, even if homeowners do most of the work themselves.

Types of Housing

Homes come in all shapes and sizes, providing housing alternatives for a range of budgets and lifestyles.

Single-Family Dwellings The most popular type of housing in the United States is the single-family house. A single-family house usually stands on a separate lot with a lawn and some outdoor living space. The home is not attached to any other buildings. Because a single-family **dwelling,** or shelter, provides the most privacy of any type of housing, it is often the most expensive.

Multiunit Dwellings This category of housing includes duplexes and townhouses. A duplex is a single building divided into living spaces for two families—or two units. A building divided into three units is a triplex. A townhouse is one of many single-family units attached to other units. For these types of housing, each unit has its own outside entrance.

Express Yourself
Being able to remodel your home is just one benefit of home ownership. *What are some other benefits that might come with home ownership?*

Careers That Count!

Javier Salinas • Real Estate Agent

One of the most significant events in peoples' lives is the purchase or sale of a home. I have a knack for putting people at ease during this complex process, and I enjoy my job as a real estate agent. My primary function is to act as matchmaker between buyers and sellers. I advise sellers on how to make homes more appealing to potential buyers, and I advise buyers on the suitability and value of the homes they visit. To get this job, I earned a real estate certificate from a community college, and I got my license after passing a written examination on basic real estate transactions and laws. My job can be affected by swings in the economy and by interest rates, but real estate agents like me keep at it because we enjoy the challenge of making our clients happy, and the satisfaction of closing a deal.

EXPLORE CAREERS

Real estate agents work with real estate brokers. Conduct research to learn more about the jobs real estate agents and brokers do.

1. What are the differences between a broker and an agent?
2. How do a broker and an agent work together?

Skills	Education	Career Path
Sales, marketing, administration, time management, communication, negotiation, and math skills, and knowledge of real estate laws	High school diploma or equivalent; training through a real estate company or organization; and state license	Real estate agents can become sales managers in a firm, brokers, appraisers, assessors, property managers, and may enter real estate investment counseling.

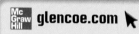

glencoe.com

Activity Download a Career Exploration Activity.

Condominiums A condominium is one of a group of apartments or townhouses that people own instead of rent. Condominium owners pay a monthly fee to cover the cost of maintenance, repairs, improvements, and insurance for the building and its common spaces. The unit owners form a condominium association, which manages the housing complex. Common spaces, such as hallways, lawns, and elevators, belong to the association, not to individual owners. A condominium is not a type of building structure; it is a legal form of home ownership.

Cooperative Housing Cooperative housing is another apartment-style living arrangement in which a building that contains a number of units is owned by a nonprofit organization. The shareholders purchase stock to obtain the right to live in a unit in the building. Members of the organization do not actually own the property, but they have the legal right to occupy a unit for as long as they own stock in the corporation. Members pay a monthly fee which covers their rent and the operating expenses of the organization.

Prefabricated Homes Prefabricated houses are manufactured and partially assembled at a factory. The pieces are then transported to a building site and put together there. Prefabricated homes are often cheaper than other single-family houses because the mass production of their pieces and partial assembly at the factory help keep costs down.

Mobile Homes Another type of manufactured home is known as a mobile home. Most mobile homes are not truly mobile because they are rarely moved from their original sites. Mobile homes are fully assembled in factories. They contain many of the features of larger houses, such as fully equipped kitchens, bathrooms, and even fireplaces. Some mobile-home owners purchase the land on which their houses are located. Spaces can also be rented in mobile-home parks where access to community recreation facilities is often included.

Compared with other housing choices, mobile homes are relatively inexpensive. However, they are not as well constructed or as safe as many other types of housing, and they usually do not increase in value at the same rate as single-family houses do.

Affordability and Your Needs

Selecting a type of dwelling is only one part of determining your home ownership needs. You will also need to consider the price of a home, its size, and its quality.

Price and Down Payment To determine how much you can afford to spend on a home, you will need to examine your income, your savings, and your current living expenses. Can you afford to make a large down payment when you buy a home? A down payment is a portion of the total cost of an item that is required at the time of purchase. You will need to make monthly payments on a loan, pay property taxes, and buy homeowners insurance. The exact amounts will depend on interest rates and local economic conditions. Is your income enough to cover these costs as well as other current expenses?

Before you look for the home of your dreams, it is smart to know exactly what you can afford to pay. To determine how much you can afford to spend on a home and if you will be approved for a loan, talk to a loan officer at a mortgage company or other financial institution. Many companies and banks will prequalify loan applicants so that prospective home buyers will know in advance if they can get a mortgage loan. This service is usually provided without charge.

Size and Quality Ideally, the home you buy will be big enough for your needs and will be in good condition. If you are a first-time buyer, though, you may not be able to get everything you want.

Consider the Options
Condominiums are a popular choice of home for people who want the financial benefits of ownership without all the responsibility of maintenance and repairs. *Who manages the maintenance and insurance for condominium owners?*

Financial advisors suggest you get into the housing market by purchasing what you can afford. As you move up in the housing market, your second or third home can include more of the features you want.

Trading Up Most financial experts recommend buying what you can afford, even if you have to sacrifice the size and features you would love to have. As you advance in your career and your income increases, you may be able to "trade up" and purchase a home with some extra comforts. For example, eight years ago, Kanya bought a condominium that had only a tiny garden and one small bathroom. Last week she sold it, made a profit, and moved into a larger house, where she will be able to plant a vegetable and flower garden and enjoy the convenience of two full baths.

Reading Check

Identify What are six types of housing to choose from when buying a home?

Step 2: Find and Evaluate a Property to Purchase

Why is the location of your home important?

When you know what type of residence you would prefer and what you can afford, you will be able to start searching for a property to purchase.

Selecting a Location

The location of your home is very important. Ask yourself if you would rather live in a city, in the suburbs, or in a small-town or country setting. Perhaps you want a neighborhood with parks and trails that accommodate cyclists and runners. If you commute to work by bus, you will have to make sure that your house is close to the bus lines. The distance between home and work, the quality of the local school system, your interests and lifestyle, and other factors all help determine where you will want to live.

Local Zoning Laws Some communities have strict zoning laws, which are regulations that limit how property in a given area can be used. The existence of such laws may also affect your housing decisions. William wanted to live in an all-residential area, so he bought a duplex in a neighborhood where local zoning laws ban any commercial construction of stores or business buildings. In contrast, Alicia bought a condominium in a much less restrictive community because she wanted to be able to walk to nearby restaurants and businesses.

Calculating a Mortgage Payment

You may not realize all of the expenses you incur each month. Therefore, when considering purchasing a home, you must carefully calculate your cash flow to be sure you are not overestimating your ability to pay for expenses. A worksheet to calculate an affordable mortgage payment contains the following information:

- Your monthly income
- Your monthly expenses
- Difference between your monthly income and expenses

Name: LeBron	
Monthly Income (cash flow)	
Wages and salary	$5,500
Investment income	300
Other income	0
Total Monthly Income	**$5,800**
Monthly Expenses	
Groceries	$300
Car payments	350
Car maintenance	50
Gasoline	75
Clothing	125
Student loan payments	200
Medical expenses not covered by insurance	55
Automatic deposit, savings account	200
Retirement account	200
Credit card payments	350
Insurance payments (car, life, health, etc.)	550
Income taxes, including Social Security	1,925
Restaurants	50
Charitable contributions	25
Vacations	150
Entertainment	75
Other expenses	0
Total Monthly Expenses	**$4,680**
Affordable Mortgage Payment (Monthly Income – Expenses)	**$1,120**

Key Points A mortgage payment for a house is usually the single largest monthly expense you will incur. It is important that you are able to pay it each month. By determining your monthly income and expenses, you will be able to calculate how much you can afford to pay each month for a mortgage.

FIND the Solutions

Review Key Concepts

1. What are some other possible expenses?
2. Why are income taxes monthly expenses?
3. Does LeBron have enough money to cover monthly mortgage payments and closing and other costs?
4. Should LeBron spend all of the money he has left after paying his monthly expenses on a mortgage payment?
5. What expenses would you be willing to cut if your mortgage payment was $1,500 per month? Why?

Hiring a Real Estate Agent

Real estate agents are people who arrange the sale and purchase of homes as well as other buildings and land. They are good sources of information about the location, availability, prices, and quality of homes. Potential home buyers often use real estate agents to help them find housing. The agents can also negotiate the purchase price between buyer and seller. They help buyers arrange financing for the purchase, and they can recommend lawyers, insurance agents, and home inspectors to serve the buyers' needs.

Real estate services are usually free to the buyer. The agents may represent the sellers, who pay them a commission of 3 to 6 percent when the property is sold. Some real estate agents also represent buyers. In this case, the agent may be paid by either the buyer or the seller.

Conducting a Home Inspection

Before you make a final decision to buy property, it is important to get an evaluation of the house and land by a qualified home inspector. (See **Figure 6.**) When Josh Samuels called in a home inspector to check the house he wanted to buy, the inspector found cracks in the foundation, an overloaded electrical system, and problems with the water quality. Josh still wanted the house, and he was able to negotiate a lower price because he had the inspector's report. A home inspection costs money, but it can save you from problems and unplanned expenses in the future.

Some states, cities, and lenders require inspection documents. The mortgage company will usually conduct an appraisal to determine the fair market value of the property. An appraisal is not a detailed inspection. It is an estimation of the value of the property usually in comparison with other similar properties that have recently sold in the particular area.

Reading Check

Summarize For what type of information is a real estate agent a good source?

Step 3: Price the Property

What price should you offer to pay?

After you have checked out the property as thoroughly as possible, it is time to consider making an offer to the current owner. This is usually done through a real estate agent, unless the owner is acting as his or her own agent.

FIGURE 6 **Conducting a Home Inspection**

Protect Yourself A detailed home inspection will let a prospective buyer know if there are problems with the construction of a home. *How can this information help protect a buyer?*

Taking steps to evaluate a home before you buy it may save you unplanned expenses and disappointments later.

1 **The Exterior** The buyer does a "walk-through" of the neighborhood to check the condition of streets and sidewalks. It is also important to check the exterior features of the home.

2 **The Interior** The buyer looks at the interior design of the home to be sure that it will meet his or her needs.

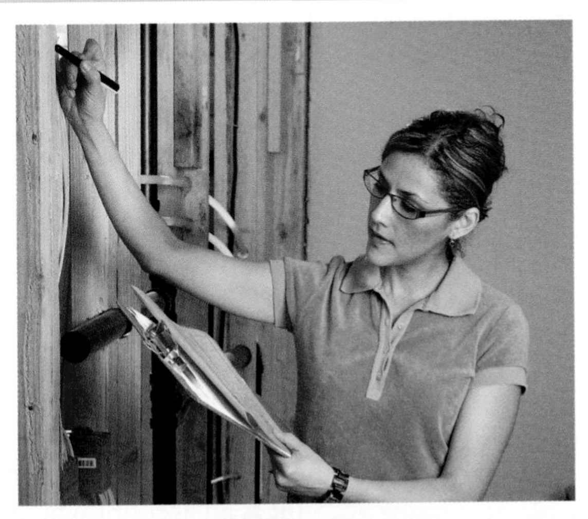

3 **Professional Home Inspection** The buyer hires a home inspector who checks the exterior: windows, foundation, chimney, and roof. The home inspector will also look at the interior construction: wiring, plumbing, heating system, walls, and floors.

Apple Pie Home Inspection Service
21044 Manitowoc Avenue
Woodland Hills, CA 91364

Inspection No: 099422909
Inspection Date: 09/29/--
Inspector: Michelle Cabalu
Client: Peggie Thompson
Address: 6301 Glade Rd. Carlsbad, CA 91335

The house is a single-family dwelling, one-story structure built on a flat lot. Estimated age is approximately 35 to 40 years old. Weather at time of inspection was sunny.

100 EXTERIOR

101 Driveway: Concrete with cracks noted.
102 Walks: Concrete and brick with cracks noted. Missing bricks noted.
103 Fence/Gates: Wood and chain links. Detached wood fence noted.
104 Siding: Stucco and wood with cracks noted.
105 Trim: Wood.
106 Window Frames: Metal and wood.
107 Elec. Fixtures: S
108 Gutters/Downspouts: S

4 **Inspection Report** The buyer reviews the home inspector's report to decide whether this is the right home to buy.

Determining the Price of the Home

Every home that is for sale has a listing price. That price is not necessarily the price you will pay. You are free to make a lower offer. What should you offer? Here are some questions to consider:

- How long has the home been on the market? If a home is on the market for a while, the owner may accept a lower price.
- What have similar homes in the neighborhood sold for recently? If a listing price is too high, you should offer less.
- In a "seller's market," homes are in high demand, and sellers can get the highest prices. In a "buyer's market," there is an abundant supply of homes for sale, and buyers can pay lower prices.
- Do the current owners need to sell in a hurry? If so, they may be willing to accept less than they feel the home is worth.
- How well does the home meet your needs? If a home fits your needs, you may be willing to pay more.
- How easily can you arrange financing?

Negotiating the Purchase Price

Once you have decided on a reasonable amount to offer, the real estate agent will notify the seller, who may either accept or reject it.

Sometimes the seller will not accept your offer. In that case, you will have to make a second, higher offer, or start looking for a different home. A seller may also make a counteroffer in response to your bid. For example, Jian Wang offered $178,900 for a condominium that was listed at $186,000. The sellers rejected his offer but made a counteroffer of $184,500. Jian thought that the price was still too high, so he submitted a bid of $182,000. They eventually settled on a purchase price of $183,000.

When the buyer and seller agree on a price, they must sign a purchase agreement, or purchase contract, that states their intention to complete the sale. Most purchase contracts are conditional; that is, they take effect only if certain other events occur. For example, the contract may be valid only if the buyers can obtain financing, or only if they can sell their current home in a specified period of time.

At this point in the process, the buyer sometimes must pay the seller a portion of the purchase price, called *earnest money*. This money shows that the offer is serious. It is held in an escrow account until the sale is completed. An **escrow account** is an account where money is held in trust until it can be delivered to a designated party. The earnest money is applied toward the down payment.

Reading Check

Define What is *earnest money*?

Around the World

Italy

Stable Approach to Home Ownership

It is not uncommon for many people to think of homes as investment vehicles, to be exchanged for something more valuable or more prestigious. These people may live in a house only a few years before moving to another property. This way of thinking is rare in Italy, though, where there is a much more conservative view of home ownership. Italians stay in their homes for an average of 20 years. Moreover, 68 percent of Italians own their homes, compared to 59 percent of Americans.

In spite of the higher rate of home ownership, mortgages tend to be fewer and smaller than those in other countries. Mortgage lending is commonly only 60 percent of the property value, and more homes are paid for in cash rather than financed by mortgages. Italy has fewer types of mortgages available than does the United States, and higher taxes and fees make it less likely to get rich from buying and selling houses. This approach has kept property values relatively steady, and though Italy has not experienced property booms that other countries have in the past few decades, Italians also have not suffered the mortgage debt and overdevelopment that some other countries have.

Critical Thinking

1. **Expand** How do Italy's real estate policies encourage people to keep their homes for so long?
2. **Relate** Do you think the Italian model of home buying and selling would be popular in the United States? What might the advantages and disadvantages be?

DATABYTES

Capital
Rome

Population
58,090,681

Languages
Italian (official), German (parts of Trentino-Alto Adige region are predominantly German speaking), French (small French-speaking minority in Valle d'Aosta region), Slovene (Slovene-speaking minority in the Trieste-Gorizia area)

Currency
euro

Gross Domestic Product (GDP)
$2.114 trillion

GDP per capita
$30,300

Industry
Tourism, machinery, iron and steel, chemicals, food processing, textiles, motor vehicles, clothing, footwear, ceramics

Agriculture
Fruits, vegetables, grapes, potatoes, sugar beets, soybeans, grain, olives; beef, dairy products; fish

Exports
Engineering products, textiles and clothing, production machinery, motor vehicles, transport equipment, chemicals; food, beverages and tobacco; minerals, and nonferrous metals

Natural Resources
Coal, mercury, zinc, potash, marble, barite, asbestos, pumice, fluorspar, feldspar, pyrite (sulfur), natural gas and crude oil reserves, fish, arable land

COMMON CENTS

On Your Own
Sharing an apartment or a house with a roommate is a great way to cut costs and can be fun. It is a good idea to have a trial period to make sure you get along before making a long-term commitment.

Concept Application
Why do you think sharing an apartment or a house might be financially beneficial?

Step 4: Obtain Financing

What are the costs involved in purchasing property?

After you have decided to purchase a specific home and have agreed on a price, you will have to think about how you will pay for your purchase. First, you will have to come up with money for the down payment. Next, you will probably have to get a loan to help pay for the remainder of the purchase price. Finally, you will be responsible for fees and other expenses related to the settlement of the transaction.

Determining Amount of Down Payment

As a general rule, the greater the portion of the total purchase price you can pay up front, the easier it will be to obtain a loan. Many lenders suggest that you put 20 percent or more of the purchase price as a down payment. For example, if the purchase price of the house is $100,000, the down payment would be $20,000. The most common sources of funds for down payments are personal savings accounts, sales of investments or other assets, or gifts or loans from relatives.

Private Mortgage Insurance If the down payment is less than 20 percent of the purchase price, most lenders will require you to obtain private mortgage insurance. **Private mortgage insurance (PMI)** is a special policy that protects the lender in case the buyer cannot make payments or cannot make them on time. When the borrower has paid between 20 to 25 percent of the purchase price, the insurance can be dropped. The Homeowners Protection Act requires that a PMI policy be terminated automatically when the equity in the home reaches 22 percent of the property value at the time the mortgage was executed. Homeowners can request early termination of the insurance if they can provide proof that the equity in the home has grown to 22 percent of the current market value.

Qualifying for a Mortgage

A **mortgage** is a long-term loan extended to someone who buys property. The buyer borrows money from a bank, credit union, savings and loan association, or mortgage company, which pays the full amount of the loan to the seller. In return, the buyer makes monthly payments to the lender. These monthly payments are usually made over a period of 15, 20, or 30 years.

The home you buy serves as collateral, a type of guarantee that the loan will be repaid. If you fail to repay the mortgage or make regular payments, the lender can **foreclose,** or take possession of the property.

Financial Qualifications To take out a mortgage, you need to meet certain criteria, just as you would to qualify for any other type of loan. Lenders look at your income, your debts, and your savings to decide whether you are a good risk. These figures are put into a formula to determine how much you can afford to pay.

Interest Rate Factors The size of your mortgage will also depend on the current interest rate. The higher the rate, the more you will need to pay in interest each month. That means that less of your money will be available to pay off the purchase price. When interest rates rise, fewer people are able to afford the cost of an average-priced home. In contrast, low rates increase the size of the loan that you can receive.

For example, Bernadette qualifies for a monthly mortgage payment of $700. If interest rates are 7 percent, she will be able to take out a 30-year loan of $105,215. However, if interest rates increase to 12 percent, she will qualify for a 30-year loan of only $68,053. Both of these loans will carry the same monthly payment of $700. The differences can be quite surprising.

Paying Points

Different lenders may offer slightly different interest rates for mortgages. In addition, when you compare the cost of doing business with various lenders, you will have to consider other factors. If you want a lower interest rate, you may have to pay a higher down payment and **points**—extra charges that must be paid by the buyer to the lender in order to get a lower interest rate. Each point equals 1 percent of the loan amount. For example, suppose that a bank offers you a $100,000 mortgage with two points, or 2 percent. Since 2 percent of $100,000 is $2,000, you will have to pay an extra $2,000 when you get the loan to purchase your home.

Comparing Points How does a high interest rate with no points compare to a low interest rate with points? A lower interest rate results in a lower monthly payment, but you pay more money up front.

Mortgage Application
A bank representative will help you determine if you can qualify for a loan, and how much the payments on that loan will be. *What are three things the lender looks at to decide if you are a good risk?*

Economics and You

Money and Inflation

Money has three main functions. It acts as a medium of exchange, a unit of value, and a store of value. The United States Federal Reserve System (the Fed) attempts to maintain money stability to ensure that money functions in those three ways. When there is inflation, the stability of money is in jeopardy, so the Fed may increase interest rates to curb inflation. If the Fed does not take action and inflation gets out of hand money loses value. If you have been paying $2.50 for a loaf of bread and inflation occurs, you may end up paying $2.75 for that same loaf of bread. If your income does not increase in proportion to inflation, you will have less money to spend. Thus people on fixed incomes find it difficult financially during an inflationary period.

Consumer Price Index of Selected Categories

	2007	2008	2009
Food	203.3	214.2	218.2
Apparel	118.9	119.0	120.1
Housing	209.6	216.2	217.1
Medical	351.1	364.1	375.6

Personal Finance Connection If you want to buy a home in an inflationary period, the higher interest rates will make your mortgage loan payments high. In addition, you will be paying more for food, clothing, and other essential items.

Critical Thinking Explain the three main functions of money with regard to buying a home during a recession. What do you think happens to housing prices and mortgage rates when the economy is in a recession?

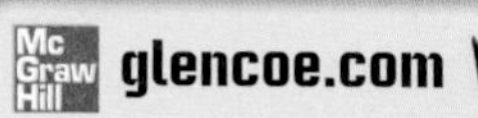

Activity Download an Economics and You Worksheet Activity.

If you keep your home for only a short time, you may lose money with the lower rate because the monthly savings will not add up to what you had to pay in points. If you keep the home for several years, however, your monthly savings will eventually make up for what you paid in points. As a rule, the longer you keep the home, the better off you are when paying the points in exchange for a lower interest rate.

The Loan Application Process

Most lenders charge home buyers a fee of between $100 and $300 to apply for a mortgage, which is added into the loan amount. To apply, the buyer must fill out forms, giving details of his or her income, employment, debts, and other information. The lender will verify this information by obtaining a buyer's credit report.

After a careful examination of the buyer's financial history and the size, location, and condition of the property, the lender decides to approve or deny the application. If it is approved, the purchase contract between seller and buyer becomes legally binding.

Reading Check

Explain Why would a buyer pay points on a loan?

Types of Mortgages

How do the various types of mortgages differ?

For most people, a mortgage is the greatest financial obligation of their lives. There are several types of mortgages. Depending on the loan, a homeowner will make monthly payments for many years.

The monthly payments on a mortgage are set at a level that allows amortization of the loan. **Amortization** is the reduction of a loan balance through payments made over a period of time. So the balance is reduced every time you make a payment. The amount of your payment is applied first to the interest owed and then to the principal, which is the original amount you borrowed. In the first years of the loan, only a small part of each monthly payment goes to reduce the principal. Most goes toward paying off the interest. Near the end of the loan period, almost all of each payment goes toward reducing the principal.

It is possible to pay off a mortgage early. Paying a little extra each month and applying that amount to the principal will save interest charges over the long run. For example, paying $25 extra a month on a 30-year, 10 percent mortgage of $75,000 will save more than $34,000 in interest charges—and will repay the loan in about 25 years. Some lenders charge an extra fee for prepaying.

Fixed-Rate Mortgages

A **fixed-rate mortgage,** or conventional mortgage, is a mortgage with a fixed interest rate and a fixed schedule of payments. A fixed rate is an interest rate that does not change. For example, if the interest rate is 8.75 percent when the loan is granted, the homeowner will continue to pay 8.75 percent throughout the life of the loan, even if interest rates for new loans rise. Conventional mortgages typically run for a period of 15, 20, or 30 years. They offer peace of mind because monthly payments always remain the same.

Adjustable-Rate Mortgages

Fixed-rate loans guarantee a particular interest rate for the life of the loan. An **adjustable-rate mortgage (ARM),** also known as a variable-payment mortgage, is a mortgage with an interest rate that increases or decreases during the life of the loan. The rate changes according to economic indicators, such as rates on U.S. Treasury securities, the Federal Home Loan Bank Board's mortgage rate index, or the lender's own cost-of-funds index. As a result, your loan payments may go up or down.

Your rates will change according to the terms of your agreement with the lender. Generally, if interest rates decline and stay low, an ARM will save you money. However, if rates increase and stay high, it may cost you money because your monthly payment will go up.

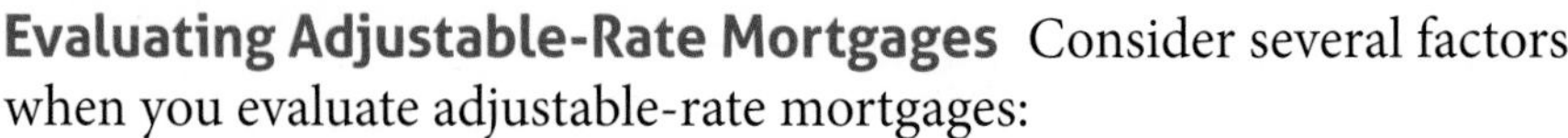

Evaluating Adjustable-Rate Mortgages Consider several factors when you evaluate adjustable-rate mortgages:

1. Determine the frequency of and restrictions on allowed changes in interest rates.
2. Consider the frequency of and restrictions on changes in the monthly payment.
3. Find out what index the lender will use to set the mortgage interest rate over the term of the loan.

Rate Caps Most adjustable-rate mortgages have a rate cap, which limits the amount the interest rate can rise or fall. Rate caps generally limit increases (or decreases) of the interest rate to one or two percentage points in a year—or no more than five points over the life of the loan.

Some ARMs also carry payment caps, which limit the size of monthly payments. That may seem like good protection for the buyer, but it has drawbacks. When interest rates rise while monthly payments remain the same, the payments will not cover the interest. As a result, the loan balance increases, and payments may have to be extended over a longer time.

Convertible ARMs Some lenders also offer convertible ARMs. Convertible ARMs permit a borrower to convert, or change, an adjustable-rate mortgage to a fixed-rate mortgage during a certain period of time. If you decide to make the change, your interest rate will be 0.25 to 0.50 percent higher than current rates for conventional 30-year mortgages. You will also have to pay a conversion fee.

Government Financing Programs

The Federal Housing Administration (FHA) and the Veterans Administration (VA) help home buyers obtain low-interest, low-down-payment loans. VA loans are available to eligible veterans of the armed services. These agencies do not actually lend money. Instead, they help qualified buyers obtain loans from regular lenders.

Typically, an agency guarantees repayment to the lender if the borrower defaults, or is unable to make payments. Although extra insurance fees may be added on to these loans, government-backed mortgages are a good deal for those who qualify for them.

Home Equity Loans

A second mortgage is also called a **home equity loan,** which is a loan based on the difference between the current market value of a home and the amount the borrower owes on the mortgage. To determine the amount of this type of loan, the financial institution will find out the current market value of a home and how much equity is in the property. Such loans can provide money for education, home improvements, or other purposes. However, some states limit the ways in which the money may be used.

Second mortgages are one source of extra cash for homeowners. However, taking out additional loans can keep a homeowner continually in debt. Also, if the borrower cannot make the payments on a second mortgage, the lender can take the home.

Refinancing

Many homeowners need extra money or want to reduce their monthly payments. These options are possible when they **refinance,** which is obtaining a new mortgage to replace an existing one. For example, Esther Aquino originally took out a fixed-rate mortgage at 11 percent interest, and then watched interest rates fall to 6 percent. Fortunately, she was able to refinance her home, and take out a new mortgage at the lower 6 percent interest rate. In Esther's case, her monthly payment decreased considerably.

Refinancing is not always a good choice. To refinance, a homeowner usually pays extra fees, which may reduce any savings from a small drop in interest rates. Moreover, refinancing may extend the life of a loan. In general, refinancing is an advantage when the interest rate drops two or more points below the current rate and when the owner plans to stay in his or her present home for at least two or more years. To decide if refinancing is financially advantageous, divide the costs of refinancing by the amount saved each month to determine the number of months it would take to recover all of your refinancing costs.

Reading Check

Paraphrase Identify three factors to consider when evaluating an adjustable-rate mortgage.

Step 5: Close the Transaction

What are closing costs?

The final step in the home-buying process is the **closing,** a meeting of the seller, the buyer, and the lender of funds, or representatives of each party, to complete the transaction. At the closing, documents are signed, last-minute details are settled, and money is paid. The seller and buyer must also pay a number of fees and charges, which are called *closing costs.*

Closing Costs

Most closing costs involve the legal details related to purchasing a home. For example, a title company researches the property to make sure that no disputes exist over its ownership or that there are no unpaid real estate taxes for the property. The title company also offers **title insurance,** a type of insurance that protects the buyer if problems with the title are found later.

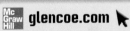

Planning

Planning is often a strength for effective leaders and productive workers. Planning is also an essential part of financial planning. People who effectively plan are able to set and meet goals even in the face of problems and opposing pressures. Effective planning will help you to multitask while still producing high-quality results. You can benefit from effective planning both personally and academically.

Write About It

Think of a scenario in which planning would help you at school. Write one or more paragraphs to describe the scenario and explain how effective planning would have positively impacted the results.

Activity Download a Career and College Readiness Worksheet Activity.

FIGURE 7 **Closing Costs**

Calculating Cost Closing costs can add to the purchase price of a home and should be considered when making an offer. *Who pays for the bulk of the closing costs?*

Item	Cost Range Buyer	Seller
Title search fee	\$ 50 – \$ 100	\$ 300 – \$ 900
Title insurance	\$ 300 – \$ 900	\$ 50 – \$1000
Attorney's fee	\$ 50 – \$1000	\$ 100 – \$ 500
Property survey	–	–
Appraisal fee	\$ 100 – \$ 350	–
Recording fees	\$ 30 – \$ 65	\$ 35 – \$ 65
Credit report	\$ 35 – \$ 75	–
Termite inspection	\$ 100 – \$ 250	–
Lender's origination fee	1–5% of loan	–
Real estate agent's commission	–	5–7% of purchase price
Insurance, taxes, and interest	varies	–

Another typical closing cost is a fee for recording the **deed,** which is the official document transferring ownership from seller to buyer. See **Figure 7.** The Real Estate Settlement Procedures Act (RESPA) requires that loan applicants be given an estimate of the closing costs before the actual closing.

Escrow Account

After the closing, your lender might require that you deposit money into an escrow account. The money, usually held by the lender, is set aside to pay for taxes and insurance. The lender does not have to worry whether the borrower is paying these obligations because the money is available. See **Figure 8** for a list of home-buying issues.

Taxes and Insurance Homeowners must pay property taxes and homeowners insurance in addition to their mortgage payments. In most states, property taxes generally cover the cost of public services, such as police and fire protection, schools, and street repair. Homeowners insurance protects the lender's investment in case of damage to the home from fire or other hazards.

Reading Check

Recall What is money in an escrow account used for?

FIGURE 8 **The Elements of Buying a Home**

Careful Considerations When purchasing a home, you must consider more than just the price and location. *Why is it important to determine the down payment and closing costs before making an offer on a home?*

It is important to consider these factors when making a home purchase:

- **Location** Consider both the surrounding community and the geographic region. The same home may vary greatly in cost depending on where it is located: in Kansas or California, on a busy highway or a quiet street, in a landscaped suburb or an urban neighborhood.
- **Down Payment** A large down payment reduces your mortgage costs, but how much can you afford to pay up front?
- **Mortgage Rates and Points** You will have to choose between a lower mortgage rate with points and a higher mortgage rate without points. You will also need to consider what type of mortgage to arrange. When you apply for the loan, be prepared to provide the lender with copies of your financial records and other relevant information.
- **Closing Costs** Settlement costs may range anywhere from 2 to 6 percent of the total amount you borrow. That is in addition to the down payment.
- **Monthly Payments** Your monthly payment for interest, principal, insurance, and taxes will be among your largest, most enduring expenses. Beware of buying a home that costs more than you can afford.
- **Maintenance Costs** Homes require a lot of repair and maintenance. Be sure to set aside funds for these necessities.

Selling a Home

What can an owner do to get the best selling price?

As your needs change, you may decide to sell your home. You will have to get it ready for the market, set a price, and decide whether to sell it on your own or get professional help from a real estate agent.

Preparing a Home for Selling

The nicer your home looks, the faster it will sell at the price you want. Real estate salespeople recommend that homeowners make needed repairs and paint worn exterior and interior areas when preparing a home for selling. For example, Dora and Dennis Muldoon repainted several rooms, replaced some light fixtures, and changed the living room carpet before they put their house on the market. They kept the house as clean, neat, bright, and airy as possible while prospective buyers were visiting. They also made sure that the lawn was cut regularly and that their children did not leave toys in the yard. Their work paid off: They sold their home within a few months of listing their home.

Determining the Selling Price

Setting a price on a home can be difficult. A price that is too high may scare off potential buyers. Setting the price too low will result in lost profit. Some sellers will pay for an **appraisal**—an estimate of the current value of the property—and use that as a basis for a listing price. If you ever sell a home, find out whether the current market favors buyers or sellers. Then decide how quickly you need to sell.

You will also need to evaluate any improvements you have made to the property. Adding certain features—such as a deck or an extra bathroom—may or may not increase a home's value. Certain features may have no value for potential buyers. Among the most desirable improvements are a remodeled kitchen, an additional or remodeled bathroom, added rooms, a converted basement, a fireplace, and an outdoor deck or patio.

Choosing a Real Estate Agent

Many sellers put the sale of their home into the hands of a licensed real estate agent who is affiliated with an agency. There is a wide choice of firms, from small local real estate agencies to nationally known companies. When choosing an agent, pick someone who knows your neighborhood and is eager to sell your home.

Real Estate Agent Services Real estate agents provide various services. They can help determine a selling price, attract buyers, show your home, and handle the financial aspects of the sale. They are paid a commission, or fee, upon the sale of a home—usually 5 to 7 percent of the purchase price.

Sale by Owner

Each year about 10 percent of home sales are made directly by homeowners without the help of real estate agents. Selling your home yourself can save you thousands of dollars, but it will cost you time and energy. Advertising the home will be up to you. Showing the home to prospective buyers will also be your responsibility. Be sure to use the services of a lawyer or a title company to help you with the contract, closing, and other legal matters.

Making Choices

Your housing decisions will be affected by many factors, including your lifestyle and financial situation. By carefully reviewing your options, making educated decisions, and following the appropriate processes, you will make the best housing choice to suit your needs.

After You Read

React With the information provided in this chapter, do you feel that you could make a wise decision about whether to rent or buy a home? Why or why not?

Assessment

Review Key Concepts

1. **Summarize** What are the benefits of owning your residence?
2. **Explain** How do you evaluate a property?
3. **List** What are the three basic steps involved in financing a new home?
4. **Identify** What activities can you do to prepare your home for selling?

Higher Order Thinking H.O.T.

5. **Assess** Suppose you were applying for a home loan for $150,000. Decide whether you would rather have a 6.5 percent fixed-rate mortgage or an adjustable-rate mortgage at 5.5 percent. Explain your reasoning.

English Language Arts

6. **Sell Your Home** Imagine that you would like to sell your home. (If you live in an apartment, imagine it to be a condominium for this exercise.) Write an advertisement that you could post online to attract buyers to your home. Be sure to include information about location, features, and asking price. Use a word processing program to type up your ad and add photos, if available.

NCTE 12 Use language to accomplish individual purposes.

Mathematics

7. **Loan Amortization** Tara has recently purchased a house for $200,000. She made a 10 percent down payment on the house and took a mortgage out on the remaining amount. The annual interest rate on her loan is 7 percent. Her monthly mortgage payment is $1,198 which includes interest and principal. Calculate the amount of Tara's loan. Then calculate the total amount of principal paid on the loan after 3 months. What is Tara's loan balance after the third month?

Math Concept **Calculate Loan Amortization** To calculate the amortization on a loan, first determine the monthly interest amount. Subtract this amount from the payment to acquire the principal applied to the balance. Subtract the principal amount from the loan balance.

Starting Hint Determine the ending balance after month 1 by first multiplying the loan amount by the monthly interest rate. Subtract the result from the payment to get the principal. Subtract the principal from the loan balance.

NCTM Problem Solving Build new mathematical knowledge through problem solving.

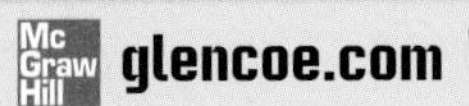

Check your answers.

Visual Summary

The Finances of Housing

Rental Options

There are distinct advantages and disadvantages to consider before renting a house or an apartment.

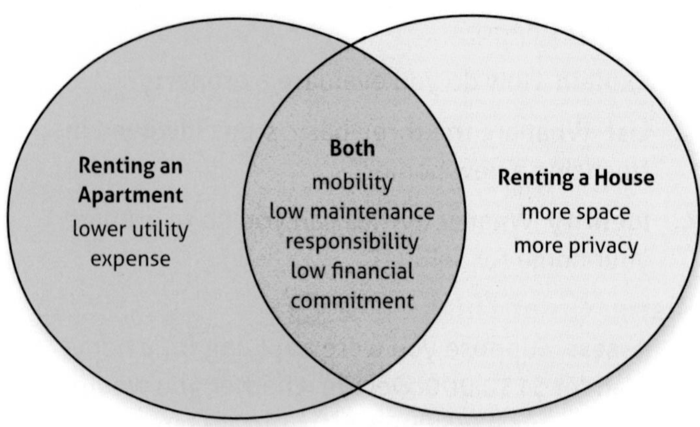

The Price of Renting

When renting a home, there is more to the cost than just the monthly rent payments.

Try It!

Draw a diagram like the one shown to outline the steps involved in the home-buying process.

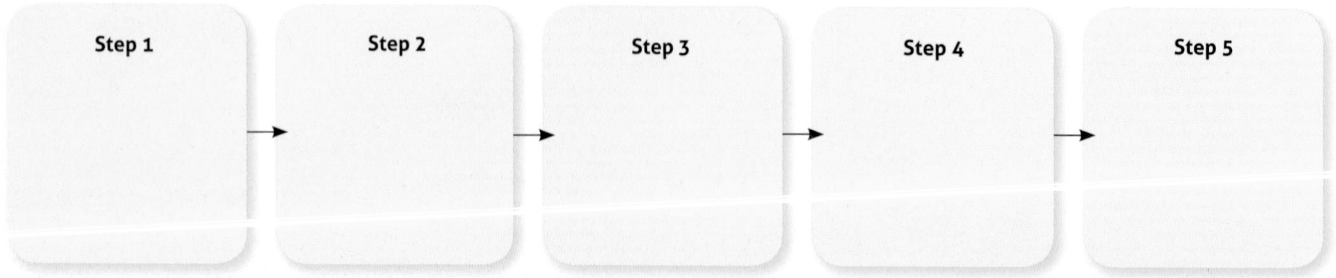

Chapter Review and Assessment

Chapter Summary

- Renting tends to be less expensive than buying and offers more flexibility.
- Home ownership offers stability, financial benefits, and increased value over time.
- Renting a residence has the advantages of mobility, few maintenance responsibilities, and relatively low initial costs. Disadvantages include rent increases, few tax benefits, and restricted activities.
- The cost of renting is affected by the neighborhood, space, monthly rent, security deposit, and renters insurance.
- Advantages of owning a residence include stability, individual expression, tax benefits, and increased value. Disadvantages include financial risk, the possibility of value not increasing, limited mobility, and high expenses.
- When evaluating property, walk through the neighborhood, check the home exterior and interior, and get a home inspection.
- A down payment is needed to purchase a home.
- Then a buyer must get a long-term loan, or mortgage, to pay for the remaining purchase price. Closing costs must also be paid.
- To sell a home, decide whether to use a real estate agent, prepare the home, set a fair price, and keep the home neat and clean.

Vocabulary Review

1. With a partner, role-play a real estate agent and a client discussing preparations for closing on a house. Write a script of the conversation you would have, using at least 10 of the terms below.

- mobility
- tenant
- landlord
- lease
- security deposit
- renters insurance
- equity
- escrow account
- private mortgage insurance (PMI)
- mortgage
- points
- amortization
- fixed-rate mortgage
- adjustable-rate mortgage (ARM)
- home equity loan
- refinance
- closing
- title insurance
- deed
- appraisal
- lifestyle
- consideration
- complex
- sublet
- dwelling
- foreclose

Higher Order Thinking 

2. **Predict** Do you think you will purchase renters insurance when you rent a home? Why or why not?
3. **Weigh** Consider the advantages and disadvantages of renting versus owning a home. Which do you think would be more appropriate for you within the next five years?
4. **Deduce** What are the basic responsibilities of a tenant and a landlord?
5. **Conclude** Review the criteria to consider when selecting an apartment. Choose which factors will be most important to you.
6. **Formulate** Explain the process you might use to find a real estate agent who suits you.
7. **Theorize** Why might a young couple expecting a child decide to buy a home rather than continue renting?
8. **Evaluate** Think about the various housing information sources. Which do you think will be most helpful for you?
9. **Assess** Consider the advantages of selling your home and using the services of an agent to sell your home. Which method do you prefer?

College and Career Readiness

Social Studies

10. Cultural Differences In the United States, it is often seen as a sign of independence and maturity for children to live on their own. Conversely, adult children are sometimes viewed differently if they live with their parents. This is not true in all cultures though. Many cultures believe it is a sign of respect, and often an obligation, for grown children to live with and help take care of their parents. Conduct research into the advantages and disadvantages of living with family members or inviting them to live with you. Why do you think different cultures view this differently? Write a summary of your findings.

NCSS I F Interpret patterns of behavior reflecting values and attitudes that contribute or pose obstacles to cross-cultural understanding.

Mathematics

11. Refinance a Loan Marcus has a mortgage with an annual interest rate of 7.75 percent. The current balance on his loan is $150,000. Since the time of his original purchase, interest rates have decreased. Marcus has an option to refinance the loan at an annual interest rate of 6.75 percent. The bank will charge Marcus $5,000 in closing costs in order to refinance. If Marcus is planning to keep his house for 5 more years, is the refinance a good financial option?

Math Concept Calculate Break-Even Point To calculate the break-even point you must first estimate the annual interest savings. Divide the closing costs of the refinance by the annual interest savings to determine the break-even.

Starting Hint Determine an estimate for the annual interest savings in order to calculate the break-even point. Do this by first subtracting the new interest rate from the current interest rate on the loan. Multiply this rate change by the current balance on the loan in order to determine the annual interest savings.

NCTM Number and Operations Compute fluently and make reasonable estimates.

English Language Arts

12. Housing Options Edward is graduating this year and plans to attend a local school while working part-time. He is trying to decide if he should continue living with his parents or if he should rent a home with his friends. Evaluate the advantages and disadvantages and decide which you would recommend to Edward. Write two separate monologues in which Edward explains his decision. One explanation is to his friends and the other is to his parents. Be sure to consider what reasons Edward would use for each audience to best support his decision.

NCTE 4 Use written language to communicate effectively.

Ethics

13. ARM Loans Imagine you are opening your own mortgage company with some investors. You have learned from previous jobs that adjustable-rate mortgages (ARMs) can sometimes force homeowners into foreclosure when the rates go up. However, because ARMs will make money for the company, your investors are urging you to offer them as an option to your clients. Consider the responsibilities you have to both your clients and your investors. How could you offer ARMs and still help your clients be financially responsible? Write a business plan to explain how you will market ARMs.

Real-World Applications

14. Lease Agreements Isabella is looking for her first apartment. She knows that she will have to sign a lease agreement. She is concerned though, about the legal language used in these forms and fears she might not fully understand the terms in the lease and what her rights and responsibilities are. Conduct online research to find a sample apartment lease agreement. Carefully read through and evaluate each section of the lease agreement. Then paraphrase each section in simpler language to help explain what it means in terms of Isabella's rights and responsibilities.

Your Financial Portfolio

Renting or Buying Your Home

Atul and Elena have saved enough money to buy a townhouse and have found one they like, but they need to consider how much it will actually cost to live there. The rent on their apartment is $700 a month ($8,400 a year), and the townhouse costs $85,000. They will need to consider any additional costs.

Atul and Elena's Dilemma

Rental Costs	
Annual rent payments	$8,400
Renters insurance	170
Total annual cost of renting	**$8,570**
Buying Costs	
Down payment (at 10%)	8,500
Annual mortgage payments	8,060
Property taxes (annual costs)	1,275
Mortgage insurance (annual premium)	536
Homeowners insurance (annual premium)	400
Estimated maintenance costs	**850**
Financial Benefits of Home Ownership	
Less: Tax savings for mortgage interest	–1,820
Less: Tax savings for property taxes	–357
Total cost of buying first year	**$17,444**
Less: one-time down payment	–8,500
Estimated annual appreciation (4%)*	–3,400
Total long-term annual cost of buying	**$5,544**

*Nationwide average; actual appreciation varies by geographic area and economic conditions.

Atul and Elena compared the annual costs of renting ($8,570) and buying ($5,544) and decided that it would be a good investment to buy the townhouse.

Compare

On a separate sheet of paper, compare renting versus buying your place of residence using a table like the one above. Check a newspaper for a rental price for a two-bedroom apartment and selling price for a two-bedroom house. Use those figures to complete your comparison.

Unit 5

Unit Project
Preparing for Home Ownership

Ask Yourself...

Have you ever thought about the type of home you would want to live in? Have you ever considered how much credit you would need to buy a home? What sacrifices would you be willing to make in order to own your own home? Responses to these questions can help you prepare for home ownership.

Your Objective

The goal of this project is to understand and practice the decisions and planning that must be done prior to purchasing a home to ensure that you get a home you are happy with and can afford.

Skills You'll Use

Success in defining goals and preparing financially for those goals depends on your skills. Some skills you might use include:

Academic Skills—Reading, writing, and mathematics.

21st Century Skills—Decision making, financial literacy, communication, and interpersonal skills

Technology Skills—Word processing, keyboarding, Internet research, calculator, spreadsheet, and presentation software

Standards

NCTE 4 Use written language to communicate effectively.

NCTE 7 Conduct research and gather, evaluate, and synthesize data to communicate discoveries.

NCTE 12 Use language to accomplish individual purposes.

NCTM Numbers and Operations Compute fluently and make reasonable estimates.

STEP 1 Explore Housing Options

As with any purchase, before you can buy a house you must decide what exactly you want. Answer the following questions to determine what your ideal house would be:

- What type of home would you prefer? (e.g., condominium, single-family dwelling, etc.)
- What area or neighborhood do you want to live in?
- How much space do you want or need?
- Do you want a yard?
- Do you need a garage or covered parking?
- Are there amenities that you would like to have, such as a fireplace or wood floors?

Create a list of all the factors you would like to have in your ideal house. Order the items in the list by priority. How important is the location or the inclusion of a garage? Would you refuse a house without a certain factor?

STEP 2 Analyze Cost

Once you know what you want in a house, you need to calculate how much you can actually afford to pay. Find and use an online calculator to help you determine how much you can afford to pay for a home. For this exercise, suppose that you are earning $45,000 per year. Be sure to factor in each of the following, even though some of these costs will not be included in the online calculator:

- Down payment
- Closing costs
- Monthly mortgage payments (including escrow and taxes)
- Monthly utility bills
- Repairs and maintenance

You might want to speak to an adult family member or friend to get a good estimate of how much you might spend on utility bills and general repairs and maintenance. Develop a spreadsheet to show each of the costs and how much you would need on a monthly basis as well as in savings in order to purchase a home.

STEP 3 Build Relationships

How can a good real estate agent help you with the home-buying process? Arrange an interview with a local real estate agent. Find out if your desires from Step 1 are realistic with the pricing you calculated in Step 2. If not, ask the realtor to help you revise your options. Also ask the agent how he or she would help you to find the right house and what the next steps would be once you found a house.

- Have your priority list and spreadsheet available to review with the realtor.
- Prepare interview questions before your meeting and have paper and pen to take notes.
- Practice active listening skills.
- Ask for clarification if you do not understand anything the realtor tells you.
- Be respectful of the realtor's time and thank him or her for meeting with you.
- Type up your interview questions and answers in a question and answer essay.

STEP 4 Develop Your Presentation

Use the Unit 5 Project Checklist to plan and create your presentation.

STEP 5 Evaluate Your Presentation

Your presentation will be evaluated based on the following:

- Evaluation Rubric
- Thoroughness of priority list and cost research
- Mechanics—spelling and grammar of essay and presentation
- Interview skills

Project Checklist

Plan

- ✔ Consider the features you want in your home and prioritize them.
- ✔ Analyze the cost of home ownership and determine how much you can afford to spend on a house.
- ✔ Meet with a realtor in your community to help explain his or her role in the home buying process.

Write

- ✔ List all the features you would like to see in your house.
- ✔ Prioritize the factors in your list.
- ✔ Create a spreadsheet to organize and tally all the various costs you will need to consider when buying a house. Include the monthly payments determined from an online calculator.
- ✔ Write a list of interview questions.
- ✔ Key a question and answer essay with the information gained from your interview.

Present

- ✔ Create an outline for your presentation.
- ✔ Create visuals and use technology to enhance your presentation.
- ✔ Speak clearly and concisely.
- ✔ Present your priorities and your cost evaluation and explain how they relate to one another.
- ✔ Share the findings from your interview and tell how they might change your priorities.
- ✔ Respond to questions raised by the class.

 **glencoe.com**

Evaluate Download a rubric you can use to evaluate your project.

UNIT
6 Investing Financial Resources

Visual Literacy

Stock market indices such as Dow Jones, NASDAQ, and the S&P 500 are used to measure and track the average performance figures of selected groups of mutual funds and stocks. ***How is this information helpful to investors and portfolio managers?***

In Your World

Profits and Pitfalls of Mutual Funds

A mutual fund is a company that professionally manages investment portfolios. There are over 8,000 mutual funds using various investment strategies. Because of the specialized tasks involved, there are more than 80 million people who believe the convenience of having experts manage their portfolios is worth the cost. However, having mutual fund experts on your side does not guarantee instant income. You are ultimately responsible for how you reach your personal financial goals.

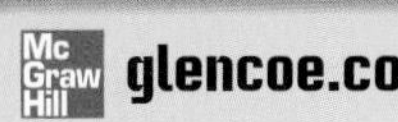

Video Watch the Unit 6 video to learn more about the benefits and drawbacks of mutual funds.

Portfolio Managers Choosing a portfolio manager is an important decision when considering mutual funds. The position of portfolio manager requires significant experience, education, training, and licensing. What skills should a portfolio manager possess? What personal qualities would you hope to find in a portfolio manager?

Economics and You

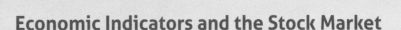

Economic Indicators and the Stock Market

So how do investors know when to buy and when to sell? Many investors study economic indicators that give them an idea of the health of the economy. They look at changes in inflation and unemployment rates, as well as how other economies are doing internationally. Investors also study corporate financial reports to make investment decisions. Even with all of this information there is still risk involved. If you purchase stock at $100 a share and a month later the stock price goes down to $40 a share, what would you do? Why do you think people invest in the stock market? Why is investing in the stock market important to our economy?

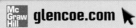

Activity Download an Economics and You Worksheet Activity.

CHAPTER 17

Saving and Investing

Visual Literacy

With careful planning and research, you can make your money work for you. ***Why might you invest your money instead of putting it in a savings account?***

Discovery Project

Planning for the Future

Key Question

Why is it impossible to create a "one size fits all" investment plan for everyone?

Project Goal

Alexa, a college freshman, works as part-time office assistant. She has a checking account for regular expenses and a savings account to earn interest. She has started researching stocks, bonds, and mutual funds, and she found investment plans that will earn more interest than a savings account. Although a little nervous, she is excited about making her money work for her. She hopes to invest in real estate after she graduates.

- Put yourself in the role of a financial planner. Assuming she is financially stable, develop an investment plan specific to Alexa's situation.
- Use online resources to learn more about what financial planners do.
- If possible, contact a financial planner for more information.

Ask Yourself ...

- *What is Alexa's primary investment goal?*
- *What factors would you tell Alexa to consider before she makes long-term investment decisions?*
- *Which types of investments would you recommend based on her personality and this stage in her life?*
- *How would you suggest Alexa evaluate her plan over time?*

Use and Manage Information

What questions would you ask Alexa during a consultation to determine her financial stability?

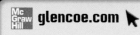

glencoe.com

Evaluate Download an assessment rubric.

THE BIG IDEA

Informed investors know how to save and plan wisely for reaching goals and achieving financial security.

ASK STANDARD & POOR'S

Investments

Q *After paying my bills, I do not have much money left over. I save any extra that I get. Since I do not have a lot of money, why should I even consider investing?*

A If inflation increases at a higher rate than your savings account return, you can lose purchasing power. To stay ahead of inflation and taxes, the money you set aside for long-term goals will need to earn more than the rates usually paid on savings accounts. Consider other investments that can earn a higher return.

Writing Activity

Aside from investing some of your money, what are some other things that you could do to help you reach your long-term financial goals? Imagine that you write a blog (short for "Web log," an online journal) for new college students. Come up with five tips that can help new students to economize.

CHAPTER 17

Reading Guide

Before You Read

The Essential Question What research and planning can you do now to help secure your financial future?

Main Idea

When you know about different investment opportunities and the financial planning process, you will be able to select a savings or investment program tailored to your goals.

Content Vocabulary

- emergency fund
- speculative investment
- dividends
- retained earnings
- investment liquidity
- equity capital
- common stock
- preferred stock
- corporate bond
- government bond
- mutual fund
- diversification
- financial planner
- tax-exempt income
- tax-deferred income
- capital gain
- capital loss
- prospectus

Academic Vocabulary

You will see these words in your reading and on your tests.

- resort
- elective
- maturity
- diversity
- commissions
- discriminating

Graphic Organizer

Before you read this chapter, create a K-W-L-H chart like the one below. As you read, take notes about what you know, what you want to know, what you learned, and how you can learn more about investing your money.

What I Know	What I Want to Know	What I Learned	How I Can Learn More

glencoe.com Print this graphic organizer.

Academic

Mathematics

NCTM Number and Operations Understand meanings of operations and how they relate to one another.

NCTM Problem Solving Apply and adapt a variety of appropriate strategies to solve problems.

NCTM Connections Recognize and apply mathematics in contexts outside of mathematics.

English Language Arts

NCTE 12 Use language to accomplish individual purposes.

Science

NSES C Develop an understanding of the cell; molecular basis of heredity; biological evolution; interdependence of organisms; matter, energy, and organization in living systems; and behavior of organisms.

NCTM *National Council of Teachers of Mathematics*
NCTE *National Council of Teachers of English*
NCSS *National Council for the Social Studies*
NSES *National Science Education Standards*

Common Core

Reading Determine central ideas or themes of a text and analyze their development; summarize the key supporting details and ideas.

Reading Read and comprehend complex literary and informational texts independently and proficiently.

Writing Write routinely over extended time frames (time for research, reflection, and revision) and shorter time frames (a single sitting or a day or two) for a range of tasks, purposes, and audiences.

Establishing Your Financial Goals

Why are financial goals important to your future?

When you think about the future, do you picture yourself owning your own home, starting your own small business, or retiring at age 50? You might want to travel or start a family. No matter how much you may want to have something, you will not acquire it if you cannot pay for it.

To gather the funds, you need to plan carefully—and have self-discipline along the way. If you are saving or investing to meet a goal that will make you happy and financially secure, the sacrifices you make will be worth it.

A savings or investment plan starts with a specific, measurable goal. For example, you may want to save $15,000 to make a down payment on a house five years after graduating from school. To reach that goal, a savings account provides safety but does not increase in value quickly. An investment may be safe or risky and increase in value slowly or quickly—or it may lose value.

You might also decide that you should begin saving money in an **emergency fund**—a savings account that you can access quickly to pay for unexpected expenses or emergencies. For example, if you had to pay for an unexpected car repair or if you lost your job, you could use the money you put away in your emergency fund.

Your Goals and Values

Your goals should correspond with your values. At one extreme, some people save or invest as much of each paycheck as possible. The satisfaction they get from fulfilling long-term financial goals is more important to them than spending a lot of money on something temporary, such as a weekend trip. At the other extreme, some people spend every cent they earn, and then run out of money before they receive their next paycheck.

Remember there are three types of goals: short-term, intermediate, and long-term. These classifications are also useful in planning your investment program.

Outlining Goals

It is probably wise to take a middle-of-the-road approach. You can spend money on some things you enjoy and still save enough for a savings or investment program. As you will learn, even a small amount of money saved or invested on a regular basis can add up to a large amount over time.

Section Objectives

- **Outline** your financial goals and evaluate how they align with your values.
- **Summarize** ways to prepare for and survive a financial crisis.
- **Identify** sources of money you can invest.
- **Describe** the factors that affect your investment choices.

As You Read

Consider How will your personality and goals affect your choices for investment and savings plans?

Careers That Count!

Juliana Shepherd • Investment Analyst

Some people find the world of finance a bit daunting, but I am fascinated by it. After receiving a bachelor's degree in economics, I became an investment analyst to help companies and individuals make decisions about buying and selling securities. On any given day, I track stock performance and prepare reports on a stock's financial health, and I analyze financial information to forecast business, industry, and economic conditions. I use this information to interpret data concerning price, yield, stability, and future trends of investments. I collect and evaluate financial statements, industry, regulatory and economic information, and financial periodicals and newspapers. I enjoy finding connections between the news and economics, and I like searching for patterns in the unpredictable world of finance. If you want to pursue a career like mine, go for a bachelor's degree in a financial field, and look into summer internship opportunities before you graduate.

EXPLORE CAREERS

Go online to learn more about the responsibilities and requirements of an investment analyst.

1. Why would an investment analyst need to be aware of world news and current events?
2. What certifications are useful to an investment analyst? What are the certification requirements?

Skills	Education	Career Path
Math, statistics, economics, and teamwork skills	Bachelor's in finance, economics, or business; MBA or professional certification	Investment analysts can become financial advisors, stockbrokers, and securities sales agents.

Activity Download a Career Exploration Activity.

To be useful, investment goals must be specific and measurable. They must also be tailored to your particular financial needs. As you outline your financial goals, ask yourself these questions:

- How do I want to spend my money?
- How much money do I need to satisfy my goals?
- How will I get the money?
- How long will it take to save the money?
- How much risk am I willing to take when I invest?
- What conditions in the economy or in my life could change my investment goals?
- Are my goals reasonable, considering my circumstances or future circumstances?
- Am I willing to make sacrifices to save?
- What will happen if I do not meet my goals?

Reading Check

Explain Why is it wise to establish an emergency fund?

Performing a Financial Check-Up

How can you assess the health of your finances?

Before you think about investing for the future, you must take steps to be sure your personal finances are in good shape. Then you will be prepared to handle any unexpected expenses and ready to move ahead with your financial plan. See **Figure 1** for tips on how to perform your own financial check-up.

Surviving a Financial Crisis

The recent financial and banking crisis underscores the importance of managing your personal finances and your savings and investment program. As a result of the nation's economic problems, many people were caught off guard and had to scramble to find the money to pay their monthly bills. Many of these same individuals had to borrow money or use credit cards to survive from one payday to the next. Some individuals were forced to sell some or all of their investments at depressed prices just to pay for everyday necessities.

To prepare for and survive a financial crisis, many experts recommend that you take action to make sure your financial affairs are in order. Here are some steps you can take:

1. Establish a larger than usual emergency fund. Under normal circumstances, an emergency fund or three months' living expenses is considered adequate, but you may want to increase your fund in anticipation of a crisis. You may consider saving six month's worth of expenses in your emergency fund.
2. Know what you owe. Make a list of all your debts and the amount of the required monthly payments, and then identify the debts that must be paid. Typically these include the mortgage or rent, medicine, utilities, food, and transportation costs.
3. Reduce spending. Cut back to the basics and reduce the amount of money spent on entertainment, dining at restaurants, and vacations. Although this is not pleasant, the money saved from reduced spending can be used to increase your emergency fund or pay for everyday necessities.
4. Pay off credit cards. Get in the habit of paying your credit card bills in full each month. If you have credit card balances, begin by paying off the balance on the credit card with the highest interest rate.
5. Apply for a line of credit at your bank, credit union, or financial institution. A line of credit is a preapproved loan and will provide access to cash for future emergencies.
6. Notify credit card companies and lenders if you are unable to make payments. Although not all lenders are willing to help, many will work with you and lower your interest rate, reduce your monthly payment, or extend the time for repayment.

7. Monitor the value of your investment and retirement accounts. Tracking the value of your stock, mutual fund, and retirement accounts, for example, will help you decide which investments to sell if you need cash for emergencies. Continued evaluation of your investments can also help you reallocate your investments to reduce investment risk.

Above all, do not panic. While financial problems are stressful, staying calm and considering all the options may help reduce the stress. Keep in mind that bankruptcy should be a last **resort,** or choice. The reason is simple. A bankruptcy will remain on your credit report for up to ten years.

Reading Check

List Identify the steps you should take to survive a financial crisis.

Getting the Money Needed to Start an Investment Program

What are some sources of money to invest?

After you have set your goals and completed your financial check-up, you are almost ready to start saving or investing. But first you have to get the money. Here are a few ways to do that.

Pay Yourself First

People often save or invest money that is left over after they have paid all of their other expenses. As you might guess, in many cases, nothing is left over. Here is a better approach:

1. Include the amount you want to save in your monthly expenses. Pay that amount first. Consider it as a bill that you owe to yourself.
2. Pay your monthly living expenses, such as rent and food.
3. Use money that is left over for personal expenses, such as going to the movies or buying a new CD.

Employer-Sponsored Retirement Plans

If your employer offers a retirement plan, usually a 401(k) or 403(b) plan, you can take advantage of a ready-made investment program. Saving is simple because an amount you choose is deducted automatically from each paycheck. Many employers match part or all of the money you save. For example, for every dollar you contribute, your employer may put in 25 cents, 50 cents, or even a dollar, which would double your savings. In addition, money put in a retirement fund is not taxed until you withdraw it—usually at retirement age.

FIGURE 1 **Your Financial Checkup**

Get Organized Keeping your personal finances in order is an important step in meeting your long-term financial goals. *What are some other reasons to keep your finances in order?*

1 **Balance your budget.** Spend less money than you make; stay out of debt; and limit your credit card use. Eventually, the amount of cash remaining after you pay your bills will increase. You will be able to use that money to start a savings program.

2 **Have insurance.** When you are on your own, you should have enough insurance to cover losses from events such as a car accident, a medical emergency, or theft.

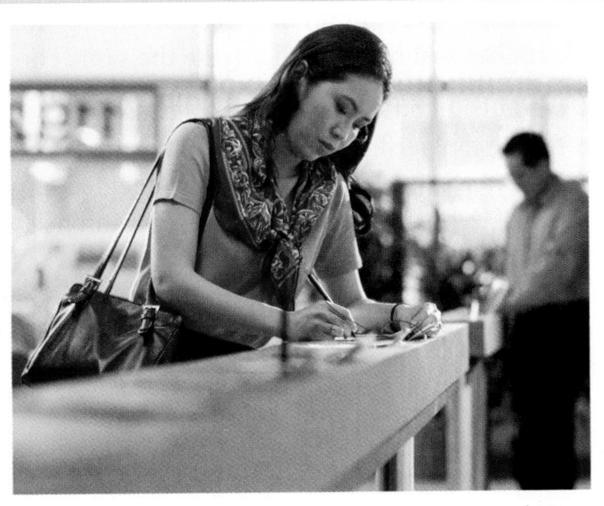

3 **Start an emergency fund.** Save money that you can access quickly to help you pay for unexpected situations, such as not being able to work. You should have enough money to cover living expenses for three to nine months.

4 **Have other sources of cash.** A source might be a line of credit with a financial institution or cash advance capability from a credit card company. Use it only for serious emergencies.

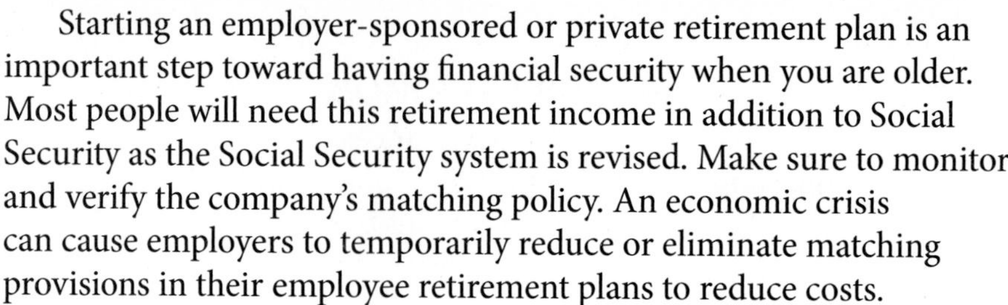

Starting an employer-sponsored or private retirement plan is an important step toward having financial security when you are older. Most people will need this retirement income in addition to Social Security as the Social Security system is revised. Make sure to monitor and verify the company's matching policy. An economic crisis can cause employers to temporarily reduce or eliminate matching provisions in their employee retirement plans to reduce costs.

Elective Savings Programs

Some employers provide the option of having money automatically withheld from your paycheck and deposited in a standard savings account.

On your own, you can also arrange with a mutual fund or brokerage firm to take a certain amount from your bank account every month and invest it. This is an easy way to save because you do not have to think about it. You may be less tempted to use the money if you never see it. An **elective,** or optional, savings program is an excellent way to fund a traditional IRA or Roth IRA account.

Special Savings Effort

Another way to save is to set aside a specific time each year when you cut back sharply on what you spend and put the money you save in an investment fund. Many financial planners recommend that you cut back to the basics for one or two months each year.

Gifts, Inheritances, and Windfalls

During your lifetime, you might receive gifts of money, or you might inherit some money. You may also receive bonuses at work, tax refunds, and salary raises. What would you do with that money? Often people choose to spend this extra money on something they could not afford under normal circumstances. Others may choose to add this money to their savings program or investment program. Consider Jihwan's plan and whether you would make the same choice.

When Jihwan received his income tax refund, his friends suggested that this would be the perfect time to buy a big-screen television. Jihwan's friends were disappointed when he decided to put the money in a certificate of deposit that earned 6 percent interest. Jihwan did not mind watching television on his parents' smaller television screen because his savings deposit was increasing. No one can make you save money to finance a savings or investment program. You have to choose to do it.

Reading Check

Describe What does it mean to pay yourself first?

Document Detective

A Savings Goals Worksheet

In order to make large purchases or achieve lofty financial goals, you need a savings plan. A savings plan will help you determine how much you need to reach your goals and how long it will take to achieve them. A savings goals worksheet contains this information:

- Your savings goal
- Amount you have
- Amount you need to achieve your goal
- Target date to goal

Savings Goals Worksheet						
Name: Susan Sharpe						
Goals	Target Dates	Cost	Current Assets	Amount Still Needed	Years to Target Date	Amount to Save This Year
Down payment to purchase a house	2015	$30,000	$5,000	$25,000	5 years	$5,000
Buy a new car	2013	$22,000	$7,000	$15,000	3 years	$5,000
Save for retirement	2040	$500,000	$10,000	$490,000	30 years	$10,000

Key Points A savings plan should be ambitious but not unrealistic. Do not try to set goals that you know you cannot reach. You should also reevaluate your savings plan at least once each year to make sure your savings plan is on track with your goals.

FIND the Solutions

Review Key Concepts

1. How much should Susan save to reach her goal?
2. What should Susan save this year to be on track to achieve her goals?
3. What assets other than savings might Susan use to help pay for a new car?
4. Why might Susan need to adjust her plan each year?
5. Susan's retirement savings plan calls for saving $10,000 each year for 30 years to save $300,000. However, she needs $490,000. What missing factor will enable Susan to achieve her savings goal?

Long-Term Investment Programs

Why should you invest in a long-term program?

Many people do not start investing because they have only a small amount of money. Others believe that they are too young to invest. However, having a small amount of money in a bank account should not stop you. Remember that small amounts of money add up because of the *time value of money.*

Figure 2 shows the growth of $2,000 during different time periods and at different rates of return. A rate of return is the percentage of increase in the value of your savings due to earned interest. Remember that you must continue to add money to your investments to see the growth that is represented in **Figure 2.**

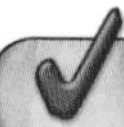

Reading Check

Explain What is a rate of return?

FIGURE 2 **Long-Term Investing and Growth**

Growing Wild The growth shown in this table at different rates of return assumes that you will invest $2,000 at the end of each year. *Would you be willing to invest $2,000 a year for a long term? Why or why not?*

	Balance at End of Year					
Rate of Return	**1**	**5**	**10**	**20**	**30**	**40**
4%	$2,000	$10,832	$24,012	$59,556	$112,170	$190,052
5%	2,000	11,052	25,156	66,132	132,878	241,600
6%	2,000	11,274	26,362	73,572	158,116	309,520
7%	2,000	11,502	27,632	81,990	188,922	399,280
8%	2,000	11,734	28,974	91,524	226,560	518,120
9%	2,000	11,970	30,386	102,320	272,620	675,780
10%	2,000	12,210	31,874	114,550	328,980	885,180
11%	2,000	12,456	33,444	128,406	398,040	1,163,660
12%	2,000	12,706	35,098	144,104	482,660	1,534,180

FIGURE 3 **Investment Levels**

Build a Foundation Without a solid foundation, you risk losing your investment. *Is it appropriate for every investor to include investments from all four levels? Why or why not?*

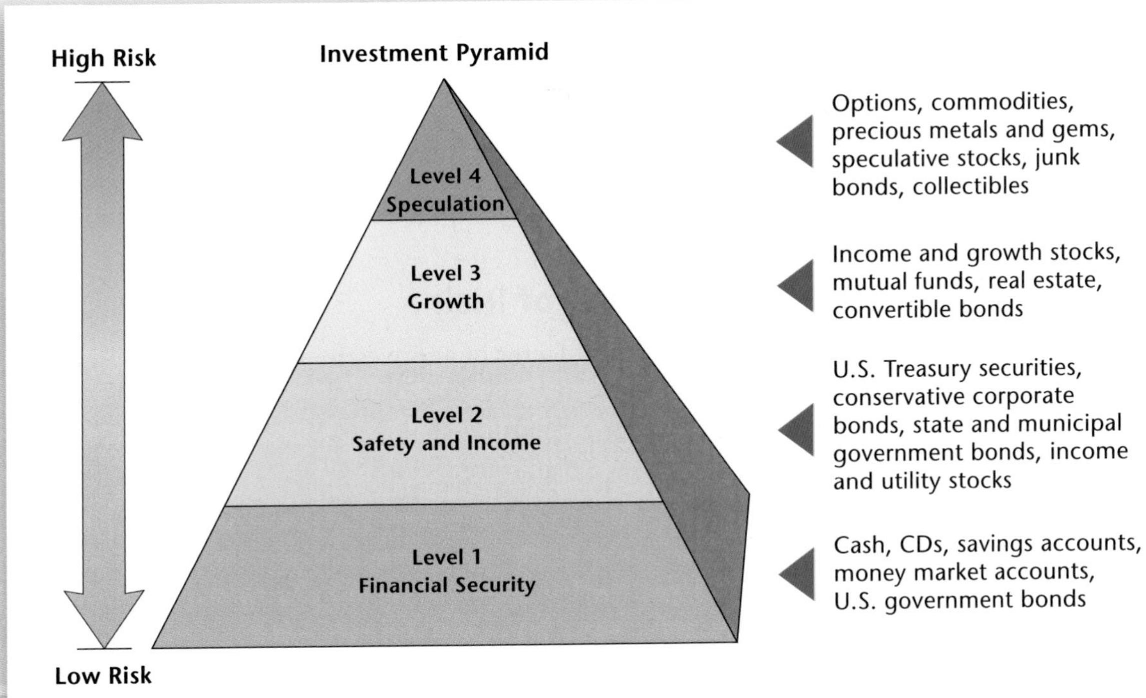

Making Investment Decisions

What are the factors you should consider when choosing investments?

Once you know how much money you need to meet your goals, you then have to think about where to invest it. To make that decision, you need to understand the different risk factors. Also, you should consider each investment's potential for income and growth as well as its liquidity.

Safety and Risk

In the financial world, the words *safety* and *risk* have specific meanings. Safety means the chance of losing your money in an investment is fairly small. Risk indicates that you cannot be certain about the profit of your investment.

Generally, if you choose a safe investment, your rate of return will be low. On the other hand, a **speculative investment** is considered a high-risk investment that might earn a large profit in a short time. The disadvantage of a speculative investment is the possibility that you could lose most or all of the money you invest. See **Figure 3.**

One basic rule sums up the relationship between the factors of safety and risk: The potential return on any investment should be directly related to the risk you, the investor, take. Your attitude toward risk will vary according to your circumstances. For example, when you are young, you may be more willing to take risks because you have long-term investment goals. When you are older and close to retirement, you may decide to shift your investments from speculative to conservative investments to be sure that you will not lose your life savings.

Beginning investors may be afraid of the risk associated with some investments. The key is to determine how much risk you are willing to take. Then choose quality investments that offer higher returns without an extremely high risk.

Five Components of Risk

Evaluate the overall risk factor of an investment by examining what creates the risk in the investment. Five different components of risk are inflation, interest rate, business failure, financial market, and global investment.

Inflation Risk Inflation is a persistent economic condition that affects everyone. For example, when Harry Majors opened his deli in 1990, he framed the first dollar he earned and hung it on the wall. Twenty years later, one of his customers reminded him that his 1990 dollar could now buy less than 50 cents' worth of salami. The loss of value to Harry's dollar was a result of inflation, which is a general rise in prices that affects everybody.

Investing your money can help you stay ahead of inflation. However, during periods of rapid inflation, the return from your investments might not keep up with the inflation rate. When that happens, you lose buying power, and your money will buy less.

You can calculate the effect of inflation on your investments. First, subtract your rate of interest from the inflation rate. This is your loss of buying power converted to a percentage. Then multiply that percentage by the original amount of your investment. The result is your loss of buying power in dollars. (See the **Go Figure** box.)

In addition, you can find out the current price of your investment, based on the rate of inflation during the period that you held the investment. Multiply the original price of the investment by the rate of inflation. Add that figure to the original price of the investment. The result is how much it would cost you to purchase the same investment today. Some investments will protect you from inflation better than others. For example, over the period from 1926 to 2002, the compounded rate of return on common stocks adjusted for inflation was 7 percent. Concurrently, U.S. Treasury bills (T-bills) had an inflation-adjusted compounded rate of return of only 0.6 percent. During that time, common stocks provided a better protection against inflation than did T-bills.

Ethiopia

Investing at Home

Emigration may benefit individuals, but it can diminish a country's economy and society. When talented citizens leave to make a living in another country, they remove themselves from their home country's workforce and communities. This has an especially damaging effect on developing nations.

Ethiopia has found a way to stem the damage by encouraging people who leave to continue investing in their home country. As a result, Ethiopia's economy has grown despite the loss of valuable workers. The Ethiopian government has worked to encourage this investment. Tax and investment policies have been made clearer, and there are fewer government regulations. The government also issues a diaspora bond, or certificate of debt, to its emigrating citizens to encourage them to invest their money at home. Money from these bonds goes toward development projects in Ethiopia. Emigrants also often bring what they learn back home. One economist used her American education and experience at the World Bank to create the Ethiopia Commodity Exchange, which links farmers to a computerized national market to gauge food production, and which in turn is connected internationally. Investment has helped this developing country cultivate one of the healthiest economies in Africa.

Critical Thinking

1. **Expand** Research the Ethiopia Commodity Exchange. How has it helped agricultural development among the nation's farmers?
2. **Relate** The Ethiopian government can offer confidence and simplicity for investors. But investors might find these same things in other countries, with possibly a better rate of return. Why would an emigrant care to invest his money at home?

DATABYTES

Capital
Addis Ababa

Population
88,013,491

Languages
Amarigna, Oromigna, Tigrigna, Somaligna, Guaragigna, Sidamigna, Hadiyigna

Currency
Ethiopian birr

Gross Domestic Product (GDP)
$34.32 billion

GDP per capita
$900

Industry
Food processing, beverages, textiles, leather, chemicals, metals processing, cement

Agriculture
Cereals, pulses, coffee, oilseed, cotton, sugarcane, potatoes, cut flowers; hides, cattle, sheep, goats; fish

Exports
Coffee, gold, leather products, live animals, oilseeds

Natural Resources
Coffee, gold, leather products, live animals, oilseeds

GO FIGURE Mathematics

Inflation Rate and Investments

When prices and the cost of living rise in one year, your money will buy less and be worth less than it was during the prior year. For example, $500 this year will buy less than it did last year.

EXAMPLE Nina put $500 in a certificate of deposit for one year at 3 percent interest. The inflation rate during that year was 5 percent. How much of her buying power did she lose? How much money would she need at the end of the year to buy what she bought a year ago with $500?

A. Calculate the percentage of the loss of buying power:
Formula Inflation Rate − Interest Rate = Loss-of-Buying-Power Percentage
Solution 5% − 3% = 2% Loss of Buying Power

B. Calculate the loss of buying power in dollars:
Formula Original Price of Investment × Loss of Buying Power Percentage = Loss of Buying Power in Dollars
Solution $500 × 2% or .02 = $10 Nina lost $10.

C. Calculate the cost of the same investment today:
Formula (Original Price of Investment × Inflation Rate) + Original Price of Investment = Current Price of Investment
Solution ($500 × 5% or .05) + $500 = $525

Nina would need $525 at the end of the year to buy what she bought a year ago with $500.

Your Turn

A year ago, you worked part-time and put $1,000 in a savings account. The interest rate for one year was 6 percent. The inflation rate during that year was 4 percent. How much money would you need at the end of the year to buy what you bought a year ago with $1,000?

Interest Rate Risk If you put money in an investment that gives you a fixed rate of return (stable rate), such as government or corporate bonds, the value of your investment will go down if interest rates go up. If you have to sell your bonds, you will get less than you originally paid.

To figure out the market price of a $1,000 bond if interest rates go up, divide one year of interest at a fixed rate of 8 percent by the new higher interest rate of 10 percent. (See the **Go Figure** box.) If you hold onto the bond until maturity, you will get your full $1,000 back, but you will receive only 8 percent annual interest.

Business Failure Risk This type of risk applies to common stock, preferred stock, and corporate bonds. When you buy stocks or corporate bonds, you are investing in a particular company. You are betting that the company will succeed. However, it could fail, especially if the company is managed poorly. Even if the company offers a valuable product or service, positive response from customers is not guaranteed. Lower profits usually mean lower **dividends,** which are distributions of money, stock, or other property that a corporation pays to stockholders. If the company declares bankruptcy, your investment may become worthless. Your best protection is to do careful research on companies in which you might invest. Another good idea is to invest your money in more than one company.

Financial Market Risk Economic growth is not as predictable as most investors believe. Sometimes the prices of stocks, bonds, mutual funds, and other investments go up or down because of the overall state of financial markets. The value of a stock may decrease, even though a company is financially healthy. Factors that affect financial markets include social and political conditions. For example, the price of oil stocks may be affected by the political situation in the Middle East, where much of the world's oil supply is produced.

Global Investment Risk Today many investors are investing their money in stocks and bonds issued by companies in other countries in an effort to diversify their portfolios. When the U.S. markets are in decline, other markets around the world may be increasing. Because these types of investments may be risky, financial analysts advise small investors to invest in global mutual funds, instead of individual international stocks. U.S. firms offer global mutual funds. These mutual funds specialize in companies that operate in another nation or region of the world. A mutual fund includes stocks or bonds from many companies and may offer more safety than one company's stocks or bonds. If you plan to invest in companies outside the United States, take these steps:

1. **Evaluate international investments as if they were U.S. investments:** Be aware that because of different accounting standards in other countries, it may be hard to discover the true financial condition of foreign companies.
2. **Consider the currency exchange rate:** This rate may affect the return on your investment, favorably or unfavorably. For example, if you buy stock in a French company, stock dividends will be paid to you in euros and then converted to dollars.

GO FIGURE Mathematics

A Bond's Market price When Interest Rates Go Up

A bond's interest earnings can be reduced if you sell it before the maturity date when bond rates are higher than those at time of purchase.

EXAMPLE You buy a $1,000 corporate bond that pays a fixed rate of 8 percent interest. You earn $80 a year ($1,000 × 8% or .08 = $80) until maturity. What price would you get if you sold it before the maturity date when bond rates were 10 percent?

Formula Annual Interest Earned/New Interest Rate = Market Price

Solution 80/10% or .10 = $800

You would get $800, which equals a loss of $200. ($1,000 – $800 = $200).

Your Turn

You buy a $1,500 corporate bond that pays a fixed rate of 8.5 percent interest. You earn $127.50 a year ($1,500 × .085 or 8.5% = $127.50) until maturity. What price would you get if you sold it before the maturity date when bond rates were 11 percent?

GO FIGURE Mathematics

A Bond's Market Price When Interest Rates Go Down

You may profit from selling a bond before maturity when bond interest rates are lower than those at time of purchase.

EXAMPLE Your \$1,000 corporate bond pays a fixed rate of 8 percent interest, or \$80 a year (\$1,000 × 8% or .08 = \$80). What price would you get if you sold it before maturity when bond rates were 6 percent?

Formula Annual Interest Earned/New Interest Rate = Market Price

Solution \$80 /6% or .06 = \$1,333.33

You would receive \$1,333.33, which equals a profit of \$333.33 (\$1,333.33 – \$1,000 = \$333.33).

Your Turn

Your \$1,200 corporate bond pays a fixed rate of 8.5 percent interest, or \$102 a year (\$1,200 × 8.5% or .085 = \$102). What price would you get if you sold it before maturity when bond rates were 6 percent?

Also, keep in mind that the economic and political stability of a country can affect the value of your investment. It is risky to invest in stocks and bonds issued by individual companies in other countries. Only experienced investors should consider this option.

Investment Income

There are a variety of other types of investments for income. If you want a dependable source of income, you have several choices. The safest investments include: savings accounts, certificates of deposit (CDs), U.S. Savings Bonds, and U.S. Treasury bills. These options are also the most predictable sources of income. With these programs, you know the interest rate and how much interest income you will receive on a specific date.

Other sources of investment income include government bonds, corporate bonds, preferred stocks, utility stocks, certain common stocks, annuities, and stable mutual funds. If investment income is a primary objective these investments are viable options. Before investing in stocks or corporate bonds, obtain information about the company's overall profits, its history of dividend payments, and its outlook for the future. Be sure to check out the costs associated with annuities before investing.

Real estate rental property also offers income, but it is not guaranteed. For example, your profits from a rental property may be lower than expected if you have vacancies or expensive repairs. In addition, Real Estate Investment Trusts, or REITs, also offer income that is not guaranteed. These trusts are similar to mutual funds.

Speculative investments, such as commodities, options, precious metals and gems, and collectibles, offer little potential for income and are risky. These types of investments are more appropriate for investors who have expertise and experience in these markets.

Investment Growth

To investors, growth means that their investments will increase in value. The best opportunities for growth usually come from common stocks and growth stocks. A growth stock is a common stock issued by a corporation. This type of stock has the potential to earn above-average profits in comparison to other corporate stocks.

Growth companies usually reinvest their profits rather than pay dividends. **Retained earnings** are profits that a company reinvests, usually for expansion or to conduct research and development. Growth that is financed by retained earnings usually contributes to increasing the stock's value. Therefore, stock in a growth company may not provide immediate cash dividends, but you will benefit because your stock may increase in value.

Investment Liquidity

A final factor to consider when choosing investments is **investment liquidity**—the ability to buy or sell an investment quickly without substantially reducing its value. You may be able to sell some investments quickly, but conditions or other factors may prevent you from regaining your original investment.

A savings account is an example of a high-liquidity investment. A low-liquidity investment requires more time to sell your investment. An investment in real estate is usually a low-liquidity investment because finding a buyer takes time.

Taking Chances
It often makes good sense to avoid certain risks. *Why should inexperienced investors hold off on investing their money in commodities?*

Review Key Concepts

1. **Identify** List sources of money you can invest.
2. **Explain** Describe the factors that affect your investment choices.
3. **Summarize** Describe the steps you should take to prepare for and survive a financial crisis.
4. **Relate** Outline your financial goals and describe how they align with your values.

Higher Order Thinking H.O.T.

5. **Consider** Reread the section "Gifts, Inheritances, and Windfalls." If you received a substantial income tax refund, would you make the same choice Jihwan made? Explain your answer.

English Language Arts

6. **Offshore Investing** It is commonly thought that choosing an offshore, or foreign, investment is more complicated than choosing a domestic investment. However, offshore investing is much the same as domestic investing. When searching for a foreign mutual fund, for example, you should look for the characteristics you would look for in a domestic one, such as strong relative performance over time and reasonable expenses. Research offshore investments and write a brief report describing the benefits and drawbacks.

NCTE 1 Read texts to acquire new information.

Mathematics

7. **Building Savings** Nina and her friends are planning a trip at the end of the year. In order to go on the trip, she will need to save $5,000. Nina earns $50,000 per year and has monthly expenses of $3,500. She also wants to invest her earnings surplus each month. Will Nina be able to save enough in 12 months to go on the trip assuming no additional expenses? If so, how much will she have available to invest each month?

Math Concept **Calculate Savings Potential** To calculate savings potential, you subtract your savings need from your net income to determine the surplus available for investment. Net income is the amount of income left after all expenses have been paid.

Starting Hint Divide the annual salary and total trip cost by number of months to determine monthly income and monthly trip savings needed, respectively.

NCTM Connections Recognize and apply mathematics in contexts outside of mathematics.

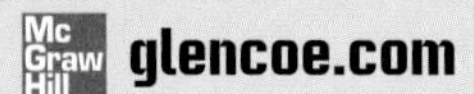
Mc Graw Hill glencoe.com Check your answers.

Types of Investments

How would you invest your money?

When you have your personal finances in order, an emergency fund, and money for investments, and you know how much risk you can take, you can begin to research investment alternatives. Investment alternatives include: stocks, corporate bonds, government bonds, mutual funds, and real estate.

Section Objectives

- **Describe** the two basic types of stock.
- **Compare** corporate bonds and government bonds.
- **Identify** the main goal of real estate investing.
- **Explain** the purpose of diversification.
- **List** the steps involved in developing a personal investment plan.

Stocks

A business that is owned by one person gets operating money from that one owner, who is the sole proprietor. In a partnership, the partners provide the money, or equity capital. **Equity capital** is money that a business gets from its owners in order to operate. A corporation gets its equity capital from its stockholders, who become owners when they buy shares of stock in the company. The two basic types of stock are common and preferred.

As You Read

Decide As you learn about savings and investment options, decide if you would be willing to invest in stock, or if you would prefer to keep your money in a CD.

Common Stock **Common stock** is a unit of ownership of a company, and it entitles the owner, or stockholder, to voting privileges. Common stock can sometimes provide a source of income if the company pays dividends. Stock can provide growth profits if the dollar value of the stock increases. In addition, if the company "splits" its stock, or divides shares into a larger number of shares, the stockholder gains because he or she will get more shares. Most large corporations generate money they need by selling common stock.

Preferred Stock A corporation may also issue preferred stock. **Preferred stock** is a type of stock that gives the owner the advantage of receiving cash dividends before common stockholders receive cash dividends. This is important if a company is having financial problems. If a company fails, preferred stockholders receive dividends first and any assets that are left before common stockholders receive anything.

Stock can be an attractive investment because, as owners, stockholders share in the success of the company. However, you should consider several facts before you invest in stock.

1. A corporation does not have to repay you what you paid for the stock. If you want to sell your stock, another investor must buy your shares through a stockbroker.
2. The current value of your stock is partially determined by how much another investor is willing to pay for your shares.
3. The corporation does not have to pay dividends. If the company has a bad year or decides to reinvest earnings, the board of directors can vote to eliminate dividend payments.

Information Literacy

Information literacy is the ability to access, analyze, and evaluate information efficiently and effectively. Information literacy involves using information accurately and creatively to address a particular issue or problem. Information literacy will help you to manage information from a variety of sources and evaluate the information critically and proficiently. Understanding ethical and legal issues concerning the access and use of information is an important aspect of information literacy.

Write About It

Think of a scenario in which you recently accessed information for a report or project. Write one or more paragraphs summarizing the information. Evaluate the source(s). Is the source(s) reliable and credible? Was the information useful?

 **glencoe.com** 

Activity Download a Career and College Readiness Worksheet Activity.

Corporate and Government Bonds

You may also consider investing in bonds. There are two types of bonds an investor can consider: a corporate bond and a government bond. A **corporate bond** is a corporation's written pledge to repay a specific amount of money, along with interest. A **government bond** is the written pledge of a government or a municipality, such as a city, to repay a specific sum of money with interest. When you purchase bonds, you are lending money to a corporation or government for a period of time.

The Value of a Bond Two key factors affect the value of a bond: (1) whether the bond will be repaid at maturity and (2) whether the corporation or government entity will be able to pay interest until **maturity,** or the state of a financial arrangement when it falls due for payment. Maturity dates range from 1 to 30 years, and interest on bonds is usually paid every six months. You can keep a bond until maturity and then redeem it, or you can sell it to another investor. In either case, the value of the bond is closely tied to the ability of the corporation or government agency to repay the bond at maturity. If a corporation or government agency cannot pay the interest on its bonds, the value of those bonds will decrease.

Funds

A **mutual fund** is an investment in which investors pool their money to buy stocks, bonds, and other securities selected by professional managers who work for an investment company. Their knowledge is an advantage for inexperienced investors. If one of the fund stocks or other securities performs poorly, the loss can be offset by gains in another stock or security within the mutual fund.

Real Estate

The goal of real estate investing is to own property that increases in value so that you can sell it at a profit—or to receive rental income. When you invest in real estate, you need to find out if the property is priced as similar properties. You also need to know what financing is available and the cost of property taxes.

Before making a decision to purchase any property, ask the following questions: Why are the present owners selling? Is the property in good condition? What is the condition of other properties in the area? Is there a chance that the property will decrease in value? When you sell real estate, consider these questions: Can you find an interested buyer? Can the buyer get financing to buy the property?

Reading Check

Explain How can inexperienced investors benefit from putting their money in mutual funds?

Evaluating Investment Alternatives

How would you diversify your investments?

You have learned how safety, risk, income, growth, and liquidity affect investment choices. You have also examined different investment possibilities. Which ones would you choose?

As you make your choices, remember it is wise to diversify. **Diversification** is the process of spreading your assets among several different types of investments to reduce risk. You should avoid "putting all your eggs in one basket." Diversification is often expressed in percentages. For example, what percentage of my assets do I want to put in stocks and mutual funds? What percentage do I want to put in bonds or certificates of deposit? Some brokerage firms construct model portfolios like those, illustrated in **Figure 4.** This strategy provides both financial growth and protection no matter what your age, circumstances, or level of financial knowledge. Some brokerage firms allow you to purchase the securities as a package known as portfolio investing. Remember the rule: The potential return on any investment should be directly related to the risk the investor assumes.

FIGURE 4 **Investment Portfolios**

Diversify The bottom row in this figure represents a very aggressive portfolio. *Why does this allocation of assets have the most potential for a large return?*

Model Name	Assets Allocated	
Conservative portfolio	Stocks and mutual funds Bonds and CDs Cash and equivalents	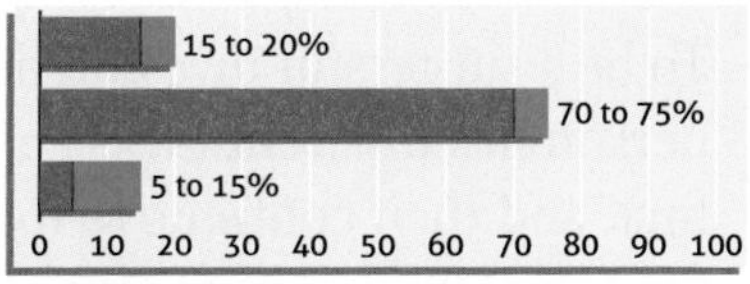 15 to 20% 70 to 75% 5 to 15% 0 10 20 30 40 50 60 70 80 90 100
Aggressive portfolio	Stocks and mutual funds Bonds and CDs Cash and equivalents	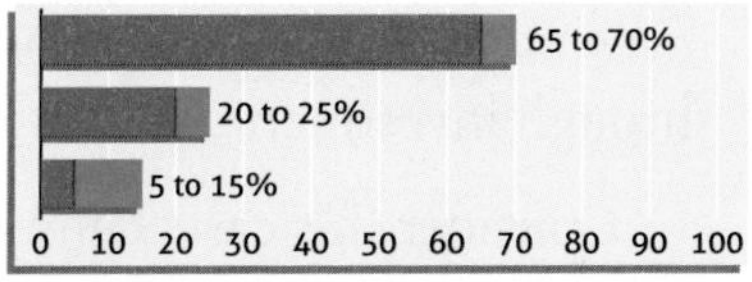 65 to 70% 20 to 25% 5 to 15% 0 10 20 30 40 50 60 70 80 90 100
Very aggressive portfolio	Stocks and mutual funds Bonds and CDs Cash and equivalents	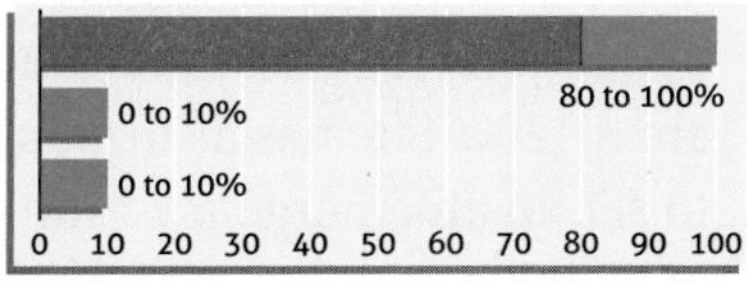 80 to 100% 0 to 10% 0 to 10% 0 10 20 30 40 50 60 70 80 90 100

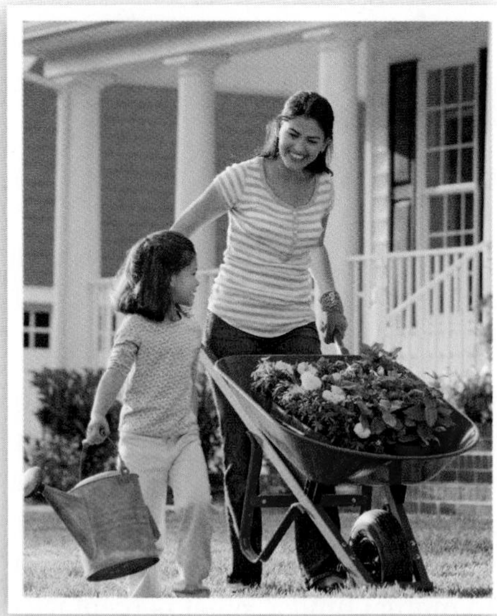

Curb Appeal
Real estate agents may offer suggestions on how a seller can improve the appeal of a home. *Do you think it is worth spending money for improvements when you are selling a house?*

Look at each portfolio illustrated in **Figure 4.** Which portfolio is the best for you? The answer to that question is often connected to your tolerance for risk. Remember the basic rule: The potential return on any investment should be directly related to the risk the investor assumes. While investors often say they want larger returns, they must be willing to assume larger risks to obtain larger returns.

Reading Check

Decide How can you determine which type of investment portfolio is best for you?

Developing a Personal Investment Plan

How do you create an investment plan?

To be a successful investor, develop a plan and put it into action. Each person has different ideas and goals. Establish your investment goals first, and then continue to follow through. Often following through is the most important component of a successful, long-range, personal investment plan. Follow a series of steps and begin earning money through investment.

Consider this case: Ginny is single and has recently started her first full-time job after graduation. Her monthly take-home pay (after deductions for taxes and other items) is $1,600. Her monthly expenses are $1,200. She has a surplus of $400 a month. She is using her surplus to set up an emergency fund. She recently received an inheritance of $5,000 when her grandfather died. She plans to use this money to fund her investments. **Figure 5** illustrates how Ginny developed her individual investment plan. Your plan may be quite different, but the steps will be the same.

FIGURE 5 **Ginny's Personal Investment Plan**

Master Plan After reviewing all of her options, Ginny decided on CDs and mutual funds. *Why do you think she made this decision?*

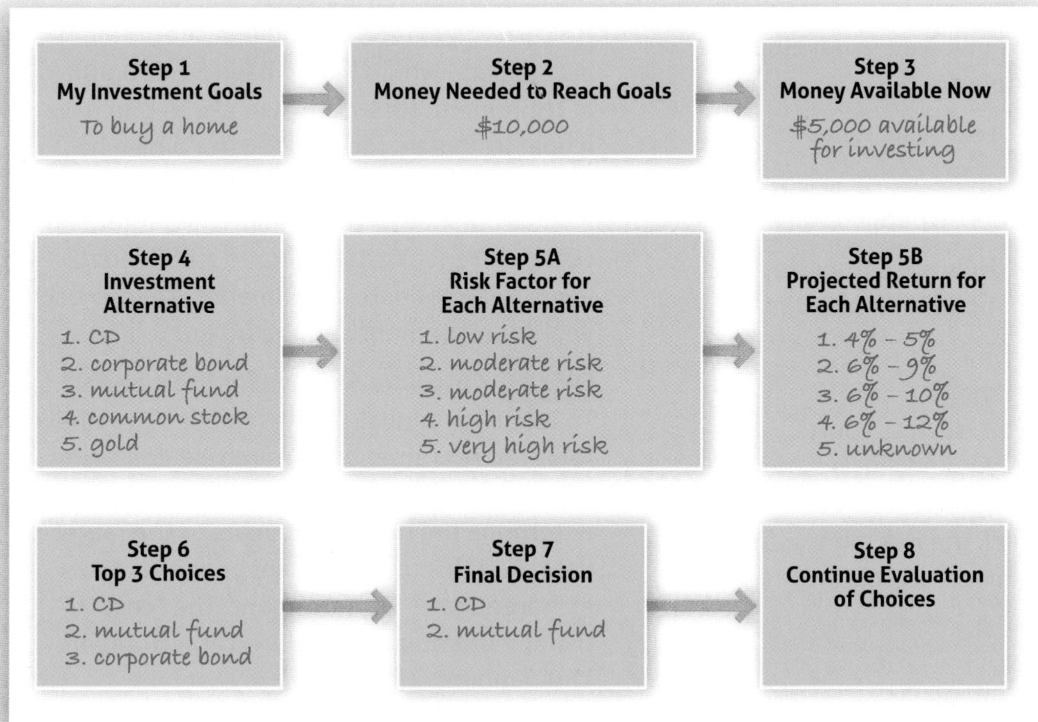

You may find these steps helpful to get started:

1. Establish investment goals.
2. Decide how much money you will need to reach those goals.
3. Determine the amount of money you have to invest.
4. List all the investments you want to evaluate.
5. Evaluate the risks and potential return for each investment.
6. Reduce your list of possible investments to a reasonable number.
7. Choose at least two investments so that you have some **diversity,** or variety. You may want to add more investments as the value of your holdings grows.
8. Because your investment goals may change as you go through life, recheck your investment program regularly. Remember that changes in the economy can affect your investments. For example, if interest rates on certificates of deposit are high, you might invest some of your money in a CD.

To develop your personal investment plan, establish your goals, and then follow through. If your goals are important to you, you will be willing to work to attain them.

Assessment

Review Key Concepts

1. **Identify** What is the main goal of real estate investing?
2. **List** What are the steps involved in developing a personal investment plan?
3. **Describe** What are the two basic types of stock?
4. **Explain** What is the purpose of diversification?
5. **Compare and contrast** How are corporate bonds and government bonds similar? How are they different?

Higher Order Thinking H.O.T.

6. **Assess** Collectible items, such as sports memorabilia, comic books, and vintage toys, can be valuable and may make for a good investment. Do you think the risk of investing in collectibles is high, moderate, or low? Explain your answer.

21st Century Skills

7. **Analyze Media** The media can have a tremendous impact on everything from which shoes you buy to what foods you eat. In the financial world, the *media effect* theory states that stories in newspapers, magazines, on television, and online influence or intensify current economic trends. Go online or the library to find recent news stories about the economy. Using the topics in this chapter as a guide, gather examples of stories that might influence investors to act on financial news. As a class, discuss the pros and cons of using the media as a financial resource.

Mathematics

8. **Retirement Planning** In 2010, Pierre is 40 years old and wants to retire at age 55. He currently has $500,000 in his retirement account and would like to have $1,000,000 at retirement. He would also like to purchase a boat in 3 years for $30,000, for which he already has $10,000 saved. Setup a savings goals worksheet to determine the target dates, costs, current assets, amounts still needed, years to target date, and amounts to save each year for retirement and the boat.

Math Concept **Calculate Savings for Retirement** To calculate annual savings needed to achieve targeted retirement and purchase goals first subtract current age from retirement age to determine the number of years to the target date. Add this to the current year to arrive at "target date" of retirement. The "cost" is the amount of money desired at retirement. The "amount still needed" is cost less current assets.

Starting Hint Divide the amounts still needed by the years to the target date to determine the amount to save this year. Follow the same procedure for the boat goal.

NCTM Problem Solving Apply and adapt a variety of appropriate strategies to solve problems.

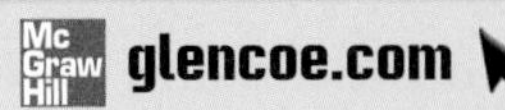

Check your answers.

Reducing Risk and Sources of Information

Financial Planners

What is the role of a financial planner?

When making your investment decisions, you may want to consult a **financial planner,** a specialist who is trained to offer specific financial help and advice.

There are two main factors to consider when deciding if you need a financial planner: (1) your income level and (2) your willingness to make your own financial decisions. If you make less than $45,000 a year, you may not need a planner's services.

Section Objectives

- **Explain** the role of a financial planner.
- **Describe** the actions you should take when managing your investments.
- **Identify** sources of investment information.

As You Read

Predict Would you prefer to manage your investments alone, have a stockbroker assist you, or hire a financial advisor?

Types of Financial Planners

Financial planners work for various insurance companies, investment companies, real estate agencies, and law firms. Some are self-employed. There are four main types of financial planners:

1. **Fee-only planners** charge an hourly rate from $75 to $200 or a flat fee, ranging from about $500 to several thousand dollars. They may also charge an annual fee ranging from 0.04 percent to 1 percent of the value of the investments they manage.
2. **Fee-offset planners** charge an hourly or annual fee, but they reduce, or offset, it with the **commissions,** or earnings, they make by buying or selling investments.
3. **Fee-and-commission planners** charge a fixed fee for a financial plan and earn commissions from the products they sell.
4. **Commission-only planners** earn all their money through the commissions they make on sales of insurance, mutual funds, and other investments.

Consumers must be cautious about the fees charged and how these fees are communicated. When hiring a financial planner, find out the exact fees for specific services. Also discuss how and when the fees will be collected from you. There should be no hidden commission charges if the financial planner provides "fee only" services.

Selecting a Financial Planner

Look for a financial planner who will provide these basic services:

- Assess your current financial situation
- Offer a clearly written plan with investment recommendations
- Discuss the plan with you and answer questions
- Help you keep track of your progress
- Guide you to other financial experts and services as needed

You can find a financial planner by looking in the yellow pages, by contacting financial institutions, and by getting recommendations from friends, coworkers, or professional contacts. **Figure 6** suggests questions that you might ask a financial planner to help you make a decision.

Certification of Financial Planners

The requirements for becoming a financial planner vary from state to state. Some states require that financial planners pass an exam. Other states issue licenses to individual planners and planning companies. Some states have no regulations at all. The federal government requires that the Securities and Exchange Commission (SEC) monitor the largest financial planning companies.

A financial planner may have credentials, such as Certified Financial Planner (CFP) or Chartered Financial Consultant (ChFC). Not all planners are licensed, however. You should research and investigate any financial planner you might be considering.

Reading Check

Name What are the four types of financial planners?

FIGURE 6 **Selecting a Financial Planner**

Investigate Qualifications to work as a financial planner vary from state to state. *Why do you think it is worthwhile to spend the time and effort to research a potential planner for your finances?*

When evaluating a financial planner, ask the following questions:

- What are your areas of expertise?
- Are you affiliated with a major financial services company, or do you work independently?
- Are you licensed or certified?
- What is your education and training?
- How is your fee determined? (Is this amount something I can afford?)
- Am I allowed a free initial consultation?
- May I see a sample of a written financial plan?
- May I contact some of your clients as references?
- Is financial planning your primary activity?

Managing Your Investments

What should you do to manage your investments?

Most people do not have professional financial planners and need to learn how to manage their own finances. Managing your savings and investments requires ongoing attention. You can take an active role by taking these steps: Evaluate investments; monitor investments; keep accurate records; and consider tax consequences.

Evaluating Investments

Always research and evaluate before you invest so that you can make an informed decision. Suppose that you invest $2,000. With a 5 percent return the first year, you will earn $100. While your money is earning, you also need to continue to evaluate your current investment. Evaluate future investment opportunities as well.

Monitoring Your Investments

Many people forget to or choose not to keep track of or monitor the value of their investments. They do not know if their investments have increased or decreased in value. In addition, since they do not monitor their investments, they do not know if they should sell their investments or continue to hold them. Always keep track of the value of your stocks, bonds, or mutual funds by checking price quotations reported on the Internet, in newspapers, and on financial news programs. Keep a chart of the value of your investments to check their progress over time. Also track the percentage of increase or decrease as well.

Looking Ahead
Even if you choose to allow an investment company to handle your money, it is your responsibility to track and evaluate your investments on a regular basis. *What records should you keep, and what are some ways to keep them organized?*

Keeping Accurate Records

Accurate recordkeeping helps you notice opportunities to increase your profits or reduce losses. It can also help you decide whether to put more money in other investments—or to sell a particular investment. Keep purchase records that list the cost of the investment and commissions or fees you have paid. With these records, you will know where to begin your research when it is time to reevaluate the investments you own.

reality bytes

From Ticker Tape to Smart Phones

In 1870, Thomas Edison invented the first practical ticker-tape machine. With a printing speed of one character per second, it enabled people to track changes in the prices of stocks and bonds. Information was printed on long thin strips of paper called *ticker tape*. Used ticker tape was cut into a form of confetti and tossed in ticker-tape parades. Today you can have data from the world's markets, streaming charts, and analysis downloaded to handheld devices such as a Smart Phone through applications such as QuoTrek.

Tax Considerations

It is your responsibility to determine how taxes may affect your investments. The city, state, and federal governments charge various amounts of tax to individuals and businesses for income they earn.

In general, investment income falls into three categories: tax-exempt, tax-deferred, and taxable. **Tax-exempt income** is income that is not taxed. For example, the interest you can receive from most state and municipal bonds is exempt from federal income tax. **Tax-deferred income** is income that is taxed at a later date. The most common type of tax-deferred income is earned from a traditional individual retirement account (IRA). When you withdraw earnings from your IRA, you must pay federal income tax. The 401(k) and 403(b) retirement plans offered by your employer or privately are also tax-deferred. Income from most other investments is taxable.

Dividends, Interest Income, and Rental Income You must report cash dividends on your tax return as ordinary income. You also have to pay tax on the interest from banks, credit unions, and savings and loan associations. In addition, interest you receive from bonds (unless tax-exempt), promissory notes, loans, and U.S. securities must be reported as income. Income from rental property is also taxable.

Capital Gains and Capital Losses A **capital gain** is the profit from the sale of assets such as stocks, bonds, or real estate. Capital gains are taxed according to how long you own an asset—over a short term or a long term.

Under current law, a short-term capital gain is profit you make when you sell an asset owned for 12 months or less. It is taxed as ordinary income. For example, if you are in the 15 percent tax bracket for general income taxes, you will also pay 15 percent tax on your short-term capital gains.

The profit from selling investments owned for more than 12 months is considered a long-term capital gain. Long-term capital gains are usually taxed at the rate of 5 to 15 percent. Investors in low tax brackets are taxed at only 5 percent. As of 2008, these investors pay no tax on long-term capital gains. Some personal property, such as collectibles, is taxed at a higher rate. Examples of collectible assets include rare books and stamp collections.

A **capital loss** is the sale of an investment for less than its purchase price. You can subtract up to $3,000 a year in capital losses from your ordinary income. If your losses are greater than $3,000, you can subtract the rest of the loss in later tax years.

Reading Check

Connect What do you need to know about capital gains and capital losses in terms of your taxes?

Economics and You

Economic Institutions

All legal forms of business that provide goods and services are needed in a market economy to satisfy the needs and wants of consumers. Individuals and groups have goals that economic institutions help them to achieve. For example, banks offer financial services. You can save your money, use their checking account services, and even purchase a safe-deposit box for your valuables. Not-for-profit organizations raise money to help others. For example the Susan B. Komen Foundation uses its donations to fund breast cancer research. Labor unions negotiate working conditions and wages for groups of workers. Corporations provide goods and services, as well as the means to invest in their companies.

Overview of the Financial System

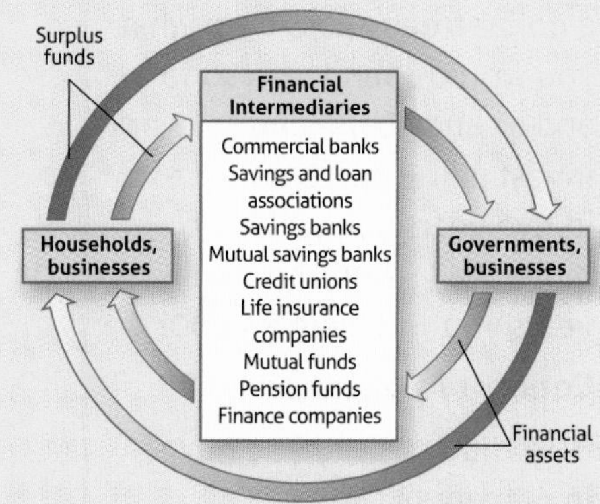

Personal Finance Connection There are several economic institutions that can help with your personal savings and investing goals. For example, public corporations sell stock in their companies, which may offer dividends. Stock brokers offer advice and act on an individual's behalf when purchasing and selling securities. Individuals can also invest in real estate. Real estate agents perform the task of bringing buyers and sellers together to negotiate a sale. Financial advisors provide advice on how to plan for one's financial future.

Critical Thinking Identify three economic institutions in your community that offer savings and/or investing services and explain why they are important in a market economy.

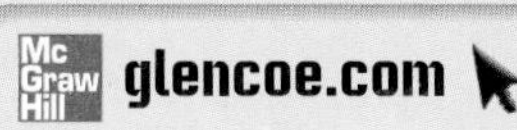

Activity Download an Economics and You Worksheet Activity.

Sources of Investment Information

Where can you find information about investments?

Because there is so much investment information available, both complex and basic, you need to be **discriminating,** or selective. The important thing is to be sure that the source of advice and information that you receive is accurate and reliable.

The Internet and Online Services

The Internet provides access to a wealth of information on most personal finance topics and investment alternatives. For example, you can obtain interest rates for certificates of deposit; prices of stocks, bonds, and other securities; and advice on starting and managing an investment program including recommendations from brokers on investments. You can even trade securities through online brokers. You can also use financial planning software and financial calculators available on many personal finance Web sites to develop a personal financial plan.

COMMON CENTS

A Dollar a Day

Do you know that if you save a dollar a day—less than what you would spend on a soda and a candy bar—and save or invest it at 5 percent interest, in five years you will have more than $2,000? In ten years you will have $4,600!

Concept Application

How much would you have in 40 years?

One of the best ways to access information is to use a search engine. Search engines such as Yahoo! or Google allow you to do a word search for either the personal finance topic or investment you want to explore. For example, topics of interest might include "financial planning," "asset allocation," or "growth stocks."

Federal, state, and local governments; brokerage firms and investment companies; financial institutions; and corporations also have Web sites where you can obtain valuable investment information.

Newspapers and News Programs

The financial page of your metropolitan newspaper or *The Wall Street Journal* is another source of investment information that is easy to access. In addition, many radio and television stations broadcast investment market summaries and economic information as part of their regular news programs. Several television channels are also dedicated to financial news.

Business and Government Publications

Barron's, Forbes, Fortune, Harvard Business Review, and similar business publications provide general news about the economy as well as information about individual companies. In addition, magazines, such as *Money, Smart Money,* and *Kiplinger's Personal Finance,* provide information and advice designed to improve your investment skills. In addition, national news magazines often feature stories on the economy and finance.

The United States federal government is also an excellent resource of information—and much of it is free. *The Federal Reserve Bulletin,* published by the Federal Reserve System, and the *Survey of Current Business,* published by the Department of Commerce, are just two sources of useful financial information.

In the Know

Staying informed is one way to ensure you are in control of your finances. *Name at least three sources of financial news and information that can help you reach your goals.*

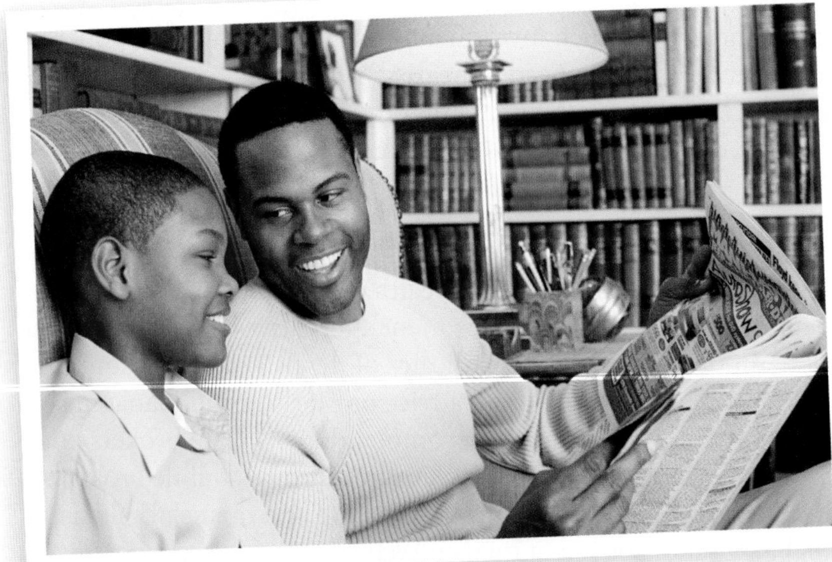

FIGURE 7 Statistical Averages for Evaluating Investments

Trend Watchers You can locate these statistical averages in the newspaper and on the Internet. *How would you use this information when monitoring your investments?*

Statistical Average	Type of Investment
Dow Jones Industrial Average	Stocks
Standard & Poor's 500 Stock Index	Stocks
Value Line Stock Index	Stocks
New York Stock Exchange Index	Stocks on New York Stock Exchange
American Stock Exchange Index	Stocks on American Stock Exchange
NASDAQ Composite Stock Index	Over-the-counter stocks
Lipper Mutual Funds Index	Mutual funds
Dow Jones Bond Average	Corporate bonds
The Wall Street Journal Consumer Rates Index	Interest and finance rates
New Residential Sales Index	Real estate
Dow Jones Spot Market Index	Commodities
Sotheby's Art Sales Index	Art/paintings
Linn's Trends of Stamp Values	Stamps

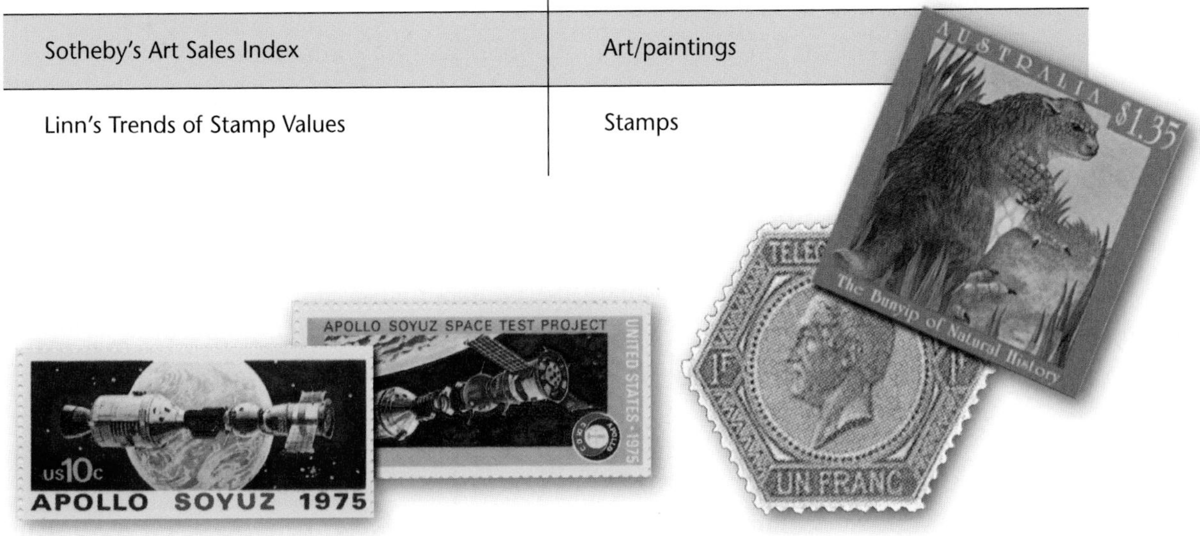

Corporate Reports

As required by the federal government, any corporation selling new issues of securities must provide investors with a prospectus. A **prospectus** is a document that discloses information about a company's earnings, assets and liabilities, its products or services, a particular stock, and the qualifications of its management. All publicly owned corporations also send investors quarterly reports and annual reports that contain detailed financial data. Annual reports contain a statement of the corporation's financial position, including assets, liabilities, and the owner's equity, and an income statement, including dollar amounts for sales, expenses, and profits or losses.

Statistical Averages

You can keep track of the value of your investments by following one or more recognized statistical averages, such as the Standard & Poor's 500 Stock Index or the Dow Jones Industrial Average. These averages are reported daily online and in newspapers. The average indicates whether the category it measures is increasing or decreasing in value. It will not pinpoint the value of a specific investment, but it will show the general direction of stocks, bonds, mutual funds, and other investments. **Figure** 7 lists some of the most widely used statistical averages.

Investor Services

Many stockbrokers and financial planners mail free newsletters to their clients. In addition, investor services, such as Moody's Investors Service, sell subscription newsletters that are available in print and on the Internet.

Some widely used and useful publications are:

- *Standard & Poor's Stock and Bond Guide*
- *Value Line Investment Survey®*
- *Handbook of Common Stocks (information on companies)*
- *Morningstar Mutual Funds™*

In addition to these publications, securities exchanges provide information in print and on the Internet. They include the American Stock Exchange, the Chicago Mercantile Exchange, the New York Stock Exchange, and the NASDAQ market. All of these sources of financial information are most often used by professionals. Many individual private investors also refer to them to become well-informed when making investment decisions.

After You Read

Summarize What is your role in your personal financial program, even if you have outside help?

Assessment

Review Key Concepts

1. **Identify** sources of investment information.
2. **Describe** the actions you should take when managing your investments.
3. **Explain** the role of a financial planner.

Higher Order Thinking H.O.T.

4. **Judge** Earned interest and dividends from savings accounts, investments, and rental income are taxed like ordinary income. Explain whether or not you think this is fair.

21st Century Skills

5. **Information Literacy** You have decided that now is the perfect time to start some serious, long-term financial planning. However, you are overwhelmed by the amount of information available. Choose one investment topic that you want to research, such as interest rates on CDs or stock information from a particular company. Use at least three of the investment information sources you learned about to find articles about your topic. How can you ensure that the sources of information are accurate and reliable? Present your articles and your conclusion to your class.

Mathematics

6. **Capital Loss** Eric purchased 500 shares of XYZ Company stock for $54.00 per share. Two years later, he sold the stock at $45.00 per share. Calculate the capital loss Eric will be able to subtract from his ordinary income for tax purposes at the end of the year. If applicable, what is the additional loss he will be able to subtract from his ordinary income the year after?

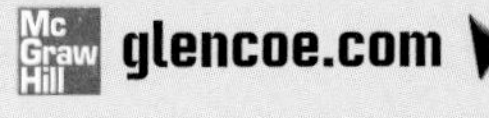

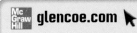

Calculate Capital Loss To calculate the capital loss on the sale of stock, subtract the proceeds from the sale of stock from the cost basis to determine the capital loss.

Starting Hint Multiply the number of shares by the purchase price to determine the cost basis of the investment. Then multiply the number of shares by the selling price to determine the proceeds from sale of stock.

NCTM Problem Solving Solve problems that arise in mathematics and in other contexts.

Mc Graw Hill glencoe.com Check your answers.

Visual Summary

Saving and Investing

Risk Factors

Without risk, it is impossible to obtain the returns that make investments grow. The key is knowing your personal tolerance for risk.

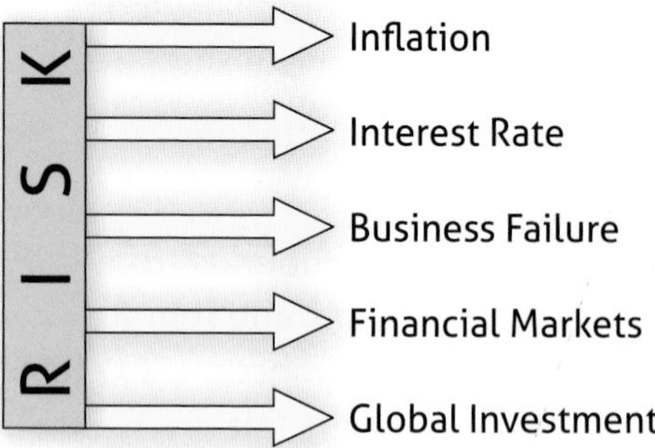

Interview Your Planner

Not all states have requirements or regulations for financial planners. Have a list of questions ready to ask potential planners.

Financial Planner Evaluation Questions	
✓	What are your areas of expertise?
✓	Are you affiliated with a major financial services company, or do you work independently?
✓	Are you licensed or certified?
✓	What is your education and training?
✓	How is your fee determined? (Is this amount something I can afford?)
✓	Am I allowed a free initial consultation?
✓	May I see a sample of a written financial plan?
✓	May I contact some of your clients as references?
✓	Is financial planning your primary activity?

Try It!

Draw a pyramid like the one shown. Record the types of investments that would be appropriate for each level of the investment pyramid.

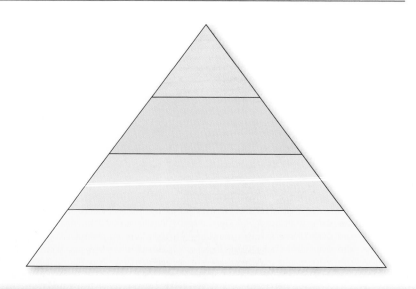

Chapter Review and Assessment

Chapter Summary

- Before investing, set financial goals that are compatible with your values.
- Obtain money to start investing by setting aside funds before you buy other things; by contributing to employer-sponsored retirement plans and savings programs; and by saving gifts of money and unexpected windfalls.
- Consider an investment's safety or degree of risk, income potential, and liquidity.
- Also, diversifying your investments is wise.
- Saving and investment alternatives include savings accounts, CDs, stocks, bonds, some annuities, mutual funds, and real estate.
- Steps in developing a personal investment plan include establishing goals, determining funds needed and available, evaluating investments, and choosing at least two investments.
- Check your investments for yourself, keep track of them, keep accurate records, and consider the tax consequences of buying and selling.
- A great deal of investment information is available on the Internet, in books, magazines, newspapers, government publications, as well as from individual corporations and investment companies.

Vocabulary Review

1. Imagine you are a financial advisor, use at least ten of the vocabulary terms below to write a letter to a client describing investment strategies and the need for a financial plan.

- emergency fund
- speculative investment
- dividends
- retained earnings
- investment liquidity
- equity capital
- common stock
- preferred stock
- corporate bond
- government bond
- mutual fund
- diversification
- financial planner
- tax-exempt income
- tax-deferred income
- capital gain
- capital loss
- prospectus
- resort
- elective
- maturity
- diversity
- commissions
- discriminating

Higher Order Thinking 

2. **Explain** How could owning real estate cause you to lose money every month? How could it make money for you every month?
3. **Pose** If you have debts, such as credit cards or student loans, how can you put money in savings or investments?
4. **Compare** Describe a demographic group that may not prefer investment risk. Describe another demographic group that may be more comfortable with a greater degree of risk.
5. **Conclude** If you want to buy a house in ten years, should you put your money in a CD or invest it in growth stocks? Explain your answer.
6. **Assess** Explain which level of the investment pyramid would be most appropriate for: gold, stock in a hydroelectric power company, and beachfront rental property.
7. **Evaluate** Would it be useful to follow the Dow Jones Industrial Average and/or the Standard & Poor's 500 Stock Index before making investments? Explain your answer.
8. **Justify** Asses and defend the importance of personal investment monitoring.
9. **Relate** How does the currency exchange rate affect the return on an international investment?

College and Career Readiness

Science

10. Risky Behavior Adrenaline is a chemical produced in humans and animals in response to stressful or dangerous situations. Some people intentionally participate in risky activities, such as skydiving, because they enjoy the physical feeling produced by adrenaline.

Procedure Research individuals whose occupations include significant risks, such as extreme athletes or police officers. Then research individuals who take investment risks. Choose one person from each category.

Analysis Compare the behaviors of the individuals you selected. What do they have in common? How are their risky actions similar? How are they different? Present your conclusions in a brief report to share with your classmates.

NSES C Develop an understanding of the cell; molecular basis of heredity; biological evolution; interdependence of organisms; matter, energy, and organization in living systems; and behavior of organisms.

Mathematics

11. Savings and Tax on Capital Gains Tima earns $5,000 per month and is saving 8 percent of her earnings in an investment account on a monthly basis. After twelve months, she purchased stock with the saved money in her investment account for $24.00 per share. Six months later, she sold all of her shares for $26.45 per share. Tima is in the 15 percent tax bracket. How many shares of stock did Tima purchase? What was the capital gains tax on her sale of stock?

Math Concept **Calculate Savings and Taxes** To calculate savings based on a percentage of income multiply monthly income by savings percentage to determine monthly savings.

Starting Hint Calculate the proceeds from the sale by multiplying the sale price by the number of shares purchased. Subtract the proceeds from the sale from the total purchase price to determine the taxable amount of the proceeds.

NCTM Number and Operations Understand meanings of operations and how they relate to one another.

English Language Arts

12. Owning Property Real estate often can be a more comfortable investment for some because they probably grew up hearing their parents talk about the value of "owning a home." Stocks, bonds, and commodities may not have been general topics of discussion. The result is that they are more open to buying land than many other investments. When you invest in real estate, you invest in something tangible. For many people, this is important to their feeling of security. However, it is important to be realistic. Create a poster, pamphlet, comic strip, or other visual depiction that represents the benefits and drawbacks of being a property owner.

NCTE 12 Use language to accomplish individual purposes.

Ethics

13. Altering Records Imagine you are a small business owner. You are considering expanding. You have asked your financial planner to help. While she is preparing the paperwork, your financial planner suggests altering the way some transactions are recorded to lower your taxes. What she is suggesting is not illegal, but it is questionable. Some business owners would appreciate the financial planner's suggestion. Others would consider the suggestion unethical. How would you respond to the financial planner's suggestion? Would you keep your financial planner? Write a one-page memo to your financial planner explaining your reasoning.

Real-World Applications

14. Retirement Plans Many employers offer 401(k) retirement savings plans. Many companies match a certain percentage of each employee's deposits. Go online to find Web sites of a few companies you might want to work for in the future. Search for at least three companies that offer 401(k) plans, profit sharing, or other savings programs. Find out if your relatives, neighbors, or friends participate in such plans, and ask them why or why not. How will this information affect your career decisions?

Your Financial Portfolio

Avoiding Future Shock

Mackenzie is already showing signs of being a great scholar at age three. At least that is what her dad, Jasper, thinks. He wants Mackenzie to be able to continue her education, so he has decided to start a college fund for her now. Jasper has $2,000 to start and has decided to invest $175 a month. He has developed an investment plan to reach his goal.

Jasper figures he has 15 years to invest and will invest in an aggressive stock mutual fund. He feels that the diversity of a mutual fund will be safer and give greater returns. Jasper has plenty of time to take a fair amount of risk and is comfortable that he will have Mackenzie's college money when she needs it.

Goal Tending					
Established Goal: College					
Amount of money needed: $50,000					
Initial amount to invest: $2,000					
Possible investment alternatives	savings account	CD	money market account	mutual fund	stock
Risk factor for each alternative	low risk	low risk	low risk	moderate risk	high risk
Expected return on each alternative	1%–3%	4%–5%	4%–6%	6%–10%	6%–12%
Top 3 choices		3		1	2
Final choice: mutual fund					

Prepare

Choose a short-term or long-term financial goal you would like to reach. On a separate sheet of paper, prepare an investment plan for yourself using the same guidelines as shown above. Research some of the available investments and come up with your own investment alternatives. Explain the reasons for your final choice.

CHAPTER 18

Stocks

Visual Literacy

The stock market is a complex investing mechanism. ***How can a new investor find information and tools to make the stock market less overwhelming and complicated?***

Discovery Project

Virtual Stock Market

Key Question

Why is playing a stock market game a good tool for beginning investors?

Project Goal

One of the best ways to learn about how the stock market works without risking any of your money is to play a stock market simulation game. These games teach new investors, about economics, finance, and the American economic system in a safe environment. In a simulation game, players work in teams and create a stock portfolio using virtual money. Based on their research of market trends, economic conditions, and business news, the teams select and trade common or preferred stocks. Portfolios "earn" interest and "pay" commissions—and make and lose virtual money.

- Find these games online. Use search terms like "stock market simulation game" or "virtual stock exchange."
- Explore the games with a partner, then work together to choose one game to evaluate.
- Present your evaluation to your class in an oral report.

Think About ...

- *What is the purpose of the game?*
- *Is the site user-friendly and appropriate for beginning investors?*
- *Are there fees associated with playing the game?*
- *What prior knowledge do players need to play?*
- *What real-life stock trading skills will players learn?*
- *What other skills are improved or learned?*
- *Who would most benefit from the game?*

Analyze Media

Why would a for-profit company offer stock market simulation games for free?

glencoe.com

Evaluate Download an assessment rubric.

THE BIG IDEA

Exploring stock markets can help you understand your choices, risks, and benefits when investing in stock.

ASK STANDARD &POOR'S

Stock Certificates

Q *My parents gave me stock certificates for a graduation present. Is it a good idea to put them in a safe-deposit box and save them for retirement?*

A A safe-deposit box is a good way to store important documents, but a better option for stock certificates would be to place them in a brokerage account with a bank or brokerage firm. This will make it easier for you to buy or sell shares of these or other stocks. Also, you will receive statements showing the value of your shares and dividends.

Writing Activity

Consider a few corporate sectors you are interested in such as banking, real estate, or electronics. Research stocks of companies in these fields. Write a short report summarizing the companies and detailing the risks and benefits of investing in these stocks.

Reading Guide

Before You Read

The Essential Question What do you need to know about stocks before you invest your hard-earned money?

Main Idea

You can make the best investments for your financial situation when you understand the stock markets and learn how to evaluate, buy, and sell stocks.

Content Vocabulary

- securities
- private corporation
- public corporation
- par value
- blue-chip stock
- income stock
- growth stock
- cyclical stock
- defensive stock
- large-cap stock
- capitalization
- small-cap stock
- penny stock
- bull market
- bear market
- current yield
- total return
- earnings per share
- price-earnings (PE) ratio
- securities exchange
- over-the-counter (OTC) market
- portfolio

Academic Vocabulary

You will see these words in your reading and on your tests.

- return
- appreciates
- engaged
- prospects
- floor
- executed

Graphic Organizer

Before you read this chapter, create an organizer like the one below. As you read, take note of the seven classifications of stocks.

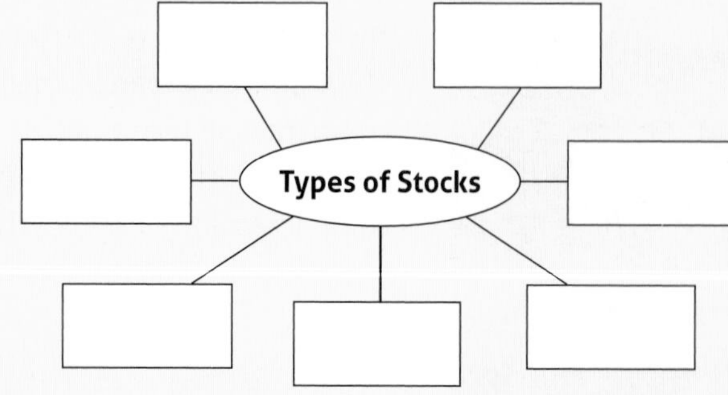

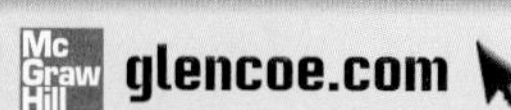

Print this graphic organizer.

Standards

Academic

Mathematics

NCTM Number and Operations Understand meanings of operations and how they relate to one another.

NCTM Connections Recognize and apply mathematics in contexts outside of mathematics.

NCTM Problem Solving Solve problems that arise in mathematics and in other contexts.

English Language Arts

NCTE 6 Apply knowledge of language structure and conventions to discuss texts.

NCTE 7 Conduct research and gather, evaluate, and synthesize data to communicate discoveries.

Social Studies

NCSS VII H Apply economic concepts and reasoning when evaluating historical and contemporary social developments and issues.

NCTM *National Council of Teachers of Mathematics*
NCTE *National Council of Teachers of English*
NCSS *National Council for the Social Studies*
NSES *National Science Education Standards*

Common Core

Reading Determine central ideas or themes of a text and analyze their development; summarize the key supporting details and ideas.

Reading Read and comprehend complex literary and informational texts independently and proficiently.

Writing Write routinely over extended time frames (time for research, reflection, and revision) and shorter time frames (a single sitting or a day or two) for a range of tasks, purposes, and audiences.

Common Stock

Why do companies offer common stock?

Section Objectives

- **Explain** why companies offer common and preferred stock.
- **Discuss** the reasons for investing in common stock.
- **Discuss** the reasons for investing in preferred stock.

Investors have a choice of **securities,** which are all investments—stocks, bonds, mutual funds, options, and commodities—that are bought and sold on the stock market.

When investors buy shares of stock in a company, the company uses that money to make and sell its products, fund its operations, and expand. If the company earns a profit, the stockholders (owners of shares of stock in the company) earn a **return,** or gain, on their investment. People buy and sell stocks for one reason: They want larger returns than they can get from more conservative investments.

As You Read

Discover What do you think it means to own stock in a company?

Why Corporations Issue Common Stock

Companies issue common stock to raise money to start up their businesses and then to help pay for ongoing activities. A **private corporation,** or a closely held corporation, is a company that issues stock to a small group of people. A private corporation's stocks are not traded openly in stock markets. On the other hand, a **public corporation,** or publicly held corporation, is one that sells its shares openly in stock markets, where anyone can buy them. Some large corporations, such as AT&T, General Electric, and Procter & Gamble have thousands or even millions of stockholders.

A Form of Equity Because corporations do not have to repay the money a stockholder pays for stock, they are able to use that money to fund their ongoing activities. For the stockholder to make money on the stock, he or she sells the stock to another investor. The price is set according to how much the buyer is willing to pay. As the demand for a certain company's stock increases or decreases, the price goes up or down accordingly. News on expected sales revenues, earnings, or mergers can make demand for the stock go up or down.

Dividends Not Mandatory It is up to the corporate board of directors, a group elected to make the major decisions for the corporation, to decide whether any profits will be paid to stockholders as dividends. Companies that are growing quickly might pay low or no dividends instead using profits to expand the company. Of course, the board of directors can reduce or stop dividend payments when a corporation has a bad year.

Why Investors Purchase Common Stock

Most investors purchase common stock to make money in three different ways: when they receive dividends, when the dollar value of their stock increases, and when the stock splits and increases in value.

reality bytes

E-trading

Can you imagine that the average person did not have access to the Internet for their personal use before 1979? That was the year CompuServe became a leader in providing services to the financial industry by providing quotes and financial information electronically to Wall Street. Today, in addition to instantly downloading music and sending text messages, you can research, evaluate, buy, sell, and trade stocks and other securities entirely online. You can even hire an online brokerage service. This is called electronic trading, or e-trading. Type any of these terms in a search engine and you will find a supply of information that would have been virtually impossible to gather before the Internet.

Income from Dividends A corporation's board members do not have to pay dividends, but they do want to keep stockholders happy because those same stockholders are funding the corporation's business. As a result, board members often vote to pay dividends if possible, unless they decide to place the profits back into the company. With a cash dividend, each common stockholder receives an equal amount per share. Most dividends are paid quarterly. Some companies that have large increases in earnings might declare a special cash dividend at the end of the year. You might also receive a dividend of company stock—or of company products.

Appreciation of Stock Value If the market value of the stock **appreciates,** or increases, you must decide whether to sell your stock at the higher price or continue to hold it. If you sell, the difference between the price that you paid and the price at which you sell is your profit or loss if the value of the stock falls. **Figure 1** provides tips for tracking your stock investment. If a company's board decides to place profits back into the company, it might reward its stockholders through dollar appreciation of stock value instead of dividends.

Increased Value from Stock Splits Your profits can also increase through a stock split. This occurs when the shares of stock owned by existing stockholders are divided into a larger number of shares.

For example, in a two-for-one stock split, the corporation doubles the number of outstanding shares. Suppose that a corporation has 10,000 shares of stock valued at $50 a share. If the corporation splits its stock, the value of each share decreases to $25, but the number of outstanding shares increases to 20,000.

	Before	After
Shares issued	10,000	20,000
Value	50	25
Your shares	200	400
Your value	$10,000	$10,000

The Stock Pages

Savvy investors follow stock information on a regular basis. *What information should an investor be aware of that could have an impact on his or her investments?*

Why do corporations split their stock? Often the management believes that the stock should be trading within an ideal price range. If the market value is a lot higher than this range, a stock split brings the market value back into line. The lower price of stocks often attracts more investors. As a result, the price starts to rise again. The public wants to buy because of the belief that most corporations split their stock only when the company's financial future looks very good. Be aware that a stock's value is not guaranteed to go up after a stock split.

Voting Rights and Control of the Company In addition to the profit that stockholders may make on their investments, they are also given certain rights in return for the money they invest. For example, a corporation is required by law to hold a yearly meeting at which stockholders can vote on company business. Stockholders usually get one vote for each share they own.

Some states require that corporations offer existing stockholders a preemptive right. A preemptive right gives current stockholders the right to buy any new stock a corporation issues before its stock is offered to the public. By buying more shares, a stockholder can keep the same proportion of ownership in the company. This can be important when a corporation is small and control is critical.

Reading Check

Explain Why do people buy and sell stocks?

FIGURE 1 **Tracking Your Stock Investments**

Time and Patience *Why should you take the time to keep up with information about the companies that issue stock you own?*

1. Monitor.

Graph the dollar value of your stock on a daily or weekly basis.

2. Watch the financials.

Continually evaluate the company's current sales and profits and those projected for the future. Compare its progress to the performance of other companies in the same industry. If it cannot compete, sell.

3. Track the products.

Poor-quality products or a lack of new or up-to-date products can make the value of a company's stock drop.

4. Watch the economy.

The inflation rate, the state of the overall economy, and other economic factors can affect your company's stock price.

5. Be patient.

If you think that you have bought into a good company, hang on. Over time, your investment will usually increase in value.

Preferred Stock

Is preferred stock preferable?

You could buy preferred stock in addition to, or instead of, common stock. If a company is struggling financially, then the preferred stockholder might get the dividends. Preferred stockholders should know the amount of the dividend they will receive. It is either a specific amount of money or a percentage of the par value of the stock. The **par value** is an assigned dollar value that is printed on a stock certificate. If the par value is $30 and the dividend rate is 5 percent, then the dollar amount of the dividend is $1.50 per share ($30 × 5% = $1.50). Unlike market value, par value does not change.

Few corporations use preferred stock as a way of raising money. However, for some companies it is another method of financing, which may attract more conservative investors who do not want to buy common stock. Preferred stockholders receive limited voting rights and usually vote only if the corporation is in financial trouble.

Why Investors Purchase Preferred Stock

Preferred stock is considered a "middle investment." The yield on preferred stock is generally lower than the yield on corporate bonds but higher than the yield on common stock. Preferred stock is considered a safer investment than common stock, but not as safe as bonds. Preferred stocks lack the potential for growth that common stocks offer. As a result, preferred stocks are not considered a good investment for most people. These stocks are often purchased by individuals who need a predictable source of income greater than what is offered by common stock investments. To make preferred stocks more attractive, some corporations may offer cumulative preferred stock, convertible preferred stock, or a participation feature.

Cumulative Preferred Stock Cumulative preferred stock is stock whose unpaid dividends build up and must be paid before any cash dividend is paid to the common stockholders. This means that if a corporation decides to omit dividend payments to preferred stockholders, people who hold cumulative preferred stock will still receive those dividend payments during a later payment period.

Convertible Preferred Stock Convertible preferred stock is stock that can be exchanged for shares of common stock. This feature provides an investor with the safety of preferred stock and the possibility of greater returns through conversion to common stock.

Participation Feature Some corporations offer a participation feature, which allows preferred stockholders to share in the corporation's earnings with the common stockholders. After a required dividend is paid to preferred stockholders and a stated dividend is paid to common stockholders, the remainder of earnings is shared by preferred and common stockholders. This feature is rare.

Document Detective

A Stock Confirmation Report

When you buy or sell stock, you will receive a confirmation report that the purchase or sale has occurred. Be sure to check that the transaction was completed correctly. Check to see that the correct number of shares was purchased or sold, and that the fees for completing the transaction are reasonable. A stock confirmation report contains the following information:

- Name and address of the stock owner
- Account number
- Name of the stock purchased or sold
- Price of the stock
- Number of shares held
- Commission and fees

Taylor Financial Services
175 Montrose Avenue
Cincinnati, OH 52549

Account Number: DR 199704

Hector Gonzales
3482 Mayfair Lane
Cincinnati, OH 52546

Trade date:	04/29/20--
Date processed:	04/29/20--
Payment Date:	05/04/20--

SOLD:

Quantity	Description	Price	Gross Amount	Commission	Fees	Total Amount
160	Analog Devices	$43.90	$7,024.00	$159.20	$5.42	$6,859.38

Key Points When you own stock, there will be times when you want to sell or buy more. You may also want to purchase stocks from other companies. When you make these transactions, you will receive a stock confirmation report to track of all your stock transactions.

FIND the Solutions

Review Key Concepts

1. Who performed the stock transaction?
2. Did Hector purchase or sell stock?
3. How many shares were involved in the transaction?
4. Why is there a difference between the gross amount and the total amount Hector received?
5. When will Hector be sent his money?

SECTION 1 Assessment

Review Key Concepts

1. **Summarize** Explain why companies offer common and preferred stock.
2. **Explain** Discuss the reasons for investing in common stock.
3. **Describe** Discuss the reasons for investing in preferred stock.

Higher Order Thinking H.O.T.

4. **Justify** Defend a corporation's decision to split its stock when the stock price has risen significantly.

English Language Arts

5. **Investing** Sonja thinks investing in stocks is something only older or wealthy people are able to do. However, thanks to the Internet, she has discovered that anyone can have access to stock information. She is intrigued, but she is intimidated and overwhelmed. Think of something you did that made you nervous at first. For example, have you ever auditioned for a play, had a first day at work, or initiated a friendship? Drawing on your own experiences, write a paragraph to explain why you think many people are reluctant to invest in stocks. Write a second paragraph with suggestions for making sound stock investments decisions.

NCTE 3 Apply strategies to interpret texts.

Mathematics

6. **Preferred Stock Dividend** Karma has been given 95 shares of preferred stock of XYZ Co. from her parents. She is interested in determining how much she will receive in dividends each year from the stock. The stock certificates show that the par value of the stock is $52.00 and the dividend rate of the stock is 4.25 percent. What is the actual dollar amount of the dividend Karma will receive each year? Assume the par value and dividend rate stay the same each year.

Math Concept **Calculate Preferred Stock Dividend** To calculate the annual dividend received on preferred stock you must determine the par value and dividend rate of the stock.

Starting Hint Determine the annual dividend received for each share of preferred stock by multiplying the par value of the stock by the dividend rate.

NCTM Connections Recognize and apply mathematics in contexts outside of mathematics.

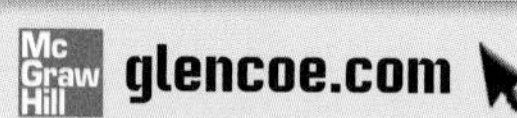

Check your answers.

Types of Stock Investments

How are stocks classified?

Financial professionals classify most stocks into the following categories: blue-chip stocks, income stocks, growth stocks, cyclical stocks, defensive stocks, large-cap stocks, small-cap stocks, and penny stocks.

Blue-Chip Stocks

A **blue-chip stock** is considered a safe investment that generally attracts conservative investors. These stocks are issued by the strongest and most respected companies, such as AT&T, General Electric, and Kellogg. If you are interested in a blue-chip stock, look for a company that shows leadership in an industry, a history of stable earnings, and consistency in the payment of dividends.

Income Stocks

An **income stock** pays higher-than-average dividends compared to other stock issues. The buyers of preferred stock are also attracted to this type of common stock because the dividends are predictable. Stocks issued by companies such as Bristol-Myers Squibb and Dow Chemical are classified as income stocks. This is also the type of stock issued by gas and electric companies.

Section Objectives

- **Classify** and describe the types of stock investments.
- **Identify** sources of information for evaluating stock investments.
- **Discuss** the factors that affect stock prices.
- **Compare** investment theories.

As You Read

Determine What are some ways to research stocks to make wise buying decisions?

Industry Leaders
Strong, respected, and financially sound companies issue blue-chip stocks. *What other companies can you name that are likely to offer blue-chip stocks?*

Cyclical Stock
When the economy is doing well, people have more money to spend, which allows the economy to grow even more. *Why is cyclical stock most closely linked with the state of the economy?*

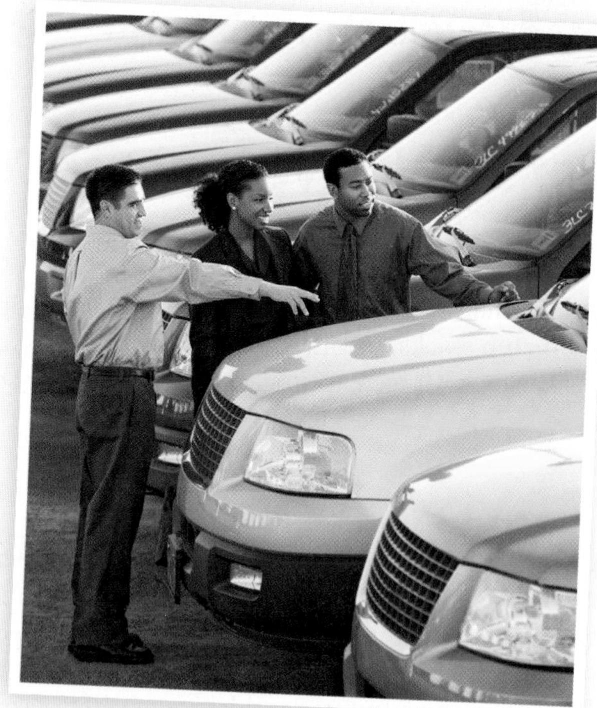

Growth Stocks

A **growth stock** is issued by a corporation whose potential earnings may be higher than the average earnings predicted for all the corporations in the country. Stocks issued by these corporations generally do not pay dividends. Look for signs that the company is **engaged,** or involved, in activities that produce higher earnings and sales revenues: building new facilities; introducing new, high-quality products; or conducting recognized research and development. Growth companies in the early 2000s included Home Depot and Southwest Airlines.

Cyclical Stocks

A **cyclical stock** has a market value that tends to reflect the state of the economy. When the economy is improving, the market value of a cyclical stock usually goes up. During an economic decline, the market value of a cyclical stock may decrease. This is because the products and services of these companies are linked directly to the activities of a strong economy. Investors try to buy these stocks when they are still inexpensive, just before the economy starts to improve. Then they seek to sell them just before the economy declines. Stocks issued by Ford and Centex (a construction firm) are considered cyclical stocks.

Defensive Stocks

A **defensive stock** is a stock that remains stable during declines in the economy. The companies that issue such stocks have steady earnings and can continue dividend payments even in periods of economic decline. Many blue-chip stocks and income stocks, such as those issued by Procter & Gamble, are defensive stocks.

Large-Cap and Small-Cap Stocks

A **large-cap stock** is stock from a corporation that has issued a large number of shares of stock and has a large amount of capitalization. **Capitalization** is the total amount of stocks and bonds issued by a corporation. The stocks listed in the Dow Jones Industrial Averages, a stock indicator which measures the overall condition of the stock market, are typically large-cap stocks. These stocks appeal to conservative investors because they are considered secure.

A **small-cap stock** is a stock issued by a company with a capitalization of $500 million or less. Since these stocks are issued by smaller, less-established companies, they are considered to be a higher investment risk.

Penny Stocks

A **penny stock** typically sells for less than $1 a share, although it can sell for as much as $10 a share. These stocks are issued by new companies or companies whose sales are very unsteady. The prices of these stocks can go up and down wildly. It is difficult to keep track of a penny stock's performance because information about them is hard to find. Penny stocks should be purchased only by investors who understand the risks.

Reading Check

Generalize Which type of stock generally appeals to conservative investors? Why?

Sources for Evaluating Stocks

How do you assess a stock investment?

There are many sources where you can find information about stocks before making investment decisions. Some sources include: newspapers, the Internet, stock advisory services, and corporate news publications.

Today's Trading
Search engines are examples of Web sites that can be used to find financial information. *How has the Internet changed the trading of stocks?*

FIGURE 2 **Common Stock Information**

Interpreting the Financial News Many major financial Web sites and newspapers offer a wealth of financial information. *What is represented in the column "Net Chg"?*

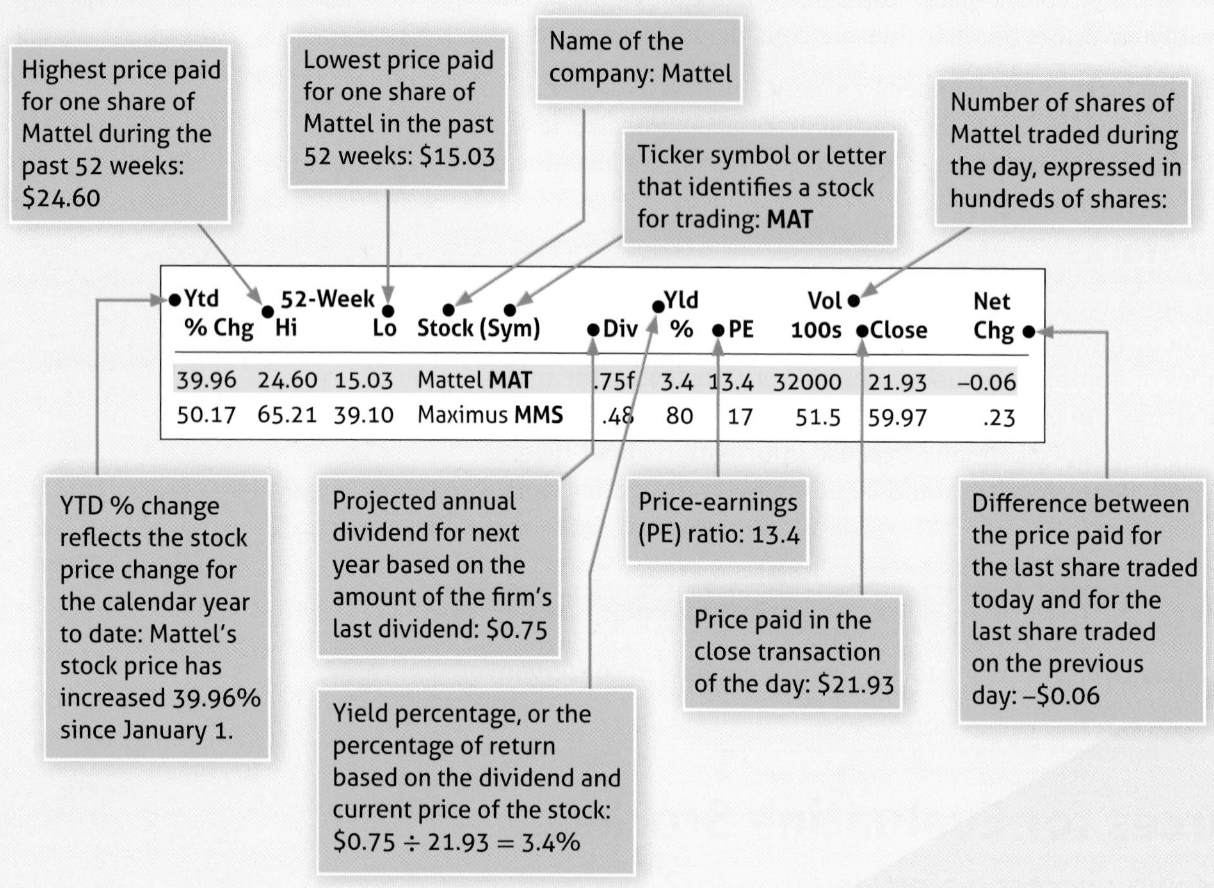

Newspapers

Most major newspapers have financial sections that contain information about stocks that are listed on major stock exchanges, such as the New York Stock Exchange (NYSE) and the American Stock Exchange (AMEX). Newspapers may also cover stocks of local interest. **Figure 2** illustrates the detailed information provided in *The Wall Street Journal* about common stock.

The Internet

Today most corporations have their own Web sites. The information may be more up to date and detailed than material from the corporation's printed publications. You can also use search engines to find information about investing in stocks. Sites provide general financial news and specific information about a company and its stock's performance.

Stock Advisory Services

In addition to newspapers and the Internet, you can use stock advisory services to evaluate potential stock investments. Many stock advisory services, such as Moody's Investors Service, charge fees for their information, which can vary from simple alphabetic listings to detailed financial reports. As mentioned previously, three widely used sources for information on companies' stock are *Standard & Poor's Stock and Bond Guide, Value Line Investment Survey*, and Mergent's *Handbook of Common Stocks.*

As shown in **Figure 3,** basic financial report from *Mergent's Handbook of Common Stocks* consists of six sections. One section contains information about stock prices and capitalization, earnings, and dividends. A background section, "Business Summary," provides a detailed description of the company's major operations, such as the products they produce. A third section, "Recent Developments," offers current information about net income and sales revenue. A "Prospects" section describes the company's **prospects,** or outlook, for the future. The "Financial Data" section provides important statistics on the company for a specific length of time in the past. A final section lists information such as important officers in the corporation and the location of its headquarters.

Corporate News Publications

Annual and quarterly reports offer a summary of a corporation's activities as well as detailed financial information. You do not have to be a stockholder to get an annual report. Simply call, write, or e-mail to request a copy from the company's headquarters. Financial publications such as *Barron's*, *BusinessWeek*, *Fortune*, *Kiplinger's Personal Finance*, *Money*, and *Smart Money* also provide information about specific companies.

Reading Check

Identify What are the six sections of a basic financial report?

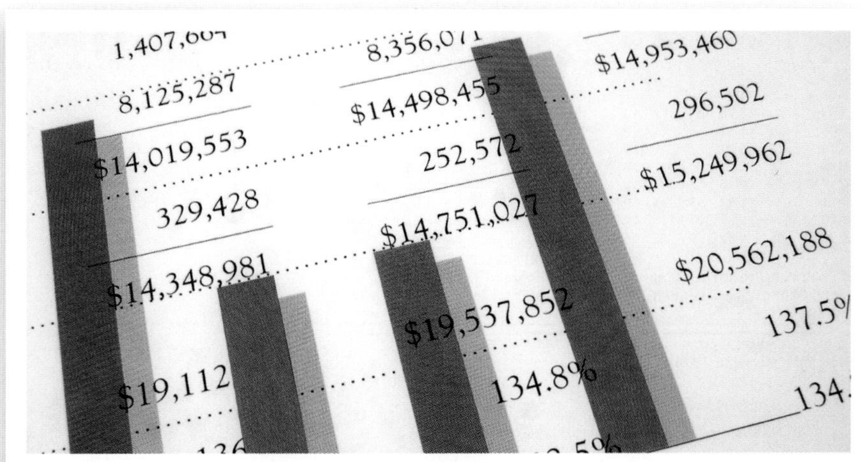

Summaries and Details Annual and quarterly reports provide a great deal of information for investors. *Where can you find this information?*

FIGURE 3 A Basic Financial Report

Up and Down This financial report from Mergent's *Handbook of Common Stocks* provides information about PepsiCo, Inc. *What is reported in the lower section of the graph?*

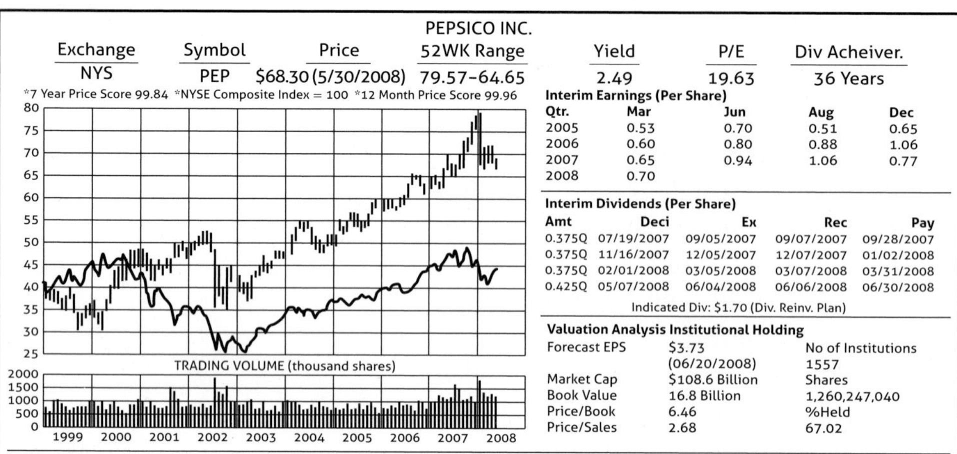

PEPSICO INC.

Exchange	Symbol	Price	52WK Range	Yield	P/E	Div Acheiver.
NYS	PEP	$68.30 (5/30/2008)	79.57-64.65	2.49	19.63	36 Years

*7 Year Price Score 99.84 *NYSE Composite Index = 100 *12 Month Price Score 99.96

Interim Earnings (Per Share)

Qtr.	Mar	Jun	Aug	Dec
2005	0.53	0.70	0.51	0.65
2006	0.60	0.80	0.88	1.06
2007	0.65	0.94	1.06	0.77
2008	0.70			

Interim Dividends (Per Share)

Amt	Deci	Ex	Rec	Pay
0.375Q	07/19/2007	09/05/2007	09/07/2007	09/28/2007
0.375Q	11/16/2007	12/05/2007	12/07/2007	01/02/2008
0.375Q	02/01/2008	03/05/2008	03/07/2008	03/31/2008
0.425Q	05/07/2008	06/04/2008	06/06/2008	06/30/2008

Indicated Div: $1.70 (Div. Reinv. Plan)

Valuation Analysis Institutional Holding

Forecast EPS	$3.73 (06/20/2008)	No of Institutions 1557
Market Cap	$108.6 Billion	Shares
Book Value	16.8 Billion	1,260,247,040
Price/Book	6.46	%Held
Price/Sales	2.68	67.02

Business Summary: Food (MIC: SIC: 2086 NAIC: 312111)
Pepsico is engaged in manufacturing, marketing and selling a range of salty, sweet and grain-based snacks as well as carbonated and non-carbonated beverages and foods. Co. is organized into four divisions; Frito-Lay North America (FLNA); PepsiCo Beverages North America (PBNA); PepsiCo International (PI); and Quaker Foods North America (QFNA). FLNA branded snacks include Lay's potato chips, Doritos tortilla chips and Rold Gold pretzels. PBNA's brands include Pepsi, Mountain Dew, Gatorade, Tropicana Pure Premium, and Dole. PI's brands include Lay's, Walkers, Cheetos; Doritos, Ruffles, Gamesa and Sabritas, QFNA's brands include Quaker oatmeal, Rice-A-Roni and Near East side dishes.

Recent Developments: For the quarter ended Mar 22 2008, net income increased 4.7% to US$1.15 billion from US$1.10 billion in the year-earlier quarter. Revenues were US$8.33 billion, up 13.4% from US$7.35 billion the year before. Operating income was US$1.55 billion versus US$1.42 billion in the prior-year quarter, an increase of 9.4%. Direct operating expenses rose 16.7% to US$3.83 billion from US$3.29 billion in the comparable period the year before. Indirect operating expenses increased 11.3% to US$2.95 billion from US$2.65 billion in the equivalent prior-year period.

Prospects: For full-year 2008; Co.expects 3.0% to 5.0% volume growth, high-single-digit net revenue growth and earnings per share of at least $3.72. Meanwhile, on May 6 2008. The Pepsi Bottling Group, Inc. and Co. announced that, through their PR Beverages Limited joint venture in Russia, they have completed their acquisition of Sobol-aqua JSC, a beverage manufacturing company based in Novosibirsk, Russia Separately, on Apr 30 2008. Co. announced the acquisition of V Water, a vitamin water brand in the U.K. This acquisition reflects Co.'s strategy to transforming its portfolio of products and extending its range of healthier beverages, and should provide Co.with significant opportunities.

Financial Data (US$ in Thousands)	**3 Mos**	**12/29/2007**	**12/30/2006**	**12/31/2005**	**12/25/2004**	**12/27/2003**	**12/28/2002**	**12/29/2001**
Earnings Per Share	3.48	3.41	3.34	2.39	2.44	2.05	1.85	1.47
Cash Flow Per Share	4.27	4.29	3.70	3.45	2.99	2.53	2.65	2.39
Tang Book Value Per Share	6.01	6.30	5.50	5.20	4.84	3.82	4.93	2.17
Dividends Per Share	1.500	1.425	1.160	1.010	0.850	0.630	0.595	0.575
Dividend Payout %	43.13	41.79	34.73	42.26	34.84	30.73	32.16	39.12
Income Statement								
Total Revenue	8,333,000	39,474,000	35,137,000	32,562,000	29,261,000	26,971,000	25,112,000	26,935,000
EBITDA	1,926,000	9,092,000	8,399,000	7,732,000	6,848,000	6,269,000	6,077,000	5,189,000
Depn & Amortn	303,000	1,362,000	1,344,000	1,253,000	1,209,000	1,165,000	1,067,000	1,008,000
Income Before Taxes	1,566,000	7,631,000	6,989,000	6,382,000	5,546,000	4,992,000	4,868,000	4,029,000
Income Taxes	418,000	1,973,000	1,347,000	2,304,000	1,372,000	1,424,000	1,555,000	1,367,000
Net Income	1,148,000	5,658,000	5,642,000	4,078,000	4,212,000	3,568,000	3,313,000	2,662,000
Average Shares	1,632,000	1,658,000	1,687,000	1,706,000	1,729,000	1,739,000	1,789,000	1,807,000
Balance Sheet								
Current Assets	11,065,000	10,151,000	9,130,000	10,454,000	8,639,000	6,930,000	6,413,000	5,853,000
Total Assets	35,699,000	34,628,000	29,930,000	31,727,000	27,987,000	25,327,000	23,474,000	21,695,000
Current Liabilities	8,587,000	7,753,000	6,860,000	9,406,000	6,752,000	6,415,000	6,052,000	4,998,000
Long-Term Obligations	4,884,000	4,203,000	2,550,000	2,313,000	2,397,000	1,702,000	2,187,000	2,651,000
Total Liabilities	18,985,000	17,394,000	14,562,000	17,476,000	14,464,000	13,453,000	14,183,000	13,021,000
Stockholders'Equity	16,806,000	17,325,000	15,447,000	14,320,000	13,572,000	11,896,000	9,298,000	8,648,000
Shares Outstanding	1,590,000	1,605,000	1,638,000	1,656,000	1,679,000	1,705,000	1,722,000	1,756,000
Statistical Record								
Return on Assets %	17.47	17.58	18.35	13.44	15.84	14.66	14.71	13.34
Return on Equity %	35.51	34.62	38.01	28.77	33.17	33.76	37.02	33.58
EBITDA Margin %	23.11	23.03	23.90	23.75	23.40	23.24	24.20	19.26
Net Margin %	13.78	14.33	16.06	12.52	14.39	13.23	13.19	9.88
Asset Turnover	1.24	1.23	1.14	1.07	1.10	1.11	1.11	1.35
Current Ratio	1.29	1.31	1.33	1.11	1.28	1.08	1.06	1.17
Debt to Equity	0.29	0.24	0.17	0.16	0.18	0.14	0.24	0.31
Price Range	79.57-62.89	78.69-62.16	65.91-56.77	59.90-51.57	55.55-45.39	48.71-37.30	53.12-35.50	50.28-41.26
P/E Ratio	22.85-18.07	23.08-18.23	19.73-17.00	25.06-21.58	22.77-18.60	23.76-18.20	28.71-19.19	34.20-28.07
Average Yield %	2.15	2.09	1.90	1.82	1.66	1.43	1.29	1.25

Address: 700 Anderson Hill Road, Purchase, NY 10577-1444 Telephone: 914-253-2000 Fax: 914-253-2070	Web Site: www. pepsico. com Officers: Indra K. Nooyi-Chairman, President, Chief Executive Officer Michael D. White-Vice-Chairman	Auditors: KPMG LLP Investor Contact: 914-253-3035 Transfer Agents: The Bank of New York

Source: *Mergent's Handbook of Common Stocks*, Summer 2008 (New York: Mergent, 2008).

Economics and You

Economic Growth

For an economy to grow and for the standard of living to improve businesses and the government must invest. Businesses need to invest in new machinery and technology. For example, advanced computer systems that link companies with their suppliers improve inventory control and reduce costs. New medical technology shortens hospital stays and improves the quality of life for many individuals. Government support of educational programs through grants and allocations create an educated and skilled work force. How a nation makes use of its factors of production (land, labor, capital and entrepreneurship) will determine how well it will grow in the future.

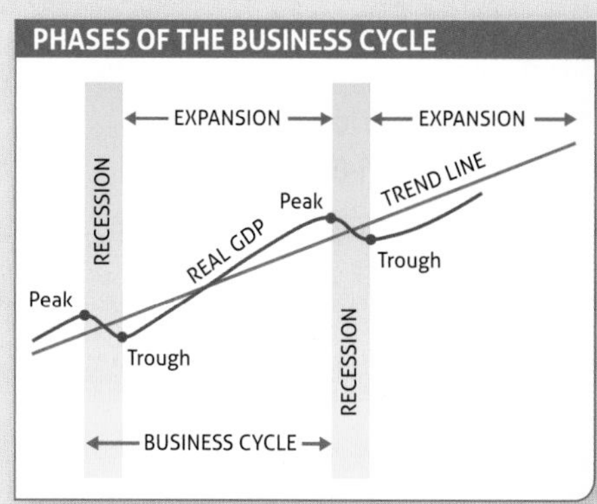

Personal Finance Connection When purchasing stock in a corporation, look at its growth potential. Find out if it is investing in new technology, employee training, and research and development. Study its earnings potential and see if its products and services are affected by the economy. Also note how well it does in relation to its competition.

Critical Thinking Analyze two competing stocks to determine in which one you would invest. Provide the reasoning for your decision and include analysis of your personal risk comfort zone.

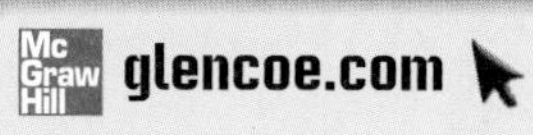

Activity Download an Economics and You Worksheet Activity.

Factors that Influence the Price of Stock

How would you determine whether your investment is increasing or decreasing in dollar value?

When you are deciding whether it is the right time to buy or sell a particular stock, you must first consider the overall condition of the stock market. A **bull market** is a market condition that occurs when investors are optimistic about the economy and buy stocks. Because of the greater demand for stock, the value of many stocks and the value of the stock market as a whole increases. A **bear market** is a market condition that occurs when investors are pessimistic about the economy and sell stocks. As a result of this decline in demand, the value of individual stocks and the stock market as a whole decreases.

Next you should consider the company's profits, losses, and other numerical measures of its financial situation. To be a successful investor, you must learn the numbers game. Many calculations can help you gauge the value of a potential stock investment. These same calculations can help you decide if the time is right to sell a stock investment. Examples of these valuable calculations include: current yield, total return, earning per share, and price-earnings (PE) ratio.

Beasts of Finance
Knowing the current market is important when you make decisions as an investor. *How do bull markets and bear markets affect stocks?*

Numerical Measures for a Corporation

Using numerical measures such as current yield, total return, earnings per share, and the price-earnings ratio is a good way to find out about the health of a corporation.

Current Yield One of the most common calculations investors use to track the value of their investments is the current yield. **Current yield** is the annual dividend or interest of an investment divided by the current market value. The current yield is expressed as a percentage. As a general rule, an increase in current yield is a healthy sign for any investment.

Total Return The current yield calculation is useful, but you also need to know whether your investment is increasing or decreasing in dollar value. **Total return** is a calculation that includes the annual dividend as well as any increase or decrease in the original purchase price of the investment.

GO FIGURE Mathematics

Current Yield of a Stock Investment

Computing the current yield of your stocks will help you to determine the value of your investment.

EXAMPLE Suppose that Tanika purchases stock in EatGrapes.com. Assume that EatGrapes.com pays an annual dividend of $1.20 and is currently selling for $24 a share. What is Tanika's current yield?

Formula Annual Dividend/Current Market Value = Current Yield
Solution $1.20/$24.00 = 0.05 = 5%
Tanika's current yield would be 5 percent.

Your Turn

If your stock pays an annual dividend of $.80 and is currently selling for $18 a share, what is your current yield?

GO FIGURE Mathematics

Total Returns

Calculating the total return of your investment will let you know whether your investment is increasing or decreasing in value.

EXAMPLE Two years ago Mark bought 40 shares of Ferguson's Motor Company for $70 a share. The stock pays an annual dividend of $1.50. Mark is going to sell his stock at the current price of $120 a share. What would be the total return on his investment?

Formula Current Return + Capital Gain = Total Return
Solution
A. Find the current return:
Dividend × Number of Shares × Years Held = Current Return
$1.50 × 40 × 2 = $120
The current return is $120.
B. Calculate the capital gain:
(Selling Price per Share − Purchase Price per Share) ×
Number of Shares Held = Capital Gain
($120 − $70) × 40 = $2,000
The capital gain is $2,000
C. Find the total return:
Current return + Capital Gain = Total Return
$120 + $2,000 = $2,120
The total return on Mark's investment would be $2,120.

Your Turn

If your current return on a stock is $60 and your capital gain is $1,280, what is your total return?

To calculate total return, add the current return on your investment to its capital gain. The current return is the total amount of dividends paid to you, based on the number of shares you own and how long you have held them. To figure out your current return, multiply your dividend amount per share by the number of shares and the length of time that you have held the shares.

Next determine your capital gain. As you learned previously, capital gain is the profit you make from the sale of an asset, or the difference between the selling price and the purchase price. To compute capital gain, subtract the purchase price per share from the selling price per share. Then multiply that number by the number of shares held.

Once you have determined your current return and your capital gain, add those two figures to arrive at your total return. Also keep in mind that commissions and fees can reduce your total return.

In the **Go Figure** example, Mark's investment in Ferguson's Motor Company increased in value, so the total return was greater than the current return. For an investment that decreases in value, the total return will be less than the current return. And while it may be obvious, the larger the dollar amount of the total return, the better.

Earnings Per Share Another measurement of a company's performance is **earnings per share.** Earnings per share are a corporation's net, or after-tax, earnings divided by the number of outstanding shares of common stock. This calculation measures the amount of corporate profit assigned to each share of common stock. This figure gives a stockholder an idea of a company's profitability. In general, an increase in earnings per share is a good sign for any corporation and its stockholders.

Price-Earnings Ratio The **price-earnings (PE) ratio** is the price of one share of stock divided by the corporation's earnings per share of stock over the last 12 months. This measurement is commonly used to compare the corporate earnings to the market price of a corporation's stock. The PE ratio is a key factor that serious investors as well as beginners can use to decide whether to invest in a stock. A low PE ratio indicates that a stock may be a good investment: The company has a lot of earnings when compared to the price of the stock. A high PE ratio tells you that it might be a poor investment. The company has little earnings when compared to the price of the stock. Generally, you should study the PE ratio for a corporation over a period of time so that you can see a range. Although PE ratios vary by industry, they range between 5 and 35 for most corporations.

Projected Earning Both earnings per share and the price-earnings ratio are based on historical numbers, or how a company has performed in the past. With this fact in mind, many investors will also look at the earnings estimates, or projections, for a corporation. For an investor, a projected increase in earning is a good sign. Of course, you should remember that these projections are just estimates. Changes in the economy, for example, may cause analysts to revise their estimates.

Reading Check

List What are four numerical measures to help determine the health of a company?

GO FIGURE Mathematics

Earnings Per Share

Figuring out the earnings per share can help you find out a company's profits. This information can help you determine the general health of the company in which you are investing.

EXAMPLE EFG Corporation had net earnings of $800,000 last year. EFG had 100,000 outstanding shares of common stock. What were EFG's earnings per share?

Formula Net Earnings/Common Stock Outstanding = Earnings Per Share
Solution $800,000/100,000 = $8
The corporation's earnings per share were $8.

Your Turn

You recently invested in an up-and-coming home improvement company and you want to know about the company's health. If the company had net earnings of $400,000 last year and had 80,000 outstanding shares of common stock, what were the company's net earnings per share?

GO FIGURE Mathematics

Price-Earnings Ratio

The price-earnings ratio is the most common measure of how expensive a stock is. Determining the price-earnings ratio can help you decide whether a stock is worth purchasing.

EXAMPLE EFG's stock is selling for $96 a share. EFG's earnings per share are $8. What is EFG's price-earnings ratio?

Formula Market Price Per Share/Earnings Per Share = Price-Earnings Ratio
Solution $96/$8 = 12
The corporation's price-earnings ratio is 12.

Your Turn

If a company's market price per share is $67 and its earnings per share is $6, what is the company's price-earning ratio?

Investment Theories

Which investment theory makes the most sense to you?

Over the years theories have developed about ways to evaluate possible investments. Three investment theories dominate:

- The fundamental theory
- The technical theory
- The efficient market theory

The Fundamental Theory

The *fundamental theory* assumes that a stock's real value is determined by looking at the company's future earnings. If earnings are expected to increase, then the stock's price should go up. Fundamental theorists look at the financial strength of the company, the type of industry the company is in, its new products, and the state of the economy.

The Technical Theory

The *technical theory* is based on the idea that a stock's value is really determined by forces in the stock market itself. Technical theorists look at factors such as the number of stocks bought or sold over a certain period or the total number of shares traded.

The Efficient Market Theory

In the *efficient market theory,* sometimes called the random walk theory, the argument is that stock price movements are purely random. This theory declares that all investors have considered all of the available information on a stock as they make their decisions. Therefore, according to the efficient market theory, it is impossible for an investor to outperform the stock market average over a long period of time.

Review Key Concepts

1. **Identify** List sources of information for evaluating stock investments.
2. **Explain** Discuss the factors that affect stock prices.
3. **Compare** What are the investment theories? How are they similar?
4. **Classify** Describe the types of stock investments.

Higher Order Thinking H.O.T.

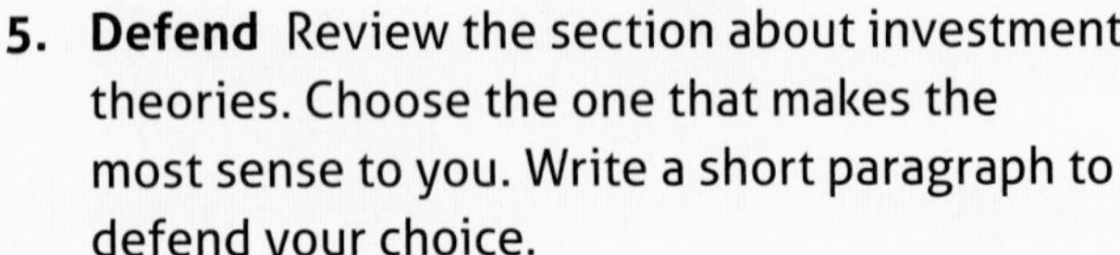

5. **Defend** Review the section about investment theories. Choose the one that makes the most sense to you. Write a short paragraph to defend your choice.

21st Century Skills

6. **Interact Effectively** Sometimes the best career information comes from informational interviews with people working in the real world. An informational interview is a scheduled conversation with a professional to gain information about his or her job, the skills and education required for the job, and details about day-to-day activities. It is not a job interview; however, informational interviews are good tools for establishing contacts for future networking. Interview a financial services professional, such as a stockbroker or other financial services sales agent. Ask him or her about the background, education, training, and experience needed to work in that profession. Write an article based on the interview for your school or class newsletter.

Mathematics

7. **Price-Earnings Ratio** You are researching companies in order to determine which stocks to purchase. One of the companies you are looking at is ABC Corp. Using online tools you found that the company's net earnings were $1,250,000 last year. You also found that they had 120,000 outstanding shares. Using this information determine ABC Corp.'s earnings per share. You decided that another measurement tool would be helpful to analyze stocks. If the current stock price is $56.50 what is ABC Corp.'s price-earnings ratio?

Math Concept **Calculate Price-Earnings Ratio** To calculate the earnings per share divide a company's net earnings by their common stock outstanding. To calculate the price-earnings ratio, divide the company's market price per share by their earnings per share.

Starting Hint Determine the earnings per share of ABC Corp. by first acquiring the company's net earnings and common stock shares outstanding.

NCTM Problem Solving Solve problems that arise in mathematics and in other contexts.

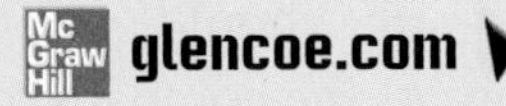

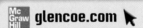

Mc Graw Hill glencoe.com Check your answers.

Markets for Stocks

What are the markets for stocks?

To buy common or preferred stock, you usually have to go through a brokerage firm. In turn, the brokerage firm must buy the stock in the primary or secondary markets.

Section Objectives

- **Explain** primary and secondary markets.
- **Describe** the ways to buy and sell stock.
- **Evaluate** long-term and short-term investment strategies.

The Primary Markets

The primary market is a market in which investors purchase new security issues from a corporation through an investment bank or some other representative of the corporation. An investment bank is a financial firm that helps corporations to raise funds, usually by helping to sell new securities. The investors are commercial banks, insurance companies, pension funds, mutual funds, and the general public.

An initial public offering (IPO) occurs when a company sells stock to the general public for the first time. Companies use IPOs to fund new business start-ups or to finance new corporate growth and expansion. IPOs are considered a high-risk investment.

A corporation can also get financing through the primary market by selling directly to its current stockholders. By doing so, the corporation bypasses the investment bank, avoids any fees it might have had to pay, and therefore obtains financing at a lower cost.

As You Read

Choose Would you hire a brokerage firm to handle your portfolio, or would you prefer to manage it yourself?

The Secondary Markets

Once a company's stocks have been sold on the primary market, they can then be sold in the secondary market. The secondary market is a market for existing financial securities currently traded among investors.

Securities Exchanges A **securities exchange** is a marketplace where brokers who represent investors meet to buy and sell securities. Many securities issued by national corporations are first registered and then traded at either the NYSE or AMEX. There are also regional exchanges in San Francisco, Boston, Chicago, and other cities that trade stocks of companies in their respective regions. For example, American firms that do business abroad may also trade on the Tokyo, London, or Paris exchanges.

The NYSE is one of the largest securities exchanges in the world, listing more than 4,000 corporations with a total market value of about $30 trillion. Most of the NYSE members, or seats, represent brokerage firms that charge commissions on security trades made by their representatives for their customers.

Before a corporation is approved for listing on the NYSE, the corporation must meet specific listing requirements. Various regional exchanges also have listing requirements, though they are typically less stringent than the NYSE requirements. A corporation must have a very large capitalization and trade many shares in order to be listed on the NYSE. Companies that cannot meet the NYSE requirements can use AMEX or regional exchanges.

Over-the-Counter Market Not all stocks are traded on organized exchanges. Several thousand companies trade their stock in the over-the-counter market. The **over-the-counter (OTC) market** is a network of dealers who buy and sell the stocks of corporations that are not listed on a securities exchange.

Most over-the-counter stocks are traded through NASDAQ (pronounced "NAZZ-dack"), an electronic marketplace for more than 4,000 different stocks. NASDAQ stands for the National Association of Securities Dealers Automated Quotation System. The association was established in 1939 to regulate the OTC. When you want to buy or sell a stock that trades on NASDAQ, such as Microsoft® your brokerage firm sends your order in to the NASDAQ computer system. It shows up on a screen with all the other orders from people who want to buy or sell Microsoft. Then a NASDAQ dealer matches the orders of those who want to buy and those who want to sell Microsoft. Once a match is found, your order is completed.

Typically, NASDAQ handles trades for many forward-looking companies, many of which are fairly small. However, some very large companies such as Microsoft, Intel, and MCI are also traded on NASDAQ.

Reading Check

Define What is a securities exchange?

On Wall Street
The New York Stock Exchange (NYSE) is one of the largest securities exchanges in the world. *What can a company do if it cannot meet the NYSE requirements?*

How to Buy and Sell Stock

Why is it important to be directly involved in your investment program?

There are many decisions that you need to make before beginning to buy and sell stock. You must decide on a brokerage firm, an account executive, and on what type of order—market order, limit order, or stop order—you want to use to make your transaction.

Brokerage Firms

Today you can choose a full-service or discount brokerage firm or trade stocks online. The biggest difference is the amount of the commissions you will be charged when you buy or sell securities. A commission is a fee charged to an investor by a brokerage firm for the buying and/or selling of a security. Generally, full-service and discount brokerage firms charge higher commissions than online brokerage firms. Full-service firms usually charge the highest commissions in exchange for personalized service and free research information. However, there may be other differences among the types of firms.

First, consider the amount of research information that will be available to you and how much it costs. All of these firms offer excellent research materials, but you are more likely to pay extra for information if you choose a discount brokerage or online firm. Although most discount brokerage firms do not charge a lot of money for research reports, the fees can add up. Second, consider how much help you will need in order to make an investment decision. The full-service account executive may not have a lot of time to spend with each client, but you can expect him or her to answer questions and make recommendations.

Discount and online firms generally believe that you alone are in charge of your investment plan and that the most successful investors are totally involved in their programs. They usually have printed materials or information on their Web sites to help you become a better investor.

COMMON CENTS

Listen Up

It is smart to shop at music stores that let you listen to CDs or online stores that allow you to listen to songs before you purchase them. You can also check out your friends' music to see if you like it. You will save money by not buying CDs or downloading songs you will not use.

Concept Application

What are some other types of purchases to which you could apply this method?

NASDAQ

The NASDAQ was the first electronic stock exchange in the world. *Why was it was created?*

Problem Solving
Effective problem solving is often a characteristic of successful people. Problem solving is the ability to tackle challenging situations and find a solution. Frequently you will encounter both common and unique problems that must be addressed. Effective problem solvers utilize conventional and innovative ways to resolve issues. In order to find the best answer, you will often need to ask essential questions and clarify different points of view to arrive at the best solution.

Write About It
Think of a challenging situation in school which required problem-solving skills. What questions did you ask? Did you gather input from other sources? Write one or more paragraphs to describe the scenario and explain how the problem was resolved.

glencoe.com

Activity Download a Career and College Readiness Worksheet Activity.

An account executive, or stockbroker, is a licensed individual who buys or sells securities, or stocks, for clients. Account executives usually work for brokerages.

Whether he or she is called an account executive or stockbroker, this person deals with all types of securities, not just stocks, and can handle your entire portfolio. A **portfolio** is a collection of all the securities held by an investor. Some account executives will take risks, while others are more conservative. When you are choosing an account executive, be sure that you can clearly describe your short- and long-term financial goals so that you will receive the best service for your needs.

Remember that account executives can make errors, so be sure to stay actively involved in decisions concerning your investments. Never let the stockbroker take action on your account without your permission. Brokerage firms are usually not responsible for financial losses that are the result of a recommendation by your account executive.

Be aware of a practice known as "churning." Churning occurs when an account executive does a lot of buying and selling of stocks within your portfolio to generate more commissions. Although churning is illegal, it is difficult to prove. Note that the value of your portfolio does not increase through churning; rather, it stays about the same.

Most traditional brokerage firms have a minimum commission that ranges from $25 to $55 for buying and selling stocks. However, commissions for online brokerage firms can be as low as $10. Additional fees based on the number of shares and the value of the stock can also be charged. On the **floor,** or the physical area where securities are exchanged, stocks are traded in round lots, which are 100 shares or multiples of 100 shares of a particular stock. An odd lot contains fewer than 100 shares of a stock.

Types of Orders

When you are ready to trade a stock, you will execute an order to buy or sell. Many people still prefer to use telephone orders to buy and sell stocks, but a growing number are using computers to complete transactions. You can also go to a brokerage firm and place your order in person.

The types of orders used to trade stocks include market orders, limit orders, and stop orders.

Market Orders A market order is a request to buy or sell a stock at the current market value. Because the stock market is essentially an auction, the account executive's representative will try to get the best price possible and make the transaction as soon as possible. **Figure 4** illustrates how a typical market order on the NYSE would be **executed,** or carried out.

FIGURE 4 **The Stock Floor**

1.46 Billion Shares a Day The New York Stock Exchange (NYSE) is the leading stock exchange in the world. *Who are the major players on the floor of the NYSE?*

1 **Receiving an Order** Your account executive receives your order to sell stock and relays the order electronically to the brokerage firm's representative at the stock exchange.

2 **Signal to Floor Broker** A clerk for the firm signals the transaction to a floor broker on the stock exchange floor.

3 **Trading** The floor broker goes to the trading post at which this stock is traded and trades with a floor broker (from another firm) who has an order to buy.

4 **To the Ticker System** The floor broker signals the transaction back to the clerk. Then a floor reporter—an employee of the NYSE—collects the information and inputs it into the ticker system.

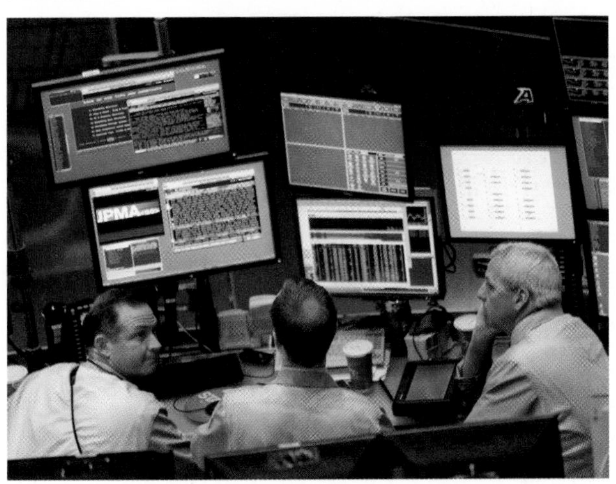

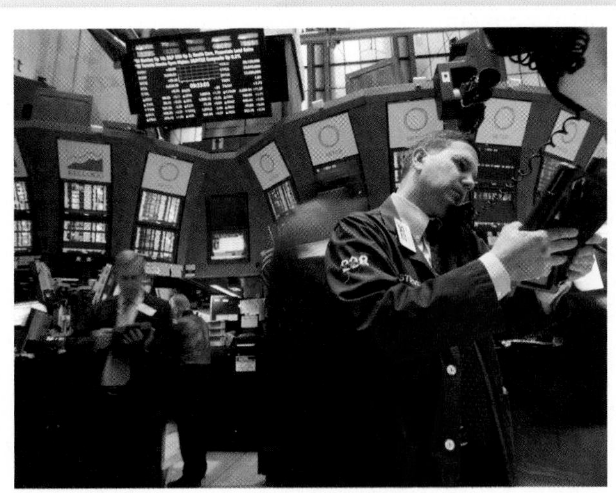

5 **On the Board** The sale appears on the price board, and a confirmation is relayed to your account executive, who notifies you of the completed transaction.

Note that every stock listed on the NYSE is traded at a computer-equipped trading post on the floor of the exchange. A computer monitor above the trading post indicates current price information for all stocks traded at each post.

Then each transaction is recorded, and the necessary information—the ticker symbol (the letters that identify a stock for trading), number of shares, and price—is transmitted through a communications network called the *ticker system*. The NYSE also uses the Super Display Book or SDBK system, which transmits orders electronically.

Payment for stocks is generally required within three business days of the sale. About four to six weeks later, the broker sends a stock certificate (proof of ownership) to the purchaser. A sample of a common stock certificate is shown below. However, the investor's brokerage firm can receive the certificate and hold it, which is convenient when it comes time to sell the stock. The phrase *left in the street name* is used to describe investor-owned securities held by a brokerage firm.

Limit Orders A limit order is a request to buy or sell a stock at a specified price. You agree to buy the stock at the best price up to a certain dollar amount. When you are selling, the limit order ensures that you will sell at the best price and not below a certain price.

A Common Stock Certificate
This is an example of a common stock certificate. Stock certificates may be a prized collector's item for fans of a particular product. *Practically speaking, why is a common stock certificate valuable?*

For example, if you place a limit order to buy Kellogg common stock for $34 a share, the stock will not be purchased until the price drops to $34 or lower. If you place a limit order to sell a stock, the Kellogg stock will not be sold until the price rises to $34 or higher.

However, a limit order does not guarantee that the purchase or sale will be made when the desired price is reached. Limit orders are filled in the order in which they are received, so other investors may get orders filled before you do. If the price of Kellogg, for example, continues to rise while purchase orders ahead of yours are being filled, then when your turn comes, the price may reach $36, and you will miss the chance to buy the stock at $34.

Brazil

Trading on Ethanol

Many people today are promoting the idea of "going green" to help save the environment. One of the largest threats to the environment is greenhouse gases, caused in part by auto emissions. Brazil has perhaps found a new way to encourage people to "go green" with a monetary incentive. The Brazilian Mercantile and Futures Exchange was the first financial market to offer trading on the future production of ethanol, an alternative fuel for vehicles. The refining of biofuels, such as ethanol, is a growing industry in the resource-rich nation of Brazil.

Carbon credits are used on both a national and international level to try and control the rise in greenhouse gases. A carbon credit would be equal to, for example, one ton of greenhouse gases. Companies and government entities with programs in place to reduce greenhouse gases can apply for carbon credits. Some of these companies then sell the credits to polluters. The city of São Paulo has chosen to auction off 800,000 tons worth of its carbon-emission credits through the new stock system.

Critical Thinking

1. **Expand** How can buying carbon credits actually reduce the emission of greenhouse gases?
2. **Relate** Do you agree with the carbon credit system? Should companies who are awarded credits be allowed to sell them?

DATABYTES

Capital
Brasilia

Population
201,103,330

Languages
Portuguese (official and most widely spoken language); note-less common languages include Spanish, German, Italian, Japanese, English, and a large number of minor Amerindian languages

Currency
Brazilian real

Gross Domestic Product (GDP)
$1.499 trillion

GDP per capita
$10,200

Industry
Textiles, shoes, chemicals, cement, lumber, iron ore, tin, steel, aircraft, motor vehicles and parts, other machinery and equipment

Agriculture
Coffee, soybeans, wheat, rice, corn, sugarcane, cocoa, citrus, beef

Exports
Transport equipment, iron ore, soybeans, footwear, coffee, autos

Natural Resources
Bauxite, gold, iron ore, manganese, nickel, phosphates, platinum, tin, uranium, petroleum, hydropower, timber

Careers That Count!

Gary Houseman • Stockbroker

Each day, billions of dollars change hands on the United States securities exchanges. This money is invested in stocks, bonds, and other securities, which are bought and sold by institutional investors, mutual funds, pension plans, and the general public. Most trades are arranged through stockbrokers, whether they are between individuals with a few hundred dollars or large institutions with millions of dollars. This is what I do. As a stockbroker, I serve as the agent between clients and the stock exchange. I assist clients with trades, quotes, and account inquiries via phone and e-mail. Simply put, I help people buy and sell stocks. I work long hours, travel, and endure a high stress level. Many firms hire summer interns, and the most successful interns are often offered full-time jobs after college graduation. Turnover can be high for newcomers, but if you work hard and get beyond the level of junior stockbroker, there is a potential for high earnings.

EXPLORE CAREERS

Brokerage firms seek stockbroker applicants who have excellent communication skills, a strong work ethic, and the ability to work as part of a team.

1. Explain why employers would also look for stockbroker applicants who have a good credit history.
2. What certifications are required for a stockbroker?

Skills	Education	Career Path
Communication, organizational, math, customer service, computer, data-entry, and multitasking skills; ability to make split-second decisions and work under pressure	Bachelor's degree in finance, business, or a related field; MBA or professional certification; current Series 7 and Series 60 or 63 licenses	Stockbrokers can become personal financial advisors, investment advisors, and brokerage team managers.

glencoe.com

Activity Download a Career Exploration Activity.

Stop Orders You can also place a stop order, which is used for selling stock. Sometimes called a stop-loss order, a stop order is a type of limit order to sell a particular stock at the next available opportunity when the market price reaches a specified amount. A stop order does not guarantee that your stock will be sold at the price you want, but it does guarantee that it will be sold at the next available opportunity. Both stop and limit orders can be good for a day, a week, a month, or until you cancel them.

Computerized Transactions

More and more people are using their computers to make securities transactions. To meet the demand for this service, discount brokerage firms and some full-service firms allow investors to trade online. You can use a software package or the brokerage's Web site to help you evaluate stocks, track your portfolio and monitor its value, and buy and sell securities online. The more active the investor is, the more sense it makes to trade online. Of course, you are still responsible for doing research and analyzing the information you get.

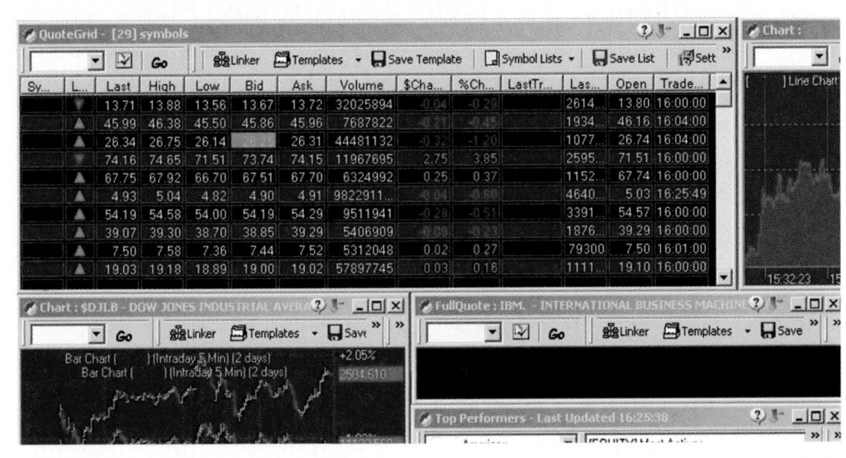

Virtual Broker
Internet brokerage companies offer instant access to your account information and the ability to evaluate, buy, and sell securities online. *Does this mean you can eliminate the responsibility of researching and analyzing your portfolio?*

Reading Check

Connect Explain the connection between a limit order and a stop order.

Investment Strategies

Which type of investment strategy would you use: a long-term or short-term strategy?

Once you purchase stock, the investment may be categorized as long term (held for ten years or more), or short term (held for one year or less). Generally, if you hold investments for at least a year, you are considered an investor. If you buy and sell investments within short periods of time, you are a speculator or a trader.

Long-Term Techniques

Long-term techniques such as the buy-and-hold technique, dollar cost averaging, direct investment, and dividend reinvestment are used by all investors who are interested in avoiding losses in their investments.

Buy-and-Hold Technique A typical long-term investing method is to buy stock and hold on to it for a number of years, often ten or more. During that time, you may get dividends, and the price of the stock may go up. The stock may also be split, which increases its value as well as number of shares owned.

Dollar Cost Averaging With this method, you buy an equal dollar amount of the same stock at equal intervals. For example, suppose that you invested $2,000 in Johnson & Johnson common stock each year for a period of three years. When the price of the stock went up, your $2,000 purchased fewer shares, and when it went down, your $2,000 purchased more shares. This system protects investors from buying at high prices and selling at low prices. The price you pay for the stock averages out over time.

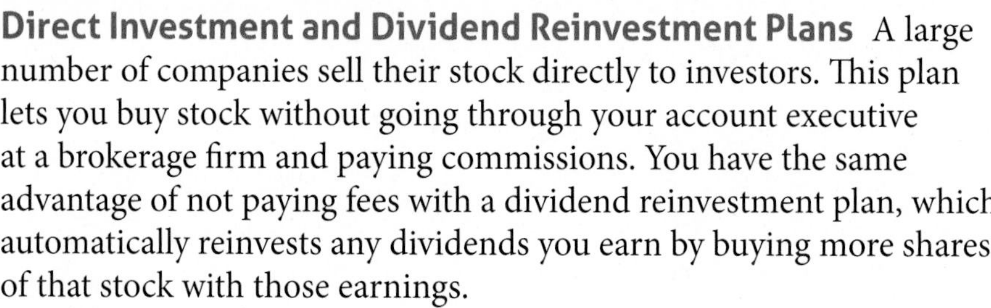

Direct Investment and Dividend Reinvestment Plans A large number of companies sell their stock directly to investors. This plan lets you buy stock without going through your account executive at a brokerage firm and paying commissions. You have the same advantage of not paying fees with a dividend reinvestment plan, which automatically reinvests any dividends you earn by buying more shares of that stock with those earnings.

Short-Term Techniques

Investors sometimes use more speculative, short-term techniques. These methods are quite risky. Only investors who fully understand the risks should use techniques such as buying on margin and selling short.

Buying on Margin When buying stock on margin, an investor borrows through a brokerage firm part of the money needed to purchase a stock. The Federal Reserve Board currently limits the margin requirement to 50 percent and $2,000, which means that you can borrow up to half of the purchase price as long as you have at least $2,000 in your brokerage account. Investors buy stock on margin in order to purchase more shares. If the shares go up in value, the investor makes more money. However, if the shares go down in value, the investor loses more money.

Selling Short Your ability to make money buying and selling securities is related to how well you can predict what the stock is going to do—whether it will rise or fall in value. Normally you want to buy a stock that will go up in value, and this is called buying long. Of course, the value of stocks can decrease, too.

You can actually make money by selling short when the value of a stock appears as if it may go down. Selling short is selling a stock that has been borrowed from a brokerage firm and that must be replaced at a later date. You sell the stock you have borrowed today, knowing that you will have to buy the stock again at a later date. Here is how it is done:

1. Arrange to borrow a certain number of shares of a particular stock from a brokerage firm.
2. Sell the borrowed stock, assuming that it will drop in value in a reasonably short period of time.
3. Buy the stock at a lower price than the price it sold for in Step 2.
4. Use the stock you purchased in Step 3 to replace the stock that you borrowed from the brokerage firm in Step 1.

There is usually no extra brokerage charge for selling short, since the brokerage firm receives its commission when the stock is bought and sold. Remember that when you borrow the stock, it really belongs to someone else, so if a dividend is due, you must pay it. Eventually these dividends may absorb all the profits you make on the transaction. To make money, you have to predict correctly that the value of the stock will go down. If the value increases, you lose money.

After You Read

Assess What are the advantages and disadvantages of investing in stocks?

Assessment

Review Key Concepts

1. **Explain** What are primary and secondary markets?
2. **Summarize** Describe the ways to buy and sell stock.
3. **Evaluate** Explain the benefits and drawbacks of long-term and short-term investment strategies.

Higher Order Thinking H.O.T.

4. **Assess** Stockbrokers are trained and licensed to manage your portfolio. Given this expertise, why is it risky to allow a stockbroker to act on your behalf without consulting you first?

English Language Arts

5. **Choosing Your Broker** Hiring an account executive, or stockbroker, is a lot like hiring an employee. You need to interview several before making a decision. After all, you are entrusting this person or firm with your money, your financial future, and your personal information. Follow your teacher's instructions to form groups. With your group, brainstorm a list of questions and topics for discussion with the account executive candidates. Then, choose two representatives from your group. One person should act as the investor, and the other should act as the potential broker. Using your list, act out a question-and-answer scenario for the class.

NCTE 7 Conduct research and gather, evaluate, and synthesize data to communicate discoveries.

Mathematics

6. **Dollar Cost Averaging** Angela has been putting aside money to invest each year for four years. She saves $3,000 each year and purchases IBM stock with her saved money. In 2007 the stock price for IBM was $97.42. In 2008 the stock price was $97.67. The price was $84.92 in 2009, and it was $130.85 in 2010. Calculate how many shares Angela has accumulated over the past 4 years. Also calculate the average dollar cost of the IBM stock for Angela over this time.

Math Concept **Calculate Dollar Cost Averaging** To calculate the dollar cost average of a stock over a period of time add the product of the shares purchased by the stock price for each year and divide by the total number of shares accumulated.

Starting Hint Determine the shares purchased each year by identifying the dollars invested and the stock price at the time of purchase. Divide the dollars invested by the stock price for each year.

NCTM Connections Recognize and apply mathematics in contexts outside of mathematics.

Check your answers.

CHAPTER REVIEW

Visual Summary

Stocks

Use Money to Make Money

Investors purchase stock to make money in a variety of ways.

Why Investors Purchase Stock

- **Common Stock**
  - Income from Dividends
  - Appreciation of Stock Value
  - Increased Value from Stock Splits
  - Voting Rights and Control of the Company
- **Preferred Stock**
  - Cumulative
  - Convertible
  - Participation Feature

Do Your Research

Before making any investment decisions, take advantage of the many sources available for information.

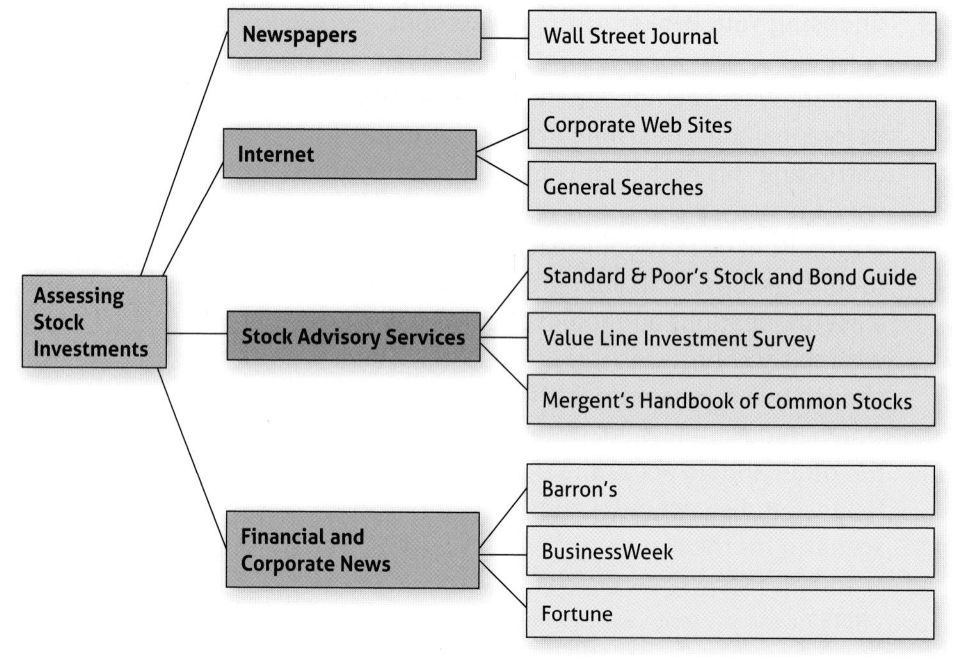

Try It!

Create a step-by-step organizer like the one shown to record the steps involved in trading on the floor of the New York Stock Exchange.

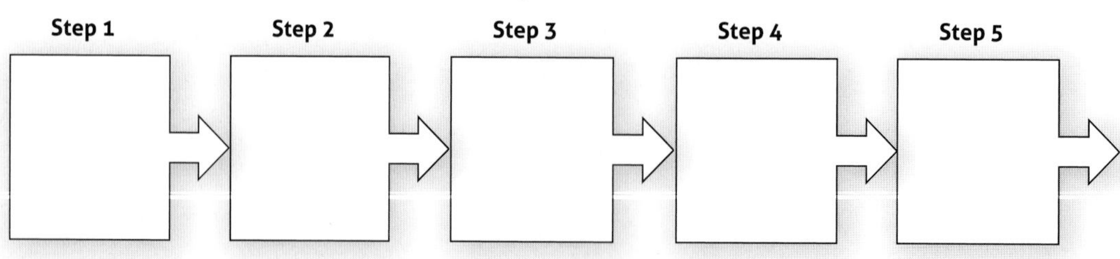

Chapter Review and Assessment

Chapter Summary

- Investors choose common stock because stocks provide a greater potential return than bank savings accounts and government bonds.
- Investors choose preferred stocks because they are less risky than common stocks and because they provide a steady income in the form of dividends.
- Types of stock investments include blue-chip stocks, income stocks, growth stocks, cyclical stocks, defensive stocks, large- and small-cap stocks, and penny stocks.
- Information about stocks' risk can be found in newspapers, stock advisory services, corporate reports, and on the Internet.
- Factors affecting stock prices include general attitudes about current economic conditions and corporate performance.
- Stocks are bought and sold in primary markets, such as in an initial public offering (IPO), and in secondary markets, such as securities exchanges and the over-the-counter (OTC) market.
- Long-term investors buy and hold stocks, use dollar-cost averaging to smooth out the prices they pay for stocks they buy regularly, and reinvest their dividends and buy more stock directly from companies in which they have already invested to avoid stockbroker commissions.
- Short-term speculators use techniques such as buying stock on margin and selling short.

Vocabulary Review

1. Find or create visual examples for at least ten of these vocabulary terms. Use the examples to create a collage.

- securities
- private corporation
- public corporation
- par value
- blue-chip stock
- income stock
- growth stock
- cyclical stock
- defensive stock
- large-cap stock
- capitalization
- small-cap stock
- penny stock
- bull market
- bear market
- current yield
- total return
- earnings per share
- price-earnings (PE) ratio
- securities exchange
- over-the-counter (OTC) market
- portfolio
- return
- appreciates
- engaged
- prospects
- floor

Higher Order Thinking 

2. **Compare and contrast** Identify advantages and disadvantages of a stock advisory service to evaluate a stock.
3. **Extend** Explain why corporations prefer to issue common stock to raise funds.
4. **Conceive** Describe a situation in which a stockholder might wish to exercise his or her voting rights.
5. **Role Play** Describe a situation in which preemptive rights would benefit a business owner.
6. **Theorize** The Internet enables individuals to trade their own stocks. Why might people continue to use the services of a stockbroker?
7. **Assess** Explain why a small-cap stock is more likely to be a growth stock.
8. **Defend** Should a person use long-term investment strategies to obtain a tax advantage? Why or why not?
9. **Evaluate** Is the stock market a good place to "get rich quick"? Why or why not?

College and Career Readiness

Social Studies

10. Road to Recovery When the stock market crashed in October 1929, public confidence in the markets plummeted. Investors and banks lost great amounts of money in the Great Depression that followed. For the economy to recover, it was clear that the public's faith in the capital markets needed to be restored. Congress held hearings to find solutions. Congress passed the Securities Act of 1933 and the Securities Exchange Act of 1934, which created the Securities and Exchange Commission (SEC). Research the acts and the SEC, and then write a summary that explains the mission of the SEC and what these laws were intended to do. Do you think these acts will prevent a repeat of the Great Depression? Explain your answer.

NCSS VII H Apply economic concepts and reasoning when evaluating historical and contemporary social developments and issues.

Mathematics

11. Total Return Three years ago Aryana purchased 75 shares of Toy Company for $32.00 per share. Toy Company stock pays an annual dividend of $1.25 per share each year. Aryana is willing to sell her shares only if she can realize a total return of at least $1,000. If the current market price of Toy Company is $45.00, should Aryana sell her stock based on her requirements? What would Aryana's total return be if she sold the stock at $45.00 per share?

Math Concept **Calculate Total Return** To calculate the total return on an investment, determine the sum of the current return and capital gain.

Starting Hint Subtract the purchase price per share from the selling price per share to determine the gain/loss per share.

NCTM Number and Operations Understand meanings of operations and how they relate to one another.

English Language Arts

12. Word Origins Etymology is the study of the history of words. Etymologists use text written in and about various languages to gather knowledge about how words and phrases became part of the language. For example, the early meaning of "bear market" was the practice of selling stock before actually owning it. These speculators would hope for the prices to fall before making the purchase. Eventually, the term came to mean pessimism about stock prices. Create an etymological dictionary of terms and phrases used in or inspired by the stock market: blue-chip stocks, ticker tape parade, hedging, and melting. Add any others that you find.

NCTE 6 Apply knowledge of language structure and conventions to discuss texts.

Economics

13. Institutional Investors Businesses, governments, and other institutions face decisions similar to those faced by individual investors. An institutional investor is a person or organization that trades securities in share quantities or dollar amounts so large that they qualify for preferential treatment and lower commissions. Institutional investors also face fewer regulations. What are some typical institutional investors? What is their role in the economy? What costs and benefits do they have to consider? What can you say about their tolerance for risk?

Real-World Applications

14. Risk Tolerance As you start to earn money, you should not rush into complicated investments before you are ready. Investing in low-risk choices can protect your money and help you to learn about investing. Hannah, a high school senior, has been saving money from her barista job in a savings account for two years. Her parents have suggested that she invest it to earn a greater return than she is earning on her bank account. What steps can Hannah take next in her financial planning, and what advice would you offer as she awaits her returns?

Your Financial Portfolio

Investing in Stock

Rick would like to invest in the stock market. Before he invests any money, Rick is researching a company he thinks has potential. He picked eSongz, an online music store that lets you rent or purchase mp3 players and buy songs from the company directly from its Web site. Along with the price of stock, he watches for any announcements or industry changes that may affect the stock.

Rick has studied the company's financial reports and also keeps tabs on its financial news reports. He believes eSongz will continue to be successful, but he plans to watch the stock a little longer before he makes his decision to invest.

Rick's Research
eSongz

Highest price paid per share during the past 52 weeks	$41.80
Lowest price paid per share in the past 52 weeks	$19.89
Current price paid per share	$35.35
Price-earnings (PE) ratio	20
Earnings per share	$1.78

Research

Choose a stock you would like to buy and research it. On a separate sheet of paper, create a spreadsheet using the information from your research. You can get information about a company in the financial section of major newspapers, the Internet, and from the companies themselves. You can also find information from *Standard & Poor's Stock and Bond Guide*, *Mergent's Handbook of Common Stocks*, or *Value Line Investment Survey*. What type of stock would you be interested in purchasing? Explain why. Using the financial figures you researched, do you think the company you chose to research would be a wise investment choice? Explain your answer.

CHAPTER 19

Bonds and Mutual Funds

Visual Literacy

Bonds are often used to help finance new projects. ***What types of new projects do you think are completed thanks to bonds?***

Discovery Project

Interpreting a Prospectus

Key Question

Why should you read a mutual fund prospectus before investing?

Project Goal

A good financial planner will tell you to always consult a mutual fund's prospectus before handing over your money. However, this document can be a bit overwhelming to new investors. A mutual fund prospectus provides information about the investment objectives and strategies, and details about the fund's past performance, managers, and financial information. Choose a company that offers mutual funds, such as Fidelity Investments or American Funds Investment Company, and obtain a prospectus by e-mailing, writing, calling, or searching the company's Web site for a PDF version. Thoroughly read the prospectus. Then, using the bullet list under the section Mutual Fund Prospectuses as a guide, write a summary of the information in the prospectus that a person new to investing could understand.

Ask Yourself...

- *What are the fund's investment objectives and strategies?*
- *What are the risks of investing in the fund?*
- *What should you look for in the fund's past performance?*
- *How are distributions made?*
- *What kind of fees or expenses can you expect?*
- *What can you learn about the fund's manager?*

Access and Evaluate Information

If you still need more information after reading a prospectus, what other steps can you take?

Evaluate Download an assessment rubric.

THE BIG IDEA

Understanding bonds and mutual funds will give you more choices to consider when investing your money.

ASK STANDARD & POOR'S

Mutual Funds

Q *I have about $50 a month to invest. What is a good investment choice for me?*

A Many mutual fund companies offer systematic investment programs in which you invest the same amount each month regardless of changes in the share price. As a result, your money buys more shares when prices are low and fewer shares when prices are high. Over time, this strategy can result in a lower average cost per share; however, it does not guarantee a profit or protect against a loss.

Writing Activity

Write a short persuasive report that explains why it is a good idea to invest even a small amount of money each month. Include examples of how someone who does not have a lot of money can still find ways to set aside investment money.

Reading Guide

Before You Read

The Essential Question How can reading, understanding, and analyzing bond information and mutual funds increase your potential for higher investment returns?

Main Idea

Learning how to differentiate, evaluate, and calculate the different types of bonds and mutual funds will help you make smart investment choices.

Content Vocabulary

- maturity date
- face value
- debenture
- mortgage bond
- convertible bond
- sinking fund
- serial bonds
- registered bond
- coupon bond
- bearer bond
- zero-coupon bond
- municipal bond
- investment-grade bonds
- yield
- closed-end fund
- exchange-traded fund
- open-end fund
- net asset value (NAV)
- load fund
- no-load fund
- income dividends

Academic Vocabulary

You will see these words in your reading and on your tests.

- premium
- default
- metropolitan
- speculative
- compensated
- holding
- exhausted
- liquidate

Graphic Organizer

Before you read this chapter, create an organizer like the one shown. As you read, write down the five questions you need to consider when identifying your investment goals.

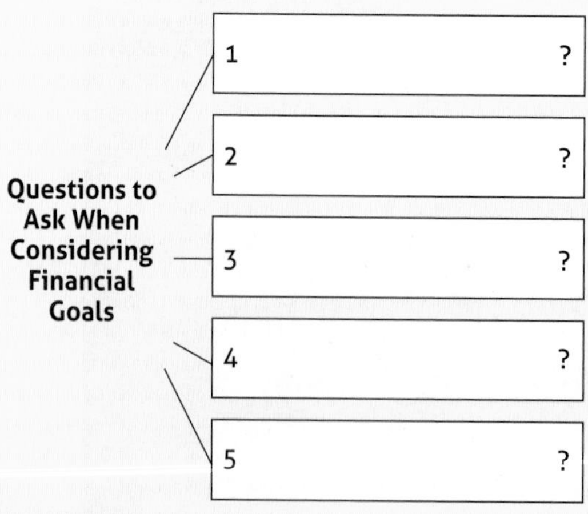

 glencoe.com Print this graphic organizer.

Standards

Academic

Mathematics

NCTM Number and Operations Compute fluently and make reasonable estimates.

NCTM Connections Recognize and apply mathematics in contexts outside of mathematics.

NCTM Problem Solving Solve problems that arise in mathematics and in other contexts.

English Language Arts

NCTE 4 Use written language to communicate effectively.

NCTE 5 Use different writing process elements to communicate effectively.

NCTE 12 Use language to accomplish individual purposes.

Science

NSES F Develop an understanding of personal and community health; population growth; natural resources; environmental quality; natural and human-induced hazards; science and technology in local, national, and global challenges.

NCTM *National Council of Teachers of Mathematics*
NCTE *National Council of Teachers of English*
NCSS *National Council for the Social Studies*
NSES *National Science Education Standards*

College & Career READINESS

Common Core

Reading Determine central ideas or themes of a text and analyze their development; summarize the key supporting details and ideas.

Writing Write routinely over extended time frames (time for research, reflection, and revision) and shorter time frames (a single sitting or a day or two) for a range of tasks, purposes, and audiences.

Corporate and Government Bonds

Corporate Bonds

What is a corporate bond?

When you buy a corporate bond, you are basically loaning money to a corporation. As discussed previously, a corporate bond is a corporation's written pledge to repay a bondholder (the person who bought the bond) a specified amount of money with interest. The bond's interest rate, maturity date, and face value are stated on the bond. The **maturity date** is the date when a bond will be repaid. The **face value** is the dollar amount that the bondholder will receive at the bond's maturity. Typically, the face value of a corporate bond is $1,000. However, corporate bonds can have face values as high as $50,000. Between the date when you buy a bond and the maturity date, the corporation pays you annual interest at the rate stated on the bond. Interest is usually paid semiannually (twice a year). By multiplying the face value by the interest rate, you can calculate how much interest you would earn each year.

At the maturity date, you can cash in the bond and receive a check in the amount of the bond's face value. Maturity dates for bonds can range from 1 to 30 years. Maturities for corporate bonds are classified as short term (less than 5 years), intermediate term (5 to 15 years), and long term (more than 15 years).

Why Corporations Sell Bonds

Corporations sell bonds to raise money when it is difficult or impossible to sell stock. Companies also often use bonds simply to finance regular business activities. Selling bonds can also reduce the amount of tax a corporation must pay because the interest paid to bondholders is tax-deductible.

A corporation may sell both bonds and stocks to help pay for its activities. However, the corporation's responsibility to investors is different for bonds and for stocks. Bondholders must be repaid at a future date for their investments. Stockholders do not have to be repaid. Companies are required to pay interest on bonds. They can choose whether to pay dividends to their stockholders. Finally, if a corporation files for bankruptcy, bondholders' claims to assets are paid before the claims of stockholders.

Reading Check

Distinguish How is a corporation's responsibility to investors different for bonds and for stocks?

Section Objectives

- **Describe** the types of corporate bonds.
- **Identify** the reasons corporations sell bonds.
- **Explain** why investors buy corporate bonds.
- **Discuss** the reasons governments issue bonds.
- **Classify** the types of government bonds.

As You Read

Consider Would investing in corporate bonds be a good way to reach your financial goals? Why or why not?

GO FIGURE Mathematics

A Bond's Annual Interest

The interest on a bond is paid twice a year. By calculating the annual interest on your bond, you will be able to determine how much money you will earn on the bond each year.

EXAMPLE Suppose that you purchase a $1,000 Mobil Corporation bond. The interest rate for the bond is 8.5 percent (8.5%). How much annual interest would you earn on this bond?

Formula Face Value × Interest Rate = Annual Interest

Solution $1,000 × 8.5% or .085 = $85

You would receive interest of $85 a year from Mobil, paid in two installments of $42.50.

Your Turn

If you purchased two $2,000 bonds that had an interest rate of 7 percent, how much annual interest would you earn?

Types of Corporate Bonds

What are the advantages of the various bond types?

There are several types of corporate bonds including: debentures, mortgage bonds, subordinated debentures, and convertible bonds.

Debentures

Most corporate bonds are debentures. A **debenture** is a bond that is backed only by the reputation of the issuing corporation, rather than by its assets. Investors buy this type of bond because they believe that the company, or corporation, that issues them is on solid financial ground. Investors expect the company to repay the face value of the bond and make interest payments until the bond matures.

Subordinated Debenture A subordinated debenture is a type of unsecured bond that gives bondholders a claim to interest payments and assets of the corporation only after all other bondholders have been paid. Because the level of risk is higher, investors usually receive higher interest rates.

Mortgage Bonds

A bond issue occurs when a company makes available a quantity of bonds at one time. To make these bonds more appealing to conservative investors, a corporation may also issue mortgage bonds. A **mortgage bond**, sometimes referred to as a secured bond, is a bond that is backed by the assets of a corporation. A mortgage bond is safer because it is backed by corporate assets. These assets, such as equipment, can be sold to repay the mortgage bondholders if necessary. Mortgage bonds usually earn less interest than debentures because their risk to the investor is lower.

Russia

First Bond Issued in 12 Years

Government bonds in the United States are often attractive to people because they come with such a low risk of default. This is not the case for all governments though. In fact, Russia had a financial crisis in 1998 and defaulted on all of its domestic debt. However, in the last decade, the country has followed a policy of saving oil profits and has found itself in a cash-strong position. In fact, the government has no need to borrow money as it has enough in gold and foreign currency reserves to finance its deficit. However, in 2010, the government decided to borrow to diversify its sources of deficit financing, to set a low benchmark for commercial borrowing, and to leave intact the sovereign wealth fund's role as a shock absorber for future oil price collapses. This was done by selling Eurobonds, an international bond that is denominated in a currency not native to the country where it is issued, worth $5.5 billion. This significant event marks the return of Russia to international capital markets.

Critical Thinking

1. **Expand** Do you think the bonds issued by Russia would be attractive to foreign investors? Explain your answer.
2. **Relate** If you were going to buy government bonds, would you consider purchasing them from a foreign country to get better percentage points?

DATABYTES

Capital
Moscow

Population
139,390,205

Language
Russian

Currency
Russian ruble

Gross Domestic Product (GDP)
$1.232 trillion

GDP per capita
$15, 100

Industry
Mining and coal production, oil, gas, chemicals, and metals; machine building from rolling mills to high-performance aircraft and space vehicles; defense industries including radar, missile production, and advanced electronic components, shipbuilding; road and rail transportation equipment; communications equipment; agricultural machinery, tractors, and construction equipment; electric power generating and transmitting equipment; medical and scientific instruments; consumer durables, textiles, foodstuffs, handicrafts

Agriculture
Grain, sugar beets, sunflower seed, vegetables, fruits; beef, milk

Exports
Petroleum and petroleum products, natural gas, grain, wood and wood products, metals, chemicals

Natural Resources
Oil, natural gas, coal, and many strategic minerals, timber

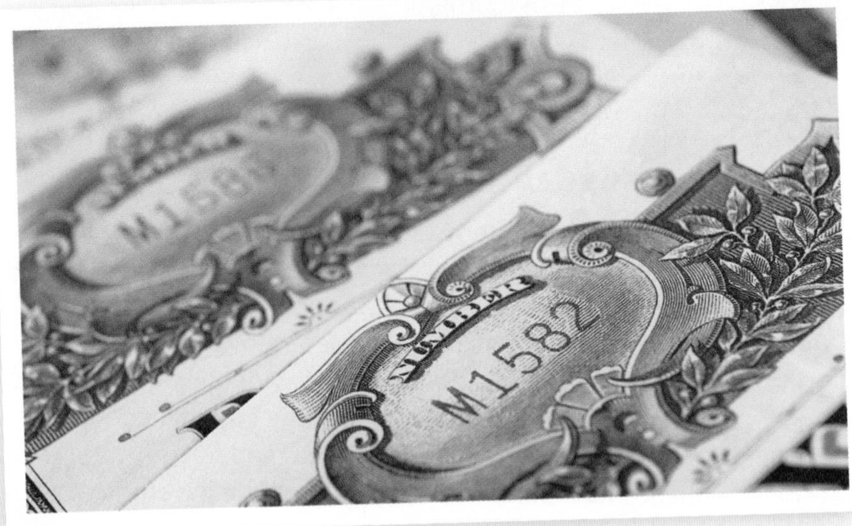

A Corporate Bond
Most corporate bonds are held electronically for faster transactions. *Why would someone want an actual corporate bond certificate?*

Convertible Bonds

A **convertible bond** is a bond that an investor can trade for shares of the corporation's common stock. Because of the unique flexibility that it offers, the interest rate on a convertible bond is often 1 to 2 percent lower than interest rates on other corporate bonds. Many bondholders choose not to convert their bonds into stock even when stock values are high. As the market value of a company's common stock increases, the market value of the company's convertible bonds also increases.

Methods Corporations Use to Repay Bonds

Today most corporate bonds are "callable," which means they have a call feature that allows a corporation to "call in" or buy back bonds from current bondholders before the maturity date. Corporations may sell stock, use profits, or sell new bonds to fund a call. For example, suppose that Mobil Corporation issued bonds at 8.5 percent, but later, interest rates on comparable bonds dropped to 4.5 percent. Mobil might decide to call the bonds issued at 8.5 percent, and they would not have to pay bondholders interest at that high rate.

Premiums Usually, companies agree not to call their bonds for the first five to ten years after the bonds are issued. When they do call their bonds, they may have to pay bondholders a **premium,** or an additional amount above the face value of the bond. The amount of the premium is stated in a *bond indenture*, which details all the conditions pertaining to a particular bond issue.

Sinking Funds A corporation may use one of two methods to make sure that it has enough funds to pay off a bond issue. First, the corporation may set up a sinking fund. A **sinking fund** is a fund to which a corporation makes deposits for the purpose of paying back a bond issue. If the bond indenture states that the corporation will deposit money in a sinking fund, the company will be able to repay its bonds.

Serial Bonds Second, a corporation may issue serial bonds. **Serial bonds** are bonds issued at the same time but which mature on different dates. For example, Seaside Productions issued $100 million of serial bonds for a 20-year period. None of the bonds matured during the first ten years. Therefore, during that time the company did not have to pay anything but the interest owed on the outstanding bonds. Instead, Seaside Productions used the funds raised by selling the bonds to grow its business. After that, only 10 percent of the bonds matured each year until all the bonds were retired at the end of 20 years. That allowed Seaside Productions to repay its bonds a few at a time instead of having to repay all $100 million at once.

Reading Check

Recall What is meant by the term "callable"?

Why Investors Buy Bonds

Why are bonds considered safe investments?

Many corporate and government bonds are considered safe investments. Some investors use corporate and government bonds to diversify their investment portfolios (all the securities held by an investor). Bonds offer you three other benefits:

- Most bonds provide interest income.
- Bonds may increase in value, depending on the bond market, overall interest rates in the economy, and the reputation and assets of the issuer.
- The face value of a bond is repaid when it reaches maturity.

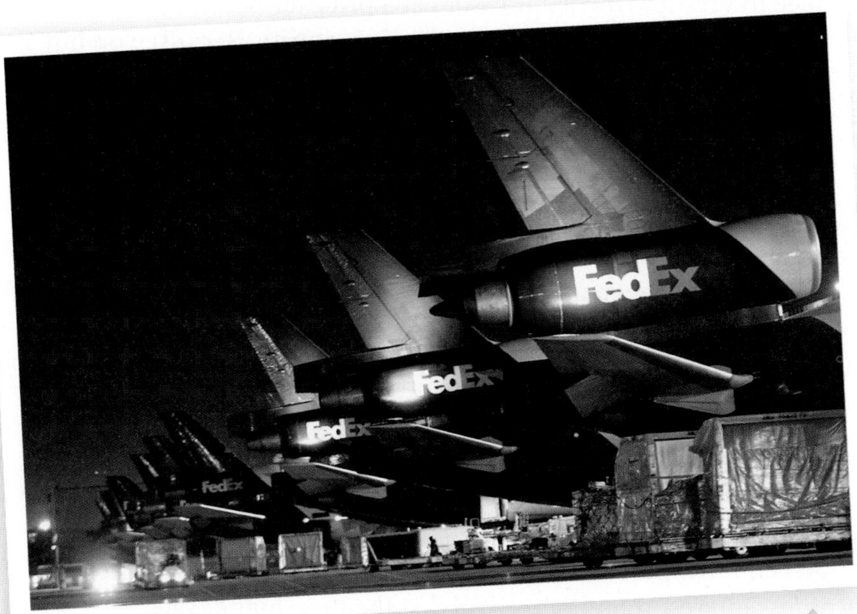

Back-Up Plan
Mortgage bonds are backed by all of a company's assets, like these planes. The average mortgage bond tends to yield a lower rate of return than debenture bonds that are backed only by the corporation's reputation. *Why would an investor want to buy a mortgage bond?*

COMMON CENTS

Savings Mind-Set
It is exciting when you get a raise or finally pay off a loan. You know you have more money available. Be a smart saver—stick to your current budget and stash that newfound money in your savings or investment account.

Concept Application

If you received a $30 per week raise in net pay and were paid four times per month, how much "extra" money would you have in ten months from February to November? Would you save or invest that money? Why or why not?

Interest Income

Bondholders usually receive interest payments every six months. The dollar amount of annual interest is determined by multiplying the interest rate by the face value of the bond. The method used by a company to pay you interest depends on the type of corporate bond you purchase:

- Registered bond
- Coupon bond
- Bearer bond
- Zero-coupon bond

Registered Bonds A **registered bond** is a bond registered in the owner's name by the company that issues the bond. This ensures that only the owner can collect money from the bond. Interest checks for registered bonds are mailed directly to the bondholder.

Coupon Bonds A registered **coupon bond** is a bond that is registered in the owner's name for only the face value and not for interest. This type of bond comes with detachable coupons. Because the face value of the bond is registered, only the bond's owner can collect the face value. However, anyone who holds the coupons can collect the interest. To collect an interest payment on a registered coupon bond, you simply present one of the detachable coupons to the issuing corporation or to the appropriate bank or broker.

Bearer Bonds A **bearer bond** is a bond that is not registered in the investor's name. As with registered coupon bonds, the owner of a bearer bond must present coupons in order to collect interest payments. Anyone who has physical possession of the bonds or their coupons can collect on them. A few bearer bonds are still in circulation, but they are no longer issued by corporations.

Zero-Coupon Bond A **zero-coupon bond** is a bond that does not produce interest payments. It is sold at a price far below its face value, but it is redeemed for its full face value at maturity. Because you buy it for less than its face value, you automatically make a profit when your zero-coupon bond is repaid.

Market Value of a Bond

Many beginning investors think that a $1,000 bond is always worth $1,000. Actually, the market value of a corporate bond may fluctuate before its maturity date. Usually, shifts in bond prices result from changes in overall interest rates in the economy.

For example, suppose that Vanessa has a bond with a 7.5 percent interest rate. If overall interest rates fall below 7.5 percent, Vanessa's bond will go up in market value because it earns more interest than bonds issued at the new lower rate. If overall interest rates rise above 7.5 percent, the market value of Vanessa's bond will fall because it earns less interest than bonds issued at the new, higher rate.

When a bond is selling for less than its face value, it is said to be selling at a *discount*. When a bond is selling for more than its face value, it is said to be selling at a *premium*. You can calculate a bond's approximate market value by using a formula that compares the bond's interest rate to that of similar new corporate bonds. (See **Go Figure.**) Find the dollar amount of the bond's annual interest by multiplying the face value by the annual interest rate. Then, compute the bond's approximate market value by dividing the dollar amount of annual interest by the interest rate of comparable new corporate bonds.

The market value of a bond may also be affected by the financial condition of the company that issues it. In addition, the law of supply and demand changes in the economy and can affect a bond's value.

Repayment at Maturity

Corporate bonds are repaid at maturity. After you purchase a bond, you have two choices. You can keep the bond until its maturity date and then cash it in. You can also sell the bond at any time to another investor. In either case, the value of the bond is closely tied to the corporation's ability to repay it. Other investors will pay more money to get a quality bond that has solid prospects of repayment.

Reading Check

Define Explain *discount* and *premium* in terms of face value.

reality bytes

Security in an Uncertain Time

Just like paper money, stock certificates, corporate bonds, and U.S. Treasury bills have value and can be counterfeited. Since 1877, the Bureau of Engraving and Printing (BEP) has been the sole maker of U.S. currency and other financial instruments, including U.S. Treasury bills, notes, and savings bonds. The BEP has been committed to advanced security for more than a century.

A Typical Bond Transaction

Where can you purchase corporate bonds?

Most bonds are sold through full-service brokerage firms, discount brokerage firms, or online. If you use a full-service brokerage firm, your account executive should provide information and advice about bond investments. If you use a discount brokerage firm or buy bonds online, you must do your own research. However, you will probably pay a lower commission. If you buy or sell a bond through an account executive or brokerage firm, you should expect to pay a commission, and you should also expect to pay commissions when you sell bonds.

Purchasing in Primary and Secondary Markets

Bonds are purchased in the same way as stocks. Corporate bonds may be purchased in the primary or secondary markets. In the primary market, you purchase financial securities from an investment banker representing the corporation that issued them. In the secondary market, you trade financial securities with other investors. Corporate bonds issued by large companies are traded on the New York Bond Exchange and American Bond Exchange.

GO FIGURE Mathematics

Approximate Market Value of a Bond

The market value of a bond can change many times before its maturity date. Calculating the approximate market value of a bond can help you determine what your bond will be worth at its maturity date.

EXAMPLE Shawn purchased a New York Telephone bond that pays 4.5 percent interest based on a face value of $1,000. Comparable new corporate bond issues are paying 7 percent. How much is Shawn's bond worth?

Formula Dollar Amount of Annual Interest/Interest Rate of Comparable New Corporate Bonds = Approximate Market Value

Solution

A. Find the dollar amount of annual interest.
Face Value of Bond × Annual Interest Rate = Dollar Amount of Annual Interest $1,000 × 4.5% or .045 = $45 The dollar amount of annual interest is $45.

B. Solve for approximate market value.
Dollar Amount of Annual Interest/Interest Rate of Comparable New Corporate Bonds = Approximate Market Value
$45/7% or .07 = $642.86

The approximate market value of Shawn's New York Telephone bond is $642.86.

Your Turn

You bought two $1,000 bonds, each with an interest rate of 5.5 percent. New corporate bonds being issued are paying 8 percent interest. What is the approximate market value of your bonds?

Sample Bond Transaction **Figure 1** shows an example of a bond transaction—Ms. Mansfield's Borden bond transaction. On October 8, 1995, Ms. Mansfield purchased an 8.375 percent corporate bond issued by Borden, Inc. She paid $680 for the bond plus a $10 commission. On October 8, 2006, she sold it at its current market value of $1,030 minus a $10 commission ($1,030 − $10 = $1,020). After paying commissions, Ms. Mansfield had a capital gain of $330. The market value of the bond increased because overall interest rates declined during the time she owned the bond. Borden also established a good business reputation during this period, making the bond more secure and, therefore, more valuable.

Ms. Mansfield also made money on her Borden bond by collecting interest payments. For each year she owned the bond, Borden paid her $83.75. When she sold the bond, she had received interest payments totaling $921.25. In total, she had a total return of $1,251.25.

Reading Check

List What are three options for purchasing corporate bonds?

Government Bonds and Securities

Why does the government issue bonds and securities?

Like private corporations, federal, state, and local governments issue bonds to help raise the money they need to operate.

The federal government sells bonds and other securities to help fund its regular activities and services, and to finance the national debt. U.S. government securities are considered to be almost risk-free. They are backed by the full faith and credit of the United States government. However, because they have a low risk of **default,** failure to pay debts, government bonds offer lower interest rates.

Treasury Bills, Notes, and Bonds

The U.S. Department of the Treasury issues five basic types of securities: Treasury bills (T-bills), Treasury notes, Treasury bonds, Treasury Inflation-Protected Securities (TIPS), and U.S. government savings bonds.

You can buy Treasury bills, bonds, notes, and TIPS online through Treasury Direct, which is a Web site operated by the Department of the Treasury. When you buy through Treasury Direct, you do not have to pay a commission. You can also buy these securities through banks or brokers, which charge a commission for their services. U.S. government savings bonds can also be purchased through Treasury Direct, commercial banks, savings and loan associations, or other financial institutions.

FIGURE 1 **Ms. Mansfield's Borden, Inc., Bond Transaction**

Transaction Fees Ms. Mansfield paid a commission fee when she bought her bond and again when she sold it. *How did these fees affect the cost of her investment and the profit she made from selling the bond?*

Interest, 8.375 percent; maturity date, 2019; purchased October 8, 1995; sold October 8, 2006.

Costs when purchased	
1 bond @ $680	$680
Plus commission	+ 10
Total investment	$690
Return when sold	
1 bond @ $1,030	$1,030
Minus commission	– 10
Dollar return	$1,020

Transaction summary	
Dollar return	$1,020.00
Minus total investment	– 690.00
Profit from bond sale	$330.00
Plus interest ($ 83.75 for 11 years)	+ 921.25
Total return on the transaction	$1,251.25

Treasury Securities
The Treasury Direct Web site provides information on United States Treasury securities. *Why might United States Treasury securities be a good investment option?*

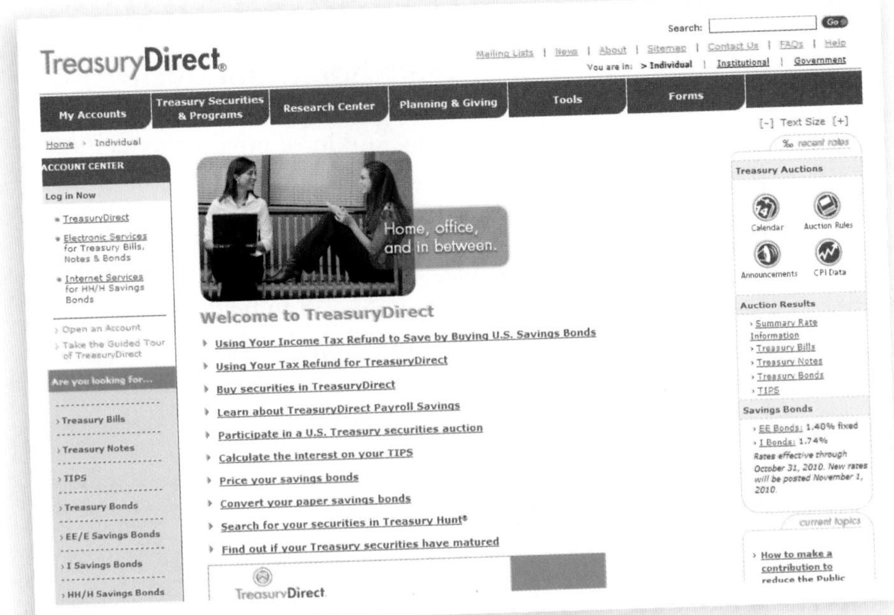

You can hold U.S. government securities until maturity or sell them before maturity. You must pay federal income tax on the interest; however, this interest is exempt from state and local taxation.

Treasury Bills Treasury bills are sold in units of $1,000. They may reach maturity in 4 weeks, 13 weeks, 26 weeks, or 52 weeks. T-bills are discounted securities. That means that the actual purchase price you pay when you buy a T-bill is less than the face value of the T-bill. On the maturity date, you receive the full face value of the T-bill. A T-bill held until maturity can be reinvested in another bill or can be paid to the owner. To figure out the dollar amount of return on a T-bill, just subtract the purchase price of the T-bill from the face value.

After you have determined the dollar amount of return on your T-bill, you can calculate the rate of return by dividing the dollar amount of return by the purchase price. (See **Go Figure.**)

Treasury Notes Treasury notes are issued in $1,000 units with a maturity of between one and ten years. Interest rates for Treasury notes are slightly higher than those for Treasury bills because investors must wait longer to get their money back. Interest for Treasury notes is paid every six months.

Treasury Bonds Treasury bonds are issued in minimum units of $100 and have a 30-year maturity. Because of the length of time to maturity, interest rates for Treasury bonds are usually higher than those for Treasury bills or Treasury notes. Like interest on Treasury notes, interest on Treasury bonds is paid every six months.

Treasury Inflation-Protected Securities (TIPS) Treasury inflation-protected securities (TIPS) are sold in minimum units of $100 with additional increments of $100 above the minimum. Currently, TIPS are sold with 5-, 10-, or 20-year maturities.

The principal of Treasury inflation-protected securities increases with inflation and decreases with deflation, as measured by the consumer price index (CPI). When TIPS mature you are paid the adjusted or original principal, whichever is greater.

Series EE Savings Bonds As you learned previously, the federal government also offers savings bonds called Series EE Savings Bonds. The purchase price for a Series EE bond is one-half of its face value. For example, a $100 bond costs $50. You can redeem a savings bond anytime from 6 months to 30 years after you purchase it. You receive the amount that you paid for it plus interest. Series EE bonds can accumulate interest for up to 30 years. The interest on Series EE bonds is not taxed by state or local governments. You do not pay federal taxes on the interest until you cash in the bond.

Series I Savings Bonds The federal government offers other types of savings bonds, too. The most popular bonds, Series I bonds, are inflation-indexed. This means that Series I bonds pay a fixed interest rate that is lower than the rate of traditional savings bonds, but they also pay a variable rate that increases with inflation.

The inflation rate is measured by the Consumer Price Index, which measures the change in cost of a fixed group of products and services such as gasoline, food, and automobiles. The inflation rate for Series I bonds is recalculated twice a year. Series I bonds pay interest for up to 30 years. If you redeem the bond less than five years from the date purchased, there is a penalty of three months of earnings.

Reading Check

Summarize How can you purchase Treasury bills, Treasury notes, Treasury bonds, TIPS, and U.S. government savings bonds?

GO FIGURE Mathematics

Dollar Amount of Return on a T-Bill

The purchase price of a Treasury bill is less than its full face value. By calculating the return you will receive at the T-bill's maturity date, you will be able to determine how much money you earned on your investment.

EXAMPLE Suppose that you buy a 52-week T-bill for $950. On the maturity date, you receive $1,000. What is the dollar amount of return on the T-bill?

Formula Face Value − Purchase Price = Dollar Amount of Return

Solution $1,000 − $950 = $50

The dollar amount of return on your T-bill would be $50.

Your Turn

The maturity date of your 13-week T-bill is coming up. If you paid $1,500 for a T-bill with a face value of $2,000, what is the dollar amount of your return?

GO FIGURE Mathematics

Rate of Return on a T-Bill

Calculating the rate of return on your T-bill will help you determine whether the T-bill is a good addition to your investment portfolio.

EXAMPLE The dollar amount of return on your T-bill is $50. What is the rate of return on the T-bill?

Formula Dollar Amount of Return ÷ Purchase Price = Rate of Return

Solution $50 ÷ $950 = .0526 or 5.26%

The rate of return on your T-bill is 5.26 percent.

Your Turn

If the dollar amount of return on your T-bill is $500 and you paid $1,500 for it, what is the rate of return on your T-bill?

Bonds Issued by Federal Agencies

What are agency bonds?

In addition to the securities issued by the Department of the Treasury, bonds are issued by other federal agencies as well. Agency bonds, such as the participation certificates issued by the Federal National Mortgage Association (sometimes referred to as *Fannie Mae*) and the Government National Mortgage Association (sometimes referred to as *GinnieMae*), are almost completely risk-free. However, they offer a slightly higher interest rate than securities issued by the treasury department and have an average maturity of about 12 years. Generally, their minimum denomination is $25,000. Securities issued by federal agencies have maturities ranging from 1 year to 30 years, with an average life of about 12 years.

Reading Check

Name What are the two federal agencies that issue bonds?

Bonds Issued by State and Local Governments

What are the two classifications of municipal bonds?

A **municipal bond,** sometimes called a *muni*, is a security issued by a state or local government (town, city, or county) to pay for its ongoing activities. These bonds may also pay for major projects, such as the building of airports, schools, and highways. You can buy municipal bonds directly from the government that issues them or through an account executive.

State and local government securities are classified as either general obligation bonds or revenue bonds. A general obligation bond is a bond that is backed by the full faith and credit of the government that issued it. A revenue bond is a bond that is repaid from the income generated by the project it is designed to finance. For example, a municipal sports arena would generate profits that would repay the investors who bought the bond to build the arena.

Although these bonds are relatively safe, on rare occasions, governments have defaulted, or failed to repay, their bonds. If a government defaults, investors could lose millions of dollars.

Insured Municipal Bonds

If the risk of default worries you, you might consider buying insured municipal bonds. Some states offer to guarantee payments on these selected securities. Also, three large private insurers guarantee such bonds: MBIA, Inc.; the Financial Security Assurance Corporation; and the American Municipal Bond Assurance Corporation. Because of the reduced risk of default, insured municipal securities usually carry a slightly lower interest rate than uninsured bonds.

The interest on municipal bonds may be exempt from federal taxes. Tax-exempt status depends on how the funds generated by the bonds are used. Before you invest in a particular municipal bond, find out whether the interest that you will receive from it is taxable.

Like a corporate bond, a municipal bond may be callable by the government that issued it. In most cases, the municipality that issues the bond agrees not to call it for the first ten years. If your municipal bond is not called, you can hold the bond until the maturity date or sell it to another investor.

New and Improved State and local governments often finance major projects, such as schools, airports, and highways, by selling municipal bonds. *What is a possible disadvantage of investing in municipal bonds?*

Assessment

Review Key Concepts

1. **List** Describe the types of corporate bonds.
2. **Identify** Why do corporations sell bonds?
3. **Explain** Why do investors buy corporate bonds?
4. **Describe** Discuss the reasons the government issues bonds.
5. **Classify** What are the types of government bonds?

Higher Order Thinking H.O.T.

6. **Relate** Why do you think yields on callable bonds tend to be higher than yields on non-callable bonds?

English Language Arts

7. **Personal Goals and the Community** The county in which Saundra lives is selling bonds to finance a new sports arena. Saundra knows that a lot of people would enjoy the arena, and it could bring in much needed revenue to help her financially unstable community. However, she is not sure that bonds are a good investment. Use what you have learned about personal satisfaction and financial goals in previous chapters to help Saundra decide what to do. Should she buy the bonds to help improve her community and her own personal living conditions, or should she invest her money in another way that has a better chance of helping her meet her financial goals? Explain your reasoning.

NCTE 12 Use language to accomplish individual purposes.

Mathematics

8. **Bond Market Value** Julian owns two corporate bonds with face values of $2,000 each. The bonds pay interest twice per year at an annual interest rate of 7.5 percent. What is the total interest that Julian will earn each year from his bond holdings? If comparable new bond issues are paying 6.75 percent annual interest, did Julian's bonds increase or decrease in value? Explain your answer. Based on the interest rates of the new bond issues, what is the approximate market value of Julian's bonds now?

Math Concept **Calculate Annual Interest and Approximate Market Value** To calculate the annual interest, multiply the face value by the annual interest rate. Approximate market value can be calculated by dividing the dollar amount of annual interest by the interest rate on comparable new bond issues.

Starting Hint Determine the annual interest earned by first multiplying the face value of the bond by its annual interest rate. Repeat this process for each bond held and add the sum of interest earned for all bonds.

NCTM Number and Operations Compute fluently and make reasonable estimates.

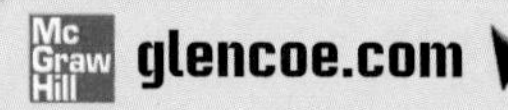

Check your answers.

Determining Investment Value

How do you determine the investment value of a bond?

Before you make a decision to include bonds in your investment portfolio, you must learn how to accurately determine the investment value of a bond. By understanding bond price quotations, researching various sources of information on bonds, checking bond ratings, and calculating the yield of your bond investment, you will be able to determine whether a bond is a good investment.

Section Objectives

- **Define** bond price quotations.
- **List** information resources for selecting bond investments.
- **Categorize** and describe bond ratings.
- **Explain** how to determine a bond's yield.

As You Read

Examine Do you think buying government bonds would free you from watching your investments?

Bond Price Quotations

Before you buy or sell bonds, you should become familiar with bond price quotations. Not all local newspapers contain bond price quotations, but many **metropolitan,** or large urban area, newspapers publish complete information on the subject. Two other valuable sources for bond information are *The Wall Street Journal and Barron's.*

In a bond price quotation, the price of a bond is given as a percentage of its face value. Remember that a bond's face value is usually $1,000. To find the current market value, or price, for a bond, you must multiply the face value ($1,000) by the price quotation given in the newspaper. For example, a price quoted as "84" means that the current market value is 84 percent of the face value. Therefore, the selling price is $840 ($1,000 × 84% = $840). Purchases and sales of bonds are reported in tables. (See **Figure 2.**)

For government bonds, most financial publications include two price quotations: the bid price and the asked price. The bid price is the price a dealer is willing to pay for a government security. It represents the amount that a seller could receive for a government bond. The asked price is the price at which a dealer is willing to sell a government security. It represents the amount for which a buyer could purchase the bond. Newspaper bond sections also provide information about interest rates, maturity dates, and yields.

Sources of Information on Bonds

As a bondholder, you should always be aware of the financial stability of the issuer of your bonds. The most important questions are:

- Will the bond be repaid at maturity?
- Will you receive interest payments until maturity?

To help answer these questions, annual reports, the Internet, business magazines, and government reports are good resources.

FIGURE 2 Corporate Bond Information

Bond Values Newspaper bond quotations indicate a bond's interest, yield, and price. *What was the last price of the Target (TGT) bond?*

Corporate Bonds

Monday, January 10, 2005

Forty most active fixed-coupon corporate bonds

COMPANY (TICKER)	COUPON	MATURITY	LAST PRICE	LAST YIELD	*EST SPREAD	UST	EST $ VOL (000's)
General Motors Acceptance (GM)	6.750	Dec 01, 2014	97.856	7.053	278	10	245,352
General Motors (GM)	8.375	Jul 15, 2033	101.029	8.280	346	30	242.397
General Motors Acceptance (GM)	5.625	May 15, 2009	98.754	5.953	222	5	111,727
Ford Motor Credit (F)	7.000	Oct 01, 2013	103.380	6.484	221	10	104,831
Encana Holdings Finance (ECACN)	5.800	May 01, 2014	106.151	4.965	67	10	96,000
Target (TGT)	5.875	Mar 01, 2012	109.037	4.385	10	10	95,148
General Motors Acceptance (GM)	6.875	Sep 15, 2011	100.858	6.711	298	5	94,355
General Electric (GE)	5.000	Feb 01, 2013	102.338	4.648	37	10	93,211

Look at the bond quotation highlighted above. Each column includes information about this bond. Reading from left to right:

Column 1: Company (Ticker)—The name of the issuing firm is Target. Its abbreviated name is TGT.

Column 2: Coupon—This bond's current yield, or return, based on today's market price is 5.875 percent.

Column 3: Maturity—The date this bond matures is March 1, 2012.

Column 4: Last Price—The current market price of this bond at the close of trading on this day was 109.037 percent of the bond's face value.

Column 8: Estimated $ Volume—On this day, 95,148,000 bonds of this issue were traded.

Annual Reports Annual reports provide detailed financial information about a company and its products, services, activities, goals, and future plans. You will also find news about the company's position in its industry and the industry's major trends. A typical annual report contains the following sections:

- Letter to stockholders from the chief executive officer
- Company highlights for the year
- Detailed company review for the year
- Financial statements

Economics and You

Bonds

The United States government provides many services, such as protection, regulation, and assistance for those who need help. To provide protection the government finances all branches of military service and special programs such as the Central Intelligence Agency (CIA). Regulatory agencies set standards for worker and consumer safety and food consumption. They also provide the guidelines for a competitive market place. Social programs, like Medicare and Medicaid provide assistance. All of these services cost money. Money is generated through taxation and the sale of government bonds. The Securities and Exchange Commission is the regulatory agency that oversees the bond market.

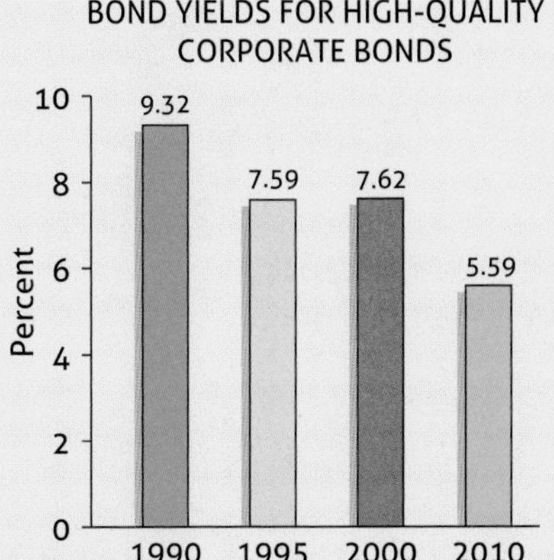

Personal Finance Connection You can elect to buy bonds issued by corporations and/or by the government. Since bonds are loans made to companies and to the government, you will earn interest on them. Federal government bonds are virtually risk free, which makes them a good investment for younger people without investment experience.

Critical Thinking A bridge in your town is very old, so the town wants to issue a municipal bond to finance its reconstruction. You also have three elementary schools that have old, leaking roofs that pose a safety hazard for children; so the school board wants to issue a bond to replace them. If you only had enough money to invest in one of those projects, which bond would you purchase? Explain your decision.

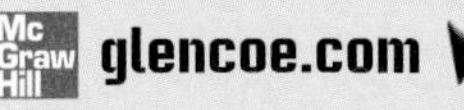

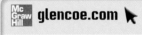

Activity Download an Economics and You Worksheet Activity.

- Notes to financial statements
- Independent auditors' report
- List of directors and officers
- Investor information

To receive an annual report, call, e-mail, or write to the corporation's headquarters and request one. Many large companies have toll-free telephone numbers for customers. You may also find annual reports for major corporations on the Internet or in the reference section of some large libraries.

As you read an annual report, look for signs of financial strength or weakness and ask:

- Is the firm profitable?
- Are sales increasing?
- Are long-term liabilities increasing?
- How might the company's current activities and future plans affect its ability to repay bonds?

The Internet You can access a wealth of information about bond investments on the Internet. You will find answers to many of your questions on corporate Web sites, which typically offer information about the particular company's financial performance. Some sites even include financial information from past years, which allows you to compare one year's performance with another's.

Other sites are devoted to general information about bonds. However, some bond Web sites charge a fee for their research and recommendations.

When investing in bonds, you can use the Internet to obtain price information on specific bond issues to track investments. If you live in a small town or rural area without access to newspapers that provide bond coverage, the Internet can be a good source of current bond prices. You also might visit Web sites operated by Standard & Poor's, Moody's, or Mergent to obtain detailed information about both corporate and government bonds. While you may be asked to pay a fee to access some information on these sites, much of the same information may be available in printed form at a college or public library.

Once your research is completed, you can even use the Internet to purchase bonds, to monitor the value of your bonds, and to manage your investments. If you trade bonds online, you might pay lower commissions than you would if you used a full-service brokerage firm.

Business Magazines Another way to research possible bond investments is by reading business magazines. They provide information about the overall economy and give detailed financial data about companies that issue bonds.

Government Reports and Research You can also consult reports and research published by the government to track the nation's economy. This information is available in printed form and on the Internet. If you want to buy United States Treasury bills or notes, or U.S. savings bonds, check Web sites run by the Federal Reserve System or Treasury Direct. In addition, you can review information from the Securities and Exchange Commission by accessing its Web site. State and local governments will also give you information about municipal bond issues upon request.

Bond Ratings

Before you invest in a particular corporate or municipal bond, you should check its rating. This rating will give you a good idea of the quality and risk associated with that bond. Bond issues are rated or evaluated by independent rating companies. These companies assign to each bond a rating based on the financial stability of its issuer. Two of the best-known sources of bond ratings are *Moody's Bond Survey*, published by Moody's Investors Service, Inc., and *Standard & Poor's Stock and Bond Guide*, published by Standard & Poor's. Investors rely on this information when making investment decisions. You can also find bond ratings on the Internet, in financial magazines, and at your public library.

FIGURE 3 **Bond Ratings**

Know Your AAABC's Savvy investors check a bond's rating before they make any purchasing decisions. *Is there any reason an investor might consider bonds rated C or D? Why or why not?*

Quality	Standard & Poor's	Description
High-grade	AAA	Bonds that are judged to be of the best quality. They have the lowest risk and the most secure interest and principal payments.
	AA	Bonds that are judged to be of high quality by all standards. Protection of principal and interest payments is only slightly less than the best.
Medium-grade	A	Bonds that have many favorable investment attributes and adequate security.
	BBB	Bonds that are neither highly protected nor poorly secured.
Speculative	BB	Bonds that have some risky elements. Often their protection of principal and interest payment is very moderate.
	B	Bonds that lack the characteristics of a desirable investment. Investors cannot be sure that interest and principal will be paid in the future.
Default	CCC	Bonds that are of poor standing. They are currently unlikely to be repaid.
	CC	Bonds that are highly risky.
	C	Standard & Poor's rating given to bonds whose issuers have filed for bankruptcy.
	D	Bond issues that are in default, or are failing to make payments.

As you can see in **Figure 3,** bond ratings are generally categorized from AAA (the highest—the best) to D (the lowest—the worst). The top four categories (Standard & Poor's AAA, AA, A, and BBB, comparable to Moody's Aaa, Aa, A, and Baa) include investment-grade bonds. **Investment-grade bonds** are bonds that are issued by financially stable companies or municipalities. They are suitable for conservative investors because they are considered safe investments that will provide a predictable source of income.

Bonds in the next two categories (Standard & Poor's BB and B, comparable to Moody's Ba and B) are considered **speculative,** or riskier, in nature and are often referred to as "junk" bonds. Bonds in the C and D categories are used to rank bonds where there are poor prospects for repayment. Bonds in categories C and D may be in default or cannot continue interest payments to bondholders.

GO FIGURE Mathematics

Current Yield of a Bond Investment

Yield is the rate of return an investor earns. By calculating the current yield of a bond, you can determine the return on a bond.

EXAMPLE Suppose that you own a $1,000 AT&T corporate bond that pays 7.5 percent interest per year. This means that each year you will receive $75 in interest ($1,000 × 7.5% = $75). Assume that the current market value of the AT&T bond is $960. What is the current yield of your bond investment?

Formula Dollar Amount of Annual Interest Income/ Current Market Value = Current Yield of a Bond

Solution $75/$960 = 0.078 or 7.8%

The current yield is 7.8 percent.

Your Turn

You receive $120 in interest each year on your $2,000 corporate bond. What is the current yield of your bond?

U.S. government securities are usually not rated because they are basically risk-free. Long-term municipal bonds are rated in much the same way as corporate bonds. However, short-term municipal bonds are rated differently. Standard & Poor's rates municipal bonds that have maturity dates of three years or less with the following system:

- SP-1: Strong ability to pay face value and interest (Bonds with very safe characteristics get a plus (+) sign.)
- SP-2: Satisfactory ability to pay face value and interest
- SP-3: Doubtful ability to pay face value and interest

Yield of a Bond Investment To determine the return a bond may produce, investors calculate its yield. The **yield** is the rate of return, usually stated as a percentage, earned by an investor who holds a bond for a certain period of time.

The simplest way to measure a bond's yield is to calculate its current yield. To find the current yield of a bond, divide the dollar amount of annual interest income by its current market value.

This calculation lets you compare the yield on a bond investment with the yields of other investment alternatives such as savings accounts, certificates of deposit, common stocks, preferred stocks, and mutual funds. If the current market value is higher than the bond's face value, the current yield decreases. If the current market value is less than the bond's face value, the current yield increases. The higher the current yield, the better the return is for the investor.

Investors may also consider the yield to maturity of a bond. This calculation takes into account the relationship between a bond's maturity value, the time to maturity, the current price, and the dollar amount of interest. Like the current yield, the yield to maturity allows you to compare returns on a bond investment with other investments, which is another strategy to track and evaluate your investment finances.

SECTION 2 Assessment

Review Key Concepts

1. **Identify** List information resources for selecting bond investments.
2. **Explain** How do you determine a bond's yield?
3. **Summarize** Define bond price quotations.
4. **Classify** Categorize and describe bond ratings.

Higher Order Thinking H.O.T.

5. **Relate** Explain the meaning of bond ratings and the impact they have on the way investors make their decisions.

21st Century Skills

6. **Solve Problems** Andrew is an aspiring architect, and he is looking to add new investments to his portfolio to help him pay for computer-aided drafting classes. Every day Andrew looks at the bond section of *The Wall Street Journal* to see if he can get a good deal on a $1,000 bond and add it to his portfolio. This morning a price quotation of 98 for a high-tech architectural design firm caught his interest. What should Andrew to do figure out the current market value of that bond?

Mathematics

7. **Bond Price and Yield** Samir would like to invest some of his money in bonds in order to better diversify his portfolio. He has decided to look through the newspaper as a part of his research. One of the bonds he found has a face value of $1,000. The price in the newspaper was quoted at "86." What is the selling price of this bond? The same bond pays 6.75 percent interest per year. Using the price quoted in the newspaper, calculate this bond's current yield.

Math Concept **Calculate Bond Price and Yield** To calculate the price of a bond multiply the face value by the price quoted as a percentage. The yield can be calculated by dividing the annual interest of the bond by the bond price.

Starting Hint Determine the price of the bond by first identifying the amount quoted. This amount should be converted to a percentage and then multiplied by the face value of the bond.

NCTM Connections Recognize and apply mathematics in contexts outside of mathematics.

Mc Graw Hill glencoe.com Check your answers.

Section Objectives

- **Define** mutual funds.
- **Explain** why investors buy mutual funds.
- **Identify** types of mutual funds.
- **Categorize** the three main groups of mutual funds.

As You Read

Infer Based on its name, how would you define a mutual fund?

Defining Mutual Funds

What is a key benefit of purchasing a mutual fund?

Mutual funds are an excellent choice for many investors. A mutual fund is an investment alternative in which investors pool their money to buy stocks, bonds, and other securities based on the selections of professional fund managers who work for an investment company. By buying shares in a mutual fund, even an investor with limited resources can own part of an entire portfolio of diverse securities. These funds can also be used for retirement accounts, such as 401(k) and 403(b) plans, individual retirement accounts (IRAs), and Roth IRAs.

Why Investors Buy Mutual Funds

One major reason for purchasing a mutual fund is professional management. Investment companies employ professional fund managers who try to pick the best securities for their mutual fund portfolios. However, this can lead some investors to become careless. Many mutual fund investors assume that their investments will increase in value. They might not research and evaluate funds carefully before they buy. They may also neglect to keep track of the performance of the funds they own. Even the best portfolio managers make mistakes. Therefore, wise investors should monitor and review their mutual funds regularly.

Another key reason for buying a mutual fund is diversification. Mutual funds include a variety of securities, which reduces the shareholders' risk. An occasional loss from one investment in a mutual fund is usually **compensated,** or made up for, by gains from other investments in the same fund. Researching and tracking the right mutual fund can provide great results with less effort than it would take to maintain such a diverse portfolio on your own.

Because of these advantages, mutual funds have become extremely popular investments. In 1970, there were 361 mutual funds. By 2003, there were more than 8,300 mutual funds, and the combined assets owned by mutual funds in the United States were worth more than $6 trillion. In the month of April 2003 alone, investors poured more than $16.1 billion into mutual fund investments. Read the material in this section to see if mutual funds are right for you.

Reading Check

Generalize Why might some investors become careless about their portfolios?

Types of Mutual Funds

What are the differences among the various types of mutual funds?

An investment company is a firm that invests the pooled funds of many investors in various securities. The firm receives a fee for this service. Mutual funds are classified as either closed-end funds, exchange-traded funds, or open-end funds.

Closed-End Funds

About six percent of all mutual funds are closed-end funds offered by investment companies. A **closed-end fund** is a mutual fund with a fixed number of shares that are issued by an investment company when the fund is first organized. After all the original shares have been sold, an investor can buy shares only from another investor. Closed-end funds are actively managed by professional fund managers, who select stocks and securities included in a fund, and are traded (bought and sold) on the floors of stock exchanges or in the over-the-counter market. A special section of *The Wall Street Journal* provides information about closed-end funds.

Exchange-Traded Funds

Increasing in popularity, an **exchange-traded fund (ETF)** is a fund that invests in stocks or other securities contained in a specific stock or securities index. ETFs are traded in the same manner as closed-end funds. Exchange-traded funds track various indexes including:

- Dow Jones Industrial Average, S&P 500 Index, Nasdaq 100 Index
- Midcap and Small-cap stocks
- Stocks issued by companies in specific industries
- Stocks issued by corporations in different countries

Know Your Funds
Mutual funds can be a great option for many investors, but there are many types of mutual funds to choose from. *How would you begin your research?*

GO FIGURE Mathematics

Net Asset Value

Investors can buy and sell shares in an open-end mutual fund at the net asset value (NAV). The net asset value is the amount that one share of a mutual fund is worth. Investors use the net asset value formula to assess the real worth of their portfolios and make buying decisions.

EXAMPLE Beth owns shares in the New American Frontiers Mutual Fund. The value of the fund's portfolio is $124 million, and its liabilities total $4 million. If this mutual fund has 6 million shares outstanding, what is the net asset value of each of Beth's shares?

Formula (Value of the Fund's Portfolio − Liabilities)/ Number of Shares Outstanding = Net Asset Value

Solution ($124 million − $4 million)/6 million shares =$20 per share. The NAV of Beth's shares is $20.

Your Turn

You own shares in an open-end mutual fund that has a portfolio value of $220 million. Its liabilities are $6 million, and it has 8 million shares outstanding. What is the net asset value of your shares?

Although exchange-traded funds are similar to closed-end funds, there is one significant difference. Most closed-end funds are actively managed by a fund manager. An ETF, on the other hand, has less of a need for a professional to make investment decisions. ETFs invest in the securities included in a specific index, and often mirror the performance of that index. Because of this, fees for ETFs are often lower. Some other advantages include: no minimum investment and shares can be bought or sold anytime during regular market hours.

Open-End Funds

Most mutual funds are open-end funds. An **open-end fund** is a mutual fund with an unlimited number of shares that are issued and redeemed by an investment company at the investors' request. Shares of open-end funds are bought and sold on any business day by contacting the investment company that manages the mutual fund.

Services If you buy shares of an open-end fund, you gain access to a variety of services including: payroll deduction programs, automatic reinvestment programs, and automatic withdrawal programs.

Net Asset Value Investors are free to buy and sell shares at the net asset value. The **net asset value (NAV)** is the amount that one share of a mutual fund is worth. To calculate the net asset value of a mutual fund, subtract the fund's liabilities from the value of the fund's portfolio, and divide the result by the number of shares outstanding. Shares outstanding are the number of shares held by all the investors.

Load Funds

Before investing in mutual funds, compare the costs of the investment options. Mutual funds are classified as either load or no-load funds.

Careers That Count!

Elisa Hing • Certified Financial Planner

As a certified financial planner, I help people reach their financial goals. I advise people about effective money management. On a daily basis, I determine clients' assets, liabilities, cash flow, insurance coverage, tax status, and financial objectives. Then I identify and analyze their income, spending, investment patterns, and risk tolerance to develop a customized financial plan that may include investment and tax strategies, securities, insurance, pension plans, real estate, and education goals. I also spend a lot time marketing my services. I often meet potential clients by giving seminars or through networking. Finding clients and building a customer base is important to my success. A formal education is not required to pursue this career, but a bachelor's degree in accounting, finance, economics, business, mathematics, or law is preferred, and you may need to be licensed and/or registered. I also suggest taking courses in investments, taxes, estate planning, and risk management.

EXPLORE CAREERS

Visit the Web site of the U.S. Department of Labor's Bureau of Labor Statistics and obtain information about a career as a certified financial planner.

1. What are some circumstances that would make you consider hiring a certified financial planner?
2. What factors would you consider when selecting a financial planner?

Skills	Education	Career Path
Communication, math, analytical, sales, and customer service skills; ability to build a client base	Bachelor's degree preferred; Certified Financial Planner (CFP) or Chartered Financial Consultant (ChFC) designation	Certified financial planners can become tax preparers, investment advisors, estate planners, and branch office owners for securities firms.

glencoe.com 

Activity Download a Career Exploration Activity.

A **load fund** (or an "A" fund) is a mutual fund for which you pay a commission every time you buy or sell shares. The commission, or sales charge, can be as high as 8.5 percent. The average load charge for mutual funds is between 3 and 5 percent. The stated advantage of load funds is that the representatives, such as financial planners, will offer advice and guidance about when to buy or sell shares of the fund.

No-Load Funds

A **no-load fund** is a mutual fund that has no commission fee. No-load funds do not charge commissions when you buy shares because they have no salespeople. No-load funds offer the same investment opportunities as load funds. If you have a choice between a load fund and a no-load fund, and both offer the same investment opportunities, choose the no-load fund.

Management Fees and Other Charges The investment companies that sponsor mutual funds also charge management fees. This fee is a fixed percentage of the fund's asset value. The fees generally range from 0.5 to 1.25 percent.

Instead of charging investors a fee when they purchase shares, some mutual funds charge a back-end load, which is a fee that is charged for withdrawing money from the fund. Fees range from 1 to 5 percent and are based on how long you own shares of the mutual fund. A back-end load is designed to discourage early withdrawals. A 12b-1 fee is a fee that an investment company charges to help pay for the marketing and advertising of a mutual fund. It is approximately 1 percent of a fund's assets per year.

Reading Check

Explain If you have a choice between a load fund and a no-load fund and both offer the same investment opportunities, which one should you choose and why?

Categories of Mutual Funds

What are the three main groups of mutual funds?

The managers of mutual funds match their investment portfolios to the investment objectives of their customers. Usually a fund's objectives are clearly explained in its prospectus. You can sort mutual funds into three main groups: stock, bond, and mixed. Different sources may use different categories for the same mutual fund.

Stock Mutual Funds

Most mutual funds are part of the stock mutual funds group. Stock mutual funds are made up of stocks. These funds fall into categories, which describe the fund objectives and types of stock.

Aggressive Growth Funds Aggressive growth funds (sometimes called *capital appreciation funds*) seek to grow money rapidly by investing in stocks whose prices will increase greatly in a short period of time. Because the stocks are often risky, the market value of shares in this type of fund frequently swings between low and high.

Equity Income Funds Equity income funds include stocks issued by companies with a long history of paying dividends. The major objective of these funds is to provide steady income. These funds are investment choices for conservative or retired investors.

Global Stock Funds Global stock funds invest in stocks of companies throughout the world, including the United States.

Growth Funds Growth funds buy shares of companies expecting higher-than-average revenue and earnings growth. Growth funds tend to invest in larger, less risky companies that may pay some dividends. As a result, the market value of shares in a growth fund is more stable when compared to aggressive growth funds.

Index Funds Index funds include stocks of companies that are listed in an index such as Standard & Poor's 500 Stock Index or Russell 3000 Index. Fund managers select stocks issued by companies included in the index. Thus, an index fund should perform almost the same as the index. Index funds may have lower management fees.

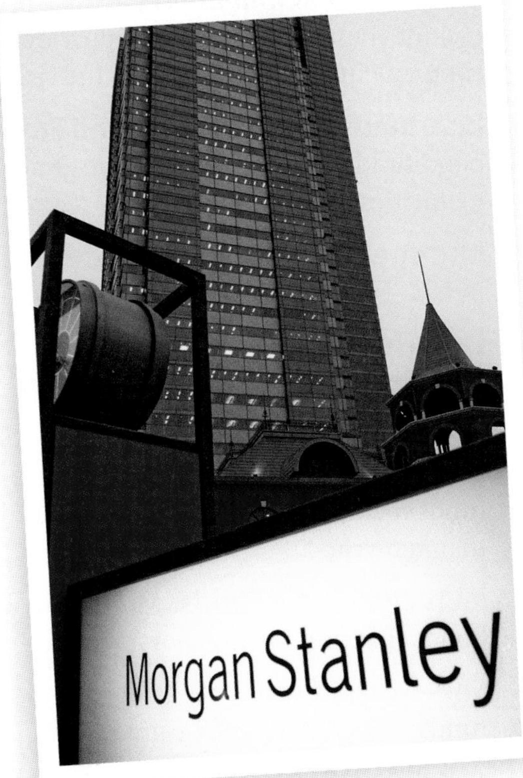

International Funds International funds include foreign stocks that are sold in securities markets throughout the world. That way, if the economy in one region or nation is in a decline, profits can still be earned in others. Such funds invest outside of the United States.

Large-Cap Funds Large-cap funds invest in companies with total capitalization, or the total market value of a company's outstanding shares, greater than $10 billion. A large-cap fund is a long-term **holding,** or legally-owned security, used for retirement savings.

Mid-Cap Funds Mid-cap funds include stocks of companies with total capitalization of $2 billion to $10 billion. Mid-cap funds offer more security than small-cap funds and more growth potential.

Small-Cap Funds Small-cap funds include shares of small, innovative companies with total capitalization less than $2 billion. They offer high growth potential but are riskier.

Regional Funds Regional funds include stocks that are traded within one region of the world. Examples include the European region, the Latin American region, and the Pacific region.

Sector Funds Sector funds invest in companies within the same industry. Examples of sectors include health and biotechnology, science and technology, computers, and natural resources.

Bond Mutual Funds

Bond mutual funds invest only in bonds. The bond fund categories are based on the type of bond the mutual funds purchase.

High-Yield (Junk) Bond Funds High-yield (junk) bond funds invest in high-yield, high-risk corporate bonds.

World-Class Opportunities
Investment firms that create international and global mutual funds are always looking for stocks in countries that are experiencing growth. *Why would an American investor choose a fund that includes stocks from India, China, Brazil, or another emerging market?*

Interpersonal Skills

Successful people and effective leaders often possess strong interpersonal skills. Interpersonal skills include the ability to manage your emotions and behaviors during social or professional interactions. Knowing when it is appropriate to listen and when you should speak is another aspect of interpersonal skills. People with strong interpersonal skills are able to interact with people from a wide range of social and cultural backgrounds and thrive in a diverse environment. This type of environment can often lead to new ideas and an increase in the quality of work produced.

Write About It

Think of a situation in which you or someone you know exhibited strong interpersonal skills. Write one or more paragraphs to describe the situation and explain how interpersonal skills had a positive impact. How do you think interpersonal skills could benefit you in the future?

 **glencoe.com** 

Activity Download a Career and College Readiness Worksheet Activity.

Insured Municipal Bond Funds Insured municipal bond funds include municipal bonds that provide tax-exempt income. An outside company insures them against the risk of default, or nonpayment.

Intermediate Corporate Bond Funds Intermediate corporate bond funds invest in investment-grade corporate bonds that have maturities between five and ten years.

Intermediate U.S. Government Bond Funds These funds invest in U.S. Treasury securities with maturities between five and ten years.

Long-Term Corporate Bond Funds Long-term corporate bond funds buy investment-grade corporate bonds that have maturities of more than ten years.

Long-Term U.S. Government Bond Funds Long-term U.S. bond funds include U.S. Treasury securities that have maturities of longer than ten years.

Municipal Bond Funds Municipal bond funds invest in municipal bonds that provide investors with tax-exempt interest income.

Short-Term Corporate Bond Funds Short-term corporate bond funds include investment-grade corporate bond issues that have maturities of between one and five years.

Short-Term U.S. Government Bond Funds Short-term U.S. bond funds invest in U.S. Treasury securities that have maturities of less than five years.

Mixed Mutual Funds

Other mutual funds are part of a third group—mixed mutual funds. These funds invest in a mix of stocks and bonds or in various other types of securities. The funds fall into three categories: balanced funds, money-market funds, and stock/bond blend funds.

Balanced Funds Balanced funds include both stocks and bonds to provide income while avoiding excessive risk. Often the percentage of stocks and bonds is stated in the fund's prospectus.

Money-Market Funds Money-market funds invest in certificates of deposit, government securities, and other safe investments. It is relatively easy to withdraw money from a money-market fund.

Stock/Bond Blend Funds Stock/bond blend funds invest in both stocks and bonds, enabling investors to diversify their holdings with a single fund.

Variety of Funds A variety of mutual funds managed by one investment company is called a *family of funds*. Each mutual fund within the family has a different financial objective. For instance, one fund may be a short-term U.S. bond fund and a growth stock fund. Most investment companies make it easy for shareholders to switch among the mutual funds within a family. This allows investors to adjust their investments conveniently.

Assessment

Review Key Concepts

1. **Summarize** Define mutual funds.
2. **Explain** Why do investors buy mutual funds?
3. **Identify** List types of mutual funds.
4. **Classify** Identify the three main categories of mutual funds and provide an example of each.

Higher Order Thinking H.O.T.

5. **Role Play** Consider the fees charged by mutual funds, and look at them from the perspectives of both the investors and the fund managers. Write a brief essay to discuss why these fees are charged, whether they are justified, and if it is reasonable for investors not to expect to pay fees.

English Language Arts

6. **Fund Objectives** Kaylee wants to invest her savings in a mutual fund, but she is concerned about the risk of investing. She wants a fund that is stable and safe. Her friend Ana recommends that she consider equity income funds and money-market funds. Her friend Jack says she should explore aggressive growth funds and high-yield (junk) bond funds. Review the characteristics of equity income funds, money-market funds, aggressive growth funds, and high-yield (junk) bond funds. Write down a list of the objectives for these funds. Then explain who is offering the best advice to Kaylee, and why.

NCTE 5 Use different writing process elements to communicate effectively.

Mathematics

7. **Load Fund** Gabriel has saved $2,250 which he would like to invest. He is thinking about putting the money into a global stock mutual fund. The fund he is considering includes a charge for a front-end load of 5.5 percent. (Note: Front-end loads are deducted from the total investment amount; the remainder is invested in the fund). How much will Gabriel be charged for the load? If the mutual fund's net asset value is $23.00, how many shares will he end up purchasing?

Math Concept **Calculate Front-end Load** To calculate the front-end load charge on a mutual fund first determine the percentage charge of the load and then multiply this by the total dollar amount that is invested.

Starting Hint Determine the front-end load charge on the mutual fund by multiplying the charge percentage by the total dollar amount invested. Subtract this amount from the total dollar amount invested in order to determine the actual amount used to purchase shares.

NCTM Problem Solving Solve problems that arise in mathematics and in other contexts.

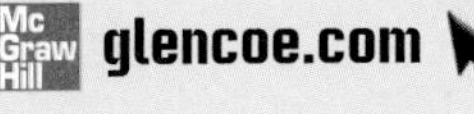

Check your answers.

Section Objectives

- **Identify** sources of information for selecting mutual funds.
- **Differentiate** between capital gain and capital gain distribution.
- **Summarize** the ways in which mutual fund earnings are taxed.
- **Discuss** ways to buy and sell mutual funds.

As You Read

Predict Read the list of questions under "Considering Your Financial Goals." As you read the rest of this chapter, think about how your answers to these questions will affect your investment decisions, both now and in years to come.

Making an Informed Decision

What steps can you take to decide on mutual fund investments?

Which mutual funds are best for you? When should you buy or sell your shares? By considering your financial goals and consulting various sources of information, you will be able to determine the best approach for investing in mutual funds.

Considering Your Financial Goals

You can consider several questions when you are in the process of identifying your investment goals:

- How old are you?
- What is your family situation?
- How much risk do you want to take?
- How much money do you make now? In the future?

After you have considered these factors and answered these questions, you can set your investment goals. Once you know your goals, find a mutual fund with investment objectives that match your own.

Information on Mutual Funds

You will find a great deal of information that can guide you through the decision-making process of buying or selling shares in a mutual fund. The main sources of information on mutual funds include:

- Newspapers
- Quotations
- Prospectuses
- Annual reports
- Financial publications
- Professional advice
- Internet

Newspapers Metropolitan newspapers and financial newspapers, such as *The Wall Street Journal* and *Barron's*, provide a wealth of information.

Quotations As shown in **Figure 4,** mutual fund quotations contain information about a fund's net asset value, objective, performance, and cost. When you read mutual fund quotations, remember to note any letters beside the name of a specific fund. Then look up their meanings in the quotation footnotes.

FIGURE 4 Mutual Fund Information in *The Wall Street Journal*

Decoding Quotations When you read newspaper quotations, notice the letter(s) beside the name of a specific fund and refer to the quotation footnotes. *What does the letter "p" indicate about a fund?*

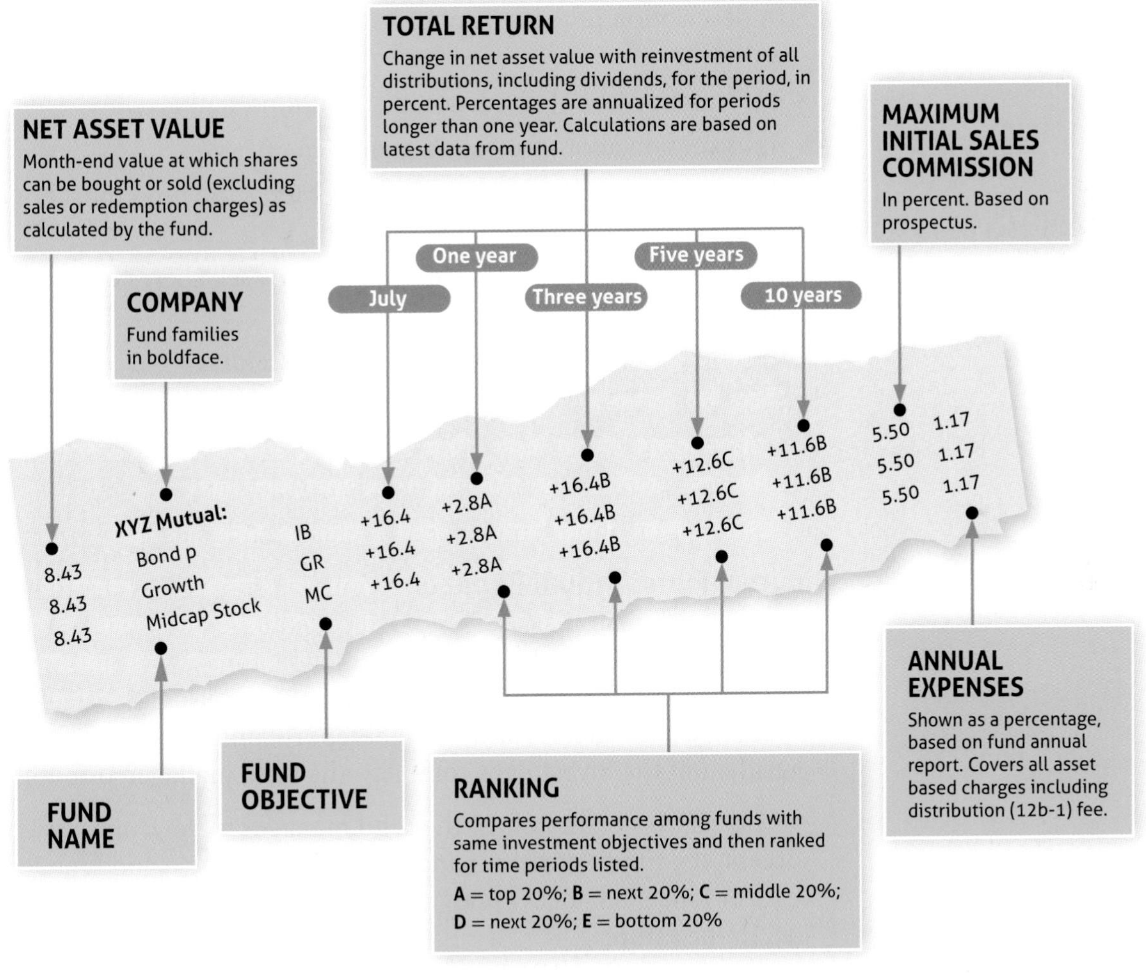

How to Read the Monthly Performance Tables
Performance tables are provided by Lipper, Inc. These tables include all primary funds listed by NASDAQ. Bond performance numbers are preliminary. Though verified, the data cannot be guaranteed by Lipper or its data sources. Double-check with funds before investing.
Performance calculations assume reinvestment of all distributions and are after subtracting annual expenses. But figures do not reflect sales charges ("loads") or redemption fees.
TOTAL RETURN
Change in net asset value with reinvestment of all distributions, including dividends, for the period, in percent. Percentages are annualized for periods longer than one year. Calculations are based on latest data from fund.
NET ASSET VALUE
Month-end value at which shares can be bought or sold (excluding sales or redemption charges) as calculated by the fund.
MAXIMUM INITIAL SALES COMMISSION
In percent. Based on prospectus.
COMPANY
Fund families in boldface.
One year
Five years
July
Three years
10 years
8.43 XYZ Mutual:
8.43 Bond p IB +16.4 +2.8A +16.4B +12.6C +11.6B 5.50 1.17
8.43 Growth GR +16.4 +2.8A +16.4B +12.6C +11.6B 5.50 1.17
Midcap Stock MC +16.4 +2.8A +16.4B +12.6C +11.6B 5.50 1.17
ANNUAL EXPENSES
Shown as a percentage, based on fund annual report. Covers all asset based charges including distribution (12b-1) fee.
FUND NAME
FUND OBJECTIVE
RANKING
Compares performance among funds with same investment objectives and then ranked for time periods listed.
A = top 20%; B = next 20%; C = middle 20%; D = next 20%; E = bottom 20%
–Quotation Footnotes–
e–Ex-distribution. f–Previous day's quotation. g–Footnotes x and s apply. j–Footnotes e and s apply. p–Distribution costs apply, 12b-1. r–Redemption charge may apply. s–Stock split or dividend. t–Footnotes p and r apply. v–Footnotes x and e apply. x–Ex-dividend. z–Footnotes x, e, and s apply.
NA–Not available due to incomplete price performance or cost data. NE–Not released by Lipper; data under review. NN–Fund not tracked. NS–Fund didn't exist at start of period.

Mutual Fund Prospectuses After you have narrowed your search, check out the prospectuses of the mutual funds that most interest you. To get a copy of a prospectus, call, write, or e-mail the investment company that manages the mutual fund. Many investment companies have toll-free telephone numbers that you can find by calling the toll-free information number (1-800-555-1212). An investment company sponsoring a mutual fund must give a potential investor a prospectus when requested. Read the prospectus completely before you invest. The prospectus summarizes the fund and lists any fees you will have to pay. The prospectus usually provides the following information:

- A description of the fund's objective
- The risk factor associated with the fund
- A fee table
- A description of the fund's past performance
- A description of the type of investments contained in the fund's portfolio
- Information about dividends, distributions, and taxes
- Information about the fund's management
- Information on limitations or requirements the fund must honor when choosing investments
- The process by which investors can buy or sell shares of the mutual fund
- A description of services provided to investors
- Fees for services
- Information about how often the fund's investment portfolio changes (sometimes referred to as turnover ratio)
- Information about how to open a mutual fund account

Mutual Fund Annual Reports If you are a potential investor, you may request an annual report by mail, telephone, or e-mail. When you become a shareholder, the investment company will automatically send you an annual report. Annual reports may also be posted on a company's Web site. A fund's annual report contains a letter from the president of the investment company, the fund manager, or both.

Do not forget the role of the fund manager in determining a fund's success. If a fund's present manager has been doing a good job for five years or longer, chances are that he or she will continue to perform well in the future.

The annual report contains detailed financial information about the fund's assets and liabilities. It also includes a statement of operations that describes expenses and day-to-day operating costs of the fund, a statement of changes in net assets, and a schedule of investments.

Finally, most annual reports include a letter from the fund's independent auditors. This letter backs up the accuracy of the information contained in the report.

Document Detective

A Mutual Fund Account Statement

When you invest in a mutual fund, you need to monitor how effectively your investment is growing. Periodically, you may find it necessary to sell a mutual fund and place your money in another mutual fund that has a potential to grow faster. A mutual fund account statement contains the following information:

- Name of the fund
- Account number
- Beginning and ending share balance
- Activity since the last statement

President's Group
P.O. Box 605, Springfield, NY 12345

Tanya Sawyer
5744 Pioneer Trail, Harrison, UT 54321

Account number: 6875430001 Account statement: DECEMBER 31, 2010

JEFFERSON MUTUAL INVESTORS FUND

Trade Date	Description	Dollar Amount	Share Price	Shares This Transaction	Share Balance
10/1/10	Beginning share balance		$34.20		721.273
10/19/10	Income dividend	$104.58	$34.20	3.058	724.331
11/11/10	Income dividend	$105.03	$33.45	3.140	727.471
11/28/10	Direct investment	$1,000.00	$34.70	28.818	756.289
12/05/10	Direct investment	$700.00	$32.26	21.699	777.988
Ending share balance					777.988

Ending value as of 12/31/10 was $25,097.89

Key Points An account statement for a mutual fund will list your contributions and any dividends your account has earned. It will also tell you how many shares of the mutual fund you own and what the value of each is on a given day.

FIND the Solutions

Review Key Concepts

1. How many shares did Tanya have at the beginning of the period?
2. How is the Shares This Transaction amount calculated?
3. Why is the share price different for each transaction?
4. How is the ending value calculated?
5. Did the value of Tanya's account grow or decline during this time period?

FIGURE 5 Mutual Fund Resources

Fund Data There are various resources that provide mutual fund information and research. *Beside ratings, what other types of information does this resource provide?*

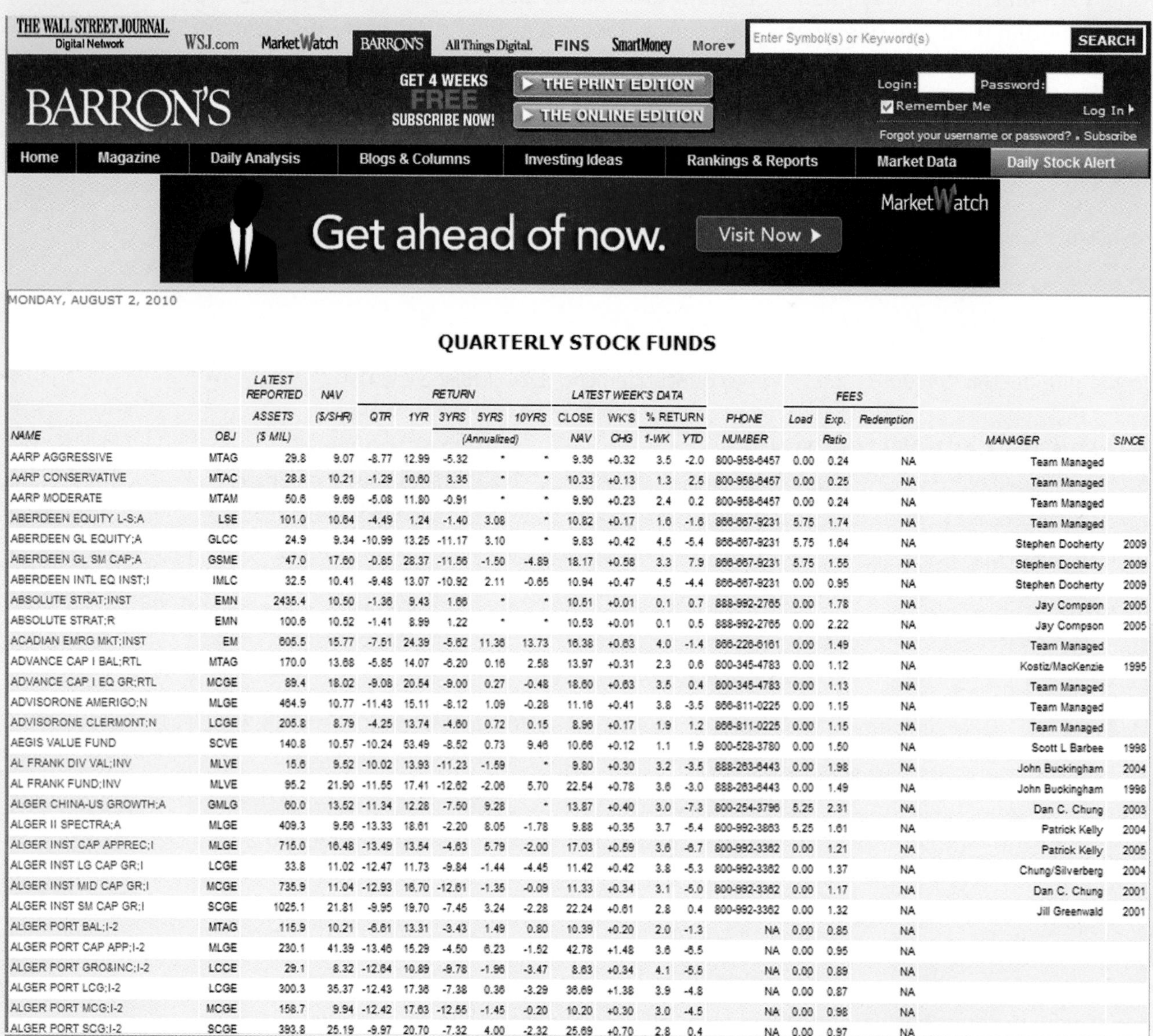

QUARTERLY STOCK FUNDS

NAME	OBJ	LATEST REPORTED ASSETS ($ MIL)	NAV ($/SHR)	RETURN QTR	1YR	3YRS (Annualized)	5YRS	10YRS	LATEST WEEK'S DATA CLOSE NAV	WK'S CHG	% RETURN 1-WK	YTD	PHONE NUMBER	FEES Load	Exp. Ratio	Redemption	MANAGER	SINCE
AARP AGGRESSIVE	MTAG	29.8	9.07	-8.77	12.99	-5.32	*	*	9.36	+0.32	3.5	-2.0	800-958-6457	0.00	0.24	NA	Team Managed	
AARP CONSERVATIVE	MTAC	28.8	10.21	-1.29	10.60	3.35	*	*	10.33	+0.13	1.3	2.5	800-958-6457	0.00	0.25	NA	Team Managed	
AARP MODERATE	MTAM	50.6	9.69	-5.08	11.80	-0.91	*	*	9.90	+0.23	2.4	0.2	800-958-6457	0.00	0.24	NA	Team Managed	
ABERDEEN EQUITY L-S;A	LSE	101.0	10.64	-4.49	1.24	-1.40	3.08	*	10.82	+0.17	1.6	-1.6	866-667-9231	5.75	1.74	NA	Team Managed	
ABERDEEN GL EQUITY;A	GLCC	24.9	9.34	-10.99	13.25	-11.17	3.10	*	9.83	+0.42	4.5	-5.4	866-667-9231	5.75	1.64	NA	Stephen Docherty	2009
ABERDEEN GL SM CAP;A	GSME	47.0	17.60	-0.85	28.37	-11.56	-1.50	-4.89	18.17	+0.58	3.3	7.9	866-667-9231	5.75	1.55	NA	Stephen Docherty	2009
ABERDEEN INTL EQ INST;I	IMLC	32.5	10.41	-9.48	13.07	-10.92	2.11	-0.65	10.94	+0.47	4.5	-4.4	866-667-9231	0.00	0.95	NA	Stephen Docherty	2009
ABSOLUTE STRAT;INST	EMN	2435.4	10.50	-1.36	9.43	1.66	*	*	10.51	+0.01	0.1	0.7	888-992-2765	0.00	1.78	NA	Jay Compson	2005
ABSOLUTE STRAT;R	EMN	100.6	10.52	-1.41	8.99	1.22	*	*	10.53	+0.01	0.1	0.5	888-992-2765	0.00	2.22	NA	Jay Compson	2005
ACADIAN EMRG MKT;INST	EM	605.5	15.77	-7.51	24.39	-5.62	11.36	13.73	16.38	+0.63	4.0	-1.4	866-226-6161	0.00	1.49	NA	Team Managed	
ADVANCE CAP I BAL;RTL	MTAG	170.0	13.68	-5.85	14.07	-6.20	0.16	2.58	13.97	+0.31	2.3	0.6	800-345-4783	0.00	1.12	NA	Kostiz/MacKenzie	1995
ADVANCE CAP I EQ GR;RTL	MCGE	89.4	18.02	-9.08	20.54	-9.00	0.27	-0.48	18.60	+0.63	3.5	0.4	800-345-4783	0.00	1.13	NA	Team Managed	
ADVISORONE AMERIGO;N	MLGE	464.9	10.77	-11.43	15.11	-8.12	1.09	-0.28	11.16	+0.41	3.8	-3.5	866-811-0225	0.00	1.15	NA	Team Managed	
ADVISORONE CLERMONT;N	LCGE	205.8	8.79	-4.25	13.74	-4.60	0.72	0.15	8.96	+0.17	1.9	1.2	866-811-0225	0.00	1.15	NA	Team Managed	
AEGIS VALUE FUND	SCVE	140.8	10.57	-10.24	53.49	-8.52	0.73	9.46	10.66	+0.12	1.1	1.9	800-528-3780	0.00	1.50	NA	Scott L Barbee	1998
AL FRANK DIV VAL;INV	MLVE	15.6	9.52	-10.02	13.93	-11.23	-1.59	*	9.80	+0.30	3.2	-3.5	888-263-6443	0.00	1.98	NA	John Buckingham	2004
AL FRANK FUND;INV	MLVE	95.2	21.90	-11.55	17.41	-12.62	-2.06	5.70	22.54	+0.78	3.6	-3.0	888-263-6443	0.00	1.49	NA	John Buckingham	1998
ALGER CHINA-US GROWTH;A	GMLG	60.0	13.52	-11.34	12.28	-7.50	9.28	*	13.87	+0.40	3.0	-7.3	800-254-3796	5.25	2.31	NA	Dan C. Chung	2003
ALGER II SPECTRA;A	MLGE	409.3	9.56	-13.33	18.61	-2.20	8.05	-1.78	9.88	+0.35	3.7	-5.4	800-992-3863	5.25	1.61	NA	Patrick Kelly	2004
ALGER INST CAP APPREC;I	MLGE	715.0	16.48	-13.49	13.54	-4.63	5.79	-2.00	17.03	+0.59	3.6	-6.7	800-992-3362	0.00	1.21	NA	Patrick Kelly	2005
ALGER INST LG CAP GR;I	LCGE	33.8	11.02	-12.47	11.73	-9.84	-1.44	-4.45	11.42	+0.42	3.8	-5.3	800-992-3362	0.00	1.37	NA	Chung/Silverberg	2004
ALGER INST MID CAP GR;I	MCGE	735.9	11.04	-12.93	16.70	-12.61	-1.35	-0.09	11.33	+0.34	3.1	-5.0	800-992-3362	0.00	1.17	NA	Dan C. Chung	2001
ALGER INST SM CAP GR;I	SCGE	1025.1	21.81	-9.95	19.70	-7.45	3.24	-2.28	22.24	+0.61	2.8	0.4	800-992-3362	0.00	1.32	NA	Jill Greenwald	2001
ALGER PORT BAL;I-2	MTAG	115.9	10.21	-6.61	13.31	-3.43	1.49	0.80	10.39	+0.20	2.0	-1.3	NA	0.00	0.85	NA		
ALGER PORT CAP APP;I-2	MLGE	230.1	41.39	-13.46	15.29	-4.50	6.23	-1.52	42.78	+1.48	3.6	-6.5	NA	0.00	0.95	NA		
ALGER PORT GRO&INC;I-2	LCCE	29.1	8.32	-12.64	10.89	-9.78	-1.96	-3.47	8.63	+0.34	4.1	-5.5	NA	0.00	0.89	NA		
ALGER PORT LCG;I-2	LCGE	300.3	35.37	-12.43	17.36	-7.38	0.36	-3.29	36.69	+1.38	3.9	-4.8	NA	0.00	0.87	NA		
ALGER PORT MCG;I-2	MCGE	158.7	9.94	-12.42	17.63	-12.55	-1.45	-0.20	10.20	+0.30	3.0	-4.5	NA	0.00	0.98	NA		
ALGER PORT SCG;I-2	SCGE	393.8	25.19	-9.97	20.70	-7.32	4.00	-2.32	25.69	+0.70	2.8	0.4	NA	0.00	0.97	NA		

Financial Publications Financial publications, both print and electronic, such as *Forbes*, *Kiplinger's Personal Finance*, *Barron's*, and *Money*, and their Web sites, are sources of information about mutual funds. These publications provide research, results, annual surveys, and rankings of mutual funds, such as the information shown in **Figure 5.**

In addition to annual surveys, a number of mutual fund guidebooks are available at bookstores, through company Web sites, or at your local public library.

GO FIGURE Mathematics

Capital Gain per Share

Capital gain is the amount by which a share's selling price exceeds its purchase price. Determining the capital gain that you will receive when you sell the shares of your mutual fund will tell you how much the return on your investment will be.

EXAMPLE Sani purchased shares in the Fidelity Stock Selector Fund at $17 per share. Two years later, Sani sold the shares at $19.50 per share. What was the capital gain per share on Sani's mutual fund?

Formula Sales Price – Purchase Price = Capital Gain per Share

Solution $19.50 – $17.00 = $2.50

The capital gain per share on Sani's mutual fund was $2.50.

Your Turn

If you purchased mutual fund shares at $8.50 each and sold them for $11 per share, what would be your capital gain per share?

Professional Advice Professional advisory services also provide detailed information on mutual funds (see **Figure 6**). Popular sources include Standard & Poor's, Lipper Analytical Services, Morningstar, Inc., and Value Line. In addition, various mutual fund newsletters provide financial information to subscribers for a fee. These publications are expensive, but you may be able to obtain copies of them from brokerage firms or public libraries.

Professional advisory services, such as Morningstar, also offer online research reports for mutual funds. Many investors find that the research reports provided by such companies are worth the fees they charge. The information is similar to the printed reports; however, the ability to access the information quickly can be a real advantage.

Internet Many investors research mutual fund investments on the Internet. You may access this information online by one of several methods. If you know the name or the four- or five-letter symbol for a fund, you may obtain current market values, price history, and profile.

Most investment companies that sponsor mutual funds have Web sites. These sites are another source of useful information. To obtain information, use a search engine and type in the name of the fund. You will find information regarding statistics about individual funds, procedures for opening an account, promotional literature, and investor services. However, investment companies want you to become a shareholder, and therefore, their site's material may read like a sales pitch. Look at the facts before you invest your money.

Reading Check

List What information is contained in a mutual fund quotation?

FIGURE 6 Morningstar Mutual Fund Research

Online Information This report from June 2010 shows the type of information that Morningstar.com provides to an investor who is interested in the Dodge & Cox Balanced Fund. *What can you learn by reading the sections titled "Risk Measures" to the right of the Web Page?*

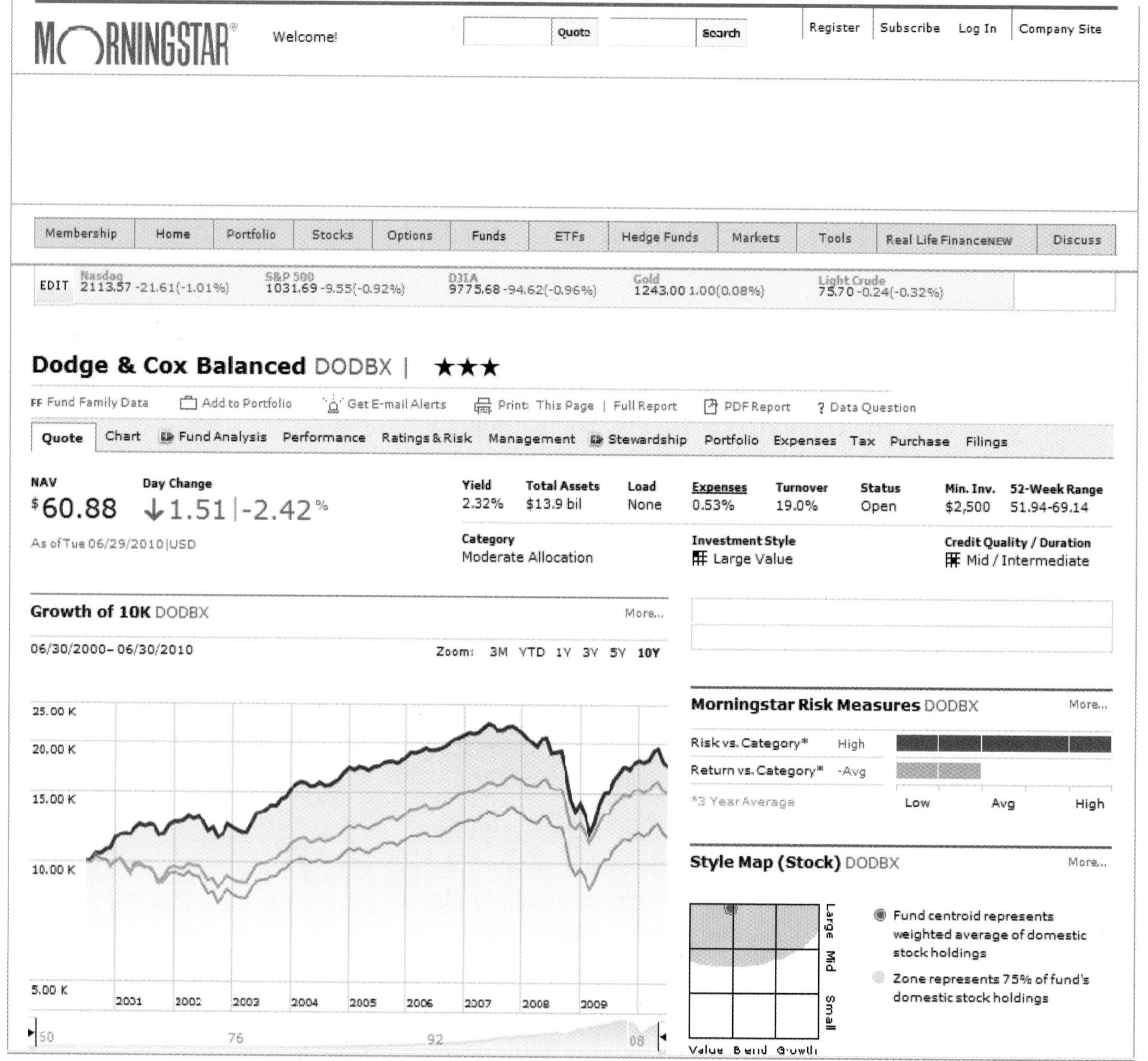

Return on Investment

What is the difference between a capital gain distribution and a capital gain?

Whether you choose a closed-end fund or an open-end fund, the purpose of investing in a mutual fund is to receive income. As a mutual fund shareholder, you may gain income in one of three ways.

First, you may receive income dividends. **Income dividends** are the earnings a fund pays to shareholders. Second, you may earn capital gain distributions. Capital gain distributions are payments made to shareholders that result from the sale of securities in the fund's portfolio. Third, you may make a good return by buying shares at a low price and then selling them after the price increases.

When you sell shares in a mutual fund, the profit that results from an increase in value is referred to as a capital gain. As discussed previously, a capital gain is the profit from the sale of an asset such as stocks, bonds, or real estate. Of course, if the price of a fund's shares goes down between the time of purchase and the time of sale, you lose money. Note the difference between a capital gain distribution and a capital gain. A capital gain distribution occurs when the fund sells securities within the fund's portfolio and distributes profits to shareholders. A capital gain occurs when the shareholder sells some of his or her shares in the mutual fund.

Reading Check

Define What are income dividends?

Taxes and Mutual Funds

How are mutual fund earnings taxed?

Income dividends, capital gain distributions, and capital gains are all taxable earnings. At the end of every year, investment companies and brokerage firms send each shareholder a statement detailing the income dividends and capital gain distributions he or she received. Usually, this information is provided on the IRS Form 1099DIV. However, the investor is responsible for maintaining clear and accurate records of the purchase and sale prices. The following are some general guidelines on how mutual fund transactions are taxed:

- Income dividends are reported along with all other dividend amounts you have received. They are taxed as regular income.
- Capital gain distributions are reported on your federal income tax return.
- Capital gains or losses that result from the investor selling shares in a mutual fund are reported on your federal income tax return.

You should be aware of two factors concerning taxes on mutual funds. First, most investment companies allow you to reinvest the capital gain distributions and income dividends you earn instead of receiving cash. These earnings are taxable and must be reported on your income tax return. Second, you decide when to sell your stocks or bonds.

Thus, you can pick the tax year when you pay tax or deduct losses on these investments. Mutual funds, on the other hand, buy and sell securities on a regular basis during any 12-month period. Unlike investments that you manage, you have no control over when the mutual fund sells securities. Therefore, you have no control over when you are taxed on capital gain distributions.

Reading Check

Identify What are two factors you should be aware of when you pay taxes on your mutual funds?

Buying and Selling Mutual Funds

How do you buy and sell mutual funds to help you meet your financial goals?

The main reason for investing is the opportunity to make money on your investment. Mutual funds can provide investors with income dividends, capital gain distributions, and profits that result from their decision to sell their shares. Various purchase options and withdrawal options allow you to manage your mutual fund investments and profits to help you meet your financial goals.

Purchase Options

Before you buy shares in a fund, you will need to consider several different purchase options. As discussed earlier in this chapter, different types of funds are sold by different means. Closed-end funds are traded through stock exchanges, such as the New York Stock Exchange or in the over-the-counter market. You can purchase shares of an open-end fund from a brokerage firm or by contacting the investment company that sponsors the fund.

A wide variety of both no-load and load funds can also be bought from mutual fund supermarkets that are available through brokerage firms such as Charles Schwab and E*Trade. Mutual fund supermarkets offer at least two advantages. First, instead of dealing with several investment companies, you can make one toll-free phone call to buy or sell a large number of mutual funds. Second, you receive one statement from the brokerage firm instead of receiving a statement from each investment company. This statement provides the information that you need to monitor all of your investments in one place and in the same format.

When you buy shares in an open-end mutual fund from an investment company, you have several purchase options: a regular account transaction, a voluntary savings plan, a payroll deduction plan, a contractual savings plan, or a reinvestment plan.

Regular Account Transactions A regular account transaction is the most popular and least complicated way to buy shares. With this method you decide how much money to invest and when to invest it. Then you simply buy as many shares as possible.

Voluntary Savings Plans A voluntary savings plan lets you make smaller purchases than the minimum required by the regular account transaction. However, when you make your first purchase, you also must commit to making regular minimum purchases of the fund's shares. Such small monthly investments can be a great way to save for long-term objectives. For most voluntary savings plans, the minimum purchase ranges from $25 to $100.

Payroll Deduction Plans Most voluntary savings plans also offer payroll deduction plans. This means that with your approval, the investment company will deduct a certain amount from your paycheck each month and invest it in your mutual fund. Mutual fund savings plans can also be used to invest money that is contributed to tax-deferred 401(k) and 403(b) retirement plans or individual retirement accounts (IRAs).

Contractual Savings Plans Contractual savings plans require you to make regular purchases of shares over a specific period of time, usually 10 to 20 years. You will pay penalty fees if you do not make the required purchases. Financial experts and government agencies disapprove of contractual savings plans because many investors lose money with these plans.

Reinvestment Plans You can also buy shares in an open-end fund by using the fund's reinvestment plan. With a reinvestment plan, your income dividends and capital gain distributions are automatically reinvested to buy additional shares of the fund. Most reinvestment plans allow shareholders to reinvest without having to pay additional sales charges or commissions. This is a great way to add to a portfolio.

Withdrawal Options

If you choose to invest in mutual funds, you will also need to know how you can take your money out of a fund. You can sell shares of closed-end funds to another investor any time you want on the stock exchange or in the over-the-counter market. Shares in an open-end fund can be sold to the investment company that sponsors the fund. In this case, provide proper notification, and the fund will send you a check for the net asset value of your shares. With some funds, you can write checks to withdraw money. If you have at least $5,000 worth of shares in a mutual fund, most funds will offer you four additional ways of withdrawing money.

GO FIGURE Mathematics

Percentage of Asset Growth Withdrawal

Most mutual funds will allow an investor to withdraw a prearranged percentage of his or her investment's asset growth—or the amount that the investment has grown during a period.

EXAMPLE Marco invested $1,500 in a green energy mutual fund. This first period, his investment was reported to be worth $1,800. He is allowed to withdraw 60 percent of the asset growth per period. How much can he withdraw?

> **Formula** Current Portfolio Value – Original Portfolio Value = Asset Growth
> Asset Growth × Prearranged Percentage = Withdrawal Amount
>
> **Solution** $1,800 – $1,500 = $300
> $300 × 60% or .60 = $180
> Marco can withdraw $180.

Your Turn

You invested $1,000 in a mutual fund specializing in cell phone technology. During the first period, your portfolio has a value of $1,235. Your prearranged withdrawal percentage is 40 percent of net asset growth. How much can you withdraw?

Investment Period Withdrawal First, you may withdraw a certain amount each investment period until your fund has been **exhausted,** or completely used up. Typically, an investment period is three months, and most funds require investors to withdraw a minimum amount, usually $50, if the investor chooses to withdraw funds.

Investment Period Liquidation A second option is to **liquidate,** or sell off, a certain number of shares each investment period. Of course the net asset value of shares in a fund varies from one period to the next. Therefore, the amount of money you receive will also vary.

After You Read

Decide Which mutual fund purchasing plans would you suggest for a young investor and for a retired investor? Why?

Asset Growth Withdrawal A third choice lets you withdraw a prearranged percentage of your investment's asset growth, which is the amount by which your portfolio has increased in value.

For example, suppose that you arrange to receive 60 percent of the asset growth of your portfolio. The asset growth of your portfolio was $800 in a particular investment period. For that period you will receive a check for $480 ($800 × 60% or .60 = $480). If the value of your portfolio does not increase, you receive no payment. See the **Go Figure** box for an additional example.

Under this option, your principal (the amount of your original investment) remains untouched, and assuming you withdraw less than 100 percent of asset growth, your fund will continue to grow.

Dividend and Distribution Withdrawal A final option allows you to withdraw all income that results from income dividends and capital gains distributions earned during an investment period. Like the asset growth withdrawal mentioned above, under this option, your principal remains untouched.

SECTION 4 Assessment

Review Key Concepts

1. **Identify** What are the sources of information for selecting mutual funds?
2. **Explain** Discuss ways to buy and sell mutual funds.
3. **Summarize** Describe the ways in which mutual fund earnings are taxed.
4. **Differentiate** What is the difference between capital gain distribution and a capital gain?

Higher Order Thinking H.O.T.

5. **Recommend** Many people see mutual funds as a convenient and relatively easy way to save for their retirement. Why do you think this is so, and what advice would you offer to a young adult about when to start investing in his or her retirement?

21st Century Skills

6. **Make Judgments and Decisions** Erik, an auto repair technician, has invested in a mutual fund. He wants to add to his investment on a regular basis and is trying to decide which purchase option to use. His mutual fund offers a voluntary savings plan, a contractual savings plan, and a reinvestment plan. What are the advantages and disadvantages of the three purchase options available to Erik? Which purchase option would you suggest to him? Explain your answer.

Mathematics

7. **Capital Gain and Percentage of Asset Growth Withdrawal** Ella purchased an international equity mutual fund that had a net asset value of $43.50 at the time of purchase. She was able to purchase 125 shares at this price. She arranged to have 45 percent of the asset growth withdrawn on an annual basis. If the net asset value is $46.25 one year after her purchase, what amount will she withdraw? At the end of the second year, Ella sells her shares for $52.90, what is her capital gain per share?

Math Concept **Calculate Capital Gain and Percentage of Asset Growth Withdrawal** To calculate the capital gain, subtract the original net asset value from the net asset value at sale. The percentage of asset growth withdrawal is calculated by multiplying the annual capital gain by the percentage designated for withdrawal.

Starting Hint Determine the capital gain on sale of the mutual fund by first subtracting the sale price from the purchase price. This figure provides the gain per share. Multiply the result by the number of shares purchased.

NCTM Connections Recognize and apply mathematics in contexts outside of mathematics.

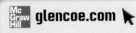

Check your answers.

Visual Summary

Bonds and Mutual Funds

Corporate Bonds

When you buy a corporate bond, you are basically loaning money to a company. There are four types of corporate bonds that you can evaluate to best suit your investment goals.

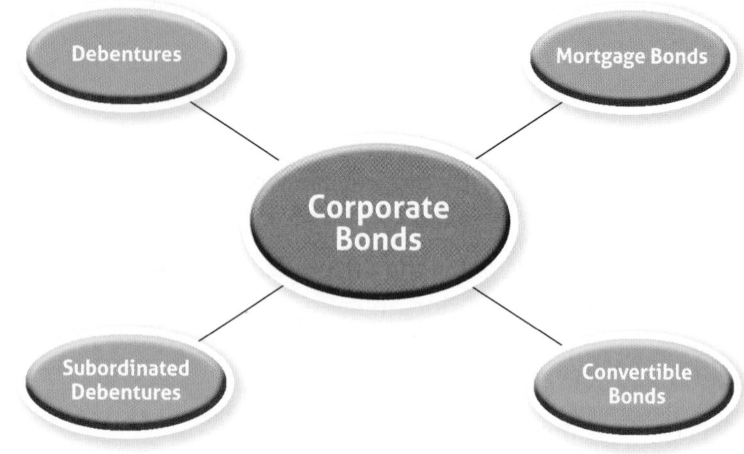

Bond Ratings

There are four quality ratings used for judging the security of a bond investment. Understanding these ratings can go a long way in making smart investments.

Try It!

Bond mutual funds invest only in bonds, and stock mutual funds are made up of stocks. Create an organizer like the one shown to categorize the types of stocks and bonds that mutual funds purchase.

Stock Mutual Funds	Bond Mutual Funds
1.	1.
2.	2.
3.	3.
4.	4.
5.	5.
6.	6.
7.	7.
8.	8.
9.	9.
10.	
11.	
12.	

Chapter Review and Assessment

Chapter Summary

- Corporate bonds have the following characteristics: interest rates, maturity dates, and face values.
- Corporations sell bonds to raise funds for operations, expansions, or purchases.
- Investors buy bonds because they provide regular income, plus the principal must be repaid by maturity.
- Governments sell bonds for reasons similar to corporations: to fund regular activities and finance the national debt. Government bonds include Treasury bills, Treasury notes, Treasury bonds, Treasury inflation-protected securities, and U.S. savings bonds (Series EE).
- Information on bonds is available in the financial press, corporate annual reports, bond rating reports, and online.
- Types of mutual funds include closed-end mutual funds, open-end mutual funds, load funds, and no-load funds.
- Mutual fund information is found in newspapers, annual reports, and financial publications, and through Web sites and advisors.
- Methods of buying and selling include regular account transactions, voluntary savings plans, payroll deduction plans, contractual savings plans, reinvestment plans, and withdrawal options.

Vocabulary Review

1. Write each of the vocabulary terms below on an index card, and the definitions on separate index cards. Work in pairs or small groups to match each term to its definition.

- maturity date
- face value
- debenture
- mortgage bond
- convertible bond
- sinking fund
- serial bonds
- registered bond
- coupon bond
- bearer bond
- zero-coupon bond
- municipal bond
- investment-grade bonds
- yield
- closed-end fund
- exchange-traded fund
- open-end fund
- net asset value (NAV)
- load fund
- no-load fund
- income dividends
- premium
- default
- metropolitan
- speculative
- compensated
- holding
- exhausted
- liquidate

Higher Order Thinking 

2. **Explain** Describe the type of investor who would be interested in a zero-coupon bond.
3. **Summarize** What are the factors that influence the price of a fund's shares?
4. **Compare and contrast** How are securities issued by state and local governments and corporate bonds similar? How are they different?
5. **Hypothesize** Bonds rated B and BB are considered speculative. Explain why someone might consider investing in such bonds.
6. **Defend** Explain why mutual funds can be a wise choice for inexperienced investors who have limited time and limited funds to invest.
7. **Justify** Explain why the high commission charged for a load fund is reasonable or not reasonable.
8. **Judge** If you want to diversify your portfolio, would you add corporate bonds? Why or why not?
9. **Evaluate** There are seven main sources of information on mutual funds. Review these sources, and then organize them in the order that you would use them. Explain your reasoning for the order.

College and Career Readiness

Science

10. Health Care Mutual Funds According to the *Occupational Outlook Handbook*, employment of medical professionals, from records and health information technicians to cancer researchers, is expected to increase by 20 percent, much faster than the average for all occupations through 2018.

Procedure Research the reasons for this projected job increase, and research what investment experts say about investing in health care mutual funds.

Analysis Prepare a report that explains the connection between health care jobs and investing in health care mutual funds.

NSES F Develop an understanding of personal and community health; population growth; natural resources; environmental quality; natural and human-induced hazards; science and technology in local, national, and global challenges.

Mathematics

11. Net Asset Value Troy has purchased some shares in a large-cap equity mutual fund. The fund's assets are made up of $20 million in agricultural stocks, $56 million in automotive stocks, $50 million in financial stocks, $45 million in telecommunication stocks, and $15 million in all other industries. The fund's liabilities include payable for investment securities purchased in the amount of $25 million, investment management fees payable of $15 million, and all other liabilities totaling $5 million. If there are 12 million common shares outstanding, what is the fund's net asset value?

Math Concept Calculate Net Asset Value To calculate the net asset value for a mutual fund, subtract the total liabilities from the total assets and then divide the result by the total number of common shares outstanding.

Starting Hint Subtract the total liabilities from the total assets to acquire the total net assets of the fund.

NCTM Number and Operations Compute fluently and make reasonable estimates.

English Language Arts

12. Mutual Fund Imagine that you are the manager of a large mutual fund. Think about the information potential investors would need to know. Then think about how you can organize the information in a creative, professional way to be presented to investors. Research the Web sites or publications from other mutual fund companies for inspiration. Prepare a flyer or pamphlet that will convince people to invest in your fund. Name your fund, and give several reasons to explain why investing in your mutual fund would be a wise investment. Make your item appealing by including pictures, charts, and graphs. Remember your flyers should be professional and polished.

NCTE 4 Use written language to communicate effectively.

Economics

13. Bond Markets One of the world's largest and most liquid bond markets is comprised of debt securities issued by the U.S. Treasury, by U.S. government agencies, and by U.S. government-sponsored enterprises. Governments issue bonds to help make the money they need to function. Identify and evaluate the benefits and costs of government-issued treasury securities, municipal bonds, and U.S. savings bonds. How does the government use bonds and securities? Who enjoys the benefits, and who bears the costs? Summarize your research in a report.

Real-World Applications

14. Investment Companies Go online and review several Web sites for investment firms that sponsor mutual funds. Just like any other business, investment companies want you to become a paying customer. Choose one of the Web sites to analyze. What is their mission statement? What services do they offer? What do they do to capture your attention? What do they want you to believe they can do for you as an investor? Find at least three unbiased sources you can use to confirm that the information on a company Web site is accurate. Summarize your findings and present them to the class.

Evaluating Mutual Funds

Eric is looking at a mutual fund because it might earn a greater return than a CD. He used the following chart as a way to evaluate the Pacific Sun Growth Fund, a stock mutual fund.

After evaluating Pacific Sun Growth Fund, Eric has decided that he likes the potential for a high return. He may go with the fund, even though he needs $1,000 to make his initial investment.

	Pacific Sun Growth Fund
1. Name of mutual fund	1. Pacific Sun Growth Fund
2. Mutual fund group and category	2. Stock mutual fund/aggressive growth
3. Mutual fund's objective (Aggressive growth, moderate growth, income and safety, and income)	3. Aggressive growth of capital
4. Yield in the last twelve months	4. 15%
5. Average return or yield for last five years	5. 11%
6. Average return or yield for last ten years	6. 18%
7. Load fees or redemption fees	7. no fees
8. What is the minimum investment?	8. $1,000
9. Is the fund closed to new investors?	9. No
10. Morningstar rating (in stars and risk)	10. Three-star rating and moderate risk

Research

Call an investment company for a prospectus of a mutual fund. You can also visit your local library and look in *Morningstar Mutual Funds* or the *Weisenberger Investment Companies Yearbook*, or see if company Web sites offer a PDF version of their prospectuses. On a separate sheet of paper or in a spreadsheet, create a chart similar to the one shown. Fill in the information on the chart to evaluate the fund. Use the figures and information to determine whether or not this fund would be a wise investment.

CHAPTER 20

Real Estate and Other Investments

Visual Literacy

Buying and selling collectibles can be a fun way to invest, but these investments can be riskier than stocks and bonds. ***What are some benefits of investing in collectibles?***

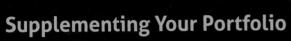

Discovery Project

Supplementing Your Portfolio

Key Question

What is a smart way to include risky investments in your portfolio?

Project Goal

You love to spend your weekends at yard sales, swap meets, thrift shops, pawnshops, and antique dealers to look for out-of-print books and records, classic comic books, rare toys, and celebrity memorabilia. You have a knack for knowing what items are in demand, so you supplement your income by buying and selling those items through online auctions. The Internet makes it easy for you to sell to people near and far, and you have built an excellent online reputation. Collectibles can be a good investment, but you know that they are riskier than other investments. Therefore, you want to make sure you maintain a sensible portfolio. Research real estate and precious metal and gem investments. Develop a strategy to add real estate and precious metal and gem investments to your portfolio.

Ask Yourself...

- *How can you participate in real estate investment with your limited funds?*
- *How will you narrow down your real estate options?*
- *Which precious metals and gems make the most sense to include in your portfolio?*
- *What will you do to monitor your investments?*

Make Judgments and Decisions

You just found out that your parents are planning to pay for your college education by selling some family jewelry. You appreciate this, but you have some concerns about this plan. Write a paragraph that explains your concerns.

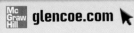

glencoe.com

Evaluate Download an assessment rubric.

THE BIG IDEA

Real estate, precious metals, gems, and collectibles can be a fun and challenging way to expand your investments.

ASK STANDARD & POOR'S

Collecting

Q *Are collectible action figures a smart investment for retirement?*

A Although collecting can be an enjoyable and sometimes profitable pursuit, collectibles are not a mainstay of retirement planning. It would be best if you focused your retirement planning efforts on building a diversified portfolio that may include stock and bond investments. You could still use collectibles as a small part of your portfolio, but their returns are very unpredictable.

Writing Activity

Write a full-page report about the pros and cons of investing in precious metals and gems. After you have finished, trade papers with a classmate. Proofread and edit each other's work. Look for errors in spelling, grammar, and punctuation, and offer suggestions for content improvement. Be willing to offer and accept constructive criticism. Revise your paper based on the feedback you received.

Reading Guide

Before You Read

The Essential Question Stocks and bonds are the foundation of most portfolios, but what are some other worthwhile investments?

Main Idea

Knowing the risks and rewards of investing in real estate, precious metals, gems, and collectibles can help you build a sound, diversified portfolio.

Content Vocabulary

- direct investment
- commercial property
- indirect investment
- syndicate
- participation certificate (PC)
- financial leverage
- precious metals
- precious gems
- collectibles

Academic Vocabulary

You will see these words in your reading and on your tests.

- liable
- handsome
- hedge
- soar

Graphic Organizer

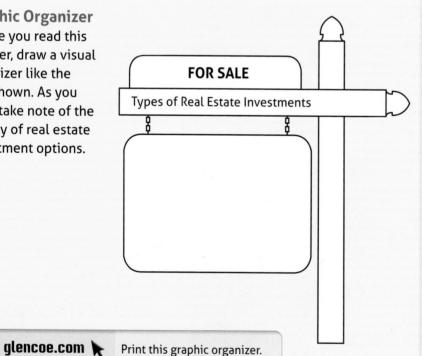

Before you read this chapter, draw a visual organizer like the one shown. As you read, take note of the variety of real estate investment options.

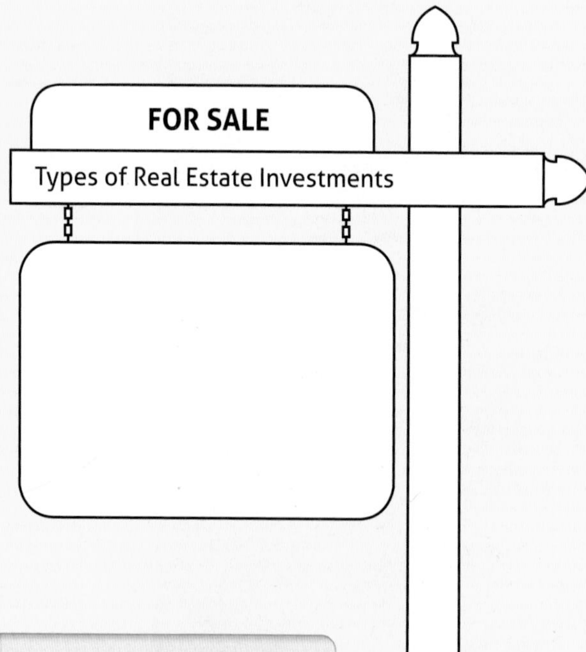

glencoe.com Print this graphic organizer.

Standards

Academic

Mathematics

NCTM Problem Solving Apply and adapt a variety of appropriate strategies to solve problems.

NCTM Problem Solving Solve problems that arise in mathematics and in other contexts.

NCTM Connections Organize and consolidate their mathematical thinking through communication.

English Language Arts

NCTE 5 Use different writing process elements to communicate effectively.

NCTE 7 Conduct research and gather, evaluate, and synthesize data to communicate discoveries.

Science

NSES B Students should develop an understanding of the structure of atoms, structure and properties of matter, chemical reactions, motions and forces, conservation of energy and increase in disorder, and interactions of energy and matter.

NCTM *National Council of Teachers of Mathematics*
NCTE *National Council of Teachers of English*
NCSS *National Council for the Social Studies*
NSES *National Science Education Standards*

Common Core

Reading Read and comprehend complex literary and informational texts independently and proficiently.

Speaking and Listening Present information, findings, and supporting evidence such that listeners can follow the line of reasoning and the organization, development, and style are appropriate to task, purpose, and audience.

Real Estate Investments

What is the difference between direct and indirect investment in real estate?

Unlike stocks and bonds, real estate is often something you can see and touch and take pride in. However, if you are new to the real estate market, you may be confused by all the different choices you have.

Section Objectives

- **Describe** the different types of direct real estate investments.
- **Describe** the different types of indirect real estate investments.
- **Discuss** the advantages and disadvantages of real estate investments.

As You Read

Predict Imagine that you have a relative who owns a 16-unit complex building and has offered you free rent in return for managing it. How long would you manage the building?

Direct Real Estate Investments

Real estate investments can be direct or indirect. The owner of a **direct investment** holds legal title to the property he or she has purchased. Direct investments include single-family houses, duplexes, apartments, land, and commercial property.

A Home as an Investment What is a home? Obviously, it is the place where you and your family live. However, owning a home can also be a good investment. According to Mortgage Bankers Association of America, home ownership is most Americans' largest financial asset. The estimated market value of homes in the United States is nearly $13 trillion.

During periods of inflation, the purchasing power of your money declines. Investing your money can help you stay ahead of inflation. Housing will continue to be an investment that promises steady returns over time. Generally, home prices have risen steadily over the years. (See **Figure 1.**) However, in recent years housing prices across the country have tumbled. While near-term increases are not expected to match the gains of the past, economists expect prices to gain 5.5 to 6 percent in the coming decade. During the past 150 years, owning a home has produced an average rate of return after inflation of about 2.5 percent. That is about the same rate of return you would expect from a bond.

Most homeowners have mortgages, which can provide certain tax benefits. Homeowners can report the interest charges on mortgage payments as well as property taxes as deductions on their tax returns.

Vacation Homes Second-home mortgages may also provide certain tax benefits. How much depends largely on whether the Internal Revenue Service views the property as your second home or as a rental property. As long as you do not rent out the property more than 14 days a year, it is considered a second home by the government. In this case you are able to write off mortgage interest and property tax on your federal income tax return. If you rent the vacation home regularly, the size of your deduction is determined by whether you actively manage the property and the size of your income.

FIGURE 1 **Average Sales Prices of New Single-family Homes**

Up and Away The average selling price of homes in the United States has risen steadily from 1980 until 2006, and then began to drop in certain regions. *Which region experienced the greatest gain through 2006? The lowest? Why do you think homes began to drop in certain regions after 2006?*

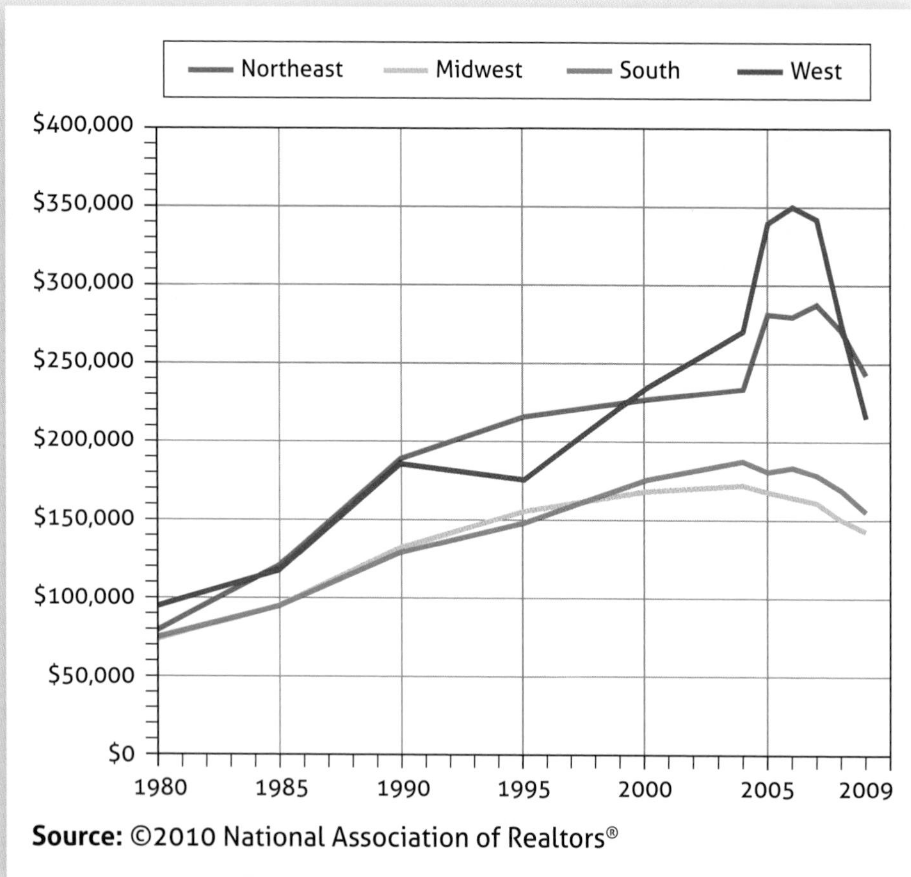

Source: ©2010 National Association of Realtors®

For example, Kevin's parents own a vacation home. It is a good investment because the family uses it year-round and never rents it out to others which qualifies it as a second home. Therefore, Kevin's parents can take advantage of certain tax deductions.

Commercial Property In addition to the vacation home, Kevin's parents also own commercial property. **Commercial property** is land and buildings that produce rental income. Kevin's parents own an apartment building that adds to their income. Other examples of commercial property include duplexes, hotels, office buildings, and stores. Most small investors favor duplexes, four-plexes, or small apartment buildings. Many investors start by purchasing a small commercial property. Then they buy larger properties as the equity in their original investment increases.

Document Detective

County Real Estate Valuation

Real estate property, such as a house or land, is taxed based on its value. The higher the value, the more taxes you pay to the local government. You will need to make sure that your property is valued correctly so that you do not pay excessive taxes. A county real estate valuation contains the following information:

- Property parcel ID number
- Description of the property
- Appraised value
- Assessed value

Parcel Number:	30-05655	
Owner:	Milo Lucky	
Property Address:	6731 Williamsburg Circle	
Legal Description:	Williamsburg Colony Phase C Lot 73	
Land Description:	100 ft. by 200 ft.	
Description of Primary Building(s)		
Colonial frame 2.0 story 2,251 sq. ft. built about 1988 with 8 total rooms with 4 bedrooms with 2 bathrooms with 1 half bath with full basement with no attic with 0 car basement garage with 1 fireplace.		
Description OBY Building(s) Value	**Proposed 2010 Appraised Value**	**2010 Assessed Value**
WD1: Wood Deck $1,330	Land: $42,900 Building(s): $162,870 Total: $205,770	Total: $205,770 Land: $15,020 Building(s): $57,010 Total: $72,020

Key Points The county government assesses the value of real estate property to determine how much tax should be paid for the property. County auditors review the value of recent real estate purchases and any improvements made to the property. The auditors then determine an appraised value for the property and an assessed value. The assessed value determines the amount of tax. Then a statement is sent to the property owner explaining the valuation.

FIND the Solutions

Review Key Concepts

1. What is the parcel ID number?
2. How many square feet of interior space does the building have?
3. What style is the building?
4. What is the appraised value of the wood deck?
5. What is the total square footage of the lot?

Land In 1986, Kevin's parents received quite a shock. Tax laws in the United States were rewritten so that many popular real estate investments, such as apartment buildings, lost some of their tax advantages. Owning commercial property became less appealing to some real estate investors. Many of these investors began investing in land that was ready to be developed.

Kevin's parents talked to an investment banker before they purchased land. She told them that while land investments often promise tremendous gains, they also pose enormous risks. If construction in general slowed or business activity declined, Kevin's parents might not be able to sell their property at a profit. Even worse, they might not be able to get the price that they had paid for it. Furthermore, the banker reminded them that unlike an apartment building, land in urban areas usually does not produce any income.

The banker also cautioned Kevin's parents about buying land and then dividing it into smaller lots to build single-family houses. They must be certain that water, sewers, and other utilities would be available. Otherwise, they would have to supply those services. The most common and least expensive way to obtain water and sewer service is to connect to existing services in a nearby city or town.

Indirect Real Estate Investments

Suppose that you want to invest in real estate, but you do not have enough money to purchase property on your own. The answer may be an indirect real estate investment. An **indirect investment** is an investment in which a trustee is appointed to hold legal title to the property on behalf of an investor or group of investors. Indirect investments include real estate syndicates, real estate investment trusts, high-risk mortgages, and participation certificates.

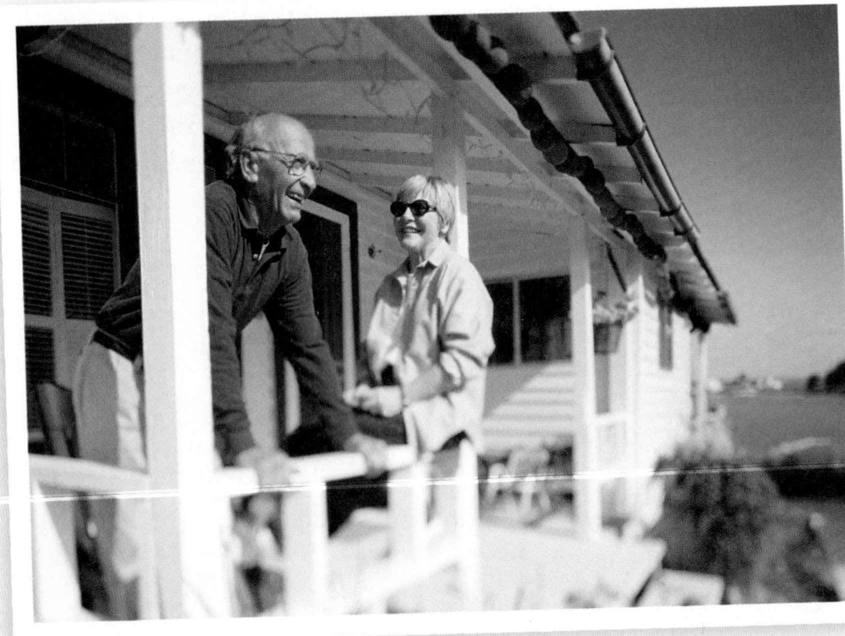

Invest in Leisure
A family vacation home can be part of a sensible investment strategy. *How can vacation homes be smart investments?*

Real Estate Syndicates or Limited Partnerships A **syndicate** is a temporary association of individuals or business firms organized to perform a task that requires a large amount of funds. A real estate syndicate invests in real estate. A syndicate may be organized as a corporation or as a trust. Most commonly, however, a syndicate is organized as a limited partnership.

Here is how a limited partnership works: A general partner, who takes complete responsibility for all of the partnership's liabilities, forms the partnership. The general partner then sells participation units, or shares, to a number of limited partners, or investors. Suppose that you decide to join the syndicate. As a limited partner, you are **liable,** or responsible, for only the amount of money you have invested, perhaps $5,000 or $10,000. This limited liability is an important condition of a real estate syndicate because the syndicate's mortgage debt may be more than your personal net worth or that of the other limited partners.

A real estate syndicate offers you and the other partners a variety of benefits. For example, if the syndicate purchases several types of property, your investment will be diversified. That is, you will be part owner of different types of property. In addition, the property owned by the syndicate is professionally managed. You do not need to care for it yourself.

At one time, people would join a real estate syndicate to create a tax shelter, which is a legal arrangement to take advantage of income tax deductions. However, the Tax Reform Act of 1986 limits the tax advantages available to syndicate investors. For example, investors can no longer use losses from their syndicate investments to offset, or reduce, their income from other sources. The 1986 law limits deductions for interest and for depreciation, which is the cost of general wear and tear. It also raised the tax on capital gains.

Real Estate Investment Trusts (REITs) Joshua's grandfather gave him $3,000 for graduation. Joshua would like to invest that money in real estate, but he realizes that he cannot buy an apartment building or condominium for that much money. One real estate investment choice Joshua could consider is a real estate investment trust (REIT). A REIT works much like a mutual fund. Like mutual funds, REITs combine money from many investors. However, while mutual funds are investments in stocks, bonds, and other securities, REITs are investments of the investors' money in real estate or in construction or mortgage loans. Shares in REITs are traded on stock exchanges or in the over-the-counter market.

There are three types of REITs: equity, mortgage, and hybrid. If you choose an equity REIT, your money will be invested in properties. Choosing a mortgage REIT will put your money to work financing construction loans and mortgages on developed properties. If you want to combine the investment goals of equity and mortgage REITs, you can choose a hybrid REIT.

Communication

One characteristic of successful people is possessing strong communication skills. People with strong communication skills are able to express thoughts and ideas effectively in a variety of forms and contexts. Communication skills can be used to inform, persuade, or motivate. Good communicators are also able to listen effectively, determining the meaning and intention of the message. Developing strong communication skills will help you to communicate effectively in diverse environments and achieve desired results.

Write About It

Think of a situation in which you or someone you know exhibited strong communication skills. Write one or more paragraphs to describe the situation and explain how communication skills impacted the scenario. How do you think communication skills could benefit you in the future?

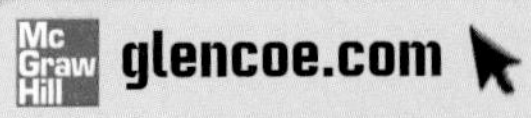

Activity Download a Career and College Readiness Worksheet Activity.

Careers That Count!

Tim Sandoval • Commercial Property Manager

When commercial property owners lack the time or expertise needed for the day-to-day management of their real estate investments, they often hire a commercial property manager like me. I monitor and maintain the building systems, vendor contracts, tenant relations, and profit and loss responsibilities for the buildings I manage. I visit the sites regularly and attend weekly or monthly tenant meetings. I take care of the properties' bills, licenses, and any emergencies or complaints, and I negotiate contracts for janitorial, security, landscaping, trash removal, and other services. Sometimes I purchase supplies and equipment for the property and make arrangements with professionals for repairs. The best opportunities in my field will be available to those with a degree in business administration or real estate, or with professional certification. To see if you would like this kind of work, look for opportunities to be the onsite manager of a small apartment complex.

EXPLORE CAREERS

Research the variety of job descriptions and duties that fall under the category of property management.

1. How can property managers affect the value of the properties they manage?
2. What are some of the duties of property managers?

Skills	Education	Career Path
Communication, multitasking, math, computer, management, customer service, organization, and time-management skills	Bachelor's degree or master's degree in business administration, finance, real estate, or related fields	Commercial property managers can become real estate asset managers, real estate brokers, land developers, and specialists in certain types of buildings, such as renovation projects and health care facilities.

glencoe.com

Activity Download a Career Exploration Activity.

According to federal government regulations, REITs are required to:

- Distribute at least 90 percent of their net annual earnings to shareholders.
- Avoid investing in risky, short-term real estate holdings in the hope of selling them for quick profits.
- Hire independent real estate professionals to carry out certain management activities.
- Have at least 100 shareholders, with no more than half the shares owned by five or fewer people.

If you are interested in finding out more about REITs, you can contact the National Association of Real Estate Investment Trusts.

High-Risk Mortgages Some investors accept high risk in exchange for possible profits. For example, Mr. Moy is a wealthy investor who purchases high-risk mortgages and other debt contracts. Because he is wealthy, Mr. Moy is willing to take risks that financial institutions, such as banks and savings and loan associations, will not. For example, Mr. Moy might purchase the mortgage on a property that is not in demand because the title to the property may not be legally clear or insurable. Because of such risks, Mr. Moy and other similar investors might receive a high rate of return on their investments. Even though Mr. Moy is not guaranteed a high rate of return, he hopes that the demand for his property will increase so he will make a **handsome,** or higher than expected, profit in the future. On the other hand, if the demand does not increase, Mr. Moy may lose most or all of his investment.

Participation Certificates Unlike Mr. Moy, investors cannot afford to take such risks with their money. If you are looking for a risk-free real estate investment, then participation certificates might be a good choice for you. A **participation certificate (PC)** is an investment in a group of mortgages that have been purchased by a government agency. Because the investment is made in a group of mortgages, it is considered a mutual fund. You can buy participation certificates from these federal agencies:

- Government National Mortgage Association (Ginnie Mae)
- Federal Home Loan Mortgage Corporation (Freddie Mac)
- Federal National Mortgage Association (Fannie Mae)
- Student Loan Marketing Association (Sallie Mae)

A few states also issue participation certificates. You can purchase PCs from the State of New York Mortgage Agency (Sonny Mae) and the New England Education Loan Marketing Corporation (Nellie Mae).

Agencies with close ties to the federal government guarantee Maes and Macs. The PCs they issue are as secure as U.S. Treasury securities. You can invest as little as $1,000 to buy shares. Each month, you can receive a check for the principal and interest or reinvest the profits.

Reading Check

Define What is commercial property, and what are some examples?

World-Class Opportunities
Giant corporate complexes can cost millions of dollars to build and maintain.
How can someone who is not wealthy invest in such properties?

Real Estate Investment: Pros and Cons

What should you know when considering real estate investment?

Before you invest in real estate, you will want to weigh the advantages and disadvantages.

Advantages of Real Estate Investments

There may be several advantages enjoyed by certain types of real estate investments:

Hedge Against Inflation When inflation rises, your purchasing power decreases. Both direct and indirect investments in areas such as real estate may provide some protection against inflation. Historically, real estate continues to increase in value over time or at least hold its value, thus protecting investors from declining purchasing power.

Easy Entry By making an indirect investment in a real estate syndicate, you can easily become a part owner of an apartment building or a shopping center. For example, you may have the opportunity to invest $5,000 as a limited partner to gain entry to an apartment building. As a limited partner your liability is restricted by the amount you invested. The minimum capital requirements for the purchase of commercial property such as an apartment building may be as high as $1 million or more. This is often beyond the limits of a typical real estate investor. By combining your money with that of other investors, you can purchase commercial property.

Limited Financial Liability An indirect investment in a real estate syndicate allows you to be a limited partner. That means you are not liable for losses beyond your original investment. This advantage is important if the syndicate is investing in a risky venture.

Financial Leverage **Financial leverage** is the use of borrowed funds for direct investment purposes. By using borrowed money, you can purchase more expensive property. If property values and incomes are rising, this can be an advantage.

For example, suppose that Deborah buys a building for $100,000 with no borrowed funds. She then sells the building for $120,000. Deborah's $20,000 profit equals a 20 percent return on her $100,000 investment ($20,000 ÷ $100,000 = 0.20 or 20%).

On the other hand, suppose that Deborah invested just $10,000 of her own money and had a $90,000 mortgage with an interest rate of 8.5 percent. After three years, she sells the property for $120,000, with a profit of $7,721 ($20,000 – $12,279 in interest = $7,721). Her profit would represent a 77 percent return on her $10,000 investment ($7,721 ÷ $10,000 = 0.7721 or 77.21%).

Australia

Opals

Many people choose gems as an investment because not only are they valuable but they are things of beauty that can be enjoyed. Of course there are many gems to choose from, including diamonds, rubies, and sapphires. One gem that has a history to go along with its beauty is the opal. Australia is often considered to be the origin of the opal. Different varieties of opal have present and historic sources throughout Australia. For example, the Lightning Ridge district is famous as a source for the black opal, Queensland is a source for sandstone boulder opal, and New South Wales offers up light and crystal opals.

Australia is also home to the oldest continuous culture in the world, the Aborigines. The opal plays an important role in the legends of the Aborigines. The Pitjanjatjara tribe in Central Australia believes that a giant rainbow serpent created the world. As he did so, scales fell from his skin and those scales became opals. The Wangkumara tribe passes on the legend of a pelican pecking at an opal rock to create fire, which was then believed to be a gift from the creator.

Critical Thinking

1. **Expand** What is opal made up of? What other countries produce opal?
2. **Relate** Would the history of a gem influence your decision to invest in it?

DATABYTES

Capital
Canberra

Population
21,515,754

Languages
English 78.5%, Chinese 2.5%, Italian 1.6%, Greek 1.3%, Arabic 1.2%, Vietnamese 1%, other 8.2%, unspecified 5.7%

Currency
Australian dollar

Gross Domestic Product (GDP)
$930.8 billion

GDP per capita
$38,800

Industry
Mining, industrial and transportation equipment, food processing, chemicals, steel

Agriculture
Wheat, barley, sugarcane, fruits; cattle, sheep, poultry

Exports
Coal, iron ore, gold, meat, wool, alumina, wheat, machinery and transport equipment

Natural Resources
Bauxite, coal, iron ore, copper, tin, gold, silver, uranium, nickel, tungsten, mineral sands, lead, zinc, diamonds, natural gas, petroleum

Common Cents

Collectible Gifts

Suggest to your family and friends that you make gifts for each other instead of buying them for special days and holidays. You will all save money, and your gifts may become family heirlooms.

Concept Application

How much money do you think you could save each year by making gifts instead of buying them?

Disadvantages of Real Estate Investments

Unfortunately, investors such as Deborah cannot be certain that their real estate investments will pay off. There are several possible disadvantages to real estate investments:

Illiquidity Perhaps the most significant drawback to real estate investment is illiquidity. Real estate is an illiquid investment, which means that it cannot be easily converted into cash without a loss in value. It may take months or even years to sell commercial property or shares in a limited partnership.

Declining Property Values As discussed earlier, real estate investments may offer some protection against inflation. However, when interest rates fall, or if the economy is in a decline, the value of real estate investments may decrease. If you own property, you may have to make the difficult decision to sell your property for less than you paid for it and accept a loss.

Lack of Diversification Because real estate is expensive, many investors can afford only one or two properties. Subsequently, it may be difficult to build a diversified real estate investment portfolio. Keep in mind, however, that REITs, PCs, and syndicates do offer various levels of diversification.

Lack of a Tax Shelter In the past, real estate syndicates were tax shelters for investors. However, the Tax Reform Act of 1986 eliminated that advantage. Syndicate investors cannot deduct real estate losses from the income they receive through other sources, such as wages, dividends, and interest.

Other provisions of the 1986 act affect real estate investments and reduce the value of the tax credits for such investments. For example, investors are not allowed to take losses in excess of the actual amounts they invested. In addition, the investment tax credit has been eliminated entirely for all real estate except low-income housing.

Management Problems When you invest in REITs, syndicates, or PCs, property management is provided as a part of your investment. When you invest in mortgages, property management is not an issue. However, when you buy your own properties, you must manage them. That means that you are responsible for such things as finding reliable tenants, replacing worn carpeting, and fixing the furnace. Property management can be a full-time job, and many investors are not willing to take on that much responsibility.

Investment Options

If you consider all the advantages and disadvantages of investing in real estate and you believe it is too risky or too complicated, you might consider other tangible investments. Gold and other precious metals, gems, and collectibles are options that some investors choose. However, these investments also carry risk with the reward, as discussed in the next section.

SECTION 1 Assessment

Review Key Concepts

1. **Identify** Describe the different types of direct real estate investments.
2. **List** Describe the different types of indirect real estate investments.
3. **Compare** Discuss the advantages and disadvantages of real estate investments.

Higher Order Thinking H.O.T.

4. **Assess** The Tax Reform Act of 1986 limits the tax advantages available to syndicate investors. For example, investors can no longer use losses from their syndicate investments to offset their income from other sources, it limits deductions for interest and for depreciation, and it raised the tax on capital gains. Discuss the impact of this act on real estate investments.

21st Century Skills

5. **Create Media Products** Participation certificates are considered risk-free investments. This makes them appealing to investors who are looking for protection against inflation but who do not have a lot of money to invest. How would you interest potential investors in these certificates? Using illustration software, create a persuasive advertisement for a financial magazine. Point out the benefits of participation certificates, and include information that highlights the risk-free nature of these investments. Include attention-getting graphics and appropriate images.

Mathematics

6. **Financial Leverage** Evan purchased an apartment building as an investment for $140,000. He pays for it without borrowing any funds. If he sells the building for $165,000 what is his return on the building? Now assume Evan had taken out a mortgage in the amount of $125,000 to help pay for the building. The mortgage has an interest rate of 5.5 percent. If he sells the building after 3 years for $165,000, what is his return now? Assume Evan pays $5,500 per year in interest on the loan.

   Math Concept **Calculate Financial Leverage** To calculate financial leverage you must first calculate the total profit from the sale. Divide this result by the initial investment to determine the return on the investment with borrowed funds.

   Starting Hint Determine the net profit on the sale of the building by subtracting the sale price from the original purchase price. Subtract the total interest paid on the loan from the result.

NCTM Problem Solving Apply and adapt a variety of appropriate strategies to solve problems.

Check your answers.

Section Objectives

- **Identify** the different types of precious metal and gem investments.
- **Explain** the appeal of investing in precious gems.
- **Discuss** collectibles as a type of investment.
- **Analyze** the disadvantage and risks of investing in precious metals, gems, and collectibles.

As You Read

Relate Think about jewelry you possess that might be made from precious metals or gems. Do you consider them ornaments or investments?

Gold

Why do people invest in gold and other precious metals?

Precious metals include such valuable ores as gold, platinum, and silver. Many people invest their money in precious metals as a **hedge,** or protection, against inflation. If you are interested in purchasing gold, you have several choices, as shown in **Figure 2.**

The price of gold rises when people believe that war, political unrest, or inflation may be just around the corner. As international tensions ease or the political situation stabilizes, the price of gold falls. **Figure 3** shows how the price of gold rose and fell from 1980 to 2009.

Reading Check

Restate In times of peace, does the value of gold increase or decrease? Why?

Other Precious Metals

What is one disadvantage of investing in precious metals such as platinum?

Other precious metals that rise in value during times of political or economic trouble are silver, platinum, palladium, and rhodium. Silver prices have ranged from a historic low of 24.25 cents an ounce in 1932 to more than $16.99 an ounce in December 2009.

Platinum, palladium, and rhodium, which are three lesser-known precious metals, are also popular investments. All of these metals have industrial uses, particularly in automobile production. In December 2009, platinum sold for about $1,461 an ounce, palladium for about $393 an ounce, and rhodium for about $2,266 an ounce.

Storing precious metals can be tricky. Twenty thousand dollars' worth of gold, for example, is about the size of a paperback book. That same amount in silver weighs more than 200 pounds. Also, remember that while stocks and other interest-bearing investments are earning money for you, precious metals sit in vaults, and earn nothing. In order to make a profit, you must correctly predict the market and sell the metals when their value is higher than what you paid.

Reading Check

Recall In what industry are precious metals often used?

FIGURE 2 Investing in Gold

Golden Value When the economy weakens or political unrest develops, some people believe that gold is the safest investment they can make. *What might be some drawbacks of investing in gold?*

1 **Bullion** You can purchase gold bullion, which is offered in bars and wafers, from dealers of precious metals and from banks. The seller's commission can range from 1 to 8 percent. If you do not store the gold with the dealer, you must have it reassayed (tested for quality) before you can resell it.

2 **Coins** Gold coins represent a simple way to invest in this precious metal. Most coin dealers require a minimum order of ten coins and will charge you a seller's commission of at least 2 percent.

3 **Stocks** You can diversify your investment portfolio by purchasing common stock in mining companies. When the economy is healthy, the price of gold stocks tends to fall while the value of other investment rises. When the economy falters so that traditional investments lose value, gold stocks tend to rise in value.

Precious Gems

What is one of the advantages of investing in precious gems?

When the Queen of England opens the British Parliament, she wears a crown and carries a scepter, both of which are covered with diamonds, rubies, sapphires, and other glittering gems. As soon as the ceremony is over, the royal ornaments are quickly locked up again in the Jewel House at the Tower of London.

Throughout world history people have valued the precious gems that lie below the earth's surface. **Precious gems** are rough mineral deposits (usually crystals) that are dug from the earth by miners and then cut and shaped into brilliant jewels. These gems include diamonds, sapphires, rubies, and emeralds. They appeal to investors because of their small size, ease of storage, great durability, and their potential as a protection against inflation.

The inflation that occurred in the United States during the 1970s prompted investors to put more of their money into tangible assets such as gemstones. The result was a 40-fold increase in the price of diamonds. A few lucky investors made fortunes during that time.

Whether you are buying precious gems to store in a safe-deposit box or to wear as jewelry, keep in mind the risks associated with this type of investment. First, you cannot easily convert diamonds and other precious gems into cash. Also, as a beginning investor, you may have difficulty determining whether the gems you are purchasing are

FIGURE 3 **Changing Price of Gold Since 1980**

Gold's Wild Ride The value of gold fluctuated widely during the last quarter of the 1900s. *What might explain the spike in gold prices during 1980 and again in 2009?*

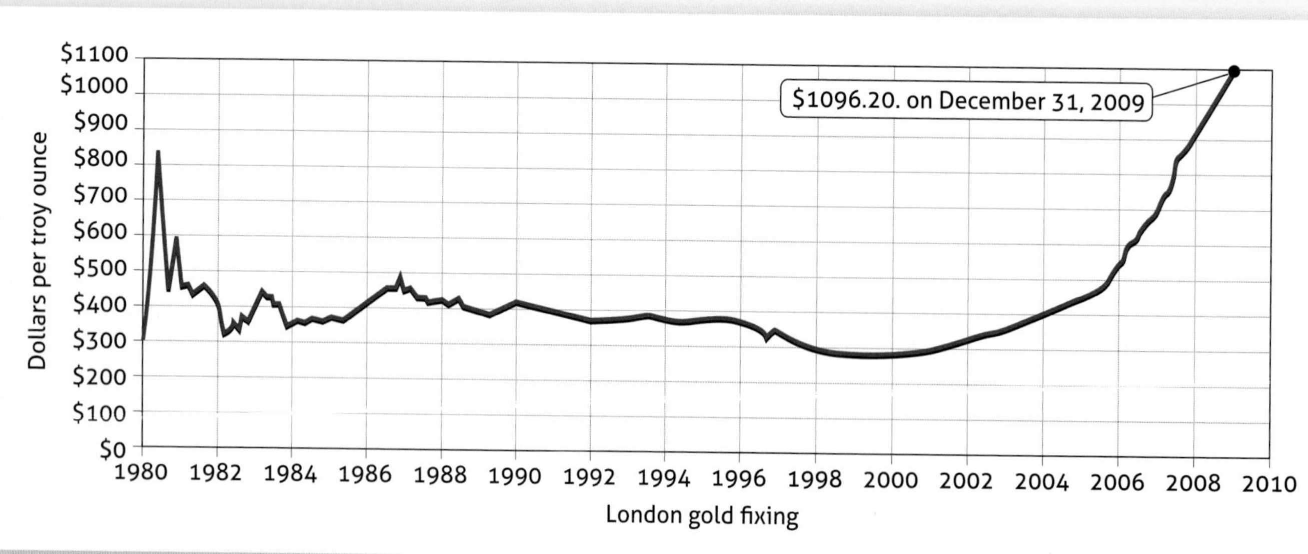

of high quality. Political unrest in gem-producing countries can affect supply and pricing. In addition, you will likely have to buy your gems at higher retail prices and sell them at lower wholesale prices. The difference is usually 10 to 15 percent and can be as high as 50 percent.

Crown Jewels
Throughout history, precious gems have been associated with royalty and wealth. *What gives diamonds, sapphires, rubies, and other precious stones their value today?*

The best way to know exactly what you are getting in an expensive precious gem is to have the stone certified by an independent geological laboratory, such as the Gemological Institute of America. The certificate should list the stone's characteristics, including its weight, color, clarity, and quality of cut. The grading of gems, however, is not an exact science. Experiments have shown that the same stone submitted twice to the same laboratory may get two different ratings.

Despite the attraction of precious metals and gems, the investment risks are sizable. The primary risk is the great fluctuation in prices, which can be influenced by global, economic, and political factors. For example, in 1980, world events caused the prices of precious metals and gems to **soar,** or rise quickly. Investors bought gold for as much as $850 an ounce, and a one-carat diamond for $62,000.

Reading Check

Define What are precious gems?

Collectibles

What are collectibles?

Collectibles are another type of investment. **Collectibles** include rare coins, works of art, antiques, stamps, rare books, comic books, sports memorabilia, paintings, and other items that appeal to collectors and investors. Each of these items offers the knowledgeable collector or investor both pleasure and an opportunity for profit. Many collectors have been surprised to discover that items they bought for their own enjoyment have increased greatly in value while they owned them.

For example, when Hannah was a little girl, her Aunt Sylvia bought her two collectible dolls. As she grew up, Hannah received more dolls as gifts and also bought some of her own. She now has an extensive collection of over 100 different dolls. Although Hannah never really thought of her dolls as an investment, she recently discovered that several of them are worth $500 each, which is more than three times what she paid for them.

Economics and You

Market Pricing

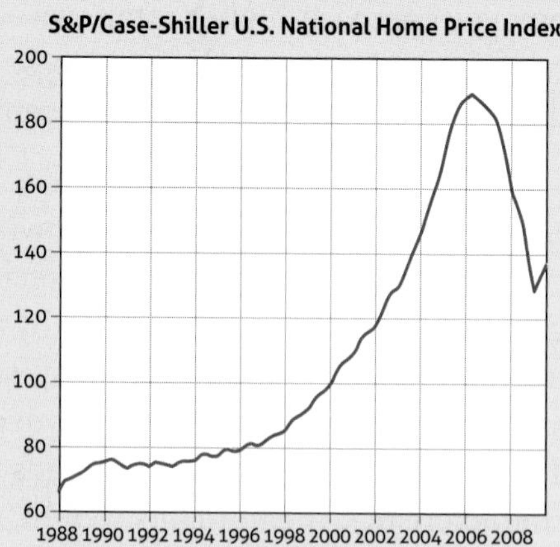

Product surpluses and shortages influence prices. When there is a surplus of products, prices are reduced to encourage more people to buy. For example, when there is an abundance of broccoli, the price is less than when a business has just enough for its customers. When there is a shortage, sellers know they can charge more because there are a lot of potential customers, many of whom are willing and able to buy the product at the higher price. The real estate market is a perfect example of how surpluses and shortages affect the market. When there are many sellers and few buyers, real estate prices are lower than normal. When there are many buyers, prices can be higher.

Personal Finance Connection If you have been given vintage collectibles you may be surprised to learn that they are worth a lot of money. There are very few of those items in circulation so there is a shortage, which results in higher prices for people who want to add them to their collection. You must keep them in mint condition for them to be worth anything to a collector.

Critical Thinking Compare and contrast real estate and collectibles with regard to their respective markets and the price each commands currently. To accomplish this task, you need to research both markets and consider the current economy.

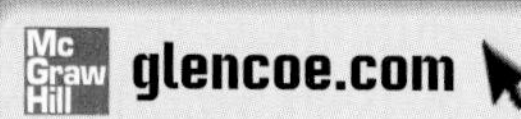

Activity Download an Economics and You Worksheet Activity.

Collectibles on the Internet

Before the era of the World Wide Web, finding items to add to your collections could be very time-consuming. You would have to pore over collectors' trade magazines to research the value of items you wished to buy. Then you would have to go to shows, sometimes far away, where collectors met to buy and sell their merchandise.

That process has changed. The Internet has made buying and selling collectibles efficient and convenient, and the number of Web sites for collectors has exploded. In 1999, when Guernsey's Auction House offered Mark McGwire's 70th home run baseball to bidders, they opened the bidding process to online buyers as well. Although the baseball went to an anonymous telephone bidder (later known to be the famed comic book artist Todd McFarlane) for $3 million, the use of the Internet as an auction site was firmly established.

It is easy to see why the Internet appeals to collectors. As a buyer, you can search for items to add to your collection with a few keystrokes, and sellers can reach people all around the world. Prices are not necessarily lower on the Internet, but comparison shopping is easier, and most sites do not charge buyer's a commission.

Selling collectibles on the Internet is best suited to smaller items, such as books, coins, stamps, buttons, and textiles that can be easily scanned for viewing and shipped by mail.

Of course, collecting through the Internet has its drawbacks. As an online buyer, you cannot assess a dealer face-to-face or examine the objects for flaws or trademarks. Furthermore, fraud is an ever-present danger.

A more serious concern is the security risk of buying online when you do not know who is getting your cash or credit card number. While the security risks of online collecting grab headlines, actual fraud is relatively low.

Let the Collector Beware

Collecting can be a satisfying hobby and a good investment. Nevertheless, a wise collector must always be alert for scams—on or off the Internet. For example, how do you know that the fielder's glove you bought was actually signed by Mickey Mantle? Could your Civil War-era postage stamps be counterfeit? Is that Barbie® doll, Lionel® locomotive, or Darth Vader™ action figure really as rare and valuable as you have been told?

When you trade collectibles, be aware that some online auction and exchange sites are more reliable than others. According to figures from Internet Fraud Watch, which is sponsored by the National Consumers League (NCL), 76 percent of the fraud complaints it received during a previous six-month period were related to online auctions. Consumers can report suspected Internet fraud by calling the NCL Fraud Hotline. The safest way to steer clear of collectibles-related fraud is to learn everything you can about the items you collect and to buy and sell only with reputable dealers and auction Web sites.

reality bytes

Collectibles

Are you interested in antiques or other collectibles? In order to make sure your initial investment grows, you have to buy items at the right price. To better understand what objects sell for and what makes something valuable, you can visit the Web site of an auction house and view collectible objects and their suggested prices.

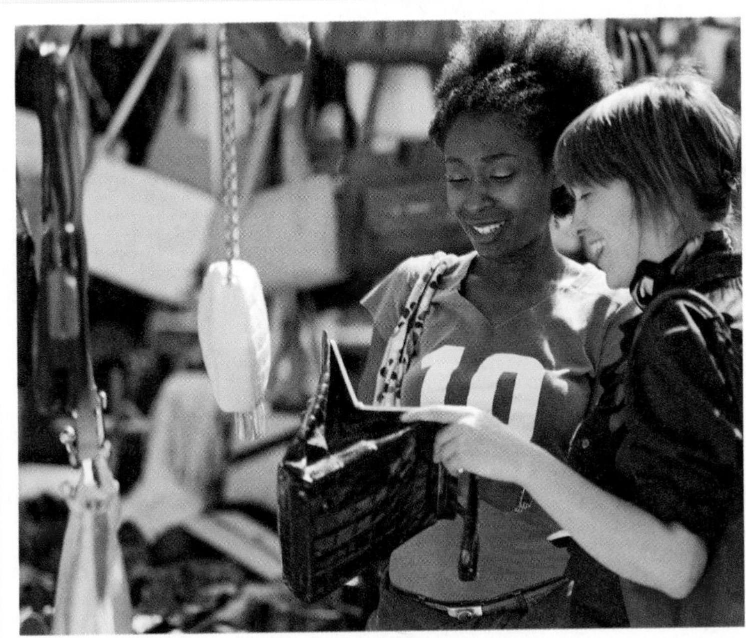

Unexpected Riches
Collecting can be an enjoyable and sometimes profitable pastime. *Are collectibles a wise investment? What are some items you might enjoy collecting as an inestment?*

FIGURE 4 **Stocks for the Long Term**

Best Investments According to this table, stocks and bonds offered investors the highest average annual return over the long term. *After one year, which asset provided the highest average annual return? After five years?*

Average Annual Return After . . .

Asset	1 Year	5 Years	10 Years	20 Years
Stocks	2.6%	10.4%	15.5%	13.1%
Bonds	0.7%	9.9%	14.1%	10.2%
3-Month Treasury Bills	4.3%	5.6%	6.7%	8.3%
Diamonds	0.0%	1.4%	5.9%	7.9%
Housing	1.8%	2.9%	4.1%	6.3%
Gold	4.7%	1.3%	−0.2%	4.5%

Remember that collectibles do not offer interest or dividends. Also, you may have a hard time selling items at a good price on short notice. If your collection grows significantly in value, you will have to purchase insurance against damage and theft.

Reading Check

Connect How has the Internet affected the buying and selling of collectibles?

After You Read

Predict How can you use the information provided in this chapter to make a wise investment in precious metals, gems, or collectibles?

Planning Investments

How do you choose the best types of investments for you and your financial goals?

Investments such as stocks and bonds may not be very interesting or exciting, but as you can see in **Figure 4,** they have proven to be the most stable types of investments in the long run. Investing in collectibles may seem interesting, but it may not be the best way for you to achieve your financial goals.

Wise planning is the best way to get the most out of your investments. Be sure to research the types of investments that are available so you can make an informed decision. Weigh the advantages and disadvantages of each type of investment. Ask yourself how much risk and responsibility you are willing to assume. By taking these steps, you will be able to make a decision that is best for your financial future.

Assessment

Review Key Concepts

1. **Identify** What are the different types of precious metal and gem investments?
2. **Explain** What is the appeal of investing in precious gems?
3. **Summarize** Discuss collectibles as a type of investment.
4. **Analyze** What are the disadvantages and risks of investing in precious metals, gems, and collectibles?

Higher Order Thinking H.O.T.

5. **Determine** How can you protect yourself from fraud when buying and selling collectibles through online auctions?

English Language Arts

6. **Show and Tell** Think about your personal collections, or the collections of a family member. What do you or your family have that might be considered collectibles? Go online to research the value of these items. What can you learn about their history? How, if at all, are they traded? If you or your family members do not have such a collection, think of something you would like to collect, such as action figures, porcelain dolls, toy automobiles, and so on, and do the same research. Present your findings to the class, and bring in a sample or photo of the collectible if possible.

NCTE 7 Conduct research and gather, evaluate, and synthesize data to communicate discoveries.

Mathematics

7. **Buying Gold** Leela purchased 15 ounces of gold in 2005 for $422 per ounce in order to try to diversify her investment portfolio. She sold a third of her holdings in gold in 2009 at a price of $944 per ounce. She sold the rest of her gold holdings in 2010 for $1,254 per ounce. What is Leela's profit in 2009 and 2010? What would her profit have been if she sold all of the gold holdings in 2009? What if she sold everything in 2010?

Math Concept **Calculate Return on Gold** To calculate the return on gold subtract the sale price from the purchase price and multiply the result by the number of ounces sold. Divide this by the total investment at the time of purchase.

Starting Hint Determine the number of ounces sold in 2009. Subtract the price per ounce in 2009 from the price per ounce in 2005 and multiply the result by the number of ounces sold.

NCTM Problem Solving Solve problems that arise in mathematics and in other contexts.

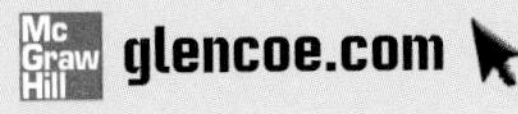

Check your answers.

Visual Summary

Real Estate and Other Investments

Mortgage Participation Certificates

A participation certificate (PC) is an investment in a group of mortgages that have been purchased by a government agency.

Name of Federal Agency	Agency Nickname
Government National Mortgage Association	Ginnie Mae
Federal Home Loan Mortgage Corporation	Freddie Mac
Federal National Mortgage Association	Fannie Mae
Student Loan Marketing Association	Sallie Mae
State of New York Mortgage Agency	Sonny Mae
New England Education Loan Marketing Corporation	Nellie Mae

Investing in Gold

Gold, available in many forms, can be a good investment choice if you have the ability to predict the behavior of the market.

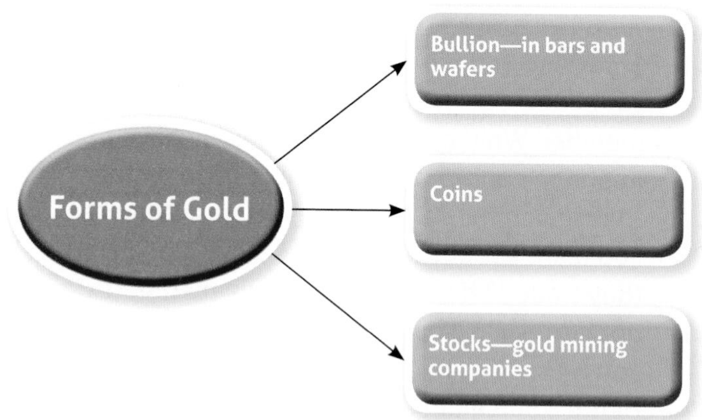

Try It!

Create a pros and cons diagram like the one shown, and write down the benefits and drawbacks of investing in collectibles.

The Pros and Cons of Investing in Collectibles

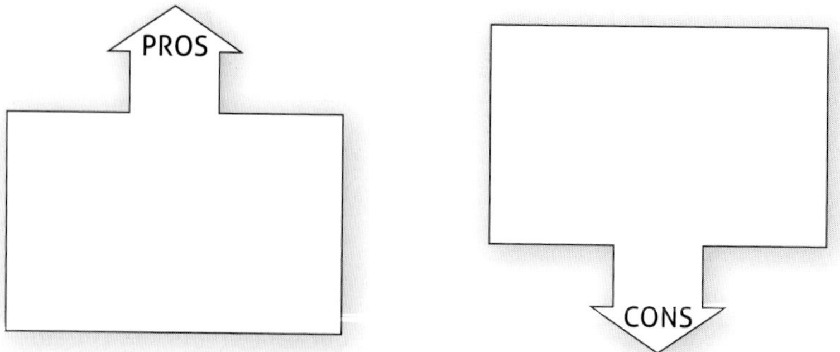

Chapter Review and Assessment

Chapter Summary

- The owner of a direct investment in real estate directly holds the legal title to the residential or commercial property and is responsible for its maintenance and management.
- An indirect investment is similar to investing in mutual funds. A group of investors buys property, and a trustee holds legal title.
- Real estate syndicates, limited partnerships, and real estate investment trusts (REITs) are examples of indirect investments.
- The advantages of investments (syndicates and REITs) in real estate are: use as a hedge against inflation, ease of entering the market, and limited liability.
- Lack of liquidity and diversification, risk of declining property values, fewer tax incentives, and potential management problems are disadvantages.
- Precious metals include gold, silver, platinum, palladium, and rhodium.
- Precious gems include diamonds, sapphires, rubies, and emeralds.
- Collectibles include rare coins, works of art, antiques, stamps, rare books, comic books, sports memorabilia, rugs, ceramics, and other items.
- The value of precious metals and gems can fluctuate greatly, making them a risky investment. It is also difficult to predict the value of collectibles.

Vocabulary Review

1. Write a short story using two or more of these vocabulary terms. The story should clearly show how the terms are related.

- direct investment
- commercial property
- indirect investment
- syndicate
- participation certificate (PC)
- financial leverage
- precious metals
- precious gems
- collectibles
- liable
- handsome
- hedge
- soar

Higher Order Thinking 

2. **Analyze** It has long been said that homeownership is a big part of "the American dream." Do you think this is still true? Why or why not?
3. **Explain** Why do people join limited partnerships and REITs?
4. **Defend** Do you agree with the notion that it is not a waste of time for a young person to consider investing in real estate? Explain.
5. **Examine** Investing in real estate can be a good way to diversify your portfolio, but real estate investment lacks diversification. Explain this apparent contradiction.
6. **Assess** Your friend thinks that investing in collectibles is a waste of time and money. What would you say to her?
7. **Recommend** Samantha inherited a diamond-and-ruby necklace from her grandmother's estate. Unfortunately, the settings for the stones are damaged beyond repair. Samantha is trying to decide what to do with her inheritance. Create a strategy that will help Samantha determine the value of her inheritance and how she might increase that value.

College and Career Readiness

Science

8. All That Glitters Although the United States is the largest consumer of gem-quality diamonds, it has no commercial mine production. At depths of over 100 miles, under specific temperature and pressure conditions, inorganic carbon forms into a solid with a specific crystalline structure. Most diamonds come to the earth's surface via volcanic channels.

Procedure Print a world map and mark the places where gem-quality diamonds are mined.

Analysis What geological feature do these locations have in common?

NSES B Students should develop an understanding of the structure of atoms, structure and properties of matter, chemical reactions, motions and forces, conservation of energy and increase in disorder, and interactions of energy and matter.

Mathematics

9. Portfolio Hedging Jack holds 150 shares of an international equity fund which he bought at $24.75 per share in 2008. He decided to purchase stock in a gold mining company in order to hedge against his other holdings. Jack decided to purchase 50 shares of ABC Gold Mining Co. for $12.50 per share. In 2010 the international equity fund's market value is $29.50 per share and ABC's market value is $9.75 per share. If Jack sells both investments in 2010 what is his total profit and return? What options does he have in order to try to increase his gains?

Math Concept **Calculate Return on Portfolio** To calculate the return on a portfolio divide the total profit from the portfolio by the total investment amount.

Starting Hint Determine the total investment amount of the portfolio by first multiplying the number of shares of the international equity fund by the price per share in 2008. Multiply the number of shares purchased of ABC Gold Mining Co. by the price per share in 2008. Add the two amounts to get the total investment.

NCTM Connections Organize and consolidate their mathematical thinking through communication.

English Language Arts

10. Investment Options Your friend Jerry, who lives in another state, is the sole heir of his grandmother's estate. After setting aside some items that he wants to keep for sentimental reasons, Jerry needs to figure out what to do with the rest of his inheritance: a piece of land in an urban area, several REITs and Ginnie Mae certificates, and a 1957 Cadillac that needs some work. Jerry just sent you an email to ask your advice in determining which of his grandmother's investments he should keep and which he should sell. Write an email to Jerry with your suggestions.

NCTE 5 Use different writing process elements to communicate effectively.

Ethics

11. Reproductions There are many antiques and collectibles that have been reproduced. Some are reproduced and marked as such, but others are not authorized, and they are sold as originals. In fact, some items are so close to the originals that, short of an expert, there are few ways that a collector and even some dealers can tell the difference. Explain whether it is acceptable in some situations for a dealer to represent a reproduction as an authentic antique or collectible. How might such a practice affect the antiques industry?

Real-World Applications

12. Real Estate Imagine that you started your first full-time job about eight months ago. Your new job offers benefits to employees after six months of employment, so you have just enrolled in the 401(k) program. You rent half of a duplex and the owner is selling the property. A married couple rents the other half of the duplex. The building is in a nice area, close to your job. You are considering purchasing the building. Use the newspaper or search the Internet to find current prices for duplexes. What factors would you need to consider? What are the pros and cons of buying the building?

Collecting Treasures

Russell inherited three diamonds from his grandmother and needs to decide whether to keep them or sell them. He already had them evaluated for the "4 Cs"—clarity, color, cut, and carat weight—but not their actual dollar value. He took the diamonds and the evaluation papers to the Diamond Mart downtown.

A sales representative at the Diamond Mart appraised them. The four- carat diamond was the most valuable because it was beautifully cut in a marquise shape, and it also had good clarity, meaning it had few microscopic bits of other elements embedded in it. Its color, which was very close to the whitest end of the scale, also added to its value. The other two diamonds, a matched set of one-carat gems cut as round brilliants, were of a higher quality in clarity but more yellow. The appraiser told Russell that the three diamonds could be worth $5,000, but gem dealers would probably offer him about half that. He also told him that the Diamond Mart would not be interested in buying them.

Russell went to another store that had a sign, "We Buy Diamonds," but the most the store could offer was $2,350. Rather than settling for a price well below the actual worth of the diamonds, Russell decided to keep them in a safe-deposit box. By keeping them, he had the option of turning them into cash in the future, possibly selling them for more money. He also liked the idea of making them into jewelry someday. After researching his grandmother's diamonds, Russell is now interested in finding out more about other gems. One day he would like to start a gem collection.

Apply

On a separate sheet of paper, list five things you might enjoy collecting that will keep their value or possibly be worth more in the future. Choose one and describe why each appeals to you. Describe how an expert could appraise its value, using such criteria as age, quality, rarity, and popular demand. Why would this collectible be interesting for you to keep? Do you think it would be a good or bad long-term investment? Explain why.

Unit 6

Unit Project

Developing an Investment Plan

Ask Yourself...

Have you considered how you will accumulate wealth and achieve financial success? Perhaps you have thought about playing the stock market? Would you like to invest in real estate? Do you have a high or low tolerance for risk? Responses to these questions can guide you in developing an investment plan.

Your Objective

The goal of this project is to perform a financial check-up, analyze investment options, determine how to begin your personal investment portfolio, and create a short presentation for your class on your investment decisions.

Skills You'll Use

Success in defining goals and preparing financially for those goals depends on your skills. Some skills you might use include:

Academic Skills—Reading, writing, and mathematics

21st Century Skills—Financial literacy, decision making, critical thinking, information management, speaking, listening, and interpersonal skills

Technology Skills—Word processing, keyboarding, spreadsheet or budgeting software, presentation software

Standards

NCTE 4 Use written language to communicate effectively.

NCTE 7 Conduct research and gather, evaluate, and synthesize data to communicate discoveries.

NCTE 12 Use language to accomplish individual purposes.

NCTM Numbers and Operations Compute fluently and make reasonable estimates.

STEP 1 Assess Your Finances

The first step toward a successful investment plan is to perform a financial check-up. Ask yourself:

- What is your current income?
- What are your current or expected expenses?
- Do you have adequate insurance protection?
- How much money do you have in savings? Would you have enough to cover living expenses for three to nine months?
- What other sources of cash are available to you?

Use your responses to these questions to develop a balanced budget, using either spreadsheet or budgeting software. Also prepare a document to outline your current insurance, your emergency fund savings program, and other liquid assets.

STEP 2 Explore Investment Options

How much money do you have to begin investing? What short- and long-term goals do you need to plan for? For example, do you need to start saving for a down payment to buy a home in a few years or do you want to start saving for retirement? Consider these questions as well as risk factors, investment growth, and liquidity to determine which investments might be best for you. Consider building a diverse portfolio with varying asset classes, such as:

- Stocks
- Bonds
- Gems
- Collectibles
- Real estate
- Mutual funds
- CDs

Keep in mind that you may not be able to invest in all of these now, but it is still helpful to develop a plan. Perhaps you have just enough income now to make one investment and in another year or two, you will begin to diversify and grow your investment portfolio. Write a summary of which investments appeal to you, both for current and future investing. Explain your choices.

STEP 3 Build Relationships

Arrange to speak with a financial planner in your community, perhaps from your local bank or an investment firm. How do financial planners determine which investments are best for their clients? How do they evaluate each client's risk tolerance?

- Prepare interview questions to clarify any questions you had when evaluating your investment options.
- Share your budget as well as your investment plan with the financial planner. Does the professional recommend a different course of action?
- Take notes and record the interview responses.
- Listen attentively and respond appropriately.
- Ask for further explanations if you do not understand something.
- Write a summary of the information learned in the interview.
- Adjust your budget and investment plan, if appropriate.

STEP 4 Develop Your Presentation

Use the Unit 6 Project Checklist to plan and create your presentation.

STEP 5 Evaluate Your Presentation

Your presentation will be evaluated based on the following:

- Evaluation rubric
- Accuracy and organization of your information
- Mechanics—presentation and logic
- Speaking and listening skills

Project Checklist

Plan

- ✔ Perform a personal financial check-up by balancing your budget, obtaining adequate insurance protection, establishing an emergency fund, and assessing liquid assets.
- ✔ Evaluate various investment options to determine the ones best suited to your financial goals and risk tolerance.
- ✔ Meet with a professional financial planner to review your investment plan.

Write

- ✔ Develop a balanced budget.
- ✔ Outline your current insurance, your emergency fund savings program, and other liquid assets.
- ✔ Summarize your preferred investment options and why you feel they are the best choices.
- ✔ Create a list of interview questions.
- ✔ Write a summary of the financial planner's advice and information.

Present

- ✔ Create an outline for your presentation.
- ✔ Create visuals and use technology to enhance your presentation.
- ✔ Speak clearly and concisely.
- ✔ Present your budget and explain how you were able to balance it.
- ✔ Share your investment plan and why you chose the options you did.
- ✔ Present the findings from your interview.
- ✔ Respond to questions from your classmates.

glencoe.com

Evaluate Download a rubric you can use to evaluate your project.

UNIT 7 Protecting Your Finances

Visual Literacy

Effective financial planning should include a plan to protect your finances from unexpected problems or events. ***Why is it important to have a plan to protect your finances?***

In Your World

Employee Benefits

If you think you are too young to think about tax strategies, worry about insurance, or plan for retirement, think again. Time is on your side when it comes to building and protecting your finances. Having a job means getting a paycheck, but it can be much more. Your job can work for you by providing unemployment and disability insurance, workers' compensation, social security, and retirement funding.

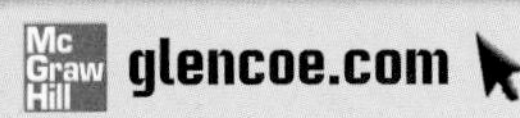

Watch the Unit 7 video to learn more about employee benefits.

Social Security and Retirement Have you ever thought of how you would like to spend retirement? As you build your career, there are many things you need to consider in order to meet your future financial goals. Social Security is a tax that finances federal programs that provide retirement, disability, and life insurance benefits. With this tax on your pay, why should you invest in retirement plans such as a 401(k)?

Economics and You

Government Protection of Young Employees

The Fair Labor Standards Act (FLSA) covers provisions for child labor, minimum wage, and overtime pay. For example, the FLSA prohibits employment of minors in dangerous jobs and limits the hours they may work. In a recent year the FLSA set the minimum wage at $7.25 per hour. If you have a job in which you earn tips, and you earn at least $30 in tips, your minimum wage may be as low as $2.13. There are also exemptions for full-time students and student learners whereby employees may pay less than the minimum wage. The U.S. Department of Labor enforces minimum wage laws. Why do you think the government allows exceptions to the minimum wage law? How would businesses be affected if these exceptions were removed?

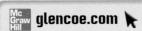

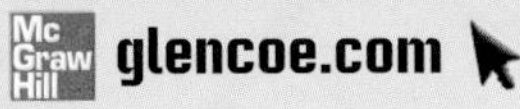

Activity Download an Economics and You Worksheet Activity.

CHAPTER 21

Planning Your Tax Strategy

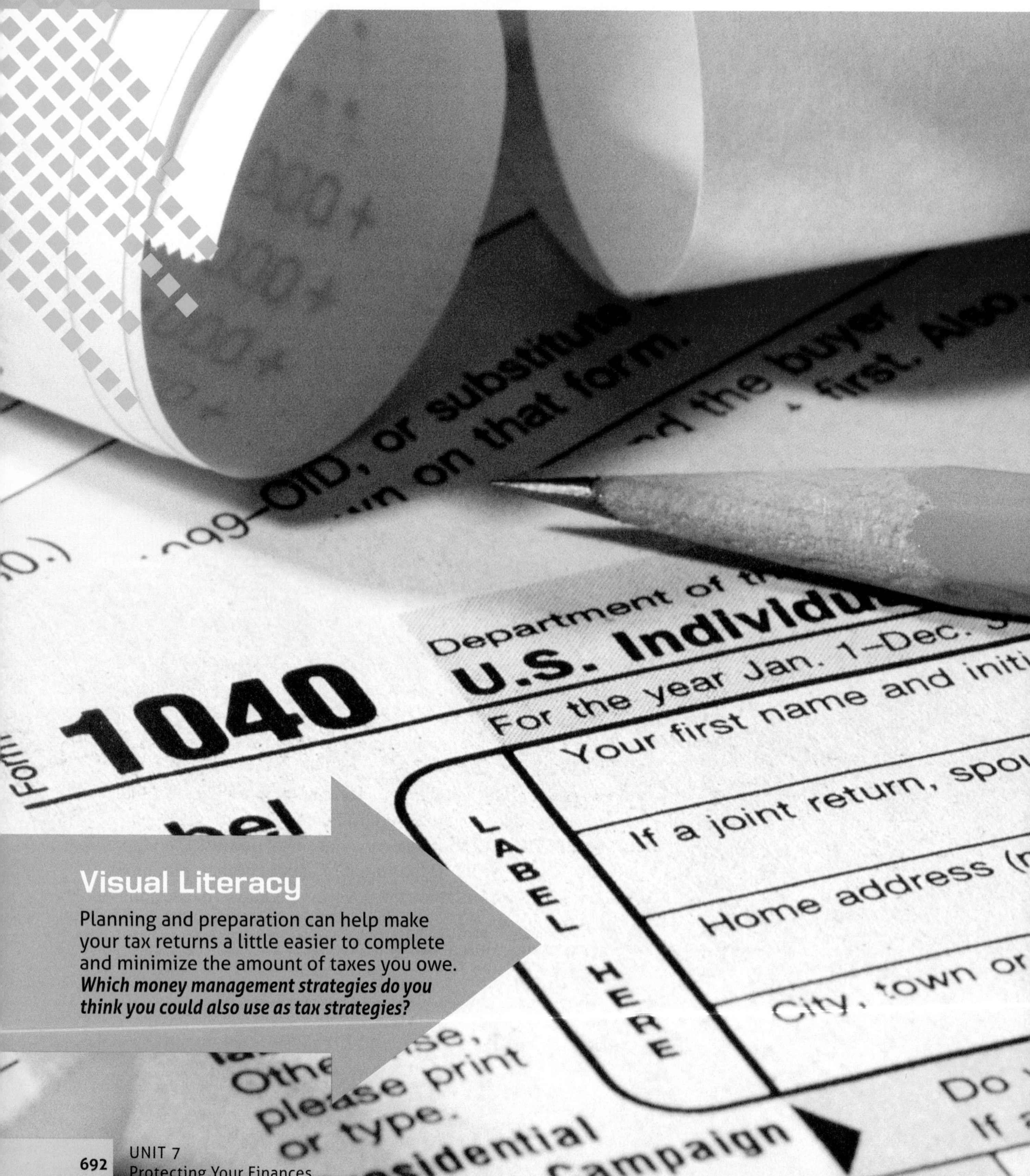

Visual Literacy

Planning and preparation can help make your tax returns a little easier to complete and minimize the amount of taxes you owe. ***Which money management strategies do you think you could also use as tax strategies?***

Discovery Project

Comparing Tax Rates

Key Question

Why do sales tax rates vary from one city to another?

Project Goal

While the tax rate is obviously not the only factor in deciding where to live, it should be one of the factors you consider. Sales tax rates will vary not only from state to state, but also between counties and cities. The difference in these rates will affect your cost of living. By knowing what the sales tax rates are ahead of time, you can help minimize the amount of taxes you will pay. Choose a state or area that you might like to live in some day and research what the total sales tax rate is for three different towns in that area. Prepare a brief presentation to share your findings. Include a visual aid to show the different tax rates and how they are totaled.

Ask Yourself...

- *Is the new area you researched more or less than where you currently live?*
- *What is the difference between the highest and lowest rates you found?*
- *Is the difference enough to rule out one town as a possible place of residence?*
- *What other purchasing strategies can help minimize your taxes?*

Reason Effectively

Many people shop online to avoid paying sales tax. But as online purchases increase, many states are fighting for the right to collect sales tax. Do you think online purchases should be taxed? Why or why not?

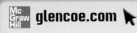

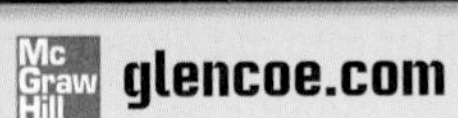

glencoe.com

Evaluate Download an assessment rubric.

THE BIG IDEA

There are strategies available to help you lower the amount of taxes you owe.

ASK STANDARD & POOR'S

Electronic Taxes

Q *I would like to file my income tax form electronically. Is it risky to file through the Internet?*

A If you are concerned about being charged late penalties if your tax return is not received by the IRS via the Internet, you can protect yourself by using filing services that offer a receipt, such as a confirmation number or e-mail confirmation.

Writing Activity

In recent years it has become increasingly popular to use tax preparation software and file income tax forms electronically. Write a question and answer essay to explain the advantages and drawbacks of filing income tax forms electronically instead of by mail.

CHAPTER 21

Reading Guide

Before You Read

The Essential Question What actions can you take throughout the year to help reduce the amount of taxes you owe?

Main Idea

There are several types of taxes. When preparing your tax return, you will need to understand the terms and have the correct forms and documents. You should follow basic strategies to reduce the amount of taxes you owe.

Content Vocabulary

- tax liability
- estate tax
- inheritance tax
- income tax
- income tax return
- exclusion
- adjusted gross income
- taxable income
- tax deduction
- standard deduction
- itemized deduction
- exemption
- tax credit
- allowance
- extension
- tax audit

Academic Vocabulary

You will see these words in your reading and on your tests.

- excise tax
- dependent
- negligence
- levies
- clarification
- jeopardizing

Graphic Organizer

Before you read this chapter, draw a T-chart like the one below. As you read, note the types of income that make up your total, or gross, income.

Type of income	Description

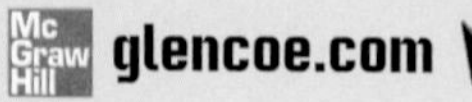

Print this graphic organizer.

Standards

Academic

Mathematics

NCTM Connections Recognize and apply mathematics in contexts outside of mathematics.

English Language Arts

NCTE 5 Use different writing process elements to communicate effectively.

NCTE 7 Conduct research and gather, evaluate, and synthesize data to communicate discoveries.

NCTE 8 Use information resources to gather information and create and communicate knowledge.

Science

NSES E Develop abilities of technological design, understandings about science and technology.

NCTM *National Council of Teachers of Mathematics*

NCTE *National Council of Teachers of English*

NCSS *National Council for the Social Studies*

NSES *National Science Education Standards*

Common Core

Reading Read and comprehend complex literary and informational texts independently and proficiently.

Speaking and Listening Present information, findings, and supporting evidence such that listeners can follow the line of reasoning and the organization, development, and style are appropriate to task, purpose, and audience.

Speaking and Listening Adapt speech to a variety of contexts and communicative tasks, demonstrating command of formal English when indicated or appropriate.

Taxes and You

Why are taxes so important?

Taxes are an everyday expense of life that allow your local, state, and federal governments to provide important services. Taxes pay the bills for those services such as Medicare, Medicaid, the military, the national debt, police and fire protection, public schools, road maintenance, parks, libraries, and safety inspection of foods, drugs, and other products.

You pay some type of tax every time you get a paycheck, buy a new CD or pair of shoes, or fill up your car's gas tank. Each year the Tax Foundation, an independent public policy research group, determines how much of the year the average person works to pay taxes. In recent years, "Tax Freedom Day" came in early April. This means that from January 1 until early April, all the money you earn goes toward paying taxes.

Effective tax planning can help you to have money left after paying taxes and living expenses. Use several strategies to plan for taxes. First, find out how the current tax laws and regulations affect you. Second, maintain complete and accurate tax records. Third, learn how to make decisions that can reduce your **tax liability,** which is the total amount of taxes owed. If you follow these strategies, you will pay a fair share of taxes while taking advantage of tax benefits that allow you to owe less money.

Reading Check

Recall Why is effective tax planning important?

Section Objectives

- **Discuss** the importance of tax planning.
- **Identify** your taxable income.
- **Explain** deductions and tax credits.
- **Explain** the W-4 form.

As You Read

Consider Why is it important for you to keep accurate and organized tax records?

Types of Taxes

What are the different types of taxes?

Throughout your life, you will pay different types of taxes in four major categories: purchases, property, wealth, and earnings.

Taxes on Purchases

You probably already pay sales tax each time you buy a product. These taxes are added to the prices of most products you purchase and are collected by state and local governments. Many states do not charge sales tax on food and medicine. Another type of sales tax is an **excise tax,** a tax on specific goods and services (such as gasoline, air travel, and telephone service) collected by federal and state governments.

reality bytes

E-commerce Tax

Should all online transactions be taxed? Buying and selling on the internet has steadily increased over the years. In fact, retail sales of goods on the internet reached nearly $142 billion dollars in a recent year. Those in favor of taxing e-commerce note the potential revenue generated from taxing online transactions, as well as the revenue lost as customers choose to shop online in greater numbers. Opponents of the tax point out the barrier to entry and growth for small businesses that would be created by such a tax.

Taxes on Property

Real estate property tax is a major source of income for local governments. This tax is based on the value of land and buildings. As the value of real estate goes up, the amount of property tax may increase as well. In some areas, state and local governments may assess taxes on property such as boats and farm equipment.

Taxes on Wealth

An **estate tax** is a federal tax collected on the value of a person's property at the time of his or her death. Unfortunately, that is not always the end of tax liability. States may collect an inheritance tax. An **inheritance tax** is a state tax collected on the property left by a person to his or her heir(s) in a will. Therefore, before heirs can claim their inheritance, they have to pay the inheritance tax. Another type of federal tax on wealth is the gift tax. A gift tax is collected on money or property valued at more than $11,000, given by one person to another in a single year. Gifts that are designated for educational or medical expenses are not subject to gift taxes.

Taxes on Earnings

Income tax is the tax on wages, salaries, and self-employed earnings. Wages are payments received for hourly work, but salaries are payments received for weekly or monthly work, regardless of the number of hours worked. The personal income tax, or tax you pay on the income you receive, is the federal government's main source of revenue. Social Security funds are also collected as a tax. These funds finance retirement, disability, and life insurance benefits of the federal government's Social Security program. Current and future revisions to the Social Security program may affect the amount of benefits.

The Internal Revenue Service (IRS) The Internal Revenue Service (IRS) is the federal agency, part of the Department of Treasury, that collects these taxes, or tax revenues. The primary missions of the IRS are to collect federal income taxes and to enforce the nation's tax laws.

Taxes on earnings are collected on a pay-as-you-earn basis. Your employer must withhold Social Security and income tax payments from your paycheck and send the money to the IRS. If you are self-employed, own your own business, or are retired, you could be required to make your own estimated tax payments. When you complete your federal income tax return, you determine if you have paid too much or too little income tax. At that time you either pay more tax or you receive a refund from the IRS.

Reading Check

Cite What are the four categories of taxes that you will pay?

Document Detective

A Form W-2

The Form W-2 provides much of the information that you need to file your yearly federal income tax return. You must save this form and attach copies to your income tax return. A Form W-2 contains the following information:

- Employer's name and address
- Employee's name, address, and Social Security number
- Wages the employee earned
- Taxes withheld from earnings

a Control number 22222	Void ☐	For Official Use Only ▶ OMB No. 1545-0008	
b Employer identification number (EIN) 26 - 8310024		1 Wages, tips, other compensation 86.411.75	2 Federal income tax withheld 21,880.59
c Employer's name, address, and ZIP code Group Transportation 37 Main Street Tampa, FL 33606		3 Social security wages 87,900.00	4 Social security tax withheld 5449.80
		5 Medicare wages and tips 88,775.00	6 Medicare tax withheld 1287.24
		7 Social security tips	8 Allocated tips
d Employee's social security number XXX - XX-7822		9 Advance EIC payment	10 Dependent care benefits
e Employee's first name and initial Theresa C.	Last name Alvarez	11 Nonqualified plans	12a See instructions for box 12
1335 Smith Lane Tampa, FL 33605		13 Statutory employee ☐ Retirement plan ☐ Third-party sick pay ☐	12b
		14 Other	12c
f Employee's address and ZIP code			12d

15 State	Employer's state ID number	16 State wages, tips, etc.	17 State income tax	18 Local wages, tips, etc.	19 Local income tax	20 Locality name
FL	61 - 281517	86411.75	5326.50	88775.00	887.75	Tampa

Form **W-2** Wage and Tax Statement **20--**

Department of the Treasury—Internal Revenue Service

For Privacy Act and Paperwork Reduction Act Notice, see back of Copy D.

Copy A For Social Security Administration — Send this entire page with Form W-3 to the Social Security Administration; photocopies are **not** acceptable.

Cat. No. 10134D

Do Not Cut, Fold, or Staple Forms on This Page — Do Not Cut, Fold, or Staple Forms on This Page

Key Points A Form W-2 is a document that employers are required to prepare and distribute to each employee and the IRS by the end of January each year. The form details the wages earned by the worker as well as all taxes withheld for the year. The Form W-2 is labeled and numbered to coincide with the IRS Form 1040 and Form 1040EZ income tax form.

FIND the Solutions

Review Key Concepts

1. What are Theresa's wages, tips, and other compensation?
2. How much was withheld from her wages for Social Security?
3. How much state income tax was withheld from her wages?
4. What is the employer's identification number?
5. What are Theresa's total Social Security wages?

Tax Dollars at Work
State and federal governments use tax dollars to provide services to the community, such as public parks, museums, libraries, and road construction. *Why does a government continue to require taxes for existing parks and libraries?*

Understanding Income Taxes

How do you determine how much tax you owe?

Every year, millions of taxpayers in the United States prepare income tax returns and send their completed forms to the IRS. An **income tax return** is a form, such as 1040 or 1040EZ, on which a taxpayer reports how much money he or she received from work and other sources and the exact taxes that are owed.

You determine the amount of tax you owe when filling out the returns. Then you compare that amount to the total income tax your employer withheld from your paychecks during the year. If the income tax you paid through your employer was greater than your tax liability, you will receive a refund. However, if your tax liability is greater than the tax you paid, you will need to pay the difference to the U.S. Treasury because you owe more taxes than were withheld.

Gross and Adjusted Gross Income

Most, but not all, income is subject to taxation. Gross income, or total income, can include one, two, or three main components:

1. **Earned income**—the money you receive for work, such as wages, salary, commissions, tips, bonuses, and self-employed earnings
2. **Interest income**—the interest that you receive from banks, credit unions, and savings and loan associations
3. **Dividend income**—the cash dividends that you receive from investments

Your gross income can also be affected by exclusions—amounts of income that do not have to be included in your gross income. An **exclusion** is also called tax-exempt income, or income that is not subject to taxes. For example, interest earned on most municipal bonds is exempt from federal income tax.

Another kind of income is tax-deferred income, or income that will be taxed at a later date. The earnings on an individual retirement account (IRA) are tax-deferred income. Although these earnings are credited to your account now, you do not have to pay tax on this money until you withdraw it from the account, usually at retirement.

You pay income tax on your adjusted gross income, not on your gross income. Your **adjusted gross income** is your gross income after calculating certain reductions, or adjustments to income. They include items such as contributions to an IRA or student loan interest. The correct amount of your adjusted gross income is important because it is the basis for other tax calculations.

Try Layaway

Some stores offer layaway plans. If you want to buy that special dress, pair of pants, or coat, ask the store about its layaway plan. You make installment payments and get the item when the last payment is made. This is a no-interest way of paying that does not require a credit card.

Concept Application

If you want to buy a pair of skis that costs $240, how long will you make monthly payments of $30?

Your Taxable Income

When you determine your adjusted gross income, you can figure out your taxable income. Your **taxable income** is your adjusted gross income less any allowable tax deductions and exemptions. Your income tax is calculated based on the amount of your taxable income.

Tax Deductions A **tax deduction** is an expense that you can subtract from your adjusted gross income to figure your taxable income. Every taxpayer receives at least the **standard deduction,** an amount of money set by the IRS that is not taxed. In 2009, a single person's standard deduction was $5,700. A married couple filing a joint tax return could deduct $11,400. People over age 65 or people who are blind are entitled to higher standard deductions.

You may qualify for other deductions that can reduce your taxable income. An **itemized deduction** is a specific expense, such as a medical expense, that you deduct from your adjusted gross income. You can take the standard deduction or itemize your deductions, but you cannot take both. You would take the standard deduction if it were greater than your total itemized deductions. You must keep records to document tax deductions. Common deductions include:

- **Medical and Dental Expenses** These include doctors' fees, prescription medications, hospital expenses, medical insurance premiums, eyeglasses, hearing aids, and medical travel that has not been reimbursed or paid by others, such as a health insurance provider. You can deduct only the amount of your medical and dental expenses that is more than 7.5 percent of your adjusted gross income (as of 2009). Therefore, if your adjusted gross income is $10,000, you can deduct only the amount that exceeds $750.
- **Taxes** You can deduct state and local income tax, real estate property tax, and state and local personal property tax.
- **Interest** You can deduct home mortgage interest and home equity loan interest.
- **Contributions** You can deduct contributions of cash or property to qualified charities. If your contribution is more than 20 percent of your adjusted gross income, it is subject to certain limitations.

Careers That Count!

Christina Schaeffer • Tax Preparer

I enjoy math, and I have always been able to manipulate and make sense of numbers. I also enjoy working with people, so I became a self-employed tax preparer. Because tax laws change annually and can be confusing, many individuals and small businesses hire a tax preparer. I use computer programs, adding machines, tax form instructions, and tax tables to compute taxes owed or overpaid, and I apply appropriate adjustments, deductions, and credits to keep clients' taxes to a minimum. January through April is my busiest time. A typical client meeting may include reviewing wage statements and previous tax returns, asking about income, expenses, investments, and other financial information, and printing out the appropriate forms to send to the IRS. Unusual returns may require more time and the consultation of tax law handbooks or bulletins. You can pursue a career like mine by taking online courses, community college classes, or training offered by established tax preparation chains.

EXPLORE CAREERS

Visit the Web site of the U.S. Department of Labor's Bureau of Labor Statistics to obtain information about a career as a tax preparer and an accountant.

1. How do you think the careers of a tax preparer and accountant have been impacted by advancements in technology?
2. Why do CPAs earn a higher income than tax preparers?

Skills	Education	Career Path
Communication, math, computer, interpersonal, time-management, active learning, critical thinking, problem solving, and judgment and decision-making skills	High school diploma; tax preparation training online or in vocational schools; on-the-job experience; associate's degree; courses through tax preparation companies	Tax preparers can become Certified Income Tax Preparers (CTPs), Certified Public Accountants (CPAs), credit checkers, actuaries, and financial advisors.

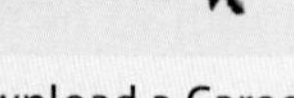

Activity Download a Career Exploration Activity.

Exemptions An **exemption** is a deduction from adjusted gross income for the taxpayer, the spouse, and qualified dependents. A **dependent** is someone you support financially, such as a child.

To qualify as a dependent, a person must meet all of the following requirements:

1. A dependent must not earn more than a set amount unless he or she is under age 19 or is a full-time student under age 24.
2. He or she must be a specified relative or live in the home of the taxpayer who claims him or her on the tax return.
3. More than half of a dependent's support must be provided by the taxpayer who claims him or her on the tax return.
4. A dependent must meet certain citizenship requirements.

Calculating Your Tax Once you know your taxable income, you can calculate how much income tax you owe. Most taxpayers use either a

Tax Table or a Tax Rate Schedule to figure income tax. The Tax Rate Schedules are based on the six rates from 2009 shown in **Figure 1.** The Tax Rate schedule changes from year to year.

Your income tax may be reduced by a **tax credit,** which is an amount of money that can be subtracted directly from taxes you owe. A tax credit is different than a deduction. A tax deduction is an expense that you can subtract from your adjusted gross income. However, a tax credit results in a dollar-for-dollar reduction in the amount of taxes you owe. If you owe $300 in taxes and get a $100 tax credit, you can subtract that and owe only $200.

Lower-income workers can benefit from a tax credit called earned income credit (EIC). This federal tax credit is for people who work and whose taxable income is less than a certain amount. People who do not earn enough to owe federal income tax are also eligible for it.

Reading Check

Recognize What are the two types of tax deductions?

Making Tax Payments

How do you make income tax payments to the IRS?

You can pay your income taxes to the federal government in different ways: through estimated payments or payroll withholding payments. People who are self-employed may pay estimated taxes each quarter.

FIGURE 1 **The Six-Rate System for Federal Income Taxes**

Higher Income, Higher Rates The six-rate system is a progressive tax, meaning the more taxable income you have, the higher your tax rate. *Using this system, what tax rate would apply to a single person who earned $55,000?*

Rate	Single Taxpayer	Rate	Married Taxpayers Filing Jointly
10%	Up to $8,350	10%	Up to $16,700
15% of amount over $8350, plus $835	$8,350 – $33,950	15% of amount over $16,700, plus $1,670	$16,700 – $67,900
25% of amount over $33,950, plus $4,675	$33,950 – $82,250	25% of amount over $67,900, plus $9,350	$67,900 – $137,050
28% of amount over $82,250, plus $16,750	$82,250 – $171,550	28% of amount over $137,050, plus $26,637.50	$137,050 – $208,850
33% of amount over $171,550, plus $41,754	$171,550 – $372,950	33% of amount over $208,850, plus $46,741.50	$208,850 – $372,950
35% of amount over $372,950, plus $108,216	$372,950 and up	35% of amount over $372,950, plus $100,894.50	$372,950 and up

Payroll Withholding

When James Irving began his job at a company, his employer asked him to complete a W-4 form, or the Employee's Withholding Allowance Certificate. (See **Figure 2.**) The amount of federal income tax an employer withholds to send to the IRS, depends on the number of allowances you claim on a W-4 form. An **allowance** is an adjustment to the tax withheld from your paycheck, based on your marital status and whether you have dependents. An allowance can reduce the amount of income taxes your employer withholds.

Completing a W-4 Form To fill out the W-4 form, follow these simple instructions:

1. Fill in your name and address.
2. Fill in your Social Security number.
3. Indicate whether you are single or married by checking the appropriate box.
4. Check the box if your last name is different from the name shown on your Social Security card.
5. Write the number of allowances you are claiming. To figure out how many allowances you can claim, complete the Personal Allowances Worksheet at the top of the W-4 form.
6. Indicate how much additional money, if any, you wish to have withheld.
7. If you meet the conditions listed on the form and indicate that you are exempt, or excused, from paying income tax, no income tax will be withheld.
8. Sign and date the form.

Estimated Payments

Every summer, John earns money by running his own landscaping business. How does he pay his taxes since he does not have an employer? Like other self-employed workers, John makes estimated payments to the government. These payments are due April 15th, June 15th, September 15th, and January 15th (the last payment is for the previous year). John's payments are based on his estimate of taxes due at the end of the year. Estimated payments must be at least equal to the taxes he owed last year or be at least 90 percent of the current year's taxes to avoid penalties for underpayment.

Claiming Allowances

Some employees claim fewer allowances on their W-4 forms than they actually have and, consequently, more tax money is withheld from their paychecks. Some employees claim no allowances. In both of these cases, employers withhold more money than is required from each paycheck. As a result, the employees look forward to receiving

FIGURE 2 **The W-4 Form**

Tax Allowances The W-4 Form lets employers know how much tax to withhold from an employee's paycheck. *Why might you request for additional money to be withheld?*

Personal Allowances Worksheet (Keep for your records.)

A Enter "1" for **yourself** if no one else can claim you as a dependent . . . . A 1

B Enter "1" if: { • You are single and have only one job; or • You are married, have only one job, and your spouse does not work; or • Your wages from a second job or your spouse's wages (or the total of both) are $1,000 or less. } . . B 1

C Enter "1" for your **spouse.** But, you may choose to enter "-0-" if you are married and have either a working spouse or more than one job. (Entering "-0-" may help you avoid having too little tax withheld.) . . . . C 0

D Enter number of **dependents** (other than your spouse or yourself) you will claim on your tax return . . . . . D 0

E Enter "1" if you will file as **head of household** on your tax return (see conditions under **Head of household** above) . E 0

F Enter "1" if you have at least $1,500 of **child or dependent care expenses** for which you plan to claim a credit . . F 0

(**Note:** *Do* **not** *include child support payments. See* **Pub. 503,** *Child and Dependent Care Expenses, for details.*)

G **Child Tax Credit** (including additional child tax credit):
• If your total income will be between $15,000 and $42,000 ($20,000 and $65,000 if married), enter "1" for each eligible child plus **1 additional** if you have three to five eligible children or **2 additional** if you have six or more eligible children.
• If your total income will be between $42,000 and $80,000 ($65,000 and $115,000 if married), enter "1" if you have one or two eligible children, "2" if you have three eligible children, "3" if you have four eligible children, or "4" if you have five or more eligible children. G 0

H Add lines A through G and enter total here. **Note:** *This may be different from the number of exemptions you claim on your tax return.* ▶ H 2

For accuracy, complete all worksheets that apply.
• If you plan to **itemize or claim adjustments to income** and want to reduce your withholding, see the **Deductions and Adjustments Worksheet** on page 2.
• If you have **more than one job** or are **married and you and your spouse both work** and the combined earnings from all jobs exceed $35,000, see the **Two-Earner/Two-Job Worksheet** on page 2 to avoid having too little tax withheld.
• If **neither** of the above situations applies, **stop here** and enter the number from line H on line 5 of Form W-4 below.

Cut here and give Form W-4 to your employer. Keep the top part for your records.

Form **W-4** Department of the Treasury Internal Revenue Service

Employee's Withholding Allowance Certificate

▶ **For Privacy Act and Paperwork Reduction Act Notice, see page 2.**

OMB No. 1545-0010 20––

1 Type or print your first name and middle initial: JAMES A. Last name: IRVING

2 Your social security number: 123 XX XXXX

Home address (number and street or rural route): 23 CEDAR GLENN

3 ☐ Single ☐ Married ☐ Married, but withhold at higher Single rate.
Note: *If married, but legally separated, or spouse is a nonresident alien, check the "Single" box.*

City or town, state, and ZIP code: ARLINGTON, ILLINOIS 61312

4 **If your last name differs from that shown on your social security card, check here. You must call 1-800-772-1213 for a new card.** ▶ ☐

5 Total number of allowances you are claiming (from line **H** above **or** from the applicable worksheet on page 2) 5 2

6 Additional amount, if any, you want withheld from each paycheck . . . . 6 $

7 I claim exemption from withholding for 20––, and I certify that I meet **both** of the following conditions for exemption:
Last year I had a right to a refund of **all** Federal income tax withheld because I had **no** tax liability **and**
This year I expect a refund of **all** Federal income tax withheld because I expect to have **no** tax liability.
If you meet both conditions, write "Exempt" here . . . . ▶ 7

Under penalties of perjury, I certify that I am entitled to the number of withholding allowances claimed on this certificate, or I am entitled to claim exempt status.

Employee's signature (Form is not valid unless you sign it.) ▶ James A. Irving Date ▶ 1/3/20––

8 Employer's name and address (Employer: Complete lines 8 and 10 only if sending to the IRS.) | 9 Office code (optional) | 10 Employer identification number

Cat. No. 10220Q

large refunds from the government when they file their tax returns. Claiming few or no allowances on their W-4 forms is one way to get that refund. They may view the extra tax withheld as a "forced savings account." However, as employees, they might use a payroll deduction plan for savings instead. They may be forgetting the opportunity cost of withholding excessive amounts of their money. These taxpayers may not realize that the extra deducted money is like providing an interest-free loan to the government. The government does not have to return that extra money for up to a year until tax returns are filed, usually by April 15th of each year. Wise taxpayers claim all the allowances to which they are entitled when preparing the W-4 form. That puts the money into their pockets.

Assessment

Review Key Concepts

1. **Summarize** What are three basic strategies to use in planning for taxes?
2. **Describe** What is taxable income?
3. **Compare and contrast** How are a tax deduction and a tax credit similar or different?
4. **Relate** How is a W-4 form used by employers?

Higher Order Thinking

5. **Evaluate** Many people enjoy having more taxes withheld from their paychecks in order to receive a larger refund on their income taxes. Decide whether or not this is a good idea. Explain your conclusion.

English Language Arts

6. **The Tax Foundation** One mission of the Tax Foundation is to educate taxpayers about tax policy. It is considered to be a nonpartisan tax research group. Use online sources to learn more about the research areas that the Tax Foundation is involved in, such as income taxes, tax brackets, and job creation. Choose one of these areas that interests you and research to find out more. Prepare a summary of the information available from the Tax Foundation on your chosen topic to share with your classmates.

NCTE 7 Conduct research and gather, evaluate, and synthesize data to communicate discoveries.

Mathematics

7. **Federal Income Taxes** Tyree has just started his career as an architect at XYZ Architecture, Inc. He is not married and has no dependents that he would claim on his taxes. Tyree also cannot be claimed as a dependent on anyone else's taxes. His annual salary in his new position is $30,000, and he has no other sources of income. Per the table in **Figure 1** what is Tyree's tax rate. How much federal income tax will he owe at the end of the year?

Math Concept **Calculate Tax Owed** To calculate the federal income tax owed first use the annual salary to identify the rate on taxable income. Follow the rate formula to calculate the income tax owed.

Starting Hint Determine the total annual salary as well as the marital status of the individual. Use this information to determine the rate on taxable income from the table in **Figure 1.**

NCTM Connections Recognize and apply mathematics in contexts outside of mathematics.

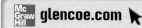

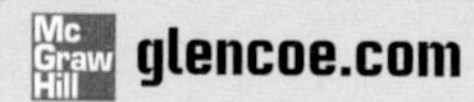

Check your answers.

The W-2 Form

What information does the W-2 form provide?

Each year, when it is time for James to file his annual income tax return, his employer sends him a W-2 form, or the Wage and Tax Statement. This form lists his annual earnings and the amount withheld from his paychecks for federal income taxes, Social Security, and any applicable state and local income taxes. By law, your employer must send you this form by January 31st each year.

Reading Check

Recognize What is a W-2 form?

Section Objective

- **Describe** the types of federal income tax forms.

As You Read

Predict What factors might determine whether you have to file income taxes?

The Federal Income Tax Return

What should you know about the federal income tax return?

When you know how to compute your taxable income, you are ready to begin the yearly task of filling out your income tax return and sending it to the IRS. Before you begin, consider some basic information: who must file, deadlines and penalties, and tax forms.

Who Must File?

Are you a citizen or a resident of the United States or a U.S. citizen who resides in Puerto Rico? If so, then you are required to file a federal income tax return if your income is above a certain amount. That amount is based on your filing status and other factors. For example, a single person under the age of 65 with a gross annual income of more than $7,700 or a single person over age 65 with a gross income of more than $8,850 is required to file an income tax return. Even if Kerry did not meet the filing requirements, she should still file a tax return to obtain a refund of the income tax withheld from her paycheck.

These are the five filing status categories:

- **Single**—an individual who never married, or is divorced or legally separated with no dependents
- **Married, filing a joint return**—a married couple with combined income
- **Married, filing separate returns**—each spouse paying for his or her own tax

- **Head of household**—an unmarried individual or a surviving spouse who maintains a household, paying more than one-half of the costs for a child or other dependent relative
- **Qualifying widow or widower**—an individual whose spouse died within the last two years and who has a dependent

Deadlines and Penalties

You are required to file an income tax return each year by April 15th, unless that date falls on a Saturday or Sunday. In that case, you must file by the following Monday. If you have a refund owed to you, file your return as early as possible to avoid a long wait. You may have to pay financial penalties if you do not file on time, even if you are just one day late.

If you cannot meet the deadline, you can file Form 4868 by April 15th to receive a four-month **extension,** which is an extended deadline for filing an income tax return, but it does not delay your tax liability. When you submit Form 4868, you must also send a check for the estimated amount of the tax you may owe.

If you make quarterly estimated tax payments, they must be on time. If you underestimate the amount owed, you have to pay interest plus the amount you should have paid. Underpayment due to **negligence** (lack of attention) or fraud can result in large penalties. Failing to file a required tax return is a serious violation of the tax code and can result in a substantial penalty.

The good news is that if you claim a refund several months or years late, perhaps because you discovered a calculation error or you did not take an allowable deduction, the IRS will pay you interest plus your refund. You must claim your refund and interest within three years of filing a return or within two years of paying the tax.

Choosing the Tax Form

The IRS offers about 400 tax forms and schedules. However, you have a choice of three basic forms: the short forms known as *Form 1040EZ* and *Form 1040A*, and the long form known as *Form 1040*.

Form 1040EZ Form 1040EZ is the simplest tax form to complete. You may use this form if you meet the following qualifications:

- Your taxable income is less than $100,000.
- You are single or married (filing a joint tax return).
- You are under age 65.
- You claim no dependents.
- Your income consisted of only wages, salaries, and tips, and no more than $1,500 of taxable interest.
- You will not itemize deductions, claim any adjustments to income, or claim any tax credits.

For example, Yasmeen is a high school senior who works part time at a health clinic. She is single, earned less than the amount needed to file, and had only $11 in interest income last year. So, Yasmeen was able to use Form 1040EZ to obtain a tax refund.

Form 1040A You may use this form if any of the following apply:

- You have less than $100,000 in taxable income.
- You have capital gains distributions but not capital gains or losses.
- You claim the standard deduction.
- You claim deductions for IRA contributions.
- You claim a tax credit for child and dependent care, education, earned income, adoption, or retirement savings contributions.
- You have deductions for IRA contributions, student loan interest, educator expenses, or higher education tuition and fees.
- You have no itemized deductions.

Form 1040 Form 1040 is an expanded version of Form 1040A. It includes sections covering all types of income. You are required to use this form if your taxable income is more than $100,000. Also, if you have income from interest or dividends over a set limit, self-employment income, or income from the sale of property you are required to use form 1040. Many taxpayers who earn less than $100,000 use this form and find Form 1040 offers tax advantages.

Itemize deductions on this form by using Schedule A. Deduct expenses, such as medical and dental expenses, home mortgage interest, and real estate property tax. These deductions will reduce your taxable income and, therefore, reduce the amount of tax you must pay.

Reading Check

Name What are the five filing status categories?

Completing the Federal Income Tax Return

What do you need to complete the three main income tax forms?

Filling out a federal income tax return does not have to be difficult as long as you are prepared, have the correct documents and information, and understand the forms you are using. See **Figure 3** for a list of all the documents and information you will want to have on hand before you begin to fill out your return. Make a rough draft of your tax return before you complete a final draft. Whether you file electronically or by mail, a rough draft will allow you to double-check your calculations before you submit your return.

Saudi Arabia

Zakat Taxes

Taxes are generally accepted as a way of life. We pay sales tax on most of our goods and services. We have taxes deducted from our paychecks. And once a year, we pay income taxes. Citizens in Saudi Arabia follow a different system though. They still pay taxes to the government, but there is no sales tax and no income tax. Instead, Saudis pay a *zakat* tax, or a religious wealth tax. Established in 1975, the zakat tax is calculated based on the taxable income of individuals and businesses. The zakat is an annual flat rate of 2.5 percent and is collected by the Department of Zakat and Income Tax (DZIT).

While Saudis are responsible for the zakat tax, non-Saudi individuals and companies are responsible for paying personal income taxes to the DZIT. These tax rates range from 5 percent up to 30 percent, depending on the amount of the taxable income. The government also collects corporate taxes, though the rules on how the rates are determined vary based on the industry and the amount of profit.

Critical Thinking

1. **Expand** Research the zakat tax and non-Saudi income tax. How are the corporate tax for petroleum and other hydrocarbon producing companies in Saudi Arabia determined?
2. **Relate** Do you think it is fair that foreigners are taxed differently from Saudi citizens? Why or why not?

DATABYTES

Capital
Riyadh

Population
29,207,277

Language
Arabic

Currency
Saudi riyal

Gross Domestic Product (GDP)
$384 billion

GDP per capita
$20,400

Industry
Crude oil production, petroleum refining, basic petrochemicals, ammonia, industrial gases, sodium hydroxide (caustic soda), cement, fertilizer, plastics, metals, commercial ship repair, commercial aircraft repair, construction

Agriculture
Wheat, barley, tomatoes, melons, dates, citrus; mutton, chickens, eggs, milk

Exports
Petroleum and petroleum products

Natural Resources
Petroleum, natural gas, iron ore, gold, copper

Gathering Information and Documents

Being prepared at tax time means you have all the necessary documents. The following checklist of documents will help you complete a successful tax return:

- **Tax Forms and Instruction Booklets** Be sure that you have the most current forms and instruction booklets that contain the latest tax information. After you have filed your first tax return, the IRS will send these to you each year in January. If you need different or additional forms, you can download them from the Internal Revenue Service's Web site. You can also find them at some post offices, libraries, banks, and at your local IRS office.
- **Copies of Your Tax Returns** Have copies of your tax returns from previous years for reference—unless, of course, you are filing for the first time.
- **Your W-2 Form** You must attach a copy of your W-2 form to your tax return if you are filing by mail. If you worked for more than one employer during the tax year, you will receive more than one W-2.
- **Interest and Dividend Forms** You may also receive Form 1099-INT, which reports your interest income, (see **Figure 4**), and Form 1099-DIV, which reports your dividend income.

After you complete your returns, be sure to save copies of these forms and all supporting documents in a safe place for at least six years.

Completing the Form 1040EZ

After you have collected all the necessary tax documents, it is time to begin filling out your tax return. Take a look at **Figure 5,** which illustrates a sample tax return.

FIGURE 3 Tax Records

Recordkeeping System You will be more organized and prepared if you maintain a recordkeeping system with the documents and information shown here. *When would you have more than one W-2 form?*

Tax Forms and Tax Filing Information

- Current tax forms and instruction booklets
- Reference books on current tax laws and tax-saving techniques
- Social Security numbers of household members
- Copies of federal tax returns from previous years

Income Records

- W-2 forms reporting salary, wages, and taxes withheld
- W-2P forms reporting pension income
- 1099 forms reporting interest, dividends, and capital gains and losses from savings and investments
- 1099 forms for self-employment income, royalty income, and lump-sum payments from pension or retirement plans

Expense Records

- Receipts for medical, dependent care, charitable donations, and job-related expenses
- Mortgage interest (Form 1098) and other deductible interest
- Business, investment, and rental-property expense documents

FIGURE 4 **The Interest Income Form**

Earned Interest You will receive a 1099-INT from any financial institution that paid you interest on an account. *What type of income requires a form 1099-DIV?*

9292 ☐ VOID ☐ CORRECTED

PAYER'S name, street address, city, state, ZIP code, and telephone no.	Payer's RTN (optional)	OMB No. 1545-0112	
BAILEY'S BANK 1155 DARNESTOWN ROAD ARLINGTON, IL 61312		20–– Form 1099-INT	Interest Income

PAYER'S Federal identification number	RECIPIENT'S identification number	1 Interest income not included in box 3		Copy A For Internal Revenue Service Center
521283179	123XXXXXX	$ 45.00		
RECIPIENT'S name: JAMES A. IRVING		2 Early withdrawal penalty $ .00	3 Interest on U.S. Savings Bonds and Treas. obligations $ .00	File with Form 1096.
Street address (including apt. no.): 23 CEDAR GLENN LANE		4 Federal income tax withheld $ .00	5 Investment expenses $ .00	For Privacy Act and Paperwork Reduction Act Notice and instructions for completing this form, see the 20–– Instructions for Forms 1099, 1098, 5498, and W-2G.
City, state, and ZIP code: ARLINGTON, IL 61312		6 Foreign tax paid	7 Foreign country or U.S. possession	
Account number (optional): 894-6210	2nd TIN Not. ☐	$ .00		

Form **1099-INT** Cat. No. 14410K Department of the Treasury - Internal Revenue Service

Do NOT Cut or Separate Forms on This Page — Do NOT Cut or Separate Forms on This Page

As shown in **Figure 5,** here is how James Irving would complete Form 1040EZ:

1. After printing his name, address, and Social Security number, James enters the total wages from his W-2 form on line 1.
2. James earned $45 in interest on his savings account. (This was reported on Form 1099-INT.) He enters this amount on line 2.
3. James has nothing to report on line 3, so he leaves it blank.
4. James adds lines 1, 2, and 3 to get his adjusted gross income. He records it on line 4.
5. James's parents claim him as a dependent on their income tax return, so James uses the worksheet on the back of Form 1040EZ to calculate his maximum standard deduction. He enters $4,850 on line 5. (See Figure 5.)
6. He subtracts his deduction from his adjusted gross income and computes his taxable income: $5,445. He writes it on line 6.
7. On line 7, in the payments and tax section, James enters the amount of income tax that was withheld from his paychecks ($1,375) as reported on his W-2 form.
8. James cannot claim any earned income credit, so he leaves line 8 blank.

GO FIGURE Mathematics

1040EZ Tax Due

You can find out if you owe tax or if you will get a refund by using tax tables.

EXAMPLE Jacqui works part-time in a bookstore. Her year's adjusted gross income was $10,840. Her standard deduction is $4,850. She is using the tax table in Figure 6. How much is her tax?

Formula Adjusted Gross Income – Standard Deduction = Taxable Income
Taxable Income bracket on Tax Table to find Tax Due

Solution $10,840 – $4,850 = $5,990 Taxable Income
$5,959 to $6,000 for single person is $598 tax due.

Your Turn

Your adjusted gross income is $9,438. If you are single and claimed by someone else as a dependent, how much tax do you owe?

9. He adds lines 7 and 8 to find his total payments ($1,375). He enters this amount on line 9.
10. Now James finds out how much tax he owes. He knows from line 6 that his taxable income is $5,445. He checks the tax table in the Form 1040EZ instruction booklet (see **Figure 6**) and finds the column that says "If Form 1040EZ, line 6, is" and the row that corresponds with "At least" $5,400 "But less than" $5,450. Because he is single, he owes $543. He enters this amount on line 10.
11. James's employer withheld more tax than James owed. By subtracting his tax owed (line 10) from his tax withheld (line 9), James finds that the IRS owes him a refund of $832, which he enters on line 11a. If he fills in lines 11b, 11c, and 11d, he can have his refund deposited directly into his bank account. He leaves the lines blank so that he will receive a refund check.
12. He then signs and dates his income tax return and enters his occupation. James makes a photocopy of his tax return for his records, attaches his W-2 to the original tax return, and mails the completed return to the IRS.

Completing the Form 1040A

James used Form 1040EZ because his tax situation was uncomplicated. Some taxpayers, however, will benefit from using Form 1040A, shown in **Figure 7.** Form 1040A enables taxpayers to claim deductions that will reduce the amount of tax they must pay.

Filing Your Federal Income Tax return

You may be able to file the return using one of several options. You can file the traditional paper return by filling out the forms and mailing them to the IRS. If you file electronically through the Internet, your return is transmitted directly to an IRS computer.

FIGURE 5 **Form 1040EZ**

Tax Return Be sure to always write legibly and to double check all numbers that you enter on your tax return. *Why should you make a photocopy of your return before mailing it?*

Form **1040EZ** | Department of the Treasury—Internal Revenue Service | **Income Tax Return for Single and Joint Filers With No Dependents** (99) **20--** | OMB No. 1545-0675

Label (See page 11.) **Use the IRS label.** Otherwise, please print or type. LABEL HERE

Your first name and initial	Last name	Your social security number
JAMES A.	IRVING	123 XX XXXX
If a joint return, spouse's first name and initial	Last name	Spouse's social security number
Home address (number and street). If you have a P.O. box, see page 11. 23 CEDAR GLENN	Apt. no.	
City, town or post office, state, and ZIP code. If you have a foreign address, see page 11. ARLINGTON, ILLINOIS 61312		

▲ Important! ▲ You **must** enter your SSN(s) above.

Presidential Election Campaign (page 11) **Note.** Checking "Yes" will not change your tax or reduce your refund. Do you, or your spouse if a joint return, want $3 to go to this fund? You: ☐ Yes ☒ No Spouse: ☐ Yes ☐ No

Income Attach Form(s) W-2 here. Enclose, but do not attach, any payment.	1	Wages, salaries, and tips. This should be shown in box 1 of your Form(s) W-2. Attach your Form(s) W-2.	1	10,250 00
	2	Taxable interest. If the total is over $1,500, you cannot use Form 1040EZ.	2	45 00
	3	Unemployment compensation and Alaska Permanent Fund dividends (see page 13).	3	
	4	Add lines 1, 2, and 3. This is your **adjusted gross income.**	4	10,295 00
Note. You **must** check Yes or No.	5	Can your parents (or someone else) claim you on their return? **Yes.** ☒ Enter amount from worksheet on back. **No.** ☐ If **single,** enter $7,950. If **married filing jointly,** enter $15,900. See back for explanation.	5	4,850 00
	6	Subtract line 5 from line 4. If line 5 is larger than line 4, enter -0-. This is your **taxable income.** ▶	6	5,445 00
Payments and tax	7	Federal income tax withheld from box 2 of your Form(s) W-2.	7	1,375 00
	8a	**Earned income credit (EIC).**	8a	
	b	Nontaxable combat pay election. 8b		
	9	Add lines 7 and 8a. These are your **total payments.** ▶	9	1,375 00
	10	**Tax.** Use the amount on **line 6 above** to find your tax in the tax table on pages 24–32 of the booklet. Then, enter the tax from the table on this line.	10	543 00
Refund Have it directly deposited! See page 18 and fill in 11b, 11c, and 11d.	11a	If line 9 is larger than line 10, subtract line 10 from line 9. This is your **refund.** ▶	11a	832 00
	▶ b	Routing number ▶ c Type: ☐ Checking ☐ Savings		
	▶ d	Account number		
Amount you owe	12	If line 10 is larger than line 9, subtract line 9 from line 10. This is the **amount you owe.** For details on how to pay, see page 19. ▶	12	

Third party designee Do you want to allow another person to discuss this return with the IRS (see page 19)? ☐ **Yes.** Complete the following. ☒ **No**
Designee's name ▶ Phone no. ▶ ( ) Personal identification number (PIN) ▶

Sign here Joint return? See page 11. Keep a copy for your records.
Under penalties of perjury, I declare that I have examined this return, and to the best of my knowledge and belief, it is true, correct, and accurately lists all amounts and sources of income I received during the tax year. Declaration of preparer (other than the taxpayer) is based on all information of which the preparer has any knowledge.

Your signature	Date	Your occupation	Daytime phone number
James A Irving	2/2/--	ASSISTANT MGR.	(815) 555-1941
Spouse's signature. If a joint return, **both** must sign.	Date	Spouse's occupation	

Paid preparer's use only
Preparer's signature ▶ | Date | Check if self-employed ☐ | Preparer's SSN or PTIN
Firm's name (or yours if self-employed), address, and ZIP code ▶ | EIN | Phone no. ( )

For Disclosure, Privacy Act, and Paperwork Reduction Act Notice, see page 23. Cat. No. 11329W Form **1040EZ** (20--)

Use this form if

- Your filing status is single or married filing jointly. If you are not sure about your filing status, see page 11.
- You (and your spouse if married filing jointly) were under age 65 and not blind at the end of 2004. If you were born on January 1, 1940, you are considered to be age 65 at the end of 2004.
- You do not claim any dependents. For information on dependents, use TeleTax topic 354 (see page 6).
- Your taxable income (line 6) is less than $100,000.
- You do not claim any adjustments to income. For information on adjustments to income, use TeleTax topics 451-458 (see page 6).
- The only tax credit you can claim is the earned income credit. For information on credits, use TeleTax topics 601-608 and 610 (see page 6).
- You had only wages, salaries, tips, taxable scholarship or fellowship grants, unemployment compensation, or Alaska Permanent Fund dividends, and your taxable interest was not over $1,500. But if you earned tips, including allocated tips, that are not included in box 5 and box 7 of your Form W-2. you may not be able to use Form 1040EZ (see page 12). If you are planning to use Form 1040EZ for a child who received Alaska Permanent Fund dividends, see page 13.
- You did not receive any advance earned income credit payments.
If you cannot use this form, use TeleTax topic 352 (see page 6).

Filling in your return

For tips on how to avoid common mistakes, see page 20.

If you received a scholarship or fellowship grant or tax-exempt interest income. Such as on municipal bonds, see the booklet before filling in the form. Also, see the booklet if you received a Form 1099-INT showing federal income tax withheld or if federal income tax was withheld from your unemployment compensation or Alaska Permanent Fund dividends.
Remember, you must report all wages, salaries, and tips even if you do not get a Form W-2 from your employer. You must also report all your taxable interest, including interest from banks, savings and loans, credit unions, etc., even if you do not get a Form 1099-INT.

Worksheet for dependents who checked "Yes" on line 5

(keep a copy for your records)

Use this worksheet to figure the amount to enter on line 5 if someone can claim you (or your spouse if married filing jointly) as a dependent, even if that person chooses not to do so. To find out if someone can claim you as a dependent, use TeleTax topic 354 (see page 6).

A. Amount, if any, from line I on front 10,250
\+ 250.00 Enter total ▶ **A.** 10,500.00

B. Minimum standard deduction . . . . **B.** 800.00

C. Enter the **larger** of line A or line B here . . . . **C.** 10,500.00

D. Maximum standard deduction. If **single**, enter $4,850; if **married filing jointly,** enter $9,700 . . . . **D.** 4,850.00

E. Enter the **smaller** of line C or line D here. This is your standard deduction . . . . **E.** 4,850.00

F. Exemption amount.
- If single, enter -0-.
- If married filing jointly and—
  —both you and your spouse can be claimed as dependents, enter-0-.
  —only one of you can be claimed as a dependent, enter $3,100.

F. -0-

G. Add lines E and E Enter the total here and on line 5 on the front. **G.** 4,850.00

If you checked "No" on line 5 because no one can claim you (or your spouse if married filing jointly) as a dependent, enter on line 5 the amount shown below that applies to you.

- Single, enter $7,950. This is the total of your standard deduction ($4,850) and your exemption ($3,100).
- Married filing jointly, enter $15,900. This is the total of your standard deduction ($9,700), your exemption($3,100), and your spouse's exemption ($3,100).

Mailing return

Mail your return by **April 15, 20--.** Use the envelope that came with your booklet. If you do not have that envelope or if you moved during the year, see the back cover for the address to use.

Form **1040EZ** (20--)

The IRS provides two ways for individuals to file electronically. First, you can use an authorized IRS e-file provider. With this method, either you or a tax professional would prepare your tax return. The tax professional would transmit it to the IRS. Second, you can file by using your personal computer and tax software.

Today most taxpayers use personal computers for tax recordkeeping and tax form preparation. Software packages such as *H&R Block At Home* and *TurboTax* allow you to complete needed tax forms and schedules to either print for mailing or file online. Electronic filing of federal taxes now exceeds 60 million returns annually. With e-file, taxpayers usually receive their refunds within three weeks.

FIGURE 6 **Sample Tax Table**

Tax Owed The tax form instruction booklet will contain a current tax table for you to use in determining how much tax you should have paid for the year based on your taxable income. *How much tax would you owe if you were single with a taxable income of $6,825?*

20- - Tax Table

Example. Mr. Brown is single. His taxable income on line 6 of Form 1040EZ is $26,250. First, he finds the $26,250–26,600 income line. Next, he finds the "Single" column and reads down the column. The amount shown where the income line and filing status column meet → is $6,584. This is the tax amount he should enter on line 10 of Form 1040EZ.

At least	But less than	Single	Married filing jointly
		Your tax is—	
26,200	26,250	3,576	3,219
26,250	26,300	(3,584)	3,226
26,300	26,350	3,591	3,234
26,350	26,400	3,599	3,241

If Form 1040EZ, line 6, is—		And you are—	
At least	But less than	Single	Married filing jointly
		Your tax is—	
3,000			
3,000	3,050	303	303
3,050	3,100	308	308
3,100	3,150	316	316
3,150	3,200	318	318
3,200	3,250	323	323
3,250	3,300	328	328
3,300	3,350	333	333
3,350	3,400	338	338
3,400	3,450	343	343
3,450	3,500	348	348
3,500	3,550	353	353
3,550	3,600	358	358
3,600	3,650	363	363
3,650	3,700	368	368
3,700	3,750	373	373
3,750	3,800	378	378
3,800	3,850	383	383
3,850	3,900	388	388
3,900	3,950	393	393
3,950	4,000	398	398

If Form 1040EZ, line 6, is—		And you are—	
At least	But less than	Single	Married filing jointly
		Your tax is—	
4,000			
4,000	4,050	403	403
4,050	4,100	408	408
4,100	4,150	416	416
4,150	4,200	418	418
4,200	4,250	423	423
4,250	4,300	428	428
4,300	4,350	433	433
4,350	4,400	438	438
4,400	4,450	443	443
4,450	4,500	448	448
4,500	4,550	453	453
4,550	4,600	458	458
4,600	4,650	463	463
4,650	4,700	468	468
4,700	4,750	473	473
4,750	4,800	478	478
4,800	4,850	483	483
4,850	4,900	488	488
4,900	4,959	493	493
4,959	5,000	498	498

If Form 1040EZ, line 6, is—		And you are—	
At least	But less than	Single	Married filing jointly
		Your tax is—	
5,000			
5,000	5,050	503	503
5,050	5,100	508	508
5,100	5,150	516	516
5,150	5,200	518	518
5,200	5,250	523	523
5,250	5,300	528	528
5,300	5,350	533	533
5,350	5,400	538	538
5,400	5,450	543	543
5,450	5,500	548	548
5,500	5,550	553	553
5,550	5,600	558	558
5,600	5,650	563	563
5,650	5,700	568	568
5,700	5,750	573	573
5,750	5,800	578	578
5,800	5,850	583	583
5,850	5,900	588	588
5,900	5,959	593	593
5,959	6,000	598	598

If Form 1040EZ, line 6, is—		And you are—	
At least	But less than	Single	Married filing jointly
		Your tax is—	
6,000			
6,000	6,050	603	603
6,050	6,100	608	608
6,100	6,150	616	616
6,150	6,200	618	618
6,200	6,250	623	623
6,250	6,300	628	628
6,300	6,350	633	633
6,350	6,400	638	638
6,400	6,450	643	643
6,450	6,500	648	648
6,500	6,550	653	653
6,550	6,600	658	658
6,600	6,650	663	663
6,650	6,700	668	668
6,700	6,750	673	673
6,750	6,800	678	678
6,800	6,850	683	683
6,850	6,900	688	688
6,900	6,959	693	693
6,959	7,000	698	698

Using tax software can save you ten or more hours when preparing your Form 1040 and accompanying schedules.

When selecting tax software, consider the following factors:

1. Your personal situation—are you employed or do you operate your own business?
2. Special tax situations with regard to types of income, unusual deductions, and various tax credits.
3. Features in the software, such as "audit check," future tax planning, and filing your federal and state tax forms online.
4. Technical aspects, such as the hardware and operating system requirements, and online support that is provided.

Electronic Filing In recent years, the IRS has made online filing easier and less expensive. Through the Free File Alliance, online tax preparation and e-filing are available free to millions of taxpayers. This partnership between the IRS and the tax software industry encourages more e-filing. Taxpayers who do not qualify for the Free File Alliance program may still be able to file online for a nominal fee. You do not have to purchase the software; simply go to the software company's Web site and pay a fee to use the tax program.

Taxpayers who qualify to use the Free File Alliance are cautioned to be careful consumers. A company may attempt to sell other financial products to inexperienced taxpayers, such as expensive refund anticipation loans. Also, taxpayers using the free file service must be aware that their state tax return might not be included in the free program.

Completing State Income Tax Returns

If you live in a state that **levies**, or collects, income tax, you will have to complete a state income tax return. Only seven states do not have a state income tax:

- Alaska
- Florida
- Nevada
- South Dakota
- Texas
- Washington
- Wyoming

In most states, the tax rate ranges from 1 to 10 percent and is based on your adjusted gross or taxable income reported on your federal tax return. States usually require their income tax returns to be filed at the same time as federal income tax returns. To find out more about state income tax forms and preparation, contact your state's department of revenue or tax board.

Self-Management

One characteristic of many successful people is self-management. Self-management is the ability to assess your knowledge, skills, and abilities and to motivate yourself to achieve personal goals. People who possess strong self-management skills are able to manage change and utilize strategies to complete difficult tasks. Self-managements skills will also help you to apply and transfer strategies and information you have learned to overcome challenges.

Write About It

Think of a situation in which you did use or could have used self-management skills. Write one or more paragraphs to describe the scenario and explain how self-management skills had a positive influence on the situation. How do you think self-management skills could help you achieve future personal goals?

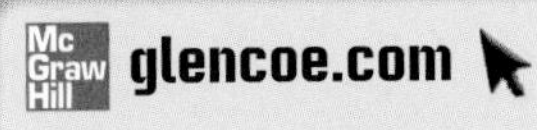

Activity Download a Career and College Readiness Worksheet Activity.

FIGURE 7 **Form 1040A**

Keep It Simple Form 1040A is more complex than the 1040EZ but still simpler than the Form 1040. *When should you use Form 1040 instead of 1040A?*

Form **1040A** Department of the Treasury—Internal Revenue Service
U.S. Individual Income Tax Return (99) **20--** IRS Use Only—Do not write or staple in this space.

OMB No. 1545-0085

Label (See page 18.)
Use the IRS label. Otherwise, please print or type.
LABEL HERE

Your first name and initial: ROBERT S. Last name: PARK
Your social security number: 129 XX XXXX
If a joint return, spouse's first name and initial: JI SUN Last name: PARK
Spouse's social security number: 156 XX XXXX
Home address (number and street). If you have a P.O. box, see page 18.: 140 OAK LANE Apt. no.
City, town or post office, state, and ZIP code. If you have a foreign address, see page 18.: CHARLOTTESVILLE VA 22901

▲ **Important!** ▲ You **must** enter your SSN(s) above.

Presidential Election Campaign (See page 18.)
Note. Checking "Yes" will not change your tax or reduce your refund.
Do you, or your spouse if filing a joint return, want $3 to go to this fund? . . . ▶
You: ☐ Yes ☒ No Spouse: ☐ Yes ☒ No

Filing status Check only one box.
1 ☐ Single
2 ☒ Married filing jointly (even if only one had income)
3 ☐ Married filing separately. Enter spouse's SSN above and full name here. ▶
4 ☐ Head of household (with qualifying person). (See page 19.) If the qualifying person is a child but not your dependent, enter this child's name here. ▶
5 ☐ Qualifying widow(er) with dependent child (see page 19)

Exemptions
6a ☒ **Yourself.** If someone can claim you as a dependent, **do not** check box 6a.
b ☒ **Spouse**
Boxes checked on 6a and 6b: 2
c **Dependents:**

If more than six dependents, see page 20.

(1) First name Last name	**(2)** Dependent's social security number	**(3)** Dependent's relationship to you	**(4)** √ if qualifying child for child tax credit (see page 21)
LILY SUN PARK	201 XX XXXX	DAUGHTER	☐
MICHAEL JOON PARK	401 XX XXXX	SON	☐
			☐
			☐
			☐
			☐

No. of children on 6c who: • lived with you: 2
• did not live with you due to divorce or separation (see page 21)
Dependent's on 6c not entered above
d Total number of exemptions claimed. Add numbers on lines above ▶ 4

Income
Attach Form(s) W-2 here. Also attach Form(s) 1099-R if tax was withheld.
If you did not get a W-2, see page 22.
Enclose, but do not attach, any payment.

7	Wages, salaries, tips, etc. Attach Form(s) W-2.	7	47,500 00
8a	**Taxable** interest. Attach Schedule 1 if required.	8a	325 00
b	**Tax-exempt** interest. **Do not** include on line 8a. 8b		
9a	Ordinary dividends. Attach Schedule 1 if required.	9a	
b	Qualified dividends (see page 23). 9b		
10	Capital gain distributions (see page 23).	10	
11a	IRA distributions. 11a — **11b** Taxable amount (see page 23).	11b	
12a	Pensions and annuities. 12a — **12b** Taxable amount (see page 24).	12b	
13	Unemployment compensation and Alaska Permanent Fund dividends.	13	
14a	Social security benefits. 14a — **14b** Taxable amount (see page 26).	14b	
15	Add lines 7 through 14b (far right column). This is your **total income.** ▶	15	47,825 00

Adjusted gross income

16	Educator expenses (see page 26). 16		
17	IRA deduction (see page 26). 17 — 00		
18	Student loan interest deduction (see page 29). 18		
19	Tuition and fees deduction (see page 29). 19		
20	Add lines 16 through 19. These are your **total adjustments.**	20	
21	Subtract line 20 from line 15. This is your **adjusted gross income.** ▶	21	

Cat. No. 11327A Form **1040A** (20--)

Taxpayer indicates filing status and the number of exemptions claimed.

Taxpayer can enter income from a variety of sources.

IRA contributions, student loan interest, and certain other items can be deducted, lowering the taxpayer's adjusted gross income.

Several types of tax credits, estimated tax payments, and withheld taxes add up to the total taxes.

If someone other than the taxpayer is paid to complete the form, he or she must also sign the form and provide additional information.

Form 1040A (20--) Page 2

Tax, credits, and payments

22	Enter the amount from line 21 (adjusted gross income).	22	43,825 00
23a	Check if: ☐ **You** were born before January 2, 1940. ☐ Blind; ☐ **Spouse** was born before January 2, 1940. ☐ Blind. **Total boxes checked** ▶	23a	
b	If you are married filing separately and your spouse itemizes deductions, see page 30 and check here ▶	23b ☐	
24	Enter your **standard deduction** (see left margin).	24	9,700 00
25	Subtract line 24 from line 22. If line 24 is more than line 22, enter -0-.	25	34,125 00
26	If line 22 is $107,025 or less, multiply $3,100 by the total number of exemptions claimed on line 6d. If line 22 is over $107,025, see the worksheet on page 32.	26	12,400 00
27	Subtract line 26 from line 25. If line 26 is more than line 25, enter -0-. This is your **taxable income.** ▶	27	21,725 00
28	**Tax,** including any alternative minimum tax (see page 31).	28	2,544 00
29	Credit for child and dependent care expenses. Attach Schedule 2.	29	
30	Credit for the elderly or the disabled. Attach Schedule 3.	30	
31	Education credits. Attach Form 8863.	31	
32	Retirement savings contributions credit. Attach Form 8880.	32	
33	Child tax credit (see page 36).	33	
34	Adoption credit. Attach Form 8839.	34	
35	Add lines 29 through 34. These are your **total credits.**	35	-0-
36	Subtract line 35 from line 28. If line 35 is more than line 28, enter-0-.	36	
37	Advance earned income credit payments from Form(s) W-2.	37	
38	Add lines 36 and 37. This is your **total tax.** ▶	38	
39	Federal income tax withheld from Forms W-2 and 1099.	39	4,550 00
40	2004 estimated tax payments and amount applied from 2003 return.	40	
41a	**Earned income credit (EIC).**	41a	
b	Nontaxable combat pay election.	41b	
42	Additional child tax credit. Attach Form 8812.	42	
43	Add lines 39, 40, 41a, and 42. These are your total payments. ▶	43	4,550 00

Standard Deduction for—
• People who checked any box on line 23a or 23b or who can be claimed as a dependent, see page 31.
• All others:
Single or Married filing separately, $4,850
Married filing jointly or Qualifying widow(er), $9,700
Head of household, $7,150

If you have a qualifying child, Attach Schedule EIC.

Refund

44	If line 43 is more than line 38, subtract line 38 from line 43. This is the amount you **overpaid**.	44	2,006 00
45a	Amount of line 44 you want **refunded to you**. ▶	45a	2,006 00
▶ b	Routing number ☐☐☐☐☐☐☐☐☐ ▶ c Type: ☐ Checking ☐ Savings		
▶ d	Account number ☐☐☐☐☐☐☐☐☐☐☐☐☐☐☐☐☐		
46	Amount of line 44 you want applied to your **2005 estimated tax.**	46	

Direct deposit? See page 50 and fill in 45b, 45c, and 45d.

Amount you owe

47	**Amount you owe.** Subtract line 43 from line 38. For details on how to pay, see page 51. ▶	47	
48	Estimated tax penalty (see page 51).	48	

Third party designee
Do you want to allow another person to discuss this return with the IRS (see page 52)? ☐ Yes. Complete the following. ☒ No
Designee's name ▶ Phone no. ▶ ( ) Personal Identification numer (PIN) ▶

Sign here
Joint return? See page 18. Keep a copy for your records.

Under penalties of perjury, I declare that I have exemined this return and accompanying schedules and statements, and to the best of my knowledge and belief, they are true, correct, and accurately list all amounts and sources of income I received during the tax year. Declaration of preparer (other than the taxpayer) is based on all information of which the preparer has any knowledge.

Your signature	Date	Your occupation	Daytime phone number
Robert S. Park	3/8/--	LANDSCAPER	804 555-9394
Spouse's signature. If a joint return, **both** must sign.	Date	Spouse's occupation	
Ji Sun Park	3/8/--	FLORIST	

Paid preparer's use only
Preparer's signature ▶ Date Check if self-employed ☐ Preparer's SSN or PTIN
Firm's name (or yours if self-employed), address, and ZIP code ▶ EIN Phone no. ( )

Form **1040A** (20--)

Assessment

Review Key Concepts

1. **Describe** What are the three basic tax forms available?
2. **Summarize** What documents are needed to help you complete your tax return?
3. **Identify** What factors should be considered when selecting tax preparation software?

Higher Order Thinking H.O.T.

4. **Hypothesize** Why might you want to hire a professional tax preparer rather than using tax software to prepare your own return?

21st Century Skills

5. **Access and Evaluate Information** When preparing a tax return, it is important to understand all the current laws. Changes to tax laws occur fairly frequently. In addition to reviewing the current tax forms and instruction booklets, you can visit online resources that describe the tax changes from one year to the next. Conduct online research to see what changes occurred in the previous tax year. Write a paragraph to share the information you find. Would any of these changes affect you if you were filing a tax return from your summer job?

Mathematics

6. **Deductions** Niko earned $25,000 this past year. He is not claimed on anyone else's tax returns as a dependent nor does he have any dependents to claim. Niko lives in an apartment so he does not have any home mortgage interest or tax deductions to claim. He does however have student loans and has paid $3,750 in interest for the year. He has also donated $575 to charity during the year. Determine Niko's deductions and calculate his adjusted gross income. Should Niko use the itemized or standard deduction?

Math Concept **Calculate Adjusted Gross Income** To calculate the adjusted gross income, first determine the appropriate deduction to use. The appropriate deduction should be subtracted from the total annual salary to acquire the adjusted gross income.

Starting Hint Determine the total itemized deduction by calculating the sum of all qualified deductions. Compare this to the standard deduction based on marital status and apply the greater number to your taxable income.

NCTM Connections Recognize and apply mathematics in contexts outside of mathematics.

glencoe.com Check your answers.

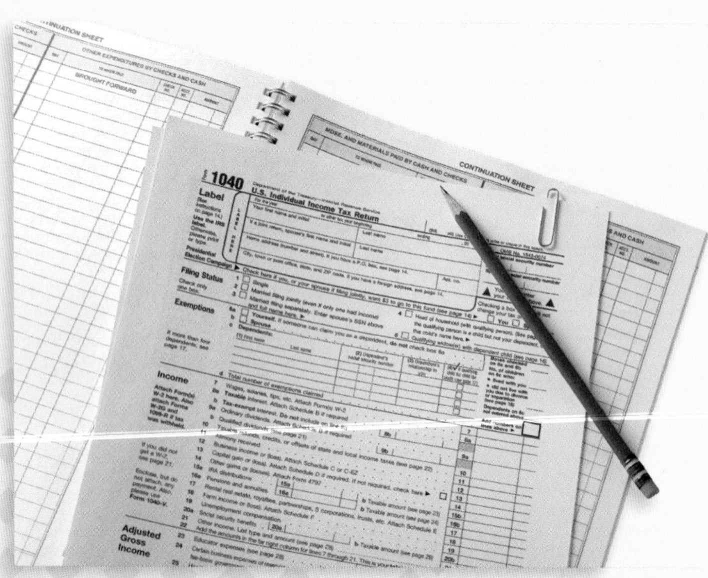

Tax Assistance

Is help available to prepare tax returns?

If your personal finances become more complex, your tax preparation will also become more complicated. All the rules and regulations can be confusing, but assistance is available. You will find many professionals and agencies willing to answer your questions and offer good advice. In addition, you can choose from a variety of software programs for tax preparation. A visit to a bookstore will uncover shelves of how-to books about tax planning and completing tax forms. Personal finance magazines also offer tax information. **Figure 8** shows you some of the available options.

When evaluating tax assistance services consider:

- What training and experience does the tax professional possess?
- How will the fee be determined?
- Does the preparer suggest you report various deductions that might be questioned?
- Will the preparer represent you if your return is audited?
- Is tax preparation the main business activity, or does it serve as a front for selling other financial products and services?

In addition, like all government agencies, the IRS is online. You can download forms and obtain important tax information and advice. You will find the same services at your local IRS office.

Reading Check

Summarize Where can you go for assistance with preparing your tax return?

Tax Audits

What does it mean to be audited?

The IRS reviews all tax returns for completeness and accuracy. If your math is incorrect, the IRS will refigure your tax return and send you either a bill or a refund. In some cases, the IRS may audit your tax return and request additional information. A **tax audit** is a detailed examination of your tax return by the IRS. The IRS does periodic audits to determine whether taxpayers are paying all of their required taxes. The IRS does not discuss reasons for auditing returns; however, the agency may look for unusually large deductions or for deductions that you cannot claim.

Section Objective

- **Identify** tax strategies.

As You Read

Question What are some job-related expenses that you can deduct from your taxes?

FIGURE 8 Tax Assistance Is There for You

Ask for Help Tax laws can often be confusing and a little scary to the average taxpayer. *If you use tax software, why should you buy new software each year?*

When you must file your income tax returns, take advantage of these tax assistance products and services.

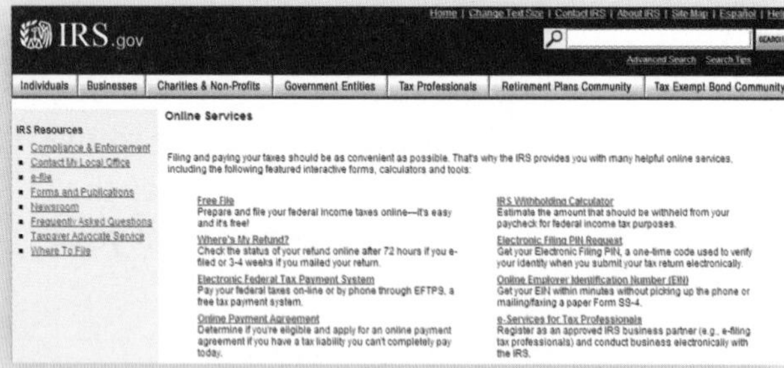

IRS Web Site Like all government agencies, the IRS is online. You can download forms and obtain important tax information and advice. You will find the same services at your local IRS office.

Books Visit a bookstore to uncover shelves of how-to books about tax planning and completing tax forms. Personal finance magazines offer tax information as well.

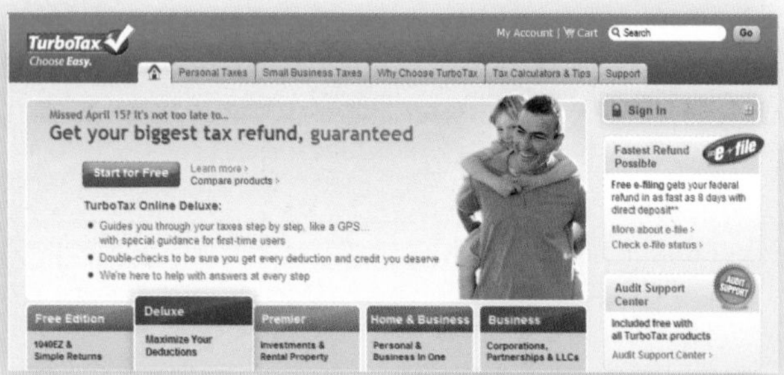

Software Tax preparation software is updated yearly to reflect changes in the tax laws.

Professionals Tax professionals can help you with your tax preparation, answer questions, and determine if you are eligible for deductions and credits.

If you receive an audit notice, you have the right to request time to prepare. You may also ask the IRS for **clarification,** or an explanation, of items they are questioning. On the day of your audit, arrive on time for the appointment and bring only the documents that are relevant and consistent with the tax law. Be sure to answer the auditor's questions clearly, completely, and briefly. Maintain a positive attitude during the audit. If you prefer, your tax preparer, accountant, or lawyer may be present. If you have kept complete and accurate financial records, the audit should go smoothly.

Reading Check

Define What is a tax audit?

Planning Tax Strategies

What are some strategies to reduce the tax you owe?

Smart taxpayers know how to legally minimize the amount of tax they have to pay. You must pay your fair share, but you do not have to pay more. Various strategies related to purchases, investments, and retirement help reduce the amount of tax you owe.

Consumer Purchasing Strategies

The buying decisions you make can affect the amount of taxes you pay. For example, if you purchase a house, the interest you pay on your mortgage and your real estate property taxes are deductible. You can also deduct the interest on a home equity loan. The IRS allows you to deduct the interest on home equity loans up to $100,000.

Some job-related expenses may also be deducted. Union dues, some travel and education expenses, business tools, and certain job-search expenses qualify. Only the portion of these expenses that exceeds 2 percent of your adjusted gross income is deductible. However, expenses related to finding your first job or obtaining work in a different field are not deductible.

Job Expenses
Many job-related expenses, including training classes, can often be deducted on your taxes. *What portion of job-related expenses can be deducted?*

Economics and You

Fact of Scarcity

All nations face the "fact of scarcity." Scarcity occurs due to limited economic resources and unlimited wants and needs. Each nation is forced to make economic decisions on what should be produced, how it should be produced, and for whom it should be produced. In the United States the government chooses to allow the people of the nation to decide on what should be produced by what they purchase in the market place. How it should be produced is left up to businesses. For whom it should be produced is based on an individual's income. The government must make similar decisions on how to use taxpayers' money as well as other revenue. The government must consider how best to serve the people and the country with regard to protection, regulation, and assistance.

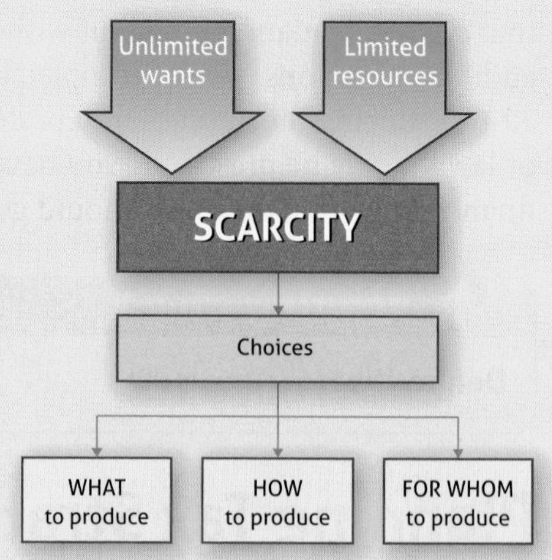

Personal Finance Connection Most people have limited resources and unlimited wants and needs. This scarcity of economic resources forces you to make decisions about how to save, invest, and spend your money.

Critical Thinking Explain the fact of scarcity by using a recent situation involving you, your local community, or the federal government.

Activity Download an Economics and You Worksheet Activity.

Investments

Certain investment decisions may reduce your income tax. Moreover, some investment decisions can increase your income—and lower your taxes. Other investments may be tax-deferred, meaning the income is taxed at a later date.

Retirement Plans Regardless of your age, whether you are 16 or 26, now is the time to start planning for your retirement. To encourage early planning, the government allows you to defer paying taxes on money that you invest in retirement plans. If you open an Individual Retirement Account (IRA) this year, the money you invest, up to a certain amount and under certain conditions, may qualify as a tax deduction. You do not have to pay any income tax on this money or the interest it earns until you withdraw it—perhaps in 50 years.

After You Read

Judge How does the government encourage early saving for retirement? Do you think starting to save for retirement when you are young is a good idea? Why?

Changing Your Tax Strategy

People pay taxes because they are required to do so by law. The government tries to find ways to minimize the taxes you owe without **jeopardizing,** or placing in danger, the important services it provides. This is one reason why the tax laws are always changing. Your tax strategies should change too. As the government allows new deductions or as deductible amounts change, you should review your financial plans to always take full advantage of new tax laws.

Assessment

Review Key Concepts

1. **Describe** What are your rights if you receive an audit notice from the IRS?
2. **Identify** What are the three areas you should look at when considering strategies to reduce the amount of taxes you owe?
3. **Explain** How does the government encourage retirement planning with tax strategies?

Higher Order Thinking H.O.T.

4. **Compile** Fred owns a small advertising agency. Compile a list of possible job-related expenses that Fred could deduct from his taxes.

English Language Arts

5. **Retirement Plans** Many businesses and organizations offer retirement plans to their employees. These can be used as alternatives or in addition to opening an IRA on your own. The most common retirement plans are the 401(k) Plan and the 403(b) Plan. Though these plans are offered through the organization, the employee still maintains control of the account should he or she leave the company. Conduct research to find out more about these retirement plans and write a paragraph explaining the advantages for an employee of using the offered retirement plan.

NCTE 8 Use information resources to gather information and create and communicate knowledge.

Mathematics

6. **Purchasing Strategies** Gail has an adjusted gross income of $41,000 from her job as an engineer for an automobile manufacturer. She has a home in which she has paid $12,350 in home equity interest. Her job requires that she incur some expenses. In the past year, these included $450 for travel, $350 for union dues, $400 for educational expenses, and $500 for business tools. These are the only deductions Gail can make for her year end taxes. Calculate the deductions that Gail will be able to use on her taxes.

Math Concept **Calculate Deductions** To calculate the total deductions allowable first identify all job-related expenses which exceed 2 percent of adjusted gross income. Add the result to any other deductions to determine total deductions.

Starting Hint Determine the job-related expenses allowable as deductions by first multiplying the adjusted gross income by 2 percent.

NCTM Connections Recognize and apply mathematics in contexts outside of mathematics.

Check your answers.

Visual Summary

Planning Your Tax Strategy

Taxes for Life

Understanding the types of taxes that you will pay throughout your life can help you to control how much you pay.

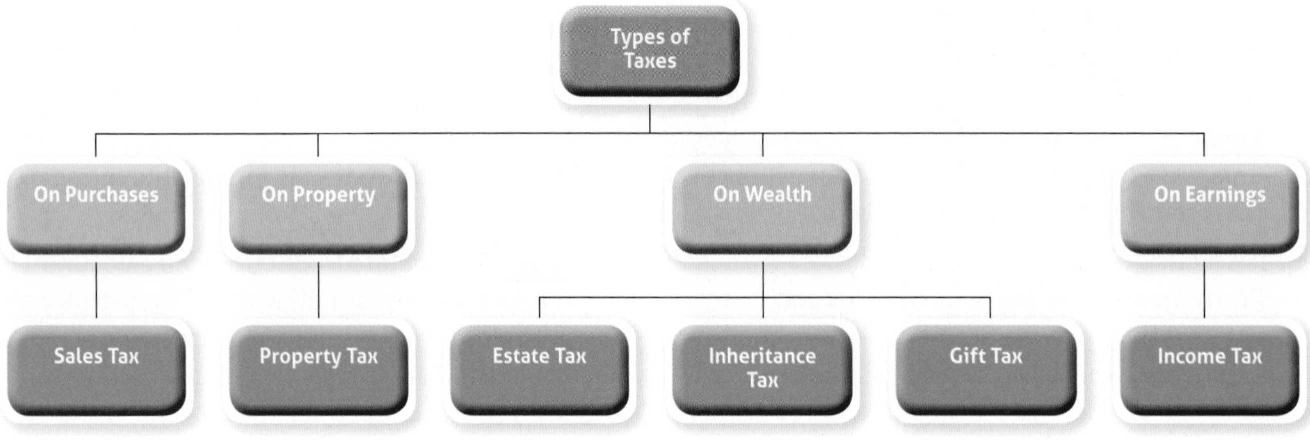

Be Prepared

Before filling out your tax return, be sure you have gathered all the information and documents you will need to accurately complete the form.

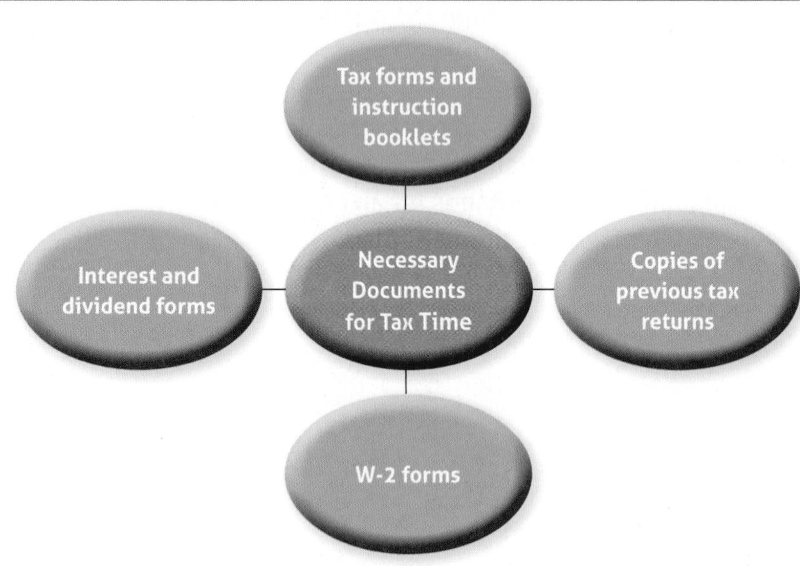

Try It!

Create a checklist like the one shown to describe the various tax strategies you can use to reduce the amount of taxes you owe.

Tax Strategies

Chapter Review and Assessment

Chapter Summary

- Financial planning involves taxes because they reduce your take-home pay.
- Other financial decisions also affect the amount of taxes you pay.
- Your taxable income is earned income plus interest and dividend income minus exclusions, deductions, and exemptions.
- Tax deductions are expenses you are allowed to subtract from your adjusted gross income to arrive at your taxable income.
- The standard deduction is determined by the Internal Revenue Service.
- Tax credits are subtracted directly from the tax you owe.
- An employee fills out a W-4 form, which determines the tax withheld.
- Preparing the W-4 form correctly ensures an employer will withhold the right amount of money owed to the IRS and state and local taxing authorities.
- Form 1040EZ is for filers with no dependents and less than a certain amount in taxable income.
- Form 1040A allows filers to claim deductions for IRA contributions and tax credits.
- Form 1040 must be filed if you are itemizing deductions and/or have more than a certain amount in taxable income.
- You can make strategic decisions that may reduce your tax liability, such as buying a home or saving money in an IRA.

Vocabulary Review

1. Use at least 10 of these vocabulary terms in a short essay explaining to a foreign exchange student how people pay taxes in the United States.

- tax liability
- estate tax
- inheritance tax
- income tax
- income tax return
- exclusion
- adjusted gross income
- taxable income
- tax deduction
- standard deduction
- itemized deduction
- exemption
- tax credit
- allowance
- extension
- tax audit
- excise tax
- dependent
- negligence
- levies
- clarification
- jeopardizing

Higher Order Thinking 

2. **Identify** Consider your personal finances. What types of taxes have you paid recently?
3. **Evaluate** Progressive tax means that the more you earn, the higher rate of taxes you owe. Analyze whether you feel this is a fair system for taxation.
4. **Assess** Sarah wants to claim few deductions on her W-4 so that she can get a bigger tax refund. What would you recommend to Sarah?
5. **Conclude** Ishaan is single, 26 years old, earned $45,000 last year, and regularly contributes to an IRA account and has no itemized deductions. Should he use Form 1040EZ or Form 1040A?
6. **Classify** Would you classify yourself as a taxpayer if you have not yet filed income taxes? Explain your answer.
7. **Predict** Why might it be useful for tax preparation software to have tax professionals available via phone or online chats to answer questions?
8. **Role Play** If you were a financial planner, would you advise most of your clients to consult a professional accountant? Why or why not?

College and Career Readiness

Science

9. **Tax Preparation Software** Advances in technology have made tax preparation easier for and more accessible to the average citizen. Many people who previously felt they had to pay a professional tax preparer to file their returns each year are now realizing that they can save time and money by doing their tax returns at home with the help of tax preparation software.

   Procedure Conduct research to find out the benefits of using tax preparation software and why it is becoming more and more popular.

   Analysis Prepare a list of your findings to share the information with your classmates.

   NSES E Develop abilities of technological design, understandings about science and technology.

Mathematics

10. **Form 1040EZ** Christen earned $11,500 in total wages, salaries and tips last year from her job. Her company withheld $650 for federal income tax purposes. Christen is not able to claim anyone as a dependent, and no one is able to claim her as a dependent for tax purposes. She earned taxable interest of $97 during the year from her savings account. Use the table in **Figure 6** to determine how much Christen's tax payment or credit will be.

    Math Concept **Calculate Tax Payment or Credit** To calculate the tax payment or credit, identify the taxable income and use the table in **Figure 6**.

    Starting Hint Identify the total annual salary and add any taxable interest to determine the adjusted gross income. Subtract the standard deduction from the adjusted gross income to determine Christen's taxable income.

    NCTM Connections Recognize and apply mathematics in contexts outside of mathematics.

English Language Arts

11. **Tax Preparation** When you hire a professional to help you prepare your taxes, you will be sharing a lot of personal information. You must be careful when hiring a professional tax preparer to avoid financial fraud. Use online resources to find warning signs that you should look for to help identify a fraudulent tax preparer. Use the information you find to create a flyer illustrating the warning signs.

    NCTE 5 Use different writing process elements to communicate effectively.

Economics

12. **Tax System** Even taxpayers with equal incomes pay different amounts of taxes due to deductions and credits. The government tries to make taxation fairer by offering tax breaks to certain groups. When too many people take advantage of tax breaks, the government loses money and must raise taxes or cut back on programs. Lobbyists try to influence government decisions about tax laws. Often, there will be multiple lobbyists, representing different groups, trying to influence lawmakers on a single issue. Conduct research into the Fair Tax Bill that was first introduced in 1999. Write a one-page report summarizing how this bill would change our tax system if it were passed. How does it relate to any recent legislation?

Real-World Applications

13. **Charitable Contributions** Jace makes regular donations to local charities. His tax preparer tells him that the IRS allows you to deduct contributions of cash or property to qualified charities. While you cannot deduct your time if you volunteer for these charities, you can deduct your travel expenses. There are limits on how much you can deduct and rules you must follow in order to claim these deductions. Visit the IRS Web site to find out more about the rules and limits, including what records you need to keep and where you indicate the deductions on your tax return. Write a letter to Jace to share your findings.

Take It EZ

Using a photocopy of this form, complete your income tax return. You may also download the form from the IRS Web site. Assume that your wages for the year were $13,220 and you earned $137 in interest. Your W-2 form shows that you had $1,003 in federal income tax withheld. Your parents cannot claim you on their income tax return. Find your tax using the tax table in **Figure 6,** and then calculate your refund or the amount you owe.

Form **1040EZ** Department of the Treasury—Internal Revenue Service
Income Tax Return for Single and Joint Filers With No Dependents (99) **20--** OMB No. 1545-0675

Label (See page 11.) **Use the IRS label.** Otherwise, please print or type.

LABEL HERE

Your first name and initial | Last name | **Your social security number**

If a joint return, spouse's first name and initial | Last name | **Spouse's social security number**

Home address (number and street). If you have a P.O. box, see page 11. | Apt. no.

City, town or post office, state, and ZIP code. If you have a foreign address, see page 11.

▲ **Important!** ▲ You **must** enter your SSN(s) above.

Presidential Election Campaign (page 11) **Note.** Checking "Yes" will not change your tax or reduce your refund. Do you, or your spouse if a joint return, want $3 to go to this fund? . . . . . . ▶ You ☐ Yes ☐ No Spouse ☐ Yes ☐ No

Income **Attach Form(s) W-2 here.** Enclose, but do not attach, any payment.	1	Wages, salaries, and tips. This should be shown in box 1 of your Form(s) W-2. Attach your Form(s) W-2.	1
	2	Taxable interest. If the total is over $1,500, you cannot use Form 1040EZ.	2
	3	Unemployment compensation and Alaska Permanent Fund dividends (see page 13).	3
	4	Add lines 1, 2, and 3. This is your **adjusted gross income.**	4
Note. You **must** check Yes or No.	5	Can your parents (or someone else) claim you on their return? **Yes.** ☐ Enter amount from worksheet on back. **No.** ☐ If **single,** enter $7,950. If **married filing jointly,** enter $15,900. See back for explanation.	5
	6	Subtract line 5 from line 4. If line 5 is larger than line 4, enter -0-. This is your **taxable income.** ▶	6
Payments and tax	7	Federal income tax withheld from box 2 of your Form(s) W-2.	7
	8a	**Earned income credit (EIC).**	8a
	b	Nontaxable combat pay election. 8b	
	9	Add lines 7 and 8a. These are your **total payments.** ▶	9
	10	**Tax.** Use the amount on **line 6 above** to find your tax in the tax table on pages 24–32 of the booklet. Then, enter the tax from the table on this line.	10
Refund Have it directly deposited! See page 18 and fill in 11b, 11c, and 11d.	11a	If line 9 is larger than line 10, subtract line 10 from line 9. This is your **refund.** ▶	11a
	▶ b	Routing number ☐☐☐☐☐☐☐☐☐ ▶ c Type: ☐ Checking ☐ Savings	
	▶ d	Account number ☐☐☐☐☐☐☐☐☐☐☐☐☐☐☐☐☐	
Amount you owe	12	If line 10 is larger than line 9, subtract line 9 from line 10. This is the **amount you owe.** For details on how to pay, see page 19. ▶	12

Third party designee Do you want to allow another person to discuss this return with the IRS (see page 19)? ☐ **Yes.** Complete the following. ☐ **No**
Designee's name ▶ Phone no. ▶ ( ) Personal identification number (PIN) ▶

Sign here Joint return? See page 11. Keep a copy for your records.
Under penalties of perjury, I declare that I have examined this return, and to the best of my knowledge and belief, it is true, correct, and accurately lists all amounts and sources of income I received during the tax year. Declaration of preparer (other than the taxpayer) is based on all information of which the preparer has any knowledge.
Your signature | Date | Your occupation | Daytime phone number ( )
Spouse's signature. If a joint return, **both** must sign. | Date | Spouse's occupation

Paid preparer's use only
Preparer's signature ▶ | Date | Check if self-employed ☐ | Preparer's SSN or PTIN
Firm's name (or yours if self-employed), address, and ZIP code ▶ | EIN | Phone no. ( )

For Disclosure, Privacy Act, and Paperwork Reduction Act Notice, see page 23. Cat. No. 11329W Form **1040EZ** (20--)

CHAPTER 22

Home and Motor Vehicle Insurance

Visual Literacy

Though monthly insurance rates may seem high, the cost is minimal when compared to the price of repairs when an accident occurs. ***Why do you think age is a factor in the price of auto insurance?***

Discovery Project

Explore Insurance Options

Key Question

Why is it important for tenants to buy renters insurance?

Project Goal

Taylor is ready to move out on his own for the first time. He has found an apartment that is close to school and work. He knows he needs to obtain renters insurance to protect himself but is not sure what he needs or how much it will cost.

- Help Taylor begin by creating a list of the property he owns and determining an approximate replacement value.
- Consider items such as a computer, stereo, or sports equipment, as well as any furniture or clothing that would need to be replaced if a natural disaster occurred.
- Choose three companies that offer renters insurance and compare what each company covers and the costs of coverage.
- Use a spreadsheet to compare your findings. Then choose which company you believe offers the best deal.

Ask Yourself...

- *How would you create an inventory of your personal property?*
- *How should I determine the value of my property?*
- *Would you prefer a policy with actual cash value or replacement value method of settlement?*
- *How can you lower the monthly premiums on your policy?*

Make Judgments and Decisions

Where should you store your inventory, photos, and related documents? Why?

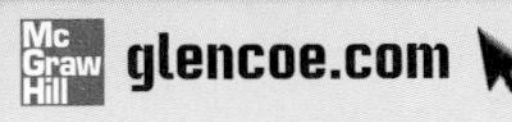

Evaluate Download an assessment rubric.

THE BIG IDEA

Home and motor vehicle insurance offer financial protection for both you and your property.

ASK STANDARD & POOR'S

Insurance Rates

Q *My brother is 17 and has an excellent driving record. Why are his motor vehicle insurance rates higher than rates for females in his same age group?*

A Insurance rates are based on an analysis of accident statistics for all types of drivers. Since young men have a higher incidence of being involved in accidents than young women have, insurance rates for young men are more expensive. Some insurance companies offer discounts for young adults covered on a parent's policy.

Writing Activity

Consider all the factors that determine your auto insurance rate. Then write a letter to the editor of your local newspaper with specific actions that teens can take to help keep insurance rates as low as possible.

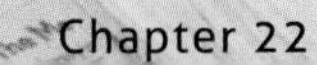

CHAPTER 22 **Reading Guide**

Before You Read

The Essential Question What types of risk can lead to the need for home or motor vehicle insurance?

Main Idea

Having the right insurance program and risk management plan can protect you from financial loss. The goal of an insurance program is to get the best protection at the lowest cost, and there are many factors that affect the cost of insurance.

Content Vocabulary

- insurance
- policy
- premium
- risk
- peril
- hazard
- negligence
- deductible
- liability
- homeowners insurance
- personal property floater
- medical payments coverage
- actual cash value
- replacement value
- bodily injury liability
- uninsured motorist's protection
- property damage liability
- collision
- no-fault system
- assigned risk pool

Academic Vocabulary

You will see these words in your reading and on your tests.

- assume
- vandalism
- appraised
- endorsement
- stiff
- mandatory

Graphic Organizer

Before you read this chapter, draw a pie chart like the one shown. As you read, note the five areas of coverage included in a homeowners policy.

Homeowners Policy Coverage

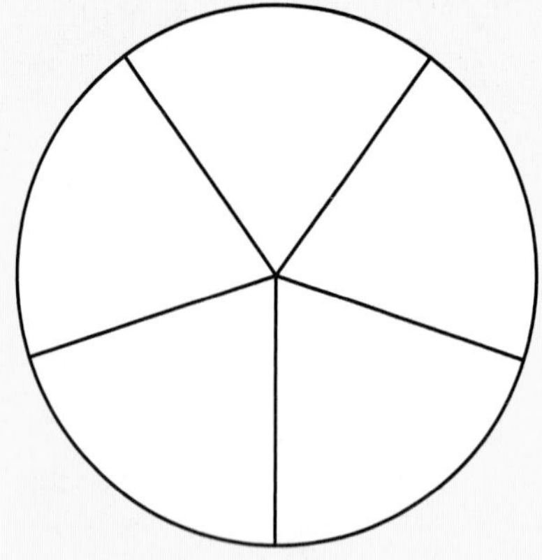

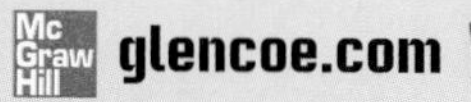

Print this Organizer.

Academic

Mathematics

NCTM Connections Organize and consolidate their mathematical thinking through communication.

English Language Arts

NCTE 4 Use written language to communicate effectively.

NCTE 8 Use information resources to gather information and create and communicate knowledge.

NCTE 12 Use language to accomplish individual purposes.

Social Studies

NCSS I A Analyze and explain the ways groups, societies, and cultures address human needs and concerns.

NCTM *National Council of Teachers of Mathematics*
NCTE *National Council of Teachers of English*
NCSS *National Council for the Social Studies*
NSES *National Science Education Standards*

Common Core

Speaking and Listening Present information, findings, and supporting evidence such that listeners can follow the line of reasoning and the organization, development, and style are appropriate to task, purpose, and audience.

Speaking and Listening Adapt speech to a variety of contexts and communicative tasks, demonstrating command of formal English when indicated or appropriate.

What Is Insurance?

Why is it important to have insurance?

Insurance is protection against possible financial loss. Since you cannot predict the future, you never know when something might happen to you or your property. Insurance allows you to be prepared for the worst. It provides protection against risks, such as unexpected property loss, illness, and injury. Although many kinds of insurance exist, they all have several characteristics in common. For example, they give you peace of mind and protect you from financial loss.

An insurance company, or insurer, is a risk-sharing business that agrees to pay for losses that may happen to someone it insures. A person joins the risk-sharing group by purchasing a contract known as a **policy.** The purchaser of the policy is called a policyholder. Under the policy, the insurance company agrees to take on the risk of the policyholder. In return, the policyholder pays the company a **premium,** which is a fee for insurance. The protection provided by the terms of an insurance policy is known as *coverage*, and the person protected by the policy is known as the *insured.*

Reading Check

Identify What is an *insurer*?

Types of Risks

What are the most common types of risks?

Risk, peril, and *hazard* are important terms in insurance. In everyday use, these terms have almost the same meanings. In the insurance business, however, each word has a distinct and special meaning.

Risk is the chance of loss or injury. You face risks every day. For example, if you cross the street, there is some danger that a motor vehicle might hit you. If you own property, there is risk that it will be lost, stolen, damaged, or destroyed.

In the insurance business, risk refers to the fact that no one can predict trouble. This means that an insurance company is taking a chance every time it issues a policy. Insurance companies frequently refer to the insured person or property as the risk.

Peril is anything that may possibly cause a loss. It is the reason that someone takes out insurance. People buy policies for protection against a wide range of perils, including fire, windstorms, explosions, robbery, and accidents.

Section Objectives

- **Identify** types of risks and risk management methods.
- **Explain** how an insurance program can help manage risks.
- **Describe** the importance of property and liability insurance.

As You Read

Determine Why do most people want to have their cars, homes, and personal property insured?

Hazard is anything that increases the likelihood of loss through peril. For example, defective electrical wiring in a house is a hazard that increases the chance that a fire will start.

The most common risks are personal risks, property risks, and liability risks. Personal risks involve loss of income or life due to illness, disability, old age, or unemployment. Property risks include losses to property caused by perils, such as fire or theft, and hazards. Liability risks involve losses caused by negligence that leads to injury or property damage. **Negligence** is the failure to take ordinary or reasonable care to prevent accidents from happening. If a homeowner does not clear the ice from the front steps of her house, for example, he or she creates a liability risk because visitors could fall on the ice.

Personal risks, property risks, and liability risks are types of pure, or insurable, risk. The insurance company will have to pay only if some event that the insurance covers actually happens. Pure risks are accidental and unintentional. Although no one can predict whether a pure risk will occur, it is possible to predict how much it will cost if it does.

A speculative risk is a risk that carries a chance of either loss or gain. Starting a small business that may or may not succeed is an example of speculative risk. Speculative risks are not insurable.

Reading Check

Recall What are the three most common types of risk?

Risk-Management Methods

Why is risk management important?

Risk management is an organized plan for protecting yourself, your family, and your property. It helps reduce financial losses caused by destructive events. Risk management is a long-range planning process. Your risk-management needs will change at various points in your life. If you understand how to manage risks, you can provide better protection for yourself and your family. See **Figure 1.** Most people think of risk management as buying insurance. However, insurance is not the only way of dealing with risk.

Risk Avoidance

You can avoid the risk of a traffic accident by not driving to work. A car manufacturer can avoid the risk of product failure by not introducing new cars. These are both examples of risk avoidance. They are ways to avoid risks, but they involve serious trade-offs. You might have to give up your job if you cannot get there by driving a car. The car manufacturer might lose business to competitors who take the risk of producing exciting new cars.

In some cases, though, risk avoidance is practical. For example, by taking precautions in high-crime areas, you might avoid the risk of being robbed. By installing a security system in your car, you might avoid the risk of having it stolen. A business owner who manages a jewelry store may avoid losses from robbery by locking his or her merchandise in a vault. Obviously, no person or business can completely avoid risk.

Risk Reduction

You cannot avoid risks completely. However, you can decrease the likelihood that they will cause you harm. For example, you can reduce the risk of injury in a car accident by wearing a seat belt. You can reduce the risk of developing lung cancer by not smoking. By installing fire extinguishers in your home, you can reduce the damage that could be caused by a fire. In addition, you can lower your risk of illness by eating properly and exercising regularly.

Risk Assumption

Risk assumption means taking on responsibility for the negative results of a risk. It makes sense to **assume,** or take upon yourself, a risk if you know that the possible loss will be small. It also makes sense when you have taken all the precautions you can to avoid or reduce the risk.

FIGURE 1 Risks and Risk Management Strategies

Cost of Risk While most types of risk come with a cost, there are strategies to help reduce the financial impact. *How might maintaining your property help reduce the financial impact of liability?*

Risks		
Personal Events	Financial Impact	Strategies for Reducing Financial Impact
Disability	• Loss of income • Increased expenses	• Savings and investments • Disability insurance
Death	• Loss of income	• Life insurance • Estate planning
Property Loss	• Catastrophic storm damage to property • Repair or replacement • Cost of theft	• Property repair and upkeep • Motor vehicle insurance • Homeowners insurance • Flood or earthquake insurance
Liability	• Claims and settlement costs • Lawsuits and legal expenses • Loss of personal assets and income	• Maintaining property • Homeowners insurance • Auto insurance

Lower the Risk
While no one can completely avoid risks, you can take steps to reduce the impact of unavoidable risks. *How can you lower the risk of your home being burglarized?*

When insurance coverage for a particular item is expensive, it may not be worth insuring. For instance, older cars are generally worth less than new cars. So even if an accident happens and the car is wrecked, you may be better off financially by not paying for the insurance coverage since the car was not worth much anyway.

Self-insurance is another option for risk assumption. By setting up your own special fund, perhaps from savings, you can cover the cost of loss. Self-insurance does not eliminate risks, but it does provide a way of covering losses as an alternative to an insurance policy. Some people self-insure because they cannot obtain insurance from an insurance company.

Risk Shifting

The most common method of dealing with risk is to shift it, which means to transfer it to an insurance company. In exchange for the fee you pay, the insurance company agrees to pay for your losses.

Most types of insurance policies include deductibles. Deductibles are a combination of risk assumption and risk shifting. A **deductible** is the set amount that the policyholder must pay per loss on an insurance policy. For example, if a falling tree damages your car, you may have to pay $200 toward the repairs. Your insurance company will pay the rest.

Reading Check

Recognize What are four risk-management methods?

Planning an Insurance Program

What factors will affect your insurance goals?

Because all people have their own needs and goals, many of which change over the years, a personal insurance program should be tailored to those changes. Your personal insurance program should change along with the changes of your needs and goals. For example, Kirk and Luanne are a young married couple. The following four steps outline how they will plan their insurance program to meet their needs and goals.

STEP 1 Set Insurance Goals

Kirk and Luanne's main goal should be to minimize personal, property, and liability risks. They also need to decide how they will cover costs resulting from a potential loss. Income, age, family size, lifestyle, experience, and responsibilities are important factors in determining the goals they set. The insurance that they buy must reflect those goals.

Document Detective

Auto Insurance Declaration

In most states the law requires that you insure your automobile. To protect yourself from financial loss, it is important to know exactly what your auto insurance covers and how much it will cost. The declaration lists this information:

- Policy identification number
- Time period of insurance policy
- Amount of insurance coverage
- Premium amount

The Premier Global Insurance Company Auto Declarations

Policy Number A02 0076215
Policy Period: From 12/27/20-- To 12/27/20--
12:01 Standard Time at the Address of the Named Injured

Coverages and Limits of Liability

Coverages	Vehicle 1		Vehicle 2	
	Limit	Premium	Limit	Premium
A Bodily Injury and Property Damage		$265.00		$339.00
Each Accident	**$1,000,000**		**$1,000,000**	
B Medical Payments	**$5,000**	$9.00	**$5,000**	$11.00
C Uninsured Motorists Bodily Injury		$76.00		$76.00
Each Accident	**$1,000,000**		**$1,000,000**	
D Damage to Your Auto Other Than Collision		$63.00		$126.00
Actual Cash Value Less Deductible	**$500.00**		**$500.00**	
Collision		$155.00		$271.00
Actual Cash Value Less Deductible	**$500.00**		**$500.00**	
Additional Coverages				
Transportation Expense		Included		Included
Per Day/Maximum	**$20/$600**		**$20/$600**	
Towing and Labor Costs		$10.00		$10.00
Each Disablement	**$50**		**$50**	
Theft Coverage - Electronic				
Tapes, Records & Discs				
GAP Coverage				
Total		**$578.00**		**$833.00**

Key Points An auto insurance declaration details what is covered by the policy. It states what the policy will pay in the event of an accident. This includes damage to the car(s) and injury to people. The declaration also explains how the premium is determined.

FIND the Solutions

Review Key Concepts

1. What is the policy identification number?
2. What is the bodily injury payment limit?
3. How much will the policy pay for transportation expenses, such as renting a car?
4. How many vehicles are covered by this policy?
5. What is the cost of this policy?

COMMON ¢ENTS

Student Discounts

Many places, such as theaters, zoos, and museums, offer discount prices to students. You can also get discounts for buses and subways, movies, and cultural and sporting events. You may even qualify for a discount on your car insurance. Be sure to ask before paying full price.

Concept Application

Why do you think businesses offer discounts to students?

Kirk and Luanne should try to come up with a basic risk-management plan that achieves the following goals:

- Reduces possible loss of income caused by premature death, illness, accident, or unemployment
- Reduces possible loss of property caused by perils, such as fire or theft, or hazards
- Reduces possible loss of income, savings, and property caused by personal negligence

STEP 2 Develop a Plan

Planning is a way of taking control of your life instead of just letting life happen to you. Kirk and Luanne need to determine what risks they face and what risks they can afford to take. They also have to determine what resources can help them reduce the damage that could be caused by serious risks.

Furthermore, they need to know what kind of insurance is available. The cost of different kinds of insurance and the way the costs vary among companies will be key factors in their plan. Finally, this couple needs to research the record of reliability of different insurance companies.

Kirk and Luanne must ask four questions as they develop their risk-management plan:

- What do they need to insure?
- For how much should they insure it?
- What kind of insurance should they buy?
- Which insurance company should they choose?

STEP 3 Put Your Plan into Action

After they have developed their plan, Kirk and Luanne need to follow through by putting it into action. During this process, they might discover that they do not have enough insurance protection. If that is the case, they could purchase additional coverage. Kirk and Luanne could also change the kind of coverage they have. Another alternative would be to adjust their budget to cover the cost of additional insurance. Finally, Kirk and Luanne might expand their savings plans or investment programs and use those funds in the case of an emergency.

The best risk-management plans will be flexible enough to allow Kirk and Luanne to respond to changing life situations. Their goal should be to create a plan that can grow or shrink as needs change.

STEP 4 Review Your Results

You should take time to review a risk-management plan every two or three years, or whenever family circumstances change. Among the questions you should ask yourself are: Does it work? Does it adequately protect my plans and goals?

For example, Kirk and Luanne have been satisfied with the coverage provided by their insurance policies. However, when the couple bought a house six months ago, it was time for them to review their insurance plan. With the new house, the risks became much greater. After all, what would happen if a fire destroyed part of their home?

The needs of a couple who rent an apartment differ from the needs of a couple who own a house. Both couples face similar risks, but their financial responsibilities differ greatly. When you are developing or reviewing a risk-management plan, consider if you are providing the financial resources you will need to protect yourself; your family, if you have one; and your property.

Reading Check

Recall What four questions should you ask as you develop a risk-management plan?

Property and Liability Insurance

Why is it important to include property and liability insurance in a financial plan?

Major natural disasters have caused catastrophic amounts of property loss in the United States and other parts of the world. In 2004, the damage caused by Hurricane Charley resulted in $6.8 billion in insurance claims in the state of Florida alone. In 2005 Hurricanes Katrina, Rita, and Wilma caused $50 billion in damages. Insurance claims are requests for payment to cover financial losses. Without the money they received from their insurance, the people affected by the hurricane may not have been able to make repairs to their homes.

The price of insurance is an investment in the protection of your most valuable possessions. The cost may seem high, but the financial losses against which it protects could be much higher. There are two main types of risks related to your home and vehicle. One is the risk of damage to or loss of your property. The second type of risk involves your responsibility for injuries to people or damage to their property.

Liability

Liability is legal responsibility for the financial cost of another person's losses or injuries. You can be judged legally responsible even if the injury or damage was not your fault. Suppose that Terry falls and gets hurt while playing in Lisa's yard. Terry's family could sue Lisa's parents even though they did nothing wrong. Similarly, suppose that Sanjay accidentally damages a painting while helping Ed move. Ed may sue Sanjay to pay for the cost of the painting.

Usually, if you are found liable in a situation, it is because negligence on your part caused the mishap. Examples of such negligence include letting young children swim in a pool without supervision or cluttering a staircase causing someone to slip and fall.

Professional Liability Professional liability, or malpractice insurance, covers a business or professional in the event a client claims that an error caused a financial loss. Common reasons for claims are negligence, misrepresentation, and inaccurate advice. Doctors, lawyers, architects, engineers, and home inspectors may have this insurance. The coverage will vary depending on the profession. For example, a tax professional would be covered if an error on a client's tax return caused the client a financial loss. These policies are typically issued in increments of $1,000,000 in coverage with deductibles from $1,000 per claim to $25,000.

Property Damage or Loss

People spend large amounts of their money on personal property such as homes, vehicles, furniture, and clothing. Property owners face two basic types of risks. The first is physical damage caused by perils such as fire, wind, and flooding. These perils can damage or destroy your property. For example, a windstorm might cause a tree branch to smash the windshield of your car. As a result, you would have to get your car repaired. Because you could not drive your car while you waited for the repair, you would have to find another way to get to work or to get home. Insurance could help cover the costs of transportation while your car is being repaired.

The second type of risk that property owners face is loss or damage caused by criminal behavior, such as robbery and **vandalism** (deliberate destruction of private or public property). Insurance can protect you from loss of or damage to your property.

reality bytes

Reducing Car Insurance Costs
High auto-theft rates lead to high auto insurance rates. Australia has one of the highest auto-theft rates in the world—twice that of the United States. Scientists there have developed a high-tech solution to keep insurance rates down. Tiny microdots called "DataDots" are laser-etched with vehicle identification numbers and spray-glued on engines and most other parts. This makes it difficult to resell stolen cars and parts.

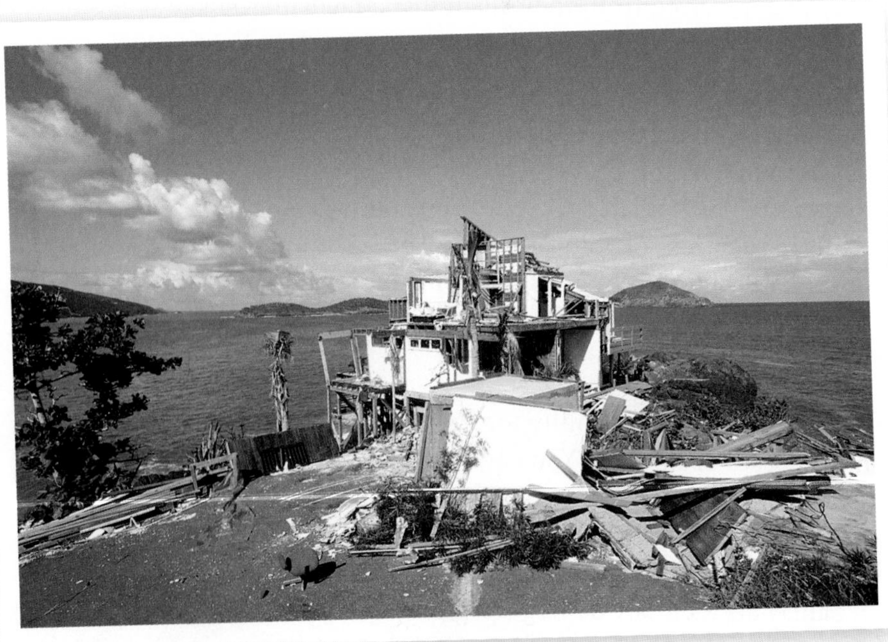

Natural Disasters
While you cannot prevent a natural disaster, such as a hurricane, you can take steps to protect your property in such an event. *What other types of risks are there to your property?*

SECTION 1 Assessment

Review Key Concepts

1. **Distinguish** What are the differences between risk, peril, and hazard as used in the insurance business?
2. **Paraphrase** What is the role of an insurance program in risk assumption and risk shifting?
3. **Summarize** What is the importance of property and liability insurance in a financial plan? What are the costs and benefits of professional liability insurance?

Higher Order Thinking

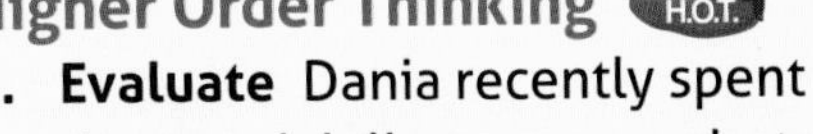

4. **Evaluate** Dania recently spent several thousand dollars on new photography equipment, using most of her savings. Consider whether you would recommend self-insurance or an insurance policy for Dania.

English Language Arts

5. **My Favorite Things** Make a list of your most valuable possessions. Consider how much it might cost to replace these items. Note that some of your possessions may have more personal value than monetary value or may not be replaceable, such as photographs. Write a journal entry discussing the personal and financial consequences of having the items on your list lost, stolen, or damaged. Also describe how an insurance policy on those items might affect the consequences.

NCTE 12 Use spoken, written, and visual language to accomplish one's own purposes.

Mathematics

6. **Liability Insurance** Devan's son had a sleepover at his house. Unfortunately, one of the children at the sleepover fell down some stairs due to negligence on Devan's part. The injured child's parents are suing Devan in order to cover all the medical expenses incurred which totaled $3,200. Devan has liability insurance in which his deductible is $350; he also pays a monthly premium of $25 for this insurance. How much did Devan save over the course of the year by having this insurance?

Math Concept **Calculate Insurance Savings** To calculate the savings from insurance first identify the total expense that would have been incurred without the insurance. Next determine the sum of all insurance premiums and deductibles.

Starting Hint Determine the total cost of the insurance over the course of the year by calculating the annual premiums paid and adding this figure to the deductible owed. Premiums paid over the year equals the monthly amount times the number of months.

NCTM Number and Operations Compute fluently and make reasonable estimates.

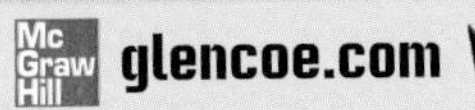

Check your answers.

Section Objectives

- **Identify** the types of insurance coverages and policies available to homeowners and renters.
- **Analyze** the factors that influence the amount of coverage and cost of home insurance.

As You Read

Infer Why do you think lenders will require you to buy homeowners insurance when you take out a mortgage to buy a home?

Homeowners Insurance Coverage

What does a homeowners insurance policy cover?

Insuring your residence and its contents is absolutely necessary to protect your investment. **Homeowners insurance** is coverage that provides protection for your residence and its associated financial risks, such as damage to personal property and injuries to others.

A homeowners policy provides coverage for the home, building, or any other structures on the property; additional living expenses; personal property, personal liability and related coverages; and specialized coverages.

Buildings and Other Structures

The main purpose of homeowners insurance is to protect you against financial loss in case your home is damaged or destroyed. Detached structures on your property, such as a garage or tool shed, are also covered under a homeowners' policy. In fact, the insurance coverage even includes trees, shrubs, and other plants, which are landscaping.

Additional Living Expenses

If a fire or other event damages your home, additional living expense coverage pays for you to stay somewhere else. For example, you may need to stay in a motel or rent an apartment while your home is being repaired or rebuilt. These extra living expenses will be paid for by your insurance. Some policies limit additional living expense coverage to 10 to 20 percent of the home's total coverage amount. They may also limit the payment period to a maximum of six to nine months. Other policies may pay additional living expenses for up to a year.

Personal Property

Household belongings, such as furniture and clothing, are covered by the personal property portion of a homeowners policy up to a portion of the insured value of the home. That portion is usually 55, 70, or 75 percent. For example, a home insured for $80,000 might have $56,000 (70 percent) worth of coverage for household belongings.

Personal property coverage typically includes limits for the theft of certain items, such as $1,000 for jewelry. It also provides protection against the loss or damage of articles that you take with you when you are away from home. For example, items you take on vacation or use at school are usually covered up to the policy limit. Personal property coverage even extends to property that you rent, such as a rug cleaner, while it is in your possession.

Most homeowners policies also include optional coverage for personal computers, including stored data, up to a certain limit. Your insurance agent can determine whether the computer equipment is covered against data loss as well as damage from spilled drinks or power surges.

Household Inventories If something does happen to your personal property, you must prove how much it was worth and that it belonged to you. To make the process easier, you can create a household inventory. A household inventory is a list or other documentation of personal belongings, with purchase dates and cost information. You can get a form for an inventory from an insurance agent. **Figure 2** provides a list of items you might include if you decide to compile your own household inventory. For items of special value, you should have receipts, serial numbers, brand names, model names, and proof of value.

In addition, keep a video recording or photographs of your home and its contents with your inventory list. Make sure that closet and storage area doors are photographed open. On the backs of the photographs, indicate the date and the value of the objects pictured. Update your inventory, photos, and related documents on a regular basis. Keep a copy of each document in a secure location, such as a safe-deposit box.

Additional Property Insurance If you own valuable items, such as expensive musical instruments, or need added protection for computers and related equipment, you can purchase a personal property floater. A **personal property floater** is additional property insurance that covers the damage or loss of a specific item of high value. The insurance company will require a detailed description of the item and its worth. You will also need to have the item **appraised,** or evaluated, by an expert from time to time to make sure that its value has not changed. In addition, keep photographs of valuable items as well as descriptions, receipts, and appraisals.

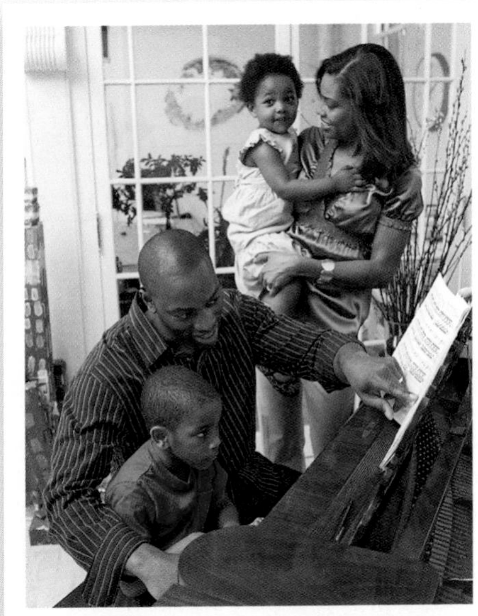

Protecting Investments
Valuable items such as musical instruments and computer equipment are investments that may require a personal property floater. *Why should you have these items appraised from time to time?*

FIGURE 2 **Household Inventory**

Personal Possessions Having a household inventory can help prove the worth of your property should your possessions be stolen, damaged, or destroyed. *Why should you also keep a video or photograph of the items listed?*

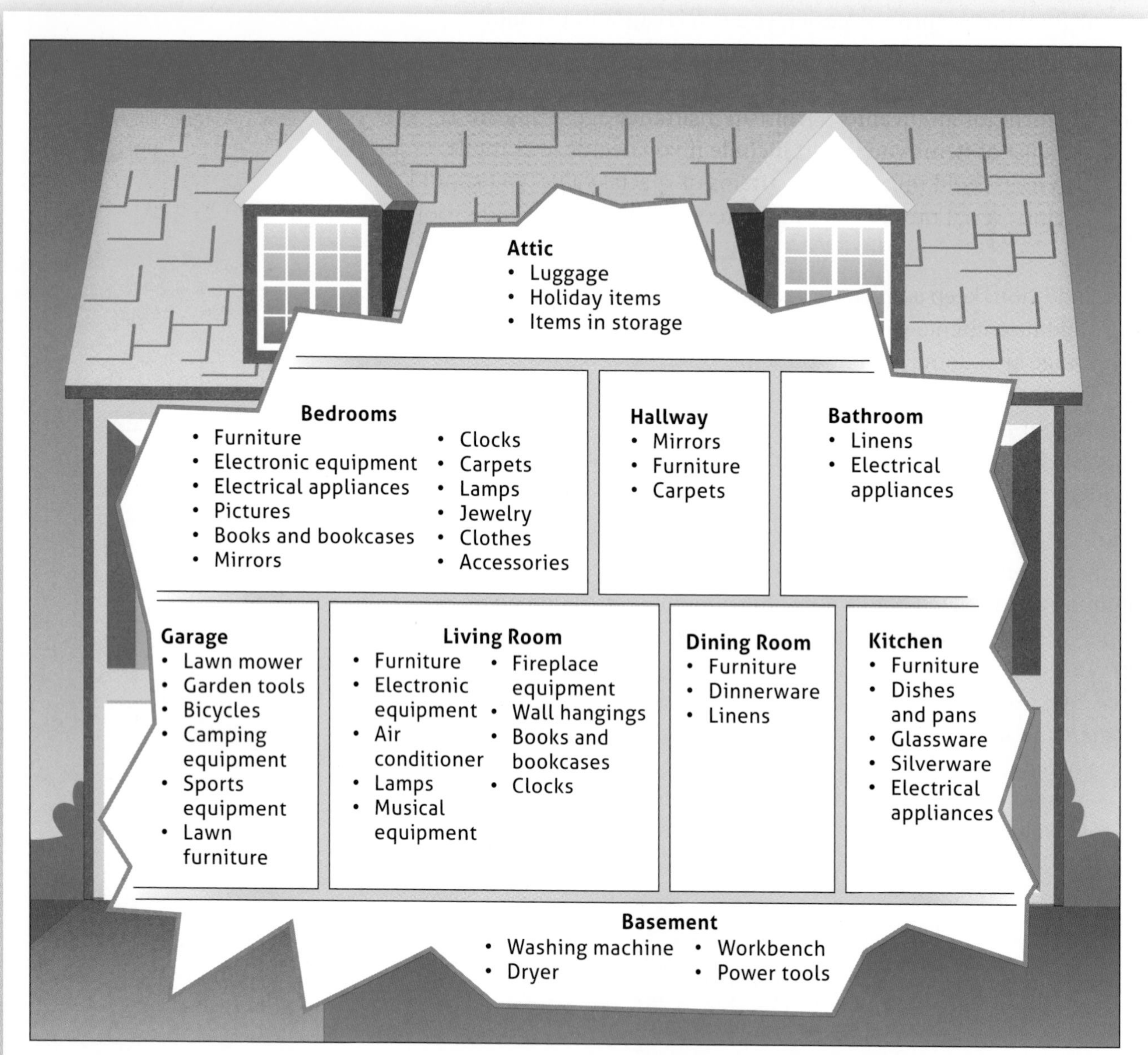

Personal Liability and Related Coverages

Every day people face the risk of financial loss due to injuries to other people or their property. For example, a guest could fall on a patch of ice on your steps and break his arm, or your son or daughter could accidentally break an antique lamp while playing at a neighbor's house.

Careers That Count!

Alan Bhargava • Insurance Claims Adjuster

I want to help people when disasters strike, whether it is a car accident or damages caused by extreme weather. As an insurance claims adjuster, I plan and schedule the work required to process a claim. I investigate claims by interviewing the claimant and witnesses, consulting police and hospital records, and inspecting property damage to determine how much the insurance company should pay for the loss. Sometimes I may consult with other professionals, such as accountants, architects, construction workers, engineers, lawyers, and physicians, who can offer a more expert evaluation of a claim. The information gathered is put in a report used to evaluate the claim. When the policyholder's claim is approved, then I negotiate with the claimant and settle the claim. Helping claimants is one of my favorite parts of the job. I provide a high level of customer service when I review policies with claimants and investigate claims-coverage questions.

EXPLORE CAREERS

Visit the Web site of the U.S. Department of Labor's Bureau of Labor Statistics to obtain information about a career as a claims adjuster.

1. How do the duties of a claims examiner differ from those of a claims adjuster?
2. Research job postings for a claims adjuster. What qualifications do employers require? What qualifications do they prefer?

Skills	Education	Career Path
Interpersonal, problem-solving, negotiation, computer, and math skills; comprehensive knowledge of codes, construction, repair techniques, and legal terminology	High school diploma; insurance-related work experience or vocational training; some states require licensing	Insurance claims adjusters can become private investigators, insurance appraisers, underwriters, actuaries, and investigations department managers.

glencoe.com

Activity Download a Career Exploration Activity.

In these situations, you could be held responsible for paying for the damage. The personal liability portion of a homeowners policy protects you and members of your family if others, except regular employees, sue you for injuries they suffer or for damage to their property. This coverage includes the cost of legal defense.

Amounts of Coverage Most homeowners policies provide basic personal liability coverage of $100,000, but often that is not enough. An umbrella policy, also called a personal catastrophe policy, supplements basic personal liability coverage. This added protection covers all kinds of personal injury claims. For example, an umbrella policy will cover you if someone sues you for saying or writing something negative or untrue, damaging his or her reputation.

Extended liability policies are useful for wealthy people and for businesses. The policies are sold in amounts of $1 million or more. If you are a business owner, you may need other types of liability coverage as well.

Medical payments coverage pays the costs of minor accidental injuries to visitors on your property. It also covers minor injuries caused by you, members of your family, or even your pets, away from home. Settlements under medical payments coverage are made without determining who was at fault. This makes it fast and easy for the insurance company to process small claims, generally up to $5,000. If the injury is more serious, the personal liability portion of the homeowners policy covers it. Medical payments coverage does not cover injury to you or the other people who live in your home.

If you or a family member should accidentally damage another person's property, the supplementary coverage of homeowners insurance will pay for it. This protection is usually limited to $500 or $1,000. Again, payments are made regardless of fault. If the damage is more expensive, it is handled under the personal liability coverage.

Specialized Coverages

Homeowners insurance usually does not cover losses from floods and earthquakes. If you lived in an area that had frequent floods or earthquakes, you would need to purchase special coverage. In some places the National Flood Insurance Program, run by the federal government, makes flood insurance available. This protection is separate from a homeowners policy. An insurance agent or the Federal Emergency Management Agency (FEMA) of the Federal Insurance Administration can give you additional information.

You may be able to get earthquake or flood insurance as an **endorsement** (addition of coverage) to a homeowners policy or through a state-run insurance program. The most serious earthquakes occur in the Pacific Coast region. However, earthquakes can happen in other regions, too. If you purchase a home in an area that has a high risk of earthquakes or floods, you may have to buy insurance for those risks.

Reading Check

Recall What is covered under buildings and other structures in an insurance policy?

Renters Insurance

Why is it important for a renter to get renters insurance?

For people who rent, home insurance coverages include personal property protection, additional living expenses coverage, and personal liability and related coverages. Renters insurance does not provide coverage on the building or other structures.

Economics and You

Competition

Competition is the struggle among companies for customers. It plays an essential role in a market economy. Companies strive to produce better quality products at lower prices to attract and keep their customers. Besides price competition, there is nonprice competition which allows companies to charge more and still regain customer loyalty, as well as attract new customers. With nonprice competition, companies provide special services or excellent quality, expertise, and reliability that set them apart from their competitors.

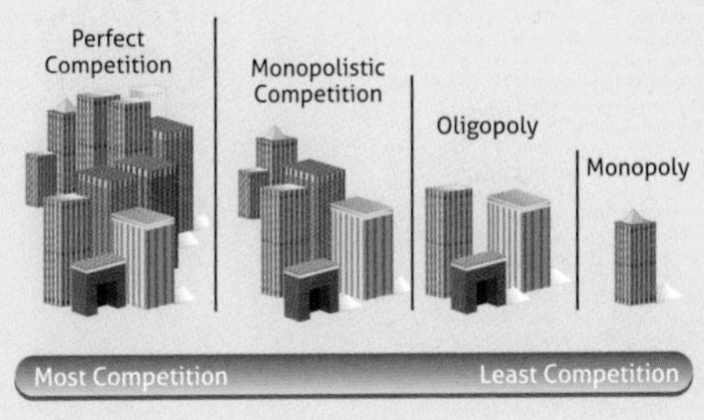

Personal Finance Connection When shopping around for home and motor vehicle insurance, it is wise to consider both price and nonprice competition. A lower priced insurance policy may not always provide the coverage or services you need to insure your home or vehicle.

Critical Thinking Describe the nonprice competition tactics you have experienced. What nonprice competition factors might you consider when selecting an insurance company and policy for your home or vehicle?

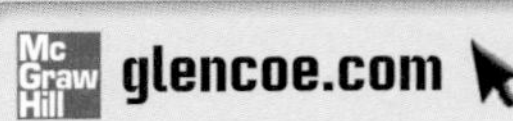

Activity Download an Economics and You Worksheet Activity.

The most important part of renters insurance is protection for personal property. Many renters believe that they are covered under their landlords' policies. However, that is true only when the landlord is liable for damage. For example, if bad wiring causes a fire and damages a tenant's property, he or she may be able to collect money from the landlord. Renters insurance is relatively inexpensive and provides protection similar to homeowners insurance.

Reading Check

Summarize What types of insurance coverages are included in a renters insurance policy?

Home Insurance Policy Forms

What coverage is offered by each type of policy form?

Home insurance policies are available in several forms. The forms provide different combinations of coverage. Some forms are not available in all areas.

The basic form (HO-1) protects against perils such as fire, lightning, windstorms, hail, volcanic eruptions, explosions, smoke, theft, vandalism, glass breakage, and riots. The broad form (HO-2) covers an even wider range of perils, including falling objects and damage from ice, snow, or sleet.

The special form (HO-3) covers all basic- and broad-form risks, plus any other risks except those specifically excluded from the policy. Common exclusions are flood, earthquake, war, and nuclear accidents. Personal property is covered for the risks listed in the policy.

The tenants' form (HO-4) protects the personal property of renters against the risks listed in the policy. It does not include coverage on the building or other structures.

The comprehensive form (HO-5) expands the coverage of the HO-3. The HO-5 includes endorsements for replacement-cost coverage on contents and guaranteed replacement-cost coverage on buildings.

Condominium owners insurance (HO-6) protects personal property and any additions or improvements made to the living unit. These might include bookshelves, electrical fixtures, wallpaper, or carpeting. The condominium association purchases insurance on the building and other structures.

Manufactured housing units and mobile homes usually qualify for insurance coverage with conventional policies. However, some mobile homes may need special policies with higher rates that are dependent on the home's location and the way it is attached to the ground. Mobile home insurance is quite expensive: A \$50,000 mobile home can cost as much to insure as a \$150,000 house.

Though some risks are not covered by home insurance (see **Figure 3**), home insurance policies do include coverage for additional costs:

- Credit card fraud, check forgery, and counterfeit money
- Removal of damaged property
- Emergency removal of property to protect it from damage
- Temporary repairs after a loss to prevent further damage
- Fire department charges in areas with such fees

Reading Check

Recall Which homeowners insurance policy form(s) does not include coverage of the building or other structures?

How Much Coverage Do You Need?

What is the actual cash value method?

You can get the best insurance value by choosing the right amount of coverage and knowing the factors that affect insurance costs. Your insurance should be based on the amount of money you would need to rebuild or repair your house, not the amount you paid for it. As construction costs rise, you should increase the amount of coverage. In fact, today most insurance policies automatically increase coverage each year as construction costs rise.

FIGURE 3 Not Everything Is Covered

Included or Not? Be sure you know what property is covered by your homeowners insurance so you can purchase separate coverage if necessary. *Why do you think a policy does not cover property rented by the homeowner to other people?*

Certain personal property is not covered by homeowners insurance:	
• Items insured separately, such as jewelry, furs, boats, or expensive electronic equipment	• Aircraft and parts
• Animals or fish	• Property belonging to tenants
• Motorized vehicles not licensed for road use, except those used for home maintenance	• Property contained in a rental apartment
• Sound devices used in motor vehicles, such as radios and CD players	• Property rented by the homeowner to other people
	• Business property

In the past, many homeowners' policies insured a building for only 80 percent of the replacement value. If the building were destroyed, the homeowner would have to pay for part of the cost of replacing it. Today most companies recommend full coverage.

If you are borrowing money to buy a home, the lender will require that you have property insurance. The amount of insurance on your home determines the coverage on your personal belongings. Coverage for personal belongings is usually between 55 and 75 percent of the amount of insurance you have on your home.

Insurance companies base claim settlements on one of two methods. Under the **actual cash value** method, the payment you receive is based on the replacement cost of an item minus depreciation. Depreciation is the loss of value of an item as it gets older. You would receive less for a five-year-old bicycle than you originally paid for it.

Under the **replacement value** method for settling claims, you will receive the full cost of repairing or replacing an item. Depreciation is not considered when settling the claim. Many companies limit the replacement cost to 400 percent of the item's actual cash value. Replacement value coverage is more expensive than actual cash value coverage.

Reading Check

Define What is depreciation?

Home Insurance Cost Factors

Why do the location and type of construction of your home affect your home insurance costs?

The cost of your home insurance will depend on factors such as the location of the home, type of structure and construction materials used, and amount of coverage and type of policy you choose.

Location of Home

The location of your home affects your insurance rates. Insurance companies offer lower rates to people whose homes are close to a water supply or fire hydrant—or are located in an area that has a good fire department. Rates are higher in areas where crime is common. People living in regions that experience severe weather, such as tornadoes and hurricanes, may pay more for insurance.

Type of Structure

The type of structure and its construction influence the price of insurance coverage. A brick house, for example, will usually cost less to insure than a similar structure made of wood. However, earthquake coverage is more expensive for a brick house than for a wooden dwelling because a wooden house is more likely to survive an earthquake. Also, an older house may be more expensive to restore to its original condition. That means that it will cost more to insure.

Price, Coverage Amount, Policy Type

The purchase price of a house directly affects how much you pay for insurance. Therefore, it costs more to insure a $300,000 home than a $100,000 home. Also, the type of policy you choose and the amount of coverage you select affect the amount of premium you pay.

Replacement Costs
Insurance policies may use actual cash value or replacement value method for claim settlements.
Why do you think a policy with replacement value coverage is more expensive than one with actual cash value coverage?

Construction Matters
The materials used to construct your house can affect the cost of insurance coverage. *Why might a brick house be less expensive to insure than a house made of wood?*

The deductible amount listed on the policy also affects the cost of insurance. If you increase the amount of the deductible, the premium will be lower because the company will pay out less in claims. The most common deductible amount is $250. Raising the deductible from $250 to $1,000 can reduce the premium by 15 percent or more.

Home Insurance Discounts

Most companies offer discounts if a homeowner takes action to reduce risks to a home. Your premium may be lower if you have smoke detectors or a fire extinguisher. If your home has dead-bolt locks and alarm systems, which make it harder for thieves to get in, insurance costs may be lower.

Company Differences

A homeowner can save up to 25 percent on homeowners insurance by comparing rates from several companies. Some insurance agents work for only one company. Others are independent agents who represent several different companies.

Do not select a company on the basis of price alone. Also consider service and coverage. Not all companies settle claims in the same way.

For example, suppose that all of the homes on Evergreen Terrace are hit on one side by large hailstones. They all have the same kind of siding. Unfortunately, the homeowners discover that this type of siding is no longer available. So all the siding on all the houses will need to be replaced. Some insurance companies will pay to replace all the siding. Others will pay only to replace the damaged parts.

State insurance commissions and consumer organizations can give you information about different insurance companies. *Consumer Reports*, a magazine that provides unbiased information on a variety of goods and services, rates insurance companies on a regular basis.

Review Key Concepts

1. **Describe** What are the five basic areas of coverage on a homeowners insurance policy?
2. **Identify** What home insurance policy forms are available?
3. **Explain** What factors will affect the cost of home insurance?

Higher Order Thinking H.O.T.

4. **Infer** Many insurance companies will not want to sell homeowners insurance policies to everyone in the same neighborhood. Infer why this might be the case.

21st Century Skills

5. **Analyze Media** Larger insurance companies will use several media forms for advertising, such as billboards, direct mail flyers, radio advertisements, magazine ads, and television ads. Locate ads for at least three different insurance companies. Evaluate the ads to determine the message, or purpose of each ad. Is the company promoting its services, its price, its customer service, or something else? Write a brief report explaining your analysis. Would you be likely to choose one company over another based on these ads? Why or why not?

Mathematics

6. **Homeowners Insurance** Eva's house has recently burned down. Luckily she has a homeowners insurance policy in which the house was insured for $150,000. The homeowners policy provides coverage for personal belongings up to 55 percent of the insured value of the house. Eva's lost household items include $25,000 of furniture, $10,000 of appliances, $5,000 of electronics, and $3,500 of other items. How much is Eva covered for under her policy for household items? Will she recover all of her losses? If not, how much of the loss will not be covered?

Math Concept **Calculate Insurance Coverage** To calculate the amount of personal belongings covered under a homeowners policy first identify the insured amount of the home. Multiply the percent of personal belongings coverage by this amount.

Starting Hint Determine the total loss incurred of personal belongings by adding the values for all individual items. Subtract this amount from the amount of personal belongings covered under the policy to determine if all losses will be covered.

NCTM Problem Solving Solve problems that arise in mathematics and in other contexts.

 glencoe.com  Check your answers.

The Need for Auto Insurance

Why is it a good idea for drivers to have motor vehicle insurance?

Motor vehicle accidents cost more than $150 billion in lost wages and medical bills every year. They can destroy people's lives physically, financially, and emotionally. Buying insurance cannot eliminate the pain and suffering that vehicle accidents cause. However, insurance can reduce the financial impact.

Every state in the United States has a financial responsibility law, which is a law that requires a driver to prove he or she can pay for damage or injury caused by an automobile accident if he or she is at fault. As of 2003, more than 45 states had laws requiring people to carry motor vehicle insurance. When injuries and property damage occur in an accident, the driver(s) is required to file a report with the state. In the remaining states, most people buy motor vehicle insurance by choice. Very few people have the money they would need to meet the financial responsibility requirements on their own.

The coverage provided by motor vehicle insurance falls into two categories: protection for bodily injury and protection for property damage. (See **Figure 4.**)

Reading Check

Describe What is a financial responsibility law?

Section Objectives

- **Identify** important types of motor vehicle insurance coverage.
- **Explain** factors that affect the cost of motor vehicle insurance.

As You Read

Discover Does your state require car owners to carry motor vehicle insurance? If so, what type?

FIGURE 4 **Motor Vehicle Insurance Coverage**

Protect Yourself Having motor vehicle insurance protects the driver financially in case of an accident. *Why would you want bodily injury coverage rather than relying on your medical insurance?*

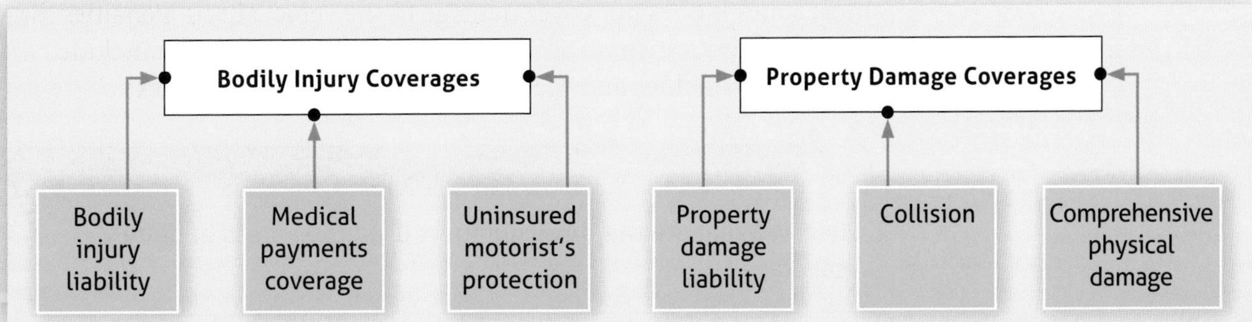

Leadership

A characteristic of many successful people is leadership. Leadership is the ability to motivate a group of people to achieve a common goal or complete a task. People who possess strong leadership skills use interpersonal and problem-solving skills to lead others toward a common goal. Strong leaders utilize the strengths of others and lead by example with integrity to help others reach their full potential. Developing strong leadership skills will help you to overcome challenges and succeed in school, in the community, and in your career.

Write About It

Think of a situation that required strong leadership skills. Write one or more paragraphs to describe the scenario and explain how leadership skills impacted the results. How do you think developing leadership skills could help you achieve future success?

Activity Download a Career and College Readiness Worksheet Activity.

Motor Vehicle Bodily Injury Coverages

Who is covered by bodily injury liability insurance?

Most money motor vehicle insurance companies pay in claims goes for legal and medical expenses, and other costs that occur if someone is injured. The main types of bodily injury coverages are: bodily injury liability, medical payments, and uninsured motorist's protection.

Bodily Injury Liability

Bodily injury liability is insurance that covers physical injuries caused by a vehicle accident for which you are responsible. If pedestrians, people in other vehicles, or passengers in your vehicle are injured, this coverage pays for expenses related to the crash.

Liability coverage is usually expressed by three numbers, such as 100/300/50. These amounts represent thousands of dollars of coverage. The first two numbers refer to bodily injury coverage. In the 100/300/50 example, $100,000 is the maximum amount that the insurance company will pay for the injuries of any one person in any one accident. The second number, $300,000, is the maximum amount the company will pay for all injured parties (two or more) in any one accident. The third number, $50,000, indicates the limit for payment for damage to the property of others. (See **Figure 5.**)

Medical Payments Coverage

Medical payments coverage is insurance for medical expenses of anyone injured in your vehicle, including you. This coverage also provides medical benefits for you and members of your family while riding in another person's vehicle or if any of you are hit by a vehicle.

Uninsured Motorist's Protection

You can guard yourself and your passengers against the risk of getting into an accident with someone who has no insurance by having uninsured motorist's protection. **Uninsured motorist's protection** is insurance that covers you and your family members if you are involved in an accident with an uninsured or hit-and-run driver. In most states it does not cover damage to the vehicle itself. Penalties for driving without insurance vary by state, but they generally include **stiff,** or harsh, fines and the suspension of driving privileges.

Reading Check

Recall What are the three numbers used to express liability coverage?

FIGURE 5 **Motor Vehicle Insurance Liability Coverage**

Know the Numbers The three numbers used to describe liability coverage refer to the limits on three different payments. *Why are there two numbers to represent bodily injury liability payments?*

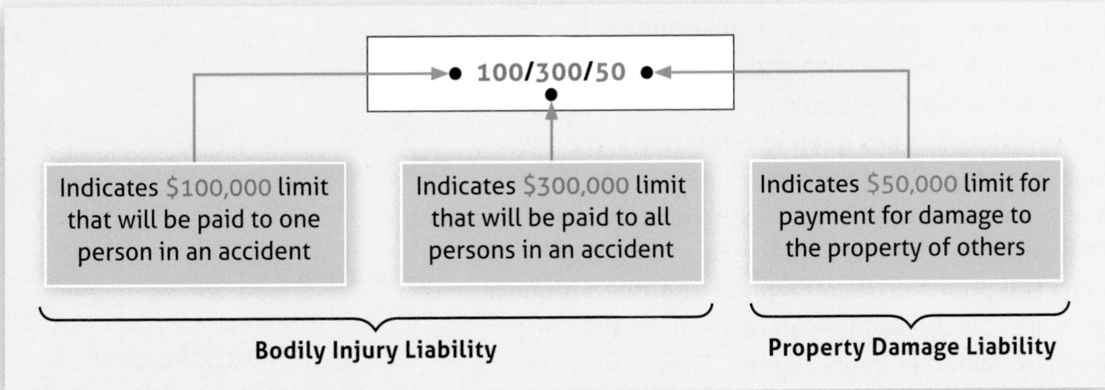

Motor Vehicle Property Damage Coverage

What is the significance of each type of property damage coverage?

One afternoon, during a summer storm, Carrie was driving home from her job as a hostess at a pancake house. The rain was torrential, and she could not see very well. As a result, she did not realize that the car in front of her had stopped to make a left turn, and she hit the car. The crash totaled Carrie's new car. Fortunately, she had purchased insurance with property damage coverage. Property damage coverage protects you from financial loss if you damage someone else's property or if your vehicle is damaged.

Property damage coverage includes:

- property damage liability
- collision
- comprehensive physical damage

Property Damage Liability

Property damage liability is motor vehicle insurance that applies when you damage the property of others. In addition, it protects you when you are driving another person's vehicle with the owner's permission. Although the damaged property is usually another car, the coverage also extends to buildings and to equipment such as street signs and telephone poles.

Mexico

Green Angels

Many people purchase a membership to an automobile club for the benefit of emergency road service rather than adding this coverage to their motor vehicle insurance. In Mexico, the government has stepped in to fill this need for both natives and tourists. The roadside assistance program known as the *Angeles Verdes*, or Green Angels, is a federally funded program that has been in operation since the 1970s, patrolling and servicing all federal and toll highways. You are advised to open your hood if you are forced to stop on the side of the road so they will know that you need assistance. In addition, you can phone "078" from any cell phone or TELMEX phone booth to request aid. The Green Angels are tow trucks that can take you to a service station, but they are also trained in minor repairs. They carry gasoline, motor oil, spare tires, and parts for minor repairs, as well as maps and brochures for lost tourists (drivers are usually fluent in English as well as their native Spanish). They are also capable of performing first aid in the case of an accident or medical emergency. All services are free, though motorists are expected to pay for gasoline, oil, or parts.

Critical Thinking

1. **Expand** Conduct additional research to learn how expansive the Green Angels service is. How can motorists identify the Green Angels?
2. **Relate** How does the Green Angels program relate to the roadside services offered by auto clubs, such as AAA, in the U.S.?

DATABYTES

Capital
Mexico City

Population
112,468,855

Languages
Spanish only 92.7%, Spanish and indigenous languages 5.7%, indigenous only 0.8%, unspecified 0.8%

Currency
Mexican peso

Gross Domestic Product (GDP)
$1.017 trillion

GDP per capita
$13,500

Industry
Food and beverages, chemicals, iron and steel, petroleum, mining, textiles, clothing, motor vehicles, consumer durables, tourism

Agriculture
Corn, wheat, soybeans, rice, beans, cotton, coffee, fruit, tomatoes; beef, poultry, dairy products; wood products

Exports
Manufactured goods, oil and oil products, silver, fruits, vegetables, coffee, cotton

Natural Resources
Petroleum, silver, copper, gold, lead, zinc, natural gas, timber

Collision

Collision insurance is insurance that covers damage to your vehicle when it is involved in an accident. You collect money no matter who is at fault. However, the amount that you can collect is limited to the actual cash value of your vehicle at the time of the accident. So keep a record of your car's condition and value.

Comprehensive Physical Damage

Comprehensive physical damage insurance protects you if your vehicle is damaged in a non-accident situation. It covers your vehicle against risks such as fire, theft, falling objects, vandalism, hail, floods, tornadoes, earthquakes, and avalanches.

Reading Check

Summarize What is covered by property damage liability coverage?

No-Fault Insurance

Why are some states adopting the no-fault system?

To reduce the time and cost of settling vehicle injury cases, some states are trying a number of alternatives, including the no-fault system. The **no-fault system** is an arrangement whereby drivers who are involved in accidents collect money from their own insurance companies. It does not matter who caused the accident. Each company pays the insured up to the limits of his or her coverage. No-fault systems and coverages vary by state.

Reading Check

Define What is a no-fault system?

Other Motor Vehicle Insurance Coverages

When is wage loss insurance required?

In addition to bodily injury and property damage, other kinds of motor vehicle insurance are available. For example, rental reimbursement coverage pays for a rental car if your vehicle is stolen or is being repaired. Wage-loss insurance pays for any salary or income you might have lost due to being injured in a vehicle accident. States that have adopted a no-fault insurance system usually require auto owners to carry wage-loss insurance. It is available by choice in other states.

Towing and emergency road service coverage pays for mechanical assistance in the event that your vehicle breaks down. This can be helpful on long trips or during bad weather. If necessary, you can get your vehicle towed to a service station. However, once your vehicle arrives at the repair shop, you are responsible for paying the bill. If you belong to an automobile club, your membership may include towing coverage. If that is the case, paying for emergency road service coverage could be a waste of money. Rental reimbursement coverage pays for a rental car if your vehicle is stolen or being repaired.

Reading Check

Recognize What is wage-loss insurance?

Motor Vehicle Insurance Costs

Why is bodily injury liability coverage of 100/300 recommended?

Motor vehicle insurance is not cheap. The average household spends more than $1,200 for motor vehicle insurance yearly. The premiums are related to the amount of claims that insurance companies pay out each year. Your automobile insurance cost is directly related to factors such as the vehicle, your place of residence and your driving record.

Frank is a high school junior who recently got his driver's license. At his part-time job, he earns minimum wage. Frank's situation provides an example of what to consider to get the best insurance value—amount of coverage, insurance premium factors, and ways to reduce insurance premiums.

Amount of Coverage

The amount that Frank will pay for insurance depends on the amount of coverage he requires. He needs enough coverage to protect himself legally and financially.

Legal Concerns As discussed earlier, most people who are involved in motor vehicle accidents cannot afford to pay an expensive court settlement with their own money. For this reason, most drivers buy liability insurance.

Many basic insurance policies provide 10/20 coverage for bodily injury liability. However, some accident victims have been awarded millions of dollars in bodily injury cases; therefore, coverage of 100/300 is usually recommended.

Property Values Just as amounts of medical expenses and legal settlements have increased, so has the cost of vehicles. Therefore, Frank should consider a policy with a limit of $50,000 or even $100,000 for property damage liability.

Motor Vehicle Insurance Premium Factors

Vehicle type, rating territory, and driver classification are three other factors that influence insurance costs.

Vehicle Type The year, make, and model of a vehicle affect insurance costs. High-priced vehicles and vehicles that have expensive replacement parts and complicated repairs cost more to insure. Also, premiums can be higher for those vehicles that are frequently stolen.

Rating Territory In most states the rating territory, or owner's place of residence, is used to determine the vehicle insurance premium. Different locations have different costs. For example, accidents and incidents of theft occur less frequently in rural areas. Your insurance would probably cost less than if you lived in a large city.

Driver Classification Driver classification is based on age, sex, marital status, driving record, and driving habits. In general, young drivers (under 25) and elderly drivers (over 70) have more frequent and more serious accidents. As a result, these groups pay higher premiums. Your driving record will also influence how much you pay. If you have accidents or receive traffic tickets, your rates will increase.

The cost and number of claims that you file will also affect your premium. If you file expensive claims, your rates will increase. If you have too many claims, your insurance company may cancel your policy, and it may be difficult to get coverage from another company. To deal with this problem, every state has an **assigned risk pool,** which is a group of people who cannot get motor vehicle insurance who are assigned to each insurance company operating in the state. These policyholders pay several times the normal rates. If they establish a good driving record, they can reapply for regular rates.

Insurance companies may also consider your credit score. However, an insurer cannot refuse to issue you an insurance policy solely based on your credit report.

Shop Around
As with any other goods or services, you should get insurance quotes from several companies before deciding who to use. *What factors will affect the cost of motor vehicle insurance?*

All About Statistics
Because statistics show that drivers under age 25 have more frequent and more serious accidents, insurance is generally more expensive for this age group. *How will your driving record affect your rates?*

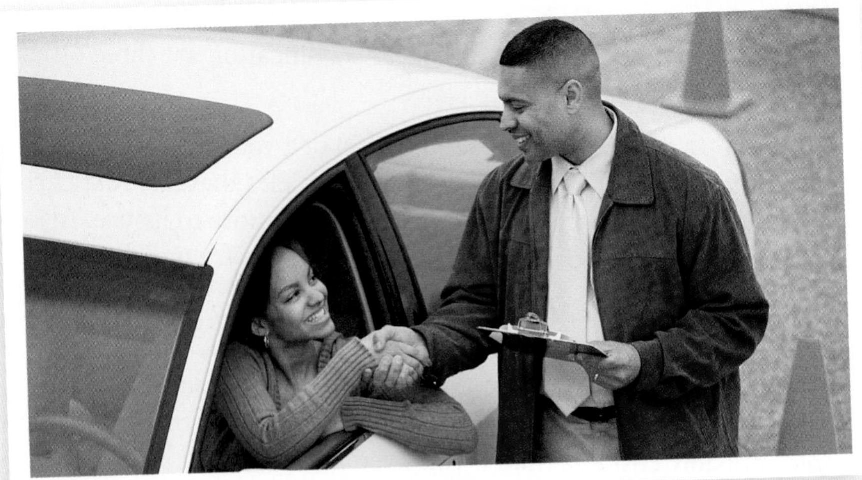

Reducing Vehicle Insurance Premiums

Two ways in which Frank can reduce his vehicle insurance costs are by comparing companies and by taking advantage of discounts.

Comparing Companies Rates and services vary among motor vehicle insurance companies. Even among companies in the same area, premiums can vary by as much as 100 percent. Frank should compare the services and rates of local insurance agents. Most states publish this type of information. Furthermore, Frank can check a company's reputation with sources such as *Consumer Reports* or his state insurance department.

Premium Discounts The best way for Frank to keep his rates down is to maintain a good driving record by avoiding accidents and traffic tickets. In addition, most insurance companies offer various types of discounts.

Because Frank is under 25, he can qualify for reduced rates by taking a driver training program or maintaining good grades in school. In addition, installing security devices in his vehicle will decrease the chance of theft and lower Frank's insurance costs. Being a nonsmoker can qualify him for lower motor vehicle insurance premiums as well. Discounts are also offered for insuring two or more vehicles with the same company. Increasing the amounts of deductibles will also lead to a lower premium. For example, an older car may not be worth the cost of carrying collision and comprehensive coverage.

No matter what coverage you choose, motor vehicle insurance is a valuable and **mandatory,** or required, protection to include in any personal finance plan.

After You Read

Decide Do you think states should require all drivers to have motor vehicle insurance? Why?

Review Key Concepts

1. **List** Name the two categories of motor vehicle insurance.
2. **Identify** In addition to bodily injury and property damage, identify three other types of motor vehicle insurance available.
3. **Explain** Recognize the three main factors that influence the cost of motor vehicle insurance.

Higher Order Thinking H.O.T.

4. **Assess** Insurance is typically more expensive for a sports car than for a sedan. Assess why this is the case.

English Language Arts

5. **Don't Drink and Drive** Avoiding accidents can help your driving record and lower your insurance rates. Many accidents are caused by drinking and driving. Conduct research to find out more about what can be done to reduce alcohol-related traffic accidents. Consider asking classmates and parents for their ideas, as well as contacting groups such as MADD or SADD. Use the ideas you collect to create a public service announcement. Write your script in the form of a radio ad, lasting no more than 60 seconds.

NCTE 4 Use written language to communicate effectively.

Mathematics

6. **Motor Vehicle Insurance** Gabe has motor vehicle insurance which includes liability coverage with terms of 100/300/50. He was talking on his mobile phone while driving and accidentally ran into another car. The accident was Gabe's fault and resulted in injuries for 3 people. These people incurred medical costs of $150,000, $75,000 and $175,000, respectively. The other driver's car incurred damages of $15,500. Is Gabe's coverage enough to pay for all the medical expenses? If not, how much will he have to pay out of pocket? Is he covered enough for the vehicle damage?

Math Concept **Calculate Liability Coverage** To calculate whether motor vehicle liability coverage is sufficient for damages incurred first determine the coverage amount for medical and property damages. Subtract the medical and property costs incurred from the respective coverage amounts.

Starting Hint Determine the amount of liability coverage for medical expenses and property by reviewing the policy terms. The first, second and third numbers represent damages for one person, damages for up to 3 people, and damages to property.

NCTM Connections Organize and consolidate their mathematical thinking through communication.

Check your answers.

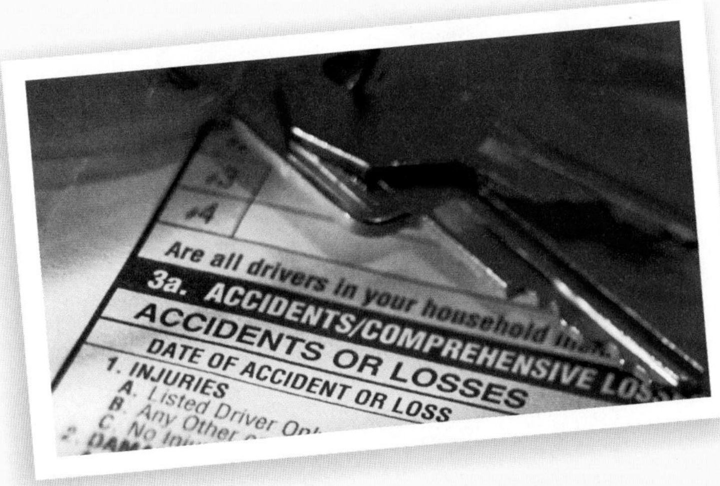

Visual Summary

Home and Motor Vehicle Insurance

Program Planning

By planning your insurance program, you can ensure that you find one to meet your needs and goals.

Steps to Plan an Insurance Program

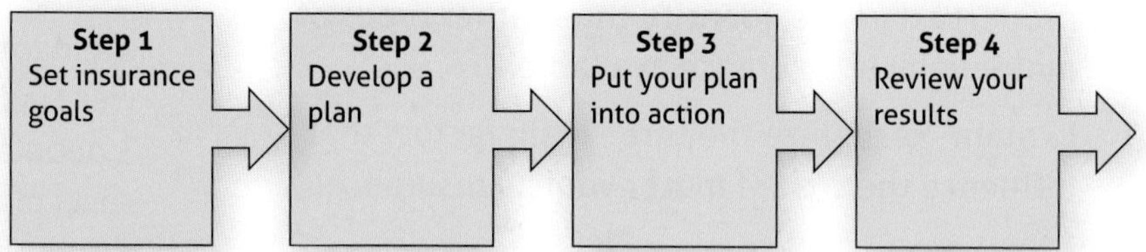

Policy Preferences

Understanding the different insurance policy forms can help you choose the one that is best suited for your needs.

Home Insurance Policy Forms		
HO-1	Basic Form	perils such as fire, lightning, windstorms, hail, volcanic eruptions, explosions, smoke, theft, vandalism, glass breakage, riots
HO-2	Broad Form	same as HO-1 plus falling objects and damage from ice, snow, sleet
HO-3	Special Form	everything covered in HO-1 and HO-2 plus other risks specifically excluded, such as flood, earthquake, war, and nuclear accidents. Includes personal property coverage.
HO-4	Tenants' Form	personal property of renters
HO-5	Comprehensive Form	expands HO-3 by including endorsements for replacement-cost coverage on contents and guaranteed replacement-cost coverage on buildings
HO-6	Condominium Owners Form	protects personal property and any additions or improvements made to the living unit

Try It!

Draw a web diagram like the one shown to help you organize the various types of motor vehicle insurance coverage that are available.

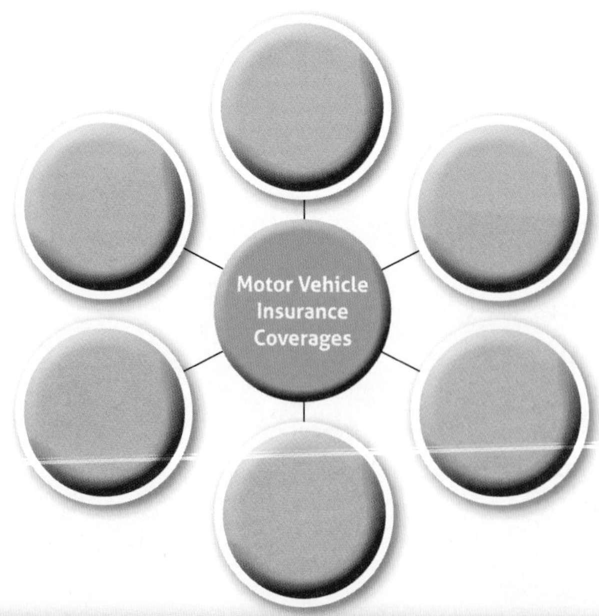

Chapter Review and Assessment

Chapter Summary

- Risk is the probability of loss or injury; peril is something that may cause a loss; hazards increase the probability of loss; and negligence is failing to take reasonable care to prevent accidents.
- Risk avoidance, risk reduction, risk assumption, and risk shifting are ways of managing risk.
- Insurance involves the risk management method of shifting risk: In exchange for fees, the insurance pays for losses.
- Property insurance protects from losses resulting from natural causes, fire, and criminal activity.
- Liability insurance covers legal responsibility for the cost of losses to others.
- Homeowners insurance covers the building, living expenses, personal property, and personal liability.
- Renters insurance covers personal possessions, living expenses, and personal liability.
- Factors affecting the cost of homeowners insurance are home location, structural type, coverage amount and policy type, discounts, and differences among insurance companies.
- The types of motor vehicle insurance include bodily injury liability, medical payments coverage, uninsured motorist's protection, property damage liability, collision, and comprehensive physical damage coverage.
- Factors affecting the cost of motor vehicle insurance include the amount of coverage, type of vehicle, rating territory, and driver classification.

Vocabulary Review

1. Use these content and academic vocabulary terms to create a crossword puzzle on graph paper. Use the definitions as clues.

- insurance
- policy
- premium
- risk
- peril
- hazard
- negligence
- deductible
- liability
- homeowners insurance
- personal property floater
- medical payments coverage
- actual cash value
- replacement value
- bodily injury liability
- uninsured motorist's protection
- property damage liability
- collision
- no-fault system
- assigned risk pool
- assume
- vandalism
- appraised
- endorsement
- stiff
- mandatory

Higher Order Thinking 

2. **Interpret** Suppose you purchase an insurance policy with 10/20/10 liability coverage. Explain what this means.
3. **Differentiate** What are the differences between pure and speculative risks?
4. **Examine** Explain why your driving record affects your car insurance rates.
5. **Conclude** Renters insurance covers personal property but not buildings. Conclude why.
6. **Formulate** Predict two scenarios in which you might need personal and professional liability insurance coverage. Identify the costs and benefits of each.
7. **Construct** Develop a list of motor vehicle risks that could be caused by negligence.
8. **Judge** Suppose that Rick tripped and fell, breaking his arm, while visiting your home. Judge whether Rick should have the right to sue your family.
9. **Consider** Think about the personal possessions you own. Which items do you think might require a personal property floater?

College and Career Readiness

Social Studies

10. FEMA The Federal Emergency Management Agency (FEMA) was founded in 1979 and is responsible for managing the National Flood Insurance Program. This program is intended to help fight the rising costs of repairing and replacing damaged buildings and property. In order to participate in the program, communities must adhere to special management requirements that help reduce flood damage. Homeowners who live in these communities are required to buy flood insurance when they purchase their homes. Use print or online resources to find out more about the floodplain management requirements a community must follow. Write a brief report to outline the requirements.

NCSS I A Analyze and explain the ways groups, societies, and cultures address human needs and concerns.

Mathematics

11. Home and Motor Vehicle Insurance Alia has homeowners insurance as well as motor vehicle insurance. Her monthly premium for the homeowners insurance is $50 and the monthly premium for her motor vehicle insurance is $110. Her deductibles are $1,200 and $350 for the homeowners insurance and motor vehicle insurance respectively. How much does Alia pay in total insurance per year? If Alia's home is damaged by a storm and she also has a car accident in the same year, what will her total insurance payments be for the year?

Math Concept **Calculate Total Insurance Payments** To calculate the total insurance payments per year first determine the total premiums for each type of insurance per month and multiply by the number of months. Add any deductibles.

Starting Hint Determine the total monthly premium for the homeowners insurance. Multiply this by the number of months to calculate the annual premium paid.

NCTM Number and Operations Compute fluently and make reasonable estimates.

English Language Arts

12. No-Fault Insurance Many states use a no-fault motor vehicle insurance system. In certain states, no-fault insurance policyholders are unable to sue the other driver involved in an accident. By avoiding court costs, the system can offer lower premiums. Some states allow drivers to sue one another. Some no-fault systems limit or define the type of coverage that is included. Follow your teacher's direction to work with a partner. Choose one state that uses a no-fault insurance system and conduct research with your partner to understand the system. Prepare an oral presentation to summarize the information you find.

NCTE 8 Use a variety of technological and information resources to gather and synthesize information and to create and communicate knowledge.

Economics

13. Uninsured Motorists A recent study shows that when unemployment rates rise, so do uninsured motorists. When economic conditions are challenging, some people will decide that the risks of an auto accident is less costly than the monthly insurance premiums. Other people may keep or even increase their insurance to ensure that they are financially covered in an emergency. Write a journal entry describing which stance you would take and why.

Real-World Applications

14. Safe Driving Contract In order to encourage teens to be more aware of the risks of driving, many schools and students are adopting the use of Safe Driving Contracts. These contracts are signed by the teen and the parent or guardian. By signing the contract, the adult promises to talk to the teen about safe driving practices. The teen promises to follow safety guidelines, such as wearing a seatbelt and not drinking and driving. Conduct research to find examples of Safe Driving Contracts. Use these as a basis to develop your own contract. Also include any safety risks that you have witnessed in your friends' or family's driving habits.

Your Financial Portfolio

The Price of Car Insurance

Before Mario bought the car he wanted, he needed to be sure he could afford the insurance for it. In this example he chose low liability, uninsured motorist coverage, and high deductibles to keep his insurance payments as low as possible. Clearly, Insurer B offered a lower price for the same coverage.

Investigating Insurance Companies

	Insurer A	Insurer B
Bodily Injury Coverage:		
Bodily injury liability $50,000 each person; $100,000 each accident	$472	$358
Uninsured motorist's protection	208	84
Medical payments coverage $2,000 each person	48	46
Property Damage Coverage:		
Property damage liability $50,000 each accident	182	178
Collision with $500 deductible	562	372
Comprehensive physical damage with $500 deductible	263	202
Car Rental:	40	32
Discounts: good driver, air bags, garage parking	(165)	
Annual Total	**$1,610**	**$1,272**

Research

Identify a make, model, and year of a vehicle you might like to own. Research two insurance companies and get prices using this example. You can get their rates by telephone. Many companies also have Web sites. On a separate sheet of paper, record your findings. How do they compare? Which company would you choose and why?

CHAPTER 23

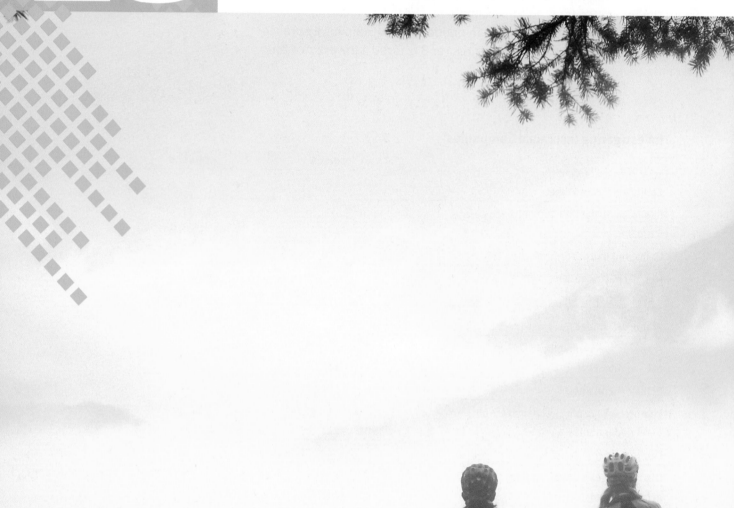

Health, Disability, and Life Insurance

Visual Literacy

Though some young adults feel they do not need health insurance, insurance can make a difference when accidents occur. ***What occurrences might cause a young adult to need health insurance?***

Discovery Project

Exploring Health Insurance Coverages

Key Question

What should you look for in a health insurance policy?

Project Goal

When choosing a health insurance policy, it is important to carefully consider your specific situation and needs before making a selection. Though you may feel that a low monthly premium is the most important factor, you must take into account the out-of-pocket expenses you will incur to determine which policy is truly the best value and fit for you. Start by considering how you would use a health insurance plan. How often do you visit the doctor? Do you participate in risky activities? Do you need vision or dental coverage? Make a list of the key items you would look for in a plan. Use brochures or Web sites from insurance companies to see what types of coverage are included to help you decide if they should be added to your list.

Ask Yourself...

- *Do you need coverage beyond basic health insurance?*
- *How much out-of-pocket expense can you afford?*
- *Would co-payments or coinsurance be more affordable?*
- *Do you have any pre-existing conditions?*
- *Are you eligible for government health care programs?*

Adapt to Change

How might your health care needs be affected by future life changes?

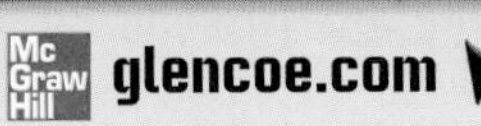

Evaluate Download an assessment rubric.

THE BIG IDEA

A good financial plan should include health and life insurance.

ASK STANDARD & POOR'S

Health Care Costs

Q *I am a high school student. Why should I be concerned about my future health care costs now?*

A Your health care costs, now and in the future, can be affected by your personal health habits. Many health problems result from poor habits, such as lack of exercise or inadequate diet, and may take years to develop. By establishing good habits now, you can reduce the likelihood of future health problems and related expenses.

Writing Activity

Create a poster with both text and art to illustrate good habits that you can establish now that will help you ensure that your health care costs will stay low in the future.

CHAPTER 23

Reading Guide

Before You Read

The Essential Question How can a life insurance policy help build a successful financial plan?

Main Idea

It is important to understand the types of health insurance coverage available, as well as the sources of health insurance when choosing the best plan for your needs. Disability income insurance is important if you become unable to work. Life insurance can relieve the financial burden of those who depend on you.

Content Vocabulary

- health insurance
- coinsurance
- stop-loss
- co-payment
- Blue Cross
- Blue Shield
- managed care
- health maintenance organization (HMO)
- preferred provider organization (PPO)
- point-of-service (POS) plan
- Medicare
- Medicaid
- disability income insurance
- beneficiary (insurance)
- term insurance
- whole life insurance
- cash value
- endowment

Academic Vocabulary

You will see these words in your reading and on your tests.

- lapse
- board
- supplemental
- hospices
- valid
- suspend
- hardship
- provisions

Graphic Organizer

Before you read this chapter, draw a chart like the one below. As you read, note the two government health care programs and what benefits are provided by each.

Government Health Care Programs	

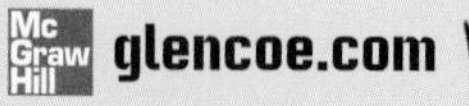

glencoe.com Print this Organizer.

Standards

Academic

Mathematics

NCTM Connections Communicate their mathematical thinking coherently and clearly to peers, teachers, and others.

NCTM Problem Solving Build new mathematical knowledge through problem solving.

English Language Arts

NCTE 4 Use written language to communicate effectively.

NCTE 8 Use information resources to gather information and create and communicate knowledge.

Science

NSES F Develop understanding of personal and community health; population growth; natural resources; environmental quality; natural and human-induced hazards; science and technology in local, national, and global challenges.

NCTM *National Council of Teachers of Mathematics*
NCTE *National Council of Teachers of English*
NCSS *National Council for the Social Studies*
NSES *National Science Education Standards*

Common Core

Reading Read closely to determine what the text says explicitly and to make logical inferences from it; cite specific textual evidence when writing or speaking to support conclusions drawn from the text.

Speaking and Listening Present information, findings, and supporting evidence such that listeners can follow the line of reasoning and the organization, development, and style are appropriate to task, purpose, and audience.

What Is Health Insurance?

Why is it important for healthy people to have health insurance?

Section Objectives

- **Explain** the importance of health insurance in financial planning.
- **Analyze** costs and benefits of various types of health insurance.

As You Read

Predict Imagine and describe a situation in which a young, healthy person would need health insurance.

Health insurance is a form of protection that eases the financial burden people may experience as a result of illness or injury. You pay a premium, or fee, to the insurer. In return, the company pays most of your medical costs.

Health insurance includes both medical expense insurance and disability income insurance. Medical expense insurance typically pays only the actual medical costs. Disability income insurance provides payments to make up for some of the income of a person who cannot work as a result of injury or illness. In this chapter the term "health insurance" generally refers to medical expense insurance. Health insurance plans can be purchased as several different plans: group health insurance, individual health insurance, and COBRA.

Group Health Insurance

Most people who have health insurance are covered under group plans. Typically, these plans are employer sponsored meaning an employer offers the plans and usually pays some or all of the premiums. Other organizations, such as professional associations, also offer group plans. Group insurance plans cover you and your immediate family. The Health Insurance Portability and Accountability Act of 1996 set new federal standards to ensure that workers will not lose their health insurance if they change jobs. For example, a parent can move from one group health plan to another plan without a **lapse,** or stop, in coverage. Also, the parent will not pay more for coverage than other employees.

The cost of group insurance is fairly low because many people are insured under the same policy, which is a contract with a risk-sharing group or insurance company. However, group insurance plans vary in the amount of protection that they provide. For example, some plans limit the amount they will pay for hospital stays and procedures.

Coordination of Benefits If your plan does not cover all your health insurance needs, you have some options. If you are married, you may be able to take advantage of a coordination of benefits (COB) provision, which is included in most group insurance plans. This provision allows you to combine the benefits from more than one insurance plan. The benefits received from all plans are limited to 100 percent of all allowable medical expenses. For example, a couple could use benefits from the wife's group plan and from the husband's group plan up to 100 percent. If this is not available, or if you are single, you can get protection by buying individual health insurance.

COMMON CENTS

Fitness Fun

Expensive exercise clothes may look good, but they usually do not improve your workout. If you cannot afford to pay to join a health club, you can get your exercise by walking or jogging in your neighborhood or at your school's track. All you need is a good pair of athletic shoes.

Concept Application

How can staying fit save you money?

Individual Health Insurance

Some people may not be offered an employer-sponsored group insurance plan or may not have access to one because they are self-employed. Others are dissatisfied with the coverage that their group plans provide. In these cases, individual health insurance may be the answer. You can buy individual health insurance directly from the company of your choice. Plans usually cover you as an individual or as a family. Individual plans can be adapted to meet your needs. You should comparison shop, because rates can vary between companies.

COBRA

The Consolidated Omnibus Budget Reconciliation Act of 1986, known as *COBRA*, allows an employee who loses his or her job to keep the former employer's group coverage for a set period of time. For example, Hakeem had a group insurance plan through his employer, but he was laid off. Fortunately for Hakeem, COBRA allowed him to keep coverage for a while. He had to pay the premiums himself, but the coverage was not canceled. When he found a new job, he was then able to switch to the new employer's group plan with no break in coverage.

To utilize COBRA you have to work for a private company or a state or local government to be eligible.

Reading Check

Recognize What is the division between the two parts of health insurance—medical expense and disability income insurance?

Types of Coverage

Why do you think basic health insurance and major medical insurance are often offered together?

Several types of health insurance coverage are available, either through an individual or group plan. Some benefits are included in nearly every health insurance plan; other benefits are less common.

Basic Health Insurance Coverage

Basic health insurance coverage includes hospital expense coverage, surgical expense coverage, and physician expense coverage.

Hospital Expense Hospital expense coverage pays for some or all of the daily costs of room and **board,** or daily meals, during a hospital stay. Routine nursing care, minor medical supplies, and the use of other hospital facilities are covered as well. For example, covered expenses would include anesthesia, dressings, related X-rays, and the use of an operating room.

Most policies set a maximum amount they will pay for each day you are in the hospital. They may also limit the number of days they will cover. Many policies may also require a deductible.

Surgical Expense Surgical expense coverage pays all or part of the surgeon's fees for an operation, whether it is done in the hospital or in the doctor's office. Policies often have a list of the services that they cover, which specifies the maximum payment for each type of operation. For example, a policy might allow $500 for an appendectomy. If the entire surgeon's bill is not covered, the policyholder has to pay the difference. People often buy surgical expense coverage in combination with hospital expense coverage.

Physician Expense Physician expense coverage meets some or all of the costs of physician care that do not involve surgery. It covers treatment in a hospital, a doctor's office, or even the patient's home. Plans may cover routine visits, X-rays, and lab tests. Like surgical expense, physician expense coverage includes maximum benefits for specific services. Physician expense coverage is usually combined with surgical and hospital coverage in a basic health insurance package.

Major Medical Expense Insurance

Most people find that basic health insurance meets their usual needs. The cost of a serious illness or accident, however, can quickly go beyond the amounts that basic health insurance will pay. For example, Chen needed emergency surgery, which meant an operation, a two-week hospital stay, lab tests, and several follow-up visits. He was shocked to discover that his basic health insurance paid less than half of the total bill, leaving him with debts of more than $10,000.

Major medical expense insurance would have better protected Chen. This coverage pays the large costs involved in long hospital stays and multiple surgeries. It takes up where basic health insurance coverage leaves off. Most types of care and treatment prescribed by a physician, in or out of a hospital, are covered. Maximum benefits can range from $5,000 to over $1 million per illness per year.

Coinsurance Of course, this type of coverage is not inexpensive. To keep premiums lower, most major medical plans require a deductible. Some plans also include a coinsurance provision. **Coinsurance** is the percentage of the medical expenses the policyholder must pay in addition to the deductible amount. Many policies require policyholders to pay 20 or 25 percent of expenses after they have paid the deductible.

For example, Ariana's policy includes an $800 deductible and a coinsurance provision requiring her to pay 20 percent of all bills. If her bills total $3,800, the insurance company will first exclude the deductible ($800) from coverage. It will then pay 80 percent of the remaining $3,000, equaling $2,400. Therefore, Ariana's total costs are $1,400 ($800 for the deductible and $600 for the coinsurance).

reality bytes

Transferable Skills
If you have a disability claim due to illness or an accident, your disability insurance carrier will require you to take a test called a Transferable Skills Analysis (TSA). The TSA determines if a disabled person has the potential to work at a job that uses his or her skills. Several software programs can perform a TSA. Insurance companies also use TSAs to detect fraudulent claims.

Stop-Loss Provisions Some major medical policies contain a stop-loss provision. **Stop-loss** is a provision that requires the policyholder to pay all costs up to a certain amount, after which the insurance company pays 100 percent of the remaining expenses covered in the policy. Typically, the policyholder will pay between \$3,000 and \$5,000 in out-of-pocket expenses before the coverage begins.

Comprehensive Major Medical Major medical expense insurance may be offered as part of a single policy that includes basic health insurance coverage, or it can be bought separately. Comprehensive major medical insurance is a type of complete health insurance that helps pay hospital, surgical, medical, and other bills. It has a very low deductible, usually \$200 to \$300. Many major medical policies set limits on the benefits they will pay for certain expenses, such as surgery and hospital room and board.

Hospital Indemnity Policies

A hospital indemnity policy pays benefits when you are hospitalized. Unlike most of the other plans mentioned, however, these policies do not directly cover medical costs. Instead, you are paid in cash, which you can spend on medical or nonmedical expenses as you choose. While such policies have limited coverage, their benefits can have wide use. Hospital indemnity policies are used as a supplement to—not a replacement for—basic health insurance or major medical insurance policies. The average person who buys such a policy, however, usually pays much more in premiums than he or she receives in payments.

Little Baby, Big Bills
The cost of having a baby can be quite high when you consider the doctors' visits and tests performed throughout pregnancy in addition to the hospital stay, medical procedures, and nursing care for the actual birth. *What part of the costs might fall under hospital expense coverage?*

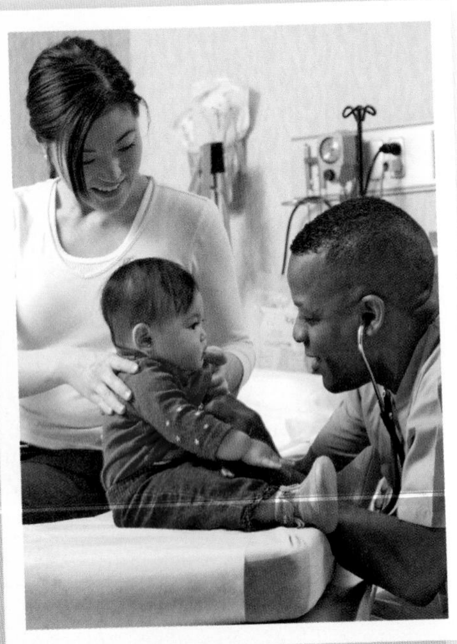

Dental Expense Insurance

Dental expense insurance provides policyholders reimbursement for the expenses of dental services and supplies. It encourages preventive dental care because it pays for maintenance care. The coverage normally provides for oral examinations, X-rays, cleanings, fillings, extractions, oral surgery, dentures, and braces. However, some dental expense policies do not cover X-rays and cleanings. As with other insurance plans, dental insurance may have a deductible and a coinsurance provision, stating that the policyholder pays from 20 to 50 percent of the dental expenses after the deductible.

Vision Care Insurance

Many insurance companies offer vision care insurance as part of group plans. Vision and eye health problems are second among the most prevalent chronic health care concerns. In considering vision coverage, you should analyze the costs and benefits. In some cases vision coverage costs more than it is worth. Vision care insurance may cover eye examinations, glasses, contact lenses, eye surgery, and the treatment of eye diseases.

Unnecessary Policies

Dread disease, trip accident, death insurance, and cancer policies are usually sold through the mail, in newspapers, and magazines. These policies play upon unrealistic fears, and they are illegal in many states. They only cover very specific conditions, which are already fully covered under a major medical plan.

Long-Term Care Insurance

Long-term care insurance provides coverage for the expense of daily help that you may need if you become seriously ill or disabled and are unable to care for yourself. It covers a lengthy stay in a nursing home and help at home with daily activities such as dressing, bathing, and household chores. Annual premiums range from $1,000 up to $16,000, depending on age and the amount of coverage. The older you are when you enroll, the higher your annual premium will be. Typically, individual insurance plans are sold to the 50-to-80 age group, pay benefits for a maximum of two to six years, and carry a dollar limit on the total benefits that the insurance company will pay. Long-term care insurance is not for everyone and is rarely recommended for people under 60.

Another option is to explore services in your community to help meet long-term care needs. Care given by family members can be supplemented by visiting nurses, home health aides, home-delivered meals, and services for caregivers who need a break from the daily responsibilities. These services are becoming more widely available and may or may not be available in your community.

Reading Check

Identify List the three basic coverages that are usually included in basic health insurance policies.

Major Provisions in a Health Insurance Policy

What are the benefits and limits of the major provisions in a health insurance policy?

All health insurance policies have certain provisions in common. You must be sure that you understand what your own policy covers. What are the benefits? What are the limits? Even the most comprehensive policy may be of little value if a provision in small print limits or denies benefits.

An insurance company usually allows you a minimum of ten days to review your health insurance policy, so be sure to check the major provisions that affect your coverage.

Health Literacy

Whether you are setting money aside for emergency medical expenses, or simply paying health insurance premiums, planning for health care costs will play a major role in establishing and achieving your financial goals. Heath literacy is the ability to obtain, interpret, and understand basic health information. Health literacy also involves understanding preventative health actions and making appropriate health-related decisions. Mastering health literacy will help you not only enhance your overall health but also manage your medical and health care expenses.

Write About It

Research preventative health measures and other aspects of health literacy. Write about the impact these measures could have on health care costs and medical expenses. How would these steps help you to achieve your future financial goals?

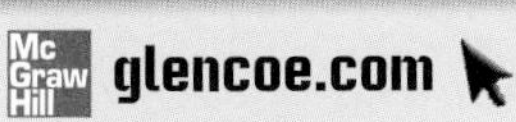

Activity Download a Career and College Readiness Worksheet Activity.

The following provisions are included in most health insurance plans:

- **Eligibility** This provision defines the people covered by the policy. That usually includes the policyholder, a spouse, and children up to a certain age.
- **Assigned Benefits** You are reimbursed for payments when you submit your bills and claim forms. When you assign benefits, you let your insurer make direct payments to your doctor or hospital.
- **Internal Limits** A policy with internal limits sets specific levels of repayment for certain services. Even if your hospital room costs $400 a day, you will not be able to get more than $250 if an internal limit specifies that maximum.
- **Co-payment** A **co-payment** is a flat fee that you pay every time you receive a covered service. The fee is usually between $5 and $20, and the insurer pays the balance of the cost of the service. This is different from coinsurance, which is the percentage of your medical costs for which you are responsible after paying your deductible.
- **Service Benefits** Policies with this provision list coverage in terms of services, not dollar amounts. For example, you are entitled to X-rays, instead of $40 worth of X-rays per visit. Service benefits provisions are always preferable to dollar amount coverage because the insurer pays all of the costs for a particular service.
- **Benefit Limits** This provision defines a maximum benefit, either in terms of a dollar amount or in terms of number of days spent in the hospital.
- **Exclusions and Limitations** This provision specifies services that the policy does not cover. That may include preexisting conditions (conditions diagnosed before the insurance plan took effect), cosmetic surgery, and more.
- **Coordination of Benefits** As discussed earlier, the coordination of benefits provision prevents you from collecting benefits from two or more group policies that would in total exceed the actual charges. Under this provision, the benefits from your own and your spouse's policies are coordinated to allow you up to 100 percent payment of your covered charges.
- **Guaranteed Renewable** With this provision, the insurer cannot cancel the policy unless you fail to pay the premiums. It also forbids insurers from raising your premiums unless they raise all premiums for all members of your group.
- **Cancellation and Termination** This provision explains the circumstances under which the insurer can cancel your coverage. It also explains how you can convert your group insurance policy into an individual insurance policy.

Reading Check

Define What is a co-payment?

Choosing Coverage

What type of health insurance coverage should you choose?

Now that you are familiar with the available types of health insurance and some of their major provisions, how do you choose one? The type of coverage you choose will be affected by the amount you can afford to spend on the premiums and the level of benefits that you feel you want and need. It may also be affected by the kind of coverage your employer offers, if you are covered through your employer.

You can buy basic health coverage, major medical coverage, or both basic and major medical coverage. Any of these three choices will take care of at least some of your medical expenses. Ideally, you should get a basic plan and a major medical supplement. Another option is to purchase a comprehensive major medical policy that combines the value of both plans in a single policy. See **Figure 1** for a description of the basic features you should look for in a health insurance plan. You should also consider the trade-offs of the various benefits.

Health Insurance Trade-Offs

Different health insurance policies may offer very different benefits. As you decide which insurance plan to buy, you should consider the following trade-offs.

Reimbursement Versus Indemnity A reimbursement policy pays you back for actual expenses. An indemnity policy pays specified amounts, regardless of how much the actual expenses may cost.

Benefits and Limits
It is important to carefully read and understand all the provisions of your health insurance policy. *Why is a policy with a service benefits provision preferred?*

For example, Katy and Seth were each charged $200 for an office visit to the same specialist. Katy's reimbursement policy has a deductible of $300. Once she has met the deductible, the policy will cover the full cost of subsequent visits. Seth's indemnity policy will pay him $125, which is what his plan provides for each specialist visit.

Internal Limits Versus Aggregate Limits A policy with internal limits covers only a fixed amount for an expense, such as the daily cost of room and board during a hospital stay. A policy with aggregate limits may limit only the total amount of coverage (the maximum dollar amount paid for all benefits in a year), such as $1 million in major expense benefits, or it may have no limits.

Deductibles and Coinsurance The cost of a health insurance policy is affected by the size of the deductible, which is the set amount that the policyholder must pay toward medical expenses before the insurance company pays benefits. The cost can also be affected by the terms of the coinsurance provision.

Out-of-Pocket Limits Some policies limit the amount of money you must pay for the deductible and coinsurance. After you have reached that limit, the insurance company covers 100 percent of any additional expenses. Having out-of-pocket limits may help you lower your financial risk, but they may also increase your premiums.

Benefits Based on Reasonable and Customary Charges Some policies consider the average fee for a service in a particular geographical area. They use that amount to set a limit on payments to policyholders. If the standard cost of a procedure is $1,500 in your geographic area, then your policy will not pay more than that amount.

FIGURE 1 Health Insurance Must-Haves

Necessities When choosing a health insurance policy, there are basic features that you should look for in the coverage. *What provisions might you desire in addition to these basic necessities?*

A health insurance plan should:
• Offer basic coverage for hospital and doctor bills.
• Provide at least 120 days' hospital room and board in full.
• Provide at least a $1 million lifetime maximum for each family member.
• Pay at least 80 percent for out-of-hospital expenses after a yearly deductible of $500 per person or $1,000 per family.
• Impose no unreasonable exclusions.
• Limit your out-of-pocket expenses to no more than $3,000 to $5,000 a year, excluding dental, vision care, and prescription costs.

Review Key Concepts

1. **Identify** Describe the benefits provided by hospital expense coverage, surgical expense coverage, and physician expense coverage.
2. **List** Identify five health insurance policies that you might want to consider purchasing in addition to basic health insurance coverage.
3. **Relate** Explain how health insurance relates to your financial planning.

Higher Order Thinking H.O.T.

4. **Analyze** Describe the pros and cons of a reimbursement policy versus an indemnity policy.

English Language Arts

5. **Physical and Financial Health** Your friend Bryan is 25 years old and leads an active healthy life. He is rarely sick so he does not feel that he should spend the money for health insurance. Write a script in which you discuss the benefits of health insurance and explain to Bryan why he should purchase basic health insurance coverage, regardless of his current situation. Your script should be a dialogue, including Bryan's protests or questions and your answers based on the information in the text.

NCTE 12 Use language to accomplish individual purposes.

Mathematics

6. **Coinsurance or Stop-loss?** Cameron is looking into purchasing an insurance policy. She has limited her choices down to two options. One policy includes a coinsurance provision with a $600 deductible and requires the policy holder to pay 20 percent of all bills. The other policy contains a stop-loss provision which requires the policy holder to pay all costs up to $1,000 after which the insurer will pay 100 percent of the remaining expenses. Which policy would result in the least out-of-pocket expenses if Cameron incurred $3,000 of medical expenses?

Math Concept Calculate Medical Expenses
To calculate the medical expenses incurred first determine the total amount of medical bills or expenses. Identify the amount of coverage received from the insurance policy and subtract this from the total expense.

Starting Hint Determine the total expense incurred from the insurance policy with a coinsurance provision by subtracting the deductible from the total expense and multiplying the result by 20 percent. Add this result to the deductible.

NCTM Problem Solving Solve problems that arise in mathematics and in other contexts.

Check your answers.

Section Objective

- **Differentiate** between private and government health care plans.

As You Read

Discover What is the difference between insurance provided by private organizations and insurance provided by the government?

Private Health Care Plans

What is the difference between an HMO and a PPO?

Most health insurance in the United States is provided by private organizations rather than by the government. Private health care plans may be offered by a number of sources: private insurance companies; hospital and medical service plans; health maintenance organizations; preferred provider organizations; home health care agencies; and employer self-funded health plans. In addition, there are now health care accounts available through some employers to help manage health care costs.

Private Insurance Companies

Insurance companies sell health insurance through either group or individual policies. Of these two types, group health insurance represents about 90 percent of all medical expense insurance and 80 percent of all disability income insurance.

Several hundred private insurance companies are in the health insurance business. They provide mostly group health plans to employers. These employers then provide the options to their employees as an employment benefit. Premiums may be fully or partially paid by the employer, with the employee paying any remainder.

These policies typically pay for medical costs by sending payments directly to the doctor, hospital, or lab that provides the services.

Hospital and Medical Service Plans

Blue Cross and Blue Shield are statewide organizations similar to private health insurance companies. Each state has Blue Cross and Blue Shield. **Blue Cross** is an insurance company that provides hospital care benefits. **Blue Shield** is an insurance company that provides benefits for surgical and medical services performed by physicians. The "Blues" provide health insurance to millions of Americans.

Managed Care

Rising health care costs have led to an increase in managed care plans. According to a recent industry survey, 23 percent of employed Americans are enrolled in some form of managed care. **Managed care** refers to prepaid health plans that provide comprehensive health care to their members. Managed care is designed to control the cost of health care services by controlling how they are used.

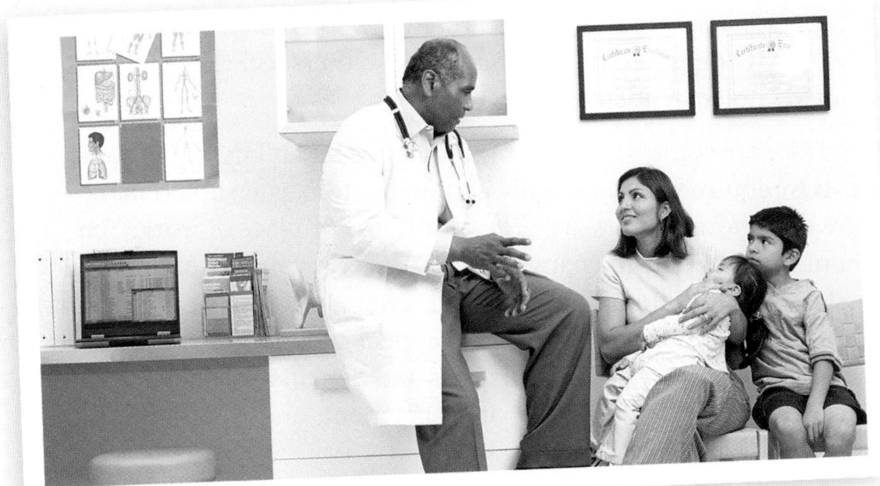

Controlled Cost
By helping to keep the cost of health care down, managed care plans help make health insurance available to more people. *Which managed care plan(s) require you to choose a primary care physician?*

Managed care companies now provide information that helps members better manage their health care needs. Health plans have launched Internet programs that allow you to access medical research, support groups, and professional advice. Managed care is offered by health maintenance organizations, preferred provider organizations, and point-of-service plans.

Health Maintenance Organizations One managed-care option is a **health maintenance organization (HMO),** which is a health insurance plan that directly employs or contracts with selected, or preapproved, physicians and other medical professionals to provide health care services in exchange for a fixed, prepaid monthly premium. HMOs are an alternative to basic health insurance and major medical expense insurance.

HMOs are based on the idea that preventive services will minimize future medical problems. Therefore, these plans typically cover routine immunizations and checkups, screening programs, and diagnostic tests. They also provide coverage for a wide range of other health services. These services are divided into two categories: basic and supplemental. Basic health services include inpatient and outpatient procedures; surgery; and emergency care. If you have an HMO, you usually pay a small co-payment for each covered service, such as a doctor's office visit. **Supplemental,** or extra, services may include vision care and prescription services, which are typically available for an additional fee.

When you first enroll in an HMO, you must choose a plan physician from a list of doctors provided by the HMO. This physician provides or arranges for all your health care services. If you receive care from a physician outside your HMO's approved physician list, you are responsible for the cost of the service. The only exception to this rule is in the case of a medical emergency. If you experience a sudden illness or injury that would threaten your life or health if not treated immediately, you may go to the nearest emergency room. All other care must be provided by hospitals and doctors under contract with the HMO.

HMOs are not for everyone. Many HMO customers complain that their HMO denies them necessary care. Others feel restricted by the limited choice of doctors.

Here are some tips on using and choosing an HMO. Because HMOs require you to use only certain doctors, you should make sure that those doctors are near your home or place of work. You should also be able to change doctors easily if you do not like your first choice. Second opinions should always be available at the HMO's expense, and you should be able to appeal any case in which the HMO denies care. Finally, look at the costs and benefits—whether you will incur out-of-pocket expenses or co-payments and what services the plan will provide.

Preferred Provider Organizations A variation on the HMO is a **preferred provider organization (PPO),** which is a group of doctors and hospitals that agree to provide specified medical services to members at prearranged fees. PPOs offer these discounted services to employees either directly or indirectly through an insurance company. The premiums for PPOs are slightly higher than the premiums for HMOs.

PPO plan members often pay no deductibles but may have minimal co-payments. While HMOs require members to receive care from HMO providers only, PPOs allow members greater flexibility. Members can either visit a preferred provider (a physician selected from a pre-approved list) or go to their own physicians. Patients who decide to use their own doctors do not lose coverage as they would with an HMO. However, they must pay deductibles and larger co-payments.

Point-of-Service (POS) Plan A **point-of-service (POS) plan** combines features of both HMOs and PPOs. POS plans use a network of participating physicians and medical professionals who have contracted to provide services for certain fees. As with an HMO, you choose a plan physician who manages your care and controls referrals to specialists. As long as you receive care from a pre-approved provider, you pay little or nothing, just as you would with an HMO. However, you are allowed to seek care outside the network at a higher charge, as with a PPO. While with POS plans you are not locked into a network of doctors, POS plans cost more than HMOs.

Home Health Care Agencies

Rising hospital costs, new medical technology, and the increasing number of elderly people have helped make home care one of the fastest-growing areas of the health care industry. Home health care consists of home health care agencies; home care aide organizations; and **hospices,** which are facilities and organizations that provide care for the terminally ill. These providers offer medical care in a home setting in agreement with a medical order, often at a fraction of the cost charged by hospitals for similar services.

Taiwan

Smart Card System

With the rising costs of medical care, health insurance is necessary for most people. The United States government has developed programs like Medicare and Medicaid for people who otherwise could not afford or be eligible for health insurance. Taiwan is using technology to take a different approach to meeting the health care needs of its citizens. This technology comes in the form of Smart Cards.

The National Health Insurance (NHI) system in Taiwan covers 99 percent of the population and each person carries a Smart Card. Each person's Smart Card serves as his or her patient ID and contains the entire medical history for that person. Unlike many nations with national health care, Taiwan reports having little to no wait times and doctors brag that they regularly see 50 percent more patients in a week than doctors in the United States. The system is paid for through a payroll tax. Premiums are paid by a combination of individuals, employers, and the government. Most claims are processed electronically, also using the Smart Card technology. Thus, the Smart Card helps keep administration costs down, as well as helping to prevent over-treatment which can lead to costlier bills.

Critical Thinking

1. **Expand** Research to find additional information on Smart Cards. How does the use of the Smart Card help prevent over-treatment? How does it prevent individuals from over-using health care?
2. **Relate** Do you think the Smart Card technology would be beneficial in a public health care system? What might be some drawbacks to implementing this technology?

DATABYTES

Capital
Taipei

Population
23,024,956

Languages
Mandarin Chinese (official), Taiwanese (Min), Hakka dialects

Currency
Taiwan dollar

Gross Domestic Product (GDP)
$361.5 billion

GDP per capita
$29,800

Industry
Electronics, communications and information technology products, petroleum refining, armaments, chemicals, textiles, iron and steel, machinery, cement, food processing, vehicles, consumer products, pharmaceuticals

Agriculture
Rice, corn, vegetables, fruit, tea; pigs, poultry, beef, milk; fish

Exports
Electronics, flat panels, machinery; metals; textiles, plastics, chemicals; optical, photographic, measuring, and medical instruments

Natural Resources
Small deposits of coal, natural gas, limestone, marble, and asbestos

Employer Self-Funded Health Plans

Some companies choose to self-insure. The company runs its own insurance plan, collecting premiums from employees and paying medical benefits. These companies must cover any costs that exceed the income from premiums. Unfortunately, some corporations do not have the financial assets necessary to cover these situations, which can cause a financial disaster for the company and its employees.

New Health Care Accounts

Health savings accounts (HSAs) are the newest addition to the alphabet soup of health insurance available to American workers. Now you and your employer must sort through HSAs, health reimbursement accounts (HRAs), and flexible spending accounts (FSAs). Each has its own rules about how money is spent, how it can be spent, and how it is taxed.

FSAs allow you to contribute pretax dollars to an account managed by your employer. You use the money for health care spending but forfeit anything left over at the end of the year.

HRAs are tied to high-deductible policies. They are funded solely by your employer and give you a pot of money to spend on health care. You can carry over unspent money from year to year, but you lose the balance if you switch jobs. Premiums tend to be lower than for traditional insurance but higher than for HSAs. You can invest the funds in stocks, bonds, and mutual funds. The money grows tax-free but can be spent only on health care.

HSAs allow you to contribute money to a tax-free account that can be used for out-of-pocket health care expenses if you buy high-deductible health insurance policies to cover catastrophic expenses. For example, your health insurance policy offers a deductible of at least $1,150. You can put pretax dollars into an HSA each year up to the amount of the deductible—but no more than $5,950 for family coverage or $3,000 for individual coverage, plus a $1,000 catch-up contribution for those who are over 55. You withdraw money from the HSA tax-free, but it can be used only for your family's medical expenses. After the deductible and co-payments are met, insurance still covers eighty percent of health costs. HSA plans are required to have maximum out-of-pocket spending limits. That is when your company's insurance kicks in again at 100 percent coverage. Like an HRA, you can invest the funds in stocks, bonds, and mutual funds, and the money grows tax-free. Unlike an HRA, if you switch jobs, money from an HSA can be taken with you.

Reading Check

Distinguish What are the two statewide organizations that offer health care plans and how do they differ?

Government Health Care Programs

Who benefits most from government health care programs?

The health insurance coverages discussed so far are normally purchased through private companies. Some consumers, however, are eligible for health insurance coverage under programs offered by federal and state governments. The federal program is Medicare, and the federal and state program is Medicaid.

Medicare

Perhaps the best-known government program is Medicare. **Medicare** is a federally funded health insurance program available to people over 65 or with certain disabilities. Medicare has four parts: hospital insurance (Part A), medical insurance (Part B), Medicare Advantage (Part C), and Prescription Drug Coverage (Part D).

Medicare Part A is funded by part of the Social Security payroll tax. Part A helps pay for inpatient hospital care, inpatient care in a skilled nursing facility, home health care, and hospice care. Part A pays for all covered services for inpatient hospital care after program participants pay a single annual deductible. Most people over the age of 65 are eligible for free Medicare hospital insurance.

Medicare medical insurance Part B helps pay for doctors' services and a variety of other medical services and supplies not covered, or not fully covered, by Part A. Part B has a deductible and a 20 percent coinsurance provision. This means that once a person meets the annual medical insurance deductible, medical insurance will pay 80 percent of the approved charges for the covered services that the person receives during the rest of the year. Medicare medical insurance is a supplemental program paid for by individuals who feel that they need additional coverage. A regular monthly premium is charged. The federal government matches this amount.

The Balanced Budget Act of 1997 created the Medicare + Choice program, which was renamed Medicare Advantage (Part C) in 2003. Part C combines Parts A and B. Private insurance companies approved by Medicare provide this coverage. The costs may be lower than the original Medicare plan, and extra benefits may be provided.

Part D covers prescription drugs. Private, approved, companies run these plans. Medically necessary drugs must be covered by all plans. Part C plans also often cover prescription drugs.

Medicare Finances Medicare is at risk financially. Health care costs continue to grow, and the population of senior citizens in the United States is increasing. This situation puts Medicare in danger of running out of funds. According to projections, the program will be bankrupt by the year 2019 if no changes are made.

Living Longer
The number of people living past the age of 65 is growing thanks in part to active, healthy lifestyles and improved medical services. *Why might older people need government programs to help pay for health insurance?*

Careers That Count!

Akayla Sall • Insurance Agent

I have natural sales abilities, and I care about my clients. I sell insurance policies to individuals, families, business firms, and other groups to protect them from future financial loss due to injury, illness, death, property damage, or theft. On a typical day, I interview prospective clients to obtain data about their financial resources and needs, as well as the physical condition of the person or property to be insured. I then work out an insurance program suited to that client, explain the program's costs and benefits, and write a policy. I follow up regularly with my clients so I can handle any changes and renewals to his or her policy. The Internet has made it easier for me to take on more clients and to be better informed about new products. Developing a satisfied client base that will recommend my services to other potential clients is essential to my success.

EXPLORE CAREERS

Visit the Web site of the U.S. Department of Labor's Bureau of Labor Statistics to obtain information about a career as an insurance agent.

1. What job duties might an insurance agent perform, in addition to selling an insurance policy?
2. How has this job changed due to technological advancements? How might it change in the future?

Skills	Education	Career Path
Sales, negotiation, communication, interpersonal, math, computer, and time-management skills; legal and financial knowledge	High school diploma or equivalent, but a college degree in business, finance, or economics is preferred; a state-issued license; continuing education	Insurance agents can become sales managers and independent agency or brokerage firm owners.

 **glencoe.com** 

Activity Download a Career Exploration Activity.

What Is Not Covered by Medicare? Medicare effectively covers many medical costs, but there are some medical expenses that Medicare will not cover at all. These expenses include:

- Certain types of skilled or long-term nursing care
- Care received outside of the United States, except in Canada and Mexico, and then only in limited circumstances
- Private-duty nursing
- Out-of-hospital prescription drugs
- Routine checkups
- Dental care
- Most screening tests and some diabetic supplies
- Most immunizations

Medicare also limits the types of services it will cover and the amount it will pay for those services. If a doctor does not accept Medicare's approved amount as payment in full, the patient is responsible for paying the difference.

Medigap People who are eligible for Medicare and who would like to have more coverage may buy Medigap insurance. Medigap insurance supplements Medicare by filling the gap between Medicare payments and medical costs not covered by Medicare. Medigap insurance is not sold or serviced by federal or state governments. It is offered by private companies. All supplement insurance policies must cover certain gaps in Medicare coverage, such as the daily coinsurance amount for hospitalization.

Medicaid

The other well-known government health program is **Medicaid,** a medical assistance program offered to certain low-income individuals and families. Medicaid is administered by the individual states, but it is financed by a combination of state and federal funds. Unlike Medicare, Medicaid coverage is so comprehensive that people with Medicaid do not need supplemental insurance. Typical Medicaid benefits include:

- Physicians' services
- Inpatient hospital services
- Outpatient hospital services
- Lab services
- Skilled nursing and home health services
- Prescription drugs
- Eyeglasses
- Preventive care for people under 21

Government Consumer Health Information Web Sites

The Department of Health and Human Services operates more than 60 Web sites that contain a wealth of reliable information related to health and medicine.

Healthfinder Healthfinder includes links to more than a thousand Web pages operated by government and nonprofit organizations. The site lists topics according to subject.

MedlinePlus MedlinePlus is the world's largest Internet collection of published medical information. It was originally designed for health professionals and researchers, but it is also valuable for students and others who are interested in health care and medical issues.

NIH Health Information The National Institutes of Health (NIH) operates a Web site that can direct you to the consumer health information in NIH publications and on the Internet.

FDA The Food and Drug Administration (FDA), a federal consumer protection agency, provides a Web site with information about the safety of various foods, drugs, cosmetics, and medical devices.

SECTION 2 Assessment

Review Key Concepts

1. **Identify** List six sources for private health care plans.
2. **Distinguish** What are the differences between the government health care programs Medicare and Medicaid?
3. **Summarize** Describe three types of health care accounts.

Higher Order Thinking H.O.T.

4. **Judge** Do you think people over the age of 65 who can afford private health insurance should be eligible for Medicare? Explain.

21st Century Skills

5. **Make Judgments and Decisions** You have always had health insurance through your parents. Suppose you have just started work at your first full-time job and you must now get your own health insurance policy. The company you are working for offers two managed-care options for its employees: an HMO and a PPO. Consider the benefits and drawbacks of each type of plan, along with your personal situations and needs. Which health insurance plan do you feel would best fit your health and financial needs?

Mathematics

6. **PPOs** Kris was experiencing back problems and decided to go to the hospital. Kris has a PPO under which care at a network hospital is 85 percent covered after the policy holder has met a $400 annual deductible. Assume that Kris went to a hospital within his PPO network. His total medical expense was $1,200, and Kris has not paid anything toward his annual deductible in the current year. How much did Kris have to pay out-of-pocket? How much of the medical expense was covered under the PPO?

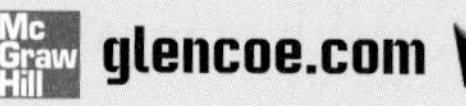
Math Concept **Calculate Coverage Costs** To calculate the coverage on a PPO subtract the annual deductible from the total medical expenses and multiply the result by the percent of coverage. Out-of-pocket cost is the covered amount subtracted from the total medical expense.

Starting Hint Calculate the amount of coverage received by first determining the total annual deductible required. Subtract this from the total medical expenses incurred and multiply the result by the coverage percentage.

NCTM Number and Operations Compute fluently and make reasonable estimates.

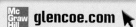

McGraw Hill glencoe.com Check your answers.

Disability Income

Why is it important to have disability insurance?

Before disability insurance existed, people who were ill often lost more money from missed paychecks than from paying medical bills. Disability income insurance was set up to protect against such loss of income. **Disability income insurance** provides regular cash income when an employee is unable to work due to pregnancy, a non-work-related accident, or an illness. It protects your earning power, which is your most valuable resource. This kind of coverage is very common today, and several hundred insurance companies offer it.

The exact definition of the word *disability* varies from insurer to insurer. Some insurers will pay you when you are unable to work at your regular job. Other insurers will pay only if you are so ill or badly hurt that you cannot work at any job. A violinist with a hand injury, for example, might have trouble doing his or her regular work but might be able to perform a range of other jobs. A good disability income insurance plan pays you if you cannot work at your regular job. A good plan will also pay partial benefits if you are able to work only part-time.

Many people make the mistake of ignoring disability insurance, not realizing that it is very important to have. A disability can cause even greater financial problems than death because disabled persons lose their earning power but still have to pay for their living expenses. In addition, they often face huge costs for the medical treatment and special care that their disabilities require.

Section Objectives

- **Explain** the importance of disability insurance in financial planning.
- **Describe** different sources of disability income.

As You Read

Infer What might disability insurance cover?

Sources of Disability Income

Before you buy disability income insurance from a private insurance company, remember that you may already have some form of this insurance. This coverage may be available through worker's compensation if you are injured on the job. Disability benefits may also be available through your employer or through Social Security in case of a long-term disability.

Worker's Compensation If your disability is the result of an accident or illness that occurred on the job, you may be eligible to receive worker's compensation benefits. The amount of benefits will depend on your salary and your work history.

Employer Many employers provide disability income insurance through group insurance plans. In most cases, your employer will pay part or all of the cost of such insurance. Some policies may only provide continued wages for several months, while others will provide long-term protection.

Social Security Social Security may be best known as a source of retirement income, but it also provides disability benefits. If you are a worker who pays into the Social Security system, you are eligible for Social Security funds if you become disabled. How much you get depends on your salary and the number of years you have been paying into Social Security. Your dependents also qualify for certain benefits. However, Social Security has very strict rules. Workers are considered disabled if they have a physical or mental condition that prevents them from working for at least 12 months, or if they have a condition that may result in death. Benefits start at the sixth full month the person is disabled. They stay in effect as long as the disability lasts.

Private Income Insurance Programs Privately owned insurance companies offer many policies to protect people from loss of income resulting from illness or disability. Disability income insurance gives weekly or monthly cash payments to people who cannot work due to illness or accident. The amount paid is usually 40 to 60 percent of a person's normal income. Some plans pay as much as 75 percent.

Be Prepared
Though accidents can happen to anyone at anytime, you can be prepared to deal with them financially by ensuring that you have disability income insurance. *When does a person become qualified for Social Security disability benefits?*

Disability Insurance Trade-Offs

When you purchase health or disability insurance, you must make certain trade-offs when you decide among different private disability insurance policies. You should consider several factors as you look for a plan.

Waiting or Elimination Period Your benefits will not begin the day you become disabled. You will have to wait between one and six months before you can begin collecting. This span of time is called a waiting, or elimination, period. Usually a policy with a longer elimination period charges lower premiums.

Duration of Benefits Every policy names a specified period during which benefits will be paid. Some policies are **valid,** or good, for only a few years. Others are automatically canceled when you turn 65.

Risky Business
Some jobs contain a much higher risk of injury than others. *What type of coverage would provide disability income if one of these workers was injured on the job?*

Still others continue to make payments for life. You should look for a policy that pays benefits for life. If a policy stops payments when the policyholder is age 65, then having a permanent disability could be a major financial burden.

Amount of Benefits You should aim for a benefit amount that, when added to other sources of income, will equal 70 to 80 percent of your take-home pay. Of course, greater benefits cost more money.

Accident and Sickness Coverage Some disability policies pay only for accidents. However, accidents are not the only cause of disability, so coverage for sickness is also important.

Guaranteed Renewability If your health becomes poor, your disability insurer may try to cancel your coverage. Look for a plan that guarantees coverage as long as you continue to pay your premiums. Some plans may even **suspend,** or stop, premiums if you become disabled.

Reading Check

Recall What are four sources for disability income?

Your Disability Income Needs

How do you determine your disability income needs?

After you find out what your benefits would be from the numerous public and private sources, you should determine whether those benefits would meet your disability income needs. Ideally, you want to replace all the income you otherwise would have earned. This money should enable you to pay your day-to-day expenses while you are recovering. You will not have work-related expenses, and your taxes will be lower during the time that you are disabled. In some cases, you may not have to pay certain taxes at all.

Review Key Concepts

1. **Describe** Why should you have disability insurance?
2. **Explain** What type of disability would not be covered by worker's compensation insurance? Why?
3. **Identify** What five factors should you consider when purchasing disability insurance?

Higher Order Thinking H.O.T.

4. **Theorize** Which professions might have a greater need for disability income insurance? Explain your answer.

English Language Arts

5. **Inclusive Insurance** Most people understand the importance of insuring their possessions, such as their house, car, or jewels. Unfortunately, many people fail to consider their earning power as a resource and therefore do not realize the need for disability income insurance. Suppose that you are a magazine journalist for a publication in the entertainment industry. Write an article explaining the importance of disability income insurance to people who work in the entertainment industry, such as actors, writers, and musicians.

NCTE 4 Use written language to communicate effectively.

Mathematics

6. **Workers' Compensation** Rita was injured at work when she slipped on some ice in the parking lot. Her company provides long-term workers' compensation benefits in which they pay 100 percent of annual salary for up to 4 months, then 65 percent of annual salary up to one year. If Rita was out of work for 9 months, how much in workers' compensation would she collect? How much would she have earned over the same time period had she not been injured? Assume Rita earns a monthly salary of $3,500.

Math Concept Calculate Workers' Compensation Benefits To calculate workers' compensation benefits determine the monthly salary and multiply this amount by the percentage of salary paid out by the benefit for each month of the out of work time period.

Starting Hint Calculate the amount of benefit received for the first 4 months of disability by multiplying the percentage of total salary paid out for the first 4 months by the monthly salary.

NCTM Connections Recognize and apply mathematics in contexts outside of mathematics.

McGraw Hill glencoe.com Check your answers.

What Is Life Insurance?

Why is it important to include life insurance in your financial planning?

When a person buys life insurance, he or she is making a contract with the company issuing the policy. He or she agrees to pay a certain amount of money—the premium—periodically. In return, the company agrees to pay a death benefit, or a stated sum of money upon his or her death, to his or her beneficiary. A **beneficiary** is a person named to receive the benefits from an insurance policy. In the case of an endowment policy, the money is paid to the policyholder if he or she is alive on the future, or maturity, date named in the policy.

Section Objectives

- **Describe** various types of life insurance coverage.
- **Identify** the key provisions in a life insurance policy.

As You Read

Consider Imagine your life 5, 10, and 15 years from now. At what point would you want a good life insurance policy?

The Purpose of Life Insurance

Buying life insurance can help you protect the people who depend upon you from financial losses caused by your death. Those people could include a spouse, children, an aging parent, or a business partner. Life insurance benefits may be used to

- Pay off a home mortgage or other debts at the time of death.
- Provide lump-sum payments as an endowment for children when they reach a certain age.
- Provide an education or income for children.
- Pay uncovered medical expenses and funeral costs.
- Make charitable donations after death.
- Provide a retirement income.
- Accumulate savings.
- Establish a regular income for survivors.
- Set up an estate plan.
- Pay estate and death taxes.

Life insurance is one way to provide liquidity at the time of death.

The Principle of Life Insurance

No one can say with any certainty how long a particular person will live. However, insurance companies are able to make some educated guesses. Over the years they have compiled tables that show an estimate of how long people live. Using these tables, the companies make a rough guess about a person's life span and set the price of insurance premiums for him or her accordingly. The sooner a person is likely to die, the higher the premium he or she will pay to have life insurance. For example, life insurance will cost more for a 65-year-old woman than for a 25-year-old woman.

FIGURE 2 **Life Expectancy Table**

Years to Go Insurance companies use life expectancy tables to help determine prices for life insurance policies. *Does history show that males or females typically live longer?*

Age	Total	Male	Female	Age	Total	Male	Female
0	77.7	75.1	80.2	45	35.2	33.1	37.0
1	77.2	74.7	79.7	50	30.7	28.8	32.5
5	73.3	70.8	75.8	55	26.5	24.7	28.0
10	68.4	65.8	70.8	60	22.4	20.7	23.8
15	63.4	60.9	65.9	65	18.5	17.0	19.7
20	58.6	56.1	61.0	70	14.9	13.6	15.9
25	53.9	51.5	56.1	75	11.6	10.4	12.3
30	49.2	46.9	51.3	80	8.7	7.8	9.3
35	44.4	42.2	46.4	85	6.4	5.7	6.8
40	39.7	37.6	41.7				

Life Expectancy

If history is any guide, you will live longer than your ancestors lived. In 1900, the life expectancy of an American male was 46.3 years, and it was 48.3 years for an American female. In contrast, by the year 2000, the life expectancy increased to 74 years for men and 80 years for women. **Figure 2** shows an estimate of how many years a person can be expected to live today. This type of table guides insurance companies when they set prices. For example, a 30-year-old woman can be expected to live another 51.3 years. This is the average number of additional years a 30-year-old woman may expect to live.

Do You Need Life Insurance?

Before you buy life insurance, you will have to decide whether you need it at all. Generally, if your death would cause financial **hardship,** or suffering, for somebody, then life insurance is a wise purchase. Households with children usually have the greatest need for life insurance. Single people who live alone or with their parents, however, usually have little or no need for life insurance unless they have a great deal of debt or want to provide for their parents or a friend, relative, or charity.

Reading Check

Define What is a beneficiary?

Types of Life Insurance Policies

When do you think it is most important to have life insurance?

You can purchase life insurance from two types of life insurance companies: stock life insurance companies, which are owned by shareholders, and mutual life insurance companies, which are owned by their policyholders. About 95 percent of life insurance companies in the United States are stock companies. Insurance policies can be divided into two major types: temporary insurance, such as term insurance, and permanent insurance, such as whole life insurance.

Term Insurance

Term insurance, which is sometimes called *temporary life insurance*, is insurance that provides protection against loss of life for only a specified term, or period of time. A term insurance policy pays a benefit only if you die during the period it covers, which may be 1, 5, 10, or 20 years, or up to age 70. If you stop paying the premiums, your coverage stops. Term insurance is often the best value for most consumers. The premiums for people in their 20s and 30s are less expensive than those for whole life insurance. You need life insurance coverage most while you are raising children. As your children become independent and your assets increase, you can reduce your coverage. Term insurance comes in many different forms.

Renewable Term The coverage of term insurance ends at the conclusion of the term, but you can continue it for another term, such as five years, if you have a renewable option. However, the premium will increase because you will be older. It also usually has an age limit, which means you cannot renew your coverage after you reach a certain age.

Multiyear Level Term A multiyear level term, or straight term, policy guarantees that you will pay the same premium for the duration of your policy.

Conversion Term This type of policy allows you to change from term to permanent coverage. If you have conversion term insurance, you can exchange it for a whole life policy without a medical examination. This change will require a higher premium. However, the whole life premium will stay the same for the rest of your life.

Decreasing Term Term insurance is also available in a form that pays less to the beneficiary as time passes. The premiums are usually the same over the entire period of coverage. The insurance period you select might depend on your age or on how long you want to be covered. For example, if you have a mortgage on a house, you might buy a 25-year decreasing term policy as a way to make sure that the debt could be paid if you died. The coverage would decrease as the balance on the loan decreased.

Name Your Terms
Term insurance provides coverage for a specified length of time. *When are people most likely to need life insurance?*

Economics and You

Your Tax Dollars

The government uses your tax dollar to provide services needed for the health, welfare, and safety of the country. Government officials decide on the allocation of tax dollars for government programs by analyzing their costs and benefits. The Federal Insurance Contributions Act (F.I.C.A.) is a tax that funds Social Security. Social Security provides benefits for old, disabled, and low-income citizens in the United States. It includes health insurance for the elderly (Medicare) and low-income citizens (Medicaid).

Personal Finance Connection Before you vote, research the candidates to see if any share your opinion on the costs/benefits of particular government programs. Ask yourself if the candidate agrees with your ideas on how your taxes should be spent.

Critical Thinking Use cost/benefit analysis to discuss the pros and cons of universal health care, which is government-run health care for all people in a nation. Prepare a brief report and share it with the class.

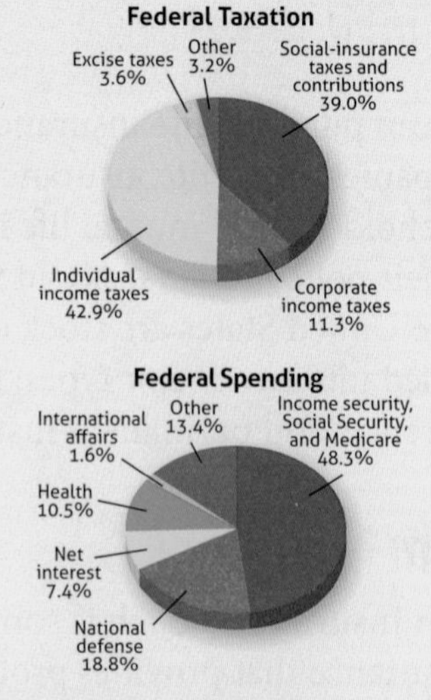

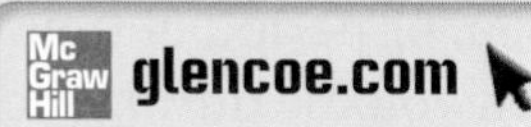

Activity Download an Economics and You Worksheet Activity.

Whole Life Insurance

The most common type of permanent insurance is whole life insurance (also called a straight life policy, a cash value policy, or an ordinary life policy). **Whole life insurance** is a permanent policy for which you pay a specified premium each year for the rest of your life. The insurance company pays your beneficiary a stated sum when you die. The amount of your premium depends mostly on the age at which you purchase the insurance.

Whole life insurance can also serve as an investment. Part of each premium you pay is set aside in a savings account. When and if you cancel the policy, you are entitled to the accumulated savings, which is known as the **cash value.** Whole life policies are popular because they provide both a death benefit and a savings component.

Cash value policies may make sense for people who intend to keep the policies for the long term or for people who want a more structured way to save. However, the Consumer Federation of America Insurance Group suggests that you explore other strategies before investing your money in a permanent policy.

The premium on a term insurance policy will increase each time you renew your insurance. In contrast, whole life policies have higher annual premiums at first, but the payment amount remains the same for the rest of your life. Several types of whole life policies have been developed including: the limited payment policy, the variable life policy, the adjustable life policy, and universal life insurance.

Limited Payment Policy Limited payment policies charge premiums for only a certain length of time, usually 20 or 30 years or until the insured reaches a certain age. At the end of this time, the policy is "paid up" and the policyholder remains insured for life. When the policyholder dies, the beneficiary receives the full death benefit. The annual premiums are higher for limited payment policies because the premiums have to be paid within a shorter period of time. A special form of the limited payment plan is the single-premium policy. In this type of contract, you make only one very large premium payment.

Variable Life Policy With a variable life policy, premium payments are fixed. As with a cash value policy, part of the premium is placed into a separate account; this money is invested in a stock, bond, or money market fund. The death benefit is guaranteed, but the cash value of the benefit can vary considerably according to the ups and downs of the stock market. Your death benefit can also increase if the earnings of that separate fund increase. Thus, policyholders, not insurance companies, assume the investment risk. The premium payments for a variable life policy are fixed. Life insurance agents selling variable life policies must be registered representatives of a broker-dealer licensed by the National Association of Securities Dealers and registered with the Securities and Exchange Commission.

Adjustable Life Policy An adjustable life policy allows you to change your coverage as your needs change. For example, if you want to increase or decrease your death benefit, you can change either the premium payments or the period of coverage.

Universal Life Universal life insurance is essentially a term policy with a cash value. Part of your premium goes into an investment account that grows and earns interest. You are able to borrow or withdraw your cash value. With universal life you are able to control and change your premium without changing your coverage.

Other Types of Life Insurance Policies

Other types of life insurance policies include group life insurance, credit life insurance, and endowment life insurance.

Group Life Insurance Group life insurance is a variation of term insurance. It covers a large number of people under a single policy. The people included in the group do not need medical examinations to get coverage. Group insurance is usually offered by employers, who pay part or all of the costs for their employees. It may also be offered by professional organizations, which allow members to obtain coverage. It can be more expensive than similar term policies.

Credit Life Insurance Credit life insurance pays off debts, such as auto loans or mortgages, in the event that you die before they are paid in full. These types of policies are not the best buy for the protection they offer. Decreasing term insurance is a better option.

Endowment Life Insurance **Endowment** is life insurance that provides coverage for a specific period of time and pays a sum of money to the policyholder if he or she is living at the end of the endowment period. If the policyholder dies before that time, the beneficiary receives the money.

Reading Check

Identify Name four types of whole life insurance policies.

Key Provisions in a Life Insurance Policy

Why should you consider adding provisions to your life insurance policy?

Study the **provisions,** or conditions, in your policy carefully and be sure to update the necessary information as changes in your life occur. The following are the most common provisions:

Beneficiary Designation

You decide who receives the benefits of your life insurance policy. The beneficiary could be your spouse, your child, or even your business partner. You can also name *contingent beneficiaries*, those who will receive the money if your primary beneficiary dies before or at the same time as you do. You will need to update your list of beneficiaries as your needs change.

Incontestability Clause

The incontestability clause says that the insurer cannot cancel the policy if it has been in force for a specified period, usually two years. After that time the policy is considered valid during the lifetime of the insured. The clause protects the beneficiaries from financial loss if the insurance company refuses to meet the terms of the policy.

The Grace Period

When you buy a life insurance policy, you agree to pay a certain premium regularly. The grace period allows 28 to 31 days to elapse, during which time you may pay the premium without penalty. After the grace period, the policy lapses if you have not paid the premium.

Policy Reinstatement A lapsed policy can be put back in force, or reinstated, if it has not been turned in for cash. To reinstate the policy, you must again qualify as an acceptable risk, and you must pay overdue premiums with interest. There is a time limit on reinstatement, usually one or two years.

Document Detective

A Life Insurance Policy Statement

If a person who holds a life insurance policy dies, the people who depended upon that policyholder can be protected from financial losses by the life insurance policy. By obtaining a life insurance policy, you are ensuring that your loved ones, or your beneficiaries, will not be stuck with your debts. A life insurance policy statement contains the following information:

- Policy identification number
- Name of insured
- Death benefit amount
- Cash value
- Cost of the premium

GHL *GENERAL HOME LIFE*

Policy Anniversary Statement

Juan Ramirez
21 First Street
Smithville, Florida 55523

Policy number:	2–615–879
Date prepared:	May 18, 20--
Insured:	Juan Ramirez
Plan name:	Whole Life
Face amount:	$36,364
Premium:	$41.87 monthly
Issued:	June 23, 2003
Paid to:	June 23, 2016

This policy will provide the following benefits up to June 23, 2016, assuming premiums are paid to that date and no other changes occur.

	DEATH BENEFIT	*CASH VALUE*
Basic policy	$36,364.00	$4,253
Paid-up additions	$81.39	$7.82
Option term	$63,554.61	0.00
TOTAL	**$100,000.00**	**$4,260.82**

Key Points A life insurance policy provides a predetermined payment that the insurance company will make in the event of the death of the policy owner. This amount is called the death benefit. In addition, the policy also accumulates a cash value over time as the holder of the policy pays premiums. If the owner chooses to cancel the policy before death, he or she will receive the policy's cash value.

FIND the Solutions

Review Key Concepts

1. What is the yearly cost of this policy?
2. When was this policy issued or started?
3. How much will the policy pay upon Juan's death?
4. When does Juan's insurance coverage expire?
5. If Juan decides to cancel this policy, how much will the insurance company pay him?

Suicide Clause

Many insurance policies state that in the first two years of coverage, beneficiaries of someone who dies by suicide receive only the amount of the premiums paid. After two years from the date of death, beneficiaries may receive the full value of death benefits. However, some insurance policies will not provide benefits at all if a policyholder dies by suicide.

Riders to Life Insurance Policies

An insurance company can change the conditions of an insurance policy by adding a rider to it. A rider is a document attached to a policy that changes its terms by adding or excluding specified conditions or altering its benefits. Examples of riders include a waiver of premium disability benefit, an accidental death benefit, and a guaranteed insurability option.

Waiver of Premium Disability Benefit One type of rider is a waiver of premium disability benefit. This clause allows a policyholder to stop paying premiums if he or she is totally and permanently disabled before reaching a certain age, usually 60. The insurance company will continue to pay the premiums at its own expense so that the policy remains in force.

Accidental Death Benefit Another typical rider to life insurance policies is an accidental death benefit, sometimes called *double indemnity*. Double indemnity pays twice the value of the policy if the insured is killed in an accident. Again, the accident must occur before a certain age, generally 60 or 65. Experts counsel against adding this rider to your coverage. The benefit is expensive, and your chances of dying in an accident are slim.

Guaranteed Insurability Option A third important rider is a guaranteed insurability option. This rider allows you to buy a specified additional amount of life insurance at certain intervals without undergoing medical exams. This is a good option for people who anticipate needing more life insurance in the future.

Cost of Living Protection This special rider is designed to help prevent inflation from eroding, or reducing, the purchasing power of the protection that your policy provides. A *loss, reduction,* or *erosion of purchasing power* refers to the effect that inflation has on a fixed amount of money. As inflation increases a fixed amount of money will not buy as much in the future as it does today.

Insurance Needs

Before you buy any type of insurance, you should always consider a number of factors, such as your source of income, financial responsibilities, savings, and net worth. You need to regularly evaluate your insurance needs to determine if you have the right kind of coverage to support your personal financial plan.

After You Read

Connect Using the information provided in this chapter, what insurance plans would you choose to meet both your health and financial needs?

Review Key Concepts

1. **Describe** What are the four types of term insurance?
2. **Identify** What are the three life insurance policies other than term and whole life?
3. **List** Cite four riders that are common to life insurance policies.

Higher Order Thinking

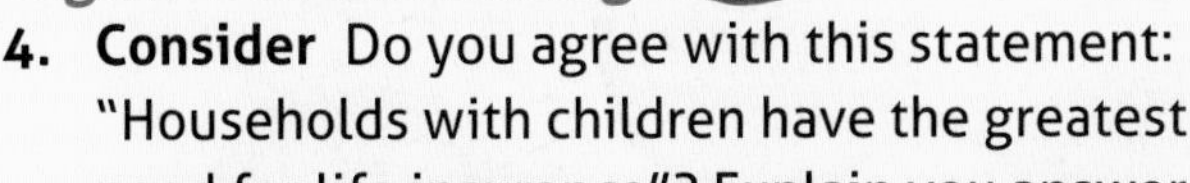

4. **Consider** Do you agree with this statement: "Households with children have the greatest need for life insurance"? Explain you answer.

21st Century Skills

5. **Analyze Media** There are companies that advertise life insurance policies for children. According to one ad, for as little as 11¢ a day, you can purchase a whole life insurance policy for a child. Identify a company that advertises children's life insurance. What are the benefits that the company places on such policies? Do you feel that these benefits are valid? Or do you agree with the text that people only need life insurance if someone else is dependent on their income or if they have a lot of debt? Write a summary of your evaluation and assessment.

Mathematics

6. **Universal Life** Terrance has decided to purchase a universal life insurance policy. On this policy, he pays $55 per month in premiums. Of this amount 25 percent is deposited into an investment account by the insurance company. After 15 years, how much money has Terrance paid in total premiums? How much money has been deposited into the investment account on his behalf? If Terrance earned 7 percent per year in the investment account, what is the balance in the account after 15 years? (Use the annuity formula provided below).

Math Concept **Calculate Benefits of Universal Life** To calculate the total investment value of a universal life insurance policy determine the total amount deposited into the investment account each year and add any returns earned on the account.

Starting Hint Calculate the balance of the investment account after "n" number of years using the following formula: balance = $P \times [((1 + r)^{(n+1)} - 1) / r] - P$, where P is the amount invested each year and r is the annual return percentage.

NCTM Problem Solving Build new mathematical knowledge through problem solving.

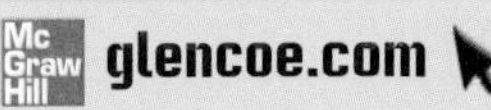

Check your answers.

Visual Summary

Health, Disability, and Life Insurance

Where to Purchase

When purchasing health insurance from a private organization, you should carefully consider the options available to you before deciding where to spend your money.

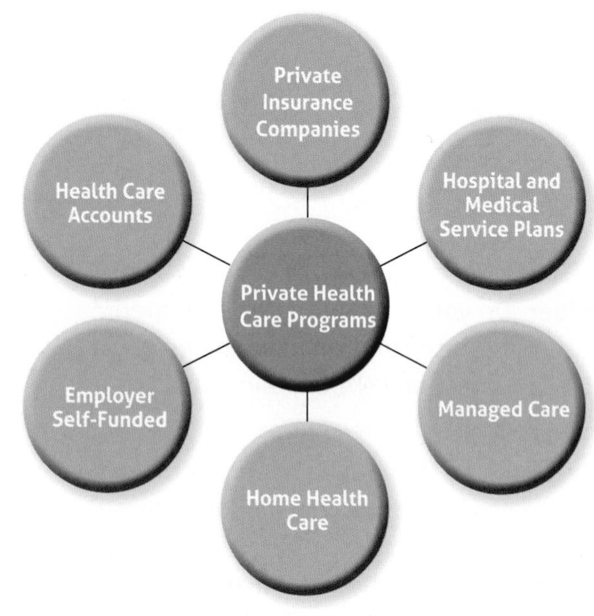

Insuring Income

You may choose to buy disability income insurance from a private company, but you may also receive disability income from other sources.

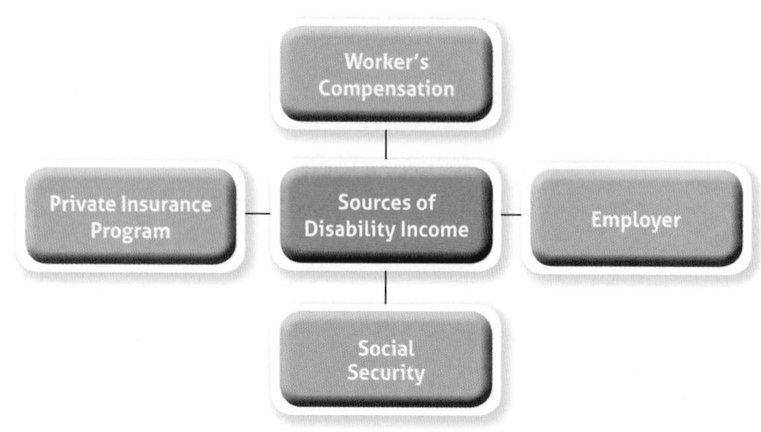

Try It!

Create a chart like the one shown to help organize and compare life insurance options.

Life Insurance	
Type	Description

Chapter Review and Assessment

CHAPTER REVIEW

Chapter Summary

- Health insurance is important for financial planning because it can help protect against the financial burden of illness or injury.
- Health insurance policies have certain similarities but can differ in terms of reimbursement versus indemnity, internal limits versus aggregate limits, deductibles and coinsurance, and out-of-pocket limits.
- Private health care plans are offered by private insurance companies and include: health maintenance organizations, preferred provider organizations, and employer self-funded plans.
- Some employers offer health care accounts in addition to a traditional health plan.
- Health care accounts can include a health savings account (HSA), health reimbursement account (HRA), or a flexible spending account (FSA).
- Government health care programs are Medicare and Medicaid.
- Disability insurance provides regular cash income for people who are unable to work due to pregnancy, a non-work-related accident, or illness.
- Sources of disability income are workers' compensation, an employer, Social Security, and private disability insurance.
- Types of life insurance policies include term insurance, whole life insurance, group life insurance, credit life insurance, and endowment life insurance.
- The key provisions in a life insurance policy include naming a beneficiary, an incontestability clause, a suicide clause, and policy riders.

Vocabulary Review

1. Create fill-in-the-blank sentences for each of these vocabulary terms. The sentences should contain enough information to help determine the missing term.

- health insurance
- coinsurance
- stop-loss
- co-payment
- Blue Cross
- Blue Shield
- managed care
- health maintenance organization (HMO)
- preferred provider organization (PPO)
- point-of-service (POS) plan
- Medicare
- Medicaid
- disability income insurance
- beneficiary (insurance)
- term insurance
- whole life insurance
- cash value
- endowment
- lapse
- board
- supplemental
- hospices
- valid
- suspend
- hardship
- provisions

Higher Order Thinking 

2. **Explain** What are some life changes that might prompt a change to your policy?
3. **Propose** Present two scenarios in which a person might need disability insurance.
4. **Consider** Jack found a job with a new company but will not be eligible for benefits for a few months. Why might he choose COBRA rather than buying an individual insurance policy?
5. **Appraise** Having a coinsurance provision can force you to pay more out-of-pocket. Assess why a policyholder might want a coinsurance provision.
6. **Evaluate** Are government health care plans necessary? Why or Why not?
7. **Assess** How can health information resources help keep health insurance costs down?
8. **Judge** Some insurers will pay you disability income only when you are unable to work at any job. Is this fair? Why or why not?
9. **Defend** Defend the right of life insurers to include a suicide clause.

College and Career Readiness

Science

10. HMOs Health maintenance organizations are based on the idea that preventive services will minimize future medical problems thus saving money. However, many people argue that while preventive services are beneficial, it does not actually save money.

Procedure Conduct research on the cost of preventive medicine and how it might affect the cost of medical care and health insurance.

Analysis Based on your findings, do you think preventive medicine can save money? Write a paragraph to share your opinion, using your research to support your conclusion.

NSES F Develop understanding of personal and community health; population growth; natural resources; environmental quality; natural and human-induced hazards; science and technology in local, national, and global challenges.

Mathematics

11. Which Policy Should I Choose? Calvin is choosing between two types of life insurance policies. The first is a 20-year term policy for $250,000 worth of insurance. The monthly premiums are $17 and the cash value at the end of the term will be $0. The second type is a whole life policy for the same amount of coverage. The monthly premiums are $92 and the cash value after 20 years is $26,000. What is the net income/expense after 20 years for the whole life policy? Which policy would you choose and why?

Math Concept **Calculate Benefits** Calculate the income/expense of a life insurance policy by subtracting the total premiums paid from the cash value at the end of the term.

Starting Hint Calculate the total expense incurred due to payment of premiums over the term of the whole life insurance policy by first identifying the monthly premium expense. Multiply this figure by 12 months to attain the annual expenditure and then multiply the result by the number of years in the term.

NCTM Connections Communicate their mathematical thinking coherently and clearly to peers, teachers, and others.

English Language Arts

12. FSAs FSAs are generally offered in addition to traditional health care insurance plans. Employees contribute money to their FSA and can then use that money for health care expenses not covered by their insurance, including co-payments, prescriptions, and deductibles. Some employers will even contribute money to match the employee's donation up to a certain dollar amount. Conduct research to learn more about the benefits and uses of a health care FSA. Design a brochure to promote an FSA to a company's employees.

NCTE 8 Use information resources to gather information and create and communicate knowledge.

Ethics

13. Health Care Costs Many health insurance plans pay an agreed-upon rate for certain services or they pay a set amount and the policyholder must pay the difference. Some doctors will accept the amount paid even if it is less. Some doctors take advantage of patients without insurance by charging more for their services claiming they are losing money on Medicare patients and must charge more of the uninsured. Do you think this is fair? Should the government regulate what doctors can charge? Write a paragraph to explain your reasoning.

Real-World Applications

14. Individual Health Insurance Bill is 22 years old and single. He currently works full-time and is a part-time graduate student. His job currently does not offer a health insurance plan so he wants to purchase individual health insurance. Use online resources to locate two companies offering basic health insurance coverage. Compare health insurance plans from the two companies, including benefits, co-payments, deductibles, and cost. Create a chart or spreadsheet to help you compare the two plans side-by-side. Based on your findings, which plan would you recommend to Bill? Write a letter to Bill explaining your recommendation.

Comparing Life Insurance

Sean Richards is investigating the cost of life insurance. He is 28 years old, married, and has two children. Sean contacted two reputable insurance companies and based his comparison on $100,000 worth of insurance. Sean chose the 20-year decreasing term insurance because of the low cost, even though he cannot convert it into cash at a future date. He purchased his policy with Company B.

Type of Policy	Company A	Company B
20-year decreasing term insurance $100,000		
Monthly premium	$14.00	$8.25
Total premiums for 20 years	$3,360.00	$1,980.00
Cash value in 20 years	none	none
Whole life insurance (limited payment) $100,000		
Monthly premium	$82.00	$62.60
Total premiums for 20 years	$19,280.00	$15,024.00
Cash value in 20 years	$25,000.00	$21,243.00

Compare

Follow Sean's chart and on a separate sheet of paper create your own chart to compare life insurance rates. Using the Internet, or by visiting, calling, or writing, get quotes from two different insurance companies. Base the quote on (1) a 20-year decreasing term insurance policy for $100,000 and (2) a whole life (limited payment) insurance policy for $100,000. Use your own age.

CHAPTER 24

Retirement and Estate Planning

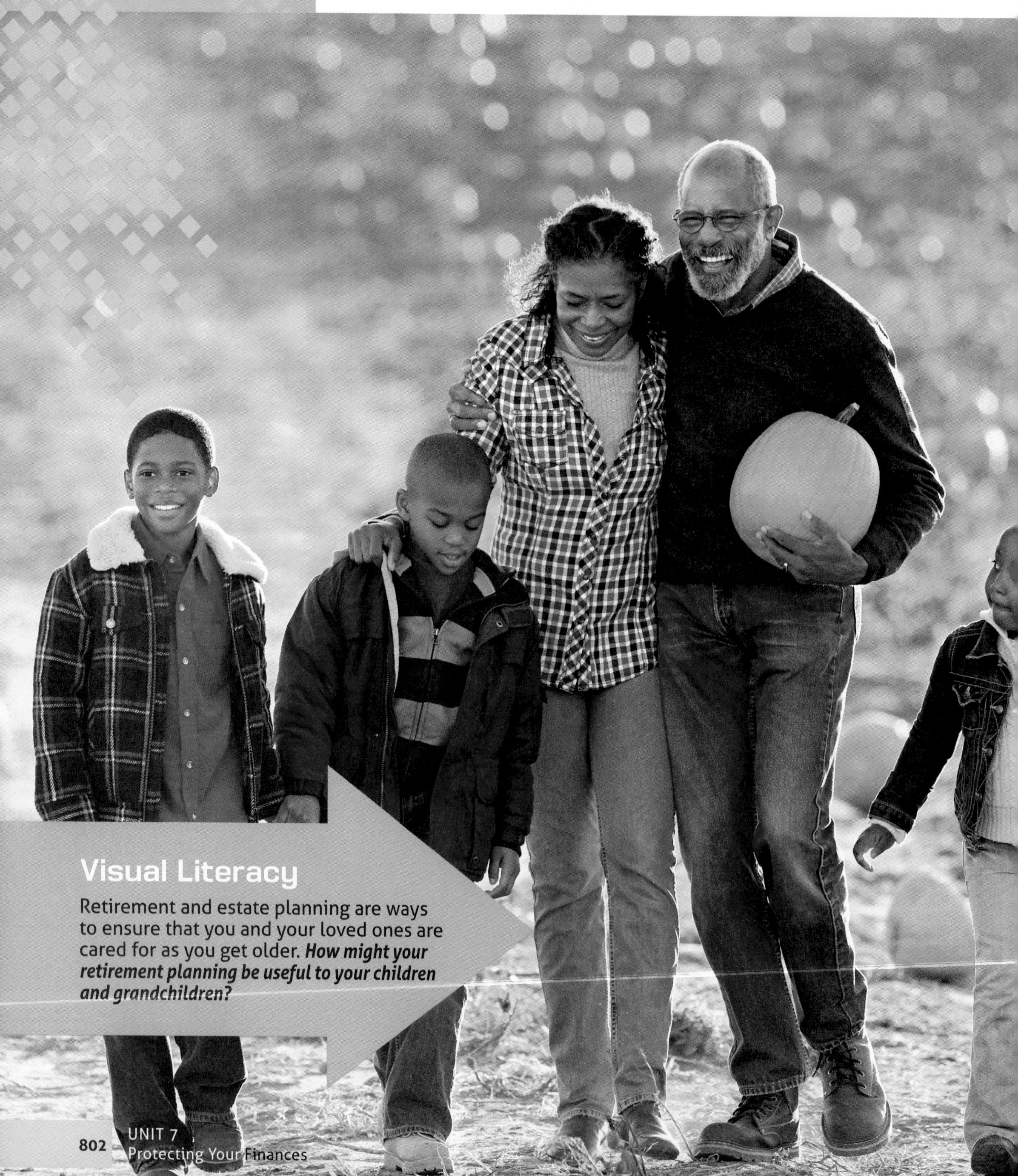

Visual Literacy

Retirement and estate planning are ways to ensure that you and your loved ones are cared for as you get older. ***How might your retirement planning be useful to your children and grandchildren?***

Discovery Project

Planning for Retirement

Key Question

Why is it important to start thinking about your retirement plans now?

Project Goal

It is never too early to start planning for retirement. Retirement planning means more than just putting a few dollars in savings though. The first step is to think about the lifestyle you want when you retire. This will help you determine how much income you will need to achieve your goals. You will need to consider what your living expenses will be, including housing, food, transportation, medical care, and more. Once you have determined your expenses, you will need to evaluate all the possible sources of income. Think about the life you expect to have when you retire, and use that to help you develop a financial analysis. Though you will not know the dollar amounts now, you can list all the assets and liabilities you expect to have when you near retirement age.

Ask Yourself...

- *Do you plan to own a home when you retire or rent?*
- *What percentage of your wages will you be willing to save for retirement?*
- *Will you purchase life insurance or annuities?*
- *Will you set up a personal retirement account, such as an IRA?*
- *Will an employer pension plan be an important benefit to look for when finding a job?*

Apply Technology Effectively

How can you use the Internet to manage your retirement accounts?

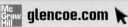

glencoe.com

Evaluate Download an assessment rubric.

THE BIG IDEA

Retirement and estate planning allow you to set the terms for your later years of life.

ASK STANDARD &POOR'S

Will Power

Q *My parents do not have a lot of money, so is it really that important for them to write up a will?*

A Even if your parents do not have a lot of money, they should have a will. If they die without a will, their state of residence will step in and control how their estate is distributed. It costs somewhere between $200 and $350 to have an attorney draft a will. The peace of mind it will provide your parents will be worth the cost.

Writing Activity

Suppose you were to write up a will now. Consider all of your possessions and any bank accounts you might have. Write an instructional paragraph detailing how to create a will and what factors to consider.

Reading Guide

Before You Read

The Essential Question At what age should people begin their retirement and estate planning?

Main Idea

Retirement planning will allow you to save or invest enough money to live comfortably during retirement. There are many types of retirement plans to meet individual needs. Different types of wills and trusts will protect your financial interests and those of your family.

Content Vocabulary

- assisted-living facility (ALF)
- defined-contribution plan
- 401(k) plan
- vesting
- defined-benefit plan
- individual retirement account (IRA)
- Keogh plan
- annuity (insurance)
- heirs
- estate
- estate planning
- beneficiary (estate)
- will
- intestate
- trust
- probate
- executor
- guardian
- codicil
- living will
- power of attorney

Academic Vocabulary

You will see these words in your reading and on your tests.

- misconceptions
- adjustments
- roll over
- distributions
- declaration
- disclaim

Graphic Organizer

Before you read this chapter, create a checklist like the one shown. As you read, look for the legal documents that will be needed to settle your estate.

Legal Documents for Estate Planning
1.
2.
3.
4.
5.
6.
7.
8.
9.
10.
11.

glencoe.com  Print this Organizer.

Standards

Academic

Mathematics

NCTM Data Analysis and Probability Develop and evaluate inferences and predictions that are based on data.
NCTM Connections Recognize and apply mathematics in contexts outside of mathematics.
NCTM Connections Understand how mathematical ideas interconnect and build on one another to produce a coherent whole.

English Language Arts

NCTE 3 Apply strategies to interpret texts.
NCTE 4 Use written language to communicate effectively.
NCTE 12 Use language to accomplish individual purposes.

Social Studies

NCSS I A Analyze and explain the ways groups, societies, and cultures address human needs and concerns.

NCTM *National Council of Teachers of Mathematics*
NCTE *National Council of Teachers of English*
NCSS *National Council for the Social Studies*
NSES *National Science Education Standards*

Common Core

Reading Read closely to determine what the text says explicitly and to make logical inferences from it; cite specific textual evidence when writing or speaking to support conclusions drawn from the text.
Writing Write informative/explanatory texts to examine and convey complex ideas and information clearly and accurately through the effective selection, organization, and analysis of content.

Planning for Retirement

What factors should you consider when planning for retirement?

A recent poll from Harris Interactive reported that 95 percent of people ages 55 to 64 years old plan to do at least some work after they have retired. Another survey reported that future retirees expected to continue to learn, try new things, and pursue new hobbies and interests. Someday, when you retire, you too may desire an active life.

Your retirement years may seem a long way off right now. You are still in high school, and after you graduate, you will probably work for many years. However, it is never too early to start planning for retirement. Planning can help you cope with sudden changes that may occur in your life, and it can give you a sense of control over your future. Planning can also help make the retirement years more comfortable.

If you have not done any research on the subject of retirement, you may have some **misconceptions,** or wrong ideas, about the "golden years." Here are some myths about retirement:

- You have plenty of time to start saving for retirement.
- Saving a small amount of money will not help.
- You will spend less money when you retire.
- Your retirement will last about 15 years.
- You can depend on Social Security and a company pension plan to pay your basic living expenses.
- Your pension benefits will increase to keep pace with inflation.
- Your employer's health insurance plan and Medicare will cover all your medical expenses.

Some of these statements may have been true in the past, but they are no longer true today. You may live for many years after you retire. If you want your retirement to be a happy and comfortable time of your life, you will need enough money to suit your lifestyle. That is why you should start planning and saving as early as possible. Saving now for the future requires tackling the trade-offs between spending and saving. It is never too late to start saving for retirement, but the sooner you start, the better off you will be.

Suppose that you want to have at least $1 million when you retire at age 65. If you start saving at age 25, you can meet that goal by putting about $127 per month into investment funds that grow at a rate of about 11 percent each year. If you wait to begin saving until age 50, the monthly amount to achieve that goal skyrockets to $2,244.

Section Objectives

- **Explain** the importance of retirement planning.
- **Identify** retirement living costs and housing needs.

As You Read

Predict When do you think you should begin planning for your retirement?

Setting Long-Range Goals

As you think about your retirement years, consider your long-range goals. What does retirement mean to you? Maybe it will be a time to stop working and to relax. Perhaps you imagine traveling the world, developing a hobby, or starting a second career. Ask yourself: Where do you want to live after you retire? What type of lifestyle would you like to have? Then analyze your current financial situation to determine what you need to do to reach your long-range goals.

Conducting a Financial Analysis

The checklist in **Figure 1** is an example of how you might analyze your financial assets and liabilities. Remember, an asset is any item of value that you own, including cash, property, personal possessions, and investments. This includes cash in checking and savings accounts, a house, a car, a television, and so on. It also includes the current value of any stocks, bonds, other investments, life insurance policies, and pension funds.

Your liabilities are the debts you owe, including the balance on an automobile loan, credit card balances, other loans, and unpaid taxes. If you subtract your liabilities from your assets, you get your net worth. Ideally, your net worth should increase each year.

FIGURE 1 **Assets, Liabilities, and Net Worth**

Know Your Worth You can calculate your net worth by subtracting your total liabilities from your total assets. *What are your liabilities?*

Assets:	
Cash:	
Checking account	$ 800
Savings account	4,500
Investments:	
U.S. Savings Bonds (current cash-in value)	5,000
Stocks, mutual funds	4,500
Life insurance:	
Cash value, accumulated dividends	10,000
Company pension rights:	
Accrued pension benefit	20,000
Property:	
House (resale value)	50,000
Furniture and appliances	8,000
Collections and jewelry	2,000
Automobile	3,000
Other:	
Loan to brother	1,000
Gross assets	$108,800

Liabilities:	
Current unpaid bills	$ 600
Home mortgage (remaining balance)	9,700
Auto loan	1,200
Property taxes	1,100
Home improvement loan	3,700
Total liabilities	$16,300

Net worth:

Assets	– Liabilities	=	Net Worth
$108,800	– $16,300	=	$92,500

Retirement Rewards Many people view retirement as a reward for a life lived well and an opportunity to travel and explore new hobbies. *What are some things you might like to do when you retire?*

Reviewing Assets

Review your assets on a regular basis. You may need to make **adjustments** (changes) in your saving, spending, and investments to stay on track with your goal. As you review your assets, consider the following factors: housing, life insurance, savings, and investments. Each asset will have an important effect on your retirement income.

Housing A house can be your most valuable asset. However, if you buy a home with large mortgage payments, you may be unable to save money for retirement. In that case, you might consider buying a smaller, less expensive place to live. A smaller house is usually easier and less expensive to maintain. You can use the money you save by having lower payments to increase your retirement fund.

Life Insurance At some point in the future, you might buy life insurance to provide for your loved ones. If you have children, life insurance can provide financial support in case you die while they are still young. As you near retirement, though, your children will probably be self-sufficient. When that time comes, you might reduce your premium payments by decreasing your life insurance coverage. This would give you extra money for living expenses or investments.

Other Investments When you review your assets, also evaluate any other investments you have. When you originally chose those investments, you may have been more interested in making your money grow over time than in getting a quick return. When you are ready to retire, you may want to use the income from those investments to cover living expenses.

 **Reading Check**

Identify What are four assets that you should review on a regular basis?

Retirement Living Expenses

What living expenses should you consider when planning for retirement?

When planning for retirement, estimate how much money you will need to live comfortably during your retirement years. You cannot predict exactly how much money you will need, but you can estimate the expense of your basic needs. To do this, think about how your spending patterns and living situation might change.

For example, when you are retired, you may spend more money on recreation, health insurance, and medical care than you will as a young adult. At the same time, you may spend less money on transportation and clothing. Your federal income taxes may be lower as well. Also, some income from various retirement plans may be taxed at a lower rate or not at all. **Figure 2** provides an example of retirement expenses. To make a realistic comparison, list your major spending categories, starting with fixed expenses. Then list your variable expenses as well as miscellaneous expenses such as medical expenses and vacation expenses. Be sure to have an emergency fund for unexpected expenses. Remember to estimate high in your calculations.

FIGURE 2 **Expenses for Older Households (65 + years)**

Cost of Retirement Part of financial planning is estimating how much money you will need to live once you retire. *Based on the graph, how much money would an older household spend on housing if their annual income was $20,000?*

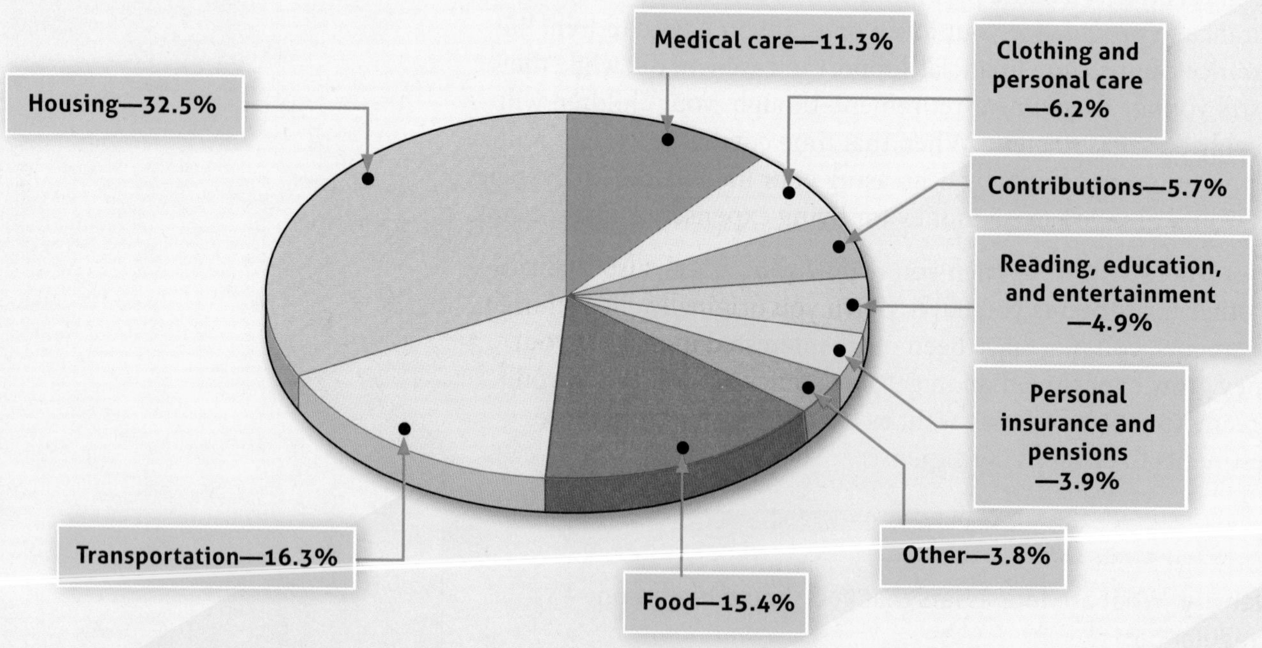

FIGURE 3 Inflation Over Time

Value of Money Because of inflation, a dollar will not buy as much in the future as it does today. *Why should you estimate high when calculating the future price of goods?*

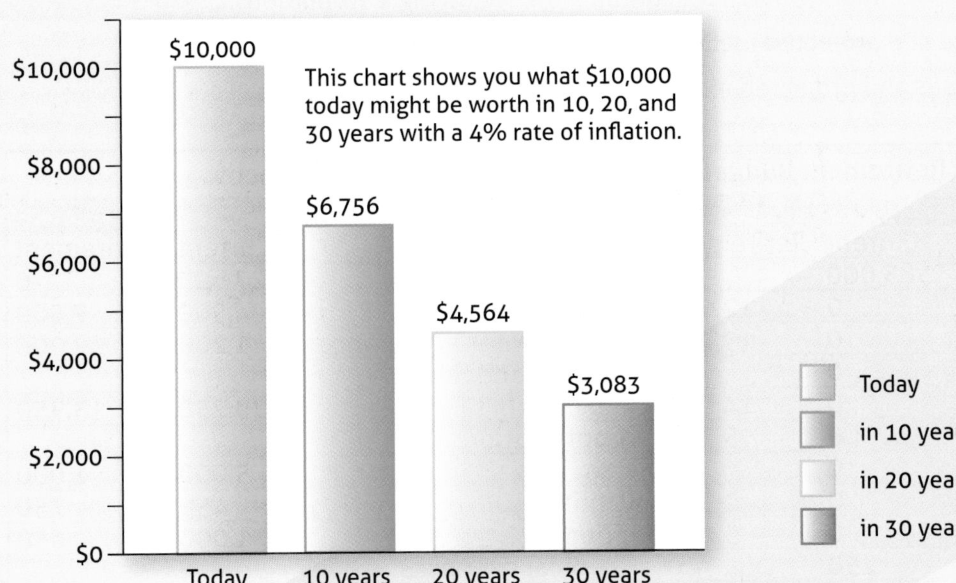

Remember to take inflation into account. Estimate high when calculating how much the prices of goods and services will rise by the time you retire. (See **Figure 3.**) Even a 3 percent rate of inflation will cause prices to double every 24 years. Also, plan for emergencies as you consider future retirement living expenses.

Reading Check

Recall What are some areas in which you might increase spending after retirement?

Retirement Housing

What factors should you consider regarding housing needs during retirement?

The place where you live can have a significant impact on your financial needs. In the years before retirement, use vacations to explore areas where you might want to settle. If you find a place you like, go there at different times of the year. That way, you will be able to experience the climate and environment. Meet people who live in the area and learn about activities, transportation, and taxes.

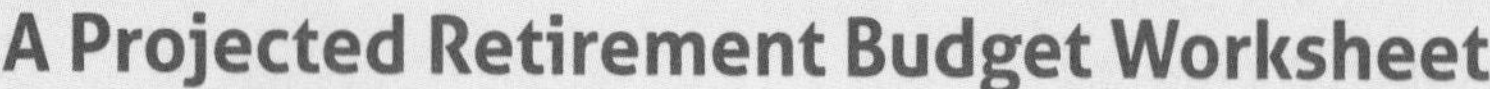

Document Detective

A Projected Retirement Budget Worksheet

The best time to plan for your retirement is when you are young. You will need to save money each month during your working career to provide you with enough money to live on when you stop working. A projected retirement budget worksheet contains the following information:

- Your current annual income and projected income
- Your current annual expenses and projected expenses

Projected Retirement Budget Worksheet —Robert & Emily Rathcliff

Annual Income	Current	Retirement	**Annual Expenses**	Current	Retirement
Wages	$85,000	$0	Mortgage/rent	$27,600	0
Pension	0	12,000	Real estate taxes	4,500	7,500
Social Security	0	19,200	Homeowner's insurance	1,200	2,000
Rental income	0	0	Income and Social Security taxes	29,750	13,750
IRAs	0	14,000	Contributions to savings	5,000	1,000
Annuities	0	5,000	Utilities	450	750
Bond interest	0	0	Food	1,000	650
Stock dividends	0	2,300	Medical expenses insurance	750	3500
Mutual fund dividends	0	3,210	Life insurance	850	0
Money market interest	250	0	Vehicle payments	1,500	750
Other	0	0	Vehicle insurance	1,400	800
Total Income	**$85,250**	**$55,710**	Vehicle maintenance and gasoline	2,500	1,500
			Charitable contributions	1,000	1,000
			Gifts	1,500	1,000
			Travel/entertainment	5,000	15,000
			Loans/credit cards	1,200	500
			Other	0	0
			Total Expenses	**$85,200**	**$49,700**
			Total Income Minus Expenses	**$50**	**$6,010**

Key Points A Projected Retirement Budget Worksheet helps you calculate the difference between your projected retirement income and your projected expenses. This worksheet will help you determine how much money you will need to save for retirement years.

FIND the Solutions

Review Key Concepts

1. What are the current annual expenses?
2. Why would they not list a mortgage or rent payment as an expense in retirement?
3. Why might food and vehicle expenses go down when they retire?
4. Why might the Rathcliffs not have a life insurance expense in retirement?
5. Do they have enough projected income?

Retirement Relocation Pitfalls

Consider the downside of moving to a new location. People sometimes find themselves stuck in a place they really do not like. Some retirees find they miss their children, grandchildren, and friends and relatives left behind. Other retired people move to the location of their dreams and discover they have made a mistake financially.

Researching Locations Here are some tips from specialists on how to research taxes and other costs before moving to a new area:

- Contact the local chamber of commerce for details on area property taxes and the local economy.
- Contact the state tax department to research income, sales, inheritance taxes, and exemptions for retirees.
- Read the Sunday edition of the local newspaper of the town or city you are considering.
- Check with local utility companies to estimate energy costs.
- Visit the area in different seasons and talk to local residents about the cost of living there.
- If you plan to buy a home, take time and rent a home first.

Types of Housing

Even if you do not move to a new location, housing needs may change during retirement. Many retirees want a home that is easy and inexpensive to maintain, such as a smaller house, a condominium, or an apartment. Having access to public transportation, stores, and recreation areas is also important. **Figure 4** presents several options.

A great majority of people prefer to grow old in their own homes in their own communities. Recognizing this trend, building suppliers offer everything from lever door handles to faucets that turn on automatically when you put your hand beneath the spout. Remodeling to accommodate aging homeowners is creating a demand for these products. In addition, contractors are building universal design homes from scratch that can accommodate people who use wheelchairs and walkers or those who simply want more convenience.

Many elderly people move into assisted-living facilities during their retirement years. An **assisted-living facility (ALF)** is a residence complex that provides personal and medical services for the elderly. Assisted-living facilities offer everything from minimal services to full, continuous nursing care. They may vary greatly in quality, but ALFs are increasingly popular with elderly retirees, some of whom are no longer able to live alone and care for themselves.

With the many choices available, determining where to live in retirement is itself a time-consuming job. Whatever retirement housing option you choose, make sure you know what you are signing and understand what you are buying.

FIGURE 4 Retirement Housing Options

No Place Like Home Some people choose to move to a new home once they retire while others enjoy the home that they have already established. *Why might a retired person decide to move in with their adult children?*

Housing options for retirement are based on personal, financial, and medical factors. The goal of most retirees is to have comfortable and affordable housing that meets their particular needs.

1 **Most retired people** decide to remain where they are and continue living in their own homes.

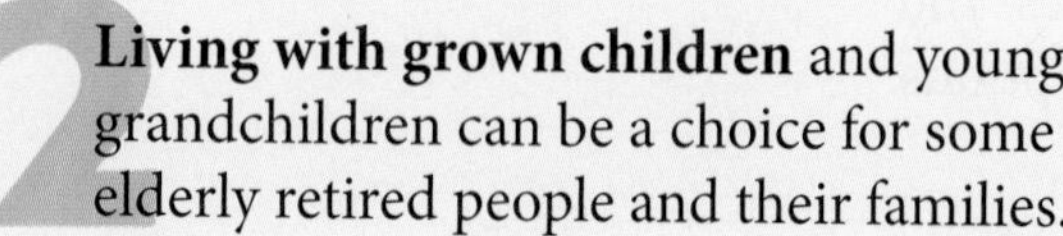

2 **Living with grown children** and young grandchildren can be a choice for some elderly retired people and their families.

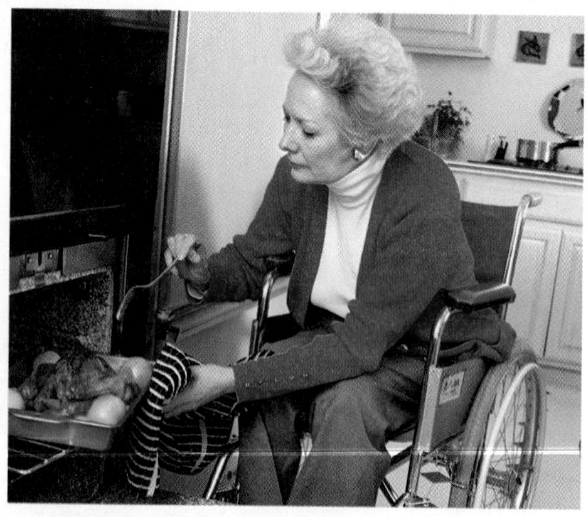

3 **For retired people with disabilities,** a universal design home built with special features, such as extra-wide doors, lower appliances, and automatic faucets, can be both appealing and practical. These homes help people with disabilities to maintain their independence.

Assessment

Review Key Concepts

1. **Identify** What three steps can you take to help you plan for retirement?
2. **List** Name four areas that should be included when estimating retirement expenses.
3. **Describe** What are some of the pitfalls of relocating after retirement?

Higher Order Thinking H.O.T.

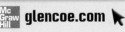

4. **Assess** One tip for researching a location before moving is to read the Sunday edition of the local newspaper. Assess how this action might help avoid a retirement pitfall.

English Language Arts

5. **Retirement Dreams** Knowing what type of lifestyle you want when you retire is the first step toward successful retirement planning. You must set some long-term goals in order to take the necessary steps to achieve them. Often visual images can help remind you of your goals and motivate you to achieve them. Imagine the type of life you would like to have when you retire. Combine pictures and words to create a collage that expresses your thoughts and feelings about your retirement dreams.

NCTE 12 Use language to accomplish individual purposes.

Mathematics

6. **Expenses for Households** Tom and Carol are retired and have an annual income of $73,000. They are trying to track their budget and need to identify how they spend their money. They have asked you to help them identify some of their expenditures. Refer to the chart in **Figure 2** which shows a breakout of the percentage of income spent on specific expenses for older households 65 years of age or older. Provide an estimate of how much of their annual salary Tom and Carol spend on medical care and housing.

Math Concept **Calculate Estimates for Household Spending** To calculate an estimate of the annual household income spent on a specific category find the estimated percentage spent for each category and multiply the percentage by the annual income.

Starting Hint Determine the estimated amount of annual salary spent on housing by identifying the percentage of expenditure from the chart in **Figure 2** and multiplying this percentage by the annual income.

NCTM Data Analysis and Probability Develop and evaluate inferences and predictions that are based on data.

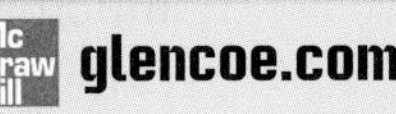

Check your answers.

Section Objectives

- **Describe** the role of Social Security in planning for retirement.
- **Discuss** the benefits offered by employer pension plans.
- **Explain** various personal retirement plans.

As You Read

Discover As you learn about retirement plans, determine which type of IRA seems more flexible—traditional or Roth.

Public Pension Plans

Who receives benefits under Social Security?

Remember, a pension plan is a retirement plan that is funded, at least in part, by an employer. Public pension plans are established by states and municipalities. Social Security is a public pension plan established by the United States government in 1935. The government agency that manages the program is called the Social Security Administration.

Social Security

Social Security is an important source of retirement income for many Americans. The program covers 97 percent of all workers, and almost one out of every six Americans currently collects some form of Social Security benefit. Social Security is a package of protection that provides benefits to retirees, survivors, and disabled persons. However, you should not rely solely on Social Security to cover all of your retirement expenses. Social Security was not designed to provide 100 percent of retirement income. In addition, current and future revisions to the program may reduce retirement benefits in years to come.

Who Is Eligible The amount of Social Security retirement benefits you receive is based on your earnings over the years. The more you earn, the greater your benefits will be, up to a maximum amount.

Each year the Social Security Administration will send you a history of your earnings and an estimate of your future monthly benefits. The statement includes an estimate, in today's dollars, of how much you would get each month if you retired at different ages. For example, your statement might list benefits for retirement at age 62, 67, and 70, based on the year you were born, your earnings to date, and your projected future earnings.

To qualify for retirement benefits, you must earn a certain number of credits. These credits are based on the length of time you work and pay Social Security tax, or contributions, on your earnings. Your credits are calculated on a quarterly basis. The number of quarters needed to qualify depends on your year of birth. For example, people born after 1928 need at least 40 quarters to qualify for benefits.

Dependent Eligibility Certain dependents of a worker may also receive benefits under the Social Security program. They include a spouse age 62 or older; unmarried children under 18 (or under 19 if they are full-time students no higher than grade 12); and unmarried individuals with disabilities aged 18 or older. Widows and widowers can receive Social Security benefits before age 62.

Social Security Retirement Benefits Most people can begin collecting Social Security retirement benefits at age 62. However, the monthly amount at age 62 is less than it would be if the person waited until full retirement age. This initial amount becomes the permanent base amount.

In the past, people could receive full retirement benefits at age 65. However, the full retirement age is being increased in gradual steps. For people born in 1960 and later, the full retirement age is 67. If you postpone applying for benefits when you are eligible, your monthly payment amount will increase slightly for each year you wait, but only up to age 70.

Social Security Information For more information about Social Security, you can visit the Social Security Web site. It provides access to forms and publications and gives links to other valuable information. To learn more about the taxability of Social Security benefits, contact the Internal Revenue Service (IRS) and ask for Publication 554, Older Americans' Tax Guide, and Publication 915, Social Security and Equivalent Railroad Retirement Benefits. These publications can also be found on the IRS Web site.

Other Public Pension Plans

Besides Social Security, the federal government provides other special retirement plans for federal government workers and railroad employees. These employees are not covered by Social Security. The Veterans Administration provides pensions for survivors of people who died while serving in the armed forces. It also offers disability pensions for eligible veterans. In addition, many state and local governments provide retirement plans for their employees.

Reading Check

Recall What are Social Security benefit credits based on?

Social Security Benefits
The amount of Social Security benefits will vary from person to person, as well as the eligible age to begin receiving them. *On what is the amount of your benefits based?*

Careers That Count!

Mitchell Cantor • Estate Planner

Estate planning is more than writing a will. It also involves financial, tax, medical, and business planning. It is not a one-time event—it is a dynamic process, and people should adjust their estate plans as needed to reflect changes in assets, relationships, health, and laws. Under the direction of the attorney responsible for estate administration, I work as an estate planner to help people through this process. I help people determine how their assets will be distributed after death. I also help them decide how their assets and health care will be managed if they become unable to care for themselves. I educate beneficiaries about procedural and tax deadlines, and I ensure compliance with the deadlines. I also calculate debts, expenses, taxes, and cash needs. Under some circumstances, I may need to reconcile conflicts between beneficiaries or family members. Every day, I balance good judgment, tact, and financial information to create the best outcome for people in difficult situations.

EXPLORE CAREERS

Visit the Web site of the U.S. Department of Labor's Bureau of Labor Statistics to obtain information about a career as an estate planner.

1. Considering the various tasks of an estate planner, why is discretion a necessary personal trait?
2. Research online postings for estate planners. For what qualifications, both preferred and required, are companies searching?

Skills	Education	Career Path
Writing, math, interpersonal, organizational, problem-solving, analytical, and multitasking skills	Bachelor's degree in accounting, finance, economics, business, or law; courses in estate planning, and risk management	Estate planners can become financial advisors, estate lawyers, investment advisors, and real estate asset managers.

glencoe.com

Activity Download a Career Exploration Activity.

Employer Pension Plans

What is one of the benefits of having an employer pension plan?

Another possible source of retirement income is an employer pension plan offered by the company for which you work. With this type of plan, your employer contributes to your retirement benefits, and sometimes you contribute, too. These contributions and their earnings remain tax-deferred until you withdraw them during retirement.

Private employer pension plans vary. If the company you work for offers one, find out what benefits you will receive and when you will become eligible to receive those benefits. You should start participating in the program as soon as possible. Most employer plans are one of two basic types: defined-contribution plans or defined-benefit plans.

Defined-Contribution Plan

A **defined-contribution plan,** sometimes called an individual account plan, is an individual account for each employee. The employer contributes a specific amount to the account annually. This type of retirement plan does not guarantee any particular benefit. When you retire and become eligible for benefits, you receive the total amount of funds (including investment earnings) that is in your account. Several types of defined-contribution plans exist.

Money-Purchase Plans With a money-purchase plan, your employer promises to set aside a certain amount of money for you each year. That amount may be a percentage of your earnings.

Stock Bonus Plans Under a stock bonus plan, your employer's contribution is used to buy stock in the company for you. The stock is held in trust until you retire. Then you can keep or sell your shares.

Profit-Sharing Plans Under a profit-sharing plan, your employer's contribution depends on the company's profits each year.

401(k) Plans A **401(k) plan,** or salary-reduction plan, is a type of retirement savings plan funded by a portion of your salary that is deducted from your gross paycheck and placed in a special account. Many employers match their employees' 401(k) contributions up to a specific dollar amount or percentage of salary.

The funds in 401(k) plans can be invested in stocks, bonds, and mutual funds. As a result, you can accumulate a significant amount of money in this type of account if you begin contributing to it early in your career. Also, the money in your 401(k) plan is tax-deferred.

403(b) Plans If you are employed by a tax-exempt institution, such as a hospital or a nonprofit organization, the salary-reduction plan is called a Section 403(b) plan. The funds in this plan are also tax-deferred. The 401(k) and 403(b) plans are known as tax-sheltered annuity (TSA) plans. The amount that can be contributed each year to 401(k) and 403(b) plans is limited by law, as is the amount of contributions to other types of defined-contribution plans.

Vesting Employee contributions to a pension plan belong to you, the employee, regardless of the amount of time that you are with a particular employer. But what happens to the contributions that the employer has made to your account if you change jobs and move to another company? One of the most important aspects of these plans is vesting. **Vesting** is the right of an employee to keep the company's contributions from company-sponsored plans, such as pensions, even if the employee no longer works for that employer. Vesting occurs at different points in time, depending on company policy. After a certain number of years with a company, you become fully vested, or entitled to receive 100 percent of the company's contributions to the plan on your behalf. Under some plans, vesting may occur in stages. For example, you might receive 20 percent of your benefits after three years and gain another 20 percent each year until you are fully vested.

Time to Save

Saving money in a savings or retirement account is the simplest way to build assets for retirement. Starting to save while you are young may even allow early retirement. However, if you have 30 or 40 years until retirement, every year without saving can subtract from one to five years off retirement.

Concept Application

At what age will you want to retire?

Defined-Benefit Plan

A **defined-benefit plan** is a retirement plan that specifies the benefits an employee will receive at retirement age, based on total earnings and years on the job. The plan does not specify how much the employer must contribute each year. Instead, your employer's contributions are based on how much money the fund will need for each participant in the plan who retires. If the fund is inadequate, the employer will have to make additional contributions.

Moving to Another Plan

Some pension plans allow "portability," which means that you can carry earned benefits from one pension plan to another when you change jobs. Workers are also protected by the Employee Retirement Income Security Act of 1974 (ERISA), which sets minimum standards for pension plans. Under this act, the federal government insures part of the payments promised by defined-benefit plans.

Reading Check

List What are five types of defined-contribution plans?

Personal Retirement Plans

What is the biggest benefit of an IRA?

In addition to employer plans, many people have personal retirement plans. Such plans are especially important to self-employed people and workers not covered by employer pension plans. Examples are individual retirement accounts (IRAs) and Keogh accounts.

Individual Retirement Accounts

An **individual retirement account (IRA)** is a special account in which a person saves a portion of income for retirement. **Figure 5** summarizes the various types of IRAs.

Regular IRA A regular IRA, which is a traditional or classic IRA, allows you to make annual contributions until age 70½. As of 2010 a person under 50 years old can contribute up to $5,000 per year. A person 50 years old and over can contribute $6,000 per year. Depending on your tax filing status and income, the contribution may be fully or partially tax-deductible. The tax deductibility also depends on whether you belong to an employer-provided retirement plan.

Roth IRA Annual contributions to a Roth IRA are not tax-deductible, but the earnings are tax-free. You may contribute the same amounts as allowed for a regular IRA if you are a single taxpayer with an adjusted gross income (AGI) of less than $95,000. For married couples, the combined AGI must be less than $150,000.

You can continue to make annual contributions to a Roth IRA even after age 70½. If you have a Roth IRA, you can withdraw money from the account without paying taxes or penalties after five years if you are at least 59½ years old or if you are using the money to help buy your first home. You may convert a regular IRA to a Roth IRA. Depending on your situation, one type of account may be better for you than the other.

Simplified Employee Pension (SEP) Plan A Simplified Employee Pension (SEP) plan, also known as a *SEP-IRA*, is an individual retirement account that is ideal for small businesses or for self-employed individuals. For a small-business SEP-IRA, each employee sets up an IRA account at a bank or other financial institution. Then the employer makes an annual contribution up to a maximum set by law. The employees' contributions, which can vary from year to year, are fully tax-deductible, and earnings are tax-deferred. The SEP-IRA for a self-employed individual works much the same way. An individual could contribute up to $42,000 a year in 2005. The limits increase yearly until 2010.

Spousal IRA You can make contributions to a spousal IRA on behalf of your nonworking spouse if you file a joint tax return. The contributions are the same as for the traditional and Roth IRAs. This contribution may be fully or partially tax-deductible depending on your income. This also depends on whether you belong to an employer-provided retirement plan.

Rollover IRA A rollover IRA is a traditional IRA that allows **roll over,** or transfer, of all or a portion of your taxable distribution from one retirement plan to another IRA without paying taxes on it.

Education IRA An Education IRA, also known as a *Coverdell Education Savings Account*, is a special IRA with certain restrictions. It allows individuals to contribute up to $2,000 per year toward the education of any individual under age 18. The contributions are not tax-deductible, but they do provide tax-free distributions for education expenses.

Even if you are covered by another type of pension plan, you can make IRA contributions that are not tax-deductible. All of the income your IRA earns will compound, tax-deferred, until you begin making withdrawals. Remember, the biggest benefit of an IRA lies in its tax-deferred earnings growth. (See **Figure 6.**)

IRA Withdrawals When you retire, you can withdraw the money from your IRA by one of several methods. You can take out all of the money at one time, but the entire amount will be taxed as income. If you decide to withdraw the money from your IRA in installments, you will have to pay tax only on the amount that you withdraw. You might also place the money that you withdraw in an annuity that guarantees payments over your lifetime. See the discussion on annuities later in this section for further information about this option.

reality bytes

Calculate Your Benefits
It is never too early to start thinking about how you will fund your retirement. One source of retirement income will probably be your Social Security benefits. The Social Security administration will help you calculate how much your Social Security benefits will be. A good way to start planning for your retirement is to make some reasonable guesses about what your yearly earnings will be when you are in your mid-20s.

FIGURE 5 Types of IRAs

Account Options You should understand all options to get the most from your contributions. *How do a regular IRA and a Roth IRA differ?*

Type of IRA	IRA Features
Regular IRA	• Tax-deferred interest and earnings • Annual limit on individual contributions • Limited eligibility for tax-deductible contributions • Contributions do not reduce current taxes
Roth IRA	• Tax-deferred interest and earnings • Annual limit on individual contributions • Withdrawals are tax-free in specific cases • Contributions do not reduce current taxes
Simplified Employee Pension Plan (SEP-IRA)	• "Pay yourself first" payroll reduction contributions • Pre-tax contributions • Tax-deferred interest and earnings
Spousal IRA	• Tax-deferred interest and earnings • Both working spouse and nonworking spouse can contribute up to the annual limit • Limited eligibility for tax-deductible contributions • Contributions do not reduce current taxes
Rollover IRA	• Traditional IRA that accepts rollovers of all or a portion of your taxable distribution from a retirement plan • You can roll over to a Roth IRA
Education IRA	• Tax-deferred interest and earnings • 10% early withdrawal penalty is waived when money is used for higher-education expenses • Annual limit on individual contributions • Contributions do not reduce current taxes

Keogh Plans

A **Keogh plan,** which is also an H.R.10 plan or a self-employed retirement plan, is a retirement plan specially designed for self-employed people and their employees. Keogh plans have various restrictions, including limits on the amount of annual tax-deductible contributions you can make. Keogh plans can be complicated to administer, so you should get professional tax advice before using this type of personal retirement plan.

Reading Check

Recall Who should consider using an SEP plan?

Limits on Retirement Plans

When must you begin to withdraw your money?

With the exception of Roth IRAs, you cannot keep money in most tax-deferred retirement plans forever. When you retire, or by age 70½ at the latest, you must begin to receive "minimum lifetime distributions." These are withdrawals from the funds you have accumulated through your plan. The amount of the **distributions,** or withdrawals, is based on your life expectancy at the time the distributions begin. If you do not withdraw the minimum distributions from a retirement account, the IRS will charge you a penalty.

Reading Check

Remember By what age must you begin to receive minimum distributions from your tax-deferred retirement plans?

Annuities

Why do people purchase annuities in addition to other retirement plans?

What if you have funded your 401(k) or profit-sharing plans up to the allowable limits and you want to put away more money? The answer may be an annuity. An **annuity** is a contract purchased from an insurance company that guarantees a future fixed or variable payment to the purchaser for a certain number of years or for life.

You might also want to purchase an annuity with the money you receive from an IRA or company pension. You can buy an annuity to supplement the income you will receive from these other types of retirement plans. You can choose to purchase an annuity that has a single payment or installment payments. You will also need to decide whether you want the insurance company to send the income from your annuity to you immediately or begin sending it to you at a later date. The payments you receive from an annuity are taxed as ordinary income. However, the interest you earn from the annuity accumulates tax-free until payments begin. Some income annuity options include:

- **Lifetime income**: you receive income payments for the rest of your life. The income ceases upon death.
- **Lifetime income with a minimum number of payments**: you receive income for life. If you die before you receive a set number of payments your beneficiary will receive the balance of the payments.
- **Lifetime income for two people**: Income payments are received for the life of the two people. Upon the death of either person, the income continues as a percentage of the original amount.

FIGURE 6 Benefits of Starting a Retirement Plan Early

Earning Potential The earlier you contribute to a retirement plan, the higher your earnings will be when you retire, even if you do not continue to add to the account. *In this example, why do you think the net earnings were greater for Saver A even though he contributed less money?*

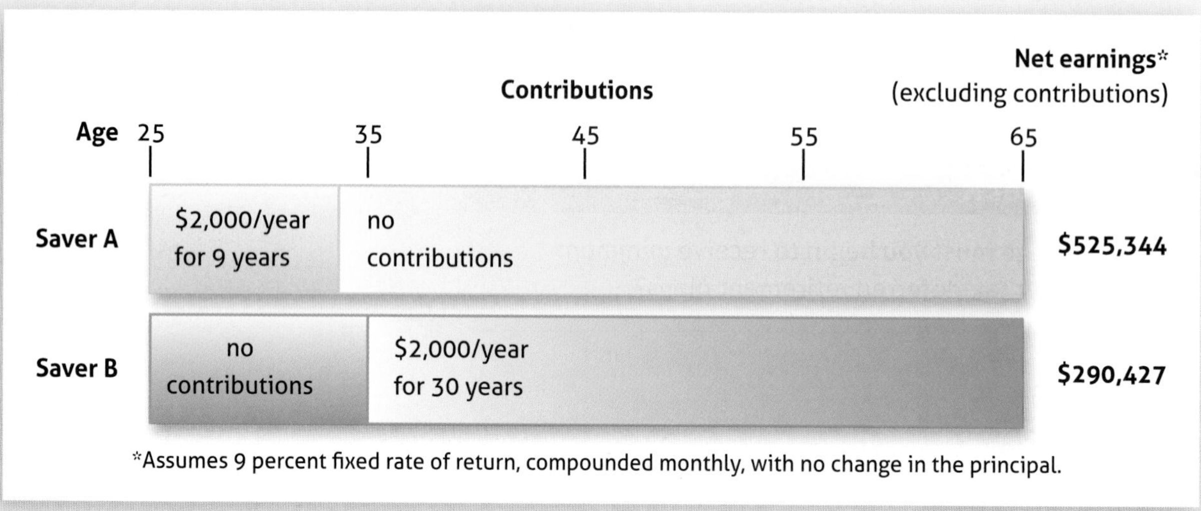

Types of Annuities

Annuities may be fixed or variable. Fixed annuities provide a certain amount of income for life. Variable annuities provide payments guaranteed above a minimum amount, depending on the rate of return on your investment.

Immediate Annuities People approaching retirement age can purchase immediate annuities. These annuities provide income payments at once. They are usually purchased with a lump-sum payment. When you are 65, you may no longer need all of your life insurance coverage—especially if you have grown children. You may decide to convert the cash value of your insurance policy into a lump-sum payment for an immediate annuity.

Deferred Annuities With deferred annuities, income payments start at some future date. Meanwhile, interest accumulates on the money you deposit. Younger people often buy such annuities to save money toward retirement. A deferred annuity purchased with a lump-sum payment is known as a *single-premium deferred annuity.* A "premium" is the payment you make. These annuities are popular because of the greater potential for tax-free growth. If you are buying a deferred annuity on an installment basis, you may want one that allows flexible premiums, or payments. That means that your contributions can vary from year to year.

Costs of Annuities

There are various choices regarding the type of annuity and the annuity income it will generate. The costs, fees, and other features of annuities differ from policy to policy, so you should discuss all of the possible options with an insurance agent. Ask about charges, fees, and interest-rate guarantees. Also, be sure to check the financial health of the insurance company that offers the annuity.

Reading Check

Summarize How does an immediate annuity differ from a deferred annuity?

Living on Retirement Income

What are some things you can do to stretch retirement income farther?

As you plan for retirement, you will estimate a budget or spending plan. When the time to retire arrives, however, you may find that your expenses are higher than you had expected. If that is the case, you will have to make some adjustments.

First, make sure that you are getting all the income to which you are entitled. Are there other programs or benefits for which you might qualify? You will also need to think about any assets or valuables you might be able to convert to cash or into other sources of income.

In addition, retirees may have to re-examine the trade-off between spending and saving. For example, instead of taking an expensive vacation, they can take advantage of free and low-cost recreation opportunities, such as public parks, museums, libraries, and fairs, which are enjoyable options. Retirees can also receive special discounts at movie theaters, restaurants, stores, and more.

Additional Income
Annuities are sold by insurance companies and offer another way to save for retirement.
What advantage does an annuity offer?

Economics and You

Gross Domestic Product

The Gross Domestic Product (GDP) is a measure of a nation's productivity. It is comprised of consumer spending, government spending, and private investment. It also takes into account a country's balance of trade and changes in inventories. To calculate GDP, add spending by consumers and the government with investments. Then subtract a trade deficit or add a trade surplus and subtract inventories that are shrinking or add inventories that are growing to that figure. To determine if the economy is doing well, compare the GDP with previous GDP figures. If the GDP is increasing, the economy is doing well. By calculating the percentage each factor contributes to the GDP, you can analyze how growth was achieved. Historically, consumer spending has been the largest percentage of the United States GDP.

GDP in Billions of Dollars

Year	GDP
2004	11,867.8
2005	12,638.4
2006	13,398.9
2007	14,077.6
2008	14,441.4
2009	14,256.3

Personal Finance Connection As an economic indicator, GDP provides insight into the health of the economy. A historical review of the United States GDP may help you determine how much money you need to start saving now in order to live well in retirement. The United States Bureau of Economic Analysis (BEA) provides figures and graphs of the U.S. GDP, including Real GDP which is seasonally adjusted.

Critical Thinking How would a ten-year graph that reports GDP indicate where in the business cycle the economy is at any given point in time? How would that information be helpful in estate planning?

Activity Download an Economics and You Worksheet Activity.

Working During Retirement

Retirees can use their skills and time instead of spending money. Some people decide to work part-time or full-time after they retire. Many people prefer to keep active and pursue new careers. Work can provide a person with a greater sense of involvement and self-worth. It is also a good source of supplementary retirement income.

Using Your Nest Egg

When should you take money out of your "nest egg," or savings, during retirement? The answer depends on your financial circumstances and how much you want to leave to your heirs. Your **heirs** are the people who will have the legal right to your assets when you die. Your savings may be large enough to allow you to live comfortably on the interest earned by your savings, or you may need to make regular withdrawals to finance your retirement. However, do so with caution. If you dip into your retirement funds, you should consider how long your savings will last if you make regular withdrawals. Whatever your situation, you should try to conserve your retirement funds to make it last.

Assessment

Review Key Concepts

1. **Identify** What are the two defined-contribution plans known as tax-sheltered annuity plans?
2. **Describe** What are the features of an education IRA?
3. **Recognize** Whom does the Social Security pension plan provide benefits to?

Higher Order Thinking

4. **Consider** Many companies now offer 401(k) plans as a benefit to employees. Unfortunately, employees do not always take full advantage of these plans. Consider ways that you can maximize the benefits of a 401(k) plan.

21st Century Skills

5. **Adapt to Change** Damon is planning for his retirement. He realizes that Social Security, his IRA, and his pension plan will not provide the same level of income that he currently has. He does not want to go back to work after retirement as he is hoping to use his time to pursue new skills and hobbies. Write a letter to Damon to offer your advice on changes that he can make to ensure he has the income necessary to support him in his retirement years.

Mathematics

6. **Early Retirement Planning** Dan recently graduated from college. His parents threw him a graduation party from which Dan received $2,500 in gifts from the guests. After speaking to his parents, Dan decided to invest this money in a retirement account. He put the money into a Roth IRA which earns 9 percent interest, compounded annually. How much money will Dan have in his Roth IRA account after 5 years assuming the interest rate remains the same and Dan does not contribute any additional money?

Math Concept **Calculate Account Balance** To calculate the balance in an account after a specific time period you must calculate the interest earned for the year and add to the beginning balance. Repeat this process for each year.

Starting Hint Determine the ending balance after year 1 by multiplying the original deposit amount by the annual interest rate in order to calculate the interest earned. Add this interest to the original deposit amount to calculate the ending balance after year 1.

NCTM Connections Recognize and use connections among mathematical ideas.

Section Objectives

- **Identify** various types of wills.
- **Discuss** several types of trusts.
- **Describe** common characteristics of estates.
- **Identify** the types of taxes that affect estates.

As You Read

Consider What situations might motivate you to change your will?

The Importance of Estate Planning

Why is it important to have an estate plan?

Many people think of estates as belonging only to the rich. However, the fact is that everyone has an estate. An **estate** is all the property and assets owned by an individual or group. During your working years, your financial goal is to build your estate for your current and future needs. However, as you grow older, your point of view will change. You will start to consider what will happen after you die.

What Is Estate Planning?

Estate planning is the process of creating a detailed plan for managing personal assets to make the most of them while you are alive and to ensure that they are distributed wisely after your death. Without a good estate plan, the assets you accumulate during your lifetime might be greatly reduced by various taxes when you die.

Estate planning is an essential part of retirement planning and financial planning. It has two stages. The first stage involves building your estate through savings, investments, and insurance. The second stage consists of making sure that your estate will be distributed as you wish at the time of your death. If you get married, your estate planning should take into account the needs of your spouse and children, if you have any. If you are single, your financial affairs should be in order for your beneficiaries. A **beneficiary (estate)** is a person who is named to receive a portion of someone's estate.

When you die, your surviving spouse, children, relatives, and/or friends will face a period of grief. One or more of these people will probably be responsible for settling your affairs. This will be a difficult time, and so your estate plan should be clear and well-organized. Otherwise, the people you have left behind may encounter problems settling your estate. One way to avoid these problems is to make sure that important documents are accessible, understandable, and legal.

Legal Documents

An estate plan involves various legal documents such as a **will**, which is a legal **declaration** (or statement) of a person's wishes regarding disposal of his or her estate after death. When you die, the person who is responsible for handling your affairs will need access to your will and other important documents. The documents must be reviewed and verified before your heirs can receive the assets to which they are entitled. If no one can find the necessary documents, your heirs may experience difficult delays or even lose a portion of their inheritance.

You should organize various important papers:

- Birth certificates for you, your spouse, and your children
- Marriage certificates and divorce papers
- Legal name changes (important for protecting adopted children)
- Military service records or veteran's documents
- Social Security documents
- Insurance policies
- Transfer records of joint bank accounts
- Safe-deposit box records
- Automobile registrations
- Titles to stock and bond certificates

Have several copies of the documents needed for processing insurance claims and settling your estate. In some cases, children whose parents have died may need to have documents proving their parents' births and marriage and/or divorce. Surviving spouses, children, and other heirs may also be required to show a death certificate.

All that You Own
All of your possessions and assets make up your estate. *What does your estate consist of at this point in your life?*

Reading Check

Paraphrase What are the two stages of estate planning?

Wills

Why is a will such an important document?

One of the most important documents that every adult should have is a written will. If you die **intestate**—which is the status of not having a valid will—your legal state of residence will step in and control the distribution of your estate without regard for your wishes.

Make sure that you have a written will. An attorney with estate planning experience can draft a will, which can help your heirs avoid many difficulties. Legal fees will vary with the size of an estate and particular family situation. A standard will costs between $200 and $500.

Types of Wills

You have several options in preparing a will. The four basic types of wills are the simple will, the traditional marital share will, the exemption trust will, and the stated dollar amount will. The differences among the types of wills can affect how your estate will be taxed.

All types of wills usually designate a beneficiary, the person who is named to receive a portion or all of an estate after your death. A beneficiary can be a spouse, relative, friend, or organization. In the following discussions, the beneficiary will be referred to as the *spouse*.

Simple Will A simple will leaves everything to the spouse. Such a will is generally sufficient for people with small estates. However, for a large or complex estate, a simple will may not meet objectives. This type of will may also result in higher overall taxation, since everything left to the spouse will be taxed as part of his or her estate.

Traditional Marital Share Will The traditional marital share will leaves one-half of the adjusted gross estate (the total value of the estate minus debts and costs) to the spouse. The other half of the estate may go to children or other heirs. It can also be held in trust for the family. A **trust** is an arrangement in which a designated person known as a *trustee* manages assets for the benefit of someone else. A trust can provide a spouse with a lifelong income and would not be taxed at his or her death. Under this type of will half of the estate is taxed at the death of the first spouse, and half is taxed at the death of the other spouse.

Exemption Trust Will With an exemption trust will, all assets go to the spouse except for a certain amount, which goes into a trust. This amount, plus any interest it earns, can provide the spouse with lifelong income that will not be taxed. In 2004 and 2005, the tax exemption amount was $1.5 million. That amount increased to $2 million for the years 2006 through 2008. In 2009, the amount increases to $3.5 million. The tax-free aspect of this type of will may become important if property values increase considerably. This type of will is beneficial for large estates.

Stated Dollar Amount Will The stated dollar amount will allows you to pass on to your spouse any amount that satisfies your family's financial goals. For tax purposes, you could pass on the exempted amount of $1.5 million (in 2004 and 2005). However, you might decide to pass on a stated amount related to your family's future income needs or related to the value of personal items.

State law may dictate how much you must leave to your spouse. Most states require that the spouse receive a certain amount, usually one-half or one-third of the value of an estate. States also have laws regarding when and how portions of an estate pass to beneficiaries.

The stated dollar amount will has one major shortcoming. The will may leave specific dollar amounts to listed heirs and the balance to the surviving spouse. Although these amounts may be reasonable when the will is drafted, they can soon become obsolete.

The stated dollar amount will has one major drawback. Suppose that you leave specific dollar amounts to your listed heirs and the balance to your spouse. Although these amounts may be fair and reasonable when the will is drafted, they can soon become outdated. What if the value of the estate decreases because of a business problem or a drop in the stock market? That decrease will not affect heirs who are left specific dollar amounts, but it will affect the value of your spouse's inheritance. For this reason, most experts recommend using percentages rather than specific amounts.

Wills and Probate

The type of will that is best for your particular needs depends on many factors, including the size of your estate, inflation, your age, and your objectives. No matter what type of will you choose, it is best to avoid probate. **Probate** is the legal procedure of proving that a will is valid or invalid. It is also the process by which your estate is managed and distributed after your death, according to the provisions of your will. A special probate court validates wills and makes sure that your debts are paid. You should avoid probate because it is expensive, lengthy, and public. As you will read later in this chapter, a living trust avoids probate and is also less expensive, quicker, and private.

Formats of Wills

Wills may be either holographic or formal. A *holographic* will is a handwritten will that you prepare yourself. It should be written, dated, and signed entirely in your own handwriting. No printed or typed information should appear on its pages. Some states do not recognize holographic wills as legal.

A *formal will* is usually prepared with the help of an attorney. It may be typed, or it may be a preprinted form that you fill out. You must sign the will in front of two witnesses; neither witness can be a beneficiary named in the will. Witnesses must sign in front of you.

A *statutory will* is prepared on a preprinted form, which is available from lawyers, office-supply stores, and some stationery stores. There are serious risks in using preprinted forms to prepare your will. The form may include provisions that are not in the best interests of your heirs. If you change the preprinted wording, part or all of the will may be declared invalid. Furthermore, the form may not remain up-to-date with current laws regarding wills. For these reasons, it is best to seek a lawyer's advice when you prepare your will.

Fair Distribution
Preparing a will can ensure that each member of your family gets a portion of your estate, according to your wishes. *Why might you not want all of your estate to go to one person?*

Decision Making

Successful people and effective leaders often possess strong decision-making skills. Decision-making skills include analyzing and evaluating evidence and arguments to select the best solution. Effective decision makers are able to make connections between information and arguments and consider various points of view. In addition, people who possess strong decision-making skills are able to assess the effectiveness of their decisions and apply their experiences and learning to future situations. Developing decision-making skills will benefit you at school, in the community, and at work.

Write About It

Think of a situation that required you to use decision-making skills. Write one or more paragraphs to describe the scenario and explain the decision that was made. Was the decision effective? Thinking back, would you have changed your decision?

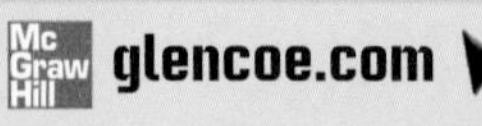

Activity Download a Career and College Readiness Worksheet Activity.

Writing Your Will

Writing a will allows you to express exactly how you want your property to be distributed to your heirs. It is the only way to make sure that all of your property will end up where you want it. Some guidelines for writing a will include:

1. Work closely with your spouse or partner to prepare your will.
2. Write your will to conform to your current wishes.
3. Do not choose a beneficiary as a witness. If such a person is called on to validate your will he or she may not be allowed to collect any inheritance.
4. Consider signing a prenuptial agreement if you are remarrying. If you sign an agreement before the wedding, you and your intended spouse can legally agree that neither of you will make any claim to the other's estate.
5. Consider using percentages instead of dollar amounts.
6. If you are married, your spouse should also write a will.
7. Be flexible.
8. Keep your original will in a safe place and a copy at home.
9. If you alter your will, prepare a new one or add a codicil.
10. Select an executor who is willing to do the needed tasks.

Selecting an Executor An **executor** is a person who is willing and able to perform the tasks involved in carrying out a will. These tasks include preparing an inventory of assets, collecting any money due, and paying off debts. An executor must also prepare and file all income and estate tax returns. In addition, he or she will be responsible for making decisions about selling or reinvesting assets to pay off debts and provide income for your family while the estate is being settled. Finally, an executor must distribute the estate and make a final accounting to beneficiaries and to the probate court. An executor can be a family member, a friend, an attorney, an accountant, or the trust department of a bank. You may also name a beneficiary as the executor. State law sets fees for executors. If you do not name an executor in your will, the court will appoint one. Naming your own executor eliminates that possibility and helps prevent unnecessary delay in the distribution of your property. It will also minimize estate taxes and settlement costs.

Selecting a Guardian If you have children, your will should name a guardian to care for them in the event that you and your spouse die at the same time and the children cannot care for themselves. A **guardian** is the person who accepts the responsibility of caring for the children of the deceased and managing an estate for the children until they reach a certain age. Many states require a guardian to post a bond (several hundred dollars) with the probate court. The bonding company will reimburse the minor's estate the amount of the bond if the guardian uses the minor's property for his or her own gain. When you name a guardian, choose someone you know who loves them and shares your beliefs about raising children. The person must also be capable and willing to accept the responsibilities of being a parent.

Altering or Rewriting Your Will There may be times when you wish to change the provisions of your will because of changes in your life or in the law. Here are some reasons to review your will:

- You have moved to a new state that has different laws.
- You have sold property that is mentioned in the will.
- The size and composition of your estate have changed.
- You have married, divorced, or remarried.
- Potential heirs have died, or new ones have been born.

Do not make any written changes on the pages of an existing will. Additions, deletions, or erasures on a will that has been signed and witnessed can invalidate the will.

If you want to make only a few minor changes, adding a codicil may be the best choice. A **codicil** is a document that explains, adds, or deletes provisions in an existing will. To be valid, it must meet the legal requirements for a will.

If you want to make major changes in your will, or if you have already added a codicil, it is best to prepare a new will. In the new will, be sure to include a clause that revokes, or cancels, all earlier wills and codicils.

Reading Check

Define What is probate?

A Living Will

Why is it important to have a living will?

At some point in your life, you may become physically or mentally disabled and unable to act on your own behalf. If that happens, a living will can help ensure that you will be cared for according to your wishes. A **living will** is a legal document in which you state if you want to be kept alive by artificial means if you become terminally ill and are unable to make such a decision. See **Figure 7**. Sign and date the document before two witnesses. Review your living will from time to time to update your decisions. To ensure effectiveness, discuss your intentions of preparing a living will with those closest to you.

You might consider writing a living will when you draw up a traditional will. Most lawyers will prepare a living will at no cost if they are already preparing a traditional will or your estate plan. You can also get the forms for a living will from nonprofit groups.

Costa Rica

Popular Destination for Expatriates

Many people consider moving to a new place for their retirement. Sometimes a new place can be a completely new country. An expatriate is defined as a person living in a foreign land. Many countries have growing communities of expatriates, or expats. American expats are often drawn to their new homes by the challenge and excitement of a new language or culture. One of the most popular countries for American expats is Costa Rica. This country is close to the U.S. so expats can keep in touch with friends and relatives left behind. In addition, Costa Rica is considered to be peaceful and beautiful, full of rain forests, beaches, and national parks. It also has a low cost of living and many tax advantages. Tax rates are low, real estate is considered a bargain compared to the U.S., and investors pay no capital gains on real estate. Many people live comfortably for less than $1,000 a month.

Critical Thinking

1. **Expand** You are not required to become a citizen when you move to another country but there are other government regulations to be considered. Research the process for becoming a citizen in another country. What paperwork will you need to obtain in addition to a passport?
2. **Relate** What precautions might you take when considering relocating to a foreign country that might be different from relocating to a new town or state?

DATABYTES

Capital
San Jose

Population
4,516,220

Languages
Spanish (official), English

Currency
Costa Rican colón

Gross Domestic Product (GDP)
$29.64 billion

GDP per capita
$10,900

Industry
Microprocessors, food processing, medical equipment, textiles and clothing, construction materials, fertilizer, plastic products

Agriculture
Bananas, pineapples, coffee, melons, ornamental plants, sugar, corn, rice, beans, potatoes; beef, poultry, dairy; timber

Exports
Bananas, pineapples, coffee, melons, ornamental plants, sugar; beef; seafood; electronic components, medical equipment

Natural Resources
Hydropower

FIGURE 7 **A Living Will**

Sound Decisions A living will ensures that your preferences about medical care are honored even if you become unable to make decisions. *Under what circumstances would you be unable to make a decision about your own medical care?*

Living Will Declaration

Declaration made this _____ day of ______ (month, year)

I, _________________________, being of sound mind, willfully and voluntarily make known my desire that my dying shall not be artificially prolonged under the circumstances set forth below, do hereby declare: if at any time I should have an incurable injury, disease, or illness regarded as a terminal condition by my physician and if my physician has determined that the application of life-sustaining procedures would serve only to artificially prolong the dying process and that my death will occur whether or not life-sustaining procedures are utilized, I direct that such procedures be withheld or withdrawn and that I be permitted to die with only the administration of medication or the performance of any medical procedure deemed necessary to provide me with comfort care.

In the absence of my ability to give directions regarding the use of such life-sustaining procedures, it is my intention that this declaration shall be honored by my family and physician as the final expression of my legal right to refuse medical or surgical treatment and accept the consequences from such refusal. I understand the full import of this declaration, and I am emotionally and mentally competent to make this declaration.

Signed _______________________

City, County, and State of Residence_______________________

The declarant has been personally known to me, and I believe him or her to be of sound mind.

Witness_______________________

Witness_______________________

Power of Attorney

A **power of attorney** is a legal document that authorizes someone to act on your behalf. If you become seriously ill or injured, you will probably need someone to take care of your needs and personal affairs. This can be done through a power of attorney.

You can assign a power of attorney to anyone you choose. The person you name can be given limited power or a great deal of power. You can give that person power to carry out only certain actions or transactions, or you may allow the person to act on your behalf in all matters, including your living will.

Letter of Last Instruction

In addition to a traditional will and a living will, it is a good idea to prepare a letter of last instruction. This document is not legally binding, but it can provide heirs with important information. It should contain preferences for funeral arrangements as well as the names of the people who are to be informed of the death. With a letter of last instruction, you can also let people know the locations of your bank accounts, safe-deposit box, and other important items.

Reading Check

Identify To whom can you assign a power of attorney?

Trusts

Why is it important that trusts avoid probate?

Basically, a trust is a legal arrangement that helps manage the assets of your estate for your benefit or that of your beneficiaries. The creator of the trust is called the *trustor*, or *grantor*. The trust is administered by the trustee, which can be a person or an institution, such as a bank. Trustee services are commonly provided by banks and in some cases life insurance companies. A bank charges a small fee for its services in administering a trust. The fee is usually based on the value of the assets in the trust. Individual circumstances determine whether it makes sense to establish a trust.

Some of the common reasons for setting up a trust are to:

- Reduce or provide for payment of estate taxes.
- Avoid probate and transfer your assets immediately to your beneficiaries.
- Free yourself from managing your assets while you receive a regular income from the trust.
- Provide income for a surviving spouse or other beneficiary.
- Ensure that your property serves a desired purpose after your death.

Types of Trusts

There are many types of trusts, including a credit-shelter trust, a disclaimer trust, a living trust, and a testamentary trust. Choose the type of trust that is most appropriate for your situation. An estate attorney can advise you about the right type of trust for your needs.

Trusts can be either revocable or irrevocable. A *revocable trust* is one in which you have the right to end the trust or change its terms during your lifetime. Revocable trusts avoid the lengthy process of probate, but they do not protect assets from federal or state estate taxes. An *irrevocable trust* is one that cannot be changed or ended.

Irrevocable trusts avoid probate and help reduce estate taxes. However, by law you cannot remove any assets from an irrevocable trust, even if you need them at some later point in your life.

Credit-Shelter Trust A credit-shelter trust is a trust that enables the spouse of a deceased person to avoid paying federal taxes on a certain amount of assets left to him or her as part of an estate. As of 2004, the exemption amount was $1.5 million. It increased to $2 million in 2006 and continues to increase to $3.5 million in 2009. As the most common estate-planning trust, the credit-shelter trust has many other names: bypass trust, residuary trust, A/B trust, exemption equivalent trust, and family trust. A single person does not need to set up a credit-shelter trust because assets passing to someone other than a spouse automatically qualify for the estate exemption amount.

Disclaimer Trust A disclaimer trust is appropriate for couples who do not have enough assets to need a credit-shelter trust but who may in the future. With a disclaimer trust, the surviving spouse is left everything, but he or she has the right to **disclaim,** or deny, some portion of the estate. Anything that is disclaimed goes into a credit-shelter trust. This approach allows the surviving spouse to protect wealth from estate taxes.

Living Trust A living trust, also known as an *inter vivos trust*, is a property management arrangement that you establish. It allows you, as trustor, to receive benefits during your lifetime. To set up a living trust, you simply transfer some of your assets to a trustee. Then you give the trustee instructions for managing the trust while you are alive as well as after your death.

A living trust has several advantages:

- It ensures privacy. A will is a public record; however, a trust is not a public record.

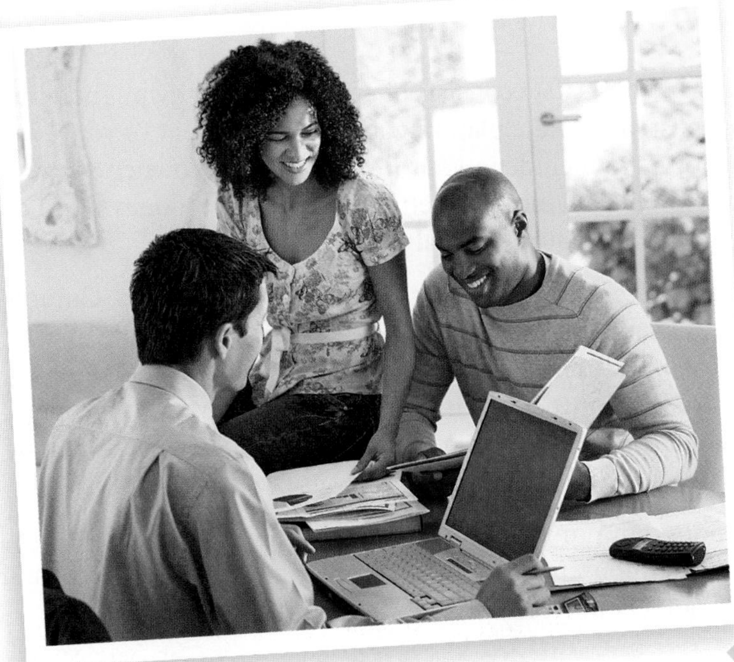

Trust Me
A trust can help manage the assets of your estate for yourself and your beneficiaries. *Why might you set up a trust for your beneficiaries?*

- The assets held in trust avoid probate at your death. This eliminates probate costs and delays.
- It is advantageous if you own property in more than one state.
- It enables you to review your trustee's performance and make changes if necessary.
- It can relieve you of management responsibilities.
- It is less likely than a will to create arguments between heirs upon your death.
- It can guide your family and doctors to follow your wishes if you become terminally ill or if you become unable to make your own decisions.

Setting up a living trust costs more money than creating a will. However, depending on your particular circumstances, a living trust can be a good estate-planning option.

Testamentary Trust A testamentary trust is established by your will and becomes effective upon your death. Such a trust can be valuable if your beneficiaries are inexperienced in financial matters. It may also be the best option if you expect your estate taxes will be high. A testamentary trust provides many of the same advantages as a living trust.

Reading Check

Summarize What is the main difference between a revocable and irrevocable trust?

Your Estate

How does the type of joint ownership affect the distribution of an estate?

Remember, your estate consists of everything you own. Therefore, an important step in estate planning is taking inventory of your assets. Do not forget to include in your inventory jointly owned property, life insurance policies, employee retirement benefits, money owed to you by others, and all your personal possessions.

Some states are known as *community-property states.* Community property is any money earned by either spouse during the marriage and any items purchased with that money. It does not include assets received as gifts or through inheritances. In community-property states, each spouse owns 50 percent of the property. Thus, half of the couple's assets are included in each spouse's estate.

In non-community-property states, property is included in the estate of the spouse who owns it. The way you own property can make a significant tax difference.

Joint Ownership

Joint ownership of property between spouses is very common. Joint ownership may also exist between parents and children or other relatives. Joint ownership may help avoid probate and inheritance taxes in some states. However, it does not avoid federal estate taxes. It may, in fact, increase the amount of federal estate taxes.

There are three types of joint ownership, each of which has different tax and estate-planning consequences.

1. You and your spouse may own property as "joint tenants with the right of survivorship."
   - The property is considered to be owned 50-50 for estate tax purposes and will pass to one spouse at the other's death.
   - No gift tax is paid on creating such ownership. Also, no estate tax is paid at the first death. However, when the surviving spouse dies, more estate taxes may be due than with a traditional marital share will.
2. You and your spouse may own property as "tenants in common."
   - Each individual is considered to own a certain share of property for tax purposes, and only your share is included in your estate.
   - Your share does not go to the other tenant in common at your death. Instead, it is included in your probate estate, and you decide who gets it.
   - Gift and estate taxes do not apply to property that belongs to spouses. However, gifts of joint interests to children, for example, can create taxation.
3. Married couples may own property under the form of "tenancy by the entirety."
   - Both spouses own the property.
   - When one spouse dies, the other gets the property automatically.
   - Neither spouse may sell property without the other's consent.

Joint ownership is a poor substitute for a will because it provides less control over how property is distributed and taxed after death. State laws govern the types and effects of joint ownership. Some states require that survivorship rights be spelled out in the deed, or at least abbreviated. An attorney should be consulted on these matters.

Life Insurance and Employee Benefits

If you have life insurance, the benefits of that insurance will be counted among the assets in your estate. Life insurance benefits are free of income tax, and they do not go through probate. They are also partially exempt from most state inheritance taxes. However, they are subject to federal estate taxes under certain circumstances, such as when you change beneficiaries, surrender the policy for cash, or make loans on the policy.

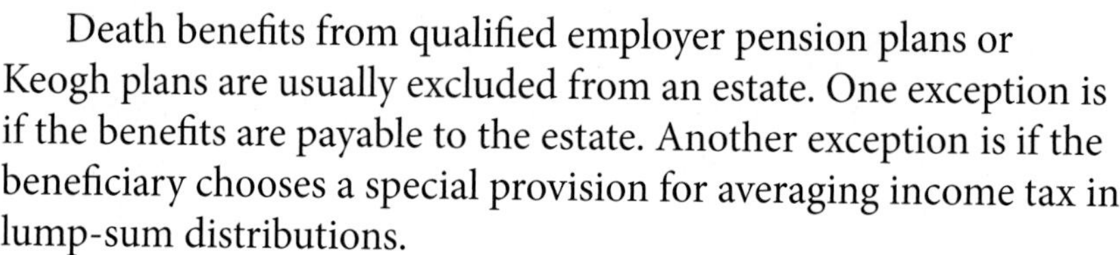

Death benefits from qualified employer pension plans or Keogh plans are usually excluded from an estate. One exception is if the benefits are payable to the estate. Another exception is if the beneficiary chooses a special provision for averaging income tax in lump-sum distributions.

Lifetime Gifts and Trusts

You may give part of your estate as a gift or set up a trust for your spouse or a child. Under certain conditions, such gifts and trusts are not included as part of your estate upon your death. However, if you keep any control or use of the gift or trust, it remains part of your estate and is subject to taxes. For example, if you transfer title of your home to a child but continue to live in it, the value of the home is taxed as part of your estate.

Similarly, if you put property in a trust but keep some control over the income or principal, it is included in your estate even though you may not be able to obtain it yourself.

Reading Check

Recognize What is community property?

Taxes and Estate Planning

Which government, state or federal, imposes inheritance taxes?

Federal and state governments impose various types of taxes that you must consider in estate planning. Four types of taxes are estate tax, estate and trust federal income tax, inheritance tax, and gift tax.

Estate Taxes

An estate tax is a federal tax collected on the value of a person's property at the time of his or her death. The tax is based on the fair market value of the deceased person's investments, property, and bank accounts, less an exempt amount.

As of 2009, the exempt amount was $3.5 million. This means that the "first" $3.5 million is not used to compute the estate tax. Only the amount in excess of $3.5 million can be considered. The tax rate applied to the remaining amount is 45 percent. With careful planning, federal estate taxes can be avoided for estates over $3.5 million.

Under present law, whatever you give your spouse as a gift is exempt from gift and estate taxes. Gift tax returns do not need to be filed for gifts to a spouse. It is still possible that such gifts will be included in your estate if they were given within three years of your death.

Estate and Trust Federal Income Taxes

In addition to the federal estate tax return, owners of estates and certain trusts must file federal income tax returns. Taxable income for estates and trusts is computed in the same manner as taxable income for individuals. Taxes must be paid quarterly on both.

Inheritance Taxes

Your heirs might have to pay a tax for the right to acquire the property that they have inherited. An inheritance tax is a tax collected on the property left by a person in his or her will.

Only state governments impose inheritance taxes. Most states collect an inheritance tax, but state laws differ widely as to exemptions and rates of taxation. A reasonable range for state inheritance taxes would be 4 to 10 percent of whatever the heir receives.

Gift Taxes

Both the federal and state governments impose a gift tax, a tax collected on money or property valued at more than $11,000 given by one person to another in a single year. One way to reduce the tax liability of your estate is to reduce the size of the estate by giving away portions of it as gifts. You are free to make such gifts to your spouse, children, or anyone else. However, when doing this, be careful that you do not give away assets that you may need in your retirement.

According to federal law, you may give up to $11,000 per person per year free of any gift tax. A married couple may give up to $22,000 per person per year without paying the tax. Gifts that exceed those amounts are subject to the tax. Gift tax rates are currently the same as estate tax rates, and they are called *unified transfer tax rates*. However, gifts might be considered as part of your estate and be taxed if they were given within three years of your death. Many states have other gift tax laws as well.

Government's Share Beneficiaries must pay taxes on the deceased person's estate. *What are the four types of taxes to consider for estate planning?*

Paying the Tax

After doing everything possible to reduce your estate taxes, you may still find that taxes are due. In that case, you will have to think about the best way to help your heirs pay the taxes.

The federal estate tax is due nine months after a death. State taxes, probate costs, debts, and other expenses are also usually due within that same period. These costs might result in a real financial problem for your survivors. Finding enough cash to pay taxes, debts, and other costs without causing financial hardship can be very difficult.

There are a number of ways this problem can be handled.

1. Obtain life insurance. A life insurance policy may be the best way to provide your heirs with the tax-free cash that they will need to settle your estate.
2. Save enough cash ahead of time to pay taxes and expenses when they are due. However, the cash may be subject to income tax during your lifetime and also subject to estate tax at your death.
3. Your heirs could sell assets to pay taxes. However, this could result in the loss of important sources of income.
4. Your heirs might borrow money. However, it is unusual to find a commercial lender that will lend money to pay taxes. Besides, borrowing money only prolongs the problem and adds interest costs in the process.
5. If your family members or beneficiaries can show they have a reasonable cause, the IRS may allow them to make deferred or installment payments on taxes that are due. However, like borrowing, making payments may prolong the problem.

Planning for the Future

Estate planning is essential not only to ensure that your assets are distributed in the way you choose, but also to make sure that your loved ones are not left with difficult or costly problems.

Planning for your estate and taxes as well as writing a will are just a few of the steps you can take to have a secure financial future for yourself and others. In addition, planning and saving for your own retirement will help ensure that your needs are met in your later years.

Remember that the trade-offs, decisions, and goals that you make for yourself today affect your personal finances, which will continue to affect your life now and in the future.

After You Read

React Has the information in this chapter convinced you to start your retirement planning sooner than you may have originally planned? Why or why not?

Review Key Concepts

1. **Describe** What are the four basic types of wills?
2. **Explain** What are the advantages of a credit-shelter trust?
3. **Identify** What are the three types of joint ownership of property?
4. **Distinguish** What are the differences between inheritance taxes and gift taxes?

Higher Order Thinking H.O.T.

5. **Assess** Stefan's will leaves his entire estate to his wife but they are getting a divorce. Assess whether Stefan should prepare a new will or add a codicil to his existing will.

English Language Arts

6. **Final Wishes** Suppose that your friend Ian tells you that he does not want to spend the money for a lawyer to help him create a will. Instead, he feels that he can leave a letter of last instruction to convey his wishes for distributing his assets. Write a dialogue between you and Ian in which you explain why he should not use a letter of last instruction in this way and what the benefits of creating a will are.

NCTE 4 Use written language to communicate effectively.

Mathematics

7. **Estate Tax** In 2010 Annette and Harold are retired and have accumulated $2.75 million in total estate value. Based on the federal estate tax laws, if Annette or Harold passes away between 2011 and 2013, the other can receive $2 million tax-free. Any amount received over that exemption is subject to the federal estate tax. If either Annette or Harold passes away during this time frame, how much federal estate tax will the other have to pay? Assume that the estate is taxed at 48 percent.

Math Concept **Calculate Estate Tax** To calculate the federal estate tax owed, first identify the amount received above the exemption defined by the estate tax laws. Multiply this amount by the federal estate tax rate.

Starting Hint Determine the amount received above the federal estate tax law defined exemption by first identifying the total amount received upon death. Subtract the exemption amount from this figure to arrive at the taxable amount.

NCTM Connections Recognize and apply mathematics in contexts outside of mathematics.

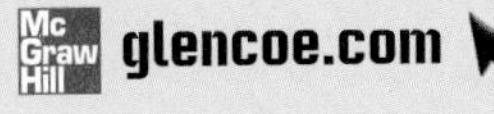

Check your answers.

Visual Summary

Retirement and Estate Planning

Plan Ahead

By thinking about the lifestyle you want for your retirement, you can evaluate where you are and determine the steps you need to take to get the desired lifestyle.

Retirement Planning
1. Setting Long-Range Goals
2. Conducting a Financial Analysis
3. Reviewing Assets

Understand Your Options

An attorney can help you choose the best type of will for your situation to ensure that your beneficiaries will pay the least amount of taxes.

Try It!

Draw a diagram like the one shown to organize the four main types of trusts that you can choose from to meet your needs.

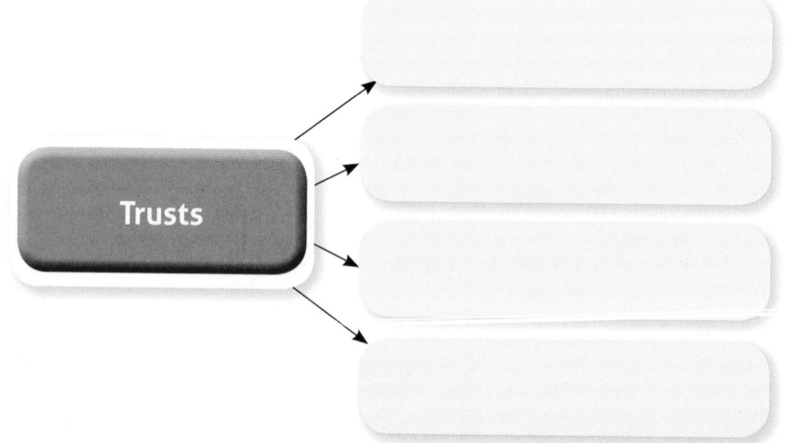

Chapter Review and Assessment

CHAPTER REVIEW

Chapter Summary

- The sooner you start planning and saving for retirement, the faster your assets will accumulate.
- Estimating your living expenses is the first step of retirement planning. Housing needs will depend on your desires and your health.
- Social Security provides a regular monthly income payment but is not meant to cover all retirement expenses.
- A defined-contribution plan is an individual account for each employee into which an employer contributes a specific annual amount; a defined-benefit plan specifies benefits based on total earnings and years on the job.
- Personal retirement accounts include regular IRAs, Roth IRAs, SEP plans, Spousal IRAs, Rollover IRAs, Education IRAs, and Keogh plans.
- The various types of wills include simple wills, traditional marital share wills, exemption trust wills, and stated dollar amount wills.
- The several types of trusts include credit-shelter trusts, disclaimer trusts, living trusts, and testamentary trusts.
- One common characteristic of many estates is joint ownership of property between spouses.
- Estates are taxed with estate taxes, estate and trust federal income taxes, inheritance taxes, and gift taxes.

Vocabulary Review

1. Write each of the vocabulary terms below on an index card, and the definitions on separate index cards. Work in pairs or small groups to match each term to its definition.

- assisted-living facility (ALF)
- defined-contribution plan
- 401(k) plan
- vesting
- defined-benefit plan
- individual retirement account (IRA)
- Keogh plan
- annuity (insurance)
- heirs
- estate
- estate planning
- beneficiary (estate)
- will
- intestate
- trust
- probate
- executor
- guardian
- codicil
- living will
- power of attorney
- misconceptions
- adjustments
- roll over
- distributions
- declaration
- disclaim

Higher Order Thinking 

2. **Explain** One of the myths about retirement is that saving a small amount of money will not help. Explain why this is a myth.
3. **Relate** How does a rollover IRA relate to a regular IRA?
4. **Determine** What are some factors you might use when selecting an executor?
5. **Theorize** Why is it beneficial to an employer to offer a retirement plan?
6. **Hypothesize** Why might an estate planner recommend newlyweds to own property as "tenants in common"?
7. **Judge** Do you think inheritance taxes are fair or unfair? Should federal and state governments do away with these taxes?
8. **Defend** Now retired, Jackson wants to use his savings to travel. His family wants him to leave the money to his children. Do you agree with Jackson or his family? Defend your position.
9. **Evaluate** A couple owns a home with no mortgage payments. They have plans to travel after retirement. Discuss whether Lauren and Tyler should keep their current home or consider other options.

College and Career Readiness

Social Studies

10. Pension Plan As life expectancies lengthen and costs of living increase, many people feel that the Social Security system needs to be revised to better serve our aging population. How do other countries provide for the elderly? Use print or online resources to conduct research to learn about Social Security, or a comparable public pension plan, in another country. How does it differ from America's Social Security? How does it meet the needs of its citizens? Prepare a brief report to share your findings. Do you feel that their system works? Would it work in the U.S.?

NCSS I A Analyze and explain the ways groups, societies, and cultures address human needs and concerns.

Mathematics

11. Savings for Retirement Marta has decided to participate in her company's 401(k) plan. She is allowed to contribute up to 25 percent of her annual salary to the plan. The company matches 50 percent of the first 5 percent of an employee's contributions ($0.50 per every $1.00). Marta has chosen to contribute 7 percent of her salary. Assume the plan earns 10 percent each year and Marta's annual salary is $75,000. Also assume that contributions are made once per year at the beginning of each year. How much will the total contributions be after 3 years? What will her balance be at the end of 3 years?

Math Concept **Calculate 401(k) Benefits** Calculate the balance of a retirement plan by determining the total contributions made as well as the gains earned and adding these to the balance.

Starting Hint Calculate the total contributions made each year by first multiplying the annual salary by the employee's contribution percentage. Next multiply the annual salary by the percentage the company will match of an employee's contribution, and multiply the result by the match percentage. Add the two contributions to determine total contributions.

NCTM Connections Understand how mathematical ideas interconnect and build on one another to produce a coherent whole.

English Language Arts

12. Social Security Many retirees find themselves returning to work. You should be aware though, that employment can affect your Social Security benefits. With your teacher's permission, visit the Web site for the Social Security administration and find the publication titled "How Work Affects Your Benefits." If there are parts you do not understand, speak to an adult or contact the Social Security administration office, to get clarification. Do you feel the policies surrounding employment during retirement are fair? Write a paragraph to summarize the key points of the publication, along with your evaluation.

NCTE 3 Apply strategies to interpret texts.

Ethics

13. Financial Decisions Greg and Beth's grandmother just passed away but left no letter of last instructions. Greg wants to have a big funeral to honor their grandmother. Beth, however, believes their grandmother would prefer them to keep it small and intimate. Greg thinks Beth is just concerned about the money. Beth insists that it is not about the money. How do you think Greg and Beth should deal with this situation? Is there a 'right' or 'wrong' thing to do? Write a paragraph with your analysis, including your recommendations for Greg and Beth.

Real-World Applications

14. Wills and Trusts You will need a lawyer to help you draw up a will and/or trusts. However, you can minimize the amount of time a lawyer will have to spend preparing the will or trust by doing some preliminary research and organization. Conduct online research to find out some of your state's requirements for a will or trust to be valid. Look for sample wills and trust documents so that you will know what to expect. Your research can also tell you what documents you will need to bring with you. Write a brief summary of your state's requirements and a list of necessary documents.

Your Financial Portfolio

Saving for Retirement

Henri has become eligible to participate in his company's 403(b) program. He can invest from 2 to 15 percent of his salary, which is $20,000 a year. The company matches the first 5 percent at a rate of 50 percent, or 50 cents for every dollar he invests. Henri has decided to save 5 percent of his salary. Based on the current investment return of 10 percent compounded annually, Henri has calculated how much he would be able to save over 10 years, including company-matching contributions.

	Contributions	Interest	Total
Henri's contribution of 5 percent of his $20,000 salary	$1,000/year	10%	
Company contribution matching 50 percent of 5 percent of his salary	$500/year		
1st Year	$1,500	$150.00	$1,650.00
2nd Year	1,500	315.00	3,465.00
3rd Year	1,500	496.50	5,461.50
4th Year	1,500	696.15	7,657.65
5th Year	1,500	915.77	10,073.42
6th Year	1,500	1,157.34	12,730.76
7th Year	1,500	1,423.08	15,653.84
8th Year	1,500	1,715.38	18,869.22
9th Year	1,500	2,036.92	22,406.14
10th Year	1,500	2,390.61	26,296.75
Total	**$15,000**	**$11,296.75**	**$26,296.75**

Calculate

On a separate sheet of paper, create a table like the one shown. Use the table to calculate how much you would have in ten years if you saved $2,000 a year at an annual interest rate of 10 percent, with the company contributing $500 a year.

Unit 7

Unit Project

Planning for Retirement

Ask Yourself...

Have you ever considered what your life will be like when you retire? Why is it important to save and invest your money, and have insurance protection? Do you know anyone who is retired and living the lifestyle you would like? Responses to these questions can help lead you to a realistic and successful retirement plan.

Your Objective

The goal of this project is to estimate expenses needed to maintain your desired lifestyle during retirement, to consider sources of income to meet those expenses, and prepare a short presentation to share your findings and solutions.

Skills You'll Use

Success in defining goals and preparing financially for those goals depends on your skills. Some skills you might use include:

Academic Skills—Reading, writing, and mathematics

21st Century Skills—Critical thinking, speaking, listening, financial literacy, and interpersonal skills

Technology Skills—Word processing, keyboarding, Internet research, and presentation software

Standards

NCTE 4 Use written language to communicate effectively.

NCTE 5 Use different writing process elements to communicate effectively.

NCTE 12 Use language to accomplish individual purposes.

NCTM Number and Operations Compute fluently and make reasonable estimates.

STEP 1 Determine Living Expenses

Knowing how much money is needed to support your desired lifestyle will help ensure that your financial plan can accommodate your retirement.

- How much income will you need for your living expenses such as housing, food, and clothing once you retire?
- How much will your insurance premiums and medical expenses require?
- What types of leisure activities do you want to be able to do?
- Will you continue to give gifts and charitable donations?

Once you have a reasonable estimate of the income needed, adjust it to allow for inflation. Assume a 4 percent rate of inflation for your calculations. Write a descriptive essay to share your desired lifestyle. Then write a paragraph to summarize your calculations of the income needed.

STEP 2 Consider Income Sources

At what age would you like to retire? How will you continue to create income once you have retired? Consider all the income sources discussed in the text.

- Do you have a savings plan in place?
- How might adequate insurance now affect your income later?
- Are you investing your money in a diverse portfolio?
- Will you have pension plans, IRAs, or annuities available to you?
- Do you want to continue to work—part-time or full-time—during your retirement years?

Though you may not have the income to invest or open an IRA now, it is important to understand all the options and have a plan in place to funnel your future income appropriately. Research as necessary to better understand your options. Then write a proposal of how you will prepare for your retirement income. Your proposal should include date estimates. For example, when do you plan to begin investing or open an IRA?

STEP 3 Build Relationships

What information can you gain from someone with personal experience? Meet with retired adults in your community to find out more about how they prepared for retirement and what they would recommend to you. Did they do enough to support the lifestyle they desired? How do their expenses now compare to their expenses prior to retirement?

- Prepare interview questions ahead of time.
- Take notes and record the responses.
- Use positive body language and ask open-ended questions.
- Be polite and respectful when asking your questions.
- Practice active listening skills.
- Write a summary of the information learned in your interview.

STEP 4 Develop Your Presentation

Use the Unit 7 Project Checklist to plan and create your presentation.

STEP 5 Evaluate Your Presentation

Your presentation will be evaluated based on the following:

- Evaluation rubric
- Thoroughness and organization of information
- Mechanics—clarity and neatness
- Interpersonal skills

Project Checklist

Plan

- ✔ Consider what your expenses will be after retirement.
- ✔ Determine what income sources you are likely to have during retirement.
- ✔ Meet with a retired member of your community to discuss his or her planning and recommendations for retirement.

Write

- ✔ Write an essay describing the lifestyle you hope to have when you retire.
- ✔ Write a summary of the expenses you will have during retirement, making sure to allow for inflation.
- ✔ Write a proposal of how you will finance your retirement lifestyle, including all likely or planned sources of income and when you plan to begin developing those sources.
- ✔ List your interview questions.
- ✔ Write a summary of the interviewee's responses.

Present

- ✔ Create an outline for your presentation.
- ✔ Create visuals and use technology to enhance your presentation.
- ✔ Speak clearly and concisely.
- ✔ Share your retirement lifestyle expectations with the class.
- ✔ Present your proposal of retirement income sources.
- ✔ Present your interview summary and describe how it might have changed your expectations or proposal.
- ✔ Respond to questions posed by the audience.

McGraw Hill **glencoe.com**

Evaluate Download a rubric you can use to evaluate your project.

Writing Numbers as Words and Rounding Numbers

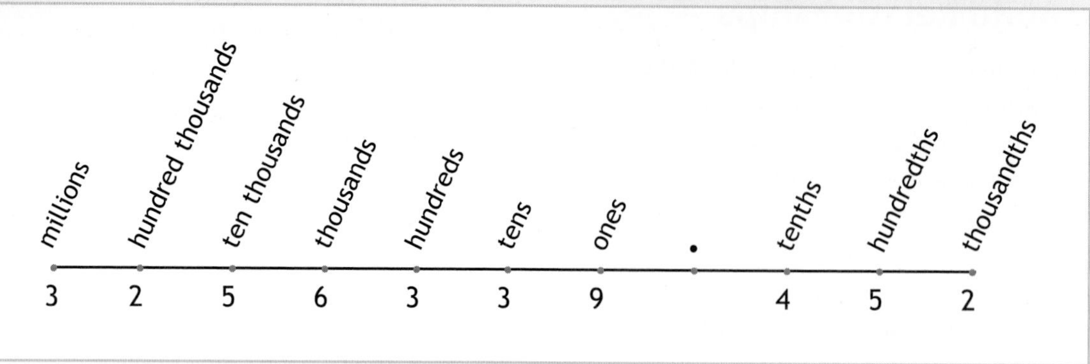

The place-value chart shows the value of each digit in the number 3,256,339.452. The place-value chart can help you write numbers.

EXAMPLE

482
8.557
$39.45

SOLUTION

four hundred eighty-two
eight and five hundred fifty-seven thousandths
thirty-nine and forty-five hundredths dollars
or thirty-nine and $^{45}/_{100}$ dollars

Place value is also used in rounding numbers. If the digit to the right of the place value you want to round is 5 or more, round up by adding 1 to the number in the place value. Then change all the digits to the right of the place value to zeros. If the number is 4 or less, round down by changing all the numbers to the right of the place value to zeros.

EXAMPLE Round 4765 to the nearest hundred.

SOLUTION

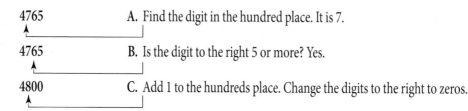

4765 — **A.** Find the digit in the hundred place. It is 7.

4765 — **B.** Is the digit to the right 5 or more? Yes.

4800 — **C.** Add 1 to the hundreds place. Change the digits to the right to zeros.

EXAMPLE Round 0.843 to the nearest tenth.

SOLUTION

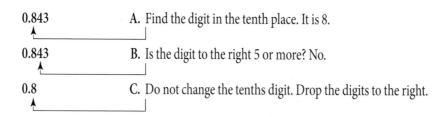

0.843 — **A.** Find the digit in the tenth place. It is 8.

0.843 — **B.** Is the digit to the right 5 or more? No.

0.8 — **C.** Do not change the tenths digit. Drop the digits to the right.

Writing Numbers as Words and Rounding Numbers

Dollar and cents amounts are often rounded to the nearest cent, or the hundredths place.

EXAMPLE $26.7443 / $683.1582

SOLUTION $26.74 / $683.16

PROBLEMS

Write as numbers.

1. three thousand four hundred ninety-nine
2. one hundred eleven and $^{32}/_{100}$ dollars
3. two hundred six and eighty-eight thousandths

Write in word form.

4. 572
5. 2.897
6. $325.10

Round to the nearest place value shown.

7. ten thousand 327,975
8. thousand 816,777
9. hundred 26,312
10. ten 6336
11. one 28.91
12. tenth 86.379
13. hundredth 5.5787

Round 23,793,611 to the place value shown.

14. millions
15. ten millions
16. thousands
17. hundreds
18. ten thousands
19. hundred thousands

Round to the nearest place value shown.

20. cent $87.2671
21. ten cents $213.432
22. one dollar $671.98
23. ten dollars $5,982
24. hundred dollars $12,785

APPLICATIONS

25. As an accountant for the advertising agency of Phillips & Phillips, Marcia Strasser writes many checks. Write each check amount in words.
    a. $27.83
    b. $121.77
    c. $569.14
    d. $8,721.65

26. Juan Sanchez, an inventory clerk for a lumber yard, often rounds inventory figures for easier handling. Round the number from the inventory list to the nearest ten.
    a. grade 1 oak 519 ft.
    b. grade 2 oak 795 ft.
    c. grade 1 pine 323 ft.
    d. grade 2 pine 477 ft.

Adding and Subtracting Decimals

When adding decimals, write the addition problem in vertical form. Be sure to line up the decimal points. When adding amounts with different numbers of decimal places, write zeros in the empty decimal places.

EXAMPLE 15.27 + 16.39 + 36.19

SOLUTION

```
  15.27
  16.39
 +36.19
 ------
  67.85
```

EXAMPLE 58.2 + 3.97 + 8 + 123.796

SOLUTION

```
   58.2          58.200
    3.97          3.970
    8.            8.000
 +123.796      +123.796
 --------      --------
                193.966
```

When subtracting decimals, write the subtraction problem in vertical form. Be sure to line up the decimal points. When subtracting amounts with different numbers of decimal places, write zeros in the empty decimal places.

EXAMPLE 78.63 − 42.41

SOLUTION

```
  78.63
 −42.41
 ------
  36.22
```

EXAMPLE 149.9 − 28.37

SOLUTION

```
 149.9      149.90
 −28.37     −28.37
 ------     ------
            121.53
```

Adding and subtracting amounts of money is just like adding and subtracting decimals. The decimal point separates the dollars and cents. Remember to put a dollar sign in the total.

EXAMPLE $74.99 + $8.76

SOLUTION

```
 $74.99
  +8.76
 ------
 $83.75
```

EXAMPLE $750 − $43.29

SOLUTION

```
 $750.00
  −43.29
 -------
 $706.71
```

PROBLEMS

```
1. 19.87      2.  4.377     3.    8.3       4.  46.65      5. $ 2.77
   32.24          6.829          12.78            3.5          35.96
  +27.55         +2.707        +322.437        +125.397       +10.37
```

6. 22.19 + 47.75 + 13.88 + 19.85
7. 0.78 + 9.82 + 36.242 + 37.4
8. 6.7 + 27.81 + 653.47 + 5.5
9. 54.32 + 0.37 + 2.5 + 0.797
10. $6.22 + $53.19 + $ .33 + $7.85
11. $4.78 + $12.50 + $22 + $17.10

```
12.  3.75     13. 376.55     14. 468.47     15. 367.05     16. $363.27
    −2.18         −27.42        −233.55        −219.87         −79.14
```

Adding and Subtracting Decimals

17. 547.7 − 127.6
18. 76.99 − 3.87
19. 695.13 − 428.1
20. 3076 − 2205.50
21. \$300 − \$5.75
22. \$445.19 − \$175.76

APPLICATIONS Complete the sales receipts by finding the subtotals and the totals.

23.

Date	Auth. No.	Identification	Clerk	Reg./Dept.	☑ Take ☐ Send
6/1/--	86430		DL		

Qty	Class	Description	Price	Amount	
1		dress		77	98
1		jacket		85	99
2		hosiery	12.99 ea	25	98
a.	Freight charges will be included with your invoice at the time of shipping. You will be billed the published rates from UPS, US Postal Service.		Subtotal	?	
	CUSTOMER SIGNATURE X *Shelley Turner*		Tax	13	30
b.	Sales Slip		Total	?	

24.

Date	Auth. No.	Identification	Clerk	Reg./Dept.	☑ Take ☐ Send
3/14/--	42		JR		

Qty	Class	Description	Price	Amount	
1		couch		599	95
1 pr		draperies		279	88
a.	Freight charges will be included with your invoice at the time of shipping. You will be billed the published rates from UPS, US Postal Service.		Subtotal	?	
	CUSTOMER SIGNATURE X *Betty Clark*		Tax	57	19
b.	Sales Slip		Total	?	

Complete the bank deposit slips by finding the subtotals and the total deposits.

25.

			DOLLARS	CENTS
CASH	CURRENCY		72	00
	COINS			
CHECKS	LIST SEPARATELY	95-76	413	12
		98-11	25	00
		95-13	211	10
a.	SUBTOTAL		?	
	LESS CASH RECEIVED		50	00
b.	TOTAL DEPOSIT		?	

26.

			DOLLARS	CENTS
CASH	CURRENCY		23	00
	COINS		7	44
CHECKS	LIST SEPARATELY	85-76	175	66
		88-11	23	33
			12	87
a.	SUBTOTAL		?	
	LESS CASH RECEIVED		75	00
b.	TOTAL DEPOSIT		?	

27.

			DOLLARS	CENTS
CASH	CURRENCY			
	COINS		4	75
CHECKS	LIST SEPARATELY	57-12	25	95
		57-10	38	11
	SUBTOTAL		?	
	LESS CASH RECEIVED		25	00
	TOTAL DEPOSIT		?	

25. a. b.
26. a. b.
27. a. b.

28. You are a cashier at a coffee shop. Compute the correct change for each of the following orders.

	Customer's Order	Customer Gives You	Change
a.	\$8.76	\$10.00	
b.	\$12.94	\$15.00	
c.	\$9.30	\$10.50	
d.	\$16.11	\$20.00	
e.	\$5.57	\$5.75	
f.	\$22.02	\$25.00	
g.	\$7.12	\$7.15	
h.	\$3.33	\$5.00	
i.	\$28.04	\$30.04	
j.	\$6.12	\$10.25	

Multiplying and Dividing Decimals

When multiplying decimals, multiply as if the decimal numbers were whole numbers. Then count the total number of decimal places in the factors. This number will be the number of decimal places in the product.

EXAMPLE

```
  18.7 ← factor
× 0.34 ← factor
   748
  561
  6358 ← product
```

SOLUTION

```
  18.7 ←   1 decimal place
× 0.34 ← + 2 decimal places
   748
  561
 6.358 ←   3 decimal places
```

If the product does not have enough digits to place the decimal in the correct position, you will need to write zeros. Start at the right of the product in counting the decimal places and write zeros at the left.

EXAMPLE

```
  0.63
× 0.05
   315
```

SOLUTION

```
  0.63 ←   2 decimal places
× 0.05 ← + 2 decimal places
0.0315 ←   4 decimal places
```

When multiplying amounts of money, round the answer to the nearest cent. Remember to put a dollar sign in the answer.

EXAMPLE

```
 $2.25
 × 1.5
 3.375
```

SOLUTION

```
 $ 2.25 ←   2 places     $2.25 × 1.5 = $3.375
  × 1.5 ← + 1 place                  = $3.38
 $3.375 ←   3 places   rounded to the nearest cent
```

When multiplying by 10, 100, or 1000, count the number of zeros. Then move the decimal point to the right the same number of spaces.

EXAMPLE 8.32 × 100

SOLUTION 8.32 × 100 = 8.32 = 832   100 has 2 zeros; move decimal 2 places.

PROBLEMS

1. 18.3 × 2.5

2. 27.5 × 8.2

3. 56.8 × 0.33

4. 88.1 × 0.23

5. 0.57 × 0.14

6. 0.88 × 0.07

7. 0.93 × 0.04

8. 0.323 × 0.005

9. $17.85 × 15.5 = $276.675 =

10. $25.24 × 6.3 = $159.012 =

11. $18.15 × 6.5 = $117.975 =

12. $14.98 × 8.7 = $130.326 =

13. 33.8 × 10 =

14. 55.399 × 100 =

15. 0.518 × 1000 =

16. 532.788 × 10,000 =

Multiplying and Dividing Decimals

APPLICATION

17. Below are partial payroll records for Fanciful Flowers. Complete the records by calculating gross earnings (hourly rate x hours worked), Social Security tax (gross earnings × 0.062), Medicare tax (gross earnings × 0.0145), federal income tax (gross earnings × 0.15), and state income tax (gross earnings × 0.045). Round each deduction to the nearest cent. Find the total deductions and subtract from gross earnings to find the net pay.

	Employee	Hourly Rate	Number of Hours	Gross Earnings	Social Security Tax	Medicare Tax	Federal Inc. Tax	State Inc. Tax	Total Deductions	Net Pay
a.	M. Smith	$8.25	24							
b.	R. Nash	$9.15	33							
c.	C. Young	$7.75	15							
d.	D. Cha	$9.15	30							

When dividing decimals, if there is a decimal point in the divisor, you must move it to the right to make the divisor a whole number. Move the decimal point in the dividend to the right the same number of places you moved the decimal point in the divisor. Then divide as with whole numbers.

divisor $6\overline{)840}$ with quotient 140 — 140 quotient; 840 dividend

EXAMPLE

$3.44\overline{)15.5488}$

SOLUTION

$3.44\overline{)15.5488}$ (decimal points moved two places)

$$\begin{array}{r} 4.52 \\ 344\overline{)1554.88} \\ -\ 1376 \\ \hline 1788 \\ -\ 1720 \\ \hline 688 \\ -\ 688 \\ \hline \end{array}$$

Add zeros to the right of the decimal point in the dividend if needed.

EXAMPLE

$0.42\overline{)0.147}$

SOLUTION

$0.42\overline{)0.147}$ (decimal points moved two places)

$$\begin{array}{r} 0.35 \\ 42\overline{)14.70} \\ -\ 126 \\ \hline 210 \\ -\ 210 \\ \hline \end{array}$$ zero added

When the dividend is an amount of money, remember to place the dollar sign in the quotient and round the answer to the nearest cent.

EXAMPLE

$48\overline{)\$95.12}$

SOLUTION

$$\begin{array}{r} \$1.981 \\ 48\overline{)\$95.120} \end{array}$$

$95.12 ÷ 48 = $1.98 rounded to the nearest cent.

Multiplying and Dividing Decimals

When dividing by 10, 100, or 1000, count the number of zeros in 10, 100, or 1000 and move the decimal point to the left the same number of places.

EXAMPLE

15,213.7 ÷ 1000

SOLUTION

15,213.7 ÷ 1000 = 15213.7 = 15.2137 1000 has 3 zeros; move decimal 3 places

PROBLEMS

Round to the nearest hundredth or the nearest cent.

18. $2.7\overline{)11.61}$ **19.** $1.3\overline{)7.67}$ **20.** $6.2\overline{)44.02}$

21. $0.3\overline{)1.62}$ **22.** $.05\overline{)1.47}$ **23.** $.04\overline{)28.4}$

24. $8.3\overline{)46.99}$ **25.** $3.4\overline{)178.3}$ **26.** $88\overline{)\$356.68}$

27. $45\overline{)\$42.79}$ **28.** $15\overline{)\$87.32}$ **29.** $14.1\overline{)7.823}$

APPLICATIONS

30. Your family is looking into buying a late model, used vehicle. Calculate (to the nearest tenth) the gas mileage for the following types of vehicles.

	Type of Vehicle	Miles	Gallons of Fuel	Miles per Gallon
a.	Subcompact	631	17.8	
b.	4-door sedan	471.4	16.6	
c.	Minivan	405.1	18.2	
d.	Compact	512.2	15.7	
e.	SUV	298.1	23.2	

Fraction to Decimal, Decimal to Fraction

Any fraction can be renamed as a decimal and any decimal can be renamed as a fraction. To rename a fraction as a decimal, use division. Think of the fraction bar in the fraction as meaning "divide by." For example, $^5/_8$ means "5 divided by 8." After the 5, write a decimal point and as many zeros as are needed. Then divide by 8.

EXAMPLE Change $^3/_8$ to a decimal.

SOLUTION

$$^3/_8 \rightarrow 8\overline{)3.000} = 0.375$$

```
      0.375
3/8 → 8)3.000
      - 24
         60
       - 56
         40
       - 40
```

EXAMPLE Change $^1/_5$ to a decimal.

SOLUTION

```
      0.2
1/5 → 5)1.0
      - 10
```

If a fraction does not divide evenly, divide to one more decimal place than you are rounding to.

EXAMPLE Change $^5/_7$ to a decimal rounded to the nearest hundredth. (Divide to the thousandths place.)

SOLUTION

```
      0.714 = 0.71
5/7 → 7)5.000
      - 49
        10
       - 7
        30
      - 28
         2
```

EXAMPLE Change $^2/_7$ to a decimal rounded to the nearest thousandth. (Divide to the ten thousandths place.)

SOLUTION

```
      0.2857 = 0.286
2/7 → 7)2.0000
      - 14
         60
       - 56
          40
        - 35
           50
         - 49
            1
```

To rename a decimal as a fraction, name the place value of the digit at the far right. This is the denominator of the fraction.

$0.83 = {}^{83}/_{100}$

3 is in the hundredths place, so the denominator is 100.

$0.007 = {}^{7}/_{1000}$

7 is in the thousandths place, so the denominator is 1000.

Note that the number of zeros in the denominator is the same as the number of places to the right of the decimal point. The fraction should always be written in lowest terms.

$0.25 = {}^{25}/_{100} = {}^{1}/_{4}$

$3.375 = 3\ {}^{375}/_{1000} = 3\ {}^{3}/_{8}$

Fraction to Decimal, Decimal to Fraction

PROBLEMS

Change the fractions to decimals. Round to the nearest thousandth.

1. $^{2}/_{5}$
2. $^{5}/_{6}$
3. $^{4}/_{9}$
4. $^{7}/_{10}$
5. $^{9}/_{25}$
6. $^{115}/_{200}$
7. $^{1}/_{7}$
8. $^{13}/_{40}$
9. $^{4}/_{15}$
10. $^{5}/_{12}$
11. $^{11}/_{16}$
12. $^{1}/_{4}$

Change the fractions to decimals. Round to the nearest hundredth.

13. $^{1}/_{8}$
14. $^{5}/_{9}$
15. $^{33}/_{35}$
16. $^{12}/_{25}$
17. $^{7}/_{20}$
18. $^{2}/_{25}$
19. $^{15}/_{16}$
20. $^{2}/_{9}$
21. $^{3}/_{7}$
22. $^{3}/_{4}$
23. $^{1}/_{6}$
24. $^{31}/_{32}$

Change the decimals to fractions reduced to lowest terms.

25. 0.275
26. 0.3
27. 0.15
28. 0.8
29. 1.125
30. 0.117
31. 0.32
32. 2.5
33. 44.755
34. 0.005
35. 5.545
36. 0.2

APPLICATIONS

37. In the past, stock prices were quoted as dollars and fractions of a dollar. Change the stock prices to dollars and cents. Round to the nearest cent.

	Stock	Price
a.	AdobeSy	$61\ ^{5}/_{16}$
b.	AirTran	$4\ ^{15}/_{32}$
c.	CNET	$50\ ^{3}/_{4}$
d.	ETrade	$20\ ^{1}/_{4}$
e.	Omnipoint	$112\ ^{5}/_{8}$
f.	Qualcomm	$142\ ^{1}/_{16}$
g.	WebLink	$17\ ^{13}/_{16}$
h.	Winstar	$70\ ^{23}/_{32}$

38. Individual bowling averages in the Southern Community League are carried to the nearest hundredth. Convert the decimals to fractions reduced to the lowest terms.

	Name	Average
a.	B. Taylor	220.13
b.	J. Scott	217.02
c.	T. Anfinson	216.97
d.	G. Ingram	212.08
e.	D. Ingram	210.50
f.	B. Jordan	209.25
g.	G. Maddux	207.88
h.	A. Jones	205.15

Percent to Decimal, Decimal to Percent

Percent is an abbreviation of the Latin words *per centum*, meaning "by the hundred." So percent means "divide by 100." A percent can be written as a decimal. To change a percent to a decimal, first write the percent as a fraction with a denominator of 100, then divide by 100.

EXAMPLE Change 31% to a decimal.

SOLUTION $31\% = {}^{31}/_{100} = 0.31$

EXAMPLE Change 17.3% to a decimal.

SOLUTION $17.3\% = {}^{17.3}/_{100} = 0.173$

When dividing by 100, you can just move the decimal point two places to the left. When you write a percent as a decimal, you are moving the decimal point two places to the left and dropping the percent sign (%). If necessary, use zero as a placeholder.

EXAMPLE

A. 31%

B. 7%

SOLUTION

31% = 31. = 0.31 ← Drop % sign. Move decimal 2 places.

7% = 07. = 0.07 ← Insert a zero as a placeholder.

To write a decimal as a percent, move the decimal point two places to the right and add a percent sign (%).

EXAMPLE

A. 0.31

B. 0.07

C. 2.5

D. 0.008

SOLUTION

0.31 = 0.31 = 31 % ← Add % sign. Move decimal 2 places.

0.07 = 0.07 = 7%

2.5 = 2.50 = 250%

0.008 = 0.008 = 0.8%

PROBLEMS

Write as decimals.

1. 35% **2.** 22% **3.** 68% **4.** 30%

5. 49.2% **6.** 88.7% **7.** 11.5% **8.** 92.9%

9. 322% **10.** 526% **11.** 663% **12.** 275%

13. 9% **14.** 5% **15.** 4% **16.** 12%

17. 7.03% **18.** 9.02% **19.** 2.0725% **20.** 3.0843%

Write as percents.

21. 0.75 **22.** 0.17 **23.** 0.44 **24.** 0.26

Percent to Decimal, Decimal to Percent

25. 0.06	**26.** 0.07	**27.** 0.01	**28.** 0.02
29. 0.003	**30.** 0.009	**31.** 0.0045	**32.** 0.0029
33. 3.12	**34.** 4.14	**35.** 6.007	**36.** 5.000
37. 0.1	**38.** 0.5	**39.** 325.5	**40.** 0.2015

APPLICATIONS

41. The percent changes in retail sales were reported as a decimal in the October issue of *Retail Monthly* magazine. Change the decimals to percents.

Retail Sales

	Month	Change
a.	February	0.012
b.	March	0.006
c.	April	0.013
d.	May	0.038
e.	June	0.043
f.	July	0.011
g.	August	0.022

42. The commission rate schedule for a stockbroker is shown. Change the percents to decimals.

Commission Rate Schedule

	Dollar Amount	% of Dollar Amount
a.	\$0–\$2,499	2.3%, minimum \$30
b.	\$2,500–\$4,999	2.0%, minimum \$42
c.	\$5,000–\$9,999	1.5%, minimum \$65
d.	\$10,000–\$14,999	1.1%, minimum \$110
e.	\$15,000–\$24,999	0.9%, minimum \$135
f.	\$25,000–\$49,999	0.6%, minimum \$175
	\$50,000 and above	negotiated

Percent to Decimal, Decimal to Percent

43. During the National Basketball Association season, the teams had these won-lost records. The Pct. column shows the percent of games won, expressed as a decimal. Change the decimals to percents.

EASTERN CONFERENCE
Atlantic Division

	W	L	Pct.	GB
a. Miami	28	16	.636	-
b. New York	27	17	.614	1
c. Philadelphia	25	21	.543	4
d. Boston	21	25	.457	8
e. Orlando	21	26	.447	8½
f. New Jersey	17	29	.370	12
g. Washington	15	31	.326	14

Central Division

	W	L	Pct.	GB
h. Indiana	29	15	.659	-
i. Milwaukee	26	21	.553	4½
j. Charlotte	24	20	.545	5
k. Toronto	24	20	.545	5
l. Detroit	22	23	.489	7½
m. Cleveland	19	26	.422	10½
n. Atlanta	17	26	.395	11½
o. Chicago	9	34	.209	19½

WESTERN CONFERENCE
Midwest Division

	W	L	Pct.	GB
p. San Antonio	30	16	.652	-
q. Utah	27	17	.614	2
r. Minnesota	25	18	.581	3½
s. Denver	21	22	.488	7½
t. Houston	19	27	.413	11
u. Dallas	18	27	.400	11½
v. Vancouver	12	32	.273	17

Pacific Division

	W	L	Pct.	GB
w. L.A. Lakers	34	11	.756	-
x. Portland	34	11	.756	-
y. Sacramento	28	16	.636	5½
z. Seattle	29	18	.617	6
aa. Phoenix	26	18	.591	7½
ab. Golden State	11	32	.256	22
ac. L.A. Clippers	11	34	.244	23

44. How many teams have won more than 75% of their games? ______
Who are they? ____________________

45. How many teams have won more than 50% of their games? ______
46. How many have won less than 30% of their games? ______

Finding a Percentage

Finding a percentage means finding a percent of a number. To find a percent of a number, you change the percent to a decimal, then multiply it by the number.

EXAMPLE 30% of 90 is what number?

SOLUTION

$30\% \times 90 = n$	In mathematics, *of* means "times" and *is* means "equals."
	Let n stand for the unknown number.
$0.30 \times 90 = n$	Change the percent to a decimal.
$27 = n$	Multiply.
30% of $90 = 27$	Write the answer.

EXAMPLE The delivery charge is 8% of the selling price of $145.00. Find the delivery charge.

SOLUTION

$8\% \times \$145.00 = n$
$0.08 \times \$145.00 = n$
$\$11.60 = n$
$8\% \times \$145.00 = \$11.60$ delivery charge

EXAMPLE The student had 95% correct out of 80 questions. How many answers were correct?

SOLUTION

$95\% \times 80 = n$
$0.95 \times 80 = n$
$76 = n$
$95\% \times 80 = 76$ correct

PROBLEMS

Find the percentage.

1. 25% of 60
2. 45% of 80
3. 40% of 30
4. 33% of 112
5. 58% of 420
6. 50% of 422
7. 3% of 100
8. 2% of 247
9. 110% of 65
10. 7% of 785
11. 1% of 819
12. 4% of 19.5
13. 185% of 95
14. 200% of 720
15. 135% of 860
16. 120% of 3.35
17. 4.5% of 50
18. 1.25% of 300
19. 33.3% of 80
20. 67.2% of 365

Round the answer to the nearest cent.

21. 7% of $35.78
22. 6.5% of $80
23. 10% of $93.20
24. 5.5% of $135
25. 4.25% of $65.00
26. 2.75% of $115
27. 125% of $98
28. 7.5% of $150
29. 0.3% of $450
30. 0.15% of $125
31. 8.2% of $19.89
32. 5.25% of $110.15

APPLICATIONS

33. The following items appeared in a sales flyer for a major department store. Calculate the amount saved from the regular price as well as the sale price for each item. Round to the nearest cent.

		Amount Saved	Sale Price
a.	Save 25% on juniors knit shirts. Reg. $18.		
b.	Save 30% on women's dresses. Reg. $69.99		
c.	Save 20% on men's shoes. Reg. $135.		
d.	Save 25% on all nursery cribs. Reg. $119.99		
e.	Save 25% on all boxed jewelry sets. Reg. $19.99		
f.	Save 30% on family athletic shoes. Reg. $59.99		

34. Student Sean Hu received these test scores. How many answers were correct on each test?

	Subject	Test Score	Number of Items	Correct Answers
a.	Math	90%	80	
b.	English	70%	90	
c.	Science	80%	110	
d.	Spanish	90%	50	
e.	Government	85%	100	

35. Sales taxes are found by multiplying the tax rate times the selling price of the item. The total purchase price is the selling price plus the sales tax. Find the sales tax and total purchase price for each selling price. Round to the nearest cent.

	Selling Price	Tax Rate	Sales Tax	Total Purchase Price
a.	$14.78	4%		
b.	$22.50	5%		
c.	$3.88	6%		
d.	$95.85	6.5%		
e.	$212.00	7.25%		
f.	$85.06	8.25%		
g.	$199.99	7.455%		

Average (Mean)

The average, or mean, is a single number used to represent a group of numbers. The average, or mean, of two or more numbers is the sum of the numbers divided by the number of items added.

EXAMPLE Find the average of 8, 5, 3, 7, and 2. Add to find the total.

SOLUTION $\frac{8+5+3+7+2}{5} = \frac{25}{5} = 5$ Divide by the number of items.

EXAMPLE Find the average of 278, 340, 205, and 235.

SOLUTION $\frac{278+340+205+235}{4} = \frac{1058}{4} = 264.5$

EXAMPLE Find the average of 4.3, 7.1, 1.5, 3.2, and 6.4. Round to the nearest tenth.

SOLUTION $\frac{4.3+7.1+1.5+3.2+6.4}{5} = \frac{22.5}{5} = 4.5$

EXAMPLE Find the average of \$12, \$35, \$19, \$23, \$11, and \$21. Round to the nearest dollar.

SOLUTION $\frac{\$12+\$35+\$19+\$23+\$11+\$21}{6} = \frac{\$121}{6} = \$20.17 = \$20$

PROBLEMS

Find the average for each group.

1. 3, 5, 7, 9, 11
2. 25, 40, 35, 50
3. 211, 197, 132
4. 416, 310, 344, 430
5. 4.4, 2.9, 3.7, 1.8, 6.5
6. 3.6, 7.1, 4.8, 4.7, 6.3, 5.3
7. $23, $21, $25, $24, $26
8. $98, $87, $79, $85, $88, $91

Find the average for each group. Round to the nearest hundredth or cent.

9. 8.1, 8.6, 7.7, 9.2, 5.5, 6.9, 7.3
10. 3.3, 5.8, 4.6, 2.8, 3.4, 5.2
11. $31.70, $33.91, $36.17, $33.85
12. $4.37, $3.74, $4.90, $5.74, $6.11
13. $55.78, $44.20, $43.95, $34.36

Average (Mean)

14. $121.19, $115.08, $135, $129.05, $111.88
15. Ben Agars had bowling scores of 187, 154, and 130. What was his average?
16. Kelley O'Reilly's tips from being a waitress were $5.00, $5.50, $4.75, $3.00, $4.50, $2.00, $5.75, and $4.50. What was her average tip?
17. Last year, Michael Legato's telephone bills averaged $66.12 a month. What was his total bill for the year?
18. Mark Purdue recorded his math test scores this quarter. What is his average?

Test Number	1	2	3	4	5	6	7	8
Score	65	77	81	79	90	86	92	98

19. What does he need on the next test to have an average of 85?
20. If Mark got a 97 on test 9 and 100 on test 10, what would be his average?

APPLICATIONS

21. As captain of the school golf team, Erica Samuelson has to complete this form after each game. Help her by computing the total and the average for each golfer. She also computes the total and the team average for each game. Round to the nearest whole number.

	Golfer	Game 1	Game 2	Game 3	Total	Average
a.	Samuelson	86	78	75		
b.	Haas	80	81	70		
c.	Sutherland	82	77	71		
d.	Beck	80	66	73		
e.	McCarron	78	81	82		
f.	Total					
g.	Team average					

Elapsed Time

To find elapsed time, subtract the earlier time from the later time.

EXAMPLE Find the elapsed time for Kaitlin Harper who worked from:
A. 4:30 P.M. to 11:45 P.M. B. 5:15 A.M. to 10:33 A.M.

SOLUTION

A.
11:45
− 4:30
7:15 = 7 hours 15 minutes
written as 7 h:15 min

B.
10:33
− 5:15
5:18 = 5 hours 18 minutes
written as 5 h:18 min

You cannot subtract 45 minutes from 30 minutes unless you borrow an hour and add it to the 30 minutes. Remember that 1 hour = 60 minutes.

EXAMPLE Find the elapsed time from 2:50 P.M. to 9:15 P.M.

SOLUTION

9:15 = 8:15 + :60 = 8:75 borrowed 1 hour
−2:50 = − 2:50 − 2:50
6:25 = 6 h:25 min

To find elapsed time when the time period goes past noon, add 12 hours to the later time before subtracting.

EXAMPLE Find the elapsed time from 6:00 A.M. to 3:15 P.M.

SOLUTION

3:15 = 3:15 + 12:00 = 15:15
−6:00 = − 6:00 − 6:00
9:15 = 9 h:15 min

EXAMPLE Find the elapsed time from 10:35 P.M. to 3:12 A.M.

SOLUTION

3:12 = 15:12 = 14:12 + :60 = 14:72
− 10:35 = − 10:35 = − 10:35 − 10:35
4:37 = 4 h:37 min

PROBLEMS

Find the elapsed time.

1. From 2:30 P.M. to 6:35 P.M.
2. From 1:18 P.M. to 7:25 P.M.
3. From 4:40 A.M. to 8:57 A.M.
4. From 3:33 A.M. to 10:47 A.M.
5. From 3:15 A.M. to 5:20 A.M.
6. From 1:25 P.M. to 9:05 P.M.
7. From 7:35 P.M. to 11:12 P.M.
8. From 8:43 A.M. to 11:30 A.M.
9. From 6:00 A.M. to 3:30 P.M.
10. From 10:30 A.M. to 6:45 P.M.
11. From 5:45 A.M. to 9:16 A.M.
12. From 1:45 A.M. to 7:05 A.M.
13. From 6:10 P.M. to 8:08 P.M.
14. From 3:28 A.M. to 11:16 A.M.
15. From 2:27 P.M. to 9:11 P.M.
16. From 3:56 P.M. to 10:22 P.M.

Elapsed Time

17. From 12:07 A.M. to 7:25 A.M.
18. From 12:35 P.M. to 6:45 P.M.
19. From 8:10 A.M. to 4:45 P.M.
20. From 7:45 A.M. to 5:30 P.M.
21. From 7:00 A.M. to 3:00 P.M.
22. From 8:30 A.M. to 5:00 P.M.
23. From 7:30 A.M. to 4:10 P.M.
24. From 8:23 A.M. to 5:04 P.M.
25. From 5:45 A.M. to 2:15 P.M.
26. From 7:43 A.M. to 4:21 P.M.
27. From 8:45 P.M. to 1:18 A.M.
28. From 9:47 A.M. to 7:08 P.M.
29. From 11:27 P.M. to 4:11 A.M.
30. From 5:55 P.M. to 1:55 A.M.

APPLICATIONS

31. Jack Keegan worked from 7:15 A.M. to 5:00 P.M. How long did he work?
32. Elena Diaz took a bus that left Cincinnati at 5:45 P.M. and arrived in Cleveland at 1:10 A.M. How long was the trip?
33. National Delivery Service (N.D.S.) ships hundreds of packages across the United States every day by air freight. Below is an N.D.S. air freight schedule. Calculate the total transit time for each shipment. (Note that all times given are Eastern Standard Time; therefore, time zones do not need to be taken into account.)

	Shipped From	Shipped To	Departure Time	Arrival Time	Total Transit Time
a.	Chattanooga, TN	Atlanta, GA	7:35 A.M.	8:20 A.M.	
b.	Chicago, IL	Houston, TX	8:10 A.M.	12:57 P.M.	
c.	Los Angeles, CA	New Orleans, LA	8:35 A.M.	2:17 P.M.	
d.	New York, NY	Cleveland, OH	5:25 P.M.	7:25 P.M.	
e.	Boston, MA	Phoenix, AZ	11:45 A.M.	7:28 P.M.	
f.	Atlanta, GA	Miami, FL	7:07 A.M.	9:00 A.M.	

Reading Tables and Charts

To read a table or chart, find the *column* containing one of the pieces of information you have. Look across the *row* containing the other piece of information. Read down the column and across the row. Read the information you need where the column and row intersect.

Shipping Costs

Not Over (lbs)	Zone 2 & 3	Zone 4	Zone 5	Zone 6	Zone 7
1	$4.00	$4.00	$4.00	$4.00	$4.00
2	$4.00	$4.00	$4.00	$4.00	$4.00
3	$5.10	$5.10	$5.10	$5.10	$5.10
4	$6.20	$6.20	$6.20	$6.20	$6.20
5	$7.30	$7.30	$7.30	$7.30	$7.30
6	$8.60	$8.90	$9.10	$9.45	$9.70
7	$8.70	$9.30	$9.70	$10.40	$10.90
8	$8.80	$9.70	$10.30	$11.35	$12.10
9	$8.90	$10.10	$10.90	$12.30	$13.30
10	$9.00	$10.50	$11.50	$13.25	$14.50

EXAMPLE What is the cost to ship a 6-lb package to Zone 5?

SOLUTION
a. Find the Zone 5 column.
b. Find the 6-lb row.
c. Read across the 6-lb row to the Zone 5 column. The cost is $9.10.

To classify an item, find the row that contains the known data. Then read the classification from the head of the column.

Men's Body Measurement

Size	S	M	L	XL	XXL
Neck	14–14 1/2	15–15 1/2	16–16 1/2	17–17 1/2	18–18 1/2
Chest	34–36	38–40	42–44	46–48	50–52
Waist	28–30	32–34	36–38	40–42	44–46
Reg. Sleeve	32–33	33–34	34–35	35–36	36–37
Tall Sleeve	33–34	34–35	35–36	36–37	37–38
Height	Reg. 5′8″–6′	Tall 6′1″–6′4″			

Talls: Measure 2″ longer overall, 1″ at sleeves

EXAMPLE What size shirt should a man with a 42-inch chest order?

SOLUTION
a. Find the row for the Chest measurements.
b. Read across the row to 42–44.
c. Read the size at the head of the column (L). A man with a 42-inch chest should order a size L, which stands for large.

PROBLEMS

Use the shipping chart above to find the cost to ship each package to the indicated zone.

1. 3 lb, Zone 3
2. 4 lb, Zone 7
3. 9 lb, Zone 4
4. 2 lb, Zone 6
5. 6 lb, Zone 2
6. 5 lb, Zone 5
7. 1.5 lb, Zone 5
8. 6.4 lb, Zone 7
9. 8.2 lb, Zone 3
10. 7.1 lb, Zone 6
11. 5.8 lb, Zone 4
12. 9.3 lb, Zone 3

Reading Tables and Charts

Use the size chart on the previous page to determine what size to order. In-between sizes should order the next size up.

13. Shorts—waist 33
14. Shirt—chest 37
15. Jacket—chest 47
16. Pants—waist 43
17. Sweater—chest 43
18. Shirt—height 6′2″ sleeves 36

APPLICATIONS

19. Use the shipping chart on the previous page to determine the maximum amount a package can weigh.

	a.	b.	c.	d.	e.	f.
Shipping Zone	2	5	7	3	6	4
Shipping Cost	$7.30	$4.00	$13.30	$8.90	$7.30	$5.10
Maximum Weight						

Use the Federal Income Tax table to find the amount of tax withheld in questions 20–25 and the amount of wages earned in questions 26–31:

Federal Income Tax Table
MARRIED Persons—WEEKLY Payroll Period

If the wages are—		And the number of withholding allowances claimed is—							
At least	But less than	0	1	2	3	4	5	6	7
		The amount of income tax to be withheld is—							
$480	$490	$63	$56	$50	$44	$38	$32	$25	$19
490	500	64	58	52	45	39	33	27	21
500	510	66	59	53	47	41	35	28	22
510	520	67	61	55	48	42	36	30	24
520	530	69	62	56	50	44	38	31	25
530	540	70	64	58	51	45	39	33	27
540	550	72	65	59	53	47	41	34	28
550	560	73	67	61	54	48	42	36	30
560	570	75	68	62	56	50	44	37	31
570	580	76	70	64	57	51	45	39	33
580	590	78	71	65	59	53	47	40	34
590	600	79	73	67	60	54	48	42	36
600	610	81	74	68	62	56	50	43	37
610	620	82	76	70	63	57	51	45	39
620	630	84	77	71	65	59	53	46	40

	20.	21.	22.	23.	24.	25.
Income	$491.77	$501.07	$617.30	$525.00	$600.00	$531.13
Allowances	2	1	3	0	4	6
Amount Withheld						

	Number of Allowances	Tax Withheld	Wages At least	Wages But less than
26.	5	$47		
27.	2	$71		
28.	3	$53		
29.	1	$62		
30.	4	$38		
31.	0	$76		

Constructing Graphs

A **bar graph** is a picture that displays and compares numerical facts in the form of vertical or horizontal bars. To construct a vertical bar graph, follow these steps:

a. Draw the vertical and horizontal axes.
b. Scale the vertical axis to correspond to the given data.
c. Draw one bar to represent each quantity.
d. Label each bar and the vertical and horizontal axes.
e. Title the graph.

Metropolitan Statistical Areas
Population (in millions)

Chicago, IL	8.6
San Francisco, CA	6.6
Philadelphia, PA	6.0
Detroit, MI	5.3

EXAMPLE Construct a vertical bar graph of the given data.

SOLUTION
a. Draw vertical and horizontal axes.
b. Scale the vertical axis.
c. Draw one bar to represent each quantity.
d. Label each bar and the vertical and horizontal axes.
e. Title the graph.

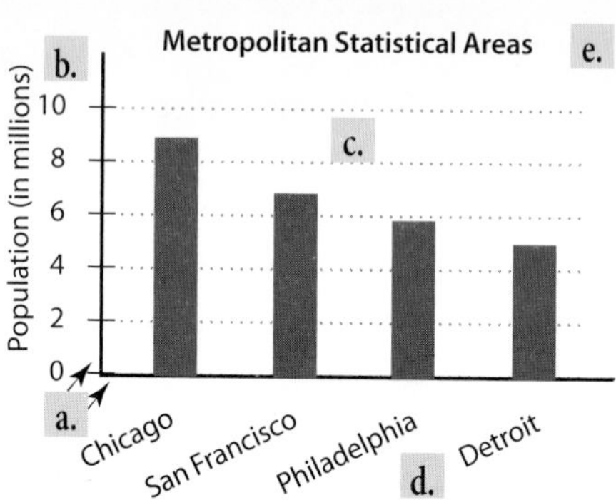

A **line graph** is a picture used to compare data over a period of time. It is an excellent way to show trends (increases or decreases). To construct a line graph, follow these steps:

a. Draw the vertical and horizontal axes.
b. Scale the vertical axis to correspond to the given data.
c. Label the axes.
d. Place a point on the graph to correspond to each item of data.
e. Connect the points from left to right.
f. Title the graph.

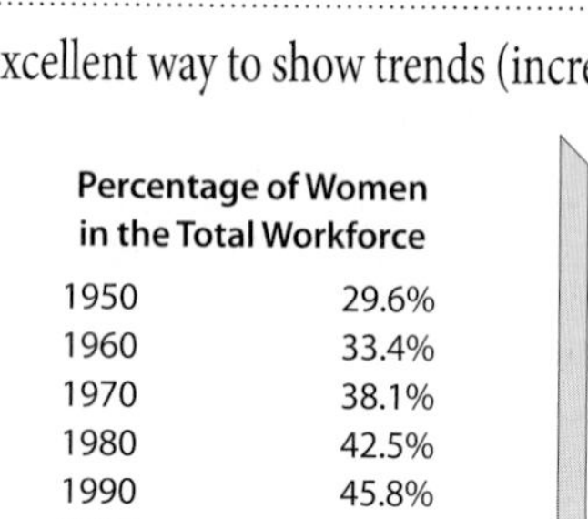

Percentage of Women in the Total Workforce

1950	29.6%
1960	33.4%
1970	38.1%
1980	42.5%
1990	45.8%
2000	47.5%

EXAMPLE Construct a line graph of the given data.

SOLUTION
a. Draw the vertical and horizontal axes.
b. Scale the vertical axis.
c. Label the axes.

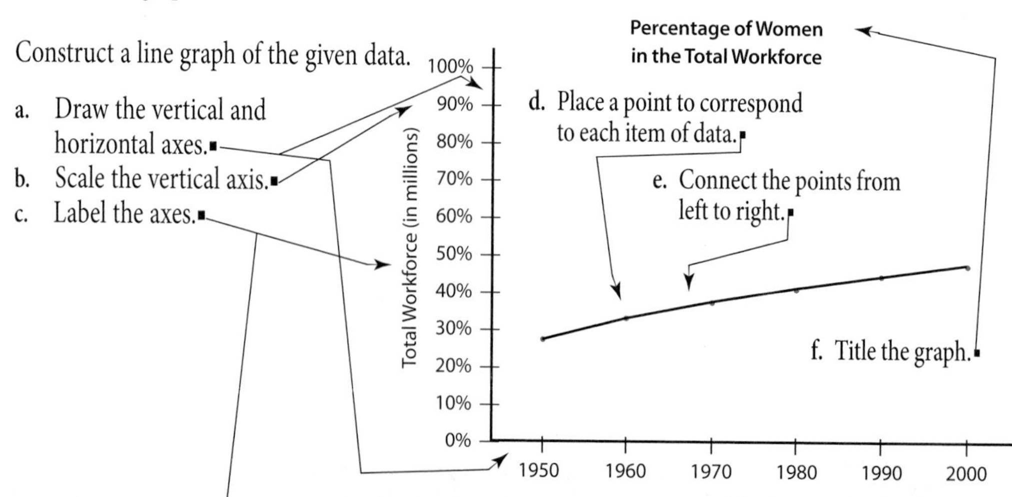

Constructing Graphs

PROBLEMS

1. Construct a vertical bar graph of the given data.

Wrenn's Department Store
Total Sales by Department (in thousands)

Housewares	122
Men's Clothing	145
Women's Clothing	160
Appliances	183
Electronics	214

2. Read the vertical bar graph.
   a. Of the metropolitan areas listed, which is projected to have the largest population in 2033?
   b. Which of the metropolitan areas listed is projected to have the smallest population in 2033?
   c. What is Chicago's projected population for 2033?

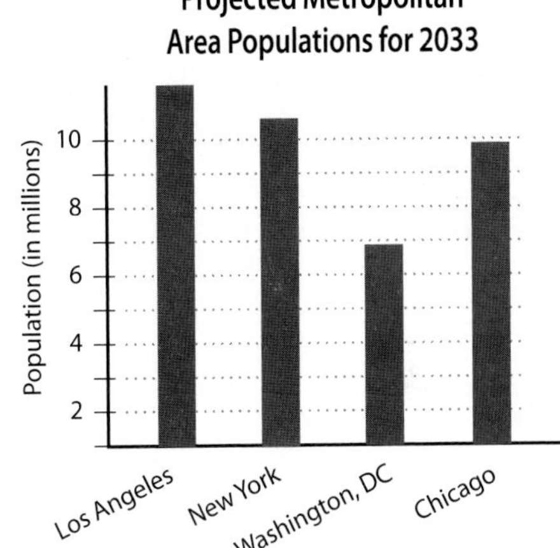

3. Construct a line graph of the given data.

Tollhouse Industries Stock

Month	Average
Jan.	16.50
Feb.	17
Mar.	16.25
Apr.	15
May	17.50
June	18

Units of Measure

Here are abbreviations and conversions for units of measure in the customary measurement system.

Length	Volume	Weight
12 inches (in) = 1 foot (ft)	2 cups (c) = 1 pint (pt)	16 ounces (oz) = 1 pound (lb)
3 ft = 1 yard (yd)	2 pt = 1 quart (qt)	2000 lb = 1 ton (t)
5280 ft = 1 mile (mi)	4 qt = 1 gallon (gal)	

Here are symbols and conversions for units of measure in the metric system.

Length

1000 millimeters (mm) = 1 meter (m)
100 centimeters (cm) = 1 m
1000 m = 1 kilometer (km)

Volume

1000 milliliters (mL) = 1 liter (L)

Mass

1000 grams (g) = 1 kilogram (kg)

To convert from one unit of measure to another, use the conversions lists above.
When converting to a smaller unit, multiply.

EXAMPLE Convert 5 feet to inches.

SOLUTION Use 12 in = 1 ft
5 ft: 5 × 12 = 60
5 ft = 60 in

EXAMPLE Convert 4 meters to centimeters.

SOLUTION Use 100 cm = 1 m
4 m: 4 × 100 = 400
4 m = 400 cm

When converting to a larger unit, divide.

EXAMPLE Convert 6 pints to quarts.

SOLUTION Use 2 pt = 1 qt
6 pt: 6 ÷ 2 = 3
6 pt = 3 qt

EXAMPLE Convert 6500 grams to kilograms.

SOLUTION Use 1000 g = 1 kg
6500 g: 6500 ÷ 1000 = 6.5
6500 g = 6.5 kg

PROBLEMS

Make the following conversions.

1. 12 yd to feet
2. 8 gal to quarts
3. 9 lb to ounces
4. 2 ft to inches
5. 3 lb to ounces
6. 5 L to milliliters
7. 2.4 km to meters
8. 24 pt to cups
9. 3.6 kg to grams
10. 99 in to yards
11. 15 qt to gallons
12. 66 oz to pounds
13. 18 qt to gallons
14. 24 oz to pounds
15. 7000 g to kilograms
16. 60 cm to meters
17. 2200 mL to liters
18. 350 cm to meters
19. 29 kg to grams
20. 17.3 L to milliliters
21. 522 g to kilograms
22. 10.122 mL to liters
23. 72 cm to millimeters
24. 432.2 cm to meters
25. 1 yd 7 in to inches
26. 5 ft 7 in to inches
27. 3 qt 1 pt to pints
28. 6 lb 9 oz to ounces
29. 4 gal 1 qt to quarts
30. 3 yd 1 ft 5 in to inches
31. 5 gal 3 qt 1 pt to pints
32. 3 m 57 cm 29 mm to millimeters

Units of Measure

APPLICATIONS

33. How many quarts will a 6-gallon bucket hold?
34. How many milliliters will a 2-liter bottle hold?
35. How many cups of coffee does a 4-quart coffeepot hold?
36. How many cups of hot chocolate will a 1.5-gallon thermos jug hold?
37. How many inches long is an 8-yard roll of aluminum foil?
38. Strawberries are sold in 1-pint containers. How many pints must be purchased to have enough for a recipe that calls for 3 cups?
39. James Jones knows that his jogging stride is about 1 meter long. The jogging trail he uses is 4.2 kilometers long. How many strides does it take him to go around the trail once?
40. The cafeteria receives 49 cases of milk each day. Each case contains 24 half-pint cartons. How many gallons of milk are received each day?
41. A soft drink is sold in 355 mL cans. How many liters are in a six-pack?
42. Katie Karanikos baked a chocolate layer cake weighing 1.5 kilograms. How many 75-gram servings can be cut from the cake?
43. Joan Baird ordered baseboard molding for the rooms of a new house. Joan needs to complete this chart to determine the total number of feet of molding needed. How much molding is needed?

	Length	Width	2 lengths	+ 2 widths	= Perimeter
	12 ft	10 ft	24 ft	+ 20 ft	= 44 ft
	11 ft	8 ft	22 ft	+ 16 ft	=
a.	11 ft	19 ft			
b.	12 ft	12 ft 2 in			
c.	15 ft	16 ft 8 in			
d.	11 ft 8 in	12 ft 2 in			
e.	12 ft 10 in	16 ft 10 in			
f.	16 ft 9 in	24 ft 3 in			
g.	9 ft 4 in	10 ft			
h.			Total		

 Making Career Choices

A career differs from a job in that it is a series of progressively more responsible jobs in one field or a related field. You will need to learn some special skills to choose a career and to help you in your job search. Choosing a career and identifying career opportunities require careful thought and preparation. To aid you in making important career choices, follow these steps:

Steps to Making a Career Decision

1. Conduct a self-assessment to determine your:
   - values
   - lifestyle goals
   - interests
   - skills and aptitudes
   - personality
   - work environment preferences
   - relationship preferences
2. Identify possible career choices based on your self-assessment.
3. Gather information on each choice, including future trends.
4. Evaluate your choices based on your self-assessment.
5. Make your decision.

After you make your decision, plan how you will reach your goal. It is best to have short-term, medium-term, and long-term goals. In making your choices, explore the future opportunities in this field or fields over the next several years. What impact will new technology and automation have on job opportunities in the next few years? Remember, if you plan, you make your own career opportunities.

 Personal Career Portfolio

You will want to create and maintain a personal career portfolio. In it you will keep all the documents you create and receive in your job search:

- Contact list
- Résumé
- Letters of recommendation
- Employer evaluations
- Awards
- Evidence of participation in school, community, and volunteer activities
- Notes about your job search
- Notes made after your interviews

 Career Research Resources

In order to gather information on various career opportunities, there are a variety of sources to research:

- **Libraries.** Your school or public library offers good career information resources. Here you will find books, magazines, pamphlets, films, videos, and special reference materials on careers. In particular, the U.S. Department of Labor publishes three reference books that are especially helpful: the *Dictionary of Occupational Titles (DOT),* which describes about 20,000 jobs and their relationships with data, people, and things; the *Occupational Outlook Handbook (OOH),* with information on more than 200 occupations; and the *Guide for Occupational Exploration (GOE),* a reference that organizes the world of work into 12 interest areas that are subdivided into work groups and subgroups.
- **The Internet.** The Internet is becoming a primary source of research on any topic. It is especially helpful in researching careers.
- **Career Consultations.** Career consultation, an informational interview with a professional who works in a career that interests you, provides an opportunity to learn about the day-to-day realities of a career.
- **On-the-Job Experience.** On-the-job experience can be valuable in learning firsthand about a job or career. You can find out if your school has a work-experience program, or look into a company or organization's internship opportunities. Interning gives you direct work experience and often allows you to make valuable contacts for future full-time employment.

The Job Search

To aid you in your actual job search, there are various sources to explore. You should contact and research all the sources that might produce a job lead, or information about a job. Keep a contact list as you proceed with your search. Some of these resources include:

- **Networking with family, friends, and acquaintances.** This means contacting people you know personally, including school counselors, former employers, and professional people.
- **Cooperative education and work-experience programs.** Many schools have such programs in which students work part-time on a job related to one of their classes. Many also offer work-experience programs that are not limited to just one career area, such as marketing.
- **Newspaper ads.** Reading the Help Wanted advertisements in your local papers will provide a source of job leads, as well as teach you about the local job market.
- **Employment agencies.** Most cities have two types of employment agencies, public and private. These employment agencies match workers with jobs. Some private agencies may charge a fee, so be sure to know who is expected to pay the fee and what the fee is.
- **Company personnel offices.** Large and medium-sized companies have personnel offices to handle employment matters, including the hiring of new workers. You can check on job openings by contacting the office by telephone or by scheduling a personal visit.
- **Searching the Internet.** Cyberspace offers multiple opportunities for your job search. Web sites, such as Hotjobs.com or Monster.com, provide lists of companies offering employment. There are tens of thousands of career-related Web sites, so the challenge is finding those that have jobs that interest you and that are up-to-date in their listings. Companies that interest you may have a Web site, which will provide valuable information on their benefits and opportunities for employment.

Applying for a Job

When you have contacted the sources of job leads and found some jobs that interest you, the next step is to apply for them. You will need to complete application forms, write letters of application, and prepare your own résumé. Before you apply for a job, you will need to have a work permit if you are under the age of 18 in most states. Some state and federal labor laws designate certain jobs as too dangerous for young workers. Laws also limit the number of hours of work allowed during a day, a week, or the school year. You will also need to have proper documentation, such as a green card if you are not a U.S. citizen.

Job Application

You can obtain the job application form directly at the place of business, by requesting it in writing, or over the Internet. It is best if you can fill the form out at home, but some businesses require that you fill it out at the place of work.

Fill out the job application forms neatly and accurately, using standard English, the formal style of speaking and writing you learned in school. You must be truthful and pay attention to detail in filling out the form.

Personal Fact Sheet

To be sure that the answers you write on a job application form are accurate, make a personal fact sheet before filling out the application:

- Your name, home address, and phone number
- Your Social Security number
- The job you are applying for
- The date you can begin work
- The days and hours you can work
- The pay you want
- Whether or not you have been convicted of a crime
- Your education
- Your previous work experience
- Your birth date
- Your driver's license number if you have one

- Your interests and hobbies, and awards you have won
- Your previous work experience, including dates
- Schools you have attended
- Places you have lived
- Accommodations you may need from the employer
- A list of references—people who will tell an employer that you will do a good job, such as relatives, students, former employers, and the like

Letters of Recommendation

Letters of recommendation are helpful. You can request teachers, counselors, relatives, and other acquaintances who know you well to write these letters. They should be short, to the point, and give a brief overview of your assets. A brief description of any of your important accomplishments or projects should follow. The letter should end with a brief description of your character and work ethic.

Letter of Application

Some employees prefer a letter of application, rather than an application form. This letter is like writing a sales pitch about yourself. You need to tell why you are the best person for the job, what special qualifications you have, and include all the information usually found on an application form. Write the letter in standard English, making certain that it is neat, accurate, and correct.

Résumé

The purpose of a résumé is to make an employer want to interview you. A résumé tells prospective employers what you are like and what you can do for them. A good résumé summarizes you at your best in a one- or two-page outline. It should include the following information:

1. **Identification.** Include your name, address, telephone number, and e-mail address.
2. **Objective.** Indicate the type of job you are looking for.
3. **Experience.** List experience related to the specific job for which you are applying. List other work if you have not worked in a related field.
4. **Education.** Include schools attended from high school on, the dates of attendance, and diplomas or degrees earned. You may also include courses related to the job you are applying for.
5. **References.** Include up to three references or indicate that they are available. Always ask people ahead of time if they are willing to be listed as references for you.

A résumé that you put online or send by e-mail is called an *electronic résumé.* Some Web sites allow you to post them on their sites without charge. Employers access these sites to find new employees. Your electronic résumé should follow the guidelines for a regular one. It needs to be accurate. Stress your skills and sell yourself to prospective employers.

Cover Letter

If you are going to get the job you want, you need to write a great cover letter to accompany your résumé. Think of a cover letter as an introduction. The cover letter is the first thing a potential employer sees, and it can make a powerful impression. The following are some tips for creating a cover letter:

- **Keep it short.** Your cover letter should be one page, no more.
- **Make it look professional.** These days, you need to type your letter on a computer and print it on a laser printer. Do not use an inkjet printer unless it produces extremely crisp type. Use white or buff-colored paper; anything else will draw the wrong kind of attention. Type your name, address, phone number, and e-mail address at the top.
- **Explain why you are writing.** Start your letter with one sentence describing where you heard of the opening. "Joan Wright suggested I contact you regarding a position in your marketing department," or "I am writing to apply for the position you advertised in the Sun City Journal."
- **Introduce yourself.** Give a short description of your professional abilities and background. Refer to your attached résumé: "As you will see in the attached résumé, I am an experienced editor with a background in newspapers, and textbooks." Then highlight specific accomplishments.

- **Sell yourself.** Your cover letter should leave the reader thinking, "This person is exactly what we are looking for." Focus on what you can do for the company. Relate your skills to the skills and responsibilities mentioned in the job listing. If the ad mentions solving problems, relate a problem you solved at school or work. If the ad mentions specific skills or knowledge required, mention your mastery of these in your letter. (Also be sure these skills are included on your résumé.)
- **Provide all requested information.** If the Help Wanted ad asked for "salary requirements" or "salary history," include this information in your cover letter. However, you do not have to give specific numbers. It is okay to say, "My wage is in the range of $10 to $15 per hour." If the employer does not ask for salary information, do not offer any.
- **Ask for an interview.** You have sold yourself, now wrap it up. Be confident, but not pushy. "If you agree that I would be an asset to your company, please call me at [insert your phone number]. I am available for an interview at your convenience." Finally, thank the person. "Thank you for your consideration. I look forward to hearing from you soon." Always close with a "Sincerely," followed by your full name and signature.
- **Check for errors.** Read and re-read your letter to make sure each sentence is correctly worded and there are no errors in spelling, punctuation, or grammar. Do not rely on your computer's spell checker or grammar checker. A spell check will not detect if you typed "tot he" instead of "to the." It is a good idea to have someone else read your letter, too. He or she might notice an error you overlooked.

Interview

Understanding how to best prepare for and follow up on interviews is critical to your career success. At different times in your life, you may interview with a teacher or professor, a prospective employer, or a supervisor. Just as having an excellent résumé is vital for opening the door, interview skills are critical for putting your best foot forward and seizing the opportunity.

Research the Company

Your ability to convince an employer that you understand and are interested in the field you are interviewing to enter is important. Show that you have knowledge about the company and the industry. What products or services does the company offer? How is it doing? What is the competition? Use your research to demonstrate your understanding of the company.

Prepare Questions for the Interviewer

Prepare interview questions to ask the interviewer. Some examples include:

- "What would my responsibilities be?"
- "Could you describe my work environment?"
- "What are the chances to move up in the company?"
- "Do you offer training?"
- "What can you tell me about the people who work here?"

Dress Appropriately

You will never get a second chance to make a good first impression. Nonverbal communication is 90 percent of communication, so dressing appropriately is of the utmost importance. Every job is different, and you should wear clothing that is appropriate for the job for which you are applying. In most situations, you will be safe if you wear clean, pressed, conservative business clothes in neutral colors. Pay special attention to grooming. Keep makeup light and wear very little jewelry. Make certain your nails and hair are clean, trimmed, and neat. Do not carry a large purse, backpack, books, or coat. Simply carry a pad of paper, a pen, and extra copies of your résumé and letters of reference in a small folder.

Exhibit Good Behavior

Conduct yourself properly during an interview. Go alone; be courteous and polite to everyone you meet. Relax and focus on your purpose: to make the best possible impression.

- Be on time.
- Be poised and relaxed.
- Avoid nervous habits.
- Avoid littering your speech with verbal clutter such as "you know," "um," and "like."
- Look your interviewer in the eye and speak with confidence.
- Use nonverbal techniques to reinforce your confidence, such as a firm handshake.
- Convey maturity by exhibiting the ability to tolerate differences of opinion.
- Never call anyone by a first name unless you are asked to do so.
- Know the name, title, and the pronunciation of the interviewer's name.
- Do not sit down until the interviewer does.
- Do not talk too much about your personal life.
- Never bad-mouth your former employers.

Be Prepared for Common Interview Questions

You can never be sure exactly what will happen at an interview, but you can be prepared for common interview questions. There are some interview questions that are illegal. Interviewers should not ask you about your age, gender, color, race, or religion. Employers should not ask whether you are married or pregnant, or question your health or disabilities.

Take time to think about your answers now. You might even write them down to clarify your thinking. The key to all interview questions is to be honest, and to be positive. Focus your answers on skills and abilities that apply to the job you are seeking. Practice answering the following questions with a friend:

- "Tell me about yourself."
- "Why do you want to work at this company?"
- "What did you like/dislike about your last job?"
- "What is your biggest accomplishment?"
- "What is your greatest strength?"
- "What is your greatest weakness?"
- "Do you prefer to work with others or on your own?"
- "What are your career goals?" or "Where do you see yourself in five years?"
- "Tell me about a time that you had a lot of work to do in a short time. How did you manage this?"
- "Have you ever had to work closely with a person you didn't get along with? How did you handle the situation?"

 After the Interview

Be sure to thank the interviewer after the interview for his or her time and effort. Do not forget to follow up after the interview. Ask, "What is the next step?" If you are told to call in a few days, wait two or three days before calling back.

If the interview went well, the employer may call you to offer you the job. Find out the terms of the job offer, including job title and pay. Decide whether you want the job. If you decide not to accept the job, write a letter of rejection. Be courteous and thank the person for the opportunity and the offer. You may wish to give a brief general reason for not accepting the job. Leave the door open for possible employment in the future.

Follow Up With a Letter

Write a thank-you letter as soon as the interview is over. This shows your good manners, interest, and enthusiasm for the job. It also shows that you are organized. Make the letter neat and courteous. Thank the interviewer. Sell yourself again.

Accepting a New Job

If you decide to take the job, write a letter of acceptance. The letter should include some words of appreciation for the opportunity, written acceptance of the job offer, the terms of employment (salary, hours, benefits), and the starting date. Make sure the letter is neat and correct.

 Starting a New Job

Your first day of work will be busy. Determine what the dress code is and dress appropriately. Learn to do each task assigned properly. Ask for help when you need it. Learn the rules and regulations of the workplace.

You will do some paperwork on your first day. Bring your personal fact sheet with you. You will need to fill out some forms. Form W-4 tells your employer how much money to withhold for taxes. You may also need to fill out Form I-9. This shows that you are allowed to work in the United States. You will need your Social Security number and proof that you are allowed to work in the United States. You can bring your U.S. passport, your Certificate of Naturalization, or your Certificate of U.S. Citizenship. If you are not a permanent resident of the United States, bring your green card. If you are a resident of the United States, you will need to bring your work permit on your first day. If you are under the age of 16 in some states, you need a different kind of work permit.

You might be requested to take a drug test as a requirement for employment in some states. This could be for the safety of you and your coworkers, especially when working with machinery or other equipment.

Important Skills and Qualities

You will not work alone on a job. You will need to learn skills for getting along and being a team player. There are many good qualities necessary to get along in the workplace. They include being positive, showing sympathy, taking an interest in others, tolerating differences, laughing a little, and showing respect. Your employer may promote you or give you a raise if you show good employability skills. You must also communicate with your employer. For example, if you will be sick or late to work, you should call your employer as soon as possible.

There are several qualities necessary to be a good employee and get ahead in your job:

- be cooperative
- possess good character
- be responsible
- finish what you start
- work fast but do a good job
- have a strong work ethic
- work well without supervision
- work well with others
- possess initiative
- show enthusiasm for what you do
- be on time
- make the best of your time
- obey company laws and rules
- be honest
- be loyal
- exhibit good health habits

Leaving a Job

If you are considering leaving your job or are being laid off, you are facing one of the most difficult aspects in your career. The first step in resigning is to prepare a short resignation letter to offer your supervisor at the conclusion of the meeting you set up with him or her. Keep the letter short and to the point. Express your appreciation for the opportunity you had with the company. Do not try to list all that was wrong with the job.

You want to leave on good terms. Do not forget to ask for a reference. Do not talk about your employer or any of your coworkers. Do not talk negatively about your employer when you apply for a new job.

If you are being laid off or face downsizing, it can make you feel angry or depressed. Try to view it as a career-change opportunity. If possible, negotiate a good severance package. Find out about any benefits you may be entitled to. Perhaps the company will offer job-search services or consultation for finding new employment.

 Take Action!

It is time for action. Remember the networking and contact lists you created when you searched for this job. Reach out for support from friends, family, and other acquaintances. Consider joining a job-search club. Assess your skills. Upgrade them if necessary. Examine your attitude and your vocational choices. Decide the direction you wish to take and move on!

Glossary

A

absolute advantage economic advantage a country has when it can produce more of a product than can any other country (p. 48)

* **accommodate** provide for (p. 274)

account a record that shows the balance for a specific item, such as cash or equipment (p. 192)

accounting systematic process of recording and reporting the financial position of a business (p. 106)

accounting cycle the activities or steps that help a business keep its accounting records in an orderly manner (p. 191)

accounting equation Assets – Liabilities = Owner's Equity; the basis for keeping all accounting records in balance (p. 192)

accounting period a block of time covered by an accounting report (p. 190)

accounts payable the total amount of money owed to the creditors of a business (p. 194)

accounts receivable the total amount of money owed to a business by customers (p. 194)

* **accumulate** collect (p. 306)

actual cash value method for settling claims in which the payment received is based on the replacement cost of an item minus depreciation (p. 747)

adjustable-rate mortgage (ARM) a mortgage with an interest rate that increases or decreases during the life of a loan (p. 525)

adjusted gross income gross income after calculating certain reductions to income (p. 699)

* **adjustments** changes or corrections (p. 807)

* **allocate** distribute (p. 9)

allowance an adjustment to the tax withheld from a paycheck (p. 702)

* **alternative** option (p. 430)

amortization the reduction of a loan balance through payments made over a period of time (p. 525)

annual percentage rate (APR) cost of credit on a yearly basis, expressed as a percentage (p. 463)

annual percentage yield (APY) amount of interest that a $100 deposit would earn, after compounding, for one year (p. 435)

annuity a series of equal regular deposits (p. 306)

annuity (insurance) a contract purchased from an insurance company that guarantees a future fixed or variable payment to the purchaser for a certain number of years, or for life (p. 821)

* **anticipate** predict (p. 268)

appraisal an estimate of the current value of a property (p. 530)

* **appraised** evaluated (p. 741)

* **appreciates** increases (p. 582)

* **approach** method (p. 380)

aptitudes natural abilities that people possess (p. 320)

arbitration a process whereby a conflict between a customer and a business is resolved by an impartial third party whose decision is legally binding (p. 400)

articles of incorporation an application to operate as a corporation (p. 77)

* **asset** benefit (p. 320)

assets owned items of value, such as cash, real estate, personal possessions, and investments (p. 354)

assigned risk pool a group of people who cannot get motor vehicle insurance who are assigned to each insurance company operating in the state (p. 757)

assisted-living facility (ALF) a residence complex that provides personal and medical services for the elderly (p. 811)

* **assume** take upon yourself (p. 733)

* **authorization** permission (p. 419)

automated teller machine (ATM) a computer terminal that allows a withdrawal of cash from an account (p. 420)

B

balance of trade difference between the value of a country's imports and exports during a period of time (p. 49)

balance sheet a report of the balances of all asset, liability, and owner's equity accounts at the end of an accounting period (p. 209)

bank reconciliation a report that accounts for the differences between a bank statement and a checkbook balance (p. 442)

bankruptcy a legal process in which some or all of the assets of a debtor are distributed among creditors because the debtor is unable to pay his or her debts (p. 490)

bartering exchanging products without the use of money (p. 10)

bear market market condition that occurs when investors are pessimistic about the economy and sell stocks (p. 593)

bearer bond a bond that is not registered in the investor's name (p. 622)

beneficiary a person named to receive benefits from an insurance policy (p. 789)

beneficiary (estate) a person who is named to receive a portion of someone's estate (p. 826)

Blue Cross an insurance company that provides hospital care benefits (p. 776)

Blue Shield an insurance company that provides benefits for surgical and medical services performed by physicians (p. 776)

blue-chip stock a safe investment that generally attracts conservative investors, usually issued by the strongest and most respected companies (p. 587)

* **board** daily meals (p. 768)

board of directors a group of individuals who are responsible for overseeing the general affairs of a corporation (p. 79)

bodily injury liability insurance that covers physical injuries caused by a vehicle accident for which one is responsible (p. 752)

break-even point the point at which total sales equal total costs (p. 266)

budget a formal, written statement of expected income and expenses for a future period of time (p. 108)
a plan for spending and investing money (p. 363)

budget deficit financial situation that occurs when more money is spent than is received (p. 36)

budget surplus financial situation that occurs when more money is received than spent (p. 36)

budget variance the difference between the budgeted amount and the actual amount spent (p. 365)

bull market market condition that occurs when investors are optimistic about the economy and buy stocks (p. 593)

business credit card a credit card that is issued to a business rather than to an individual (p. 176)

business plan a written proposal that describes a new business and strategies to launch that business (p. 93)

C

cafeteria-style employee benefits programs that allow workers to choose benefits that best meet their personal needs (p. 336)

capital money needed to establish a business (p. 121)
tools, equipment, and factories used to make goods and perform services (p. 8)

capital gain profit from the sale of assets such as stocks, bonds, or real estate (p. 568)

capitalization total amount of stocks and bonds issued by a corporation (p. 589)

capital loss sale of an investment for less than its purchase price (p. 568)

career a commitment to work in a field that is found to be interesting and fulfilling (p. 319)

cash flow the amount of cash that is available at any given time (p. 110)
the movement of cash in and out of wallets and bank accounts (p. 359)

cash value in a whole life insurance policy, the accumulated savings to which one is entitled when and if one cancels the policy (p. 792)

certificate of deposit (CD) a savings alternative in which money is left on deposit for a stated period of time to earn a specific rate of return (p. 430)

chart of accounts a list of general ledger accounts that a business will use (p. 146)

* **claim** legal right (p. 191)

* **clarification** an explanation (p. 721)

class-action suit a legal action on behalf of all the people who have suffered the same injustice (p. 401)

closed-end credit credit as a one-time loan that is paid back over a specified period of time in payments of equal amounts (p. 456)

closed-end fund a mutual fund with a fixed number of shares that are issued by an investment company when the fund is first organized (p. 639)

closing meeting of a seller, a buyer, and a lender of funds to complete a transaction (p. 527)

codicil a document that explains, adds, or deletes provisions in an existing will (p. 831)

coinsurance the percentage of medical expenses that the policyholder must pay in addition to the deductible amount (p. 769)

collateral a form of security that helps guarantee that the creditor will be repaid (p. 465)

collectibles items that appeal to collectors and investors, including rare coins, works of art, antiques, stamps, rare books, comic books, sports, memorabilia, and paintings (p. 679)

collision insurance that covers damage to one's vehicle when it is involved in an accident (p. 755)

command economy system in which a central authority controls all economic decisions (p. 10)

commercial bank a for-profit institution that offers a full range of financial services, including checking, savings, and lending (p. 423)

commercial debt financing borrowing money from a bank or other financial institution to fund a business (p. 167)

commercial finance company a firm that lends money only to businesses (p. 178)

commercial loan a loan that finances a new or ongoing business (p. 167)

commercial property the land and buildings that produce rental income (p. 666)

commission an amount of money paid to an employee based on a percentage of the employee's sales (p. 225)

* **commissions** earnings (p. 565)

common stock unit of ownership of a company entitling the stockholder to voting privileges (p. 559)

comparative advantage economic advantage that a country has when it can produce a product more efficiently and at a lower opportunity cost than another country (p. 48)

* **compensated** made up for (p. 638)

competition the struggle among businesses for customers (p. 63)

* **complex** difficult (p. 124)

* **complex** a building or group of buildings with housing units (p. 505)

* **components** parts (p. 102)

compounding the process in which interest is earned on both the principal and on any previously earned interest (p. 434)

* **condensed** summarized (p. 206)

* **confidential** private (p. 490)

* **consideration** matters for thought (p. 502)

* **consume** use up (p. 298)

consumer a person who purchases and uses goods or services (p. 301)

consumer credit use of credit for personal needs (p. 453)

Consumer Price Index (CPI) a measure of the changes in prices for commonly purchased goods and services in the United States (p. 43)

* **contingency** emergency (p. 93)

contribution margin the amount of money that the sale of a particular product contributes toward the payment of fixed costs and the profit of a business (p. 266)

convertible bond a bond that an investor can trade for shares of a corporation's common stock (p. 620)

cooperative an organization that is owned and operated by its members (p. 75)

cooperative education education that allows students to enhance classroom learning with part-time work related to their majors and interests (p. 330)

co-payment a flat fee that one pays every time one receives a covered service (p. 772)

copyright exclusive right granted by the government to an author (p. 40)

corporate bond a corporation's written pledge to repay a specific amount of money, along with interest (p. 560)

corporate bylaws rules by which a corporation must operate (p. 77)

corporate charter a license to operate a corporation (p. 77)

corporation business organization that operates as legal entity that is separate from its owners and is treated by law as if it were an individual person (p. 77)

* **correspond** agree (p. 270)

cosigning agreeing to take responsibility for loan payments if the other person fails to make them (p. 482)

cost behavior the way a cost changes in relation to a change in business activity (p. 263)

cost of merchandise sold the amount of money a business paid for the goods that it then sold to customers (p. 205)

coupon bond a bond that is registered in the owner's name for only the face value and not for interest (p. 622)

cover letter a personal letter that is presented along with a résumé (p. 332)

credit an arrangement to receive cash, goods, or services now and pay for them in the future (p. 453)

credit (accounting) an amount entered on the right side of a T account (p. 194)

credit rating a measure of a person's ability and willingness to make credit payments on time (p. 470)

credit union a nonprofit financial institution that is owned by its members and organized for their benefit (p. 424)

creditor an entity that lends money (p. 453)

* **cultivate** promote the growth of (p. 370)

current yield the annual dividend or interest of an investment divided by the current market value (p. 594)

cyclical stock a stock with market value that tends to reflect the state of the economy (p. 588)

D

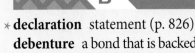

* **declaration** statement (p. 826)

debenture a bond that is backed only by the reputation of the issuing corporation, rather than by its asset (p. 618)

debit an amount entered on the left side of a T account (p. 194)

debit card a cash card that allows one to withdraw money or pay for purchases with a checking or savings account (p. 420)

deductible the set amount that the policyholder must pay per loss on an insurance policy (p. 734)

deductions the various amounts that are subtracted from an employee's gross earnings (p. 226)

deed official document transferring ownership from seller to buyer (p. 528)

* **default** failure to pay debts (p. 625)

defensive stock a stock that remains stable during declines in the economy (p. 588)

deficit financial situation that occurs when more money is spent than received (p. 361)

defined-benefit plan a retirement plan that specifies the benefits an employee will receive at retirement age, based on total earnings and years on the job (p. 818)

defined-contribution plan an individual retirement account for each employee (p. 817)

deflation decline in the level of prices for goods and services over time (p. 43)

demand the amount consumers are willing and able to buy (p. 13)

demand elasticity degree to which demand is affected by price (p. 15)

demographic trends tendencies of people that change over time, grouped by age, gender, ethnicity, education, or income (p. 322)

* **dependent** someone you support financially, as a child (p. 700)

depository institutions institutions that handle deposited money, such as commercial banks, credit unions, and saving and loan associations (p. 20)

* **depressed** disadvantaged (p. 176)

* **derivatives** involves managing financial risks (p. 19)

direct deposit an automatic deposit of net pay to an employee's designated bank account (p. 419)

direct investment real estate investment in which the owner holds legal title to the property he or she has purchased (p. 665)

direct labor the work required to convert raw materials into a finished product (p. 263)

direct materials raw materials used to make a finished product (p. 263)

disability income insurance insurance that provides regular cash income when an employee is unable to work due to pregnancy, a non-work-related accident, or illness (p. 785)

* **disclaim** deny (p. 835)

* **discretion** judgment (p. 12)

discretionary income the money left over after paying for essentials such as rent, utilities, clothing, transportation, and medications (p. 360)

* **discriminating** selective (p. 569)

* **distributions** withdrawals (p. 821)

diversification the process of spreading assets among several different types of investments to reduce risk (p. 561)

* **diversity** variety (p. 563)

dividends distributions of money, stock, or other property that a corporation pays to stockholders (p. 554)

* **document** to record (p. 398)

double-entry accounting a system of record-keeping in which each business transaction affects at least two accounts (p. 194)

down payment a portion of the total cost of an item that must be paid at the time of purchase (p. 386)

* **dwelling** shelter (p. 513)

E

earnings per share a corporation's net earnings divided by the number of outstanding shares of common stock (p. 596)

economics the study of the decisions that go into making, distributing, and using goods and services (p. 7)

economy the ways in which nations make decisions to allocate their resources (p. 10)

elastic demand demand that is affected by changes in price (p. 15)

* **elect** choose (p. 77)

* **elective** optional (p. 548)

* **eligible** qualified (p. 402)

embargo restriction on imports and exports to and from a country (p. 50)

emergency fund a savings account that can be accessed quickly to pay for unexpected expenses or emergencies (p. 543)

Employer Identification Number (EIN) a number assigned by the IRS used for income tax purposes (p. 67)

* **encounter** experience unexpectedly (p. 368)

endorsement signature of the payee (p. 441)

* **endorsement** addition of coverage to an insurance policy (p. 744)

endowment life insurance that provides coverage for a specific period of time and pays a sum of money to the policyholder if he or she is living at the end of the endowment period (p. 794)

* **engaged** involved (p. 588)

entrepreneur individual who takes the risk of starting a new business (p. 66)

entrepreneurship ability of individuals to start new businesses, introduce new products, and improve business processes (p. 8)

equilibrium point price at which consumers and producers agree (p. 14)

equity the value of a home minus the amount still owned on the money borrowed to purchase it (p. 512)

equity capital money that a business gets from its owners in order to operate (p. 559)

escrow account an account where money is held in trust until it can be delivered to a designated party (p. 520)

estate all the property and assets owned by an individual or group (p. 826)

estate planning the process of creating a detailed plan for managing personal assets to make the most of them while alive and to ensure that they are distributed wisely after death (p. 826)

estate tax a federal tax collected on the value of a person's property at the time of his or her death (p. 696)

* **estimate** make an approximate calculation of something (p. 291)

* **evaluate** assess (p. 354)

exchange-traded fund (ETF) a fund that invests in stocks or other securities contained in a specific stock or securities index (p. 639)

* **excise tax** a tax on specific goods and services such as gasoline, air travel, and telephone service) collected by federal and state governments (p. 695)

exclusion income that is not subject to taxes (p. 698)

* **executed** carried out (p. 602)

executor a person who is willing and able to perform the tasks involved in carrying out a will (p. 830)

exemption a deduction from adjusted gross income for the taxpayer, the spouse, and qualified dependents (p. 700)

* **exhausted** completely used up (p. 656)

extension an extended deadline for filing an income tax return (p. 706)

F

face value the dollar amount that a bondholder will receive at a bond's maturity (p. 617)

factors of production resources needed to produce goods and services (p. 8)

Federal Insurance Contributions Act (FICA) 1935 law that established the present Social Security system (p. 227)

fiat money money deemed to be legal tender (p. 33)

* **finance** give or get money for (p. 454)

finance charge total dollar amount paid to use credit (p. 458)

financial forecasting process of estimating a business's operating capital (p. 127)

financial leverage the use of borrowed funds for direct investment purposes (p. 672)

financial market mechanism that provides means for purchasing and selling stocks, bonds, commodities, and other financial instruments (p. 19)

financial plan a written outline of how a business will get money to start up and operate, and how it will maintain financial operations and business records (p. 94)

financial planner a specialist who is trained to offer specific financial help and advice (p. 565)

financial reports written records that summarize the results of financial transactions affecting a business and report its current financial position (p. 189)

financial statements reports that summarize changes that result from business transactions during an account period (p. 204)

first-in, first-out method (FIFO) an inventory costing method that assumes the first items purchased are the first items sold (p. 246)

* **fixed** unchanging (p. 337)

fixed costs costs that remained constant even if activity or production level changes (p. 264)

fixed expenses expenses that remain the same regardless of business activity (p. 129)

fixed-rate mortgage a mortgage with a fixed interest rate and a fixed schedule of payments (p. 525)

* **flexible** adjustable (p. 319)

* **floor** the physical area where securities are exchanged (p. 602)

* **foreclose** take possession of the property (p. 522)

* **foundation** basis (p. 361)

401(k) plan a type of retirement savings plan funded by a portion of one's salary that is deducted from the gross paycheck and placed in a special account (p. 817)

* **framework** structure (p. 146)

franchise a contractual agreement to sell a company's products or services in a designated geographic area (p. 84)

fraud dishonest business practices that are meant to deceive, trick, or gain an unfair advantage (p. 397)

free enterprise system an economic system in which people can choose what they buy, produce, and sell, as well as where they work (p. 93)

* **fungible** can be easily substituted for a good of equal value (p. 19)

future value the amount an original deposit will be worth in the future based on earning a specific interest rate over a specific period of time (p. 305)

G

general ledger a book or set of electronic files that contains the accounts used for a business (p. 198)

general partner business partner who has decision-making authority, takes an active role in the operation of the business, and has unlimited liability (p. 70)

generally accepted accounting principles (GAAP) a standard set of guidelines used in recording and reporting financial changes (p. 107)

* **generate** make (p. 71)

geographic trends tendencies of people moving from one area of the country to another as financial centers shift location (p. 324)

goals the things one wants to accomplish (p. 291)

good a physical item that is produced and can be weighed or measured (p. 297)

government bond a written pledge of a government of a municipality to repay a specific sum of money with interest (p. 560)

grace period time period during which no finance charges will be added to an account (p. 458)

Gross Domestic Product (GDP) value of all final goods and services produced inside a country in a given period of time (p. 43)

gross earnings total amount of money an employee earns in a pay period (p. 224)

gross profit on sales profit made from selling merchandise before operating expenses are deducted (p. 128)

growth stock a stock issued by a corporation whose potential earnings may be higher than the average earnings predicted for all the corporations in the country (p. 588)

guardian a person who accepts the responsibility of caring for the children of the deceased and managing an estate for the children until they reach a certain age (p. 830)

H

* **handsome** higher than expected (p. 671)

* **hardship** suffering (p. 790)

hazard anything that increases the likelihood of loss through peril (p. 732)

health insurance a form of protection that eases the financial burden people may experience as result of illness or injury (p. 767)

health maintenance organization (HMO) a health insurance plan that directly employs or contracts with selected physicians and other medical professionals to provide health care services in exchange for a fixed, prepaid monthly premium (p. 777)

⋆ **hedge** protection (p. 676)

heirs people who have the legal rights to one's assets when one dies (p. 824)

⋆ **holding** legally owned security (p. 643)

home equity loan a loan based on the difference between the current market value of a home and the amount the borrower owes on the mortgage (p. 526)

homeowners insurance coverage that provides protection for a residence and its associated financial risks, such as property damage and injuries to others (p. 740)

⋆ **hospices** facilities or organizations that provide care for the terminally ill (p. 778)

hourly wage a specific amount of money paid per hour to an employee (p. 225)

I

⋆ **impostors** people who deceive others by assuming different identities (p. 479)

impulse buying the act of purchasing items on the spur of the moment (p. 392)

incentive device that encourages specific behavior and helps motivate individuals to take specific action (p. 22)

income cash inflow, including paychecks, allowances, and interest earned (p. 359)

income dividends the earnings a fund pays to shareholders (p. 653)

income statement a report of the net income or net loss for an accounting period (p. 204)

income stock a stock that pays higher-than-average dividends compared to other stock issues (p. 587)

income tax a tax on wages, salaries, and self-employed earnings (p. 696)

income tax return a form, such as 1040 or 1040EZ, on which a taxpayer reports how much money he or she received from work and other sources, and the exact taxes that are owed (p. 698)

⋆ **indicators** statistical values (p. 43)

indirect investment real estate investment in which a trustee is appointed to hold legal title to the property on behalf of an investor group or group of investors (p. 668)

individual retirement account (IRA) a special account in which a person saves a portion of income for retirement (p. 818)

inelastic demand demand that is not affected by changes in price (p. 16)

inflation rise in the level of prices for goods and services over time (p. 43)

informational interview a meeting with someone who works in one's area of interest who can provide practical information about the career or company (p. 331)

inheritance tax a state tax collected on the property left by a person to his or her heir(s) in a will (p. 696)

insolvency the inability to pay debts when they are due (p. 358)

insurance protection against possible financial loss (p. 731)

⋆ **intellectual property** an idea or invention (p. 40)

⋆ **interdependent** they need each other to create the goods and services produced in a nation (p. 47)

interest the price that is paid for the use of another's money (p. 301)

interest inventories tests that help identify the activities that one enjoys most (p. 320)

international trade exchange of goods and services among nations (p. 47)

internship a position in which a person receives training by working with people who are experienced in a particular field (p. 329)

intestate the status of not having a valid wall (p. 827)

inventory merchandise retailers have for sale (p. 108)

investment liquidity the ability to buy or sell an investment quickly without substantially reducing its value (p. 557)

investment-grade bonds bonds that are issued by financially stable companies or municipalities (p. 635)

* **issuers** providers (p. 420)

itemized deduction a specific expense, such as a medical expense, that can be deducted from the adjusted gross income (p. 699)

J

* **jeopardizing** placing in danger (p. 722)

job work done mainly to earn money (p. 319)

journal a record of all the transactions of a business (p. 197)

K

Keogh plan a retirement plan designed for self-employed people and their employees (p. 820)

L

labor work that people do, including all of their abilities, efforts, and skills (p. 8)

land natural resources that exist and were not created by people (p. 8)

landlord the person who owns the property that is rented (p. 505)

* **lapse** stop or interruption (p. 767)

large-cap stock a stock from a corporation that has issued a large number of shares and has a large amount of capitalization (p. 589)

last-in, first-out method (LIFO) an inventory costing method that assumes the last items purchased are the first items sold (p. 247)

lease a legal document that defines the conditions of the rental agreement between the tenant and the landlord (p. 508)

legal aid society a network of community law offices that provide free or low-cost legal assistance (p. 402)

* **levies** collects (p. 715)

liabilities debts that one owes (p. 357)

liability legal responsibility for the financial cost of another person's losses or injuries (p. 738)

* **liable** responsible (p. 669)

* **lifestyle** the way you choose to spend your time and money (p. 501)

limited liability company (LLC) a business that operates and pays taxes as a partnership but has limited liability for the owners (p. 82)

limited life a situation in which a business's life span or existence is determined by the owner's life span or decision to terminate the business (p. 70)

limited partner business partner who does not take an active role in decision making or in running the business (p. 71)

line of credit an arrangement in which bank customers can borrow a certain amount of money from the bank immediately (p. 168) maximum amount of money a creditor will allow a credit user to borrow (p. 457)

liquid assets cash and items that can be quickly converted to cash (p. 354)

* **liquidate** sell off (p. 656)

liquidity the ability to easily convert financial assets into cash without loss in value (p. 295)

living will a legal document in which one states if one wants to be kept alive by artificial means if terminally ill or unable to make such a decision (p. 831)

load fund a mutual fund for which you pay a commission every time you buy or sell shares (p. 641)

LowDoc Program a government loan program that allows businesses applying for loans of less than $150,000 to submit a one-page application with a small amount of documentation (p. 175)

M

managed care prepaid health plans that provide comprehensive health care to their members (p. 776)

* **mandatory** required (p. 758)

manufacturing business a business that buys raw materials or processsed goods and transforms them into finished products (p. 261)

margin of safety the target sales minus the break-even sales, which indicates the amount of risk that sales will meet the break-even point (p. 276)

market field of exchange that takes place between buyers and sellers (p. 63)

market economy system in which supply, demand, and pricing systems allow people to make economic decisions through free interaction (p. 11)

market penetration an attempt to increase sales in a current market (p. 272)

market value the price at which property would sell (p. 356)

marketing plan a written outline of how a business will be promoted to increase customers and sales (p. 94)

markup the difference between the cost of an item to a business and the selling price of an item (p. 260)

* **maturity** the state of a financial arrangement when it falls due for payment (p. 560)

maturity date the date when a bond will be repaid (p. 617)

mediation the attempt by a neutral third party to use discussion and negotiation to resolve a conflict between a customer and a business (p. 400)

Medicaid a medical assistance program offered to certain low-income individuals and families (p. 783)

medical payments coverage coverage that pays the costs of minor accidental injuries to visitors of the policyholder's property (p. 744)

Medicare a federally funded health insurance program available mainly to people over 65 and to people with certain disabilities (p. 781)

Medicare tax tax that finances part of the Medicare program (p. 228)

mentor an experienced employee who serves as a teacher and counselor for a less-experienced person (p. 339)

merchandise goods retailers buy with the intent to resell to customer (p. 108)

* **metropolitan** large urban area (p. 631)

minimum monthly payment smallest amount that one can pay and remain a borrower in good standing (p. 468)

* **misconceptions** wrong ideas (p. 805)

mobility the ability to move easily from place to place (p. 501)

money management day-to-day financial activities necessary to get the most from one's money (p. 349)

money market account a savings account that requires a minimum balance and earns interest that varies from month to month (p. 432)

money supply total amount of money in circulation in a country (p. 35)

monopoly market condition characterized by the existence of only one supplier in a market (p. 64)

* **monotonous** boring and unchanging (p. 107)

mortgage a long-term loan extended to someone who buys property (p. 522)

mortgage bonds a bond that is backed by the assets of a corporation (p. 618)

municipal bond a security issued by a state or local government to pay for its ongoing activities (p. 628)

mutual fund an investment in which investors pool their money to buy stocks, bonds, and other securities (p. 560)

N

negative cash flow a situation that occurs when a business spends more money than it receives (p. 111)

* **negligence** lack of attention (p. 706)

negligence the failure to take ordinary or reasonable care to prevent accidents from happening (p. 732)

net asset value (NAV) the amount that one share of a mutual fund is worth (p. 640)

net income the amount of revenue that remains after expenses for the accounting period subtracted from the gross profit on sales (p. 206) income received from take-home pay, allowance, gifts, and interests (p. 462)

networking a way of making and using contacts to get job information and advice (p. 331)

net worth difference between the amount you own and the debts you owe (p. 354)

no-fault system an arrangement whereby drivers who are involved in accidents collect money from their own insurance companies (p. 755)

no-load fund a mutual fund that has no commission fee (p. 641)

non-depository institutions institutions that act as intermediaries between savers and borrowers (p. 20)

nonprice competition struggle for business that relies on factors other than price to attract and keep customers (p. 63)

O

★ **obligations** commitments (p. 231)

oligopoly market condition characterized by the existence of a few large businesses in a market (p. 63)

open dating a labeling method that indicates the freshness or shelf life of a perishable product (p. 393)

open-end credit credit as a loan with a certain limit on the amount of money that can be borrowed for a variety of goods and services (p. 457)

open-end fund a mutual fund with an unlimited number of shares that are issued and redeemed by an investment company at the investors' requests (p. 640)

★ **operate** perform or run (p. 66)

operating capital amount of capital needed to operate a business for the first few months or years (p. 127)

operating costs ongoing expenses for operating a business (p. 162)

opportunity cost what is given up when making one choice instead of another (p. 7)

overdraft protection an automatic loan made to an account if the balance will not cover checks written (p. 438)

over-the-counter (OTC) market a network of dealers who buy and sell the stocks of corporations that are not listed on a securities exchange (p. 600)

overtime rate the amount paid above the normal rate, usually 1.5 times the employee's regular hourly wage (p. 225)

par value an assigned dollar value that is printed on a stock certificate (p. 584)

participation certificate (PC) an investment in a group of mortgages that have been purchased by a government agency (p. 671)

partnership a business owned by two or more persons (p. 70)

partnership agreement written document that states how a partnership will be organized (p. 70)

patent exclusive right granted by the government to an investor to prevent anyone else from using the invention for a period of time (p. 40)

payroll a list of employees and the payments due to each employee for a specific period of time (p. 223)

penny stock a stock that typically sells for less than $1 a share (p. 589)

pension plan a retirement plan that is funded at least in part by an employer (p. 337)

peril anything that may possibly cause a loss (p. 731)

periodic inventory system a system in which inventory records are updated only after someone makes an actual physical count of the merchandise on hand (p. 245)

perpetual inventory system a system that keeps a constant, up-to-date record of merchandise on hand (p. 242)

personal balance sheet a financial statement that shows what one owns and debts that one owes (p. 354)

personal financial planning arranging to spend, save, and invest money to live comfortably, have financial security, and achieve goals (p. 291)

personal financial statement a statement that gives information about current financial position and presents a summary of income and spending (p. 354)

personal property floater additional property insurance that covers the damage or loss of a specific item of high value (p. 741)

* **pledged** promised (p. 465)

point-of-sale terminals electronic cash registers used by many businesses (p. 242)

point-of-service (POS) plan health insurance plan that uses a network of participating physicians and medical professionals who have contracted to provide services for certain fees (p. 778)

points extra charges that must be paid by a buyer to a lender in order to get a lower interest rate (p. 523)

policy contract between an insurance company and a person by which that person joins a risk-sharing group (p. 731)

portfolio a collection of all the securities held by an investor (p. 602)

* **portion** part (p. 465)

posting the process of recording transfers of amounts from the general journal to individual accounts in the general ledger (p. 199)

potential earning power the amount of money that can be earned over time (p. 320)

power of attorney a legal document that authorizes someone to act on someone else's behalf (p. 833)

precious gems rough mineral deposits (usually crystals) that are dug from the earth by miners and then cut and shaped into jewels (p. 678)

precious metals valuable ores such as gold, platinum, and silver (p. 676)

preferred provider organization (PPO) a group of doctors and hospitals that agree to provide specified medical services to members are prearranged fees (p. 778)

preferred stock a type of stock that gives an owner the advantage of receiving cash dividends before common stockholders receive cash dividends (p. 559)

* **preliminary** early (p. 138)

premium a fee for insurance (p. 731)

* **premium** additional amount above the face value of the bond (p. 620)

present value the amount of money one would need to deposit now in order to have a desired amount in the future (p. 306)

price ceiling maximum price, set by the government, that can be charged for goods and services (p. 14)

price competition struggle for business that assumes consumers will choose the lowest priced products available (p. 63)

price floor minimum price, set by the government, that can be charged for goods and services (p. 15)

price-earnings (P-E) ratio the price of one share of stock divided by the corporation's earning per share of stock over the last 12 months (p. 596)

pricing the process of assigning a selling price to a good or service (p. 259)

* **primary** most important (p. 204)

principal the original amount of money on deposit (p. 305)

private corporation a company that issues stock to a small group of people (p. 581)

private financing borrowing money from family or friends (p. 166)

private investor a person outside an entrepreneur's circle of friends and relatives who provides funding because he or she is interested in helping a new business to succeed (p. 177)

private mortgage insurance (PMI) a special policy that protects a lender in case a buyer cannot make payments at all or on time (p. 522)

private sector business not funded by the government (p. 63)

probate the legal procedure of proving that a will is valid or invalid (p. 829)

product costing the process of analyzing all costs involved in creating products (p. 262)

product cost-plus pricing the process of determining an item's selling price by adding the invoice cost of the item to a certain percentage of the cost (p. 260)

* **project** predict (p. 108)

projected financial statements reports that predict the financial position of a business in the months and years to come (p. 127)

* **promptly** on time (p. 478)

property damage liability motor vehicle insurance that applies when one damages the property of others (p. 753)

* **prospects** outlooks (p. 591)

prospectus document that discloses information about a company's earnings, assets, and liabilities (p. 572)

protectionism practice of using barriers to free trade (p. 50)

* **provisions** conditions (p. 794)

public corporation a company that sells its shares openly in stock markets where anyone can buy them (p. 581)

public sector government-funded services (p. 63)

Q

* **quarterly** every three months (p. 430)

quota restriction on the quantity or value of goods that can be imported into a country (p. 50)

R

rate of return percentage of increase in the value of savings from earned interest (p. 434)

real estate land and any structures that are on it, such as a house or any other building (p. 356)

rebate a partial refund of the price of a product (p. 394)

recession a period of economic downturn (p. 44)

refinance to obtain a new mortgage to replace an existing one (p. 527)

registered bonds a bond registered in the owner's name by the company that issues the bond (p. 622)

* **regulator** controller (p. 37)

renters insurance a type of insurance that covers the loss of a tenant's personal property as a result of damage or theft (p. 510)

replacement value method for settling claims in which one receives the full cost of repairing or replacing an item (p. 747)

* **repossess** take back (p. 487)

reserve capital money set aside for unexpected costs or opportunities (p. 135)

reserve fund money that can be made available for the future expansion of a business (p. 163)

* **resolve** reach a decision about (p. 349)

* **resort** choice (p. 546)

résumé a one- or two-page summary of a job applicant's education, training, experience, and qualifications (p. 332)

retained earnings profits that a company reinvests usually for expansion or to conduct research and development (p. 557)

* **return** gain (p. 581)

* **revenue** income (p. 128)

risk the chance of loss or injury (p. 731)

* **roll over** transfer (p. 819)

* **routine** regular (p. 168)

S

safe-deposit box a small, secure storage compartment that can be rented in a bank (p. 352)

salary a fixed amount of money paid to an employee for each pay period, regardless of the number of hours worked (p. 224)

savings and loan association (S&L) a financial institutional that traditionally specialized in savings accounts and mortgage loans, but now offers many of the same services as commercial banks (p. 424)

scarcity economic principle requiring that people decide which goods and services to use or not use due to limited resources and unlimited wants (p. 7)

* **secure** safe (p. 352)

secured loan a loan that is backed by collateral (p. 169)

securities investments bought and sold on the stock market, including stocks, bonds, mutual funds, options, and commodities (p. 581)

securities exchange a marketplace where brokers who represent investors meet to buy and sell securities (p. 599)

security deposit an amount of money paid by a tenant to the owner of a property to guard against any financial loss or damage that the tenant might cause (p. 510)

serial bonds bonds issued at the same time but which mature on different dates (p. 621)

service a task that a person or machine performs for you (p. 297)

service contract a separately purchased agreement by a manufacturer or distributor to cover the costs of repairing an item (p. 395)

service industries businesses that provide services for a fee (p. 326)

simple interest interest computed only on the principal (p. 467)

sinking fund a fund to which a corporation makes deposits for the purpose of paying back a bond issue (p. 620)

Small Business Administration (SBA) an independent agency of the federal government that offers assistance to people who are starting small businesses and to those who want to expand existing businesses (p. 174)

Small Business Investment Companies (SBICs) private investment firms that work with the Small Business Administration to provide longer-term funding for small businesses (p. 178)

small claims court a court that deals with legal disputes that involve amounts below a certain limit (p. 401)

small-cap stock a stock issued by a company with a capitalization of $500 million or less (p. 589)

⋆ **soar** rise quickly (p. 679)

Social Security tax tax that finances the federal programs that provide retirement, disability, and life insurance benefits (p. 228)

sole proprietorship business owned by one person (p. 66)

⋆ **sound** firm (p. 171)

specialization in manufacturing, a division of tasks among different workers (p. 47)

specific identification method an inventory costing method in which the exact cost of each item is determined and assigned to an item (p. 246)

⋆ **speculative** riskier (p. 635)

speculative investment a high-risk investment that might earn a large profit in a short time (p. 551)

standard deduction an amount of money set by the IRS that is not taxed (p. 699)

standard of living a measure of quality of life based on the amounts and kinds of goods and services a person can buy (p. 319)

⋆ **staple** basic (p. 249)

start-up capital money required to start a business (p. 122)

start-up costs costs or fees involved in establishing a business (p. 122)

statement of cash flows a financial statement that reports how much cash a business took in and where the cash went (p. 212)

⋆ **stiff** harsh (p. 752)

⋆ **stock** supplies & products (p. 240)

⋆ **stockholders** people who buy shares of stock and become the legal owners of a corporation (p. 78)

stop-loss a provision that requires a policyholder to pay all costs up to a certain amount, after which the insurance company pays 100 percent of the remaining expenses covered (p. 770)

stop-payment order a request made to a bank or other financial institution to not cash a particular check (p. 441)

strategic plan a written outline of business goals and the steps to take to achieve them (p. 94)

⋆ **sublet** to have a person other than the original tenant take over the rental unit and payments for the remaining term of the lease (p. 508)

⋆ **supplemental** extra (p. 777)

supply the amount producers are willing and able to produce (p. 13)

surplus extra money that you can spend or save (p. 360)

★ **suspend** stop (p. 787)

syndicate a temporary association of individuals or business firms organized to perform a task that requires a large amount of funds (p. 669)

T

T account a tool used to increase or decrease each account that is affected by a transaction (p. 194)

take-home pay amount of income left after taxes and other deductions are subtracted from gross pay (p. 360)

target profit the amount of net income that a business sets as a goal (p. 274)

target sales the number of units a business needs to sell to reach a target profit (p. 275)

tariff tax on imports (p. 50)

tax audit a detailed examination of a tax return by the IRS (p. 719)

tax credit an amount of money that can be subtracted directly from owed taxes (p. 701)

tax deduction an expense that can be subtracted from adjusted gross income to figure taxable income (p. 699)

tax liability total amount of taxes owed (p. 695)

taxable income adjusted gross income minus any allowable tax deductions and exemptions (p. 699)

tax-deferred income income that is taxed at a later date (p. 568)

tax-exempt income income that is not taxed (p. 568)

tenant a person who pays for the right to live in a residence owned by someone else (p. 505)

term insurance insurance that provides protection against loss of life for only a specified term (p. 791)

time value of money the increase of an amount of money due to earned interest or dividends (p. 304)

★ **title** document showing ownership (p. 456)

title insurance a type of insurance that protects the buyer if problems with the title are found later (p. 527)

total gross earnings amount paid to all employees before any deductions are taken out (p. 234)

total return a calculation that includes the annual dividend, as well as any increase or decrease in the original purchase price of the investment (p. 594)

trademark an indicator that protects a company's name and reputation (p. 40)

traditional economy system in which economic questions are answered by customs and tradition (p. 10)

transaction an activity that has an effect on the financial situation of a business (p. 106)

★ **transactions** dealings (p. 384)

★ **transfer** move (p. 198)

trends developments that mark changes in a particular area (p. 319)

trial balance a list of all the account names for a business and their current balances (p. 202)

trough a low point in a business cycle (p. 45)

trust an arrangement in which a trustee manages assets for the benefit of someone else (p. 828)

U

uninsured motorist's protection insurance that provides coverage for accidents involving an uninsured or hit-and-run driver (p. 752)

unit pricing the use of a standard unit of measurement to compare the prices of packages that are different sizes (p. 393)

unlimited liability situation in which the owner of a business is responsible to pay the business debts out of personal assets (p. 69)

unsecured loan a loan that does not require collateral from the borrower (p. 169)

V

★ **valid** good or effective (p. 786)

values the beliefs and principles you consider important, correct, and desirable (p. 292)

★ **vandalism** deliberate destruction to private or public property (p. 738)

variable costs costs that change in direct proportion to the activity level of production (p. 263)

variable expenses expenses that may change (p. 129)

venture capital firm a company that provides private funding for small businesses that need a substantial amount of immediate cash (p. 178)

vesting the right of an employee to keep the company's contributions from company-sponsored plans, even if the employee no longer works for that employer (p. 817)

* **voice** right to be heard (p. 178)

W

warranty a written guarantee from a manufacturer or distributor that states the conditions under which a product can be returned (p. 394)

* **wealth** large amount (p. 330)

wealth property that has a money value or an exchangeable value (p. 354)

* **weigh** consider (p. 304)

whole life insurance a permanent policy for which one pays a specified premium each year for the rest of one's life (p. 792)

will legal declaration of a person's wishes regarding disposal of his or her estate after death (p. 826

* **withheld** taken out of (p. 226)

Y

yield the rate of return earned by an investor who holds a bond for a certain period of time, usually stated as a percentage (p. 636)

* **yield** bring in (p. 259)

zero-coupon bond a bond that does not produce interest payments (p. 622)

Index

A

B

Index

D

Index

E

F

G

H

Index

J

K

L

M

N

O

P

Q

R

T

Index

U

W

Photo Credits

All Unit Videos are Courtesy of Learn360.

BPF video icon photo component credit BananaStock/PunchStock.

Cover (l)Patrick Sheandell O'Carroll/PhotoAlto/Corbis, (r)Vectorstock.com; 2-3 John Moore/Getty Images; 4-5 Sean Gallup/Getty Images; 5 Tanya Constantine/Getty Images; 11 Lanz von Horsten/Getty Images; 17 Francis Dean/Sygma/Corbis; 18 Keith Weller/USDA; 20 Siede Preis/Getty Images; 21 Michael Nagle/Bloomberg via Getty Images; 22 Getty Images; 24 BananaStock/PictureQuest; 30-31 Bob Daemmrich/PhotoEdit; 31 Tanya Constantine/Getty Images; 34 DAJ/Getty Images; 35 Alex Wong/Getty Images; 38 AFOLABI SOTUNDE/CORBIS; 42 McGraw-Hill Companies; 48 Image Source/CORBIS; 57 Sean Gallup/Getty Images; 58-59 Tony Freeman/PhotoEdit; 60-61 Royalty-Free/CORBIS; 61 Tanya Constantine/Getty Images; 69 Don Smetzer/Getty Images; 71 Steve Prezant/Getty Images; 73 Medioimages/Photodisc/Getty Images; 78 BananaStock/PunchStock; 83 (t)CORBIS, (b)Joe Raedle/Getty Images; 84 Andrew Resek/The McGraw-Hill Companies, Inc.; 85 Comstock Images/Getty Images; 90-91 Fuse/Getty Images; 91 Tanya Constantine/Getty Images; 96 Susan Van Etten/PhotoEdit; 97 Flying Colours Ltd/Getty Images; 99 Fuse/Getty Images; 100 (tl)Frances Roberts/Alamy, (tr)Fuse/Getty Images, (bl)Juice Images/Alamy, (br)Digital Vision/Getty Images; 102 Yuri Arcurs/Cutcaster; 103 Erica S. Leeds; 105 Dgital Vision/Getty Images; 109 Andersen Ross/Brand X/Corbis; 118-119 Hans Neleman/Getty Images; 119 Tanya Constantine/Getty Images; 123 (t)Patti McConville/Alamy, (c)Tetra images RF/Getty Images (b)Getty Images; 124 Ariel Skelley/Getty Images; 127 Comstock Images/Getty Images; 129 Justin Sullivan/Getty Images; 132 JGI/Daniel Grill; 136 David Schaffer/Getty Images; 137 Jeffrey Coolidge/Getty Images; 146 Mel Yates/Getty Images; 153 Hans Neleman/Getty Images; 154-155 Blend Images/Getty Images; 155-156 Ariel Skelley/Getty Images; 156 Tanya Constantine/Getty Images; 160 Fuse/Jupiter Images; 161 Blend Images/Getty Images; 163 California California/Alamy; 168 Glowimages/Getty Images; 169 Thomas Northcut/Getty Images; 170 Image Source/JupiterImages; 174 Micheline Pelletier/Corbis; 175 Image Source/Getty Images; 179 Peter Adams/Getty Images; 181 iStock Exclusive/Getty Images; 186-187 JupiterImages/Getty Images; 187 Tanya Constantine/Getty Images; 191 David Shwatal/Alamy; 197 Alexander Walter/Getty Images; 203 Image Source/Almay; 207 ICP/Alamy; 208 Fuse/Getty Images; 212 TORSTEN BLACKWOOD/AFP/Getty Images; 220-221 Andrew Harrer/Bloomberg via Getty Images; 221 Tanya Constantine/Getty Images; 227 Digital Vision/Getty Images; 234 image100 Ltd; 235 AP Photo/Charlie Collins; 236 B. O'Kane/Alamy; 239 Alistair Berg/Getty Images; 241 (tl)Alistair Berg/Getty Images, (tr)RL Productions/Getty Images, (bl)Commercial Eye/Getty Images, (br)Blend Images/Getty Images; 245 Michael Krasowitz/Getty Images; 250-257 LWA/Dann Tardif/Getty Images; 257 Tanya Constantine/Getty Images; 260 Felbert & Eickenberg/Getty Images; 261 B2M Productions/Getty Images; 262 Jamie Grill/Getty Images; 265 Monty Rakusen/Getty Images; 267 Influx Productions/Getty Images; 272 CORBIS; 275 (t)Kay Blaschke/Getty Images, (b)Tonya Constantine/Getty Images; 285 Andrew Harrer/Bloomberg via Getty Images; 286-287 altrendo images/Getty Images; 288-289 Jin Lee/Bloomberg via Getty Images; 287 Learn360; 287 Tanya Constantine/Getty Images; 293 ©Jose Luis Pelaez, Inc./Getty Images; 294 (l)CORBIS Royalty-Free; 294 (r)©BananaStock/Alamy, (l)©JupiterImages/Getty Images; 295 (c)©Ryan McVay/Getty Images, (r)©DK Stock/David Deas/Getty Images; 303 ©Jeffrey Coolidge/Getty Images; 305 ©Stephen Simpson/CORBIS; 308 ©Daniel Cheong/Getty Images; 316-317 Jeff Greenberg/PhotoEdit; 317 Tanya Constantine/Getty Images; 319 ©Kevin Dodge/CORBIS; 323 (tl)©Andy Sacks/Getty Images, (tr)©Steve Cole/Getty Images,(bl)©Peter Dazeley/Getty Images, (br)©Simon Jarratt/CORBIS; 325 ©Aero Graphics, Inc./CORBIS; 330 ©Tim Pannell/CORBIS; 331 Lars A. Niki; 331 ©Getty Images; 338 ©Justin Lane/epa/CORBIS; 339 ©Jose Luis Pelaez, Inc./CORBIS; 346-347 Thinkstock Images/Getty Images; 347 Tanya Constantine/Getty Images; 351 ©JGI/Jamie Grill/Blend Images/CORBIS; 353 ©Kit Kittle/CORBIS; 357 ©Kevin Fleming/CORBIS; 362 Brand X/PunchStock; 369 ©Ann Johansson/CORBIS; 370 ©Image Source/CORBIS; 376-377 Mike Kemp/Getty Images; 377 Tanya Constantine/Getty Images; 382 (l)©Sam Bloomberg-Rissman/Blend Images/CORBIS, (r)©Ross Anania/Getty Images; 383 (l)Consumer Reports ® issued by independent organizations and the media, (r) Bloomberg via Getty Images; 385 (t)©JGI/Jamie Grill/CORBIS, (c)©Medioimages/Getty Images, (b)©Alan Schein Photography/CORBIS; 391 Stockbyte/Getty Images; 392 ConsumerSearch.com; 394 ©Fuse/Getty Images; 397 Getty Images; 398 Michael Heinsen/Getty Images; 402 ©Jim Arbogast/Getty Images; 403 McGraw-Hill Companies; 409 Mike Kemp/Getty Images; 410-411 Andrew Sacks/Getty Images; 412-413 Andersen Ross/Getty Images; 413 Tanya Constantine/Getty Images; 419 Doug Menuez/Getty Images; 424 (l)©Ariel Skelley/CORBIS, (r)JupiterImages/Getty Images; 425 (l)A.Chederro/CORBIS, (r)Photodisc/Getty Images; 426 ©Image Source/Getty Images; 427 ©David Cumming/CORBIS; 432 CORBIS; 444 David Ashley/CORBIS; 445 Artville/Getty Images; 450-451 Michele Constantini/Corbis; 451 Tanya Constantine/Getty Images; 455 ©JupiterImages/Getty Images; 466 Image Source/Alamy; 469 ©Jose Luis Pelaez/CORBIS; 475 Ariel Skelley/Blend Images/CORBIS; 477 Alamy Images; 479 Image Source/CORBIS; 488 Dimitri Vervitsiotis/Getty Images; 493 Ariel Skelley/Getty Images; 498-499 Blend Images/Getty Images; 499 Tanya Constantine/Getty Images; 504 Photodisc/Getty Images; 507 LWA/Dann Tardif/Getty Images; 511 Royalty-Free/CORBIS; 513 ©Martin Barraud/Getty Images; 515 Panoramic Images/Getty Images; 519 (tl)©JupiterImages/Getty Images, (tr)David Sacks/Getty Images, (b)©David Buffington/Getty Images; 521 MedioImages/Getty Images; 523 ©Douglas Keister/CORBIS; 537 Andersen Ross/Getty Images; 538-539 Allan Baxter/Getty Images; 540-541 Image Source/Corbis; 541 Tanya Constantine/Getty Images; 547 (tl)Tooga/Getty Images, (tr)Francis Twitty/Getty Images, (bl)Bruce Ayres; 553 Jon Hicks/CORBIS; 557 Nicole Hill/Getty Images; 562 Ariel Skelley/Getty Images; 567 Radius Images/Alamy; 570 Image Source/Getty Images; 573 Brand X Pictures/PunchStock; 578-579 Spencer Platt/Getty Images; 579 Tanya Constantine/Getty Images; 582 BrandXPictures/PunchStock; 586 Bloomberg via Getty Images; 587 ©AFP/Getty Images; 588 ©Thinkstock/Getty Images; 589 Bloomberg via Getty Images; 591 Brand X Pictures; 594 ©Stuart Pearce/Alamy; 600 ©Mark Lewis/Getty Images; 601 ©Bloomberg via Getty Images; 603 (tl)Stephen Chernin/Getty Images, (bl)STAN HONDA/AFP/Getty Images, (br)Mario Tama/Getty Images; 604 Comstock/Getty Images; 605 ©Sergio Moraes/CORBIS; 607 Scottrade; 614-615 David Sherman/NBAE via Getty Images; 615 Tanya Constantine/Getty Images; 619 STR/AFP/Getty Images; 620 Stockbyte/Getty Images; 621 Bloomberg/Getty Images; 626 U.S. Department of the Treasury; 629 Visions of America, LLC/Alamy; 637 BrandXPictures/PunchStock; 639 JupiterImages/Getty Images; 643 Everett Kennedy+Brown/Corbis; 650 Barron's; 652 Morningstar; 657 Don Farrall/Getty Images; 662-663 GABRIEL BOUYS/AFP/Getty Images; 663 Tanya Constantine/Getty Images; 668 Keith Thomas Productions/Brand X Pictures/PictureQuest; 671 Jacobs Stock Photography/PunchStock; 673 Philippe Reichert/Getty Images; 677 (t)Gianni Cigolini/Getty Images, (b) Will Crocker/Getty Images; 679 Peter Macdiarmid - WPA Pool/Getty Images; 681 Howard Grey/Getty Images; 689 GABRIEL BOUYS/AFP/Getty Images; 690-691 BananaStock/SuperStock; 691 Joson/CORBIS; 692-693 Elizabeth Simpson/Getty Images; 693 Tanya Constantine/Getty Images; 698 Comstock Images; 708 Danita Delimont/Getty Images; 708721 Noel Hendrickson/Getty Images; 718 Digital Vision/Getty Images; 720 (t) Internal Revenue Service, (cl)Intuit, (cr)Andersen Ross/Getty Images, (b) Jill Braaten/McGraw-Hill Companies; 728-729 Bloomberg/Getty Images; 729 Tanya Constantine/Getty Images; 734 Getty Images; 738 C. Lee/PhotoLiGetty Images; 741 Jeff Randall/Getty Images; 748 Jose Luis Pelaez Inc/Blend Images/Getty Images; 749 age fotostock/SuperStock; 750 Comstock Images/Getty Images; 754 Cody Duncan/Alamy; 757 Geico; 758 Don Mason/Getty Images; 759 Comstock/JupiterImages; 764-765 John Kelly/Getty Images; 765 Tanya Constantine/Getty Images; 771 rubberball/Getty Images; 774 Jetta Productions/David Atkinson/Getty Images; 776 Ken Knudson/Getty Images; 778 Todd Pearson/Getty Images; 780 imagebroker/Alamy; 782 George Shelley Productions/Getty Images; 787 Getty Images; 788 Paul Chesley/Getty Images; 788 ©CORBIS Royalty-Free; 792 Lori Adamski Peek/Getty Images; 802-803 Image Source/Getty Images; 807 Digital Vision/Getty Images; 812 (tl)Jose Luis Pelaez Inc/Getty Images, (r)Fancy/Alamy, (bl)Larry Dale Gordon/Getty Images; 815 Digital Vision/Getty Images; 823 Image Source/Getty Images; 825 Stockbyte/Getty Images; 827 Blend Images/Getty Images; 829 Ronnie Kaufman/CORBIS; 832 Pepiera Tom/Iconotec.com; 835 moodboard/Corbis; 839 blueduck/Asia Images/Getty Images; 847 Image Source/Getty Images.